Contents

"HADLOW"
3.5 ABV
BITTER
WITH HADLOW HOPS
SUSSEX
BEST
BITTER
GRASS
HOPPER

Using the Guide

❶ **Guide Order** Pubs are listed alphabetically by name (ignoring The) under their village or town. Towns and villages are listed alphabetically within their county (a county map appears at the back of the guide). The guide has entries for England, Channel Islands, Isle of Man, Scotland and Wales in that order. Some village pubs prefer to be initially located under the nearest town, in which case the village name is included in the address and directions.

Pick of the Pubs Around 700 of the best pubs in Britain have been selected by the editor and inspectors and these are highlighted. They have longer, more detailed descriptions and a tinted background. Around 250 have a full page entry and two photographs.

A pub name shown in *italics* indicates that 2006 data has been used to create the entry.

❷ **Map Reference** The map reference number denotes the map page number in the atlas section at the back of the book and (except for London maps) the National Grid reference. The London map references help locate their position on the Central and Greater London maps.

❸ **Symbols** See Symbols in the panel on page 5.

❹ **Address and Postcode** This gives the street name and the postcode, and if necessary the name of the village is included (see 1 above). This may be up to five miles from the named location.

☎ Telephone number 🖹 Fax number, email and websites: Wherever possible we have included an email address and a website.

❺ **Directions** Directions are given only when they have been supplied by the proprietor.

❻ **Open** Indicates the hours and dates when the establishment is open and closed.

❼ **Bar meals** Indicates the times and days when proprietors tell us bar food can be ordered, and the average price of a main course as supplied by the proprietor. Please be aware that last orders could vary by up to 30 minutes.

❶ DENHAM — MAP 06 TQ08 ❷

The Falcon Inn ★★★★ INN ❸

❹ Village Rd UB9 5BE ☎ 01895 832125

e-mail: falcon.inn@btconnect.com

❺ **dir:** *Exit M40 junct 1, follow A40/Gerrards Cross signs. Approx 200yds turn right onto Old Mill Rd. Pass church on right, enter village. Pub opposite village green.*

This traditional 16th-century inn, located opposite the green in beautiful Denham Village, is an ideal base for exploring Colne Valley Country Park. Expect excellent real ales and award-winning food. Lunch could include Spanish tortilla with mixed salad, or a home-made burger with fries; in the evening, perhaps ginger king prawns and scallops with aubergine caviar, rôsti potatoes, langoustine and herb oil, or rack of lamb with marinated courgettes, straw potatoes and red wine sauce. Lots of fish. ❼

❻ **Open** 12-3 5-11 (Summer Sat/Sun 12-11) **Bar Meals** L served all week 12-2.30 D served all week 6.30–9.30 (Sun 12-4) **Restaurant** L served Mon-Sun 12-2.30 D served Mon-Sun 6.30-10 (Sun 12-4, 6.30-9.30) ❽

❾ Timothy Taylor Landlord, Bombardier, Youngs, Deuchars & Guest Ale.

❿ 11 **Facilities** Children's licence Garden **Rooms** 4 bedrooms en suite S£85 D£95 ⓫

❽ **Restaurant** Indicates the times and days when proprietors tell us food can be ordered from the restaurant. The average cost of a 3-course à la carte meal and a 3- or 4-course fixed-price menu are shown as supplied by the proprietor. Last orders may be approximately 30 minutes before the times stated.

❾ **Brewery or Company** This is the name of the Brewery to which the pub is tied, or the Company which owns it. A free-house is where the pub is independently owned and run.

The beer tankard symbol indicates the principal beers sold by the pub. Up to five cask or hand-pulled beers are listed. Many pubs have a much greater selection, with several guest beers each week.

The wine glass symbol followed by a number indicates the number of wines sold by the glass.

❿ **Facilities** Indicates if a pub has a children's licence, a garden, allows dogs on the premises, offers parking and has a children's play area.

⓫ **Rooms** Only accommodation that has been inspected is included. The AA, in partnership with the national tourist bodies (VisitBritain, VisitScotland and the VisitWales) has introduced new Quality Standards for accommodation that is inspected.

Notes As so many establishments take one or more of the major credit cards only those taking no cards are shown.

The Diamond classification for guest accommodation has been replaced by a Star rating. To differentiate, between the various types of stars, each rating also has a designator (see page 6).

AA Stars (and designators as appropriate) are shown at the beginning of an entry. Small Stars appearing under Rooms at the end of an entry indicates that the accommodation has been inspected by another organisation.

The number of ensuite bedrooms is listed. Accommodation prices indicate the minimum single and double room prices per night. Breakfast is generally included in the price, but guests should check when making a reservation.
See pages 6-7 for further explanation

Key to Symbols

	Rosettes The AA's food award. Explanation on p7
★★★	**Stars** Accommodation rating please see p6/7 Accommodation rating please see p6/7
	A fish symbol indicates that a pub serves a minimum of five main course dishes with fresh sea fish as the main ingredient.
	Indicates that at least six wines are available by the glass. For the exact number of wines served this way, see notes at the bottom of each entry.
	Denotes the principal beers sold.
NEW	Pubs appearing in the guide for the first time in 2008

AA Classifications & Awards

AA Classifications & Awards

Many of the pubs in this Guide offer accommodation. Where a Star rating appears next to an entry's name in the Guide, the establishment has been inspected by the AA under common Quality Standards agreed between the AA, VisitBritain, VisitScotland and VisitWales. Where a Star rating appears after the Room information at the end of an entry, it has been inspected by VisitBritain, VisitScotland or VisitWales using the same standards. These ratings are for the accommodation, and ensure that it meets the highest standards of cleanliness, with an emphasis on professionalism, proper booking procedures and prompt and efficient services. Some of the pubs in this Guide offer accommodation but do not belong to a rating scheme. In this case the accommodation is not included in their entry.

AA recognised establishments pay an annual fee that varies according to the classification and the number of bedrooms. The establishments receive an unannounced inspection from a qualified AA inspector who recommends the appropriate classification. Return visits confirm that standards are maintained; the classification is not transferable if an establishment changes hands.

The annual AA Hotel Guide and AA Bed & Breakfast Guide give further details of recognised establishments and the classification schemes. Details of AA recognised hotels, guest accommodation, restaurants and pubs are also available at **www.theAA.com**, along with a useful Route Planner.

AA Hotel Classification

Hotels are classified on a 5-point scale, with one star being the simplest, and five stars offering a luxurious service at the top of the range. The AA's top hotels in Britain and Ireland are identified by red stars.

In addition to the main **Hotel** (HL) classification which applies to some pubs in this Guide, there are other categories of hotel applicable also to pubs, as follows:

Town House Hotel (TH) - A small, individual city or town centre property, which provides a high degree of personal service and privacy

Country House Hotel (CHH) - Quietly located in a rural area

Small Hotel (SHL) - Has fewer than 20 bedrooms and is owner managed

Metro Hotel (MET) - A hotel in an urban location that does not offer an evening meal

Restaurants with Rooms (RR) - Most Restaurants with Rooms have been awarded AA rosettes for their food, and the accommodation meets the required AA standard (see under **Guest Accommodation** for more details)

Budget Hotel (BUD) - These are usually purpose-built modern properties offering inexpensive accommodation. Often located near motorways and in town or city centres. **They are not awarded stars**

AA Guest Accommodation

Guest accommodation is also classified on a scale of one to five stars, with one being the most simple, and five being more luxurious. Yellow stars indicate the very best B&Bs, Guest Houses, Farmhouses, Inns and Guest Accommodation in the 3, 4 and 5 star ratings. Stars have replaced the Diamond Classification for this type of accommodation, in accordance with Common Standards agreed between the AA and the UK tourist authorities of VisitEngland, VisitScotland and VisitWales. To differentiate them from Hotel Stars, they have been given a series of designators appropriate to the type of accommodation they offer, as follows:

Bed & Breakfast (B&B) – Accommodation provided in a private house, run by the owner and with no more than six paying guests

Guest House (GH) – Accommodation provided for more than six paying guests and run on a more commercial basis than a B&B. Usually more services, for example dinner, are provided by staff as well as the owner

Farmhouse (FH) – B&B or guest house accommodation provided on a working farm or smallholding

Restaurant with Rooms (RR) – Destination restaurant offering overnight accommodation. The restaurant is the main business and is open to non-residents. A high standard of food should be offered, and restaurant service should be available at least five nights a week. A maximum of 12 bedrooms

Guest Accommodation (GA) – Any establishment which meets the entry requirements for the Scheme can choose this designator

Inn (INN) – Accommodation provided in a fully licensed establishment. The bar will be open to non-residents and provide food in the evenings

U A small number of pubs have this symbol because their Star classification was not confirmed at the time of going to press

Rosette Awards

Out of the thousands of restaurants in the British Isles, the AA identifies, with its Rosette Awards, some 1,900 as the best. What to expect from restaurants with AA Rosette Awards is outlined here, for a more detailed explanation of Rosette criteria please see www.theAA.com

◎ Excellent local restaurants serving food prepared with care, understanding and skill and using good quality ingredients.

◎◎ The best local restaurants, which consistently aim for, and achieve higher standards and where a greater precision is apparent in the cooking. Obvious attention is paid to the selection of quality ingredients.

◎◎◎ Outstanding restaurants that demand recognition well beyond their local area.

◎◎◎◎ Amongst the very best restaurants in the British Isles, where the cooking demands national recognition.

◎◎◎◎◎ The finest restaurants in the British Isles, where the cooking stands comparison with the best in the world.

AA Pub of the Year for England, Scotland and Wales

Selected with the help of our AA inspectors, we have chosen three very worthy winners for this prestigious award. The winners stand out for being great all-round pubs or inns, combining a good pub atmosphere, a warm welcome from friendly, efficient hosts and staff, excellent food, well-kept beers and comfortable accommodation.

Pub of the year for England

The Durham Ox, Crayke, North Yorkshire
Page 646

The Ox is a welcoming country inn with a cosy oak-panelled bar complete with blazing fires on cooler days, and a smart restaurant. Both are ideal showcases for the pub's food, which is taken seriously and sourced as close to the pretty village of Crayke as possible. It is surrounded by lovely countryside, and opposite is the hill of nursery rhyme fame believed to have been climbed by the Grand Old Duke of York! The Ox's dedicated family owners show a sincere commitment to providing the best wines, beers and food. At least six real Yorkshire ales, like Timothy Taylor Landlord and Theakston's Old Peculier, are kept in peak condition in the bar, and the wine list offers a terrific choice with over 80 bins personally sourced from all over the world. The pub also prides itself on serving proper pub food rather than offering a trendy gastro menu.

Pub of the year for

Scotland

The Inn at Kippen, Kippen, Stirling
Page 721

Almost equidistant between Edinburgh and Glasgow, the Inn at Kippen is set scenically in the Fintry Hills on the edge of Flanders Moss. Loch Lomond is nearby, and so are the mountains of the Trossachs. The restaurant is the ideal setting for fine dining, and the bar is a comfortable and welcoming spot delicious bar meals. Other attractions which make this inn enduringly popular include a small beer festival in the summer, wine and whisky tastings and live music. It is run enthusiastically by landlord James Fletcher and his friendly, efficient team. Locals and visitors from afar are tempted by the competent, imaginative menus, and the Scottish produce includes smoked salmon from the Outer Hebrides, beef and lamb from Kippen itself, scallops from Scrabster, and bread baked in a nearby village. An authentic wood-smoked oven in the beer garden produces Italian pizzas with a Scottish twist, and hog roasts are also popular.

Pub of the year for

Wales

Glasfryn, Mold, Flintshire
Page 735

A dramatic rescue of a near-derelict old farm and former judge's residence has resulted in this award-winning pub. The original building was not only saved but renovated and extended. The large open-plan space has plenty of windows to allow the light in, warm wooden floors, a relaxed mish-mash of old wooden chairs and tables, and rugs placed here and there. Loads of pictures cover the walls. The food changes every day, but always offers a comprehensive selection of dishes sourced where possible from North Wales and the local coast. The menus are both imaginative and reassuringly traditional: crab and prawn noodles with lime and chilli; pork loin with herb crumble; and beer-battered haddock and chips with mushy peas are carefully cooked and full of flavour. Sandwiches and snacks offer an interesting choice for those in a hurry.

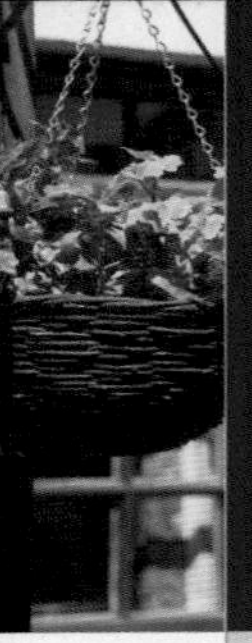

Welcome to the Guide

We aim to bring you the country's best pubs, selected for their atmosphere, great food and good beer. Ours is the only major pub guide to feature colour photographs, and to highlight the 'Pick of the Pubs', revealing Britain's finest hostelries. Updated every year, this edition includes lots of old favourites, as well as plenty of new destinations for eating and drinking, and great places to stay across Britain.

Who's in the Guide?

We make our selection by seeking out pubs that are worth making a detour - 'destination' pubs - with publicans exhibiting real enthusiasm for their trade and offering a good selection of well-kept drinks and good food. Our selected pubs make no payment for their inclusion in our guide. They are included entirely at our discretion.

Tempting Food

We are looking for menus that show a commitment to home cooking, making good use of local produce wherever possible, and offering an appetising range of freshly-prepared dishes. Pubs presenting well-executed traditional dishes like ploughman's or pies, or those offering innovative bar or restaurant food, are all in the running. In keeping with recent trends in pub food, we are keen to include those where particular emphasis is placed on imaginative modern dishes and those specialising in fresh fish. Occasionally we include pubs that serve no food, or just snacks, but are very special in other ways.

That Special Place

We look for pubs that offer something special: pubs where the time-honoured values of a convivial environment for conversation while supping or eating have not been forgotten. They may be attractive, interesting, unusual or in a good location. Some may be very much a local pub or they may draw customers from further afield, while others may be included because they are in an exceptional place. Interesting towns and villages, eccentric or historic buildings, and rare settings can all be found within this guide.

Pick of the Pubs & Full Page Entries

Some of the pubs included in the guide are particularly special, and we have highlighted these as Pick of the Pubs. For 2008 over 700 pubs have been selected by the personal knowledge of our editorial team, our AA inspectors, and suggestions from our readers. These pubs have a coloured panel and a more detailed description. From these, around 250 have chosen to enhance their entry in the 2008 Guide by purchasing two photographs as part of a full-page entry.

Smoking Regulations

A law banning smoking in public places came into force in July 2007. This covers all establishments in this guide. Some pubs provide a private area in, for example an outbuilding, for smokers. If the freedom to smoke is important to you, we recommend that you check with the pub when you book.

Walks and Cycle Rides

What could be more fun than to start or end a pub lunch with a walk or cycle ride through attractive countryside? Appetites can be whetted, and large meals worked off with some suitably pleasant exercise when you take advantage of the 10 walks and 10 rides attached to pubs in this Guide.

Tell us what you think

We welcome your feedback about the pubs included and about the guide itself.
We are also delighted to receive suggestions about good pubs you have visited and loved. Reader Report forms appear at the back of the book, so please write in or e-mail us at lifestyleguides@theAA.com to help us improve future editions. The pubs also feature on the AA website, www.theAA.com, along with our inspected restaurants, hotels and bed & breakfast accommodation.

Beer Festivals

On the Hop – a Celebration

Beer festivals, or their equivalent, are as old as the hills. The brewing of hops goes back to the beginning of human civilisation, and the combination of common crop and a fermenting process that results in alcoholic liquid has long been a cause of celebration. Beer festivals officially began in Germany with the first Munich Oktoberfest in 1810, although the history of beer and the celebration of the hop is probably nearly as old as human civilisation. Wherever in the world beer is brewed, today and for the last few millennia, admirers, enthusiasts, aficionados – call them what you will – have gathered together to sample and praise its unique properties. It happens throughout Europe, in Australia and New Zealand, and in America and Canada, and annual events are held in pubs all over Britain.

Beer festivals are often occasions for the whole family, when entertainment is laid on for children as well as adults. Summer is naturally a popular season for festivals, when the action can be taken outdoors. Other festivals are held in October, traditionally harvest time, but they can be at any time of the year. They can be large and well-advertised gatherings that attract a wide following for sometimes several days of unselfconscious consumption of unusual or award-winning ales; or they might be local but none the less enthusiastic get-togethers of neighbourhood or pub micro-breweries.

We list here a selection of pubs that appear in this guide, that hold usually annual beer festivals. For up-to-date information, please check directly with the pub. We would love to hear from our readers about their favourite beer festivals.
E-mail us at **lifestyleguides@theAA.com**

Bhurtpore Inn, Aston, Cheshire 01270 780917. Mid July. Last year 121 different beers, many from microbreweries.

The Burnmoor Inn, Boot, Cumbria 019467 23224. and Brook House Inn, Boot, Cumbria. 019467 23160. Joint beer festival held over three days in June. More than 70 real ales to sample, along with a barbecue, fish supper and black pudding bonanza.

Eagle & Child, Staveley, Cumbria 01539 821320. Gurning, hog roast, live music

The Queens Head Inn, Tirril, Cumbria 01768 863219. The Tirril Brewery's output, and other locally brewed beers, can be tasted at the annual beer and sausage festival held in August.

Wasdale Head Inn, Wasdale Head, Cumbria 019467 26229. Large numbers descend on this old drovers' inn twice a year

The Royal Hotel, Hayfield, Derbys 01663 741721. A full entertainment programme and 50 cask ales is the reward for anyone visiting the beer festival here in the second week of October.

Mildmay Colours Inn, Plymouth, Devon 01752 830248. Barrel-rolling contests are all part of the fun at the August BH weekend.

Greyhound, Corfe Castle, Dorset 01929 480205. The May BH festival involves around 50 real ales and ciders, a hog roast, a barbecue and a seafood buffet.

The Bankes Arms Hotel, Studland, Dorset 01929 450225. Morris dancing, stone carving, and a great selection of around 60 real ales.

The Hoop, Stock, Essex 01277 841137. The late Spring BH is at the centre of ten days of celebrations here, with 120 ales and ciders. Hog roast and barbecue.

The Boat Inn, Ashleworth, Glos 01452 700272. Visitors to the annual summer beer festival can choose from more than 30 different breweries

Red Shoot Inn, Linwood, Hants 01425 475792. Festivals held twice a year in April and October.

Cartwheel Inn, Whitsbury, Hants 01725 518362. The August festival includes Morris dancers, a spit-roasted pig, a barbecues and around 30 real ales.

Swan in the Rushes, Loughborough, Leicestershire 01509 217014. Two annual festivals

Cow and Plough, Oadby, Leics 0116 272 0852. The Cow & Plough hosts beer festivals and also brews its own Steamin' Billy beers.

The Victoria, Lincoln 01522 536048. Two festivals

Junction Tavern, London NW5. August BH. The pub holds regular beer festivals, with a range of 40-plus ales served straight from the cask.

Hill House, Happisburgh, Norfolk 01692 650004. Summer solstice beer festival each June, with the chance to sample over forty real ales.

Angel Inn, Larling, Norfolk 01953 717963. August. Campsite, beers from all over the country

The White Hart, Fyfield, Oxfordshire 01865 390585. Two festivals every year (May Day and August BH weekends) with at least 12 real ales, live jazz and hog roasts.

The White Horse, Petersfield 01420 588387. 3-day festival in mid- June. Bouncy castle

Sun Inn, Craven Arms, Shropshire 01584 861239. Easter & August BH

The Inn at Kippen, Kippen, Stirling 01786 871010. A small beer festival with hog roast in Aug or Sep.

The Surrey Oaks, Newdigate, Surrey 01306 631200. The late Spring BH is the time for visiting this pub, and sampling around 20 real ales and ciders.

Rose Cottage Inn, Alciston, East Sussex 01323 870377.

Kings Arms, Fernhurst, West Sussex 01428 652005. 3 days over late August BH.

The Owl, Little Cheverell, Wiltshire 01380 812263. Festivals have been held for around 12 years during June. Bouncy castle and occasional entertainer for children, with a band or singer in the later for adults.

Smoking Dog, Malmesbury, Wiltshire 01666 825823. Last weekend in May.

The Bridge Inn, West Lavington, Wilts 01380 813213. Charity Beer Festival over the August BH weekend.

Waterfront Inn, Doncaster, South Yorkshire 01427 891223. May festival.

England

Rydal Water, Lake District, Cumbria

England

BEDFORDSHIRE

BEDFORD MAP 12 TL04

Pick of the Pubs

Knife & Cleaver Inn ★★★★ INN

The Grove, Houghton Conquest MK45 3LA

☎ 01234 740387 01234 740900

e-mail: info@knifeandcleaver.com

dir: *5m S of Bedford off A6 (follow brown tourist board sign). 11m from M1 junct 12/13*

This friendly 17th-century free house is located opposite the medieval church of All Saints, Bedfordshire's largest parish church. Its many historic associations include the Jacobean oak panelling in the lounge bar, which came from nearby Houghton House, formerly the home of the Conquest family, who gave their name to the village. Light meals and hand-drawn ales are served in the bar, where leather sofas and winter log fires bring a welcome comfort. The conservatory restaurant specialises in fresh seafood, as well as a varied choice of meat and vegetarian dishes. In summer, meals are also served in the attractive cottage-style garden. Start, perhaps, with smoked haddock and leek chowder; or rabbit terrine with celeriac and carrot remoulade and toasted baguette. Main courses might include pastry-wrapped organic Scottish salmon fillet with dill butter, asparagus and pea purée; or prime pork sausages with creamy horseradish mash and red wine gravy.

Open 12-2.30 7-11 Closed: 27-30 Dec **Bar Meals** L served Mon-Fri 12-2.30 D served Mon-Fri 7-9.30 (Sat 12-2, 7-9.30 & Sun 12-2.30 only) Av main course £7.25 **Restaurant** L served Sun-Fri 12-2.30 D served Mon-Sat 7-9.30 Av 3 course à la carte £25 Av 3 course fixed price £22.50 Free House Batemans XB & Village Bike-Potton Brewery. 29 **Facilities** Garden Dogs allowed Parking **Rooms** 9 bedrooms en suite S£59 D£59

The Three Tuns

57 Main Rd, Biddenham MK40 4BD ☎ 01234 354847

e-mail: thethreetuns@btinternet.com

dir: *On A428 from Bedford towards Northampton take 1st right signed Biddenham. Into village, pub on right*

A thatched village pub with a large garden, a play area, and reputedly, a ghost. It has a friendly atmosphere, and is popular for its wide-ranging bar menu. Choose from sandwiches and snacks or popular main courses like burgers, seafood platter, and steaks with fries. There's also a range of home-made dishes such as the steak and kidney pie, curry of the day, seafood platter, steak in red wine, and peppered pork. Children's meals are also available.

Open 11-2.30 6-11 (Sun 12-3, 7-10.30) **Bar Meals** L served all week 12-2 D served Mon-Sat 6-9 Av main course £8.50 **Restaurant** L served all week 12-2 D served Mon-Sat 6-9 Greene King Greene King IPA, Abbot Ale. **Facilities** Garden Dogs allowed Parking Play Area

BLETSOE MAP 11 TL05

Pick of the Pubs

The Falcon

Rushden Rd MK44 1QN

☎ 01234 781222 01234 781222

e-mail: thefalcona6@aol.com

dir: *9m from M1 junct 13, 3m from Bedford*

See Pick of the Pubs on opposite page

BOLNHURST MAP 12 TL05

Pick of the Pubs

The Plough at Bolnhurst NEW

Kimbolton Rd MK44 2EX ☎ 01234 376274

e-mail: theplough@bolnhurst.com

dir: *On B660 N of Bedford*

The Plough is an attractive medieval building set back from the B660 in the village of Bolnhurst, five miles from Bedford. Jayne and Martin Lee took over here three years ago, bringing with them some considerable experience, having managed the Pheasant at Keystone and the Old Bridge in Huntingdon. Martin trained with top chefs Raymond Blanc, Paul Heathcote and Marc Veyrat and uses his skills to produce good value modern British dishes from carefully sourced ingredients. Fish is bought daily from day boats through Channel Fisheries, venison comes from the Denham Estate in Suffolk, chicken and ducks are from Goosnargh where the Lees used to live, and vegetables are locally grown. Typical dishes are Portland crab risotto; and roast duck with rôsti potato, bok choy and spring onion. Three real ales are kept, with Batemans XB as a regular bitter alongside featured beers such as local brew Village Bike.

Open 12-3 6.30-12 (Closed Sun eve) Closed: New Year & 2wks Jan **Bar Meals** L served Tue-Sat 12-2 D served Tue-Sat 6.30-9.30 (Sun 12-2.30) Av main course £12.50 **Restaurant** L served Tue-Sat 12-2 D served Tue-Sat 6.30-9.30 (Sun 12-2.30) Av 3 course à la carte £25 Av 3 course fixed price £16 Free House Adnams Broadside, Nethergate Azzanewt, Batemans XB, Village Bike Potton. 12 **Facilities** Children's licence Garden Dogs allowed Parking

BROOM MAP 12 TL14

The Cock

23 High St SG18 9NA ☎ 01767 314411 01767 314284

dir: *Off B658 SW of Biggleswade. 1m from A1*

Unspoilt to this day with its intimate quarry-tiled rooms with latched doors and panelled walls, this 17th-century establishment is known as 'The Pub with no Bar'. Real ales are served straight from casks racked by the cellar steps. A straightforward pub grub menu includes jumbo cod, roast chicken, gammon steak, breaded lobster, and breast of Cajun chicken. There is a camping and caravan site at the rear of the pub.

Open 12-3 6-11 (Sat 12-4, Sun 12-4) **Bar Meals** L served all week 12-2.30 D served Mon-Sat 7-9 **Restaurant** L served all week 12-2.30 D served Mon-Sat 7-9.30 (Sun 12-2.30) Av 3 course à la carte £16 Greene King Greene King Abbot Ale, IPA & Ruddles County. **Facilities** Garden Dogs allowed Parking Play Area

The Falcon

The Falcon is set in the rolling countryside of north Bedfordshire with easy access from the A6, making it a popular destination for customers from far and wide. The 17th-century coaching inn is a great place to visit at any time of the year, with welcoming log fires in winter, and a beautiful beer garden and terrace for summer dining.

Step into the relaxed ambience of the traditional country inn and you'll find an inglenook fireplace, lots of oak beams and dark wood panelling in the dining room.
As you might expect at such a venerable hostelry, there's at least one resident ghost, as well as a secret tunnel leading to nearby Bletsoe Castle. To the rear of the building, a large dining terrace overlooks mature gardens leading down to the River Great Ouse.
At lunchtime Falcon favourites include steak ciabatta and chicken Caesar wrap. There's also a choice of sandwiches, ploughman's and salads in a bowl, such as mozzarella, tomato and fresh basil, or poached salmon and crayfish with sweet chilli sauce. The main menu offers an extensive list of pub fare – fish cakes, pasta, Thai curry, steak and kidney pie – plus steaks and burgers from the grill. The Friday fish menu provides some unusual options, like pangasius fillets (a delicious white fish from Vietnam) served with prawn and mustard cream sauce; or baked Nile perch supreme topped with a pesto and parmesan crust. Further interest is inspired by the daily chef's specials, with the likes of grilled lemon sole, roast leg of lamb, or baked courgettes stuffed with Mediterranean vegetables and rice.

MAP 11 TL05
Rushden Rd MK44 1QN
☎ 01234 781222
01234 781222
e-mail: thefalcona6@aol.com
dir: *9m from M1 junct 13, 3m from Bedford*

Open 12-3 6-11 (Fri Summer, Sat 12-11, Sun 12-10.30)
Bar Meals L served all week 12-2.15 D served all week 6-9.15 Av main course £10.50
Restaurant L served all week 12-2.15 D served all week 6.30-9.15 Av 3 course à la carte £18.50
Charles Wells
Charles Wells Bombardier, Charles Wells Eagle, Fosters, Red Stripe. 13
Facilities Garden Parking

England

EATON BRAY MAP 11 SP92

The White Horse 🍷

Market Square LU6 2DG

☎ 01525 220231 📠 01525 222485

dir: *Take A5 N of Dunstable then A5050, 1m turn left & follow signs*

For almost 20 years, David and Janet Sparrow have built their reputation on great home cooked food at this traditional 300-year-old village inn. Choose from a seasonally changing menu that might include braised lamb shank; or goat's cheese on cherry tomato and rocket salad. In addition, the daily specials menu includes a choice of fresh fish dishes. It's worth booking for the restaurant, but the same menu is also available in the bar.

Open 11.30–3 6.30–11 (Fri–Sat 6.30–11.30) (Sun 12–3, 7–11) **Bar Meals** L served all week 12–2.15 D served all week 7–9.15 (Sun 7–9) Av main course £9.50 **Restaurant** L served all week 12–2.15 D served all week 7.30–9.15 (Sun 7.30–9) Av 3 course à la carte £18 Punch Taverns Greene King IPA, Shepherd Neame Spitfire, Tetley's. 🍷 8 **Facilities** Garden Parking Play Area

HARROLD MAP 11 SP95

Pick of the Pubs

The Muntjac ★★★ INN 🍷

71 High St MK43 7BJ ☎ 01234 721500

e-mail: russell@themuntjac.co.uk

Located on the borders of three shires – Bedfordshire, Buckinghamshire and Northamptonshire – the Muntjac is a 17th-century coaching inn in a picturesque village. Head chef Gary Robbins creates a menu of contemporary dishes that reflect his desire to experiment with new ideas, flavours and presentation. He prefers to offer lighter, fish-based dishes in the summer, and the likes of casseroles in the winter. A bar menu includes pick-and-mix tapas-style snacks. On the lunch menu look for moules marinière with crusty ciabattas; chargrilled Cajun chicken with spicy potato wedges and sour cream; and toasted filled paninis. The main carte offers monkfish, bacon and pea casserole with basmati and wild rice; pan-fried pork fillet with roast apple and red cabbage coleslaw; and spiced butternut squash risotto with mascarpone. Desserts include the chef's trademark crème brûlée.

Open 12–2.30 5.30–11 (Thu 12–3) (Fri*/Sat*/Sun 12–11, *Occ close at 3) Closed: 25-Dec **Bar Meals** L served Tue–Sun 12–2.30 D served Tue–Sat 6–9 (Sun 12–5) Av main course £7.95 **Restaurant** L served Tue–Sun 12–2.30 D served Tue–Sat 7–9 (Sun 12–3, Fri/Sat food untill 9.30) Av 3 course à la carte £25 Free House Bill Suttons Best Bitter, John Smith's Extra Smooth, Thwaites Thoroughbred & Village Bike (Potton Brewery). 🍷 7 **Facilities** Garden Parking

KEYSOE MAP 12 TL06

The Chequers

Pertenhall Rd, Brook End MK44 2HR

☎ 01234 708678 📠 01234 708678

e-mail: chequers.keysoe@tesco.net

dir: *On B660, 7m N of Bedford. 3m S of Kimbolton*

This peaceful 15th-century country pub has been in the same safe hands for over 25 years. No games machines, pool tables or jukeboxes disturb the simple pleasures of well-kept ales and tasty home-made food. The menu offers pub stalwarts like soup, steaks, and chicken curry, but also includes more adventurous options such as pan-fried trout with a sauce of Noilly Prat, almonds and cream. There are enough children's favourites to keep them happy too.

Open 11.30–2.30 6.30–11 **Bar Meals** L served Wed–Mon 12–2 D served Wed–Mon 7–9.45 Free House Hook Norton Best, Fuller's London Pride. **Facilities** Garden Parking Play Area **Notes**

LINSLADE MAP 11 SP92

The Globe Inn 🍷

Globe Ln, Old Linslade LU7 2TA

☎ 01525 373338 📠 01525 850551

dir: *A5 S to Dunstable, follow signs to Leighton Buzzard (A4146)*

Standing on the banks of the Grand Union Canal, this friendly inn was first licensed in 1830 to serve passing canal boats. Candles and open fires set the scene for winter evenings, and there's a large garden with children's play area for warmer days. Pub favourites range from traditional fish and chips to steak and kidney pudding, whilst restaurant diners can expect mushroom ravioli; moules marinière; and slow-roast lamb shank.

Open 11–11 (Sun 11–10.30) **Bar Meals** L served all week 12–9 D served all week 12–9 (Sun 11–8) Av main course £8 **Restaurant** L served all week 12–3 D served all week 6–9 (Sun 12–9) Av 3 course à la carte £20 Greene King Greene King Abbott Ale, Old Speckled Hen, IPA & Ruddles County Ale, Hook Norton. 🍷 16 **Facilities** Garden Dogs allowed Parking Play Area

Hare and Hounds

A traditional country pub on the Shuttleworth estate, with a warm and friendly atmosphere, near Old Warden aerodrome, home of a unique collection of aeroplanes spanning the first century of flight.

As you walk towards the pub, look up at the attractive carved bargeboarding under the projecting gables. Depending on the weather, once inside you may be greeted by the warmth from the two log fires as you head either for the bar, or one of the four separate eating areas – an indication of how seriously they take their fresh, home-cooked food here. The varied menu offers an ever-changing selection of dishes, backed by well-regarded beers from Bedfordshire's Charles Wells and Suffolk's Adnams breweries. Starter possibilities include smoked salmon risotto with crème fraîche; baked camembert with walnut toast and cranberry sauce; and chicken liver paté. Among the reasonably priced main courses are Scottish sirloin steak with pepper butter, vine tomato and red onion, rocket and basil salad; braised wild rabbit in puff pastry with shallots, wholegrain mustard and tarragon sauce; roasted sea bass with herb salad and hand-cut chips; and gnocchi with butternut squash and pine nuts. If there's pork, it has probably come from the Shuttleworth estate. During the summer fresh fish nights take place on Thursdays. Choices in the bar include sausage and mash, haddock and chips, and salmon with Caesar salad. For dessert there may be tarte tatin, caramelised lemon tart, and chocolate mousse, or one of an interesting selection of cheeses, including stilton from Nottinghamshire, and Gubbeens from Co Cork. Wines from around the world include some from the local Warden Abbey vineyard. On warmer days, enjoy the super views from the garden and patio area.

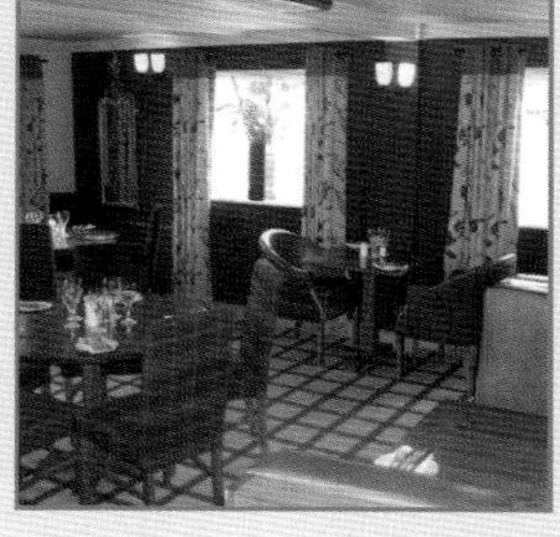

MAP 12 TL14
SG18 9HQ
☎ 01767 627225
01767 627209
dir: *From Bedford turn right off A603 (or left from A600) to Old Warden. Also accessed from Biggleswade rdbt on A1*

Open 12–3 6–11
Bar Meals L served Tue–Sun 12–2 D served Tue–Sat 6.30–9.30
Restaurant L served Tue–Sun 12–2 D served Tue–Sat 6.30–9.30
Charles Wells
Wells Bomdardier Premium & Eagle IPA, Adnams. 8
Facilities Garden Parking

MILTON BRYAN MAP 11 SP93

The Red Lion

Toddington Rd, South End MK17 9HS ☎ 01525 210044
e-mail: paul@redlion-miltonbryan.co.uk

Set in a pretty village near Woburn Abbey, this attractive brick-built pub is festooned with dazzling hanging baskets in the summer months. Comfortable, neatly maintained interior, with beams, rugs on wooden floors, and well-kept ales. Wide-ranging menu offering the likes of roast rump of lamb with potato purée, wilted spinach and ratatouille sauce; supreme of chicken stuffed with ricotta cheese, basil and Parma ham on wild rocket and roasted cherry tomato; and baked Cornish cod.

Open 11.30-3 6-11 Closed: 25-26 Dec, 1 Jan **Bar Meals** L served all week 12-2.30 D served Tue-Sat 7-9.30 Greene King Greene King IPA, Old Speckled Hen, Abbot Ale, plus Guest beers. 7 **Facilities** Garden Parking

NORTHILL MAP 12 TL14

The Crown

2 Ickwell Rd SG18 9AA ☎ 01767 627337 01767 627279
e-mail: info@thecrown-northill.com
dir: *Telephone for directions*

A delightful 16th-century pub with chocolate box setting in an acre of garden between Northill church and the village duck pond. The grounds include a children's play area, heated patio, wooden gazebos and lighting. Inside, the unique copper-covered bar leads to an informal dining area, where the bar menu of pub favourites applies. The candlelit split-level restaurant boasts much locally-sourced produce served in home-cooked dishes such as spicy citrus scallops, Cumberland sausages, and Caribbean pork steak.

Open 11.30-3 6-11 (Fri-Sat 6-12, Summer: all day Sat-Sun) Closed: 25 Dec eve **Bar Meals** L served all week 12-3 D served Mon-Sat 6.30-9.30 Av main course £11.95 **Restaurant** L served all week 12-2.30 D served all week 6.30-9.30 Greene King Greene King IPA, Abbot Ale, Old Speckled Hen, Olde Tripplus & Guest ales. 8 **Facilities** Garden Dogs allowed Parking Play Area

ODELL MAP 11 SP95

The Bell

Horsefair Ln MK43 7AU ☎ 01234 720254

A Grade II listed 16th-century thatched pub, refurbished throughout. There is a patio and aviary outside, next to a spacious garden leading down to the River Ouse. The lunch menu offers a wide choice of sandwiches, baguettes, filled jacket potatoes and light options also suitable for children. The main menu is also available at lunch or dinner, and features the likes of poached fillet of salmon with white wine sauce; home-made steak and Abbott pie, and mushroom stroganoff.

Open 11-3 6-11 (Sun 12-2.30, 7-10.30) **Bar Meals** L served all week 12-2 D served Tue-Sat 7-9 Av main course £7 **Restaurant** 12-2 6.30-9 Greene King Greene King IPA, Abbot Ale, Ruddles County & seasonal beers. 6 **Facilities** Garden Parking

OLD WARDEN MAP 12 TL14

Pick of the Pubs

Hare and Hounds

SG18 9HQ ☎ 01767 627225 01767 627209
dir: *From Bedford turn right off A603 (or left from A600) to Old Warden. Also accessed from Biggleswade rdbt on A1*

See Pick of the Pubs on page 19

SHEFFORD MAP 12 TL13

The Black Horse

Ireland SG17 5QL ☎ 01462 811398 01462 817238
e-mail: countrytaverns@aol.com
dir: *From S: M1 junct 12, A5120 to Flitwick. Onto A507 by Redbourne School. Follow signs for A1, Shefford (cross A6). Left onto A600 towards Bedford*

This traditional pub is set in a lovely garden surrounded by peaceful countryside. The name of the tiny hamlet is thought to be derived from the Irish navvies who built the local railway line in the 1850s. The memorable menu draws a devoted following, with imaginative meals that might include leg of lamb roasted with garlic and thyme; locally farmed pork loin with prune and apple sauce; and fillet of sea bass with warm fennel and red onion salad.

Open 11.30-3 6-11 (Sun 12-6) Closed: 25-26 Dec, 1 Jan
Bar Meals L served all week 12-2.30 D served Mon-Sat 6.30-10 (Sun 12-5) **Restaurant** L served all week 12-2.30 D served Mon-Sat 6.30-10 (Sun 12-5) Av 3 course à la carte £22.95 Av 3 course fixed price £25.95 Green King IPA, London Pride, Village Bike, Stella & Carling Black Label. 14 **Facilities** Garden Parking

SOUTHILL MAP 12 TL14

The White Horse 🍷

High St SG18 9LD ☎ 01462 813364
e-mail: jack@ravenathexton.f9.co.uk

A village pub retaining traditional values, yet happily accommodating the needs of children and those who like sitting outside on cool days (the patio has heaters). Locally renowned for its chargrilled steaks from the Duke of Buccleuch's Scottish estate. Other main courses include Cajun chicken, chargrilled pork loin steaks, Whitby Bay scampi, and stuffed breaded plaice. Greene King beers, with London Pride up from Chiswick. Old Warden Park and its Shuttleworth Collection of old planes is nearby.

Open 11–3 6–11 (Sun 12–10.30, all day BH's) **Bar Meals** L served all week 12–2 D served all week 6–9 (Sun 12–9, Wed–Sat dinner 6–10) Enterprise Inns Greene King IPA, London Pride, Speckled Hen, Flowers. 🍷 22 **Facilities** Garden Parking Play Area

STANBRIDGE MAP 11 SP92

Pick of the Pubs

The Five Bells 🍷

Station Rd, Stanbridge LU7 9JF
☎ 01525 210224 📠 01525 211164
dir: *Off A505 E of Leighton Buzzard*

A stylish and relaxing setting for a drink or a meal is offered by this white-painted 400-year-old village inn, which has been delightfully renovated and revived. The bar features lots of bare wood as well as comfortable armchairs and polished, rug-strewn floors. The modern decor extends to the bright, airy 75-cover dining room. There's also a spacious garden with patio and lawns. The inn offers bar meals, set menus and a carte choice for diners. The bar menu typically includes dishes such as smoked chicken, sun-dried tomato and pine nut salad; battered fish, chips and mushy peas; baked courgettes stuffed with goat's cheese and mint with a mixed salad; rib-eye steak with fries; and chicken, ham, leek and mushroom pie.

Open 12–9.30 (Sun 12–9) **Bar Meals** L served all week 12–9.30 D served all week Av main course £7.50 Traditional Free House Greene King IPA, Timothy Taylors Landlord, London Pride. 🍷 8 **Facilities** Garden Dogs allowed Parking Play Area

SUTTON MAP 12 TL24

John O'Gaunt Inn 🍷

30 High St SG19 2NE ☎ 01767 260377
dir: *Off B1040 between Biggleswade & Potton*

Situated in one of Bedfordshire's most picturesque villages, the John O'Gaunt is a traditional village inn where a guest ale features alongside the regular beers supplied in rotation from various breweries. Piped music is notable by its absence, though you may be encouraged to join in the occasional informal folk music sessions. The pub offers a large garden, and welcoming winter fires. A wide choice of good food is available most lunchtimes and evenings.

Open 12–3 7–11.30 **Bar Meals** L served all week 12–2 D served Mon–Sat 7–9 Admiral Taverns Rotating Real Ales. 🍷 8 **Facilities** Garden Dogs allowed Parking Play Area **Notes**

TILSWORTH MAP 11 SP92

The Anchor Inn 🍷

1 Dunstable Rd LU7 9PU
☎ 01525 210289 📠 01525 211578
e-mail: tonyanchorinn@aol.com

The only pub in a Saxon village, the Anchor dates from 1878. The restaurant is a recent addition to the side of the pub, and the whole building has been refurbished. The licensees pride themselves on their fresh food and well-kept ales. Hand-cut steaks are particularly popular (they buy the meat at Smithfield, butcher it and hang it themselves). An acre of garden includes patio seating, an adventure playground and a barbecue.

Open 12–11 **Bar Meals** L served all week 12–2.30 D served Mon–Sat 6–10 (Sun 12–7) Av main course £9 **Restaurant** L served all week 12–2.30 D served Mon–Sat 6–10 (Sun 12–7) Av 3 course à la carte £25 Greene King Green King IPA, Abbot Ale, Wadworth 6X, Guest Beers. 🍷 12 **Facilities** Garden Parking Play Area

BERKSHIRE

ALDERMASTON MAP 05 SU56

Hinds Head

Wasing Ln RG7 4LX ☎ 0118 971 2194 📠 0118 971 4511
e-mail: hindshead@accommodating-inns.co.uk
dir: *A4 towards Newbury, then left on A340 towards Basingstoke, 2m to village*

This 17th-century inn with its distinctive clock and bell tower still incorporates the village lock-up, which was last used in 1865. The former brew house behind the pub has been refurbished to create an additional dining area. Menu choices range from jacket potatoes and filled baguettes to whole baked sea bass; carbonara pasta; and cauliflower cheese.

Open 11.30–2.30 5–11 (Sat 11.30–2.30, 6–11 Sun 12–3, 7–10.30) **Bar Meals** L served all week 12–2 D served all week 6.30–9 (Sun 12–2, 7–9) Av main course £7.95 **Restaurant** L served all week 12–2 D served all week 6.30–9.30 Fullers Gales Best, HSB. **Facilities** Garden Parking

England

ALDWORTH MAP 05 SU57

Pick of the Pubs

The Bell Inn

RG8 9SE ☎ 01635 578272

dir: *Just off B4009 (Newbury-Streatley road)*

One might be surprised to discover that an establishment offering no meals at all can hold its own in a world of smart dining pubs and modish gastropubs. Well, be surprised. The Bell not only survives, it positively prospers and, to be fair, it does serve some food, if only hot, crusty, generously filled rolls. And since it is one of the few truly unspoiled country pubs left, and serves cracking pints of Arkell's, West Berkshire and guest real ales, this alimentary limitation has been no disadvantage. The Bell is old, very old, beginning life in 1340 as a five-bay cruck-built manor hall. It has reputedly been in the same family for 200 years: ask Mr Macaulay, the landlord – he's been here for thirty of them, and he has no plans to change it from the time warp it is. A 300-year-old, one-handed clock still stands in the taproom, and the rack for the spit-irons and clockwork roasting jack are still over the fireplace. Taller customers may bump their heads at the glass-panelled bar hatch.

Open 11-3 6-11 (Sun/Good Fri 12-3, 7-10.30) Closed: 25 Dec **Bar Meals** L served Tue-Sun 11-2.30 D served Tue-Sun 6-10.30 Free House Arkell's Kingsdown, 3B, West Berkshire Old Tyler & Maggs Magnificent Mild, Guest Beer. **Facilities** Garden Dogs allowed Parking **Notes**

ASCOT MAP 06 SU96

The Thatched Tavern

Cheapside Rd SL5 7QG ☎ 01344 620874 01344 623043

e-mail: thethatchedtaverns@4cinns.co.uk

dir: *Follow Ascot Racecourse signs. Through Ascot 1st left (Cheapside). 1.5m, pub on left*

Just a mile from the racecourse, a 17th-century building of original beams, flagstone floors and very low ceilings. In summer the sheltered garden makes a fine spot to enjoy real ales and varied choice of food. In the same safe hands for over ten years, the kitchen produces dishes like pan-fried chicken breast with cheddar mash, black pudding, Muscat and thyme sauce, seared calves' liver on bubble and squeak and steak and kidney pudding with mustard mash.

Open 12-3 5.30-11 (Fri-Sun open all day) **Bar Meals** L served all week 12-3 D served all week 7-10 (Sun 12-3, 7-9) Av main course £8 **Restaurant** L served all week 12-3 D served all week 7-10 (Sun 12-3, 7-9) Av 3 course à la carte £25 Free House Fuller's London Pride, IPA. 8 **Facilities** Garden Parking

ASHMORE GREEN MAP 05 SU56

The Sun in the Wood

Stoney Ln RG18 9HF ☎ 01635 42377 01635 528392

e-mail: suninthewood@aol.com

dir: *From A34 at Robin Hood Rdbt left to Shaw, at mini-rdbt right then 7th left into Stoney Ln 1.5m, pub on left*

This family-friendly refurbished pub occupies a delightful woodland setting only a stone's throw from Newbury's centre. Stone floors and plenty of wood panelling within, and swings, slides, climbing frame and crazy golf outside for children. Sample a pint of Wadworth's or one of 17 wines by the glass while choosing starters like three slices of hot garlic bread topped with mozzarella, and mains of duck, lamb, pork, beef or chicken cooked with today's European flavours.

Open 12-2.30 6-11 **Bar Meals** L served Tue-Sun 12-2 D served Tue-Sat 6-9.30 Av main course £11.50 **Restaurant** L served Tue-Sun 12-2 D served Tue-Sat 6-9.30 Av 3 course à la carte £20 Wadworth Wadworth 6X & Henrys Original IPA, Badger Tanglefoot. 17 **Facilities** Garden Parking Play Area

BOXFORD MAP 05 SU47

The Bell at Boxford

Lambourn Rd RG20 8DD

☎ 01488 608721 01488 608749

e-mail: paul@bellatboxford.com

dir: *A338 toward Wantage, right onto B4000, take 3rd left to Boxford*

Mock Tudor country pub at the heart of the glorious Lambourn Valley, noted for its pretty villages and sweeping Downland scenery. Cosy log fires add to the appeal in winter, and the patio is popular throughout the year with its array of flowers and outdoor heating, hog roasts, barbecues and parties. Starters range from baked goats' cheese to oriental tiger prawns, while main courses might include sea bass with wild mushrooms, and poached hake with lobster sauce.

Open 11-3 6-11 (Sat 6.30-11, Sun 7-10.30) **Bar Meals** L served all week 12-2 D served all week 7-10 (Sun 12-3, 7-9) **Restaurant** L served all week 12-2 D served all week 7-10 Free House Interbrew Bass, Scottish Courage, Courage Best, Wadworth 6X, Henrys IPA. 60 **Facilities** Garden Dogs allowed Parking

See advertisement under NEWBURY

BRAY MAP 06 SU97

Pick of the Pubs

Hind's Head Hotel NEW

High St SL6 2AB ☎ 01628 626151 01628 623394

e-mail: info@hindsheadhotel.co.uk

See Pick of the Pubs on opposite page

Hind's Head Hotel

The Hinds Head was built in the 15th century, though its original purpose has been lost in rumour and hearsay. It may have been a royal hunting lodge, or perhaps a guesthouse for the local Abbot of Cirencester.

Whatever its origins, as a much-loved village tavern, The Hinds Head has been at the heart of life in Bray for over 400 years. It's had an illustrious cast of customers over the centuries, hosting the engagement party of Princess Margaret and Lord Snowdon, as well as the stag night of Prince Philip. In recent years, the pub has been taken over by the celebrity chef Heston Blumenthal, who also owns the famous Fat Duck, just over the street. The interior has everything you'd expect from a traditional English inn, from sturdy oak panelling and beams to leather chairs and crackling fires. The short, inviting menu presents an equally alluring sense of days gone by. Blumenthal has been working with staff at the Tudor Kitchens at Hampton Court Palace to create a range of traditional British dishes, some lost from menus for over 500 years. Sample starters include rabbit and bacon terrine with cucumber pickles; potted shrimp; and soused herrings with beetroot and horseradish. Main courses are equally simple and hearty: oxtail and kidney pudding; Lancashire hotpot; or Gloucester Old Spot pork chop with pease pudding. Snacks include such recherché pleasures as devils on horseback or Scotch quail egg, while for dessert you could try banana Eton Mess, or the delightfully named quaking pudding. The pea and ham soup is justifiably famous, the perfect partner to a pint of Marlow Rebellion or Abbot Ale.

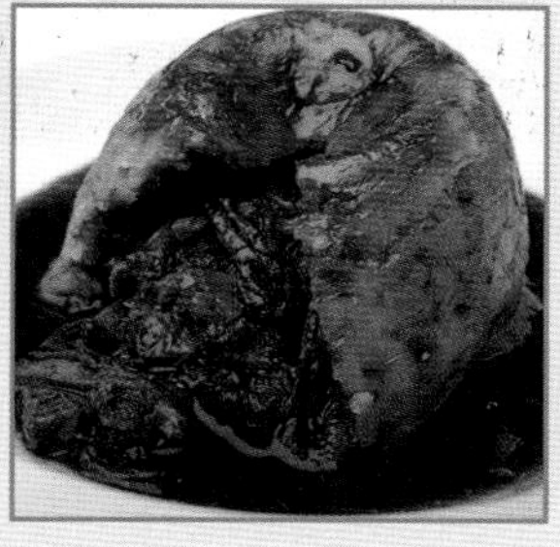

NEW

MAP 06 SU97

High St SL6 2AB

☎ 01628 626151

01628 623394

e-mail:

info@hindsheadhotel.co.uk

Open 11–11 Closed: 25–26 Dec

Bar Meals L served all week 12–2.30 (Sun 12–3) D served all week 6.30–9.30

Restaurant L served all week 12–2.30 (Sun 12–4) D served Mon–Sat 6.30–9.30 Av 3 course à la carte £25

Free House

Greene King IPA, Greene King Abbot Ale, Marlow Rebellion, Amstel. 8

Facilities Parking

England

BURCHETT'S GREEN MAP 05 SU88

The Crown

SL6 6QZ ☎ 01628 822844
e-mail: admin@thecrownatburchettsgreen.co.uk
dir: *From M4 take A404(M), then 3rd exit*

Set amid a large rose garden overlooking the village green, this popular local has a welcoming interior with low-beamed ceilings, striking whitewashed walls and a restaurant. Head chef Michael Field uses local and organic ingredients to produce fresh, unfussy dishes including pan-fried pork chop with creamed parmesan leeks and mashed potato; traditional battered haddock and French fries; and roasted red pepper, sunblushed tomato and leek risotto.

Open 12–2.30 6.30–11 **Bar Meals** L served Tue–Sun 12–2.30 D served Tue–Sat 6.30–9.30 **Restaurant** L served Tue–Sun 12–2.30 D served Tue–Sat 6.30–9.30 Greene King Greene King IPA, Ruddles Best. 10 **Facilities** Garden Parking

See advert on opposite page

CHADDLEWORTH MAP 05 SU47

The Ibex

Main St RG20 7ER ☎ 01488 638311 01488 639458
dir: *A338 towards Wantage, through Great Shefford then right, then 2nd left, pub on right in village*

Originally two cottages forming part of a 17th-century farm, this Grade II listed building was later used as a bakery and then an off-licence before eventually becoming a pub. In more recent years it was run by ex-jockey Colin Brown who partnered the legendary Desert Orchid for many years, and kept the cosy lounge bar with low ceilings and bench seats. Popular bar menu includes chicken and leek pie; beef and ale casserole; liver and onions; and halibut with red wine and wild mushrooms.

Open 11–11 (Sun 12–11) **Bar Meals** L served all week 12–3 D served all week 6–10 **Restaurant** L served all week 12–3 D served all week 6–10 Av 3 course à la carte £25 Greene King Regularly changing guest ales. 7 **Facilities** Children's licence Garden Dogs allowed Parking

CHIEVELEY MAP 05 SU47

The Crab at Chieveley ★★★★ RR

North Heath, Wantage Rd RG20 8UE
☎ 01635 247550 01635 247440
e-mail: info@crabatchieveley.com
dir: *Off B4494 N of Newbury, Junction 13 off the M4 signed to Chieveley*

Break that tedious M4 journey with a pit-stop at this old thatched dining pub, one of the best seafood restaurants in England. Specialising in mouth-watering fish dishes, with fresh deliveries daily, the Fish Bar offers, for example, hot Irish oysters with chorizo as a starter, and Cornish fish curry with coconut and cardamom-scented rice as a main. In the elegant, maritime-themed restaurant, try the unfishy saltmarsh lamb confit accompanied by goats' cheese and shallot tart.

Open 11–11 (Sun 12–10.30) **Bar Meals** L served all week 12–2.30 D served all week 6–10 **Restaurant** L served all week 12–2.30 D served all week 6–10 Free House Fullers London Pride, Boddingtons, West Berkshire, Black Sheep. 14 **Facilities** Garden Dogs allowed Parking **Rooms** 15 bedrooms en suite S£90 D£120

COOKHAM DEAN

Pick of the Pubs

Chequers Brasserie

Dean Ln SL6 9BQ ☎ 01628 481232 01628 481237
e-mail: info@chequersbrasserie.co.uk
dir: *From A4094 in Cookham High St towards Marlow, over rail line. 1m on right*

Kenneth Grahame, who wrote *The Wind in the Willows*, spent his childhood in these parts. He'd surely have enjoyed this historic pub, tucked away between Marlow and Maidenhead in one of the prettiest villages in the Thames Valley. Striking Victorian and Edwardian villas around the green set the tone, whilst the surrounding wooded hills and dales have earned Cookham Dean a reputation as a centre for wonderful walks. Today, the

Chequers offers carefully chosen wines and a good selection of real ales to go with an Anglo-French menu dedicated to the use of fresh, excellent produce. Sample the likes of seared king scallops with crayfish tail risotto; fillet of smoked haddock topped with a poached egg; whole black bream with citrus beurre blanc; and roast rack of lamb with wilted spinach and redcurrant jus.

Open 12-3.30 5.30-12 (Fri, Sat, Sun 11-12) **Restaurant** L served all week 12-2.30 D served all week 6-9.30 (Fri & Sat 12-2.20, 6-10) Av 3 course à la carte £24.95 Free House Guinness, Heineken Export, Greene King IPA, Rebellion Marlow Brewery. 10 **Facilities** Garden Parking

CRAZIES HILL MAP 05 SU78

Pick of the Pubs

The Horns

RG10 8LY ☎ 0118 9401416 0118 9404849
e-mail: reservations@thehornspub.com
dir: *Off A321 NE of Wargrave*

At the end of the 19th century there were only 15 houses in Crazies Hill, the hamlet in which The Horns occupies a central position. Since then it has expanded rapidly and, incredibly, at one time supported six pubs. This beautifully restored, 16th-century pub has three interconnecting terracotta-coloured, oak-beamed rooms full of old pine tables, with stripped wooden floors, open fires and rugby memorabilia. It started life in Tudor times as a hunting lodge, to which a barn (now the dining area) was added some 200 years ago. Today's peaceful atmosphere is untroubled by music or electronic games. Dishes on offer include coq au vin with spring onion mash; pork tenderloin with black pudding and light Dijon mustard gravy; and salmon and haddock fishcakes with prawn and smoked salmon sauce. Freshly-filled baguettes and home-made desserts are also available.

Open 11-11 **Bar Meals** L served all week 12-3 D served all week 7-9.30 **Restaurant** L served all week 12-3 D served Mon-Sun 7-9.30 Brakspear Brakspear Bitter. **Facilities** Garden Dogs allowed Parking Play Area

CURRIDGE MAP 05 SU47

The Bunk Inn 🍷

RG18 9DS ☎ 01635 200400 📠 01635 200336

e-mail: thebunkinn@btconnect.com

dir: *M4 junct 13, A34 N towards Oxford. Take 1st slip rd then right for 1m. Right at T-junct, 1st right signed Curridge*

Owned by the Liquorish family since 1991, this village free house is renowned for its cuisine and friendly atmosphere. Stay in the log fire-warmed bar in winter or, in summer, head for the attractive garden and patio. The only question is, where to dine – stylish restaurant or lovely conservatory? All food is fresh, and wherever possible, seasonal and local. An impressive carte menu, plus specials that usually include fresh Brixham fish.

Open 11–11 **Bar Meals** L served all week 12–2.30 D served all week 6–9.30 **Restaurant** L served all week 12–2.30 D served all week 6–9.30 Free House Arkells 3B, Fuller's London Pride, plus 2 guest ales. 🍷 9 **Facilities** Garden Dogs allowed Parking Play Area

See advert on page 25

EAST GARSTON MAP 05 SU37

Pick of the Pubs

The Queen's Arms Country Inn

★★★ INN 🍷

RG17 7ET ☎ 01488 648757 📠 01488 648642

e-mail: info@queensarmscountryhotel.co.uk

dir: *4m from junct 14 off the M4, then join A338 to Great Shefford, follow country road to East Garston*

This 18th-century inn is pleasantly located in a small village in the Lambourn Valley, with its many racehorse training yards. It is also an excellent area for walking, being quite close to the Ridgeway. As a freehouse the Queen's Arms can offer a selection of cask-conditioned real ales, and there is also a good wine list. Bar snacks are available, and there is also a good selection of traditional country food made from fresh local ingredients. On the main menu are dishes such as goats' cheese and black pudding salad; wild boar and leek sausages; lamb cutlets; and roast peppers stuffed with brie, mushrooms and red onion served with tagliatelle. The terrace and large garden are popular in the summer, when barbecues and hog roasts take place.

Open 11–11 (Closed on 25 Dec at 2pm) **Bar Meals** L served all week 12–3 D served all week 7–10 **Restaurant** L served all week 11–3 D served all week 7–10 Free House Fuller's London Pride, Brakspears, Carling, Stella. 🍷 12 **Facilities** Garden Dogs allowed Parking **Rooms** 14 bedrooms en suite S£70 D£80

HARE HATCH MAP 05 SU87

The Queen Victoria 🍷

The Holt RG10 9TA ☎ 0118 940 2477 📠 0118 940 2477

e-mail: kempjo@aol.com

dir: *On A4 between Reading & Maidenhead*

A country cottage-style pub dating back over 300 years, handily placed between Reading and Maidenhead. It offers excellent draught beers and an interesting choice of wines. The menu mainly features satisfying and traditional pub grub, but there is also a more adventurous specials board which usually includes a vegetarian option. The location of the Queen Victoria on the edge of the Chilterns means that there are some good countryside walks nearby.

Open 11–3 6–11 (Sun 12–10.30) Closed: Dec 25–26 **Bar Meals** L served all week 12–2.30 D served all week 6–10 (Sun 12–9.30) Av main course £7.50 **Restaurant** L served all week 12–2.30 D served all week 6–10 (Sun 12–9.30) Brakspear Brakspear Bitter & Special. 🍷 11 **Facilities** Garden Parking

HERMITAGE MAP 05 SU57

The White Horse of Hermitage 🍷

Newbury Rd RG18 9TB ☎ 01635 200325

e-mail: thewh@btconnect.com

This refurbished village pub lies close to the former home of writer DH Lawrence who regularly explored much of the area on foot. The extensive range of refreshments includes Greene King ales, gourmet coffees, a garden snack menu, outrageous cocktails, a grill menu and a good selection of fresh fish specials. Outside there is a large garden area with a children's play area, plus a covered patio with seating for 30 guests.

Open 11–11 (Sun 11–8) **Bar Meals** L served all week 11.30–3 D served all week 11.30–9 (Sun 11.30–4 Winter, 11.30–8 Summer) **Restaurant** L served all week 11.30–3.30 D served all week 11.30–9 (Sun 11.30–4 Winter, 11.30–8 Summer) Greene King Abbot Ale, Greene King IPA, Fosters Super Chilled, Guinness & Kronenbourg. 🍷 9 **Facilities** Garden Dogs allowed Parking Play Area

HUNGERFORD MAP 05 SU36

Pick of the Pubs

The Crown & Garter ★★★★ INN 🍷

Inkpen Common RG17 9QR ☎ 01488 668325

e-mail: gill.hern@btopenworld.com

dir: *From A4 to Kintbury & Inkpen. At village store turn left into Inkpen Rd, stay on road to Inkpen Common about 2m*

See Pick of the Pubs on opposite page

The Crown & Garter

A family-owned, personally run 17th-century inn in a really pretty part of Berkshire. James II allegedly used to stop off here on his way to visit one of his mistresses – perhaps he wasn't in such a hurry to see her.

The inn's barn was used to lay out the bodies of two lovers hanged at nearby Combe Gibbet for killing the woman's husband. There have been four of these gruesome constructions: the original rotted away, its replacement was struck by lightning, the third lasted a hundred years or so until felled by a gale in 1949, and then there's the one you see today. The inn's ancient charm can best be seen in the bar area, where there's a huge inglenook fireplace and criss-crossing beams. You can eat here, in the restaurant, or outside in the enclosed beer garden, choosing from a variety of dishes all freshly prepared on the premises from local produce. First courses include oak-smoked salmon with horseradish cream; wild mushroom risotto with red chard salad; and oriental duck spring roll and chilli dip. Among the main courses are likely to be half a roast duck with brandy and fresh orange sauce; pan-fried lambs' liver with onions and bubble and squeak; or daily fish and seafood specials from the blackboard feature. There's also a Thai and Indonesian selection, including green, red and rendang curries. White peach soup with raspberry sherbet should slip down easily afterwards. Eight spacious en suite bedrooms have been built around a pretty cottage garden. Nearby Hungerford has some good antique shops, and Bath, Oxford and Winchester are less than an hour away. But why drive when the stunning countryside surrounding the inn is so perfect for walking, cycling, fishing or simply chilling out?

★★★★ INN 🍷
MAP 05 SU36
Inkpen Common RG17 9QR
☎ 01488 668325
e-mail:
gill.hern@btopenworld.com
dir: *From A4 turn to Kintbury & Inkpen. At village store turn left into Inkpen Rd, stay on road to Inkpen Common about 2m*

Open 12–3 5.30–11 (Sun eve 7–10.30)
Bar Meals L served Wed–Sun 12–2 D served Mon–Sat 6.30–9.30 (Sun 12–2.30) Av main course £14
Restaurant L served Wed–Sun 12–2 D served all week 6.30–9.30 (Sun 12–2.30) Av 3 course à la carte £25
Free House
Mr Chubbs, Good Old Boy, Guinness, Boddingtons. 🍷 9
Facilities Garden Parking Play Area
Rooms 8 bedrooms en suite S£59.50 D£90

England

HUNGERFORD continued

Pick of the Pubs

The Swan Inn ★★★★ INN

Craven Rd, Lower Green, Inkpen RG17 9DX

☎ 01488 668326 📠 01488 668306

e-mail: enquiries@theswaninn-organics.co.uk

dir: *S down Hungerford High St (A338), under rail bridge, left to Hungerford Common. Turn right signed Inkpen 3m.*

Local organic beef farmers Mary and Bernard Harris preside over this rambling 17th-century free house, which stands in fine walking country just below Combe Gibbet and Walbury Hill. An attractive terraced garden sets the scene for al fresco summer dining, in contrast to the heavily beamed interior with its old photographic prints and open winter fires. As you'd expect, almost everything on the menu is prepared on the premises using fresh, GMO-free organic produce. The bar menu features traditional English favourites alongside more adventurous fare, such as garlic roasted Mediterranean vegetables with couscous and spicy tomato dressing. In the restaurant, expect dishes like grilled cod fillet with a herb crust; and fillet steak with red wine sauce. The inn also boasts ten comfortable en-suite bedrooms and a well-stocked farm shop, which offers an extensive selection of quality local organic beef, groceries and other produce.

Open 12-2.30 7-11 (Open all day wknds summer) Closed: 25-26 Dec **Bar Meals** L served all week 12-2 D served all week 7-9.30 (Sat 12-2.30, Sun 12-3) Av main course £10 **Restaurant** L served Wed-Sun 12-2.30 D served Wed-Sat 7-9.30 (Sun lunch only 12-3) Av 3 course à la carte £28.50 Free House Butts Traditional, Butts Jester Bitter, Maggs Magnificent MIld, guest ales. **Facilities** Garden Parking Play Area **Rooms** 10 bedrooms en suite S£60 D£80

HURST MAP 05 SU77

The Green Man 🍷

Hinton Rd RG10 0BP ☎ 0118 934 2599 📠 0118 934 2939

e-mail: admin@thegreenman.uk.com

dir: *Off the A321 next to Hurst Cricket Club*

Once part of Windsor Great Park, this building dates from 1646. Low ceilings and log fires make for a cosy interior, where good beers and some value-for-money wines can be enjoyed. Food choices are varied and include light bites, salads and more elaborate specials such as roast monkfish cooked in Vermouth crème fraîche; or Caribbean coconut chicken curry. Look out for regular themed menus. The garden has a heated patio and a popular children's play area.

The Green Man

Open 11-3 5.30-11 (Sun 12-3, 6-10.30) **Bar Meals** L served all week 12-9 D served all week **Restaurant** L served all week 12-9 D served all week Brakspear Brakspear Bitter, Special & Seasonal Ales. 🍷 7 **Facilities** Children's licence Garden Parking Play Area

KINTBURY MAP 05 SU36

Pick of the Pubs

The Dundas Arms

53 Station Rd RG17 9UT

☎ 01488 658263 📠 01488 658568

e-mail: info@dundasarms.co.uk

dir: *M4 junct 13 take A34 to Newbury, then A4 to Hungerford, left to Kintbury. Pub 1m by canal & rail station*

Set in an area of outstanding natural beauty on the banks of the Kennet and Avon canal, this free house has been welcoming travellers since the end of the 18th century. The pub has been in the same family for many years, and proprietor David Dalzell-Piper has worked and cooked here throughout that time. Traditional beers like West Berkshire and Cornish Coaster are served in the convivial bar, whilst the simply styled restaurant is redolent of a French aubèrge. On warmer days, outdoor tables offer views of the narrow boats and wildlife on the canal. On the bar's blackboard menu, oxtail casserole in red wine sauce jostles with grilled halibut on saffron and fennel risotto. Meanwhile, a typical restaurant meal might start with home-potted shrimps, before moving on to grilled Kilravock pork chop with root mash and sage gravy, followed by raspberry crème brûlée.

Open 11-2.30 6-11 Closed: 25 & 31 Dec **Bar Meals** L served Mon-Sat 12-2 D served Tue-Sat 7-9 (Sun 12-2.30) Av main course £12 **Restaurant** D served Tue-Sat 7-9 Av 3 course à la carte £28 Free House West Berkshire, Mr Chubbs Lunchtime Bitter, Adnams, Sharps Cornish Coaster. **Facilities** Children's licence Parking **Rooms** 5 bedrooms en suite S£80 D£90 (★★★ INN)

KNOWL HILL MAP 05 SU87

Pick of the Pubs

Bird In Hand Country Inn

Bath Rd RG10 9UP
01628 826622 & 822781 01628 826748
e-mail: sthebirdinhand@aol.com
dir: *On A4, 5m W of Maidenhead, 7m E of Reading*

Parts of this charming building date from the 14th century, and legend has it that in the late 1700s George III wet his regal whistle here while his horse was being re-shod at the forge next door. The wood-panelled Oak Lounge Bar has a striking tartan carpet, while a new development is the Buffet Bar. The restaurant menu offers an appealing mix of exotic and traditional dishes, with typical starters of fresh artichoke heart with wild mushroom and chive cream sauce; and sautéed quail breast with bread sauce and thyme jus. Follow with rosette of lamb on parsnip mash with mint jus; fillet of sea bass with crispy skin, celeriac mash and lobster sauce; or tagliatelle in cream sauce with tiger prawns. All bedrooms are en suite and generously equipped. If you're staying the night, listen out for the phantom coach and horses.

Open 11-3 6-11 (Sun 12-10.30) **Bar Meals** L served all week 12-2.30 D served all week 6.30-10 (Sun 12-9.30) Av main course £9.95 **Restaurant** L served all week 12-2.30 D served all week 7-10 (Sun 7-9.15) Av 3 course à la carte £25 Av 3 course fixed price £15.50 Free House Brakspear Bitter, Hogsback TEA. 12 **Facilities** Garden Dogs allowed Parking **Rooms** 15 bedrooms en suite S£70 D£90 (★★★ HL)

LECKHAMPSTEAD MAP 05 SU47

Pick of the Pubs

The Stag

Shop Ln RG20 8QG 01488 638436
e-mail: enquiries@stagleckhampstead.co.uk
dir: *6m from Newbury on B4494*

See Pick of the Pubs on page 30

MAIDENHEAD MAP 06 SU88

The Belgian Arms

Holyport SL6 2JR 01628 634468 01628 777952
e-mail: enquiries@thamessideevents.com
dir: *In Holyport village, 2m from Maidenhead, off Ascot road*

Originally known as The Eagle, the Prussian eagle inn sign attracted unwelcome attention during the First World War. As a result, the name was changed to reflect an area where the fiercest fighting was taking place. Things are more peaceful now, and details of local walks are listed outside the pub. The attractive menu includes snacks and light lunches, as well as hot dishes like sausages, mash and onion gravy, and spicy beanburger and chips.

Open 11-3 5.30-11 (Fri-Sat 11-11, Sun 12-10.30) Closed: Dec 25 eve **Bar Meals** L served all week 12-2 D served Mon-Sun 6.30-9 Av main course £9 Brakspear Brakspear Best, Brakspear Special. 8 **Facilities** Garden Dogs allowed Parking

The White Hart

Moneyrow Green, Holyport SL6 2ND
01628 621460 01628 621460
e-mail: info@whitehartholyport.com
dir: *2m S of Maidenhead. Exit M4 junct 8/9, follow signs for Holyport and then Moneyrow Green. Located next to petrol stn halfway along Moneyrow Green.*

A busy, good-humoured 19th-century coaching inn offering quality home-made food, with most vegetables and herbs used – 36 varieties at the last count – freshly picked from its own organic allotment. Typical mains are caramelised breast of duck, calves' liver and bacon, venison sausages, grilled fillet of plaice, and slow-roasted tomato tart with Somerset brie. The wood-panelled lounge bar is furnished with leather chesterfields and warmed by an open fire. Poltergeists have been reported.

Open 11-12 (Fri & Sat 11am-12.30am) Closed: 1 Jan **Bar Meals** L served all week 12-2.30 D served Mon-Sat 6-9.30 Av main course £12 **Restaurant** L served all week 12-2.30 D served Mon-Sat 6-9.30 Av 3 course à la carte £25 Greene King Guinness, IPA, Morland Original, Fosters & Stella Artois. 8 **Facilities** Garden Dogs allowed Parking Play Area

The Stag

To look at, the privately owned, white-painted Stag could only be a pub. It lies just off the village green in a sleepy downland village, and close by are the Ridgeway long-distance path and Snelsmore Common, home to nightjar, woodlark and grazing Exmoor ponies.

Needless to say, with such beautiful countryside all around, muddy wellies and wet dogs are expected – in fact, the latter are as genuinely welcome as their owners. During the winter months the wood-burning stove is always ready with its dancing flames. The bar and restaurant walls are painted in warm red, or left as bare brick, while old black and white photographs tell of village life many years ago. Surrounding farms and growers supply all produce, including venison, pheasant and fresh river trout. These fish often appear on the specials board, courtesy of a regular customer who barters them for a few glasses of Rioja, depending on their size. Aberdeen Angus beef from cattle raised next door may also feature as a special, and those lucky enough to find it there agree that its taste and texture are sublime. Other possibilities, depending on the prevailing menu, are Cornish mussels in cream, white wine and herbs; field mushroom topped with mozzarella, olives and pesto; Thai red chicken curry and sticky lemon rice; pork fillet with sautéed chorizo and baby broad beans; beer battered fish and chips with mushy peas and home-made tartare sauce; and a daily vegetarian special. Home-made desserts include apricot bread and butter pudding with cream, and chocolate and Cointreau cheesecake. There are around 20 red and white wines, among them varieties from Australia, California and France. Compulsive workers can take advantage of a wireless internet connection, although in a pub like this it would have to be pretty urgent work.

🍷
MAP 05 SU47
Shop Ln RG20 8QG
☎ 01488 638436
e-mail: enquiries@stagleckhampstead.co.uk
dir: *6m from Newbury on B4494*

Open 12–2.30 6–11
Bar Meals L served all week 12–2 D served all week 6–9.30 Av main course £10
Restaurant L served all week 12–2 D served all week 6–9.30 Av 3 course à la carte £18
Brakspears, Guest beers. 🍷 8
Facilities Children's licence Garden Dogs allowed Parking

MARSH BENHAM MAP 05 SU46

Pick of the Pubs

The Red House

RG20 8LY ☎ 01635 582017 01635 581621
e-mail: annattheredhouse@btconnect.com
dir: *5m from Hungerford, 3m from Newbury, 400yds off A4*

Very much a gastro-pub, but the spacious bar's stripped wooden floors and warmly painted walls also welcome drinkers, as does the sun-trap terrace outside. Previously known as the Water Rat, this striking 18th-century brick-and-thatch pub lies close to the banks of the River Kennet, one of Britain's prettiest chalk streams; the book-lined dining room overlooks water-meadows. A strong kitchen brigade prepares good English produce with French flair. You may find starters such as ham hock and foie gras terrine on toasted brioche, or seared scallops with thyme and lemon jam. Main courses again feature the European twist: Gressingham duck with an Italian marinade; free-range chicken breast with taleggio and pancetta; and shank of lamb in Moroccan spices with fresh potato gnocchi. Classic desserts include chocolate brownie or sticky toffee pudding, and a range of ice creams and sorbets. After lunch take a stroll along the towpath of the nearby Kennet and Avon Canal.

Open 11.30–3 6–11 (Sun 11.30–3.30) Closed: 25–26 Dec & 31 Dec–1 Jan **Bar Meals** L served Mon–Sat 11.30–2.30 D served Mon–Sat 7–9.30 Av main course £15 **Restaurant** L served Mon–Sat 12–2.30 D served Mon–Sat 7–9.30 Av 3 course à la carte £24 Free House Bombardier, Stella, Amstel, Murphy's, London Pride. 7 **Facilities** Garden Parking

NEWBURY MAP 05 SU46

Pick of the Pubs

The Yew Tree Inn

Hollington Cross, Andover Rd, Highclere RG20 9SE
☎ 01635 253360 01635 255035
e-mail: gareth.mcainsh@theyewtree.net
dir: *A34 toward Southampton, 2nd exit bypass Highclere, onto A343 at rdbt, through village, pub on right*

This 16th-century inn belongs to the celebrated chef-turned restaurateur, Marco Pierre White. His famed perfectionism is evident everywhere, from the immaculate styling that blends original 17th-century features with the refinement of white tablecloths and sparkling glassware, to the menu, which performs

CONTINUED

NEWBURY continued

a similar trick, offering both traditional Britsh food and time-honoured classics from the French culinary canon. So your meal might open with a parfait of foie gras; calves' tongue with celeriac remoulade; or duck rillettes, followed by lobster thermidor; Dover sole meunière; or venison with sauce grand veneur. There is a relaxed, pick-and-choose feel to the menu, which includes lighter options such as eggs Benedict, Scotch woodcock, and various soups (game consommé en croûte; bisque of lobster Newburg). Tellingly, the desserts are described as 'puddings' and might include such familiar comforts as bread and butter pudding or rhubarb crumble. Good-value fixed-price menus are also a feature at lunchtime, early evening and on Sundays. There is an excellent wine list with eight by the glass, and a variety of guest beers. The building is beguiling, with subtle lighting, a smouldering log fire, whitewashed walls and a subtly stylish, contemporary feel running through the series of interconnecting dining areas.

Open 10–12 **Bar Meals** L served all week 12–3 D served all week 6–10 (Sun 12–4, 7–9) Av main course £14.50 **Restaurant** L served all week 12–3 D served all week 6–10 (Sun 12–3, 7–9) Av 3 course à la carte £35 Free House Guest beers, London Pride, Timothy Taylor. 8 **Facilities** Children's licence Garden Dogs allowed Parking

PALEY STREET MAP 05 SU87

Pick of the Pubs

The Royal Oak

SL6 3JN ☎ 01628 620541

dir: *From Maidenhead take A330 towards Ascot for 2m, turn right onto B3024 signed White Waltham, 2nd pub on left*

TV presenter Michael Parkinson owns this popular inn, which is run by his son. Lovers of jazz and popular music will undoubtedly be drawn by the quality of the entertainment – Jamie Cullum, Katie Melua and James Morrison have all performed at the regular music nights – and the walls are adorned with TV and sporting memorabilia. An equal lure is the accomplished and imaginative food. Starters like potted rabbit with pickles and toast; and crab and mint tagliatelle might be followed by such mains as monkfish with gnocchi, or lemon sole with capers and lemon. Look out for the daily specials which feature such rare British classics as salt beef stovey with a fried egg; dandelion salad with duck hearts and bacon; or poached turbot with samphire. Cambridge burnt cream or chocolate mousse with Agen prunes will round matters of nicely.

Open 11–3 6–11 **Bar Meals** L served all week 11–3 D served Mon–Sat 6.30–10 (Sun 11–4) Av main course £13 **Restaurant** L served all week 12–3 D served Mon–Sat 6–10 Av 3 course à la carte £26 Fullers London Pride. 10 **Facilities** Children's licence Garden Parking

READING MAP 05 SU77

The Crown NEW

Playhatch RG4 9QN ☎ 0118 947 2872 0118 946 4586

e-mail: info@thecrown.co.uk

dir: *A4155 towards Henley-on-Thames. At 1st rdbt after leaving Reading take 1st exit, pub 400mtrs on left*

This charming 16th-century country inn with its lovely garden and excellent restaurant nestles between the Thames and the Chilterns in an area of outstanding natural beauty. The Crown has become known for its food and friendly service, whilst Head Chef Nana Akuffo is behind the move to buy fresh local produce wherever possible. Typical main courses include roasted monkfish with caramelised red onion and sweet potato; and slow-roasted Welsh lamb provençale.

Open 10–11 **Bar Meals** L served all week 12–2.30 D served all week 6–9.30 (Sun 12–3, 6–9) Av main course £14 **Restaurant** L served all week 12–2.30 D served all week 6–9.30 (Sun 12–3, 6–9) Av 3 course à la carte £24 Brakspear Brakspear Bitter, Brakspear Special, Brakspear Seasonal, Guinness. 10 **Facilities** Garden Parking **Rooms** 10 bedrooms en suite S£80 D£80 (★★★★ INN)

The Flowing Spring

Henley Rd, Playhatch RG4 9RB ☎ 0118 969 3207

e-mail: flowingspring@aol.com

dir: *3m N of Reading*

A lovely country pub overlooking the Thames flood plain at the point where the Chiltern Hills strike out north east towards Bedfordshire. The proprietor likes his establishment to be known as "a pub that serves good food, rather than a restaurant that serves lousy beer". Representative dishes on the combined bar/restaurant menu include home-made curries, shoulder of lamb, and rib-eye steaks. It's a Fullers pub, so Chiswick, London Pride and ESB are all well kept on tap.

Open 12–11 **Bar Meals** L served Mon–Sun 12–2.30 D served Wed–Sat 6.30–9.30 Av main course £7 Fullers London Pride, ESB, Chiswick, HSB. 7 **Facilities** Garden Dogs allowed Parking Play Area

The Shoulder of Mutton

Playhatch RG4 9QU ☎ 0118 947 3908

e-mail: grnwillows@hotmail.com

dir: *From Reading follow signs to Caversham, then join the A4155 to Henley. At rdbt turn left to Binfied Heath, pub on left.*

Unusually, mutton is on the menu at this characterful pub, with its atmospheric low-beamed ceilings, large open fireplace and beautiful Victorian walled garden with conservatory and terrace. It is renowned locally for good food – from the signature slow-roast local shoulder of mutton to grilled tilapia fillets or 'Fungiorama' – a mushroom and aubergine lasagne. Theme nights are popular, but need to be booked.

The Shoulder of Mutton

Open 12-3 6-11 (Mon 7-11, Sat 6.30-11) Closed: 26-28 Dec, 1-3 Jan **Bar Meals** L served all week 12-2 D served all week **Restaurant** L served all week 12-2 D served all week 6.30-9 (Sun 7-9) Greene King Greene King IPA & Old Speckled Hen. **Facilities** Garden Parking

STANFORD DINGLEY MAP 05 SU57

The Bull Country Inn

RG7 6LS ☎ 0118 974 4409 0118 974 5249

e-mail: admin@thebullatstanforddingley.co.uk

dir: *A4/A340 to Pangbourne. 1st left to Bradfield. Through Bradfield, 0.3m left into Back Lane. At end left, pub 0.25m on left*

A nook-and-cranny-rich taproom bar, smoke-blackened fireplace and exposed wattle and daub make this free house a delightfully traditional setting. Family-owned, and dating from the 15th century, it remains a hub of the village while also being a destination pub. Food choices run from snacks (nachos; salads) through to main meals such as monkfish tail with Parma ham and fresh vegetables; or rack of lamb with redcurrant jus. The landlord's passion for cars is much in evidence.

Open 12-3 6-11 (Sun 7-10.30) **Bar Meals** L served all week 12-2.30 D served all week 6.30-9.30 Av main course £8.50 **Restaurant** L served all week 12.30-2.30 D served all week 6.30-9.30 (Sun 7-9.30) Free House West Berkshire, Brakspear Bitter, West berkshire Good Old Boy. 7 **Facilities** Garden Dogs allowed Parking

The Old Boot Inn

RG7 6LT ☎ 0118 974 4292 0118 974 4292

dir: *M4 junct 12, A4/A340 to Pangbourne. 1st left to Bradfield. Through Bradfield, follow Stanford Dingley signs*

Set in the glorious Pang Valley, in a village of Outstanding Natural Beauty, the original 18th-century Old Boot has been extended to include a popular conservatory. Fresh seafood choices are announced daily, and include the likes of seabass, cod, scallops, haddock and swordfish.

Open 11-3 6-11 (Sun 12-3, 7-10.30) **Bar Meals** L served all week 12-2.15 D served all week 7-9.30 (Sun 12-2.30 7-9.30) **Restaurant** L served all week 12-2.15 D served all week 7-9.30 Free House Brakspear Bitter, Interbrew Bass, West Berkshire Dr Hexters, Archers Best. 8 **Facilities** Garden Dogs allowed Parking Play Area

SWALLOWFIELD MAP 05 SU76

Pick of the Pubs

The George & Dragon

Church Rd RG7 1TJ ☎ 0118 9884 432 0118 9886474

Don't judge a pub by its façade, at least not this one. It may look unassuming, but it has a smart, cosy interior with stripped low beams, terracotta-painted walls, log fires and rug-strewn floors, and it has earned quite a reputation for its food. Dining takes precedence over drinking, and booking for lunch or dinner would be prudent. Main courses include Caribbean jerk chicken with jollof rice and mojo salsa; fillet of sea bass with creamed spinach and aubergine ragoût; and wild mushroom and asparagus tagliatelle with gorgonzola cream. A typical specials board could offer a starter of smoked quail filled with winter fruits and nuts on poached apricots, followed by grilled cod with a smoked haddock, mussel and clam broth with champ mash.

Open 12-12 (Fri-Sat 12-1am, Sun 12-10.30) Closed: 26 Dec Rest: 25 Dec, 1 Jan Closed eve **Bar Meals** L served all week 12-2.30 D served all week 7-10 (Sun 12-3, 7-9) Av main course £10.95 **Restaurant** L served all week 12-2.30 D served all week 7-10 (Sun 12-3, 7-9) Av 3 course à la carte £23 Free House Fullers London Pride, Brakspears, Youngs. **Facilities** Garden Dogs allowed Parking

THATCHAM MAP 05 SU56

The Bladebone Inn

Chapel Row, Bucklebury RG7 6PD ☎ 0118 971 2326

e-mail: jeanclaude@thebladebone.net

dir: *5m from Newbury and the A4, 2m from the A4 at Thatcham*

Above the entrance to this historic inn hangs a bladebone, which, according to legend, originally came from a mammoth that once stalked the Kennet valley. A more probable explanation is that it was used to indicate that whale oil was sold here for use in oil-burning lamps and probably of 17th-century origin. These days the Bladebone is a stylish dining venue with a mixture of English and Mediterranean influences.

Open 12-3 6.30-11 **Bar Meals** L served Tue-Sun 12-3 D served Tue-Sat 6-10 Av main course £10 **Restaurant** L served Tue-Sun 12-3 D served Tue-Sat 6-10 Av 3 course à la carte £25 Whitbread Fuller's London Pride, Good Old Boy, Strongbow Cider, Fosters. **Facilities** Garden Dogs allowed Parking

England

THEALE MAP 05 SU67

Thatchers Arms

North St RG7 5EX ☎ 0118 930 2070 📄 0118 930 2070

Many footpaths and quiet lanes are to be found in the nearby countryside, making this warm, friendly pub something of a destination for walkers. Although in a small hamlet, the inn is also only a five-minute drive from the M4. There are good garden facilities and a separate patio area. Under new management, the food is still being taken seriously: try warm salad of bacon and poached egg; or pan-fried cod on crushed herb potatoes.

Open 12–2.30 6–11 **Bar Meals** L served all week 12–2.30 D served all week 6–9.30 Av main course £12.50 **Restaurant** L served all week 12–2.30 D served all week 6–9.30 Av 3 course à la carte £25 Punch Taverns Fuller's London Pride, Stella, Carling, Brakspears. 8 **Facilities** Garden Dogs allowed Parking

WALTHAM ST LAWRENCE MAP 05 SU87

The Bell

The Street RG10 0JJ ☎ 0118 9341788

dir: *On B3024 E of Twyford (from A4 turn at Hare Hatch)*

The Bell is a 14th-century building given to the village in 1608. It now runs as a free house with rent going to a trust to benefit village charities. The pub is renowned for its constantly changing range of real ales selected from smaller micro-breweries all over the country. It also has a growing reputation for its food: beef and pearl barley broth; king prawn, squid and chorizo couscous; and apple crumble and vanilla ice cream.

Open 12–3 5–11 (Sat 12–11, Sun 12–10.30) **Bar Meals** L served all week 12–2 D served all week 7–9.30 (Sat/Sun 12–3, 7–9.30) Av main course £10 **Restaurant** L served all week 12–2 D served all week 7–9.30 (Sat & Sun 12–3, 7–9.30) Av 3 course à la carte £20 Free House Waltham St Lawrence No.1 Ale plus 4 Guests. 7 **Facilities** Garden Dogs allowed Parking Play Area

WARGRAVE MAP 05 SU77

St George and Dragon

High St RG10 8HY ☎ 0118 940 5021

dir: *3.5m from Henley on A321*

A friendly Thames-side pub, in one of the river's most scenic locations. Heaters on the outdoor decking make it possible to enjoy the view all year round, while inside are open kitchens, stone-fired ovens and log-burning fires. The menu offers the familiar – pizza, pasta and steaks – and the not so familiar, such as duck confit with pak choi, egg noodles, black bean and chilli sauce; and swordfish with Tuscan bean cassoulet and chorizo.

Open 12–11 **Bar Meals** L served all week 12–2 D served all week 6–9.30 (Sun 12–7) **Restaurant** L served all week 12–2.30 D served all week 6–9.30 (Sun 12–3.30, 6.30–9) Free House Loddon Hulabaloo & Timothy Taylors Landlord. 14 **Facilities** Children's licence Garden Parking

WINKFIELD MAP 06 SU97

Rose & Crown

Woodside, Windsor Forest SL4 2DP

☎ 01344 882051 📄 01344 885346

e-mail: info@roseandcrownascot.com

dir: *M3 junct 3 from Ascot Racecourse on A332 take 2nd exit from Heatherwood Hosp rdbt, then 2nd left*

A 200-year-old traditional pub complete with old beams and low ceilings. Hidden down a country lane, it has a peaceful garden overlooking open fields where you can see horses and llamas at pasture. A typical menu may include pan-fried fillet steak with blue cheese gratin potatoes, with seasonal vegetables and a bourguignon sauce; pavé of halibut with rosemary sauté potatoes, chargrilled asparagus and baby leeks, with horseradish cream sauce; or asparagus tortellini with basil and parmesan cheese.

Open 11–12 (9am Royal Ascot wk) **Bar Meals** L served all week 12–4 D served Tue–Sat 7–9.30 Av main course £8 **Restaurant** L served all week 12–2.30 D served Tue–Sat 7–9.30 (Sun 12–4) Av 3 course à la carte £27.50 Greene King Morland Original, Greene King IPA & Guest Ale. 9 **Facilities** Garden Parking Play Area

WINTERBOURNE MAP 05 SU47

The Winterbourne Arms

RG20 8BB ☎ 01635 248200 📄 01635 248824

e-mail: winterbournearms@tiscali.co.uk

dir: *Exit M4 junct 13 & turn into Chieveley Services, follow Donnington signs until Winterbourne sign. Turn right down Arlington Ln, turn right at T-junct then left into Winterbourne.*

Formerly known as the New Inn, this large 300-year-old free house once also sheltered the village shop and bakery. The remains of the original bread oven still survive, whilst the beautifully kept gardens provide a safe environment for younger guests. The extensive menus reflect traditional dishes with a contemporary twist: in addition, daily specials might include grilled sea bass; wild boar terrine with toasted brioche; and pan-fried liver with bacon and onions.

Open 12–3 6–11 (Sun 12–10.30) **Bar Meals** L served all week 12–2.30 D served all week 6–10 (Sun 12–4, 6–10) Av main course £8 **Restaurant** L served all week 12–2.30 D served all week 6–10 (Sun lunch 12–4) Av 3 course à la carte £15 Free House West Berkshire Good Old Boy, 6X, Ramsbury Gold, Guinness & Carling. 12 **Facilities** Garden Dogs allowed Parking

WORLD'S END MAP 05 SU47

The Langley Hall Inn 🍷

RG20 8SA ☎ 01635 248332 📠 01635 248571

dir: *Exit M4 junct 13 north, take 1st slip rd signed Beedon & Chieveley. Turn left & immediately right, Langley Hall is 1.5m on left.*

Friendly, family-run bar/restaurant with a reputation for freshly prepared food, real ales and a good selection of wines. Fresh fish dishes vary according to the daily catch – maybe pan-fried crevettes, grilled Dover sole, salmon fishcakes with spinach and parsley sauce, or roast cod fillet with cheese and herb crust. Other favourites are braised lamb, beef stir-fry, and Thai chicken curry. Outside there is a large patio and garden, plus a petanque court for fine weather use.

Open 11-3 5.30-12 (Fri-Sat 11-12, Sun 11-7) Closed: 26 Dec-2 Jan **Bar Meals** L served Mon-Sat 12-2.30 D served Mon-Sat 6.30-10 (Sun 12.30-4) Av main course £12 **Restaurant** L served Mon-Sat 12-2.30 D served Mon-Sat 6.30-10 (Sun 12-4) Av 3 course à la carte £24 Enterprise Inns West Berkshire - Good Old Boy, Mr Chubbs, Lunchtime Bitter, Deuchars IPA. 🍷 9 **Facilities** Garden Dogs allowed Parking

YATTENDON MAP 05 SU57

Pick of the Pubs

The Royal Oak Hotel ★★ HL 🍷

The Square RG18 0UG

☎ 01635 201325 📠 01635 201926

e-mail: info@royaloakyattendon.com

dir: *From M4 junct 12, A4 to Newbury, right at 2nd rdbt to Pangbourne then 1st left. From junct 13, A34 N 1st left, right at T-junct. Left then 2nd right to Yattendon*

This quintessentially English country inn dates back to the 16th century, as the timber framework will attest. The Oak – as it was formerly known – has played host to such luminaries as King Charles I and Oliver Cromwell, but today it's rarely interrupted by anything more than the clip-clop of passing horse-riders. The village bar remains popular, though the culinary emphasis is based on a brasserie-style menu and an extensive wine list, to be taken in a charmingly formal dining room. Starters like foie gras with quince purée or prawns and prunes wrapped in pancetta are the precursor to main dishes such as pan-fried red mullet in dill sauce; grilled sirloin with feta cheese; or asparagus and langoustine risotto. Round off your meal with appetising desserts like passion fruit parfait or walnut chocolate cake. Traditionally furnished bedrooms add to the appeal.

Open 11-11 **Bar Meals** L served Mon-Sat 12-2.30 **Restaurant** L served all week 12-2.15 D served all week 7-9.30 (Sun 12-3, 7-9) Av 3 course à la carte £28 Av 3 course fixed price £15 West Berks, Good Old Boy, Mr Chubbs. 🍷 8 **Facilities** Garden Parking **Rooms** 5 bedrooms en suite S£85 D£110

BRISTOL

BRISTOL MAP 04 ST57

Cornubia

142 Temple St BS1 6EN ☎ 0117 925 4415 📠 0117 929 1523

e-mail: thecornubia@hotmail.co.uk

dir: *Opposite Bristol Fire Station*

Characterful Georgian city centre pub built as two houses, and now owned by the Hidden Brewery company. Office workers love it, not just because of its convenience, but for of its choice of seven changing real ales, two draught ciders and a serious collection of malts. And then there's the food – chicken and mushroom pie is an example – chalked up on a blackboard. Cornubia, by the way, is the Latinised name for Cornwall.

Open 11.30-11 (Sat 5.30-11) Closed: BHs **Bar Meals** L served Mon-Fri 12-8 All Hidden Brewery Beers. **Facilities** Children's licence Dogs allowed Parking

Highbury Vaults

164 St Michaels Hill, Cotham BS2 8DE ☎ 0117 973 3203

e-mail: highburyvaults@youngs.co.uk

dir: *Take main road to Cotham from inner ring dual carriageway*

Once a turnpike station, this 1840s pub retains a Victorian atmosphere in its many nooks and crannies. In days when hangings took place on nearby St Michael's Hill, many victims partook of their last meal in the vaults. Today, it's a business crowd by day and students at night feasting on chilli, meat and vegetable curries, casseroles, pasta dishes, and jacket potatoes. No fried foods, no music or fruit machines and a heated garden terrace.

Open 12-12 (Sun 12-11) **Bar Meals** L served all week 12-2.30 (Sat-Sun 12-3) D served Mon-Fri 5.30-8.30 Av main course £4.95 Young & Co Bath Ales Gem, St Austells Tribute, Brains SA, Young's Special & Bitter. **Facilities** Garden

Robin Hood's Retreat NEW 🍷

197 Gloucester Rd BS7 8BG ☎ 078750 20590

dir: *At main rdbt at Broad Mead take Gloucester Rd exit, St Pauls. Road leads into Gloucester Rd, pub straight on after 10 mins*

In the heart of Bristol this Victorian red-brick pub is popular with real ale lovers, who usually have eight to choose from. The interior has been superbly refurbished, keeping original features and adding to the richly coloured wood panelling and furniture. There's plenty of attention to detail in the food too, which is all prepared on the premises. Favourites are slow-cooked British dishes with a French accent, and several seafood options such as devilled crab.

Open 12-11 Closed: 25-26 Dec **Bar Meals** L served Tue-Sun 12-3 (Sun 12-4) D served Tue-Sun 6-9.30 Av main course £13.25 **Restaurant** 12-3 (Sun 12-4) D served Tue-Sun 6-9.30 Av 3 course à la carte £25 Av 2 course fixed price £12.95 🍷 9 **Facilities** Garden

England

BUCKINGHAMSHIRE

AMERSHAM MAP 06 SU99

Hit or Miss Inn

Penn St Village HP7 0PX ☎ 01494 713109 01494 718010
e-mail: hit@ourpubs.co.uk
dir: *Off Amersham - High Wycombe Rd (A404)*

You'll find The Hit or Miss in lovely countryside between Amersham and Beaconsfield, overlooking the cricket pitch where the pub's namesake team plays. It is a cottage-style establishment, in business since 1798, with a country garden complete with lawn, patio and picnic tables. A good choice of dishes, freshly prepared and cooked on the premises, might include leek and feta parcel with tzatziki, and house smoked salmon with garlic mushrooms and potato gratin.

Open 11-11 (Sun 12-10.30) **Bar Meals** L served all week 12-2.30 D served all week 6.45-9.30 (Sun 12-8) **Restaurant** L served all week 12-2.30 D served all week 6.45-9.30 (Sun 12-8) Hall & Woodhouse Badger Best, Tanglefoot, Sussex, Hofbrau & Stella. 12
Facilities Garden Dogs allowed Parking

BEACONSFIELD MAP 06 SU99

Pick of the Pubs

The Royal Standard of England

Brindle Ln, Forty Green HP9 1XT ☎ 01494 673382
e-mail: theoldestpub@btinternet.com
dir: *A40 to Beaconsfield, right at church rdbt onto B474 towards Penn, left onto Forty Green Rd 1m.*

What could be the oldest free house in England, this welcoming country inn dates from the 12th century. During the Civil War, it became a Royalist headquarters, which accounts for its rather grand name. Striking stained glass windows, beams, flagstone floors, and a large inglenook fireplace set the scene for a building so haunted you are invited to record your own scary encounters in its ghost book! Hearty, traditional food includes roast Welsh Black beef, pork, venison and mountain lamb; sea bass; squid and chorizo; cod and chips; pork sausages and mash; chicken caesar salad; and wild mushroom risotto. Welsh rarebit, garlic prawns, and cheese and onion tart are lighter options. Appropriately English puddings include apple and berry crumble, jam roly poly and spotted dick. Popular wines are available by the glass and beers on tap run from Amstel to Westons Perry, by way of Rebellion IPA.

Open 11-12 (Sun 12 - 11) **Bar Meals** L served all week 12-10 D served all week 12-10 Av main course £10 **Restaurant** D served all week 12-10 Av 3 course à la carte £20 Free House Marston's Pedigree, Brakspear Bitter, Rebellion IPA & Guest Beers. 12
Facilities Children's licence Garden Dogs allowed Parking

BLEDLOW MAP 05 SP70

The Lions of Bledlow

Church End HP27 9PE ☎ 01844 343345 01844 343345
dir: *M40 junct 6 take B4009 to Princes Risborough, through Chinnor into Bledlow.*

A traditional free house with rambling low-beamed bar and log fire; frequently used as a location for the ITV series Midsomer Murders. In summer, the spacious rear garden seating overflows onto the village green. The specials board offers around eight daily-changing dishes like medallions of beef in a red wine sauce, or whole prawns in white wine and garlic, plus a separate board with vegetarian choices. The menu features many classic British favourites like lambs' liver and bacon, and game pie.

Open 11.30-3 6-11 (Sun 12-3, 7-10.30) **Bar Meals** L served all week 12-2.30 D served all week 7-9.30 (Sun 7-9) **Restaurant** L served all week 12-2.30 D served all week 7-9.30 (Sun 7-9) Free House Wadworth 6X, Scottish Courage Courage Best, Marston's Pedigree, Brakspear Bitter. 8
Facilities Garden Dogs allowed Parking

BLETCHLEY MAP 11 SP83

Pick of the Pubs

The Crooked Billet

2 Westbrook End, Newton Longville MK17 0DF
☎ 01908 373936
e-mail: john@thebillet.co.uk
dir: *Exit M1 junct 13, follow signs to Buckingham. 6m signed at Buttledump rdbt to village of Newton Longville.*

See Pick of the Pubs on opposite page

The Crooked Billet

Back in the 16th century, the Crooked Billet was a farmhouse tucked away in the depths of the Buckinghamshire countryside. These days, the sprawl of Milton Keynes has long since embraced it. Don't let that deter you – there's a large garden, and the thatched building has retained all its traditional charm.

Despite the original oak beams and open log fires, the real attraction is the food and wine. The inn is owned and run by a husband-and-wife team, and both have impeccable pedigrees. John Gilchrist, who's responsible for the inn's staggering 300-bin wine list (all available by the glass), introduced a list more than three times that length when he was the award-winning sommelier at top Mayfair hotel, Brown's, while wife Emma used to be head chef at Nicole Farhi in London's Bond Street. Emma's monthly-changing menus are based on the finest ingredients, local where possible, and the suppliers – right down to the apiarist and the cleaner – are acknowledged in the menu. The menu itself offers everything from a crispy bacon and Somerset brie sandwich as a bar snack, to a decadent 8-course tasting menu. In between, starters may include grilled English goats' cheese and raisin crostini with blood orange, beetroot, rocket and red onion; or bubble and squeak, streaky bacon, poached egg and hollandaise. You might move on to lemon poached halibut fillet with braised lettuce and sorrel consommé and poached oyster; or a study on lamb that includes lamb cutlet, braised shoulder, crispy sweetbreads, fondant potato and celeriac purée. Desserts include coffee and hazelnut mousse with hot cinnamon doughnuts; lemon and frangipane tart with St Clements ice cream; and tropical fruit trifle. The cheese board has won multiple awards and, unsurprisingly, the perfect wine can be chosen for each course. Needless to say, booking is vital.

MAP 11 SP83
2 Westbrook End, Newton Longville MK17 0DF
☎ 01908 373936
e-mail: john@thebillet.co.uk
dir: *Exit M1 Junct 13, follow signs to Buckingham. 6m signed at Buttledump rdbt to village of Newton Longville.*

Open 12–2.30 5.30–11 (Sun 12–4, 7–10.30) Closed: 25 Dec
Bar Meals L served Tue–Sun 12–2 D served Mon–Thu 7–9.30 Av main course £9
Restaurant L served Sun 12.30–3 D served Tue–Sat 7–10 Av 3 course à la carte £28 Av 8 course fixed price £60
Greene King
Old Speckled Hen, Badger Tanglefoot, Hobgoblin, Ruddles County. 300
Facilities Garden Parking

The Royal Oak

Sprawling gardens, a pétanque piste, fragrant kitchen herbs and a sunny terrace create an idyllic impression before you've even stepped inside this delightful little whitewashed pub. It stands a short way up the hill out of Marlow in the village of Bovingdon Green.

Its interior delivers all the hoped-for country charm: a wood burning stove in the snug, dark floorboards, rich fabrics and heritage colours. The front-of-house team looks after customers well – nothing is too much trouble and it shows in their smiles. Head chef James Walker has a wealth of experience and a wicked sense of humour. His passion, shared by his colleagues, is evident in the great-tasting food and beautiful presentation. Whether a 'small plate' or serious gastronomic treat, it will be based on seasonal local produce. Start with rustic breads, roast garlic and olive oil; lemon cured salmon with pickled vegetables and wheaten bread; or Italian bean cassoulet with mascarpone. Follow with grilled herb-crusted pollock on warm pickled cabbage; pan-roasted lamb rump on lemon and garlic hummus with candied beetroot and red wine jus; or roast partridge with fondant potato, bread sauce and blackberry chutney. For pudding, perhaps plum clafoutis with 'oak' aged yogurt; warm pecan pie with caramel sauce; or pear poached in red wine with a baked baby cheesecake. Beers come from the Rebellion Brewery in nearby Marlow Bottom.

🍷
MAP 05 SU88
Frieth Rd SL7 2JF
☎ 01628 488611
📠 01628 478680
e-mail:
info@royaloakmarlow.co.uk
dir: *From Marlow, take A4155. After 300 yds turn right signed Bovingdon Green. After 0.75m pub is on left through woods.*

Open 11–11 (Sun 12–10.30)
Closed: 25–26 Dec
Bar Meals L served Mon–Sat 12–2.30 (Sun 12–4) D served all week 7–10 Av main course £12.75
Restaurant L served all week 12–2.30 (Sun 12–4) D served all week 7–10 Av 3 course à la carte £23.50
London Pride, Brakspears, Rebellion IPA. 🍷 18
Facilities Garden Dogs allowed Parking

England

BOLTER END MAP 05 SU79

The Peacock

HP14 3LU ☎ 01494 881417

e-mail: andy.callen@thepeacockbolterend.co.uk

dir: *On B482 (Marlow to Stokenchurch road). 2m from M40 junct 5*

The oldest part of this pub dates from 1620, featuring original beams and a fireplace dating from the early 1800s. It is situated on top of the Chiltern Hills overlooking the common. At lunch alongside a bar snack selection of baguettes, ciabatta and ploughman's, the menu offers steak and chips, vegetable lasagne or cod and chips. At dinner you could expect beef Stroganoff, lamb dhansak, or halibut steak. A selection of pies is also available. Children are particularly welcome as there are two specially designated areas just for them. Quiz night every Thursday at 9pm.

Open 12–3 5.30–11 (Sat 11.30–11, Sun 12–10.30) Winter closed Sun eve and Mon. **Bar Meals** L served all week 12–2.30 (Sun 12–3) D served Mon–Sat 6.30–9.30 Av main course £11 **Restaurant** L served Mon–Sun 12–2.30 (Sun 12–3) D served Mon–Sat 6.30–9.30 Av 3 course à la carte £18.50 Punch Taverns Brakspear Bitter, Sheppard Neame Spitfire. 8 **Facilities** Children's licence Garden Dogs allowed Parking

BOVINGDON GREEN MAP 05 SU88

Pick of the Pubs

The Royal Oak

Frieth Rd SL7 2JF ☎ 01628 488611 01628 478680

e-mail: info@royaloakmarlow.co.uk

dir: *From Marlow, take A4155. After 300yds turn right signed to Bovingdon Green. After 0.75m pub is on left as you come out of woods.*

See Pick of the Pubs on opposite page

BRILL MAP 11 SP61

The Pheasant Inn

Windmill St HP18 9TG ☎ 01844 237104

dir: *In village centre, by windmill*

Set on the edge of Brill Common, the large garden and veranda at this 17th-century beamed inn make the most of its fine hilltop position, with stunning views over seven counties. Really a lovely spot to watch the sun set in the summer. The popular blackboard menu offers fresh salmon, plus local steaks and pheasant in season. Roald Dahl and JRR Tolkien were both frequent visitors to the pub, and the annual Brill Music Festival is on the first Saturday each July.

Open 11–11 **Bar Meals** L served all week 12–2 D served all week 7–9 (Sat 12–9, Sun 12–8) Av main course £8 **Restaurant** L served all week 12–2 (Sat/Sun 12–2.30) D served all week 7–9 (Sat 7–9.30) Av 3 course à la carte £18 Free House Spitfire, Adnams & Tetleys. 9 **Facilities** Garden Parking

The Red Lion NEW

27 Church St HP18 9RT ☎ 01844 238339 01844 238339

e-mail: info@the-red-lion-at-brill.co.uk

web: www.the-red-lion-at-brill.co.uk

dir: *Off B4011 Thame to Bicester road.*

The Red Lion dates back to the early 17th century and was originally five separate buildings. Plenty of walking and cycling routes converge upon the village, which is overlooked by a famous windmill. Simple, traditional menus change regularly and may feature pork medallions; beer-battered cod, or lamb shank braised in red wine. In summer the secluded garden is home to fierce competitions of Aunt Sally – a local form of skittles.

Open 12–3 5.30–11 (Fri–Sat 5.30–12.30, Etr–Sep open all day) **Bar Meals** L served Mon–Sun 12–4 D served Mon–Sat 6.30–9.30 Av main course £9.50 **Restaurant** L served Mon–Sun 12–2.30 (Sun 12–4) D served Mon–Sat 6.30–9.30 Av 3 course à la carte £16 Greene King Greene King IPA, Old Trip & Fireside. 7 **Facilities** Children's licence Garden Dogs allowed

BUCKINGHAM MAP 11 SP63

The Old Thatched Inn

Main St, Adstock MK18 2JN

☎ 01296 712584 01296 715375

e-mail: manager@theoldthatchedinn.co.uk

Listed in 1645, this lovely old thatched and beamed inn still boasts the traditional beams and inglenook fireplace. The spacious interior consists of a formal conservatory and a bar with comfy furniture and a welcoming atmosphere. Fresh fish is a speciality, with grilled turbot with tiger prawn ravioli a typical example – there are always two additional fish speacials on a Friday. Meat options might include roast duck breast with celeriac purée, braised chicory and griottes cherry sauce.

Open 12–3 6–11 (all day BH & wknds) **Bar Meals** L served all week 12–2.30 D served all week 6–9.30 (Sat 12–9.30, Sun 12–9) Av main course £10.95 **Restaurant** L served all week 12–2.30 D served all week 6–9.30 Av 3 course à la carte £21 Free House Hook Norton Best, Sharps Doom Bar, Tom Wood, Deuchars. 10 **Facilities** Dogs allowed Parking

England

BUCKINGHAM continued

The Wheatsheaf

Main St, Maids Moreton MK18 1QR

01280 815433 01280 814631

dir: *From M1 junct 13 take A421 to Buckingham, then A413 to Maids Moreton or M40 junct 9 take A34 to Bicester, then A421 to Buckingham then A413 to Maids Moreton.*

This traditional, thatched village inn is over three hundred years old, and offers an appetising à la carte menu in the spacious conservatory overlooking the secluded beer garden. Eating options include baked cod and prawns in cream; roast aubergine stuffed with ratatouille; and home-made Thai chicken curry. Real ales and snacks can also be enjoyed in the bar, with its cosy inglenook fireplaces. Children will be delighted with the outdoor play equipment.

Open 12-3 6-11 (Sun 6-10.30) **Bar Meals** L served Mon-Sat 12-2.15 D served Mon-Sat 7-9.30 (Sun 12-2) Av main course £7 **Restaurant** L served Mon-Sat 12-2.15 D served Mon-Sat 7-9.30 (Sun 12-2) Av 3 course à la carte £23 Free House Hook Norton,Old Speckled Hen, John Smiths, Side Pocket For A Toad & Reverend James. 10 **Facilities** Children's licence Garden Dogs allowed Parking Play Area

CHALFONT ST GILES MAP 06 SU99

Pick of the Pubs

The Ivy House ★★★★ INN

London Rd HP8 4RS 01494 872184 01494 872870

e-mail: enquiries@theivyhouse-bucks.co.uk

dir: *On A413 2m S of Amersham & 1.5m N of Chalfont St Giles*

See Pick of the Pubs on opposite page

The White Hart

Three Households HP8 4LP

01494 872441 01494 876375

e-mail: enquiries@thewhitehartstgiles.co.uk

dir: *Off A413 (Denham/Amersham)*

Oak and brown leather furniture and a refurbished bar characterise the quiet, relaxed atmosphere of this prettily-located 100-year-old inn, giving it a welcoming, contemporary feel. The menu offers the likes of loin of pork en croute, carpet bag fillet steak, supreme of chicken, lamb shank, and calves' liver. Fish dishes include baked sea bass with vegetables and Thai fish sauce, and seared blue-fin tuna.

Open 11.30-2.30 5.30-11 (All day Sun, BHs) **Bar Meals** L served all week 12-2 D served all week 6.30-9.30 (Sun all day) **Restaurant** L served all week 12-2 D served all week 6.30-9.30 (Sun all day) Av 3 course à la carte £20 Greene King Greene King Morland Original, Abbot Ale, Rev. James. 12 **Facilities** Garden Parking **Rooms** 11 bedrooms en suite S£47.50 D£67.50 (★★★★ INN)

CHALFONT ST PETER MAP 06 TQ09

Pick of the Pubs

The Greyhound Inn

SL9 9RA 01753 883404 01753 891627

e-mail: reception@thegreyhoundinn.net

dir: *M40 junct 1/M25 junct 16, follow signs for Gerrards Cross, then Chalfont St Peter*

The 14th-century Greyhound has a macabre place in English history. Not only are its grounds believed to be where the last man hanged for stealing sheep was executed, but a former patron was Sir George Jeffreys, known as the Hanging Judge for his harsh sentencing policy during the Monmouth Rebellion. While still a local magistrate he held court in a room above the restaurant, mention of which brings us neatly to the food here. The cooking style is essentially classic British with a modern twist, producing starters such as moules marinière, shallots, parsley, white wine and cream; chargrilled chicken Caesar salad; and avocado, orange and prawn salad with Marie Rose sauce. From a well balanced list of main courses choose from deep-fried haddock in beer batter; whole baked sea bass; pan-fried calves' liver; home-made shepherd's pie; or leg of duck confit, among many others.

Open 11-11 Closed: 1 Jan **Bar Meals** L served all week 12-3 D served all week 6-9 Av main course £10 **Restaurant** L served all week 12-3 D served all week 6-9 Av 3 course à la carte £22.50 Enterprise Inns London Pride. 12 **Facilities** Children's licence Garden Dogs allowed Parking

CHEDDINGTON MAP 11 SP91

The Old Swan NEW

58 High St LU7 0RQ 01296 668226 01296 663811

e-mail: enquiries@theoldswancheddington.co.uk

dir: *From Tring head towards Marsworth, take B489 0.5m. Left towards Cooks Wharf continue on to Cheddington, The Old Swan on left*

This delightful thatched 15th-century pub is known not only for its real ales and traditional charm but also for its ghost – a figure in a long dark coat who appears from a cupboard in the long room. The please-all menus include a selection of sweet and savoury pancakes and daily specials such as game pie; Singapore chicken noodles; and skate wings with parsley butter. Outside there's a large garden with a children's play area.

Open 12-3 5-11 (Fri-Sun 12-11) **Bar Meals** L served all week 12-2 (Sun 12-4) D served Mon-Thurs 6-9 (Fri-Sat 12-2.30, 6-9.30) Av main course £8 **Restaurant** L served all week 12-2 (Sun 12-4) D served Mon-Thurs 6-9 (Fri-Sat 12-2.30, 6-9.30) Av 3 course à la carte £18 Punch Taverns Greene King IPA, Brakspear Best, Everard's Tiger, Shepherd Neame Spitfire. 12 **Facilities** Garden Dogs allowed Parking Play Area

The Ivy House

Set in the heart of the Chiltern Hills with views across the Misbourne Valley and the South Bucks Way, this 17th-century brick and flint free house proves popular with cask ale fans, wine lovers and diners alike.

The atmosphere is cosy, warm and welcoming with open fires, comfy armchairs, old pictures, beams and brasses. Naturally there's the odd ghost story to be told, and there is always a new beer to sample, plus more than 50 wines to choose from with some 20 available by the glass. Whisky aficionados will appreciate the good range of malts, including some rarities favoured by the landlord. You can eat wherever you like, as the same menu is served in the bar, the former coach house and the restaurant. The award-winning food includes plenty of highlighted healthy options (oak-aged salmon with fresh dill, mustard, lemon and olive oil dressing), and vegetarian specials (roasted vegetable ratatouille bound in a rich Mediterranean tomato sauce, studded with melting mozzarella, served with penne pasta then finished with a sweet balsamic reduction). Seafood and fish dishes feature prominently (luxury seafood pie with a mix of fish fillets and seafood bound in a creamy sauce, laced with white wine and scented with lemon and fresh tarragon), but alternatives include steak with triple cooked chunky chips; and pan-fried pheasant breast with a West Country cider, cream and Bramley apple sauce, topped with apple crisps. The pub is also well known for its choice of home-made desserts, notably the classic bread-and-butter pudding with an extra touch of fruit and spice, served with cream, ice cream or hot custard. Following extensive refurbishment, accommodation is now provided in five en suite bedrooms, with a traditional cooked breakfast to look forward to in the morning.

★★★★ INN ⇨ 🍷
MAP 06 SU99
London Rd HP8 4RS
☎ 01494 872184
🖷 01494 872870
e-mail: enquiries@theivyhouse-bucks.co.uk
dir: *On A413 2m S of Amersham & 1.5m N of Chalfont St Giles*

Open 12–3 6–11 (Sat 12–11, Sun 12–10.30)
Bar Meals L served all week 12–2.30 D served all week 6.30–9.30 (Sat 12–9.30, Sun 12–9) Av main course £13.95
Restaurant L served all week 12–2.30 D served all week 6.30–9.30 (Sat 12–10, Sun 12–9) Av 3 course à la carte £25
Free House
Fuller's London Pride, Brakspear Bitter, Wadworth 6X, Hook Norton Old Hooky. 🍷 22
Facilities Garden Dogs allowed Parking Play Area
Rooms 5 bedrooms en suite S£75 D£95

The Red Lion

Chenies is a picturesque village in the Chess valley. It has a pretty green, an ancient parish church and a manor house that was once the home of the Dukes of Bedford. With 20 years' experience behind them, Mike and Heather Norris firmly believe the 17th-century Red Lion's popularity stems from being a pub that serves good food, not a restaurant that serves beer.

In the jukebox- and gaming machine-free bar, the noisiest thing to be heard, says Mike, are his protestations when an irritating mobile goes off, followed by its owner's often inane conversation. Get him talking about his real ales, one of which, Lion Pride, brewed by Rebellion in Marlow, is available here and here alone; other local beers come from Vale Brewery in Haddenham. There's no separate restaurant as such, although part of the bar is reserved for dining. Heather cooks everything, including fresh daily pastas; bangers with bubble and squeak; big chunks of oven-baked leg of lamb (much like Greek kleftiko); Orkneys rump steak; curries; sea bass with wholegrain mustard sauce; poached haddock with peppered red wine sauce; quorn lasagne; and sausage, apple and cheddar pie. Speaking of pies, brace yourself for the lamb version, which a visiting American serviceman once declared beat a rival pub's pies hands down. Ever since, its entry on the menu has acquired an additional adjective every time it is rewritten. Today, therefore, it reads (take a deep breath) 'The awesome, internationally acclaimed, world-renowned, aesthetically and palatably pleasing, not knowingly genetically modified, hand-crafted, well-balanced, famous, original Chenies lamb pie'. The Red Lion also serves some good wines, but look in vain for anything French – the boycott's all to do with their refusal to buy British beef. Outside, on the pub's sunny side, is a small seating area.

MAP 06 TQ09
WD3 6ED
☎ 01923 282722
Fax 01923 283797
dir: *Between Rickmansworth & Amersham on A404, follow signs for Chenies & Latimer*

Open 11–2.30 5.30–11 Sun 5.30–10.30 Closed: 25 Dec
Bar Meals L served all week 12–2 D served all week 7–10 Sun 6.30–9.30
Free House
Wadworth 6X, Rebellion, Lion's Pride, Vale Best. 10
Facilities Garden Dogs allowed Parking

CHENIES MAP 06 TQ09

Pick of the Pubs

The Red Lion 🍷

WD3 6ED ☎ 01923 282722 📠 01923 283797

dir: *Between Rickmansworth & Amersham on A404, follow signs for Chenies & Latimer*

See Pick of the Pubs on opposite page

CHESHAM MAP 06 SP90

The Black Horse Inn 🍷

Chesham Vale HP5 3NS ☎ 01494 784656

dir: *A41 from Berkhamstead, A416 through Ashley Green, 0.75m before Chesham right to Vale Rd, bottom of Mashleigh Hill for 1m, inn on left*

Set in some beautiful valley countryside, this 500-year-old pub is ideal for enjoying a cosy, traditional environment without electronic games or music. During the winter there are roaring log fires to take the chill off those who may spot one of the resident ghosts. An ever-changing menu includes an extensive range of snacks, while the main menu may feature steak and Stallion Ale pie, trout and almonds, various home-made pies, steaks and gammons, stuffed plaice, or salmon supreme.

Open 11-3 5.30-11 (Sun 12-4, 7-10.30) **Bar Meals** L served all week 12-2.30 D served Mon-Sat 6.30-9 (Sun 12-3) Av main course £8.95 **Restaurant** L served all week 12-2.30 D served Mon-Sat 6.30-9 (Sun 12-3) Adnams Bitter, London Pride, Speckled Hen, guest ale. 🍷 10 **Facilities** Garden Dogs allowed Parking

The Swan 🍷

Ley Hill HP5 1UT ☎ 01494 783075 📠 01494 783582

e-mail: swan@swanleyhill.com

dir: *E of Chesham by golf course*

Once three cottages, the first built around 1520, qualifying it as one of Buckinghamshire's oldest pubs. Condemned prisoners, heading for nearby gallows, would drink 'a last and final ale' here. During the Second World War, Clark Gable, James Stewart and Glenn Miller frequently drank here after cycling from Bovingdon airbase. Menus change several times monthly, and a blackboard features daily specials. Steamed fillet of salmon with lobster sauce is a typical dinner choice.

Open 12-3 5.30-11 (Sun 12-4, 7-10.30) **Bar Meals** L served Mon-Sat 12-2.15 D served Tues-Sat (Sun 12-2.30, D all wk summer) **Restaurant** L served Mon-Sat 12-2 D served Tues-Sat 7-9 (Sun 12-2.30, D all wk summer) Punch Group Adnams Bitter, Fuller's London Pride, Timothy Taylor Landlord, Brakespears. 🍷 8 **Facilities** Garden Parking

CHICHELEY MAP 11 SP94

The Chester Arms 🍷

MK16 9JE ☎ 01234 391214 📠 01234 391214

e-mail: foodjunkies@btopenworld.com

dir: *On A422, 2m NE of Newport Pagnell. 4m from M1 junct 14*

A philosophy of buying well and keeping things simple pays dividends at this comfortable roadside pub near Chicheley Hall. Bar lunches and Greene King ales are always available, and in fine weather meals are served in the pub garden. Home-made soup or mixed seafood salad support main courses like chargrilled lamb chops; whole sea bass; or chicken chasseur.

The Chester Arms

Open 11-3 6-11 **Bar Meals** L served Tues-Sat 12-2 Av main course £11 **Restaurant** L served Tues-Sun 12-2 D served Tues-Sat 6.30-9.30 Av 3 course à la carte £22 Greene King Greene King IPA & Ruddles County. 🍷 35 **Facilities** Garden Parking

CHOLESBURY MAP 06 SP90

Pick of the Pubs

The Full Moon 🍷

Hawridge Common HP5 2UH ☎ 01494 758959

e-mail: annie@alberto1142.freeserve.co.uk

dir: *At Tring on A41 take turn for Wiggington & Cholesbury. On Cholesbury Common in by windmill*

When this 17th-century former coaching inn was first built, the local Chiltern hills were overrun with alehouses. These days, only three remain. Fortunately, the Full Moon, which graduated from The Half Moon in 1812, is something of an ideal country pub, complete with beams, flagstones, winter fires and a windmill-backed setting. Thorough menus cover a range of possibilities, from baguettes and jacket potatoes to more adventurous fare. Moroccan lamb shank; pumpkin and potato rôsti; and monkfish tail wrapped in Parma ham give an indication of the range. Those looking for a Sunday lunch will find plenty of options, with chicken and porcini stroganoff; and roasted vegetable lasagne accompanying the likes of beef, turkey and lamb. In 1907, the landlord was fined for permitting drunkenness on the premises: these days the clientele is much better behaved when it comes to the eclectic selection of real ales.

Open 12-11 (Sun 12-10.30) Closed: 25 Dec **Bar Meals** L served all week 12-2 D served all week 6.30-9 (Sun 6-8) Av main course £11.10 **Restaurant** L served all week 12-2 D served all week 6.30-9 (Sun 6-8) Av 3 course à la carte £22.50 Admiral Taverns Interbrew Bass, Adnams, Fuller's London Pride, Brakspear Special, and Guest Ales. 🍷 7 **Facilities** Garden Dogs allowed Parking

England

CUDDINGTON MAP 05 SP71

Pick of the Pubs

The Crown

Spurt St HP18 0BB ☎ 01844 292222
e-mail: david@anniebaileys.com
dir: *Off A418 between Aylesbury & Thame*

See Pick of the Pubs on opposite page

DENHAM MAP 06 TQ08

The Falcon Inn ★★★★ INN

Village Rd UB9 5BE ☎ 01895 832125
e-mail: falcon.inn@btconnect.com
dir: *Exit M40 junct 1, follow A40/Gerrards Cross signs. Approx 200yds turn right onto Old Mill Rd. Pass church on right, enter village. Pub opposite village green.*

This traditional 16th-century inn, located opposite the green in beautiful Denham village, is an ideal base for exploring Colne Valley Country Park. Expect excellent real ales and award-winning food. Lunch could include Spanish tortilla with mixed salad, or a home-made burger with fries; in the evening, perhaps ginger king prawns and scallops with aubergine caviar, rôsti potatoes, langoustine and herb oil, or rack of lamb with marinated courgettes, straw potatoes and red wine sauce. Lots of fish.

Open 12-3 5-11 (Summer Sat/Sun 12-11) **Bar Meals** L served all week 12-2.30 D served all week 6.30-9.30 (Sun 12-4) **Restaurant** L served Mon-Sun 12-2.30 D served Mon-Sun 6.30-10 (Sun 12-4, 6.30-9.30) Timothy Taylor Landlord, Bombardier, Youngs, Deuchars & Guest Ale. 11 **Facilities** Children's licence Garden **Rooms** 4 bedrooms en suite S£85 D£95

Pick of the Pubs

The Swan Inn

Village Rd UB9 5BH ☎ 01895 832085 01895 835516
e-mail: info@swaninndenham.co.uk
dir: *From A40, take A412. After 200yds follow Denham village sign on right. Continue through village, over bridge, last pub on left.*

Covered in wisteria and set in the lovely village of Denham, the Swan Inn must be everyone's idea of the ideal country inn. The pub – Georgian, double-fronted and cosily welcoming – is entirely in keeping. There's a large log fire and interesting pictures inside, while outside is a sunny, secluded terrace and gardens large enough to lose the children in. Fresh, seasonal produce underpins a menu that runs from 'small plates' – perhaps ballotine of guinea fowl and foie gras with cranberry and orange chutney, or polenta cake with harissa dressing – through to main meals such as braised lamb shank on Moroccan vegetable ragout; or confit duck leg on fondant potato with jalapeno and pumpkin seed pesto and elderberry jus. A separate pudding menu offers such seductive treats as chocolate truffle doughnuts with vanilla milkshake or plum crème brûlée with pistachio tuile. The wine list includes a good selection by the glass and a long list of pudding wines.

Open 11-11 (Sun 12-10.30) Closed: 25-26 Dec **Bar Meals** L served all week 12-2.30 (Sun 12-4) D served all week 7-10 Av main course £12.75 **Restaurant** L served all week 12-2.30 (Sun 12-4) D served all week 7-10 Av 3 course à la carte £23.50 Salisbury Pubs Wadworth 6X, Courage Best, Marlow Rebellion IPA. 18 **Facilities** Garden Dogs allowed Parking

The Crown

Fans of 'Midsomer Murders' may recognise Cuddington's Crown, which has been used several times as a location for the popular TV series. There's nothing sinister about the place in real life though.

It's a delightful thatched and whitewashed pub at the heart of a picturesque village, and has made a name for itself as a great place to eat. Having successfully run Annie Bailey's bar/brasserie near by for a number of years, the Berrys turned their attention to improving the Crown. Today the characterful Grade II-listed pub functions equally well as a popular local, with a choice of Fullers and Adnams brews served in the bar, augmented by an extensive wine list; several low-beamed dining areas are filled with charming prints and the glow of evening candlelight. The small patio area provides outside seating and an opportunity for al fresco dining in the summer. The eclectic menus should please all comers. Starters might include the Crown fishcake with sweet chilli jam; linguini with prawn, chilli and spring onion; avocado, smoked chicken and pine kernel salad; and roasted red pepper with shaved parmesan and croutons. On the main course menu you will find such dishes as confit duck on puy lentil stew; Thai seafood curry with coconut and lime-scented rice; honey-glazed shank of lamb; chargrilled rib-eye steak; and vegetarian alternatives such as the Mediterranean vegetable risotto with pesto. Fish dishes are a major attraction, and could include seafood pie; smoked haddock with grilled Welsh rarebit, tomato salad and chips; sea bass with crab risotto; and scallops with pancetta, salad leaves and truffle vinaigrette. The changing selection of desserts chalked up on a blackboard is guaranteed to conclude in fine style the eating-out experience here.

🍷
MAP 05 SP71
Spurt St HP18 0BB
☎ 01844 292222
e-mail: david@anniebaileys.com
dir: *Off A418 between Aylesbury & Thame*

Open 12–3 6–11 (All day Sun)
Bar Meals L served all week 12–2.30 D served all week 6.30–10 (Sun 12–8)
Restaurant L served all week 12–2.30 D served all week 6.30–10 (Sun 12–8)
Fullers
Fullers London Pride, Adnams, Guinness. 🍷 9
Facilities Garden Parking

The Dinton Hermit

A 400-year-old, listed inn deep in the Vale of Aylesbury. A sympathetic restoration and extension programme a few years ago included a 200-year-old barn constructed of packed earth known as wychert, a building method often used in this area.

The hermit in question was John Bigg, a local eccentric, who renounced his normal lifestyle in protest at his former employer's involvement in the execution of Charles I in 1649. Adopting a cave as his home, he never changed his clothes, patching them when holes appeared; you can see one of his shoes in Oxford's Bodleian Library. In the bar, nibbles include marinated olives, and real ales come from Adnams, Fuller's, Bateman's, Wadworth and Brakspear. At lunchtime, sandwiches, the Dinton Hermit burger and a variety of main courses are served. The elegantly furnished restaurant offers imaginative contemporary British cooking, with everything sourced locally, apart from fish and seafood delivered directly from the ports. Menus change seasonally and blackboard specials are always on offer. An idea of style and choice may be gained from starters such as marinated seared scallops with brussels sprouts, bacon and horseradish potato cake; twice-roasted duck leg with chilli mash, pak choi and hoi sin; and crispy skewered salmon with oriental spicy sauce. Among the eight main courses, taken from a winter menu, might be baked John Dory with crispy pancetta, buttered spinach, ratatouille and beurre rouge; herb-stuffed corn-fed chicken supreme wrapped in Parma ham with classic jambalaya; and wild mushroom millefeuille with Boursin cheese and gratinated vegetables. Wines are modestly priced, with enough varieties by the glass to suit all tastes, and there's an extensive list of brandies and cognacs.

★ SHL
MAP 05 SP70
Water Ln HP17 8XH
☎ 01296 747473
01296 748819
e-mail:
dintonhermit@btconnect.com
dir: *Off A418 between Aylesbury & Thame*

Open 10-12 (Sun 12-11.30)
Closed: 25-26 Dec & 1 Jan
Bar Meals L served Mon-Sat 12-2 D served all week 7-9 (Sun 12-4) Av main course £16
Restaurant L served Mon-Sat 12-2 D served Mon-Sat 7-9 (Sun 12-4) Av 3 course à la carte £27
Free House
Adnams Bitter, 6X, Brakspears, London Pride, Batemans XB.
Facilities Garden Parking
Rooms 13 bedrooms en suite D£80

England

DORNEY MAP 06 SU97

The Palmer Arms

Village Rd SL4 6QW ☎ 01628 666612 📠 01628 661116
e-mail: info@thepalmerarms.com
dir: *From A4 take B3026, over M4 to Dorney*

The Palmer Arms, dating from the 15th century, is well-located in the beautiful conservation village of Dorney. Its owners are passionate about providing high standards of food and service, and like to think of their cooking as 'English with a twist'. Seasonal game dishes are always available, and fish is well represented on the menu. It is open every day of the year for lunch, afternoon tea, dinner and all-day coffee.

Open 11-11 (Sun 12-8) **Bar Meals** L served All week 12-5 (Sun 12-4) Av main course £12 **Restaurant** L served Mon-Sat 12-2.30 D served Mon-Sat 6-9.30 (Sun 12-4) Av 3 course à la carte £26 Av 2 course fixed price £12.50 Greene King Greene King Abbot Ale, Old Speckled Hen, IPA, Guinness. 20 **Facilities** Garden Parking

FARNHAM COMMON MAP 06 SU98

The Foresters

The Broadway SL2 3QQ
☎ 01753 643340 📠 01753 647524
e-mail: barforesters@aol.com

There's a great atmosphere at the Foresters, a pub dating back to the 1930s and built to replace a Victorian building. It's conveniently situated for discovering the delights of Burnham Beeches containing the world's largest collection of ancient beech. The quality daily menu might include fillet of brill colbert with parsley potatoes; pork loin steak with bubble and squeak and shallot and mustard sauce; and escalopes of veal with fondant potato and Irish cabbage.

Open 11-11 (Sun 12-10.30) **Bar Meals** L served Mon-Sat 12-2.30 D served Mon-Sat 6.30-10 (Sun all day) Av main course £14 **Restaurant** L served Mon-Sat 12-2.30 D served Mon-Sat 6.30-10 (Sun 12-9) Av 3 course à la carte £25 Punch Taverns Fullers London Pride, Draught Bass, Carling, Stella Artois. 10 **Facilities** Children's licence Garden Dogs allowed Parking

FARNHAM ROYAL MAP 06 SU98

The King of Prussia NEW

Blackpond Ln SL2 3EG ☎ 01753 643006
e-mail: gm@tkop.co.uk

This old inn has a wealth of polished wood floors and original beams running through its bar, conservatory and refurbished barn. A log fire burns in winter, and tables outside beckon on summer days. British food based on fresh seasonal fare is the overriding emphasis on the menus. You may find potted Aylesbury duck with baby leaf salad to start, followed by canon of Welsh lamb with dauphinoise potatoes, and fresh fruit meringue to finish.

Open 12-3 6-11 Closed: 1 Jan **Bar Meals** L served all week 12-2.15 D served Mon-Sat 7-9.15 (Sun 12-4.30) Av main course £10.50 **Restaurant** L served all week 12-2.15 D served Mon-Sat 7-9.15 (Sun 12-4.30) Av 3 course à la carte £22.50 Enterprise Inns Guinness, London Pride, Carling, Caffreys. 8 **Facilities** Garden Parking

FORD MAP 05 SP70

Pick of the Pubs

The Dinton Hermit ★ SHL

Water Ln HP17 8XH ☎ 01296 747473 📠 01296 748819
e-mail: dintonhermit@btconnect.com
dir: *Off A418 between Aylesbury & Thame*

See Pick of the Pubs on opposite page

FRIETH MAP 05 SU79

The Prince Albert

RG9 6PY ☎ 01494 881683
dir: *4m N of Marlow. Follow Frieth road from Marlow. Straight across x-rds on Fingest road. Pub 200yds on left*

Set in the Chilterns, close to Hambledon and Marlow, this traditional country pub prides itself on old world values. There are no televisions, juke boxes or games – just good conversation and a welcoming atmosphere. Warm open fires enhance the mood in winter. Expect baguettes, jacket potatoes and ploughman's lunches among the lunchtime light bites, while the evening menu typically offers jumbo battered cod, chilli con carne, lamb shank, and home-made steak and kidney pie.

Open 11-11 (Sun 12-10.30) **Bar Meals** L served Mon-Sat 12.15-2.30 Sun 12.30-3 (D served Fri-Sat 7-9.30) Av main course £8.50 **Restaurant** L served Mon-Sat 12.30-2.30 Sun 12.30-3 (D served Fri & Sat 7-9.30) Brakspear Brakspear Bitter, Brakspear Seasonal Ales. **Facilities** Garden Dogs allowed Parking

FRIETH continued

The Yew Tree

RG9 6PJ ☎ 01494 882330 01494 883497

e-mail: enquiries@theyewtreerestaurant.com

dir: *From M40 towards Stokenchurch, through Cadmore End, Lane End right to Frieth*

Deep in the Chiltern Hills, the 16th-century, red-brick Yew Tree manages to be both traditional rustic country pub and contemporary restaurant, its unexpected pale beams contributing to the effect. Bar meals are available, although you may prefer the dining room where main courses include crispy-skinned sea bass with stir-fried vegetables and honey and soy glaze; and lamb shank, dauphinoise potatoes and garlic and thyme jus. A paddock with three llamas adjoins the substantial rear garden.

Open 12-3 6-11 (Sun 12-5) **Bar Meals** L served all week 12-2.30 D served all week 6-10 (Sun 12-5) **Restaurant** L served all week 12-2.30 D served all week 6-10 Free House Fullers Honeydew, Rebellion, IPA, Smuggler. 4 **Facilities** Garden Dogs allowed Parking Play Area

GREAT HAMPDEN MAP 05 SP80

The Hampden Arms

HP16 9RQ ☎ 01494 488255 01494 488094

e-mail: louise@thehamptonarms.fsnet.co.uk

dir: *From M40 take A4010, right before Princes Risborough. Great Hampden signed*

Whether you're celebrating a special occasion or just want a quiet pint of real ale, you'll find a warm and friendly welcome at this mock Tudor pub restaurant in the heart of the beautifully wooded Hampden Estate. The menu features such dishes as game pie set on a rich port sauce; baked halibut steak with a watercress, mussel and cream sauce; and roasted vegetables set on a rocket and parmesan salad. Lighter snacks are available, and there is a good choice of hot puddings.

Open 12-3 6-11 (Sun 7-10.30) **Bar Meals** L served all week 12-2 (Sun 12-3) D served all week 6.30-9 (Fri-Sat 6.30-9.30, Sun 7-9) Av main course £10.95 **Restaurant** L served all week 12-2 (Sun 12-3) D served all week 6.30-9 Av 3 course à la carte £20 Free House Adnams Bitter, Hook Norton, Tetley. 7 **Facilities** Garden Dogs allowed Parking

GREAT MISSENDEN MAP 06 SP80

Pick of the Pubs

The Polecat Inn

170 Wycombe Rd, Prestwood HP16 0HJ

☎ 01494 862253 01494 868393

e-mail: polecatinn@btinternet.com

dir: *On A4128 between Great Missenden & High Wycombe*

The colourful three-acre garden with interesting herbaceous borders is a huge attraction at this charming 17th-century free house, set amidst rolling Chilterns countryside. John Gamble bought the closed and dilapidated Polecat 17 years ago, renovating and extending it to create an attractive inn that still retains many original features. Now the small low-beamed rooms that radiate from the central bar are ideal for relaxing with a pint of ale, and eating freshly prepared dishes using local ingredients and herbs from the garden. Lunchtime snacks include a range of sandwiches, warm baguettes, jacket potatoes and ploughman's. Or refer to the blackboard daily specials for a taste of something different: you may find sweet potato cakes with jalapeno chillies to start, and main courses like venison paupiettes with wild boar, juniper and apple stuffing; or breadcrumbed pork escalope rolled with Bowland cheese. Puddings include mainstays like sherry trifle, and profiteroles with chocolate sauce.

Open 11.30-2.30 6-11 (Sun 12-3) Closed: Dec 25-26, Jan 1 **Bar Meals** L served all week 12-2 D served Mon-Sat 6.30-9 Free House Marston's Pedigree, Moorland, Old Speckled Hen, Interbrew Flowers IPA & Brakspears Bitter. 16 **Facilities** Garden Dogs allowed Parking Play Area

Pick of the Pubs

The Rising Sun

Little Hampden HP16 9PS

☎ 01494 488393 & 488360 01494 488788

e-mail: sunrising@rising-sun.demon.co.uk

web: www.rising-sun.demon.co.uk

dir: *From A413, N of Gt Missenden, take Rignall Rd on left signed for Princes Risborough 2.5m. Turn right signed Little Hampden only*

You'll find this 250-year-old inn tucked away in the Chiltern Hills, close to the Ridgeway, down a single track, no-through-road, surrounded by beech woods and glorious scenery. It is just three miles from the Prime Minister's country retreat at Chequers and was once frequented by Harold Wilson and Ted Heath, although the original clientele were more likely to be farm labourers or bodgers who worked in the local beech woods. A network of footpaths begins just outside the front door, so it's a perfect base for country walks. An attractive new feature is the landscaped garden area with comfortable armchair seating and tables for outside wining and dining in beautiful surroundings. Rotisserie paprika-seasoned corn-fed chicken and chips is a speciality. There's some good seafood too, like hot dressed crab with cheese and grain mustard sauce, and pan-fried skate wings with scallop, lemon and capers.

Open 11.30-3 6.30-10 (Sun 12-3 only) Open BH lunchtime **Bar Meals** L served Tue-Sun 12-2 D served Tue-Sat 7-9 (Sun 12-2) **Restaurant** L served Tue-Sun 12-2 D served Tue-Sat 7-9 (Sun 12-2) Av 3 course à la carte £22 Free House Adnams, Spitfire, Marstons Pedigree, Brakspear Special. 10 **Facilities** Garden Dogs allowed Parking **Rooms** 5 bedrooms en suite S£55 D£80 (★★★ INN)

The Green Dragon

The Green Dragon is attractively located in the old part of Haddenham, close to the village green and 12th-century church. The pub dates back to 1650 and was once a manorial court, as the last man to be executed in Buckinghamshire discovered to his cost.

The garden offers two large lawned areas offering some shade and a mix of tables and chairs, some distance from the main building. There is also a seating area under a canopy near to the door. Over the last seven years pub co-owner and chef Paul Berry has built up a formidable reputation for his food, and the place gets very busy, so booking is strongly advised. Local produce from local suppliers is to the fore, and fresh fish arrives post haste from Devon. Local guest ales feature, along with Wychert Ale, IPA Deuchars Ale and Wadworths 6X. The menu is slightly different at lunch and dinner, offering a comprehensive range of dishes. Starters might feature salmon and prawn fishcakes served with herb salad and a lime and ginger dressing; or perhaps confit duck leg with a warm rhubarb and apple compote, cider and vanilla dressing. Main courses offer a selection of home-made delights from pies and fish and chips to dishes like braised Buckinghamshire lamb shank with vegetable tagine and pak choi. Vegetarians are well catered for with the likes of a warm terrine of potatoes, celeriac, ceps, wild mushrooms and artichokes served with parmesan cream.

MAP 05 SP70
8 Churchway HP17 8AA
☎ 01844 291403
299532
e-mail:
pete@eatatthedragon.co.uk
dir: *From M40 A329 to Thame, then A418, 1st right after entering Haddenham*

Open 12–3 6.30–11 Closed: 25 Dec & 1 Jan
Bar Meals L served all week 12–2 D served Mon–Sat 6.30–9.15 (Sun 12–3) Av main course £12.50
Restaurant L served all week 12–2 D served Mon–Sat 6.30–9.15 Av 3 course à la carte £25
Enterprise Inns
IPA Deuchars Ale, Wadworth 6X & Local Guest Ale. 10
Facilities Garden Parking

HADDENHAM MAP 05 SP70

Pick of the Pubs

The Green Dragon ◎◎ 🍷

8 Churchway HP17 8AA

☎ 01844 291403 📠 01844 299532

e-mail: pete@eatatthedragon.co.uk

dir: *From M40 A329 to Thame, then A418, 1st right after entering Haddenham*

See Pick of the Pubs on page 49

HAMBLEDEN MAP 05 SU78

The Stag & Huntsman Inn

RG9 6RP ☎ 01491 571227 📠 01491 413810

e-mail: andy@stagandhuntsman.com

dir: *5m from Henley-on-Thames on A4155 toward Marlow, left at Mill End towards Hambleden*

Warm and welcoming 400-year-old brick and flint pub in a quintessentially English village that's featured in many TV productions. Relax in the cosy snug, or choose the public bar for a game of darts or dominos. Alternatively, savour the bustling atmosphere of the L-shaped, half-panelled lounge, with low ceilings, and open fire. The dining room offers home-cooked choices such as marinated chargrilled chicken, pan-fried pheasant breast, Hambleden venison sausages, and Huntsman steak with caramelised sugar and mustard. BBQs and a beer festival in summer.

Open 11–2.30 6–11 (Sat 11–3, 6–11, Sun 12–3, 7–10.30) Closed: Dec 25–26 & 1 Jan (evening) **Bar Meals** L served all week 12–2 D served Mon–Sat 7–9.30 Av main course £10 **Restaurant** L served all week 12–2 D served Mon–Sat 7–9.30 ⊕ Free House ◀ Rebellion IPA, Wadworth 6X, Guest ales. **Facilities** Garden Parking

HEDGERLEY MAP 06 SU98

The White Horse 🍷

SL2 3UY ☎ 01753 643225

The original part of the pub is 500 years old, and over 1000 beers take their turn at the pumps during each year. At least seven real ales are always available, served by gravity. An annual beer festival is held at the end of May bank holiday. Home-made food ranges from a salad bar with pies, quiches, sandwiches and ploughman's through to curries, chilli, pasta dishes, pies and steaks.

Open 11–2.30 5–11 (Sat 11–11, Sun 12–10.30) **Bar Meals** L served all week 12–2 (wknds 12–2.30) Av main course £6.50 ⊕ Free House ◀ Constantly changing. 🍷 10 **Facilities** Garden Dogs allowed Parking

KINGSWOOD MAP 11 SP61

Crooked Billet 🍷

Ham Green HP18 0QJ ☎ 01296 770239 📠 01296 770094

e-mail: info@crookedbillet.com

dir: *On A41 between Aylesbury & Bicester*

Located in peaceful Buckinghamshire countryside, this 200-year-old pub offers an extensive and tempting choice of food. Starters may include port and stilton rarebit with date and walnut bread, and tomato Cumberland sauce, or salad of queenie scallops with smoked salmon. Among the main courses can be found pasta alla Fiorentina smothered in cream cheeses and spinach; roasted sea bass fillet with shrimp velouté and parsley mash; or gratin of fine herb gnocchi with chard, turnips and carrots.

Open 11–11 **Bar Meals** L served Mon–Sat 12–2.30 D served Mon–Sat 6–9.30 (Sun 12–3.30) **Restaurant** L served Mon–Sat 12–2.30 D served Mon–Sat 6–9.30 (Sun 12–3.30) ⊕ Free House ◀ Hook Norton, Guinness, Tetley's, Carlsberg & Carlsberg Export. 🍷 15 **Facilities** Garden Parking Play Area

LITTLE CHALFONT MAP 06 SU99

Pick of the Pubs

The Sugar Loaf Inn 🍷

Station Rd HP7 9NP ☎ 01494 765579

e-mail: info@thesugarloafinn.com

dir: *On A404 between junct 18–25 motorway and Amersham town. From junct 25 towards Amersham after 4m enter Little Chalfont. Pub on right.*

See Pick of the Pubs on opposite page

PICK OF THE PUBS

LITTLE CHALFONT-BUCKINGHAMSHIRE

The Sugar Loaf Inn

Sited within the gently rolling Chiltern hills, the Sugar Loaf Inn is a short drive from excellent walks in the Chess valley. It's a classic 1930s pub, but now endowed with a contemporary gastro feel after a major refit.

Original oak-panelled walls have been restored, and new wooden floors, bespoke lighting and blinds all contribute to the clutter-free atmosphere of the bar and two dining rooms. Locals populate the bar whatever the weather, while a private rear garden and decked seating to the front and side are popular on balmy days. A good selection of real ales and a dozen wines served by the glass are augmented by a range of whiskies, brandies, chilled vodkas and champagnes. When it comes to choosing from the menu, service is informal and an eat-anywhere policy applies. Lunchtime sandwiches include roast beef or chicken and bacon club; alternatively there's a crayfish crostini, or home-made beefburger served with Monterey Jack and fresh chips. If à la carte is preferred, starters may include grilled asparagus with prosciutto and roast fig; and Thai crab cakes with tomato and chilli dressing. The good gastro standard continues in main courses like grilled calves' liver and bacon with buttered mash; braised shank of lamb with garlic and herb mash; and roast guinea fowl with sweet potato purée. Fish and seafood lovers may plump for fillet of roast salmon with leaf spinach; or mussels steamed in white wine with garlic cream sauce. Children are spoilt for choice on their own reasonably-priced menu, which offers Amersham pork and leek sausages, home-made haddock goujons, grilled corn-fed chicken breast, and fresh pasta of the day. Finish with a pudding such as apple tarte Tatin, or treacle tart with vanilla ice cream. Excellent rail connections (tube and Chiltern main line).

🍷
MAP 06 SU99
Station Rd HP7 9NP
☎ 01494 765579
e-mail:
info@thesugarloafinn.com
dir: *on A404 between junct 18 M25 motorway and Amersham town. Towards Amersham after 4m enter Little Chalfont. Pub on right.*

Open 12–11 Closed: 26 Dec & 1 Jan
Bar Meals L served all week 12–3 5–10
Restaurant L served all week 12–3 D served all week 6–10.30 (Sun/Sat 12–4)
Adnams, Guinness, London Pride, Hoegaarden & Staropramen. 🍷 10
Facilities Children's licence Garden Parking

51

LONG CRENDON MAP 05 SP60

Pick of the Pubs

The Angel Inn

47 Bicester Rd HP18 9EE

☎ 01844 208268 01844 202497

e-mail: angelrestaurant@aol.com

dir: *A418 to Thame, B4011 to Long Crendon. Inn on B4011*

Expect great food and stylishly rustic décor at this proper gastro-pub. Wattle-and-daub walls and inglenook fireplaces attest to the age of the place, which dates from the 16th century. Real ales are served, along with cocktails, champagne and wine by the glass, but food is the main focus in the warm bar and the bright conservatory and, in finer weather, the heated sun terrace. For lunch try baguettes, open sandwiches, or something more substantial like roast fillet of local pork in Parma ham on apple mash with sage and cider sauce. There's a good choice of fish specials at lunch and dinner (seared fillet of sea bass on chargrilled vegetables with sweet chilli dressing), and vegetarian dishes (leek and smoked cheddar risotto). An evening main course could be roast fillet of English lamb and Scottish black pudding on cabbage and bacon tart with dauphinoise potato and basil jus.

Open 12-3 7-10 **Bar Meals** L served all week 12-3 D served Mon-Sat 7-9.30 **Restaurant** L served all week 12-2.30 D served Mon-Sat 7-9.30 Free House Oxford Blue, IPA, Brakspears. 11 **Facilities** Garden Parking

MARLOW MAP 05 SU88

The Kings Head

Church Rd, Little Marlow SL7 3RZ

☎ 01628 484407 01628 484407

dir: *M40 junct 4 take A4040 S, then A4155 towards Bourne End. Pub 0.5m on right*

Together with the Old Forge, this flower-adorned, 17th-century pub forms part of an attractive group of buildings a few minutes' walk from the Thames Footpath. It has an open-plan but cosy interior with original beams and open fires. In addition to sandwiches and jacket potatoes, the menu offers quite a range of more substantial meals, including salmon fillet hollandaise; mixed fish salad; lamb shank with rich minty gravy; pheasant casserole; and stir-fry duck with plum sauce.

Open 11-11 **Bar Meals** L served all week 12-2.15 D served all week 6.30-9.30 (Sun 12-7) **Restaurant** L served all week 12-2.15 D served all week 6.30-9.30 (Sun 12-7) Enterprise Inns Fuller's London Pride, Timothy Taylor Landlord, Adnam Broadside & Deuchars IPA. 9 **Facilities** Garden Parking

MENTMORE MAP 11 SP91

Pick of the Pubs

Il Maschio @ The Stag

The Green LU7 0QF

☎ 01296 668423 01296 660264

dir: *Please telephone for directions*

An imposing stone building, the Stag sits on a ridge overlooking the Vale of Aylesbury. So too does Mentmore Towers, the huge Elizabethan-style stately home built in 1855 for Baron Amschel de Rothschild. In the 1970s the contents of the house were auctioned off, in what the press called The Sale of the Century, for £6m. Following a change of ownership the renamed restaurant has taken on a different guise. The Portuguese owner and chef has introduced an altogether new menu that is available all week in both the bar and restaurant. Very much focussed on Mediterranean cuisine it features antipasti, pizzas and fresh pasta plus fish and meat dishes such as pesce rosa, grilled pink bream and fracosta fettunda, chicken in white wine. A special menu for children is available too. Check out the cocktail bar for some exotic flavoured infusions in the form of martinis, daiquiris and margaritas.

Open 12-11 **Bar Meals** L served all week 12-10 D served all week 12-10 Av main course £8 **Restaurant** L served all week 12-10 D served all week 12-10 Charles Wells Youngs Bitter, Fosters, Guinness, Bombardier. 8 **Facilities** Children's licence Garden Dogs allowed Parking

MOULSOE MAP 11 SP94

The Carrington Arms

Cranfield Rd MK16 0HB ☎ 01908 218050 01908 217850

e-mail: thecarringtonarms@4cinns.co.uk

dir: *M1 junct 14, A509 to Newport Pagnell 100yds, turn right signed Moulsoe & Cranfield. Pub on right*

This Grade II listed building is surrounded by farm land in a conservation area. Customers can 'create' their own menu from the meat and seafood counter, which the chef then cooks in full view of his expectant diners. Aberdeen beef, monkfish, tiger prawns, Colchester oysters are all on offer, along with unusual meats like ostrich, crocodile and kangaroo, plus vegetarian dishes and chef's specials. Friday night is fish night and lobster is available for pre-order.

Open 12-3 5.30-11 (Sun 7-10.30) Closed: 26-27 Dec, 1 Jan **Bar Meals** L served all week 12-2.30 D served all week (Sat 6-10, Sun 7-9.30) **Restaurant** L served all week 12-2.30 D served all week 6.30-10 (Sat 6-10, Sun 7-9.30) Free House Morland Old Speckled Hen, Greene King IPA, Fosters, Kronenbourg. 10 **Facilities** Garden Parking

OVING MAP 11 SP72

The Black Boy

Church Ln HP22 4HN ☎ 01296 641258 01296 641271

e-mail: theblackboyoving@aol.com

dir: *4.6m N of Aylesbury*

Oliver Cromwell and his soldiers camped in the Black Boy's huge garden after sacking nearby Bolebec Castle during the Civil War. Today, the 16th-century pub is a rural oasis, with spectacular views over the Vale of Aylesbury to Stowe School and beyond. Choices in the dining room include Scottish salmon with new potatoes and seasonal greens; local lamb shank with minted gravy and root vegetables; and a vegetarian cheese and onion filo parcel.

Open 12–3 6–11 **Bar Meals** L served Tue–Sun 12–2 D served Tue–Sat 6.30–9 (Sun 12–3.30) **Restaurant** L served Tue–Sun 12–2 D served Tue–Sat 6.30–9 (Sun 12–3.30) Av 3 course à la carte £25 Brakspear, Rebellion, Youngs Bitter, Batemans Bitter & Gales. 10 **Facilities** Garden Dogs allowed Parking

RADNAGE MAP 05 SU79

The Three Horseshoes Inn

Horseshoe Rd, Bennett End HP14 4EB ☎ 01494 483273

Dating from 1748, this delightful little inn is tucked away down a leafy lane. Stone floors, original beams, a bread oven and an open fire are among the features. The menu changes daily, and the award-winning chef/owner uses as much local produce as possible. Outside there are beautiful gardens.

Open 12–11 **Bar Meals** L served all week 12–2.30 D served Mon–Sat 6–9.30 (Sun 12–4) Av main course £12 **Restaurant** L served all week 12–2.30 D served all week 7–9.30 (Sun 12–4) Free House Adnams, Brakspears, Guest beers. 6 **Facilities** Garden Dogs allowed Parking

SKIRMETT MAP 05 SU79

The Frog

RG9 6TG ☎ 01491 638996 01491 638045

e-mail: jim.crowe@btinternet.com

dir: *Turn off A4155 at Mill End, pub in 3m*

This privately owned pub and restaurant is tucked away in the beautiful Hambleden valley. The simple set menu offers great value for money with options like salad of Gravadlax, followed by roast loin of pork, and sticky toffee pudding to finish. The carte offers a range of starters like soup, garlic bread or bruschetta; followed by mains like pan-seared salmon with curried lentils and coriander cream sauce.

Open 11.30–3 6.30–11 **Bar Meals** L served all week 12–2.30 D served all week 6.30–9.30 Av main course £10.50 **Restaurant** L served all week 12–2.30 D served all week 6.30–9.30 Av 3 course à la carte £25 Free House Adnams Best, Hook Norton, Rebellion, Fullers London Pride. **Facilities** Garden Dogs allowed Parking

STOKE MANDEVILLE MAP 05 SP81

The Wool Pack

Risborough Rd HP22 5UP

☎ 01296 615970 01296 615971

dir: *4m from Aylesbury*

The gardens and landscaped decking here are ideal for a summertime real ale. Inside there's a relaxed, informal atmosphere beneath the thatch and low beams, and the pub's stylish interior features open kitchens, log fires and a restaurant. The simple, up-to-the-minute menu offers lots of comfort appeal: choose from 'Sharing Plates' with Spanish tapas or Greek mezze; 'Fired Pizzas'; 'Pastas' such as rigatoni and smoked haddock; or 'Rotisserie' dishes like spit chicken with lemon and garlic confit.

Open 11–11 **Bar Meals** L served all week 12–2.30 D served all week 6–9.30 (Sun 12–7) **Restaurant** L served all week 12–2.30 D served all week 6–9.30 (Sun 12–7) London Pride, Timothy Tylor Landlord, Amstel, Staropramen. 10 **Facilities** Garden Parking

TURVILLE MAP 05 SU79

Pick of the Pubs

The Bull & Butcher

RG9 6QU ☎ 01491 638283 01491 638836

e-mail: info@thebullandbutcher.com

dir: *M40 junct 5 follow Ibstone signs. Right at T-junct. Pub 0.25m on left*

Even if you've never been to Turville or this delightful black-and-white-timbered 16th-century pub, you may well recognise them immediately you arrive here. The village has earned itself celebrity status over the years as a popular location for numerous film and television productions, most notably Midsomer Murders and The Vicar of Dibley. Several of these classics have been immortalised in the pub menu too; for example there is Dibley Pudding and Midsomer Burger. Movies shot in the area include Chitty Chitty Bang Bang and the lesser-known Went the Day Well, filmed in Turville at the height of the Second World War. After an exhilarating walk in the glorious Chilterns, relax in the pub's refurbished bar, surrounded by original floor tiles and natural oak beams. An appetising menu ranges from smoked fish platter and venison and vegetable casserole, to oven-roasted rump of lamb, and chicken, mushroom and tarragon pie.

Open 12–11 (Sun and BH 12–10.30) **Bar Meals** L served all week 12–2.30 D served all week 6.30–9.30 (Sun 12–9) Av main course £11.95 **Restaurant** L served all week 12–2.30 D served all week 7–9.45 (Sun 12–9) Av 3 course à la carte £24 Brakspear Brakspear Bitter, Brakspear Special, Hooky Dark and Brewers selections. 36 **Facilities** Garden Dogs allowed Parking Play Area

Please see walk on page 54

PUB WALKS

TURVILLE - BUCKINGHAMSHIRE

Bull & Butcher

Walk information

Distance: 3 miles (4.8km)
Map: OS Explorer 171 Chiltern Hills West
Start/finish: small parking area in centre of Turville; grid ref SU 767911
Ascent/gradient: 1
Paths: field and woodland paths, some road walking; 9 stiles
Landscape: rolling Chiltern countryside, farmland and woodland

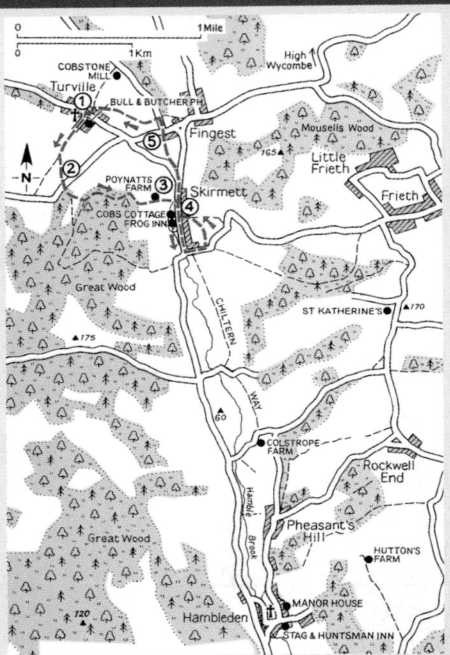

Walk directions

A Park near the Bull & Butcher and take the lane just to the left of the church entrance, with Sleepy Cottage on the corner. Pass Square Close Cottages and the school before continuing on the Chiltern Way through a tunnel of trees. Climb gently to a gate and keep ahead along the field edge to a waymark in the boundary. Branch half-left, heading diagonally down the field to a stile.

B Cross the road to a further stile and follow the track through the trees, passing a gas installation on the right. Pass a bench on the left before breaking cover from the trees. Avoid a path branching off to the right and continue up the field slope to the next belt of trees. Turville and its windmill are clearly seen over to the left. Enter the woodland and keep left at the junction. Follow the clear, wide path as it contours round the slopes, with the ground, dotted with beech trees, rippling away to the left. Descend the hillside, keeping to the woodland edge. Follow the fence and bear left at the next corner, heading to a stile by Poynatts Farm.

C Walk along the drive to the road, bear right and enter Skirmett. On the right is Cobs Cottage and next door to it is the aptly-named Ramblers. Pass the Frog Inn and follow the road south to the next junction. An assortment of houses, a telephone box and a post box line the route. Turn left, pass a stile on the right and walk along to the next left footpath. Follow the field edge to a bungalow and stile, cross over to a drive and make for the road.

D Bear right, heading out of the village to the junction with Watery Lane. 'Except for access' signs can be seen here now. Look for the stile and footpath immediately to the right of it. Cross the field to a stile in the corner and make for the boundary hedge ahead in the next field. Cross the stile and head diagonally right to a hedge by some houses. Once over the stile, take the road opposite, signposted 'Ibstone and Stokenchurch'.

E Walk up the road for about 120 yards (110m) and swing left at the first waymarked junction. Follow the Chiltern Way between trees, with teasing glimpses of the Chilterns themselves. Cross a stile and head diagonally down the field towards Turville. Make for a track and follow it to the village green and back to the pub.

While there

Visit Turville's Church of St Mary the Virgin. There was a church here in the 12th century, but it is not clear if there was one on this site before that. The first vicar of Turville recorded on the roll in the porch was a Benedictine monk who came here from St Albans in 1228. The squat tower dates from about 1340.

TYLERS GREEN MAP 06 SU99

The Old Queens Head NEW

Hammersley Ln HP10 8EY

☎ 01494 813371 📠 01494 816145

e-mail: info@oldqueensheadpenn.co.uk

dir: *B474 (Penn road) through Beaconsfield New Town towards Penn, after approx 3m left into School Rd, left again after 500yds into Hammersley Ln. Pub on corner opposite church*

Tucked away between the villages of Penn and Tylers Green, and worth seeking out for its character and hospitality. Here you'll find lots of cosy corners, real fires, a dining room dating from 1666, and a sunny terrace with views to the village church. The menu tempts with classic dishes prepared with modern British flair such as pan-fried pigeon breast, or creamy fish pie with leek and cheddar mash.

Open 11-11 (Sun 12-10.30) Closed: 26 Dec **Bar Meals** L served all week 12-2.30 D served all week 7-10 (Sun 12-4) Av main course £12.50 **Restaurant** L served all week 12-2.30 D served all week 7-10 (Sun 12-4) Av 3 course à la carte £23.50 Morlands Original, Greene King IPA, Heineken, Fosters. 17 **Facilities** Garden Dogs allowed Parking

WEST WYCOMBE MAP 05 SU89

Pick of the Pubs

The George and Dragon Hotel

High St HP14 3AB ☎ 01494 464414 📠 01494 462432

e-mail: sue.raines@btconnect.com

dir: *On A40, close to M40*

Built on the site of a 14th-century hostelry, this 18th-century former coaching inn in a National Trust village has welcomed generations of visitors. Indeed, some from a bygone era are rumoured still to haunt its corridors – notably Sukie, a beautiful servant girl with ideas above her station, who met her fate at the hands of three spurned locals. The hotel is reached through a cobbled archway and comprises a delightful jumble of whitewashed, timber-framed buildings. The range of real ales is excellent, and the eclectic menu draws influences from all over the globe. Varied and freshly-prepared dishes include spinach timbale; sea bass with rôsti; mushroom stroganoff; lamb tagine; tandoori chicken; and a range of grills. A lengthy dessert list covers all the classics. Visitors to the area will enjoy exploring West Wycombe Caves, and the stately houses at Cliveden and Hughenden Manor.

Open 11-3 5.30-11 (Sun 12-3, 6-10.30) **Bar Meals** L served all week 12-2.30 D served all week 6-9.30 (Sun 7-9) Enterprise Inns Courage Best, Wells Bombardier, Timothy Taylor Landlord. **Facilities** Children's licence Garden Dogs allowed Parking Play Area

WHEELEREND COMMON MAP 05 SU89

The Chequers

Bullocks Farm Ln HP14 3NH ☎ 01494 883070

e-mail: thechequers.inn@virgin.net

dir: *4m N of Marlow*

This picturesque 17th-century inn, with its roaring winter fires and two attractive beer gardens, is ideally located for walkers on the edge of Wheeler End Common. A solid choice of mouth-watering sandwiches and bar meals supplements the main menu, which features plenty of fresh fish and local estate game. Warm pigeon and apple salad; venison pie with red wine and juniper; and roast salmon on crushed potato tartare are typical choices.

Open 12-3 5.30-11 (Fri-Sun all day) **Bar Meals** L served all week 12-2.30 D served Tue-Sat 7-10 (Sun 12-4) Av main course £12.50 **Restaurant** L served all week 12-2.30 D served Tue-Sat 7-10 (Sun 12-4) Av 3 course à la carte £17.50 Av 3 course fixed price £9.50 Fullers Fuller's ESB, London Pride, Jack Frost & Summer Ale, Guest ale. 7 **Facilities** Garden Dogs allowed Parking

WHITELEAF MAP 05 SP80

Red Lion

Upper Icknield Way HP27 0LL

☎ 01844 344476 📠 01844 273124

e-mail: tim_hibbert@hotmail.co.uk

dir: *A4010 through Princes Risborough, turn right into The Holloway, at T-junct turn right, pub on left*

Family-owned 17th-century inn in the heart of the Chilterns, surrounded by National Trust land and situated close to the Ridgeway national trail. There are plenty of good local walks with wonderful views. A cosy fire in winter and a secluded summer beer garden add to the appeal. Hearty pub fare includes prawn marie-rose, rib-eye steak, sausage and mash, vegetarian lasagne, haddock and chips, warm baguettes and jacket potatoes.

Open 12-3 5-11 (All day wkds) **Bar Meals** L served all week 12-2 D served Mon-Sat 5-9 Av main course £6.95 **Restaurant** L served all week 12-2 D served Mon-Sat 7-9 Av 1 course fixed price £9.95 Free House Brakspear Bitter, Hook Norton, Guinness, Carlsberg. **Facilities** Garden Dogs allowed Parking

WOOBURN COMMON MAP 06 SU98

Pick of the Pubs

Chequers Inn ★★★ HL

Kiln Ln HP10 0JQ ☎ 01628 529575 01628 850124
e-mail: info@chequers-inn.com
dir: *M40 junct 2 through Beaconsfield towards High Wycombe. 1m left into Broad Ln. Inn 2.5m*

Located in one of the prettiest areas of England, the Chilterns, this 17th-century inn has lovely views of open countryside. Historic features include oak posts and beams, flagstone floors and a wonderful open fireplace in the bar, blackened by countless blazing logs. Bar food takes in sandwiches, home-made burgers, chicken Caesar salad and slow roasted lamb shank. The restaurant, attractively presented with displays of plants, palms and memorabilia, offers award-winning classic French and English cuisine from a choice of fixed-price and carte menus. Fresh local ingredients are used where possible in dishes such as red snapper, artichoke, green beans and crushed new potatoes; or saddle of rabbit stuffed with chicken mousse wrapped in bacon, with Savoy cabbage and lyonnaise potatoes. For those in a hurry a fixed-price 45-minute lunch menu is available Monday to Saturday. Outside is a large garden area with tables and chairs, and a barbecue in summer.

Open All day **Bar Meals** L served all week 12–2.30 D served all week 6.30–9.30 **Restaurant** L served all week 12–2.30 D served all week 7–9.30 Av 3 course à la carte £25 Av 2 course fixed price £13.95 Free House Ruddles, IPA, Abbot, Guest bitter. 12 **Facilities** Children's licence Garden Parking **Rooms** 17 bedrooms en suite S£82.50 D£87.50

CAMBRIDGESHIRE

BABRAHAM MAP 12 TL55

Pick of the Pubs

The George Inn at Babraham

High St CB2 4AG ☎ 01223 833800
e-mail: george@inter-mead.com
dir: *In High St, just off A11/A505 & A1307*

See Pick of the Pubs on opposite page

BARRINGTON MAP 12 TL34

The Royal Oak

West Green CB2 5RZ ☎ 01223 870791 01223 870791
dir: *From Barton off M11 S of Cambridge*

One of the oldest thatched pubs in England is this rambling, timbered 13th-century building overlooking what is (coincidentally) the largest village green in England. Yet it is only six miles from Cambridge, three miles from the M11 and a mile from Shepreth Station. A wide range of fish dishes includes scallops, trout, scampi, tuna, swordfish, tiger prawns, squid and other seasonal offerings. There is also a carvery on Sunday.

Open 11.30–2.30 6–11 (Sun 12–10.30) **Bar Meals** L served all week 12–2.30 D served Mon–Thu 6.30–9 (Fri&Sat 6.30–9.30) Av main course £7.50 **Restaurant** L served Sun 6.30–9 Av 3 course à la carte £25 Old English Inns IPA Potton Brewery, Adnams, Elgoods, Nethergates. 6 **Facilities** Garden Parking

BROUGHTON MAP 12 TL27

Pick of the Pubs

The Crown

Bridge Rd PE28 3AY ☎ 01487 824428 01487 824912
e-mail: simon@thecrownbroughton.co.uk
dir: *Just off A141 between Huntingdon & Warboys, by church in village centre*

An idyllic, 18th-century village pub in a picturesque setting next to the church. In 1857, according to an insurance policy, it also incorporated a saddler's shop, thatched stables and piggeries. After it closed in 2000, around 40 villagers raised enough money to buy and renovate it, reopening in 2001. It is now run as a village-owned tenancy, with real ales from Greene King, Elgood's and other local breweries. Menus offer a lunchtime selection of filled ciabattas; and you'll find bangers and mash, fish and chips, and contemporary dishes like pork and apple sausages, savoy cabbage, black pudding mash and onion gravy; and Mediterranean vegetable lasagne. The main menu might come up with steamed Scottish steak and ale pudding with horseradish crushed potatoes and swede purée; roast cod with olive oil mash, roast fennel and caponata; or chargrilled vegetable skewer with couscous, coriander and harissa sauce.

Open 12–3 6–11 Closed: 1–11 Jan **Bar Meals** L served Wed–Sun 12–2 D served Tue–Sat 6.30–9 (Sun 12–4.30) Av main course £14 **Restaurant** L served Wed–Sat 12–2 D served Tue–Sat 6.30–9 (Sun 12–4.30) Av 3 course à la carte £25 Av 3 course fixed price £14.50 Free House Adnams Broadside, Elgoods Black Dog, Greene King IPA, City of Cambridge Hobson Choice. 10 **Facilities** Children's licence Garden Dogs allowed Parking

The George Inn at Babraham

Following a devastating fire in 2004, the pub was closed by its brewery owner; when George Wortley saw the ruin, he recognised an opportunity and lovingly rebuilt it. A team of craftsmen incorporated new kitchens and three restaurant areas in this now beautifully furnished and decorated village dining pub.

It has become firmly established in the area (the head chef trained with Jamie Oliver), serving dishes complete with home-made stocks, jus and sauces. The house motto is 'a passion for detail', which pairs traditional English ingredients with worldwide influences. The lunch menu offers a choice of freshly-baked ciabattas, such as warm bacon, brie and cranberry, or buffalo mozzarella, cherry tomato and rocket pesto, all served with a side salad. For larger appetites, there's traditional steak and kidney pie, or grilled Newmarket sausages on a horseradish mash. In the evening the choice broadens to include first courses of tempura-fried Mediterranean prawns on crispy seaweed with a Japanese dressing; or herbed tagliatelle with marinated artichokes, cannelloni beans and walnuts in green basil pesto. Main courses are no less punctilious: English pork on sautéed wild mushrooms with mustard and truffle dressing; or grilled fillet of plaice topped with crayfish, capers, lemon zest and wild rocket. Desserts finish nicely with banana and toffee sponge pudding with maple walnut ice cream; or dark chocolate, Baileys and Amaretto mousse on a framboise sauce. If all this sounds soporific, you'll be happy to know that plans are in place to convert barns alongside the pub into accommodation.

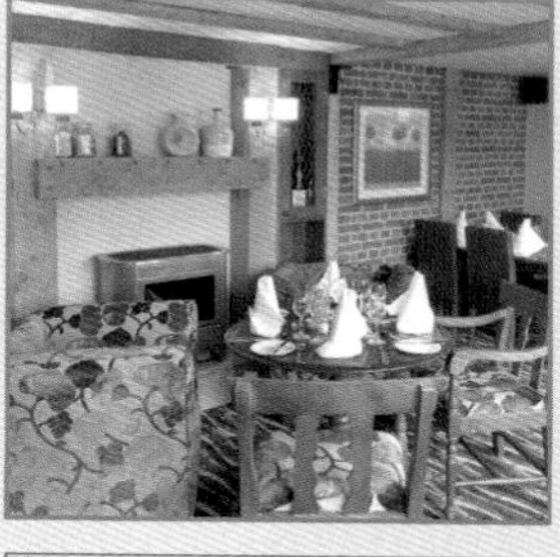

MAP 12 TL55
High St CB2 4AG
☎ 01223 833800
e-mail: george@inter-mead.com
www.georgeinn.babraham.co.uk
dir: *In High St, just off A11/A505 & A1307*

Open 11.30–3 5.30–11 (Open all day summer w/ends)
Bar Meals L served all week 12–2.15 D served all week 6.30–9 Av main course £12
Restaurant L served all week 12–2.15 D served all week 6.30–9 Av 3 course à la carte £25
Free House
Old Speckled Hen, Guinness, Greene King Abbot Ale. 8
Facilities Garden Parking

England

BYTHORN MAP 12 TL07

Pick of the Pubs

The White Hart 🍷

PE28 0QN ☎ 01832 710226 📠 01832 710226
e-mail: hartofby-thorn@btconnect.com
dir: *0.5m off A14 (Kettering-Huntingdon road)*

The White Hart, located in a peaceful village just off the A1/M1 link, is now under the new ownership of Jayne Masters and Justin Ackrill. The restaurant, The Hart of Bythorn (formerly known as Bennett's), has re-opened following an extensive refit. The menu is Anglo-French and changes on a monthly basis to take advantage of seasonal produce, supplemented by regular specials. Only the best quality ingredients are used by the team of chefs, and these are locally sourced wherever possible. There is a lot of history associated with the pub, beginning with John Brown who brewed his own beer on the premises in the early 19th century, where the ladies' toilets are now situated. Several people have seen a grey lady in old-fashioned dress walk in through the front wall of the pub, cross the bar and exit through the rear wall of the private dining/meeting room.

Open 12–3 6–11 (Sun 12–3, 6–10.30) **Bar Meals** L served Tue–Sat 12–2 D served Tue–Sat 6–9 (Sun 12–2.30 6–8) Av main course £10 **Restaurant** L served Tue–Sat 12–2 D served Tue–Sat 6–9 (Sun 12–2.30, 6–8) Av 3 course à la carte £27.50 Av 3 course fixed price £17.95 Free House Guinness, Becks Vier, Stella, Boddingtons. 🍷 6 **Facilities** Children's licence Garden Dogs allowed Parking

CAMBRIDGE MAP 12 TL45

Pick of the Pubs

The Anchor 🍷

Silver St CB3 9EL ☎ 01223 353554 📠 01223 327275

Situated at the end of the medieval lane that borders Queens' College in the heart of the university city, this attractive waterside pub appeals to students and visitors alike. Hard by the bridge over the River Cam, in fine weather the riverside patio is an ideal spot for enjoying one of a range of good ales including guest beers while watching the activities on the water. The more adventurous can hire a punt for a leisurely trip to Grantchester (of Rupert Brooke and Jeffrey Archer fame), and on return sample a choice of hearty meals from a range that includes lasagne, home-made pie, and roast beef.

Open 11–11 (Thurs-Sat 11–12 Sun 12–11.30) Closed: 25 Dec **Bar Meals** L served 12–3 D served Mon–Sat Av main course £5.50 Greene King Greene King, IPA Abbotts Ale. 🍷 12 **Facilities** Dogs allowed

Cambridge Blue

85 Gwydir St CB1 2LG ☎ 01223 361382 📠 01223 505110
e-mail: c.lloyd13@ntlworld.com
dir: *Town centre*

Rowing memorabilia and pictures cover the walls of this convivial, community-spirited pub. There's an unexpectedly huge rear garden at the back, and noisy machines, including mobile phones, have no place within. Daily papers and local publications are provided, and the inn is presided over by Ajax, the resident Greek cat. Hearty regulars include Zorba pie (lamb, black olive and spinach); local sausages, mash and gravy; and Texas chilli.

Open 12–2.30 5.30–11 (Sat–Sun 12–3, Sun 6–10.30) **Bar Meals** L served all week 12–2.30 D served all week 6–9.30 (No food 25-Dec) Av main course £7 Free House Woodforde's Wherry, Hobson's Choice, Adnams, Elgoods Black Dog Mild. **Facilities** Garden Dogs allowed Play Area

Free Press 🍷

Prospect Row CB1 1DU ☎ 01223 368337

Students, academics, locals and visitors rub shoulders in this atmospheric and picturesque back-street pub near the city centre. Non-smoking for over a decade, it has open fires and a beautiful walled garden – but no music, mobile phones or gaming machines. Punters are attracted by first-rate real ales and nourishing home-made food such as chilli with garlic bread; goats' cheese salad; filled toasted ciabattas; venison sausages; salmon filled with couscous and vegetables; and fresh pasta.

Open 12–2.30 6–11 (Sat 12–11, Sun 12–3, 7–10.30) Closed: 25–26 Dec, 1 Jan **Bar Meals** L served all week 12–2 D served Mon–Sat 6–9 (Sat/Sun 12–2.30) Av main course £6.25 Greene King Greene King IPA, Abbot Ale, Dark Mild plus Guest ales. 🍷 10 **Facilities** Garden

DUXFORD MAP 12 TL44

The John Barleycorn

3 Moorfield Rd CB2 4PP
☎ 01223 832699 📠 01223 832699
dir: *Turn off A505 into Duxford*

Traditional thatched and beamed English country pub situated close to Cambridge. Originally built as a coaching house in 1660, it was renamed once or twice until 1858, when the current name was attached. The same menu is served throughout and ranges from a cheese sandwich to tournedos Rossini. Typical dishes are large leg of lamb in mint gravy, and chicken breast with garlic and herbs.

Open 11–11 (Sun 12–10.30) **Bar Meals** L served all week 12 D served all week 10 Av main course £8 Greene King Greene King IPA, Abbot Ale, Old Speckled Hen, Ruddles Best & County. **Facilities** Garden Parking

The Black Horse

Antique furnishings and open log fires crank up the old world charm in this 17th-century inn, while the delightful one-acre rear garden overlooks Elton's famous church and rolling open countryside.

Although it is located within easy lunching distance of the Peterborough business park, there's no doubting its credentials as a genuine village inn. The warm country atmosphere is somewhat at odds with parts of its history: Harry Kirk, the landlord here in the 1950s, was an assistant to Tom and Albert Pierrepoint, Britain's most famous hangmen; Harry's son is now said to haunt the bar. The pub was also once the village jail, and the building later became a morgue. But today's clientele are very much alive, and its current landlord has had to extend the car park to meet growing demand. The real ales include Everards Tiger, seasonal Nethergate brews, and Barnwell Bitter, which is brewed locally. The superb selection of food ranges from bar snacks to a full à la carte. Among the 'snacks' are sandwiches, filled baguettes jacket potatoes, a home-made pie of the day, and seasonal salads. If you opt for the à la carte, you might start with portobello mushrooms topped with bacon and cheese gratin; fresh dressed crab with brown bread and salad; or chef's paté with salad, onion marmalade and toasted brioche. Typical main courses include guinea fowl stuffed with black pudding and chorizo sausage, wrapped in Parma ham and served with a rich red wine jus; fillet of sea bass with braised pak choi, pesto and sun-blushed tomatoes; and bangers and mash.

MAP 12 TL09
14 Overend PE8 6RU
☎ 01832 280240 & 280875
dir: *Off A605 (Peterborough to Northampton road)*

Open 12 -11.30
Bar Meals L served all week 12-2 D served Mon-Sat 6-9 (Sun 12-3) Av main course £13.50
Restaurant L served all week 12-2 D served Mon-Sat 6-9 Av 3 course à la carte £25
Free House
Bass, Everards Tiger, Nethergate, Barnwell Bitter. 14
Facilities Garden Dogs allowed Parking Play Area

ELSWORTH MAP 12 TL36

The George & Dragon

41 Boxworth Rd CB3 8JQ

☎ 01954 267236 01954 267080

e-mail: www.georgeanddragon-elsworth.co.uk

dir: *SE of A14 between Cambridge & Huntingdon*

Set in a pretty village just outside Cambridge, this pub offers a wide range of satisfying food to locals and visitors alike. After a refurbishment there are even more fish dishes, daily specials and prime Scottish steaks on offer. Expect Mediterranean king prawns, and fresh cod, haddock or plaice from Lowestoft. For a lighter meal, ploughman's lunches and sandwiches are available. The Monday Night menus are always popular so booking is advised.

Open 11-3 6-11 (Sun 12-3, 6.30-10.30) **Bar Meals** L served all week 12-2 D served Mon-Sat 6.30-9.30 (Sun 12-3, 6-9) Av main course £10 **Restaurant** L served all week 12-2 D served Mon-Sat 6.30-9.30 (Sun 12-2.30, 6-9) Av 3 course à la carte £18.50 Free House Greene King IPA, Ruddles County, Greene King Old Speckled Hen. 8 **Facilities** Garden Parking

ELTISLEY MAP 12 TL25

The Leeds Arms

The Green PE19 6TG ☎ 01480 880283 01480 880379

dir: *On A428 between Cambridge & St Neots*

Built towards the end of the 18th century and named after a local landowner, the Leeds Arms is a Charles Wells pub. A sample menu includes lamb shank with a mint jus, medallions of pork with Calvados sauce, chicken breast wrapped in bacon on mashed potatoes, and wild mushroom and avocado hotpot. Meat is sourced from an organic farm.

Open 11.30-2.30 6.30-11 **Bar Meals** L served all week 12-2 D served all week 6.30-9.45 Av main course £7.95 **Restaurant** L served all week 12-2 D served all week 6.30-9.45 (Sun 12-2, 7-9) Av 3 course à la carte £15 Charles Wells Charles Wells Smooth, 3 Guest Ales. **Facilities** Garden Dogs allowed Parking Play Area

ELTON MAP 12 TL09

Pick of the Pubs

The Black Horse

14 Overend PE8 6RU ☎ 01832 280240 & 280875

dir: *Off A605 (Peterborough to Northampton road)*

See Pick of the Pubs on page 59

ELY MAP 12 TL58

Pick of the Pubs

The Anchor Inn

Sutton Gault CB6 2BD

☎ 01353 778537 01353 776180

e-mail: anchorinn@popmail.bta.com

dir: *From A14, B1050 to Earith, take B1381 to Sutton. Sutton Gault on left*

See Pick of the Pubs on opposite page

FEN DITTON MAP 12 TL46

Pick of the Pubs

Ancient Shepherds

High St CB5 8ST ☎ 01223 293280 01223 293280

dir: *From A14 take B1047 signed Cambridge/Airport*

Named after the ancient order of Shepherders who used to meet here, this heavily-beamed pub and restaurant was built originally as three cottages in 1540. The two bars, a lounge and a dining room all boast inglenook fireplaces. Located three miles from Cambridge in the riverside village of Fen Ditton, it provides a welcome escape for those who like to enjoy their refreshments without the addition of music, darts or pool. Among the fish dishes on the menu are fillet of sea bass on a bed of creamed leaks and home-made fishcakes. Meat eaters are equally well catered for with, among other items, half a casseroled guinea fowl in Burgundy with roast vegetables, Barnsley lamb chops, and pork loin steaks in cream and mustard sauce to choose from.

Open 12-3 6-11 (Fri-Sat 12-3, 6.30-11 Sun 12-5) Closed: 25-26 Dec **Bar Meals** L served all week 12-2 D served Mon-Sat **Restaurant** L served all week 12-2 D served Mon-Sat 6.30-9 Punch Taverns Adnams Bitter, Greene King IPA. 8 **Facilities** Garden Parking

FENSTANTON MAP 12 TL36

King William IV

High St PE28 9JF ☎ 01480 462467 01480 468526

e-mail: kingwilliam@thefen.fsnet.co.uk

dir: *Off A14 between Cambridge & Huntingdon (junct 27)*

Originally three 17th-century cottages, this rambling old inn stands next door to the clock tower in the heart of the village. Inside are low beams, a lively bar and the appropriately named Garden Room. Fresh food is cooked daily, with pork and leek sausages and King Bill vegetarian burger among the lunchtime options, while the à la carte menu offers the likes of lemon sole fillet, mignons of chicken fillet, and risotto of butternut squash.

Open 11-11 (Sun 12-10.30) **Bar Meals** L served all week 12-2.15 D served Mon-Sat 6.30-9.45 (Sun 12-3.30) **Restaurant** L served all week 12-2 D served Mon-Sat 7-9.45 (Sun 12-3.30) Greene King Greene King Abbot Ale & IPA, Guest Ales. 9 **Facilities** Garden Dogs allowed Parking

The Anchor Inn

Sutton Gault lies on the western edge of the Isle of Ely, whose ancient cathedral stands high above the flat surrounding fens. Today this is rich agricultural country, but until the mid–17th century the fens were lawless and disease-ridden swamps, which is why, in 1630, the Earl of Bedford commissioned the Dutch engineer Cornelius Vermuyden to drain them.

Using a large contingent of Scottish prisoners of war, captured in a skirmish by Oliver Cromwell, he dug the Old and New Bedford Rivers. The Anchor was built to provide them with shelter, and it's been an inn ever since. Enter this family-run free house for a cosy atmosphere of scrubbed pine tables on gently undulating floors, evening candleglow and winter log fires. Adam Pickup and Carlene Bunten bought The Anchor in December 2006 having previously been head chef and manager. The inn continues to win wide recognition for its modern British cuisine with an emphasis on seasonal, traditional and local ingredients, notably hand-dressed Cromer crabs, Brancaster oysters and mussels, samphire, asparagus, smoked products from Bottisham and venison from the Denham Estate, together with pheasant, partridge, pigeon and wild duck in the winter. Menus may be adjusted daily to reflect a delivery of something special. The main menu is available lunchtimes and evenings and offers a typical three-course meal (taken on the riverside terrace, maybe) of grilled dates wrapped in bacon with mild grain mustard cream sauce; pork fillet with ginger cake stuffing in Parma ham with savoy cabbage and sage and onion sauce; home-made lemongrass pannacotta with sweet chilli and coconut sorbet; or unusual British farmhouse cheeses such as oven-baked Bottisham smoked camembert. Lighter lunches are available on weekdays. Plenty of wines by the glass from a long list. Some of the recently redecorated suites and rooms overlook the river.

MAP 12 TL58
Sutton Gault CB6 2BD
☎ 01353 778537
01353 776180
e-mail:
anchorinn@popmail.bta.com
dir: *From A14, B1050 to Earith, B1381 to Sutton. Sutton Gault on left*

Open 12-3 7-11
Bar Meals L served all week 12–2 D served all week 7–9 (Sat 6.30–9.30) Av main course £13.50
Restaurant L served all week 12–2 D served all week 7–9 (Sat 6.30–9.30)
Free House
City of Cambridge Hobson's Choice, Boathouse Bitter. 12
Facilities Garden Parking
Rooms 4 bedrooms en suite S£59.50 D£79.50 (★★★★ RR)

FORDHAM MAP 12 TL67

White Pheasant

CB7 5LQ ☎ 01638 720414
e-mail: whitepheasant@whitepheasant.com
dir: *From Newmarket A142 to Ely, approx 5m to Fordham. Pub on left in village*

Standing in a fenland village between Ely and Newmarket, the White Pheasant's already considerable appeal has been subtly enhanced by improvements that preserve its 17th-century period charm. To a large extent it is food driven, with the kitchen producing globally influenced, traditional British food, including seared king scallops with black pudding and citrus butter sauce; halibut wrapped in smoked salmon with onion confit; marmalade-glazed breast of Gressingham duck; and dishes featuring rare-breed beef.

Open 12-3 6-11 (Sun 7-10.30) Closed: 26-29 Dec & 1 Jan **Bar Meals** L served all week 12-2.30 D served all week 7-9 Av main course £10.50 **Restaurant** L served all week 12-2.30 D served all week 6-9.30 (Sun 7-9) Av 3 course à la carte £25 Free House Brandon Gunflint, Fenland Rabbit Poacher. 14 **Facilities** Garden Parking

FOWLMERE MAP 12 TL44

The Chequers

High St SG8 7SR ☎ 01763 208369 01763 208944
dir: *From M11, A505, 2nd right to Fowlmere. 8m S of Cambridge, 4m E of Royston*

This pub's sign, blue and red chequers honouring the British and American squadrons that were based nearby during World War II, belies 16th-century origins that include a visit from Samuel Pepys in 1660. Today the Chequers is known for its imaginative cooking served formally in the smart, galleried restaurant or in the more relaxed surroundings of the bar or attractive garden. The extensive seasonal menu includes prawn and mango curry, pigeon breasts on baby spinach and rocket, and moules marinière.

Open 12-3 6-11 Closed: 25 Dec & 1 Jan eve **Bar Meals** L served all week 12-2 D served all week 7-9.30 (Sun 7-9) **Restaurant** L served all week 12-2 D served all week 7-9.30 (Sun 7-9) Av 3 course à la carte £20 Free House Adnams, Nethergate , Cottage, Archers & Guest Ales. 14 **Facilities** Garden Parking

GOREFIELD MAP 12 TF41

Woodmans Cottage

90 High Rd PE13 4NB ☎ 01945 870669 01945 870631
e-mail: magtuck@aol.com
dir: *3m NW of Wisbech*

This friendly, family-run village pub stands in Cambridgeshire's Fenland, a mere 2m above the level of the sea nearly 10 miles away. It offers a good range of pub food, from lunchtime baguettes and jacket potatoes to bar snacks (chicken nachos with a salsa dip, beef teriyaki with mixed leaf salad), and main courses such as seared tuna steak with garlic, sage, rosemary, lime and Lyonnaise potatoes, or steak and chips.

Open 11-2.30 7-11 Closed: 25 Dec **Bar Meals** L served all week 12-2 D served all week 7-10 (Sun 12-8) Av main course £8.50 **Restaurant** L served all week 12-2 D served all week 7-10 (Sun 12-8) Av 3 course à la carte £20 Av fixed price £12.50 Free House Greene King IPA , Speckled Hen, Interbrew Worthington Bitter. **Facilities** Garden Parking

GREAT CHISHILL MAP 12 TL43

The Pheasant

24 Heydon Rd SG8 8SR ☎ 01763 838535
dir: *Off B1039 between Royston & Saffron Walden*

Stunning views and roaring log fires characterise this traditional village free house, where Nethergates' and Greene King ales easily outsell lager. There are no gaming machines or piped music to disturb the friendly, sociable bar, and children under 14 are not allowed in. In summer, bird song holds sway in the idyllic pub garden. Freshly-made sandwiches come complete with chips and salad garnish, whilst home-made dishes like rabbit casserole, poached haddock, or wild mushroom lasagne cater for larger appetites.

Open 12-3 6-11 (Sat 12-12, Sun 12-10.30) **Bar Meals** L served all week 12-2 D served all week 6-9.30 Av main course £9 **Restaurant** L served all week 12-2 D served all week 6-9.30 Free House Nethergates IPA & Umbel Ale, Greene King IPA. 8 **Facilities** Garden Dogs allowed Parking

HEMINGFORD GREY MAP 12 TL27

The Cock Pub and Restaurant

47 High St PE28 9BJ ☎ 01480 463609 01480 461747
e-mail: cock@cambscuisine.com
dir: *2m S of Huntingdon and 1m E of A14*

There's been a spring in the step of this village pub since Oliver Thain and Richard Bradley arrived a few years ago. Transforming it into an award-winning dining pub, they've retained traditional values, with well kept real ales, log fires blazing when the weather demands, and a welcome for walkers, children and dogs. In the wooden-floored restaurant fresh fish, including pan-fried halibut fillets, and chef's various home-made sausages, may prove irresistible.

Open 11.30-3 6-11.30 (Sun 12-4, 6.30-10.30) **Restaurant** L served all week 12-2.30 D served all week 6.30-9 (Fri-Sat 6.30-9.30, Sun 6.30-8.30) Av 3 course à la carte £23 Av 3 course fixed price £12.95 Free House Woodfordes Wherry, Golden Jackal, Wolf Brewery, Victoria Bitter. 13 **Facilities** Children's licence Garden Dogs allowed Parking

HILDERSHAM MAP 12 TL54

The Pear Tree

CB1 6BU ☎ 01223 891680 01223 891970
e-mail: jamieson_diane@yahoo.co.uk

Popular with walkers and locals alike, the Pear Tree is every inch the traditional village pub, set opposite the village green with beams and a stone floor inside and a country garden outside. It has a well-deserved reputation for its home-cooked food – perhaps deep-fried brie wedges wrapped in filo pastry with a gooseberry dip, followed by oven-baked fresh trout with fresh vegetables. Typical desserts are Bakewell tart, and bread and butter pudding.

Open 11.45-2 6.30-11 **Bar Meals** L served Tue-Sun 12-2 D served all week 6.30-9.30 (Sun 7-9) Av main course £5.99 Greene King Greene King IPA & Abbot Ale. **Facilities** Garden Parking

HILTON MAP 12 TL26

The Prince of Wales ★★★ INN

Potton Rd PE28 9NG ☎ 01480 830257 01480 830257
e-mail: princeofwales.hilton@talk21.com
dir: *On B1040 between A14 & A428 S of St Ives*

The Prince of Wales is a traditional, 1830s-built, two-bar village inn with four comfortable bedrooms. Food options range from bar snacks to full meals, among which are grills, fish, curries brought in from a local Indian restaurant, and daily specials, such as lamb hotpot. Home-made puddings include crème brûlée and sherry trifle. The village's 400-year-old grass maze was where locals used to escape the devil.

Open 11–2.30 6–11 **Bar Meals** L served all week 12–2 D served Tue–Sat 7–9 (Winter closed lunch Mon–Thu) **Restaurant** L served all week 12–2 D served Tue–Sun 7–9 (Winter closed lunch Mon–Thu) Free House Adnams, Timothy Taylor Landlord, Smoothflow, Worthingtons. 9 **Facilities** Children's licence Garden Parking **Rooms** 4 bedrooms en suite S£50 D£70

HINXTON MAP 12 TL44

The Red Lion

32 High St CB10 1QY ☎ 01799 530601 01799 531201
e-mail: info@redlionhinxton.co.uk
dir: *1m from M11 junct 9.*

The Red Lion has been in Hinxton, a conservation village, since the 16th century. The bar is in the oldest part, while the spacious oak-built extension is the dining room. Pub policy is always to use fresh local produce where possible to create amply-proportioned dishes such as maize-fed chicken breast with tomato confit, purple-sprouting broccoli and sweet potato fondant; and fillet of turbot with oyster and sorrel sauce, lentil and spinach fritter and tarragon wild rice.

Open 11–3 6–11 (Sun 12–4.30, 7–10.30) **Bar Meals** L served all week 12–2 D served all week 6.45–9 (Sun 12–2.30, Fri–Sat 6.45–9.30) Av main course £11 **Restaurant** L served all week 12–2 D served all week 6.45–9 (Sun 12–2.30, Fri–Sat 6.45–9.30) Av 3 course à la carte £20 Free House Adnams, Greene King IPA, Woodforde's Wherry, plus Guest ales including Nethergates & Hobsons Choice. 12 **Facilities** Children's licence Garden Dogs allowed Parking

HOLYWELL MAP 12 TL37

The Old Ferryboat Inn ★★ HL

Back Ln PE27 4TG ☎ 01480 463227 01480 463245
dir: *A14 then right onto A1096, then A1123, right to Holywell*

Renowned as England's oldest inn, built some time in the 11th century, but with a hostelry history that goes back to the 6th. The Old Ferryboat has immaculately maintained thatch, white stone walls, and cosy interior. A pleasant atmosphere – despite the resident ghost of a lovelorn teenager – in which to enjoy hot chicken curry, roast rack of lamb, steak and ale pie, fish and chips, and Greene King ales.

Open 11.30–11 **Bar Meals** L served all week 12–2.30 D served all week 6–9.30 (Sun 12–2.30, 6–9) Av main course £8.95 Old English Inns Greene King Abbot Ale/IPA, Old Speckled Hen, Guest ales. 6 **Facilities** Garden Parking **Rooms** 7 bedrooms en suite S£50 D£60

HUNTINGDON MAP 12 TL27

The Three Horseshoes ★★★ INN

Moat Ln, Abbots Ripton PE28 2PA
☎ 01487 773440 01487 773440
e-mail: abbotsripton@aol.com

Dating back to1654 and retaining many original features, the picturesque Three Horseshoes once had the lowest ceiling of any pub in the county. Stepping inside today, customers are greeted by three bar areas, a restaurant and a range of hand pumped Adnams real ales. Typical food includes Sunday roasts like rib of beef with Yorkshire pudding, roast loin of pork with crackling and apple sauce; and grilled tuna steak.

Open 11.30–3 6–11 **Bar Meals** L served Tue–Sat 12–2 D served Tue–Sat 6.30–9.30 (Sun 12–2.30 & 6.30–9) **Restaurant** L served Tue–Sat 12–2 (Sun 12–2.30) D served Tue–Sat 6.30–9.30 Av 3 course à la carte £25 Adnams Bitter, Adnams Broadside, Oakhams & JHB. 12 **Facilities** Garden Parking **Rooms** 5 bedrooms en suite S£55 D£70

KEYSTON MAP 11 TL07

Pick of the Pubs

Pheasant Inn

Village Loop Rd PE28 0RE
☎ 01832 710241 01832 710340
e-mail: thepheasant@cyberwave.co.uk
dir: *Signed from A14, W of Huntingdon*

The Pheasant is a charming 15th-century, thatched free house in a sleepy farming village. Here you will find a large traditional bar featuring a mixture of oak beams, big open fires and simple wooden furniture. Three distinct dining areas offer a choice of comfortable, intimate and relaxed places to eat and drink. The latest addition is a garden at the rear of the pub, and there are also tables outside at the front. The food is an eclectic mix, with favourite influences coming from the south of France. Whet your appetite with a rhubarb Bellini before embarking on a starter like warm duck salad with chicory, green beans, lardons, poached duck egg and mustard. Then move on to braised ox cheek with horseradish dauphinoise and Swiss chard, and ginger and whisky parfait with poached pears and madeleines. Three Suffolk real ales are always on offer, alongside a widely acclaimed wine list with extensive tasting notes, created by Master of Wine, John Hoskins. New owners for 2007.

Open 12–3 6–11 **Bar Meals** L served all week 12–2 D served all week 6.30–9.30 Av main course £10.95 **Restaurant** L served all week 12–2 D served all week 6.30–9.30 Av 3 course à la carte £23 Huntsbridge Adnams, Village Bike Potton Brewery, Augustinian Nethergate Brewery. 16 **Facilities** Garden Parking

KIMBOLTON MAP 12 TL16

The New Sun Inn 🍷

20–22 High St PE28 0HA

☎ 01480 860052 📠 01480 869353

e-mail: newsunninn@btinternet.com

dir: *From A1 N, B645 for 7m, from A1 S B661 for 7m, from A14 B660 for 5m*

An impressive array of flowers greets visitors to this 16th-century inn near Kimbolton Castle. As well as being a real ale pub, it offers a good choice of wines by the glass. Dishes from the restaurant menu include king prawns in hot garlic and ginger oil, or whole baked camembert to start, then venison sausages with grain mustard mash or home-made steak and kidney pudding as mains. Lighter meals, such as jacket potatoes or sandwiches are also available.

Open 11–2.30 6–11 (All day Sun) **Bar Meals** L served all week 12–2.15 D served Tue–Sat 7–9.30 **Restaurant** L served Tue–Sun 12–2 D served Tue–Sat 7–9.30 Charles Wells Wells Bombardier & Eagle IPA, Greene King Old Speckled Hen. 🍷 12 **Facilities** Garden Dogs allowed

LITTLE WILBRAHAM MAP 12 TL55

Hole in the Wall NEW 🍷

2 High St CB1 5JY ☎ 01223 812282

When only the gentry were allowed entry to this pub, local farm workers had to order and collect their beer through a hole in the wall. Today the pub welcomes all comers with a regular real ale and changing guests from local micro-breweries. The same honest menu applies whether customers choose to eat in the bar with open fire, the snug with coal range, or the main dining room. Try the Welsh rarebit with Fulbourn ham.

Open 11.30–3 6.30–11 **Bar Meals** L served Tue–Sun 12–2 D served Tue–Sat Av main course £11 **Restaurant** L served Tue–Sun 12–2 D served Tue–Sat Av 3 course à la carte £21 Av 3 course fixed price £18.50 Free House Woodforde's Wherry, Brewers Gold, Cambridge Bitter, Sparta. 🍷 9 **Facilities** Garden Dogs allowed Parking

MADINGLEY MAP 12 TL36

Pick of the Pubs

The Three Horseshoes 🍷

High St CB3 8AB ☎ 01954 210221 📠 01954 212043

e-mail: thethreehorseshoes@huntsbridge.co.uk

dir: *M11 junct 13, 1.5m from A14*

Inside this picturesque thatched inn you'll find a bustling bar and a pretty conservatory-restaurant, while outside a large garden extends toward local meadowland. Chef patron Richard Stokes is a local from the fens who has eaten his way around the world, and his success can be gauged by the long queues for tables. Richard's own style is a modern take on Italian cuisine, characterised by intensely seasonal and imaginative dishes with lots of flavour and flair. Starters might include cured shoulder of pork with beetroots, or hand-made ravioli stuffed with ricotta, spinach, pecorino and sage butter. To follow, try Loch Duart salmon with olive oil braised leeks; roast saddle of venison with creamed cannellini beans; or orecchiette pasta with purple sprouting broccoli. Tempting desserts like white chocolate pannacotta with passionfruit toasted pandoro bread round things off nicely. Prior booking is advisable.

Open 11.30–3 6–11 (Sun 6–8.30) **Bar Meals** L served all week 12–2 D served Mon–Fri 6.30–9.30 (Sat & Sun 12–2.30, 6–8.30) Av main course £17.50 **Restaurant** L served Mon–Fri 12–2 D served Mon–Sat 6.30–9.30 (Sat & Sun 12–2.30) Av 3 course à la carte £35 Huntsbridge Inns Adnams Bitter, Hook Norton Old Hooky, Smile's Best, Cambridge Hobsons Choice. 🍷 20 **Facilities** Garden Parking

MILTON MAP 12 TL46

Waggon & Horses

39 High St CB4 6DF ☎ 01223 860313

e-mail: winningtons.waggon@ntlworld.com

dir: *A14/A10 junct. Past Tesco, through village, approx 1m set back on left*

Famed for its large collection of hats, this imposing mock-Tudor roadhouse also boasts an impressive array of games, from a pétanque terrain in the large garden to bar billiards and shove ha'penny in the one-room bar. Other delights include a good range of draught beers, and a simple, satisfying menu. Try bean stew and crusty bread; haddock and chips; or spinach and ricotta cannelloni. Thursday is balti night, and Wednesday is the notorious quiz.

Open 12–2.30 5–11 (Fri 5–12, Sat 6–11.30 & Sun 7–10.30) **Bar Meals** L served all week 12–2 D served all week 7–9 Av main course £5 **Restaurant** L served all week 12–2 D served all week 7–9 Elgood & Sons Elgoods Cambridge Bitter, Black Dog Mild, Golden Newt, and Seasonal Ales. **Facilities** Garden Dogs allowed Parking

NEWTON MAP 12 TL44

The Queen's Head 🍷

Fowlmere Rd CB22 7PG ☎ 01223 870436

dir: *6m S of Cambridge on B1368, 1.5m off A10 at Harston, 4m from A505*

Best described as 'quintessentially English' this 17th-century pub has been run by the same family since 1962. They continue to steadfastly ban fruit machines and piped music from the two small bars. Lunches are limited to home-made soup, Aga-baked potatoes, toast with beef dripping, and sandwiches. In the evening it's just soup and cold platters. There's no specials board since, as the landlord says, 'We have no specialist'!

Open 11.30–2.30 6–11 (Sun 12–2.30, 7–10.30) Closed: 25–26 Dec **Bar Meals** L served all week 11.30–2.15 D served Mon–Sat 7–9.30 (Sun 7–9.30) Av main course £4 Free House Adnams Southwold, Broadside, Fisherman, Bitter & Regatta. 🍷 8 **Facilities** Dogs allowed Parking **Notes**

PETERBOROUGH MAP 12 TL19

The Brewery Tap 🍷

80 Westgate PE1 2AA ☎ 01733 358500 📠 01733 310022

e-mail: brewerytap@hotmail.com

dir: *Opposite bus station*

This is the home of multi-award-winning Oakham Ales, moved here from their home in Rutland when Peterborough's spacious old labour exchange opened its doors as the Brewery Tap in 1998. Visitors to this striking pub can see the day-to-day running of the brewery through a glass wall spanning half the length of the bar. As if the appeal of the beer range were not enough, Thai chefs beaver away producing delicious snacks, soups, salads, stir-fries and curries.

Open 12–11 Closed: Dec 25–26, Jan 1 **Bar Meals** L served all week 12–2.30 D served all week 6–9.30 (Fri–Sat 12–10.30) **Restaurant** L served all week 12–2.30 D served all week 6–9.30 (Fri–Sat 12–10.30) Free House Oakham, Jeffery Hudson Bitter, Bishops Farewell & White Dwarf, Elgoods Black Dog & 7 Guest Beers. 7 **Facilities** Dogs allowed

Charters Bar & East Restaurant

Town Bridge PE1 1FP

☎ 01733 315700 & 315702 01733 315700

e-mail: manager@charters-bar.co.uk

dir: *A1/A47 Wisbech, 2m for city centre & town bridge (River Nene). Barge moored at Town Bridge (west side)*

Charters is a 176ft long barge which was sailed over from Holland in 1991 and moored right in the heart of the city, on the River Nene. The East part of the name applies to the upper deck, which is an oriental restaurant with dishes from Vietnam, Japan, Thailand, Malaysia and elsewhere. Twelve hand pumps dispense a continually changing repertoire of real ales, and a good selection of foreign beers is always available. Friday and Saturday nights are a treat for blues lovers, with a late night live blues club.

Open 12–11.30 (Fri–Sat 12–12) Closed: 25–26 Dec, 1 Jan **Bar Meals** L served all week 12–2.30 **Restaurant** L served all week 12–2.30 D served all week 6–10.30 (Sun 6–10) Av 2 course fixed price £8.95 Free House Oakham JHB, Oakham White Dwarf & Bishops Farewell, Elgoods Black Dog. 10 **Facilities** Children's licence Garden Dogs allowed Parking

SPALDWICK — MAP 12 TL17

Pick of the Pubs

The George Inn

High St PE28 0TD ☎ 01480 890293 01480 896847

dir: *6m W of Huntingdon on A14, junct 18 towards Spaldwick/Stow Longa*

Recently refurbished to create a pleasing blend of traditional and modern, this fine old building retains historic features such as original beams and fireplaces. It started life as a large private residence belonging to the Dartington family, and became a coaching inn in 1679. Today it remains a serene presence beside the manor house, overlooking the village green. The bar is relaxing with its comfortable leather sofas, while the restaurant, set in a beautifully converted barn, offers a pleasing selection of traditional British and Mediterranean-influenced dishes. Typical choices include a starter of crispy duck salad with spicy chorizo, bacon lardons, croutons and plum dressing, followed by wood pigeon breasts with herb dumplings, mash, red cabbage and a chocolate red wine sauce. Finish with apple crumble tart or a delightful selection of cheeses. A good choice of wines is available by the glass, and there are plenty of well-kept real ales.

Open 12–11 (Fri–Sat 12–12) **Bar Meals** L served all week 12–2.30 D served all week 6–9.30 Av main course £11.95 **Restaurant** L served all week 12–2.30 D served all week 6–9.30 Av 3 course à la carte £25 Punch Taverns Adnams Broadside, Greene King IPA, Youngs Special. 25 **Facilities** Children's licence Garden Parking

STILTON — MAP 12 TL18

Pick of the Pubs

The Bell Inn Hotel ★★★ HL

Great North Rd PE7 3RA

☎ 01733 241066 01733 245173

e-mail: reception@thebellstilton.co.uk

dir: *From A1 follow signs for Stilton. Hotel on main road in village centre*

Stilton cheese made in the village was first served at The Bell in the early 1700s, but the inn's claims to fame do not rest there. Dick Turpin, the highwayman, hid from the law here, and more recently the inn was visited by Clark Gable and Joe Louis, when they were with the American Air Force during World War II and were stationed nearby. The inn has been brought up to date without losing any of its historic charm; the galleried restaurant is very atmospheric, while the bistro has a more contemporary feel. Dishes range from flame seared yellow fin tuna steak with sweet 'n' sour tomatoes, new potatoes, chilli salsa and mint crème fraiche from the bar/bistro carte, to roasted quails stuffed with thyme brioche and served with honey jus, baby vegetables and lyonnaise Jersey royals from the fixed price restaurant menu.

Open 12–2.30 6–11 (Fri–Sat 6–12, Sat–Sun 12–3, Sun 7–11) Closed: Dec 25 **Bar Meals** L served all week 12–2 D served all week 6.30–9.30 (Sun 12–2.30, 7–9) Av main course £8 **Restaurant** L served Sun–Fri 12–2 D served all week 7–9.30 Av 3 course fixed price £26.95 Free House Greene King Abbot Ale, Oakham JHB, Interbrew Boddingtons, Fullers London Pride. 8 **Facilities** Garden Parking **Rooms** 23 bedrooms en suite S£72.50 D£89.50

STRETHAM MAP 12 TL57

The Lazy Otter 🍷

Cambridge Rd CB6 3LU ☎ 01353 649780 📠 01353 649314
e-mail: swilkilazyotter@aol.com
dir: *Telephone for directions*

With a large beer garden and riverside restaurant overlooking the marina, the Lazy Otter lies just off the A10 between Ely and Cambridge. The pub's location beside the Great Ouse river makes it very popular in summer. Typical dishes include jumbo cod, lemon sole topped with crab meat, and fisherman's medley, as well as a selection of steaks and grills. The marina holds 30 permanent boats, as well as up to 10 day boats.

Open 11–11 **Bar Meals** L served all week 12–2.30 D served all week 6–9.30 (Sun 12–4) **Restaurant** L served all week 12–2.30 D served all week 6–9.30 (Sun 12–4) Marston's Pedigree, Scottish Courage John Smith's & Courage Best. 🍷 8 **Facilities** Garden Parking Play Area

CHESHIRE

ALDFORD MAP 15 SJ45

Pick of the Pubs

The Grosvenor Arms 🍷

Chester Rd CH3 6HJ
☎ 01244 620228 📠 01244 620247
e-mail: grosvenor.arms@brunningandprice.co.uk
dir: *On B5130 S of Chester*

The landlords describe their pub as a 'large, rather austere Victorian governess of a building'. In fact they regard its locally famous mid-Victorian architect as a bit of a vandal who, in the name of progress, destroyed many of the fine medieval buildings in and around Chester. But there's much to be positive about, and the locals are very fond of it. From the garden it's a delight of higgledy-piggledy rooflines and soft, warm Cheshire brick. The spacious, open-plan interior includes an airy conservatory and a panelled, book-filled library. On the bistro-style menu are duck breast with parsnip dauphinoise and red wine sauce; salmon and smoked haddock fishcakes with tomato and spring onion salad; Thai red curry with king prawns and sweet potatoes; and spaghetti bolognaise. A great outside terrace leads into a small but pleasing garden which, in turn, takes you out to the village green.

Open 11.30–11 (Sun 12–10.30) **Bar Meals** L served all week 12–10 D served all week 12–10 (Sun 12–9) Av main course £10 Free House Weetwood-Eastgate, Caledonian Deuchars IPA, Phoenix Arizona, Thwaites Original. 🍷 16 **Facilities** Garden Dogs allowed Parking

ASTON MAP 15 SJ64

Pick of the Pubs

The Bhurtpore Inn 🍷

Wrenbury Rd CW5 8DQ ☎ 01270 780917
e-mail: simonbhurtpore@yahoo.co.uk
dir: *Between Nantwich & Whitchurch just off A530. Turn towards Wrenbury at crossroads in village on the A530*

See Pick of the Pubs on opposite page

BARTHOMLEY MAP 15 SJ75

The White Lion Inn

CW2 5PG ☎ 01270 882242

Dating from 1614, this half-timbered and thatched inn with character bars is in a lovely rural setting, and has associations with the English Civil War. It offers home-cooked food like hotpot, lasagne, cottage pie, 'hot beef' baguettes, sirloin and stilton on French stick, and a selection of sandwiches.

Open 11.30–11 (Sun 12–10.30) **Bar Meals** L served all week 12–2 (Sun 12–2.30) Av main course £5 Burtonwood Marstons Bitter, Marstons Pedigree, Mansfield Banks, plus Monthly Guest. **Facilities** Garden Dogs allowed Parking

BOLLINGTON MAP 16 SJ97

The Church House Inn 🍷

Church St SK10 5PY ☎ 01625 574014 📠 01625 562026
e-mail: info@the-church-house-inn.co.uk
dir: *From A34 take A538 towards Macclesfield. Through Prestbury, then follow Bollington signs*

Exposed beams, log fires and agricultural decorations lend a homely feel to this stone-built village free house, which hit the headlines when it was bought by a group of local residents. The varied menu includes home-made soup, the inn's own sausages and pies, and other traditional British favourites. Vegetarian options feature on the daily specials board. The pub also has a small enclosed beer garden.

Open 12–3 5.30–11 (Fri–Sun all day) **Bar Meals** L served all week 12–2.30 D served all week 6.30–9.30 **Restaurant** L served all week 12–2.30 D served all week 6–9.30 Av 3 course à la carte £15 Av 3 course fixed price £7.50 Free House Greene King IPA, Black Sheep, Stella, Interbrew Boddington's. 🍷 18 **Facilities** Parking

The Bhurtpore Inn

The George family has a bit of a thing about this traditional village pub. In 1849 James George leased it from the local Combermere estate, from which descendant Philip George bought it in 1895, only to sell it six years later to a Crewe brewery.

Ninety years later, in 1991, Simon and Nicky George were looking to buy their first pub and came across the boarded-up, stripped-out Bhurtpore. It ticked just about every box. Although it has been a pub since at least 1778, it was the 1826 Siege of Bhurtpore in India, where Lord Combermere had distinguished himself, that inspired its current name. With eleven real ales always available, a large selection of bottled beers and seven continental beers on tap, it is truly a free house. The award-winning food is fresh, home made and reasonably priced, both in the bar and the restaurant. Starters include spicy lamb samosas with yogurt and mint dip; potato skins with grilled cheese and bacon topping; and pork and black pudding patties with coarse grain mustard and apple sauce. In addition to typical mains such as steak, kidney and real ale pie, and breaded wholetail scampi, there is a good choice of specials, such as lamb fillet wrapped in pastry with port and cranberry sauce; fish and king prawn pie with mushrooms, egg and spring onion mash; and buffalo mozzarella with garlic bread. Finish with spiced raisin and ginger pudding with toffee sauce, or a local farmhouse ice cream. Behind the pub is a lawn with countryside views. Very much at the centre of the local community, the pub is home to an enthusiastic cricket team, a group of cyclists known as the Wobbly Wheels and, once a month, folk musicians.

MAP 15 SJ64
Wrenbury Rd CW5 8DQ
☎ 01270 780917
e-mail: simonbhurtpore@yahoo.co.uk
dir: *Between Nantwich & Whitchurch just off A530. Turn towards Wrenbury at crossroads in village on the A530*

Open 12–2.30 6.30–11.30 (Sun 12–11.30) Closed: 25–26 Dec, 1 Jan
Bar Meals L served all week 12–2 D served all week 6.45–9.30 (Sun 12–9) Av main course £9.50
Restaurant L served all week 12–2 D served all week 6.45–9.30 (Sun 12–9) Av 3 course à la carte £17.50
Free House
Salopian Golden Thread, Abbeydale Absolution, Weetwood Oasthouse Gold, Copper Dragon Golden Pippin. 10
Facilities Garden Dogs allowed Parking

The Pheasant Inn

This 300-year-old sandstone and half-timbered former farmhouse is set in beautiful rural surroundings. It attracts walkers, golfers, anglers and visitors to the nearby Chester racecourse and Oulton Park racing circuit, as well as locals.

During the winter, meals and drinks are served at one of the tables standing on polished wooden floorboards, or those grouped around the brick pillars warmed by open fires – one of them is reputedly the largest log fire in the county. There's also a stone-flagged conservatory and flower-filled courtyard, ideal for enjoying the well-kept ales and sophisticated cooking during the warmer summer weather. The owners aim to provide the best of food, with friendly service in a relaxed environment; children are welcome during the day, but evenings are carefully preserved for adults. Featured on the menu are ranges of sandwiches, ploughman's, paninis and salads, or light bites such as braised field mushrooms with garlic tomato sauce and melted cheddar; and confit of crispy duck leg with honey and ginger. 'Home comforts' lists the likes of lambs' liver and smoked bacon, or smoked haddock and salmon fish pie. More substantial main courses range from Cholmondley Estate hand-reared rump of beef; and Goosnargh chicken breast simmered in white wine; to grilled fillet of Anglesey sea bass with buttered leaf spinach and new potatoes. Puddings follow traditional lines with the Pheasant's own Eton Mess; home-made banoffee pie with lashings of cream; and home-made apple and sultana crumble with custard. If it seems a shame to drive home, you can always opt to stay in one of the en suite country-style bedrooms.

★★ HL ◉ 🍷
MAP 15 SJ55
CH3 9PF
☎ 01829 770434
🖷 01829 771097
e-mail:
info@thepheasantinn.co.uk
dir: *A41 (Chester to Whitchurch), after 4m left to Burwardsley. Follow 'Cheshire Workshops' signs*

Open 11–11
Bar Meals L served all week 12–10 D served all week 12–10 (Sun 12–8.30)
Restaurant L served all week D served all week
Free House
Weetwood Old Dog, Eastgate, Best, Hoegarden and guest Bitter. 🍷 8
Facilities Children's licence Garden Dogs allowed Parking Play Area
Rooms 12 bedrooms en suite S£65 D£85

BROXTON MAP 15 SJ45

The Copper Mine

Nantwich Rd CH3 9JH ☎ 01829 782293

e-mail: geoff@the-coppermine.freeserve.co.uk

dir: *At Sainsbury's rdbt take A41 (Whitchurch), left at next rdbt onto Nantwich A534 1m, pub on right.*

A well known food venue, this pub is convenient for Cheshire Ice Cream Farm, Beeston Castle, and the Candle Factory at Cheshire Workshops. Sit in the conservatory to make the most of the beautiful views, or in summer, enjoy the patio and lawn with mature trees. Meals range from salads, sandwiches and omelettes through to main meals such as salmon and broccoli fish cakes with a pink Caesar dressing or home-made steak burger with chips.

Open 12-3 6-11 **Bar Meals** L served Tue-Sun 12-2.30 D served Tue-Sun 6.30-9.30 Av main course £7.95 **Restaurant** L served Tue-Sun 12-2.30 D served Tue-Sun 6.30-9.30 Free House Marstons Cream Flow, Pedigree & Banks Real Ale. **Facilities** Garden Parking Play Area

BUNBURY MAP 15 SJ55

Pick of the Pubs

The Dysart Arms

Bowes Gate Rd CW6 9PH

☎ 01829 260183 01829 261286

e-mail: dysart.arms@brunningandprice.co.uk

dir: *Between A49 & A51, by Shropshire Union Canal, opposite church*

A truly classic English village pub, built as a farmhouse in the mid-18th century, and licensed since the late 1800s. Around its central bar are several airy rooms with solid wooden tables and chairs, tiled and wooden floors, lovely open fires and a couple of large bookcases. From the terrace and immaculate garden there are views of Peckforton Castle one way, and Beeston Castle the other. Home-grown herbs are used in an appetising menu offering starters like black olive and artichoke tart, and warm goats' cheese with honey dressing. Among the main courses are steak, kidney and oyster pudding; seafood gratin; locally made Bunbury bangers; and pan-fried duck breasts. Ask for the menu again and consider apple and cinnamon crumble with custard, or chocolate pecan pie with clotted cream. The amusingly named Struggling Monkey from Manchester's Phoenix brewery is among the beers on offer.

Open 11.30-11 (Sun 12-10.30) **Bar Meals** L served all week D served all week (Sat 12-9.30, Sun 12-9) Av main course £10.95 Free House Phoenix Struggling Monkey, Weetwood Eastgate, Thwaites Bitter, Roosters Yankee. 14 **Facilities** Garden Dogs allowed Parking

BURLEYDAM MAP 15 SJ64

The Combermere Arms

SY13 4AT ☎ 01948 871223 01948 661371

e-mail: combermere.arms@brunningandprice.co.uk

dir: *From Whitchurch take A525 towards Nantwich, see signs for Newcastle, Audlem & Woore, turn right at junct. 100yds on right*

Popular with local shoots, walkers and town folk alike, this busy 17th-century inn retains great character and warmth. Three roaring fires complement the wealth of oak, pictures and old furniture. Dishes include haddock, leek and Appleby Cheshire tart to start, followed by roast topside of Welsh black beef; or wild mushroom, chestnut and spinach suet pudding. Especially popular at weekends, so do book ahead to enjoy the good country food.

Open 12-11 **Bar Meals** L served all week 12-9.30 D served all week 12-9.30 **Restaurant** L served all week Free House Woodlands Oak Beauty, Weetwood Cheshire Cat, Thornbridge Jaipur Monsoon, St Austells Tribute & Storm Hurricane Hubert. 15 **Facilities** Garden Dogs allowed Parking

BURWARDSLEY MAP 15 SJ55

Pick of the Pubs

The Pheasant Inn ★★ HL

CH3 9PF ☎ 01829 770434 01829 771097

e-mail: info@thepheasantinn.co.uk

dir: *A41 (Chester to Whitchurch), after 4m left to Burwardsley. Follow 'Cheshire Workshops' signs*

See Pick of the Pubs on opposite page

CHESTER MAP 15 SJ46

Pick of the Pubs

Albion Inn

Park St CH1 1RN ☎ 01244 340345

e-mail: christina.mercer@tesco.net

dir: *In city centre adjacent to Citywalls & Newgate*

The home fires still burn on winter nights at this living memorial to the 1914-18 war. It is a traditional Victorian street corner pub, with a splendid cast-iron fireplace, enamelled advertisements and World War I memorabilia. Trench rations are locally and regionally

CONTINUED

England

CHESTER continued

sourced, including Staffordshire oatcakes, Lincolnshire sausages, award-winning haggis and meat from local butchers. Organic pasta, local market fish and meats cooked on the premises include boiled gammon and pease-pudding served with parsley sauce. Please note: Children are not welcome.

Open 11-3 5-11 (Sat 11.30-3 6-11, Sun 12-2.30 7-10.30) Closed: 25-26 Dec, 1-2 Jan **Bar Meals** L served all week 12-2 D served Mon-Sat 5-8 Av main course £7.80 **Restaurant** L served all week D served Mon-Sat Punch Taverns Black Sheep, Batemans, Deuchars & Guest Beers. **Facilities** Dogs allowed **Notes**

Old Harkers Arms

1 Russell St CH1 5AL ☎ 01244 344525 01244 344812
e-mail: harkers.arms@brunningandprice.co.uk
dir: *Follow steps down from City Road onto canal path*

A buzzy, almost clubby meeting place with the feel of a London boozer, this former Victorian warehouse on the Shropshire Union Canal is one of Chester's more unusual pubs. The bar offers over 100 malt whiskies and a changing range of cask ales supported by blackboard tasting notes while the impressive menu runs from sandwiches and snacks (cottage pie; mushroom and tarragon soup) to mains such as duck breast with potato and celeriac rôsti.

Open 11.30-11 (Sun 12-10.30) Closed: 25 Dec **Bar Meals** L served all week 12-9.30 D served all week 12-9.30 (Sun 12-9) Av main course £11.50 Brunning & Price Weetwood Cheshire Cat, Flowers Original, Wapping Bitter, Titanic Stout & Spitting Feathers. 24 **Facilities** Dogs allowed

CHOLMONDELEY — MAP 15 SJ55

Pick of the Pubs

The Cholmondeley Arms ★★★ INN

SY14 8HN ☎ 01829 720300 01829 720123
e-mail: guy@cholmondeleyarms.co.uk
dir: *On A49, between Whitchurch & Tarporley*

See Pick of the Pubs on opposite page

CONGLETON — MAP 16 SJ86

The Plough At Eaton ★★★★ INN

Macclesfield Rd, Eaton CW12 2NH
☎ 01260 280207 01260 298458
e-mail: theploughinn@hotmail.co.uk
dir: *On A536 (Congleton to Macclesfield road)*

Like a giant jigsaw puzzle, an ancient Welsh barn was transported here in hundreds of pieces to become a marvellously atmospheric restaurant adjoining this Elizabethan inn. From the specials menu come poached fresh salmon and prawn salad; chicken Madras with rice; and lamb Henry with mash. The carte offers lightly grilled turbot with lemon butter, and fillet steak cooked at the table. Apple crumble and custard and chocolate fudge cake are typical desserts.

The Plough at Eaton

Open 11-11 (Sun 12-10.30) **Bar Meals** L served all week 12-2.30 D served all week 6-9.30 (Sun 12-8) Av main course £8.95 **Restaurant** L served all week 12-2.30 D served all week 6-9.30 (Sun 12-8.30) Free House Boddingtons, Hydes, Moore Houses, Storm Brew. 10 **Facilities** Garden Parking **Rooms** 17 bedrooms en suite S£55 D£70

HANDLEY — MAP 15 SJ45

The Calveley Arms

Whitchurch Rd CH3 9DT
☎ 01829 770619 01829 770901
e-mail: calveleyarms@btconnect.com
dir: *5m S of Chester, signed from A41*

First licensed in 1636, the Calveley is chock full of old timbers, jugs, pots, pictures, prints and ornaments. The food is a big attraction, with daily changing specials supplementing a menu offering fresh fish, Madras curry, classic moules à la crème, and more unusual dishes such as tarte flambée (like they make it in Alsace). Sandwiches, baguettes and special salads are among the lighter options.

Open 12-3 6-11 (Sun 7-10.30) Closed: 25 Dec eve **Bar Meals** L served all week 12-2.15 D served all week 6-9.30 **Restaurant** L served all week 12-2.15 D served all week 6-9.30 (Sun 12-2.30, 7-9.30) Enterprise Inns Castle Eden Ale, Marston's Pedigree, Black Bull, Deucars Caledonian. 10 **Facilities** Garden Dogs allowed Parking

HAUGHTON MOSS — MAP 15 SJ55

The Nags Head

Long Ln CW6 9RN ☎ 01829 260265 01829 261364
e-mail: rorykl@btinternet.com
dir: *Turn off A49 S of Tarporley at Beeston/Haughton sign into Long Ln, continue for 1.75m*

This typical 16th-century Cheshire black and white building, once a smithy, is every inch the traditional pub. Inside are low ceilings, crooked beams, exposed brickwork and real fires. A comprehensive set of menus offers everything from pizza, jacket potatoes and panini through to full meals such as mussels in white wine and cream followed by duck in orange sauce. Ask owner Debbie Keigan about the Cash Trap board game she devised.

Open 12-12 (Closed: 25 Dec eve) **Bar Meals** L served all week 12-10 D served all week 12-10 Av main course £8 **Restaurant** L served all week 12-10 D served all week 12-10 Free House Flowers IPA, Abbot Ale, Guest ales. 20 **Facilities** Children's licence Garden Dogs allowed Parking Play Area

The Cholmondeley Arms

Where once village children got to grips with the three Rs, grown-ups now get to grips with pints of Marston's Pedigree and Everard's Tiger Best. For until 1982 this attractive and elegant pub was the village school, as those with an architectural eye will detect.

It remained closed until 1988 when the current owners, with the help of Lord and Lady Cholmondeley, residents of the nearby castle, embarked on its conversion. And not a moment too soon for many of the villagers, for the development at last reversed a late 19th-century, passionately teetotal Cholmondeley's decision to close all the licensed premises on the 25,000-acre estate. Since reopening it has won many regional, and even national, trade and newspaper awards. The menu is such that one could dine here frequently without repeating one's order too often, and without breaking the bank. All food is freshly prepared, wherever possible using local produce. From its daily changing menu come hot baked prawns in sour cream and garlic; Jerusalem artichoke hummus with rosemary bruschetta; and, at lunchtimes only, devilled kidneys on toast. Usually appearing in the main courses section are braised oxtail in red wine sauce; smoked haddock fishcakes with devilled tomato sauce; leek and cheddar soufflé; hot Madras beef curry with rice and chutneys; and rack of lamb with onion and mint sauce. Going on a Sunday? Then expect roast rib-eye of beef with Yorkshire pudding and horseradish cream. Home-made puddings are a speciality, with hot baked syrup sponge, sticky toffee pudding and ice soufflé Grand Marniér. Children are always made welcome. Across the former playground is the secluded School House, which now provides six comfortable, individually designed bedrooms.

★★★ INN 🍷
MAP 15 SJ55
SY14 8HN
☎ 01829 720300
📠 01829 720123
e-mail:
guy@cholmondeleyarms.co.uk
dir: *On A49, between Whitchurch & Tarporley*

Open 11-3 6-11 Closed: 25 Dec
Bar Meals L served all week 12-2.30 D served all week 6.30-10 Av main course £10
Restaurant L served all week 12-2.30 D served all week 6.30-10 Av 3 course à la carte £20
Free House
Marston's Pedigree, Adnams Bitter, Banks's, Everards Tiger Best. 🍷 7
Facilities Garden Dogs allowed Parking Play Area
Rooms 6 bedrooms en suite S£50 D£70

KNUTSFORD MAP 15 SJ77

Pick of the Pubs

The Dog Inn

Well Bank Ln, Over Peover WA16 8UP
☎ 01625 861421 📠 01625 864800
e-mail: thedog-inn@paddockinns.fsnet.co.uk
dir: *S from Knutsford take A50. Turn into Stocks Ln at The Whipping Stocks pub 2m.*

In its lifetime The Dog Inn has been a row of cottages, a grocer's shop, a shoemaker's and a farmstead. In 1860 it became a beer house. The timbered building is located in Over Peover (pronounced Peever) in the heart of the Cheshire countryside between Knutsford and Holmes Chapel. In summer it is bedecked with dazzling flowerbeds, tubs and hanging baskets. The pub attracts a faithful following with its interesting guest ales and impressive use of local produce. Typical starters include home-made curried apple and parsnip soup; and home-made breaded crab and salmon fishcakes. You could follow with pork loin cutlets with apple fritters and a Dijon and Calvados sauce; or half a roasted crispy duck with a red wine, mushroom and black cherry sauce. More pubby options include steaks, steak and ale pie, and fish and chips, while dessert might be bread and butter pudding or pecan and lemon cheesecake.

Open 11.30-3 4.30-11 (Sun 11-11) **Bar Meals** L served all week 12-2.30 D served all week 6-9 (Sun 12-8.30) Av main course £10 **Restaurant** L served all week 12-2.30 D served all week 6-9 (Sun 12-8.30) Av 3 course à la carte £20 Free House Hydes Traditional Bitter, Weetwood Best, Skipton Brewery, Moorhouses. 8 **Facilities** Garden Dogs allowed Parking **Rooms** 6 bedrooms en suite S£60 D£80 (★★★ INN)

LACH DENNIS MAP 15 SJ77

The Duke of Portland NEW

Penny's Ln CW9 7SY ☎ 01606 46264
e-mail: info@dukeofportland.com

Located in the heart of the glorious Cheshire plain, the Duke is a new venture from the owners of Knutsford's Belle Époque Brasserie. The sunny, landscaped garden complements the newly-refurbished building, and the owners have a genuine commitment to local producers, many of whom have never supplied other commercial customers. Menu choices might include pan-fried pheasant with chestnut and oregano gravy; or whole roast sea bass with soy, lemon grass and vegetable salad.

Open 12-3 5.30-11 (Sat 12-11, Sun 12-10.30) **Bar Meals** L served all week 12-2.30 D served all week 5.30-9.30 (Sun 12-8) Av main course £7.95 **Restaurant** L served all week 12-2.30 D served all week 5.30-9.30 (Sun 12-8) Av 3 course à la carte £19.95 Av 2 course fixed price £9.95 Staropramen, Twaites Bomber, Marstons Pedigree, Banks Original. 7 **Facilities** Children's licence Garden Parking

LANGLEY MAP 16 SJ97

Leathers Smithy

Clarke Ln SK11 0NE ☎ 01260 252313 📠 01260 252313
e-mail: leatherssmithy@supanet.com

Splendidly located pub overlooking the Ridgegate Reservoir and Macclesfield Forest with a country park at the rear, offering what the landlord describes as 'the most beautiful views in Cheshire'. The name commemorates both William Leather, a 19th-century licensee, and the building's previous role as a village forge. Food options range from beef tips hoi-sin, wild mushroom risotto, and pan-fried fresh Cajun salmon fillet and lime butter, to sandwiches, baguettes and salads.

Open 12-3 7-11 (Sat-Sun all day) **Bar Meals** L served all week 12-2 D served all week 7-10 (Sat 12-9.30, Sun 12-8) Av main course £8 **Restaurant** L served all week 12-2 D served all week 7-10 (Sat 12-9.30, Sun 12-8) Theakstons Best, Bombardier, Timothy Taylor's Landlord & Guest cask ale. **Facilities** Garden Parking

LOWER WHITLEY MAP 15 SJ67

Pick of the Pubs

Chetwode Arms

St Lane WA4 4EN ☎ 01925 730203 📠 01925 730870
e-mail: info@chetwodearms.com
dir: *On A49 2m S from M56 junct 10, 6m S of Warrington*

See Pick of the Pubs on opposite page

Chetwode Arms

Adorned with window boxes and built from Cheshire brick, this 400-year-old former coaching inn is a welcoming sight in the heart of this small village. The inn's interior is as cosy and rambling as you could wish for.

There's the tap room, which welcomes walkers and their dogs; the bar room, which is tiny and has an open fire; and, leading off the bar, a warren of small, intimate dining rooms and passageways. It is said that somewhere underground, a tunnel leads from the pub to the vicarage, and then on to St Luke's church, which is believed to be the oldest brick church still standing in England. From the main dining room you can step onto a terrace overlooking the pub's own crown bowling green, one of the best kept greens in the country. There, with the wall heated gently by the sun, you can while away the hours late into the evening supping a pint of Marston's Pedigree or Jennings Cumberland. The pub's owners are English and Austrian, so expect a continental touch to the cooking.

Snacks, available until 3.30pm from Monday to Sunday, include crusty baguettes served with chips and filled with the likes of lobster tails, Marie Rose sauce and rocket, or brie, bacon and cranberry. For a more warming snack, opt for a panini filled with roasted vegetables or sirloin steak and fried onions. Dishes from the main menu include starters such as black pudding and stilton rarebit on rôsti; and asparagus spears wrapped in Parma ham topped with hollandaise sauce. Follow with mains such as vegetarian Thai curry; lobster and salmon ravioli in a creamy sauce with lemon and sun dried tomatoes; and osso buco. A selection of steaks cooked on volcanic stone is also available, and there are always plenty of seafood options.

MAP 15 SJ67
St Lane WA4 4EN
☎ 01925 730203
Fax 01925 730870
e-mail:
info@chetwodearms.com
dir: *On A49 2m S from M56 junct 10, 6m S of Warrington*

Open 12–11 (Winter 12–4, 5.30–11)
Bar Meals L served all week 12–3 D served all week 6–9
Restaurant L served all week 12–3 D served all week 6–9.30 (Sun 12–8)
Punch Taverns
Marston's Pedigree, Banks Original, Adnams Broad, Jennings Cumberland & Guest Ale. 🍷 12
Facilities Garden Dogs allowed Parking Play Area

England

MACCLESFIELD MAP 16 SJ97

The Windmill Inn

Holehouse Ln, Whitely Green, Adlington SK10 5SJ

☎ 01625 574222

e-mail: thewindmill@dsl.pipex.com

dir: *Between Macclesfield & Poynton. Follow brown tourist signs on main road 1.5m*

A beamed former farmhouse set in lovely Cheshire countryside with a landscaped garden. The pub is close to the Macclesfield Canal and fantastic walks including the Middlewood Way. Sandwiches and side orders like home-made chips are supplemented by such daily specials as beef casserole with wholegrain mustard mash and chopped parsley. Main courses include the likes of gateau of aubergines with Nantwich goats' cheese, plum tomatoes and basil.

Open 12-3 5-11 (Sat 12-11, Sun 12-10.30) **Bar Meals** L served all week 12-2.30 D served all week 6-9 (Sat 12-9.30, Sun 12-8) **Restaurant** L served all week 12-2.30 D served all week 6-9 (Sat 12-9.30, Sun 12-8) Six Continents Retail Timothy Taylor Landlord, Black Sheep, Old Speckled Hen, Tetleys & Guest. **Facilities** Garden Dogs allowed Parking

MARTON MAP 15 SJ86

Pick of the Pubs

The Davenport Arms NEW

Congleton Rd SK11 9HF

☎ 01260 224269 01260 224565

e-mail: enquiries@thedavenportarms.co.uk

dir: *3m from Congleton off A34*

Marton's 14th-century, half-timbered church is probably the oldest of its type still in use in Europe. Opposite is this 18th-century pub, formerly a farmhouse, and nearby is the ancient Marton Oak, still producing acorns after more than a millennium. The traditional bar has cushioned settles and leather armchairs by a log fire, while in the middle of the restaurant is a well, although purely decorative these days. Upstairs, criminals were once tried, the really bad ones ending up on a gibbet over the road. Food – and this includes chutneys, sauces and desserts – is all freshly made on the premises from locally supplied ingredients. The menu, incorporating a light lunch selection, offers fishcakes; tenderloin of pork wrapped in bacon with blue cheese and cider sauce; and breast of duck marinated with ginger, garlic and chilli, noodles and stir-fried vegetables. The lovely beer garden contains a discreet children's play area.

Open 12-3 6-close (Fri-Sun all day) **Bar Meals** L served Tue-Sat 12-2.30 D served Tue-Sat 6-9 (Sun 12-3, 6-8.30) Av main course £11.50 **Restaurant** L served Tue-Sat 12-2.30 D served Tue-Sat 6-9 (Sun 12-3, 6-8.30) Av 3 course à la carte £22.50 Free House Copper Dragon, Storm Brewing, Directors, Websters Yorkshire Bitter & Weetwood. 9 **Facilities** Children's licence Garden Parking Play Area

MOULDSWORTH MAP 15 SJ57

Pick of the Pubs

The Goshawk

Station Rd CH3 8AJ ☎ 01928 740900 01928 740965

dir: *A51 from Chester onto A54. Left onto B5393 towards Frodsham. Enter Mouldsworth, pub on left opposite rail station*

There is a professional yet relaxed atmosphere at The Goshawk, with its friendly staff, log fires in winter and stripped pine floors. The wide-ranging menu should have something for everyone, with light snacks such as smoked mackerel bruschetta with roast peppers; or steak burgers; meat dishes like chicken stuffed with chorizo; or steak and kidney pie; up to twelve fish dishes, including Thai baked sea bass; monkfish with mussel and clam chowder; and lobster thermidor; vegetarian choices like goats' cheese in filo pastry with Mediterranean vegetables; and several traditional desserts such as spotted dick; chocolate fudge cake; and Bakewell tart. A wide choice of wines is on offer as well as real ales like Timothy Taylors Landlord. There is a good play area for children, and the decked area to the rear overlooks one of the finest crown bowling greens in the area.

Open 12-11 Closed: 25 Dec & 1 Jan **Bar Meals** L served all week D served all week 12-9.30 (Sun 12-9) **Restaurant** L served all week D served all week 12-9.30 (Sun 12-9) Timothy Taylors Landlord, Greene King IPA, Deuchars & Speckled Han. 14 **Facilities** Garden Parking Play Area

NANTWICH MAP 15 SJ65

The Thatch Inn

Wrexham Rd, Faddiley CW5 8JE

☎ 01270 524223 01270 524674

e-mail: thethatchinn@aol.com

dir: *Follow signs for Wrexham from Nantwich, inn is 4m from Nantwich*

The black-and-white Thatch Inn is believed to be the oldest as well as one of the prettiest pubs in south Cheshire. It has a three quarter acre garden, and inside you'll find oak beams, and open fires in winter. The menu is divided between options from the grill; traditional favourites (pies, roasts and casseroles); tastes from afar (nachos, lasagne, curry); and fish, summer salads, light bites and a children's menu. Speciality coffees are a feature.

Open 11-11 (Sun 12-10.30) **Bar Meals** L served all week 11-9.30 D served all week 11-9.30 (Sun 12-9.30) Av main course £7.95 **Restaurant** L served all week 12-9.30 D served all week 12-9.30 Free House Marston Pedigree, Timothy Taylor Landlord, Weetwoods, Archers. 24 **Facilities** Garden Parking Play Area

NORTHWICH — MAP 15 SJ67

The Red Lion NEW ★★★ INN

277 Chester Rd, Hartford CW8 1QL ☎ 01606 74597

e-mail: cathy.iglesias@tesco.net

dir: *M6 junct 19, at rdbt take 3rd exit onto A556, 5m. Turn off at Hartford onto School Lane, left onto The Green-Pub at junct*

Originally a malt house attached to a fire station, this pub retains its old well, stables and pump, plus a fire bell in the beer garden. Enjoy glowing log fires in the winter or relaxed summer evenings spent in the flower-bedecked, enclosed beer garden. Drinks include a good choice of real ales; food-wise there is a hearty 'steak bar' menu and traditional comforts such as home-made lamb hotpot; liver and onions; and fish and chips.

Open 12–11 (25 Dec 12–2) **Bar Meals** L served Mon–Sat 12–2 D served Mon–Sat 6–8 Av main course £4 Punch Taverns John Smiths Cask, Marston Pedigree Cask, Tetleys Cask, Stella & Guinness. **Facilities** Garden Parking **Rooms** 3 bedrooms en suite S£40 D£60

PENKETH — MAP 15 SJ58

The Ferry Tavern 🍷

Station Rd WA5 2UJ ☎ 01925 791117 01925 791116

e-mail: ferrytavern@aol.com

dir: *From Widnes A562 pass Fiddlers Ferry power station & golf driving range. Turn into Tannery Ln. Right at Three Elms nursing home into Station Road*

Set on its own island between the Mersey and the St Helen's canal, this 12th-century ale house has been an inn since 1762, and welcomes walkers and cyclists from the trans-Pennine Way. Beneath the low beams in the stone-flagged bar you'll find a range of unusual guest beers and over 300 different whiskies, including 60 Irish. Lunch only is served and includes home-made dishes such as soup, burgers and paté, plus sandwiches and jacket potatoes.

Open 12–3 5.30–11 (Fri–Sat 12–11.30, Sun 12–10.30) **Bar Meals** L served Mon–Fri 12–2 Av main course £5 Free House Interbrew Boddingtons Bitter, Abbot Ale, Boddingtons Cask & Ruddles County. 🍷 10 **Facilities** Garden Dogs allowed Parking

PLUMLEY — MAP 15 SJ77

The Golden Pheasant Hotel 🍷

Plumley Moor Rd WA16 9RX

☎ 01565 722261 01565 722125

dir: *From M6 junct 19, take A556 signed Chester. 2m turn left at signs for Plumley/Peover. Through Plumley, after 1m pub opposite rail station.*

In the heart of rural Cheshire, the hotel has a large restaurant, bar area, public bar, children's play area and bowling green. The menu offers substantial choice, from bar snacks such as nachos or panninis, to a more elaborate restaurant menu, including pork medallions in apricot and tarragon reduction. Real ales are pulled from the attractive handpumps installed by J.W. Lees, one of the country's few remaining independent family breweries with its own cooperage.

Open 11–11 (Sun 12–10.30) **Bar Meals** L served all week 12–2.30 D served all week 6–9.30 (Sat 12–9.30, Sun 12–8.30) Av main course £6.95 **Restaurant** L served all week 12–2.30 D served all week 6–9.30 (Sat 12–9.30, Sun 12–8.30) Av 3 course à la carte £20 Av 2 course fixed price £12.95 J W Lees J W Lees Bitter, GB Mild & Moonraker. 🍷 10 **Facilities** Children's licence Garden Dogs allowed Parking Play Area

The Smoker 🍷

WA16 0TY ☎ 01565 722338 01565 722093

e-mail: smoker@plumley.fsword.co.uk

dir: *From M6 junct 19 take A556 W. Pub 1.75m on left*

The name of this 400-year-old coaching inn derives from a white racehorse bred by the Prince Regent. The pub's striking wood-panelled interior provides a traditional, welcoming atmosphere, with its log fires, beams and assortment of horse brasses. The menu has an appealing and lengthy array of starters and main courses, including battered black pudding; hock of ham; smoked haddock and eggs; and Mediterranean risotto.

Open 10–3 6–11 (all day Sun) **Bar Meals** L served all week 11.30–2.30 D served all week 6–9.15 (Sun 12–9) Av main course £8.95 **Restaurant** L served all week 11.30–2.30 D served all week 6.30–9.30 (Sun 12–9) Frederic Robinson Robinson's Best & Hatters Mild, Double Hop, Old Stockport, Robinsons Smooth. 🍷 10 **Facilities** Garden Parking Play Area

PRESTBURY — MAP 16 SJ87

Pick of the Pubs

The Legh Arms & Black Boy Restaurant 🍷

SK10 4DG ☎ 01625 829130 01625 827833

dir: *From M6 through Knutsford to Macclesfield, turn to Prestbury at Broken Cross. Pub in village centre.*

A smart country pub with a large suntrap garden, The Legh Arms is located in one of Britain's most prosperous and charming villages. The original 15th-century inn on this site was called The Saracen's Head, to commemorate the Crusades. In 1627, when the current inn was built, the sign maker mistakenly painted a black boy's head and the image is still used today. Bonnie Prince Charlie is believed to have stayed here on his way to Derby during the ill-fated 1745 rebellion. An extensive menu in the oak-beamed

CONTINUED

PRESTBURY continued

restaurant ranges through pot roast pheasant, triple tomato risotto with spinach and asparagus, and grilled fillet steak. Fresh fish, delivered six days a week, is a notable feature, along with herbs from the inn's walled garden. A private dining/conference room is available.

The Legh Arms & Black Boy Restaurant

Open 12–11 **Bar Meals** L served all week 12–2 D served all week 7–10 (Sun 12–10) **Restaurant** L served all week 12–2 D served all week 7–10 (Sun all day) Av 3 course à la carte £30 Frederic Robinson Robinsons Bitter, Hatters Mild, Grolsch, Guinness. 8 **Facilities** Garden Parking

SHOCKLACH MAP 15 SJ44

Bull Inn Country Bistro

Worthenbury Rd SY14 7BL ☎ 01829 250239

e-mail: jaws@fsbdial.co.uk

This welcoming mid-19th-century pub is located in a quiet village 20 minutes from Chester. Exposed beams, many other original features, and often a cosy log fire greet visitors heading for a pint of Mansfield Cask, or a traditional pub meal. Popular are fish, chips and mushy peas, 'big and hearty' pies, curries, braised beef, pork loin with black pudding, grills, poached salmon, and vegetarian pancakes. For the kids there are burgers, pizzas and nuggets.

Open 12–3 6.30–11 (Sun 7–10.30) **Bar Meals** L served Fri–Sun 12–2.30 D served Tue–Sun 6.30–9 (Sun 7–9) Av main course £8.95 **Restaurant** L served Fri–Sun 12–2.30 D served Tue–Sun 6.30–9 (Sun 12–2.30, 7–9) Mansfield Cask, Pedigree, Guinness. **Facilities** Children's licence Garden Parking

SWETTENHAM MAP 15 SJ86

Pick of the Pubs

The Swettenham Arms

Swettenham Ln CW12 2LF

☎ 01477 571284 01477 571284

e-mail: info@swettenhamarms.co.uk

web: www.swettenhamarms.co.uk

dir: *M6 junct 18 to Holmes Chapel, then A535 towards Jodrell Bank. 3m right (Forty Acre Lane) to Swettenham.*

A riot of flowers covers the stone frontage of The Swettenham Arms, idyllically situated behind a 13th-century church. The pub itself dates back almost as far: it was once a nunnery, linked to the church by an underground passage where corpses 'rested' before burial. Expect ghost stories: indeed, in 2005, after seeing a lady apparently floating in the restaurant, a customer had to seek urgent counselling from the vicar. Following starters of home-made duck liver paté, or sautéed queen scallops, the extensive menu progresses to steamed steak and kidney pudding or cod fillet rolled with spinach, before hitting the heights of Chef's Specialities. These include roasted grey mullet filed with prawn duxelle; and beef stroganoff served with pilaff rice. Vegetarians are well catered for, and each of the specialities has a suggested wine and beer. The pub's lavender and sunflower meadow is a delight in summer.

The Swettenham Arms

Open 12–3 6.30–11 (open all day Sun) **Bar Meals** L served all week 12–2.30 D served all week 7–9.30 (Sun 12–9.30) **Restaurant** L served all week 12–2.30 D served all week 7–9.30 (Sun 12–9) Free House Landlord, Hydes, Beartown, Pride of Pendle. 8 **Facilities** Garden Parking

TARPORLEY MAP 15 SJ56

Alvanley Arms Inn ★★★★ INN

Forest Rd, Cotebrook CW6 9DS ☎ 01829 760200

e-mail: info@alvanleyarms.co.uk

dir: *On A49, 1.5m N of Tarporley*

There's a strong shire horse theme throughout this charming 16th-century coaching inn. Photographs, rosettes, harnesses and horseshoes decorate the walls, linking the inn to the landlords' Cotebrook Shire Horse Centre next door. Hand-pulled ales in the oak-beamed bar complement a range of freshly prepared dishes, based on ingredients from local family businesses. A typical lunchtime selection includes steak and ale pie; mushroom stroganoff with rice and crusty bead; and grilled North Sea cod.

Open 12–3 5.30–11 (Sun all day) **Bar Meals** L served all week 12–2 D served all week 6–9 (Sun 12–9) Av main course £9.95 **Restaurant** L served all week 12–2 D served all week 6–9 (Sun 12–9) Av 3 course à la carte £22 Frederic Robinsons Robinsons Best & Guest Beers. 12 **Facilities** Garden Parking **Rooms** 7 bedrooms en suite S£52 D£75

Pick of the Pubs

The Boot Inn

Boothsdale, Willington CW6 0NH ☎ 01829 751375

dir: *Off A54 Kelsall by-pass or off A51(Chester-Nantwich), follow signs to Willington*

A charming row of red brick and sandstone cottages, which was once a small beer house, has been converted into an inviting pub and restaurant offering good, freshly-prepared food. The quarry tiled floors, old beams and open fires enhance the welcome. The food comes from local suppliers wherever possible and includes home produced Cumberland sausage; Barnsley lamb chops; and baked Spanish omelette. For something lighter try salad platters, sandwiches, fresh baguettes and hot paninis.

Open 11-3 6-12 (All day Sat-Sun & BHs) Closed: 25 Dec **Bar Meals** L served all week 11-2.30 D served all week 6-9.30 (Sat-Sun & BHs food all day) **Restaurant** L served all week 11-2.30 D served all week 6-9.30 Weetwood, Timothy Taylor Landlord, Bass. 8 **Facilities** Garden Dogs allowed Parking

Pick of the Pubs

The Fox & Barrel

Forest Rd, Cotebrook CW6 9DZ

☎ 01829 760529 01829 760192

e-mail: info@thefoxandbarrel.com

dir: *On A49 between Tarporley & Sandiway.*

Originally known as the King's Head, the pub's name was changed after a former landlord sheltered a hunted fox in his cellar. This thriving food pub now offers a genuine welcome, interesting seasonal menus and a tip-top pint of Bass. Beyond the snug bar, with its huge log fire, china jugs and daily newspapers, the half-panelled dining area sports a rug-strewn wood floor and rustic farmhouse tables topped with church candles. Interesting menus list bar meals such as roast ham platter; smoked chicken Caesar salad; and chicken fajita. More inventive restaurant meals take in smoked haddock and chorizo risotto with pesto; Thai king prawn curry; and lamb rump with champ and Mediterranean vegetables. Desserts include spiced raisin and ginger pudding with local Snugbury's ice cream. There's a good choice of wines, and a secluded summer patio for alfresco dining.

Open 12-3 5.30-11 Closed: 25 Dec **Bar Meals** L served all week 12-2.30 D served Mon-Sat 6.30-9.30 Av main course £13.50 **Restaurant** L served all week 12-2.30 D served all week 6-9.30 (Sun 12-8) Av 3 course à la carte £25 Pubmaster Scottish Courage John Smith's, Marston's Pedigree, Jennings Cumberland Ale, Timothy Taylor Landlord. 15 **Facilities** Garden Parking

TUSHINGHAM CUM GRINDLEY — MAP 15 SJ54

Pick of the Pubs

Blue Bell Inn

SY13 4QS ☎ 01948 662172 01948 662172

dir: *A41, 4m N of Whitchurch, signed Bell O'the Hill.*

A lovely black-and-white building that oozes character with its abundance of beams, open fires and horse brasses. In what must be a unique tale from the annals of pub-haunting, it was once occupied by a duck whose spirit is reputedly sealed in a bottle buried in the bottom step of the cellar. Believe that or not, the Blue Bell remains a charming and characterful pub. Its oldest part dates to approximately 1550, and the main building was completed in 1667. It has all the features you'd expect of a timber-framed building of this date, including one of the largest working chimneys in Cheshire and a priest hole. Curios that have been discovered from within the wall structure are on show in the pub. The menu is based on traditional English fare, with specials prepared daily. Drink options include well-kept ales plus a selection of wines.

Open 12-3 6-11 (Sun 12-3, 7-11) **Bar Meals** L served Tue-Sun 12-2 D served Tue-Sun 6-9 **Restaurant** L served Tue-Sun 12-2 D served Tue-Sun 7-9 Free House Carlins, Shropshire Gold, Golden Pippin, Thirst Quencher. **Facilities** Garden Dogs allowed Parking

WARMINGHAM — MAP 15 SJ76

The Bear's Paw ★★★★ INN

School Ln CW11 3QN ☎ 01270 526317 & 526342

e-mail: enquiries@thebearspaw.co.uk

dir: *From M6 junct 18 take A54 then A533 towards Sandbach. Follow signs for village*

Delightful country house hotel conveniently situated within easy reach of many Cheshire towns and some of the county's prettiest countryside. Wide-ranging menus offer an extensive selection of starters, including chicken liver paté, smoked haddock fish cake, and bacon and black pudding salad, followed by breast of chicken stuffed with spinach and brie, and red mullet on a crab mash. Beef lasagne, cod supreme and Cumberland sausage are other options.

Open 5-11 (all day Sat-Sun) Closed: 25-26 Dec & 1 Jan **Bar Meals** L served Sat-Sun 12-6 D served all week 6-9 (Fri-Sat 6-9.30) Av main course £10 **Restaurant** L served Sat-Sun 12-6 D served all week 6-9 (Fri-Sat 6-9.30) Av 3 course à la carte £19 Free House Tetley Cask, Carling, Stella, Erdinger & Guest ales. **Facilities** Garden Parking **Rooms** 12 bedrooms en suite S£60 D£70

WRENBURY MAP 15 SJ54

The Dusty Miller

CW5 8HG ☎ 01270 780537

A beautifully converted 16th-century mill building beside the Shropshire Union Canal. A black and white lift bridge, designed by Thomas Telford, completes the picture postcard setting. The menu, which tends to rely on ingredients from the region, offers light bites including filled rolls and a cheese platter, alongside the more substantial baked hake with buttery mash and a white wine and parsley sauce, and home-made Aberdeen Angus burger with pear and apple chutney.

Open 11.30–3 6.30–11 (Fri/Sat 6.30–12) **Bar Meals** L served Tue–Sun 12–2 D served all week 6.30–9.30 (Sun 12–2.30, 7–9) Av main course £10 **Restaurant** L served Tue–Sun 12–2 D served all week 6.30–9.30 Frederic Robinsons Robinsons Best Bitter, Double Hop, Old Tom, Hatters Mild & Hartleys XB. 12 **Facilities** Garden Dogs allowed Parking

WYBUNBURY MAP 15 SJ64

The Swan

Main Rd CW5 7NA ☎ 01270 841280 01270 841200

e-mail: bistrobonsamis@btconnect.com

dir: *M6 junct 16 towards Chester & Nantwich. Turn left at lights in Wybunbury*

The Swan, a pub since 1580, is situated in the village centre next to the church. All the food is freshly prepared on the premises and includes glazed lamb shoulder, Cumberland sausage, basil-crusted cod fillet, crispy half roast duckling, and beef, mushroom and Jennings ale pie. The menu also features hot baps, thick-cut sandwiches and salads. Sit in the garden below the church tower.

Open 12–11 **Bar Meals** L served Tue–Sun 12–2 D served all week 6.30–9.30 (Sun & BHs 12–8) Av main course £10 **Restaurant** L served Tue–Sun 12–2 D served all week 6.30–9.30 (BHs 12–8) Av 3 course à la carte £20 Av 2 course fixed price £6.95 Jennings Jennings Bitter, Cumberland Ale, Abbot Ale & Townhouse Ales. Guest beers. 9 **Facilities** Children's licence Garden Dogs allowed Parking

CORNWALL & ISLES OF SCILLY

BLISLAND MAP 02 SX17

The Blisland Inn

PL30 4JF ☎ 01208 850739

dir: *5m from Bodmin towards Launceston. 2.5m off A30 signed Blisland. On village green*

An award-winning inn in a very picturesque village on the edge of Bodmin Moor. The superb parish church was a favourite of John Betjeman who wrote about it extensively. Most of the traditional pub fare is home cooked, including a variety of puddings. Leek and mushroom bake is a perennial favourite, while lasagne, sausage and mash, and traditional farmhouse ham, egg and chips are also popular.

Open 11.30–11 (Sun 12–10.30) **Bar Meals** L served all week 12–2.15 D served all week 6.30–9.30 (Sun 12–2, 6.30–9) Av main course £6.95 **Restaurant** L served all week 12–2.15 6.30–9.30 Av 3 course à la carte £15 Guest ales. **Facilities** Garden Dogs allowed

BODINNICK MAP 02 SX15

Old Ferry Inn

PL23 1LX ☎ 01726 870237 01726 870116

e-mail: royce972@aol.com

dir: *A38 towards Dobwalls, left onto A390. After 3m left onto B3359 then right to Bodinnick/Polruan for 5m.*

This friendly, family-run free house stands just 50 yards from the scenic River Fowey, where the car ferry still makes regular crossings to Fowey itself. Inside the 400-year-old building, old photographs and nautical bric-a-brac set the scene for sampling Sharp's Bitter and an extensive bar menu. Choices range from snacks to home-cooked dishes like steak and stilton pie; fresh Dover sole with prawn and lemon butter; and creamy garlic mushrooms with pasta and melted cheese.

Open 11–11 (Nov–Feb 12–10.30) Closed: 25 Dec **Bar Meals** L served all week 12–3 D served all week 6–9 (Winter 12–2, 6.30–8.30) Av main course £7.50 **Restaurant** L served Sun 12–2.30 D served all week 7–9 (Winter 7–8.30) Av 3 course à la carte £20 Free House Sharp's Bitter, Stella, Guinness, Becks Vier. **Facilities** Children's licence Garden Dogs allowed Parking **Rooms** 8 bedrooms en suite S£60 D£60 (★★★ INN)

BOLVENTOR — MAP 02 SX17

Jamaica Inn 🍷

PL15 7TS ☎ 01566 86250 📠 01566 86177
e-mail: enquiry@jamaicainn.co.uk
web: www.jamaicainn.co.uk

The setting for Daphne du Maurier's famous novel of the same name, this 18th-century inn stands high on Bodmin moor. Its Smugglers' Museum houses fascinating smuggling artefacts, while the Daphne de Maurier room honours the great writer. The place is big on atmosphere, with a cobbled courtyard, beamed ceilings and roaring fires. Lunch includes Cornish pasties; a daily roast; and jacket potatoes. Typical restaurant dishes are steaks, curry of the day, and home-made vegetable lasagna.

Open 9 –11 **Bar Meals** L served all week 12–2.30 D served all week 2.45–9 **Restaurant** L served all week 2.30–9 D served all week 2.45–9 Free House Doom Bar, Tribute, Budweiser & Jamaica Inn Ale. 🍷 8 **Facilities** Children's licence Garden Parking Play Area **Rooms** 17 bedrooms en suite S£65 D£70 (★★★ B&B)

BOSCASTLE — MAP 02 SX09

The Wellington Hotel ★★ HL 🍷

The Harbour PL35 0AQ ☎ 01840 250202 📠 01840 250621
e-mail: info@boscastle-wellington.com
dir: *In Boscastle follow signs to harbour, into Old Road, hotel ahead*

Set in a glorious wooded valley, this listed 16th-century coaching inn has beamed ceilings and real log fires. With such a cosy and intimate atmosphere, it's easy to believe – as the locals do – that many ghostly guests and staff still linger. Food options range from traditional ploughman's lunches through to hearty main courses such as a home-made cheeseburger with onion marmalade; mussels in white wine sauce; or sausages and mash.

Open 11–11 (Sun 10–10.30) **Bar Meals** L served all week 12–3 D served all week 6–10 (Sun 12–9, Summer 12–10) Av main course £7 **Restaurant** D served Fri–Wed 6.30–9 Av 3 course à la carte £25 Free House St Austell HSD, St Austell Tribute, Skinners Ales-Spriggan, Wooden Hand Brewery & Cornish Blonde. 🍷 8 **Facilities** Garden Dogs allowed Parking **Rooms** 15 bedrooms en suite S£40 D£80

CADGWITH — MAP 02 SW71

Pick of the Pubs

Cadgwith Cove Inn

TR12 7JX ☎ 01326 290513 📠 01326 291018
e-mail: enquiries@cadgwithcoveinn.com
dir: *10m from Helston on main Lizard road*

See Pick of the Pubs on page 80

CALLINGTON — MAP 03 SX36

The Coachmakers Arms 🍷

6 Newport Square PL17 7AS
☎ 01579 382567 📠 01579 384679
dir: *Between Plymouth & Launceston on A388*

Traditional stone-built pub on the A388 between Plymouth and Launceston. Clocks, plates, pictures of local scenes, old cars and antique trade advertisements contribute to the atmosphere, as do the fish tank and aviary. There's plenty of choice on the menu, from chargrilled steaks, steak and kidney pie or hot-pot, to oven-baked plaice, vegetable balti or salads. Regulars range from the local football team to the pensioners dining club. On Wednesday there's a charity quiz night, and Thursday is steak night.

Open 11–11.30 (Sun 12–10.30) **Bar Meals** L served all week 12–2 D served all week 7–9.30 Av main course £4.95 **Restaurant** L served all week 12–2 D served all week 7–9.30 Av 3 course à la carte £15 Enterprise Inns Doom Bar, Worthing Best Bitter, Abbot Ale, Tetley. 🍷 7 **Facilities** Dogs allowed Parking

Cadgwith Cove Inn

This traditional, whitewashed Cornish inn transports you right back the days when Cadgwith Cove was a smuggler's haunt. The atmospheric bars are adorned with relics that record a rich seafaring history.

It's easy to imagine that the ghosts of smugglers still gather within these cosy walls. The inn occupies an idyllic spot on the Lizard peninsular, right on the coastal path and overlooking the cove. Appealing to both locals and tourists alike, it offers a warm welcome and authentic local colour. Ramblers with their well-behaved dogs gather here all year round, relaxing with pints of ale and listening to sea shanties sung by the Cadgwith Singers late into Friday night. On Tuesday nights the inn hosts a thriving folk club when guests are invited to join in or just sit back and enjoy the music. On any night of the week you might find yourself swapping tales with one of the fishermen whose catches feature on the popular menus. As may be expected, these are positively laden with seafood – lobster and crab of course, but also grilled red mullet or bass, moules marinière, the special Cadgwith fish casserole, and traditional fish and chips. Meat eaters and vegetarians are alsowell provided for, with ingredients coming from local butchers and surrounding farms. Meals can be served in the garden in clement weather, and the large terrace with sea views is an ideal spot during the summer gig races, or for one of the regular seafood barbeques prepared by local fishermen.

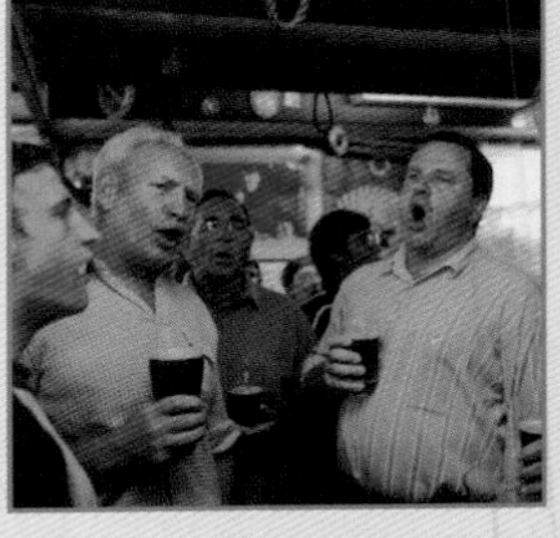

MAP 02 SW71
TR12 7JX
☎ 01326 290513
01326 291018
e-mail:
enquiries@cadgwithcoveinn.com
dir: *10m from Helston on main Lizard road*

Open 12-3 7-11 (Jul-Aug & Sat-Sun open all day)
Bar Meals L served all week 12-2 D served all week 6.30-9 Av main course £8
Restaurant L served all week 12-2 D served all week 6-9 Av 3 course à la carte £15
Punch Taverns
Interbrew Flowers IPA, Sharp's, Skinners, Guest Ales.
Facilities Garden Dogs allowed Parking

CONSTANTINE
MAP 02 SW72

Pick of the Pubs

Trengilly Wartha Inn ★★★ INN

Nancenoy TR11 5RP
☎ 01326 340332 📠 01326 340332
e-mail: reception@trengilly.co.uk
dir: *From Constantine follow signs to Nancenoy*

See Pick of the Pubs on page 82

CRACKINGTON HAVEN
MAP 02 SX19

Coombe Barton Inn

EX23 0JG ☎ 01840 230345 📠 01840 230788
e-mail: info@coombebarton.co.uk
dir: *S from Bude on A39, turn off at Wainhouse Corner, then down lane to beach*

The inn, parts of which are over 200 years old, was built for the 'captain' of the quarry in the days when slate was shipped out from this small port. Expect a good choice of locally caught fish and seafood, home-baked Cornish pasties, toasted sandwiches and home-made chef's specials. The Sunday lunchtime carvery offers roast ribs of local beef, leg of pork and chicken.

Open 11 -11 (Fri-Sat 11-12, Sun 12-11) **Bar Meals** L served all week 11-2.30 D served all week 6.30-9.30 (Sun 12-2.30, 6.30-9 booking required for Sun lunch) **Restaurant** L served all week 11-2.30 D served all week 6-10 Free House St Austell Tribute & Hick's Special Draught, Sharp's Doom Bar Bitter, Sharp's Safe Haven, Skinners Betty Stogs. **Facilities** Dogs allowed Parking

CUBERT
MAP 02 SW75

The Smuggler's Den Inn

Trebellan TR8 5PY ☎ 01637 830209 📠 01637 830580
e-mail: hankers@aol.com
dir: *From Newquay take A3075 to Cubert x-rds, then right, then left signed Trebellan 0.5m*

A thatched, undoubtedly haunted, 16th-century pub in a valley leading down to the coast. Features include a long bar, family room, children's play area, courtyards and huge beer garden. The Smuggler's is well known for its daily specials, as well as pastas, chargrills, liver and bacon casserole, Falmouth Bay moules marinière, toad-in-the-hole, and butternut squash, chickpea and basil gratin. Real ales, including local brew Betty Stogs, are served from barrels behind the bar.

The Smuggler's Den Inn

Open 11-3 6-11 (Winter 12-2) **Bar Meals** L served all week 12-2 D served all week 6-9.30 Av main course £10 **Restaurant** L served all week 12-2 D served all week 6-9.30 Free House Skinner's Smugglers Ale, Betty Stogs Bitter, Sharp's Doom Bar, Trebellan Tipple. 12 **Facilities** Garden Dogs allowed Parking Play Area

DULOE
MAP 02 SX25

Ye Olde Plough House Inn

PL14 4PN ☎ 01503 262050 📠 01503 264089
e-mail: alison@ploughhouse.freeserve.co.uk
dir: *A38 to Dobwalls, take turn signed Looe*

A welcoming 18th-century free house set in the heart of the Cornish countryside yet only three miles from the coastal town of Looe. The building features slate floors, wood-burning stoves, settles and old pews, with a fenced, grassy garden outside. Lunchtime brings local pasties and home-made spaghetti bolognese, while the restaurant menu might offer goats' cheese cannelloni, beer battered cod or steak cooked on hot stones.

Open 12-2.30 6.30-11 (Sun 7-10.30) Closed: 25-26 Dec **Bar Meals** L served all week 12-2 D served all week 6.30-9.30 Av main course £6.95 **Restaurant** L served all week 12-2 D served all week 6.30-9.30 Av 3 course à la carte £20 Free House Sharp's Doom Bar, Butcombe Bitter, Worthington. 9 **Facilities** Garden Dogs allowed Parking

DUNMERE
MAP 02 SX06

The Borough Arms

PL31 2RD ☎ 01208 73118
e-mail: borougharms@aol.com
dir: *From A30 take A389 to Wadebridge, 1m from Bodmin*

Built in the 1850s for train crews taking china clay from the moors down to the port at Padstow, but it seems much older. Walkers, cyclists and horseriders drop in for refreshment as they follow the disused railway line, now the 17-mile Camel Trail. The menus offer steak and ale pie, Spanish chicken, fish and chips, tender meats from the carvery, and snacks. Specials, mostly home made, are on the chalkboards.

Open 11-11 (Sun 12-10.30) **Bar Meals** L served all week 12-9 D served all week 12-9 Av main course £6.95 **Restaurant** L served all week 12-9 D served all week 12-9 Spirit Group Sharp's Bitter, Skinner's, John Smith's Smooth. **Facilities** Garden Dogs allowed Parking Play Area

Trengilly Wartha Inn

This unusually named inn is situated in the hamlet of Nancenoy, in an area designated as being of outstanding natural beauty, about a mile from the village of Constantine. The name is actually Cornish and means a settlement above the trees, in this case the wooded valley of Polpenwith Creek, an offshoot of the lovely Helford River.

The six acres of gardens and meadows that surround the inn include a vine-shaded pergola just perfect for summer dining. There's a small restaurant, which boasts an AA Rosette for its food, on one side of the inn, and plenty more space for eating in the informal bar area, where a conservatory extension houses the family room. Talented chefs prepare everything from scratch using the best locally produced meats and game, and fish and shellfish from local waters. The bar menu offers pub favourites like lasagne al forno, steak and chips, and wholetail scampi, as well as less traditional choices such as courgette and rosemary pancakes stuffed with Cornish feta, cashew nuts, spinach and smoked cherry tomatoes; chicken breast with chilli and cranberry butter with creamed savoy cabbage and crispy pancetta; and warm fillet of lightly smoked, locally caught pollock with herb butter. The fixed price menu in the restaurant always has a good seafood selection, but watch out, because in summer the day's boatload of fresh fish can sell out fast. Fresh home-made steak and kidney puddings are sold at a discount on Wednesday nights. Since it's a free house, there's a good selection of real ales, over 40 malt whiskies and 150 wines, with 15 available by the glass. Six en suite cottage bedrooms are located in the main building, with two more in the Garden Annexe overlooking the lake.

★★★ INN

MAP 02 SW72
Nancenoy TR11 5RP
☎ 01326 340332
01326 340332
e-mail: reception@trengilly.co.uk
dir: *From Constantine follow signs to Nancenoy*

Open 11–3 6.30–11 (Summer 5.30–11)
Bar Meals L served all week 12–2.15 D served all week 6.30–9.30 Av main course £10
Restaurant D served all week 7.30–9.30 (No food 25 & 31 Dec) Av 3 course fixed price £29
Free House
Sharps Cornish Coaster, Skinners, Lizard Ales, Greene King. 15
Facilities Garden Dogs allowed Parking Play Area
Rooms 8 bedrooms en suite S£50 D£80

FEOCK MAP 02 SW83

The Punch Bowl & Ladle

Penelewey TR3 6QY ☎ 01872 862237 📠 01872 870401

dir: *Off Truro to Falmouth road, after Shell garage at 'Playing Place' rdbt follow signs for King Harry Ferry to right. 0.5m, pub on right.*

This cob-built former customhouse is full of atmosphere, and even houses a resident ghost. There are delightful rural views from the inn's patio, and in warmer weather you can enjoy a drink in the walled garden. The owners offer daily fish and seafood specials, while meat dishes might include beef lasagne or pan-fried lambs' liver. Look out for the fish pie, a medley of freshly caught fish covered in creamed potato and melted cheese.

Open 11.30–11 (Fri–Sat 11.30–12 Sun 12–10.30, Sun Summer 12–11) **Bar Meals** L served all week 12–2.30 D served all week 6–9.15 Av main course £8.95 **Restaurant** L served all week 12–2.30 D served all week 6–9.15 Av 3 course à la carte £25 IPA Tribute, HSD & Cornish Cream. 8 **Facilities** Garden Dogs allowed Parking

FOWEY MAP 02 SX15

The Ship Inn

Trafalgar Square PL23 1AZ

☎ 01726 832230 📠 01726 834931

e-mail: a1dwd@msn.com

dir: *From A30 take B3269 & A390*

One of Fowey's oldest buildings, The Ship was built in 1570 by John Rashleigh, who sailed to the Americas with the as yet unknighted Walter Raleigh. Given Fowey's riverside position, assume a good choice of fish, including Thai fishcakes; prawn risotto; and home-made crab and mussel soup. Other options include Cornish sausages, or beef and Guinness pie. St Austell ales, real fires and a long tradition of genial hospitality add the final touches.

Open 10–12 10–1am (Winter times vary, please telephone) **Bar Meals** L served all week 12–2.30 D served all week 6–9 **Restaurant** L served all week 12–2.30 D served all week 6–9 Av 3 course à la carte £20 St Austell Brewery St Austell Tinners Ale, Tribute & HSD. 16 **Facilities** Children's licence Dogs allowed

GOLDSITHNEY MAP 02 SW53

The Trevelyan Arms

Fore St TR20 9JU ☎ 01736 710453

e-mail: mikehitchens@hotmail.com

dir: *5m from Penzance. A394 signed to Goldsithney*

The former manor house for Lord Trevelyan, this 17th-century property stands at the centre of the picturesque village just a mile from the sea. It has also been a coaching inn and a bank/post office in its time, but these days is very much the traditional family-run Cornish pub. Food is fresh and locally sourced, offering good value for money. Typical dishes are rib-eye steaks, chilli, fisherman's pie, beef burger, curry or Cumberland ring sausage.

The Trevelyan Arms

Open 12 –12 **Bar Meals** L served all week 12–2 D served all week 6–9 (Sun 12–2.30) Av main course £7.50 **Restaurant** L served all week 12–2 D served all week 6–9 Punch Taverns Morland Speckled Hen, Flowers IPA, Guinness, & St Austell Tribute. **Facilities** Garden Dogs allowed

GUNNISLAKE MAP 03 SX47

The Rising Sun Inn

Calstock Rd PL18 9BX ☎ 01822 832201

dir: *From Tavistock take A390 to Gunnislake, through village. Left at lights, pub 0.25m on right*

A traditional two-roomed picture postcard pub set in award winning terraced gardens overlooking the beautiful Tamar Valley. Great walks start and finish at the Rising Sun, which is understandably popular with hikers and cyclists, locals and visitors. This pub is currently not serving food.

Open 12–2.30 5–11 Free House Spitfire, Otter, Sharp's Cornish Coaster, Skinner's Betty Stogs Bitter. **Facilities** Garden Dogs allowed Parking **Notes**

GUNWALLOE MAP 02 SW62

Pick of the Pubs

The Halzephron Inn

TR12 7QB ☎ 01326 240406 📠 01326 241442

e-mail: halzephroninn@gunwalloe1.fsnet.co.uk

dir: *3m S of Helston on A3083, right to Gunwalloe, through village. Inn on left.*

Halzephron is derived from Als Yfferin, old Cornish for Cliffs of Hell, the name given to this hazardous stretch of coastline.

CONTINUED

GUNWALLOE continued

Once a haunt of smugglers, the pub stands just 300 yards from the famous South Cornwall footpath and is the only pub on the stretch between Mullion and Porthleven. It was originally called The Ship, and changed its name in the late 1950s when, after 50 'dry' years, it regained its licence. Today it offers a warm welcome, a wide selection of ales and whiskies, and meals prepared from fresh local produce. Lunch brings a choice of platters accompanied by home-made rolls, plus heartier dishes such as tagliatelli bolognaise. The evening menu shifts comfortably from the classic (seared venison haunch steak on Puy lentils) to the modern: perhaps steamed fillet of sea bass with tiger prawns, rice noodles, wilted vegetables and a lemon grass and lime velouté.

Open 11-2.30 6.30-11 (Summer 6-11) Closed: 25 Dec **Bar Meals** L served all week 12-2 D served all week 7-9 (Summer 6.30-9.30) Av main course £12 **Restaurant** L served all week 12-2 D served all week 7-9 (Summer 6.30-9.30) Av 3 course à la carte £24 Free House Sharp's, Wills Resolve, Doom Bar & Special, St Austell Tribute. 6 **Facilities** Garden Parking

GWEEK — MAP 02 SW72

The Gweek Inn

TR12 6TU ☎ 01326 221502 01326 221502

e-mail: info@gweekinn.co.uk

dir: *2m E of Helston near Seal Sanctuary*

The lovely location of this traditional family-run village pub at the mouth of the pretty Helford River makes booking a table a wise precaution. It is known for value-for-money food, typically steak, kidney and ale pie; tagliatelle con pollo; filled jacket potatoes; and a range of salads. The chalkboard lists locally caught seafood.

Open 12-2.30 6.30-11 **Bar Meals** L served all week 12-2 D served all week 6.30-9 **Restaurant** L served Sun 12-2 D served 6.30-9 Av 3 course à la carte £14 Punch Taverns Old Speckled Hen, Sharps Doom Bar, Skinners Betty Stogs, 3 guest beers. **Facilities** Garden Dogs allowed Parking Play Area

HAYLE — MAP 02 SW53

The Watermill

Old Coach Rd, Lelant Downs TR27 6LQ ☎ 01736 757912

e-mail: watermill@btconnect.com

dir: *Exit A30 at junct for St Ives/A3074, turn left at 2nd mini rdbt*

Built in the 1700s to mill grain for the local estate, the watermill was converted into a pub/restaurant in the 1970s. Old mill machinery is still in place and the iron waterwheel still turns, gravity fed by the mill stream. It is a family friendly establishment, with extensive gardens and fantastic views up the valley towards Trencrom Hill. Bar meals are served, and there is a separate restaurant where steaks and fish (sea bass, sardines and mackerel perhaps) are specialities.

Open 12-11 **Bar Meals** L served all week 12-2 D served all week 6-9 **Restaurant** D served all week 6-9 Free House Sharp's Doom Bar, Ring 'o' Bells Dreckly, Skinners Betty Stogs, Carling & Stella Artois. **Facilities** Garden Play Area

HELFORD — MAP 02 SW72

Pick of the Pubs

Shipwright Arms

TR12 6JX ☎ 01326 231235

dir: *A390 through Truro, A394 to Helston, before Goonhilly Down left for Helford/Manaccan*

Superbly situated on the banks of the Helford River in an idyllic village, this small thatched pub is especially popular in summer when customers relax on the three delightful terraces, complete with palm trees and glorious flowers, which lead down to the water's edge. Summer buffet offers crab and lobster subject to availability, alongside various ploughman's lunches, salads, home-made pies, marinated lamb fillet, steaks and a wide range of international dishes. Barbecues in summer on the terrace.

Open 11-2.30 6-11 Rest: Winter closed Sun & Mon nights **Bar Meals** L served all week 12-2 D served all week 7-9 Av main course £8.75 **Restaurant** L served Sun 12-2 D served Tue-Sat 7-9 Free House Castle Eden, Greene King IPA, Sharps Doom Bar. **Facilities** Garden Dogs allowed Parking

Please see walk on opposite page

Shipwright Arms

Walk information

Distance: 5 miles (8km)
Map: OS Explorer 103 The Lizard
Start/finish: large car park at Helford; grid ref SW 759261
Ascent/gradient: 2
Paths: good woodland paths and tracks and field paths; short section of quiet lane; 10 stiles
Landscape: wooded creekside and fields
Note: only authorised cars are allowed beyond the car park into Helford village

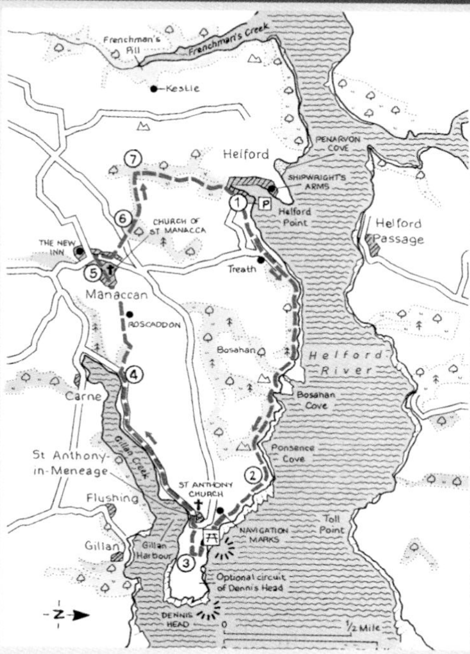

Walk directions

A As you leave the car park, turn left along a path, signed 'Coast Path'. Go through a metal gate and follow a sunken track. Descend steps, then turn right along a lane. At a steep right-hand bend, bear off ahead along a track. Follow this permissive path trough trees, keeping left at any junctions.

B Leave the wooded area via a metal gate, then turn left along a field edge to a stone stile. Follow the bottom edge of the next two fields. Cross a fence at a field gap beside a white pole and a red post and triangle (these are navigation marks). Follow the field edge ahead. Go through a kissing gate, then follow the field edge (there's a seat and viewpoint on the left), to where it ends at the beginning of a wide track (to make the short circuit of Dennis Head, follow the tack ahead to a stile on the left).

C Turn sharply right at the start of the wide track and follow the left-hand field edge and then a path across the open field. Join a track behind a house, then go through a kissing gate and descend to St Anthony's Church. Follow the road alongside Gillan Creek.

D Just past where the road curves round a bay, go up right between granite gate posts by a public footpath sign. Follow a broad track through trees to houses at Roscadden. Keep ahead along a track that leads to Manaccan at a T-junction opposite Manaccan Church.

E Go through the churchyard and on through the gate opposite to a road (the village shop is to the left). Keep ahead to a junction, then go up right, past the school. Keep uphill, then turn left along Minster Meadow, go over a stile, and through two fields to reach a road.

F Go diagonally left to the stile opposite, cross a field, then go left following signposts to reach woods. Follow the path ahead. At a junction keep ahead, go over a stile and reach a second junction. (The extended walk starts here.)

G Bear down right and follow a broad track through trees to reach some buildings at Helford. Keep ahead on reaching a surfaced road and follow the road uphill to the car park.

While there

At the green heart of the Helford River lies the impossibly romantic Frenchman's Creek. More properly known as Frenchman's Pill, this thin finger of tidal water has become famous through its association with the romantic novel Frenchman's Creek, by Daphne du Maurier; but the writer Arthur Quiller Couch had written a short story with the same title long before du Maurier's novel appeared and the source of the name is not certain. It was recorded on 19th-century maps and may yet prove to be a corruption of an old usage, or simply a longstanding reference to French ships that must, at one time, have visited the Helford quite regularly.

The Crown Inn

The Crown Inn is one of Cornwall's oldest pubs, dating back to the 12th century. It was built to house the stonemasons building the next-door church of St Brevita, and stands on the ancient Saint's Way.

This meandering path takes the walker past chapels, standing stones and holy wells and through varied Cornish scenery, for the 30 miles from Padstow to Fowey. Needless to say, with such a history everything about this charming pub oozes tradition. It has flagstone floors, low beams, open fireplaces, and thick stone walls, as well as a large and unusual bread oven. The pub is only a few miles away from Fowey harbour, and local produce features strongly on the menu, including Cornish crab, Cornish pasties and local pork and beef. The many fish dishes may be based on calamari, sea bass, plaice, whitebait, sole, scallops and crab (depending on availability). A typical meal could start with locally smoked salmon served with organic brown bread, or Cornish smoked mackerel paté, followed by tomato, pesto and rocket pasta, or chargrilled Cornish steak with all the traditional trimmings; a scoop of blackcurrant Callestick ice cream might finish a meal off. The beers come from Sharps in Rock or one of the many Cornish microbreweries, and one of them, Skinners' Betty Stogs ale, can also be found in the steak and ale pie. A reasonably priced wine list offers seven wines by the glass. The pretty front garden is a lovely spot to enjoy a summer evening, perhaps with a glass of Pimms and a plate of Fowey crab.

★★★ INN

MAP 02 SX05

PL30 5BT

☎ 01208 872707

Fax 01208 871208

e-mail: thecrown@wagtailinns.com

dir: *Signed off A390 via brown sign about 1.5m W of Lostwithiel*

Open 12–11

Bar Meals L served all week 12–2.30 D served all week 6–9.30 Av main course £8

Restaurant L served all week 12–2.30 D served all week 6.30–9 (Summer 12–3, 5.30–9.15)

Free House

Sharp's Doom Bar, Skinners Betty Stogs, Skinners Cornish Knocker, Cornish Coaster glory.

7

Facilities Garden Dogs allowed Parking

Rooms 4 bedrooms en suite S£39.95 D£39.95

KINGSAND — MAP 03 SX45

The Halfway House Inn

Fore St PL10 1NA ☎ 01752 822279 01752 823146
e-mail: info@halfwayinn.biz
dir: *From Torpoint Ferry or Tamar Bridge follow signs to Mount Edgcumbe*

Set among the narrow lanes and colour-washed houses of a quaint fishing village, this family-run inn has been licensed since 1850, and has a pleasant stone-walled bar with low-beamed ceilings and a large central fireplace. Locally caught seafood is a feature of the small restaurant, including crab cocktail; sautéed scallops with white wine, cream and parsley sauce; whole sea bass with toasted almonds; and baked monkfish with Mediterranean vegetables. For the lunchtime visitor there's a good selection of bar snacks.

Open 12-3 7-11 (All day in summer) **Bar Meals** L served all week 12-2 D served all week 7-9 (Winter 12-2, 7-9) Av main course £10.50 **Restaurant** L served all week 12-2 D served all week 7-9 (Sun 12-2, 7-9) Av 3 course à la carte £17 Free House Sharp's Doom Bar Bitter, Sharp's Own, Marstons Pedigree, Guinness. 10 **Facilities** Dogs allowed

LAMORNA — MAP 02 SW42

Lamorna Wink

TR19 6XH ☎ 01736 731566
dir: *4m on B3315 towards Land's End 0.5m turning on left*

This oddly-named pub was one of the original Kiddleywinks, a product of the 1830 Beer Act that enabled any householder to buy a liquor licence. Popular with walkers and not far from the Merry Maidens standing stones, the Wink provides a selection of local beers and a simple menu that includes sandwiches, jacket potatoes and fresh local crab. The management have been at the Wink for over thirty years, and prides itself on providing diners with as much local produce as possible.

Open 11-11 (Winter 11-4, 6-11) **Bar Meals** L served all week 11-3 D served all week 6-9 Free House Sharp's Doom Bar, Skinners, Cornish Ale, Heligan Honey & Cornish Storm Lager. **Facilities** Garden Dogs allowed Parking **Notes**

LANLIVERY — MAP 02 SX05

Pick of the Pubs

The Crown Inn ★★★ INN

PL30 5BT ☎ 01208 872707 01208 871208
e-mail: thecrown@wagtailinns.com
dir: *Signed off A390 via brown sign about 1.5m W of Lostwithiel*

See Pick of the Pubs on opposite page

LERRYN — MAP 02 SX15

The Ship Inn Lerryn

PL22 0PT ☎ 01208 872374 01208 872614
e-mail: shiplerryn@aol.com
dir: *3m S of A390 at Lostwithiel*

The Ship dates from the 16th century and is the sole pub in the idyllic riverside village of Lerryn. The River Lerryn joins the Fowey River a mile or so further down stream, and the wooded banks inspired Kenneth Graham to write *The Wind in the Willows*. It's still a great area for walkers. Typical dishes include local plaice cooked with cheddar and cider; vegetarian tagliatelle; venison, pheasant and rabbit pie; and for dessert: Cornish nog.

Open 11-11 (Sun 12-3, 6-10.30) **Bar Meals** L served all week 12-3 D served all week 6.30-9.30 Av main course £10 **Restaurant** L served all week 12-3 D served all week 6.30-9.30 Av 3 course à la carte £16 Free House Interbrew Bass, Sharp's, Skinner's. 9 **Facilities** Garden Dogs allowed Parking Play Area

LOSTWITHIEL — MAP 02 SX15

The Royal Oak

Duke St PL22 0AG ☎ 01208 872552 01208 872922
e-mail: mail@royaloakrestaurant.co.uk
dir: *A30 from Exeter to Bodmin then onto Lostwithiel. From Plymouth take A38 towards Bodmin left onto A390 to Lostwithiel*

There is believed to be a secret tunnel connecting this 12th-century inn to Restormel Castle a short way up the River Fowey. The tunnel was some kind of escape route, perhaps for smugglers. Though there is a strong emphasis on the restaurant side of the business, The Royal Oak also has a stone-flagged public bar, cosy and welcoming with a log fire, and separate lounge bar, both serving real ales and ten malt whiskies. Quality Cornish produce is used wherever possible in a menu

CONTINUED

England

LOSTWITHIEL continued

of largely traditional fare, with dishes such as deep-fried haddock with hand-cut chips, pea purée and tartare sauce, and slow-cooked belly pork with black pudding and Bramley apple sauce. Vegetarian options are also available, like baked aubergine herb salad with wild Cornish Yarg and basil dressing.

Open 11–12 (Fri–Sat 11–1am, Sun 12–11.30) **Bar Meals** L served all week 12–2 D served all week 6.30–9 **Restaurant** L served all week 12–2 D served all week 6.30–9 Punch Taverns Interbrew Bass, Fuller's London Pride, Sharp's Own, Doom Bar. 8 **Facilities** Garden Dogs allowed Parking

LUDGVAN MAP 02 SW53

White Hart

Churchtown TR20 8EY ☎ 01736 740574

dir: *From A30 take B3309 at Crowlas*

Built somewhere between 1280 and 1320, the White Hart retains the peaceful atmosphere of a bygone era and offers splendid views across St Michael's Mount and Bay. Fresh fish is a feature from Thursday to Saturday, and other popular dishes are toad-in-the-hole, steak and kidney pie and home-made lasagne (including a vegetarian version). The bar offers a good choice of malts and Irish whiskies.

Open 11–2.30 6–11 **Bar Meals** L served Tue–Sun 12–2 (Mon–Sun Etr–Oct) D served Tue–Sun 7–9 (Mon–Sun Etr–Oct) **Restaurant** L served Tue–Sun 12–2 (Mon–Sun Etr–Oct) D served Tue–Sun (Mon–Sun Etr–Oct) 7–9 Punch Taverns Sharps Doom Bar, Interbrew Flowers & Bass, Abbots. **Facilities** Garden Dogs allowed Parking **Notes**

MALPAS MAP 02 SW84

The Heron Inn

Trenhaile Ter TR1 1SL ☎ 01872 272773 01872 272773

Set in an Area of Outstanding Natural Beauty, this Cornish inn overlooks the River Fal where you might spot herons from the riverside patio. Choose from a range of seafood dishes and specials to enjoy as you birdwatch: fresh Cornish crab, cod mornay, smoked haddock and more. Real ales to wash it down include St Austell's Duchy and I.P.A.

Open 11–3 6–11 **Bar Meals** L served all week 12–2 D served all week 6–9 (Sun 7–9) Av main course £7.50 **Restaurant** L served all week 12–2 D served all week 7–9 St Austell Brewery HSD, Tribute, IPA, Duchy & Carlsberg. 8 **Facilities** Children's licence Garden Dogs allowed Parking

MANACCAN MAP 02 SW72

The New Inn

TR12 6HA ☎ 01326 231323

e-mail: penny@stmartin.wanadoo.co.uk

dir: *7m from Helston*

Thatched village pub, deep in Daphne du Maurier country, dating back to Cromwellian times, although obviously Cromwell forbade his men to drink here. Attractions include the homely bars and a large, natural garden full of flowers. At lunchtime you might try a locally made pasty or moules marinière, and in the evening perhaps sea bass and chive fishcakes with tomato coulis and sautéed vegetables, or slow-roasted lamb shank with red wine and redcurrant gravy.

The New Inn

Open 12–3 6–11 (Sat–Sun all day in summer) **Bar Meals** L served all week 12–2.30 D served all week 6–9.30 (Sun 12–2, 7–9) **Restaurant** L served all week D served all week Punch Taverns Flowers IPA, Sharp's Doom Bar. 10 **Facilities** Garden Dogs allowed Parking Play Area

MARAZION MAP 02 SW53

Pick of the Pubs

Godolphin Arms ★★ SHL

TR17 0EN ☎ 01736 710202 01736 710171

e-mail: enquiries@godolphinarms.co.uk

dir: *From A30 just outside Penzance follow Marazion signs. Pub 1st large building on left in Marazion*

Locations don't come much more spectacular than this: the Godolphin Arms stands atop a sea wall directly opposite St Michael's Mount, and has superb views across the bay. It's so close that the sea splashes at the windows in the winter, and you can watch the movement of seals, dolphins, ferries, and fishing boats returning to Newlyn with their daily catch. From the traditional bar and beer terrace to the more homely restaurant and most of the stylishly-decorated bedrooms, the Mount is clearly visible. Seafood figures prominently in the restaurant -the specials blackboard lists daily choices such as lemon sole pan fried in butter and capers; moules; scallops; or seafood tagliatelle. Aside from the view, the highlight of any stay is breakfast, which includes everything from a full English breakfast to kippers on toast.

Open 10.30–11 (Sun 12–10.30) **Bar Meals** L served all week 12–2.30 D served all week 6.30–9 (Summer 12–3, 6–9.30) **Restaurant** L served all week 12–2.30 D served all week 6.30–9 (Summer 12–3, 6–9.30) Av 3 course à la carte £25 Free House Sharp's Doom Bar, Sharp's Special, St Austell Tribute, Tetley's Smooth. 9 **Facilities** Children's licence Garden Dogs allowed Parking **Rooms** 10 bedrooms en suite S£64 D£80

MEVAGISSEY MAP 02 SX04

The Rising Sun Inn

Portmellon Cove PL26 6PL ☎ 01726 843235

e-mail: cliffnsheila@tiscali.co.uk

Built partly from shipwreck timber, this listed building is superbly situated in a beautiful cove on the Southwest Coastal Path. The inn has a cosy beamed bar, snug and cellar bar serving real ale, an impressive list of speciality bottled beers, malt whiskies and wines by the glass. The kitchen offers a host of local seafood dishes – teriyaki scallops, and crispy skinned sea bass among them – plus alternatives like Cornish duck breast or stuffed aubergine.

Open 11-3 6-12 (BHs, Apr-Oct 11-12) Closed: 1 Nov–28 Feb **Bar Meals** L served all week 12.30-3 (Sun 12.30-4) Av main course £6 **Restaurant** L served all week 12.30-3 D served all week 6-9 (Sun 12.30-4) Av 3 course à la carte £25 Free House Adnams Bitter, Fuller's London Pride, Skinners, Greene King Abbot Ale & Spitfire. 12 **Facilities** Dogs allowed Parking

The Ship Inn ★★★ INN

Fore St PL26 6UQ ☎ 01726 843324 01726 844368

e-mail: reservations@smallandfriendly.co.uk

dir: *7m S of St Austell*

The inn stands just a few yards from Mevagissey's picturesque fishing harbour, so the choice of fish and seafood dishes comes as no surprise: moules marinière, beer-battered cod, and oven-baked fillet of haddock topped with prawns and Cornish Tiskey cheese and served with a lemon and dill sauce. Other options take in baguettes, burgers, jacket potatoes, steaks, and trio of Cornish sausages served with creamy mash and rich red onion gravy.

Open 11–12 **Bar Meals** L served all week 12–3 D served all week 6–9 (Sun 12–3, 5–9) Av main course £7.95 St Austell Brewery St Austell Ales. 8 **Facilities** Dogs allowed **Rooms** 5 bedrooms en suite S£35 D£50

MITCHELL MAP 02 SW85

Pick of the Pubs

The Plume of Feathers

TR8 5AX ☎ 01872 510387 01637 839401

e-mail: enquiries@theplume.info

Since its establishment in the 16th century, the Plume of Feathers has accommodated various historical figures – John Wesley preached Methodism from the pillared entrance, and Sir Walter Raleigh used to live locally. The present owners took over the inn some years ago and have turned it into a successful destination pub restaurant; the imaginative kitchen has an excellent reputation for its food, based on a fusion of modern European and classical British dishes, with an emphasis on fresh fish and the best Cornish ingredients. There is always a daytime specials board, which changes at 6pm to include an extensive choice of 'on the night' creations. Dinner could start with chicken liver parfait with spiced pear chutney, or salmon and cod fishcake. Mains choices include grilled Angus rib-eye steak with tomato and onion salad; and penne pasta in a wild mushroom sauce. Specials include roasted whole sea bass with crispy fennel and basil salad, and chargrilled Moroccan rack of lamb with basmati rice.

Open 9–11 **Bar Meals** L served all week 12–5 D served all week 6–10 **Restaurant** L served all week 12–5 D served all week 6–10 Free House Doom Bar, John Smiths Smooth & Stella. **Facilities** Garden Parking Play Area

MITHIAN MAP 02 SW75

Miners Arms

TR5 0QF ☎ 01872 552375 01872 552375

dir: *From A30 take B3277 to St Agnes. Take 1st right to Mithian*

A 16th-century character pub with slate floors, wall paintings, a cobbled courtyard, exposed beams and ornate plasterwork ceilings that were made for a visit by Edward VII in 1896. Claiming to be the second oldest pub in Cornwall, this was previously used as a courtroom and a pay house for local miners.

Open 12–11 Closed: Mon lunch Oct–Feb **Bar Meals** L served all week 12–2.30 D served all week 6–9.30 **Restaurant** 12–2.30 6–9.30 Pubmaster Sharp's Doom Bar, Guinness, Old Speckled Hen. **Facilities** Garden Dogs allowed Parking

MORWENSTOW MAP 02 SS21

Pick of the Pubs

The Bush Inn

EX23 9SR ☎ 01288 331242 01288 331630

e-mail: info@bushinn-morwenstow.co.uk

dir: *10m from Bude. Exit 3m N of Kilkhampton, 2nd right into village of Shop. 1.5m to hamlet of Crosstown. Inn on left on far side of village green.*

The Bush is reputedly one of Britain's oldest pubs, originally built as a chapel in 950 for pilgrims from Wales en route to Spain. Set in an isolated cliff-top hamlet close to bracing coastal path walks, it became a pub some 700 years later. The unspoilt interior, with stone-flagged floors and old stone fireplaces, has a Celtic piscina carved from serpentine set into a wall behind the bar where real Cornish ales are served. Food is served from 11am until 9.30pm: robust and warming winter dishes of game from local shoots or meat from neighbouring farms; and summertime plates of seafood from the local waters. Children are not forgotten: sturdy wooden equipment in the garden keeps them amused, while food from the same fresh ingredients is prepared, such as mini pizzas, pasta sauces and freshly crumbed goujons of plaice. A traditional roast is served on Sundays.

Open 11 –12 **Bar Meals** L served all week 12–6 D served all week 6–9 Av main course £11.50 **Restaurant** L served all week 12–3 D served all week 6–9 (Sun 12–4.30) Free House St Austell HSD, Sharp's Doom Bar & Skinners Betty Stogs. **Facilities** Children's licence Garden Dogs allowed Parking Play Area

MOUSEHOLE — MAP 02 SW42

Ship Inn ★★★★ INN

TR19 6QX ☎ 01736 731234 01736 732259

e-mail: reservations@smallandfriendly.co.uk

Beautifully located on the harbour, this old-world inn lies at the hub of the community, attracting many of the village's more colourful characters and seadogs. Seafood landed at nearby Newlyn figures prominently, with dishes such as cod in crispy beer batter, home-made fish pie, whole Dover sole, fresh Newlyn crab and fillets of sea bass stuffed with crab and wine cream sauce. Other options feature game pie, locally-made burgers, casseroles and doorstep sandwiches.

Open 11–11 (Sun 12–10.30) **Bar Meals** L served all week 12–2.30 D served all week 6–9 St Austell Brewery St Austell's HSD & Tinners Ale, Tribute, IPA. **Facilities** Dogs allowed **Rooms** 8 bedrooms en suite S£40 D£65

MYLOR BRIDGE — MAP 02 SW83

Pick of the Pubs

The Pandora Inn

Restronguet Creek TR11 5ST

☎ 01326 372678 01326 378958

dir: *From Truro/Falmouth follow A39, left at Carclew, follow signs to pub*

Rather romantically, you can reach this thatched, white-painted inn by foot, bicycle and boat. It has a breathtaking location, set right on the banks of the Restongruet Creek, with panoramic views across the water. There's seating right outside, and also at the end of the pontoon, where up to twenty boats can moor at high tide. The inn itself dates back in part to the 13th century, and its flagstone floors, low-beamed ceilings and thatched roof suggest little can have changed since. The name stems from the good ship Pandora, sent to Tahiti to capture the Bounty mutineers. Sadly, it was wrecked and the captain court-martialled. Forced into early retirement, he bought the inn. Call in for a casual lunch: perhaps smoked mackerel fillets with creamed horseradish. In the evening make a meal of grilled sea bass with spinach risotto; or home-made Cornish crab cakes in saffron dressing.

Open 10–12 (Winter 10.30–11) **Bar Meals** L served all week 12–3 D served all week 6.30–9 (Fri–Sat 6.30–9.30) Av main course £12 **Restaurant** L served all week 12–3 D served all week 7–9 (Fri–Sat 7–9.30) Av 3 course à la carte £23 Av 3 course fixed price £24 St Austell Brewery St Austell Tinners Ale, HSD, Bass, Tribute. 12 **Facilities** Garden Dogs allowed Parking

PENZANCE — MAP 02 SW43

Dolphin Tavern

Quay St TR18 4BD ☎ 01736 364106 01736 364194

A 600-year-old harbourside pub overlooking Mounts Bay and St Michael's Mount. In this building, apparently, Sir Walter Raleigh first smoked tobacco on English soil and, the following century, Judge Jeffreys held court. Haunted by not one but several ghosts. A good choice of seafish is among the options on the menu.

Open 10–12 **Bar Meals** L served all week 11–9.30 D served all week 11–9.30 Av main course £6.95 St Austell Brewery St Austell HSD, Tinners, Tribute, Cornish Cream. **Facilities** Garden Dogs allowed

The Turks Head Inn

Chapel St TR18 4AF ☎ 01736 363093 01736 360215

e-mail: turkshead@gibbards9476.fsworld.co.uk

Dating from around 1233, making it Penzance's oldest pub, it was the first in the country to be given the Turks Head name. Sadly, a Spanish raiding party destroyed much of the original building in the 16th century, but an old smugglers' tunnel leading directly to the harbour, and priest holes, still exist. Typically available are fresh seafood choices like mussels, sea bass, John Dory, lemon sole, and tandoori monkfish, along with others such as pan-fried venison, chicken stir-fry, pork tenderloin, steaks, mixed grill and salads. A sunny flower-filled garden lies at the rear.

Open 11–3 5.30–12 (Sun 12–3, 5.30–10.30) **Bar Meals** L served all week 11–2.30 D served all week 6–10 (Sun 12–2.30, 6–10) **Restaurant** L served all week 11–2.30 D served all week 6–10 Punch Taverns Betty Stogs, 6X, Sharp's Doom Bar Bitter & Guest Ale. 14 **Facilities** Garden Dogs allowed

PERRANUTHNOE — MAP 02 SW52

The Victoria Inn ★★★ INN

TR20 9NP ☎ 01736 710309 01736 719284

dir: *Off A394 (Penzance to Helston road), signed Perranuthnoe*

Queen Victoria stares sternly from the sign outside this pink-washed, 12th-century inn, reputedly Cornwall's oldest, and first used as a hostelry by masons building the village church. Fresh seafood is its forte, the selection changing daily according to the local catch. Among the possibilities are megrim sole stuffed with Newlyn crab and baby bay prawns, and halibut steak with avocado salsa and Moroccan orange dressing. In the garden imagine you're by the Med.

Open 11.30–2.30 6.30–11 Summer 6–11 **Bar Meals** L served all week 12–2 D served all week 6.30–9 (Sun 7–9) **Restaurant** L served all week 12–2 D served all week 6.30–9 (Sun 7–9) Av 3 course à la carte £18 Bass, Doom Bar, Abbot Ale. 8 **Facilities** Garden Dogs allowed Parking **Rooms** 3 bedrooms en suite S£35 D£60

POLKERRIS MAP 02 SX05

The Rashleigh Inn

PL24 2TL ☎ 01726 813991 01726 815619
e-mail: jonspode@aol.com
dir: *Off A3082 outside Fowey*

A 300-year-old, stone-built pub on the beach, once a boathouse and coastguard station. Panoramic views across St Austell Bay can be enjoyed from the multi-level sun terrace, with a giant sun parasol on the top terrace, and heaters and glass panels for cool evenings. Real ale selections vary according to season, and there is a good choice of malt whiskies. The pub specialises in freshly caught fish and offers sandwiches, steaks and specials like fish pie or curry.

Open 11–11 (Sun 12–10.30) **Bar Meals** L served all week 12–2 D served all week 6–9 Av main course £8 **Restaurant** L served all week 12–2 D served all week 6–9 Free House Sharp's Doom Bar, Cotleigh Tawny , Blue Anchor Spingo, Timothy Taylor Landlord. 8 **Facilities** Garden Parking

POLPERRO MAP 02 SX25

Old Mill House Inn

Mill Hill PL13 2RP ☎ 01503 272362
e-mail: oldmillhouseinn@btconnect.com

In the heart of historic Polperro, this 16th-century inn has been extensively refurbished. Here you can sample well-kept local ales and 'scrumpy' cider beside a log fire in the bar, or sit out over lunch in the riverside garden during fine weather. Local ingredients, with an emphasis on freshly caught fish, are the foundation of dishes on the restaurant menu. Traditional roasts are served on Sundays.

Open 11–11 **Bar Meals** L served all week 12–2.30 (Sun carvery 12–3) **Restaurant** D served Mon–Sat 7–9.30 Free House Carling, Skinners, Erdinger Weiss Beer, Skinners Mill House Ale & Becks Vier. **Facilities** Garden Dogs allowed Parking

PORT GAVERNE MAP 02 SX08

Pick of the Pubs

Port Gaverne Hotel ★★ HL

PL29 3SQ ☎ 01208 880244 01208 880151
dir: *Signed from B3314, S of Delabole via B3267 on E of Port Isaac*

Just up the lane from a beautiful little cove, this delightful 17th-century inn is a magnet for both locals and holidaymakers. It's a meandering building with plenty of period detail, evocative of its long association with fishing and smuggling. Bread is home made, and locally supplied produce includes plenty of fresh fish. Along with a selection of ploughman's and children's favourites, the lunchtime bar menu offers a half pint of prawns with mayonnaise; seafood pie served with new potatoes and vegetables; or a chargrilled chicken salad. At dinner you might try tomato, red onion and Cornish goats' cheese salad; pan-fried fillet of John Dory served on saffron mash with a white wine and parsley sauce; and a selection of West Country cheeses. Walkers from the Heritage Coast Path can pause for a pint of St Austell Tribute in the small beer garden, or at a table in front of the hotel.

Open 11–11 **Bar Meals** L served all week 12–2.30 D served all week 6.30–9.30 **Restaurant** D served all week 7–9.30 Free House Sharp's Doom Bar, Bass, St Austell Tribute. 9 **Facilities** Garden Dogs allowed Parking **Rooms** 15 bedrooms en suite S£52.50 D£85

PORTHLEVEN MAP 02 SW62

The Ship Inn

TR13 9JS ☎ 01326 564204 01326 564204
dir: *From Helston follow signs to Porthleven, 2.5m. On entering village continue to harbour head. Take W side road by side of harbour to inn*

Dating from the 17th century, this smugglers' inn is actually built into the cliffs, and is approached by a flight of stone steps. The terraced garden has wonderful views over the harbour, and inside there's a bar with a log fire and a family room converted from a smithy. An extensive menu ranges through toasties, ploughman's and sandwiches to daily fish specials and favourites like smoked fish platter, steak, and minted leg of lamb casserole.

Open 11.30–11 (Sun 12–10.30) **Bar Meals** L served all week 12–2 D served all week 7–9 Av main course £11 Free House Scottish Courage Courage Best, Sharp's Doom Bar, Old Speckled Hen, Sharp's Special. **Facilities** Garden Dogs allowed

PORTREATH MAP 02 SW64

Basset Arms

Tregea Ter TR16 4NG ☎ 01209 842077 🖷 01209 843936

e-mail: bas.bookings@ccinns.com

dir: *From Redruth take B3300 to Portreath*

Typical Cornish stone cottage, built as a pub in the early 19th century to serve the harbour workers, with plenty of tin mining and shipwreck memorabilia adorning the low-beamed interior. As you'd expect, seafood dominates the menu. Look out for grilled seabass fillet, tuna steak with sweet chili sauce, turbot stuffed with prawns and mushrooms, large grilled fillet of plaice Veronique, and whole trout with almonds.

Open 11.30–3 6–11 (all day in summer) **Bar Meals** L served all week 12–2 D served all week 6–9 Av main course £6 **Restaurant** L served all week 12–2 D served all week 6–9 Free House Sharp's Doom Bar, Worthington 6X, Courage & John Smith's Smooth. **Facilities** Children's licence Garden Dogs allowed Parking Play Area

RUAN LANIHORNE MAP 02 SW84

The Kings Head

TR2 5NX ☎ 01872 501263

e-mail: contact@kings-head-roseland.co.uk

dir: *3m from Tregony Bridge on A3078*

Deep in the Roseland countryside, there's a warm welcome at this rural free house. Roaring winter fires, beamed ceilings and mulled wine contrast with summer days relaxing on the terrace with a jug of Pimms. But whatever the time of year, the chef responds with seasonal menus that might include hot or cold soups, pheasant, venison and shellfish in season. Look out for the signature dish, too – slow-roasted Ruan duckling with a warm pepper sauce.

Open 12–2.30 6–11 Closed: Mon Nov–Mar **Restaurant** L served all week 12.30–2 D served all week 6.30–9 Av 3 course à la carte £23 Free House Skinners Kings Ruan, Cornish Knocker, Betty Stogs. **Facilities** Garden Dogs allowed Parking

ST AGNES MAP 03 SW75

Driftwood Spars

Trevaunance Cove TR5 0RT

☎ 01872 552428 & 553323 🖷 01872 553701

e-mail: driftwoodspars@hotmail.com

dir: *A30 onto B3285, through St Agnes, down steep hill, left at Peterville Inn, onto road signed Trevaunance Cove*

Previously a tin miners' store, a chandlery and a sail loft, this 300-year-old building's whitewashed perfection is today enhanced by baskets of flowers. An old smugglers' tunnel ends in the back bar, where brass and lanterns add to its salty charm. Sit by the fire and try ales from its micro-brewery, or dine on moules marinière; roasted sea bass stuffed with apricots and hazelnuts; or chargrilled fillet of beef with a forest mushroom gratin.

Driftwood Spars

Open 11–1 **Bar Meals** L served all week 12–2.30 D served all week 6.30–9.30 (all day Aug) **Restaurant** L served all week 12–2.30 D served all week 6.30–9.30 Free House Carlsberg-Tetley Bitter, Sharp's Own, St Austell HSD, Cuckoo Ale. 🍷 15 **Facilities** Garden Dogs allowed Parking **Rooms** 15 bedrooms en suite S£43 D£86

ST AGNES (ISLES OF SCILLY) MAP 02 SV80

Turks Head

TR22 0PL ☎ 01720 422434

dir: *By boat or helicopter to St Mary's & boat on to St Agnes*

Named after the 16th-century Turkish pirates who arrived from the Barbary Coast, the Turks Head is Britain's most southwesterly inn. Noted for its atmosphere and superb location overlooking the island quay, this former coastguard boathouse is now packed with fascinating model ships and maritime photographs. Lunchtime brings soup, salads and open rolls, while evening dishes might include blackened swordfish steak in Cajun spices, or sirloin steak with all the trimmings.

Open 10.30–11.30 Closed: Nov–Feb **Bar Meals** L served all week 12–2.30 D served all week 6–9 Free House Skinners Betty Stogs, Sharp's Doom Bar, Ales of Scilly, Scuppered. **Facilities** Garden Dogs allowed

ST BREWARD MAP 02 SX07

The Old Inn & Restaurant

Churchtown, Bodmin Moor PL30 4PP

☎ 01208 850711 🖷 01208 851671

e-mail: darren@theoldinn.fsnet.co.uk

dir: *A30 to Bodmin. 16m, right just after Temple, follow signs to St Breward. B3266 Bodmin to Camelford road take turn to St Breward, follow brown signs.*

Located high up on Bodmin Moor, one of Cornwall's oldest inns is now owned and run by local man Darren Wills, the latest licensee in its

1,000-year history. The pub is well-known throughout this glorious area for its wholesome home-cooked food, frequented by many regulars who are drawn by its Moorland Grills and Sunday roasts. Sizzling platters, home-made curries and an array of new fish and vegetarian options add to the menu's appeal. Check out the local Cornish wines.

The Old Inn & Restaurant

Open 11–11 **Bar Meals** L served all week 11–2 D served all week 6–9 (Sun 12–2, 6–9) Av main course £8.95 **Restaurant** L served all week 11–2 D served all week 6–9 (Sun 12–2, 6–9) Av 3 course à la carte £24.50 Free House Sharp's Doom Bar Bitter, Sharp's Special, Guest Ales. 20 **Facilities** Garden Dogs allowed Parking

ST EWE MAP 02 SW94

The Crown Inn

PL26 6EY ☎ 01726 843322 01726 844720

e-mail: linda@thecrowninn737.fsnet.co.uk

dir: *From St Austell take B3273. At Tregiskey x-rds turn right. St Ewe signed on right*

Hanging baskets add plenty of brightness and colour to this delightful 16th-century inn, just a mile from the famous 'Lost gardens of Heligan', which Crown chef John Nelson co-founded and helped to restore. Well-kept St Austell ales complement an extensive menu and daily specials. Expect cod in beer batter, local steaks, rack of lamb, and liver and bacon among other favourites. Try a glass of Polmassick wine from the vineyard only half a mile away.

Open 12–3 5–11 Rest: Winter 6–11 **Bar Meals** L served all week 12–2 D served all week 6–9 **Restaurant** L served all week 12–2 D served all week 6–9 St Austell Brewery Tribute, Hicks Special, Tinners, plus Guest ale. 8 **Facilities** Garden Dogs allowed Parking Play Area

ST JUST (NEAR LAND'S END) MAP 02 SW33

Pick of the Pubs

Star Inn

TR19 7LL ☎ 01736 788767

dir: *Telephone for directions*

Plenty of tin mining and fishing stories are told at this traditional Cornish pub, located in the town of St Just, near Lands End. It dates back a few centuries, and was reputedly built to house workmen constructing the 15th-century church. John Wesley is believed to have been among the Star's more illustrious guests over the years, but these days the pub is most likely to be recognised for having featured in several television and film productions. A choice of local beers is served alongside some good bar food. Dishes on offer include home-made pies (beef, and chicken and ham), soups, pasties and crab dishes, notably crab Averock – white crab meat with a cream and mustard sauce. Monday night is folk night, and there's live music on Thursdays and Saturdays, too, in a whole range of styles.

Open 11 –11 (Sat 11–12, Sun 12–11) **Bar Meals** L served all week 12–2.30 Av main course £6 St Austell Brewery St Austell HSD, Tinners Ale, Tribute, Dartmoor. 7 **Facilities** Garden Dogs allowed **Notes**

ST MAWES MAP 02 SW83

Pick of the Pubs

The Rising Sun ★★ HL

The Square TR2 5DJ ☎ 01326 270233 01209 270198

e-mail: info@risingsunstmawes.com

dir: *From Truro & St Austell 21m*

At the heart of Cornwall's yachting community, The Rising Sun stands by the picturesque harbour at St Mawes. The Lizard Peninsula shelters this popular yet dignified resort from the vagaries of the Atlantic, and the mild climate makes the terrace an ideal spot to relax with a drink and watch the world sail by. Innovative English cooking is offered from a flexible daily changing menu, taking account of the freshest local ingredients available. The emphasis is on wholesome food, flavour and attractive presentation so that diners enjoy every aspect of their meal. Seafood is strongly represented with crab bisque, hot smokie crumble, and grilled sea bass fillets with redcurrant dressing. Other options might be pink organic West Country duck breast with red wine sauce, and comfort food like cottage pie, beef burgers, fishcakes and chicken curry.

Open 10–11 **Bar Meals** L served all week 12–2.30 D served all week 6.30–9 (all day in Summer) Av main course £10.50 **Restaurant** L served all week 12–2.30 D served all week 6.45–9 (Oct–Mar 12–2) St Austell Brewery Hicks Special Draught, St Austell Tinners Ale, Tribute. 11 **Facilities** Garden Dogs allowed Parking **Rooms** 8 bedrooms en suite S£60 D£60

England

ST MAWES continued

Pick of the Pubs

The Victory Inn

Victory Hill TR2 5PQ
☎ 01326 270324 📠 01326 270238
e-mail: contact@victory-inn.co.uk
web: www.victory-inn.co.uk
dir: *Take A3078 to St Mawes, located up Victory Steps adjacent to harbour*

Close to St Mawes Harbour on the Roseland Peninsula is this friendly fishermen's local, named after Nelson's flagship. These days it doubles as a modern dining pub, offering the freshest of local seafood, and harbour views. There is a heated and covered sea view terrace. The blackboard specials change daily, with dishes such as rabbit terrine and toast to start; and home baked ham with free range egg and chips to follow. Fish choices are understandably extensive. Look out for sea bass fillets with balsamic-baked cherry tomatoes; lobster thermidore; or grilled razor clams with coriander and orange pesto. In addition to the range of real ales, there's a decent selection of wines by the glass, plus speciality spirits – malt whiskies, Cognac and Calvados.

Open 11 -11 Closed: Nov–Mar Rest: Mar–Oct, 11–12 **Bar Meals** L served all week 12–2.30 D served all week 6.30–9.30 Av main course £8.95 **Restaurant** L served Mon–Sun 12–2.15 D served Mon–Sun 6.30–9 Av 3 course à la carte £17.50 Punch Taverns Sharp's, Bass, Ringwood, IPA. 8 **Facilities** Dogs allowed

ST MAWGAN — MAP 02 SW86

Pick of the Pubs

The Falcon Inn ★★★★ INN

TR8 4EP ☎ 01637 860225 📠 01637 860884
e-mail: enquiries@thefalconinn-newquay.co.uk
dir: *From A30 8m W of Bodmin, follow signs to Newquay/St Mawgan Airport. After 2m turn right into village, pub at bottom of hill*

Nestling in the sheltered Vale of Lanherne, the Falcon has a large, attractive garden with a lovely magnolia tree and walls covered with wisteria. plus a cobbled courtyard. Inside it is cosy and relaxed, with flagged stone floors and log fires in winter. The beers come from the St Austell brewery, and there are plenty of wines available by the glass with a choice of ten malt whiskies. At lunchtime, you'll find home-made soup; garlic bread made with sun-dried tomatoes and basil ciabatta; sandwiches, jacket potatoes; and bigger dishes such as seafood and broccoli mornay; tortelloni al pesto; chicken, mushroom and ale pie; and vegetable and five bean chilli. The evening menu is more substantial and may feature starters of fresh scallops; Cornish smoked salmon and shell-on prawns; antipasto misto; or roast vegetable bruschetta. Among the main courses there are always fish dishes such as red mullet, hake or trout.

The Falcon Inn

Open 11–3 6–12 (Sun 12–5, 7–11) **Bar Meals** L served all week 12–2 D served all week 6–9 (Summer 12–2.30, 6–9.30) **Restaurant** L served all week 12–2 D served all week 6–9 St Austell Brewery St Austell HSD, Tinners Ale & Tribute. 7 **Facilities** Garden Dogs allowed Parking Play Area **Rooms** 2 bedrooms en suite D£78

ST NEOT — MAP 02 SX16

The London Inn

PL14 6NG ☎ 01579 320263 📠 01579 321642
e-mail: lon.manager@ccinns.com

Dating back to the 18th century, this pub was the first coaching inn on the route from Penzance to London. The bar and dining areas have old beamed ceilings and polished flagstone floors. Seafood platter, salmon, and halibut are among the fish dishes, while other main courses include lamb shank in a spiced port sauce. Lighter fare ranges from ciabatta bread with a variety of fillings, including roast beef, chicken, bacon and cheese, to a choice of ploughman's lunches.

Open 12–3 6.30–11 **Bar Meals** L served all week 12–2 D served all week 7–9 Av main course £9.95 **Restaurant** L served all week 12–2 D served all week 7–9 Av 3 course à la carte £25 Coast & Country Inns Doom Bar, Courage Best, John Smiths & Guest Ales. 16 **Facilities** Dogs allowed Parking

SALTASH — MAP 03 SX45

The Crooked Inn ★★★ INN

Stoketon Cottage, Trematon PL12 4RZ
☎ 01752 848177 📠 01752 843203
e-mail: info@crooked-inn.co.uk

Overlooking the lush Lyher Valley, a family-run inn that once housed staff from Stoketon Manor, whose ruins lie the other side the courtyard. Traditional, home-made dishes include pie, pasta or curry of the day; battered fresh cod; breaded wholetail scampi; and 'generous, hefty, ample or copious' steaks. Boards list lunchtime, evening and vegetarian specials and there's a special Little Horrors menu. The children's playground has friendly animals, swings, slides, a trampoline and a treehouse.

Open 11–11 (Sun 11–10.30) Closed: 25 Dec **Bar Meals** L served all week 12–2.30 D served all week 6–9.30 Av main course £6.95 **Restaurant** L served all week 12–2.30 D served all week 6–9.30 Free House Hicks Special Draught, Sharp's Own Ale, Skinner's Cornish Knocker Ale. **Facilities** Children's licence Garden Dogs allowed Parking Play Area **Rooms** 18 bedrooms 15 en suite S£45 D£70

The Weary Friar Inn ★★★★ INN

Pillaton PL12 6QS ☎ 01579 350238 01579 350238
e-mail: info@wearyfriar.co.uk
dir: *2m W of A388 between Callington & Saltash*

This whitewashed 12th-century inn with oak-beamed ceilings, an abundance of brass, and blazing fires lies next to the Church of St Adolphus, tucked away in a small Cornish village. A typical selection from the menu includes venison pie, spit roasted chicken, fillet steak with wild mushroom sauce, spinach and mushroom bake, and Cornish crab cakes. Salads, sandwiches, afternoon cream teas and ploughman's are also available. Curry and other themed nights are popular.

Open 11–11 (Sun 12–10.30) **Bar Meals** L served all week 11–3 D served all week 5–9 (Sun 12–3, 5–9) **Restaurant** L served all week 11–3 D served all week 5–9 Free House St Austell Tribute, Tinners, Interbrew Bass, Fullers London Pride. **Facilities** Garden Parking **Rooms** 12 bedrooms en suite

SENNEN — MAP 02 SW32

The Old Success Inn ★★ HL

Sennen Cove TR19 7DG ☎ 01736 871232 01736 871457
e-mail: oldsuccess@sennencove.fsbusiness.co.uk

Once the haunt of smugglers and now a focal point for the Sennen Lifeboat crew, this 17th-century inn enjoys a glorious location overlooking Cape Cornwall. Its name comes from the days when fishermen gathered here to count their catch and share out their 'successes'. Fresh local seafood is to the fore, and favourites include cod in Doom Bar batter, steaks, chilli, and vegetable lasagne. Live music every Saturday night in the bar.

The Old Success Inn

Open 11–11 **Bar Meals** L served all week 12–2.30 D served all week 6.15–9.30 **Restaurant** L served Sun 12–2.15 D served all week 7–9.30 Av 3 course à la carte £18.50 Av 3 course fixed price £17 Free House Doom Bar, Skinners, Heligan Honey, Headlaunch Special. **Facilities** Garden Dogs allowed Parking **Rooms** 12 bedrooms en suite S£32 D£80

TINTAGEL — MAP 02 SX08

The Port William ★★★ INN

Trebarwith Strand PL34 0HB
☎ 01840 770230 01840 770936
e-mail: theportwilliam@btinternet.com
dir: *Off B3263 between Camelford & Tintagel, pub signed*

Occupying one of the best locations in Cornwall, this former harbourmaster's house lies directly on the coastal path, 50 yards from the sea. There is an entrance to a smugglers' tunnel at the rear of the ladies' toilet. Focus on the daily-changing specials board for such dishes as artichoke and roast pepper salad, warm smoked trout platter, and spinach ricotta tortelloni. Recent change of owner.

Open 11–11 (Sun 12–10.30) Rest: 12 opening in winter **Bar Meals** L served all week 12–2.30 D served all week 6.30–9.30 Av main course £8.50 **Restaurant** L served all week 12–2.30 D served all week 6–9.30 Av 3 course à la carte £15 Free House St Austell Tinners Ale & Hicks, Interbrew Bass. 8 **Facilities** Garden Dogs allowed Parking **Rooms** 8 bedrooms en suite S£42.50 D£60

The Mill House Inn

Set in seven acres of wooded gardens on the north Cornish coast, the Mill House dates back to 1760 and was a working mill until the late 1930s. Hardly surprising, then, that it's a beautifully atmospheric stone building with log fires in the bar, dining room and residents' lounge.

Surfing beaches, the coastal path and numerous tourist attractions are dotted around the surrounding area; King Arthur's legendary castle of Tintagel is in the very next valley. Originally known as Treknow Mill, the building became a public house in 1960; since then, it has been progressively refurbished and upgraded by a number of different owners. Today, this welcoming free house provides first-class food. The slate-floored bar with its wooden tables and chapel chairs has a relaxed, family-friendly feel. In contrast, the dining room over the old millstream is light and airy during the day, yet intimate and romantic at night. Lunches, evening drinks and barbeques can be enjoyed outside on the attractive split-level terraces in fine weather. Sharp's local ales and an unusual and creative wine list complement the regularly changing lunch and dinner menus, which make use of the best locally sourced ingredients. At lunchtime, traditional pub favourites such as sausages and mash or battered haddock and chips appear alongside more adventurous dishes like Tuscan bean cassoulet with dressed leaves, parmesan and ciabatta. In the restaurant, typical starters include pan-fried medallions of monkfish with local bacon and dressed leaves; and oven-baked stuffed mushrooms. You could follow with chargrilled Cornish venison steak on potato wedges with creamy wholegrain mustard sauce; or roast supreme of local chicken wrapped in Parma ham and served on couscous. Round things off with a choice of home-made traditional and contemporary desserts, or a selection from the local cheeseboard. The Mill House is licensed for weddings and civil ceremonies.

MAP 02 SX08
PL34 0HD
☎ 01840 770200
01840 770647
e-mail: management@themillhouseinn.co.uk
dir: *From Tintagel take B3263 S, right after Trewarmett to Trebarwith Strand. Pub 0.5m down valley on right.*

Open 12 –11 Closed: 25 Dec
Bar Meals L served all week 12–2.30 (Sun 12–3) Av main course £9
Restaurant L served all week 12–2 (Sun 12–3) D served all week 6.30–9 Av 3 course à la carte £28
Free House
Sharps Doom Bar, Sharps Special, Red Stripe, Carlsberg.
Facilities Children's licence Garden Dogs allowed Parking Play Area

TORPOINT
MAP 03 SX45

Pick of the Pubs

Edgcumbe Arms ★★★★ INN

Cremyll PL10 1HX ☎ 01752 822294 01752 822014
e-mail: edgcumbe-arms@btconnect.com
dir: *Please phone for directions*

The inn dates from the 15th century and is located right on the Tamar estuary, next to the National Trust Park, close to the foot ferry from Plymouth. Views from the bow window seats and waterside terrace are glorious, taking in Drakes Island, the Royal William Yard and the marina. Real ales from St Austell like Cornish Cream, Tribute HS, and Tinners, and quality home-cooked food are served in a series of rooms, which are full of character with American oak panelling and stone flagged floors. A good choice of bar snacks is also offered. The inn has a first floor function room with sea views, and a courtyard garden; it also holds a civil wedding license. A bridal suite is included in the range of pretty bedrooms.

Open 11-11 (Sun 12-10.30) **Bar Meals** L served all week 12-6 D served all week 6-9.30 **Restaurant** L served all week 12-6 D served all week 6-9.30 St Austell Brewery St Austell HSD, Tribute HS, IPA, Cornish Cream. 10 **Facilities** Garden Dogs allowed Parking **Rooms** 6 bedrooms en suite

TREBARWITH
MAP 02 SX08

Pick of the Pubs

The Mill House Inn

PL34 0HD ☎ 01840 770200 01840 770647
e-mail: management@themillhouseinn.co.uk
dir: *From Tintagel take B3263 S, right after Trewarmett to Trebarwith Strand. Pub 0.5m down valley on right.*

See Pick of the Pubs on opposite page

TREBURLEY
MAP 03 SX37

Pick of the Pubs

The Springer Spaniel

PL15 9NS ☎ 01579 370424
e-mail: enquiries@thespringerspaniel.org.uk
dir: *On A388 halfway between Launceston & Callington*

See Pick of the Pubs on page 98

TREGADILLETT
MAP 03 SX28

Eliot Arms (Square & Compass)

PL15 7EU ☎ 01566 772051
e-mail: eli.bookings@ccinns.com
dir: *From Launceston take A30 towards Bodmin. Then follow brown signs to Tregadillett*

This old coaching inn is built from Cornish stone and boasts a huge collection of clocks, Masonic regalia and horse brasses. It was believed to have been a Masonic lodge for Napoleonic prisoners, and even has its own friendly ghost! Customers can enjoy real fires in winter and lovely hanging baskets in summer. Fish features strongly, with delicacies such as moules marinière and grilled sardines. Other options include Cajun-style chicken, and home-made vegetable curry.

Open 11.30-3 6-11 (Fri-Sun all day) **Bar Meals** L served all week 12-2 D served all week 7-9 Av main course £11 **Restaurant** L served all week 12-2 D served all week 7-9 Av 3 course à la carte £20 Free House Doom Bar, Scottish Courage Courage Best. 9 **Facilities** Dogs allowed Parking

TRESCO (ISLES OF SCILLY)
MAP 02 SV81

Pick of the Pubs

The New Inn ★★ HL

New Grimsby TR24 0QQ
☎ 01720 422844 01720 423200
e-mail: newinn@tresco.co.uk
dir: *By New Grimsby Quay*

If you want a drink on Tresco, you'll end up here – it's the only pub. Awash with maritime history, even the pub's signboard was salvaged from a wreck. Locally caught seafood tends to steal the limelight, with crab, lobster, line-caught sea bass, and whole megrim sole among many species likely to make an appearance. Non-fishy counterbalance comes from Tresco beef and ale pie, and asparagus risotto. Many rooms have ocean views.

Open 11-11 Rest: Nov-Feb 11-2.30 & 6-11 **Bar Meals** L served all week 12-2 D served all week 6-9 (Limited menu Apr-Sep) **Restaurant** D served all week 7-9 Av 3 course à la carte £22 Free House Skinner's Betty Stogs Bitter, Tresco Tipple, Ales of Scilly Natural Beauty, St Austell IPA. 8 **Facilities** Garden **Rooms** 16 bedrooms en suite S£112.50 D£150

The Springer Spaniel

Reputedly a pub for the last 200 years, with old creeper-clad walls concealing a cosy bar with high-backed wooden settles, farmhouse-style chairs, and a woodburning stove. The atmosphere is friendly, and there's bound to be a local willing to reveal an interesting nugget or two about the area.

Food is a big draw here, with bar blackboards listing daily specials such as warm smoked duck salad, pan-fried scallops, and decent soups. Game might appear among the daily specials, along with fresh fish from Fowey, and organic beef and lamb from the owners' organic farm, a 100-hectare holding that raises South Devon cattle and Lleyn sheep on lush pastureland. Dishes in the separate beamed dining room again depend on the seasons, with spiced winter vegetable casserole an obvious example. You could start with goats' cheese and caramelised apple tart; a warm salad of sweet potato and crayfish; or a pot of mushrooms sautéed with bacon and cream, flamed in brandy and topped with melted cheese.

Main courses have just the same hearty and appetising appeal. Try pan-fried Cornish beef in rich, creamy stilton and brandy sauce; breast of Barbary duck with ginger and orange; fillet of salmon in a Thai spice crust; or roast chicken breast with a field mushroom, sage and pine nut sauce. There is an extensive home-cooked bar menu, and children will have fun with the 'Little Jack Russell' menu, which serves up chicken goujons, sausages, chips and beans, and fresh penne bolognaise, using the same well-sourced ingredients as appear in the adults' dishes. A serious wine list features guests of the month.

MAP 03 SX37
PL15 9NS
☎ 01579 370424
e-mail: enquiries@thespringerspaniel.org.uk
dir: *On A388 halfway between Launceston & Callington*

Open 12–3 6–11 (wknds 6–12)
Bar Meals L served Mon–Sat 12–1.45 D served all week 6.30–8.45 Av main course £10
Restaurant L served all week 12–1.45 D served all week 6.30–8.45 Av 3 course à la carte £20
Free House
Sharp's Doom Bar, Skinners Betty Stogs, St Austel Tribute & Guest. 7
Facilities Garden Dogs allowed Parking

TRURO MAP 02 SW84

Old Ale House

7 Quay St TR1 2HD ☎ 01872 271122 📠 01872 271817
e-mail: old.ale.house@btconnect.com
dir: *A30, Truro City centre*

Olde-worlde establishment with a large selection of real ales on display, as well as more than twenty flavours of fruit wine. Lots of attractions, including live music and various quiz and games nights. Food includes 'huge hands of hot bread', oven-baked jacket potatoes, ploughman's lunches and daily specials. Vegetable stir fry, five spice chicken and sizzling beef feature among the sizzling skillets.

Open 11–11 (Sun 12–10.30) Closed: 25 Dec, 1 Jan **Bar Meals** L served all week 12–2.45 D served Mon–Fri 6.30–8.45 Enterprise Inns Skinners Kiddlywink, Shepherd Neame Spitfire, Scottish Courage Bass, Greene King Abbot Ale. 9

The Wig & Pen Inn

Frances St TR1 3DP ☎ 01872 273028 📠 01872 277351
dir: *City centre near Law Courts, 10 mins from railway station*

A listed city centre pub originally known as the Star, that became the Wig & Pen when the county court moved to Truro. There is a ghost called Claire who lives in the cellar, but she is friendly! The choice of food includes such home-made dishes as steak and ale pie, curry, casseroles, steaks and vegetarian dishes, and a range of fish options such as sea bass, John Dory, mullet or monkfish.

Open 11–11 **Bar Meals** L served all week 12–9 D served all week Av main course £6 St Austell Brewery St Austell, Tribute, IPA, HSD & Guest ales. **Facilities** Garden Dogs allowed

TYWARDREATH MAP 02 SX05

The Royal Inn NEW

66 Eastcliffe Rd PL24 2AJ ☎ 01726 815601 📠 01726 816415
e-mail: info@royal-inn.co.uk
dir: *A3082 Par, follow brown tourist signs for 'Newquay Branch line' or railway station. Pub opposite railway station*

Named by royal assent after a visit by King Edward VII to a local copper mine, this 19th-century inn hosted travellers and employees of the Great Western Railway. It was completely refurbished a few years ago, and today supports many Cornish micro-breweries and food producers. The open-plan bar with large log fire is a great place for, say, simple sausages and mash, while the restaurant and conservatory serves delicious local seafood such as Fowey River mussels.

Open 11.30–11 (Sun 12–10.30) **Bar Meals** L served all week 12–2 D served all week 6.30–9 (Sun 7–9) Av main course £7.25 **Restaurant** L served all week 12–2 D served all week 6.30–9 (Sun 7–9) Av 3 course à la carte £21 Free House Sharpe's Doom Bar, Skinners Heligan Honey, Cotleigh Barn Owl, Skinners Cornish Knocker. 11 **Facilities** Children's licence Garden Dogs allowed Parking **Rooms** S£30 D£50 (★★★★ INN)

VERYAN MAP 02 SW93

The New Inn ★★★★ INN

TR2 5QA ☎ 01872 501362 📠 01872 501078
e-mail: jack@newinn-veryan.fsnet.co.uk
dir: *From St Austell take Truro road, after 2m bear left to Tregony, through Tregony follow signs to Veryan.*

Based in a pair of 16th-century cottages, this unspoilt pub is found in the centre of a pretty village on the Roseland Peninsula. It has a single bar, open fires and a beamed ceiling, and the emphasis is on good ales and home cooking. Simple, satisfying dishes abound, with seafood featuring heavily: expect pan-fried bass fillet and Dover sole grilled on the bone, plus jumbo rump steak or a special like Louisiana jambalaya.

Open 12–3 6–11 (Winter 12–2.30) **Bar Meals** L served all week 12–2 D served Mon–Sat 7–9 Av main course £10 St Austell Brewery St Austell HSD, Dartmoor Ale & Tribute. 8 **Facilities** Children's licence Garden **Rooms** 3 bedrooms 2 en suite S£32 D£65

WADEBRIDGE MAP 02 SW97

The Quarryman Inn

Edmonton PL27 7JA ☎ 01208 816444
dir: *Off A39 opposite Royal Cornwall Showground*

Close to the famous Camel Trail, this friendly 18th-century free house has evolved from a courtyard of cottages once used by slate workers at the nearby quarry. Several bow windows, one of which features a stained-glass quarryman panel, add character to this unusual inn. Sandwiches and freshly-baked baguettes are favourites on the regular lunchtime menu, which also includes chargrilled local steaks. Watch the blackboards for daily specials and delicious puddings.

Open 12–11 (Sun 12–10.30) **Bar Meals** L served all week 12–2.30 D served all week 6–9 Av main course £11.50 **Restaurant** L served all week 12–2.30 D served all week 6–9 Av 3 course à la carte £16 Free House Sharps, Skinners, Timothy Taylor Landlord, various Guest ales. **Facilities** Garden Dogs allowed Parking

England

WADEBRIDGE continued

Swan ★★★★ INN

9 Molesworth St PL27 7DD

☎ 01208 812526 01208 812526

e-mail: reservations@smallandfriendly.co.uk

dir: *In centre of Wadebridge on corner of Molesworth St and The Platt*

A town centre hotel that is family friendly, it was originally called the Commercial Hotel, and sits alongside the old Padstow Railway Branch Line. Typical pub food includes doorstep sandwiches and baguettes, light snacks like cheesy chips, salads, chargrill dishes, full Cornish breakfast and main courses like Tribute beer-battered cod, or curry of the day. Children's dishes include chicken nuggets made of 100% chicken breast; pizza or pork sausage.

Open 10–11 **Bar Meals** L served all week 12–3 D served all week 6–9 Av main course £6.50 St Austell Brewery HSD, Tribute, Carlsberg, Guinness & Carling. 13 **Facilities** Children's licence Garden Dogs allowed **Rooms** 6 bedrooms en suite S£30 D£60

WIDEMOUTH BAY MAP 02 SS20

Bay View Inn NEW

EX23 0AW ☎ 01288 361273 01288 361145

e-mail: thebayviewinn@aol.com

dir: *On Marine Drive adjacent to beach in Widemouth Bay*

The Bay View Inn, as its name implies, enjoys wonderful vistas of the rolling Atlantic from its Surf Bar restaurant and the large raised decking area outside. About a hundred years old, it was a guest house for many years before transformation to an inn in the 1960s. The appetising menu makes excellent use of Cornish produce in such dishes as smoked pilchard and St Marwenne cream cheese paté, and locally farmed rump steak cooked to your liking.

Open 9–1am (Sun 9–11.30) **Bar Meals** L served all week 12–2.30 D served all week 6.30–9.30 (Sun 12–3 & 6–9) Av main course £12.50 **Restaurant** L served all week 12–2.30 D served all week 6.30–9.30 (Sun 12–3 6–9) Free House Skinner's Spriggan Ale, Sharp's Doom Bar, Sharps Own. 17 **Facilities** Garden Dogs allowed Parking Play Area

ZENNOR MAP 02 SW43

Pick of the Pubs

The Gurnards Head ★★★ INN

Treen, Zennor TR26 3DE

☎ 01736 796928 01736 795313

e-mail: gur.bookings@ccinns.com

dir: *5m from Penzance. 5m from St. Ives on B3306.*

An imposing colour-washed building that dominates the coastal landscape above Gurnard's Head, this traditional Cornish pub (stone-flagged bar, open fires) is just the place to get stranded on a wind-swept winter's night. Here you can see Cornwall at its most brutal, but on warmer days there are some great walks along the coastal path or the rugged Penwith Moors, strewn with wild flowers and studded with ancient Celtic remains. The owners of the highly successful Felin Fach Griffin in Brecon have taken over recently, and have already stamped their upmarket brand on the place. The bar and eating areas have been refurbished, everywhere has been brightened by a few coats of paint, and the food has been given a lift as well.

Open 12–3 6–11 (Sun 7–10.30) **Bar Meals** L served all week 12–2.30 D served all week 6.30–9 Av main course £12 **Restaurant** L served all week 12–2.30 D served all week 6.30–9 Av 3 course à la carte £25 Free House Betty Stogs, Tribute, Cornish Knocker. 10 **Facilities** Children's licence Garden Dogs allowed Parking

The Tinners Arms

TR26 3BY ☎ 01736 796927

e-mail: tinners@tinnersarms.com

dir: *Take B3306 from St Ives towards St Just. Zennor, approx 5m*

With the popular South West coastal path nearby, and being the only pub in the village, this 13th-century, granite-built free house is particularly popular with walkers. Its unspoilt main bar has open fires at both ends, and outdoors is a large seating area with sea views. Menus make the most of local fresh fish. Try Tinners fish or cottage pies at lunch, or confit of duck with orange and ginger in the evening.

Open 11–11 (Sun 12–10.30) (Nov–Etr wkdays 11–3 6.30–11) **Bar Meals** L served all week 12–2.30 D served Fri–Sat 6.30–9 (Summer times vary) Av main course £10.50 Free House Doom Bar, Zennor Mermaid, Tinners Ale, Carlsberg & Skinners Cornish Lager. **Facilities** Garden Dogs allowed Parking

CUMBRIA

AMBLESIDE MAP 18 NY30

Pick of the Pubs

Drunken Duck Inn ★★★★★ INN

Barngates LA22 0NG

☎ 015394 36347 015394 36781

e-mail: info@drunkenduckinn.co.uk

dir: *From Kendal A591 to Ambleside, then follow Hawkshead sign, 2.5m on right, 1m up hill*

See Pick of the Pubs on opposite page

Drunken Duck Inn

In the heart of the Lake District, this traditional whitewashed Lakeland inn has been owned by the same family for three decades. They have always regarded good service, excellent food and drink, comfortable accommodation, and a friendly atmosphere as the combined holy grails of hospitality – and the tradition continues.

It stands in sixty acres of private land high above Lake Windermere, with breathtaking views of the fells. The amusing name stems from a flock of comatose ducks found by a former landlady. Thinking of her guests' stomachs, she began to pluck them for the pot, unaware that they were not dead but merely legless from drinking beer that had leaked into their feed. No such risk today – the adjoining Barngates Brewery takes good care of its award-winning real ales, which are served in the oak-floored and beamed bar, with open fire, numerous pictures, leather club chairs and beautiful Brathay Black slate bar top from the local quarry. Excellent locally sourced food is attentively served in three informal restaurant areas – two traditional, one more modern. Inventive is not a puffed up word to use for starters like twice-baked organic Kendal cheese soufflé with parmesan cream; marinated scallop ceviche with roasted pineapple and curried slaw; and crispy duck leg with rhubarb, green bean and goats' cheese salad. Nor indeed for main courses such as fillet of venison with sautéed potatoes, celeriac purée and pan juices; sea bass with sherry vinegar lentils and bacon; and caramelised Italian onion tart with roasted figs and parmesan. Desserts too are no less resourceful: melting chocolate fondant with white chocolate and apricot trifle; and honeycomb brûlée with thyme sablé and pan-roasted plums are just two. You'd expect an excellent wine list – and there is. Each of the sixteen bedrooms come complete with antique furniture, prints and designer fabrics.

★★★★★ INN

MAP 18 NY30
Barngates LA22 0NG
☎ 015394 36347
015394 36781
e-mail:
info@drunkenduckinn.co.uk
dir: *From Kendal on A591 to Ambleside, then follow Hawkshead sign. In 2.5m inn sign on right, 1m up hill*

Open 11.30–11
Bar Meals L served all week 12–2.30 6–9
Restaurant L served all week 12–2.30 D served all week 6–9
Free House
Barngates Cracker Ale, Chesters Strong & Ugly, Tag Lag, Catnap & Guest Beer. 20
Facilities Children's licence Garden Dogs allowed Parking
Notes
Rooms 16 bedrooms en suite S£75 D£100

Tufton Arms Hotel

Appleby-in-Westmorland is a medieval market town nestled in the heart of a valley so magically unspoilt that the only possible name for it is Eden. This 16th-century family-run coaching inn is something of a local landmark, renowned for its hospitality.

It's an ideal base from which to enjoy the many countryside pursuits available locally, including fell walking, fly-fishing, pony-trekking and golf. Less hearty types will also find much to engage them, including discovering the charms of this former county town of Westmorland, and touring the Lake District or Yorkshire Dales National Parks, both easily reached. The present owners, the Milsom family, have lovingly restored the Tufton Arms with rich drapes, period paintings and antique furniture. The elegant conservatory restaurant overlooks a cobbled mews courtyard; light and airy in the daytime, this room takes on an attractive glow in the evening when the lighting is low. Chef David Milsom and his kitchen team have won many accolades for their superb food: a selection of delicious dishes made from the finest and freshest local ingredients. The resulting cuisine is an appealing blend of the classical and the modern, with fresh local meat, game, fish and seafood appearing on the menu. Typical starters include smoked haddock and prawn chowder; or hot pot of wild mushroom and chorizo sausage. Move on to grilled fillets of sea bass with asparagus spears and lemon butter; pan-fried breast of pheasant with sloe gin sauce; salmon fillet with braised fennel and roast cherry vine tomatoes; or a traditional steak and kidney pie. Round off with a home-made dessert: milk chocolate cheesecake; raspberry mousse; or pannacotta with vanilla and grenadine ice cream. Twenty two en suite rooms round off the package

🍷
MAP 18 NY62
Market Square CA16 6XA
☎ 017683 51593
017683 52761
e-mail:
info@tuftonarmshotel.co.uk
dir: *In town centre*

Open 11–11 Closed: 25–26 Dec
Bar Meals L served all week 12–2 D served all week 6.30–9
Restaurant L served all week 12–2 D served all week 6.30–9 Av 3 course à la carte £27.50 Av 3 course fixed price £27.50
Free House
Tufton Arms Ale, Flower IPA, Tennants. 🍷 15
Facilities Dogs allowed Parking
Notes
Rooms 22 bedrooms en suite S£69.50 D£115 (★★★ HL)

AMBLESIDE continued

Wateredge Inn NEW ★★★★ INN

Waterhead Bay LA22 0EP

☎ 015394 32332 📠 015394 31878

e-mail: stay@wateredgeinn.co.uk

dir: *M6 junct 36, A591 to Ambleside, 5m from Windermere station*

At the most northerly tip of Lake Windermere, the inn's name sums up its idyllic position on the outskirts of Ambleside. The family-run establishment, developed from two 17th-century fishermen's cottages, has real fires to warm the body and a range of real ales to warm the heart; it also offers dedicated menus of European bottled beers and cocktails. Enjoy classic pub fare augmented by some gastro dishes, either indoors or on the lakeside terrace.

Open 10.30–11 Closed: 25–26 Dec **Bar Meals** L served all week 12–4 D served all week 5–9 Av main course £10 Free House Black Sheep, Coniston Bluebird, Colly Wobbles, Tag Lag. 13 **Facilities** Children's licence Garden Parking **Rooms** 22 bedrooms en suite

---

APPLEBY-IN-WESTMORLAND MAP 18 NY62

The Royal Oak

Bongate CA16 6UN ☎ 017683 51463 📠 017683 52300

dir: *M6 junct 38 take B6260 to Appleby-in-Westmorland*

The Royal Oak has a long and venerable history, with parts of the building dating back to 1100 and the rest to the 17th century. Today, sympathetically modernised and offering good food and ale, it comprises a classic tap-room with blackened beams, oak panelling and an open fire; a comfortable beamed lounge with a real fire and plenty of reading material.

Open 8–12 **Bar Meals** L served all week 12–2.30 D served all week 6–9 (Sat–Sun all day) Av main course £8.50 **Restaurant** L served Mon–Sun D served Mon–Sun Av 3 course à la carte £18 Free House Hawkshead, Blacksheep, Timothy Taylor. 8 **Facilities** Garden Dogs allowed Parking **Rooms** 11 bedrooms en suite S£39 D£69 (★★★★ INN)

Pick of the Pubs

Tufton Arms Hotel

Market Square CA16 6XA

☎ 017683 51593 📠 017683 52761

e-mail: info@tuftonarmshotel.co.uk

dir: *In town centre*

See Pick of the Pubs on opposite page

ARMATHWAITE MAP 18 NY54

The Dukes Head Inn ★★★ INN

Front St CA4 9PB ☎ 016974 72226

e-mail: info@dukeshead-hotel.co.uk

dir: *9m from Penrith, 10m from Carlisle between junctions 41 & 42 off M6*

Set in the pretty red sandstone village of Armathwaite, this family-run establishment is just minutes from the M6. The River Eden runs through the village and provides wonderful walks along its banks and up into the woods beyond. Originally a farm, the pub was licensed during the construction of the Settle to Carlisle railway, and offers two comfortable bars and an airy dining room. Typical dishes are hot potted Solway shrimps, and roast duckling.

Open 11.30–12 Closed: Dec 25 **Bar Meals** L served all week 12–1.45 D served all week 6.15–9 Av main course £9.50 **Restaurant** L served all week 12–1.45 D served all week 6.15–9 Av 3 course à la carte £16 Punch Taverns Jennings Cumberland Ale,Tetley's Bitter, Black Sheep Bitter, Guinness. 6 **Facilities** Garden Dogs allowed Parking **Rooms** 3 bedrooms en suite S£38.50 D£58.50

BARBON MAP 18 SD68

The Barbon Inn

LA6 2LJ ☎ 015242 76233 📠 051242 76233

e-mail: info@barbon-inn.co.uk

dir: *3.5m N of Kirkby Lonsdale on A683*

A 17th-century coaching inn with oak beams and open fires, the Barbon is situated in a quiet village between the lakes and dales. Pockmarks in a settle tell of a 19th-century shooting, and there's also a tale of a hanged highwayman. A good choice of wines and real ales is offered alongside dishes like Morecambe Bay potted shrimps and roast fillet of pork with Marsala sauce and apricot compote. Special diets are happily catered for.

Open 12–3 6.30–11 (Sun 6.30–10.30) **Bar Meals** L served all week 12–2 D served all week 6.30–9 **Restaurant** L served all week 12–2 D served all week 7–9 Av 3 course à la carte £22 Av 4 course fixed price £14.95 Free House Theakston, Barngates Westmorland Gold, Speckled Hen, York Brewery. 20 **Facilities** Garden Dogs allowed Parking

---

BASSENTHWAITE MAP 18 NY23

Pick of the Pubs

The Pheasant ★★★ HL

CA13 9YE ☎ 017687 76234 📠 017687 76002

e-mail: info@the-pheasant.co.uk

dir: *A66 to Cockermouth, 8m N of Keswick on left*

See Pick of the Pubs on page 104

The Pheasant

First a farmhouse then a coaching inn, this Lake District favourite dates back some 500 years and now enjoys international repute. Set in its own attractive gardens and woodland close to Bassenthwaite Lake, it combines the charm of a traditional Cumbrian hostelry with the appeal of a comfortable modern hotel.

Huntsman John Peel was a regular and the Cumbrian painter Edward Thompson bartered for beer in the pub, and two of his originals hang in the bar to this day. The interior is beautifully decorated, with period furnishings set against polished parquet flooring, fresh floral arrangements and blazing log fires. The mellow bar is richly inviting with panelled walls and oak settles, and stocks an extensive selection of malt whiskies and wines by the glass. Light lunches are served in the lounge or bar, including open sandwiches, potted Silloth shrimps, and pan-fried crab cakes with pickled cucumber. Or why not treat yourself to Cumbrian afternoon tea in one of the lounges, with home-made scones and rum butter. A more formal lunch and dinner menu is offered in the beamed dining room, where fine local produce is featured in dishes such as casserole of wild pheasant with shallots, winter vegetables, leek mash and red wine sauce, followed perhaps by warm apricot and frangipane flan with crème anglaise. A private dining room is available for parties of up to 12 people, and there are 15 individually decorated bedrooms with attractive fabrics and fine antique pieces. The en suite bathrooms are particularly impressive.

★★★ HL

MAP 18 NY23

CA13 9YE

017687 76234

017687 76002

e-mail: info@the-pheasant.co.uk

dir: *A66 to Cockermouth, 8m N of Keswick on left*

Open 11.30–2.30 5.30–10.30 (Sun 6–10.30) Closed: 25 Dec

Bar Meals L served all week 12–2

Restaurant L served all week 12.30–2 D served all week 7–9

Free House

Theakston Best, Interbrew Bass, Jennings Cumberland Ale. 12

Facilities Garden Dogs allowed Parking

Rooms 15 bedrooms en suite S£74 D£135

BEETHAM MAP 18 SD47

Pick of the Pubs

The Wheatsheaf at Beetham

LA7 7AL ☎ 015395 62123 015395 64840
e-mail: info@wheatsheafbeetham.com
dir: *On A6 5m N of junct 35*

This 16th-century former coaching inn, now a freehouse, stands in the village centre, close to the little River Bela. Fallow deer wander neighbouring fields and thousands of pheasants are reared locally every year. A small bar services dining areas, all with fresh flowers and candles in the evening. Well-behaved children may eat from their own menu in a small upstairs room before 7pm. As far as possible, seasonal menus use the freshest and finest local produce. Lunchtime bar meals include sandwiches and light dishes such as home-cured salmon, and mushroom and stilton pepper pot. The carte includes garlicky tomato, leek, mushroom and parmesan tart; cod and prawn fishcakes with coriander, chilli and ginger on toasted pinenut salad; and pot-roasted beef brisket with root vegetables on creamed horseradish mash. Charlie the Yellow-Headed Amazon parrot keeps youngsters amused. New owners January 2007.

Open 11.30-3 5.30-11 (Sun 12-3, 6.30-10.30) Closed: Dec 25 **Bar Meals** L served all week 12-2 D served all week 6-9 (Sun 12-2, 6.30-8.30) Av main course £8.95 **Restaurant** L served all week 12-2 D served all week 6-9 (Sun 12-2, 6.30-8.30) Av 3 course à la carte £20 Free House Jennings Cumberland Ale & Bitter, Tirrel, Brougham & Guest Ales. 10 **Facilities** Garden Parking

BLENCOGO MAP 18 NY14

The New Inn

CA7 0BZ ☎ 016973 61091 016973 61091
dir: *From Carlisle, take A596 towards Wigton, then B5302 towards Silloth. After 4m Blencogo signed on left*

This late Victorian sandstone pub has superb views of the north Cumbrian fells and Solway Plain. It is located in a farming hamlet, and the impressive menu makes good use of produce from the region – perhaps Cumbrian venison with blueberry and Drambuie sauce and wholegrain mustard mash or lamb from Dearham, chargrilled and topped with a mustard and herb crust and served with colcannon. A selection of malt whiskies is kept.

Open 7-11 (Sun 12-3, 6.30-10.30) Closed: 1st 2 wks in Jan **Bar Meals** L served 12-2 Sun D served Thu-Sun 7-9 Av main course £12 **Restaurant** L served Sun 12-2 D served Thu-Sun 7-9 Free House Yates, Carlisle State Bitter, Hesketh New Market, Black Sheep. 10 **Facilities** Garden Parking

BOOT MAP 18 NY10

Pick of the Pubs

The Boot Inn

CA19 1TG ☎ 019467 23224 019467 23337
e-mail: enquiries@bootinn.co.uk
dir: *From A595 follow signs for Eskdale then Boot*

See Pick of the Pubs on page 106

Brook House Inn ★★★★ INN

CA19 1TG ☎ 019467 23288 019467 23160
e-mail: stay@brookhouseinn.co.uk
dir: *M6 junct 36, A590 follow Barrow signs. A5092, then A595. Past Broughton-in-Furness, right at lights to Ulpha. Cross river, next left signed Eskdale, & on to Boot. (NB not all routes to Boot are suitable in bad weather conditions)*

Family-run country inn located in the heart of Eskdale with glorious views and fabulous walking country all around. Five or six real ales are kept during the summer and three in winter, along with an extensive selection of malt whiskies. Home-made food is available all day in the restaurant, bar and snug, with daytime sandwiches and salads, and main courses such as Cumberland sausage, king prawn curry and Moroccan vegetable and bean casserole.

Open 11-11 (8-12 during high season) Closed: 25 Dec **Bar Meals** L served all week 12-5.30 D served all week 5.30-8.30 Av main course £9.95 **Restaurant** L served all week 12-4.30 D served all week 6-8.30 Av 3 course à la carte £22.50 Free House Theakstons Best, Timothy Taylors Landlord, Guest ales. 8 **Facilities** Children's licence Garden Parking **Rooms** 7 bedrooms en suite S£47.50 D£70

The Boot Inn

The name is appropriate, as this award-winning traditional 16th-century inn is set in some of England's finest walking country. The Boot actually gets its name from the pretty pink granite village in which it is set, which also boasts England's oldest working watermill.

A beck wends its way through the valley, crossed by a 17th-century packhorse bridge. Scafell Pike (England's highest mountain) and Wastwater (England's deepest lake) are within rambling distance and, naturally enough, the pub attracts many cold and hungry climbers. Fortunately there's a roaring fire to warm them on cooler days, and plenty of hearty home-made Cumberland dishes to fill them up. The restaurant itself dates back to 1578, but there's also a modern conservatory and dining area with spectacular all-year-round views of the western fells. Tattie pot, a Cumbrian speciality made of local lamb, sliced potatoes and gravy, will soon get the circulation flowing again. Other wholesome dishes include fish pie; pork escalope Wienerschnitzel (a speciality of Heidi, the Austrian cook); and local sausages on a bed of buttery mash. Soups and jacket potatoes are available for those who haven't worked up such an appetite. Local produce is taken seriously here, with lamb, beef, eggs, cheese and sausages all coming from local suppliers. Fruit, salad and herbs have even less far to travel, arriving straight from the inn's own garden. The Eskdale valley was described by John Ruskin as 'the gateway to Paradise'.

MAP 18 NY10
CA19 1TG
☎ 019467 23224
🖷 019467 23337
e-mail: enquiries@bootinn.co.uk
dir: *From A595 follow signs for Eskdale then Boot*

Open 11–11
Bar Meals L served all week 11–5 D served all week 6–9 (Sun 11–5, 6–8.30 Summer all week) Av main course £8.95
Restaurant L served all week 11–5 D served all week 6–9 (Sun 6–8.30) Av 3 course à la carte £20
Hartleys
Hartleys XB, Old Stockport, Wards Best , Double Hop, Cumbria Way & Unicorn.
Facilities Garden Dogs allowed Parking Play Area

BORROWDALE MAP 18 NY21

The Langstrath Country Inn NEW 🍷

CA12 5XG ☎ 017687 77239

e-mail: info@thelangstrath.com

dir: *B5289 past Grange, through Rosthwaite, left to Stonethwaite. Inn on left after 1m*

Well over four hundred years old and originally a miner's cottage, the Langstrath today maintains the best traditions of Lake District hospitality and refreshment. It's ideally positioned for hikers, sitting as it does on the coast-to-coast and Cumbrian Way walks. The family-run inn offers a good range of real ales, an extensive wine list, and a small but perfectly formed menu that may include smoked Borrowdale trout, slow-roasted Rosthwaite Herdwick lamb, and fruit crumble.

Open 12–11 Closed: Nov–Mar, Mon–Wed **Bar Meals** L served all week 12.30–2.30 D served all week 6.30–9 Av main course £9.50 **Restaurant** D served all week 6.30–9 Av 3 course à la carte £20 Free House Jennings Bitter, Black Sheep, Doris 90th, Coniston Bluebird. 🍷 9 **Facilities** Garden Parking

BOUTH MAP 18 SD38

The White Hart Inn 🍷

LA12 8JB ☎ 01229 861229 01229 861229

e-mail: nigelwhitehart@aol.com

dir: *1.5m from A590, 10m M6 junct 36*

Bouth today reposes quietly in the Lake District National Park, although once it housed an occasionally noisy gunpowder factory. When this closed in 1928 villagers turned to woodland industries and farm labouring instead, and some of their tools now adorn this 17th-century coaching inn. Ever-changing specials are served in the upstairs restaurant that looks out over woods, fields and fells, or the horseshoe-shaped bar, with six real ales, including Cumbrian brews, 35 malts and real cider.

Open 12–2 6–11 **Bar Meals** L served Wed–Sun 12–2 D served Mon–Sun 6–8.45 **Restaurant** Lunch served 12–2 D served Wed–Sun 6–8.45 Free House Black Sheep Best, Jennings Cumberland Ale, Tetley, Yates Bitter. 🍷 7 **Facilities** Children's licence Garden Parking

Please see cycle ride on page 110

BOWLAND BRIDGE MAP 18 SD48

Pick of the Pubs

Hare & Hounds Country Inn 🍷

LA11 6NN ☎ 015395 68333 015395 68777

dir: *M6 onto A591, left after 3m onto A590, right after 3m onto A5074, after 4m sharp left & next left after 1m*

See Pick of the Pubs on page 109

BRAITHWAITE MAP 18 NY22

Coledale Inn

CA12 5TN ☎ 017687 78272 017687 78272

e-mail: info@coledale-inn.co.uk

dir: *From M6 junct 50 take A66 towards Cockermouth for 18m. Turn to Braithwaite then on towards Whinlatter Pass, follow sign on left and over bridge*

Built as a woollen mill in about 1824, this traditional pub was converted for pencil making before becoming an inn. Peacefully set above Braithwaite village, it is full of attractive Victorian prints, furnishings and antiques, with a fine cellar that includes cask-conditioned local ales. Its terrace and garden are very popular with walkers. Expect the likes of chicken breast with stilton and leek sauce, red Thai curry, and grilled Borrowdale trout finished with toasted almonds.

Open 11–11 **Bar Meals** L served all week 12–2 D served all week 6–9 **Restaurant** L served all week 12–2 D served all week 6–9 Free House Yates, Theakstons, Jennings Best, John Smiths. **Facilities** Garden Dogs allowed Parking Play Area

The Royal Oak NEW ★★★★ INN 🍷

CA12 5SY ☎ 017687 78533 017687 78533

e-mail: theroyaloak@hotmail.co.uk

dir: *Exit M6 junct 40, A66 to Keswick 20m. Bypass Keswick & Portinscale juncts, next left, pub in village centre*

In Braithwaite's village centre and surrounded by high fells, the Royal Oak is ideal for walkers. Taken over and refurbished some 15 years ago, the pub is a traditional country inn with oak beams, log fires, and walls decorated with a huge collection of book matches, bank notes and coins – enough to keep children counting for hours. The owners' strong Portuguese connection means bar snacks and main meals combine good home-grown produce with tasty European flavours.

Open 11–12 **Bar Meals** L served all week 12–2 D served all week 6–9 Av main course £9 **Restaurant** L served all week 12–2 D served all week 6–9 Av 3 course à la carte £17.50 W'hampton & Dudley Jennings Lakeland Ale, Jennings Cumberland Ale, Jennings Cocker Hoop, Jennings Sneck Lifter & Fosters. 🍷 7 **Facilities** Children's licence Garden Dogs allowed Parking **Rooms** 9 bedrooms en suite S£37 D£64

BRAMPTON MAP 21 NY56

Blacksmiths Arms ★★★★ INN

Talkin Village CA8 1LE ☎ 016977 3452 016977 3396
e-mail: blacksmithsarmstalkin@yahoo.co.uk
dir: *From M6 take A69 E, after 7m straightover rdbt, follow signs to Talkin Tarn then Talkin Village*

The original smithy, dating from 1700, remains part of this attractive village inn standing in some of northern Cumbria's most scenic countryside. The Old Forge Restaurant's evenly-balanced menu lists sweet and sour chicken; shepherds and steak and kidney pies; spinach and ricotta cannelloni; fresh fillet of haddock; tuna mayonnaise salad; and specialities such as beef stroganoff; loin of lamb; and fresh salmon steak. The eight bedrooms are all en suite.

Open 12-3 6-11 **Bar Meals** L served all week 12-2 D served all week 6-9 Av main course £7.50 **Restaurant** L served all week 12-2 D served all week 6-9 Av 3 course à la carte £15 Free House Copper Dragon, Yates, Jennings Cumberland, Hawkeshead. 20 **Facilities** Garden Parking **Rooms** 8 bedrooms en suite S£40 D£55

BROUGHTON-IN-FURNESS MAP 18 SD28

Pick of the Pubs

Blacksmiths Arms

Broughton Mills LA20 6AX ☎ 01229 716824
e-mail: blacksmithsarms@aol.com
dir: *A593 from Broughton-in-Furness towards Coniston, in 1.5m left signed Broughton Mills, pub 1m on left.*

The Blacksmiths Arms, set in a secluded Lakeland valley, dates back to 1577 and was originally a farmhouse called Broadstones. The interior is beautifully preserved, with the old farmhouse range, oak-panelled corridor, worn slate floors sourced from local quarries, and low beams. Gaslights in the dining room and bar still work when the electricity fails. The chef proprietor uses local suppliers who guarantee the quality produce, and serves beer from local micro-breweries. You will often find Herdwick lamb, which is reared in the Lickle Valley, on the menu, along with traditional steak pie in suet pastry made from local beef. Dishes might include Morecambe Bay potted shrimps; Cajun chicken salad; a choice of sandwiches or baguettes or a ploughman's at lunch. The dinner menu offers main courses like oven-baked Cumberland sausage served with creamy chive mash and red onion gravy; or deep-fried cod or haddock with Cumberland beer batter, chips and mushy peas.

Open 12-11 Closed: Dec 25 Rest: Oct-Jun, Mon- Fri, 12-2.30, 5-11, Winter closed Mon lunch **Bar Meals** L served Tue-Sun 12-2 D served Mon-Sun 6-9 Av main course £9.50 **Restaurant** L served Tue-Sun 12-2 D served Mon-Sun 6-9 Av 3 course à la carte £16.95 Free House Jennings Cumberland Ale, Dent Aviator, Barngates Tag Lag, Moorhouses Pride of Pendle. 7 **Facilities** Garden Dogs allowed Parking

BUTTERMERE MAP 18 NY11

Bridge Hotel ★★★ HL

CA13 9UZ ☎ 017687 70252 017687 70215
e-mail: enquiries@bridge-hotel.com
web: www.bridge-hotel.com
dir: *Take B5289 from Keswick*

The 18th-century former coaching inn is set between Buttermere and Crummock Water in an area of outstanding natural beauty surrounded by the Buttermere fells. There are wonderful walks right from the front door. Good food and real ales are served in the character bars (Cumbrian hot pot, jewel of lamb, traditional fish and chips), and a five-course dinner in the dining room (pan-fried calves' liver and mash, chargrilled rib-eye with pomme Anna and watercress salad).

Open 9.30-12 (all day summer) **Bar Meals** L served all week 12-6 D served all week 6-9.30 **Restaurant** L served Sun 12-2 D served all week 7-8.30 Av 5 course fixed price £29.50 Free House Theakston's Old Peculiar, Black Sheep Best, Buttermere Bitter, Boddingtons. 12 **Facilities** Children's licence Garden Parking **Rooms** 21 bedrooms en suite S£75 D£150

CALDBECK MAP 18 NY34

Oddfellows Arms

CA7 8EA ☎ 016974 78227 016974 78056

This 17th-century former coaching inn is set in a scenic conservation village in the northern fells. Popular with coast-to-coast cyclists and walkers on the Cumbrian Way, the Oddfellows serves Jennings Bitter and Cumberland Ale. Lunchtime snacks include jacket potatoes, sandwiches, or hot beef in a roll, whilst specials and vegetarian blackboards supplement the regular menu. Expect bacon chops with stilton; sirloin steaks; and local trout fillets. There's a daily curry, too.

Open 11-12 **Bar Meals** L served all week 12-2 D served all week 6-8.30 Av main course £7.50 **Restaurant** L served all week 12-2 D served all week 6.30-8.30 Av 3 course à la carte £14 Marstons Jennings Bitter, Cumberland Ale. **Facilities** Garden Dogs allowed Parking

Hare & Hounds Country Inn

This 17th-century coaching inn is set in the pretty little hamlet of Bowland Bridge, not far from Bowness. It is wonderfully located below Cartmel Fell and has the beautiful and peaceful Winster Valley almost to itself.

A traditional country pub atmosphere is fostered by the flagstone floors, exposed oak beams, ancient pews warmed by open fires, and cosy niches. The bar serves a good selection of well-kept real ales, including Jennings and Black Sheep, as well as a dozen or so wines by the glass. Food is another good reason for a visit: the bar menu offers local Cumberland sausage with egg and chips; mussels, either Thai style or marinière; toasted muffin with smoked haddock; confit of duck; and king prawns in filo pastry. The seasonal main menu could offer asparagus and saffron risotto; grilled goats' cheese and pancetta; and smoked salmon and prawn roulade as starters, followed by main courses like fillet of sea bass with crayfish tails; braised shank of lamb with honey; pork tenderloin with black pudding and mini Cumberland sausage; butternut squash, spinach and mozzarella strudel; fresh cod in batter with home-made chips; steak and ale pie; or a whole kilo of mussels. There is also a specials board with fresh fish and game always available. A safe garden with play area and swings for the children makes this pub particularly family friendly, and there are gorgeous views all round, especially of Cartmel Fell. The Hare and Hounds is only ten minutes from Lake Windermere and on the edge of the Lake District National Park. New owners Joanne and Kevin Regan have recently taken over the running of this Jennings pub.

🍷
MAP 18 SD48
LA11 6NN
☎ 015395 68333
Fax 015395 68777
dir: *M6 onto A591, left after 3m onto A590, right after 3m onto A5074, after 4m sharp left & next left after 1m*

Open 11–11
Bar Meals L served all week 12–2.30 D served all week 6–9
Restaurant L served all week 12–2.30 D served all week 6–9
Free House
Black Sheep, Jennings, Boddingtons, Marstons Pedigree.
🍷 10
Facilities Garden Parking Play Area

White Hart Inn

Cycle information

Distance: 7.75 miles/12.5km (2h)
Map: OS Explorer OL 7 The English Lakes (SE)
Start/finish: lane north of Bouth; grid ref: SD 328859
Trails/tracks: quiet lanes; rough tracks on longer ride, short challenging descents
Landscape: mix of woods and pasture, many small hills, views to higher fells
Public toilets: none on route
Tourist information: Ulverston, tel 01229 587120
Cycle hire: South Lakeland Mountain Bike Sales & Hire, Lowick Bridge, Ulverston, tel 01229 885210; Wheelbase, Staveley, tel 01539 821443
The pub: White Hart Inn, Bouth
Steep gradients on both loops. Shorter loop, suitability: children 7+. *On longer loop, off-road descents require experience and skill, or walk short sections, suitability: children 12+. Mountain bike recommended*

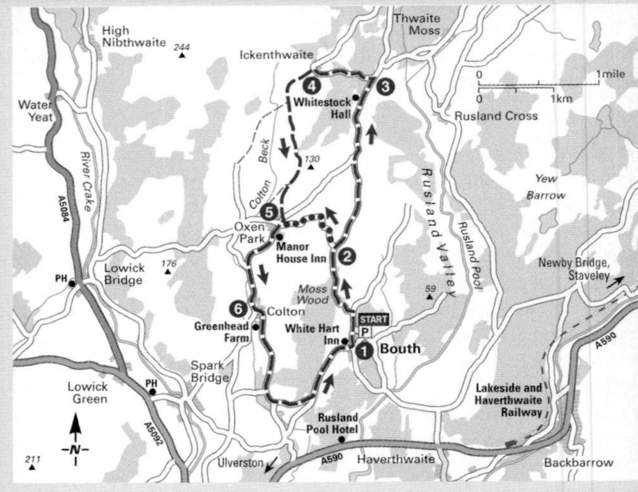

Cycle directions

1. Follow the lane north, away from Bouth. Keep left at the first junction, signed to Oxen Park. The lane twists up through woodland, with a couple of quite sharp sections of climbing, passing the entrance to Moss Wood, before levelling out. At the next junction there is a triangle of grass.

2. Keep right signposted 'Rusland: Gated Road'. Follow this lane until it drops to a ford just before a T-junction. Turn right on the wider road, signed to Grizedale, and follow it for 0.75 mile (1.2km). Shortly after passing the elegant Whitestock Hall, look for a sharp left turn, signed to Ickenthwaite.

3. This leads immediately into a very steep climb, so engage low gear in advance. The gradient eventually eases and then the woods give way to fields.

4. Just after Low Ickenthwaite turn left on to a bridleway signed to Oxen Park. The track is initially stony with a good ribbon of grass down the middle. After a second gate it becomes stonier but is still straightforward. Stay close to the wall on the left, ignoring a couple of branch tracks. The track then climbs a bit on to an open, bracken-covered area. The best riding is generally in the centre of the track as the sides are quite rough. Go through another gate, and a little more climbing leads to the crest. Keep straight ahead at another fork and the track levels off. A short steep section at the start of the descent calls for some skill. If in doubt, walk down this. Then descend more steeply to another gate. The twisting descent beyond this is steep and loose and requires great care. Again, walk down rather than risk a nasty fall. Just beyond its foot is another gate.

5. Emerge on to a road and turn right into Oxen Park. Keep straight ahead through the village. The road begins a sweeping descent into the soft green Vale of Colton.

6. Just after the Old Vicarage turn left, signposted 'Colton Church and Bouth', up a short steep climb. At the crest another sign to Colton Church and Bouth points left, up a further climb. But this is an off-road route, so continue straight on. Descend to pass Greenhead Farm, and the road is fairly level along the valley side. Keep left through two junctions. The road curves and makes a steep final drop to a T-junction (take care). Go left for an almost level run along a broader road back through Bouth.

CARTMEL MAP 18 SD37

Pick of the Pubs

The Cavendish Arms

LA11 6QA ☎ 015395 36240 015395 35082
e-mail: food@thecavendisharms.co.uk
dir: *M6 junct 36 take A590 signed for Barrow-in-Furness. In Cartmel village take 1st right*

Situated within the village walls, this 450-year-old coaching inn is Cartmel's oldest hostelry. Many traces of its long history remain, from the mounting block outside the main door to the bar itself, which used to be the stables. Oak beams, uneven floors and an open fire create a traditional, cosy atmosphere, and outside there's a tree-lined garden overlooking a stream. Lunchtime sandwiches are served on locally-baked bread with a portion of chips, while hot options include home-made soup; Morecambe Bay shrimps with herb butter; and tiger prawn piri piri. An evening meal might begin with pressed game terrine with home-made apple and pistachio chutney, followed by supreme of chicken with a goats' cheese and sun dried tomato stuffing, or braised lamb shank with orange, mint and redcurrant jus. Desserts include sticky toffee pudding and chocolate and brandy mousse.

Open 11.30–11 **Bar Meals** L served all week 12–2 D served all week 6–9 (Sun 12–9) Av main course £10.50 **Restaurant** L served all week 12–2 D served all week 6–9 (Sun 12–9) Av 3 course à la carte £18 Free House Greene King IPA, Cumberland, Bombardier, Theakstons. 8 **Facilities** Garden Dogs allowed Parking **Rooms** 10 bedrooms en suite S£45 D£60 (★★★ INN)

COCKERMOUTH MAP 18 NY13

The Trout Hotel ★★★ HL

Crown St CA13 0EJ ☎ 01900 823591 01900 827514
e-mail: enquiries@trouthotel.co.uk

Overlooking the River Derwent, the Trout's well-appointed rooms make a good base for horse riding, cycling, fell walking, climbing and fishing trips. The patio of the Terrace Bar and Bistro, with its large heated parasols, offers al fresco dining any time of the year, while the Derwent Restaurant, dominated by a classic fireplace and ornate mirrored sideboard, offers daily changing menus featuring the best local produce, such as pheasant and pigeon breast, grilled sea bass, and mushroom risotto.

Open 11–11 **Bar Meals** L served all week 9.30–9.30 D served all week Av main course £8.95 **Restaurant** L served Sat–Sun 12–2 D served all week 7–9.30 Av 3 course à la carte £28.50 Av 4 course fixed price £15.95 Free House Jennings Cumberland Ale, Theakston Bitter, John Smiths, Marston's Pedigree. 24 **Facilities** Garden Parking **Rooms** 43 bedrooms en suite S£59.95 D£109

CONISTON MAP 18 SD39

Pick of the Pubs

The Black Bull Inn & Hotel

1 Yewdale Rd LA21 8DU
☎ 015394 41335 015394 41168
e-mail: i.s.bradley@btinternet.com
dir: *From M6 junct 36 onto A590, 23m from Kendal via Windermere & Ambleside*

Originally a coaching inn, this friendly, family-run establishment nestles in the shadow of the 803m Old Man mountain, whose big toe is said to be the large stone set in the wall of the residents' lounge. It's often been a port of call for artistic types, from Coleridge and Turner to Anthony Hopkins, in these parts to film *Across the Lake*, a dramatisation of Donald Campbell's ill-fated attempt to beat the water speed record on nearby Coniston Water. Regular dishes make the most of local produce, including fresh potted shrimp; Cumbrian hotpot; and roast leg of lamb stuffed with apricot and mint. Bar snacks and children's meals are also served. Prize-winning ales from the inn's microbrewery can be savoured in the bar, along with frequently changing guest beers and ciders.

Open 11–11 (Sun 12–10.30) Closed: 25 Dec **Bar Meals** L served all week 12–9.30 D served all week 12–9.30 **Restaurant** D served all week 6–9 Free House Coniston Bluebird, Old Man Ale, Opium, Blacksmith & XB. 10 **Facilities** Children's licence Garden Dogs allowed Parking

Pick of the Pubs

Sun Hotel & 16th Century Inn

LA21 8HQ ☎ 015394 41248 015394 41219
e-mail: thesun@hotelconiston.com
dir: *From M6 junct 36, A591, beyond Kendal & Windermere, then A598 from Ambleside to Coniston. Pub signed from bridge in village*

A 16th-century inn with a 10-room hotel attached, this was Donald Campbell's base during his final water speed record attempt. Coniston Bluebird is one of the ales behind the bar, along with guest ales like Black Cat, Black Sheep Special and Speckled Hen. The menu offers seafood paella; pan-roasted pheasant with baby spinach ragout; and Hungarian goulash with dumplings. Outside is a large quiet garden with benches, and the conservatory offers exceptional views that can be enjoyed whatever the weather.

Open 12–11 **Bar Meals** L served all week 12–2.30 D served all week 6–9 Av main course £13.50 **Restaurant** L served all week 12–2.30 D served all week 6–9 Av 3 course à la carte £23 Coniston Bluebird, Hawkshead, Speckled Hen & 3 Guest beers. 7 **Facilities** Children's licence Garden Dogs allowed Parking Play Area **Rooms** 10 bedrooms 9 en suite S£40 D£80 (★★ HL)

CROOK MAP 18 SD49

The Sun Inn 🍷

LA8 8LA ☎ 01539 821351 📠 01539 821351

dir: *Off B5284*

A welcoming inn which has grown from a row of cottages built in 1711, when beer was served to travellers from a front room. The same pleasure is dispensed today by the winter fires or on the summer terrace. The bar and regular menus feature Cumbrian fell-bred meats and fresh seasonal produce. Choices are supplemented by daily specials such as marinated fresh sardines with olives and feta, and grilled halibut steak with pesto and roasted vegetables.

Open 12-2.30 6-11 (Sat 12-11, Sun 11.30-10.30) **Bar Meals** L served all week 12-2.15 D served all week 6-8.45 (Sat all day, Sun 12-8) **Restaurant** L served all week 12-2.30 D served all week 6-9 (Sun 12-8) Av 3 course à la carte £18 Theakston, Scottish Courage John Smith's, Courage Directors, Coniston Bluebird. 🍷 14 **Facilities** Garden Dogs allowed Parking

CROSTHWAITE MAP 18 SD49

Pick of the Pubs

The Punch Bowl Inn ★★★★★ INN

LA8 8HR ☎ 015395 68237 📠 015395 68875

e-mail: info@the-punchbowl.co.uk

dir: *From M6 junct 36 take A590 towards Barrow, then A5074 & follow signs for Crosthwaite. Pub next to church on left*

See Pick of the Pubs on opposite page

ELTERWATER MAP 18 NY30

Pick of the Pubs

The Britannia Inn

LA22 9HP ☎ 015394 37210 📠 015394 37311

e-mail: info@britinn.co.uk

dir: *From Ambleside take A593 3m, turn right at Skelwith Bridge onto B5343. After 2m turn left into Elterwater village. Inn in village centre*

See Pick of the Pubs on page 114

ENNERDALE BRIDGE MAP 18 NY01

Pick of the Pubs

The Shepherd's Arms Hotel

CA23 3AR ☎ 01946 861249 📠 01946 861249

e-mail: shepherdsarms@btconnect.com

dir: *A66 to Cockermouth 25m, A5086 to Egremont 5m then follow sign to Ennerdale.*

Located on one of the most beautiful stretches of Wainwright's Coast to Coast footpath, this informal free house is a favourite with walkers. Bike hire and pony trekking can also be arranged for an enjoyable alternative day out. Shepherd's Arms own brew heads a list of beers that includes Jennings Bitter and a regular guest ale; during colder months, welcoming open fires warm the bar, which is a venue for local musicians. A nicely varied menu is served throughout, with plenty of choice for vegetarians, as well as daily specials and à la carte options in the dining room. Dinner might begin with fresh home-made soup, or deep-fried brie with a hot redcurrant sauce, before moving on to nut and mushroom fettuccine; breaded haddock with lemon; or local sirloin steak with brandy and black pepper sauce. After finishing, perhaps, with raspberry meringue, diners can relax in the comfortable lounge.

Open 11-2 6-11 (Fri & Sat 6-12am, Apr-Oct open all day) **Bar Meals** L served all week 12.15-1.45 D served all week 6.15-8.45 Av main course £7.50 **Restaurant** D served all week 6.30-8 Av 3 course fixed price £17.50 Free House Jennings Bitter, Cumberland & Guests **Facilities** Garden Dogs allowed Parking

The Punch Bowl Inn

Not only is the Punch Bowl a bar, restaurant and hotel, it also serves as the village post office, with reception manager Linsey doubling her duties as Crosthwaite's post mistress. Set in the unspoilt Lyth Valley, the inn is going great guns.

The slate-floored bar, with its open fires, original beams and low ceilings, is the perfect spot to enjoy a pint of Tag Lag, brewed with fell water by the nearby Barngates Brewery. Leather chairs, gleaming wooden floors and a beautiful pale stone fireplace make for an elegant dining room. When it comes to the food, local and seasonal are the watchwords. The menu, which is available in both bar and restaurant, lists an extraordinary range of suppliers, many of them organic. Start with baked Cumbrian cheddar cheese and spring onion soufflé with wilted spinach and parmesan cream; or naturally smoked haddock, herb risotto and poached egg. Main courses might include herb-crusted rack of lamb with a cassoulet of summer beans and rosemary; slow-cooked shin of beef with wild mushroom gratin and red wine jus; or for fish lovers, perhaps pan-seared seabass with crab and chilli mash and petit pois à la Francaise. The puddings are straightforward but alluring: poached rhubarb and pannacotta, for example, or ginger crème brûlée with toffee-grilled figs and shortbread. Each of the nine stylish bedrooms boasts flat-screen TV, Roberts Revival radios and a freestanding roll top bath. The pub is affiliated to the Drunken Duck in Ambleside, where the Barngates Brewery is located.

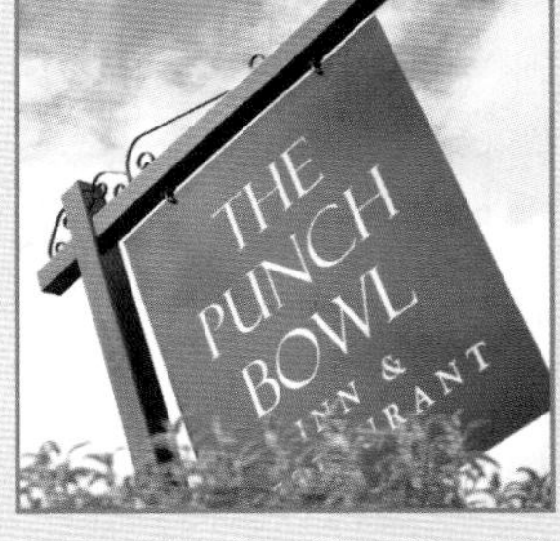

★★★★★ INN
MAP 18 SD49
LA8 8HR
☎ 015395 68237
015395 68875
e-mail:
info@the-punchbowl.co.uk
dir: *From M6 junct 36 take A590 towards Barrow, then A5074 & follow signs for Crosthwaite. Pub next to church on left.*

Open 12–11
Bar Meals L served all week 12–6 D served all week 6–9
Av main course £13.50
Restaurant L served all week 12–2.30 D served all week 7–8.45
Av 3 course à la carte £30
Free House
Tag Lag, Cat Nap & Erdinger.
21
Facilities Garden Dogs allowed Parking
Rooms 9 bedrooms en suite D£110

The Britannia Inn

Situated in the very heart of Beatrix Potter country, The Britannia Inn is sure to see an even greater influx of tourists this summer after the film* Miss Potter *starring Renée Zellweger showcased a neighbouring hill! Built over 400 years ago, this is the quintessential Lakeland inn.

It's set in the centre of the picturesque village of Elterwater, overlooking the village green beneath the dramatic fells of the Langdale valley. Footpaths lead away in all directions from the door, and Grasmere, Ambleside and Lake Windmere are all in easy reach for those who fancy a ramble. The Britannia really comes to life in summer when colourful hanging baskets dazzle the eye and the garden fills up with customers (and occasionally Morris dancers). In colder weather, the thick stone walls, log fires and beamed ceilings come into their own, and at any time the inn offers a big selection of real ales and a wide choice of fresh home-cooked food. There is something on the menu to please everyone, from popular favourites to the more unusual with an emphasis on local produce and Lakeland specialities. Informal bar lunches might take in Cumberland sausage and mash, or home-made steak and ale pie – just the thing after a morning admiring Wordsworth's daffodils. In the evening, start with oak-smoked salmon and prawn platter perhaps, followed by local fillets of trout, or red pesto and sweet pepper tart. Fresh daily specials might include pan-seared scallops with balsamic dressing; roast breast of Gressingham duck with black pudding, leeks and wild mushroom sauce; and pea and shallot risotto with parmesan shavings.

MAP 18 NY30
LA22 9HP
☎ 015394 37210
Fax 015394 37311
e-mail: info@britinn.co.uk
dir: *From Ambleside take A593, 3m, turn right at Skelwith Bridge onto B5343. After 2m turn left into Elterwater village. Inn in village centre*

Open 9–11 (25–26 Dec 10–4)
Bar Meals L served all week 12–2 D served all week 6.30–9.30 Av main course £12
Restaurant L served all week 12–2 D served all week 6.30–9.30 (Snacks 2–5.30) Av 3 course à la carte £25
Free House
Jennings Bitter, Coniston Bluebird, Timothy Taylor Landlord, Harviestoun's Bitter & Twisted Isle of Skye's Coruisk.
Facilities Children's licence Garden Dogs allowed Parking

England

ESKDALE GREEN MAP 18 NY10

Pick of the Pubs

Bower House Inn ★★ HL

CA19 1TD ☎ 019467 23244 019467 23308
e-mail: info@bowerhouseinn.freeserve.co.uk
dir: *4m off A595, 0.5m W of Eskdale Green*

This fine 17th-century stone-built former farmhouse surrounded by gardens and next to the village cricket pitch, overlooks Muncaster Fell in a scenic and unspoilt part of Cumbria. The Bower House's traditional appeal is irresistible: the oak beamed bar, warm fires and warren of rooms welcome locals and visitors alike, and the charming candlelit restaurant offers a varied selection of hearty, imaginative dishes. At dinner you could try a starter of Morecambe Bay shrimps with dressed leaves and chutney, followed perhaps by a game dish like a trio of game birds with a redcurrant and mushroom jus. Fish dishes are equally tempting with the likes of Russian fish pie with eggs, capers and a puff pastry top. The inn has lovely rooms serving the leisure and business customer. There is a conference room and various breaks, including some with a golfing theme, are offered during the year.

Open 11–2.30 6–11 **Bar Meals** L served all week 12.30–2.30 D served all week 6–9 Av main course £9.95 **Restaurant** D served all week 7–9 Av 3 course à la carte £23 Av 4 course fixed price £20 Free House Theakston Bitter, Jennings Bitter, Coniston Blue Bird, Hawkshead Bitter & Dent Ales. **Facilities** Garden Dogs allowed Parking **Rooms** 28 bedrooms en suite S£45 D£56

Please see walk on page 116

King George IV Inn

CA19 1TS ☎ 019467 23262 019467 23334
e-mail: info@kinggeorge-eskdale.co.uk
dir: *A590 to Greenodd, A5092 to Broughton-in-Furness then over Ulpha Fell towards Eskdale*

What we see today is a 17th-century coaching inn, although Roman origins are likely. It lies in one of Lakeland's finest hidden valleys, close to the narrow gauge Ravenglass & Eskdale steam railway, known affectionately as La'al Ratty. Inside are open fires, oak beams, low ceilings, flagged floors and antiques. Dishes include home-made steak and ale, curry, pan-fried liver and onions, ostrich fillet, and salmon in Martini, orange and ginger sauce. Vegetarian dishes and a children's menus, pizzas and sandwiches also served.

Open 11–11 **Bar Meals** L served all week 12–8.30 D served all week 12–8.30 **Restaurant** L served all week 12–2 D served all week 6–9 Free House Coniston Bluebird, Black Sheep Special, Jennings Cumberland Ales, Jennings Sneck Lifter & changing Cask Ales. **Facilities** Garden Dogs allowed Parking

GARRIGILL MAP 18 NY74

The George & Dragon Inn 🍷

CA9 3DS ☎ 01434 381293 01434 382839
e-mail: info@garrigill-pub.co.uk

Once serving the local zinc and lead mining communities, this 17th-century coaching inn is popular with walkers who enjoy log fires that stave off that brisk North Pennine weather. Look on the menu to find local Cumberland sausage, steak and ale pie, gammon steak, battered cod or Whitby scampi. There are plenty of Yorkshire puddings, jacket potatoes or sandwiches for a lighter meal.

Open 12–11 (Tue 5–11, Fri–Sat 12–12, Sun 12–10.30 Winter: Mon–Wed 5–11, Thu 12–2, 5–11) **Bar Meals** L served all week 12–2 D served all week 7–8.45 Av main course £6.95 **Restaurant** L served all week 12–2 D served all week 6–8.45 Free House Black Sheep Bitter, Bombardier, Guest ales. 🍷 9 **Facilities** Children's licence Dogs allowed

GOSFORTH MAP 18 NY00

The Globe Hotel

CA20 1AL ☎ 01946 725235
e-mail: gosglobel@aol.com
dir: *On A595, 15m S of Whitehaven*

Over a pint of Jennings Bitter in this friendly, traditionally furnished village pub, contemplate a walk round the shores of nearby Wast Water, England's deepest lake. Or, better still, walk first and get back here in time for that pint to accompany home-made fellman's steak, mushroom and brown ale pie with shortcrust pastry; grilled Cumberland sausages with pickled red cabbage and rich onion gravy; or deep-fried Whitby scampi with salad, chips and peas.

Open 12 –11 **Bar Meals** L served Tue–Sun 12–2 D served Tue–Sun 6–9 Av main course £7 **Restaurant** L served Tue–Sun 12–2 D served Tue–Sun 6–9 Av 3 course à la carte £13 T&P Inns Jennings Bitter, John Smiths Smooth, Stella, Cumberland Ale & Fosters. **Facilities** Children's licence Garden Dogs allowed

Bower House Inn

Walk information

Distance: 8 miles (12.8km)
Map: OS Explorer OL 6 The English Lakes (SW)
Start/finish: car park at Ravenglass, close to station; grid ref SD 085964; Eskdale Green, grid ref SD 145998
Ascent/gradient: 3
Paths: clear tracks and paths (muddy after rain); 1 stile
Landscape: woodlands, moderately rugged fell, gentle valley

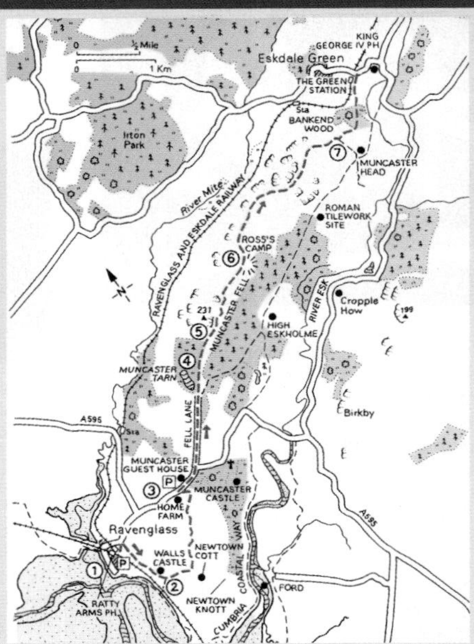

Walk directions

A Leave Ravenglass by crossing the mainline and miniature railway line on the footbridges, then follow a narrow path to a road junction. Turn right along a narrow road signposted 'Walls Castle'. The bathhouse is soon found on the left.

B Continue along the access road and turn left along a track signposted 'Newtown Cottage'. Turn left again before the cottage and follow another track up a little wooded valley. Go through four gates, following the track from the wood, across fields and into another wood. Turn left to reach Home Farm and a busy main road.

C Cross the road and turn right, passing Muncaster Castle car park and the Muncaster Guest House. The road leads up to a bend, where Fell Lane is signposted straight uphill. Follow the clear track uphill, cross a little wooded dip, then fork right and left, noticing Muncaster Tarn on the left. Go through a gate at the top of the lane to reach Muncaster Fell.

D A path forges through boggy patches and bracken along the edge of a coniferous plantation, then runs free across the rugged slopes of Muncaster Fell. A path rising to the left leads to the summit of the fell, otherwise keep right to continue.

E Views develop as the path winds about on the slope overlooking Eskdale. A panorama of fells opens up as a curious structure is reached at Ross's Camp. Here, a large stone slab was turned into a picnic table for a shooting party in 1883.

F Continue along the footpath, looping round a broad and boggy area to reach a corner of a dry stone wall. Go down through a gateway – take care, the path can be wet and muddy. There is a short ascent on a well-buttressed stretch, then the descent continues on a sparsely wooded slope, through a gate, ending on a track near another gate.

G Go through the gate and turn left, crossing a field to reach a stone wall seen at the edge of Bankend Wood. Keep to the right side of the wall to reach a stile and a stream. A narrow track continues, becoming better as it draws close to a road. Turn left at the end to reach the Green Station. Follow the road for 1 mile (1.6km) to the Bower House Inn.

While there

Don't forget to explore the little village of Ravenglass. It's essentially a fishing village at the confluence of the rivers Irt, Mite and Esk. Apart from being a Roman port, by 1280 it once had charters for a weekly market and annual fair. As trade diminished (eclipsed by the port of Whitehaven) it became a centre for rum smuggling.

Look for

The Ravenglass estuary is a haunt of wildfowl and waders. Oystercatchers and curlews probe the mudflats and there are sometimes raucous flocks of gulls. On Muncaster Fell there may be grouse in the heather and it's usual to notice buzzards circling overhead.

GRASMERE MAP 18 NY30

The Travellers Rest Inn

Keswick Rd LA22 9RR ☎ 015394 35604 📠 017687 72309
e-mail: stay@lakedistrictinns.co.uk
dir: *From M6 take A591 to Grasmere, pub 0.5m N of Grasmere*

Located on the edge of picturesque Grasmere and handy for touring and exploring the ever-beautiful Lake District, the Travellers Rest has been a pub for more than 500 years. Inside a roaring log fire complements the welcoming atmosphere of the beamed and inglenooked bar area. An extensive menu of traditional home-cooked fare is offered, ranging from Westmorland terrine and eggs Benedict, to wild mushroom gratin and rump of Lakeland lamb.

Open 12–11 (Sun 12–10.30) **Bar Meals** L served all week 12–3 D served all week 6–9.30 (Mar–Oct, 12–9.30) Av main course £9.95 **Restaurant** L served all week 12–3 D served all week 6–9.30 (Mar–Oct, 12–9.30) Av 3 course à la carte £15 Free House Jennings Bitter, Cumberland Ale, & Sneck Lifter, Jennings Cocker Hoop. 10 **Facilities** Garden Dogs allowed Parking **Rooms** 8 bedrooms 7 en suite D£50 (★★★ INN)

GREAT LANGDALE MAP 18 NY20

The New Dungeon Ghyll Hotel ★★ HL

LA22 9JY ☎ 015394 37213 📠 015394 37666
e-mail: enquiries@dungeon-ghyll.com
dir: *From M6 into Kendal then A591 into Ambleside onto A593 to B5343, hotel 6m on right*

Traditional Cumberland stone hotel dating back to medieval times, and full of character and charm. The hotel stands in its own lawned grounds in a spectacular position beneath the Langdale Pikes and Pavey Ark. Local specialities, expertly cooked, are served in the smart dining room. A sample dinner menu offers pan-fried venison in port wine, steak on haggis mash, chargrilled salmon fillet on asparagus spears, roasted vegetable risotto, whole baked rainbow trout, and crispy local lamb with mint and rosemary.

Open 11–11 (Sun 11–10.30) **Bar Meals** L served all week D served all week **Restaurant** D served all week 6.30–8.30 Av 3 course à la carte £25 Free House Thwaites Bitter, Thwaites Smooth, Thwaites Thoroughbred. 7 **Facilities** Garden Dogs allowed Parking **Rooms** 20 bedrooms en suite D£45

GREAT SALKELD MAP 18 NY53

Pick of the Pubs

The Highland Drove Inn and Kyloes Restaurant

CA11 9NA ☎ 01768 898349 📠 01768 898708
e-mail: highlanddroveinn@btinternet.com
dir: *Exit M6 junct 40, take A66 E then A686 to Alston. After 4m, left onto B6412 for Great Salkeld & Lazonby*

A 300-year-old country inn deep in the lovely Eden Valley, on one of the old drove roads from Scotland into England. Father and son team Donald and Paul Newton have turned it into the area's social hub by maintaining their well-deserved reputation for high quality food. Traditional local dishes usually feature, alongside daily specials reflecting the availability of local game and fish, and meat from herds reared and matured in Cumbria. On most days you're likely to find sea bass, brill or wild salmon sharing the menu with innovative chicken dishes, succulent steaks, and even mallard. Typical meals might be rabbit and bacon pie baked in a double crust with cider and cream; honeyed duck breast with black pudding; pan-fried plaice fillet with spiced melon and lime butter; vegetarian meze of Mediterranean appertizers; then pannacotta and stewed rhubarb. The area's many attractions include Hadrian's Wall.

Open 12-3 6–11 (Sat 12–11) **Bar Meals** L served Tue–Sun 12–2 D served all week 6.30–9 (Sun 12–2, 6–8.30) Av main course £11.45 **Restaurant** L served Tue–Sun 12–2 D served all week 6.30–9 (Sun 6.30–8.30) Av 3 course à la carte £22.50 Free House Theakston Black Bull, John Smiths Cask, John Smiths Smooth, Theakstons Best. 14 **Facilities** Children's licence Garden Dogs allowed Parking

HAWKSHEAD MAP 18 SD39

Kings Arms ★★★ INN

The Square LA22 0NZ ☎ 015394 36372 📠 015394 36006
e-mail: info@kingsarmshawkshead.co.uk
dir: *Exit M6 junct 36, follow A590 to Newby Bridge, right at 1st junct past rdbt, over bridge follow road for 8m to Hawkshead*

This 500-year-old oak-beamed inn, which presides over the main square of Hawkshead, would have been a familiar sight to William Wordsworth and Beatrix Potter alike. Mulled wine and local damson gin supplement the range of ales, whilst the lunchtime menu features an attractive selection of soups, sandwiches and hot meals. Dinner

CONTINUED

HAWKSHEAD continued

options include roast guinea fowl wrapped in Cumbrian pancetta; and, more unusually, kangaroo steak with sweet potato game chips.

Open 10–12 Rest: 25 Dec Closed eve **Bar Meals** L served all week 12–2.30 D served all week 6–9.30 Av main course £7.50 **Restaurant** L served all week 12–2.30 D served all week 6–9.30 Free House Carlsberg-Tetley Bitter, Black Sheep Best, Hawkeshead Gold, Hawkshead Bitter. **Facilities** Children's licence Garden Dogs allowed **Rooms** 9 bedrooms en suite S£37 D£64

Pick of the Pubs

Queens Head Hotel ★★ HL

Main St LA22 0NS ☎ 015394 36271 015394 36722
e-mail: enquiries@queensheadhotel.co.uk
dir: *M6 junct 36, A590 to Newby Bridge, 1st right, 8m to Hawkshead*

The Queens Head is an Elizabethan pub located in the centre of Hawkshead village, where William Wordsworth was schooled and Beatrix Potter created Peter Rabbit. Traditional features include low oak-beamed ceilings, wood-panelled walls, an original slate floor and a welcoming fire. The atmosphere within reflects the relaxed style of the village, with guests mixing effortlessly with locals. An extensive wine list and a selection of real ales is offered, along with a full carte menu with an ever changing specials board. Dishes draw from the wealth of quality produce on the doorstep: trout from Esthwaite Water, pheasant from Graythwaite, traditionally cured hams and Cumberland sausage from Waberthwaite, and slow-maturing Herdwick lamb. Dishes include game terrine wrapped in Cumbrian air dried ham; and fillet of sea bass with buerre noisette garnished with watercress. There is a good choice of light bites at lunchtime, including bruschetta and croque monsieur.

Open 11–12 **Bar Meals** L served all week 12–2.30 D served all week 6.15–9.30 (Sun 12–5, 6.15–9.30) Av main course £13.50 **Restaurant** L served all week 12–2.30 D served all week 6.15–9.30 (Sun 12–5, 6.15–9.30) Av 3 course à la carte £23.50 Frederic Robinson Robinsons Unicorn, Hartleys Cumbria Way, Double Hop. 11 **Facilities** Children's licence Garden **Rooms** 12 bedrooms en suite S£55 D£75

The Sun Inn ★★★ INN

Main St LA22 0NT ☎ 015394 36213 015394 36747
e-mail: rooms@suninn.co.uk
dir: *N on M6 junct 36, take A591 to Ambleside, then B5286 to Hawkshead. S on M6 junct 40, take A66 to Keswick, A591 to Ambleside, then B5286 to Hawkshead*

The Sun is a listed 17th-century coaching inn at the heart of the charming village where Wordsworth went to school. Inside are two resident ghosts – a giggling girl and a drunken landlord – and outside is a paved terrace with seating. Hill walkers and others will enjoy the log fires, real ales and locally-sourced food.

Open 11am–12am **Bar Meals** L served all week 12–2.30 D served Mon–Fri 6.15–9.30 (Sat–Sun all day) Av main course £9 **Restaurant** D served all week 6.30–9.30 Free House Jennings, Taylors Landlord, Hawkshead Bitter, Cocker Hoop. plus two guest ales. **Facilities** Children's licence Garden **Rooms** 8 bedrooms en suite S£40 D£50

HESKET NEWMARKET MAP 18 NY33

The Old Crown

CA7 8JG ☎ 016974 78288
e-mail: louhogg@daisybroadband.co.uk
dir: *From M6 take B5305, left after 6m towards Hesket Newmarket*

Both the pub and its associated micro-brewery are owned by co-operatives of local people and other supporters, so regulars know that their favourite pints will always be waiting for them. Aside from the real ales, there are seven Indian curries to choose from, including chicken korma, lamb Madras, and pork in a rich lentil sauce. Other meals include wild mushroom strudel with brandy sauce; Doris's steak and ale pie; and ham, egg and chips.

Open 12–3 5.30–11 **Bar Meals** L served Wed–Sun 12–2 D served Wed–Sun **Restaurant** L served Wed–Sun 12–2 D served Wed–Sat 6.30–8.30 Free House Doris, Skiddaw, Blencathra, Helvellyn Gold. **Facilities** Garden Dogs allowed

HEVERSHAM MAP 18 SD48

Blue Bell Hotel

Princes Way LA7 7EE ☎ 015395 62018 015395 62455
e-mail: stay@bluebellhotel.co.uk
dir: *On A6 between Kendal & Milnthorpe*

Originally a vicarage for the old village, this hotel dates back as far as 1460. Heversham is an ideal base for touring the scenic Lake District and Yorkshire Dales, but pleasant country scenery can also be viewed from the hotel's well-equipped bedrooms. The charming lounge bar, with its old beams, is the perfect place to relax with a drink or enjoy one of the meals available on the menu, including potted shrimps, sirloin steak, Cumbrian game pie and Isle of Man crab.

Open 11–11 **Bar Meals** L served all week 12–9 D served all week 6–8.30 (Sat 12–3, 6–9) Av main course £7.95 **Restaurant** L served all week 11–9 D served all week 7–9 (Sun 11–8) Av 3 course à la carte £15 Samuel Smith Samuel Smith Old Brewery Bitter. **Facilities** Garden Dogs allowed Parking

KENDAL MAP 18 SD59

Gateway Inn 🍷

Crook Rd LA8 8LX ☎ 01539 724187 📠 01539 720581

dir: *From M6 junct 36 take A590/A591, follow signs for Windermere, pub on left after 9m*

Located within the Lake District National Park, this Victorian country inn offers delightful views, attractive gardens and welcoming log fires. A good range of appetising dishes includes chicken casserole with red wine and herb dumplings, grilled fillets of sea bass with ratatouille and mussels, and roasted butternut squash filled with leeks and stilton. Traditional English favourites of liver and onions or rabbit pie are also a feature.

Open 11–11 **Bar Meals** L served all week D served all week Av main course £9 Thwaites Thwaites Bitter, Thwaites Smooth & Cask Ales. 🍷 11 **Facilities** Garden Dogs allowed Parking Play Area

Gilpin Bridge Inn ★★★ INN

Bridge End, Levens LA8 8EP

☎ 015395 52206 📠 015395 52444

e-mail: info@gilpinbridgeinn.co.uk

dir: *M6 junct 36, follow A590 towards Barrow*

Good food is the chief attraction at this popular pub which takes its name from a Norman knight who resided here after fighting the crusades. An extensive menu and a selection of daily specials are available in the lounge or restaurant, ranging from Bo-peep pie – tender pieces of lamb braised in a root vegetable and rosemary sauce under a golden pastry cover, to grilled lamb cutlets, bubbling hot lasagne, and grilled Dover sole.

Open 11.30–2.30 5.30–11 (Open all day Summer, BHs) **Bar Meals** L served all week 11.30–2 D served all week 5.30–9 (Sun 12–9) Av main course £9 **Restaurant** L served all week 11.30–2 D served all week 5.30–9 (Sun 12–9) Av 3 course à la carte £15.50 Frederic Robinson Unicorn, Cumbria Way, Hartleys XB & Guest ales. **Facilities** Children's licence Garden Dogs allowed Parking Play Area **Rooms** 10 bedrooms en suite S£45 D£65

KESWICK MAP 18 NY22

The Farmers

Portinscale CA12 5RN ☎ 01768 773442

dir: *Exit M6 junct 40 (Penrith) onto A66, pass Keswick B5289 junct, turn left to Portinscale*

Revitalised as one of Keswick's foremost food-led pubs, everything from stocks, soups and breads to the after-dinner mints is freshly prepared. A typical starter might be mushroom risotto with charred asparagus and parmesan crisps, followed by roast chicken thighs stuffed with haggis on bubble and squeak, or a more traditional combination like grilled lemon sole with lemon and coriander butter.

Open 12–11 **Bar Meals** L served all week 12–2 D served all week 6–9 Av main course £8.50 **Restaurant** L served all week 12–2 D served all week 6–9 Av 3 course à la carte £17.50 T&P Inns Jennings Bitter, Jennings Cumberland Ale, Jennings Cumberland Cream. **Facilities** Children's licence Garden

Pick of the Pubs

The Horse & Farrier Inn 🍷

Threlkeld Village CA12 4SQ

☎ 017687 79688 📠 017687 79823

e-mail: info@horseandfarrier.com

web: www.horseandfarrier.com

dir: *M6 junct 40 follow Keswick (A66) signs, after 12m, turn right signed Threlkeld. Pub in village centre*

See Pick of the Pubs on page 120

Pick of the Pubs

The Kings Head 🍷

Thirlspot CA12 4TN ☎ 017687 72393 📠 017687 72309

e-mail: stay@lakedistrictinns.co.uk

dir: *From M6 take A66 to Keswick then A591, pub 4m S of Keswick*

The view surrounding this 17th-century former coaching inn is truly sublime. On warm days and in summer, the garden is the best place to enjoy a meal or drink. Inside, old beams and inglenook fireplaces are traditional features of the bar, while a separate games room offers pool, snooker and darts. Popular real ales include beers from Theakstons, the Jennings brewery in nearby Cockermouth, and there is a fine selection of wines and malt whiskies. In the elegant restaurant try choosing between spicy citrus-crusted pork roast; stuffed roast poussin; and oven-baked sea bass, which might be preceded by filo wrapped prawns, or mushroom and thyme soup, and followed by home-made lemon and lime tartlet. On the bar menu you'll find Cumberland chargrill, beef stroganoff, wild mushroom gratin, Borrowdale trout stuffed with prawns, and Waberthwaite sausages, and there are sandwiches, cold platters and salads.

Open 12–11 (Sun 12–10.30) **Bar Meals** L served all week 12–3 D served all week 6–9.30 Av main course £9.95 **Restaurant** L served all week 12–3 D served all week 7–9 Av 3 course à la carte £15 Av 4 course fixed price £20 Free House Scottish Courage Theakston Best Bitter & Old Peculier, Jennings Bitter, Bluebird Bitter, Greene King Abbot Ale. 🍷 10 **Facilities** Garden Dogs allowed Parking

The Horse & Farrier Inn

Within its thick, whitewashed stone walls are all the essential features of an inn built over 300 years ago – slate-flagged floors, beamed ceilings, open fires – and that's just for starters. It stands in the picturesque village of Threlkeld, at the foot of 868-metre Blencathra, with views of the even higher Skiddaw in the west and Helvellyn to the south.

Fell walkers like to make the most of this lovely setting with a beer in the garden – a case of up hill and down ale, perhaps. Hunting prints decorate the traditional-style bars, warmed in winter by crackling log fires. The inn has an excellent reputation for good food in these parts, from hearty Lakeland breakfasts to home-cooked lunches and dinners served in either the bar, or the charming period restaurant. Making full use of local, seasonal produce, the chefs beaver away in their gleaming kitchen preparing the wide range of menu choices. At lunch there are open sandwiches, baguettes and salads, as well as more substantial pan-fried 10oz steaks; poached smoked haddock; and spinach and ricotta cannelloni. The bar menu offers deep-fried breaded Whitby scampi; Mediterranean vegetable lasagne, and plenty more. At dinner, start with roasted fennel risotto; warm oriental duck leg confit; or duck liver and brandy paté. Then, should your eyes fail to alight on the house speciality of lamb shoulder, where the meat is slowly braised in Jennings Cumberland ale, maybe they'll settle instead on seared yellow fin tuna steak in olive oil and fresh lime marinade; pan-roasted maize-fed chicken supreme with herb risotto; or warm red onion and cherry tomato tartlet. Typical desserts include chocolate pudding with chocolate sauce and ice cream; and American style vanilla cheesecake. The wine list ranges far and wide. Nine well-appointed guest rooms all have super views.

MAP 18 NY22
Threlkeld Village CA12 4SQ
☎ 017687 79688
Fax 017687 79823
e-mail: info@horseandfarrier.com
web: www.horseandfarrier.com
dir: *M6 junct 40 follow Keswick (A66) signs, after 12m, turn right signed Threlkeld. Pub in village centre*

Open 8am–12am
Bar Meals L served all week 12–2 D served all week 6–9 (Sat & Sun all day. Summer all day every day) Av main course £8
Restaurant L served all week 12–2 D served all week 6–9 (Sat & Sun all day. Summer all day every day) Av 3 course à la carte £20
Jennings
Jennings Bitter, Cocker Hoop, Sneck Lifter, Cumberland Ale & Guest Ale. 9
Facilities Children's licence Garden Dogs allowed Parking
Rooms 9 bedrooms en suite S£35 D£70 (★★★★ INN)

KESWICK continued

The Swinside Inn

Newlands Valley CA12 5UE ☎ 017687 78253
e-mail: info@theswinsideinn.com
dir: *1m from A66, signed for Newlands/Swinside*

Situated in the quiet Newlands Valley, the Swinside Inn is a listed building dating back to about 1642. From the pub there are superb views of Causey Pike and Cat Bells – among other landmarks. Nearby is the market town of Keswick, a good base for visiting the area's many attractions. Inside are two bars, traditional open fires and oak-beamed ceilings. From Easter to late October food is now served all day. Extensive bar menu may offer lamb Henry, Cumberland sausage, Swinside chicken, and fresh, grilled Borrowdale trout. Friday fish night specials.

Open 11–11 **Bar Meals** L served all week 12–2 D served all week 6–8.45 Av main course £8 **Restaurant** L served all week 12–2 D served all week 6–8.45 Scottish & Newcastle Jennings Cumberland Ale, Scottish Courage, John Smith's Smooth, Deuchars. **Facilities** Garden Dogs allowed Parking

KIRKBY LONSDALE MAP 18 SD67

Pick of the Pubs

The Pheasant Inn

Casterton LA6 2RX ☎ 01524 271230 01524 274267
e-mail: pheasantinn@fsbdial.co.uk
dir: *From M6 junct 36, A65 for 7m, left onto A683 at Devils Bridge, 1m to Casterton village centre*

This whitewashed 18th-century inn is run by Annette, Ian and William Dixon. In the welcoming oak-beamed bar, with its wood-burning fireplace, you'll find a choice of real ales and wines by the glass, while meals are served in the oak-panelled restaurant, where the menu offers mostly traditional English fare. Typical main courses are roast crispy duckling with sage and onion stuffing and apple sauce; breaded scampi; tournedos Rossini with Madeira sauce; halibut steak cooked in dairy butter; seafood mixed grill; and, for vegetarians, cannelloni stuffed with finely chopped button mushrooms, asparagus spears and parsley cream sauce. There is also a daily changing selection of specials that makes the most of the markets and the seasons. In fine weather you can sit outside on the patio or lawn, which has beautiful views of the fells.

Open 12–3 6–11 (Sun 6–10.30) **Bar Meals** L served all week 12–2 D served all week 6–9 Av main course £6.50 **Restaurant** L served all week 12–2 D served all week 6–9 Av 3 course à la carte £18 Free House Theakston Best & Cool Cask, Black Sheep Best, Dent Aviator, Timothy Taylor Landlord & John Smiths. 7 **Facilities** Garden Parking **Rooms** 10 bedrooms en suite S£37 D£76 (★★★ INN)

The Sun Inn

Market St LA6 2AU ☎ 015242 71965 015242 72489
e-mail: sunhotel@totalise.co.uk
dir: *From M6 junct 36 take A65*

Ruskin's View, famously painted by Turner, is only a few minutes' walk from this popular 17th-century pub. Rumoured to have a resident ghost, the bar is a convivial spot to enjoy a pint of such guest ales as Timothy Taylor or Coniston. Simple furniture, oak floors and open log fires to add to the atmosphere. A contemporary European-influenced menu is available in the bar, the wine library, and the intimate formal restaurant.

Open 11–11 **Bar Meals** L served all week 12–2.30 D served all week 7–9 (Fri–Sat 7–9.30) **Restaurant** L served all week 12–2.30 D served all week 7–9 (Fri–Sat 7–9.30) Free House Jennings Cumberland Ale, Timothy Taylors Landlord, Guest ales. 7 **Facilities** Dogs allowed

The Whoop Hall ★★ HL

Skipton Rd LA6 2HP ☎ 015242 71284 015242 72154
e-mail: info@whoophall.co.uk
dir: *From M6 take A65. Pub 1m SE of Kirkby Lonsdale*

16th-century converted coaching inn, once the kennels for local foxhounds. In an imaginatively converted barn you can relax and enjoy Yorkshire ales and a good range of dishes based on local produce. Oven baked fillet of sea bass with tagliatelle verde and tiger prawns, and stir-fried honey roast duck with vegetables and water chestnuts are among the popular favourites. The bar offers traditional hand-pulled ales and roaring log fires, while outside is a terrace and children's area.

Open 7–11 **Bar Meals** L served all week 12–6 D served all week 6–10 Av main course £7.95 **Restaurant** L served all week D served all week Av 3 course à la carte £16.20 Free House Black Sheep, Greene King IPA, Tetley Smooth. 14 **Facilities** Children's licence Garden Dogs allowed Parking Play Area **Rooms** 24 bedrooms en suite S£69.50 D£87.50

KIRKBY STEPHEN MAP 18 NY70

The Bay Horse

Winton CA17 4HS ☎ 017683 71451
e-mail: kingotty@hotmail.com
dir: *M6 junct 38, A685 to Brough via Kirkby Stephen, 2m N*

Refurbished 16th-century coaching inn specialising in seasonally changing beers – up to 300 different types each year including Hawkeshead Bitter and Titanic Iceberg – plus Corney and Barrow wines. A simple menu is offered at lunchtime with sandwiches, light dishes and mains like home-made burgers or lasagne. The dinner

CONTINUED

KIRKBY STEPHEN continued

menu might list half a succulent roast corn-fed chicken with rich gravy, new potatoes and fresh market vegetables. The specials board changes daily.

Open 12-3 6-11 **Bar Meals** L served Tue-Sun 12-2.30 D served Tue-Sun 6-9 Av main course £8 Free House Hawkeshead Bitter plus Guest ales. 14 **Facilities** Garden Dogs allowed Parking

LITTLE LANGDALE MAP 18 NY30

Pick of the Pubs

Three Shires Inn ★★ HL

LA22 9NZ ☎ 015394 37215 015394 37127

e-mail: enquiries@threeshiresinn.co.uk

dir: *Turn off A593, 2.3m from Ambleside at 2nd junct signed for The Langdales. 1st left 0.5m. Hotel 1m up lane*

See Pick of the Pubs on opposite page

LOWESWATER MAP 18 NY12

Pick of the Pubs

Kirkstile Inn ★★★★ INN

CA13 0RU ☎ 01900 85219 01900 85239

e-mail: info@kirkstile.com

See Pick of the Pubs on page 124

MELMERBY MAP 18 NY63

The Shepherds Inn

CA10 1HF ☎ 01768 881919

e-mail: theshepherdsinn@btopenworld.com

dir: *On A686 NE of Penrith*

Well-known in the North Pennines, this unpretentious sandstone pub looks across the village green towards remote moorland country, close to miles of spectacular walks. An interesting mix of well-kept real ales is constantly rotated, with regulars like Jennings Cumberland Ale, Black Sheep Best, and Courage Directors.

Open 11-3 6-11 (Sun 12-3, 7-10.30) Closed: 25 Dec **Bar Meals** L served all week 11.30-2 D served all week 6-9 Av main course £8.50 **Restaurant** L served all week 11.30-2 D served all week 6-9 Enterprise Inns Jennings Cumberland Ale, Black Sheep Best, Courage Directors. 8 **Facilities** Children's licence Dogs allowed Parking

MUNGRISDALE MAP 18 NY33

The Mill Inn ★★★ INN

CA11 0XR ☎ 017687 79632 017687 79981

e-mail: margaret@the-millinn.co.uk

dir: *From Penrith A66 to Keswick, after 10m right to Mungrisdale, pub 2m on left*

Set in a peaceful village, this 16th-century coaching inn is handy for spectacular fell walks. Charles Dickens and John Peel once stayed here. The inn has an annual pie festival which raises money for charity with its huge selection of pies. At lunchtime, hungry walkers could tuck into local Cumberland sausages or home-made fishcakes. Evening specials always include tempting pies with fillings such as local lamb and apricot; steak with roasted onions; and spiced chicken.

Open 12-11 (Sun 12-10.30) Closed: 25-26 Dec **Bar Meals** L served all week 12-2.30 D served all week 6-8.30 (Summer 6-9) Av main course £6 **Restaurant** L served all week 12-2.30 D served all week 6-8.30 Av 3 course à la carte £20 Free House Jennings Bitter & Cumberland plus guest ale. 7 **Facilities** Garden Dogs allowed Parking **Rooms** 6 bedrooms 5 en suite S£42.50 D£65

NEAR SAWREY MAP 18 SD39

Tower Bank Arms

LA22 0LF ☎ 015394 36334

e-mail: enquiries@towerbankarms.com

dir: *On B5285 SW of Windermere. 1.5m from Hawkshead. 2m from Windemere via Ferry.*

This 17th-century Lakeland inn was immortalised in Beatrix Potter's *Tales of Jemima Puddleduck*. The author's former home, Hilltop, now a National Trust property, is just behind the pub. Food based on local produce is served in the bar or restaurant, and children are made welcome. Typical dishes include steamed mussels with chilli, lime and lemongrass; casseroled beef cooked in Cumbrian ale, and rhubarb and ginger teacup trifle. There is also an excellent cheese slate.

Open 11-11 (Winter Nov-Feb 11-3, 5.30-11) **Bar Meals** L served all week 12-2 D served Mon-Sat 6-9 (Sun 6-8) Av main course £11.50 **Restaurant** L served all week 12-2 D served Mon-Sat 6-9 (Sun 6-8) Av 3 course à la carte £20 Free House Barngates Tag Lag, Hawkshead Bitter, Brodies Prime, Keswick. 7 **Facilities** Children's licence Garden Dogs allowed Parking

Three Shires Inn

This 19th-century hotel five miles west of Ambleside stands in the beautiful valley of Little Langdale near the meeting point of three county shires – Westmorland, Cumberland and Lancashire.

The inn is a perfect stop for lunch or a beer, or afternoon tea) on nany circular low level walks in the angdale and Skelwith area. The raditional Cumbrian slate and stone uilding was erected in 1872, when t provided a much-needed resting lace and watering hole for travellers n the journey over the high passes f Hardknott and Wrynose. The ars boasting bare beams and slate valls are warmed in winter by osy log fires, and floral country-ouse décor in other rooms further romotes the homely and welcoming tmosphere. Summertime sees locals nd visitors happily ensconced at icnic tables under parasols by a akeland stream in the landscaped arden, enjoying views over the ilberthwaite Fells. Refreshments nclude excellent real ales from earby and regional breweries Jennings Best and Cumberland, Coniston Old Man and Black Sheep), and a splendid selection of malt whiskies. Food is served in two bars and the restaurant; evening booking is advisable. Light lunches start with a range of sandwiches, baguettes and soups, or larger plates of hot food such as the home-made pie of the day. Hearty evening fare may be chosen from the specials menu: a warm fillet of smoked mackerel or home tea-smoked duckling breast can be followed by locally-made Cumberland sausage studded with black pudding and served with spiced apple sauce; or oven-roasted breast of wood pigeon served on a herb mash. Desserts like sticky toffee pudding are home made, and children are well catered for with a separate menu of dishes such as whole breaded Whitby scampi with tartare sauce. The hotel offers ten prettily furnished bedrooms with lovely views of the valley.

★★ HL
MAP 18 NY30
LA22 9NZ
☎ 015394 37215
Fax 015394 37127
e-mail:
enquiries@threeshiresinn.co.uk
dir: *Turn off A593, 2.3m from Ambleside at 2nd junct signed for The Langdales. 1st left 0.5m. Hotel 1m up lane.*

Open 11–11 (Dec–Jan 12–3, 8–10.30) Closed: Dec–25
Bar Meals L served all week 12–2 D served all week 6–8.45 (Ltd evening meals Dec–Jan) Av main course £11
Restaurant D served all week 6–8.30 (Ltd evening meals Dec–Jan) Av 3 course à la carte £23
Free House
Jennings Best & Cumberland, Coniston Old Man, Hawkshead Bitter, Blacksheep Bitters.
Facilities Children's licence Garden Parking
Rooms 10 bedrooms en suite D£74

Kirkstile Inn

The Kirkstile Inn is located between Loweswater and Crummock Water, and for some four hundred years has offered shelter and hospitality amidst the stunning Cumbrian fells. The inn stands in the shadow of Melbreak and makes an ideal base for walking, climbing, boating and fishing in the area, or for simply relaxing over a beer from one of the local breweries.

If you're a fan of real ale, be sure to try something from the Loweswater Brewery, which is attached to the inn: maybe Melbreak Bitter, Grasmere Dark Ale, or Kirkstile Gold at the bar, or stock up on bottles of Dark Ale and Gold to take home as a souvenir. The dining room is the oldest part of the inn, dating back to 1549, and faces south down the Buttermere Valley. Here the food matches the views in quality, with plenty of choice from lunch and dinner menus. A third menu of specials is also offered, listed on a blackboard. A sample includes starters such as home-made country vegetable soup served with a slice of home-made loaf; Crofton Farmhouse goats' cheese 'Stumpy'; or Brougham Hall smoked salmon. These might be followed by main courses of baked lamb shoulder with a rosemary and red wine sauce; home-made pork, apple and sage pudding; or feta, spinach, ricotta and vegetable lasagne. Desserts include traditional sticky toffee pudding, marbled chocolate marquise, and Cumberland rum nicky. The friendly atmosphere extends through to the accommodation, comprising seven en suite rooms and a family suite. Two private lounges ensure guests enjoy total relaxation.

★★★★ INN 🍷
MAP 18 NY12
CA13 0RU
☎ 01900 85219
📠 01900 85239
e-mail: info@kirkstile.com

Open 11–11 Closed: 25 Dec
Bar Meals L served all week 12–2 D served all week 6–9 Av main course £10.95
Restaurant D served all week 6–9 Av 3 course à la carte £17.50
Free House
Kirkstile Gold, Coniston Bluebird, Yates Bitter, Melbreak.
🍷 10
Facilities Children's licence Garden Dogs allowed Parking
Rooms 8 bedrooms en suite S£57.50 D£83

NETHER WASDALE MAP 18 NY10

The Screes Inn

CA20 1ET ☎ 019467 26262 📠 019467 26262

e-mail: info@thescreesinnwasdale.com

dir: *To Gosforth on A595. Through Gosforth for 3m, turn right signed Nether Wasdale. In village on left*

The pub is situated in the picturesque village of Nether Wasdale and makes an excellent base for walking, mountain biking or diving in this lovely area. It dates back 300 years and offers a log fire, real ales and large selection of malt whiskies. There is a good choice of sandwiches at lunchtime and dishes include chick pea and sweet potato curry, Cumberland sausage with apple sauce, and roast leg of lamb with mint gravy.

Open 12-11 Closed: 25 Dec, 1 Jan **Bar Meals** L served all week 12-3 D served all week 6-9 Av main course £8 **Restaurant** L served all week 12-3 D served all week 6-9 Free House Black Sheep Best, Yates Bitter, Coniston Bluebird, Derwent. **Facilities** Children's licence Garden Dogs allowed Parking

OUTGATE MAP 18 SD39

Outgate Inn

LA22 0NQ ☎ 015394 36413

e-mail: outgate@outgate.wanadoo.co.uk

dir: *Exit M6 junct 36, by-passing Kendal, A591 towards Ambleside. At Clappersgate take B5285 to Hawkshead then Outgate 3m*

A smallholding in the 18th century, and now home to Robinson's and Hartley's Brewery, whose ales are served in the bar. The poet Wordsworth went to school just down the road. During the winter a real fire warms guests coming in from the cold, while a peaceful beer garden offers warmth (one hopes) in summer. Daily specials supplement an extensive menu of dishes such as deep-fried breaded camembert; braised shoulder of Lakeland lamb; and tempura-battered vegetables.

Open 11-3 6-11 (Sat 11-11, Sun 12-10.30) **Bar Meals** L served all week 12-2 D served all week 6-9 (Sun 12-9) **Restaurant** L served all week 12-2 D served all week 6-9 (Sun 12-9) Frederic Robinson Hartleys XB, Old Stockport Bitter, Robinsons Smooth. **Facilities** Children's licence Garden Dogs allowed Parking

RAVENSTONEDALE MAP 18 NY70

The Black Swan ★★★★ INN

CA17 4NG ☎ 015396 23204

e-mail: enquiries@blackswanhotel.com

dir: *M6 junct 38 take A685 E towards Brough*

A grand, solid-looking Victorian hotel set in a peaceful village in the upper Eden valley. The sheltered garden leads across a bridge over a beck to a natural riverside glade. Local ales are served in the bar, while meals are taken in the lounge or the popular restaurant – examples include local trout fishcake; Moroccan lamb tagine with couscous; and local Cumberland sausage with colcannon mash and rich onion gravy.

Open 8-12 (Fri-Sat 8-1) **Bar Meals** L served all week 12-2 D served all week 6-9 Av main course £10 **Restaurant** L served all week 12-2 D served all week 6-9 Av 3 course à la carte £18 Free House Black Sheep, John Smith's, Dent, Tirril Brewery. 7 **Facilities** Garden Dogs allowed Parking **Rooms** 10 bedrooms en suite S£40 D£60

Pick of the Pubs

The Fat Lamb Country Inn ★★ HL

Crossbank CA17 4LL

☎ 015396 23242 📠 015396 23285

e-mail: fatlamb@cumbria.com

web: www.fatlamb.co.uk

dir: *On A683 between Sedbergh & Kirkby Stephen*

See Pick of the Pubs on page 127

Pick of the Pubs

King's Head ★★★ INN

CA17 4NH ☎ 015396 23284

e-mail: enquiries@kings-head.net

dir: *On A685, 7m from M6 junct 38 (Tebay)*

See Pick of the Pubs on page 128

England

SEATHWAITE MAP 18 SD29

The Newfield Inn 🍷

LA20 6ED ☎ 01229 716208

e-mail: paul@seathwaite.freeserve.co.uk

dir: *From Broughton-in-Furness take A595 0.5m, turn right before lights at Duddon Bridge. Follow 6m signed Seathwaite*

Located in Wordsworth's favourite Duddon Valley, this 17th-century free house has at times been a farm and a post office and still has a real fire, oak beams and a wonderful slate floor. The sheltered garden enjoys stunning views of the surrounding fells. A daily changing special board offers home-made dishes prepared from local ingredients. Favourites from the regular menu are grilled steaks, a vegetarian spicy bean casserole, and apple pie.

Open 11–11 **Bar Meals** L served all week 12–9 D served all week 12–9 Av main course £8.50 **Restaurant** L served all week 12–9 D served all week 12–9 Free House Scottish Courage, Theakston Old Peculier, Jennings Cumberland Ale, Blacksheep Bitter. 🍷 6 **Facilities** Garden Dogs allowed Parking Play Area

SEDBERGH MAP 18 SD69

The Dalesman Country Inn 🍷

Main St LA10 5BN ☎ 015396 21183 015396 21311

e-mail: info@thedalesman.co.uk

dir: *M6 junct 37, follow signs to Sedbergh, 1st pub in town on left*

Restored 16th-century coaching inn, noted for its dazzling floral displays and handy for a choice of glorious walks along the River Dee or up to the Howgill Fells. The menu changes every fortnight, and among the main courses are trio of chargrilled lamb chops, wild salmon fillet, home-made mushroom stroganoff, fresh swordfish nicoise, and organic chicken breast. Popular patio and garden, and a good wine selection.

Open 11–11 (Sun 12–10.30) **Bar Meals** L served all week 12–2.30 D served all week 6–9.30 (Sat–Sun 12–9) **Restaurant** L served all week 12–2.30 D served all week 6–9.30 (Sat–Sun 12–9) Free House Carlsberg-Tetley, Theakston Best Bitter, Black Sheep. 🍷 9 **Facilities** Children's licence Garden Parking **Rooms** 7 bedrooms en suite S£25 D£70 (★★★★ INN)

SHAP MAP 18 NY51

Greyhound Hotel 🍷

Main St CA10 3PW ☎ 01931 716474 01931 716305

e-mail: postmaster@greyhoundshap.demon.co.uk

dir: *Telephone for directions*

Built as a coaching inn in 1684, the Greyhound is a welcoming sight for travellers after crossing Shap Fell. It offers a choice of up to eight real ales and a good selection of wines. From the evening menu expect vegetable and mascarpone lasagne; lamb Henry in wine, redcurrant and onion gravy; and home-made steak and ale pie. All meats are locally sourced. There's a good choice of children's dishes, and a snack menu at lunchtime.

Greyhound Hotel

Open 11–11 (Sun 12–10.30) **Bar Meals** L served all week 12–2 D served all week 6–9 Av main course £8.50 **Restaurant** L served all week 12–2 D served all week 6–9 Av 3 course à la carte £16 Free House Carlsberg-Tetley Bitter, Young's Bitter, Greene King, Old Speckled Hen, Jennings Bitter plus Guest Ales. 🍷 10 **Facilities** Children's licence Garden Dogs allowed Parking

TIRRIL MAP 18 NY52

Queen's Head Inn ★★★★ INN 🍷

CA10 2JF ☎ 01768 863219 01768 863243

e-mail: bookings@queensheadinn.co.uk

dir: *A66 towards Penrith then A6 S toward Shap. In Eamont Bridge turn right just after Crown Hotel. Tirril 1m on B5320.*

Dating from 1719, this privately owned, traditional free house is chock-full of beams, flagstones and memorabilia. Look in the bar for the Wordsworth Indenture, signed by the great poet himself, his brother, Christopher, and local wheelwright John Bewsher, to whom the Wordsworths sold the pub in 1836. Food includes pasta dishes, steaks, and mains such as chicken fajitas; Whitby wholetail scampi; or steamed steak and ale pudding.

Open 12–3 6–11 (Fri–Sun all day) (Apr–Oct all day) Rest: Dec 25 closed evening **Bar Meals** L served all week 12–2 D served all week 6–9.30 (Sun 6.30–8.30) Av main course £9 **Restaurant** L served all week 12–2 D served all week 6–9.30 (Sun 6.30–8.30) Av 3 course à la carte £25 Free House Tirril Bewshers Best, Thomas Slee's Academy Ale & Charles Gough's Old Faithful, Brougham Ale & Cumbrian guest ales. 🍷 10 **Facilities** Children's licence Dogs allowed Parking **Rooms** 7 bedrooms en suite S£40 D£70

The Fat Lamb Country Inn

There are magnificent uninterrupted views in all directions from this 17th-century former coaching inn, built solidly of local stone in open countryside midway between the Lake District and Yorkshire Dales National Parks.

As if this isn't enough, it has its own eleven-acre private nature reserve. An old Yorkshire range, with an open fire when it's needed, has survived in the small bar from the days when it was once the kitchen and main living area. If a local or a visitor doesn't hear what someone says, it won't be because of noise from the pool table, video games or juke box – there aren't any. Snacks and meals can be eaten here, or for something more elaborate there's the print- and plate-decorated restaurant. All dishes are produced on the premises from the best local ingredients available – nothing comes in ready-made, not even the bar snacks. Try cutlets of local lamb in mint jus; roast half guinea fowl with caramelised onion and apple sauce; or pan-fried tuna steak with black olive and red onion dressing. All bedrooms are centrally heated with en-suite bathrooms and tea and coffee making facilities. Outside are informal gardens and wildlife areas with a patio and picnic tables. The nature reserve calls for more comment: it arose from the interest of long-term landlord, Paul Bonsall, in bird watching and wildlife. In 1989, concerned that the land behind the pub might fall into the hands of a shooting syndicate, he bought it at auction. Over the years, with the help of the Countryside Commission and many others, he has created a splendid wildlife haven which visitors may wander round and admire those magnificent uninterrupted views.

★★ HL
MAP 18 NY70
Crossbank CA17 4LL
☎ 015396 23242
015396 23285
e-mail: fatlamb@cumbria.com
web: www.fatlamb.co.uk
dir: *On A683 between Sedbergh & Kirkby Stephen*

Open 11–2 6–11
Bar Meals L served all week 12–2 D served all week 6–9
Restaurant L served all week 12–2 D served all week 6–9
Free House
Black Sheep Bitter.
Facilities Children's licence Garden Dogs allowed Parking Play Area
Rooms 12 bedrooms en suite S£52 D£84

King's Head

One of the oldest buildings in Ravenstonedale, this traditional, 17th-century Cumbrian inn offers everyone a warm welcome. It stands in an unspoilt village in the upper Eden valley, an Area of Outstanding Natural Beauty between two National Parks – the Yorkshire Dales and the Lake District.

Over the years it has served as inn, courthouse, jail, cottages and temperance hotel, before becoming an inn again. In January 2005, Cumbria's worst floods in living memory devastated it – these were the floods that paralysed Carlisle. During four months' closure for extensive refurbishment, the owners took the opportunity to discreetly modernise the interior, without compromising its old-world charm. The log fire-warmed main bar and snug, for example, still feel very friendly, especially with a pint from the Black Sheep or Dent breweries, or a guest ale from another part of the country. The 50-seater Candlelight Restaurant, where one of northern England's largest collections of whisky jugs is displayed, offers extensive lunchtime and evening menus and frequently changing 'specials', all based on local produce. Begin with paté Cumberland or prawn platter, and follow with a chargrilled steak; Ravenstonedale salmon in garlic butter; turkey and ham pie; chicken korma; seafood tagliatelle; or vegetable crumble. Steaks are cooked as you like them, from 'blue – still mooing' to 'cremated – like eating the chef's shoes'. Cumbria is red squirrel country and the proprietors support and encourage the local population. You can watch them display their acrobatic skills on aerial runs and feeding stations in the beer garden on the banks of the nearby beck. Squirrel pictures on the website were all taken here or nearby. Pool, darts, dominoes, bar skittles and shove ha'penny are available in the games room.

★★★ INN 🍷
MAP 18 NY70
CA17 4NH
☎ 015396 23284
e-mail:
enquiries@kings-head.net
dir: *on A685, 7m from M6 junct 38 (Tebay)*

Open 11-3 6-11 (Fri-Sat Open all day Spring & Summer)
Bar Meals L served all week 12-2 D served all week 6-9 Av main course £10.50
Restaurant L served all week 12-2 D served all week 6-9 Av 3 course à la carte £18.50
Free House
Black Sheep, Dent, Carlsberg-Tetley Tetley's Imperial, Over 100 Guest Ales. 🍷 6
Facilities Children's licence Garden Dogs allowed Parking
Rooms 3 bedrooms 2 en suite S£45 D£60

TROUTBECK MAP 18 NY40

Pick of the Pubs

Queens Head ★★★★ INN

Townhead LA23 1PW

☎ 015394 32174 015394 31938

e-mail: enquiries@queensheadhotel.com

web: www.queensheadhotel.com

dir: *M6 junct 36, A590/591, W towards Windermere, right at mini-rdbt onto A592 signed Penrith/Ullswater. Pub 2m on right*

The lovely undulating valley of Troutbeck, with its maze of footpaths and felltop views, is a magnet for ramblers the world over. True to its roots, this smart 17th-century coaching inn offers sustenance and comfortable accommodation to the hungry, weary and footsore. The views across to the Garburn Pass are stunning, and the rambling bars are full of character, with open fires and ancient carved settles. Accomplished cooking is the watchword here. The lunch menu offers hearty but innovative fare – from rustic filled rolls to Lakeland lamb hotpot, or beetroot gravadlax with blini. The à la carte menu, available at lunch or dinner, could include mussel, king prawn and saffron risotto; roast breast and leg of Magret duck; or ravioli of wild mushrooms with poached egg and smoked paprika foam. Children can tuck into beef meatballs and creamed potatoes, with the promise of treacle tart and clotted cream to encourage hearty appetites.

Open 11–11 (Sun 12–10.30) Closed: 25 Dec **Bar Meals** L served all week 12–5 D served all week 5–9 Av main course £13.95 **Restaurant** L served all week 12–2 D served all week 6.30–9 Av 3 course à la carte £23 Av 4 course fixed price £18.50 Free House Interbrew Boddingtons Bitter, Coniston Bluebird, Old Man Bitter, Jennings Cumberland Ale. 9 **Facilities** Children's licence Parking **Rooms** 15 bedrooms en suite S£67.50 D£100

ULVERSTON MAP 18 SD27

The Devonshire Arms

Victoria Rd LA12 0DH

☎ 01229 582537 & 480287 01229 480287

This popular pub is located on the outskirts of the bustling market town of Ulverston, and is home to a wide range of cask beers and guest ales, as well as two dart teams. The menu focuses on classic pub grub, with plenty in the way of light bites: baguettes, burgers, jackets and the like, as well as some more filling mains. These range from home-made mince and onion pie to vegetable korma curry.

Open 11–2.30 5.30–11 (Autumn-Winter 6–11) **Bar Meals** L served Thu–Tue 12–2 D served Thu–Tue 6–8.30 Tetley Smooth, Jennings Cumberland, Carling Lager & Tetley Dark Mild. 8 **Facilities** Children's licence Garden Parking

Farmers Arms

Market Place LA12 7BA ☎ 01229 584469 01229 582188

e-mail: roger@farmersulufreeserve.com

dir: *In town centre*

A warm welcome is extended at this lively 16th-century inn located at the centre of the attractive, historic market town. The visitor will find a comfortable and relaxing beamed front bar with an open fire in winter. Landlord Roger Chattaway takes pride in serving quality food; his Sunday lunches are famous, and at other times there's a varied and tempting specials menu, and lunchtime choice of hot and cold sandwiches, baguettes or ciabatta, and various salads.

Open 10–11 **Bar Meals** L served all week 11–3 D served all week 5.30–8.30 Av main course £8.95 **Restaurant** L served all week 11–3 D served all week 5.30–8.30 Av 3 course à la carte £14.95 Free House Hawkshead Best Bitter, Hoegarden, John Smiths. 12 **Facilities** Children's licence Garden

WASDALE HEAD MAP 18 NY10

Wasdale Head Inn

CA20 1EX ☎ 019467 26229 & 26333 019467 26334

e-mail: wasdaleheadinn@msn.com

dir: *From A595 follow Wasdale signs. Inn at head of valley*

Famous mountain inn dramatically situated at the foot of England's highest mountains and beside her deepest lake. Oak-panelled walls are hung with photographs reflecting a passion for climbing. Exclusive real ales are brewed in the pub's own micro brewery and celebrated by annual beer festivals. Menus specialising in Herdwick lamb and mutton suit outdoor appetites, and there's a choice of 25 malt whiskies.

Open 11–11 (Winter 11–10) **Bar Meals** L served all week 11–9 D served all week 11–9 (Winter 12–8) **Restaurant** D served 7–8 Av 4 course fixed price £28 Free House Great Gable, Wasd Ale, Burnmoor, Yewbarrow. 15 **Facilities** Garden Dogs allowed Parking

WATERMILLOCK MAP 18 NY42

Pick of the Pubs

Brackenrigg Inn ★★★★ INN

CA11 0LP ☎ 017684 86206 017684 86945

e-mail: enquiries@brackenrigginn.co.uk

dir: *M6 junct 40 take A66 signed Keswick. Then take A592 signed Ullswater. Turn right at lake. Inn 6m from M6 & Penrith*

See Pick of the Pubs on page 130

Brackenrigg Inn

This white-painted roadside inn dates from the 18th century and occupies a breathtakingly beautiful position with sweeping views over Ullswater and Helvellyn. Inside there is a traditional bar with plenty of wood panelling and an open fire.

A welcoming atmosphere is engendered by relaxed and friendly owners Garry Smith and John Welch. They offer a good choice of real ales, such as Coniston Bluebird, Jennings Cumberland and Copper Dragon 1816, as well as lagers and continental beers. The wine list is well-balanced and full of interest, with helpful suggestions on food and wine pairing and a very good selection by the glass. Fresh local produce is to the fore on the comprehensive menus, which include a bar and an à la carte choice. Typical choices from the bar menu include starters of smoked haddock chowder; game terrine; and French onion soup, followed perhaps by Herdwick mutton shank on a bed of mash with a white onion sauce; or local venison cobbler. From the à la carte, you could start with monkfish tail wrapped in Cumbrian air dried ham, served with pineapple risotto cake or a caramelised red onion tart, followed by honey roasted Barbary duck breast on caramelised swede with baby vegetables and a port wine reduction; or a light garlic fish stew of locally-sourced fish and shellfish. For those who can't tear themselves away from the peace and beauty of the place, there are smart bedrooms, some housed in the tastefully-refurbished Stables Cottages, where a good night's sleep and a traditional Cumbrian breakfast are too tempting to ignore. The breakfasts are open to non-residents too. Food is served to visitors all day. Excellent wheelchair access throughout.

★★★★ INN 🍷
MAP 18 NY42
CA11 0LP
☎ 017684 86206
📠 017684 86945
e-mail:
enquiries@brackenrigginn.co.uk
dir: *M6 junct 40 take A66 signed Keswick. Then take A592 signed Ullswater. Turn right at lake. Inn 6m from M6 & Penrith*

Open 12–11 (Nov–Mar, Mon–Fri closed 3–5pm)
Bar Meals L served all week 12–3 D served all week 5–9 Av main course £12
Restaurant L served all week 12–2.30 D served all week 6–9 Av 3 course à la carte £25
Free House
Jennings Cumberland, Coniston Bluebird, Copper Dragon 1816. 🍷 12
Facilities Children's licence Garden Dogs allowed Parking
Rooms 17 bedrooms en suite S£38 D£69

WHITEHAVEN MAP 18 NX91

The Waterfront

West Strand CA28 7LR ☎ 01946 691130 01946 695987

e-mail: thewaterfront@aol.com

dir: *From M6 follow A66 towards Workington. Take A595 towards Whitehaven then A5094. Pub in town centre on harbourside*

Set on Whitehaven's historic harbourside, once the third busiest port in the country. The Waterfront serves both food and drink outside in summer, where unrivalled views across the Solway can be enjoyed. There's a contemporary feel to the interior, and the friendly, knowledgeable staff are eager to make you feel at home. Modern and traditional dishes are sourced locally and prepared carefully – the evening menu is particularly strong on chargrilled steaks with a choice of sauces.

Open 12 -11 **Bar Meals** L served all week 12-2 D served all week 6-9.30 Av main course £5.75 **Restaurant** L served all week 12-2 D served all week 6-9.30 Av 3 course à la carte £20 Av 4 course fixed price £15 T&P Inns Jennings Bitter, Cumberland Ale, Cocker Hoop, Fosters & Stella. 16 **Facilities** Children's licence

WINDERMERE MAP 18 SD49

Eagle & Child Inn ★★★ INN

Kendal Rd, Staveley LA8 9LP ☎ 01539 821320

e-mail: info@eaglechildinn.co.uk

dir: *Exit M6 junct 36 then A590 towards Kendal join A591 towards Windermere. Staveley approx 2m*

The rivers Kent and Gowan meet at the gardens of this friendly inn, and it's surrounded by miles of excellent walking, cycling and fishing country. Several pubs in Britain share the same name, which refers to a legend of a baby found in an eagle's nest. Dishes include Fleetwood mussels in tomato, garlic and white wine sauce, followed by local rump steak braised with onions; or roast cod in in anchovy and parsley butter.

Open 11-11 **Bar Meals** L served all week 12-2.30 D served all week 6-9 Av main course £10 **Restaurant** L served Mon-Fri 12-2.30 D served Mon-Fri 6-9 Black Sheep Best Bitter, Coniston, Hawkshead Bitter, Dent Ales. 8 **Facilities** Garden Dogs allowed Parking **Rooms** 5 bedrooms en suite S£40 D£60

New Hall Inn

Lowside, Robinson Place, Bowness LA23 3DH

☎ 015394 43488

A listed building dating from 1612, the pub retains many original features, including oak beams, flagstone floors and open fires. It was originally a coaching inn, and one of its best-known visitors was Charles Dickens. The smaller bar was once a blacksmith's, where beer was passed through the hole in the wall. Along with baked potatoes, sandwiches and ploughman's, the menu includes fisherman's pie; nachos; and mussels.

Open 11-11 Closed: 25 Dec **Bar Meals** L served all week 12-2.30 D served Sun-Fri 6-8.30 (Sat 12-7) Av main course £7.50 Frederic Robinson Hartleys XB, Robinsons Unicorn, Double Hop. **Facilities** Children's licence Garden

WORKINGTON MAP 18 NY02

The Old Ginn House

Great Clifton CA14 1TS ☎ 01900 64616 01900 873384

e-mail: enquiries@oldginnhouse.co.uk

dir: *Just off A663m, 4m from Cockermouth*

The Ginn Room was where farm horses were harnessed to a grindstone to crush crops. Today the unique rounded room is this 17th-century inn's main bar. The butter yellows, bright check curtains and terracotta tiles of the dining areas exude a warm Mediterranean glow. A menu of the usual bar food is supplemented by larger dishes such as a Ginn House steak, which is stuffed with ham and onion and topped with stilton or cheddar.

Open 11-12 Closed: 24-26 Dec, 1 Jan **Bar Meals** L served all week 12-1.45 D served all week 6-9.15 Av main course £7 **Restaurant** L served all week 12-1.45 D served all week 6-9.15 Av 3 course à la carte £15 Free House Jennings Bitter, John Smiths Bitter, Murphys, and 4X. **Facilities** Children's licence Garden Parking **Rooms** 19 bedrooms en suite S£50 D£65 (★★★★ INN)

YANWATH MAP 18 NY52

Pick of the Pubs

The Yanwath Gate Inn

CA10 2LF ☎ 01768 862386 01768 899892

e-mail: enquiries@yanwathgate.com

The Yanwath Gate Inn has been offering hospitality in the North Lakes since 1683. Today the ethos of owner Matt Edwards is to

CONTINUED

YANWATH continued

offer good quality informal dining based on produce which is usually local and organic if possible. While choosing from the regularly changing seasonal menu, enjoy a pint of Doris's 90th Birthday Ale or one of the other Cumbrian ales on offer. Fish is delivered fresh every morning so there are always half a dozen fish and seafood specials on the à la carte menu. A typical dinner choice could be smoked halibut and crème fraîche cheesecake; rolled marinated local lamb shoulder with goats' cheese mash; and brûlée of the day. A cosy reading area in the bar ensures a relaxed mood for diners who can choose to eat here by the log fire or at a table in one of the two dining rooms.

Open 11–11 **Bar Meals** L served all week 12–2.30 D served all week 6–9 Av main course £16 **Restaurant** L served all week 12–2.30 D served all week 6–9 Free House Jennings Bitter Smooth, Hesket Brewery, Doris 90th Birthday Ale, Tirril. 9 **Facilities** Children's licence Garden Dogs allowed Parking

DERBYSHIRE

ALFRETON MAP 16 SK45

White Horse Inn

Badger Ln, Woolley Moor DE55 6FG
☎ 01246 590319 01246 590319
e-mail: info@the-whitehorse-inn.co.uk
dir: *From A632 (Matlock/Chesterfield road) take B6036. Pub 1m after Ashover. From A61 take B6036 to Woolley Moor*

Situated on an old toll road, close to Ogston Reservoir, this 18th-century inn has outstanding views over the Amber Valley. The bar food menu offers such dishes as Thai fish cakes, braised belly pork and black pudding, or chicken stroganoff – as well as an extensive range of sandwiches. From the main menu, expect Moroccan chicken tagine; winter game casserole; or sweet pepper, mushroom and mozzarella bruschetta. There is a good choice of real ales and wines.

Open 12–3 6–11 (Sun 12–10.30, Sat–Sun all day summer) **Bar Meals** L served Tue–Sun 12–2 D served Tue–Sat 6–9 Av main course £7.50 **Restaurant** L served all week 12–2 D served Tue–Sat 6–9 (Sun 12–4) Free House Jennings Cumberland, Adnams Broadside, Blacksheep, 1744. 8 **Facilities** Children's licence Garden Parking Play Area

ASHBOURNE MAP 10 SK14

Barley Mow Inn

Kirk Ireton DE6 3JP ☎ 01335 370306

On the edge of the Peak District National Park, this imposing 17th-century inn has remained largely unchanged over the years. Close to Carsington Water, ideal for sailing, fishing and bird watching. There are also good walking opportunities on nearby marked paths. Ales from the cask and traditional cider; fresh granary rolls at lunchtime, and evening meals for residents only.

Open 12–2 7–11 (Sun 7–10.30) Closed: Dec 25 & 31 **Bar Meals** 12–2 (Rolls only at lunch) Free House Hook Norton, Burton Bridge, Whim Hartington, Archers. **Facilities** Garden Dogs allowed Parking **Notes**

Dog & Partridge Country Inn ★★

Swinscoe DE6 2HS ☎ 01335 343183 01335 342742
e-mail: info@dogandpartridge.co.uk
dir: *From Ashbourne take A52 to Leek. 3m, pub on left in Swinscoe*

This country free house was extended in 1966 to accommodate the Brazilian World Cup football team, who practised in a nearby field. Nowadays the pub scores highly for its extensive menus, offering a good selection of grills, fish, poultry and vegetarian dishes. Start, perhaps, with seafood pancake, followed by pan-fried liver with apple and cranberry; or local trout with a creamy stilton sauce. To finish, there's a wide choice of sweets, ice creams and cheeses.

Open 11–11 **Bar Meals** L served all week 11–11 D served all week Av main course £9 **Restaurant** L served all week 11–11 D served all week Av 3 course à la carte £27.50 Av 3 course fixed price £21.50 Free House Greene King Old Speckled Hen, Ruddles County, Hartington Best, Wells Bombardier, Scottish Courage Courage Directors. **Facilities** Garden Dogs allowed Parking Play Area **Rooms** 29 bedrooms en suite S£40 D£75

BAKEWELL MAP 16 SK26

Pick of the Pubs

The Bull's Head NEW

Church St, Ashford-in-the-Water DE45 1QB
☎ 01629 812931
e-mail: bullshead.ashford@virgin.net
dir: *Off A6, 2m N of Bakewell, 5m from Chatsworth Estate*

See Pick of the Pubs on opposite page

The Bull's Head

Formerly a coaching inn, The Bull's Head has been under the stewardship of tenant Debbie Shaw's family since 1953. It was first run by her grandparents, before passing to an uncle who stewarded it for an impressive 27 years, before passing the baton on to Debbie and her chef husband, Carl.

These days, the London and Manchester stage coaches have long gone, and the cast of customers is a friendly mixture of locals and tourists, many keen to view the village's famous well dressing. Everything about this cosy pub is smartly turned out, from the roses climbing round the door to the shiny brassware hanging around the bar. The interior is cosy and comfortable, with dark wooden beams, open brick fires and cosy banquettes to cluster into. The menu changes frequently, using local, seasonal produce and offering plenty of home-made treats. Genetically modified produce is never knowingly used. A typical starter could be Parma ham salad with stilton dressing, or chicken and pistachio terrine with raspberry vinaigrette. Moving on to main courses, bold, thoughtful combinations include rabbit and pear sausages and celeriac mash; fennel and goats' cheese tartlet topped with Greek yoghurt; and baked cod and smoked bacon with white wine and coriander sauce. Not all the dishes are so ambitious, and simple combinations like pan-fried calves' liver with bubble and squeak, or steak and Old Stockport pie will appease the traditionalists. There are usually at least two real ales on tap and a short list of wines available by the bottle. Outside there is a boules court for temperate days.

NEW
MAP 16 SK26
Church St, Ashford-in-the-Water
DE45 1QB
☎ 01629 812931
e-mail:
bullshead.ashford@virgin.net
dir: *Off A6, 2m N of Bakewell, 5m from Chatsworth Estate*

Open 11-3 6-11 (Sun 12-3, 7-10.30)
Bar Meals L served all week 12-2 D served all week 6.30-9 (Sun 7-9) Av main course £10
Old Stockport, Wards, Unicorn & Double Hop.
Facilities Garden Parking

PUB WALKS

BAKEWELL - DERBYSHIRE

Lathkill Hotel

Walk information

Distance: 5 miles (8km)
Map: OS Outdoor Leisure 24 White Peak
Start/finish: Over Haddon car park (pay); grid ref SK 203657
Ascent/gradient: 984ft (300m)
Paths: generally well-defined paths; lots of stiles
Landscape: partially wooded limestone dales Note: limestone dale sides can be slippery after rain

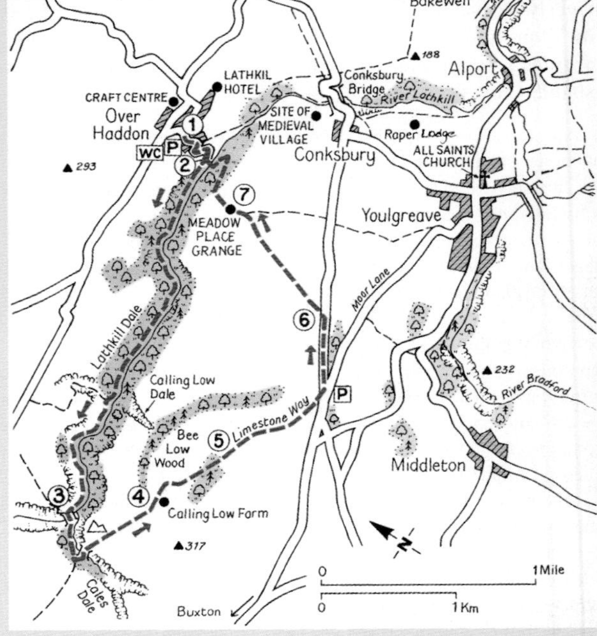

Walk directions

A Turn right out of the car park, and descend the narrow tarmac lane, which winds down into Lathkill Dale.

B Just before reaching Lathkill Lodge and the river, turn right along a concessionary track that runs parallel to the north bank. The path passes several caves and a mineshaft as it weaves its way through woodland and thick vegetation. South of Haddon Grove the trees thin out to reveal the fine limestone crags and screes of the upper dale. The path now is rougher as it traverses an area of screes.

C Go over the footbridge and follow a little path sneaking into Cales Dale. Take the left fork down to a footbridge across the stream, which could well be dry outside the winter months. You now join the Limestone Way long distance route on a stepped path climbing eastwards out of the dale and onto the high pastures of Calling Low.

D The path heads east of south-east across the fields then, just before Calling Low Farm, diverts left (waymarked) through several small wooded enclosures. The path swings right beyond the farm, then half left across a cow-pocked field to its top left-hand corner and some woods.

E Over steps in the wall the path cuts a corner through the woods before continuing through more fields to reach a tarmac lane, where you turn left.

F After about 500 yards (457m), follow a signposted footpath from a stile in a dry-stone wall on the left. Head north-east across fields to the huge farming complex of Meadow Place Grange. Waymarks show the way across the cobbled court-yard, where the path continues between two stable blocks into another field.

G After heading north across the field to the brow of Lathkill Dale, turn right through a gate onto a zig-zag track descending to the river. Cross the old clapper bridge to Lathkill Lodge and follow the outward route, a tarmac lane, back to the car park and refreshment at the well-placed Lathkill Hotel.

While there

Nearby Haddon Hall, home of the Dukes of Rutland, is well worth a visit. This 14th-century country house is as impressive as Chatsworth in its own way, with beautifully laid out gardens surrounding a Gothic-style main building. See the magnificent medieval Banqueting Hall, and the Long Gallery, with its Renaissance panelling.

Look for

Calling Low Grange and Meadow Place Grange were once farmed by monks – the former by the Cistercian order of Roche Abbey in Yorkshire, and the latter by the Augustinian order of Our Lady of Meadows (Leicester). The monks would have tended sheep for the wool trade. Today, both farms concentrate on dairy produce.

BAKEWELL continued

The Lathkil Hotel

Over Haddon DE45 1JE ☎ 01629 812501 📠 01629 812501
e-mail: info@lathkil.co.uk
dir: *2m SW of Bakewell off B5055*

Delicious home-cooked food is served at this charming small hotel. Choose from the hot or cold lunchtime buffet in summer, or ponder a menu that embraces lemon sole with grapes; feta, brie and spinach parcel; and venison haunch with Cumberland sauce. Until the end of the 19th century the hotel was known as the Miners Arms, reflecting the local lead mining industry. Today, Lathkill Vale is more tranquil, with spectacular views of the nearby Dales.

Open 11.30–3 6.30–11 (Sat–Sun, & Summer all day) Rest: Dec 25 no lunch **Bar Meals** L served all week 12–2 (Sat–Sun 12–2.30, Rest: Dec 25 no lunch) **Restaurant** D served all week 7–8.30 (Bookings only Sun in Winter) Av 3 course à la carte £22 Lathkil Hotel Ltd Whim Hartington, Everards Tiger, Black Thorn, Peak Ales. **Facilities** Garden Dogs allowed Parking

Please see walk on opposite page

Pick of the Pubs

The Monsal Head Hotel ★★ HL

Monsal Head DE45 1NL
☎ 01629 640250 📠 01629 640815
e-mail: enquiries@monsalhead.com
dir: *A6 from Bakewell towards Buxton. 1.5m to Ashford. Follow Monsal Head signs, B6465 for 1m*

See Pick of the Pubs on page 137

BAMFORD MAP 16 SK28

Pick of the Pubs

Yorkshire Bridge Inn ★★ HL

Ashopton Rd S33 0AZ
☎ 01433 651361 📠 01433 651361
e-mail: info@yorkshire-bridge.co.uk
dir: *A57 from M1, left onto A6013, pub 1m on right*

See Pick of the Pubs on page 138

BARLOW MAP 16 SK37

The Tickled Trout

33 Valley Rd S18 7SL ☎ 0114 289 0893

A few miles outside Chesterfield, this quaint country pub is located at the gateway to the superb Peak District, renowned for its walking and splendid scenery. Within the pleasant, cosy atmosphere you can sample the inn's straightforward menu: among the fishy choices are fresh local trout with almond butter, beer-battered cod, and grilled monkfish with a tomato and basil sauce on a bed of couscous. The specials board offers choices for those not inclined towards seafood.

Open 12–3 6–11 (Sun 7–10.30) **Bar Meals** L served all week 12–2.30 D served all week 6.30–9 (Sun 12–3) Av main course £6.50 **Restaurant** L served all week 12–2.30 D served all week 6.30–9 Free House Marstons Pedigree, Mansfield Smooth, Marstons Finest Creamy & Guest. **Facilities** Garden Dogs allowed Parking

BASLOW MAP 16 SK27

Rowley's NEW

Church Ln DE45 1RY ☎ 01246 583880 📠 01246 583818
e-mail: susan@fischers.baslowhall.co.uk
dir: *A619/A623 signed Chatsworth. Baslow on edge of Chatsworth Estate*

Close to the Chatsworth estate in a prime village location, Rowleys is a new venture opened in 2006. The emphasis on good eating is unmistakable, yet does not detract from its appeal as a watering hole; the building was formerly a pub and drinkers are welcome to enjoy the preserved stone-flagged bar and open fire. Alternatively the terrace with lovely church views is where a classy light bite can be relished, along with a pint of local cask ale.

Open 11–11 Closed: 1st wk Jan **Bar Meals** L served Tue–Sun 12–2.30 Av main course £14 **Restaurant** L served Tue–Sun 12–2.30 D served Tue–Sun 7–9 (Sat 7–10) Av 3 course à la carte £28 Free House London Pride, Local Cask, Guinness, 1664 Kronenburg. **Facilities** Parking

BELPER MAP 11 SK34

Pick of the Pubs

The Bluebell Inn and Restaurant

Farnah Green DE56 2UP
☎ 01773 826495 📠 01773 829102
e-mail: bluebell.inn@btinternet.com
dir: *In Farnah Green, 0.5m off A517*

The Amber Valley contains such diversely beautiful countryside that it has been classified a world heritage site. This recently refurbished 18th-century coaching inn is nestled right at the heart of it, affording some wonderful walks and, for the less energetic, far-reaching views. The bar maintains a traditional, low-beamed feel, while the restaurant is sleekly modern, with polished oak tables and high-backed leather chairs giving a feel of relaxed elegance. Smart dishes match the surrounds: fresh linguini with crab, chilli and chives as a starter; pan-fried sea bass fillets on sweet potato purée with broad beans and lemon butter; or breast of Gressingham duck with marmalade glazed cocotte potatoes, pancetta wrapped shallots and Grand Marnier flavoured jus as a main. Everything is cooked in house, and the well-balanced wine list will appeal to a variety of palates.

Open 11.30–3 6–11 **Bar Meals** L served Tues–Sun 12–2 D served Tues–Sat 6.30–9 Av main course £11 **Restaurant** L served Tue–Sun 12–2 D served Tue–Sat 6.30–9 Av 3 course à la carte £25 Av 3 course fixed price £23 John Smiths Keg, Guinness, rotating cask ales. 7 **Facilities** Garden Parking

England

BIRCHOVER MAP 16 SK26

Pick of the Pubs

The Druid Inn 🍷

Main St DE4 2BL ☎ 01629 650302

dir: *From A6 between Matlock & Bakewell take B5056, signed Ashbourne. Take 2nd left to Birchover*

A popular, friendly, ivy-clad dining pub in the heart of the Peak District. The old bar has plenty of character, with an original tiled floor and real log fires. A simple, one-page menu serves the bar and two restaurants, with starters including country terrine with prune and apricot chutney; and curried smoked haddock, garden pea risotto and poached egg. Main courses on offer might be rib-eye steak with stilton, onion rings and chunky chips; rump of lamb with confit of Mediterranean vegetables and basil pesto mash; and polenta cake with halloumi cheese and garlic mushrooms. Real ales include a Druid-badged brew from Leatherbritches in Ashbourne. Especially popular on summer weekends, this pub has many visitors who walk up to the Nine Ladies Stone Circle on Stanton Moor, or Rowtor Rocks, reached by a steep uphill path behind the inn.

Open 11-11 **Bar Meals** L served all week 12-2 D served Mon-Sat 6-9.30 (Sun 12-3) Av main course £11 **Restaurant** L served all week 12-2 (Sun 12-3) (Tue-Sat Winter) D served Mon-Sat 6-9.30 Av 3 course à la carte £22 Free House Druid Bitter & Guest ale. 🍷 12 **Facilities** Garden Parking

The Red Lion NEW

Main St DE4 2BN ☎ 01629 650363

e-mail: matteo@frau36.fsnet.co.uk

dir: *5.5m from Matlock, off A6 onto B5056*

Many people visit the village of Birchover to see the famous Rowter Rocks where druids once gathered. The Red Lion's history began in 1680 when it was built as a farmhouse, which brewed its own beer using water from its well. These days the pub welcomes villagers and visitors alike, and retains traces of its past in its bare beams, stone walls and glass-topped well. Expect reasonably priced home-cooked food made with local ingredients.

Open 12-2.30 7-11 (Mon 7-9) **Bar Meals** L served all week 12-2.30 D served all week 7-9 (Fri-Sat 7-10) Av main course £8.95 Boddingtons, Nine ladies, Timothy Taylor Landlord, Black Sheep. **Facilities** Garden Dogs allowed Parking **Notes**

BIRCH VALE MAP 16 SK08

Pick of the Pubs

The Waltzing Weasel Inn ★★★ INN 🍷

New Mills Rd SK22 1BT

☎ 01663 743402 📠 01663 743402

e-mail: w-weasel@zen.co.uk

dir: *W from M1 at Chesterfield*

See Pick of the Pubs on page 140

BRADWELL MAP 16 SK18

The Old Bowling Green Inn ★★★★ INN 🍷

Smalldale S33 9JQ ☎ 01433 620450 📠 01433 620280

dir: *Off A6187 onto B6049 towards Bradwell*

A 16th-century coaching inn with impressive views over glorious countryside. Traditional country cooking and good value daily specials supplemented by weekly changing ales produce grilled goats' cheese with sun-dried tomatoes and caramelised onions; chicken breast in mushroom, white wine and mustard grain cream sauce; sea bass fillets on celeriac mash; and meat and potato pie. Bakewell tart and apple crumble feature among a range of tempting home-made puddings.

Open 12-11 **Bar Meals** L served all week 12-2 D served all week 6-8.30 (Sun 12-3, 6-8) Av main course £8 **Restaurant** L served all week 12-2 D served all week 6-9 (Sun 12-3, 6-8) Av 3 course à la carte £16.50 Free House Stones, Timothy Taylor, Tetleys, Kelham Gold. 🍷 8 **Facilities** Children's licence Garden Parking Play Area **Rooms** 6 bedrooms en suite S£45 D£65

BRASSINGTON MAP 16 SK25

Pick of the Pubs

Ye Olde Gate Inne

Well St DE4 4HJ ☎ 01629 540448 📠 01629 540448

e-mail: theoldgateinn@supanet.com

dir: *2m from Carsington Water off A5023 between Wirksworth & Ashbourne*

Oak beams, black leaded ranges, an antique clock, charmingly worn tiled floors and a delightful mishmash of scrubbed pine furniture – this inn has no shortage of character. It was built in 1616 out of local stone and salvaged Armada timbers, and stands beside an old London to Manchester turnpike in the heart of Brassington, a hill village on the southern edge of the Peak District. Hand pumped Marston's Pedigree Bitter takes pride of place behind the bar, alongside guest ales such as Jennings Sneck Lifter. The menu, written daily on blackboards, features a wealth of local produce. At lunch, try fresh soups, sandwiches, filled baguettes or the house speciality, the Derbyshire fidget. The evening menu might open with warm potted shrimps on buttered granary toast with lemon, and move on to braised steak in stout with chopped celery, carrots, shallots and fresh thyme.

Open 12-2.30 6-11 (Sat 12-3, Sun 12-3, 7-10.30)
Bar Meals L served Tue-Sun 12-1.45 D served Tue-Sun 7-8.45 (Sun 12-2) Av main course £10.50 W'hampton & Dudley Marstons Pedigree, Hobgoblin & Guest beers. **Facilities** Garden Dogs allowed Parking

The Monsal Head Hotel

This distinctive balconied hotel in the heart of the Peak District National Park enjoys lovely views over Monsal Dale. With its seven en suite bedrooms, the hotel complex is ideally located for touring and walking; it's just three miles outside Bakewell, and Chatsworth House and Haddon Hall are a ten-minute drive away.

Originally built in the 19th century as the Bull's Head, it was later rebuilt as a railway hotel. A stone carving of a bull's head is still in place, while the hotel's real ale pub, the Stables, reflects its earlier role as the home of railway horses which collected passengers from Monsal Dale station. Today this delightful venue features original flagstone floors and seating in the former horse stalls, with horse tack on the walls and a hay rack at the back of the bar. There's a welcoming fire in winter, and a row of eight hand pumps that delivers a range of cask ales including guest brewers, speciality German bottled beers, Kelham Island, Abbeydale and Thornbridge. Lagers, wheat beers and wines by the bottle or glass are also on offer. Food from a single menu covers both the bar and restaurant, and is also served in the large enclosed garden in summer. Meat (including local lamb) and game are provided by an award-winning butcher, and fresh fish on the specials blackboard may proffer roasted whole black bream, or fillet of pollock. Light lunches feature hot or cold sandwiches, fajitas, and jacket potatoes. Cheesy garlic bread or a bowl of olives with warm ciabatta will help fill the odd corner, whilst a full three-course meal could commence with spicy Japanese fishcake; continue with Monsal Wellington or chicken Hartington; and conclude with raspberry pavlova.

★★ HL 🍷
MAP 16 SK26
Monsal Head DE45 1NL
☎ 01629 640250
📠 01629 640815
e-mail:
enquiries@monsalhead.com
dir: *A6 from Bakewell towards Buxton. 1.5m to Ashford. Follow Monsal Head signs, B6465 for 1m*

Open 11.30–11 Closed: 25 Dec
Bar Meals L served all week 12–9.30 D served all week (Sun 12–9) Av main course £10.50
Restaurant L served all week 12–9.30 D served all week 7–9.30 (Sun 12–9) Av 3 course à la carte £19.50
Free House
Ales from Theakston, Whim, Abbeydale & Thornbridge breweries. 🍷 15
Facilities Garden Dogs allowed Parking
Rooms 7 bedrooms en suite S£50 D£60

Yorkshire Bridge Inn

Against a magnificent Peak District backdrop, this old inn stands surrounded by wonderful walking country, woodlands and a profusion of wildlife. Dating back to at least 1826, it takes its name from the old packhorse bridge that crossed the River Derwent here on the border with Yorkshire.

A short stroll away are the Ladybower and other Derwent Valley reservoirs, famed for the RAF's Dambuster training runs in 1943. The bars, plentifully beamed and with attractive chintz curtains, are cosy and welcoming in winter, although in warmer weather you might want to be in the stone-built conservatory, or outside in the courtyard or spacious beer garden. Food is prepared to order using fresh local produce and the standard menu, complemented by daily specials, lists sandwiches and filled jacket potatoes (lunchtime only), and salads, grills and other hot dishes available throughout the day. Starters include large Yorkshire pudding with creamy onion sauce and gravy, and prawn cocktail, while among the main courses are home-made steak and kidney pie; roast chicken breast; lasagne verde and, from the blackboard, halibut, sea bream, salmon or whatever fish have just been caught in the North Sea. Among the desserts expect warm French apple tart; lemon and lime bavarois; and passion fruit and mango sorbet. Children are likely to go for the pork sausages, mini chicken kiev or cheese and tomato pizza on their own menu. The en suite bedrooms, including one with a four-poster, make a good base for touring nearby attractions like Chatsworth, Haddon Hall, Peveril Castle and the Blue John Caves. The Derwent Valley reservoirs caused heated controversy when they were created in the first half of the 20th century, but have matured into beautiful attractions in their own right.

★★ HL

MAP 16 SK28

Ashopton Rd S33 0AZ

☎ 01433 651361

01433 651361

e-mail:
info@yorkshire-bridge.co.uk

dir: *A57 from M1, left onto A6013, pub 1m on right*

Open 10–11

Bar Meals L served all week 12–2 D served all week 6–9 (Sun 12–8.30)

Restaurant L served all week 12–2 D served all week 6–9

Free House

Blacksheep, Old Peculier, Golden Pippen, Copper Dragon IPA.

Facilities Garden Dogs allowed Parking

Rooms 14 bedrooms en suite S£50 D£36

BROUGH MAP 16 SK18

Travellers Rest NEW ★★★ INN

Brough Ln Head S33 9HG

☎ 01433 620363 01433 623338

e-mail: elliottstephen@btconnect.com

dir: *Old A625/B6147 between Sheffield & Castleton*

A long-established family-owned stone inn only a few yards from a Roman encampment which exploited the local lead mines. The pub has undergone refurbishment and now offers rooms with lovely views. Real ales include a couple of local brews, and the good value menu may feature Thai-style fishcakes followed by beef and local ale pie with chips and mushy peas. A large garden with benches is popular in summer.

Open 12–12 (Nov–Feb 12-3, 5–12) Closed: 25–26 Dec **Bar Meals** L served all week 12–2 D served Mon–Sat 6–9 (Sun 12–6) Av main course £8 **Restaurant** 12–2 6–9 (Sun 12–6) Free House Farmers Blonde, Acorn Barnsley Bitter, Boddingtons, Worthingtons & Carling. **Facilities** Children's licence Garden Parking Play Area **Rooms** 5 bedrooms en suite S£35 D£65

CASTLETON MAP 16 SK18

The Castle BUD

Castle St S33 8WG ☎ 01433 620578 622902

dir: *Exit M1 for Chesterfield and follow Chatsworth House signs. At Chatsworth House follow Castleton signs. Pub in village centre*

The Castle in the heart of the Peak District has been a coaching inn since Charles II's reign. The four resident ghosts may go back that far too! Open fires ensure that entering on a chilly day after some brisk fell-walking is like getting into a bed that's had the electric blanket on. As for eating, you could start with black pudding and bacon salad, or salmon and broccoli fishcakes, and proceed to minted lamb cutlets or chilled Cajun salmon steak salad.

Open 12–11 (Sun 12–10.30) **Restaurant** L served all week D served all week Vintage Inns Cask Bass, Black Sheep, Bombardier, Speckled Hen. 22 **Facilities** Garden Parking **Rooms** 12 bedrooms en suite D£59.95

The Peaks Inn ★★★★ INN

How Ln S33 8WJ ☎ 01433 620247 01433 623590

e-mail: info@peaks-inn.co.uk

dir: *On A625 in town centre*

An attractive, stone-built village pub standing below the ruins of Peveril Castle, after which Castleton is named. The bar is warm and welcoming, with leather armchairs for weary walkers, and open log fires for their wet socks. The menu offers old favourites of steak and ale pie; bangers and mash, ham, egg and chips; and a range of steaks. Rest over in one of the four en suite bedrooms.

Open 12–12 (Fri/Sat 12–1am) **Bar Meals** L served all week 12–3 D served all week 5–9 (Summer 12–9) Punch Taverns Black Sheep, Deuchars IPA, Tetley Smooth & 1 Guest on rotation. 9 **Facilities** Garden Dogs allowed Parking **Rooms** 4 bedrooms en suite D£65

Ye Olde Nag's Head

Cross St S33 8WH ☎ 01433 620248

e-mail: nigel@yeoldenagshead.com

dir: *A625 from Sheffield, W through Hope Valley, pass through Hathersage & Hope. Pub on main road in Castleton*

A traditional, family-run 17th-century coaching inn offering a cosy bar with a real fire. After an energetic walk or cycle ride, there's food from county-based suppliers to be enjoyed, including beef stroganoff; pan-fried pork steak; fresh cod and chips; brie and broccoli pithiviers; an all-day breakfast, or a hot filled bap.

Open 9–11 **Bar Meals** L served all week 12–6 D served all week 6–9 (Carvery 12–8) Av main course £7.95 **Restaurant** L served all week 12–6 D served all week 6–9 (Carvery 12–8) Av 3 course à la carte £15 Free House Timothy Taylor Landlord, Black Sheep, Worthingtons, Carling & Guest ale. 12 **Facilities** Dogs allowed Parking **Rooms** 10 bedrooms en suite S£40 D£50 (★★★ INN)

DERBY MAP 11 SK33

The Alexandra Hotel

203 Siddals Rd DE1 2QE ☎ 01332 293993

Two-roomed hotel filled with railway memorabilia. Noted for its real ale (11 hand pumps and 450 different brews on tap each year), range of malt whiskies, and friendly atmosphere. A typical menu offers chilli con carne, liver and bacon, home-baked ham with free range egg and chips, filled Yorkshire puddings, ploughman's lunches, omelettes and freshly-made filled hot and cold cobs.

Open 11–11 (Sun 12–3, 7–10.30) Closed: Dec 25 **Bar Meals** L served Tues-Sat 12–2 Av main course £3.75 Tynemill Ltd Castle Rock, Nottingham Gold, Elsie Mo. 6 **Facilities** Garden Dogs allowed Parking **Notes**

DOE LEA MAP 16 SK46

Hardwick Inn

Hardwick Park S44 5QJ ☎ 01246 850245 01246 856365

e-mail: batty@hardwickinn.co.uk

dir: *M1 junct 29 take A6175. 0.5m L (signed Stainsby/Hardwick Hall). After Stainsby, 2m, left at staggered junct. Follow signs*

This pleasantly situated inn, on the south gate of the National Trust's Hardwick Hall, dates from the 15th century. It is built from locally quarried sandstone and retains its historic atmosphere with open coal fires in winter. The bar menu offers Hardwick Estate lamb dishes, a selection from the grill, and ploughman's lunches, with specials like fresh sea bass stuffed with kumquat, oranges and fresh dill.

Open 11.30–11 **Bar Meals** L served all week 11.30–9.30 D served all week 11.30–9.30 (Sun 12–9) **Restaurant** L served Tue–Sun 12–2 D served Tue–Sat 7–9 Free House Scottish Courage, Theakston Old Peculier & XB, Greene King Old Speckled Hen, Ruddles County, Black Sheep. 24 **Facilities** Children's licence Garden Parking Play Area

The Waltzing Weasel Inn

This intriguingly named and award-winning pub was built of local stone some 400 years ago, and is surrounded by Peak District hills. This is walking country beloved of outdoor enthusiasts, and owners Brian Jordan and Jon Sanderson are ready to welcome them.

Business people are welcome too, though they are asked to turn off their mobile phones in keeping with house policy prohibiting gaming machines and music, apart from the odd live jazz session. Country antiques are a feature of the bar, while from the garden and mullion-windowed restaurant there are dramatic views of Kinder Scout. The food is produced from local produce where possible, and Fair-Trade items are also used when appropriate. Bar menu regulars include vegetarian dishes such as leek and Hartington Blue stilton bread and butter pudding, or vegetable lasagne; and meat dishes such as rabbit with lavender, apricots and Galliano, loin of pork with pink peppercorns, and rare breed beef roast with parsnip chips and Yorkshire pudding. There are fish dishes like pan-seared scallops wrapped in smoked bacon with a white wine, cream and brandy sauce, salmon fillet, served with mushrooms and a white wine sauce or tuna loin Mediterranean style. Be sure and try some of the Weasel's own sausages – Harvey Bangers. Menus are regularly changed so that even regular diners don't always know what to expect. Look out for occasional special events, such as the popular 'lobster night'.

MAP 16 SK08
New Mills Rd SK22 1BT
☎ 01663 743402
01663 743402
e-mail: w-weasel@zen.co.uk
dir: *W from M1 at Chesterfield*

Open 12-11 (Sun 12-10.30)
Bar Meals L served all week 12-9 D served all week 7-9 Av main course £12
Restaurant L served all week 12-2 D served all week 6-9 Av 3 course fixed price £27.50
Free House
Marston's Best & Pedigree, Jennings Sneck Lifter, Greene King IPA, Old Speckled Hen. 10
Facilities Garden Parking

EYAM MAP 16 SK27

Miners Arms

Water Ln S32 5RG ☎ 01433 630853

dir: *Off B6521, 5m N of Bakewell*

This welcoming 17th-century inn and restaurant in the famous plague village of Eyam gets its name from the local lead mines of Roman times. Fish features strongly on the menu, with the likes of seafood pie, tuna steak on a bed of ratatouille, and grilled salmon fillet with a herb crust and sweet chilli sauce. Wash it all down with a pint of Theakston's Best, or Old Peculier.

Open 12-11 Closed: 26 Dec eve **Bar Meals** L served all week 12-2 D served Mon-Sat 6-9 (Mon 6-8, Sat 7-9, Sun 12-3) Av main course £9 **Restaurant** L served all week 12-2 D served Mon-Sat 6-9 (Sun 12-3) Worthington's Creamflow, Theakstons Best Pedigree, John Smiths, Old Peculier. **Facilities** Garden Dogs allowed Parking

FENNY BENTLEY MAP 16 SK14

Pick of the Pubs

Bentley Brook Inn ★★★ INN

DE6 1LF ☎ 01335 350278 01335 350422

e-mail: all@bentleybrookinn.co.uk

See Pick of the Pubs on page 143

The Coach and Horses Inn

DE6 1LB ☎ 01335 350246 01335 350178

e-mail: coachnhorses@aol.com

Beautifully located on the edge of the Peak District National Park, this award-winning, family-run, 17th-century coaching inn is a cosy refuge in any weather. Inside you'll find stripped wood furniture and low beams. Expect real ales and good home cooking along the lines of seared halibut steak with beurre blanc sauce; pan-fried red snapper fillet with sweet peppers and pesto dressing; and sliced venison haunch with port and forest fruits.

Open 11-11 **Bar Meals** L served all week 12-9 D served all week 12-9 Av main course £9.75 **Restaurant** L served all week 12-9 D served all week 12-9 Free House Marston's Pedigree, Timothy Taylor Landlord, Black Sheep Best, Oakham JHB. 6 **Facilities** Garden Parking

FROGGATT MAP 16 SK27

Pick of the Pubs

The Chequers Inn ★★★★ INN

Froggatt Edge S32 3ZJ

☎ 01433 630231 01433 631072

e-mail: info@chequers-froggatt.com

dir: *On A625, 0.5m N of Calver*

This traditional 16th-century country pub nestling in the Hope Valley is hard to pass by. And it really does 'nestle' below beautiful Froggatt Edge with its westward panorama of the Peak District National Park, reached by a steep, wild woodland footpath from the elevated secret garden. Reminders of former times include a horse-mounting block, and the old stables housing logs for the crackling winter fires. The interior has rag-washed yellow walls, bare board floors, Windsor chairs and bookcases – ideal surroundings for a contemplative beer. If the dining room beckons and seafood is preferred, try tasty dishes such as smoked haddock and parsley fishcake; swordfish with wild mushroom and artichoke; or seafood risotto with saffron. Other examples from the blackboard may include starters such as herb and garlic crusted field mushroom with ratatouille; main courses like pan-fried calves' liver and mash, pancetta and fruit chutney; and such desserts as Bakewell pudding and custard.

Open 12-2 6-9.30 (Open all day Sat-Sun) Closed: 25 Dec **Bar Meals** L served all week 12-2 D served all week 6-9.30 (Sun 12-9) Av main course £13 Free House Charles Wells Bombardier Premium Bitter, Greene King IPA & Black Sheep. 9 **Facilities** Garden Parking **Rooms** 5 bedrooms en suite D£70

GREAT HUCKLOW MAP 16 SK17

The Queen Anne Inn ★★★ INN

SK17 8RF ☎ 01298 871246

e-mail: mal@thequeen.net

dir: *A623 turn off at Anchor pub toward Bradwell, 2nd right to Great Hucklow*

A warm welcome awaits at this traditional country free house with its log fires, good food, and an ever-changing range of cask ales. The inn dates from 1621, and a licence has been held for over 300 years; names of all the landlords are known and one is said to haunt the premises. Comfortable en suite bedrooms make an ideal base for exploring the spectacular Peak District National Park. Bar food ranges from freshly-made sandwiches to grills, and includes favourites like steak and ale pie, beef stew and Yorkshire pudding, and chicken jalfrezi.

Open 12-2.30 6-11 (Sun 7-10.30) **Bar Meals** L served Wed-Mon 12-2 D served all week 6.30-8.30 Free House Adnams Bitter, Shaws, Storm Brewery, Kelham Island. 10 **Facilities** Garden Dogs allowed Parking **Rooms** 2 bedrooms en suite D£60

England

GRINDLEFORD MAP 16 SK27

Pick of the Pubs

The Maynard ★★★★ GA

Main Rd S32 2HE ☎ 01433 630321 01433 630445
e-mail: info@themaynard.co.uk
dir: *From M1 take A619 into Chesterfield, then onto Baslow. A623 to Calver, right into Grindleford*

This fine stone-built inn stands grandly in immaculately kept grounds overlooking the Derwent Valley, in the heart of the Peak District National Park. You may eat in either the Longshore Bar or in the Padley Restaurant, with its large windows facing the gardens. Choose the bar and the menu may well offer seared breast of chicken with mushroom risotto and balsamic oil; Moroccan-spiced braised lamb with couscous; or grilled sea bass on champ with tomato and olive salsa. Opt for the restaurant and discover other possibilities, such as eggs Benedict with chive oil, or smoked haddock fishcake as starters; main courses of fillet of beef with fondant potato, wild mushrooms and caramelised red wine onion; pan-fried calves' liver with olive oil mash, onion fritters and grilled pancetta; and pan-seared red mullet with shellfish paella and lobster oil. For dessert, try sticky toffee parkin pudding with stem ginger ice cream.

Open 11-3 5.30-11 (Sun 12-10.30) **Bar Meals** L served all week 12-2 D served all week 6-9.30 Av main course £9 **Restaurant** L served Sun-Fri 12-2 D served all week 7-9.30 Av 3 course à la carte £27 Free House Abbey Dale Moonshine, Bakewell Bitter. **Facilities** Children's licence Garden Dogs allowed Parking **Rooms** 10 bedrooms en suite S£80 D£90

HARTSHORNE MAP 10 SK32

The Mill Wheel NEW ★★★★ INN

Ticknall Rd DE11 7AS ☎ 01283 550335 01283 552833
e-mail: info@themillwheel.co.uk
dir: *A511 from Burton-on-Trent towards Leicester. Left at island signed A514/Derby. Pub a short distance*

Amazingly this old building's huge mill wheel has not only survived for 250-odd years, but also, since restoration in 1987, still slowly turns, powered by recirculated water. The wheel is very much the focus of attention in the bar and restaurant, where freshly prepared dinner might comprise leek, spinach and coriander soup; roasted red sea bream with a tapenade; and a hot or cold dessert. En suite rooms are furnished to a high standard.

Open 12-2.30 6-11 (Sun 12-11) **Bar Meals** L served all week 12-2.15 D served all week 6-9.15 (Sun 12-7) Av main course £8.95 **Restaurant** L served all week 12-2.15 D served all week 6-9.15 (Sun 12-7) Av 3 course à la carte £22 Av 2 course fixed price £12 Free House Abbot Ale, Oakham Ale, Summer Lightning, Bass & Pedigree. 8 **Facilities** Garden Parking **Rooms** 4 bedrooms en suite D£49.95

HASSOP MAP 16 SK27

Eyre Arms

DE45 1NS ☎ 01629 640390
e-mail: nick@eyrearms.com
dir: *On B6001 N of Bakewell*

Formerly a farmstead and 17th-century coaching inn, this traditional free house stands in one of the most beautiful parts of rural Derbyshire. Oak settles, low ceilings and cheery log fires create a cosy atmosphere, while the secluded garden overlooks the rolling Peak District countryside with its lovely local walks. Typical dishes include local venison pie; Grand Marnier duckling; and local trout baked with butter and almonds.

Open 11.30-3 6.30-11 Closed: 25 Dec **Bar Meals** L served all week 12-2 D served all week 6.30-9 Av main course £8.50 Free House Marston's Pedigree, Scottish Courage, Theakstons Black Bull Bitter, Black Sheep Special. 9 **Facilities** Garden Parking

HATHERSAGE MAP 16 SK28

Millstone Inn ★★★★ INN

Sheffield Rd S32 1DA ☎ 01433 650258 01433 650276
e-mail: jerry@millstone.co.uk

Tastefully furnished former coaching inn with striking views over the picturesque Hope Valley. Chatsworth House, Ladybower Reservoir and the Blue John Mines are among nearby attractions. An atmospheric bar, traditional and innovative dishes, and a popular terrace restaurant specialising in seafood add to the appeal. Try chargrilled salmon with braised lentils; or calves' liver with saffron mash and chick pea relish.

Open 11.30-3 6-11 (Sat 11-11, Sun 12-10.30) **Bar Meals** L served all week 12-2 D served all week 6-9 Av main course £8 **Restaurant** D served Thu-Sat 6.30-10 (Jun-Aug Sun 6-10) Av 3 course à la carte £17.50 Free House Timothy Taylor Landlord, Black Sheep, Guest Beers. 16 **Facilities** Garden Dogs allowed Parking **Rooms** 8 bedrooms en suite S£45 D£70

Pick of the Pubs

The Plough Inn ★★★★ INN

Leadmill Bridge S32 1BA
☎ 01433 650319 & 650180 01433 651049
e-mail: sales@theploughinn-hathersage.com

See Pick of the Pubs on page 144

Bentley Brook Inn

Part of this charming, atmospheric old building was originally a thatched medieval farmhouse. Its near neighbour was the manor house, whose fortifications included five square towers – you can see the only one remaining from the inn's car park.

In the 1800s the farmhouse, made mainly of wattle and daub, was twice extended and, on the second occasion, re-roofed with slate. Between the World Wars, two elderly ladies lived here in considerable style, attended to by five servants, a gardener, an under-gardener and a coachman. The house became a restaurant in 1954, although it was the early 1970s before a full drinks licence was granted. Now open all day, the bar serves a selection of real ales, some brewed by the on-site Leatherbritches brewery, and a cider called Scrumpi from an Italian winemaker in Batley. Both the bar and award-winning Fenny's Restaurant, which overlooks the terrace and garden, serve meals ranging from soups, sandwiches, baguettes and small savoury dishes, to substantial home-cooked dishes. These include Derbyshire lamb hotpot; breast of Gressingham duck; steak and ale pie; mussels marinière; fish and chips; and vegetarian nut roast. The menus are changed with the seasons and in response to the usually plentiful supply of local game. Delicious home-made desserts include raspberry Bakewell tart and chocolate terrine. Traditional English Sunday lunch is served as a three-course, three-roast carvery, and during the summer the barbecue in the garden is fired up. Accompanied children may enter the bar area, but there's plenty of room outside for them to play in safety. In the winter, snuggle up by the central open log fire and play dominoes, cards or chess – just ask at the bar. A wide range of Derbyshire produce is on sale in reception, including home-cured bacon, sausages, black pudding, salamis, biscuits, chutneys, pickles and preserves.

★★★ INN 🍷
MAP 16 SK14
DE6 1LF
☎ 01335 350278
📠 01335 350422
e-mail:
all@bentleybrookinn.co.uk

Open 11–12
Bar Meals L served all week 12–9 D served all week 12–9 (Sun 12–8)(Oct 1- Mar 31 kicthen closed 3–5.30) Av main course £9
Restaurant L served all week 12–9 D served all week 12–9 (Sun 12–8) Av 3 course à la carte £20
Leatherbritches Bespoke, Leatherbritches Hairy Helmet, Goldings, Marstons Pedigree. 🍷 7
Facilities Garden Dogs allowed Parking Play Area
Rooms 11 bedrooms en suite S£40 D£60

The Plough Inn

A corn mill was erected first on this site in the Peak District over five hundred years ago. In 1600 smelting was started – the oldest part of today's Plough Inn was a smelting house in 1640. With nine acres of grounds by the River Derwent, the buildings then became a farmstead.

It started to sell ale to weary travellers when its first licence was granted in 1766. With this pedigree you would rightly expect the public rooms to be charming, with plenty of exposed beams and brickwork; in winter welcoming log fires blaze in the grates. The sheltered garden is a delight in summer – with tea served in the afternoons – and a pretty array of flower-filled baskets adorns the inn's external walls. When it comes to hospitality for today's customers, 'choice' is the Plough's byword in both food and drink. A good range of hand-pulled beers is backed up by 50 malt whiskies and over a dozen wines by the glass. The extensive menu has something for everybody – from traditional British (chargrilled rump steak with chunky chips) to modern European dishes such as stuffed vine leaves with antipasti; breast of corn-fed chicken stuffed with Taleggio cheese wrapped in Parma ham; and baked figs with pistachio nuts. A good range of fish dishes completes the wealth of choice on offer, from simple sardines to sea bream, smoked haddock and salmon. This family owned establishment prides itself on the quality of its food and service, and offers five en suite rooms to maximize guests' enjoyment of a stay in this Area of Outstanding Natural Beauty.

★★★★ INN

MAP 16 SK28

Leadmill Bridge S32 1BA

☎ 01433 650319 & 650180

01433 651049

e-mail: sales@theploughinn-hathersage.com

Open 11–11 Closed: 25 Dec

Bar Meals L served all week 11.30–2.30 D served all week 6.30–9.30 (Sun 12–9)

Restaurant L served all week 11.30–2.30 D served all week 6.30–9.30 (Sun 12–9) Av 3 course à la carte £24.95 Av 3 course fixed price £18.95

Free House

Theakstons Old Peculier, Batemans, Adnams Bitter, Smiles Best. 14

Facilities Garden Parking

Rooms 5 bedrooms en suite S£59.50 D£79.50

HAYFIELD MAP 16 SK08

The Royal Hotel

Market St SK22 2EP ☎ 01663 742721 01663 742997
e-mail: enquiries@theroyalhayfield.co.uk
dir: *Off A624*

A fine-looking, 1755-vintage building in a High Peak village that itself retains much of its old-fashioned charm. The oak-panelled Windsor Bar has log fires when you need them, and serves a constantly changing roster of real ales, bar snacks and selected dishes, while the dining room usually offers a traditional menu. Hydes, Howard Town and Taylors are some of the beer choices. Kinder Scout and the fells look impressive from the hotel patio.

Open 11–1am **Bar Meals** L served all week 12–2.15 D served all week 6–9.15 Av main course £9 **Restaurant** L served all week 12–2.15 D served all week 6–9.15 Av 3 course à la carte £17 Free House Hydes, Howard Town, Taylors, Stella Artois. 8 **Facilities** Children's licence Garden Parking

HOGNASTON MAP 16 SK25

The Red Lion Inn

Main St DE6 1PR ☎ 01335 370396 01335 370396
e-mail: redlion@w3z.co.uk
dir: *Approx 5m from Ashbourne to Wirksworth road. Follow signs for Carsington Water. Turn off to Hognaston*

John F Kennedy once stayed at this whitewashed inn, located in a picturesque Peak District village overlooking Carsington Water. There's a traditional pub atmosphere, with beamed ceilings, open fireplaces and church pew seating. The food options range from baguettes or light snacks in the bar to a comprehensive restaurant à la carte. Expect to be offered beef stroganoff; seared salmon; and stuffed aubergine topped with Dovedale blue cheese.

Open 12–3 6–11 Rest: (Closed Mon lunch, Sun eve) **Bar Meals** L served all week 12–2.45 D served all week 6.30–9 Av main course £7.50 **Restaurant** L served all week 12–2.45 D served all week 6.30–9 Av 3 course à la carte £22.50 Free House Marston's Pedigree, Burton Bitter, & Guest Ales. 8 **Facilities** Garden Parking

HOLLINGTON MAP 10 SK23

Pick of the Pubs

The Red Lion Inn

Main St DE6 3AG ☎ 01335 360241 01335 361209
e-mail: redlionholl@aol.com
dir: *On A52 between Ashbourne & Derby, turn off at Ednaston/Hollington sign. Pub 2m on right*

In a beautiful country setting, this spectacular 18th-century coaching inn is known for its warm and friendly atmosphere and award-winning food. Start a meal with salt and pepper cuttlefish with sweet chilli noodles; or pheasant and thyme ravioli poached in game and vegetable broth. Main courses include crispy honey-glazed Gressingham duck breast with salsify; braised osso buco of veal with root vegetables, red wine and fine herb dumplings; venison fillet medallions set on swede mash with shallot and cep marmalade; roasted loin of lamb with Puy lentil vinaigrette and ratatouille; fresh halibut fillet steak on wilted spinach with warm chive butter sauce; and chargrilled plaice with Sauvignon Blanc dressing. For dessert see if steamed bitter chocolate sponge with hot chocolate fudge sauce is available. On a fine day the gated beer garden is just the place for a pint of Adnams Broadside.

Open 12–3 6–11 **Bar Meals** L served all week 12–2 D served all week 6.30–9 (Sun 12–2.30) Av main course £7.50 **Restaurant** L served all week 12–2 D served all week 6.30–9 (Sun 12–2.30) Av 3 course à la carte £23 Av 2 course fixed price £9.95 Free House Pedigree, Abbot Ale, Bass, Adnams Broadside. 8 **Facilities** Garden Dogs allowed Parking

HOPE MAP 16 SK18

Cheshire Cheese Inn

Edale Rd S33 6ZF ☎ 01433 620381 01433 620411
e-mail: tcheese@gmail.com
dir: *On A6187 between Sheffield & Chapel-en-le-Frith*

Located on the old trans-Pennine salt route in the heart of the Peak District, this 16th-century inn owes its name to the tradition of accepting cheese as payment for lodgings. It has a reputation for good home-made food and hand-pulled beer served in a relaxed atmosphere with open fires. There is a choice of light bites and main meals, ranging from toasted sandwiches or jacket potatoes to a mixed grill or roasted lamb shank.

Open 12–3 6.30–11 (all day at wknds) **Bar Meals** L served all week 12–2 D served all week 6.30–9 (Sun 12–8.30) **Restaurant** L served all week 12–2 D served all week 6.30–9 (Sun 12–8.30) Free House Slaters Toptotty, Wentworthy Pale Ale, Black Sheep Best, Hartington Bitter. 13 **Facilities** Garden Dogs allowed Parking

LITTON MAP 16 SK17

Red Lion Inn

SK17 8QU ☎ 01298 871458 01298 871458
e-mail: theredlionlitton@yahoo.co.uk
dir: *Just off A623 (Chesterfield -Stockport rd), 1m E of Tideswell*

The Red Lion is a beautiful traditional pub on the village green, very much at the heart of the village community. With its roaring fires, selection of real ales and friendly atmosphere, it's a favourite with walkers and holiday-makers too. The menu offers hearty pub food, such as sausage and mash; ham, egg and chips, and a selection of stews and casseroles. Sandwiches, snacks and vegetarian dishes are also available, including a fabulous home-made vegeburger.

Open 12–3 6–11 (Fri–Sun 11–11) **Bar Meals** L served all week 12–2 D served Mon–Sat 6–8.30 (Sun 12–6) Av main course £7 **Restaurant** L served all week D served Mon–Sat Free House Barnsley Bitter, Timothy Taylors, Thornbridge Hall, Kelham Island. 8 **Facilities** Garden Dogs allowed

LONGSHAW MAP 16 SK27

Fox House BUD

Hathersage Rd S11 7TY ☎ 01433 630374 📠 01433 637102

dir: *From Sheffield follow A625 towards Castleton.*

A delightfully original 17th-century coaching inn and, at 1,132 feet above sea level, one of the highest pubs in Britain. The Longshaw dog trials originated here, after an argument between farmers and shepherds as to who owned the best dog. A simple menu lists sandwiches, starters, Sunday roasts, and mains like chicken and ham pie, ground Scottish beefsteak burger, and spicy prawn pasta.

Open 11–11 (Sun 11.30–10.30) **Bar Meals** L served all week 12–5 D served all week 5–10 (Sun 12–9.30) Av main course £9 **Restaurant** L served all week 12–5 D served all week 5–10 (Sun 12–9.30) Av 3 course à la carte £18 Vintage Inns Cask Stones, Cask Tetleys. 20 **Facilities** Garden Parking **Rooms** 10 bedrooms en suite S£49.95 D£49.95

MARSTON MONTGOMERY MAP 10 SK13

Pick of the Pubs

The Crown Inn NEW ★★★★ INN

Riggs Ln DE6 2FF ☎ 01889 590541 📠 01889 591576

e-mail: info@thecrowninn-derbyshire.co.uk

dir: *From Ashbourne take A515 towards Lichfield, 5m. Turn right at Cubley x-rds, follow signs to Marston Montgomery, 1m. Pub in village centre*

Standing on the southern edge of the Peak District in the small hamlet of Marston Montgomery, the Crown Inn retains its original charm and character. Low ceilings, beams and leather sofas make the bar a comfortable place in which to unwind and enjoy the selection of beers and real ales, or choose from the carefully selected wine list. Outside, you'll find an elevated patio and garden area for hot summer days. The menu changes weekly, and the daily specials board often includes a selection of fresh fish. Lunchtime brings sandwiches on speciality breads and bagels, as well as a light bites menu and traditional Sunday roast. Typical dishes include twice-baked stilton soufflé and pickled pear salad; blade of beef and braised red cabbage; and pan-fried sea bass on black pudding and pink peppercorn mash. Seven individually designed and refurbished en suite bedrooms are available.

Open 12–3 6.30–11 Closed: 25 Dec & 1 Jan **Bar Meals** L served all week 12–2.30 **Restaurant** L served all week 12–2.30 D served Mon–Sat 7–9 (Fri–Sat 7–9.30) Av 3 course à la carte £24 Av 3 course fixed price £14.95 Free House Carling, Timothy Taylor Landlord, Marstons Pedigree, Guinness & Grolsch. 7 **Facilities** Garden Parking **Rooms** 7 bedrooms en suite S£50 D£60

MATLOCK MAP 16 SK35

The Red Lion ★★★★ INN

65 Matlock Green DE4 3BT ☎ 01629 584888

dir: *From Chesterfield, A632 into Matlock, on right just before junct of A615*

This friendly, family-run free house makes a good base for exploring local attractions like Chatsworth House, Carsington Water and Dovedale. Spectacular walks in the local countryside help to work up an appetite for bar lunches, steaks and a wide selection of home-cooked meals. In the winter months, open fires burn in the lounge and games room, and there's a boules area in the garden for warmer days.

Open 11–12 **Bar Meals** L served Tue–Fri (Sun 12–4) D served Tue–Sun 7–9 **Restaurant** L served Tue–Fri (Sun 12–4) D served Tue–Sat 7–9 Scottish Courage Courage Directors, John Smiths & Theakstons Bitter, Peak Ales & Guest Ales. **Facilities** Garden Parking **Rooms** 6 bedrooms en suite S£30 D£60

MILLTOWN MAP 16 SK36

The Nettle Inn NEW

S45 0ES ☎ 01246 590462

The Nettle Inn is a traditional 16th-century hostelry nestling in countryside bordering the Peak District. All the sought-after qualities of cosiness and character are here, from the flower-filled hanging baskets outside to the log fires and stone-flagged taproom floor within. Locals and visitors alike rejoice in the choice of real ales, and appreciate fully the head chef who will only serve dishes and breads, sauces, pickles and sweets if he has made them.

Open 12–3 5.30–11.30 **Bar Meals** L served all week 12–2.30 D served all week 6.30–9.30 (times vary Sat–Sun) Av main course £7.95 **Restaurant** L served all week 12–2.30 (Sun 12–4) D served all week 6.30–9.30 (Sat 6.30–10) Av 3 course à la carte £24 Free House Bradfield Farmers Best Bitter, Bradfield Farmers Blonde, Hardy & Hansons, Olde Trip. 9 **Facilities** Children's licence Garden Dogs allowed Parking

RIPLEY MAP 16 SK35

The Moss Cottage Hotel ★★ HL

Nottingham Rd DE5 3JT ☎ 01773 742555 📠 01773 741063

This red-brick free house specialises in carvery dishes, with four roast joints each day. The Moss Cottage also offers regular 'two for the price of one' weekday meals, as well as blackboard specials and a selection of home-made puddings. Expect popular menu choices like prawn cocktail or mushroom dippers; ham, egg and chips; liver and onions; or battered haddock. Hot puddings include rhubarb crumble and chocolate fudge cake.

Open 12–3 6–11 (All day Sun) **Bar Meals** L served all week 12–2.15 D served Mon–Sat 6–9 (Sun 12–5) **Restaurant** L served all week 12–2.15 D served Mon–Sat 6–9 Free House Old Tripp, Guinness, Old Rose Scrumpy Cider & Guest Beer. **Facilities** Parking **Rooms** 14 bedrooms en suite S£49.95 D£49.95

ROWSLEY MAP 16 SK26

The Grouse & Claret ★★★ INN

Station Rd DE4 2EB ☎ 01629 733233 📠 01629 735194

dir: *On A6 between Matlock & Bakewell*

A popular venue for local anglers, this pub takes its name from a fishing fly. It is also handy for touring the Peak District or visiting the stately homes of Haddon Hall and Chatsworth House. A meal from the cosmopolitan menu might include crispy duck salad with hoi sin sauce, and chicken and seafood paella or, for the more traditionally minded, prawn cocktail followed by steak and ale pie.

Open 7.30–11 (Sun 7.30–10.30) **Bar Meals** L served all week 7.30–9 D served all week 7.30–9 **Restaurant** L served all week 7.30–9 D served all week 7.30–9 W'hampton & Dudley Marston's Pedigree, Mansfield, Bank's Bitter. 12 **Facilities** Garden Parking Play Area **Rooms** 8 bedrooms en suite S£65 D£65

SHARDLOW MAP 11 SK43

The Old Crown

Cavendish Bridge DE72 2HL ☎ 01332 792392

e-mail: bjohns5@aol.com

dir: *M1 junct 24 take A6 towards Derby. Left before river bridge into Shardlow*

A family-friendly pub on the south side of the River Trent, where up to seven guest ales are served. It was built as a coaching inn during the 17th century, and retains its warm and atmospheric interior. Several hundred water jugs hang from the ceilings, while the walls display an abundance of brewery and railway memorabilia. Traditional food is lovingly prepared by the landlady, including sandwiches, jackets, omelettes, ham and eggs, and Cumberland sausages.

Open 11–12 (Fri-Sat 11-1, Sun 10.30–12) **Bar Meals** L served all week 12-2 D served Mon–Thu & Sat 5–8 (Sun 12–3) Av main course £6.50 Marston's Pedigree, Camerons Strongarm & 7 Guest Ales. **Facilities** Children's licence Garden Dogs allowed Parking Play Area

SOUTH WINGFIELD MAP 16 SK35

The White Hart

Moorwood Moor DE55 7NU

☎ 01629 534229 01629 534229

e-mail: allanwhitehart@w32.co.uk

dir: *Near Wingfield Manor*

Classic award-winning country pub at the gateway to the Derbyshire Peak District, superbly situated for walkers and cyclists and offering wonderful views across to Wingfield Manor where Mary Queen of Scots was held captive. A good reputation for locally-sourced food and home-grown ingredients guarantees everything from bread to truffles are made in the White Hart's kitchen. Expect chicken and locally-supplied black pudding roulade, natural-smoked haddock, Bakewell pudding, and a range of Derbyshire cheeses.

Open 12-3 5-12 (Sat 12-11, Sun 12–10.30) **Bar Meals** L served Sat–Sun 12-2 D served Mon–Sat 6–10 (Sun 12–6) Av main course £9.95 **Restaurant** L served Sat–Sun 12–2 D served Mon–Sat 5–10 (Sun 12–4) Av 3 course à la carte £15.95 Pedigree, Guinness, Bass, guest beer. 10 **Facilities** Garden Dogs allowed Parking Play Area

TIDESWELL MAP 16 SK17

The George Hotel

Commercial Rd SK17 8NU

☎ 01298 871382 01298 871382

e-mail: georgehoteltideswell@yahoo.co.uk

dir: *A619 to Baslow, A623 towards Chapel en le Frith, 0.25m*

A 17th-entury coaching inn in a quiet village conveniently placed for exploring the National Park and visiting Buxton, Chatsworth and the historic plague village of Eyam. Quality home-cooked food includes venison cooked in red wine sauce, roast pheasant with bacon, potatoes and mushrooms, seafood crumble, and rainbow trout with almonds.

Open 12-3 6-11 (Open all day Sat–Sun) **Bar Meals** L served all week 12-2 D served all week 6-9 (All day Sat–Sun (summer)) Av main course £6 **Restaurant** L served all week 12-2 D served all week 6-9 (All day Sat–Sun (summer)) Av 3 course à la carte £12 Hardy & Hansons Kimberley Cool, Olde Trip Bitter, Best Bitter. 12 **Facilities** Garden Dogs allowed Parking

Three Stags' Heads

Wardlow Mires SK17 8RW ☎ 01298 872268

dir: *At junct of A623 & B6465 on Chesterfield - Stockport road.*

Grade II listed 17th-century former farmhouse, designated by English Heritage as one of over 200 heritage pubs throughout the UK. It is located in the limestone uplands of the northern Peak District, and is now combined with a pottery workshop. Well-kept real ales and hearty home-cooked food for ramblers, cyclists and locals includes chicken and spinach curry; pork, leek and stilton pie, and game in season. No children under eight.

Open 12-11 (Fri 7-11) **Bar Meals** L served Sat–Sun 12.30–3 D served Fri–Sun 7.30–9.30 Free House Abbeydale Matins, Absolution, Black Lurcher & Brimstone Bitter. **Facilities** Dogs allowed Parking **Notes**

WESSINGTON MAP 16 SK35

The Three Horseshoes

The Green DE55 6DQ ☎ 01773 834854

e-mail: scott@3horseshoes-wessington.info

dir: *A615 towards Matlock, 3m after Alfreton, 5m before Matlock*

A century ago horses were still being traded over the bar at this late-17th-century former coaching inn and associated blacksmith's forge, to both of which activities it no doubt owes its name. For a true taste of the Peak District try Derbyshire chicken with black pudding and apple; or braised lamb shank with celeriac purée. Several local walks start or end at the pub – why not order a picnic for refreshment, or even a hamper?

Open 11.30–11 (Sun 12–10.30) Closed: Mon in winter **Bar Meals** L served Tue–Sat, BHs 12–2 D served Tue–Thu, BHs 5.30–8.30 (Sun 12.30–4.45) **Restaurant** L served Sun in winter 12.30–3 D served Fri–Sat 7–9 (Sun 12.30–5) Av 3 course à la carte £21 Guinness, Hardys & Hansons Olde Trip, Carling H & H Cool & Monthly Guest Beer. **Facilities** Garden Dogs allowed Parking Play Area

DEVON

ASHBURTON MAP 03 SX77

The Rising Sun ★★★★ INN

Woodland TQ13 7JT ☎ 01364 652544 01364 654202

e-mail: risingsun.hazel@btconnect.com

dir: *E of Ashburton from A38, take lane signed Woodland/ Denbury. Pub on left approx 1.5m*

A former drovers' inn, largely rebuilt following a fire in 1989, The Rising Sun is set in beautiful Devon countryside, convenient for Exeter,

CONTINUED

ASHBURTON continued

Plymouth and Torbay. Regularly changing real ales are served and an extensive wine list, including local Sharpham wine. The menu offers a good choice of fish and excellent West Country cheeses. The pub is also well known for its home-made pies (available to take home), and its monthly Pie Club evening.

Open 11.45-3 6-12 (Sun 12-3, 7-10.30) Closed: 25 Dec **Bar Meals** L served Tue-Sat 12-2.15 D served Tue-Sat 6-9.15 (Sun 12-3, 7-9.15) **Restaurant** L served Tue-Sun 12-2.15 D served Tue-Sun 6-9.15 (Sun 12-3, 7-9.15) Av 3 course à la carte £20 Free House Princetown Jail Ale, IPA, Teignworthy Reel Ale & guest ales. 10 **Facilities** Garden Dogs allowed Parking Play Area **Rooms** 4 bedrooms en suite S£38 D£65

AVONWICK MAP 03 SX75

The Avon Inn

TQ10 9NB ☎ 01364 73475

e-mail: rosec@beeb.net

There's a distinctly Gallic flavour to this handsome whitewashed free house, just off the busy Exeter to Plymouth trunk road. In the colder months, a cheery wood-burning stove sets the scene for sea bass and salmon on spinach and crayfish rosti with lobster bisque; and galette of chestnuts, mushrooms and leeks with boursin filo parcels. Chef/proprietor Dominique Prandi also offers more traditional English fare, including braised lamb on celeriac mash with rosemary jus.

Open 11.30-3 6-11 (Sun 12-2.30, 6-10.30) **Bar Meals** L served all week 12-2 D served Mon-Sat 6.30-9.30 **Restaurant** L served all week 12-2 D served Mon-Sat 6.30-9.30 Free House Teignworth Reel Ale, Otter Bitter, Sharp's Doom Bar. **Facilities** Garden Parking

Pick of the Pubs

The Turtley Corn Mill NEW

TQ10 9ES ☎ 01364 646100 01364 646101

e-mail: mill@avonwick.net

The setting of this sprawling former corn mill is decidedly idyllic, comprising six acres of grounds bordered by the River Glazebrook, as well as a lake with its own small island. A lot of loving attention has been lavished on the old building recently, with new wood and slate floors, bookcases and plenty of images of the former residents. Menus change monthly, and local produce is used where possible. There's a wide selection of dishes to suit all tastes, including a few designed especially for children. A typical menu might include Dartmouth smoked and poached salmon with dill dressing; baked field mushrooms with black olive tapenade; sea bass fillets with chorizo mash; or 8oz steak burger with gruyère and bacon. The cellar is well stocked with a range of local beers, nearby Summerskills Brewery the main supplier.

Open 11.30-11 (Sun 12-10.30) Closed: 25 Dec **Bar Meals** L served all week 12-9.30 D served all week 12-9.30 (Sun 12-9) Free House Tamar Ale, Jail Ale, Tribute, Dartmoor IPA. 11 **Facilities** Garden Dogs allowed Parking

AXMOUTH MAP 04 SY29

Pick of the Pubs

The Harbour Inn NEW

Church St EX12 4AF ☎ 01297 20371

e-mail: garytubb@yahoo.com

dir: *Main street opposite Church, 1m from Seaton*

The River Axe meanders through its valley into Lyme Bay, but just before they meet is Axmouth harbour, which accounted for one sixth of Devon's trade during the 16th century. This cosy, oak-beamed, harbourside inn was built four centuries earlier, however. Since taking over in 2005, Gary and Graciela Tubb have maintained three principles – local ingredients bought from small family businesses, nothing frozen, and everything home made. A bar and bistro menu offers scampi and chips, lasagne, sausages or faggots with mash and gravy, jacket potatoes, baguettes and sandwiches. From a daily updated blackboard menu, you might want to consider pork tenderloin with prunes and bacon; swordfish steak with niçoise salad; or tagliatelle, wild mushrooms and spicy tomato sauce. The Harbour makes a great stop if you are walking the South West Coast Path between Lyme Regis and Seaton.

Open 11-3 6-11 (All day in Summer, Sun 12-10.30) **Bar Meals** 12-2 6.30-9 (Sun 7-9) Av main course £11 **Restaurant** L served all week 12-2 D served all week 6.30-9 (Sun 7-9) Av 3 course à la carte £20 Hall & Woodhouse Badger 1st Gold, Tanglefoot, Sussex & Otter Bitter. **Facilities** Garden Dogs allowed Parking Play Area

The Ship Inn

EX12 4AF ☎ 01297 21838

dir: *1m S of A3052 between Lyme & Sidmouth. Signed to Seaton at Boshill Cross*

There are long views over the Axe estuary from the beer garden of this creeper-clad family-run inn. It was built soon after the original Ship burnt down on Christmas Day 1879, and is able to trace its landlords back to 1769; the current ones have been there for over 40 years. Well kept real ales complement an extensive menu including daily blackboard specials where local fish and game feature, cooked with home-grown herbs.

Open 11-3 6-11.30 (Jan & Feb closed Sun eve) **Bar Meals** L served all week 12-2 D served all week 6-9.30 (Summer 12-3) **Restaurant** L served all week 12-2 (Summer 12-3) D served all week 6-9 (Summer 6-9.30) Pubmaster Otter Bitter, Guinness, 6X, Carling & Stowford Press. 10 **Facilities** Garden Dogs allowed Parking Play Area

England

BARBROOK MAP 03 SS74

The Beggars Roost NEW

EX35 6LD ☎ 01598 752404
e-mail: info@beggarsroost.co.uk
dir: *A39 1m from Lynton*

Originally a manor farmhouse with attached cow barn, the buildings were converted into a hotel in the 1970s with the barn becoming the Beggars Roost. The long, low bar has tables around a warm log-burner; the restaurant on the floor above extends up into the beamed apex and is popular for parties. The pub menu offers a great range of reasonably priced favourites such as casseroles, terrines and ploughman's, while the restaurant focuses on more sophisticated fare.

Open 12-3 6-12 **Bar Meals** L served all week 12-3 D served all week 6-9 Av main course £6.95 **Restaurant** D served all week 6-9.30 Av 3 course à la carte £25 Free House Exmoor Ale, Cotleigh Barn Owl, Exmoor Silver Stallion, Cotleigh Tawny. **Facilities** Children's licence Garden Dogs allowed Parking

BEER MAP 04 SY28

Anchor Inn NEW

Fore St EX12 3ET ☎ 01297 20386 01297 24474
e-mail: 6403@greeneking.co.uk
dir: *A3052 towards Lyme Regis. At Hangman's Stone take B3174 into Beer. Pub on seafront*

Fish from local boats feature strongly on the menu at this pretty colourwashed hotel, which overlooks the sea in the equally picture-perfect Devon village of Beer. Dine on beer-battered cod and chips; local crab with salad; smoked haddock on cheddar cheese mash with a mustard cream sauce; or chicken breast stuffed with brie, wrapped in bacon and served with a cranberry and red wine sauce.

Open 8-11 **Bar Meals** L served all week 12-3 D served all week 6-9 (Apr-Oct food all day) Av main course £9 **Restaurant** L served all week 12-3 D served all week 6-9 (Apr-Oct 6-9.30) Av 3 course à la carte £18 Greene King Otter Ale, Greene King IPA, Abbot Ale. 14 **Facilities** Children's licence Garden

BERE FERRERS MAP 03 SX46

Olde Plough Inn

PL20 7JL ☎ 01822 840358
e-mail: oldeplough@btinternet.com
dir: *A386 from Plymouth, A390 from Tavistock*

Originally three cottages, dating from the 16th century, this inn has bags of character, with its old timbers and flagstones, which on closer inspection are revealed to be headstones. To the rear is a fine patio overlooking the River Tavey, and there are lovely walks in the Bere Valley on the doorstep. The area is ideal for birdwatchers. Dishes on offer range through fresh fish, crab, local pies, curries and stir-fries.

Open 12-3 7-11.30 **Bar Meals** L served all week 12-2 D served all week 7-9 Av main course £7 **Restaurant** L served all week 12-2 D served all week 7-9 Av 3 course à la carte £16 Free House Sharp's Doom Bar & Sharp's Own, Interbrew Flowers, weekly Guest ale. **Facilities** Garden Dogs allowed

BICKLEIGH MAP 03 SS90

Fisherman's Cot

EX16 8RW ☎ 01884 855237 01884 855241
e-mail: fishermanscot.bickleigh@eldridge-pope.co.uk

Well-appointed thatched inn by Bickleigh Bridge over the River Exe with food all day and large beer garden, just a short drive from Tiverton and Exmoor. The Waterside Bar is the place for snacks and afternoon tea, while the restaurant incorporates a carvery and à la carte menus. Sunday lunch is served.

Open 11-11 **Bar Meals** L served all week 12-6 D served all week 6-9.30 **Restaurant** L served all week 12-10 D served all week Eldridge Pope Wadworth 6X, Bass. 8 **Facilities** Garden Parking

BIGBURY-ON-SEA MAP 03 SX64

Pilchard Inn

Burgh Island TQ7 4BG ☎ 01548 810514 01548 810514
e-mail: reception@burghisland.com
dir: *From A38 turn off to Modbury then follow signs to Bigbury & Burgh Island*

A small 14th-century inn located on a tiny island off the Devon coast and only accessible on foot at low tide. The adjoining art deco hotel was once a favourite haunt of the likes of Noël Coward and the Windsors, and Agatha Christie set several of her popular detective novels here. A well-planned menu includes steamed mussels and garlic confit, and chargrilled minute steak with spicy sweet potato and watercress. Soup and a variety of baguettes available at lunchtime.

Open 11.30-11 (Sun 12-10.30) **Bar Meals** L served all week 12-2.30 D served Thu-Sat 7-9 Free House Sharp's, Teignworthy, St Austell. 7 **Facilities** Children's licence Garden Dogs allowed Play Area

BRANSCOMBE MAP 04 SY18

Pick of the Pubs

The Masons Arms ★★ HL

EX12 3DJ ☎ 01297 680300 01297 680500
e-mail: reception@masonsarms.co.uk
dir: *Turn off A3052 towards Branscombe, down hill, hotel at bottom of hill.*

See Pick of the Pubs on page 150

The Masons Arms

Originally a cider house, and a well-documented haunt of smugglers, this charming 14th-century, creeper-clad inn is set in the centre of picturesque Branscombe. Recent years have seen much renovation and redecoration, and the inn now offers 24 cottage bedrooms, several of which feature four-poster beds.

The Masons Arms is noted for its bar, which is full of character, with stone walls, ancient ships' beams, slate floors, and a splendid open fireplace. The latter is used for spit-roasts on a weekly basis, including Sunday lunch. In high season this is a popular family venue, when the walled terrace can seat up to 100 people. Despite heavy demand, the restaurant has maintained a high standard of cooking, which is receiving growing recognition. Children's meals are the usual favourites, while the extensive lunchtime bar menu ranges from snacks (sandwiches, paninis, ploughman's) to starters like steamed West Country mussels, or assiette of cured meats with roasted fig chutney, and mains such as a naturally smoked haddock with pecorino cheese velouté, or garlic roasted shoulder lamb. In good weather lobster and crab are landed on Branscombe beach just a ten-minute stroll away, and there is always something to tempt seafood enthusiasts, according to availability. Dinner brings a more sophisticated fixed-price menu of three courses. An introduction might be salad of marinated pink pigeon breast with fresh orange and star anise; continuing perhaps with grilled fillets of sea bass, smoked cherry tomato ratatouille and coriander pesto mash. In conclusion, you might try coconut pannacotta with pineapple and chilli syrup, or a board of fine West Country cheeses with celery, grapes and water biscuits.

★★ HL

MAP 04 SY18

EX12 3DJ

☎ 01297 680300

01297 680500

e-mail:
reception@masonsarms.co.uk

dir: *Turn off A3052 towards Branscombe, down hill, hotel at bottom of hill.*

Open 11–11 Times vary, please phone

Bar Meals L served all week 12–2 D served all week 7–9

Restaurant D served all week 7–9 Av 3 course fixed price £27.50

Free House

Otter Ale, Masons Ale, Tribute, Branoc & Guest Ales. 14

Facilities Children's licence Garden Dogs allowed Parking

Rooms 20 bedrooms en suite S£75 D£75

BRAUNTON MAP 03 SS43

The Williams Arms

Wrafton EX33 2DE ☎ 01271 812360 📠 01271 816595

dir: *On A361 between Barnstaple & Braunton*

Spacious thatched pub dating back to the 16th century, and adjacent to the popular Tarka Trail, named after the much-loved otter created by author Henry Williamson. The restaurant has a carvery serving fresh locally-sourced meat and various vegetable dishes. Breakfast is served all day.

Open 11–11 **Bar Meals** L served all week 11 D served all week 9.30 Av main course £7.95 **Restaurant** L served all week 12–2.30 D served all week 6.15–9.30 Av 3 course à la carte £11 Free House Carling, Carlsberg, Guinness, Bass. **Facilities** Children's licence Garden Parking Play Area

BRENDON MAP 03 SS74

Rockford Inn

EX35 6PT ☎ 01598 741214 📠 01598 741265

e-mail: enquiries@therockfordinn.com

dir: *A39 through Minehead follow signs to Lynmouth. Turn left off A39 to Brendon approx 5m before Lynmouth*

A traditional 17th-century country inn on the banks of the tumbling East Lyn River. Lots of old beams and Cotleigh real ales help to characterise the bar. A plate of local beef and dumplings is accompanied by onions, carrots and potatoes stewed in rich ale gravy; sirloin steak comes with traditional vegetables; and there's a Thai vegetable dish, gaeng keow waan. Two en suite rooms are popular with walkers, anglers and other fugitives from the rat race.

Open 12–3 6.30–10.30 Closed: Nov–Etr **Bar Meals** L served all week 11.30–2.30 D served all week 6.30–9.30 Av main course £6.95 Free House Real Ales & Lagers brewed on-site. **Facilities** Children's licence Garden Dogs allowed Parking

BROADHEMPSTON MAP 03 SX86

The Monks Retreat Inn

The Square TQ9 6BN ☎ 01803 812203

dir: *Exit Newton Abbot to Totnes road at Ipplepen, follow signs for Broadhempston for 3.5m.*

Apparently a friendly ghost inhabits this inn – certainly it's the sort of place you'd want to linger in: the building (listed as of outstanding architectural interest) is full of fascinating features, including a panelled oak screen typical of ancient Devon houses. Sit by one of the cosy log fires and enjoy a pint of Skinner's Cornish Knocker or other decent real ales from Butcombe.

Open 12–2.30 6–11 (Sun 12–3, 7–10.30) **Bar Meals** L served Tue–Sat 12–2 (Sun 12–2.30) D served Tue–Sat 6.30–9.30 (Sun 7–9) Av main course £9.50 **Restaurant** L served Tue–Sun 12–2 D served Tue–Sun 6.30–9.30 Av 3 course à la carte £18 Enterprise Inns Butcombe, Fosters, Kronenbourg, Guinness & Cornish Knocker. **Facilities** Children's licence Dogs allowed

BUCKFASTLEIGH MAP 03 SX76

Dartbridge Inn ★★★ INN 🍷

Totnes Rd TQ11 0JR ☎ 01364 642214 📠 01364 643839

e-mail: dartbridge.buckfastleigh@oldenglishinns.co.uk

dir: *From Exeter A38, take 1st Buckfastleigh turn, turn right to Totnes. Hotel on left*

Standing close to the River Dart, this 19th-century building was originally a simple dwelling, then a teashop before becoming a pub. Well known for its eye-catching floral displays, inside are open fires and oak beams. The lunch/bar menu includes slow-cooked Welsh lamb, and spinach and ricotta girasole, while dinner mains are typically baked rainbow trout with pan-fried tiger prawns, gammon and other steaks, sausages and mash, and chicken Caesar salad.

Open 11–11 **Bar Meals** L served all week 12–5 D served all week 5–9.30 (Sun 11–9) Av main course £8.95 **Restaurant** L served all week 12–2 D served all week 7–9.30 Old English Inns Scottish Courage, Abbot Ale, IPA, Otter Ale. 🍷 12 **Facilities** Parking **Rooms** 10 bedrooms en suite S£55 D£80

BUCKLAND MONACHORUM MAP 03 SX46

Drake Manor Inn 🍷

The Village PL20 7NA ☎ 01822 853892 📠 01822 853892

e-mail: drakemanor@drakemanorinn.co.uk

dir: *Off A386 near Yelverton*

There's a warm welcome at this picturesque pub, nestling between the village church and stream. The main building was constructed in the 16th century by the same masons who built the church. In summertime the tranquil gardens are full of colour, whilst in winter there are cosy woodburning stoves to cuddle up to. The extensive menu ranges from freshly filled baguettes to sweet potato, spicy parsnip and chestnut bake.

Open 11.30–2.30 6.30–11 (Sat 11.30–3, Sun 12–11) **Bar Meals** L served all week 12–2 D served all week 7–10 (Sun 12–2, 7–9.30) Av main course £7.50 **Restaurant** L served all week 12–2 D served all week 7–10 (Sun 7–9.30) Av 3 course à la carte £15 Punch Taverns Scottish Courage John Smiths & Courage Best, Greene King Abbott Ale, Sharp's Doom Bar. 🍷 9 **Facilities** Garden Dogs allowed Parking

England

BUTTERLEIGH MAP 03 SS90

The Butterleigh Inn

EX15 1PN ☎ 01884 855407 01884 855600

e-mail: enquiries@thebutterleighinn.com

dir: *3m from M5 junct 28 turn right by The Manor Hotel in Cullompton. Follow Butterleigh signs*

This 400-year old traditional Devonshire free house is very much a friendly local. There's a mass of local memorabilia throughout the pub, and customers can choose from a selection of real ales including Butcombe Bitter, Otter and Tawny. On fine days, the garden with its huge flowering cherry tree is very popular. Booking is recommended for the restaurant, where home-made dishes and daily specials are always available.

Open 12-2.30 6-11 (Summer 12-12, Sun 12-3 & 7-10.30) **Bar Meals** L served all week 12-2 D served all week 7-9 Av main course £7.95 **Restaurant** L served all week 12-2 D served Mon-Sat 7-9 Av 3 course à la carte £19 Free House Cotleigh Tawny Ale, Abbot Ale, Butcombe Bitter, guest ale. **Facilities** Children's licence Garden Dogs allowed Parking

CHAGFORD MAP 03 SX78

Ring O'Bells

44 The Square TQ13 8AH

☎ 01647 432466 01647 432466

e-mail: info@ringobellschagford.co.uk

dir: *From Exeter take A30 to Whiddon Down rdbt, 1st left onto A382 to Mortonhampstead. 3.5m to Easton Cross, right signed Chagford*

You won't find a juke box, games machines or television at this traditional West Country free house, but you can count on some lively conversation amid the open winter fires, beams and hand-carved bar. On warmer days, the exotic trees in the sun-drenched walled garden make a great backdrop to a drink and a bite to eat. Three carefully kept ales are on offer together with an extensive wine list. Dishes might include seafood risotto, farmhouse pies, Devon mussels, and steak and kidney pudding.

Open 9.30-3 5-11 (Sat 10-3, 6-11, Sun 12-3, 6-10.30) **Bar Meals** L served all week 12-2 D served all week 6-9 Av main course £9.25 **Restaurant** L served all week 12-2 D served all week 6-9 Free House Butcombe Bitter, Dartmoor Ale, Reel Ale, Tetley. 8 **Facilities** Children's licence Garden Dogs allowed

Pick of the Pubs

The Sandy Park Inn NEW

TQ13 8JW ☎ 01647 433267

e-mail: sandyparkinn@aol.com

dir: *From A30 exit at Whiddon Down, turn left towards Moretonhampstead. Inn 5m from Whiddon Down*

See Pick of the Pubs on opposite page

Three Crowns Hotel ★★ HL

High St TQ13 8AJ

☎ 01647 433444 & 433441 01647 433117

e-mail: threecrowns@msn.com

An impressive, 13th-century, granite-built inn with a wealth of historical associations to investigate. Take young poet and Cavalier Sydney Godolphin, for example, who was shot in the hotel doorway in 1643 and who continues to 'appear', making him the hotel's oldest resident. Period features include mullioned windows, sturdy oak beams and a massive open fireplace. Among chef's specialities are sautéed fillet of pork with mango salsa; roasted breast of duck with plum sauce; and lemon sole poached in white wine with mixed seafood sauce.

Open 8am-12.30am **Bar Meals** L served all week 12-3 D served all week 6-9.30 Av main course £6 **Restaurant** L served all week 12-2.30 D served all week 6-9.30 Av 3 course à la carte £22.50 Av 3 course fixed price £19.50 Free House Flowers Original, Boddingtons, Bass, Whitbread. **Facilities** Children's licence Dogs allowed Parking **Rooms** 17 bedrooms en suite S£55 D£85

CHARDSTOCK MAP 04 ST30

The George Inn

EX13 7BX ☎ 01460 220241

e-mail: info@george-inn.co.uk

dir: *A358 from Taunton through Chard towards Axminster, left at Tytherleigh. Signed from A358.*

Graffiti from 1648 can be seen in the snug of this 700-year-old pub, which was once a parish house. A friendly parson named Copeland haunts the cellar, while cheerful locals who've been drinking in the George for the past 40 years preside over 'Compost Corner'. Hearty dishes include feta, spinach and mozzarella pie; pan-fried lambs' liver or beer battered cod. Four cottage-style bedrooms are available for those who can't quite tear themselves away.

Open 11-2.30 6-11 (Sat 11-3 6-11, Sun 12-3 7-10.30) **Bar Meals** L served all week 12-2 (Sun 12-2.30) D served all week 7-9 (Sat 7-9.30) Av main course £8.50 **Restaurant** L served all week 12-2 D served all week 7-9 Av 3 course à la carte £12 Free House Branoc & Guest ale. **Facilities** Garden Dogs allowed Parking

The Sandy Park Inn

almon and brown trout fishing, horse riding and moorland walks are all available almost from ie door of this pretty thatched inn, which is hidden away in the beautiful Dartmoor National ark. But once you've stepped through the lintel, you might find it hard to tear yourself away om the cosy bar and romantic restaurant.

verything about the Sandy Park just as it should be. Dogs are equently to be found slumped ı front of the fire, horse-brasses nd sporting prints adorn the alls, and the beamed bar attracts ɔcals and tourists alike, all happily etting the world to rights with ie help of an eclectic wine list nd good range of traditional local es, including Otter Ale, St Austell ribute and Sharps Doom Bar. he candlelit restaurant is equally ppealing, offering a brasserie-yle menu that changes daily to ıake the most of local produce. tarters might include deep-fried rie with redcurrant jelly, or moked mackerel, to be followed y venison casserole, roast cod, r spinach and mushroom pie the perfect fare after a day spent stomping the moors. Should you really not be able to muster the will to leave, check in to one of the five newly refurbished bedrooms. In keeping with the inn's ethos, they're appealingly cottagey in style, without losing anything in the way of modern luxuries. Expect flat screen televisions, CD players and stunning views, not to mention your shoes cleaned in the morning, ready for another day spent tramping the moors.

NEW 🍷
MAP 03 SX78
TQ13 8JW
☎ 01647 433267
e-mail: sandyparkinn@aol.com
dir: *From A30 exit at Whiddon Down, left towards Moretonhampstead. Inn 5m from Whiddon Down*

Open 11–11
Bar Meals L served all week 12–2.30 D served all week 6.30–9 Av main course £9
Restaurant L served all week 12–2.30 D served all week 6.30–9 Av 3 course à la carte £20
Free House
Otter Ale, O'Hanlons, St Austel Tribute, Exe Valley XX1. 🍷 14
Facilities Garden Dogs allowed Parking

The Merry Harriers

Standing high on the Blackdown Hills, the pub was built as a longhouse in 1492, the year Christopher Columbus 'discovered' America. The exact location is Forches Corner, a junction of three lanes that, in the 17th and 18th centuries, highwaymen used to patrol, at least until they were caught, when they were hanged outside the pub.

Such summary justice is said to be the explanation for the resident ghost of a headless horseman. Two of the pub's three acres are pasture, but this still leaves plenty of space for a large beer garden and a recently reopened five-lane skittle alley, one of the longest in the county. Inside the characterful bar are beamed ceilings, a cosy inglenook and attractive dining areas. Peter and Angela Gatling have worked tirelessly since taking over in 2005, building the local drinks trade while expanding the food operation. More than 90 per cent of kitchen ingredients are from the surrounding hills, or further afield in the West Country, and the Gatlings plan to nudge this figure even higher. The regularly changing menus offer a wide choice, including game casserole with baby onions and rich red wine gravy; free range chicken breast with wild mushroom duxelle and port and shallot sauce; pan-fried Brixham scallops with Parma ham, ginger, chilli and coriander linguine; and whole Combe St Nicholas rainbow trout with almond butter. Among the bar snacks, which also double as starters, are mini salmon fishcakes with lemon and black pepper vinaigrette; warm wood-pigeon breast with toasted pine nut salad and raspberry dressing; and mixed tempura vegetables with satay sauce. Children can select from a menu that contains mambo Italiano, which is mezzaluna pasta filled with goats' cheese; and mad cow (steak and kidney) pie.

NEW
MAP 04 ST11
Forches Corner EX15 3TR
☎ 01823 421270
Fax 01823 421270
e-mail:
peter.gatling@btinternet.com
dir: *A38, turn onto Ford Street (marked by brown tourist sign). At top of hill turn left, 1.5m on right*

Open 12-3 6.30-11
Bar Meals L served all week 12-2 D served all week 6.30-9 (Sun 12-2.30) Av main course £9
Restaurant L served all week 12-2 D served all week 6.30-9 (Sun 12-2.30) Av 3 course à la carte £16.50
Free House
Otter Head, Cotleigh Harrier, Exmoor Gold, St Austell Tinners & Exe Valley Devon Pride. 14
Facilities Garden Dogs allowed Parking Play Area

:HAWLEIGH MAP 03 SS71

he Earl of Portsmouth

he Square EX18 7HJ ☎ 01769 580204
-mail: suzy42@aol.com

former coaching inn on the old road from Barnstaple to London. ntil it burnt down in 1869, it was the London Inn, but when the estate wner, the Earl of Portsmouth, rebuilt it no-one dared oppose the new ame. Much of the food, and most of the real ales, are locally sourced. aked pork tenderloin is served with stilton and broccoli; flaked salmon omes in pesto sauce on fresh penne pasta.

pen 11–3.30 5.30–11 (Fri–Sat 12–2am) **Bar Meals** L served Tue–Wed & i–Sun 12.30–2.30 D served Tue–Wed & Fri–Sun 6.30–8.30 Av main course 5.95 **Restaurant** L served Tue–Sat 12.30–2.30 D served Tue–Sun 6.30–9 ;un 12.30–3) Av 3 course à la carte £23 Free House Rail Ale, Firing quad. **Facilities** Children's licence Garden Dogs allowed Parking

:HERITON BISHOP MAP 03 SX79

'he Old Thatch Inn

X6 6HJ ☎ 01647 24204 01647 24584
-mail: mail@theoldthatchinn.f9.co.uk
ir: *0.5m off A30, 7m SW of Exeter*

his charming 16th-century free house once welcomed stagecoaches n the London to Penzance road. It passed into private hands and then ecame a tea-room before its licence was again renewed in the early 970s. A major refurbishment during the winter of 2006 following a re has preserved the period appeal, and included a complete refit for ne kitchen. Expect a high standard, with Devon seafood in abundance: ome-made fresh crab open ravioli, or pan-fried medallions of nonkfish with fresh fennel are likely choices.

pen 11.30–3 6–11 Closed: 25–26 Dec **Bar Meals** L served all week 2–2 D served all week 6.30–9 Av main course £8 **Restaurant** L served all week 12–2 D served all week 6.30–9 Av 3 course à la carte £23 Free House Sharp's Doom Bar, Otter Ale, Princetown's Jail Ale, Port Stout. 9 **Facilities** Garden Dogs allowed Parking

CLAYHIDON MAP 04 ST11

Pick of the Pubs

The Merry Harriers NEW

Forches Corner EX15 3TR
☎ 01823 421270 01823 421270
e-mail: peter.gatling@btinternet.com
dir: *A38, turn onto Ford Street (marked by brown tourist sign). At top of hill turn left, 1.5m on right*

See Pick of the Pubs on opposite page

CLEARBROOK MAP 03 SX56

The Skylark Inn

PL20 6JD ☎ 01822 853258
e-mail: skylvic@btinternet.com
dir: *5m N of Plymouth, just off A386 to Tavistock road. 2nd right signed for Clearbrook.*

The beamed bar with its large fireplace and wood-burning stove characterises this attractive village inn. Although only ten minutes from Plymouth, the Skylark is set in the Dartmoor National Park and the area is ideal for cyclists and walkers. Good wholesome food is served from an extensive menu that features rainbow trout with new potatoes and salad; vegetable stew with dumplings; and a range of shortcrust pastry pies.

Open 11.30–3 6–11 (Summer 11.30–11.30) **Bar Meals** L served all week 11.30–2 D served all week 6.30–9 Unique Interbrew Bass, Scottish Courage Courage Best, Sharp's Special. **Facilities** Garden Dogs allowed Parking Play Area

CLOVELLY MAP 03 SS32

Pick of the Pubs

Red Lion Hotel ★★ HL

The Quay EX39 5TF ☎ 01237 431237 01237 431044
e-mail: redlion@clovelly.co.uk
dir: *From Bideford rdbt, follow A39 to Bude for 10m. At Clovelly Cross rdbt turn right, past visitor centre entrance, bear left. At bottom of hill on sea front*

Clovelly, the famously unspoilt 'village like a waterfall', descends down broad steps to a 14th-century harbour and this charming hostelry is located right on the quay. Guests staying in the whimsically decorated bedrooms can fall asleep to the sound of waves lapping the shingle and wake to the cries of gulls squabbling for scraps. Seafood, unsurprisingly, is a priority on the modern French-influenced menu, which could offer grilled Cornish oysters with champagne sabayon, or home-made wild rabbit terrine with red onion marmalade to start, followed by chargrilled turbot steak; cod fillet in tempura batter with minted

CONTINUED

England

CLOVELLY continued

pea purée, or pan-seared tuna steak with grilled foie gras and shallots. Desserts are equally artful: frozen mango parfait with grapefruit confit and black peppercorn meringue sounds especially intriguing. Daytime visitors can tuck into a locally-made Cornish pasty, or a plate of cod and chips.

Open 11–1am **Bar Meals** L served all week 11–2.30 D served all week 6–8.30 Av main course £7 **Restaurant** D served all week 7–8.30 Av 3 course à la carte £25 Free House Doom Bar, Old Appledore, Guinness, Carlsberg Export. **Facilities** Children's licence Parking **Rooms** 11 bedrooms en suite S£54.50 D£109

CLYST HYDON MAP 03 ST00

Pick of the Pubs

The Five Bells Inn

EX15 2NT ☎ 01884 277288

e-mail: info@fivebellsclysthydon.co.uk

dir: *10m from Exeter. B3181 towards Cullompton, turn right at Hele Cross towards Clyst Hydon. Continue 2m turn right to Clyst Hydon. Sharp right left band at village sign*

Originally a 16th-century thatched farmhouse, this attractive country pub in rolling east Devon countryside started serving ale about a hundred years ago, and takes its name from the five bells hanging in the village church tower. It's gone from strength to strength in recent years, thanks to its family-friendly owners and a focus on real ales, good food and cheerful hospitality. The well-stocked and maintained garden is a delight in summer, with twenty tables enjoying lovely views, and a children's play area. The interior boasts two wood fires, numerous prints and watercolours, and brass and copper artefacts; children are welcome here too, with books and games provided for their amusement. Excellent real ales are augmented by draught lagers, cider and bottled beers. The menu offers firm favourites like steak and kidney pudding and treacle tart alongside specials such as roast pheasant or fish pie, and the children's menu also includes tasty home-made dishes.

Open 11.30–3 6.30–11 (Winter 7–11 Sun 12–3, 7–10.30) **Bar Meals** L served all week 11.30–2 D served all week 7–9 (Sun 12–2) Av main course £9 **Restaurant** L served all week 11.30–2 D served all week 7–9 (Sun 12–2) Av 3 course à la carte £20 Free House Cotleigh Tawny Ale, Otter Bitter, O'Hanlon's. 8 **Facilities** Garden Parking Play Area

COCKWOOD MAP 03 SX9

Pick of the Pubs

The Anchor Inn

EX6 8RA ☎ 01626 890203 01626 890355

dir: *Off A379 between Dawlish & Starcross*

Overlooking a small landlocked harbour on the River Exe, this 460-year-old former Seamen's Mission has been a haven to many sailors and smugglers over the years. It is said to be haunted by a friendly ghost and his dog. Real fires and low beams make the interior cosy and inviting in winter, while in summer customers spill out onto the verandah and harbour wall. The truly comprehensive menu offers everything from sandwiches and traditional Devon dishes like steak and wassail pie, to venison with Guinness and pickled walnut sauce, or home-smoked pheasant in bacon and Madeira sauce. Extensive sections of the menu are devoted to mussels, scallops and oysters. Mussels, for instance, might come in korma sauce, leek mornay sauce or Guinness, to name just three of the thirty options. Finish with local cheeses or one of 12 different treacle tarts.

Open 11–11 (Sun 12–10.30) **Bar Meals** L served all week 12–10 D served all week 12–10 (Sun 12–9.30) Av main course £7.50 **Restaurant** L served all week 12–2.15 D served all week 6.30–10 (Sun 6.30–9.30) Av 3 course à la carte £30 Heavitree Interbrew Bass, Timothy Taylor Landlord, Fuller's London Pride, Otter Ale. 10 **Facilities** Garden Dogs allowed Parking

COLEFORD MAP 03 SS7

Pick of the Pubs

The New Inn ★★★★ INN

EX17 5BZ ☎ 01363 84242 01363 85044

e-mail: enquiries@thenewinncoleford.co.uk

dir: *From Exeter take A377, 1.5m after Crediton turn left for Coleford, continue for 1.5m*

See Pick of the Pubs on opposite page

The New Inn

/hen you enter this pretty, thatched and cob-built free house, listen for a greeting from Captain, ıe blue-fronted Amazon parrot; he was a somewhat unusual fixture and fitting when Simon and ⁄lelissa Renshaw bought the inn.

ıilt in the 13th century, The ew Inn still serves the sleepy ɔnservation village of Coleford ith its ales. After so many years in rvice, new it most certainly is not, ıt despite changes over the years still retains original black beams ıd fireplaces. The ground floor divided into three – a restaurant ırtitioned by a timber and glass reen, a central bar servery, and bar around the fireplace in e oldest section. There are six ːdrooms, three in the old linney ›nce an open-sided barn) and three the main building. Three chefs e dedicated to creating a changing lection of locally sourced fresh ;h, meat and vegetarian dishes, ːch as starters of feta cheese and ،n-dried tomato salad; marinated ،illi king prawns; and grilled ›ats' cheese on a rum and raisin mixed leaf salad. Main courses include West Country faggots with wholegrain mustard mash; roast duck breast with blackcurrant jus; grilled sea bass on roasted fennel; and slow roast lamb shank with pearl barley. Desserts range from poached blackcurrants topped with cream, yoghurt and muscovado sugar, to white chocolate cheesecake with orange jelly topping. West Country cheeses are always available, as is a delicious selection of ice creams from the farm down the road. During the summer, make the most of the idyllic garden, bordered by the Cole Brook, for drinking and dining alfresco. The patio also plays host to pig-roasts between late April and October. A comprehensive wine list completes the picture.

★★★★ INN ☞ 🍷
MAP 03 SS70
EX17 5BZ
☎ 01363 84242
01363 85044
e-mail: enquiries@thenewinncoleford.co.uk
dir: *From Exeter take A377, 1.5m after Crediton turn left for Coleford, continue for 1.5m.*

Open 12-3 6-11 (Sun 7-10.30)
Closed: 25-26 Dec
Bar Meals L served all week 12-2 D served all week 7-10 (Sun 12-2, 7-9.30) Av main course £10
Restaurant L served all week 12-2 D served all week 7-10 (Sun 12-2, 7-9.30) Av 3 course à la carte £20
Free House
Doom Bar, Otter Ale, Exmoor Ale, Wells Bombardier & Tanglefoot. 🍷 8
Facilities Garden Parking
Rooms 7 bedrooms en suite S£60 D£75

England

CORNWORTHY MAP 03 SX85

Hunters Lodge Inn 🍷

TQ9 7ES ☎ 01803 732204
e-mail: gill.rees@virgin.net
dir: *Off A381, S of Totnes*

Built in 1740, this country local is at the hub of village life, sponsoring a football team, charity events and a dog show (it's a dog friendly pub). There's even a Christmas party for children. Other notable features are the real log fire and resident ghost. An extensive menu offers dishes from the sea (sesame battered Brixham cod fillet), and from the land (gammon steak, Cornworthy hens' eggs) as well as a selection of pasta dishes (spaghetti carbonara).

Open 11.30–2.30 6.30–11 **Bar Meals** L served all week 12–2 D served all week 7–9 **Restaurant** L served all week 12–2 D served all week 7–9 Free House Teignworthy Reel Ale & Springtide, Guest Ales. 🍷 14 **Facilities** Garden Dogs allowed Parking Play Area

CULMSTOCK MAP 03 ST11

Culm Valley Inn 🍷

EX15 3JJ ☎ 01884 840354 📠 01884 841659

A former station hotel in which the owners exposed a long-hidden bar during a renovation re-creating a 'between the wars' look. The ever-changing blackboard menu displays a lengthy list of home-made dishes, mostly using locally-grown or raised ingredients, including chicken breast, duck breast and spiced orange reduction, and Aberdeen Angus sirloin steak. Fish and shellfish mostly come from South Devon or Cornwall, including Cornish fix mix, hand-dived scallops, large lemon sole with quince alioli, and three sorts of Loch Fyne smoked salmon.

Open 12–3 6–11 (Open all day Sun) Closed: 25 Dec **Bar Meals** L served all week 12–2 D served Mon–Sat 7–9 Av main course £10 **Restaurant** L served all week 12–2 D served Mon–Sat 7–9 Av 3 course à la carte £21.50 Free House Otter Bright, Oakhill, Exmoor Ale. 🍷 50 **Facilities** Garden Dogs allowed Parking **Notes**

DALWOOD MAP 04 ST2

Pick of the Pubs

The Tuckers Arms 🍷

EX13 7EG ☎ 01404 881342 📠 01404 881138
e-mail: davidbeck@tuckersarms.freeserve.co.uk
dir: *Off A35 between Honiton & Axminster*

Dating back 800 years or so, this Devon longhouse originally provided accommodation for the artisans constructing the local church across the way. Today it is a popular and hospitable village inn providing good quality sustenance for modern travellers. It enjoys a pretty setting between two ridges of the Blackdown Hills, a few yards from the Corry brook and overlooked by the ancient Viking fort of Danes Hill. Inside it is everything you would expect of a traditional, thatched inn – it has inglenook fireplaces, low beams and flagstone floors. Real ales such as Otter Bitter and Old Speckled Hen are on tap. Fish and shellfish from local fishermen (the pub is only 15 minutes from Lyme Regis) and Brixham market are shown on the daily specials board, and will generally include scallops, monkfish, lemon sole, with sea bass and seafood roast when available. Outside there is a lovely olde-English country garden and, more recently created, a covered patio with heaters.

Open 12–3 6.30–11 (Sun 12–10.30) **Bar Meals** L served all week 12–2 D served all week 7–8.30 (Sun 12–7.30) **Restaurant** L served all week 12–2 D served all week 7–9 Av 3 course à la carte £20.95 Av 2 course fixed price £18.95 Free House Otter Bitter, Courage Best, Old Speckled Hen. 🍷 8 **Facilities** Garden Parking

DARTMOUTH MAP 03 SX8

The Cherub Inn 🍷

13 Higher St TQ6 9RB ☎ 01803 832571
e-mail: enquiries@the-cherub.co.uk

The Cherub Inn is Dartmouth's oldest building, dating from about 1380. It survived the threats of fire in 1864, World War II bombing an proposed demolition in 1958 to be finally restored and Grade II listec The bar and restaurant menus offer a selection of steak, poultry, gam and fish dishes. Expect pan-fried prime Exmoor venison steak, duck magret teriyaki, prime West Country best end of lamb, and a Tuscan vegetable tart.

Open 11–11 (Sun 12–10.30) **Bar Meals** L served all week 12–2 D served all week 7–9.30 **Restaurant** L served all week D served all week 7–9.30 Free House Cherub Best Bitter, Brakspear Bitter, Shepherd Neame Best, Exmoor Ale. 🍷 10 **Facilities** Dogs allowed

Pick of the Pubs

Royal Castle Hotel ★★★ HL 🍷

11 The Quay TQ6 9PS
☎ 01803 833033 📠 01803 835445
e-mail: enquiry@royalcastle.co.uk
dir: *In town centre, overlooking Inner Harbour*

In the 1630s two merchants built their neighbouring quayside houses in commanding positions on the Dart estuary. A century later, one had become The New Inn, and by 1782 it had been combined with its neighbour to become The Castle Inn. Further rebuilds incorporated the battlemented turrets and cornice that gave it an appearance worthy of its name. Opposite the bar is the Lydstone Range, forged in Dartmouth over 300 years ago, and on which you can still have your meat roasted during the winter. There is also a bell-board in the courtyard, with each room's bell pitched to a different note. In the upstairs Adam Room Restaurant fish and seafood dishes are always available – typically dishes will be based on red mullet, lemon sole, turbot and red snapper to name but a few. Other options might be pan-fried chicken breast on green pea and trompette mushroom risotto; rich lamb casserole; and baby pumpkins served with slow-roasted tomato sauce, filled with fresh local vegetables.

Royal Castle Hotel

Open 8–11.30 **Bar Meals** L served all week 11.30–11 D served all week 11.30–11 Av main course £8.50 **Restaurant** L served all week 12–2 D served all week 7–9.30 Av 3 course à la carte £25 Free House Dartmoor IPA, Directors, Becks Vier, Bass. 12 **Facilities** Dogs allowed Parking **Rooms** 25 bedrooms en suite S£85 D£125

DENBURY — MAP 03 SX86

The Union Inn

Denbury Green TQ12 6DQ
☎ 01803 812595 Fax 01803 814206
e-mail: unioninn@hotmail.co.uk
dir: *2m form Newton Abbot, signed Denbury*

At least 400 years old and counting. Inside are the original stone walls that once rang to the hammers of the blacksmiths and cartwrights who worked here many moons ago. Choose freshly prepared, mouth-watering starters such as moules marinière or smoked chicken in mango vinaigrette, and follow with slow-roasted shoulder of lamb with mint garlic and redcurrant jelly, or a rib-eye steak on a bed of haggis with stilton and whisky sauce.

Open 12–3 6–11 (Sat 12–11, Sun 12–10.30) **Bar Meals** L served all week 12.30–2.30 D served all week 6.30–9.30 Av main course £10 **Restaurant** L served all week 12.30–2.30 D served all week 6.30–9.30 Av 3 course à la carte £18 Enterprise Inns Otter, 6X & London Pride. 9 **Facilities** Garden Dogs allowed Parking

DITTISHAM — MAP 03 SX85

Pick of the Pubs

The Ferry Boat

Manor St TQ6 0EX ☎ 01803 722368

This quiet traditional pub is the only riverside inn on the River Dart, and continues to prove popular with sailors, walkers and their dogs, and families. There are tables by the waterfront with views across the river to Greenway House and Gardens, a National Trust property that was once Agatha Christie's home. In the winter months, open log fires crackle in the grates, making it a snug place to go for a pint of Hobgoblin or Adnams Broadside.

Open 11–12 (Sun 12–11) **Bar Meals** L served all week 12–2.30 D served all week 7–9 Av main course £8.25 Punch Taverns Bass, Stella Artois, Youngs, Hobgoblin, Adnams Broadside. 9 **Facilities** Children's licence Dogs allowed

DODDISCOMBSLEIGH — MAP 03 SX88

Pick of the Pubs

The Nobody Inn

EX6 7PS ☎ 01647 252394 Fax 01647 252978
e-mail: info@nobodyinn.co.uk
dir: *3m SW of Exeter Racecourse (A38)*

Dating from around 1591, for many years this building served as the village's unofficial church house and meeting place, becoming a de facto inn along the way. It was officially licensed as the New Inn in 1838; the name was changed in 1952 after the innkeeper's death, when his body was accidentally left in the mortuary whilst the funeral took place around an empty coffin. The present family has run the place since 1970, spoiling customers with unusual local ales, 240 whiskies, 600 wines and an extensive cheeseboard. All the food is home made from local ingredients, and vegetables are organic if possible. An appealing bar menu is available at lunch and in the evening, with nibbles like spicy roasted broad beans, salads such as crispy duck and chorizo, and favourites like casserole of venison with red wine and chestnuts. The restaurant, open for dinner, extends the food's complexity but prices remain refreshingly reasonable.

Open 12–2.30 6–11 (Sun 7–10.30) Closed: 25–26 & 31 Dec **Bar Meals** L served all week 12–2 D served all week 7–10 Av main course £8.50 **Restaurant** D served Tue–Sat 7.30–9 Av 3 course à la carte £20 Free House Branscombe Nobody's Bitter, Sharp's Doom Bar, RCH East Street Cream, Exmoor Gold. 20 **Facilities** Garden Parking

DOLTON — MAP 03 SS51

Rams Head Inn ★★★ INN

South St EX19 8QS ☎ 01805 804255 Fax 01805 804509
e-mail: ramsheadinn@btopenworld.com
dir: *8m from Torrington on A3124*

The inn dates from the 15th century, possibly earlier, and is located in a quiet North Devon village, in the heart of the farming community

CONTINUED

DOLTON continued

between Dartmoor and Exmoor. Huge fireplaces complete with bread ovens and pot stands lend original character. Traditional bar food is served at lunchtime, with a restaurant menu in the evening offering the likes of whitebait or garlic crevettes to start, followed by beef stroganoff or chicken imperial.

Open 10–12 (Mon 5–12) **Bar Meals** L served Tue–Sat 12–2.30 D served all week 6.30–9 (Sun 7–8.30) Av main course £9 **Restaurant** L served Tue–Sun 12–2.30 D served all week 6.30–9 (Sun 7–8.30) Av 3 course à la carte £15 Free House Flowers IPA Cask, Flowers Original. 7 **Facilities** Garden Dogs allowed Parking **Rooms** 6 bedrooms en suite S£35 D£50

The Union Inn

Fore St EX19 8QH ☎ 01805 804633 01805 804633

e-mail: theunioninn@dolton.wanadoo.co.uk

dir: *From A361 take B3227 to S Moulton, then Atherington. Left onto B3217 then 6m to Dalton. Pub on right*

A 17th-century free house built as a Devon longhouse. Traditionally constructed of cob, the building was converted to a hotel in the mid-19th century to serve the local cattle markets, and it remains a traditional village pub with a cosy atmosphere. There's a homely beamed bar, oak settles and sturdy wooden tables, plus good home cooking, especially Sunday roasts and traditional dishes washed down with West Country ales.

Open 12–3 6–11 Closed: 1st 2 wks Feb **Bar Meals** L served Thu–Tue 12–2 D served Thu–Tue 7–10 (Sun 12–2.30, 7–9) Av main course £6.95 **Restaurant** L served Sun 12–2.30 D served Thu–Tue 7–9 Free House Sharp's Doom Bar, Jollyboat Freebooter, Clearwater Cavalier, St Austell Tribute. **Facilities** Children's licence Garden Dogs allowed Parking

DREWSTEIGNTON MAP 03 SX79

Pick of the Pubs

The Drewe Arms

The Square EX6 6QN ☎ 01647 281224

e-mail: fiona@thedrewearms.co.uk

dir: *W of Exeter on A30 for 12m. Left at Woodleigh junct follow signs for 3m to Drewsteignton*

See Pick of the Pubs on opposite page

Please see walk on page 162

EXETER MAP 03 SX99

Red Lion Inn

Broadclyst EX5 3EL ☎ 01392 461271

dir: *On B3181 Exeter to Cullompton*

A 16th-century inn set at the heart of a delightful National Trust village, next to the church. Typical examples of the restaurant menu include monkfish medallions with bacon and tomato jus; seafood gratin; pan-fried pigeon; roast pheasant with redcurrant and red onion jus; and a range of steaks. In the bar expect ham, egg and chips; venison sausages with colcannon; and Thai curry.

Open 11–3 5.30–11 (Sun 12–3, 7–10.30) **Bar Meals** L served all week 12–2.30 D served all week 6–9.30 (Sun 7–9) **Restaurant** L served all wee 12–2.30 D served Mon–Sat 6–9.30 (Sun 7–9) Free House Bass, Fullers London Pride, O'Hanlons Local Blakelys Red, Speckled Hen. 7 **Facilities** Garden Parking

The Twisted Oak

Little John's Cross Hill EX2 9RG

☎ 01392 273666 01392 277705

e-mail: martin.bullock@virgin.net

dir: *A30 to Okehampton, follow signs for pub*

Set in a beautiful part of Ide just outside Exeter, this large pub has be turned into a quality, food-driven venue in the last few years. There is a choice of dining area – an informal place where you can relax on th leather sofas and eat; a separate lounge bar restaurant; and a more formal conservatory area, which is adult only in the evenings. During the summer months the huge garden provides seating and a childrer play area.

Open 11–3 6–11 (Sun 6–10.30) **Bar Meals** L served all week 12–2.30 D served all week 6–9.30 **Restaurant** L served all week 12–2.30 D servec all week 6–9.30 O'Hanlons Firefly, Cotleighs 25, Bass, Pedigree. 11 **Facilities** Garden Parking Play Area

EXMINSTER MAP 03 SX9

Swans Nest

Station Rd EX6 8DZ ☎ 01392 832371

dir: *From M5 junct 30 follow A379 (Dawlish road)*

A much extended pub in a pleasant rural location whose facilities, unusually, extend to a ballroom, dance floor and stage. The carvery is a popular option for diners, with a choice of meats served with freshl prepared vegetables, though the salad bar is a tempting alternative, with over 39 items, including quiches, pies and home-smoked chicke A carte of home-cooked fare includes grilled lamb steak, Devon pork chop, and five-bean vegetable curry.

Open 10.30–2.30 6–11 (Sun 12–2.30, 7–10.30) Closed: 26 Dec **Bar Meals** L served all week 12–2 D served all week 6–9.45 Av main course £8 **Restaurant** L served all week 12–2 D served all week 6–9.30 Free House Otter Bitter. 8 **Facilities** Garden Parking Play Area

The Drewe Arms

ucked away in a sleepy village square close to the National Trust's Castle Drogo, this uintessentially English thatched inn is an ideal place for refreshments after a country walk in he surrounding Dartmoor National Park.

he timeless atmosphere that ervades both the pub and the illage are undoubtedly a key to its uccess. Built in 1646, the inn was riginally known as the Druid Arms ut in the 1920s the Drewe family, or whom Castle Drogo was built, ersuaded the brewery to change ne pub's name. Their family coat of rms is still on the sign. The pub's nique historical charm makes it rare find these days. It was taken ver in 1919 by Ernest and Mabel ludge, and after Ernest's death label continued to run the pub lone, eventually retiring in 1994 the age of 99. Even today, the iterior remains largely unaltered by me. Traditional ales are still drawn irect from the cask, housed in the riginal 'tap bar' and served through a hatchway into the snug. The Card Room has a log fire for cold winter days, and in summer you can relax in the attractive gardens. Other alternatives are Mable's Kitchen, kept cosy by an original Rayburn stove, or the Dartmoor Room, hidden away behind the tap room. The chef provides good food, using locally sourced produce. The Long Room to the rear of the pub is a large function room opening onto the garden, ideal for weddings, parties, live music etc. And for all its country idyll, the inn is just a short drive from the A30.

MAP 03 SX79
The Square EX6 6QN
01647 281224
e-mail:
fiona@thedrewearms.co.uk
dir: *W of Exeter on A30 for 12m. Left at Woodleigh junct follow signs for 3m to Drewsteignton*

Open 11–3 6–12 (11–12 Summer)
Bar Meals L served all week 12–3 D served all week 6–9.30 Av main course £10
Restaurant L served all week 12–3 D served all week 6.30–9 Av 3 course à la carte £15
Whitbread
Otter Ale, Prince Towns Jail Ale.
Facilities Garden Dogs allowed Parking

Drewe Arms

Walk information

Distance: 5.5 miles (9km)
Map: OS Explorer 115 Exeter & Sidmouth
Start/finish: unsurfaced car park at Knowles Wood; grid ref SY 095068
Ascent/gradient: 2
Paths: country lanes, pastures and woodland paths; 7 stiles
Landscape: rolling farmland and beech woods

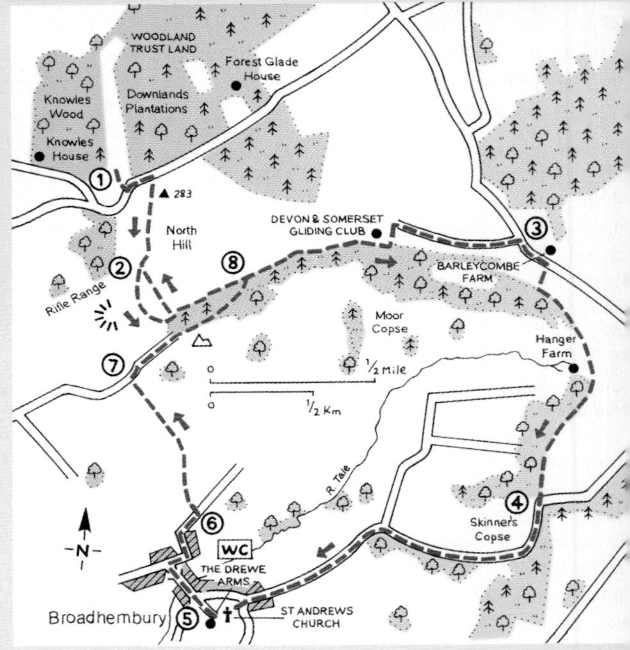

Walk directions

A Return to the road and turn left uphill. Very shortly a bridleway sign points right through another parking area. After a few minutes this narrow, level path reaches a signpost and metal gate (left), indicating that you have reached the Devon & Somerset Gliding Club. Ignore the gate, continue on the bridleway.

B Pass through the next metal gate onto the airfield. Turn left along the edge, keeping to the right of the clubhouse. Follow the tarmac drive left over a cattle grid and down the lane to join a road.

C Turn right; pass Barleycombe Farm (on the left), then follow bridleway signs right through a gate, left through another and into a field. Follow the track along the bottom of the field. The path curves right through a stand of beech trees and a metal gate, then runs straight across the next field towards a big beech tree and gate. Take the stony track through the gate. After 100 yards (91m) bear right along a grassy path (ignore the gate straight ahead) and through two metal gates, with conifers to the right.

D The path ends at a lane; turn right downhill into Broadhembury. At St Andrew's Church cross the road and go through the churchyard, then under the lychgate and downhill to find the Drewe Arms (left) for a welcome break.

E To continue the walk, from the pub, turn left down the main street to reach the bridge and ford. Turn right up the lane, past the playground and up the hill.

F Just past two thatched cottages go left over the stile in the hedge and up the field, aiming for a stile in the top left corner. Go over that and straight ahead, keeping the old farmhouse and barn conversions to your right. Over the next stile; then another; then right, round the edge of the field, and over a small stile ahead into a small copse. Another stile leads into the next field; look straight across to locate the next stile in the beech hedge opposite, which takes you into a green lane.

G Turn right and walk uphill between conifers, on the left, and fields until a metal gate leads on to an open gateway and back on to the airfield.

H Turn left along the edge of the field. Go left over the second iron gate to rejoin the bridleway which leads back to the road. Turn left downhill to find your car.

While there

Visit Broadhembury Craft Centre, which you will pass as you walk downhill towards the village after Point D. Open seven days a week and situated in an attractive courtyard setting, here you will find a range of rural craft workshops.

England

:XTON MAP 03 SX98

Pick of the Pubs

The Puffing Billy

Station Rd EX3 0PR ☎ 01392 877888 📠 01392 876232
e-mail: food@thepuffingbilly.com
dir: *3m from M5 junct 30. Take A376 signed Exmouth, through Ebford. Follow signs for Puffing Billy, turn right into Exton*

Named for its proximity to the Exeter-Exmouth branch line, the 16th-century Puffing Billy enjoys views of the Exe estuary. Diners can see the serious approach to food expressed pictorially in the original artwork on display. Enjoy mackerel rillette with marinated aubergine, pink fir potato and tapenade salad; caramelised scallops with truffled baby leek terrine; confit duck leg and fennel risotto; twice-baked Cornish Blue soufflé with walnuts and French bean salad; slow honey-roasted pork belly with creamed potato and pine nut salad; and Crediton duckling with fondant potato, turnip, apples and fig jus. Rhubarb crumble soufflé with ginger ice cream is a typical dessert.

Open 11.30-3 6-11 (Sun 12-2.30, 6.30-10.30) Closed: selected days over Christmas **Bar Meals** L served all week 12-2.30 D served Mon-Sat 6.30-9.30 Av main course £8.50 **Restaurant** L served all week 12-2.30 D served Mon-Sat 6.30-9.30 Av 3 course à la carte £29 Otter, Bass, Laffe. 12 **Facilities** Children's licence Garden Parking

IARBERTON MAP 03 SX75

'he Church House Inn

Q9 7SF ☎ 01803 863707 📠 01803 864661
·mail: churchhouseinnha@btconnect.com
ir: *From Totnes take A381 S. Take turn for Harberton on right, ıb by church in village centre*

ıilt to house masons working on the church next door (around 00), the inn has some fascinating historic features, including a Tudor ndow frame and latticed window with 13th-century glass; there's en a resident ghost. The extensive menu is supplemented by daily ecials and a traditional roast on Sundays. There's plenty of seafood/ h, and a family room is provided.

ɔen 11-2.30 6-11 (Sat 11-3, Sun 12-3, 7-10.30) **Bar Meals** L served week 12-2 D served all week 6.30-9.30 Av main course £13.50 **staurant** 12-2 6.30-9.30 (closed Sun during winter) Av 3 course à la ·te £23 Free House Skinners, Abbots, Dartmoor IPA, Church House ter & Guest ales. **Facilities** Dogs allowed

HAYTOR VALE MAP 03 SX77

Pick of the Pubs

The Rock Inn ★★ HL

TQ13 9XP ☎ 01364 661305 📠 01364 661242
e-mail: inn@rock-inn.co.uk
dir: *A38 from Exeter, at Drum Bridges rdbt take A382 for Bovey Tracey, 1st exit at 2nd rdbt (B3387), 3m left to Haytor Vale*

Old-fashioned values are as important as ever at this cheerful 18th-century coaching inn, and the old stables recall the pub's strategic position on the road between Widecombe-in-the-Moor and Newton Abbot. Modern-day travellers will find nine comfortable en suite bedrooms, all named after Grand National winners. Open fires, antique tables and sturdy furnishings lend a traditional feel to the rambling bars, but the cooking style is unashamedly modern British, using excellent produce in nicely presented dishes. Lunchtime might bring mussel and saffron tart, whole grilled dab with sauce vierge or Devon pork sausages. Dinner might include a main of herb-crusted bream or sea bass with stir-fry vegetables. The children's menu offers the likes of cottage pie and fish and chips.

Open 11-11 Closed: 25-26 Dec **Bar Meals** L served all week 12-2.30 D served all week 6.30-9.30 **Restaurant** L served all week 12-2.30 D served all week 7-9 Free House Old Speckled Hen, St Austell Dartmoor Best, Interbrew Bass. **Facilities** Garden Parking **Rooms** 9 bedrooms en suite

HOLBETON MAP 03 SX65

The Mildmay Colours Inn

PL8 1NA ☎ 01752 830248 📠 01752 830432
e-mail: mildmaycolours@btconnect.com
dir: *S from Exeter on A38, Yealmpton/Ermington, S past Ugborough & Ermington right onto A379. After 1.5m, turn left, signed Mildmay Colours/Holbeton*

A 17th-century pub, which derives its unusual name from a famous jockey, Lord Anthony Mildmay, whose portrait and silks are hung in the pub. There are simple bar snacks and children's meals, along with daily specials such as nut roast with a sherry cream sauce; Dartmouth smoked chicken salad; local mackerel and salsa sauce; Mildmay Colours beer batter cod; and whole Torbay sole.

Open 11-3 6-11 (Sun 12-3, 7-10.30) **Bar Meals** L served all week 12-2.15 D served all week 6-9 (Sun 12-2.30) Free House Mildmay Colours Bitter & Mildmay SP, Hellican Honey, Keel Over, Betty Stogs. **Facilities** Garden Dogs allowed Parking

England

HOLSWORTHY MAP 03 SS30

The Bickford Arms ★★★★ INN

Brandis Corner EX22 7XY
☎ 01409 221318 🖹 01409 220085
e-mail: info@bickfordarms.com
dir: *On A3072, 4m from Holsworthy towards Hatherleigh.*

This pub stood on the Holsworthy to Hatherleigh road for 300 years before it was gutted by fire in 2003. Now totally rebuilt, it retains much period charm, with beams, a welcoming bar and two fireplaces. The bar and restaurant menu offers food prepared with locally-sourced ingredients – perhaps free-range Devon duck breast with redcurrant and red wine sauce; home-made steak and ale pie; or seared salmon with lemon and dill butter.

Open 11–11 **Bar Meals** L served all week 12–2.30 D served all week 6.30–9.30 Av main course £9 **Restaurant** 12–2.30 D served Thu–Sat 6–9.30 Av 3 course à la carte £15 Skinners Betty Stogs, Skinners Figgy Brew, Princeton IPA & Lazy Daze. **Facilities** Children's licence Garden Parking **Rooms** 5 bedrooms en suite S£40 D£60

HONITON MAP 04 ST10

The Otter Inn

Weston EX14 3NZ ☎ 01404 42594
dir: *Just off A30 W of Honiton*

On the banks of the idyllic River Otter, this 14th-century inn is set in over two acres of grounds and was once a cider house. Enjoy one of the traditional real ales, try your hand at scrabble, dominoes or cards, or peruse the inn's extensive book collection. A wide-ranging menu caters for all tastes and includes fresh fish, game, steak, vegetarian dishes, bar meals and Sunday lunch.

Open 10–11 (Sun 12–10.30) Rest: 25–26 Dec Closed eve **Bar Meals** L served all week 12–3 D served all week 6–10 (Snacks/bar meals all day. Sun 12–8) **Restaurant** L served all week D served all week 6–9 Free House Otter Ale, London Pride, Guest Ales. **Facilities** Children's licence Garden Dogs allowed Parking

HORNDON MAP 03 SX5

The Elephant's Nest Inn

PL19 9NQ ☎ 01822 810273 🖹 01822 810273
e-mail: info@theelephantsnest.co.uk
dir: *Off A386 N of Tavistock*

The pub got its unique name in the 1950s when a regular made a humourous remark about the then rather portly landlord. An isolated inn on the flanks of Dartmoor National Park reached via narrow lanes from Mary Tavy, the 16th-century building retains its real fires, slate floors and low beamed ceilings decorated with elephant memorabilia. Meals include lunchtime baguettes, interesting vegetarian options and a good seafood selection – smoked haddock chowder, for example.

Open 12–3 6.30–11 Rest: 25–26 Dec Closed lunch **Bar Meals** L served all week 12–2.15 D served all week 6.30–9 Av main course £10.95 **Restaurant** L served all week 12–2.15 D served all week 6.30–9 Av 3 cours à la carte £21.65 Free House Palmers IPA, Copper, Otter Bright, Sail Ale & Guest ales. **Facilities** Garden Dogs allowed Parking

HORNS CROSS MAP 03 SS3

Pick of the Pubs

The Hoops Inn & Country Hotel

★★★ HL

EX39 5DL ☎ 01237 451222 🖹 01237 451247
e-mail: sales@hoopsinn.co.uk
dir: *On A39 between Bideford & Clovelly*

Having made their way along tortuous footpaths to evade the revenue men, smugglers would share out their spoils in this thatched, cob-walled, 13th-century inn. Set in 16 acres of gardens and meadows on the rugged Atlantic coast, it offers charm galore. Menus are based on the freshest produce Devon can offer, including herbs, fruit and vegetables from the gardens, and a wide choice of wines by the glass from more than 220 bins. Guests may choose to eat in the bar, morning room or restaurant, where oak-panelled walls, period furniture and tables set with crisp white napkins create just the right level of formality. Seasonal menus focus on local producers and suppliers, and house specialities include terrine of Devon game with home-made piccalilli, and Exmoor venison with griottine cherry sauce.

Open 8–11 **Bar Meals** L served all week 12–3 D served all week 6–9.30 Av main course £12.50 **Restaurant** L served all week 12–3 D served all week 6–9.30 (Sat & Sun all day) Av 3 course à la carte £25 Free House Hoops Old Ale, Hoops Special Ale, Sharps IPA, Sharp's Doom Bar & Old Appledore. 20 **Facilities** Children's licence Garden Dogs allowed Parking **Rooms** 13 bedrooms en suite S£65 D£95

HORSEBRIDGE MAP 03 SX47

The Royal Inn

PL19 8PJ ☎ 01822 870214
e-mail: paul@royalinn.co.uk
dir: *S of B3362 (Launceston-Tavistock road)*

The pub, with a façade enlivened by superb pointed arched windows, was once a nunnery. Standing near a bridge built over the Tamar in 1437 by Benedictine monks, it was the Packhorse Inn until Charles I pitched up one day – his seal is in the doorstep. Beef for the steaks, casseroles and stews, and the pheasant and venison on the specials board are all locally supplied. Chilli cheese tortillas are much appreciated. So is the absence of noisy machines.

Open 12–3 6.30–11 Rest: Dec 25 Closed eve **Bar Meals** L served all week 12–2 D served all week 7–9 Av main course £6 **Restaurant** L served all week 12–2 D served all week 7–9 Av 3 course à la carte £14 Free House Eastreet, Bass, Skinners, Sharp's. **Facilities** Garden Dogs allowed Parking

ILFRACOMBE MAP 03 SS54

The George & Dragon

5 Fore St EX34 9ED ☎ 01271 863851
e-mail: linda.quinn5@btinternet.com
dir: *Please telephone for directions*

Trading since 1360, making it the oldest pub in town. The food is of the simple, no-nonsense variety – prawn cocktail, garlic mushrooms and minestrone soup as starters; fiery chicken, boozy beef, and vegetable curry as main courses. Vegetarians have a good choice, with leek and mushroom crumble, and aubergine and apricot medley on offer. No fruit machines or pool table, but a little home-produced background music.

Open 10–12 (10–1 Jul–Aug) **Bar Meals** L served all week 12–3 D served all week 6.30–9 Av main course £7.50 Courage Directors, Courage Best, Brakspear. 7 **Facilities** Children's licence Dogs allowed **Notes**

IVYBRIDGE MAP 03 SX65

The Anchor Inn

Lutterburn St, Ugborough PL21 0NG
☎ 01752 892283 01752 690534
e-mail: theanchorinn@btinternet.com

A village inn whose origins can be traced back to the 16th century. Food is served in the bar and the à la carte restaurant, with locally farmed, organic produce being used wherever possible. Tiger prawns cooked in chilli, garlic and white wine is a likely offering among the fish dishes. Beamed ceilings, open fires and real cask ales maintain the traditional welcome, and the Anchor is ideally located for exploring the South Hams region of Devon.

Open 11.30–3 5–11 (Fri–Sat 11.30–11 Sun 12–10.30) **Bar Meals** L served all week 12–2.30 D served all week 7–10 (Sat–Sun 12–10) Av main course £7 **Restaurant** L served all week 12–2.30 D served all week 7–10 Av 3 course à la carte £22.50 Free House Bass, Courage Directors, local ales. 8 **Facilities** Garden Dogs allowed Parking

KINGSBRIDGE MAP 03 SX74

The Crabshell Inn

Embankment Rd TQ7 1JZ
☎ 01548 852345 01548 852262
dir: *A38 towards Plymouth, follow signs for Kingsbridge*

A traditional sailors' watering hole on the Kingsbridge estuary quayside (arrive by boat and you may moor free). As you would expect, the views from the outside tables and from the first-floor Waters Edge Restaurant are wonderful. The extensive menu and specials board range through grills, pies, pasta, jacket potatoes, salads and sandwiches, but the house speciality is fresh fish, with dishes such as monkfish provençale, and scallop and smoked bacon gratin.

Open 11–11 (Sun 12–10.30) **Bar Meals** L served all week 12–2.30 D served all week 6–9.30 (Winter 6–9) Av main course £6 **Restaurant** L served all week 12–2.30 D served all week 6–9.30 (Winter 6–9) Av 3 course à la carte £15 Free House Bass Bitter, Crabshell Bitter, Old Speckled Hen, Flowers IPA. **Facilities** Garden Dogs allowed Parking Play Area

England

KINGSKERSWELL MAP 03 SX86

Barn Owl Inn

Aller Mills TQ12 5AN ☎ 01803 872130 01803 875279

e-mail: barnowl@oldridge-pope.co.uk

Handy for Dartmoor and the English Riviera towns, this 16th-century former farmhouse has many charming features, including flagged floors, a black leaded range, and oak beams in a high-vaulted converted barn with a minstrel's gallery. Lunchtime snacks include toasties, wraps and baguettes, while the main menu features lots of traditional pub favourites plus an extensive tapas selection – perhaps crispy duck spring rolls, Greek lamb skewers, or chilli prawn bruschetta.

Open 11–11 (Sun 12–10.30) **Bar Meals** L served all week 12–2.30 D served all week 6–9.30 **Restaurant** L served 12–2.30 D served all week 6–9.30 Eldridge Pope 6X & Guest Ales. 14 **Facilities** Garden Parking

KINGSTON MAP 03 SX64

The Dolphin Inn

TQ7 4QE ☎ 01548 810314 01548 810314

e-mail: info@dolphininn.eclipse.co.uk

dir: *From A379 (Plymouth to Kingsbridge road) take B3233 for Bigbury-on-Sea. Follow brown inn signs*

The Dolphin is just a mile from the beautiful Erme Estuary and coastal footpath and was built in the 15th century to accommodate stonemasons constructing the neighbouring church. The inn retains its historic character, providing a cosy atmosphere for regular music and quiz nights. Locally produced home-cooked food ranges from curry and steak pie to cod Florentine and slow roasted crisp belly pork, fresh fish, mature steaks and vegetarian specials.

Open 11–3 6–11 (Sun 12–3, 7–10.30) **Bar Meals** L served all week 12–2 D served all week 6–9.30 (Sun 7–9) Punch Taverns Teignworthy Spring Tide, Four Seasons Ale, Courage Best, Sharp's Doom Bar & Otter. **Facilities** Garden Parking Play Area

KINGSWEAR MAP 03 SX85

The Ship

Higher St TQ6 0AG ☎ 01803 752348

dir: *Telephone for directions*

Historic village pub overlooking the scenic River Dart towards Dartmouth and Dittisham. Located in one of South Devon's most picturesque corners, this tall, character inn is very much a village local with a friendly, welcoming atmosphere inside. Well-prepared fresh food is the hallmark of the menu. Sandwiches, baguettes and pies are available in the bar, while the restaurant menu offers crispy duck with stir-fried vegetables on egg noodles, or oven-baked cod with lemon and lime crust.

Open 12–3 6–11 (All day in Summer) **Bar Meals** L served all week 12.30–2 D served all week 7–9.30 **Restaurant** L served all week 12.30–2 D served all week 7–9.30 Heavitree Greene King IPA, Otter, Adnams, Timothy Taylor. **Facilities** Garden Dogs allowed

LEWDOWN MAP 03 SX48

Pick of the Pubs

The Harris Arms

Portgate EX20 4PZ ☎ 01566 783331 01566 783359

e-mail: whiteman@powernet.co.uk

dir: *From A30 take Lifton turn, halfway between Lifton & Lewdown*

See Pick of the Pubs on opposite page

LIFTON MAP 03 SX38

Pick of the Pubs

The Arundell Arms ★★★ HL

PL16 0AA ☎ 01566 784666 01566 784494

e-mail: reservations@arundellarms.com

dir: *1m off A30 dual carriageway, 3m E of Launceston*

See Pick of the Pubs on page 168

LITTLEHEMPSTON MAP 03 SX86

Tally Ho Inn

TQ9 6NF ☎ 01803 862316 01803 862316

e-mail: tally.ho.inn@btconnect.com

dir: *Off A38 at Buckfastleigh. A381 between Newton Abbot & Totnes*

For the past ten years, this traditional 14th-century inn has been ably manned by four members of the Saint family. Inglenook fireplaces and a flower- and sun-filled patio make for an enchanting location. The single menu offers plenty of starters, including creamy goats' cheese mousse; and seared king scallops with pancetta; followed by lamb loin chops; chicken supreme; and myriad fish dishes, including grilled lemon sole with smoked salmon butter.

Open 12–3 6.30–11 (Sun 6–10.30) Closed: 25 Dec **Bar Meals** L served all week 12–2 D served all week 7–9 (Sun 12–2.30) Av main course £7.55 Free House Exmoor Ale, Teignworthy Brewery Ales, Whitbread Best Bitter, Guest Ales. **Facilities** Children's licence Garden Dogs allowed Parking

The Harris Arms

Iere is an establishment that certainly lives up to its promotional strapline: 'Eat Real Food and Drink Real Wine'. To the 'Drink' part could be added real beer and premium lager, which are equally important elements of this multi-award-winning gastro-pub experience.

The Harris Arms is a 16th-century nn located on the old A30 close to he boundary between Devon and Cornwall, with wonderful views o Brent Tor. Owners Rowena and Andy Whiteman are acknowledged overs of good food and wine, and have invested a great deal of ime and energy in establishing he pub's reputation as a venue for liscerning drinkers and diners. Having previously run vineyards in France and New Zealand as qualified vine-makers, the Whitemans have not resisted the urge to plant several rows of their own champagne grapes. As you might expect, heir wine list is both eclectic and extensive, with many bins from small producers or modern, ecologically sound vineyards. They operate a fair pricing policy, and if you can't finish the bottle you can take it home with you; most of their wines are also available as off-sales. They believe in honest food with substance and style, locally sourced and carefully cooked by their kitchen team. Example starters from the specials board are Fowey River mussels steamed in cream, garlic and white wine; seared scallops with sage, lemon and capers; and marinated and grilled Cornish sardines. Main courses are no less succulent, with the likes of winter cassoulet of pheasant, chicken, rare breed pork and merguez sausage; or pan-fried pigeon breast with griddled squash, smoked bacon and red wine sauce. Lunchtime dishes include home-made 100% beef burgers, fish and chips, and steak and chips. There is also a selection of West Country cheeses that should not be overlooked

🍷
MAP 03 SX48
Portgate EX20 4PZ
☎ 01566 783331
📠 01566 783359
e-mail:
whiteman@powernet.co.uk
dir: *From A30 take Lifton turn, halfway between Lifton & Lewdown*

Open 12-3 6.30-11 Closed: Sun eve & Mon
Bar Meals L served all week 12-2 D served all week 6.30-9 (Sun 12-2, 7-9) Av main course £8.95
Restaurant L served all week 12-2 D served all week 6.30-9 (Sun 12-2, 7-9) Av 3 course à la carte £25 Av 3 course fixed price £15
Free House
Guest Real Ales, San Miguel, Sharps Doom Bar, Guinness Extra Cold. 🍷 18
Facilities Garden Dogs allowed Parking

The Arundell Arms

Run by the same family for over forty years, the Arundell Arms is one of England's premier fishing hotels. Guests have access to 20 miles of private fishing along the Tamar and its tributaries, whilst walkers and bird watchers can enjoy some of England's loveliest countryside.

Formerly known as the White Horse, this 18th-century free house was renamed in about 1815 after William Arundell took over the 'best and most respectable inn in the village'. The description is still apt. Today, the Arundell Arms exudes warmth and comfort – not only in the bar, with its babble of conversation, but in the 21 individually designed en suite bedrooms, and in thoughtful touches such as home-made chocolates for after-dinner guests in the sitting room. From here you can see one of England's few remaining cockpits, now the hotel's fishing tackle room, set in the terraced garden where swifts and swallows soar overhead in the evening sunshine. Around the car park quadrangle there's a skittle alley, meeting rooms and the locals' bar, with its basic lunchtime menu. You'll find a more extensive menu in the hotel bar, with sandwiches and light snacks such as organic smoked salmon with horseradish and lemon; and avocado, goats' cheese and red onion salad. Larger appetites might choose roasted Cornish cod with saffron risotto; pork medallions with mustard mash; or home-cooked ham salad with Cumberland sauce. Five-course table d'hote and à la carte menus are served in the elegant restaurant; here, grilled fillet of Gressingham duck with lentils, leeks and saffron is a typical main course choice, followed by rhubarb desserts with saffron custard.

★★★ HL ◎◎ 🍷
MAP 03 SX38
PL16 0AA
☎ 01566 784666
📠 01566 784494
e-mail:
reservations@arundellarms.com
www.arundellarms.co.uk
dir: *1m off A30 dual carriageway, 3m E of Launceston*

Open 11–11 (Fri–Sat 11–12, Sun 12–11)
Bar Meals L served all week 12–2.30 D served all week 6–10
Restaurant L served all week 12.30–2 D served all week 7.30–9.30 Av 3 course à la carte £40 Av 5 course fixed price £36
Free House
Guest beers. 🍷 9
Facilities Garden Dogs allowed Parking
Rooms 21 bedrooms en suite S£99 D£160

LOWER ASHTON MAP 03 SX88

Manor Inn 🍷

EX6 7QL ☎ 01647 252304
e-mail: mark@themanorinn.co.uk
dir: *A38, Teign Valley turn, follow signs for B3193. Pub 5m on right, just over stone bridge*

Picturesque free house set in a Teign Valley village surrounded by countryside and attractive cottages. The Manor retains its traditional appeal with blazing log fires in winter and a sheltered garden with views of fields and hills. A selection of main courses may include pan-fried cod fillet with prawns in parsley and lemon butter; or beef, mushroom and Guinness pie. Sandwiches, baguettes, and ploughman's also available.

Open 12-2 6.30-11 (Closed Mon ex BHs) **Bar Meals** L served Tue-Sun 12-1.30 D served Tue-Sun 7-9 Av main course £7.95 Free House Teignworthy Reel Ale, Princetown Jail Ale, RCH Pitchfork, changing guest ale. 🍷 10 **Facilities** Garden Dogs allowed Parking

LUTON (NEAR CHUDLEIGH) MAP 03 SX97

The Elizabethan Inn 🍷

Fore St TQ13 0BL ☎ 01626 775425 📠 01626 775151
e-mail: nickpowell1@tesco.net
dir: *Between Chudleigh & Teignmouth*

This cosy, country free house dates back to the 16th century, with owners dedicated to serving excellent food. A list of daily specials, made with local produce wherever possible, might include Moroccan lamb with almonds and dates; chicken chasseur; and monkfish kebab with Parma ham. Local cider, Devon and guest beers, and any of 30 malt whiskies may be enjoyed next to the log fire in the bar.

Open 11-3 6-11 (Winter 12-3, 7-11) Closed: 25, 26 Dec, 1-2 Jan **Bar Meals** L served all week 12-2 D served all week 6-9.30 (Sun 7-9.30) Av main course £9.95 **Restaurant** L served all week 12-2 D served all week 6-9.30 (Sun 7-9) Free House London Pride, Teignworthy Reel Ale, Timothy Taylor's Landlord, Charles Wells Bombardier. 🍷 8 **Facilities** Garden Dogs allowed Parking

LYDFORD MAP 03 SX58

Pick of the Pubs

Castle Inn 🍷

EX20 4BH
☎ 01822 820242 & 820241 📠 01822 820454
dir: *Off A386 S of Okehampton*

This pretty, wisteria-clad inn dates from the 16th century, has a castle next door and one of the nicest beer gardens in the country. No visit would be complete without a look at the impressive Lydford Gorge nearby. The interior oozes atmosphere, with its slate floors, low, lamp-lit beams, decorative plates and huge ancient fireplace. Owners Richard and Sarah Davies offer freshly prepared dishes at lunch and dinner. Fresh fish appears daily such as fillet of salmon with coriander dressed noodles and lemon-butter sauce. Starters include warm goats' cheese salad with Parma ham or chicken liver and green peppercorn pâté. Main courses include several vegetarian dishes as well as roasts and a confit of duck. Sticky toffee or bread & butter pudding should provide enough calories for the short walk to the gorge and back. The shrub-filled garden is a lovely spot to while away time with a pint, and great for summer dining.

Open 11-11 (Sun 12-10.30) **Bar Meals** L served all week 12-2 D served all week 6.30-9 Av main course £8 **Restaurant** L served all week 12-2 D served all week 6.30-9 Heavitree Fullers London Pride, 6X, Otter Ale. 🍷 13 **Facilities** Garden Dogs allowed Parking Play Area

Dartmoor Inn 🏵🏵 🍷

EX20 4AY ☎ 01822 820221 📠 01822 820494
e-mail: info@dartmoorinn.co.uk
dir: *On A386 S of Okehampton*

Owners Karen and Philip Burgess have made their mark at this distinctive free house, which Charles Kingsley almost certainly described in his novel *Westward Ho!* The stylish, restrained décor extends through the cosy dining rooms and small bar, where an easy dining menu features dishes like bacon and egg salad with mustard dressing; and goats' cheese omelette with red onion. After your meal, you can even browse for beautiful accessories and home ware in the inn's own boutique.

Open 11.30-3 6.30-11 (6-11 in Summer) **Bar Meals** L served Tue-Sun 12-2.15 D served Tue-Sat 6.30-9.15 (Sun 12-2.30) Av main course £9.75 **Restaurant** L served Tue-Sun 12-2.15 D served Tue-Sat 6.30-9.15 (Sun 12-2.30) Free House Otter Ale, Austell Hicks Special & Dartmoor Best. 🍷 6 **Facilities** Garden Dogs allowed Parking

LYMPSTONE MAP 03 SX98

The Globe Inn 🐟 🍷

The Strand EX8 5EY ☎ 01395 263166

Set in the estuary village of Lympstone, this traditional beamed inn has a good local reputation for seafood. The separate restaurant area serves as a coffee bar during the day. Look out for bass fillets with plum sauce; monkfish kebabs; seafood platter and seafood grill. Weekend music and quiz nights are a feature.

Open 11-3 5.30-12 **Bar Meals** L served all week 12-2 D served Mon-Sat 6.30-9.30 Av main course £8 **Restaurant** L served all week D served Mon-Sat 7-9.30 Heavitree London Pride, Otter, Bass, Whitbread Best. 🍷 6 **Facilities** Dogs allowed

England

LYNMOUTH MAP 03 SS74

Pick of the Pubs

Rising Sun Hotel ★★ HL ®® 🍷

Harbourside EX35 6EG

☎ 01598 753223 📠 01598 753480

e-mail: risingsunlynmouth@easynet.co.uk

dir: *From M5 junct 25 follow Minehead signs. A39 to Lynmouth*

Overlooking Lynmouth's tiny harbour and bay is the Rising Sun, a 14th-century thatched smugglers' inn. In turn, overlooking them all, are Countisbury Cliffs, the highest in England. The building's long history is evident from the uneven oak floors, crooked ceilings and thick walls. Literary associations are plentiful: R D Blackmore wrote some of his wild Exmoor romance, *Lorna Doone*, here; the poet Shelley is believed to have honeymooned in the garden cottage; and Coleridge stayed too. Immediately behind rises Exmoor Forest and National Park, home to red deer, wild ponies and birds of prey. With sea and moor so close, game and seafood are in plentiful supply, and pheasant, venison, hare, wild boar, monkfish, crab or scallops, for example, will appear variously as starter or main course dishes. At night the oak-panelled, candlelit dining room is an example of romantic British inn-keeping at its best.

Open 11–11 (Open all day all year) **Bar Meals** L served all week 12–4 D served all week 7–9 Av main course £7 **Restaurant** L served all week 12–2 D served all week 7–9 Av 3 course à la carte £32 Free House Exmoor Gold, Fox & Exmoor Ale, Cotleigh Tawny Ale. **Facilities** Garden **Rooms** 16 bedrooms en suite S£59 D£78

LYNTON MAP 03 SS74

The Bridge Inn

Lynbridge Hill EX35 6NR

☎ 01598 753425 📠 01598 753225

e-mail: bridgeinnlynton@hotmail.co.uk

dir: *Turn off A39 at Barbrook onto B3234. In 1m pub on right just beyond Sunny Lyn camp site*

Attractive 17th-century riverside inn overlooked by National Trust woodlands. In the cellars the remains of 12th-century salmon fishermen's cottages are still visible, and the unusually shaped windows at the front originally belonged to Charles I's hunting lodge at Coombe House, salvaged following flood damage in the 1680s. The 1952 Lynmouth Flood destroyed the Lyn Bridge and car park, but most of the pub survived intact.

The Bridge Inn

Open 12–3 6–11 (Sun 7–10.30-winter) **Bar Meals** L served all week 12–2.30 D served all week 6–9.30 (Sun 7–10.30 Winter) Av main course £8.50 **Restaurant** L served all week 12–2.30 D served all week 6–9.30 Free House St. Austell Tribute, Sharp's Doom Bar, Exmoor Fox. **Facilities** Children's licence Garden Dogs allowed Parking

MARLDON MAP 03 SX86

The Church House Inn 🍷

Village Rd TQ3 1SL ☎ 01803 558279 📠 01803 664865

dir: *Take Torquay ring road, follow signs to Marldon & Totnes, follow brown signs to pub*

An ancient inn with a contemporary feel located between Torbay and the market town of Newton Abbott. The building dates from 1362, when it was a hostel for the builders of the adjoining village church, but it was rebuilt in 1750 incorporating beautiful Georgian windows. Typical dishes are poached monkfish on vegetable medley and prawn bisque; chargrilled Exmoor sirloin steak; and asparagus and parmesan risotto torte.

Open 11.30–2.30 5–11 (Sun 12–10.30) **Bar Meals** L served all week 12–2 D served all week 6.30–9.30 Av main course £12.50 **Restaurant** L served all week 12–2 D served all week 6.30–9.30 Av 3 course à la carte £24 Free House Dartmoor Best, Bass, Old Speckled Hen, Greene King IPA 🍷 10 **Facilities** Garden Dogs allowed Parking

MEAVY MAP 03 SX56

The Royal Oak Inn 🍷

PL20 6PJ ☎ 01822 852944

dir: *Off A386 between Tavistock & Plymouth*

Standing on the edge of Dartmoor, between Tavistock and Plymouth, this 12th-century brew house is a popular watering hole for those touring and exploring the National Park. Good quality fare is prepared from produce bought locally and much of the meat is free-range. A local fishmonger delivers fresh fish from Plymouth. Expect filled baguettes, local pasties and salads at lunchtime, while the evening menu consists of stuffed plaice, lemon butterfly chicken, gammon steak and salsa sardines.

Open 11.30–3 6–11 (Fri–Sat 11–11, Sun 11–10.30) **Bar Meals** L served all week 12–2 D served all week 7–9 **Restaurant** L served all week 12–2 D served Mon–Sat 7–9 Av 3 course à la carte £17 Free House Princetown Jail Ale, Dartmoor IPA, St Austell Tribute, Doom Bar & Guest. 🍷 12 **Facilities** Dogs allowed

MODBURY MAP 03 SX65

California Country Inn

California Cross PL21 0SG

☎ 01548 821449 🖹 01548 821566

e-mail: california@bellinns.entadsl.com

Oak beams and exposed stonework are features of this whitewashed 14th-century free house. Brass, copper and old photographs decorate the interior, and there's a landscaped garden for summer use. Menus are created from only locally supplied produce, with prime meats from the chargrill, and dishes ranging from lasagne and beer-battered cod in the bar to roast monk fish with Yealm mussels, or loin of Plympton venison in the restaurant.

Open 11-11 **Bar Meals** L served all week 12-2 D served all week 6-9 (Sun 6-8.30) Av main course £10 **Restaurant** D served Wed-Sat 6-9 (Sun 6-8.30) Av 3 course à la carte £25 Av 2 course fixed price £10.95 Free House Guinness, Abbot Ale, London Pride, Carling. **Facilities** Children's licence Garden Dogs allowed Parking

MOLLAND MAP 03 SS82

The London Inn

EX36 3NG ☎ 01769 550269

Just below Exmoor lies peaceful Molland, and to find its church is to find this 15th-century inn. Historic features abound, but try and picture today's spacious dining room as the original inn, and the bar as the brewhouse. The frequently-changing menu features savoury pancakes, Welsh rarebit, mixed grill, as well as ploughman's, jackets and sandwiches.

Open 11.30-2.30 6-11 (Sun 12-3, 7-10.30) **Bar Meals** L served all week 12-2 D served all week 7-9 Av main course £8 **Restaurant** L served all week D served all week Av 3 course à la carte £19.50 Free House Exmoor Ale, Cotleigh Tawny Bitter. **Facilities** Garden Dogs allowed Parking **Notes**

MORETONHAMPSTEAD MAP 03 SX78

The White Hart Hotel ★★★ HL 🍷

The Square TQ13 8NF ☎ 01647 441340 🖹 01647 441341

e-mail: enquiries@whitehartdartmoor.co.uk

web: www.whitehartdartmoor.co.uk

dir: *Off the A30 at Whiddon Down take the A382 for Chagford and Moretonhampstead. The White Hart is in centre of town*

This grade II listed building was a meeting place for French officers on parole from Dartmoor's nearby prison during the Napoleonic Wars. Today's stylish hotel provides both a well-stocked bar offering lunch and a brasserie serving up a contemporary combination of dishes: chargrilled aubergine and brie; pan fried calves' liver with red onion marmalade; or roast loin of venison with butter beans perhaps.

Open 8-12 **Bar Meals** L served all week 12.30-2.30 D served all week 6.30-9.30 (Sun 12-2.30) Av main course £9 **Restaurant** L served Sun 12-2.30 D served all week 6.30-9.30 Av 3 course à la carte £28 Av 3 course fixed price £25 Tribute, Otter Fursty Ferret, Doom Bar, O'Hanlons Brewing. 🍷 16 **Facilities** Children's licence Garden Dogs allowed Parking **Rooms** 29 bedrooms en suite S£75 D£120

NEWTON ABBOT MAP 03 SX87

The Wild Goose Inn 🍷

Combeinteignhead TQ12 4RA ☎ 01626 872241

dir: *From A380 at Newton Abbot rdbt, take B3195 Shaldon road, signed Milber, 2.5m into village then right at sign*

The name of this Devon longhouse commemorates the geese that used to leap at passers-by from a nearby field. The pub has remained virtually unchanged since it was first licensed in 1840, and has a peaceful beer garden overlooking a 14th-century church and a stream winding down to the River Teign. Dishes include boozy beef with

CONTINUED

England

NEWTON ABBOT continued

stilton, wild boar sausages with mustard mash and onion gravy, and grilled Brixham dabs with lemon and butter.

Open 11–2.30 5.30–11 (Fri–Sat 5.30–12, Sun 12–2.30, 7–11)
Bar Meals L served all week 12–2 D served all week 7–9.30 Av main course £7.50 **Restaurant** L served all week 12–2 D served all week 7–9.30 Free House Otter Ale, Cotleigh, Sharp's Bitter, Skinner's Bitter. 16
Facilities Garden Parking

NEWTON ST CYRES MAP 03 SX89

The Beer Engine

EX5 5AX 01392 851282 01392 851876
e-mail: info@thebeerengine.co.uk
dir: *From Exeter take A377 towards Crediton. Pub opposite rail station in village, signed from A377 towards Sweetham*

Striking whitewashed free house, once a railway hotel and these days acknowledged as one of Devon's first micro-breweries. There's daily fish deliveries from Brixham so expect sea bass, cod or haddock cooked in beer batter. Vegetarians can look forward to a good selection of choices including aubergine and tomato bake, vegetable curry, and spinach lasagne.

Open 11–1 **Bar Meals** L served all week 12–2.30 D served all week 6.30–9.30 (Sun 6.30–9) Av main course £9.50 **Restaurant** L served all week 12–2.30 D served all week 6.30–9.30 (Sun 6.30–9) Free House Beer Engine Ales: Piston Bitter, Rail Ale, Sleeper Heavy. **Facilities** Garden Dogs allowed Parking

NORTH BOVEY MAP 03 SX78

Pick of the Pubs

The Ring of Bells Inn

TQ13 8RB 01647 440375 01647 440746
e-mail: info@ringofbellsinn.com
dir: *1.5m from Moretonhampstead off B3212. 7m S of Whiddon Down junct on A30.*

The Ring of Bells is one of Dartmoor's most historic inns, an attractive thatched property located just off the village green. It was built in the 13th century as lodgings for the stonemasons who were working on the construction of the nearby church, and remains very much at the heart of the village's social life. Visitors too are attracted by the good Devon pub food and West Country ales, and there is certainly plenty to do and see in the area, particularly walking, cycling, fishing, riding and bird watching in this beautiful moorland countryside. Hearty appetites are happily catered for with Ring of Bells classics like steak and ale pie, local bangers and mash, and lambs' liver and bacon. Alternatives range through local rabbit braised in red wine, fishcakes with sweet chilli sauce, and charred aubergine rolls stuffed with mushroom, olives and pine nuts.

The Ring of Bells Inn

Open 11–11 **Bar Meals** L served all week 12–2.30 D served all week 6.30–9.30 (Sun 12–3) Av main course £9.95 **Restaurant** L served all week 12–2.30 D served all week 7–9.30 (Sun 12–3, 7–9) Av 3 course à la carte £25 Av 3 course fixed price £12.95 Otter Ale, Wadworth 6x, Dartmoor Best Bitter, Butcombe Best Bitter, Bass. **Facilities** Garden Dogs allowed

NOSS MAYO MAP 03 SX5

The Ship Inn

PL8 1EW 01752 872387 01752 873294
e-mail: ship@nossmayo.com
web: www.nossmayo.com
dir: *5m S of Yealmpton on River Yealm estuary*

The 16th-century Ship's tidal location is superb, especially for those arriving by boat. The pub has been completely renovated using English oak, local stone and reclaimed materials, and appears spacious yet remains cosy, thanks to the wooden floors, old furniture and bookcases, log fires and dozens of local pictures. A complete lack of music, fruit machines and pool tables leads many to call it a 'real pub'. The cellar has a good range of regional and local brews.

Open 11–11 **Bar Meals** L served all week 12–9.30 D served all week Free House Tamar, Jail Ale & Butcombe Blonde. 10
Facilities Garden Dogs allowed Parking

OTTERY ST MARY MAP 03 SY1

The Talaton Inn

Talaton EX5 2RQ 01404 822214 01404 822214

Timber-framed, well-maintained 16th-century inn, run by a brother and sister partnership. A strong seafood emphasis means that the menu may feature poached salmon hollandaise, cod and chips, seafood platter, or scampi. Blackboard specials change regularly, and may include chicken Wellington or fillet steak Rossini, for example. Good selection of real ales and malts, and a fine collection of bar games.

Open 12–3 7–11 (6–11 Summer) **Bar Meals** L served all week 12–2 D served Tue–Sat 7–9.15 **Restaurant** L served all week 12–2.15 D served Tue–Sat 7–9.15 Free House Otter, Fuller's London Pride, O'Hanlon's, Badger Tanglefoot. **Facilities** Dogs allowed Parking

The Fox & Goose

)riginally this charming free house was no more than a couple of tiny thatched cottages serving he local farming community. The landlord enlarged the building to compete with nearby hotels fter the narrow gauge Lynton & Barnstaple Railway linked Parracombe with the outside world n 1898.

'hen, in 1925, the village's narrow treet was sidelined by an early ypass, which may have contributed ɔ the closure of the railway just en years later. Through all this, he village has remained unspoilt nd the pub has continued to velcome visitors and locals alike. Nowadays, the Fox also enjoys a ound reputation for its home-made ood, with meals served in the bar, s well as in the restaurant and aved courtyard garden overlooking ne river. There's a wide selection f dishes to suit all tastes, based on roduce from the surrounding farms nd the Devon coast. The menus eep pace with daily changes, and night include starters of chicken ver paté with green peppercorns erved with granary bread; or nussels with shallots, white wine nd cream. The generous list of main courses takes in fish (lemon sole fillets with broccoli and lemon and parsley butter; halibut steak on creamed leeks); meat dishes such as Exmoor venison casserole or prime lamb leg steak with seasonal vegetables, tomatoes and mint gravy; and vegetarian choices (perhaps butternut squash risotto or mixed vegetable tagine). Desserts include an excellent range of traditional puddings and a selection of local cheeses. Sandwiches are also available at lunchtime. Real ale lovers can enjoy local ales such as Cotleigh Barn Owl, Dartmoor Best, and Exmoor Fox; and train enthusiasts should note that nearly seventy years after the railway's closure, a short section of line near Parracombe has been reopened. There are ambitious plans for future extensions

MAP 03 SS64
EX31 4PE
☎ 01598 763239
01598 763621
dir: *1m from A39 between Blackmoor Gate (2m) & Lynton (6m). Signed to Parracombe. Fox & Goose sign on approach*

Open 12–3 6–11 Rest: (Sun in Winter, 7–10.30)
Bar Meals L served all week 12–2 D served all week 6–9 (Sun 7–9) Av main course £11.95
Restaurant L served all week 12–2 D served all week 6–9 (Sun 7–9)
Free House
Cotleigh Barn Owl, Carlsberg, Dartmoor Best, Exmoor Fox. 10
Facilities Garden Dogs allowed Parking

Jack in the Green Inn

An inn has been on this site for several centuries, but the name is even older. It refers to a Green Man-like figure of pagan origins associated with spring fertility celebrations. This whitewashed pub stands just a few minutes' drive from Exeter airport.

Wood-burning stoves and leather armchairs create a cosy, welcoming interior. There are several rooms geared towards meetings and celebrations, but overall the inn is best known as a dining destination. Paul Parnell has been here for many years, and holds a simple philosophy: to serve the best of Devon's artisan produce in stylish surrounds with a dash of good old fashioned hospitality. The success of his culinary efforts has been recognised with two AA rosettes. Whether you're stopping by for a bar snack, or a fuller meal in the restaurant, the quality is evident in everything produced. Start with seared sesame tuna with chive crushed potatoes; or braised belly pork with pickled vegetables; then continue with rack and braised shoulder of Fishleigh Estate organic lamb, cos lettuce, chicken jus and hazelnut; pan-fried fillet of brill with provençal vegetables and pistou; or roast breast of chicken with smoked bacon tortellini and Jerusalem artichoke purée. Tempting desserts include apple and Calvados brûlée, and a much lauded sticky toffee pudding. The wine list offers over 100 bins, selected for character and excellent value.

MAP 03 SY09
London Rd EX5 2EE
☎ 01404 822240
01404 823445
e-mail:
info@jackinthegreen.uk.com
dir: *From M5 take old A30 towards Honiton, signed Rockbeare*

Open 11–2.30 6–11 (Sun 12–10.30) Closed: 25 Dec–5 Jan
Bar Meals L served all week 11–2 D served all week 6–9.30 (Sun 12–9.30) Av main course £13.50
Restaurant L served all week 11–2 D served all week 6–9.30 (Fixed price menu Sun 12–9.30) Av 3 course à la carte £25
Free House
Cotleigh Tawny Ale, Thomas Hardy Hardy Country, Otter Ale, Royal Oak. 12
Facilities Parking

ARRACOMBE MAP 03 SS64

Pick of the Pubs

The Fox & Goose

EX31 4PE ☎ 01598 763239 01598 763621

dir: *1m from A39 between Blackmoor Gate (2m) & Lynton (6m). Signed to Parracombe. Fox & Goose sign on approach*

See Pick of the Pubs on page 173

ATTERY MAP 03 SX76

hurch House Inn

)10 9LD ☎ 01364 642220 01364 642220

mail: ray12@onetel.com

r: *1m from A38 Exeter to Plymouth Rd & 0.75m from A385 tnes to South Brent road*

ɔwn to date from 1028, this is not only Devon's oldest inn, but ɔ one of England's. The bar features large open fireplaces, sturdy ‹ beams, a plethora of nooks and crannies, and a painting of a nk. Move this picture and misfortune will befall you! In the equally racterful dining room, the menu offers fisherman's pie; citrus and e lamb shank; rump steak and scampi combo; stilton and vegetable mble; burgers, jackets and salads.

en 11–3 6–11 (Winter 11–2.30, 6.30–10.30) **Bar Meals** L served veek 12–2 D served all week 7–9 Av main course £8.50 **staurant** L served all week 12–2 D served all week 7–9 Av 3 course à la e £20 Free House St Austell Dartmoor Best, Princetown Jail Ale, nner's Betty Stogs Bitter & Otter Ale. 8 **Facilities** Children's licence den Dogs allowed Parking

ɔCKBEARE MAP 03 SY09

Pick of the Pubs

ack in the Green Inn

ondon Rd EX5 2EE

☎ 01404 822240 01404 823445

-mail: info@jackinthegreen.uk.com

ir: *From M5 take old A30 towards Honiton, signed ockbeare*

See Pick of the Pubs on opposite page

SALCOMBE MAP 03 SX73

Pick of the Pubs

The Victoria Inn

Fore St TQ8 8BU ☎ 01548 842604 01548 844201

e-mail: info@victoriainnsalcombe.co.uk

dir: *Town centre, overlooking estuary*

When owner Andy Cannon introduced a new menu focusing on locally sourced ingredients, his trade dramatically increased. The achievement won him a competition run by St Austell Brewery, the pub's owner, which has since announced a commitment to using local produce throughout its large estate. From the first floor restaurant there are stunning views of the pretty harbour and the fishing boats bringing in the catch for the kitchen. Deciding which fresh fish dish to choose could be difficult, although one in particular merits attention – Andy's signature dish. This is a delicious chowder starter of handpicked Salcombe white crabmeat, prawns and other shellfish, white wine, fresh dill and Devon double cream. He offers a main course 'signature' too – slowly roasted half shoulder of new season Devon lamb encrusted with garlic and fresh herbs and served with a redcurrant and fresh mint sauce., served over a wholegrain mustard mash. Desserts include home-made apple and blackberry crumble and custard, and Devon ice creams and cheeses.

Open 11–11 (may close 3–6pm during Winter) **Bar Meals** L served all week 12–2.30 D served all week 6–9 **Restaurant** D served all week 7–9 St Austell Brewery St Austell Tribute, Dartmoor Best, St Austell HSD, Black Prince & Tinners Tribute. 9 **Facilities** Garden Dogs allowed Play Area

The Tower Inn

The Tower Inn dates from the 14th century and is very much a part of the historic South Hams village of Slapton, which lies almost equidistant between Kingsbridge and Dartmouth, half a mile from the coast and Slapton Sands.

The inn owes its name to the ruined tower that overlooks the walled garden, which is all that remains of the Collegiate Chantry of St Mary. In 1347 the builders of the chantry constructed cottages for their own accommodation, so it seems likely that the inn may have been the College's guesthouse, dispensing alms and hospitality even then. The pub is approached by a narrow lane, and entered through a rustic porch. The interior comprises a fascinating series of low-ceilinged, interconnecting rooms with stone walls and fireplaces, beams, pillars and pews. These in turn are decorated with plants, a giant cartwheel, brasses, pictures and violins. An excellent range of beers is augmented by local cider and mulled wine in winter. Traditional Sunday lunch with roast sirloin of beef, Yorkshire pudding and horseradish sauce is offered on a separate menu from the daily lunch and dinner selections. Lunchtime options range through sandwiches, a vegetarian pasta, local sausages, and herb crusted cod with cheese sauce. The dinner menu extends to medallions of pork tenderloin set on sautéed sugar snap peas served with pear, rosemary and lemon. Daily specials provide an additional choice of mainly fresh fish and game dishes, and a children's menu is also available. To finish choose between pudding – maybe treacle orange tart or chocolate and pecan brandy cake – or a platter of West Country cheeses with Bath Olivers and oatcakes.

MAP 03 SX84
Church Rd TQ7 2PN
☎ 01548 580216
e-mail: towerinn@slapton.org
web: www.thetowerinn.com
dir: *Off A379 S of Dartmouth, turn left at Slapton Sands*

Open 12–2.30 6–11 (Sun 7–10.30) Closed: 25 Dec
Bar Meals L served all week 12–2.30 D served all week 6–9.30 Av main course £8
Restaurant L served all week 12–2.30 D served all week 7–9.30 Av 3 course à la carte £20
Free House
Butcombe Bitter, Badger Tanglefoot, St Austell, Tower. 8
Facilities Garden Dogs allowed Parking

England

HEEPWASH MAP 03 SS40

alf Moon Inn

21 5NE ☎ 01409 231376 01409 231673

mail: lee@halfmoon.demon.co.uk

r: *From M5 take A30 to Okehampton then A386, at Hatheleigh, t onto A3072, after 4m right for Sheepwash*

ery popular venue for anglers, this white-painted inn overlooking village square in a remote Devon village is a Grade II listed lding with fishing rights for ten miles of the River Torridge. Inside u'll find slate floors and a huge inglenook fireplace where a log fire ns in cooler weather. Bar snacks are available at lunchtime and a menu of traditional English fare at dinner.

en 11.30–2.30 6–11 (Sun 12–2.30, 7–10.30) Closed: 20–27 Dec **r Meals** L served Mon–Sat 12–1.45 D served Mon–Sat 6.30–8.30 main course £8 **Restaurant** L served all week D served all week 8 Av 3 rse à la carte £20 Free House Scottish Courage Courage Best, rp's Own, Greene King Ruddles Best Bitter. **Facilities** Parking

APTON MAP 03 SX84

Pick of the Pubs

The Tower Inn

hurch Rd TQ7 2PN ☎ 01548 580216

-mail: towerinn@slapton.org

veb: www.thetowerinn.com

ir: *Off A379 S of Dartmouth, turn left at Slapton Sands*

See Pick of the Pubs on opposite page

SOURTON MAP 03 SX59

The Highwayman Inn

EX20 4HN ☎ 01837 861243 01837 861196

e-mail: info@thehighwaymaninn.net

dir: *On A386 (Okehampton to Tavistock road). Exit A30 towards Tavistock. Pub 4m from Okehampton, 12m from Tavistock*

A fascinating old inn full of eccentric furniture, unusual architectural designs, and strange bric-a-brac. Since 1959 the vision of Welshman John 'Buster' Jones, and now run by his daughter Sally, it is made from parts of sailing ships, wood hauled from Dartmoor's bogs, and Gothic church arches. Popular with holidaymakers and international tourists, the menu consists of light snacks including pasties, platters and organic nibbles. In the garden, the kids will enjoy Mother Hubbard's Shoe, and the Pumpkin House.

Open 11–2 6–10.30 (Sun 12–2, 7–10.30) Rest: Jan & Feb Closed Mon **Bar Meals** L served all week 11–1.45 D served all week Free House St Austell Duchy, Teignworthy. **Facilities** Garden Dogs allowed Parking Play Area

SOUTH POOL MAP 03 SX74

The Millbrook Inn

TQ7 2RW ☎ 01548 531581

e-mail: cjstarkey@hotmail.com

dir: *Take A379 from Kingsbridge to Frogmore then E*

This quaint 16th-century village pub is cosy and unspoilt inside, with open fires, fresh flowers, cushioned wheelback chairs, and beams adorned with old banknotes and clay pipes. Fish is a speciality, and there's a peaceful sunny rear terrace overlooking a stream with ducks.

Open 12–3 6–11 (Open all day Aug) (Sun 12–3, 6–10.30) **Bar Meals** L served all week 12–2 D served all week 7–9 Av main course £7.95 Free House Bass, Sharp's Doom Bar, Otter Ale, Teignworthy Reel Ale. 12 **Facilities** Garden Dogs allowed

SOUTH ZEAL MAP 03 SX69

Oxenham Arms

EX20 2JT ☎ 01837 840244 01837 840791

e-mail: theoxenhamarms@aol.com

dir: *Just off A30 4m E of Okehampton, in village centre*

Probably built by monks in the 12th century, this building is scheduled as an Ancient Monument. In the lounge is a stone shaped by prehistoric man, which archaeologists believe the monks built around. First licensed in 1477, the pub retains a historical feel, with beams and blazing fires. Traditional and international dishes are available in the bar and dining room, from sausage and mash to lobster thermidor. The garden overlooks Cosdon Hill and Cawsand Beacon.

Open 11–2.30 5–11 (Sun 12–2.30, 7–10.30) **Bar Meals** L served all week 12–1.45 D served all week 6.30–8.45 (Summer all day Sat) **Restaurant** L served all week 12–1.45 D served all week 6.30–8.45 (Summer 6–8.45) Free House Sharp's Doom Bar Bitter, Sharp's Special Ale, Archer's Golden, Sharp's Own. **Facilities** Garden Dogs allowed Parking

England

SPREYTON MAP 03 SX69

The Tom Cobley Tavern

EX17 5AL ☎ 01647 231314

dir: *From A30 at Whiddon Down take A3124 N. Right at Post Inn, then 1st right over bridge*

From this pub one day in 1802 a certain Thomas Cobley and his companions set forth for Widecombe Fair, recorded and remembered in the famous song. Today, this traditional village local offers a good selection of bar snacks, lighter fare and home-made main meals, including pies, salads, duck and fish dishes, as well as a good vegetarian selection. Finish off with one of the great ice creams or sorbets, including white chocolate and vodka! The garden is in a pretty setting.

Open 12–2 6–11 (Mon open Summer, BHs) **Bar Meals** L served Tue–Sat 12–2 D served Tue–Sun 7–9 **Restaurant** L served Sun 12–2 D served Wed–Sat 7–8.45 Free House Cotleigh Tawny Ale, Interbrew Bass, Tom Cobley Bitter, Doom Bar, Tribute & Guest Ales. **Facilities** Garden Parking

STOCKLAND MAP 04 ST20

Pick of the Pubs

The Kings Arms Inn 🍷

EX14 9BS ☎ 01404 881361 📠 01404 881732

e-mail: info@kingsarms.net

dir: *Off A30 to Chard, 6m NE of Honiton*

A traditional 16th-century coaching inn tucked away in the Blackdown Hills, where real ales and good food are served in a lively atmosphere. The Grade II-listed thatched and whitewashed inn boasts an impressive flagstoned walkway entrance, a medieval oak screen and an original bread oven, as well as an old grey-painted phone box. The atmospheric Farmers bar is a popular meeting place with locals and visitors united in their liking for local real ales. The Cotley restaurant bar and dining room offers a wide range of blackboard specials. A great selection of starters includes devilled whitebait; Denhay ham with melon; and smoked ostrich fillet. There's a good balance of fish, meat and vegetarian dishes: lobster or king prawn thermidor; John Dory meunière; half a crispy roast duck; venison medallions; vegetable curry; mushroom stroganoff – to name just a few. Regular skittles matches and live music add to the vibrant feel.

Open 12–3 6.30–11.30 Closed: Dec 25 **Bar Meals** L served Mon–Sat 12–2 D served all week 6.30–9 Av main course £7.50 **Restaurant** L served all week 12–2 D served all week 6.30–9 Av 3 course à la carte £25 Free House Otter Ale, Exmoor Ale, O'Hanlon's Yellowhammer, Firefly & Port Stout. 🍷 15 **Facilities** Garden Dogs allowed Parking

STOKE FLEMING MAP 03 SX8

The Green Dragon Inn 🍷

Church Rd TQ6 0PX ☎ 01803 770238 📠 01803 770238

e-mail: pcrowther@btconnect.com

dir: *Off A379 (Dartmouth to Kingsbridge coast road) opposite church*

Legend has it a smuggler's tunnel runs from this 12th-century inn down to the sea at Blackpool Sands. The pub, if not the tunnel, was built by masons labouring on the nearby church, and was first recorded as purveying ales in 1607. Lunchtime snacks include baguettes and beefburgers, while the dinner menu offers such hearty dishes as steak and ale pie; spicy venison and pork kofta kebabs; or crabcakes with saffron tartare sauce.

Open 11–3 5.30–11 **Bar Meals** L served all week 12–2.30 D served all week 6.30–9 **Restaurant** L served all week 12–2.15 D served all week 6.30–8.30 (No food Sun eve in Winter) Heavitree Otter, Flowers IP Bass, 6X. 🍷 10 **Facilities** Garden Dogs allowed Parking Play Area

STOKENHAM MAP 03 SX8

Pick of the Pubs

The Tradesman's Arms 🍷

TQ7 2SZ ☎ 01548 580313 📠 01548 580313

e-mail: nick@thetradesmansarms.com

dir: *Just off A379 between Kingsbridge & Dartmouth*

See Pick of the Pubs on opposite page

STRETE MAP 03 SX8

Pick of the Pubs

Kings Arms 🍷

Dartmouth Rd TQ6 0RW

☎ 01803 770377 📠 01803 771008

e-mail: kingsarms_devon_fish@hotmail.com

dir: *On A379 (Dartmouth-Kingsbridge road), 5m from Dartmouth*

See Pick of the Pubs on page 18

The Tradesman's Arms

he Tradesman's Arms is a fine part-thatched pub and restaurant, with beams, log-burning fires nd a lovely atmosphere, tucked away on the edge of Stokenham's large, sheep-grazed village reen.

/hen Henry VIII gave the village Anne of Cleves, for a mere six onths his fourth wife, the building originally three cottages and a ewhouse – was already 150 years d, having been built around 390. Over the years it has been any things including, until a few ars back, a restaurant, but now is most definitely a pub – a pub at serves excellent food, for that atter. Real ales come from the uth Hams brewery in nearby ngsbridge, and there are local ders too, as well as a wide range malt whiskeys, bourbons and od wines from Europe and the ew World, all served in a cosy mosphere of old beams and log es. The kitchen uses fresh and, erever possible, locally sourced ingredients extensively, and that would include a typical three-course meal of smoked salmon with capers and sun-blushed tomatoes, followed by fillet steak, roasted field mushrooms stuffed with paté, onion marmalade and a red wine sauce, then tarte au citron to finish. The menu is supplemented by home-made fresh fish and meat specials, and a curry of the day, all of which change regularly. For larger groups of people, an Edwardian-style traditional buffet can be arranged. Slapton Sands, where the Americans practised for the D-Day landings, and Slapton Ley, a nature reserve, are one mile away.

MAP 03 SX84
TQ7 2SZ
☎ 01548 580313
01548 580313
e-mail: nick@thetradesmansarms.com
dir: *Just off A379 between Kingsbridge & Dartmouth*

Open 11-3 6-11 (Sun 12-10.30)
Bar Meals L served all week 12-2.30 D served Wed-Sun 6.30-9.30
Restaurant L served all week 12-2.30 D served Wed-Sun 6.30-9.30
Free House
Brakspear, Southams Devon Pride & Eddystone, Bass & Guest Ale. 18
Facilities Garden Dogs allowed Parking

PICK OF THE PUBS

STRETE-DEVON

Kings Arms

You can't go wrong with a pub whose kitchen motto is 'keep it fresh, keep it simple'. In the Kings Arms, the only pub in the village, customers are welcome to eat in the traditional terracotta-walled bar with its old photographs of the village and fish prints, or they can opt for the contemporary dining room, enlivened by specially commissioned art.

Menus are based around local and regional produce, and seafood makes up about eighty percent of it. Among the seafood dishes you might find River Yealm oysters with local chipolatas and coarse-grain mustard; grilled fillets of red mullet on warm tomato and mint vinaigrette; seared hand-dived scallops on braised Puy lentils with Pedro Xiemenes sherry dressing; Szechwan 'salt and pepper' squid with mooli and carrot salad and sweet soy sauce; Thai-style mussels with coriander, lemon grass and chili; mackerel 'escabeche' with rhubarb jelly; grilled sardines with sea salt, lemon and thyme; Spanish-style roast cod with chorizo, potatoes and peppers; grilled sea bream, pancetta, vanilla, green peppercorn and apple syrup; and Singapore crab with black pepper, steamed pak choi and sesame oil. What's more, they also bake their own bread, brioche, oatcakes and biscuits, and make their own sausages, pickles, relishes and ice creams. At lunchtime you can opt for a light meal like Caesar salad with hot smoked salmon; or warm salad of goats' cheese with roasted baby tomato and pesto; or go for a River Yealm's oysters on ice starter, followed by mixed Devon seafood poached in a thin Thai broth

🍷
MAP 03 SX84
Dartmouth Rd TQ6 0RW
☎ 01803 770377
📠 01803 771008
e-mail: kingsarms_devon_fish@hotmail.com
dir: *On A379 (Dartmouth-Kingsbridge road), 5m from Dartmouth*

Open 11.30–2.30 6.30–11 (Sun 12–3, 7–10.30)
Bar Meals L served all week 12–2 D served all week 6.30–9 (Sun 12–3) Av main course £14
Restaurant L served all week 12–2 D served all week 6.30–9 (Sun 12–3) Av 3 course à la carte £27
Otter Ale, Adnams Bitter, Guinness. 🍷 15
Facilities Children's licence Garden Dogs allowed Parking

TEDBURN ST MARY MAP 03 SX89

Kings Arms Inn

EX6 6EG ☎ 01647 61224 01647 61324

e-mail: info@kingsarmsinn.co.uk

dir: *A30 W to Okehampton, 1st exit right signed Tedburn St Mary*

Expect log fires and exposed beams in this delightful 14th-century free house, which sits just off Dartmoor's northern flanks. Until after the Civil War the pub was the Taphouse Inn, and even today locals refer to this part of the village as Taphouse. Food is local and organic where possible, and could take in crispy Somerset belly pork, home-baked ham and eggs, or Greek salad with feta cheese.

Open 11-3 6-12 (Open all day Sat-Sun) **Bar Meals** L served all week 11-2.30 D served all week 6-9.30 (Sat-Sun all day) **Restaurant** L served all week 11-2.30 D served all week 6-9.30 (Sat-Sun all day) Free House Interbrew Bass & Worthington Best, Sharp's Cornish Coaster, Whitbread Best. 8 **Facilities** Garden Parking Play Area

THURLESTONE MAP 03 SX64

The Village Inn

TQ7 3NN ☎ 01548 563525 01548 561069

e-mail: enquiries@thurlestone.co.uk

dir: *Take A379 from Plymouth towards Kingsbridge, at Bantham rdbt straight over onto B3197, then right signed Thurlestone, 2.5m*

Built in the 16th century as a farmhouse, this old pub prides itself on good service, well-kept ales and decent food. Like the nearby Thurlestone Hotel, it has been owned by the Grose family for over a century. Seafood is a speciality, with Salcombe crabmeat, River Exe mussels and other local fish and shellfish to choose from on the seasonal menus. Other possibilities are Cajun roasted chicken breast, sirloin and rump steaks, and beef burgers.

Open 11.30-3 6-11 (Sun 12-3, 7-10.30, Aug all day) **Bar Meals** L served all week 12-2.30 D served all week 6.30-9.30 Free House Palmers IPA, Interbrew Bass, Sharp's Doom Bar & Guest beer. 10 **Facilities** Children's licence Garden Dogs allowed Parking

TOPSHAM MAP 03 SX98

Pick of the Pubs

Bridge Inn

Bridge Hill EX3 0QQ

☎ 01392 873862 01392 877497

e-mail: su3264@eclipse.co.uk

dir: *4m SE of Exeter city centre, on E bank of River Clyst*

There's been a building on this site since 1083 and a pub since 1512. Four generations of the same family have run the Bridge since great grandfather moved in during 1897, and it remains eccentrically and gloriously old fashioned. It has been described as a museum with beer, with its vernacular architecture – a mix of stone and cob – small rooms, open fires, an 18th-century malting kiln and an old malt house used for parties or overflow custom. Back in 1998 it became the only pub in England to have been officially visited by Queen Elizabeth II. This is a drinking pub with all real ales from independent breweries only, naturally cellared and served straight from the cask. There are also a few wines, including two from a local organic vineyard. Traditional bar food is available: ploughman's, pasties, sandwiches and soup, all made with local ingredients.

Open 12-2 6-10.30 (Sun 7-10.30 Fri-Sat 6-11) **Bar Meals** L served all week 12-1.45 Free House Branscombe Vale-Branoc, Adnams Broadside, Exe Valley, O'Hanlons. **Facilities** Garden Dogs allowed Parking **Notes**

The Lighter Inn

The Quay EX3 0HZ ☎ 01392 875439 01392 876013

The imposing 17th-century customs house on Topsham Quay has been transformed into a popular waterside inn. A strong nautical atmosphere is reinforced with pictures, ship's instruments and oars beneath the pub's wooden ceilings, and the attractive quayside sitting area is popular in summer. Dishes may include whole sea bass or plaice, steaks, curries and salads, or steak, ale and mushroom pie.

Open 11-11 **Bar Meals** L served all week 12-2.30 D served all week 6.30-9 (Food all day Jul-Sep) Av main course £7.95 Woodhouse Inns Badger Best, Badger Tanglefoot, Sussex. 12 **Facilities** Parking

TORCROSS MAP 03 SX84

Start Bay Inn

TQ7 2TQ ☎ 01548 580553 01548 581285

e-mail: clair@startbayinn.co.uk

dir: *Between Dartmouth & Kingsbridge on A379*

The inn dates back to the 14th century and has been favoured by fishermen ever since. The landlord, now retired, continues to scuba dive for scallops for his daughters to serve at the inn. Sample the catch of the day which may include monkfish, lemon sole, Dover sole, bass, brill, skate, plaice, or John Dory. Whether or not you choose fish, the philosophy here is to source everything locally, cook it simply, and give customers value for money.

Open 11.30-2.30 6-11 (Summer 11.30-11) **Bar Meals** L served all week 11.30-2 D served all week 6-10 (Sun 11.30-2.15, Winter 6-9.30, Summer 11.30-10) Av main course £6 Heavitree Interbrew Flowers Original & Bass, Otter Ale. 8 **Facilities** Garden Parking

England

TOTNES MAP 03 SX86

Pick of the Pubs

The Durant Arms ★★★★ INN

Ashprington TQ9 7UP ☎ 01803 732240
e-mail: info@thedurantarms.com
dir: *Leave A38 at Totnes junct, proceed to Dartington & Totnes, at 1st set of lights right for Knightsbridge on A381, after 1m left for Ashprington*

See Pick of the Pubs on opposite page

Rumour

30 High St TQ9 5RY ☎ 01803 864682 📠 01803 864682
e-mail: enquiries@rumourtotnes.com
dir: *On main street above arch on left. 5 min walk from rail station, follow signs for Totnes castle/town centre*

After a chequered history as a milk bar, restaurant and wine bar, this 17th-century building was renamed after a Fleetwood Mac album in the mid-1970s. Now comprehensively refurbished, the new owners have installed innovative heating and plumbing systems to reduce the pub's environmental footprint. The ethical theme continues with Fair Trade coffee and locally-sourced soft drinks, juices and ingredients. Expect delicious pizzas; wild mushroom and parmesan risotto; and roast pork belly with Asian spices.

Open 10-12 (Fri-Sat 10-12.30, Sun 6-10.30) **Bar Meals** L served Mon-Sat 12-3 D served all week 6-10 Av main course £10.95 **Restaurant** L served Mon-Sat 12-3 D served all week 6-10 Av 3 course à la carte £20 Free House Erdinger, Lowenbrau, Abbots Ale, Heligan Honey. 15

Steam Packet Inn ★★★★ INN

St Peter's Quay TQ9 5EW
☎ 01803 863880 📠 01803 862754
e-mail: steampacket@buccaneer.co.uk
dir: *Exit A38 towards Plymouth, 18m. Take A384 to Totnes 6m. Left at mini-rdbt, pass Morrisons on left, over mini-rdbt, 400yds on left.*

The inn's sign depicts the Amelia, a steam packet ship that regularly called here with passengers, parcels and mail before the days of modern road and rail transport. These days the building is a welcoming riverside pub with great views, particularly from the restaurant, and plenty of waterside seating for sunny days. Typical dishes from the thoroughly modern menu include curried parsnip, apple and honey soup; Chinese spiced duck breast; and slow-roasted lamb with ratatouille.

Open 11-11 (Sun 12-10.30) **Bar Meals** L served all week 12-2.30 D served all week 6-9.30 (Sun 6-9) Av main course £12.50 **Restaurant** L served all week 12-2.30 D served all week 6-9.30 (Sun 6-9) Av 3 course à la carte £21 Buccaneer Holdings Courage Best, Butcombe, Otter Bright & Guest Ale. 8 **Facilities** Children's licence Garden Parking **Rooms** 4 bedrooms en suite S£59.50 D£79.50

The White Hart Bar

Dartington Hall TQ9 6EL ☎ 01803 847111 📠 01803 847107
dir: *Totnes turn onto A38 to Plymouth*

Set in a stunning location beside the 14th-century Dartington Hall, the White Hart is surrounded by landscaped gardens, ancient deer parkland and woodland. It is a stylish dining venue with flagstone floors, limed oak settles, roughcast walls and a welcoming atmosphere. Enjoy the range of West Country ales, or choose from an accessible wine list that classifies bottles by their flavours. The innovative menu uses local and organic produce where possible to create dishes with a modern twist.

Open 11-11 Closed: Dec 24-29 **Bar Meals** L served all week 12-2 D served all week 6-9.30 Av main course £10 **Restaurant** L served all week 12-2 D served all week 6-9 Free House Otter Brewery Ale & Bitter. 8 **Facilities** Children's licence Garden Parking

TUCKENHAY MAP 03 SX85

The Maltsters Arms

TQ9 7EQ ☎ 01803 732350 📠 01803 732823
e-mail: pub@tuckenhay.demon.co.uk

Accessible only through high-banked lanes, or by boat for about three hours either side of high tide, this 18th-century pub is noted for its charcoal barbeques and cream teas in summer, and live music events. The daily changing menu may feature Dartmouth smoked salmon and trout with dill mayonnaise; River Exe mussels with garlic, white wine and herbs; local rabbit and red wine pie; or lamb and aubergine moussaka.

Open 11-11 (Dec 25 12-2 only - no food) **Bar Meals** L served all week 12-3 D served all week 7-9.30 Av main course £10 **Restaurant** L served all week 12-3 D served all week 7-9.30 Av 3 course à la carte £20 Free House Princetown Dartmoor IPA, Young's Special, Teignworthy Maltsters Ale, Southams Eddystone. 18 **Facilities** Garden Dogs allowed Parking

TYTHERLEIGH MAP 04 ST30

Tytherleigh Arms Hotel

EX13 7BE ☎ 01460 220400 & 220214 📠 01460 220406
e-mail: tytherleigharms@aol.com
dir: *Equidistant between Chard & Axminster on the A358*

Beamed ceilings and huge roaring fires are notable features of this family-run, 17th-century former coaching inn. It is a food-led establishment, situated on the Devon, Somerset and Dorset borders. Fresh home-cooked dishes, using local ingredients, include lamb shank with honey and cider, steaks and fresh seafood such as sea bass, red mullet and Lyme Bay crab thermidor. Comprehensive bar snack menu also available.

Open 11-2.30 6.30-11 **Bar Meals** L served all week 12-2.30 D served all week 6.30-9 (Sun 7-9 during summer) **Restaurant** L served all week 12-2.30 D served all week 6.30-9 (Sun 7-9 during summer) Av 3 course à la carte £25 Free House Butcombe Bitter, Otter, Murphy's, Boddingtons. **Facilities** Children's licence Garden Parking

The Durant Arms

Graham and Eileen Ellis believe there will always be a market for true British hospitality, a sentiment borne out by the popularity of their award-winning 18th-century hostelry. Locally renowned as a dining pub, the Durant Arms is situated in the picturesque village of Ashprington, just outside the Elizabethan town of Totnes, and in the very heart of the South Hams.

It was originally the counting house for the neighbouring 500-acre Sharpham Estate, then for some years became The Ashprington Inn, a smaller establishment than the Durant, which has expanded into an adjoining property. The comfortable bar is fitted out in a traditional style, with work by local artists on display alongside horse-brasses, ferns and cheerful red velvet curtains. All dishes at the Durant are cooked to order, with a wide variety of meat and fish, sourced locally as often as possible. Fish, for example, all comes from Plymouth, with typical dishes likely to include whole grilled lemon sole; scallops and tiger prawns with cream and white wine; halibut topped with cheese, or grilled skate. Another speciality is the award-winning hand-made English cheeses. These come from the nearby Sharpham's organic dairy farm on the banks of the River Dart, which has been producing unpasteurised artisan cheeses for over twenty years. Among the wines are Sharpham whites, reds, and a rosé, which the Ellises always like to recommend. The terraced rear garden is quite a suntrap, a lovely spot to linger over an al fresco meal. Eight traditionally furnished en suite bedrooms complete the package.

★★★★ INN ⇨ 🍷
MAP 03 SX86
Ashprington TQ9 7UP
☎ 01803 732240
e-mail:
info@thedurantarms.com
dir: *Leave A38 at Totnes junct, proceed to Dartington & Totnes, at 1st set of lights right for Knightsbridge on A381, after 1m left for Ashprington*

Open 11.30–2.30 6.30–11
Bar Meals L served all week 12–2.30 D served all week 7–9.15
Restaurant L served all week 12–2 D served all week 7–9.15
Av 3 course à la carte £20
Free House
Dartmoor Bitter, Tetley, Tribute. 🍷 8
Facilities Garden Parking
Rooms 8 bedrooms en suite
S£45 D£80

The Digger's Rest

Originally a Devon cider house, this picturesque country inn offers traditionally drawn Otter ales plus Butcombe bitter and Scatterbrook Devonian, home-cooked food and a relaxed, welcoming atmosphere.

Its thick 500-year-old walls are built of stone and cob with heavy beams under a thatched roof. Inside, soft furnishings and lighting, and West Country art contrast with antique furniture and a skittle alley. The patio garden provides seating for up to forty people and is the perfect setting for alfresco drinking and dining, especially at night when it is attractively lit up. A single menu is offered in the bar and restaurant, along with sandwiches at lunchtime (ham, roast beef, chicken and lettuce, and prawn or crab). You'll find the likes of hot organic pork sausage and red onion ciabatta; wild and chestnut mushrooms on toast; and roast Mediterranean vegetable bruschetta for starters; followed by haddock and herb fishcakes; Digger's fish pie; steak and kidney pie; Thai green chicken curry; 8oz rump or 10oz rib-eye steak; and free range pork sausages with mash and onion gravy. A similar menu is available in the evening along with weekly changing specials that could include beef Wellington; lamb chump chops with dauphinois potatoes and red wine sauce; organic salmon roasted in Parma ham; and John Dory coated in lemon zest breadcrumbs. Desserts are not to be missed, with sticky toffee pudding, hot treacle sponge, chocolate brownie with hot chocolate sauce, crème brûlée, and chocolate sundae among the tasty options. Children have their own menu.

MAP 03 SY08
EX5 1PQ
☎ 01395 232375
01395 232711
e-mail: bar@diggersrest.co.uk
dir: *2.5m from A3052. Signed from Westpoint*

Open 11–3 6–11 (All day Sat–Sun)
Bar Meals L served all week 12–2 D served all week 6.30–9.30
Restaurant L served all week 12–2 D served all week 6.30–9.30 (Sun 12–2.30) Av 3 course à la carte £20
Free House
Otter Bitter, Otter Ale, Scatterbrook Devonian, Butcombe Bitter. 15
Facilities Children's licence Garden Parking

UMBERLEIGH MAP 03 SS62

Pick of the Pubs

The Rising Sun Inn ★★ 🍷

EX37 9DU ☎ 01769 560447 📠 01769 560764

e-mail: risingsuninn@btopenworld.com

dir: *On A377, (Exeter-Barnstaple road), at junct with B3227*

Idyllically set beside the River Taw and with a very strong fly fishing tradition, the Rising Sun dates back in part to the 13th century. The traditional flagstone bar is strewn with fishing memorabilia, comfortable chairs and daily papers and magazines for a very relaxing visit. Outside is a sunny raised terrace with beautiful rural views of the valley, and the riverside walk is equally enjoyable before or after a meal. This inn is an excellent base for the touring motorist with several National Trust properties nearby. A choice of à la carte restaurant or regularly updated bar menus feature the best of West Country produce, with seasonal delights like seafood from the North Devon coast, salmon and sea trout from the Taw, game from Exmoor, and local cheeses. The daily changing specials board is often the best place to start looking and there's a Sunday carvery.

Open 12–3 6–11 (All day May–Sep) **Bar Meals** L served all week 12–2 D served all week 6.30–9 **Restaurant** L served all week 12–2 D served all week 6.30–9 Sun 6.30–8.30 Free House Cotleigh Tawny Bitter, Barn Owl, Guinness, Speckled Hen. 🍷 9 **Facilities** Children's licence Garden Dogs allowed Parking **Rooms** 9 bedrooms en suite S£49 D£85

WIDECOMBE IN THE MOOR MAP 03 SX77

The Old Inn 🍷

TQ13 7TA ☎ 01364 621207 📠 01364 621407

e-mail: oldinn.wid@virgin.net

dir: *Telephone for directions*

Dating from the 15th century, the Old Inn was partly ruined by fire but rebuilt around the original fireplaces. Two main bars and no fewer than five eating areas offer plenty of scope for visitors to enjoy the extensive selection of home-cooked food on offer. Sustaining main courses include home-made pies; fresh local salmon; and steaks from the grill. There are plenty of vegetarian options such as mushroom stroganoff and lasagne verde.

Open 11 –11 **Bar Meals** L served all week 11.30–2.30 D served all week 6–9 (Snack menu 2.30–6, Sun all day) Av main course £7.50 **Restaurant** L served all week 11–2 D served all week 7–10 Av 3 course à la carte £11 Free House Badger & Guest Ales. 🍷 12 **Facilities** Garden Dogs allowed Parking

Rugglestone Inn

TQ13 7TF ☎ 01364 621327 📠 01364 621224

dir: *A38 Drumbridges exit towards Bovey Tracey, left at 2nd rdbt, left at sign Haytor & Widecombe, village is 5m*

Surrounded by peaceful moorland, this pretty Dartmoor inn has a large lawned garden with picnic tables. Converted from a farm cottage in 1832, it features open fires, beamed ceilings, real ales straight from the barrel and local farm cider, helping to give the pub its special atmosphere. The menu is typically British, featuring good quality produce. Dishes include steak and kidney pie, liver and bacon and fisherman's pie.

Open 11.30–3 6.30–11 (Sun 12–3, Winter 7–11, Sun 10.30) **Bar Meals** L served all week 12–2 D served all week 7–9 Free House Butcombe Bitter, St Austells Dartmoor Best. **Facilities** Garden Dogs allowed Parking

WINKLEIGH MAP 03 SS60

Pick of the Pubs

The Duke of York 🍷

Iddesleigh EX19 8BG

☎ 01837 810253 📠 01837 810253

The atmosphere of this venerable thatched inn is blissfully unsullied by juke box, fruit machine or karaoke. Set deep in rural mid-Devon, it was originally three cottages housing craftsmen who were rebuilding the parish church; local records accurately date this work to 1387. All the timeless features of a classic country pub remain – heavy old beams, scrubbed tables, farmhouse chairs and a huge inglenook fireplace with winter fires. Popular with all, it offers decent real ales (Cotleigh Tawny, for example) and hearty home cooking, with everything freshly prepared using local produce such as meat reared on nearby farms. Examples of bar meals taken from the large blackboard menu include rainbow trout, liver and bacon, and casseroles. From the dining room menu could come Dartmouth smokehouse salmon followed by pork loin with port and tarragon sauce, then a choice of more than a dozen classic home-made desserts.

Open 11–12 **Bar Meals** L served all week 12–10 D served all week 12–10 (Sun 12–9.30) Av main course £8 **Restaurant** L served all week D served all week 7–10 (Sun 7–9.30) Av 3 course fixed price £24 Free House Adnams Broadside, Cotleigh Tawny, Guest beers. 🍷 10 **Facilities** Garden Dogs allowed

The Kings Arms 🍷

Fore St EX19 8HQ ☎ 01837 83384

dir: *Village signed off B3220 (Crediton to Torrington road)*

Scrubbed pine tables and traditional wooden settles set the scene at this ancient thatched country inn in Winkleigh's central square. Wood-burning stoves keep the beamed bar and dining rooms warm in chilly weather, and traditional pub games are encouraged. Generous servings of freshly-made food include sandwiches and hot snacks, as well as roasted vegetables with goats' cheese; Lucy's fish pie; and lamb's liver with bacon. Booking is recommended at weekends.

Open 11–11 (Sun 12–10.30) **Bar Meals** L served all week 11–9.30 D served all week (Sun 12–9) Av main course £8.95 **Restaurant** L served all week 11–9.30 D served all week (Sun 12–9) Enterprise Inns Butcombe Bitter, Sharp's Doom Bar & Cornish Coaster. 🍷 7 **Facilities** Children's licence Garden Dogs allowed

WOODBURY SALTERTON MAP 03 SY08

Pick of the Pubs

The Digger's Rest 🍷

EX5 1PQ ☎ 01395 232375 📠 01395 232711

e-mail: bar@diggersrest.co.uk

dir: *2.5m from A3052. Signed from Westpoint*

See Pick of the Pubs on opposite page

YEALMPTON MAP 03 SX55

Rose & Crown NEW

Market St PL8 2EB ☎ 01752 880223 01752 881058
e-mail: info@theroseandcrown.co.uk

A major refurbishment in 2005 saw the Rose and Crown transformed. It's a stylish spot these days, elegant without being overbearing. The food is taken seriously here, and the Pacific Rim-inspired menu includes such imaginative dishes as Falmouth bay scallops, roasted cantaloupe and coriander pesto, followed by roast breast of duck, vanilla purée and Armagnac jus. Look out for the secret garden: complete with fountain, it's a lovely spot for a romantic summer meal.

Open 12–11 **Bar Meals** L served all week 12–3 D served all week 6.30–9 Av main course £12 **Restaurant** L served 12–2 D served 6.30–9 Av 3 course à la carte £20 Av 3 course fixed price £12.95 San Miguel, Fosters, Doom Bar, London Pride, Courage Best. **Facilities** Garden Dogs allowed Parking

DORSET

ABBOTSBURY MAP 04 SY58

Ilchester Arms

9 Market St DT3 4JR ☎ 01305 871243 01305 871225

Rambling 16th-century coaching inn set in the heart of one of Dorset's most picturesque villages. Abbotsbury is home to many crafts including woodwork and pottery. A good area for walkers, and handy for the Tropical Gardens and Swannery.

Open 11–11 (Sun 12–10.30) Rest: 25 Dec 12–3 **Bar Meals** L served all week 12–2 (Sun 12–2.30) D served all week 7–9 Av main course £10 **Restaurant** L served all week 12–2.30 D served all week 7–9.30 (Sun 7–9) Av 3 course à la carte £20 Gales HSB, Courage Best, Tribute, Speckled Hen. 12 **Facilities** Children's licence Garden Dogs allowed Parking

BLANDFORD FORUM MAP 04 ST80

The Anvil Inn NEW ★★★★ INN

Salisbury Rd, Pimperne DT11 8UQ
☎ 01258 453431 01258 480182
e-mail: theanvil.inn@btconnect.com

A thatched roof, crooked beams and a cavernous fireplace are just a few of the rustic charms of this 16th-century inn located in the pretty village of Pimperne, two miles from Blandford Forum. The menu starts with ploughman's lunches, simple omelettes and salads, and runs to hearty, traditional meals including grills, fish and chips, and sausages and mash. Spicier choices include Thai vegetable curry or chicken fajitas.

Open all day **Bar Meals** L served all week D served all week **Restaurant** Av 3 course à la carte £20 Free House Guinness, London Pride. **Facilities** Children's licence Garden Dogs allowed Parking **Rooms** 13 bedrooms en suite S£65 D£90

Best Western Crown Hotel ★★★ HL

West St DT11 7AJ ☎ 01258 456626 01258 451084
e-mail: thecrownhotel@blandforddorset.freeserve.co.uk
dir: *M27 W onto A31 to A350 junct, W to Blandford. 100mtrs from town bridge*

An 18th-century coaching inn which replaces an original inn destroyed by fire in 1731. Standing on the banks of the River Stour, the Crown has plenty of period atmosphere, and a separate restaurant. Begin a meal, perhaps, with cod and parsley fishcake with sweet chilli sauce, follow it with rosemary-crusted lamb cutlets with redcurrant scented gravy; or gammon steak with grilled pineapple, chips and peas. An extensive bar menu includes sandwiches and light bites.

Open 10–2.30 6–11 Closed: 25–28 Dec **Bar Meals** L served all week 12–2 D served all week 7–9 Av main course £7 **Restaurant** L served all week D served all week 7.15–9.15 (Sun 7–9) Hall & Woodhouse Badger Tanglefoot, Best, Badger 1st Gold. 20 **Facilities** Garden Dogs allowed Parking **Rooms** 32 bedrooms en suite S£78 D£99

BOURTON MAP 04 ST73

The White Lion Inn

High St SP8 5AT ☎ 01747 840866 01747 840191
e-mail: enquiries@whitelionbourton.com
dir: *Off A303, opposite B3092 to Gillingham*

A quintessentially English pub, built from stone in 1723 and packed with beams and flagstones, not to mention a log fire and a good choice of real ales. Food options are divided between light bites (baguettes; ham, egg and chips; Catalan style meatballs) and the Shoals restaurant menu. There's also a daily selection of fish specials. Typical starters include venison pâté; meatballs; tagliatelle with seafood sauce; and mushrooms stuffed with garlic, parsley and parmesan cheese. Follow with Thai green curry; steak and kidney pie; vegetable tagine with couscous; or beef escalope with port wine sauce.

Open 12–3 5–11 Closed: 26 Dec **Bar Meals** L served all week 12–2 D served all week 7–9 (Sun 12–3) **Restaurant** L served all week 12–2 D served Mon–Sat 7–9 (Sun 12–3) Admiral Taverns Fullers London Pride, Greene King IPA & Guest Beer. **Facilities** Garden Dogs allowed Parking

Shave Cross Inn

Jo amount of guessing is likely to reveal the origins of this friendly, family-run pub's name. Back ı the 13th-century, pilgrims and monks on their way to the church of St Candida and St Cross ı nearby Whitchurch Canonicorum would stop here, or so the story goes, for a quick haircut.

he churchyard contains the rave of Georgi Markov, Bulgaria's nost revered dissident', who was ssassinated by a Soviet agent with poisoned umbrella on Waterloo ridge in 1978. Tucked away down arrow lanes, this could well be ıe inn that time forgot. The bar floored with ancient blue lias agstones from Dorset's Jurassic oast (a World Heritage Site), and ıe inglenook fireplace is just right r smoking hams. Owners Roy and Iel Warburton spent a long time ı Tobago, before returning in 2003 take over and revive the pub. hey brought with them their head ıef, who is responsible for the ıthentically Caribbean touches to ıe menu. Examples include roast éole duck with cherry compote; rk chicken salad with plantain, crispy bacon and aioli; and Dorset prime fillet steak with a rum, brandy and Caribbean peppercorn sauce. Fans of traditional British food won't be disappointed though: there are plenty of other options, especially at lunchtime. These range from fresh battered haddock, and rump steak, to cheese ploughman's, and fresh crab sandwiches. Local beers come from Quay Brewery in Weymouth and Devon's Branscombe Vale. The garden has a play area for children, a thatched wishing well and a huge collection of flowers and shrubs. Ancient customs linger on in these parts. The inn houses the oldest thatched skittle alley in the country, and maintains the traditions of Morris dancing, folk singing, and ashen-faggot burning on Twelfth Night.

MAP 04 SY49
Shave Cross, Marshwood Vale
DT6 6HW
☎ 01308 868358
01308 867064
e-mail: roy.warburton@virgin.net
dir: *From Bridport take B3162 2m turn left signed 'Broadoak/Shave Cross' then Marshwood*

Open 11–3 6–11 (All day Tue–Sun Summer, BH Mons)
Bar Meals L served Tue–Sun 12–2.30 D served Tue–Sun 5–9.30 (Sun 12–3, 6–8 Summer)
Restaurant L served Tue–Sun 12–2.30 D served Tue–Sat 7–9.30 (Sun 6–8 Summer) Av 3 course à la carte £26
Free House
Local guest beers, Branoc (Branscombe Valley), Quay Brewery Weymouth. 🍷 8
Facilities Children's licence Garden Dogs allowed Parking Play Area

BRIDPORT MAP 04 SY49

The George Hotel

4 South St DT6 3NQ ☎ 01308 423187

dir: *Town centre, 1.5m from West Bay*

Handsome Georgian town house, with a Victorian-style bar and a mellow atmosphere, which bustles all day. It offers a traditional English breakfast, decent morning coffee and a good menu featuring fresh local plaice, natural smoked haddock, avacado and bacon salad, and the famous rabbit and bacon pie. Everything is home cooked using local produce.

Open 9.30–11.30 Closed: Dec 25 **Bar Meals** L served all week 12–2.30 D served Wed–Thu 6–9 Palmers Palmers - IPA, Copper & 200, Tally Ho. **Facilities** Dogs allowed

Pick of the Pubs

Shave Cross Inn

Shave Cross, Marshwood Vale DT6 6HW

☎ 01308 868358 01308 867064

e-mail: roy.warburton@virgin.net

dir: *From Bridport take B3162, 2m turn left signed Broadoak/Shave Cross then Marshwood*

See Pick of the Pubs on page 187

The West Bay

Station Rd, West Bay DT6 4EW

☎ 01308 422157 01308 459717

e-mail: info@thewestbay.co.uk

dir: *From A35 take B3157 towards West Bay. After mini-rdbt 1st left. Pub on left*

Established around 1739, this traditional bar/restaurant is located in a beautiful harbour village forming part of the impressive World Heritage Jurassic Coast. Seafood is the speciality – dressed Lyme Bay crab, fillet of sea bass en papillote, pan-fried skate wing, and classic fish pie – as is the range of steaks with classic garnishes. Comforting puddings include steamed chocolate sponge, and apple and raisin crumble. Murder mystery evenings are an occasional feature.

Open 12–3 6.15–11.30 **Bar Meals** L served all week 12–2 (Sun 12–2.15) D served Mon–Sat 6.30–9 Av main course £13.50 **Restaurant** L served all week 12–2 D served Mon–Sat 6.30–9 Av 3 course fixed price £15 Palmers Palmers IPA, Palmers Copper, Palmers 200, Carlsberg & Guinness. **Facilities** Children's licence Garden Parking

BURTON BRADSTOCK MAP 04 SY4

Pick of the Pubs

The Anchor Inn

High St DT6 4QF ☎ 01308 897228 01308 897228

e-mail: info@dorset-seafoodrestaurants.co.uk

dir: *2m SE of Bridport on B3157 in centre of Burton Bradstock*

The Anchor Inn is a 300-year-old coaching inn just inland from a stretch of the Jurassic Coast World Heritage Site, and near the amazing shingle feature known as Chesil Beach. In keeping with its name, the pub is full of marine memorabilia: fishing nets hang from ceilings, and old fishing tools and arty things made by the chef-proprietor from shellfish adorn the walls. The house speciality is seafood, and with twenty different main fish courses on the menu, plus Catch of the Day specials, choosing might be hard. Suggestions include fillet of brill stuffed with local crab; grilled Cornish mackerel; red bream and red mullet grilled with Cajun seasoning; skate wing with prawns; and lobster Americaine. In addition there are shellfish platters, fresh scallops, and moules marinière, while meat dishes include barbary duck; beef stroganoff; peppered pork fillet; and old English sirloin steak. The bar offers 60 different malt whiskies.

Open 11–11 (Sun 12–10.30) **Bar Meals** L served Mon–Sat 12–2 D served all week 6–9 Av main course £14.50 **Restaurant** L served all week 12–2 D served all week 6–9 Punch Taverns Otter Bitter, Speckled Hen, Flowers Bitter, Thatchers Cider. **Facilities** Children's licence Parking

PICK OF THE PUBS

CERNE ABBAS-DORSET

The Royal Oak

uilt in 1540 in the market square using the remains of a 9th-century abbey, the Royal Oak ***elivers all the character and atmosphere that its history suggests, thanks to a thatched roof,*** ***agstone floors, oak beams and open fireplaces.***

'he pretty village location enhances s charm. Outside there's a lovely ourtyard garden, and just inside ne pub you'll see what is believed o be its original front door omplete with its wooden lock. In 670 a previous owner sold the ub, and with the proceeds he urchased 1800 acres of land in ne United States, now the site of Capitol Hill. Fast-forward to the resent day and the pub is owned y Maurice and Sandra Ridley, 'hose son Darran is in charge of ne kitchen. Darran, a member of ne Master Chefs of Great Britain, as vast international experience ncluding stints at Buckingham alace, the Gleneagles Hotel and n board the QE2. Dine on light ites such as a filled panini (freshly baked to order), a ploughman's or a dressed local crab salad. For a more substantial meal, you could start with River Teign oysters, grilled with garlic and parmesan or served on ice; or a warm tartlet of sun-blushed tomatoes and goats' cheese. For your main course, try venison bourguignon; lamb shank, slow cooked for seven hours in red wine, tomato, garlic and rosemary; or pie of the day (beef in ale with local blue vinney cheese is very popular). Fish dishes are also a strength, and might include simple local dressed crab salad, or monkfish cheeks with braised ox tails. Also worthy of attention are the desserts, many of which come with ice cream churned to order.

MAP 04 ST60
23 Long St DT2 7JG
01300 341797
01300 341814
e-mail:
info@theroyaloak-pub.co.uk
dir: *M5/A37, follow A37 to A352 signed Cerne Abbas, midway between Sherborne & Dorchester. Pub in centre of village*

Open 11 –11
Bar Meals L served all week 12–3 D served all week 6.30–9
Av main course £9.95
Hall & Woodhouse
Tanglefoot, Badger Best, Fursty Ferret, Stowford Press. 8
Facilities Garden Dogs allowed

England

CATTISTOCK MAP 04 SY59

Fox & Hounds Inn ★★★ INN

Duck St DT2 0JH ☎ 01300 320444 🖷 01300 320444

e-mail: info@foxandhoundsinn.com

dir: *On the A37, between Dorchester & Yeovil, signed to Cattistock*

This attractive 16th-century inn is set in the beautiful village of Cattistock. Original features include beams, open fires and huge inglenooks, one with an original bread oven. It is a fascinating building, full of curiosities, such as the hidden cupboard reached by a staircase that winds around the chimney in one of the loft areas. Traditional home-made meals include locally made faggots; mushroom stroganoff; steak and kidney pudding; fisherman's pie; and Dorset apple cake.

Open 12–2.30 7–11 **Bar Meals** L served Tue–Sun 12–2 D served all week 7–9 Av main course £8 **Restaurant** L served Tue–Sun 12–2 D served all week 7–9 Palmers Brewery Palmers IPA, Copper Ale, Palmers 200 & Dorset Gold. **Facilities** Children's licence Garden Dogs allowed Parking **Rooms** 2 bedrooms S£40 D£70

CERNE ABBAS MAP 04 ST60

Pick of the Pubs

The Royal Oak

23 Long St DT2 7JG ☎ 01300 341797 🖷 01300 341814

e-mail: info@theroyaloak-pub.co.uk

dir: *M5/A37, follow A37 to A352 signed Cerne Abbas, midway between Sherborne & Dorchester. In village centre*

See Pick of the Pubs on page 189

CHIDEOCK MAP 04 SY4

The Anchor Inn

Seatown DT6 6JU ☎ 01297 489215

dir: *On A35 turn S in Chideock opp church & follow single track road for 0.75m to beach*

Originally a smugglers' haunt, The Anchor has an incredible setting in a little cove surrounded by National Trust land, beneath Golden Cap. The large sun terrace and cliff-side beer garden overlooking the beach make it a premier destination for throngs of holidaymakers in the summer, while on winter weekdays it is blissfully quiet. The wide-ranging menu starts with snacks and light lunches – three types of ploughman's and a range of sandwiches might take your fancy. For something more substantial you could try freshly caught seafood – crab salad.

Open 11–3 6–11 (Fri–Sun, Summer all day) **Bar Meals** L served all week 12–2.30 D served all week 6–9 (all day Sat–Sun & Summer) Av main cours £7.50 Palmers Palmers 200 Premium Ale, IPA, Copper Ale. 8 **Facilities** Garden Dogs allowed Parking

Please see walk on opposite pag

CHRISTCHURCH MAP 05 SZ1

Fishermans Haunt ★★★ INN

Salisbury Rd, Winkton BH23 7AS

☎ 01202 477283 🖷 01202 478883

e-mail: fishermanshaunt@accommodating-inn.co.uk

dir: *2.5m N on B3347 (Christchurch/Ringwood road)*

Dating from 1673, this inn overlooks the River Avon and is a popular place for walkers, and anglers visiting some of the local fisheries. The area is also well endowed with golf courses. The menu offers a daily fish selection, usually including trout and whole plaice, and staples such as steak and kidney pie, battered cod, and mixed grill along with sandwiches and baked potatoes. There's a more extensive carte men in the restaurant.

Open 10.30–3 5–11 (Sat 11–11, Sun 12–10.30) **Bar Meals** L served all week 12–2 D served all week 6–9 **Restaurant** L served Sat–Sun 12–2 D served Sat–Sun 6–9 Av 3 course à la carte £15 Fullers Gales GB & HSB, Ringwood Fortyniner & London Pride. 7 **Facilities** Garden Dogs allowed Parking **Rooms** 12 en suite S£49.50 D£66

The Ship In Distress

66 Stanpit BH23 3NA ☎ 01202 485123 🖷 01202 483997

e-mail: enquiries@theshipindistress.com

Once a haunt of famous Christchurch smugglers, this 300-year-old pu featured in a recent documentary film about the history of smuggling It is located close to Mudeford Quay and has an award-winning seafood and dessert restaurant. Typical dishes are moules marinière, and baked fillet of turbot with shallots, wild mushrooms and sunblush tomatoes. Fresh daily desserts include assiette of Belgian chocolate, and Cointreau orange mascarpone cheesecake with confit orange.

Open 11–11 Closed: Dec 25 **Bar Meals** L served all week 12–2 D served all week 7–9.30 (Sun 12–3) Av main course £10 **Restaurant** L served all week 12–2 D served all week 7–9.30 Av 3 course à la carte £30 Punch Taverns Ringwood Best, Fortyniner, Interbrew Bass, Courage Directors. **Facilities** Garden Dogs allowed Parking

Anchor Inn

Walk information

Distance: 4 miles (6.4km)
Map: OS Explorer 116 Lyme Regis & Bridport
Start/finish: car park (charge) above gravel beach in Seatown (may flood in stormy weather); grid ref SY 420917
Ascent/gradient: 3
Paths: field tracks, country lanes, steep zig-zag gravel path; 7 stiles
Landscape: windswept coastline of lumps and bumps

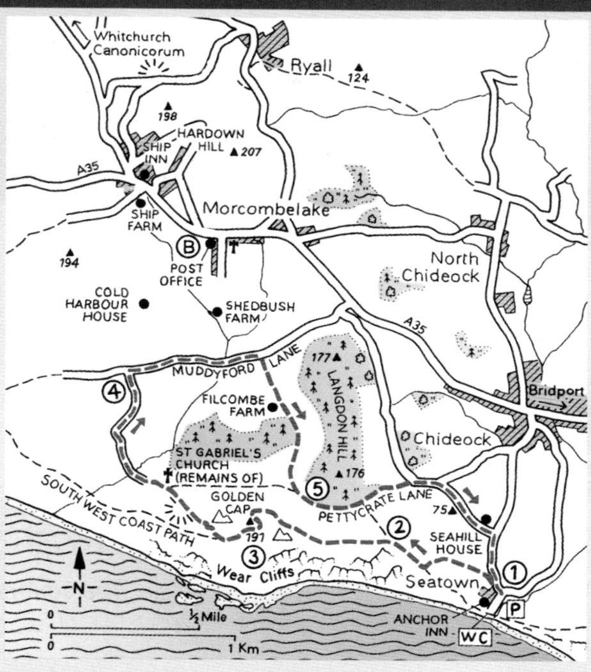

Walk directions

From the car park near the Anchor Inn, walk back up through Seatown. Cross a stile on the left, onto the footpath, signposted 'Coast Path Diversion'. Cross a stile at the end, bear left to cross a stile and footbridge into woodland. Cross a pair of stiles at the other side and bear right up the hill, signposted 'Golden Cap'.

Where the track forks keep left. Go through some trees and over a stile. Bear left, straight across the open hillside, with Golden Cap ahead of you. Pass through a line of trees and walk up the fence. Go up some steps, cross a stile and continue ahead. At the fingerpost go left through a gate to follow the path of shallow steps to the top of Golden Cap.

Pass the trig point and turn right along the top. Pass the stone memorial to the Earl of Antrim. At a marker stone turn right and follow the zig-zag path steeply downhill, enjoying views to Charmouth and Lyme Regis. Go through a gate and bear right over the field towards the ruined St Gabriel's Church. In the bottom corner turn down through a gate, passing the ruins on your right, then go through a second gate. Go down the track, passing cottages on the left, and bear right up the road, signed 'Morcombelake'. Follow this up between high banks and hedges which put the wild flowers conveniently at eye-level. Continue through a gateway.

D At the road junction, turn right down Muddyford Lane, signed 'Langdon Hill'. Pass the gate of Shedbush Farm (the extension rejoins) and continue straight up the hill. Turn right up a concreted lane towards Filcombe Farm. Follow blue markers through the farmyard, bearing left through two gates. Walk up the track, go through two more gates and bear left over the top of the green saddle between Langdon Hill and Golden Cap.

E Go left through a gate in the corner and down a gravel lane (Pettycrate Lane) beside the woods, signed 'Seatown'. Ignore a footpath off to the right. At a junction of tracks keep right, downhill, with a delectable green patchwork of fields on the hillside ahead. Pass Seahill House on the left and turn right, onto a road. Continue down this into Seatown village to return to the inn.

Look for

Moore's biscuit bakery in Morcombelake is a fascinating detour, worth a visit for the smell alone. Through a glass screen see the biscuits being hand made – and sample as you watch. There's also a gallery of artwork associated with its packaging. The famous savoury Dorset knobs, thrice-baked and explosively crisp, are a post-Christmas speciality. Open weekdays, and Saturday mornings in summer.

England

CHURCH KNOWLE MAP 04 SY98

The New Inn

BH20 5NQ ☎ 01929 480357 📠 01929 480357

dir: *From Wareham take A351 towards Swanage. At Corfe Castle turn right for Church Knowle. Pub in village centre*

A 16th-century inn of stone and thatch set in a picturesque village overlooking the Purbeck hills. Maurice and Rosemary Estop have been at this pub for over 21 years and their son Matthew is head chef. Home-made dishes feature daily-delivered fresh fish, including haddock in golden batter, roasted cod with wild mushroom and white wine sauce, fresh dressed crab, lobster, whole grilled bream or plaice, and fruits de mer. Pies, grills and sandwiches also make an appearance.

Open 11–3 6.30–11 **Bar Meals** L served all week 12–2.15 D served all week 6–9.15 Av main course £8.50 **Restaurant** L served all week 12–2.15 D served all week 6–9.15 Av 3 course à la carte £17.50 Punch Taverns Wadworth 6X, Old Speckled Hen, Interbrew Flowers Original. 8 **Facilities** Garden Parking

CORFE CASTLE MAP 04 SY98

The Greyhound Inn

The Square BH20 5EZ ☎ 01929 480205 📠 01929 480205

e-mail: eat@greyhoundcorfe.co.uk

dir: *W from Bournemouth, take A35 to Dorchester, after 5m left onto A351, 10m to Corfe Castle*

This classic old coaching inn has a lively atmosphere, encouraged by special events such as beer festivals at the end of May and the end of August, a sausage and cider festival in October, and regular live music and entertainment. Alongside real ales you'll find scrumpy ciders and home-made mulled wine. Sandwiches, salads, baguettes, baskets, chargrills, vegetarian options and light bites are served alongside a huge range of fresh seafood.

Open 11–12.30 **Bar Meals** L served all week 12–3 D served all week 6–9 (Jul–Sep & Sat–Sun food all day) Av main course £8.95 **Restaurant** L served all week 12–3 D served all week 6–9 (Jul–Sep food all day) Av 3 course à la carte £16.95 Enterprise Inns Fuller's London Pride, Timothy Taylor Landlord, Black Sheep, Ringwood Best. 13 **Facilities** Children's licence Garden Dogs allowed Play Area

CORFE MULLEN MAP 04 SY9

The Coventry Arms

Mill St BH21 3RH ☎ 01258 857284

dir: *On A31 (Wimborne-Dorchester road)*

Built in the 13th century, this friendly pub was once a watermill with its own island. Beer is served direct from the cask, while an annual spring seafood festival attracts many visitors. The inn specialises in fish and game from local estates, and most of the produce is sourced from within the area. Expect such creative dishes as open ravioli of monkfish medallions and mussels; or pan-seared Sika deer's liver with smoked bacon.

Open 11–3 5.30–11 **Bar Meals** L served all week 12–2.30 D served all week 6–9.30 (All day Sun) **Restaurant** L served all week 12–2.30 D served all week 6–9.30 (All day Sun) Av 3 course à la carte £25 Free House HSB, Timothy Taylor Landlord, Gales Best. 17 **Facilities** Garden Dogs allowed Parking

See advert on opposite page

EAST CHALDON MAP 04 SY7

The Sailors Return

DT2 8DN ☎ 01305 853847 📠 01305 851677

dir: *1m S of A352 between Dorchester & Wool*

A splendid 18th-century thatched country pub in the village of East Chaldon (or Chaldon Herring – take your pick), tucked away in rolling downland near Lulworth Cove. Seafood includes whole local plaice, scallop and mussel stroganoff, and wok-fried king prawns. Alternatives include half a big duck, local faggots, whole gammon hock, and vegetarian dishes. Choose from the blackboard in the beamed and flagstoned bar, and eat inside or in a grassy area outside.

Open 11–11 (Sun 12–10.30) **Bar Meals** L served all week 12–2 D served all week 6–9 **Restaurant** L served all week 12–2 D served all week 6–9 (Summer 12–9) Free House Ringwood Best, Hampshire Strongs Best Bitter, Badger Tanglefoot. **Facilities** Garden Parking Play Area

AST MORDEN MAP 04 SY99

Pick of the Pubs

The Cock & Bottle

BH20 7DL ☎ 01929 459238

dir: *From A35 W of Poole take right B3075, pub 0.5m on left*

Some 400 years ago this popular pub was a cob-walled Dorset longhouse. It acquired a brick skin around 1800, and remained thatched until 1966. The original interiors are comfortably rustic with quaint, low-beamed ceilings, attractive paintings and lots of nooks and crannies around the log fires. Additional to the lively locals' bar are a lounge bar and the modern rear restaurant extension; lovely pastoral views over farmland include the pub's paddock, where vintage car and motorcycle meetings are occasionally hosted during the summer. The experienced chef serves up an appealing mix of traditional and inventive cooking, with the emphasis on fresh local produce where possible. Starters could include local game terrine served with spiced pear and onion chutney. To follow try venison Wellington, or one of the fish dishes – grilled sea bass fillet with Poole Bay mussel and saffron broth or fresh local dressed crab, half a lobster and king prawn salad perhaps.

Open 11–3 6–11 (Sun 12–3, 7–10.30) **Bar Meals** L served all week 12–2 D served all week 6–9 (Sun 7–9) **Restaurant** L served all week 12–2 D served all week 6–9 (Sun 7–9) Av 3 course à la carte £23.70 Hall & Woodhouse Badger Dorset Best & Tanglefoot & Sussex. 6 **Facilities** Garden Dogs allowed Parking

VERSHOT MAP 04 ST50

Pick of the Pubs

The Acorn Inn ★★★★ INN

DT2 0JW ☎ 01935 83228 01935 83707

e-mail: stay@acorn-inn.co.uk

dir: *A303 to Yeovil, Dorchester Rd, on A37 right to Evershot*

A 16th-century coaching inn, this pub was immortalised as the Sow and Acorn in Thomas Hardy's *Tess of the D'Urbervilles*. It stands in an area of outstanding natural beauty, with walking, fishing, shooting and riding all nearby. Inside are two oak-panelled bars – one flagstoned, one tiled – with logs blazing in carved hamstone fireplaces. The skittle alley used to be the stables, and it's rumoured that the residents' sitting room was once used by Hanging Judge Jeffreys as a court room. Most of the food is sourced from within a 15-mile radius, and the interesting menus might typically include starters of smoked haddock and grain mustard chowder with chive cream, and mains of fillet of cod in beer batter with home-made tartare sauce; roasted loin of Dorset lamb with braised leeks, twice-baked mushroom and cheddar soufflé and Madeira jus; and a roasted leek, red pepper and ricotta tart.

The Acorn Inn

Open 11 –11 **Bar Meals** L served all week 12–2 D served all week 7–9 Av main course £6.95 **Restaurant** L served all week 12–2 D served all week 7–9 Free House Draymens & Guest Ale. 11 **Facilities** Garden Dogs allowed Parking **Rooms** 10 bedrooms en suite S£75 D£100

England

FARNHAM

Pick of the Pubs

The Museum Inn NEW

DT11 8DE ☎ 01725 516261 01725 516988

e-mail: enquiries@museuminn.co.uk

dir: *From Salisbury take A354 to Blandford Forum 12m. Farnham signed on right. Pub in village centre*

General Augustus Lane Fox Pitt Rivers, the father of modern archaeology, built this part-thatched country pub as accommodation for the nearby museum. All the original features have been maintained intact, from the stone flagged floors and inglenook fireplace to a traditional bread oven. The same attention to detail is displayed in the kitchens, where a commitment to sourcing local produce reared in traditional ways leads to an imaginative array of dishes arranged with pleasing intricacy. Try lightly pickled Chesil Beach mackerel with garlic aioli, or braised Longhorn oxtail, Cashmoor quail egg and sour cherry terrine, before sampling seared delice of salmon, fennel and lemon gremolata with beetroot reduction. Few could turn down rhubarb pannacotta, jelly and compote, or prune and Armagnac pudding with Cornish clotted cream.

Open 12-3 6-10.30 Closed: 25 Dec **Bar Meals** L served all week 12-2 D served all week 7-9.30 (Sat-Sun 12-2.30) Av main course £15 **Restaurant** L served all week 12-2 D served all week 7-9.30 (Sun 12-2.30) Av 3 course à la carte £28.50 Free House Ringwood Best, Hopback Summer Lightening, Timothy Taylor Landlord, Otter Gold. 14 **Facilities** Children's licence Garden Dogs allowed Parking

GILLINGHAM MAP 04 ST82

The Kings Arms Inn

East Stour Common SP8 5NB ☎ 01747 838325

e-mail: nrosscampbell@aol.com

dir: *4m W of Shaftesbury on A30*

Use this 200-year-old, family-run free house as the base for exploring Dorset's delightful countryside and coast. The restaurant its then new owners created a couple of years ago is now well into its stride, offering fillets of Poole bass on pak choi with scallop sauce; seared breast of Barbary duck with sweet plum and kirsch reduction; slow-roasted pork belly with sausagemeat; and cheese choux pastry tart with wild mushrooms and spinach cooked in madeira.

Open 12-3 5.30-11 (Sat-Sun 12-11) **Bar Meals** L served all week 12-2.30 D served all week 5.30-9.15 (Sat-Sun 12-9.15) Av main course £11 **Restaurant** L served all week 12-2.30 D served all week 5.30-9.15 (Sat-Sun 12-9.15) Av 3 course à la carte £19 Free House London Pride, Copper Ale, Carling, 6X. 8 **Facilities** Garden Dogs allowed Parking

GUSSAGE ALL SAINTS MAP 04 SU0

The Drovers Inn

BH21 5ET ☎ 01258 840084

e-mail: info@thedroversinn.net

dir: *A31 Ashley Heath rdbt, right onto B3081*

Rural 16th-century pub with a fine terrace and wonderful views from the garden. Popular with walkers, its refurbished interior retains plent of traditional appeal with flagstone floors and oak furniture. Ales include Ringwood's seasonal ales and guest beers. The menu feature home-cooked pub favourites: fresh cod in beer batter, curry, steak an kidney pie, and steak and chips.

Open 11.45 -11 **Bar Meals** L served all week 12-2 D served all week 6-9 (All day wkends) Av main course £6.95 Ringwood Ringwood Best, Old Thumper, Ringwood Seasonal Ales, Fortyniner & Guest Beers. 10 **Facilities** Garden Dogs allowed Parking

LODERS MAP 04 SY4

Loders Arms

DT6 3SA ☎ 01308 422431

e-mail: janelegg@aol.com

dir: *Off A3066, 2m NE of Bridport*

Unassuming stone-built local tucked away in a pretty thatched village close to the Dorset coast. Arrive early to bag a seat in the long cosy b or the homely dining room. A selection of mains includes scallops in Pernod and cream; fusilli with roasted vegetables, feta and pesto; wil boar sausages; and rack of lamb studded with garlic. There's a lovely garden with views of Boarsbarrow Hill, and a skittle alley that doubles as a function room.

Open 11.30-3 6-11 (Sun 11.30-11) **Bar Meals** L served all week 12.30-2 D served all week 7.15-9 **Restaurant** L served all week 12.30-2 D served all week 7.15-9 Palmers Brewery Palmers Copper, IPA, 20 **Facilities** Garden Dogs allowed Parking

England

OWER ANSTY MAP 04 ST70

he Fox Inn ★★★★ INN

T2 7PN ☎ 01258 880328 01258 881440
-mail: foxinnansty@tiscali.co.uk
r: *A35 from Dorchester towards Poole 4m, exit signed ddlehinton/Athelhampton House, turn left to Cheselbourne, en right. Pub in Ansty village, opposite post office*

oking more like a grand rectory than a pub, the 250-year-old Fox s built for brewer Charles Hall, later to co-found Blandford's Hall Woodhouse brewery, whose Badger beers are, naturally enough, ved in the bar. Typical main courses are pot-roasted half duck with erry compote and red wine jus; sautéed tiger prawn in sweet pepper d tomato sauce; and grilled fillet steak glazed with Dorset Blue Vinny eese and herb mash.

en 11–11 (Sun 12–10.30) **Bar Meals** L served all week 12–2 D served week 6.30–9 **Restaurant** L served all week 12–2 (Sun 12–3) D served all ek 6.30–9 Carvery Hall & Woodhouse Badger Tanglefoot, Badger st, Badger Smooth Seasonal Guest Ale Export. 11 **Facilities** Garden rking **Rooms** 11 bedrooms en suite S£50 D£85

YME REGIS MAP 04 SY39

ilot Boat Inn

idge St DT7 3QA ☎ 01297 443157

d smuggling and sea rescue tales are associated with this busy town ntre pub, close to the sea front. However its biggest claim to fame is the birthplace of the original Lassie, Hollywood's favourite collie. A od range of food offers sandwiches, salads and cold platters, Dorset cken with cider sauce, local crab, real scampi and chips, and other sh fish as available. There's also a good vegetarian choice, and a gan three-bean casserole.

en 11–11 Closed: Dec 25 **Bar Meals** L served all week 12–10 D served week Av main course £8.25 **Restaurant** 12–10 Palmers Palmers rset Gold, IPA, 200, Bridport Bitter. 8 **Facilities** Children's licence rden Dogs allowed

MARSHWOOD MAP 04 SY39

Pick of the Pubs

The Bottle Inn

DT6 5QJ ☎ 01297 678254 01297 678739
e-mail: thebottleinn@msn.com
dir: *On B3165 (Crewkerne to Lyme Regis road)*

The thatched Bottle Inn was first mentioned as an ale house back in the 17th century, and was the first pub in the area during the 18th century to serve bottled beer rather than beer from the jug – hence the name. Standing beside the B3165 on the edge of the glorious Marshwood Vale, its rustic interior has simple wooden settles, scrubbed tables and a blazing fire. Proprietor Shane Pym loves introducing new dishes onto the menu, and recent additions have included local pork tenderloin with a cream and stilton sauce; Highland chicken stuffed with smoked salmon and served with a whisky and mustard sauce; for vegetarians there is aubergine in oregano batter with caramelised onions and goats' cheese; and fish lovers will surely go for monkfish with a sun-dried tomato pesto, wrapped in Parma ham. Taking the organic food theme to its furthest reaches, the pub is home to the annual World Stinging-Nettle Eating Championships.

Open 12–3 6.30–11 **Bar Meals** L served all week 12–2 D served all week 6.30–9 Av main course £8.50 **Restaurant** L served all week D served all week Free House Otter Ale & 3 Guest Ales. 7 **Facilities** Garden Parking Play Area

MILTON ABBAS MAP 04 ST80

The Hambro Arms

DT11 0BP ☎ 01258 880233
e-mail: info@hambroarms.co.uk
dir: *A354 (Dorchester to Blandford road), turn off at Royal Oak*

Traditional whitewashed 18th-century thatched pub located in a picturesque landscaped village. Enjoy an appetising bar snack, or perhaps half shoulder of lamb with minted redcurrant sauce, liver and bacon, duck with orange sauce, venison sausages, or grilled sea bass, in the comfortable lounge bar or on the popular patio.

Open 11–3 6.30–11 (May–Sep 11–11) **Bar Meals** L served all week 12–2 D served all week 7–9 **Restaurant** L served all week 12–2 D served all week 7–9 Free House Abbot Ale, Ringwood. **Facilities** Parking

England

MOTCOMBE MAP 04 ST82

The Coppleridge Inn

SP7 9HW ☎ 01747 851980 01747 851858

e-mail: thecoppleridgeinn@btinternet.com

dir: *Take A350 towards Warminster for 1.5m, turn left at brown tourist sign. Follow signs to inn*

In the 1980s this 18th-century dairy farm was converted to a pub. The flagstone floors and stripped pine of the former farmhouse now add a traditional touch to the bar and restaurant. The menus offer everything from jacket potatoes and filled ciabattas to a full meal. Home-made main courses include pheasant, cranberry and bacon casserole; salmon and spinach gratin; and chicken and leek pie. Look out for the speciality dining nights each week.

Open 11–3 5–11 (All day Sat–Sun) **Bar Meals** L served all week 12–2.30 D served all week 6–9.30 Av main course £9.50 **Restaurant** L served all week 12–2.30 (All day Sat–Sun) D served all week 6–9.30 Av 3 course à la carte £20 Free House Butcombe Bitter, Greene King IPA, Wadworth 6X, Fuller's London Pride. 8 **Facilities** Garden Dogs allowed Parking Play Area **Rooms** 10 bedrooms en suite S£45 D£80 (★★★ INN)

NETTLECOMBE MAP 04 SY59

Marquis of Lorne

DT6 3SY ☎ 01308 485236 01308 485666

e-mail: enquiries@marquisoflorne.com

dir: *B3066 turn 1.5m N of Bridport. N of Gorecross Business Park, rdbt, through West Norton, 1m over junct to Nettlecombe, inn at top of hill, 300yds on left*

A 16th-century farmhouse converted into a pub in 1871, when the Marquis himself named it to prove land ownership. Membership of the Campaign for Real Food means that much local produce is used. Daily menus offer such dishes as pigeon breast with juniper and red wine sauce, home-made curry, fresh cod fillet, and mushroom and pepper stroganoff. Desserts might be rum and chocolate truffle terrine or twice baked cheesecake. Superb gardens with beautiful views.

Open 12–3 6.30–11 (Sun all day) **Bar Meals** L served all week 12–2 D served all week 7–9.30 Av main course £10 **Restaurant** L served all week 12–2 D served all week 7–9.30 Av 3 course à la carte £20 Palmers Palmers Copper, IPA, 200 Premium Ale. 12 **Facilities** Garden Dogs allowed Parking Play Area

NORTH WOOTTON MAP 04 ST6

The Three Elms

DT9 5JW ☎ 01935 812881 01935 812881

dir: *From Sherborne take A352 towards Dorchester then A3030 Pub 1m on right*

Real ales and locally produced ciders await you at this family-run free house overlooking scenic Blackmore Vale. Stunning views can be enjoyed from the pub garden, and the landlord prides himself on his impressive collection of about 1,600 model cars, as well as number plates from every state in America. Wide-ranging menu includes dishes like rosemary-crusted trout fillet, minted lamb shank, chicken Kiev and mixed grill. Extensive range of starters, snacks and sandwiches.

Open 11–2.30 6.30–11 (Sun 12–3, 7–10.30) Closed: 25–26 Dec **Bar Meals** L served all week 12–2 D served all week 6.30–10 (Sun 7–10) **Restaurant** L served all week 12–2 D served all week 6.30–10 Free House Fuller's London Pride, Butcombe Bitter, Otter Ale. 10 **Facilities** Garden Dogs allowed Parking Play Area

OSMINGTON MILLS MAP 04 SY7

The Smugglers Inn

DT3 6HF ☎ 01305 833125 01305 832219

e-mail: smugglers.weymouth@hall-woodhouse.co.uk

dir: *7m E of Weymouth, towards Wareham, pub signed*

Set on the cliffs at Osmington Mill with the South Coast Footpath running through the garden, the inn has beautiful views across Weymouth Bay. In the late 18th century it was the base of infamous smuggler Pierre Latour who fell in love with the publican's daughter, Arabella Carless, who was shot dead while helping him to escape during a raid. Typical dishes are chicken and bacon salad, chargrilled rump steak, and Sussex smokey (fish pie).

Open 11–11 (Sun 12–10.30) **Bar Meals** L served all week 11–6 D served all week 12–9 Av main course £7 **Restaurant** L served all week 11–6 D served all week 12–9 Woodhouse Inns 12 **Facilities** Children's licence Garden Dogs allowed Parking Play Area

PIDDLEHINTON MAP 04 SY7

The Thimble Inn

DT2 7TD ☎ 01300 348270

dir: *A35 W'bound, right onto B3143, Piddlehinton 4m*

Friendly village local with open fires, traditional pub games and good food cooked to order. The pub stands in a pretty valley on the banks of the River Piddle, and the riverside patio is popular in summer. The extensive menu ranges from sandwiches and jacket potatoes to fish choices like poached halibut on leek and white sauce; and grilled tro with almonds.

Open 12–2.30 7–11 (Sun 7–10.30) Closed: 25 Dec **Bar Meals** L served week 12–2 D served all week 7–9 Av main course £8 **Restaurant** L serv all week 12–2 D served all week 7–9 Free House Ringwood Best & Tanglefoot, Palmer Copper Ale & Palmer IPA, Ringwood Old Thumper. **Facilities** Garden Dogs allowed Parking

·IDDLETRENTHIDE MAP 04 SY79

·he Piddle Inn ★★★★ INN

·T2 7QF ☎ 01300 348468 📠 01300 348102
-mail: piddleinn@aol.com
ir: *7m N of Dorchester on B3143, in village centre*

ıis friendly village free house has been a pub since the 1760s, and ıs originally a stopover for prisoners in transit between the jails at orchester and Sherborne. Traditional pub games and real ales straight om the barrel accompany pub favourites like jacket potatoes; home-ade chilli con carne; and Cumberland sausage and mash. The river ddle flows past the popular beer garden.

pen 12-3 6-11 **Bar Meals** L served Tue-Sun 12-2 D served Mon-Fri 30-9 (Sat-Sun 12-9) **Restaurant** L served Tue-Sun 12-2 D served on-Sun 6.30-9 Free House Greene King IPA, Ringwood Best, ngwood 49er. 8 **Facilities** Children's licence Garden Dogs allowed ırking **Rooms** 3 bedrooms en suite S£45 D£70

·he Poachers Inn ★★★★ INN

T2 7QX ☎ 01300 348358 📠 01300 348153
-mail: thepoachersinn@piddletrenthide.fsbusiness.co.uk
ir: *6m N from Dorchester on B3143. At the Church end of ddletrenthide*

ıis family-run inn beside the River Piddle continues to provide real es, good food, fires and traditional pub games right in the heart of ıomas Hardy country. The riverside patio is especially popular in ımmer. There's an extensive menu, supported by daily specials that ay include home-made spaghetti bolognese; seafood salad with mon and dill; or pork and leek sausages with mustard mash. Leave om for traditional red and blackcurrant crumble!

pen 11-12 **Bar Meals** L served all week 12-9.30 D served all week 12-30 Av main course £9.95 **Restaurant** L served all week 12-9.30 D served week 12-9.30 Av 3 course à la carte £18 Free House **Facilities** Garden ɔgs allowed Parking **Rooms** 21 bedrooms en suite S£52 D£74

LUSH MAP 04 ST70

he Brace of Pheasants

T2 7RQ ☎ 01300 348357 📠 01300 348959
·mail: information@braceof pheasants.co.uk
ir: *A35 onto B3143, 5m to Piddletrenthide, then right to appowder & Plush*

ɔu'll find this pretty 16th-century thatched village inn tucked away in fold of the hills east of Cerne Abbas, in the heart of Hardy's beloved unty. The ambience is warm and welcoming, with an open fire, oak beams and fresh flowers. The kitchen makes good use of the lamb, beef, pork and game all reared within a 10 mile radius of the pub. An ideal place to start and end a walk.

Open 12-3 7-11 (Sun 7-10.30) Closed: Dec 25 Rest: Mon **Bar Meals** L served Tues-Sun 12.30-2.30 D served Tues-Sun 7-9.30 Av main course £9 **Restaurant** L served Tue-Sun 12-1.30 D served Tue-Sun 7-9.30 Av 3 course à la carte £23 Free House Timothy Taylors Landlord, Ringwood Best, Dorset Brewing Co. & Palmers. 8 **Facilities** Garden Dogs allowed Parking

POOLE MAP 04 SZ09

The Guildhall Tavern Ltd

15 Market St BH15 1NB ☎ 01202 671717 📠 01202 242346
e-mail: sewerynsevfred@aol.com
dir: *2 mins from Poole Quay*

This former cider house is located in the Old Town, just two minutes from Poole Quay. It is owned by Severine and Frederic Grande, whose French influence is evident throughout the bilingual menu. Snacks and sandwiches include croque monsieur and French onion soup, while main meals range through double baked cheese soufflé; wild whole sea bass flambéed with Pernod; and hazelnut meringue with fresh raspberries.

Open 11-3.30 6.15-11 Closed: 1st 2 wks in Nov **Bar Meals** L served all week 11-2.30 **Restaurant** L served all week 12-2.30 D served all week 6.30-9.30 Punch Taverns Ringwood Best. 7 **Facilities** Parking

POWERSTOCK MAP 04 SY59

Pick of the Pubs

Three Horseshoes Inn ★★★★ INN

DT6 3TF ☎ 01308 485328
e-mail: info@threehorseshoesinn.com
dir: *3m out of Bridport off A3066 (Beaminster road)*

Popularly known as the Shoes, this pretty, rural Victorian inn is surrounded by some of Dorset's finest scenery. In the restaurant, fresh local produce is used wherever possible; even the herbs, for example, are picked each day from the garden. Light lunches are available, with the main carte coming into play in the evening. From this choose starters of grilled goats' cheese salad with tomato and pinenut dressing; seared scallops with orange and fennel broth, or deep-fried prawns with chilli. Main courses include Powerstock organic lamb noisettes with roasted pepper and almond dressing; braised rabbit, wild mushroom and green

CONTINUED

England

POWERSTOCK continued

peppercorn sauce; pan-fried pigeon breasts with bourguignon sauce; Dorset crab mornay; and honey- and soy-roasted red snapper fillet with saffron potatoes, courgettes and mixed leaves. Desserts – all home made – include lime and ginger cheesecake, and strawberry and basil crème brûlée. Two of the spacious, en suite bedrooms have superb views over the river valley.

Open 11-3 6.30-11 (Sun 12-3, 6.30-10.30) **Bar Meals** L served all week 12-2.30 D served all week 7-9 (Sun 12-2.30, 7-8.30) Av main course £11 **Restaurant** L served all week 12-2.30 D served all week 7-9 (Sun 7-8.30) Av 3 course à la carte £21 Palmers Palmer's IPA, Copper Ale. 7 **Facilities** Garden Dogs allowed Parking Play Area **Rooms** 3 bedrooms en suite D£70

PUNCKNOWLE MAP 04 SY58

The Crown Inn

Church St DT2 9BN ☎ 01308 897711 01308 898282

dir: *From A35, into Bridevally, through Litton Cheney. From B3157, inland at Swyre.*

There's a traditional atmosphere within the rambling, low-beamed bars at this picturesque 16th-century thatched inn, which was once the haunt of smugglers on their way from nearby Chesil Beach to visit prosperous customers in Bath. Food ranges from light snacks and sandwiches to home-made dishes like lamb chops with mint sauce; mushroom and nut pasta with French bread; and tuna steak with basil and tomato sauce.

Open 11-3 7-11 (Sun 12-3, 7-10.30) (Summer 6.30 opening) Closed: 25 Dec **Bar Meals** L served all week 12-2 D served all week 7-9 (Summer weekdays 6.30-9) Av main course £7.60 Palmers Palmers IPA, 200 Premium Ale, Copper, Tally Ho!. 10 **Facilities** Garden Dogs allowed Parking **Notes**

SHERBORNE MAP 04 ST61

The Digby Tap

Cooks Ln DT9 3NS ☎ 01935 813148

e-mail: peter@lefevre.fslife.co.uk

Old-fashioned town pub with stone-flagged floors, old beams and a wide-ranging choice of real ale. A hearty menu of pub grub includes lasagne, steak and kidney pie, rump steak, gammon steak, and plaice or cod. The pub was used as a location for the 1990 TV drama *A Murder of Quality*, that starred Denholm Elliot and Glenda Jackson. Scenes from the film can be seen on the pub walls.

Open 11-2.30 5.30-11 (Sat 6-11, Sun 12-3, 7-10.30) Closed: 1 Jan **Bar Meals** L served Mon-Sat 12-1.45 Free House Ringwood Best, Otter Ale, Sharp's Cornish Coaster & Cornish Jack, St Austell Tinners. **Facilities** Dogs allowed **Notes**

Half Moon Inn

Half Moon St DT9 3LN ☎ 01935 812017 01935 818130

e-mail: halfmoon@eldridge-pope.co.uk

Standing opposite Sherborne Abbey in the heart of this charming Dorset town, the Half Moon is at the centre of local life. There's a choice of real ales, 11 wines served by the glass, and great food all day. Daily specials supplement the wide-ranging themed menus; typical choices include roast pork hock; chilli prawn bruschetta; Mediterranean stuffed peppers; and fisherman's crumble. Sunday roasts, desserts and children's menus are also offered.

Open 11-11 **Bar Meals** L served all week 11-6 D served all week 6-9.15 Av main course £7.95 **Restaurant** L served all week 11-3 D served all week 6-9.30 Marstons Wadworth 6X, Otter 3.6, Fosters. 11 **Facilities** Garden Parking

Queen's Head

High St, Milborne Port DT9 5DQ

☎ 01963 250314 01963 250339

dir: *On A30*

Milborne Port has no facilities for shipping, the suffix being Old English for 'borough', a status it acquired in 1249. The building came much later, in Elizabethan times, although no mention is made of it as a hostelry until 1738. Charming and friendly bars, restaurant, beer garden and skittle alley combine to make it a popular free house in these parts.

Open 12-2.30 5.30-11 (Sunday 12-10.30) **Bar Meals** L served Sat-Sun 12-1.40 D served all week 7-9.30 (Mon-Tue 7-8.40, Wed-Fri 7-9.10) Av main course £8 **Restaurant** L served Sat-Sun 12-2 D served all week 7-9.30 (Mon-Tue 7-8.40, Wed-Fri 7-9.10) Av 3 course à la carte £16 Enterprise Inns Butcombe Bitters, Fullers London Pride, Hopback Summer Lightning. **Facilities** Children's licence Garden Dogs allowed Parking

Skippers Inn

Horsecastles DT9 3HE ☎ 01935 812753

e-mail: chrisfrowde@tiscali.co.uk

dir: *From Yeovil A30 to Sherborne*

'You don't need a newspaper in Skippers, read the walls'. So says the proprietor about his end-of-terrace converted cider house, and Sherborne's self-styled premier fish restaurant. The crammed blackboard menu has everything from swordfish steak to pan-fried escolar; from duck breast with redcurrant sauce to strips of beef in Dijon mustard and wild mushroom sauce; and from sausage, egg and chips to Moroccan lamb and apricot casserole.

Open 11-12 (Winter 11-2.30, 6-11) Closed: 25 Dec **Bar Meals** L served all week 11.15-2 D served all week 6.30-9.30 (Sun 12-3, 7-10.30) Av main course £6.95 **Restaurant** L served all week 11.15-2 D served all week 6.30-9.30 (Sun 12-2, 7-9) Wadworth Wadworth 6X & Henrys IPA, Butcombe Bitter & Guest Ales. 8 **Facilities** Garden Parking

Vhite Hart 🍷

ishops Caundle DT9 5ND

☎ 01963 23301 📠 01963 23301

-mail: info@whitehartcarvery.co.uk

ir: *On A3030 between Sherborne & Sturminster Newton. 4m*

ɔcated in the heart of the Blackmore Vale, the White Hart, dating from e 16th century, was reputedly used as a courthouse by the infamous ıdge Jeffries. The large enclosed family garden offers beautiful views the wonderful Bullbarrow Hill, as well as play equipment and an dventure trail for children. The extensive menu starts with baguettes, cket potatoes and ploughman's, plus there's vegetarian options and a rvery, always with six choices. Jazz evenings.

pen 11.30–3 6.30–11 (Sun 12–3, 7–10.30) **Bar Meals** L served all week –2 D served all week 7–9 **Restaurant** L served all week 12–2 D served week 7–9 🍺 Hall & Woodhouse ⛽ Badger Gold & Hopping Hare. **cilities** Garden Dogs allowed Parking Play Area

HROTON OR IWERNE COURTNEY — MAP 04 ST81

Pick of the Pubs

The Cricketers 🍷

DT11 8QD ☎ 01258 860421 📠 01258 861800

dir: *Off A350 Shaftesbury to Blandford, signed from Shroton*

The Cricketers nestles under Hambledon Hill, which is renowned for its Iron-Age hill-forts. A classically English pub, built at the turn of the 20th century, it is above all a welcoming local. The interior comprises a main bar, sports bar and den – all light and airy rooms leading to the restaurant at the rear. This in turn overlooks a lovely garden, well stocked with trees and flowers. Inside, the cricket theme is taken up in the collection of sports memorabilia on display, and during the summer months the local cricket team really does frequent the establishment. The pub is also popular with hikers, lured from the Wessex Way, which runs conveniently through the garden. Expect an extensive food selection that ranges from traditional to modern and international. Dishes might include lamb tagine with couscous; rabbit casseroled with wine and herbs; and Malaysian beef curry.

Open 11.30–2.30 6.30–11 (Summer: Sat–Sun 12–11 Winter: Sun eve 7–11) **Bar Meals** L served all week 12–2 D served all week 6.30–9 (Sun 12–9) Av main course £9 **Restaurant** L served all week 12–2 D served all week 6.30–9 (Sun 12–9) 🍺 Free House ⛽ Greene King IPA, Ringwood 49er, Abbot Ale, Tanglefoot. 🍷 10 **Facilities** Garden Parking

STOKE ABBOTT — MAP 04 ST40

The New Inn

DT8 3JW ☎ 01308 868333

dir: *1.5m from Beaminster*

A welcoming 17th-century farmhouse turned village inn, with thatched roof, log fires and a beautiful garden. It offers three real ales, and an extensive menu of light meals such as grilled black pudding with caramelised apples, and cold smoked duck breast with plum chutney, plus a good choice of baguettes, sandwiches and vegetarian dishes. Specials might include pork schnitzel with sweet chili dip, scallops wrapped in bacon, and beef and mushroom pie. Listen out for the singing chef!

Open 12–3 7–11 (Sun 12–3) **Bar Meals** L served Tue–Sun 12–1.30 D served Tue–Sat 7–8.30 **Restaurant** L served all week 12–1.30 D served all week 7–8.30 🍺 Palmers ⛽ Palmers IPA & 200 Premium Ale, Tally Ho, Copper IPA. **Facilities** Garden Dogs allowed Parking

STOURPAINE — MAP 04 ST80

The White Horse Inn 🍷

Shaston Rd DT11 8TA ☎ 01258 453535 📠 01258 453535

dir: *From Blandford Forum on A350 towards Shaftesbury*

Typical village pub dating back to the early 18th century, sympathetically refurbished and extended. Inside, are an inglenook fireplace and two dining rooms, one opening on to the decked patio. The menu offers home-baked ham, eggs and chips; pan-fried duck breast with black cherries and brandy sauce; wholetail deep-fried scampi and chips; and mixed vegetable, pasta and blue cheese bake. Hod Hill Roman fort and the River Stour are within easy reach.

Open 12–3 6–11 (Fri–Sat 6–12) **Bar Meals** L served all week 12–2 D served Tue–Sun 6–9 **Restaurant** L served all week 12–2 D served Tue–Sun 6–9 🍺 Hall & Woodhouse ⛽ Badgers Best, Festive Pheasant, Fursty Ferret, Sussex. 🍷 8 **Facilities** Children's licence Garden Dogs allowed Parking

England

STRATTON MAP 04 SY69

Saxon Arms

DT2 9WG ☎ 01305 260020 01305 264225
e-mail: rodsaxonlamont1@yahoo.co.uk
dir: *3m NW of Dorchester on A37, pub at back of village green between church & new village hall*

A massive thatched roof, a patio overlooking the village green, solid oak beams, flagstone floors and a log-burning stove provide a great atmosphere. Menus offer steak and ale pie, local butcher's pork and herb sausages, lasagne verde, and chicken, bacon and tarragon pie, while the specials boards may conjure up scallop and tiger prawn brochette, Portland crab, or beef in Guinness casserole. Either way, leave room for one of the many desserts.

Open 11–2.30 5.30–11 (all day Sat–Sun) **Bar Meals** L served all week 11.30–2.30 D served all week 6–9.30 Free House Fuller's London Pride, Palmers IPA, Ringwood, Timothy Taylor. 14 **Facilities** Garden Parking

STUDLAND MAP 05 SZ08

The Bankes Arms Hotel

Watery Ln BH19 3AU ☎ 01929 450225 01929 450307
dir: *B3369 from Poole, across on Sandbanks chain ferry, or A35 from Poole, A351 then B3351*

Close to sweeping Studland Bay, across which can be seen the prime real estate enclave of Sandbanks, is this part 15th-century, creeper-clad inn, once a smugglers' dive. It specialises in fresh fish and seafood, but also offers game casserole; lamb noisettes in mint, honey and orange sauce; and spicy pork in chilli, coriander and caper sauce. The annual beer festival held in its large garden showcases 60 real ales, music, Morris dancing and stone carving.

Open 11–11 Closed: 25 Dec **Bar Meals** L served all week 12–9 D served all week 12–9 (Winter 12.30–3, 6–9.30) Av main course £9 **Restaurant** L served all week 12.30–3 D served all week 6–9.30 Free House Isle of Purbeck Fossil Fuel, Studland Bay Wrecked, Solar Power & IPA. **Facilities** Children's licence Garden Dogs allowed Parking

SYDLING ST NICHOLAS MAP 04 SY6

The Greyhound Inn ★★★★ INN

DT2 9PD ☎ 01300 341303 01300 341303
e-mail: info@thegreyhounddorset.co.uk
dir: *Off A37 (Yeovil to Dorchester road), turn off at Cerne Abbas/Sydling St Nicholas*

The Greyhound is a lovely 17th-century inn with a walled garden set in a picturesque village. It has a growing reputation for its food served in the cosy restaurant or the bar, where you can choose between the full menu and a light snack selection. Fresh local seafood features, including mussels with cider, leeks and cream, and fillet of sea bass in tempura batter. Other options are chicken tagine or steak and kidney pudding.

Open 11–2.30 6–11 (Sun 12–3.30) **Bar Meals** L served all week 12–2 D served all week 6.30–9 (Sun 12–2.30) Av main course £13.95 **Restaurant** L served all week 12–2 D served all week 6.30–9 Free House Palmer IPA, Wadworth 6X, St Austell Tinners, Old Speckled Hen & Spitfire 8 **Facilities** Garden Parking Play Area **Rooms** 6 bedrooms en suite S£60 D£70

TARRANT MONKTON MAP 04 ST9

The Langton Arms ★★★★ INN

DT11 8RX ☎ 01258 830225 01258 830053
e-mail: info@thelangtonarms.co.uk
dir: *A31 from Ringwood, or A357 from Shaftesbury, or A35 from Bournemouth*

An attractive 17th-century thatched inn occupying a peaceful spot in the village centre close to the church. Real ales include a couple of oft-changing guests but after a disastrous fire in 2004, the small lounge bar now serves the same à la carte menu as the Stables restaurant. Since January 2007 a new head chef has continued the tradition of sourcing seasonal food locally, seen in plates of oven-roasted Dorset Down mushrooms, game pie, venison steak, and Tarrant Valley beef.

Open 11.30–12 (Sun 12–10.30) **Bar Meals** L served all week 11.30–2.30 D served all week 6–9.30 (Sat–Sun all day) Av main course £11.45 **Restaurant** L served Sun 12–2 D served Wed–Sat 7–9 Av 3 course à la carte £30 Free House Ringwood Best Bitter, Hidden Pint, Hidden Pleasure, 2 Guest Ales. 7 **Facilities** Garden Parking Play Area **Rooms** 6 bedrooms en suite S£60 D£80

VEST BEXINGTON MAP 04 SY58

'he Manor Hotel ★★ HL 🐟 🍷

)T2 9DF ☎ 01308 897616 🖷 01308 897704

-mail: themanorhotel@btconnect.com

ir: *On B3157, 5m E of Bridport*

)verlooking the Jurassic Coast's most famous feature, Chesil Beach, arts of this ancient manor house date from the 11th century. It offers ı inviting mix of flagstones, Jacobean oak panelling, roaring fires, omfortable en suite rooms, and a cosy cellar bar serving Dorset beer ıd organic cider. Locally sourced dishes include grilled John Dory; eggy's Gloucester Old Spot sausages; butternut squash risotto; and, season, jugged hare. Muddy boots, dogs or children won't raise any yebrows.

pen 11–11 **Bar Meals** L served all week 12–2 D served all week 30–9.30 Av main course £10 **Restaurant** L served all week 12–2 served all week 7–9.30 ⊕ Free House ■ Butcombe Gold, Harbour aster. 🍷 12 **Facilities** Children's licence Garden Dogs allowed Parking ay Area **Rooms** 13 bedrooms en suite S£75 D£125

VEST LULWORTH MAP 04 SY88

'he Castle Inn 🐟 🍷

ain Rd BH20 5RN ☎ 01929 400311 🖷 01929 400415

ir: *On Wareham to Dorchester road, approx 1m from Wareham*

a delightful setting near Lulworth Cove, this family-run thatched lage inn lies close to plenty of good walks. The friendly bars offer a aditional atmosphere in which to enjoy a pint of Ringwood Best or ales' ales. Outside, you'll find large tiered gardens packed with plants, d in summer there's a giant outdoor chess set. The wide-ranging enu includes grills, poultry, fish and steak dishes and flambéed shes cooked at the table.

pen 11–3 6–11 (Winter 12–2.30, 7–11) Closed: 25 Dec **ır Meals** L served all week 11–2.30 D served all week 6–10.30 **staurant** L served all week D served Fri–Sat 7–9.30 ⊕ Free House Ringwood Best, Courage, John Smiths. 🍷 8 **Facilities** Children's licence ırden Dogs allowed Parking

VEYMOUTH MAP 04 SY67

'he Old Ship Inn 🍷

The Ridgeway DT3 5QQ

☎ 01305 812522 🖷 01305 816533

ır: *3m from Weymouth town centre, at bottom of The Ridgeway.*

)pper pans, old clocks and a beamed open fire create just the right nosphere at this historic pub, while outside the terrace offers views over Weymouth. Thomas Hardy refers to it in his novels *Under the Greenwood Tree* and *The Trumpet Major*. A good range of jacket potatoes, baguettes and salads is supplemented by traditional pub favourites, and there are fish dishes among the daily specials.

Open 12–12 (Sun 12–10.30) **Bar Meals** L served all week 12–2.30 D served all week 6–9.30 (Sun 12–4) Av main course £10.95 **Restaurant** L served Mon–Sat 12–2 D served all week 6–9.30 (Sun 12–4) Av 3 course à la carte £11.45 ⊕ Punch Taverns ■ Greene King, Old Speckled Hen, Ringwood Best & Guest Ales. 🍷 7 **Facilities** Children's licence Garden Dogs allowed Parking

WINTERBORNE ZELSTON MAP 04 SY89

Botany Bay Inne 🍷

DT11 9ET ☎ 01929 459227

dir: *A31 between Bere Regis & Wimborne Minster*

An obvious question: how did the pub get its name? Built in the 1920s as The General Allenby, it was changed about 17 years ago in belated recognition of prisoners from Dorchester jail who were required to spend a night nearby before transportation to Australia. Since no such fate awaits anyone these days, meals to enjoy at leisure include bacon-wrapped chicken breast; steak and kidney pudding; roasted Mediterranean vegetable Wellington; and fish catch of the day. Real ales are brewed locally.

Open 11.30–3 6–11 (Mon–Sat summer open 10) **Bar Meals** L served all week 12–2.15 D served all week 6.30–9.30 Av main course £7 **Restaurant** L served all week 12–2.15 D served all week 6.30–9.30 Av 3 course à la carte £17 ■ Badger Best Bitter, Tanglefoot, Botany Bay Bitter, Fursty Ferret. 🍷 7 **Facilities** Children's licence Garden Dogs allowed

CO DURHAM

AYCLIFFE MAP 19 NZ22

The County 🍷

13 The Green, Aycliffe Village DL5 6LX

☎ 01325 312273 🖷 01325 308780

dir: *Off A167 into Aycliffe*

Overlooking an award-winning village green, here is a pub/bistro that serves food from daily blackboards offering aromatic spiced mackerel, tomato and vegetable ragout; slow-roast pork belly; and provençale vegetable and goats' cheese lasagne. Owner Andrew Brown was the first Raymond Blanc scholarship winner in 1995, since when his career rise has been meteoric. Not only has The County featured on the BBC's *Food and Drink* programme, but Tony Blair famously dined here with Jacques Chirac back in 2000.

Open 12–3 5.30–11 (Sun 12–2.30 lunch only) Closed: 25–26 Dec, 1 Jan **Bar Meals** L served Mon–Sat 12–2 (Sun 12–2.30) D served Mon–Sat 6–9 Av main course £14 **Restaurant** L served Mon–Sun 12–2 D served Mon–Sat 6–9.30 (Sun 12–2.30) Av 3 course à la carte £25 Av 2 course fixed price £10 ⊕ Free House ■ Scottish Courage, Wells Bombardier, Jennings Cumberland Ale, Castle Eden & Camerons. 🍷 9 **Facilities** Parking

BARNARD CASTLE MAP 19 NZ01

Pick of the Pubs

The Morritt Arms Hotel ★★★ HL 🍷

Greta Bridge DL12 9SE

☎ 01833 627232 📠 01833 627392

e-mail: relax@themorritt.co.uk

dir: *At Scotch Corner A66 towards Penrith, after 9m turn at Greta Bridge. Hotel over bridge on left.*

Situated in rural Teesdale, The Morritt Arms has been an inn for two centuries. Here the carte offers starters of smoked haddock and potato chowder; roast pear and goats' cheese salad with a citrus reduction; seared scallops topped with a lemon crust served with a petit salad and chive oil; sweet melon and poached fruits with a port and orange syrup; and grilled black pudding with pan-fried foie gras, apricot and saffron chutney and ginger syrup. Main courses include ballantine of chicken with a wild mushroom and tarragon stuffing; cannon of lamb with a red onion crust with basil crushed potatoes and a mint and fevés jus; pan-roasted duck with parmentier potatoes and sautéed pancetta finished with honey and pepper jus; and risotto of wild mushrooms and artichokes, with deep-fried Swaledale cheese beignets. For more informal meals choose the bar, Pallatt's bistro, or the landscaped gardens.

Open 11–11 (Sun 11–10.30) **Bar Meals** L served all week 12–3 D served all week 6–9.30 (Sun 6–9) Av main course £12 **Restaurant** L served all week 12–3 D served all week 6–9.30 (Sun 7–9) Av 3 course à la carte £25 Free House John Smith's, Timothy Taylor Landlord, Black Sheep Best, Cumberland Ale. 🍷 20 **Facilities** Garden Parking Play Area **Rooms** 27 bedrooms en suite S£85 D£105

COTHERSTONE MAP 19 NZ01

The Fox and Hounds 🍷

DL12 9PF ☎ 01833 650241 📠 01833 650518

e-mail: foxenquiries@tiscali.co.uk

dir: *4m W of Barnard Castle. From A66 onto B6277, Cotherstone signed.*

Set in the heart of Teesdale, this delightful 18th-century coaching inn is the perfect outdoor holiday base. Both the restaurant and the heavily beamed bar boast welcoming winter fires in original fireplaces. Fresh local ingredients are the foundation of home-made bar meals like pork, sage and apple pie, whilst roast salmon fillet on chive mash; or curried aubergine and cashew nut loaf are typical daily specials.

Open 12–3 6.30–11 Closed: 25–26 Dec **Bar Meals** L served all week 12–2 D served all week 7–9 (Sun 7–8.30) Av main course £11 **Restaurant** L served all week 12–2 D served all week 7–9 (Sun 7–8.30) Av 3 course à la carte £19.50 Free House Black Sheep Best, Village Brewer Bull Bitter, Jennings Cumberland, Black Sheep Ale. 🍷 10 **Facilities** Garden Parking

DURHAM MAP 19 NZ2

Pick of the Pubs

Victoria Inn

86 Hallgarth St DH1 3AS ☎ 0191 386 5269

dir: *In city centre*

Small rooms with marble fireplaces, high ceilings and etched glass characterise this unspoiled Victorian free house, just five minutes' walk from Durham city centre. Here you'll find a few simple snacks to tickle the taste buds, but it's the ever-changing range of well-kept local ales and the extensive selection of malt whiskies that draws in locals, students and academics alike. The interior of the Grade II listed building has scarcely changed since it was built in 1899, and includes the unusual off-sales booth and tiny snug, where a portrait of Queen Victoria still hangs above the upright piano to keep an eye on things! Her Majesty would no doubt approve of the fact that there's no jukebox, television or pool table to spoil the traditional atmosphere, which has been carefully nurtured by the Webster family since 1975.

Open 11.45–3 6–11 Free House Wylam Gold Tankard, Durham Magus, Big Lamp Bitter, Jarrow Bitter. **Facilities** Dogs allowed Parking **Rooms** 6 bedrooms en suite S£45 D£62 (★★★ INN)

FIR TREE MAP 19 NZ1

Duke of York Inn

DL15 8DG ☎ 01388 762848 📠 01388 767055

e-mail: suggett@firtree-crook.fsnet.co.uk

dir: *On A68 N, 12m W of Durham*

Family owned and run for four generations, this pub offers an old world atmosphere enhanced by 'mouseman' Robert Thompson's furniture and bar fittings, and the proprietor's collection of African memorabilia and Stone Age flints. A former drovers' and coaching inn dating from 1749, it stands on the tourist route (A68) to Scotland. Typical dishes from the blackboard include home-made steak and kidney pie; fresh Amble cod in beer batter; and gammon in sherry and peaches.

Open 11–2.30 6.30–10.30 **Bar Meals** L served all week 12–2 D served all week 6.30–9 Av main course £8.95 **Restaurant** L served all week 12–2 D served all week 6.30–9 Av fixed price £20 Free House Black Sheep, Worthington. **Facilities** Children's licence Garden Parking Play Area

Rose & Crown

his substantial ivy-clad free house stands in the middle of three village greens, overlooking ncient stocks and a water pump, not to mention the 700-year-old St Romald's Church, also nown as the Cathedral of the Dale.

ep inside the award-winning inn, ıd you'll be met by warm smiles ıd the scent of fresh flowers. olished panelling, old beams, eaming brasses and creaking airs add to the rustic charm. The mospheric wood-panelled bar is ghly inviting with its oak settle, ily newspapers, antique prints, ırriage lamps and a crackling fire the dog-grate. In the restaurant ere's more oak panelling, crisp hite tablecloths, sparkling silver ıd soft lights: the perfect setting r a romantic supper. Lunch in e bar from the daily changing enu could start with baked ıeddar and spinach soufflé; or allop, bacon and wild mushroom sotto with garden herbs. Main ourses might include Mr Slack's ork sausages with black pudding and mustard mash; or smoked haddock kedgeree, prawns and quails' eggs. Children are well catered for, with the likes of bacon butties and spaghetti on toast, as well as smoked Scotch salmon for the more sophisticated toddlers. In the evening, a four-course dinner in the restaurant might consist of ratatouille tartlet and aubergine crisps, followed by broccoli and blue cheese soup. After a main course of pan-fried pheasant breast, apple and prune compote and Calvados cream, round off with warm apricot and almond tart and vanilla ice cream. There's a good selection of wines by the glass. Twelve beautifully furnished en suite bedrooms are available should you wish to explore the fabulous Teesdale countryside.

★★ HL ◎◎ 🍷
MAP 19 NY92
DL12 9EB
☎ 01833 650213
📠 01833 650828
e-mail: hotel@rose-and-crown.co.uk
dir: *6m NW from Barnard Castle on B6277.*

Open 11.30–3 5.30–11 Closed: 23–27 Dec
Bar Meals L served all week 12–1.30 D served all week 6.30–9.30 Av main course £11.50
Restaurant L served Sun 12–1.30 D served all week 7.30–9 Av 4 course fixed price £28
Free House
Theakston Best, Black Sheep Best, Emmerdale. 🍷 14
Facilities Children's licence Dogs allowed Parking
Rooms 12 bedrooms en suite S£80 D£130

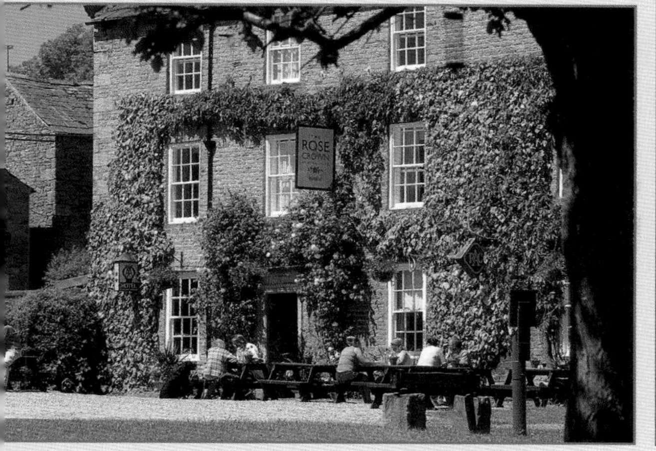

England

HUTTON MAGNA MAP 19 NZ11

Pick of the Pubs

The Oak Tree Inn

DL11 7HH ☎ 01833 627371

dir: *6.5m along A66, W from Scotch Corner*

Owners Alastair and Claire Ross provide a warm welcome at this whitewashed, part 18th-century free house. Alastair previously spent 14 years in London working at The Savoy, Leith's and, more recently, at a private members' club on the Strand. Meals in the simply furnished dining room are created from the finest local ingredients, and the menu changes daily depending on what is available. The three fish choices, in particular, rely on what comes in on the boats. The cooking style combines classic techniques and occasional modern flavours: you could start with steamed Shetland mussels in coconut, chilli, ginger and mint, or perhaps grilled fillet of sea bream with truffle celeriac remoulade and caviar crème fraîche. Typical mains include smoked haddock with a soft poached egg and a light curry mussel sauce; and roast wild duck with cabbage, bacon mashed potato and wild mushrooms. Don't miss the list of 21 whiskies.

Open 6–11 (Sun 6–10.30) Closed: 25 Dec & 1 Jan **Restaurant** D served Tue–Sun (Bookings only) Av 3 course à la carte £27 Free House Charles Wells Bombardier, Timothy Taylor Landlord & Black Sheep Best. **Facilities** Dogs allowed Parking

MIDDLESTONE MAP 19 NZ23

Ship Inn

Low Rd DL14 8AB ☎ 01388 810904

dir: *On B6287(Kirk Merrington to Coundon road)*

Beer drinkers will appreciate the string of CAMRA accolades received by this family-run pub on the village green. In the last five years regulars could have sampled well over 800 different beers. Home-cooked food is served in the bar and restaurant. The rooftop patio has spectacular views over the Tees Valley and Cleveland Hills.

Open 4–11 (Fri–Sun 12–11) **Bar Meals** L served Fri–Sun 12–2.30 D served all week 4–9 Av main course £4.50 **Restaurant** L served Fri–Sun 12–2.30 D served all week 4–9 Free House Guest Ales. **Facilities** Children's licence Dogs allowed Parking Play Area **Notes**

MIDDLETON-IN-TEESDALE MAP 18 NY92

The Teesdale Hotel ★★ HL

Market Square DL12 0QG

☎ 01833 640264 01833 640651

e-mail: enquiries@teesdalehotel.com

This family-run coaching inn is situated just off the Pennine Way, close to some of Northern England's loveliest scenery. Noted for its striking 18th-century stone exterior, the inn has been sympathetically modernised with log fires adding to the charming atmosphere. Bar snacks and meals are served in addition to the restaurant menu, and typical dishes include Thai fishcakes with chilli dip and salad, and breast of chicken topped with asparagus and cheese sauce.

Open 11–11 **Bar Meals** L served all week 12–2 D served all week 7–9 **Restaurant** L served all week 12–2.30 D served all week 7–9 Free Hou[se] Guinness, Tetley Smooth, Jennings Cumberland Ale, Jennings Red Breas[t] & Carlsberg. **Facilities** Dogs allowed Parking **Rooms** 14 bedrooms en suite S£42.50 D£75

NEWTON AYCLIFFE MAP 19 NZ2

Blacksmiths Arms

Preston le Skerne, (off Ricknall Lane) DL5 6JH

☎ 01325 314873

A former smithy dating from the 1700s, and still relatively isolated in its farmland setting. Enjoying an excellent reputation locally as a good dining pub, it offers starters of hot smoked mackerel and potato salad; cod and prawn brandade; chicken fillet goujons; and potted mushrooms. Requiring their own page on the menu are fish dishes such as grilled halibut steak with risotto, and gingered salmon. Chef's specialities include Gressingham duck breast, and pork au poivre.

Open 12–3 6–11 (Sun 2–10.30) Closed: 1 Jan **Bar Meals** L served Tue–S[at] 11.30–2 D served Tue–Sat 6–9.30 (Sun 12–10.30) Free House Guest ales. 10 **Facilities** Garden Parking Play Area

ROMALDKIRK MAP 19 NY9

Pick of the Pubs

Rose & Crown ★★ HL

DL12 9EB ☎ 01833 650213 01833 650828

e-mail: hotel@rose-and-crown.co.uk

dir: *6m NW from Barnard Castle on B6277*

See Pick of the Pubs on page 203

SEDGEFIELD MAP 19 NZ3

Dun Cow Inn

43 Front St TS21 3AT ☎ 01740 620894 01740 622163

dir: *At junct of A177 & A689, in village centre*

An interesting array of bric-a-brac can be viewed inside this splendid old village inn, which has many flower baskets bedecking its exterior in summer. It is also the pub that can claim to have been the Prime Minister's local, as Tony Blair was the local MP. This is the pub that hosted Tony's 'million pound lunch' with American President, George W Bush. Typical offerings include Angus sirloin steaks, locally-made sausages, spring lamb cutlets, fresh Shetland mussels, and mushroom stroganoff. Pudding choices often include gooseberry crumble and chocolate fudge cake with butterscotch sauce.

Open 11–3 6.30–11 (all day Sun) Rest: 25 Dec evening **Bar Meals** L served all week 12–2 D served all week 6.30–9.30 (Sun 12–8.30) Av main course £12 **Restaurant** L served all week 12–2 D served a[ll] week 7–9.30 (Sun 12–8.30) Free House Theakston Best Bitter, John Smiths Smooth, Black Sheeps Bitter & Guest Beers. 8 **Facilities** Parking

'RIMDON MAP 19 NZ33

'he Bird in Hand

alters Ln TS29 6JQ ☎ 01429 880391

illage pub nine miles west of Hartlepool with fine views over urrounding countryside from an elevated position. There's a cosy ar and games room, stocking a good choice of cask ales and guest eers, a spacious lounge and large conservatory restaurant. Traditional unday lunch goes down well, as does breaded plaice and other vourites. In summer you can sit outside in the garden, which has a ofed over area for climbing plants.

pen 12–11 (Sun 12–10.30) **Bar Meals** L served Mon–Sat 12–2.30 served Mon–Sat 5–9 Av main course £3.50 **Facilities** Garden Dogs lowed Parking

ESSEX

ARKESDEN MAP 12 TL43

Pick of the Pubs

Axe & Compasses

High St CB11 4EX ☎ 01799 550272 01799 550906

dir: *From Buntingford take B1038 towards Newport. Then left for Arkesden*

See Pick of the Pubs on page 207

BLACKMORE MAP 06 TL60

Pick of the Pubs

The Leather Bottle NEW

The Green CM4 0RL ☎ 01277 821891

e-mail: leatherbottle@tiscali.co.uk

dir: *M25 junct 8 onto A1023, left onto A128 5m. Left onto Blackmore Rd 2m. Left towards Blackmore 2m. Right and 1st left*

According to local legend, Henry VIII used to stable his horses here when he came to visit his mistress. There has been a pub on the site for over 400 years, but the original building burned down in 1954 and was rebuilt in 1956. The present day pub is a family-run affair with James and Gwen Wallace at the helm and their daughter Sarah in charge of the restaurant. The bar is a cosy, inviting place to savour real ales, while the restaurant is smart, with modern furnishings. There's also an airy conservatory which opens onto the spacious enclosed garden. Food options include a very reasonably priced lunchtime menu, which might include seafood chowder followed by sausages and mash. Typical evening dishes are pan-fried lambs' kidneys with toasted pine nuts and balsamic syrup, followed by a pork chop with roasted root vegetables, topped with apple and date chutney.

Open 11–11 (Fri–Sat 11–12, Sun 12–11) **Bar Meals** L served Sun 12–2 Av main course £10 **Restaurant** L served all week 12–2 (Sun 12–4) D served Mon–Sat 7–9 Av 3 course à la carte £20 Av 2 course fixed price £9.95 Free House Adnams Best, Adnams Broadside, Deuchars IPA, Woodford Wherry. 8 **Facilities** Garden

BRAINTREE MAP 07 TL72

Pick of the Pubs

The Green Dragon at Young's End

Upper London Rd, Young's End CM77 8QN

☎ 01245 361030 01245 362575

e-mail: info@greendragonbraintree.co.uk

dir: *M11 junct 8, A120 towards Colchester. At Braintree bypass take A131 S towards Chelmsford, exit at Youngs End on Great Leighs bypass*

See Pick of the Pubs on page 208

BURNHAM-ON-CROUCH MAP 07 TQ99

Ye Olde White Harte Hotel

The Quay CM0 8AS ☎ 01621 782106 01621 782106

dir: *Along high street, right before clocktower, right into car park*

Directly overlooking the River Crouch, the hotel dates from the 17th century and retains many original features, including exposed beams. The pub has its own private jetty. The food is mainly English-style with such dishes as roast leg of English lamb, local roast Dengie chicken and seasoning, and grilled fillet of plaice and lemon. There is also a range of bar snacks including toasted and plain sandwiches, jacket potatoes, and soup.

Open 11–11 **Bar Meals** L served all week 12–2 D served all week 7–9 **Restaurant** L served all week 12–2 D served all week 7–9 Free House Adnams Bitter, Crouch Vale Best. **Facilities** Dogs allowed Parking

England

CASTLE HEDINGHAM MAP 13 TL73

The Bell Inn

St James St CO9 3EJ ☎ 01787 460350
e-mail: bell-inn@ic24.net
dir: *On A1124 N of Halstead, right to Castle Hedingham*

Run by the same family since 1965, this former coaching inn remains quite unspoilt. Traditional features include beams, wooden floors and open fires inside and a large walled orchard garden outside. Two guest beers are served each week, and there's a beer festival every summer. Quality ingredients are carefully sourced, locally where possible, for the simple pub food including pies, coq au vin, and grilled lamb chops. Monday is fish night – try it barbecued.

Open 11.45–3 6–11 (Fri 11.45–12 Sat 12–11.30, Sun 12–11) Closed: 25 Dec (eve) **Bar Meals** L served all week 12–2 D served all week 7–9.30 (Sat–Sun 12–2.30, Sun 7–9) Grays Maldon Gold Mighty Oak, Greene King IPA, Adnams Bitter. 8 **Facilities** Garden Dogs allowed Parking Play Area

CHAPPEL MAP 13 TL82

The Swan Inn

CO6 2DD ☎ 01787 222353 01787 220012
dir: *Pub visible just off A1124 Colchester-Halstead road, from Colchester 1st left after viaduct*

This rambling low-beamed free house stands in the shadow of a magnificent Victorian railway viaduct, and boasts a charming riverside garden with overflowing flower tubs. Fresh meat arrives daily from Smithfield, and fish from Billingsgate. Typically the seafood may include crispy sole fillets, deep-fried monkfish or poached skate, while the grill comes into its own with prime steaks, platters of surf'n'turf, English pork chops and calves' liver and bacon. There are daily vegetarian specials, and home-made desserts too.

Open 11–3 6–11 (Sat 11–11, Sun 12–10.30) **Bar Meals** L served all week 12–2.30 D served all week 6.30–10 (Sun 12–8.30) Av main course £8.95 **Restaurant** L served all week 12–2.15 D served all week 7–10 (Sun 12–8.30) Av 3 course à la carte £15 Free House Greene King IPA, Abbot Ale. **Facilities** Garden Dogs allowed Parking Play Area

CHELMSFORD MAP 06 TL7

The Alma

37 Arbour Ln CM1 7RG ☎ 01245 256783 01245 25679
e-mail: the_alma@hotmail.com
web: www.thealma.biz
dir: *Please telephone for directions*

Named after the bloodiest battle of the Crimean war, The Alma was built in the late 19th century as an alehouse for soldiers recovering in the neighbouring hospital. The present owners have refurbished the pub to give it a contemporary edge, and the menu follows suit with a stylish mix of traditional and modern dishes – perhaps monkfish with Parma ham, a crab cake and asparagus tips; or parsnip tart with pumpkin risotto.

Open 11–11 Closed: 25 Dec pm, 26 Dec **Bar Meals** L served all week 12–2.30 D served all week 6–9.30 (Sun 12–8) **Restaurant** L served all week 12–2.30 D served all week (Sun 12–8) Free House Greene Kir IPA, Spitfire, Nethergate Suffolk County, Crouch Vale Brewers Gold. 11 **Facilities** Garden Parking

CLAVERING MAP 12 TL4

Pick of the Pubs

The Cricketers

CB11 4QT ☎ 01799 550442 01799 550882
e-mail: cricketers@lineone.net
dir: *From M11 junct 10, A505 E. Then A1301, B1383. At Newport take B1038*

See Pick of the Pubs on page 210

Axe & Compasses

lways just the 'Axe' in the local vernacular, this old pub stands in the centre of a pretty village ırough which runs Wicken Water, a gentle stream spanned by footbridges leading to picture-ostcard white, cream and pink-washed thatched cottages.

ne main section of the building, self also thatched, which dates om 1650, is now the comfortable unge containing easy chairs ıd settees, antique furniture and ocks, horse brasses and maybe e warming glow of an open fire. ıe part to the right is the public ır, built in the early 19th century stabling, a function it performed ıtil the 1920s. Meals in here range om sandwiches to grilled lemon le and lambs' liver and bacon. In e cosy, softly lit restaurant area, hich seats 50 on various levels, ricultural implements adorn e old beams. Here, the menu fers a good selection of starters, cluding pan-fried strips of duck east with scallions and cucumber, rved in a pancake with plum uce; and lightly baked, oat-rolled fresh mackerel fillet. There's a good choice of main courses too, examples being supreme of chicken with port wine and stilton; medallions of beef fillet with rôsti potato, soft green peppercorns, brandy and cream; and halibut steak with spinach, tomato, cheddar cheese, white wine and cream. Vegetarians may choose from breadcrumbed spinach and potato cake, with tomato and basil sauce; roasted vegetable vol au vent filled with cheese and mustard cream sauce; and mushroom, cream and cheese pancake. Round off with popular desserts from the trolley such as trifle of the day, or summer pudding. House wines are modestly priced. On a fine day many drinkers and diners head for the patio

MAP 12 TL43
High St CB11 4EX
☎ 01799 550272
01799 550906
dir: *From Buntingford take B1038 towards Newport. Then left for Arkesden*

Open 11.30–2.30 6–11
Bar Meals L served all week 12–2 D served all week 6.45–9.30 Av main course £12
Restaurant L served all week 12–2 D served all week 6.45–9.30 Av 3 course à la carte £20
Greene King
Greene King IPA, Abbot Ale & Old Speckled Hen. 14
Facilities Garden Parking

The Green Dragon at Young's En

Hosts Bob and Mandy Greybrook have been in situ at the Green Dragon for 22 years. These days the pub enjoys a quiet location on the old A131 Braintree – Chelmsford road, thanks to the building of the by-pass.

Though very much a country establishment, it is only 20 minutes from London Stansted Airport, via the A120, and next door to the Great Leighs Racecourse, the first new racecourse in the UK for 70 years. The former house and stables provide a comfortable venue for good drinking and dining, with winter fires creating a cosy atmosphere in the friendly bars, which are smartly decked out with lots of exposed beams and traditional furnishings. As their names suggest, the barn and hayloft restaurants provide plenty of space, maintaining the rustic theme with bare brick walls and wonderful old beams. Outside there's a large garden and heated patio area. Quality awards for their cask ales and hygiene standards testify to the owners' commitment to running a good-value, family-friendly hostelry. The same blackboard and extensive printed menus are available throughout, offering light snacks and full meals ranging through fresh seafood, game in season and speciality Gloucestershire Old Spot pork dishes. One of the Old Spot recipes is slow roasted belly of pork stuffed with apricots and served with cider sauce and sage mash. Seafood specials include oysters, dressed crab, moules marinière, and halibut steak with prawns and lemon and lime butter. There is also a menu for the under 10's with planet spaghetti and toad in the hole.

MAP 07 TL72
Upper London Rd, Young's End
CM77 8QN
☎ 01245 361030
01245 362575
e-mail:
info@greendragonbraintree.co.uk
dir: *M11 junct 8, A120 towards Colchester. At Braintree bypass take A131 S towards Chelmsford, exit at Youngs End on Great Leighs bypass*

Open 12–3 5.30–11 (Sun & BHs 12–11)
Bar Meals L served all week 12–2.30 D served all week 6.30–9.30 (Sat & Sun 12–9)
Restaurant L served all week 12–2.15 D served all week 6–9.30 (Sun 12–9) Av 3 course à la carte £17.50
Greene King
Greene King IPA , Abbot Ale, Ruddles County & Old Speckled Hen. 🍷 10
Facilities Garden Parking Play Area

COLCHESTER MAP 13 TL92

he Rose & Crown Hotel ★★★ HL

ast St CO1 2TZ ☎ 01206 866677 01206 866616

-mail: info@rose-and-crown.com

r: *From M25 junct 28 take A12 N.*

1400, Colchester had 13 inns, and this was one. Today, it's the oldest otel in England's oldest town, with a bar made of cell doors from the l that once stood on the site. Eating in the oak-beamed brasserie eans traditional food – fish and chips, or gammon steak, for example while in the candlelit Oak Room the style is Indian/French fusion green chicken tikka salad; spicy sea bass; and wild mushroom risotto, r example.

pen 11-2.30 6-11 (Sat-Sun all day) **Bar Meals** L served all week 12-2 served all week 6-10 (Sun 12-3) **Restaurant** L served all week 12-2 served Mon-Sat 7-9.45 Free House Carlsberg-Tetley Tetley's ter, Rose & Crown Bitter, Adnams Broadside. 7 **Facilities** Parking **ooms** 39 bedrooms en suite

DEDHAM MAP 13 TM03

larlborough Head Hotel

ill Ln CO7 6DH ☎ 01206 323250

-mail: jen.permain@tiscali.co.uk

eb: www.marlborough-head.co.uk

ir: *E of A12, N of Colchester*

cked away in glorious Constable country, a 16th-century building at was once a clearing-house for local wool merchants. In 1660, after slump in trade, it became an inn. Today it is as perfect for a pint, sofa nd newspaper as it is for a good home-cooked family meal. As well traditional favourites, such as lambs' liver and bacon, the dinner enu includes chicken arrabbiata, seafood platter, peppered steak and asted vegetable tagliatelle.

pen 11-11 **Bar Meals** L served Mon-Sat 11-11 D served Mon-Sat 11-11 un 12-10.30) Av main course £7.95 **Restaurant** L served Mon-Sat -11 D served Mon-Sat 11-11 (Sun 12-10.30) Old English Pub ompany Adnams Southwold, Greene King IPA, Adnams Broadside & uest. **Facilities** Garden Parking

Pick of the Pubs

The Sun Inn ★★★★ INN

High St CO7 6DF ☎ 01206 323351

e-mail: info@thesuninndedham.com

dir: *From A12 to Dedham for 1.5m, pub on village high street*

Owner Piers Baker has transformed the Sun from a run-down village boozer to an inn of fine repute. With open fires, oak beams, a sun-trap terrace and walled garden, you'll find character everywhere you look. Here, a quiet pint goes hand in hand with robust food and drink; there's a decent selection of real ales and a respectable wine list, with up to sixteen wines available by the glass. Locally sourced seasonal ingredients drive the menu of modern British dishes: expect roast partridge with pear, braised lentils and baked radicchio; baked organic salmon with chickpeas, Swiss chard, chilli and mint; and molten chocolate baby cake with cream. If you can't quite tear yourself away, the Sun boasts four en-suite guest rooms with large comfy beds, crisp linen, character furniture, great showers and lazy continental breakfasts.

Open 12-11 Closed: 25-27 Dec **Bar Meals** L served all week 12-2.30 (Wknds 12-3) D served all week 6.30-9.30 (Fri-Sat 6.30-10) Av main course £10 **Restaurant** L served all week 12-2.30 (Wknds 12-3) D served all week 6.30-9.30 (Fri-Sat 6.30-10) Free House Brewer's Gold Crouch Vale, Adnam's Broadside, Canary from Lowestoft, Titanic & Kaltenberg. 16 **Facilities** Children's licence Garden Dogs allowed Parking **Rooms** 4 bedrooms en suite

EARLS COLNE MAP 13 TL82

Pick of the Pubs

The Carved Angel

Upper Holt St CO6 2PG

☎ 01787 222330 01787 220013

e-mail: info@carvedangel.com

dir: *From A120 take B1024 to Coggeshall, right at junct with A1124, pub 300yds on right*

Once a haven for monks and nuns escaping persecution by Henry VIII, this 15th-century village inn is now a popular gastropub with a stylish bar and restaurant. Traditional ales from Adnams and Greene King are offered alongside continental beers and a global wine list. Frequently changing menus are created from fresh seasonal ingredients, with the aim of offering a high standard of food but in a relaxed setting at reasonable prices. The kitchen turns out well-crafted dishes such as prawn tails fried in tempura with home-made tartare sauce; confit of duck with caramelised apple and a burgundy and sage reduction; and iced rhubarb parfait with a winter berries compote. The lunch special menu is particularly good value. Special events are held on a regular basis, for Mothering Sunday, Valentine's Day and so on.

Open 11.30-3 6.30-11 (Sun 6.30-10.30) Closed: 26 Dec, 1 Jan **Bar Meals** L served all week 12-2 D served all week 7-9 (Fri-Sat 7-10, Sun 12-2.30) Av main course £10 **Restaurant** L served all week 12-2 D served all week 7-9 (Fri-Sat 7-10, Sun 12-2.30) Av 3 course à la carte £19 Free House Greene King IPA, Adnams Bitter 14 **Facilities** Garden Parking

ELSENHAM MAP 12 TL52

The Crown

The Cross, High St CM22 6DG ☎ 01279 812827

dir: *M11 junct 8 towards Takeley. Left at lights*

A pub for 200 years, with oak beams, open fireplaces and Essex pargetting at the front. The menu, which has a large selection of fresh fish, might offer baked trout with toasted almonds, steak and kidney pie, Crown mixed grill with onion rings, a choice of steaks cooked to order, or breast of duck with peppercorn sauce. There's a good choice of vegetarian dishes as well, plus lighter bites and jacket potatoes.

Open 12-11 (Sun 12-10.30) **Bar Meals** L served Mon-Sat 12-9 (Sun 12-4) D served Mon-Sat 6-9 Av main course £11 **Restaurant** L served Mon-Sat 12-9 (Sun lunch 12-3) D served Mon-Sat Av 3 course à la carte £30 Punch Retail IPA, Broadside, Spitfire. **Facilities** Garden Dogs allowed Parking

The Cricketers

Always popular, in recent years this 16th-century inn has gained renown as the place where celebrity chef Jamie Oliver first learnt to wield a spatula. Set in the heart of a beautiful and unspoilt Essex village, the pub is still run by his parents, Trevor and Sally.

It stands near the cricket pitch, and related memorabilia decorates the brick-fronted bar and green-themed restaurant. Seasonally changing menus are offered in both areas, with fixed-price in the restaurant, and carte in the bar. The cooking shows a distinctly Italian influence, and although fresh fish is served every day, Tuesdays are special fish days, with lobster and crab served up alongside whatever looks good at the market. Typical bar meals could start with home-made wild rabbit ravioli and artichoke pesto; or seared breast of wood pigeon topped with fig and red onion jam. Move on to loin of local pork with apple and sage risotto; twice-baked aubergine and basil soufflé with sun-blushed tomato and lemon polenta; or grilled turbot fillet with a Pernod butter sauce. From the restaurant menu, try roast boneless quail and Asian salad; slow braised oxtail with fresh gnocchi and Savoy cabbage; or pan-fried king scallops, sliced potatoes, leeks and bacon lardons. Main choices might be baked cod fillet with lemon, caper and chive beurre noisette; medallions of local venison, parsnip and celeriac purée and port wine jus; or Mediterranean vegetable lasagna with blue cheese sauce. The home-made dessert menu is equally mouth-watering. Beer lovers will be interested in the range of bottled English real ales and Suffolk cider.

🍷
MAP 12 TL43
CB11 4QT
☎ 01799 550442
🖷 01799 550882
e-mail: cricketers@lineone.net
dir: *From M11 junct 10, A505 E. Then A1301, B1383. At Newport take B1038*

Open 10.30–11 Closed: 25–26 Dec
Bar Meals L served all week 12–2 D served all week 7–10
Restaurant L served Sun 12–2 D served all week 7–10 Av 3 course à la carte £27 Av 3 course fixed price £27
🌐 Free House
🍺 Adnams Bitter, Carlsberg-Tetley Tetley Bitter, Greene King IPA & Adnams Broadside. 🍷 10
Facilities Garden Parking Play Area
Rooms 14 bedrooms en suite S£75 D£100 (★★★★ INN)

EERING MAP 07 TL82

he Sun Inn

eering Hill CO5 9NH ☎ 01376 570442
-mail: v2fmb@tiscali.co.uk
r: *On A12 between Colchester & Witham*

his timbered building dates from 1525, and features richly carved ecorations on the bressummer and barge boards of the three gable nds. It's a lively pub, with two log fires to welcome customers in the nter months and up to 20 constantly changing real ales. A menu of ub favourites includes a make-up-your-own ploughman's; ham, egg d chips; Ale House sausage and chips; jacket potatoes; and salads.

pen 12–3 6–11 (Sun 6–10.30) **Bar Meals** L served all week 12–2 (Sun –3) D served all week 6–9.30 Av main course £8 Free House Guest ers. 6 **Facilities** Garden Dogs allowed Parking

ELSTED MAP 06 TL62

Pick of the Pubs

The Swan at Felsted

Station Rd CM6 3DG
☎ 01371 820245 01371 821393
e-mail: info@theswanatfelsted.co.uk
dir: *Exit M11 junct 8 onto A120 signed Felsted. Pub in village centre*

Originally a Ridleys pub, the Swan was rebuilt after a disastrous fire in the early 20th century. For many years it was the village bank, and it's ideally situated for exploring the pretty Essex countryside, and only a short drive from Stansted Airport. The pub chefs design their menus to suit every palate – everything from light dishes at lunchtime to more serious fare in the evening. Fine wines and well-kept cask ales also help to achieve a balance between the traditional English pub and a high quality restaurant. Specials may feature pan-fried Scottish salmon with prawn and broccoli pasta and beurre blanc; Priors Hall Farm gammon steak with bubble and squeak and fried eggs; Swan beer-battered haddock with thick cut chips and minted mushy peas; and shepherd's pie made with Scottish mutton, roasted parsnips and sprouts. To round off, try orange and vanilla crème brûlée or apple and rhubarb custard tart.

Open 11–11 (Sun 12–4) **Bar Meals** L served all week 12–3 (Sun 12–4) D served Mon–Sat 6–10 Av main course £10 **Restaurant** L served all week 12–3 (Sun 12–4) D served Mon–Sat 6–10 Av 3 course à la carte £22.50 Greene King IPA, Fosters, Stella, Prospect. 9 **Facilities** Children's licence Garden Dogs allowed Parking

INGRINGHOE MAP 07 TM02

he Whalebone

hapel Rd CO5 7BG ☎ 01206 729307 01206 729307
mail: fburroughes1974@aol.com

is Grade II listed 18th-century free house has panoramic views of the man river valley. It also has wooden floors, aubergine walls, unique twork and sculptures, and roman blinds. The unusual name comes om bones, once fastened above the door of the pub, which came from ocally beached whale. Another unusual feature is the oak tree nearby, ought to be the largest in Essex. The menu offers hearty home-made shes like roasted poussin with ricotta, gorgonzola and mortadella; chargrilled sirloin steak and chips; roast belly of Suffolk pork; and roasted sea bass with vermouth braised fennel.

Open 12–3 5.30–11 (all day Sat–Sun) **Bar Meals** L served all week 12–2.30 D served Tue–Sat 7–9.30 Av main course £10.25 **Restaurant** L served all week D served Mon–Sat Av 3 course à la carte £18.75 Free House Greene King IPA, Caledonian Deuchars IPA & 2 Guest Beers. 7 **Facilities** Children's licence Garden Dogs allowed Parking

GOSFIELD MAP 13 TL72

The Green Man

The Street CO9 1TP ☎ 01787 472746
e-mail: greenmangosfield@tesco.net
dir: *A131 N from Braintree then A1017 to village*

A pink-washed medley of buildings housing a smart village dining pub, where Cumberland sausage, cottage pie, haddock fillet and spinach and ricotta cannelloni feature among good value lunch and dinner possibilities. Additional choices in the evening include a full rack of ribs with honey or mustard sauce, mushrooms, onion rings and chips; rump, rib-eye and fillet steaks; and chicken supreme.

Open 11–3 6.15–11 (Sun 12–4) **Bar Meals** L served all week 12–2.30 D served Mon–Sat 6.45–9 **Restaurant** L served all week 12–2.30 D served Tue–Sat 6.45–9 Greene King Greene King IPA, Old Speckled Hen & Abbot Ale. 6 **Facilities** Children's licence Garden Dogs allowed Parking

GREAT BRAXTED MAP 07 TL81

Du Cane Arms

The Village CM8 3EJ ☎ 01621 891697 01621 890009
e-mail: fred@fredrodford.com
dir: *Signed between Witham & Kelvedon on A12*

Walkers and cyclists mingle with the locals at this friendly pub, built in 1935 at the heart of a leafy village: handy for the A12 today, it is a popular spot and comes up with a variety of lively real ales and daily fresh fish. Adnams bitter boosts the beer batter for fresh cod or haddock, while the steak and kidney pie is livened up with a splash of Guinness. Thai curries, rack of lamb, and seafood curry are among the other dishes. The garden is ideal for summer eating.

Open 11.30–3 6.30–11 **Bar Meals** L served all week 12–2 D served all week 6.30–9.30 (Winter Sun 12–4.45) **Restaurant** L served all week 12–2 D served all week 7–9.30 Free House Adnams Bitter, Greene King IPA, John Smiths Smooth. 10 **Facilities** Garden Parking

England

GREAT YELDHAM MAP 13 TL73

The White Hart NEW

Poole St CO9 4HJ ☎ 01787 237250 01787 238044

e-mail: mjwmason@yahoo.co.uk

dir: *On A1017 between Haverhill & Halstead*

This impressive timber-framed inn was built in 1505 when Henry VIII was on the throne and the surrounding area was a great oak forest. These days it's a smart venue for a simple drink or a sophisticated meal – perhaps classic moules marinière followed by roasted local partridge with deep-fried cauliflower, caramelised red onion and a juniper berry and cinnamon jus.

Open 10–12 **Bar Meals** L served Mon–Sat 12–3 D served Mon–Thu 6–9.30 Av main course £8.50 **Restaurant** L served all week 12–3 D served all week 6–9.30 Av 3 course à la carte £25 Av 3 course fixed price £16.95 Free House Adnams Bitter, Black Sheep, Adnams Broadside. 12 **Facilities** Children's licence Garden Parking Play Area

HENNY STREET MAP 13 TL83

Pick of the Pubs

The Henny Swan NEW

CO10 7LS ☎ 01787 269238

e-mail: harry@hennyswan.com

dir: *From Sudbury centre take A131 to Chelmsford 1.5m, at lights turn left at Henny Street*

See Pick of the Pubs on opposite page

HORNDON ON THE HILL MAP 06 TQ68

Pick of the Pubs

Bell Inn & Hill House

High Rd SS17 8LD ☎ 01375 642463 01375 361611

e-mail: info@bell-inn.co.uk

dir: *M25 junct 30/31 signed Thurrock*

See Pick of the Pubs on page 214

LANGHAM MAP 13 TM03

The Shepherd and Dog

Moor Rd CO4 5NR ☎ 01206 272711 01206 273136

dir: *A12 from Colchester to Ipswich, 1st left signed Langham*

Situated on the Suffolk/Essex border, in Constable country, this 1928 free house has the classic styling of an English country pub. Widely renowned for its food, the Shepherd and Dog serves an extensive variety of meat, fish and poultry dishes, plus a vegetarian selection and a children's menu.

Open 11–3 5.30–11 (Sun 12–11) **Bar Meals** L served all week 12–2.15 D served all week 6–10 (Sat 11–11 Sun 12–10.30) **Restaurant** L served all week 12–2.15 D served all week 6–10 Free House Greene King IPA, Abbot Ale & Guest Beers, Stella Artois. **Facilities** Children's licence Garden Dogs allowed Parking

LITTLE BRAXTED MAP 07 TL8

The Green Man

Green Man Ln CM8 3LB ☎ 01621 891659

dir: *1.5m from A12 junct 22, B1389 signed Witham. Signs to Little Braxted, over bridge, right into Little Braxted Lane, 1.5m, right at next T-junct, pub on right*

A traditional English pub set in the picturesque village of Little Braxted. A recent addition is a fine food deli in one of the outbuildings, where you can buy fresh local produce, cheeses and organic goods. The secluded garden is popular in summer, while in winter the cosy interior and open fire draw people in. Home-made dishes include lamb shank in a minted red wine gravy, as well as lighter snacks and sandwiches.

Open 11.30–3 6–11 (Sun 12–3.30, 7–10.30) **Bar Meals** L served all week 12–2 D served all week 7–9 (No food every 1st Sun eve of month) Av main course £7.25 Greene King Greene King IPA, Morland, Old BOB & Guest Beers. **Facilities** Garden Dogs allowed Parking

LITTLE CANFIELD MAP 06 TL5

The Lion & Lamb

CM6 1SR ☎ 01279 870257 01279 870423

e-mail: info@lionandlamb.co.uk

dir: *M11 junct 8, B1256 towards Takeley and Little Canfield*

A favourite for business or leisure, this traditional country pub restaurant is handy for Stansted airport and the M11. Inside you'll find oak beams, winter log fires, and an extensive food selection. Choose sandwiches, or traditional bar food such as steak and ale pie, or go for roasted scallops on saffron scented risotto followed by breast of duck with sesame pak choi, crisp noodles and oriental dressing.

Open 11–11 (Sun 12–11) **Bar Meals** L served all week 11–10 D served all week 11–10 (Sun 12–10) **Restaurant** L served all week 11–10 D served all week 11–10 (Sun 12–10) Av 3 course fixed price £25 Greene King Old Speckled Hen, Greene King IPA, Ridleys Rumpus & Old Bob. 10 **Facilities** Garden Parking Play Area

See advertisement under STANSTED AIRPOR

The Henny Swan

ted on the Essex bank of the Stour, the Henny Swan was expensively transformed in 2004 from typical, old-fashioned rural pub into a modern dining restaurant pub. The meadows opposite its verside garden are so peaceful these days that it's hard to imagine that in AD61 Boudicca and her Iceni arriors fought a pitched battle with the Roman Army's Ninth Legion there on its way to aid Colchester.

ne interior is decidedly stylish, ith polished wood floors, soft ghting and leather armchairs. ining on the patio is a fair eather pleasure. Choice from the ıropean-influenced, regularly ıanging menus is extended by at ast three daily blackboard specials both lunch and dinner. Local oduce is used extensively. Start ith Thai-style fishcake with sweet illi sauce, or grilled avocado filled ith stilton and crushed walnuts; llowed by chargrilled rib-eye steak ith a creamy wild mushroom and ıcon sauce; seared fillet of wild lmon dusted with Cajun sauce ı sweet chilli and tiger prawn ıguine; roast chicken supreme led with brie and sundried mato, wrapped in Parma ham ith a chunky tomato sauce; and aubergine au gratin, filled with Mediterranean vegetables, flaked almonds and a parmesan and herb topping. Desserts might include home-made bakewell tart with strawberry compote and custard; fresh fruit pavlova filled with lightly whipped cream; or a selection of farmhouse cheeses. The river valley between Bures and Sudbury – in which the Henny Swan lies – is very pretty and it's a fair bet that it is still much as local artists John Constable and Thomas Gainsborough would have known it. Between Easter and October, the Rosette, an elegant electric launch designed in Edwardian style, runs on Sundays and bank holidays from Sudbury down to Henny.

NEW 🍷
MAP 13 TL83
CO10 7LS
☎ 01787 269238
e-mail: harry@hennyswan.com
dir: *From Sudbury centre A131 to Chelmsford 1.5m, left at Henny Street lights*

Open 11–3 6–11
Bar Meals L served all week 12–2.30 (Sun 12–6) D served all week 6.30–9 Av main course £7.95
Restaurant L served all week 12–2.30 (Sun 12–4) D served all week 6.30–9.30 Av 3 course à la carte £21
Greene King IPA, Adnams Broadside. 🍷 8
Facilities Garden Parking

Bell Inn & Hill House

The Bell Inn is a 14th-century coaching inn and Hill House, which is almost next door, dates from 1685. The two buildings between them provide good food and accommodation in an attractive village setting, but only ten minutes from the M25 and 35 minutes from Central London. Lakeside shopping complex is not too far away, either.

The inn has many original features including a courtyard balcony where luggage was once lifted from coach roofs. There is also an original king post that carries roof timbers over 1,000 years old. An unusual tradition takes place here every year, when someone from the village hangs a hot cross bun from a beam in the saloon bar. The two historic buildings have been modernised over the years to provide excellent facilities. Two bars serve a selection of regularly changing real ales, amounting to around 144 different cask beers in the course of a year. The wine list is very extensive and over 16 wines are available by the glass. The bar menu offers lunchtime sandwiches and light meals of roast sausages with beer battered onion rings, or grilled haddock with grilled roma tomato. From the daily changing restaurant menu you might start off with a plate of hot and cold Colchester oysters with spinach, dill hollandaise and shallot dressing, or slow roasted aromatic pork belly with honey-roast carrot and fennel purée, tempura of squid and red wine syrup. Main course options take in paupiette of Dover sole with thyme and shallots on vegetable spaghetti and chive velouté; and roast venison fillet with sautéed scallops, red onion tarte Tatin, orange reduction and shallot jus. Finish in style with a hot chocolate and almond pudding with cherry baked Alaska and Baileys parfait.

MAP 06 TQ68
High Rd SS17 8LD
☎ 01375 642463
Fax 01375 361611
e-mail: info@bell-inn.co.uk
dir: *M25 junct 30/31 signed Thurrock.*

Open 11–2.30 5.30–11 (Sun 12–4, 7–10.30) Closed: 25–26 Dec
Bar Meals L served all week 12–1.45 D served all week 6.45–9.45 (Sun 7–9.45) Av main course £13.75
Restaurant L served all week 12–1.45 D served all week 6.45–9.45 (Sun 7–9.45) Av 3 course à la carte £27.95
Free House
Greene King IPA, Interbrew Bass, Crouchvale Brewers Gold, Ruddles County. 16
Facilities Garden Dogs allowed Parking

ITTLE DUNMOW MAP 06 TL62

litch of Bacon

e Street CM6 3HT ☎ 01371 820323 01371 820338

r: *B1256 to Braintree for 10m, turn off at Little Dunmow, 0.5m b on right*

15th-century country inn whose name refers to the ancient gift of lf a salted pig, or 'flitch', to couples who have been married for a ar and a day, and 'who have not had a cross word'.

pen 12–3 5.30–11 (Sat 6–11 Sun 12–5, 7–10.30) **Bar Meals** L served e-Sat 12–2 (Sun 12–3) D served Mon–Sat 6.30–9 Av main course £6.50 Free House Fullers London Pride, Greene King IPA & Guest ales. **cilities** Garden Dogs allowed Parking

IANNINGTREE MAP 13 TM13

Pick of the Pubs

The Mistley Thorn

High St, Mistley CO11 1HE

☎ 01206 392821 01206 390122

e-mail: info@mistleythorn.com

dir: *Exit A12 at Hadleigh follow signs to E Berholt & Manningtree/Mistley*

Nowadays a casual but upscale bistro-style restaurant, this historic free house was built in 1725. It stands in the centre of Mistley, on the estuary of the River Stour near Colchester. A previous pub on the same site was the scene of 17th-century trials conducted by the self-appointed Witchfynder General, Matthew Hopkins. After a complete refurbishment a few years ago, the Mistley Thorn has a light, airy feel with terracotta-tiled floors, high quality furnishings and interesting artwork on display. Owner Sherri Singleton, who is also the proprietor of the Mistley Kitchen cookery school, serves up an accomplished menu with a strong emphasis on locally sourced and seasonal produce, organic where possible. The menu changes daily at lunch and dinner but typical dishes include lots of fish and shellfish, like rock oysters from Mersea Island, crayfish ceviche cocktail, and grilled whole lemon sole. A set-price lunch menu may offer steamed mussels and Mistley fish and chips.

Open 12–11 **Bar Meals** L served all week 12–2.30 D served all week 7–10 (all day Sat–Sun) **Restaurant** L served all week 12–2.30 D served all week 7–9.30 (all day Sat–Sun) Free House Greene King IPA, Adnams, St Peters. 10 **Facilities** Dogs allowed Parking

NORTH FAMBRIDGE MAP 07 TQ89

The Ferry Boat Inn

Ferry Ln CM3 6LR ☎ 01621 740208

e-mail: sylviaferryboat@aol.com

dir: *From Chelmsford take A130 S then A132 to South Woodham Ferrers, then B1012. Right to village*

A 500-year-old traditional weatherboard inn with beams, log fires and a resident ghost. It is tucked away at the end of a lovely village on the River Crouch, next to the marina, and was once a centre for smugglers. These days it is understandably popular with the sailing fraternity. In addition to the extensive menu, daily specials might include minted lamb chop, grilled sea bass, chicken korma or beef chilli.

Open 11.30–3 –11 (Summer all day Sun) **Bar Meals** L served all week 12–2 D served all week 7–9.30 (Sun 12–2.45, 7–9) Av main course £5.50 **Restaurant** L served all week 12–1.30 D served all week 7–9 Free House Greene King IPA, Abbot Ale, Morland. **Facilities** Garden Dogs allowed Parking

PATTISWICK MAP 13 TL82

Pick of the Pubs

The Compasses at Pattiswick NEW

Compasses Rd CM77 8BG

☎ 01376 561322 01376 564343

e-mail: info@thecompassesatpattiswick.co.uk

dir: *From Braintree take A120 E towards Colchester. After Bradwell take 1st turning left to Pattiswick*

Originally built as two estate workers cottages, this award-winning dining pub seems to be miles from any seriously populated area, although both Chelmsford and Colchester are only 20 minutes away. The owners' passion for good food translates into simple, hearty rural dishes, which you can choose from a menu jam-packed with local produce, including local estate-shot game. Lunchtime offers cottage pie with roasted parsnips and carrots; beer-battered haddock, chips and minted garden peas; and vegetable and bean casserole with herb dumplings, as well as salads, croque monsieur, jacket potatoes and other snacks. For dinner, maybe crab cakes with mixed cress and sweet chilli sauce as a starter, and braised lamb shank with crushed root vegetables and redcurrant jus to follow. Wines are selected for simplicity and clarity of flavour from both New and Old World producers.

Open 11–3 5–12 (all day Etr–Sep) **Bar Meals** L served all week 12–2.45 D served Mon–Sat 6–9.30 Av main course £11 **Restaurant** L served all week 12–2.45 D served Mon–Sat 6–9.45 Av 3 course à la carte £22 Free House Wherry-Woodforde's, Adnam's, Adnam's Broadside, St Austell Tribute. 12 **Facilities** Garden Dogs allowed Parking Play Area

RADWINTER MAP 12 TL63

The Plough Inn

CB10 2TL ☎ 01799 599222

dir: *4m E of Saffron Walden, at junct of B2153 & B2154*

An Essex woodboard exterior, old beams, open fires and a thatched roof characterise this listed inn, once frequented by farm workers.

CONTINUED

England

RADWINTER continued

Food is served in the 50-seat restaurant, making the Plough more a destination gastro-pub than a purely local village inn, without losing too much of the village pub feel. A typical menu includes the likes of smoked haddock parcels, lamb noisettes, partridge, duck breast, and a variety of home-made pies. Friday night is fish night.

Open 12-3 6-11 (Sun 12-4, 7-11) **Bar Meals** L served Mon-Sat 12-2 (Sun 12-3) D served Mon-Sat 6.30-9 Av main course £8.50 **Restaurant** L served all week 12-2 D served Mon-Sat 6.30-9 (Sun 12-3) Free House Adnams Best, IPA, Woodfordes Wherry, Archers. **Facilities** Garden Dogs allowed Parking

SAFFRON WALDEN MAP 12 TL53

Pick of the Pubs

The Cricketers' Arms ★★★★ INN

Rickling Green CB11 3YG

01799 543210 01799 543512

e-mail: reservations@cricketers.demon.co.uk

dir: *Exit B1383 at Quendon. Pub 300yds on left opposite cricket ground*

This historic inn was built as a terrace of timber-framed cottages, and overlooks the cricket green. The cricketing connection began in the 1880s when Rickling Green became the venue for London society cricket matches, and associations with the England team and the county game continue today. The pub has been beautifully refurbished in a stripped-back, modern style, retaining traditional features such as exposed beams and stone floors, but bringing in contemporary comforts such as big leather sofas and, outside, a pretty Japanese terrace garden. One modern, all-pleasing menu serves all three dining areas. Typical starters include foie gras parfait with toasted brioche, sliced apple and red onion; home-smoked tomato and parsnip soup; and risotto of crayfish, caramelized onion, fresh herbs and parmesan. Follow with monkfish wrapped in bacon with chilli, coriander and yellow pea purée; or butternut squash risotto with tempura beetroot and parmesan shavings.

Open 12-11 **Bar Meals** L served all week 12-2.30 D served all week 7-9.30 (Sun 7-9) **Restaurant** L served all week 12-2.30 D served all week 7-9.30 (Sun 7-9) Punch Taverns Greene King IPA, Jennings Cumberland & Abbott Ale. 8 **Facilities** Garden Parking **Rooms** 9 bedrooms en suite S£65 D£95

SHALFORD MAP 12 TL7

The George Inn

The Street CM7 5HH 01371 850207 01371 851355

e-mail: info@thegeorgeshalford.com

A hundred years ago there were five pubs in Shalford, but the Georg Inn, which dates back some 500 years, is the only one now. It's a traditional village pub, with oak beams and open fires, surrounded by lovely countryside. Its own George Ale is brewed at the nearby Felstar micro-brewery. The menu is written up on the blackboard dai including steaks, chicken breast specialities and popular Oriental and Indian dishes. Fish goes down well too, particularly battered plaice, c mornay, and salmon en croute.

pen 12-3 6.30-12 (Sat-Sun 12-12) **Bar Meals** L served all week -2.30 D served all week 6.30-9 (Sun 12-3) Av main course £7.95 **estaurant** L served all week 12-2.30 D served all week 6.30-9.30 (Sat 9) Free House Greene King IPA, Fullers London Pride, Woodfordes herry, George Bitter. **Facilities** Garden Parking

TANSTED AIRPORT MAP 06 TL52

ee **Little Canfield**

TOCK MAP 06 TQ69

he Hoop

High St CM4 9BD ☎ 01277 841137 01277 841137

ir: *On B1007 between Chelmsford & Billericay*

November 2006 Philip Utz and Michelle Corrigan took over this th-century free house, which stands on Stock's attractive village een. The couple brought with them a wealth of food experience, d plan to set high standards in the kitchen. But not to the detriment beer drinkers – among their objectives is a brew of the pub's own e at Brentwood. And the annual beer festival will continue, a ten-day ent spanning the last May bank holiday.

pen 11-11 (Fri 11-12.30, Sat 11-12, Sun 12-10.30) **Bar Meals** L served week 11-2.30 D served Tue-Sat 6-9 (Sun 12-7) Av main course £8.50 **estaurant** L served Tue-Sun 12-2.30 D served Tue-Sun 6-9 (Sun 12-3) 3 course à la carte £24.50 Free House Adnams Bitter & 4 Guest es. 10 **Facilities** Garden Dogs allowed

VICKHAM BISHOPS MAP 07 TL81

he Mitre

The Street CM8 3NN ☎ 01621 891378 01621 894932

ir: *Off B1018 at Witham exit A12. Right at Jack & Jenny pub. ght at end of road. 1st left over bridge. 2nd pub on left*

riginally the Carpenter's Arms, this friendly pub changed its name the mid-1890s, presumably to reflect the one-time possession the village by the Bishops of London. The pub's regular range of eat choices includes mixed grills, pies and curries, steaks, and dishes aturing duck, pork, lamb and chicken. Fish is strongly represented by shes based on haddock, cod, trout, sea bass, swordfish, plaice, Dover le, red mullet and sea halibut to name a few.

pen 11.30-12 **Bar Meals** L served all week 12-2.30 D served all eek 6.30-9.30 (all day Sat-Sun) **Restaurant** L served all week -2.30 D served all week 6.30-9.30 (all day Sat-Sun) Greene King Greene King IPA, Greene King Abbott, Fireside, Ruddles & Old Bob. **acilities** Garden Dogs allowed Parking Play Area

VOODHAM MORTIMER MAP 07 TL80

lurdle Makers Arms NEW

ost Office Rd CM9 6ST ☎ 01245 225169

-mail: hurdlemakersarms@supanet.com

ir: *From Chelmsford A414 through Maldon/Danbury 4.5m into Voodham Mortimer. Over 1st rdbt and 1st left, pub on left*

Grade II listed building dating back 400 years, the Hurdle Makers rms has been a pub since 1837. Right at the heart of village life, it has arts teams, quiz nights and regular themed food evenings. Five real es are served, two regulars plus three weekly changing guest beers. Home-made pub food is served seven days a week, and in summer there are weekend barbecues in the large beer garden.

Open 12-3 5-11 (Sat 12-3 6.30-11, Sun 12-11) **Bar Meals** L served all week 12-2.30 D served all week 6.30-9 (Sun 12-4, 7-9) Av main course £7 **Restaurant** L served all week 12-2.30 D served all week 6.30-9 (Sun 12-4 7-9) Av 3 course à la carte £15 Abbot IPA, Mighty Oak, Adnams & Guest Beers. **Facilities** Garden Dogs allowed Parking Play Area

GLOUCESTERSHIRE

ALMONDSBURY MAP 04 ST68

The Bowl ★★ HL

16 Church Rd BS32 4DT ☎ 01454 612757 01454 619910

e-mail: reception@thebowlinn.co.uk

web: www.thebowlinn.co.uk

Though The Bowl has been an inn since 1550, it was originally built for a rather more refined purpose: to house monks building the village church. The name itself derives from the shape of the valley around the nearby Severn Estuary. A good choice of meals is available in the bar, while smart Lilies Restaurant offers the likes of baked salmon, crab and asparagus mousse, and butternut squash and parmesan risotto.

Open 11-3 5-11 (Sun 12-10.30) Closed: 25 Dec **Bar Meals** L served all week 12-2.30 D served all week 6-10 (Sun 12-8) Av main course £8.95 **Restaurant** L served all week 12-2.30 D served all week 6-9.30 Av 3 course à la carte £25 Free House Scottish Courage Courage Best, Smiles Best, Wickwar BOB, Moles Best. 9 **Facilities** Garden Dogs allowed Parking **Rooms** 13 bedrooms en suite S£51.50 D£79

ANDOVERSFORD MAP 10 SP01

Pick of the Pubs

The Kilkeney Inn 🍷

Kilkeney GL54 4LN ☎ 01242 820341 📠 01242 820133

dir: *On A436 1m W of Andoversford*

See Pick of the Pubs on opposite page

The Royal Oak Inn 🍷

Old Gloucester Rd GL54 4HR ☎ 01242 820335

e-mail: bleninns@clara.net

dir: *200mtrs from A40, 4m E of Cheltenham*

The Royal Oak stands on the banks of the River Coln, one of a small chain of popular food-centred pubs in the area. Originally a coaching inn, its main dining room, galleried on two levels, occupies the converted former stables. Lunchtime bar fare of various sandwiches, lasagne and ham, egg and chips (for example), extends in the evening to Chinese crispy duck with lime and soy noodles, and roast pork fillet with rosti potato and creamy cider sauce.

Open 11–2.30 5.30–11 **Bar Meals** L served all week 12–2.30 D served all week 7–9.30 Av main course £6.50 **Restaurant** L served all week 12–2.30 D served all week 7–9.30 Av 3 course à la carte £15 Free House Hook Norton Best, Tetleys Bitter, Draught Bass. 🍷 8 **Facilities** Garden Dogs allowed Parking

ARLINGHAM MAP 04 SO71

Pick of the Pubs

The Old Passage Inn ★★★★ RR ◎◎ 🍷

Passage Rd GL2 7JR ☎ 01452 740547 📠 01452 741871

e-mail: oldpassage@ukonline.co.uk

dir: *5m from A38 adjacent M5 junct 13*

The Old Passage was for centuries a ford across the river Severn, and a ferry made the regular crossing here until 1947. Today, this delightful free house is better known for its restaurant, personally supervised by the Moore family. Head Chef Raoul Moore insists on fresh ingredients as the foundation of his fish-led menu: start, perhaps, with potted shrimps, toast and mixed leaves; or butternut and parmesan soup, before moving on to hot fruits de mer; pan-fried skate wing with crushed potatoes; or wild mushroom and asparagus ravioli. For dessert, the range includes lemon and raspberry sorbet with summer berries, Granny Smith tarte Tatin, and a selection of artisan cheeses. Traffic noise at this remote location won't be a problem if you decide to stay overnight, although geese honking their way to the neighbouring Slimbridge bird sanctuary can make a bit of a racket!

Open 12–3 7–11 Closed: 24–30 Dec **Bar Meals** L served Tue–Sun 12–2 D served Tue–Sat 7–9 Av main course £15.50 **Restaurant** L served Tue–Sun 12–2 D served Tue–Sat 7–9 Free House Moles, Wickwar. 🍷 14 **Facilities** Garden Dogs allowed Parking **Rooms** 3 bedrooms en suite S£65 D£95

ASHLEWORTH MAP 10 SO8

Boat Inn 🍷

The Quay GL19 4HZ ☎ 01452 700272 📠 01452 700272

e-mail: elisabeth_nicholls@yahoo.co.uk

This delightful free house with its tiny front parlour, flagstone floors and ancient kitchen range has been in the same family for over 300 years. The pub has a longstanding reputation for real ales, and visitors to the annual summer beer festival can choose from more than 30 different brews. A selection of traditionally filled rolls with home-made tomato chutney forms the hub of the simple but delicious food offering, available only at lunchtimes.

Open 11.30–3 6.30–11 (Winter 7–11) Closed: Mon all day & Wed lunch **Bar Meals** L served Tue–Sun 12–2 Free House Wye Valley, Church End, Arkells, RCH Pitchfork. 🍷 6 **Facilities** Garden Parking **Notes**

Pick of the Pubs

The Queens Arms 🍷

The Village GL19 4HT ☎ 01452 700395

dir: *From Gloucester N on A417 for 5m. At Hartpury, opposite Royal Exchange turn right at Broad St to Ashleworth. Pub 100yds past village green*

This 16th-century inn was given a makeover by the Victorians, but thankfully they left the original beams and iron fireplaces inside. These are now complemented by comfy armchairs and antiques. Outside, the front garden is presided over by two beautifully clipped, 200-year-old yew trees, while a flagstoned patio at the rear is decorated with white cast-iron garden furniture, flower tubs and hanging baskets. The beer list rotates 15 beers, while the bar also stocks 22 malt whiskies and a range of South African wines. The restaurant, which is really two intimate rooms, offers regular pub grub from blackboards. The daily changing specials board is influenced by South Africa, and might feature a main course of tomato bredie, a lamb stew of the Cape Malays; or carpetbagger fillet, a fillet steak stuffed with oysters. Hand-crafted desserts are also worthy of attention.

Open 12–3 7–11 Closed: 25–26 Dec **Bar Meals** L served all week 12–2 D served all week 7–9 (Fri–Sat 7–10) Av main course £12.50 **Restaurant** L served all week 12–2 D served Mon–Sat 7–9 (Fri–Sat 7–10) Av 3 course à la carte £22.50 Free House Shepherd Neame Spitfire, Donnington BB, S A Brain & Company Rev James, Young's Special. 🍷 13 **Facilities** Garden Parking

The Kilkeney Inn

igel and Jean White have owned the Kilkeney Inn on the main road outside Andoversford for a ood few years now, having already run it for two years as managers. It's very much a desirable ace to eat, but beer drinkers are obviously more than welcome and will find real ales served in ood condition.

visit to this charming country ning pub is well worth the drive ıt from Cheltenham, where the lling landscapes stretch away ı all sides. The best views of the otswolds are from the front of e pub and the mature garden at e rear with bench seating; the panse of greenery was originally x individual plots belonging to a rrace of mid–19th century stone ottages. A patio with heaters ıd seating can also be used if e weather permits. Inside, a ood-burning stove warms the eamed bar whenever there's a p in the air, and the atmosphere welcoming and cosy whatever ıe weather. The lunch menu nges from filled ciabattas, herb usages with creamy mash, and warm chicken Caesar salad, to the Kilkeney special: a slow-roasted shoulder of lamb with smashed root vegetables in a rich red wine and mint glaze. For dinner, try a starter of grilled goats' cheese on roasted sweet peppers. This can be followed by marinated breast of cornfed chicken with leeks and sweet potatoes; home-made beef, ale and stilton pie; or a fillet of sea bass on leek mash with a white wine sauce. Chocolate and orange cheesecake, or a basket of figs with raspberry coulis and cream, may appear among the pudding choices. It's best to book for any meal, especially the traditional Sunday lunch, the monthly fish supper, and occasional jazz lunches.

MAP 10 SP01
Kilkeney GL54 4LN
☎ 01242 820341
01242 820133
dir: *On A436 1m W of Andoversford*

Open 11–3 5–11
Bar Meals L served all week 12–2.30 D served all week 6.30–9 Av main course £9
Restaurant L served all week 12–2 D served all week 6.30–9 Av 3 course à la carte £18
Free House
Bombardier, Youngs Best Bitter, St Austells Tribute. 9
Facilities Garden Parking

The Red Hart Inn at Awre

Close to the beautiful River Severn, the setting is ideal for serious hikers, or for those simply seeking a relaxing, attractive place to walk off dinner – there's even a map by the front door for inspiration!

The history of this cosy, traditional free house goes back to 1483, when it was built to house the workmen who were renovating the nearby 10th-century church. The charming interior includes all the hoped-for historic features such as flagstone floors, stone fireplaces, lots of exposed beams, and an original working well, which is now attractively illuminated – it's the kind of atmospheric place where one quick post-walk drink could turn to several, or even a meal. If you do find yourself inclined to dine, rest assured that food is taken seriously here – so much so that a list of all local growers and suppliers is provided on each table. Vegetables are organic when obtainable, and the Awre family supply the inn with beef, lamb and pork, the latter cooked with Severn cider on Sundays. Look out for Red Hart favourites like Gloucester Old Spot sausages with mash and onion gravy; and local beef steak and ale casserole with mushroom mash; and from the carte, pan-roasted breast of chicken with dauphinoise potatoes, mustard and smoked bacon sauce; and chargrilled pork loin with glazed apples, mashed potato and Awre's Severn cider sauce. The four desserts can be enjoyed individually or taken all together on one Awresome plate: crème brûlée, chocolate torte with Bailey's pannacotta; syrup sponge pudding and custard; and apple cheesecake with crumble topping and caramel sauce.

MAP 04 SO70
GL14 1EW
☎ 01594 510220
dir: *E of A48 between Gloucester & Chepstow, access is from Blakeney or Newnham villages*

Open 12-3 6.30-11
Bar Meals L served Wed-Sun 12-2.30 (Summer Tue-Sun) D served Tue-Sat 6.30-9.30 (Summer Mon-Sat) Av main course £7.95
Restaurant L served all week 12-2 D served all week 6-9.30 (Sun 12-2.30, 6-9) Av 3 course à la carte £19.95
Free House
Wye Valley Hereford Pale Ale, Charles Wells' Bombardier, Whittingtons, Archers. 11
Facilities Garden Dogs allowed Parking

AWRE MAP 04 SO70

Pick of the Pubs

The Red Hart Inn at Awre

GL14 1EW ☎ 01594 510220

dir: *E of A48 between Gloucester & Chepstow, access is from Blakeney or Newnham villages*

See Pick of the Pubs on opposite page

BARNSLEY MAP 05 SP00

Pick of the Pubs

The Village Pub

GL7 5EF ☎ 01285 740421 01285 740929

e-mail: reservations@thevillagepub.co.uk

dir: *On B4425 4m NE of Cirencester.*

Light years away from the average local, this stone-built country pub with flagstones, oak floorboards, exposed timbers and open fireplaces has been decorated by internationally renowned interior designer Rupert Charles-Jones. The beautifully restored dining rooms with their eclectic mix of furniture, rug-strewn floors and open fires provide an atmospheric background to the busy free house, which enjoys a reputation as one of the best local eating places. The daily-changing menus are founded on quality ingredients, including locally sourced produce, traceable or organic meats, and fresh seasonal fish. Starters range from celery soup with coco beans to ham hock risotto with truffle oil, and mains from beer battered fish and chips with tartare sauce to grilled rib-eye of beef with salsify, mushrooms and lardons. Typical desserts are pear and almond tart with crème fraîche, and warm rice pudding with poached plums.

Open 11-3.30 6-11 (Open all day Fri, Sat & Sun) **Bar Meals** L served all week 12-2.30 D served all week 7-9.30 (Sat & Sun 12-3, Fri & Sat 7-10) Av main course £12.50 **Restaurant** L served all week 12-2.30 D served all week 7-9.30 (Sat & Sun 12-3, Fri & Sat 7-10) Av 3 course à la carte £24 Free House Hook Norton Bitter, Wadworth 6X, Cotswold Premium, Hoegarden. 12 **Facilities** Children's licence Garden Dogs allowed Parking

BERKELEY MAP 04 ST69

The Malt House ★★★ INN

Marybrook St GL13 9BA ☎ 01453 511177 01453 810257

e-mail: the-malthouse@btconnect.com

dir: *M5 junct 13/14, A38 towards Bristol. Pub on main road towards Sharpness*

Within walking distance of Berkeley Castle and its deer park, this family-run free house is also handy for the Edward Jenner museum, dedicated to the life of the founding father of immunology. Inside the heavily beamed pub you'll find a varied selection of lunchtime bar food, as well as weekly home-made specials. Pub favourites like steak and ale pie rub shoulders with vegetarian stuffed peppers; and grilled halibut, butter and lime.

Open 12-11 **Bar Meals** L served all week 12-2 D served Mon-Sat 6-9 **Restaurant** L served all week 12-2 D served Mon-Sat 6-9 Free House Courage Directors, Old Speckled Hen & Theakstons. **Facilities** Garden Parking **Rooms** 9 bedrooms en suite S£50 D£75

BIBURY MAP 05 SP10

Catherine Wheel

Arlington GL7 5ND ☎ 01285 740250 01285 740779

e-mail: catherinewheel.bibury@eldridge-pope.co.uk

Low-beamed 15th-century pub situated in a Cotswold village described by William Morris as 'the most beautiful in England'. Inside is an original ship's timber beam, as well as various prints and photographs of Old Bibury, and blazing log fires in winter. Traditional pub food includes fresh Bibury trout, salmon and prawns, and tuna steak.

Open 11-11 (Sun 12-10.30) **Bar Meals** L served all week 12-2 D served all week 6-9.30 Av main course £10 **Restaurant** L served all week 12-2 D served all week 6-9 Av 3 course à la carte £20 Eldridge Pope Wadworth 6X, Hook Norton. **Facilities** Garden Dogs allowed Parking

BIRDLIP MAP 10 SO91

The Golden Heart

Nettleton Bottom GL4 8LA

☎ 01242 870261 01242 870599

e-mail: cathstevensgh@aol.com

dir: *On A417 Gloucester to Cirencester. Pub at base of dip in Nettleton Bottom*

A centuries-old Cotswold stone inn sitting in a dip, with absolutely glorious views from its terraced gardens. The regular menu, supplemented by a daily blackboard, includes game, minted lamb steak, pork tenderloin, beef and vegetable pie, ostrich casserole, kangaroo steak and even a crocodile, zebra and rattlesnake mixed grill. For fish fans there's scampi, battered cod and chips, and pan-fried fillet of salmon. Beer-buying policy supports local breweries such as Wickwar, Archers and Goffs.

Open 11-3 5.30-11 (Fri-Sat 11-11, Sun 12-10.30) Closed: Dec 25 **Bar Meals** L served all week 12-3 D served all week 6-10 (Sun 12-10) Av main course £10 **Restaurant** L served all week 12-3 D served all week 6-10 (Sun 12-10) Free House Timothy Taylor Golden Best, Archers Golden, Young's Special, Wickwar Cotswolds Way. 10 **Facilities** Garden Dogs allowed Parking

The Kings Head Inn

Owners Archie and Nicola Orr-Ewing have worked hard to earn an excellent reputation for their free house – one built on well kept real ales, an extensive wine list and wonderful fresh produce in the kitchen.

Ingredients are locally sourced and organic as far as possible, with beef (hung for 21 days) from the family farm and fish delivered fresh from Grimsby. Set back from a perfect Cotswold village green, with its brook and stone bridge, the 16th-century, honey-coloured stone building was once a cider house. Much of the original structure has survived, leaving sturdy beams, low ceilings, flagstone floors, exposed stone walls, and big open fireplaces – all of which have been preserved and enhanced by more recent modernisations. The solid oak furniture and large black kettle hanging in an inglenook are nice touches. In the bar, Hook Norton Best is a mainstay, alongside other real ales, and guests from local micro-breweries. Organic cider and local lagers also make it into the bar, along with over 25 malts. The wine list offers a choice of more than 40 bins, including house wines by the glass. The lunch menu is quite extensive with salads, toasted panini and sandwiches supplemented by serious dishes which may also feature on the dinner menu. Here you will find the likes of roasted lamb chump with fresh herb rôsti, braised red cabbage and rosemary jus; pan-fried sea bass with herb crushed potatoes, purple sprouting broccoli and cucumber and dill relish; and fillet of beef with home-cut chips, garlic mushrooms and roquefort butter sauce. The lovely bedrooms are worth bearing in mind, with six above the pub and six more by the courtyard.

★★★★ INN ◎ 🍷
MAP 10 SP22
The Green OX7 6XQ
☎ 01608 658365
📠 01608 658902
e-mail: kingshead@orr-ewing.com
dir: *On B4450 4m from Stow-on-the-Wold*

Open 11.30–3 6–11 (Wknds & BHs 12–11) Closed: 24–25 Dec
Bar Meals L served all week 12–2 D served all week 7–9 Av main course £11.50
Restaurant L served all week 12–2 D served all week 7–9.30 (Sun & Winter exc Fri/Sat last orders 9)
Free House
Hook Norton Bitter, Shepherd Neam Spitfire, Timothy Taylor Landlord, Adnams. 🍷 8
Facilities Garden Parking
Rooms 12 bedrooms en suite S£55 D£70

BISLEY MAP 04 SO90

The Bear Inn

George St GL6 7BD ☎ 01452 770265
e-mail: kate@bearinnbisley.co.uk
dir: *E of Stroud off B4070*

The 16th-century building was originally a courthouse, and even as a pub The Bear remained a manorial court until 1838. A huge inglenook fireplace, bread oven and old priest hole are outstanding features, and the rock-hewn cellars and 58-foot well are probably Tudor. There are two distinct areas serving meals and drinks, plus a cosy family room. Food includes baguettes, burgers and Bear Essentials such as stuffed pancakes, fish and chips, and steak pie.

Open 12–3 6–11 (Sat 12–11, Sun 12–10.30) **Bar Meals** L served all week 12–2.30 D served Mon–Sat 6–9.30 (Sun lunch all afternoon) Pubmaster Tetley, Flowers IPA, Charles Wells Bombardier & Youngs Special. **Facilities** Garden Dogs allowed Parking

BLEDINGTON MAP 10 SP22

Pick of the Pubs

The Kings Head Inn ★★★★ INN

The Green OX7 6XQ
☎ 01608 658365 01608 658902
e-mail: kingshead@orr-ewing.com
dir: *On B4450 4m from Stow-on-the-Wold*

See Pick of the Pubs on opposite page

BOURTON-ON-THE-HILL MAP 10 SP13

Pick of the Pubs

Horse and Groom

GL56 9AQ ☎ 01386 700413 01386 700413
e-mail: greenstocks@horseandgroom.info
dir: *2m W of Moreton-in-Marsh on A44*

This honey-coloured Grade II-listed Georgian building retains plenty of period charm after its sympathetic refurbishment. Tom and Will Greenstock have created a contemporary feel and a serious dining pub, but also a friendly place for the locals to drink. The bar offers a selection of four cask ales, while the blackboard menu of regularly changing dishes provides plenty of appeal for the most regular of diners. With committed local suppliers backed up by the pub's own vegetable patch, the Horse and Groom's kitchen produces the likes of creamy parsnip soup, or home-made crabcakes with garden leaves; main courses like griddled Dexter rump steak with green peppercorn and tarragon butter, or pan-roasted stuffed duck breast with braised red cabbage; and puds (to use their own terminology) of apple and blueberry flapjack crumble, or vanilla pannacotta with home-grown raspberries in season. In summer, enjoy the mature garden with panoramic hilltop views.

Open 11–3 6–11 Closed: 25 Dec **Bar Meals** L served Tue–Sat 12–2 Av main course £12 **Restaurant** L served Tue–Sat 12–2 (Sun 12–2.30) D served Mon–Sat 7–9 (Fri–Sat 7–9.30) Av 3 course à la carte £25 Free House Everards Tiger, Hook Norton Hooky, & Dorothy Goodbody-Wye Valley. 9 **Facilities** Garden Parking

CHEDWORTH MAP 05 SP01

Hare & Hounds ★★★★ INN

Foss Cross GL54 4NN ☎ 01285 720288 01285 720488
e-mail: stay@hareandhoundsinn.com
web: www.hareandhoundsinn.com
dir: *On A429 (Fosse Way), 6m from Cirencester*

A 14th-century inn with various interconnecting dining areas often described as a rabbit warren. Open fires, beams and stone and polished wood floors add to the charm. It's ideally placed for touring the Cotswolds or attending Cheltenham race meetings. There's a daily changing blackboard, along with a menu typically listing breast of Gressingham duck; baked fillet of cod; and Burmese vegetable tofu curry.

Open 11–3 6–12 **Bar Meals** L served all week 12–2.30 D served all week 7–9.45 (Sun 12–3, 7–9) Av main course £12.95 **Restaurant** L served all week 11–2.30 D served all week 6.30–9.45 (Sun 12–3, 7–9) Av 3 course à la carte £15.95 Arkells Arkells 3B & JRA 2B. 10 **Facilities** Garden Dogs allowed Parking **Rooms** 10 bedrooms en suite S£60 D£75

Pick of the Pubs

Seven Tuns

Queen St GL54 4AE
☎ 01285 720242 01285 720933
e-mail: theseventuns@clara.co.uk
dir: *Exit A429 at junct to Chedworth.*

Directly opposite this creeper-covered, unmistakably Cotswold inn, are a waterwheel, a spring and a raised terrace for summer dining. The pub dates back to the 17th century, and the name derives from the seven chimney pots that deck the roof. The

CONTINUED

CHEDWORTH continued

lunch menu offers nothing too heavy – sandwiches, ploughman's, jacket potatoes and appealing Mediterranean dishes like croque monsieur, tagliatelle bolognese or minted lamb kebabs. In the evening, try chorizo, new potato and goats' cheese salad; Mexican spiced chicken supreme with avocado and tomato salsa; or home-made sage, redcurrant and beef burgers. Pudding lovers will be delighted by crunchy raspberry ripple terrine; raisin and honey bread and butter pudding; and chocolate tart with Cointreau sauce. In the beer garden there's a revolving South African barbecue and a renovated skittle alley. Handy for visiting nearby Chedworth Roman Villa, which can be reached on foot.

Open 12–3 6–11 (Sat 12–2, Sun 12–10.30) (July - Aug all day) **Bar Meals** L served all week 12–3 D served all week 6.30–9.30 Av main course £9.95 **Restaurant** L served all week 12–2.30 D served all week 6.30–9.30 (Sat 12–3, Sun 12–3, 6–9) Av 3 course à la carte £19.50 Young's Bitter, Winter Warmer, Waggledance, St Georges. 12 **Facilities** Garden Dogs allowed Parking

CHIPPING CAMPDEN MAP 10 SP13

The Bakers Arms

Broad Campden GL55 6UR ☎ 01386 840515

dir: *1m from Chipping Camden*

A small Cotswold inn with exposed stone walls, beams, an inglenook fireplace and a good atmosphere. Reasonably priced meals are served, with a choice of four, maybe five, real ales. At lunchtime there are sandwiches, warm baguettes and filled giant Yorkshire puddings, although you could also choose lamb shank, beef and Guinness pie, smoked haddock bake, or mushroom and mascarpone lasagne. These and plenty of other dishes are available in the evenings too.

Open 11.30–2.30 4.45–11 (Sun 12–10.30, Summer 11.30–11) Closed: 25 Dec **Bar Meals** L served all week 12–2 D served all week 6–9 (Apr–Oct 12–9) Av main course £6.95 **Restaurant** L served all week 12–2 D served all week 6–9 Free House Stanway Bitter, Bombardier, Timothy Taylor Landlord, Donnington BB. **Facilities** Garden Dogs allowed Parking Play Area **Notes**

Pick of the Pubs

Eight Bells

Church St GL55 6JG

☎ 01386 840371 01386 841669

e-mail: neilhargreaves@bellinn.fsnet.co.uk

This delightful little free house was built in the 14th century to house stonemasons working on the nearby church and to store the eight church bells. A cobbled entranceway leads into two atmospheric bars that retain the original oak beams, open fireplaces and a priest's hole. In summer, the exterior is hung with flower baskets, and guests spill out into the enclosed courtyard or the beautiful terraced garden that overlooks the almshouses and church. Freshly prepared local food is offered in the bar or the modern dining room. Try salads or hearty sandwiches on freshly baked bread for lunch, or order from the main menu (available lunch and evening) which offers a modern take on traditional pub food: perhaps gammon steak on Catalan bean casserole; or lamb and coriander burger with French fries and feta salad. You could finish with lemon posset with red berry coulis or apple strudel.

Eight Bells

Open 12–11 Closed: 25 Dec **Bar Meals** L served all week 12–2.30 D served all week 6.30–9.30 (Mon–Thu 6.30–9) Av main course £12 **Restaurant** L served all week 12–2.30 D served all week 6.30–9.30 (Mon–Thu 6.30–9) Av 3 course à la carte £23 Free House Hook Norton Best, Goff's Jouster, Marston Pedigree, Purity UBU & Guest Beers. 8 **Facilities** Garden Dogs allowed **Rooms** 7 bedrooms en suite S£55 D£80 (★★★★ INN)

The Kings ★★★★ GA

The Square GL55 6AW ☎ 01386 840256 01386 841598

e-mail: info@kingscampden.co.uk

Set in the square of this pretty Cotswold town, the smart 17th-century inn has an air of relaxed elegance. There are plenty of snacks, but the full menu offers some imaginative delights: tournedos Rossini with home-made chicken liver paté in a rich Madeira wine sauce; dressed crab with shell on prawns; or a gateaux of herb polenta cakes, mozzarella and plum tomatoes. Seafish comes fresh from Brixham daily. Have a look at the specials board for more choices, and take in some lovely artwork by a local painter.

Open 9–11 Closed: 25 Dec **Bar Meals** L served all week 12–2.30 D served all week 6.30–9.30 (Sat–Sun 12–3) **Restaurant** L served all week 12–2.30 D served all week 6.30–9.30 (Sat–Sun 12–3) Free House Hook Norton Best. **Facilities** Garden Dogs allowed Parking **Rooms** 12 bedrooms en suite S£75.50 D£100

Pick of the Pubs

Noel Arms Hotel ★★★ HL

High St GL55 6AT ☎ 01386 840317 01386 841136

e-mail: reception@noelarmshotel.com

dir: *On High St, opposite Town Hall*

The Noel Arms was originally a coaching inn, dating from the 1600s, and the car park is the former coaching yard accessed through the archway at the front of the building. Original oak beams and an open fire create a cosy atmosphere in the Dover's Bar, where guests can enjoy real beers and lagers from two local breweries. Produce served in both the bar and restaurant is sourced from local farms and dairies. Lunchtime sandwiches, Double Gloucester rarebit, freshly baked quiche and slow braised lamb shank are typical bar options, but you will also find authentic oriental dishes prepared by the Sri Lankan sous chef. These occur too in the restaurant selection, where chicken satay and Sri Lankan black lamb curry sit alongside pan-seared fillet of Cotswold beef, or cod with chive cream sauce. There are 26 en suite bedrooms including one with a magnificent 17th-century carved bed.

Open 11–10 (Sun 12–11) **Bar Meals** L served all week 12–2.30 D served all week 6–9.30 Av main course £13 **Restaurant** L served all week 12–2.30 D served all week 7–9.30 Av 3 course à la carte £25 Free House Hook Norton Best Bitter, Carling, Guinness. 10 **Facilities** Garden Dogs allowed Parking **Rooms** 26 bedrooms en suite S£95 D£130

he Volunteer Inn

wer High St GL55 6DY

01386 840688 01386 840543

mail: saravol@aol.com

00-year-old inn where, in the mid-19th-century, the able-bodied ed to sign up for the militia. Ramblers can set off from here to walk Cotswold Way. Unusually, there is a takeaway food menu, featuring me-made burger with coleslaw and fries; and spinach, ricotta d basil lasagne with a herby tomato sauce. The in-house menus, pplemented by daily specials, feature the likes of honey and ginger ef with stir-fried vegetables and crispy noodles.

en 11–11 (Nov–Mar weekdays 12–3, 5–11) **Bar Meals** L served all ek 12–2.30 (Sun 12–3) Av main course £8 **Restaurant** L served all ek 12–2.30 12–2.30 (Sun 12–3) Av 3 course à la carte £16 Free use Hook Norton, London Pride, Archers, Goffs & Carling. 12 **cilities** Garden Dogs allowed Play Area

INDERFORD — MAP 10 SO61

he New Inn NEW ★★★ INN

0 Ruspidge Rd, Ruspidge GL14 3AR 01594 824508

mail: thenewinnruspidge@fsmail.net

r: *1.5m from Cinderford*

raditional country pub in the heart of the Forest of Dean, The w Inn serves as a popular village local while also offering a warm lcome to visitors from further afield. A good selection of home-de pub food includes grilled steaks, an impressive choice of curries, d vegetarian dishes such as home-made spicy chilli, or butternut uash and ginger bake. Lunch is served by arrangement.

en 5–11 (Sun & BH 12–11) **Bar Meals** L served all week 5–10 D served week 5–10 Av main course £6.95 Free House 10 **Facilities** Garden gs allowed Parking **Rooms** 2 bedrooms en suite S£30 D£60

CIRENCESTER — MAP 05 SP00

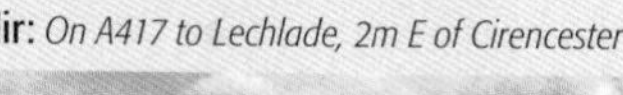

Pick of the Pubs

The Crown of Crucis ★★★ HL

Ampney Crucis GL7 5RS

01285 851806 01285 851735

e-mail: info@thecrownofcrucis.co.uk

dir: *On A417 to Lechlade, 2m E of Cirencester*

This 16th-century inn stands beside the Ampney brook in picturesque Ampney Crucis at the gateway to the Cotswolds. The name 'Crucis' refers to the Latin cross in the nearby churchyard. The inn itself retains its historical charm while feeling comfortably up-to-date. It overlooks the village cricket green, and on summer days the evocative sound of willow on leather and the quiet stream meandering past the lawns conspire to create a perfect picture of quintessential England. Bar food is served all day, with choices ranging from snacks and salads to comforting meals such as the award-winning home-made steak and kidney pie. The restaurant menu offers starters of carpaccio of beef with roast aubergines; and chicken skewers with lime and coriander marinade, followed perhaps by breast of guinea fowl and confit leg wrapped in pancetta with a celery and cranberry sauce. Typical desserts include crème brûlée and sticky toffee pudding.

Open 10.30–11 Closed: 25 Dec **Bar Meals** L served all week 12–10 D served all week 12–10 Av main course £7.50 **Restaurant** L served all week 12–2.30 D served all week 7–9.30 Av 3 course à la carte £19 Free House Doom Bar, Archers Village, Scottish Courage John Smith's. 10 **Facilities** Garden Dogs allowed Parking **Rooms** 25 bedrooms en suite S£60 D£80

CLIFFORD'S MESNE — MAP 10 SO72

Pick of the Pubs

The Yew Tree

Clifford Mesne GL18 1JS

01531 820719 01531 820912

e-mail: cass@yewtreeinn.com

dir: *From Newent High Street follow signs to Clifford's Mesne. Pub at far end of village on road to Glasshouse.*

See Pick of the Pubs on page 227

England

COATES MAP 04 SO90

Pick of the Pubs

The Tunnel House Inn

GL7 6PW ☎ 01285 770280 01285 770120

e-mail: info@tunnelhouse.com

dir: *Leave Cirencester on A433 towards Tetbury, after 2m turn right towards Coates, follow signs to Canal Tunnel & Inn.*

See Pick of the Pubs on page 228

COLESBOURNE MAP 10 SP01

Pick of the Pubs

The Colesbourne Inn

GL53 9NP ☎ 01242 870376

e-mail: info@thecolesbourneinn.co.uk

dir: *Midway between Cirencester & Cheltenham on A435.*

A handsome 17th-century stone pub on the Colesbourne estate at the heart of the Cotswolds, set between the historic towns of Cheltenham and Cirencester. It is ideally placed for exploring the villages and gentle, very English countryside of Gloucestershire. Nearby is the source of the River Thames, which can be reached on foot along delightful field and meadow paths. Dating back to 1827 and set in two acres of grounds, the Colesbourne Inn has been sympathetically restored over the years. Among the distinguishing features are a host of beams, roaring log fires, four separate dining areas, and a superb terrace and garden with stunning rural views. There is even a side entrance from the bar originally used as a chamber for smoking ham. Food is all important at the Colesbourne Inn, its reputation for excellent quality menus greatly enhanced by the appointment of licensee and chef Richard Johnson, who previously worked at Aubergine and the Oxo Tower. Fresh local produce is used wherever possible, and there is an appetising range of light bites.

Open 11-3 6-11 (Sat-Sun 11-11) (Nov-Feb 12-11) **Bar Meals** L served all week 12-1.45 D served all week 6-8.45 (Sat-Sun 12-2.30, Fri-Sat 6-9.30) Av main course £9.95 **Restaurant** L served all week 12-1.45 D served all week 6-8.45 (Sat-Sun 12-2.30, Fri-Sat 6-9.30) Wadworth Wadworth 6X, Henrys IPA, Bishops Tipple, Summersault. 20 **Facilities** Garden Dogs allowed Parking Play Area **Rooms** 9 bedrooms en suite S£55 D£75 (★★★ INN)

COLN ST ALDWYNS MAP 05 SP1

The New Inn At Coln ★★

GL7 5AN ☎ 01285 750651 01285 750657

e-mail: stay@new-inn.co.uk

dir: *Between Bibury (B4425) & Fairford (A417), 8m E of Cirencester*

The New Inn's creeper-covered façade is a welcoming sight amongst the Cotswold stone buildings of this pretty village. Flagstone floors, exposed beams and open fires characterise the bars, while outside there is a delightful flower-filled courtyard. The stylish restaurant offe acclaimed cooking: you might begin a meal with salmon and crab tartare and a caper mousse, then move on to roasted poussin with caramelized baby onions, sautéed green beans and a lardon jus.

Open 11-11 (Sun 12-10.30) **Bar Meals** L served all week 12-2 D served all week 7-9 (Sun 12-2.30, Fri-Sat 7-9.30) Av main course £9.50 **Restaurant** L served Sun 12-2 (Sun 12-2.30) D served all week 7-9 (Fri-Sat 7-9.30 Free House Hook Norton Best Bitter, Wadworth 6X, Donningtons BB. **Facilities** Garden Dogs allowed Parkin **Rooms** 14 bedrooms en suite S£109 D£126

COWLEY MAP 10 SO9

Pick of the Pubs

The Green Dragon Inn ★★★★ INN

Cockleford GL53 9NW

☎ 01242 870271 01242 870171

A handsome stone-built inn dating from the 17th century and located in the Cotswold hamlet of Cockleford. The fittings and furniture are the work of the 'Mouse Man of Kilburn' (so-called for his trademark mouse) who lends his name to the popular Mouse Bar, with its stone-flagged floors, beamed ceilings and crackling log fires. The weekly menu includes sandwiches at lunchtime, children's favourites, and a choice of starters/light meals such as smoked haddock chowder or Caesar salad. Typical fish dishes may include fillet of mackerel on ciabatta; stir-fried smoked eel with black beans and spring onions; Green Dragon fish pie; and blue swimming crab omelette. Other important features are the choice of real ales, with a monthly guest beer; the heated dining terrace; and the function room/skittle alley. Very popular at weekends.

Open 11-11 (Sun 12-10.30) Rest: 25-26 Dec, 1 Jan (closed 12-4) **Bar Meals** L served all week 12-2.30 D served all week 6-10.30 (Sat 12-3, 6-10 Sun 12-3.30, 6-9) Av main course £12.50 Free House Hook Norton, Directors, Butcombe, Guest ale. 9 **Facilities** Children's licence Garden Dogs allowed Parking **Rooms** 9 bedrooms en suite S£57 D£70

The Yew Tree

the 16th century this pretty old inn was a cider house, and in keeping with its history it still ocks a good range of local cider and perry. It's situated on the slopes of the National Trust's ay Hill.

ere you to climb to the 971ft mmit you would be able to impse the bluish outlines of e Welsh Mountains, Malvern ills and the River Severn. After years spent running a pub in ıckinghamshire, Caroline Todd me here in 2004 for what she oped would be 'a quieter life'. aditional bars are floored with ıarry tiles, and warmed by a ackling log fire. The simple pealing menu changes daily and fers a range of traditional pub shes. You could start with game ver paté with toasted brioche; arcuterie salad with fresh figs; mussels in saffron and cider, epending on what the season has offer. Follow up with fisherman's e; rabbit and bacon pudding; ixed cheese, vegetable and pine nut brioche; or a chargrilled Gloucester Old Spot loin steak. Walkers on a quest for a good Sunday lunch will be delighted by roast sirloin of local beef, followed by a bowl of steamed marmalade pudding with custard – an excellent conclusion to a morning's tramping. The wine list is lengthy, detailed and entirely French, taking in the best of regional specialities. Look out for the cider and perry festival in March, and the in-house wine shop, which sells bottles imported from France under the name of Premier Crew wines.

MAP 10 SO72
GL18 1JS
☎ 01531 820719
01531 820912
e-mail: cass@yewtreeinn.com
dir: *From Newent High Street follow signs to Clifford's Mesne. Pub at far end of village on road to Glasshouse.*

Open 12–2.30 6–11 (Sun 12–4)
Bar Meals L served Wed–Sat 12–2 D served Tue–Sat 6–9 (Sun 12–4) Av main course £10
Free House
Wye Valley Butty Bach, Fuller's London Pride, Wye Valley Best, Whittingtons Nine Lives. 8
Facilities Garden Dogs allowed Parking Play Area

The Tunnel House Inn

Between the Cotswold villages of Coates and Tarlton, the Tunnel House Inn enjoys a glorious rural location down a very bumpy track by Sapperton Tunnel on the Thames and Severn Canal; it once provided accommodation for canal construction workers, and is not far from the source of the Thames.

It was rebuilt in 1957 after a fire, and the bar has some oddities, including an upside-down table on the ceiling. In the summer or on warm spring and autumn days the garden is an ideal place for relaxing with a drink or a meal, and enjoying the views across the fields. Three log fires warm the welcoming bar in the winter months. A children's play area and spectacular walks in the surrounding countryside add to its popularity. The menu, which boasts a range of good home cooking using fresh and local produce wherever possible, is updated monthly to make the most of seasonal variety. You can dine in the restaurant area or relax in the comfortable seating in the bar. Eat lightly at lunchtime with sandwiches (bacon and brie, coronation chicken), or ploughman's. Alternatively choose from starters like moules marinière, or Gloucester Old Spot sausage with mashed potato, red onion marmalade and gravy; or spinach and ricotta cannelloni. In the evening the choices change slightly to include oven-baked field mushroom stuffed with red onion confit, spinach and blue cheese; lamb chops with rosemary roasted new potatoes, vegetables and gravy; grilled goats' cheese with crispy bacon and pinenut salad; and pan-fried calves' liver and bacon with creamy mash and onion gravy. For children there are the usual favourites: sausage and mash, fish and chips and chicken goujans.

MAP 04 SO90
GL7 6PW
☎ 01285 770280
Fax 01285 770120
e-mail: info@tunnelhouse.com
dir: *Leave Cirencester on A433 towards Tetbury, after 2m turn right towards Coates, follow signs to Canal Tunnel & Inn.*

Open 11–3 6–11 (Open all day Fri–Sun)
Bar Meals L served all week 12–2.15 D served all week 6.45–9.15
Uley Old Spot, Uley Bitter, Wye Valley Bitter, Archers Village.
Facilities Children's licence Garden Dogs allowed Parking Play Area

RANHAM MAP 10 SO81

he Black Horse Inn

.4 8HP ☎ 01452 812217

r: *A46 towards Stroud, follow signs for Cranham*

in a small village surrounded by woodland and commons, a mile m the Cotswold Way and Prinknash Abbey, this is a traditional inn h two open fires and two dining rooms upstairs. On the menu you'll d all sorts of pies, as well as chops, gammon, salads, casseroles and ariety of fish dishes including grilled salmon, and trout with garlic d herb butter. There's quite a bit of Morris dancing throughout the son, with the sloping garden offering lovely views across the valley.

en 12-3 6.30-11 (Sun 8-10.30) Closed: 25 Dec **Bar Meals** L served -Sun 12-2 D served Tue-Sun 6.45-9 Av main course £9 Free House Wickwar Brand Oak, Archers, Golden Train & Village, Hancocks HB & est Beers. **Facilities** Garden Parking

IDMARTON MAP 04 ST88

Pick of the Pubs

The Kings Arms ★★★★ INN

he Street GL9 1DT ☎ 01454 238245 01454 238249

-mail: bookings@kingsarmsdidmarton.co.uk

dir: *M4 junct 18, A46 N signed Stroud, after 8m A433 signed Didmarton 2m*

his attractively restored 17th-century coaching inn is locally amous for its annual Rook Night Supper, held after the cull on the prawling Badminton Estate. The building was originally held on 1,000-year lease from the Beaufort family at a rent of sixpence year. Today, the Edwardian-style interior is cosy and welcoming ll year round, especially when the big open fires are blazing way in winter. Both bars support local breweries, and 10 wines re available by the glass. The weekly changing seasonal menu night include smoked chicken and Moroccan salad or goats' heese and red onion charlotte, followed by wild mushroom and ed pepper tagliatelle; 10oz rib-eye steak on crushed new potato vith pepper sauce; or roast haunch of Badminton venison with utter onion mash. Fish dishes might be home-smoked scallops vith a pancetta and pinenut salad; monkfish with lime and banana urry, or red snapper with a sweet tomato and prawn risotto. The eautiful, large enclosed gardens incorporate a boules pitch.

Open 11-11.30 (Fri-Sat 11-11 Sun 12-10.30) **Bar Meals** L served ll week 12-2.30 D served all week 6-9 (Sun 7-9) Av main course 10 **Restaurant** L served all week 12-2.30 D served all week 6-9 v 3 course à la carte £21 Free House Uley Bitter, Otter, Moles rewery, Hook Norton. 10 **Facilities** Garden Dogs allowed arking **Rooms** 4 bedrooms en suite S£55 D£80

FORD MAP 10 SP02

Pick of the Pubs

The Plough Inn ★★★★ INN

GL54 5RU ☎ 01386 584215 01386 584042

e-mail: info@theploughinnatford.co.uk

dir: *4m from Stow-on-the-Wold on Tewkesbury road*

See Pick of the Pubs on page 230

FOSSEBRIDGE MAP 05 SP01

Pick of the Pubs

The Inn at Fossebridge

GL54 3JS ☎ 01285 720721 01285 720793

e-mail: info@fossebridgeinn.co.uk

dir: *From M4 junct 15, A419 towards Cirencester, then A429 towards Stow. Pub approx 7m on left*

This attractive family-run free house in the heart of the Coln Valley is ideal for visiting Bibury, Northleach and Chedworth. There's a relaxed and informal ambience here, which never undermines standards of comfort and service. The atmospheric Bridge Bar and Restaurant is located in the oldest part of the building dating back to the 15th century. Exposed beams, stone walls, flagstone floors and open fires provide the setting for the varied bar food and restaurant menus. Bar snacks range from sandwiches, baguettes and jacket potatoes to light meals, whilst the ever-changing specials board might feature steak and ale pie; or pan-fried sardines with chunky tomato sauce. The main menu offers additional choices like vegetable lasagne with garlic bread; and seared swordfish on tomato and parsley salsa with new potatoes – but leave room for tempting desserts like warm treacle tart with clotted cream.

Open 12-12 (Sun 12-11.30) **Bar Meals** L served all week 12-3 D served all week 6-10 (Sun 6-9.30) **Restaurant** L served all week 12-3 D served all week 6-10 (Sun 6-9.30) Free House Youngs, Hooky, Old Hooky & 6X. 8 **Facilities** Garden Dogs allowed Parking

The Plough Inn

Tucked away in the hamlet of Ford, this 16th-century inn is ideally situated for explorations of all that the Cotswolds have to offer. Fans of countryside activities will be particularly well serve here.

The Plough regularly hosts shooting lunches, fishing is available nearby and Cheltenham racecourse is but a short drive, while the famous racing stables of Jackdaws Castle are just across the street. Inside, the inn is steeped in history and character, providing all that one associates with a traditional English pub, from flagstone floors and log fires, to sturdy pine furnishings and lively conversation. In one of its earlier incarnations, the inn served as a local courthouse, with cellars being used as cells for sheep-stealers. Under the rear lounge window are the remnants of the indoor stocks that once held miscreants – these days seating arrangements are more hospitable! Interestingly, the literal meaning of the phrase 'you're barred' becomes clear when one sees another relic of the past – the bar that was once used to reinforce the door when court was in session. Meals made from local produce are cooked to order, and the inn is renowned for its fresh, seasonal asparagus supper. Seafood is also something of a speciality: try sea bass on a bed of wild mushroom risotto; smoked haddock with poached egg and cheese sauce; beer-battered cod; or a sumptuous lemon sole filled with crab and lobster bisque. Visitors can stay in three well-converted en suite bedrooms in what was once a stable block and hayloft.

★★★★ INN 🍷
MAP 10 SP02
GL54 5RU
☎ 01386 584215
📠 01386 584042
e-mail:
info@theploughinnatford.co.uk
dir: *4m from Stow-on-the-Wold on Tewkesbury road*

Open 11–12 (Fri–Sat 11am–1am)
Closed: 25 Dec
Bar Meals L served all week 12–2 D served all week 6.30–9 (Wknds 12–9)
Restaurant L served all week 11.30–2 D served all week 6.30–9 (Wknds 11.30–9)
Donnington
Donnington BB, SBA & XXX.
🍷 7
Facilities Garden Parking Play Area
Rooms 3 bedrooms en suite S£40 D£70

RAMPTON MANSELL MAP 04 SO90

Pick of the Pubs

The Crown Inn ★★★★ INN

GL6 8JG ☎ 01285 760601 01285 760601
e-mail: thecrown@vernons.name
dir: *A419 halfway between Cirencester & Stroud*

This 17th-century inn stands in the heart of the unspoilt village of Frampton Mansell and has views over the beautiful wooded Golden Valley. The interior is full of old world charm, with honey-coloured stone walls, beams, and open fireplaces where log fires are lit in winter. There is also plenty of seating in the large garden for the warmer months. Fresh local food with lots of seasonal specials, real ales and a good choice of wines by the glass are served in the restaurant and three inviting bars. Representative dishes include poached smoked haddock with parsley risotto and poached egg, and fillet of wild venison with apples and blackberries, served with fondant potatoes and red cabbage sauerkraut. There are some wonderful walks and cycling routes in the surrounding countryside, and the royal residences of Highgrove and Gatcombe Park are in the neighbourhood.

Open 12–11 (Sun 12–10.30) **Bar Meals** L served all week 12–10 D served all week 12–10 (Sun 12–9) Av main course £10 **Restaurant** L served all week 12–10 D served all week 12–10 (Sun 12–9) Av 3 course à la carte £25.30 Free House Bombardier, Fosters, San Miguel, Kronenbourg Blanc. 12 **Facilities** Garden Parking **Rooms** 12 bedrooms en suite S£50 D£80

Pick of the Pubs

The White Horse

Cirencester Rd GL6 8HZ ☎ 01285 760960
e-mail: emmawhitehorse@aol.com
dir: *6m from Cirencester towards Stroud on A419*

Seagrass flooring and original artwork on the walls gives this smart dining pub a fresh, inviting feel. The White Horse has a growing reputation for modern British food, and offers a warm welcome even if all you want is a quiet drink. A large sofa and comfy chairs encourage the latter, whilst the daily-changing menu will please discerning appetites. The large seawater tank ensures a good supply of fresh seafood, with oysters, clams, mussels and lobsters available in season. Restaurant diners might select potted shrimp from the monthly changing menus, before moving on to noisettes of lamb stuffed with apricots and served with chorizo mash; Cornish lobster; or slow braised pork belly with bubble and squeak. Steamed marmalade pudding with crème anglaise is a typical dessert. A good-value fixed price menu is proving highly popular, and a lengthy, thoughtful wine list will delight oeniphiles.

Open 11–3 6–11 Closed: 24–26 Dec, Jan 1 **Bar Meals** L served Mon–Sat 12–2.30 (Sun 12–3) D served Mon–Sat Av main course £8.95 **Restaurant** L served all week 12–2.30 (Sun 12–3) D served Mon–Sat 7–9.45 Av 3 course à la carte £24 Av 2 course fixed price £15.25 Free House Uley Bitter, Hook Norton Best, Arkells Summer Ale. 10 **Facilities** Garden Dogs allowed Parking

GLOUCESTER MAP 10 SO81

Queens Head

Tewkesbury Rd, Longford GL2 9EJ
☎ 01452 301882 01452 524368
e-mail: queenshead@aol.com
dir: *On A38 in Longford*

This 250 year-old pub/restaurant is just out of town but there's no missing it in summer when it is festooned with hanging baskets. Inside, there's a lovely old flagstone-floored locals' bar which proffers a great range of real ales, while two dining areas tempt with tasty menus. These may include beef stroganoff, or the pub's signature dish, Longford lamb – a kilo joint slowly cooked in mint gravy until it falls off the bone.

Open 11–3 5.30–11 **Bar Meals** L served all week 12–2 D served all week 6.30–9.30 **Restaurant** L served all week 12–2 D served all week 6.30–9.30 Free House Ringwood, Landlord, Pigswill, Butty Bach. 8 **Facilities** Parking

GREAT BARRINGTON MAP 10 SP21

The Fox

OX18 4TB ☎ 01451 844385
e-mail: info@foxinnbarrington.co.uk
dir: *3m W on A40 from Burford, N signed The Barringtons, 0.5m on right.*

Picturesque pub with a delightful patio and large beer garden overlooking the River Windrush – on warm days a perfect summer watering hole. Very popular with those attending Cheltenham racecourse. Built of mellow Cotswold stone and characterised by low ceilings and log fires, the inn offers a range of well-kept Donnington beers and a choice of food which might include beef in ale pie, local pigeon breasts casseroled with button mushrooms, chicken piri-piri, Thai tuna steak, and spinach, leek and chestnut pie.

Open 11–11 Closed: 25 Dec **Bar Meals** L served all week 12–2.30 D served all week 6.30–9.30 (Sat–Sun 12–9.30) Av main course £10 **Restaurant** L served all week 12–2.30 D served all week 6.30–9.30 (Sat–Sun 12–9.30) Av 3 course à la carte £20 Donnington Donnington BB, SBA. 7 **Facilities** Garden Dogs allowed Parking

GREAT RISSINGTON MAP 10 SP11

The Lamb Inn 🍷

GL54 2LP ☎ 01451 820388 📠 01451 820724
e-mail: enquiries@thelambinn.com
dir: *Between Oxford & Cheltenham off A40*

Make this delightful former farmhouse your base for exploring the picturesque Cotswold countryside on foot and touring the region's famous old towns by car. Among the attractions at this busy inn, some of which dates back 300 years, are part of a Wellington bomber which crashed in the garden in 1943, and a specially installed OS map of the area helpful for walkers. Home-cooked pub food might include pork loin steak on a mustard mash with apple and sage sauce, tagliatelle with spinach, blue cheese and pine nut cream, or chargrilled salmon, tuna and red mullet on noodles.

Open 11.30–2.30 6.30–11 **Bar Meals** L served all week 12–2 (Sat–Sun 12–2.30) D served all week 7–9.30 Av main course £8.95 **Restaurant** L served all week 12–2 D served all week 7–9.30 Free House Hook Norton, John Smiths & Guest ale. 🍷 9 **Facilities** Garden Dogs allowed Parking Play Area **Rooms** 14 bedrooms en suite S£50 D£70 (★★★★ INN)

GREET MAP 10 SP03

The Harvest Home 🍷

Evesham Rd GL54 5BH ☎ 01242 602430
dir: *M5 junct 9, A435 towards Evesham, B4077 & B4078 towards Winchcombe, 200yds from station.*

Set in the beautiful Cotswold countryside, this traditional country inn draws steam train enthusiasts aplenty, as a restored stretch of the Great Western Railway runs past the end of the garden. Built around 1903 for railway workers, the pub is handy for Cheltenham Racecourse and Sudeley Castle. Expect a good range of snacks and mains, including locally-reared beef and tempting seafood dishes.

Open 12–3 6–11 (Sun 6–10.30) **Bar Meals** L served all week 12–2 D served all week 6–9 Av main course £8 **Restaurant** L served all week 12–2 D served all week 6–9 Av 3 course à la carte £16.50 Av 2 course fixed price £5.95 Enterprise Inns Old Speckled Hen, Goff's Jouster, Deuchars IPA, Carling & Strongbow. 🍷 11 **Facilities** Children's licence Garden Dogs allowed Parking

GUITING POWER MAP 10 SP0

The Hollow Bottom ★★★ INN 🍷

GL54 5UX ☎ 01451 850392 📠 01451 850945
e-mail: hello@hollowbottom.com

There's a horse-racing theme at this 18th-century Cotswold free hous often frequented by the Cheltenham racing fraternity. Its nooks and crannies lend themselves to an intimate drink or meal, and there's als a separate dining room, plus outside tables for fine weather. Specials include prawn cocktail on seasonal leaves with a spicy tomato sauce; grilled salmon; breast of pan-fried chicken with stilton, olive oil, toma and spring onion; and home-made raspberry cheesecake to finish.

Open 11–12.30 **Bar Meals** L served all week 12 D served all week 9.30 Av main course £10 **Restaurant** L served all week 12 D served all week 9.30 Free House Hollow Bottom Best Bitter, Goff's Jouster, Timothy Taylor Landlord, Fullers London Pride. 🍷 7 **Facilities** Children's licence Garden Dogs allowed Parking **Rooms** 4 bedrooms 3 en suite

HINTON MAP 04 ST7

The Bull Inn 🍷

SN14 8HG ☎ 0117 9372332
dir: *From M4 junct 18, A46 to Bath 1m, turn right 1m, down hil Pub on right*

Since it was built in the 17th century, The Bull has been an inn, a farr and a dairy. Inside it retains two inglenook fireplaces and original flagstone flooring, while outside there's a front-facing terrace and a large rear garden with a children's play area. Food served in the restaurant and bar draws on locally supplied produce and home-grov fruit and vegetables. Look out for house specialities such as truffle an chive potato pancake.

Open 12–3 6–11 (Sun 7–10.30) **Bar Meals** L served Tue–Sun 12–2 D served all week 6–9 (Fri–Sat 6–9.30, Sun 12–3, 7–8.30) Av main course £10 **Restaurant** L served Tue–Sun 12–2 D served all week 6–9 (Fri–Sat 9.30, Sun 7–8.30) Av 3 course à la carte £21.50 Wadworth Wadwor 6X & Henrys IPA, Wadworth Bishops Tipple, Wadworth Summersault plus Guest ale. 🍷 12 **Facilities** Garden Dogs allowed Parking Play Area

England

ECHLADE ON THAMES MAP 05 SU29

he Trout Inn

Johns Bridge GL7 3HA
01367 252313 01367 252313
mail: chefpjw@aol.com
r: *From A40, A361 then A417. From M4 to Lechlade then A417*

ating from around 1220, a former almshouse with a large garden on e banks of the Thames. Things are generally humming here, with ctor and steam events, and jazz and folk festivals. The interior is all gstone floors and beams in a bar that overflows into the old boat-use. Appetising small snacks, and dishes like pork fillet in a stilton d bacon sauce, and supreme of salmon with warm hollandaise uce are all on offer.

pen 10–3 6–11 (Open all day summer) Closed: 25 Dec **r Meals** L served all week 12–2 D served all week 7–10 (Sun 7–9.30) main course £10.50 Unique Courage Best, John Smiths, Doom r, Bombardier & Guest. 16 **Facilities** Garden Dogs allowed Parking y Area

ITTLETON-ON-SEVERN MAP 04 ST58

Vhite Hart

35 1NR 01454 412275
mail: whitehart@youngs.co.uk
r: *M48 junct 1 towards Chepstow, left at rdbt for 3m, 1st left to tleton-on-Severn*

raditional English country pub dating back to the 1680s. It was ginally a farmhouse, from which flagstone floors and other features the old building, including two large inglenook fireplaces, survive. od ranges from home-cooked pub classics, such as beef and ale nter stew with herb dumpling and vegetables, to modern Anglo-nch dishes that usually feature among the specials. After all-day sun the front garden, watch it set over the Severn estuary.

en 12–3 6–11 (Open all day Sat–Sun) **Bar Meals** L served all week -2 D served all week 6.30–9.30 (Sat–Sun 12–2.30, 6–9) Av main course 95 Youngs Bitter, Youngs Special, Youngs Waggledance, Thatchers ritage. 18 **Facilities** Children's licence Garden Dogs allowed Parking

ITTLE WASHBOURNE MAP 10 SO93

he Hobnails Inn

20 8NQ 01242 620237 01242 620458
r: *From M5 junct 9 take A46 towards Evesham then B4077 to w-on-the-Wold. Inn 1.5m*

ablished in 1473, the Hobnails is one of the oldest inns in the unty. Inside you'll find winter log fires, and you can tuck yourself into rivate corner, or relax with a pint of ale on one of the leather sofas. good range of bar snacks is supplemented by a lunchtime carvery d a fresh fish range. Outside is a lovely large garden for warmer days h views over surrounding countryside.

en 12–2.30 6–11 **Bar Meals** L served all week 12–2 D served all week (Sun 7–9) Av main course £9.95 **Restaurant** L served all week 12–2 erved Mon–Sat 6–9 (Sun 7–9) Enterprise Inns London Pride, wers IPA, Hook Norton Best, Deuchars IPA. 6 **Facilities** Children's nce Garden Dogs allowed Parking

LONGHOPE MAP 10 SO61

The Glasshouse Inn

May Hill GL17 0NN 01452 830529
dir: *Village off A40 between Gloucester & Ross-on-Wye*

The Glasshouse is unique and its popularity confirms the need for traditional pubs with no gimmicks. The inn dates back to 1450 and gets its name from Dutch glassmakers who settled locally in the 16th century. It is located in a wonderful rural setting with a country garden outside and a tranquil and dignified interior. Home-cooked dishes now include authentic Thai choices.

Open 11.30–3 6.30–11 **Bar Meals** L served Mon–Sat 12–2 D served Mon–Sat 7–9 Free House Butcombe, Bass, Doom Bar, Brains. **Facilities** Garden Parking

LOWER APPERLEY MAP 10 SO82

The Farmers Arms

Ledbury Rd GL19 4DR 01452 780307 01452 780307
e-mail: starline.estop@btconnect.com
dir: *From Tewksbury A38 towards Gloucester/Ledbury. 2m, right at lights onto B4213 (signed Ledbury). 1.5m, pub on left*

A popular 16th-century, timber-framed pub on the village fringe and close to the River Severn. Low beams, an open fire, regular guest ales and an extensive menu are to be found within. This leans strongly towards fresh fish, roasts, grills and home-made pies, while daily fish deliveries ensure that the specials boards are usually able to offer lobster, crab, halibut and salmon, as well as game in season.

Open 11–2.30 6–11 (Open Mon eve summer hols) **Bar Meals** L served all week 12–2.15 D served all week 6.30–9.30 Av main course £8.50 **Restaurant** L served Tue–Sun 12–2.15 D served all week 6.30–9.30 Av 3 course à la carte £17.50 Wadworth Wadworth 6X, Henry's Original IPA plus guest beers. 10 **Facilities** Garden Parking Play Area

England

LOWER ODDINGTON MAP 10 SP22

Pick of the Pubs

The Fox

GL56 0UR
☎ 01451 870555 & 870669 📠 01451 870669
e-mail: info@foxinn.net
dir: *A436 from Stow-on-the-Wold then right to Lower Oddington*

Hidden away in one of the most idyllic and unspoilt village locations in the Cotswolds, this 16th-century inn is wildly popular. Its mellow stone façade is largely concealed by Virginia creeper, and with its polished flagstone floor, log fires, beams and daily papers in the convivial bar it is probably one of the area's most cosy and welcoming inns too. Candles and fresh flowers decorate the pine tables, and there are tasteful prints on the rag-washed walls. Well-kept beers are served alongside imaginative food, and there's a respectable wine list. In the summer months, sit out and enjoy supper al fresco on the awning-covered terrace or in the pretty, cottage garden. The menu combines traditional and classic influences and takes full advantage of seasonal local ingredients. Typical starters include home-cured gravadlax, or pear and roquefort tart. Follow with rabbit casserole, or seared scallops with rocket and ginger dressing.

Open 12-3 6.30-11 (Apr–Oct 12-11) Closed: 25 Dec
Bar Meals L served all week 12-2.30 D served all week 6.30-10 (Sun 6.30-9.30) **Restaurant** L served all week 12-2.30 D served all week 6.30-10 (Sun 6.30-9.30) Free House Hook Norton Best, Abbot Ale, Ruddles County, Wickwar's Old Bob. 12 **Facilities** Garden Parking

LYDNEY MAP 04 SO6

The George Inn ★★★ INN

St Briavels GL15 6TA ☎ 01594 530228 📠 01594 530260
e-mail: george_inn@tiscali.co.uk

In a quiet village high above the Wye Valley and close to the Forest of Dean, this pretty white-washed pub overlooks a moody 12th-century castle ruin. The interior includes an 8th-century Celtic coffin lid set into one of the walls. The pub is famous for braised shoulder of lamb and Moroccan lamb, along with popular dishes such as traditional steak and kidney, and beef and Guinness pies.

Open 11-2.30 6.30-11 **Bar Meals** L served all week 11-2.30 D served all week 6.30-9.30 **Restaurant** L served all week 11-2.30 D served all week 6.30-9.30 Free House RCH Pitchfork, Freeminers, London Pride, Archers. 10 **Facilities** Garden Parking **Rooms** 4 bedrooms en suite S£40 D£65

MARSHFIELD MAP 04 ST7

The Catherine Wheel

39 High St SN14 8LR ☎ 01225 891825
e-mail: bookings@thecatherinewheel.co.uk
dir: *Between Bristol and Chippenham on the A420 near A46*

Simple, stylish décor complements the clean lines of this 15th-century inn, with its exposed brick work and large open fireplaces. Menus are equally simple and well presented: try spaghetti carbonara for lunch, or grilled sardines, followed by roast leg of lamb with apple and pota purée for supper. Vegetarians might try mushroom stroganoff, and round off with chocolate marquis. A small, sunny patio is a lovely spc for the summer months.

Open 12-3 6-11 (Sun 12-10.30) **Bar Meals** L served all week 12-2 D served all week 7-9 (Sun 12-4) **Restaurant** L served all week 12-2 D served all week 7-10 (Sun 12-3) Av 3 course à la carte £22 Free Hou Scottish Courage, Courage Best, Abbey Ales Bellringer & Guest Ale. **Facilities** Garden Dogs allowed Parking

The Britannia

n impressive 17th-century former manor house occupying a delightful position on the south ›de of Nailsworth's Cossack Square. The interior is bright and uncluttered with low ceilings and ›sy fires, an open-plan design and a blue slate floor.

utside you'll find a pretty garden ith plenty of tables, chairs and nbrellas for making the most ' warm, sunny days. Whether side or out, a pint of well-kept ıller's London Pride or Greene ng Abbot Ale is sure to go down ell. The brasserie-style menu is ı interesting blend of modern ritish and continental food, with gredients bought from local ıppliers and from Smithfield arket. You can go lightly with just starter (try whole tiger prawns ith savoury rice and green pepper uce), or a small main (salmon hcakes; steak baguette with chips; sausage and mash with onion avy); sample a pasta dish such tagliatelle with creamy pesto, ın-dried tomato and mushroom sauce; or tackle a hearty main dish like steak and kidney casserole with bacon dumplings; stuffed pork tenderloin with apple, onion and bacon stuffing with a cider sauce; or haddock and prawn pancake served in a cream sauce with a mixed leaf salad. Puddings are a popular event at the Britannia, with favourites that might include fruit crumble and custard; sticky rice pudding and home-made jam; and for calorie addicts, chocolate brownie served with clotted cream, ice cream and pouring cream. The owners import their own wines, so the list is well worth browsing through.

MAP 04 ST89
Cossack Square GL6 0DG
☎ 01453 832501
Fax 01453 832010
e-mail: pheasantpluckers2003@yahoo.co.uk
dir: *From A46 S'bound right at town centre rdbt. 1st left. Pub directly ahead*

Open 11–11 Closed: 25 Dec
Bar Meals L served all week 11–2.45 D served all week 5.30–10 (all day Fri–Sun)
Restaurant L served all week 11–2.45 D served all week 5.30–10 (all day Fri–Sun)
Free House
Greene King Abbot Ale, Fuller's London pride, Bass, Deuchars IPA. 12
Facilities Garden Dogs allowed Parking

MARSHFIELD continued

The Lord Nelson Inn

1 & 2 High St SN14 8LP ☎ 01225 891820 & 891981
e-mail: thelordnelsoninn.@btinternet.com
dir: *On A420 between Bristol & Chippenham*

Located in a village on the outskirts of Bath, this 17th-century coaching inn is family run and has a good reputation for its home-made food and quality cask ales. There are log fires in winter and a patio for summer use. Dishes range from home-made burger with hand cut chips, to collops of monkfish with saffron and red pepper dressing, and timbale of white and wild rice.

Open 12–2.30 5.30–11 (all day Sun) **Bar Meals** L served all week 12–3 D served all week 6.30–9 Av main course £7.95 **Restaurant** L served all week 12–2 D served all week 6.30–9 (Sun 12–3) Av 3 course à la carte £18.95 Enterprise Inns Courage Best, Bath Gem, 6X. 9 **Facilities** Children's licence Garden Dogs allowed Play Area

MEYSEY HAMPTON MAP 05 SP10

The Masons Arms

28 High St GL7 5JT ☎ 01285 850164 01285 850164
dir: *6m E of Cirencester off A417, beside village green.*

With its origins as far back as 1725, this charming village free house is an ideal haven for travellers, and the bar remains a convivial focus of village life. A varied menu of home-made dishes, light bites and vegetarian options is served in the bar and the re-styled restaurant; daily specials might include Italian-style chicken; minted lamb chops; or fresh pan-fried swordfish. There's now a carvery on Sundays.

Open 11.30–3 6–11.30 (Sun 12–11.30) **Bar Meals** L served all week 12–3 D served all week 6.30–9.30 (Fri–Sat 6–9.30) Av main course £8.50 **Restaurant** L served all week 12–2.30 D served all week 7–9.30 (Fri–Sat 6.30–9.30) Av 3 course à la carte £16 Free House Hook Norton Best, Guest Ales. 14 **Facilities** Children's licence Garden Dogs allowed Parking Play Area

MINCHINHAMPTON MAP 04 SO8

Pick of the Pubs

The Weighbridge Inn

GL6 9AL ☎ 01453 832520 01453 835903
e-mail: enquiries@2in1pub.co.uk
dir: *Between Nailsworth & Avening on B4014*

An historic 17th-century free house located on the original London to Bristol packhorse trail. The trail is now a footpath and bridleway, ideal for exploring this Area of Outstanding Natural Beauty on foot. At one time the innkeeper also looked after the weighbridge, which served the local woollen mills; these included the long defunct Longfords Mill, memorabilia from which is displayed around the inn. Behind the scenes there has been careful renovation, but original features of the bars and upstairs restaurant, with massive roof beams reaching almost to the floor, remain untouched. The drinking areas are just as cosy while, outside, the patios and arbours offer good views of the Cotswolds. Meals include the famous '2 in 1' pies, comprising the filling of your choice (such as pork, bacon and celery; or chicken, ham and leek) topped with home-made cauliflower cheese and a pastry lid.

Open 12–11 (Sun 12–10.30) Closed: 25 Dec & 10 days in Jan **Bar Meals** L served all week 12–9.30 D served all week 12–9.30 Av main course £9 **Restaurant** L served all week 12–9.30 D served all week 12–9.30 Av 3 course à la carte £18 Free House Wadworth 6X, Uley Old Spot & Laurie Lee. 16 **Facilities** Garden Dogs allowed Parking

NAILSWORTH MAP 04 ST8

Pick of the Pubs

The Britannia

Cossack Square GL6 0DG
☎ 01453 832501 01453 832010
e-mail: pheasantpluckers2003@yahoo.co.uk
dir: *From A46 S'bound right at town centre rdbt. 1st left. Pub directly ahead*

See Pick of the Pubs on page 235

Tipputs Inn

his 17th-century pub-restaurant has been decked out in impeccable style, so that mellow otswold stone and stripped floorboards blend nicely with modern, clean-lined furniture and a uch of grandeur in the form of a giant candelabra.

ocated in the heart of the otswolds, the Tipputs Inn is vned by Nick Beardsley and hristophe Coquoin. They started t as chefs together more than 12 ars ago, but admit to spending ss time in the kitchen these ys now that they have to create enus for this and their other oucestershire food pubs. Much their time is spent on selecting d importing some of their menu gredients and wines direct from ance. The menus cater for most quirements: starters are served all y, and might include such exotic oices as sautéed Spanish chorizo th mushrooms and peppers tossed spinach leaves; pigeon breast with etroot and hazelnut salad and a port and honey dressing; and rabbit and pork terrine wrapped in Parma ham. The list of lighter meals takes in Gloucester Old Spot sausage and mash with shallot gravy; fettuccine pasta with cashew nuts and parmesan shavings; haddock in beer batter with home-made chips; and rib-eye steak sandwich on ciabatta with caramelised onions and chips. Larger mains are served for four hours at lunchtime and in the evenings: look out for whole roasted mackerel with shallots, cherry tomatoes, garlic and thyme; steak and kidney pie; farmed rabbit with a bean and vegetable casserole; pork tenderloin medallions pan fried with apples and cider on a celeriac and potato mash; wild mushroom risotto served with a mixed leaf salad; and onion and mushroom tart topped with gruyere.

🍷
MAP 04 ST89
Bath Rd GL6 0QE
☎ 01453 832466
🖷 01453 832010
e-mail: pheasantpluckers2003@yahoo.co.uk
dir: *A46, 0.5m S of Nailsworth*

Open 11–11 Closed: 25 Dec
Bar Meals L served all week 11–10 D served all week 11–10
Restaurant L served all week 11–10 D served all week 11–10
Free House
Greene King IPA, Ruddles County & Abbot Ale. 🍷 12
Facilities Garden Dogs allowed Parking

NAILSWORTH continued

Pick of the Pubs

Egypt Mill ★★ HL ❁ 🍷

GL6 0AE ☎ 01453 833449 🖷 01453 839919

e-mail: reception@egyptmill.com

dir: *M4 junct 18, A46 N to Stoud. M5 junct 13, A46 to Nailsworth*

Situated in the charming Cotswold town of Nailsworth, this converted corn mill contains many features of great character, including the original millstones and lifting equipment. The ground floor bar and bistro enjoy a picturesque setting, and its views over the pretty water gardens complete the scene. There is a choice of eating in the bistro or restaurant, and in both there is a good selection of wines by the glass. For those who like to savour an aperitif before dining, try the large Egypt Mill lounge. Tempting starters might offer ham hock and pea risotto; smoked salmon and avocado parcels; and salmon and lobster sausages. Main courses include the likes of saddle of lamb Greek style; calves' liver and bacon; breast of duck with apple and blackberry risotto; and Brixham fish and potato pie.

Open 7–11 **Bar Meals** L served all week 12–2 D served all week 6.30–9 (Sun 12–9) **Restaurant** L served all week 12–2 D served all week 7–9 (Sun 12–9) ⊕ Free House ◀ Boddingtons, Archers Best, Cats Whiskers, Wickwar Cotswold Way. 🍷 10 **Facilities** Garden Parking **Rooms** 28 bedrooms en suite S£70 D£90

Pick of the Pubs

Tipputs Inn 🍷

Bath Rd GL6 0QE ☎ 01453 832466 🖷 01453 832010

e-mail: pheasantpluckers2003@yahoo.co.uk

dir: *A46, 0.5m S of Nailsworth*

See Pick of the Pubs on page 237

NAUNTON MAP 10 SP1

The Black Horse

GL54 3AD ☎ 01451 850565

Renowned for its home-cooked food and Donnington real ales, this friendly inn enjoys a typical Cotswold village setting beloved of ramblers and locals alike. The Black Horse provides a traditional Engl menu featuring liver and bacon, cottage pie, and broccoli and cheese bake.

Open 11.30–3 6–11 **Bar Meals** L served all week 12–2 D served all wee 6.30–9.30 **Restaurant** L served all week 12–2 D served all week 6.30–9.3 ⊕ Donnington ◀ Donnington BB, SBA. **Facilities** Garden Dogs allowed Parking

NETHER WESTCOTE MAP 10 SP2

Pick of the Pubs

The Westcote Inn NEW 🍷

OX7 6SD

☎ 01993 830888 & 07976 971672 🖷 01993 831657

e-mail: julia.reed@virgin.net

dir: *2.3m from Oxford on A40 towards Cheltenham. At Burford rdbt follow signs A424 towards Stow-on-the-Wold*

See Pick of the Pubs on opposite page

NEWLAND MAP 04 SO

Pick of the Pubs

The Ostrich Inn NEW

GL16 8NP ☎ 01594 833260 🖷 01594 833260

e-mail: kathryn@theostrichinn.com

dir: *Follow Monmouth signs from Chepstow (A466), Newland signed from Redbrook*

See Pick of the Pubs on page 240

The Westcote Inn

he Westcote Inn, a 300-year-old malthouse, was extensively renovated in 2006, yet remains a ·aditional British village pub. Racehorse training country surrounds it, and an interest in the port of Kings might pay off because the Tack Room Bar is often full of trainers and jockeys nalysing the day's events at Cheltenham, Newbury or Warwick over a few pints of Old Hookie.

otswold stone slabs are plastered ith racing mementoes and the ıb even supports its own horse, Vestcote', owned by a village ·ndicate. In such a traditional :itish pub you'd expect to be :rved 'Great British Food' (to ıote the menu) and you will be, though European influences are ɔparent. Everything is freshly :oduced and makes abundant use : organic ingredients. There's a ɔmprehensive lunch and supper ·enu in the Tack Room that ıcludes cottage-, game and ale-, ıd fish pies, braised lamb shank, ıd shallot tarte Tatin, while in ıe restaurant starters include ɔast wood pigeon with puy lentils ıd wild raspberry vinaigrette; ıteau of white crab, smoked salmon, avocado and caviar; and home-made leek, potato and chive soup. Main courses here might be fillet of Scottish beef with girolle mushrooms and watercress; stuffed saddle of Cotswold rabbit with basil, sun-blushed tomatoes and garlic mash; wild Cornish sea bass and scallops with crushed new potatoes and cauliflower purée; and loin of Highland venison with savoy cabbage, bacon and red wine gravy. Snacks include sandwiches, jacket potatoes, and salads. Every bottle on the sensibly priced wine list can be served by the glass, whatever its price. Two acres of gardens include a spectacular patio overlooking what must be one of the best views in the Cotswolds.

NEW 🍷
MAP 10 SP22
OX7 6SD
☎ 01993 830888 & 07976 971672
🖷 01993 831657
e-mail: julia.reed@virgin.net
dir: *2.3m from Oxford on A40 towards Cheltenham. At Burford rdbt follow signs A424 towards Stow-on-the-Wold*

Open 11–11
Bar Meals L served all week 12–2.30 D served all week 7–9.30 Av main course £8
Restaurant L served all week 12–2.30 D served all week 7–9.30 Av 3 course à la carte £25
Free House
Hookie, Old Hookie, London Pride, Becks Vier & Guinness.
🍷 30
Facilities Garden Dogs allowed Parking Play Area

The Ostrich Inn

A 13th-century inn situated in a pretty village on the western edge of the Forest of Dean and adjoining the Wye Valley, both areas of outstanding natural beauty. The complete history of the inn has been lost, although it is known to have housed the workers who built the church opposite, known as the 'Cathedral of the Forest'.

To this day it still retains many of its ancient features, including a priest hole. The name, incidentally, comes from the emblem of the Probyn family, once prominent local landowners. With wooden beams and a welcoming log fire in the large lounge bar throughout the winter, visitors can enjoy a relaxed and friendly setting for a wide selection of cask-conditioned beers and excellent food. 'We cook everything from scratch, using local produce as much as possible,' says owner, Kathryn Horton, who took over in 2000 and has worked tirelessly ever since to create this popular free house. Diners are served in the small, intimate restaurant, the larger lounge bar, the garden and the patio. In the bar expect simpler dishes, such as salmon spinach fishcakes; steak and ale pie; and penne pasta. The monthly changing menu in the restaurant offers more sophistication in the form of fresh egg tagliatelle with dried porcini, fresh wild mushrooms and sherry cream sauce; slow-roasted spiced belly pork with pak choi; supreme of Nile perch from Lake Victoria with black tiger prawns and chive cream sauce; and wild mushroom, marinated roast red peppers and goats' cheese tart with fresh basil oil. In addition, there are weekly specials and sweets and, in harmony with everything else, an affordable wine list. No one will frown at your muddy boots, certainly not Alfie, the pub dog, who will offer to share his water bowl with you.

NEW
MAP 04 SO50
GL16 8NP
☎ 01594 833260
01594 833260
e-mail: kathryn@theostrichinn.com
dir: *Follow Monmouth signs from Chepstow (A466), Newland signed from Redbrook*

Open 12-3 6.30-11.30 (Sat 6-11.30)
Bar Meals L served all week 12-2.30 D served all week 6.30-9.30 (Sat 6-9.30) Av main course £8.50
Restaurant L served all week 12-2.30 D served all week 6.30-9.30 (Sat 6-9.30) Av 3 course à la carte £23.50
Free House
Timothy Taylor Landlord, Butty Bach, Pigs Ear, Old Hooky.
Facilities Garden Dogs allowed

ORTH CERNEY MAP 05 SP00

athurst Arms 🍷

L7 7BZ ☎ 01285 831281

mail: james@bathurstarms.com

r: *5m N of Cirencester on A435*

ntique settles, flagstone floors, stone fireplaces, beams and panelled alls characterise this former coaching inn, in a pretty village setting. e garden, including a boules pitch, stretches down to the River hurn. A special wine room offers over 100 wines with a good choice the glass. Fresh fish, and produce from ethically minded farmers ature in dishes such as roasted loin of Gloucester Old Spot pork, xury fish pie, and winter vegetable hot pot.

pen 12–3 6–11 (Sun 7–10.30) **Bar Meals** L served all week 12–2 served all week 6–9 (Sun 7–9) Av main course £11 **Restaurant** L served week 12–2 D served all week 6–9 (Fri–Sat 6–9.30, Sun 12–2.30 7–9) Av 3 urse à la carte £22 Free House Hook Norton, Cotswold Way, Guest ers. 🍷 10 **Facilities** Garden Dogs allowed Parking **Rooms** 6 bedrooms suite S£55 D£75 (★★★★ INN)

ORTHLEACH MAP 10 SP11

Pick of the Pubs

The Puesdown Inn ★★★★ INN 🏵🏵 🍷

Compton Abdale GL54 4DN

☎ 01451 860262 📠 01451 861262

e-mail: inn4food@btopenworld.com

dir: *On A40 between Oxford & Cheltenham, 3m W of Northleach*

A former coaching inn said to date from 1236. It takes its name from ancient English meaning 'windy ridge', an apposite label given its position 800ft above sea level on the old Salt Way. Apart from the risk of being 'snowed up' (an anagram of its name), the Puesdown has it all – a delightful hidden garden with wonderful views, several ghosts, a footpath leading to the Cotswold Diamond Way, two dogs and a cat, a helicopter landing pad to ferry racegoers to Cheltenham during Gold Cup week, regular tastings, live jazz, and cookery demonstrations; even the loos were featured in a national publication. Above all, it has a welcoming interior of fresh flowers, oak flooring, cosy sofas, log fires, and a cornucopia of real ales and award-winning food. Fish and shellfish are particularly plentiful (there's a regular seafood dinner event), or you could just pop in for a hearty lunch of leg of mutton stew.

Open 11–3 6–11 (Fri–Sun 11–11 Jul–Aug 11–11) **Bar Meals** L served all week 12–3 D served all week 6–10.30 (Sun 6–10) Av main course £9.50 **Restaurant** L served all week 12–3 D served Mon–Sat 6.30–10.30 (Sun 6.30–9.30) Av 3 course à la carte £28 Av 3 course fixed price £18.75 Free House Hook Norton Best Bitter, Hooky Dark, Old Hooky, Haymaker. 🍷 15 **Facilities** Garden Dogs allowed Parking **Rooms** 3 bedrooms en suite S£55 D£85

OAKRIDGE MAP 04 SO90

The Butcher's Arms

GL6 7NZ ☎ 01285 760371 📠 01285 760602

dir: *From Stroud A419, left for Eastcombe and Bisley signs. Just before Bisley right to Oakridge, brown signs for pub*

Traditional Cotswold country pub with stone walls, beams and log fires in the renowned Golden Valley. Once a slaughterhouse and butcher's shop. A full and varied restaurant menu offers steak, fish and chicken dishes, while the bar menu ranges from ploughman's lunches to home-cooked daily specials.

Open 11–3 6–11 Closed: 25–26 Dec, 1 Jan **Bar Meals** L served Tue–Sun 12–2 D served Tue–Sat 6.30–9.30 **Restaurant** L served Sun 12–3 D served Tue–Sat 7–9 Free House Greene King Abbot Ale, Wickwar Bob, Archers Best, Buttcombe Bitter. **Facilities** Garden Dogs allowed Parking

OLDBURY-ON-SEVERN MAP 04 ST69

The Anchor Inn 🐟 🍷

Church Rd BS35 1QA ☎ 01454 413331

dir: *From N A38 towards Bristol. From S A38 through Thornbury*

Parts of this Cotswold stone pub, formerly a mill, date from 1540. The large garden by a stream has plenty of seats for summer dining, and a popular boules piste. Bar snacks include filled ciabattas, crayfish mayonnaise, and home-baked ham with eggs. Crispy roast belly of pork, Oldbury sausages and mash, jalfrezi chicken curry, Devon crab and scallop gratin and smoked haddock and salmon pie feature on the main menu. New guest ales arrive every Thursday.

Open 11.30–2.30 6.30–11 (Sat 11.30–11, Sun 12–10.30) **Bar Meals** L served all week 11.30–2.30 D served all week 6.30–9 (Sun 12–3, 6–9, Fri–Sat 6.30–9.30) Av main course £9.50 **Restaurant** L served all week 11.30–2.30 D served all week 6.30–9.30 (Sun 12–3, 6–9) Free House Interbrew Bass, Scottish Courage Theakston Old Peculier, Butcombe Best & Otter Bitter. 🍷 12 **Facilities** Garden Parking

PAINSWICK MAP 04 SO80

Pick of the Pubs

The Falcon Inn 🍷

New St GL6 6UN ☎ 01452 814222 📠 01452 813377

e-mail: bleninns@clara.net

dir: *On A46 in centre of Painswick*

Boasting the world's oldest known bowling green in its grounds, the Falcon dates from 1554 and stands at the heart of a conservation village. For three centuries it was a courthouse, but today its friendly service extends to a drying room for walkers' gear. A sampling of dishes from the menu includes whole trout and almonds; gammon and egg; sirloin steak; chilli crust beef

CONTINUED

PAINSWICK continued

fillet; duck leg confit on a bed of sherry and puy lentils with Madeira sauce; penne pasta arrabiatta; stuffed pork loin with apricot and pistachios; steamed seabass fillet with scallop mousseline; and minted lamb chop with fennel, asparagus and Jerusalem artichoke garnish.

The Falcon Inn

Open 11–11 (Sun 12–10.30) **Bar Meals** L served all week 12–2.30 D served all week 7–9.30 Av main course £22 **Restaurant** L served all week 12–2.30 D served all week 7–9.30 Free House Greene King IPA, Otters Ale, Wye Valley. 10 **Facilities** Children's licence Garden Dogs allowed Parking

The Royal Oak Inn

St Mary's St GL6 6QG ☎ 01452 813129
e-mail: bleninns@clara.net
dir: *In town centre*

Tucked away behind the church of this conservation village, the Royal Oak features very low ceilings, old paintings and artefacts, and a huge, open fire. In summer, a sun-trap rear courtyard contributes to its atmosphere. Food is a mixture of old favourites (Cumberland sausage and mash; cauliflower cheese; beef curry); specials (lamb and apricot casserole; rabbit and leek pie); grills and vegetarian choices.

Open 11–3 6–11 Wed–Sun all day (trial basis) **Bar Meals** L served all week 12–2.30 D served all week 7–9.30 Av main course £6.50 **Restaurant** L served all week 12–2.30 D served all week 7–9.30 Free House Black Sheep Bitter, Spitfire, Moles plus Guest Ales. 8 **Facilities** Garden Dogs allowed

PAXFORD

MAP 10 SP1

Pick of the Pubs

The Churchill Arms

GL55 6XH ☎ 01386 594000 01386 594005
e-mail: info@thechurchillarms.com
dir: *2m E of Chipping Campden, 4m N of Moreton-in-Marsh*

Husband and wife team Sonia Kidney and Leo Brooke-Little have been running this Cotswold village inn for the past ten years. Paxford really is at the centre of this glorious region, enjoying delightful views over rolling, typically English countryside. Popular with walkers and lovers of outdoor pursuits, the pub offers refreshing ales including Hook Norton bitter, a wide and imaginative choice of wines, and quality modern pub food. Relationships with local suppliers have always been taken seriously, with an eye to seeking out new produce. Menus change daily: starters might include duck confit pancake with oyster sauce; and peppered loin of tuna with horseradish, lemon and parsley. For your main course, try such unusual and intriguing dishes as assiette of rabbit with Madeira, or lamb's kidney omelette with sherry and shallot sauce and bacon. Triple chocolate torte with raspberry parfait makes for an elegant conclusion.

Open 11–3 6–11 **Bar Meals** L served all week 12–2 D served all week 7–9 **Restaurant** L served all week 12–2 D served all week 7–9 Av 3 course à la carte £22 Free House Hook Norton Bitter, Arkells, Moonlight. 10 **Facilities** Garden

POULTON

MAP 05 SP

The Falcon Inn

London Rd GL7 5HN ☎ 01285 850844
e-mail: info@thefalconpoulton.co.uk
dir: *From Cirencester E on A417 towards Fairford*

At the heart of the Cotswold village of Poulton, the Falcon has been transformed from a straightforward village local into a stylish and sophisticated gastro pub which has become popular with drinkers an diners from far and wide. For beer drinkers this is a real ale paradise, with up to half a dozen breweries represented behind the colourful handles; the choice continues with many wines available by the glass Diners too have decisions to make. Especially good value is the fixed-price two-course lunch menu, which offers choices of three starters and three main courses.

Open 11–3 7–11 (Sun 12–3, 7–10.30. Summer 5–11) **Bar Meals** L serve Mon–Sat 12–2 **Restaurant** L served all week 12–2 D served Mon–Sat 7–9 (Summer 12–2.30, 5–9.30) Av 3 course à la carte £22 Free House Hook Norton, Wickwar BOB & Guests. 9 **Facilities** Dogs allowed Parking

OUTHROP - GLOUCESTERSHIRE

The Swan at Southrop

Cycle information

Distance: 11.25 miles/26.9km (2h30)
Map: OS Explorer OL45 The Cotswolds
Start/finish: Coln St Aldwyns; grid ref: SP 145052
Trails/tracks: minor lanes
Landscape: gently rolling Cotswold hills
Public toilets: none on route
Tourist information: Cirencester, tel 01285 654180
Cycle hire: none locally
The pub: The Swan at Southrop, Southrop
Care on the narrow lanes is required

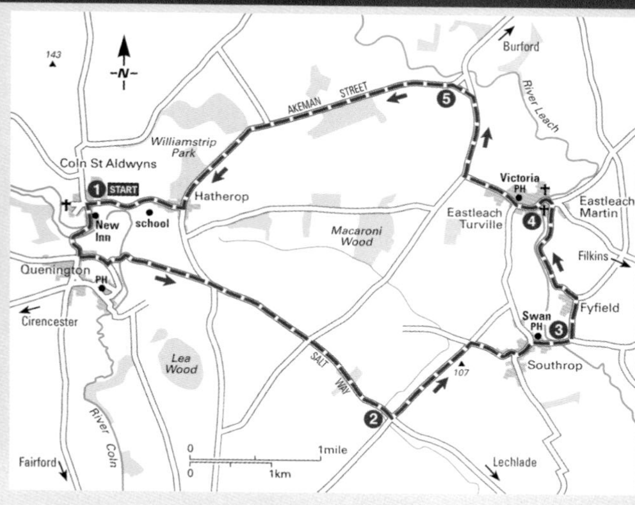

ycle directions

1 The crossroads in the middle of Coln St Aldwyns is marked by a sturdy spreading chestnut tree. Begin the ride along the lane signed to Quenington and Fairford, passing the New Inn. Leaving the village, cycle over the River Coln and climb to a crossroads at the edge of Quenington. Go left onto Fowlers Hill and drop back into the valley, following signs to Southrop and Lechlade as you bend past a junction to re-cross the Coln. The lane rises steeply then gently over open down, following an ancient salt way. Pedal on for some 2.5 miles (4km), following signs for Southrop past junctions, before eventually losing height to a 'Give Way' junction.

Go left, gaining height along a gentle fold in the rolling hillside. Stay with the main lane as it later turns to rise over the hill, winding down on the other side into Southrop. Carry on past the village hall and The Swan, the street slotted between high-kerbed pavements, signed to Filkins.

3 After dropping away and crossing the second river of the journey, the Leach, turn off left to Fyfield and Eastleach. Keep left again as the lane splits at Fyfield, following the gently rising valley to Eastleach. There are two separately named halves to the village and the lane ends at a junction by the church in Eastleach Martin. Go left, and re-cross the Leach to enter the neighbouring parish, swinging left again beneath a massive willow tree, from which a track leads off to Eastleach Turville's church.

4 The main lane winds on past the village cross and then a row of almshouses to reach a junction below The Victoria pub. Keep ahead, the way signed 'Hatherop and Burford', climbing shortly to a second junction where you should go right in the direction of Burford and Westwell. Undulate onwards across open hills that are interspersed with clumps of copse. Stay left at successive turnings to curve above the higher reaches of the Leach valley, signs now directing you to Hatherop and Coln St Aldwyns.

5 For 1.25 miles (2km), the way follows the course of Akeman Street, a Roman road, passing a turn off signed to Dean Farm before breaking away from the ancient thoroughfare into Hatherop. At a junction, go right towards Coln St Aldwyns, winding down to leave the village past Hatherop School. It is then only a short ride back to the start at Coln St Aldwyns.

Where to go from here

Experience the clack of loom-shuttles and the smell of wood-oil as fleece is transformed into woollen fabric at the Cotswold Woollen Weavers at Filkins. In Cirencester visit the Corinium Museum (www.cotswold.gov.uk), or enjoy the rare and endangered animals, children's farmyard, and adventure playground at the Cotswold Wildlife Park near Burford (www.cotswoldwildlifepark. co.uk).

The Swan at Southrop

The Swan is a creeper clad, early 17th-century Cotswold inn with a classic location on the village green at Southrop. This is an area of Gloucestershire, close to the borders of Oxfordshire and Wiltshire, which is renowned for gentle strolls and picturesque country rambles.

The inn is run by Graham Williams with Bob Parkinson as chef, both of them formerly of Bibendum in London. Their aim is to provide food of excellent quality at village inn prices. The Swan's interior, comprising a bar, snug and restaurant, is surprisingly light and airy for such a historic building, but cosy too in winter with the log fire. Another attractive feature is the skittle alley, where larger parties can be catered for. Accommodation in four bedrooms is also planned for the future. In addition to the carte there is a good-value, short, fixed-price lunch menu of two or three courses, including a vegetarian option (linguine with broccoli, red onion, pine nuts and parmesan). From the carte you might choose confit tuna salad with borlotti beans, chorizo and poached egg to start, or Thai duck salad with sour fruits, chilli, mint and coriander. Mains range through escargots de Bourgogne; grilled entrecote steak with Béarnaise sauce, pomme frites and green salad; and fillet of halibut with watercress salad, baby artichokes, courgette relish and aïoli. Meals finish with the likes of chocolate fondant with vanilla ice cream, or a selection of cheeses with leaves and fig chutney.

MAP 05 SP10
GL7 3NU
☎ 01367 850205
01367 850555
dir: *Off A361 between Lechlade & Burford*

Open 11.30–3.30 6.30–11
Bar Meals L served all week 12–2 D served all week 7–9
Restaurant L served all week 12–2.30 D served all week 7–10 (Closed Sun pm in winter) Av 3 course à la carte £28
Free House
Hook Norton, Wadworth 6X, Timothy Taylor Landlord, Marstons. 10
Facilities Dogs allowed

SAPPERTON MAP 04 SO90

Pick of the Pubs

The Bell at Sapperton

GL7 6LE ☎ 01285 760298 01285 760761
e-mail: thebell@sapperton66.freeserve.co.uk
dir: *From A419 halfway between Cirencester & Stroud follow signs for Sapperton. Pub in village centre near church*

The Bell is on the edge of the Cirencester Park, at the heart of the Cotswolds, an area popular with walkers, cyclists and horse riders. Those popping in for a light meal can enjoy something from the snack menu, perhaps washed down with a pint of locally brewed real ale. Ingredients used in the kitchen are all carefully sourced from local suppliers, and bread is made on the premises using Shipton Mill flour. Dairy products come from a local farm, and locally sourced meats might include rare breed Belted Galloway beef from the local National Trust Estate of Ebworth. Wild mushrooms, game, fruit and vegetables are also generally from the local area. Try a chalkboard special like braised Old Spot pig cheeks with parsnip mash, ginger and lime sauce; or take a good look at the dinner menu, with choices like pure bred Hereford rib-eye steak with a garnish of roast tomato, mushrooms and fries.

Open 11–2.30 6.30–11 (Sun times vary) Closed: 25 & 31 Dec, 3–10 Jan **Bar Meals** L served all week 12–2 D served all week 7–9.30 (Sun 7–9) Av main course £14.50 **Restaurant** L served all week 12–2 D served all week 7–9.30 (Sun 7–9) Av 3 course à la carte £30 Free House Uley Old Spot, Bath Ales, Buttcombe Best, Cotswold Way. 16 **Facilities** Garden Dogs allowed Parking

SHEEPSCOMBE MAP 04 SO81

Pick of the Pubs

The Butchers Arms

GL6 7RH ☎ 01452 812113 01452 814358
e-mail: mark@butchers-arms.co.uk
dir: *1.5m S of A46 N of Painswick*

Set on the sunny side of Sheepscombe valley, the pub has lovely views of beech wooded slopes on all sides, and you can take full advantage of these from the garden terrace. The building was originally used to hang the deer hunted by Henry VIII in his royal deer park – hence the name – and well-known writer Laurie Lee was once a regular. The area attracts many walkers, riders and other visitors, all made welcome by hosts Mark and Sharon and their young team. Three hand-pulled real ales are offered in the bar, served in fine condition, and a full menu is available at lunchtime and in the evening. Some of the produce on the menu comes from fields within sight of the pub. Dishes include steaks from the grill, hunter's chicken, and slow cooked lamb shank from the regular menu, which is supported by an ever-changing specials board.

The Butchers Arms

Open 11.30–2.30 6–11.30 (Open all day wkend Summer) **Bar Meals** L served all week 12–2.30 D served all week 7–9.30 (Sun 12–9) **Restaurant** L served all week 12–2.30 D served all week 7–9.30 (Sun 12–9) Free House Otter Ale, Hook Norton Bitter, Guest Ales. 10 **Facilities** Children's licence Garden Dogs allowed Parking

SOMERFORD KEYNES MAP 04 SU09

Pick of the Pubs

The Bakers Arms

GL7 6DN ☎ 01285 861298 01453 832010
e-mail: pheasantpluckers2003@yahoo.co.uk
dir: *Leave A419 signed Cotswold Water Park, cross B4696 for 1m, follow signs for Keynes Park and Somerford Keynes.*

A beautiful chocolate box pub built from Cotswold stone, with low-beamed ceilings and inglenook fireplaces. Dating from the 15th century, the building was formerly the village bakery and stands in mature gardens ideal for al fresco dining. Discreet children's play areas and heated terraces add to its broad appeal. Somerford Keynes is in the Cotswold Water Park, and the man-made beach of Keynes Park is within easy walking distance, while the nearby Thames Path and Cotswold Way make the pub popular with walkers. New owners in March are already popular with locals and visitors.

CONTINUED

England

SOMERFORD KEYNES continued

Open 11–11 (Fri–Sat 11–12) **Bar Meals** L served all week 12–2.45 D served all week 6–9.30 (Sun all day) Av main course £8.50 **Restaurant** L served all week 12–2.45 D served all week 6–9.30 (Sun all day) Av 1 course fixed price £5 Enterprise Inns Courage Best, 6X, Hook Norton, London Pride. 8 **Facilities** Children's licence Garden Dogs allowed Parking Play Area

SOUTHROP MAP 05 SP10

Pick of the Pubs

The Swan at Southrop

GL7 3NU ☎ 01367 850205 01367 850555

dir: *Off A361 between Lechlade & Burford*

See Pick of the Pubs on page 244

Please see cycle ride on page 243

STONEHOUSE MAP 04 SO80

The George Inn ★★★ INN

Peter St, Frocester GL10 3TQ

☎ 01453 822302 01453 791612

dir: *M5 junct 13, A419 at 1st rdbt 3rd exit signed Eastington, left at next rdbt signed Frocester. Inn on right in village*

An award-winning 18th-century coaching inn, unspoiled by juke box or fruit machine. Instead, crackling log fires and a sunny courtyard garden give the place all-year-round appeal. The Cotswold Way and a network of leafy paths and lanes are on the doorstep. Expect a warm welcome, a selection of real ales including three local brews, and good home-cooked food from nearby suppliers. Tuck in to half a roast chicken, or Frocester Fayre faggots with mash, peas and gravy.

Open 11.30–2.30 5–11 (Fri–Sun 11.30–11) **Bar Meals** L served all week 12–2 D served Mon–Sat 6.30–9.30 (Sun carvery 12.30–3) Av main course £9 **Restaurant** L served all week 12–2 D served Mon–Sat 6.30–9.30 (Sun 12.30–3) Deuchars IPA, Blacksheep & Guest Beers. **Facilities** Garden Parking **Rooms** 6 bedrooms en suite S£45 D£65

STOW-ON-THE-WOLD MAP 10 SP12

Pick of the Pubs

The Eagle and Child ★★★ HL

GL54 1HY ☎ 01451 830670 01451 870048

e-mail: stay@theroyalisthotel.com

dir: *From Moreton-In-Marsh train station, A429 Fosseway to Stow-On-The-Wold. At 2nd traffic lights left onto Sheep St (A436). The Royalist Hotel & Eagle & Child 500yds on the left*

See Pick of the Pubs on opposite page

The Unicorn ★★★ HL

Sheep St GL54 1HQ ☎ 01451 830257 01451 831090

e-mail: reception@birchhotels.co.uk

Attractive hotel of honey-coloured limestone, hand-cut roof tiles and abundantly flowering window boxes, set in the heart of Stow-on-the-Wold. The interior is stylishly presented with Jacobean pieces, antique artefacts and open log fires. Light meals are served in the bar (sandwiches and salads, plus beef and Guinness stew, and beer-battered fish and chips), and a dinner menu of modern British dishes is available in the elegant Georgian Shepherd's Restaurant.

Open 12 –11 (Winter 12–3, 7–11) **Bar Meals** L served all week 12–2 D served all week 7–9 **Restaurant** D served all week 7–9 **Facilities** Garden Dogs allowed Parking **Rooms** 19 bedrooms en suite

STROUD MAP 04 SO8

Pick of the Pubs

Bear of Rodborough Hotel ★★★ HL

Rodborough Common GL5 5DE

☎ 01453 878522 01453 872523

e-mail: info@bearofrodborough.co.uk

web: www.cotswold-inns-hotels.co.uk/bear

dir: *From M5 junct 13 follow signs for Stonehouse then Rodborough*

See Pick of the Pubs on page 248

The Ram Inn

South Woodchester GL5 5EL

☎ 01453 873329 01453 873329

e-mail: jewantsum@aol.com

dir: *A46 from Stroud to Nailsworth, right after 2m into South Woodchester (follow brown tourist signs)*

From the terrace of the 17th-century Cotswold stone Ram there are splendid views over five valleys, although proximity to the huge fireplace may prove more appealing in winter, with plenty of outdoor seating in summer. Rib-eye steak, at least two fish dishes, home-made lasagne and Sunday roasts can be expected, washed down by regular changing real ales such as Uley Old Spot, Wickwar BOB and Archer's Golden. The Stroud Morris Men regularly perform.

Open 11–11 (Sun 12–10.30) **Bar Meals** L served all week 12–2.30 D served all week 6–9.30 (Sun 6–8.30) **Restaurant** L served all week 12–2.30 D served all week 6–9.30 (Sun 6–8.30) Free House Uley Old Spot, Otter Brewery, Archers Village, Stroud Budding. **Facilities** Garden Dogs allowed Parking

The Eagle and Child

ertified by the Guinness Book of Records as the oldest inn in England, The Eagle and Child is art of the Royalist Hotel. The site is said to date back to 947 AD and was once a refuge on the osse Way.

istoric finds include a 10th-entury Saxon shoe, a leper hole, itches' marks in the rooms, a bear it, thousand-year-old timbers and n ancient frieze. The names of nn and hotel alike recall Stow on ne Wold's place in history as the te in 1646 of the final battle of ne English Civil War. Intriguingly, ne name Digbeth Street is thought be a derivative of 'duck bath'. ucolic as it sounds, it actually efers to the somewhat grim sight f ducks swimming in the blood of illen Royalist casualties as it flowed opiously over the cobblestones. he inn and hotel have recently een taken over by local hoteliers lark and Janine Vance, who have et about creating a luxurious ackage. In the cheerful pub, ample ham hock, curly kale pressé and apple purée; and smoked chicken with mascarpone risotto. Mains might include steak, kidney and thyme suet pudding with roast parsnips; smoked haddock, mussel and clam chowder; and slow braised lamb shank with ratatouille and garlic mash. Diners at the award-winning restaurant might start with stilton pannacotta and carpaccio of beef, followed by such assured dishes as Cornish mackerel, pomme gratin and oxtail tortellini, or braised osso buco, ox cheeks and wild mushroom. The hotel has 14 bedrooms, each a textbook example of how to blend the contemporary and tradition for maximum stylish impact.

★★★ HL

MAP 10 SP12

GL54 1HY

☎ 01451 830670

01451 870048

e-mail:

stay@theroyalisthotel.com

dir: *From Moreton-In-Marsh train station A429 Fosseway to Stow-On-The-Wold. At 2nd traffic lights left onto Sheep St. (A436). The Royalist Hotel & Eagle & Child is 500yds on the left*

Open 11 -11

Bar Meals L served all week 12–2.30 D served all week 6–9.30

Restaurant L served all week 12–2.30 D served all week 7–9.30

Av 3 course à la carte £20

Free House

Hook Norton, London Pride, Goffs & Donnington, Carlsberg.

8

Facilities Garden Dogs allowed Parking

Rooms 14 bedrooms en suite S£80 D£120

Bear of Rodborough Hotel

Built in the 17th century, this former alehouse stands 600 ft above sea level, surrounded by 300 acres of National Trust land. Its name comes from the bear-baiting that used to take place nearby. The hotel is worth seeking out for all sorts of reasons: comfortable accommodation, open log fires, stone walls and solid wooden floors.

An interesting beam over the front doors reads 'Through this wide opening gate none come too early, none return too late', reputedly carved by louche sculptor and typographer, Eric Gill. Spot the running bear design incorporated into the ceiling beams in the elegant Box Tree restaurant and Tower Room. Additional character is occasionally provided in the form, if that's the right word, of a resident ghost whose unknown identity is often discussed late at night in the Grizzly Bar (best pronounced the hillbilly way), as likely as not over pints of Gloucestershire brews from Uley and Wickwar. The restaurant offers a contemporary British menu, so one might start with baby toad-in-the-hole with red wine jus and redcurrant jelly; or poached salmon and citrus salad; continue with Bibury trout; faggots with buttered mash; or wild mushroom risotto; and finish with a dessert from the daily specials. Sandwiches include Single Gloucester cheese with Uley's Old Spot ale and apple chutney. There are two wine lists, one containing a short, modestly priced selection, the other running to the full 60 bins. Outside is a croquet lawn created in the 1920s by a former resident called Edmunds, a partner in a well-known firm of proud Stroud nurserymen.

★★★ HL 🍷
MAP 04 SO80
Rodborough Common GL5 5DE
☎ 01453 878522
📠 01453 872523
e-mail:
info@bearofrodborough.co.uk
web: www.cotswold-inns-hotels.co.uk/bear
dir: *From M5 junct 13 follow signs for Stonehouse then Rodborough*

Open 10.30–11
Bar Meals L served all week 12–2.30 D served all week 6.30–10 (Sun 12–2, 6.30–9.30) Av main course £9.95
Restaurant D served all week 7–9.30 (Sun 7–9) Av 3 course fixed price £28.95
Free House
Uley Bitter, Bob from Wickwar Brewery, Guest ale. 🍷 6
Facilities Garden Dogs allowed Parking Play Area
Rooms 46 bedrooms en suite

TROUD continued

Pick of the Pubs

Rose & Crown Inn 🍷

The Cross, Nympsfield GL10 3TU

☎ 01453 860240 📠 01453 861564

e-mail: gadros@aol.com

dir: *M5 junct 13 off B4066, SW of Stroud*

An imposing, 400-year-old coaching inn of honey-coloured local stone in the heart of the village close to the Cotswold Way and therefore a popular stop for walkers and cyclists. It could well be the highest pub in the Cotswolds, but whether it is or not is irrelevant as the views over the Severn are stunning anyway. Inside, the inn's character is preserved with natural stone, wood panelling, a lovely open fire and some local real ales. In the galleried restaurant, main courses include faggots cooked in onion gravy, enchiladas, and salmon en croûte. Just as satisfying might be Eastern Promise, a baked baguette filled with roast duck, spring onion, cucumber and hoi sin sauce. The kids will enjoy the playground area, which has a swing, slides and a climbing bridge.

Open 12–11 **Bar Meals** L served all week 12–9.30 D served all week 6–9.30 **Restaurant** L served all week 12–9.30 D served all week 6–9.30 Free House Uley, Pigs Ear & Otter. 🍷 7 **Facilities** Children's licence Garden Dogs allowed Parking Play Area

'he Woolpack Inn

lad Rd, Slad GL6 7QA ☎ 01452 813429 📠 01452 813429

ir: *2m from Stroud, 8m from Gloucester*

ituated in the Slad Valley close to the Cotswold Way, an area nmortalised by Laurie Lee in his book *Cider with Rosie*, this is a iendly local that offers good real ales and is popular with walkers and og owners.

pen 12–3 5–11 (all day Sat–Sun) **Bar Meals** L served all week 12–2.30 served all week 6–9.30 Av main course £7.95 **Restaurant** L served all eek 12–2.30 D served Mon–Sat 6–9.30 Free House Uley Pig's Ear, ld Spot, Laurie Lee. **Facilities** Garden Dogs allowed Parking

ETBURY MAP 04 ST89

Pick of the Pubs

Gumstool Inn 🍷

Calcot Manor GL8 8YJ

☎ 01666 890391 📠 01666 890394

e-mail: reception@calcotmanor.co.uk

dir: *3m W of Tetbury*

The cheerful and cosy Gumstool is part of Calcot Manor Hotel, a charmingly converted, 14th-century Cotswold stone farmhouse that was built by Cistercian monks. Depending on the month, the menu might offer starters of twice-baked Welsh rarebit cheese soufflé; gratin of Arbroath smokies; or endive, celery, apple and walnut salad with roquefort cheese and grapes. Among the main courses could well be wood-grilled salmon steak with sauté potatoes, caramelised onion and béarnaise sauce; crispy duck confit salad with pickled ginger and sweet and sour dressing; roasted half pheasant with bacon and bread sauce; and braised shoulder of lamb with mashed carrots and parsnips. Free house status means a good selection of real ales from Butcombe, Matthew's, Sharps and Wickwar. The house is set in 220 acres of countryside.

Gumstool Inn

Open 11.30–2.30 5.30–11 (Sat 11.30–11, Sun 12–10.30) **Bar Meals** L served all week 12–2 D served all week 7–9.30 (Sun 7–9) Av main course £7 **Restaurant** L served all week 12–2 D served all week 7–9.30 Free House Atlantics Sharp IPA, Matthews Bob Wool, Wickwar Cotswold Way & Butcomb Blonde. 🍷 12 **Facilities** Garden Parking Play Area

Pick of the Pubs

The Priory Inn NEW ★★★ HL 🍷

London Rd GL8 8JJ ☎ 01666 502251 📠 01666 503534

e-mail: info@theprioryinn.co.uk

dir: *M4 junct 17, A429 towards Cirencester. Left onto B4014 to Tetbury. Over mini-rdbt onto Long Street, pub 100yds around corner on right*

A complete refurbishment in 2004 saw this inn transformed into a thriving gastro pub, hotel and coffee bar at the centre of Tetbury life. The aim is to provide excellent value modern rustic cuisine with a minimum of food miles. Monthly newsletters keep customers informed of the local suppliers who have provided their supper: don't miss Westonbirt ice creams made by eighteen-year-old Harriet from cows on her father's nearby farm. Children are especially welcome, with a specialised menu of home-made dishes and junior cocktails, plus the opportunity to decorate a personalised wood-fired pizza. Adults are equally coddled with a menu that might include pinhead oat crusted herring; pan-grilled Madgett's Farm duck breast with local autumn pear sauce; and wood oven-baked plum tarte Tatin with vanilla ice cream. 14 stylish bedrooms await if you want to stay the night, while those in a rush can simple grab a takeaway gourmet pizza.

Open 11–11 **Restaurant** L served all week 12–3 D served all week 6–10 Av 3 course à la carte £21 Free House Uley Bitter, Cotswold Premium Lager, Archers Ale, Stowford Press Cider. 🍷 10 **Facilities** Children's licence Garden Parking Play Area **Rooms** 14 bedrooms en suite S£69 D£99

England

TETBURY continued

The Trouble House 🏵🏵 🍷

Cirencester Rd GL8 8SG ☎ 01666 502206
e-mail: enquiries@troublehouse.co.uk
dir: *On A433 between Tetbury & Cirencester*

An old Cotswold inn whose troubled past includes landlords who committed suicide, farmworkers who destroyed new-fangled agricultural machinery, and ghosts. Or is it named after the nearby flood-prone area known as The Troubles? No one knows. Inside are wooden floors, black beams, open fires, pastel-coloured walls and subtle lighting. Freshly prepared rustic cooking includes roasted squid stuffed with sun-dried tomatoes, mozzarella and chilli lentils; and double-cooked rib-eye of pork with mushy peas and mustard sauce.

Open 11.30–3 6.30–11 (Sun 12–3 Oct–May Tue–Sat 7–11) Closed: 25 Dec–5 Jan **Bar Meals** L served Tue–Sun 12–2 D served Tue–Sat 7–9.30 **Restaurant** L served Tue–Sun 12–2 D served Tue–Sat 7–9.30 Av 3 course à la carte £30 Wadworth Wadworth 6X & Henrys IPA. 🍷 12 **Facilities** Garden Dogs allowed Parking

TEWKESBURY MAP 10 SO83

The Fleet Inn 🍷

Twyning GL20 6FL ☎ 01684 274310 📠 01684 291612
e-mail: enquiries@fleet-inn.co.uk
dir: *M5 junct 8, M50 junct 1*

The gardens of this idyllic 15th-century pub run right down to the banks of the River Avon. The traditional bars and themed areas provide a wide range of dishes. Produce is locally sourced, and might include steak and kidney parcels; pheasant breast on colcannon mash; or half shoulder of lamb in mint and rosemary gravy. There's a boules court to keep the teenagers happy, and a pets' corner for the little ones.

Open 11–11 **Bar Meals** L served all week 12–2.30 D served all week 6–9 (Fri–Sat 6–9.30) Av main course £9 **Restaurant** L served all week 12–2.30 D served all week 6–9 (Fri–Sat 6–9.30) Av 3 course à la carte £20 Enterprise Inns Bombardier, Banks, Cat's Whiskers. 🍷 7 **Facilities** Children's licence Garden Parking Play Area

TODENHAM MAP 10 SP2

Pick of the Pubs

The Farriers Arms 🍷

Main St GL56 9PF ☎ 01608 650901 📠 01608 650403
e-mail: louise@farriersarms.com
dir: *Right to Todenham at N end of Moreton-in-Marsh 3m*

A traditional Cotswold pub dating from 1650, the Farriers Arms stands adjacent to the old village smithy, just three miles from Moreton-in-the-Marsh. It has all the features you'd associate with a country local, like a large inglenook fireplace, and exposed stone walls and beams. Horse brasses hang above the wood burner, cider flagons adorn the walls and there's a dartboard for friendly local-versus-visitor games. Award-winning food is served in the bar and restaurant, including a more secluded library area. For warmer days there is a suntrap patio garden with views of the church across the surrounding countryside. Starters range from smoked salmon with dill and caper dressing to Bury black pudding topped with rarebit and served with toast. Typical mains are local hand carved ham, topped with two eggs and served with chips, and Gressingham duck breast on braised red cabbage with port and redcurrant gravy.

Open 12–3 6.30–11.20 (Sun 7–11.20) **Bar Meals** L served all week 12–2 D served all week 7–9 (Fri–Sat 7–9.30) Av main course £11 **Restaurant** L served all week 12–2 D served all week 7–9 (Fri–Sat 7–9.30, Sun 12–2.30) Av 3 course à la carte £20 Free House Hook Norton Best, Archers Golden, Wye Valley Butty Bach, Timothy Taylor Landlord. 🍷 11 **Facilities** Garden Dogs allowed Parking

TORMARTON MAP 04 ST7

Best Western Compass Inn ★★ HL 🍷

GL9 1JB ☎ 01454 218242 📠 01454 218741
e-mail: info@compass-inn.co.uk
dir: *From M4 junct 18 take A46 N towards Stroud. After 200mtrs 1st right towards Tormarton, continue for 300mtrs*

This friendly free house has been in the same family for the past 46 years. Extensive facilities include an orangery, 26 bedrooms and space for functions, not to mention five and a half acres of beautiful grounds right on the Cotswold Way. Light bites and more fulsome meals can be taken in the bar, while the restaurant offers the likes of chicken supreme filled with basil mousse; or monkfish and spinach en croûte.

Open 7–11 Closed: 25–26 Dec **Bar Meals** L served all week 11–10 D served all week 7–10 Av main course £8.95 **Restaurant** L served all week D served all week 7–10 Av 3 course à la carte £20 Free House Interbrew Bass & Butcombe Gold. 🍷 9 **Facilities** Garden Dogs allowed Parking **Rooms** 26 bedrooms en suite S£89.50 D£99.50

The Old Fleece

)elightful coaching inn dating back to the 18th century and built of Cotswold stone with a 'aditional stone roof. The interior benefited from a complete refurbishment and makeover in the ıst couple of years.

mong the features that help to 'eate just the right atmosphere ıd ambience are wooden floors, 'ood panelling and exposed stone. he pub's surroundings are equally ıviting, with miles of stunning ɔuntryside and footpaths to explore. rom the Old Fleece, you can walk ı Rodborough, Minchinhampton ıd Selsley Commons, or go one ep further and connect eventually ith the scenic Cotswold Way ɪng-distance trail. Owners Nick ıd Christophe, who have been in ıarge here for nearly 15 years, are ıssionate about their pub and are ell-known in the Stroud valley for ıe fresh food, sharp service and ıstomer comforts. Christophe works ı the interior design, while Nick 'eates the menus. Predominantly rench chefs prepare quality, freshly roduced dishes seven days a week and ingredients are sourced locally or directly – London for meat and Bristol and Birmingham for vegetables and fish. Start perhaps with warm Greek salad with cherry tomato, focaccia bread and sweet thyme dressing; or steak and caramelised onion on toast. The main course is an event to linger over: try chicken breast with boudin noir, wrapped in bacon with an apple and cream sauce; venison fillet with rich chocolate and balsamic sauce; braised lamb shank served with rosemary jus and roasted garlic mash; or for fish lovers, salmon and tarragon fishcakes with a ginger and chilli mayonnaise; marinated chilli tuna; and fish pie. To round off you could choose banana waffle with a creamy caramel sauce; balsamic parfait with a raspberry coulis; or apple and honey tart with mascarpone cheese.

MAP 04 SO80
Bath Rd, Rooksmoor GL5 5NB
☎ 01453 872582
01453 832010
e-mail: pheasantpluckers2003@yahoo.co.uk
dir: *2m S of Stroud on A46*

Open 11–11 Closed: 25 Dec
Bar Meals L served all week 11–2.45 D served all week 5.30–10 (Sat–Sun all day)
Restaurant L served all week 11–2.45 D served all week 5.30–10 (Sat–Sun all day)
Pheasant Pluckers Ltd
Interbrew Boddington & Bass, Greene King Abbot Ale. 12
Facilities Garden Dogs allowed Parking

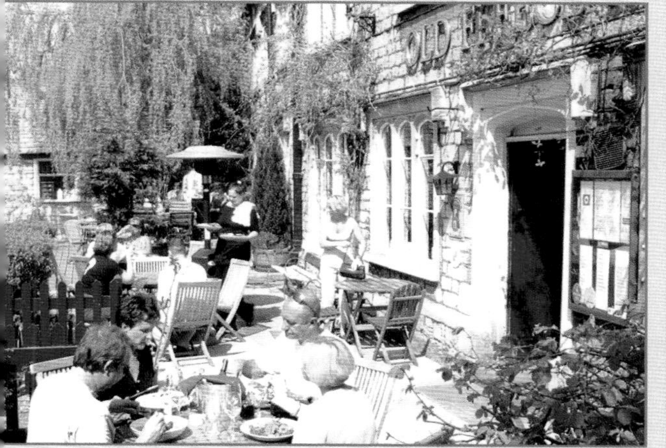

England

UPPER ODDINGTON MAP 10 SP22

Pick of the Pubs

The Horse and Groom Inn

GL56 0XH ☎ 01451 830584
e-mail: info@horseandgroom.uk.com
dir: *1.5m S of Stow-on-the-Wold, just off the A436*

In a Cotswold conservation village just a mile and a half from Stow-on-the-Wold, this immaculate 16th-century stone inn welcomes with beams, flagstone and English oak floors, and open log fires in winter. In warmer weather the terrace garden is perfect for dining outside, where tables overlook dry stone walls and pretty stone-built cottages. There's a great selection of cask ales from Wye Valley Brewery, the Wickwar Brewing Company and the Hidden Brewery, and the latest addition – the Cotswold Brewing Company – is just three miles away in Foscot. If wine is preferred, at least 25 are served by the glass. The best of regional food and drink is the head chef's quest, bringing to the table Gloucester Old Spot pork, Cotswold lamb, and Hereford beef hung for 28 days. Fresh fish from Brixham may appear on the specials board in the form of whole grilled sea bream, or seared sea bass fillets.

Open 12–3 5.30–11 (Sun 12–10.30) **Bar Meals** L served all week 12–2 D served all week 6.30–9.30 (Sun 7–9) Av main course £13 **Restaurant** L served all week 12–2 D served all week 6.30–9.30 (Sun 7–9) Av 3 course à la carte £25 Free House Wye Valley Butty Bach, Wye Valley Best, Hereford Pale Ale, Wickwar Bob Cotswold Premium Lager. 25 **Facilities** Children's licence Garden Parking Play Area

WINCHCOMBE MAP 10 SP02

The White Hart Inn and Restaurant

High St GL54 5LJ ☎ 01242 602359 01242 602703
e-mail: enquiries@the-white-hart-inn.com
dir: *In centre of Winchcombe on B4632*

A traditional 16th-century coaching inn with a Swedish twist, the White Hart has been refurbished to offer a beamed bar and Swedish-style restaurant. Enjoy snacks (antipasti, olives), a pizza or a Swedish hotdog at the bar – followed by an Italian ice-cream dessert. Dinner in the restaurant could be Scandinavian seafood platter; or pan-fried cod with red caviar mashed potato.

Open 8am-midnight Closed: 25 Dec **Bar Meals** L served all week 11–10 D served all week 6–10 **Restaurant** L served all week 11–10 D served all week 6–10 Av 3 course à la carte £25 Av 3 course fixed price £16.95 Archers Golden, Uley Old Spot, Whittingtons Cats Whiskers, Greene King IPA. 8 **Facilities** Children's licence Garden Dogs allowed Parking **Rooms** 8 bedrooms en suite S£55 D£65 (★★★ INN)

WITHINGTON MAP 10 SP0

The Mill Inn

GL54 4BE ☎ 01242 890204 01242 890195
dir: *3m from A40 between Cheltenham & Oxford*

Until 1914 the innkeeper also had to find time to grind corn in this 450-year-old inn on the banks of the River Coln. Inside are stone-flagged floors, oak panelling and log fires, while outside is a peaceful lawned garden with 40 tables. Lunch or dinner is selected from a wid selection of light meals and more substantial main courses, including blackened Cajun chicken, steak and ale pie, Barnsley chop, and Quor and vegetable chilli.

Open 11.30–3 6–11 (all day summer Sat & Sun 11.30–12) **Bar Meals** L served all week 12–2 D served all week 6–9 (Sat–Sun 12–2.3 Av main course £9 Samuel Smith Samuel Smith Old Brewery Bitter, Samuel Smith Sovereign, Alpine Lager, Pure Brew Lager. **Facilities** Garder Dogs allowed Parking

WOODCHESTER MAP 04 SO8

Pick of the Pubs

The Old Fleece

Bath Rd, Rooksmoor GL5 5NB
☎ 01453 872582 01453 832010
e-mail: pheasantpluckers2003@yahoo.co.uk
dir: *2m S of Stroud on A46*

See Pick of the Pubs on page 251

GREATER LONDON

CARSHALTON MAP 06 TQ2

Greyhound Hotel

2 High St SM5 3PE ☎ 020 8647 1511 020 8647 4687
e-mail: greyhound@youngs.co.uk
dir: *5 min from Carshalton station on foot, 20 min train journey from Victoria Station*

Standing directly opposite the ponds in Carshalton Park, this distinctiv former coaching inn has a welcoming fire in the bar in winter months Records dating back to 1706 show that the white-painted building wa formerly a centre for cock-fighters and race-goers. Today's visitors wil find an interesting range of filled ciabattas and snacks, together with more substantial options like home-made steak and kidney pudding; and hake fillet in Young's beer batter, hand cut chips and mushy peas

Open 11–12 (Sun 12–11.30) **Bar Meals** L served all week 12–3 D served all week 6.30–10 (Sun 12–9) Av main course £10 **Restaurant** D served all week 6.30–10 (Sun 12–9) Young & Co Youngs Special, Winter Warmer, PA & Waggle Dance. 17 **Facilities** Parking

ICHMOND (UPON THAMES)

ee **London Plan 2 C2**

he White Cross

/ater Ln TW9 1TH ☎ 020 8940 6844

-mail: whitecross@youngs.co.uk

censed for over two centuries, this Grade II listed pub is set right eside the River Thames. An old fireplace uniquely fitted under a ndow is still lit on winter evenings, and there's an upstairs area with balcony overlooking the river. Youngs Bitter and Winter Warmer elp to wash down home-cooked menu choices like curry, steak pie, sagne, and chilli con carne.

pen 11–11 (Fri-Sat 11–12) **Bar Meals** L served all week 12–3.30 served Mon–Fri 6.30–9.30 (Sun 12–4) Av main course £7 Young & Youngs Bitter, Winter Warmer, St Georges. 13 **Facilities** Garden ogs allowed

WICKENHAM

ee **London Plan 2 C2**

he White Swan

verside TW1 3DN ☎ 020 8892 2166

mail: whiteswan@massivepub.com

ting right by the Thames since 1690, with an outside balcony and rden on the river's edge (tides permitting), while inside there's d wood and, as you might expect in this neck of the woods, walls vered with rugby memorabilia. Food is revered too, with a 'help urself' buffet laid out in the summer, and at weekends a wonderful rbecue cooked on the patio. Winter brings out Sunday roasts and lidly traditional fare.

pen 11–11 (Sun 12–10.30) **Bar Meals** L served all week 12–2.30 served Tue–Sat 6–9.30 (Sun 12–5) Av main course £7.25 Massive IPA, Bombardier, Twickenham Ale, Deuchars. 10 **Facilities** Garden gs allowed

GREATER MANCHESTER

HEADLE HULME — MAP 16 SJ88

he Church Inn

venoak Rd SK8 7EG ☎ 0161 485 1897 0161 485 1698

mail: church_inn@yahoo.co.uk

ere's a friendly atmosphere at this old world, proprietor-run pub, ich has welcoming log fires in winter and a front patio with tables d chairs for warmer days. You'll find two guest beers in addition to binsons' ales, with a wide selection of malt whiskies and wines by e glass. Besides a good range of sandwiches and baked potatoes, ok out for home-made lasagne; peppered chicken; traditional cod d chips; and vegetarian pasta bake.

en 11–11 (Sun 12–10.30) **Bar Meals** L served all week 11.30–2.30 in 12–1.30) D served Mon–Sun 5.30–8.30 **Restaurant** L served week 11.30–2.30 D served Mon–Sat 5.30–8.30 (Sun 12–7.30) Robinsons Robinsons Best Bitter, Hatters Mild, Robinsons Old ckport plus Guests. 18 **Facilities** Garden Parking

DENSHAW — MAP 16 SD91

The Rams Head Inn

OL3 5UN ☎ 01457 874802 01457 820978

e-mail: ramsheaddenshaw@aol.com

dir: *From M62 junct 22, 2m towards Oldham*

From its position 1212 feet above sea level, this 400-year-old country inn offers panoramic views over Saddleworth. Log fires and collections of memorabilia are features of the interior, where blackboard menus list everything available and food is cooked to order. Seafood figures strongly, with dishes such as crayfish tails with ginger crème fraîche, and monkfish wrapped in Parma ham. Another attraction is 1212 at The Rams Head, a farm shop, deli, bakery, tearooms and pattisserie.

Open 12–2.30 6–11 (Sun 12–10.30) Closed: 25 Dec **Bar Meals** L served Tue–Sun 12–2.30 D served Tue–Sun 6–10 (BH Mon 12–3, Sun 12–8.30) **Restaurant** L served Tue–Sun 12–2.30 D served Tue–Sun 6–10 (BH Mon 12–3, Sun 12–8.30) Free House Carlsberg-Tetley Bitter, Timothy Taylor Landlord, Black Sheep Bitter. 8 **Facilities** Parking

DIDSBURY — MAP 16 SJ89

Pick of the Pubs

The Metropolitan

2 Lapwing Ln M20 2WS

☎ 0161 374 9559 0161 282 6544

e-mail: info@the-metropolitan.co.uk

dir: *M60 junct 5, A5103 turn right onto Barlow Moor Rd, then left onto Burton Rd. Pub at the x-rds. Right onto Lapwing Lane for car park.*

See Pick of the Pubs on page 254

LITTLEBOROUGH — MAP 16 SD91

The White House

Blackstone Edge, Halifax Rd OL15 0LG ☎ 01706 378456

Old coaching house, built in 1671, standing high on the Pennines 1,300 feet above sea level, with panoramic views of the moors and Hollingworth Lake far below. The pub is on the Pennine Way, attracting walkers and cyclists who sup on Theakstons and regular guest ales. Fresh fish is a feature of the blackboard specials: cheddar topped grilled haddock, lobster thermidor and chargrilled tuna with balsamic glaze. Alternatives include steaks or lamb Henry.

Open 12–3 6–11 (Sun 12–11) Closed: 25 Dec **Bar Meals** L served all week 12–2 D served all week 6.30–9 (Sun 12–9) Free House Timothy Taylor Landlord, Theakstons Bitter, Exmoor Gold, Black Sheep. **Facilities** Parking

The Metropolitan

Built as a hotel by the old Midland Railway for passengers on its route into Manchester, the 'Me still punches above its weight architecturally, but then that's how Victorian railway companies liked to gain a competitive edge over their rivals.

Look in particular at the decorative floor tiling, the ornate windows, the impressive roof timbering, and the delicate plasterwork. Sadly, during the latter part of the 20th century the building became very run down, until in 1997 it was given a sympathetic renovation, reopening as a gastropub, now one of several eating and drinking places in this buzzy southern city suburb. Its huge, airy interior is well filled with antique tables and chairs, which suit the mainly young, cosmopolitan clientele. Indeed, the Met does get very busy at peak times, but the addition of an outside bar with attractive furniture and patio heaters helps to spread the load. The lunchtime menu will almost certainly offer grilled Cumberland sausage on a ragout of smoked bacon, tomato, baby onions and herb potatoes; and the 'famous' 100 per cent prime beef burger with hand-cut chunky chips. In the evening look for oven-baked whole sea bream stuffed with spring onion, ginger, red pepper and basil, and passion fruit and chilli coulis; pan-fried English fillet steak with horseradish and Meaux mustard mash, parmentier carrots and tarragon jus; and baked coconut and sweet chilli risotto cakes with coriander, beansprout and spring onion salad. There are also pies big enough for two – braised steak, mushroom and stout; and smoked haddock with salmon and prawn. Ploughman's can be assembled from a wide choice of cheeses, and sandwiches are all garnished with salad and coleslaw.

MAP 16 SJ89
2 Lapwing Ln M20 2WS
☎ 0161 374 9559
Fax 0161 282 6544
e-mail: info@the-metropolitan.co.uk
dir: *M60 junct 5, A5103 right onto Barlow Moor Rd, then left onto Burton Rd. Pub at x-rds. Right onto Lapwing Lane for car park.*

Open 11–11.30 (Fri–Sat 11.30–12am) Closed: Dec 25
Bar Meals L served all week 12–6 D served all week 6–7 (Sun 12–6) Av main course £9
Restaurant L served all week 12–6 D served all week 6–9.30 (Fri–Sat 12–10, Sun 12–9, Summer 3–9) Av 3 course à la carte £20
Timothy Taylor Landlord, Deuchars IPA, Hoegarden, Staropramen & Guinness. 8
Facilities Garden Parking

IANCHESTER MAP 16 SJ89

ukes 92

 Castle St, Castlefield M3 4LZ

 0161 839 8646 0161 832 3595

mail: info@dukes92.com

r: *Town centre*

autifully-restored 19th-century stable building with a vast patio side the 92nd lock of the Duke of Bridgewater canal, opened in 62. The interior is full of surprises, with minimalist décor downstairs d an upper gallery displaying local artistic talent. The renowned eese and paté counter is a great draw, offering a huge range of itish and continental cheeses, along with a salad selection, and a oice of platters for sharing.

en 11–11 (Fri–Sat 11–1, Sun 12–10.30) Closed: 25–26 Dec, 1 1 **Bar Meals** L served all week 12–3 D served Sun–Thurs 5–8 **staurant** L served all week 12–3 D served Mon–Fri 5–8 Free House Interbrew Boddingtons Bitter. **Facilities** Garden Parking

larble Arch NEW

 Rochdale Rd M4 4HY

 0161 832 5914 0161 819 2694

r: *Located in city centre, northern quarter of Manchester*

isted building with a strikingly original interior, the Marble Arch is ine example of Manchester's Victorian heritage. It's also home to award-winning organic Marble Brewery, with six regular and eight asonal house beers. Snacks and more substantial meals are served the bar – the pies are deservedly popular. Sample the likes of steak d Marble ale pie; black pudding and potato salad; and pot-roast icken in Marble ginger beer.

en 11.30–11 (Thu–Fri 11.30–12, Sat–Sun 12–12) Closed: 25–26 Dec **r Meals** L served all week 12–7 D served all week 12–7 (Sun 12–6) main course £7.50 Free House GSB, Marble Best, Marble Ginger, gonda.

he Queen's Arms

Honey St, Cheetham M8 8RG 0161 835 3899

e Queen's is part of a loose grouping of real ale pubs in anchester's Northern Quarter. The original tiled frontage shows at it was once allied to the long-vanished Empress Brewery. Its entele spans the socio-economic spectrum from 'suits' to bikers to nsioners, all seemingly happy with the heavy rock on the jukebox. od is available, but it's the brewed, distilled and fermented products at attract, including an impressive 'menu' of bottled lagers, fruit ers, vodkas and wines.

en 12–11 (Sun 12–10.30, 25 Dec 12–3, 7.30–10.30) **Bar Meals** L served week 12–8 D served all week Av main course £3.50 Timothy Taylors ndlord, Phoenix Bantam, Guest beers. **Facilities** Children's licence rden Dogs allowed Play Area **Notes**

MELLOR MAP 16 SJ98

The Moorfield Arms ★★★★ INN

Shiloh Rd SK6 5NE 0161 427 1580 0161 427 1582

e-mail: moorfieldarms.co.uk

dir: *From Marple Bridge at lights to Mellor. 2.5m left signed Chisworth, 0.5m from New Mills follow Chisworth, Rowarth, Mellow signs, right at top of hill for Chisworth*

This pub enjoys picturesque views of Kinder and the surrounding Pennine hills from its secluded position on the edge of the moors. The building dates from 1640 and retains plenty of old world charm and atmosphere, including a log fire. Its accommodation makes it an ideal base for outdoor activities. The menu includes hot sandwiches, lunchtime snacks, an extensive selection from the grill, and signature dishes such as steak and ale pie or lamb Henry.

Open 12–3 6.30–11.30 **Bar Meals** L served all week 12–2 D served all week 6.30–10 (Sun 12–9) Av main course £9 **Restaurant** L served all week 12–2 D served all week 6.30–10 (Sun 12–9) Av 3 course à la carte £20 Free House Pedigree Bitter, Guinness, Marsden, & Guest Beers. 16 **Facilities** Garden Parking **Rooms** 4 bedrooms en suite S£55 D£70

The Oddfellows Arms

73 Moor End Rd SK6 5PT 0161 449 7826

e-mail: amollimited@hotmail.co.uk

A friendly welcome can be expected in this c1650 building, which has had a liquor licence since 1805. It changed its name from 'The Angel Inn' in 1860 to accommodate the Oddfellows Society, a forerunner of the Trades Unions. Seafood options include lobster and tiger prawn linguini, and Basque seabass with crispy rocket salad.

Open 12–3 5.30–11 (Sun 12–7) Closed: 25–26 Dec, 31 Dec–1 Jan **Bar Meals** L served Tue–Sun 12–2 D served Tue–Sat 6.30–9.30 Av main course £12 **Restaurant** L served Sun 12–2 D served Tue–Sat 7–9.30 (Sun 12–4) Free House Adnams Southwold, Marston's Pedigree, Bitter, Fennicks Arizona & Guest. 8 **Facilities** Garden Dogs allowed Parking

OLDHAM MAP 16 SD90

The Roebuck Inn

Strinesdale OL4 3RB 0161 624 7819 0161 624 7819

e-mail: smhowarth1@aol.com

dir: *From Oldham Humps Bridge, Huddersfield Rd, right at 2nd lights into Ripponden Rd, after 1m right at lights into Turfpit Ln for 1m.*

Historic inn located on the edge of Saddleworth Moor in the rugged Pennines, 1,000 feet above sea level. Part of the pub was once used as a Sunday School, while the upstairs lounge served as a morgue. This may explain the presence of the ghost of a girl who drowned in the local reservoir. The menu offers an extensive choice from vegetarian dishes and steaks to fish dishes; from the fish board perhaps smoked haddock with poached egg and hollandaise sauce.

Open 12–2.30 5–12 (Sun–Fri all day) **Bar Meals** L served all week 12–2.15 D served all week 5–9.30 (Fri 12–9.15 Sun 12–8.15) **Restaurant** L served all week 12–2.15 D served all week 5–9.30 (Fri 12–9.15 Sun 12–8.15) Av 3 course à la carte £20 Av 3 course fixed price £9.95 Free House Tetleys, Guest beer. 8 **Facilities** Garden Dogs allowed Parking Play Area

England

OLDHAM continued

Pick of the Pubs

The White Hart Inn

Stockport Rd, Lydgate OL4 4JJ

☎ 01457 872566 01457 875190

e-mail: bookings@thewhitehart.co.uk

dir: *From Manchester A62 to Oldham. Right onto bypass, A669 through Lees. In 500yds past Grotton brow of hill turn right onto A6050*

There are two major elements to this attractive 18th-century coaching inn's appeal: an award-winning restaurant, and the fact that Compo, Clegg and Bramire from the *Last of the Summer Wine* were based on former regulars here. Over the years, the inn has served as a brewery, kennels, prison, school and weaver's cottage, before returning at last to its original purpose as a hostelry. There are several different eating areas: the brasserie, the contemporary restaurant, the intimate library, and the new Oak Room for larger functions. Beer comes from local breweries and there's also a very extensive wine list. The food itself is thoughtful and creative. You might start with terrine of venison with cured loin, and follow it with roast saddle of rabbit with chestnuts, prunes and smoked bacon. Vegetarians are well taken care of: asparagus and girolles mille-feuille with truffle leeks; or ricotta and spinach lasagne with intense tomato compote.

Open 12–12 (Sun 12–11) **Bar Meals** L served all week 12–2.30 D served all week 6–9.30 (Sun 1–7.30) **Restaurant** L served Sun 1–3.30 D served Tue–Sat 6.30–9.30 Free House Timothy Taylor Landlord, J W Lees Bitter, Carlsberg-Tetley Bitter. 16 **Facilities** Garden Parking

STALYBRIDGE MAP 16 SJ99

Stalybridge Station Buffet Bar

The Railway Station, Rassbottom St SK15 1RF

☎ 0161 303 0007

Unique Victorian railway station refreshment rooms dating from 1885 and including original bar fittings, open fire and a conservatory. Decorated throughout with railway memorabilia, much donated by the regulars. There's always a good choice of real ales, and the bar hosts regular beer festivals and folk nights. Expect the pub's famous black pudding and black peas, pasta bake, pies, liver and onions, and sausage and mash on the bar menu.

Open 11–11 **Bar Meals** L served all week 11–8 Free House Boddingtons, Bass & Flowers IPA. **Facilities** Garden Dogs allowed Parking **Notes**

STOCKPORT MAP 16 SJ89

The Arden Arms NEW

23 Millgate SK1 2LX ☎ 0161 480 2185

e-mail: steve@ardenarms.com

dir: *M60 junct 27 to town centre. Across mini-rdbt, at lights turn left. Pub on right of next rdbt behind Asda*

Eighteenth-century cookery writer Elizabeth Raffald was aunt to the man who built this lovely old coaching inn. Its present incarnation is a haven for real ale lovers; and, as the landlady previously ran a well-reviewed eating establishment, it also offers good food, though only a lunchtime. Choices range from sandwiches to sausages with red wine gravy and mash. The courtyard, which still boasts stables and a haylof makes a pleasant summer drinking and eating area.

Open 12–12 **Bar Meals** L served all week 12.30–2.30 (Sat–Sun 12.30–4) Robinsons Robinsons: Unicorn Bitter, Hatters Mild, Robin Bitter, Old Town. 7 **Facilities** Garden Dogs allowed **Notes**

The Nursery Inn

Green Ln, Heaton Norris SK4 2NA

☎ 0161 432 2044 0161 442 1857

e-mail: nurseryinn@hydes37.fsnet.co.uk

dir: *Green Ln off Heaton Moor Rd. Pass rugby club and cobbled road, pub 100yds on right.*

Originally the main headquarters of Stockport County Football Club, with players changing in what is now the pub's interior, and the pitch at the rear. The Nursery dates back to 1939, with the wood panelling in the lounge/dining room reflecting the period. Food is available at lunchtime only – jacket potatoes, sandwiches and baguettes in the bar, and hot dishes such as smoked haddock and tuna steak in the restaurant.

Open 11.30–3 5.30–11 (Fri–Sun 11.30–12) **Bar Meals** L served all week 12–2.30 (Sun 12–4) **Restaurant** L served all week 12–2.30 (Sun 2 sittings 12.30 & 2.30) Hydes Bitter, Hydes Jekylls Gold, Harp Irish, Guest Ales **Facilities** Garden Parking **Notes**

WIGAN MAP 15 SD5

Bird I'th Hand

Gathurst Rd, Orell WN5 0LH ☎ 01942 212006

Handy for Aintree races, this lively pub may well have once been the home of Dr Beecham of 'powders' fame. Home-made food, freshly prepared from market produce, characterises the imaginatively designed menu which offers the likes of stuffed chicken breast, beef stroganoff, Great Grimsby fish pie, Bird special farmhouse stew, liver and onions, and Brixham plaice. Extensive range of starters.

Open 12–11 (Fri–Sat 12–3am) **Bar Meals** L served all week 12–9 D serve all week 12–9 **Restaurant** L served all week 12–9 D served all week 12–9 (Sun 12–8) Av 3 course fixed price £6.95 John Smiths, Directors Bitter, Foster Chesnut Mild, Guest beer. **Facilities** Garden Dogs allowed Parkin Play Area

HAMPSHIRE

ANDOVER MAP 05 SU3

Wyke Down Country Pub & Restaurant

Wyke Down, Picket Piece SP11 6LX

☎ 01264 352 048 01264 324 661

e-mail: info@wykedown.co.uk

dir: *3m from Andover town centre/A303. Follow signs for Wyke Down Caravan Park.*

The pub has been in its time a family farm and a base for Irish navvie building a railway cutting on the Waterloo line outside Andover. The restaurant, which opened over a decade ago, stands on the site of the old farm buildings. A good selection of dishes includes home-made urgers prepared from 100% beef steak, steaks, slow roast lamb shank, ıushroom stroganoff, and fresh fish from the blackboard specials.

pen 12-3 6-11 (Sun 6-10.30) Closed: 25 Dec- 2 Jan **ar Meals** L served all week 12-2 D served all week 6-9 (Fri-Sat 6-9.30, ɹn 6.30-8.30) **Restaurant** L served Sun-Fri 12-2 D served all week -9 (Fri-Sat 6-9.30, Sun 6.30-8.30) Free House Fosters, Guinness, ronenburg & Strongbow. 6 **Facilities** Children's licence Garden arking Play Area

XFORD MAP 05 SU64

he Crown at Axford

G25 2DZ 01256 389492 01256 389149
-mail: thecrowninn.axford@virgin.net

ıe Crown is a small country inn set at the northern edge of the pretty andover Valley. Here you can enjoy your choice from a selection of al ales and wines, with some bread and olives to keep you going, ıd order dishes like pork, beer and watercress sausages. The food all home cooked from local produce wherever possible, including h, game, and veggie dishes from the board. Organic specials are a ature.

pen 12-3 6-11 (Sat 12-11 Sun 12-10.30) **Bar Meals** L served week 12-2.30 D served all week 6.30-9.30 Av main course £9.50 **estaurant** L served all week 12-2.30 D served all week 6.30-9 (Fri Sat 30-9.30, Sun 6.30-8.30) Av 3 course à la carte £16.50 Free House London Pride, Youngs Bitter, Triple FFF, Fosters. 7 **Facilities** Children's ence Garden Dogs allowed Parking

ASINGSTOKE MAP 05 SU65

oddington Arms

pton Grey RG25 2RL 01256 862371 01256 862371
-mail: monca777@aol.com
ir: *Telephone for directions*

ıere is no shortage of traditional charm at this country pub with log fires, 18th-century beams and location near the village duck ɔnd. Hoddington pies and puddings are the house speciality, and addition to a choice of bar snacks and a set price menu of the day, ackboard specials offer the likes of Mediterranean risotto with roasted eppers, baked fillet of cod with basil and parmesan crust, and slow aised lamb shank.

pen 12-3 6-11 (Sun 7-10.30) **Bar Meals** L served all week 12-2 served Mon-Sat 6-9 **Restaurant** L served all week 12-2 D served on-Sat 6-9 Greene King Greene King IPA, Old Speckled Hen, ddles Best. 7 **Facilities** Garden Dogs allowed Parking Play Area

AUGHURST MAP 05 SU56

Pick of the Pubs

The Wellington Arms

Baughurst Rd RG26 5LP 0118 982 0110
e-mail: info@thewellingtonarms.com
dir: *Exit M4 junct 12 follow signs to Newbury along A4. At rdbt take left turn to Aldermaston. At rdbt at top of hill take 2nd exit, at T-junct turn left, pub 1m on left.*

See Pick of the Pubs on page 258

BEAUWORTH MAP 05 SU52

The Milburys

SO24 0PB 01962 771248 01962 7771910
e-mail: info@themilburys.co.uk
dir: *A272 towards Petersfield, after 6m turn right for Beauworth*

A rustic hill-top pub dating from the 17th century and named after the Bronze Age barrow nearby. It is noted for its massive, 250-year-old treadmill that used to draw water from the 300ft well in the bar, and for the far-reaching views across Hampshire that can be savoured from the lofty garden. The African Oasis restaurant has a distinctly South African flavour.

Open 11-3 6-11 (Sun 6-10.30) **Bar Meals** L served all week 12-2 D served all week 6.30-9.30 Av main course £9 **Restaurant** L served all week 12-2 D served all week 6.30-9.30 Av 3 course à la carte £10 Free House Theakstons Old Peculier, Triple FFF Altons Pride, Deuchars, Guest ale. 8 **Facilities** Garden Dogs allowed Parking

BENTLEY MAP 05 SU74

The Bull Inn

GU10 5JH 01420 22156 01420 520772
dir: *2m from Farnham on A31 towards Winchester*

15th-century beamed coaching inn in a Hampshire village made famous by a reality TV show called 'The Village'. Inside are open log fires, two separate bars and a restaurant. Extensive selection of pub food complemented by braised shank of lamb with sweet potato mash and rosemary sauce; pan-fried fillet of salmon with a lemon and chive butter; and roasted hock of ham with swede and potato purée.

Open 11-11 **Bar Meals** L served all week 12-2.30 D served all week 6.30-9.30 (Sun 12-3, 6-8.45) Av main course £10.95 **Restaurant** L served all week 12-2.30 D served all week 6.30-9.30 Av 3 course à la carte £25 Free House Scottish Courage Courage Best, Ringwood Best, Young's Bitter, Fullers London Pride. 8 **Facilities** Garden Dogs allowed Parking

England

The Wellington Arms

An oh-so-pretty whitewashed building with large lawned garden surrounded by fields and woodland. It's an ideal setting for 35 free-range rare breed chickens, whose eggs are used in the kitchen and sold on the bar.

There are beehives too, with over 200,000 inhabitants on a warm summer's day, and herbs are grown just outside the kitchen door. Owners Jason King and Simon Page previously operated a boutique catering company, and this is their first gastro-pub venture. Jason, a gold medal winner for Australia in the Culinary Olympics, has worked for Paul Bocuse in Melbourne and Lyon, Terence Conran in London, and also led a very successful restaurant, La Bodega, in Hong Kong for six years. They've already made their mark here with impressive menus, not to mention a new coffee machine which heralds the serving of morning coffee and afternoon tea at the bar. Attention to detail is reflected in the punctilious use of sometimes unique ingredients, such as Murray River pink salt flakes. Bread is baked by a craft baker, three fish deliveries arrive weekly direct from Brixham, all their beef comes from Orkney, and Henwood Farm in Ashford Hill delivers fresh organic vegetables and salads daily. They even serve Husk teas, an Australian blend of herbal infusions that are free from artificial additives. A good value simple lunch menu is available from Wednesday to Friday, offering choices from three starters, three main courses and two desserts at a fixed price: potted pork rillettes with dill pickles could be followed by twice-baked goats' cheese soufflé on sautéed spinach, and completed with steamed chocolate and hazelnut sponge. At other times, the blackboard may offer Cornish mussels steamed in olde English cider to start, and a main course of Orkney Island beef, shallot and red wine.

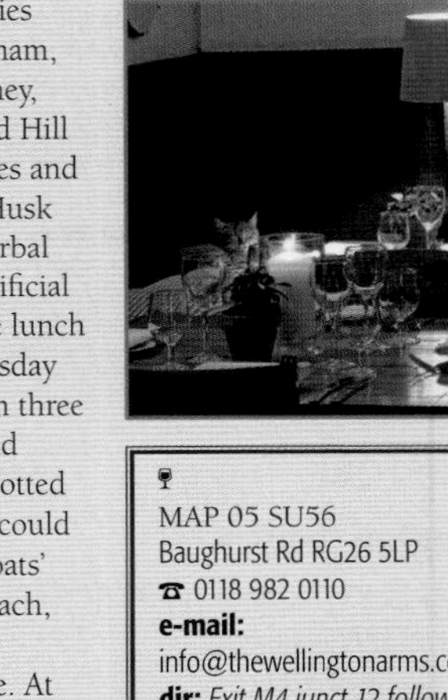

🍷
MAP 05 SU56
Baughurst Rd RG26 5LP
☎ 0118 982 0110
e-mail:
info@thewellingtonarms.com
dir: *Exit M4 junct 12 follow signs to Newbury along A4. At rdbt take left turn to Aldermaston. At rdbt at top of hill take 2nd exit, at T-junct turn left, pub 1m on left.*

Open 12–3 6.30–11.30
Restaurant L served Wed–Sun 12–2.30 D served Tue–Sat 6.30–9.30 Av 3 course à la carte £24
Punch Taverns
6X, Stella, Carlsberg & Guinness. 🍷 12
Facilities Garden Parking

ENTWORTH MAP 05 SU64

he Star Inn

J34 5RB ☎ 01420 561224
mail: matt@star-inn.com
r: *Just off A339 signed from Lasham x-rds.*

ndy for the Woodland Trust's property at Home Farm, The Star cupies a charming spot in prime Hampshire countryside. It's an ractive pub, with eye-catching floral displays in summer and a e, secluded garden. Foodwise, you can choose from good value ourites such as sandwiches, baked potatoes and omelettes; or larger eals like home-made steak and kidney pie; Mexican style enchiladas; a wide variety of fish dishes.

en 12-3 5-11 (Open all day Fri, Sun) (Sat 12-4, 6-11) **r Meals** L served all week 12-2 D served all week 6.30-9 Av main urse £10 **Restaurant** L served all week 12-2 D served all week 6.30-9 un 7-9) Free House Fullers London Pride, Ringwood Best, Doom , ESB. **Facilities** Garden Parking

Pick of the Pubs

The Sun Inn

Sun Hill GU34 5JT ☎ 01420 562338

See Pick of the Pubs on page 261

OLDRE MAP 05 SZ39

he Hobler Inn NEW

uthampton Rd, Battramsley SO41 8PT ☎ 01590 623944
mail: hedi@alcatraz.co.uk
r: *2m from Brockenhurst, towards Lymington on main road*

the main road between Brockenhurst and Lymington, with large ssed area and trestle tables ideal for families visiting the New Forest. cently taken over and refurbished, it's more London wine bar than al, but still serves a well-kept pint of Ringwood. Hot lunchtime acks like Welsh rarebit or Boston baked beans on toast are good ue. Mains include a variation on the classic shepherd's pie but with ded Nepalese spices.

en 11-11 **Bar Meals** L served all week 12-6 D served all week 9.30 Av main course £6 **Restaurant** L served all week 12-6 D served week 6-9.30 Av 3 course à la carte £18 Av 2 course fixed price 95 Ringwood, Ringwood Best, Timothy Taylor, Carlsberg. 10 cilities Garden Parking

Pick of the Pubs

The Red Lion

Rope Hill SO41 8NE ☎ 01590 673177 01590 674036
e-mail: www.theredlionboldre.co.uk
dir: *1m outside Lymington off A337. From M27 junct 1 through Lyndhurst & Brockehurst towards Lymington, follow signs for Boldre off A337*

The quintessential New Forest pub, the Red Lion even has a mention in the Domesday Book, although today's inn only dates from the 15th century, when it was created from a stable and two cottages. Inside you'll find a rambling series of beamed rooms packed with rural memorabilia. Head chef Richard West delights in

CONTINUED

BOLDRE continued

creating traditional, home-made dishes that make excellent use of local and seasonal produce, including venison from Forest herds, and fish from local catches. Start off with red onion and goats' cheese tartlet, or pan-fried black pudding with caramelised apple, before sampling such popular dishes as steak and Ringwood ale pie; twice-roasted pork belly, apple and cinnamon gravy; wild rabbit risotto; venison steak with juniper syrup; or whole plaice grilled with citrus butter. Booking is recommended, as are Angela's infamous home-made puddings.

Open 11–11 (Sun 12–10.30) **Bar Meals** L served all week 12–2.30 D served all week 6–9.30 (Sun 12–4, 6–9) Av main course £9 **Restaurant** L served all week 12–2.30 D served all week 6–9.30 (Sun 12–4, 6–9) Free House Wadworths 6X, Ringwood Best, Ringwood Fortyniner, Isle of Purbeck. 18 **Facilities** Garden Dogs allowed Parking

See advert on page 259

BRAMDEAN MAP 05 SU62

The Fox Inn

SO24 0LP ☎ 01962 771363

e-mail: thefoxinn@callnetuk.com

dir: *A272 between Winchester & Petersfield*

The crest fixed to the exterior of this 400-year-old pub commemorates the day when the Prince of Wales (later king George IV) stopped by for refreshments. Situated in the beautiful Meon Valley surrounded by copper beech trees, The Fox serves locally sourced food including a good blackboard selection of fresh fish dishes – perhaps supreme of halibut with lime and chilli butter. Other typical choices include pork fillet with stilton and brandy sauce.

Open 11–3 6–11 (Winter 6.30–11) **Bar Meals** L served all week 12–2 D served all week 7–9 Av main course £12.95 Greene King Ruddles County & IPA Smooth. 7 **Facilities** Garden Parking Play Area

BROOK MAP 05 SU21

The Bell Inn ★★★ HL

SO43 7HE ☎ 023 80812214 023 80813958

e-mail: bell@bramshaw.co.uk

web: www.bellinnbramshaw.co.uk

dir: *From M27 junct 1 (Cadnam) take B3078 signed Brook, 0.5m on right*

Since it was established in 1782 the Bell has been owned continuously by the same family. Features of the handsome building include white-painted window shutters, an imposing inglenook fireplace and beamed bedrooms. Bar food ranges from hot and cold snacks (omelettes, sandwiches, burgers) to daily specials featuring fresh fish and local game in season. A daily menu offers a wider choice.

Open 11–11 **Bar Meals** L served all week 12–9.30 D served all week Av main course £11 **Restaurant** L served all week 12–3 D served all week 7.30–9.30 Free House Ringwood Best, Fosters, Kronenbourg, Guinness & Guest Ale. 10 **Facilities** Garden Parking Play Area **Rooms** 25 bedrooms en suite S£55 D£100

BUCKLERS HARD MAP 05 SU4

The Master Builders House Hotel

★★★ HL

SO42 7XB ☎ 01590 616253 01590 616297

e-mail: res@themasterbuilders.co.uk

dir: *From M27 junct 2 follow signs to Beaulieu. Turn left onto B3056. Left to Bucklers Hard. Hotel 2m on left hand side*

This fine 18th-century building was once home to master shipbuilder Henry Adams, and has been carefully refurbished to create a smart hotel and the beamed Yachtsman's Bar. The bar offers ploughman's, sandwiches and a short lunch and evening menu with the likes of chicken, ham and leek pie; and braised lamb shank with red wine and rosemary jus. Don't forget to explore this historic ship-building village and the Beaulieu River, which runs by the hotel.

Open 11–11 (Nov–Mar Sun–Thu 11–6) **Bar Meals** L served all week 12–2.30 D served all week 7–9 **Restaurant** L served all week 12–3 D served all week 7–10 Free House Greene King IPA, Abbots, Old Hooky. **Facilities** Garden Dogs allowed Parking **Rooms** 25 bedrooms en suite S£99 D£180

BURLEY MAP 05 SU2

The Burley Inn

BH24 4AB ☎ 01425 403448

e-mail: info@theburleyinn.co.uk

dir: *4m from Ringwood*

If you think the Burley Inn, lying at the heart of the New Forest, might have been a spacious family home during the Edwardian era, you'd be right. Before it became a pub, this is where the local doctor practised, with the waiting room now the bar and dining areas. The menu ranges from Old English fish pie and steak and kidney pudding, to traditional lasagne and cheesy vegetable cakes.

Open 9–11 (Sun 9–10.30) **Bar Meals** L served all week 12–6 D served all week 12–9.30 **Restaurant** L served all week 12–6 D served all week 12–9.30 Free House Ringwood Best, Ringwood Old Thumper. 11 **Facilities** Garden Dogs allowed Parking **Rooms** 10 bedrooms en suite S£35 D£70 (★★★ INN)

The Sun Inn

his delightful flower-decked pub is either the first building you pass as you enter Bentworth om the Basingstoke-Alton road, or the last one out, depending on which way you are travelling, nd it always seems to come as a surprise.

riginally two cottages, it now has ree interconnecting rooms, each ith its own log fire and brick and ood floors. The bar is the middle om, right in front of the door. ws, settles, scrubbed pine tables ith lit candles in the evening add the homely atmosphere. Food hearty and traditional, with beef roganoff; minted lamb; a range of eat and vegetarian curries; liver d bacon; cheesy haddock bake; led Yorkshire puddings; braised eak in red wine and mushroom uce; and Mediterranean lamb. ame in season includes venison, oked in Guinness with pickled alnuts, and pheasant. Everything, om the soup to the dessert, is ome made. A thriving free house, offers eight hand-pumped real es, including Cheriton Brewhouse Pots Ale, Ringwood's Best and Old Thumper, both from Hampshire breweries, and Brakspear Bitter and Fuller's London Pride. There is much to see and do in the area: Gilbert White's House and the Oates Museum in Selborne are not far away, and neither is Jane Austen's House at Chawton, nor the Watercress Line at Alresford. Also within easy reach is Basing House in Old Basing, on the outskirts of Basingstoke.

MAP 05 SU64
Sun Hill GU34 5JT
☎ 01420 562338

Open 12-3 6-11 (Sun 12-10.30)
Bar Meals L served all week 12-2 D served all week 7-9.30
Free House
Cheriton Pots Ale, Ringwood Best & Old Thumper, Brakspear Bitter, Fuller's London Pride.
Facilities Garden Dogs allowed Parking

England

CADNAM

Sir John Barleycorn NEW 🍷

Old Romsey Rd SO40 2NP

☎ 01202 746162 📠 01202 743080

e-mail: hedi@alcatraz.co.uk

dir: *From Southampton M27 junct 1 into Cadnam*

Reputedly the oldest inn in the New Forest, this friendly establishment is formed from three 12th-century cottages, one of which was once home to the charcoal burner who discovered the body of King William Rufus. A thorough menu covers all the options from quick snacks and sandwiches to toad-in-the-hole; chicken, leek and bacon pie; and Thai chicken curry. The name derives from a folksong celebrating the transformation of barley to beer.

Open 11–11 **Bar Meals** L served all week 12–7 D served all week 6–9.30 Av main course £6 **Restaurant** L served all week 12–7 D served all week 6–9.30 Av 3 course à la carte £17 Av 2 course fixed price £9.95 Ringwood, Ringwood Best, London Pride, Carlsberg. 🍷 10 **Facilities** Garden Parking

CHALTON MAP 05 SU71

Pick of the Pubs

The Red Lion 🍷

PO8 0BG ☎ 023 9259 2246 📠 023 9259 6915

e-mail: redlionchalton@fullers.co.uk

dir: *Just off A3 between Horndean & Petersfield. Follow signs for Chalton*

Built of wood, white daub and thatch, this ancient inn blends effortlessly into the hills and trees of the South Downs. Believed to be the oldest pub in Hampshire, it was originally established in 1147 as a workshop and residence for the craftsmen working on the Norman church across the road. By 1460 it had expanded to become a hostel for church dignitaries, and in 1503 it was granted a licence to sell ale. Spectacular views can be enjoyed from the large garden and modern dining room. Under new management, the popular snack menu includes the likes of barbecued ribs; home-made Thai fishcakes; beef sandwiches; and ploughman's with mature cheddar or home-cooked gammon. The main specials board changes daily: look out for the famous steak and HSB ale pie; lamb and apricot casserole; and smoked brie and asparagus tart.

Open 11.30–11 (Sun 11.45–10.30) **Bar Meals** L served all week 12–9 D served all week 12–9 (Fri–Sat 12–9.30, Sun 12–8) Av main course £8.95 **Restaurant** L served all week 12–9 D served all week 12–9 (Fri–Sat 12–9.30, Sun 12–8) Av 3 course à la carte £18 Fullers Butser, Winter Brew, GB & HSB, Fullers London Pride. 🍷 20 **Facilities** Garden Dogs allowed Parking

CHARTER ALLEY MAP 05 SU

The White Hart Inn

White Hart Ln RG26 5QA

☎ 01256 850048 📠 01256 850524

e-mail: enquiries@whitehartcharteralley.com

dir: *From M3 junct 6 take A339 towards Newbury. Turn right to Ramsdell. Right at church, then 1st left into White Hart Lane*

Tucked away on the outskirts of the village overlooking open farmland and woods, this pub draws everyone from cyclists and walkers to real ale enthusiasts. Dating from 1819, it originally catered for local woodsmen, and coaches visiting the farrier's next door. These days the refreshments typically include local game pie; venison steak in re wine sauce; chicken madras; and filled ciabatta or burgers.

Open 12–2.30 7–11 (Sun 12–3, 7–10.30) Closed: 25–26 Dec, 1 Jan **Bar Meals** L served all week 12–2 D served Tue–Sat 7–9 Av main course £8.95 **Restaurant** L served all week 12–2 D served Tue–Sat 7–9 Av 3 course à la carte £20 Free House West Berkshire Mild, Palmers IPA, Triple FFF Alton Pride, Guest Ales. **Facilities** Garden Dogs allowed Park

CHAWTON MAP 05 SU

The Greyfriar

Winchester Rd GU34 1SB ☎ 01420 83841

e-mail: info@thegreyfriar.co.uk

dir: *Off A31 near Alton. Access to Chawton via A31/A32 junct. Follow Jane Austen's House signs.*

A terrace of cottages in the 16th century, a 'beer shop' by 1847, and from 1871 a proper pub, known as the Chawton Arms. The simple lunch menu offers baguettes, ploughman's, quiches, burgers and breaded scampi tails. The evening menu, which changes most days, might well come up with milk-fed lamb with leeks; fillet of gurnard w tomatoes and olive sauce; and gammon steak with bubble and sque Jane Austen's house is opposite.

Open 12–11 (Sun 12–10.30) **Bar Meals** L served all week 12–2 D served all week 7–9.30 (Sun 12–3, 6–8.30) Av main course £10.95 **Restaurant** L served all week 12–2 D served all week 7–9.30 (Sun 12–3, 6–8.30) Fuller's London Pride, Chiswick & ESB, Discovery & Seasonal Ales. **Facilities** Garden Dogs allowed Parking Play Area

HERITON MAP 05 SU52

Pick of the Pubs

The Flower Pots Inn

SO24 0QQ ☎ 01962 771318 01962 771318

dir: *A272 toward Petersfield, left onto B3046, pub 0.75m on right*

The Flower Pots Inn is a friendly red brick village pub, originally a farmhouse built in the 1840s by the head gardener of nearby Avington Park. It serves award-winning beers like Pots Ale or Goodens Gold, brewed in the micro-brewery across the car park. There are two bars: the rustic, pine-furnished public bar and the cosy saloon with its comfy sofa, both with welcoming open fires in winter. A large, safe garden allows young ones to let off steam. Wednesday night is Punjabi curry night, otherwise simple home-made bar food is the order of the day: toasted sandwiches, jacket potatoes and tasty hotpots – beef, spicy mixed bean, and lamb and apricot – served with a choice of crusty bread, basmati rice, garlic bread or jacket potato. There are also ploughman's (with cheese, ham or beef), and giant baps filled with a choice of beef, pork steak and onions, bacon and mushroom, cheese, or coronation chicken.

Open 12-2.30 6-11 (Sun 12-3, 7-10.30) **Bar Meals** L served all week 12-2 D served Mon-Sat 7-9 (Wed eve curry only, no dinner BHs) Free House Flower Pots Bitter & Goodens Gold. **Facilities** Garden Dogs allowed Parking **Notes**

CRAWLEY MAP 05 SU43

The Fox and Hounds

SO21 2PR ☎ 01962 776006 01962 776006

e-mail: liamlewisairey@aol.com

dir: *A34 onto A272 then 1st right into Crawley*

Just north west of Winchester, at the heart of a peaceful Hampshire village, this mock Tudor inn enjoys a burgeoning reputation for simple well-cooked food. Restored to former glories, it features beamed rooms warmed by log fires that create a welcoming, lived-in atmosphere. Typical menu choices include Old English sausages on bubble and squeak, steak and ale pie, salmon fillet with hollandaise sauce, dressed crab salad, and pork fillet with black pudding.

Open 12-3 6-11 (Sun 12-4) **Bar Meals** L served all week 12-2 D served all week 6-9 Av main course £6.95 **Restaurant** L served all week 12-2 D served all week 7-9 Av 3 course à la carte £15 Free House Wadworth 6X, Ringwood Best, Gales HSB, Fullers London Pride. 15 **Facilities** Children's licence Garden Parking Play Area

CRONDALL MAP 05 SU74

Pick of the Pubs

The Hampshire Arms

Pankridge St GU10 5QU

☎ 01252 850418 01252 850418

e-mail: dining@thehampshirearms.co.uk

dir: *From M3 junct 5 take A287 S towards Farnham. Follow signs to Crondall on right*

See Pick of the Pubs on page 264

DAMERHAM MAP 05 SU11

The Compasses Inn ★★★★ INN

SP6 3HQ ☎ 01725 518231 01725 518880

e-mail: info@compassesinn.net

web: www.compassesinn.net

dir: *From Fordingbridge (A338) follow signs for Sandleheath/ Damerham. Signed from B3078*

The Compasses is a perfect example of the traditional family-run country free house. Set next to the village green, it is an ideal spot for a tranquil summer pint or a winter warmer round the welcoming open fires. The ales are augmented by over 100 malt whiskies and a good selection of wines. Freshly prepared food is served in the bar, dining room or garden: it ranges from a simple home-baked bread ploughman's to pan-fried sea bass with prawns.

Open 11-3 6-11 (Sat all day Sun 12-4, 7-10.30) **Bar Meals** L served all week 12-2.30 D served all week 7-9.30 (Sun 7-9) **Restaurant** L served all week 12-2.30 D served all week 7-9.30 (Sun 7-9) Av 3 course à la carte £20 Free House Ringwood Best, Hop Back Summer Lightning, Courage Best, Palmers IPA. 8 **Facilities** Children's licence Garden Dogs allowed Parking **Rooms** 6 bedrooms en suite S£45 D£79

DOWNTON MAP 05 SZ29

The Royal Oak

Christchurch Rd SO41 0LA ☎ 01590 642297

e-mail: royaloak@alcatraz.co.uk

dir: *On A337 between Lymington & Christchurch*

Two miles south of the New Forest and just one mile from the beach at Lymington, this renovated pub is renowned for its food. Snack on a traditional ploughman's platter or daytime sandwiches such as warm chicken, chorizo and rocket or brie and bacon. Main meals include salmon fish cakes with tomato and chilli jam; sirloin steak with peppercorn sauce; and gourmet burgers.

Open 11-11 (Sun 11.30-11) Closed: 25 Dec **Bar Meals** L served all week 12-6 D served all week 6-9.30 **Restaurant** L served all week 12-6 D served all week 6-9.30 Enterprise Inns Ringwood Best Bitter, Gales HSB, Fullers London Pride. 15 **Facilities** Garden Parking

The Hampshire Arms

Alan and Margaret Piesse have been at the Hampshire Arms since February 2005, since when they have had the restaurant tastefully refurbished. The bar is now light and elegant, as are the two main dining areas and intimate alcoves.

Throughout the public rooms open fires, exposed beams and candlelight combine to create a delightfully welcoming atmosphere. The building dates from the 18th century and began as two cottages, but over the years it has also been a courthouse, a post office and a bakery. Outside there is a large landscaped garden with a patio area perfect for al fresco dining in the warmer weather. For a leisurely lunch in the bar or cosy dining room you might be tempted by the chef's special chicken liver parfait with red onion marmalade, freshly made brioche and sultanas soaked in jasmine tea, as a starter. Smoked salmon and haddock fishcakes with buttered spinach and French butter sauce are an established favourite, as is the classic dessert, French lemon tart, served with chocolate chip shortbread. The mid-week fixed-price menu aims to offer value for money but the same high quality of food, with choices such as seared scallops with apple and ginger purée and soft herb salad; roast rump of lamb with three mustards, wilted greens and lamb reduction; and caramelised banana cheesecake with chocolate sauce and crème Chantilly. Alternatively finish with the chef's selection of cheese and biscuits.

🍷
MAP 05 SU74
Pankridge St GU10 5QU
☎ 01252 850418
📠 01252 850418
e-mail:
dining@thehampshirearms.co.uk
dir: *From M3 junct 5 take A287 S towards Farnham. Follow signs to Crondall on right*

Open 11-3 6-11.30 (all day Sat, Sun 12-10.30)
Bar Meals L served Tue-Sun 12-2.30 D served Tue-Sat
Av main course £8
Restaurant L served Tue-Sun 12-2.30 D served Tue-Sat 6.30-9.30 Av 3 course à la carte £31.50
Greene King
Greene King IPA, Abbot Ale, Ruddles County,. 🍷 10
Facilities Garden Parking

UMMER MAP 05 SU54

he Queen Inn

own St RG25 2AD ☎ 01256 397367 01256 397601
mail: richardmoore49@btinternet.com
r: *M3 junct 7, follow Dummer signs*

u can dine by candlelight from the restaurant menu at this h-century village pub with low beams and huge open log fire. ernatively you'll find lunchtime savouries like Welsh or Scottish ebits alongside the sandwiches and jackets. A bar menu offers erything from starters and healthy options to flame grills, house ourites, and specials like chargrilled half chicken peri peri and ef bourguignon. Beers include guest ales, and the wine list is mmendably unpretentious.

en 11-3 6-11 (Sun 12-3 7-10.30) **Bar Meals** L served all week -2 D served all week 6-9.30 (Sun 7-9) **Restaurant** L served all week -2 D served all week 6-9.30 Enterprise Inns Courage Best & n Smiths, Fuller's London Pride, Old Speckled Hen & Guest ales. 10 **ilities** Garden Parking

AST END MAP 05 SZ39

Pick of the Pubs

The East End Arms

Main Rd SO41 5SY ☎ 01590 626223 01590 626223
-mail: joanna@eastendarms.co.uk
dir: *From Lymington past Isle of Wight ferry for 3m.*

ucked down quiet lanes near Beaulieu and historic Buckler's Hard, his New Forest inn has a growing reputation as a gastro-pub. It etains the authenticity of a proper local in the Foresters Bar, with s stone floors and open fires, where Ringwood ales are drawn traight from the wood. It is in the atmospheric lounge bar that the nteresting range of modern, brasserie-style dishes is offered from daily changing menu. Locally sourced fish/seafood make a strong howing in dishes such as catch of the day with mixed salad and rench fries; or brochette of monkfish with sun-blushed tomato rackwheat and pesto dressing. An alternative might be home-nade linguini with salami, plum tomatoes and goats' cheese; or risp slow-cooked belly pork with roast root vegetables, poached ear and walnut jus. The pub is well worth the short diversion om the nearby Solent Way long distance footpath.

pen 11.30-3 6-11 (Sun 12-9) **Bar Meals** L served Mon-Sat 2-2.30 D served Tue-Sat Av main course £5.50 **Restaurant** L served ues-Sun 12-2.30 D served Tue-Sat 7-9.30 (Mon baguettes only) Av 3 ourse à la carte £20 Free House Ringwood Best, Archers & ortyniner. **Facilities** Garden Dogs allowed Parking

EAST MEON MAP 05 SU62

Ye Olde George Inn

Church St GU32 1NH ☎ 01730 823481 01730 823759
e-mail: yeoldgeorge@aol.com
dir: *S of A272 (Winchester/Petersfield). 1.5m from Petersfield turn left opposite church*

This 15th-century inn is located in a lovely old village on the River Meon, close to a magnificent Norman church. Its open fires, heavy beams and rustic artefacts create an ideal setting for a good choice of real ales and freshly prepared food in the bar or restaurant. Fish features strongly with dishes of baked sea bass with samphire and balsamic olive dressing, or poached halibut with mussel sauce.

Open 12-3 (Sat 11-3 6-11) **Bar Meals** L served all week 12-2 D served all week 7-9 Av main course £9.50 **Restaurant** L served all week 12-2 D served all week 7-9 Av 3 course à la carte £16.95 Hall & Woodhouse Badger Best, Tanglefoot & King & Barnes Sussex. 8 **Facilities** Garden Dogs allowed Parking

EASTON MAP 05 SU53

Pick of the Pubs

The Chestnut Horse

SO21 1EG ☎ 01962 779257 01962 779037
dir: *From M3 junct 9 take A33 towards Basingstoke, then B3047. Take 2nd right, then 1st left*

See Pick of the Pubs on page 267

The Cricketers Inn

SO21 1EJ ☎ 01962 779353 01962 779010
e-mail: thecricketersinn@btconnect.com
dir: *M3 junct 9, A33 towards Basingstoke, right at Kingsworthy onto B3047. In 0.75m turn right.*

Standing on a corner in the heart of a popular village, this 1904 pub is a real local, with a single L-shaped bar and cricketing memorabilia on the walls. Its owners maintain its famous crusty doorstep sandwiches and open toasties, in addition to offering filled Yorkshires and specials of ribs, sweet and sour chicken and cottage pie.

Open 12-2.30 6-11 (Sun 12-3, 7-11) **Bar Meals** L served all week 12-2 D served Mon-Sat 7-9 Av main course £7 **Restaurant** L served all week 12-2 D served Mon-Sat 7-9 Marstons Ringwood, Guest ales. **Facilities** Garden Dogs allowed Parking

England

EAST TYTHERLEY MAP 05 SU22

Pick of the Pubs

The Star Inn Tytherley ★★★★ INN

SO51 0LW ☎ 01794 340225 01794 340225
e-mail: info@starinn-uk.com
dir: *5m N of Romsey off A3057, left for Dunbridge on B3084. Left for Awbridge & Kents Oak. Through Lockerley then 1m*

See Pick of the Pubs on page 268

EMSWORTH MAP 05 SU70

The Sussex Brewery

36 Main Rd PO10 8AU ☎ 01243 371533 01243 379684
dir: *On A259 between Havant & Chichester*

A fresh 'carpet' of sawdust is laid daily in the bars of this traditional 17th-century pub that boasts wooden floors, large open fires and a typically warm welcome. Fully 15 sausage recipes are on offer containing all kind of fillings, from traditional to exotic. Non sausage-related daily specials include fresh local fish, steaks, or rack of lamb.

Open 11–11 **Bar Meals** L served all week 12–2.30 D served all week 7–9.30 Av main course £8 **Restaurant** L served all week 12–2.30 D served all week 7–9.30 Young & Co Youngs Special, Youngs Ordinary, Waggle Dance, Bombardiers Tribute. 9 **Facilities** Garden Dogs allowed Parking

EVERSLEY MAP 05 SU76

The Golden Pot

Reading Rd RG27 0NB ☎ 0118 973 2104 0118 973 4042
e-mail: jcalder@goldenpot.co.uk
web: www.golden-pot.co.uk
dir: *Between Reading & Camberley on B3272 approx 0.25m from Eversley cricket ground*

Dating back to the 1700s, this welcoming pub has a warming fire connecting the bar and restaurant, and both offer wide-ranging menus: look out for baguettes at lunchtime, and bar dishes like escalope of venison with crème fraîche borscht. The restaurant menu offers the likes of seared king scallops followed by chicken and mozzarella roulade. Monday evenings are Swiss rôsti night with live music.

Open 11.30–3 5.30–11 Closed: 25–26 Dec, 1 Jan **Bar Meals** L served all week 12–2.15 D served Mon–Sat 6–9.15 (Sun lunch 12–2) **Restaurant** L served Sun–Fri 12–2 D served Mon–Sat 7–9 Greene King Greene King Ruddles Best, Abbot Ale, Greene King IPA. 8 **Facilities** Garden Dogs allowed Parking

FORDINGBRIDGE MAP 05 SU1

The Augustus John

116 Station Rd SP6 1DG ☎ 01425 652098
e-mail: enquiries@augustusjohn.com

The renowned British portrait painter lived in the village and drank here, long before it became known as a smart dining pub. Lunches range from sandwiches and baguettes to salads, by way of jackets and light meals. The carte offers Aberdeen Angus steaks, broccoli an cauliflower bake, rack of Welsh lamb, and fillet of pork tenderloin, wi fresh fish and daily specials on the blackboard. There is also a tempti Thai menu.

Open 11.30–3.30 6–12 **Bar Meals** L served all week 11.30–2 D served a week 6.30–9 (Sun 7–9) **Restaurant** L served all week 11.30–2 D served week 6.30–9 Eldridge Pope Flowers IPA, Ringwood Best, John Smi & Courage Directrors. 8 **Facilities** Garden Dogs allowed Parking

FRITHAM MAP 05 SU

The Royal Oak

SO43 7HJ ☎ 02380 812606 02380 814066
e-mail: royaloakfritham@btopenworld.com
dir: *Exit M27 junct 1, B3078 signed Fordingbridge. 2m left at x-rds signed Ocknell & Fritham.*

In a village where most buildings were probably once thatched, this small, 17th-century traditional country pub deep in the New Forest is the only one remaining. Known as the Parliament of the Forest because of all the local issues debated in the back bar. Unaltered for some 100 years, and with no jukebox or fruit machines, it doesn't of a wide range of food, although home-made evening meals are serve two nights per week in winter and by arrangement.

Open 11–3 6–11 (Summer Sat 11–11, Sun 12–10.30) **Bar Meals** L serv all week 12–2.30 Free House Ringwood Best & Fortyniner, Hop Ba Summer Lightning, Palmers Dorset Gold, Bowman Ales Swift One. 12 **Facilities** Garden Dogs allowed **Notes**

The Chestnut Horse

st a few miles from the City of Winchester, hidden in the idyllic village of Easton in the equally vely Itchen valley, this 16th-century dining pub has gained a well-earned local reputation for e quality of its food.

d tankards and teapots hang)m the low-beamed ceilings in the 'o bar areas, where a large open e is the central focus through e winter months. The romantic ndlelit restaurants are equally viting: plates adorn the light, nelled Green Room, and there's a)od-burning stove in the darker v-beamed Red Room. Fans of od food on a shoestring will want seek out the excellent value set ice menu that opens with Thai hcakes, or chicken, cream cheese d chive paté, and goes on to nb navarin with pomme purée; ared salmon darne with red ıtil dahl; beef chilli; or the pub's mous' fish and chips. From the ırte, you might start with a tian fresh Dorset crab and crayfish tails or pan-seared loin and rillette of rabbit with horseradish cream and hazelnut oil, then continue with marinated ostrich fillet with tomato and marjoram polenta, sea bass fillet with tarragon crushed new potatoes, or a prime Scotch sirloin with peppercorn sauce. Dessert choices include plum tart tatin with butterscotch sauce, or blackberry and kirsch crème brûlée. There's also a traditional roast available on Sunday. Beers such as Chestnut Horse Special and Badger Tanglefoot take some beating, and there's a choice of 30 malt whiskies. Outside is a heated decked area.

🍷
MAP 05 SU53
SO21 1EG
☎ 01962 779257
📠 01962 779037
dir: *From M3 junct 9 take A33 towards Basingstoke, then B3047. Take 2nd right, then 1st left*

Open 11–3 5.30–11 (All day Sat) (Sun eve Winter closes at 6pm)
Bar Meals L served all week 12–2.30 D served all week 6–9.30 (Sun 12–4 winter, 12–8 summer) Av main course £12.95
Restaurant L served all week 12–2.30 D served all week 6–9.30 (Sun 12–4 winter, 12–8 summer) Av 3 course à la carte £24 Av 2 course fixed price £10
Hall & Woodhouse
Chestnut Horse Special, Badger First Gold, Tanglefoot. 🍷 9
Facilities Garden Dogs allowed Parking

The Star Inn Tytherley

Set in the smallest village in the Test Valley, in the heart of the Hampshire countryside, the 17th century Star Inn stands overlooking the village cricket green. Matches are still played here on Tuesday evenings and Saturday afternoons in season.

The area is also popular with walkers, and for the enthusiastic fly fisherman the Star makes a perfect watering hole after a day on the world-famous River Test, or the Holbury Lakes. To the back of the cricket green is Lockerley Manor, the estate to which the inn belonged until 1933. You'll find seasonal Ringwood beers and other guest ales behind the bar, plus an extensive international wine list, carefully compiled to offer a selection of good 'quaffing' wines as well as fine bottles for a special occasion. Dine where you like, in the bar, in the main dining room, or outside on the patio in summer, where you can also play chess on a king-sized board. The menu features interesting British dishes, making good use of local and regional produce. Starters range from spiced pumpkin soup to pan-fried pigeon breast with pearl barley and red pepper risotto and chocolate sauce. Interest doesn't wane through the mains, with a vegetarian option of parsnip bread and butter pudding, or a meatily robust roast saddle of venison with carrot and celeriac strudel, stilton polenta and damson jus. Seafood is also featured, maybe poached halibut fillet with red rice, braised fennel and gribiche sauce. Appetising flavour combinations among the desserts include baked figs with clotted cream and pistachio shortbread, or chocolate and orange torte with cardamom crème anglaise.

★★★★ INN ◎◎ ➪ 🍷
MAP 05 SU22
SO51 0LW
☎ 01794 340225
📠 01794 340225
e-mail: info@starinn-uk.com
dir: *5m N of Romsey off A3057, left for Dunbridge on B3084. Left for Awbridge & Kents Oak. Through Lockerley then 1m*

Open 11-3 6-11
Bar Meals L served Tue-Sun 12-2.30 D served Tue-Sat 7-9
Restaurant L served Tue-Sun 12-2.30 D served Tue-Sat 7-9
Free House
Ringwood Best, Seasonal Ringwood Beers, Hidden Quest & Guest Beers. 🍷 8
Facilities Children's licence Garden Dogs allowed Parking Play Area
Rooms 3 bedrooms en suite S£60 D£90

AMBLEDON MAP 05 SU61

e Vine at Hambledon

est St PO7 4RW ☎ 02392 632419
nail: landlord@vinepub.com
: *Just off B2150*

osy little pub with a welcoming atmosphere, tucked away in the n street of the pretty village of Hambledon. Over the past few years n and Vicki Faulkner have made an impression with their modern nus built around traditional British cooking. Look out for starters scallops wrapped in Parma ham with a truffle scented green n salad, and mains such as pan-fried fillet of turbot with braised terbean and chorizo ragout.

en 11.30-3 6-11 (Sun 12-4, 7-10.30) **Bar Meals** L served veek 12-2 D served Mon-Sat 7-9 (Sun 12-4) Av main course **Restaurant** L served all week 12-2 D served Mon-Sat 7-9 Av 3 rse à la carte £19 W'hampton & Dudley Ringwood Best, nings Cockerhoop, Ringwood 49er, "Vine" House Bitter. 11 **ilities** Children's licence Garden Dogs allowed

AMBLE-LE-RICE MAP 05 SU40

Pick of the Pubs

he Bugle

igh St SO31 4HA
☎ 023 8045 3000 023 8045 3051
-mail: manager@buglehamble.co.uk
ir: *M27 junct 8, follow signs to Hamble. In village centre rn right at mini-rdbt into one-way cobbled street, pub at nd*

See Pick of the Pubs on page 271

ARTLEY WINTNEY MAP 05 SU75

e Phoenix Inn

ndon Rd, Phoenix Green RG27 8RT
01252 842484 01252 845508
: *On A30 between Hook & Hartley Wintney. 3m from M3, 7m n M4*

y and Alex Owen have taken over at this 17th-century former ching inn. Andy is the chef, whose experience includes time served ordon Ramsay's restaurant at Claridges. Food choices range from d baguettes with chunky chips, and the prime grilled beef Phoenix burger, to braised lamb shank with herb mash, and West Country chicken with a herb stuffing. The inn also has a large beer garden with mature trees and scattered picnic benches.

Open 12-3 5.30-11 **Bar Meals** L served all week 12-2.30 (Sun 12-3) D served Mon-Sat 6.30-9.30 Av main course £6.95 **Restaurant** L served all week 12-2.30 (Sun 12-3) D served Mon-Sat 6.30-9.30 Av 3 course à la carte £22 Punch Taverns Ringwood Best, London Pride, Guest Beers. **Facilities** Children's licence Garden Parking

HAVANT MAP 05 SU70

The Royal Oak

19 Langstone High St, Langstone PO9 1RY
☎ 023 92483125 023 9247 6838

Occupying an outstanding position overlooking Langstone Harbour, this historic 16th-century pub is noted for its rustic, unspoilt interior. Flagstone floors, exposed beams and winter fires contrast with the waterfront benches and secluded rear garden for alfresco summer drinking. Light lunches such as rich tomato soup or chicken Caesar salad support a dinner menu that includes slow-cooked Welsh lamb; baked salmon fillet; and British ham hock glazed with honey mustard.

Open 11-11 Rest: 25 Dec Closed eve **Bar Meals** L served all week 12-6 D served all week 6-9 Av main course £6.95 **Restaurant** L served all week 12-6 D served all week 6-9 Av 3 course à la carte £13.95 Laurel Pub Partnership Interbrew Flowers, Greene King IPA, Ruddles County, Speckled Hen. 16 **Facilities** Garden Dogs allowed

HOOK MAP 05 SU75

Crooked Billet

London Rd RG27 9EH ☎ 01256 762118 01256 761011
e-mail: richardbarwise@aol.com
dir: *From M3 take Hook ring road. At 3rd rdbt turn right onto A30 towards London, pub on left 0.5m by river*

The present pub dates back to 1935, though there has been a hostelry on this site since the 1600s. Food to suit all appetites includes half a shoulder of lamb in mint gravy; Billet toad in the hole with mash and onion gravy; home-made steak and kidney pie; fresh cod fillets in beer batter; and a range of ploughman's with hot baguette.

Open 11.30-3 6-11 (Fri-Sat 6-1) **Bar Meals** L served all week 12-2.30 D served all week 7-9.30 (Fri-Sat 7-10 Sun 12-3) **Restaurant** L served all week 12-2.30 D served all week 7-9.30 (Fri-Sat 7-10) Free House Scottish Courage Courage Best & Directors & John Smith's, Hogs Back TEA, Timothy Taylors Landord. 8 **Facilities** Garden Dogs allowed Parking Play Area

England

HORSEBRIDGE MAP 05 SU33

John O'Gaunt Inn

SO20 6PU ☎ 01794 388394
e-mail: johnogaunt@aol.com
dir: *A3057 Horsebridge 4m from Stockbridge, right at brown information board.*

Walkers from the nearby Test Way, fishermen from the River Test and the winter shooting fraternity all frequent this small country inn, six miles north of Romsey. It provides a great atmosphere for well-kept ales and generously priced food. The menu showcases fresh local produce, with dishes such as home-made steak and kidney pudding, and liver and bacon, followed by a good selection of puddings. A traditional roast at Sunday lunchtime too.

Open 11-3 6-11 (Sat-Sun all day) Closed: 4-5 Jan **Bar Meals** L served all week 12-2.45 D served Tue-Sat 6-9.30 Av main course £7 **Restaurant** L served Tue-Sun 12-2.45 D served Tue-Sat 6-9.45 Free House Ringwood Best Bitter, Ringwood Fortyniner, Palmers IPA, Carlsberg & Thatchers. 8 **Facilities** Children's licence Garden Dogs allowed Parking

IBSLEY MAP 05 SU10

Old Beams Inn NEW

Salisbury Rd BH24 3PP ☎ 01425 473387 01202 743080
e-mail: hedi@alcatraz.co.uk
dir: *On A338 between Ringwood & Salisbury*

Old Beams is a beautiful old thatched and timber framed village inn located at the heart of the New Forest with views of countryside and ponies. It has a beer garden with a decked area and patio, and a cosy old world interior with lots of nooks and crannies. Pub food favourites range from sandwiches and salads to cod and chips, Thai chicken curry, and roast shoulder of lamb with rosemary and red wine.

Open 11-12 **Bar Meals** L served all week 12-6 D served all week 6-9.30 Av main course £6 **Restaurant** L served all week 12-6 D served all week 6-9.30 Av 3 course à la carte £17 Av fixed price £9.95 IPA, Speckled Hen. 10 **Facilities** Garden Parking

See Cycle Rides on page 272

ITCHEN ABBAS MAP 05 SU53

The Trout

Main Rd SO21 1BQ ☎ 01962 779537 01962 791046
e-mail: thetroutinn@aol.com
dir: *Exit M3 junct 9, follow A34 to A33 and Itchen Abbas, pub 2m on left.*

A 19th-century coaching inn located in the Itchen Valley close to the river itself. Originally called The Plough, it is said to have been the location that inspired Charles Kingsley to write *The Water Babies*. Freshly cooked, locally sourced produce is served in the bar and restaurant: trout, of course, perhaps pan fried, home-made fishcakes, and a lunchtime selection that includes baguettes, wraps, foccacias and salads.

The Tr

Open 12-3 6-11 (all day Sat-Sun Mar-Oct) Closed: 26 Dec & 1 Jan **Bar Meals** L served all week 12-2.15 D served all week 6.30-9 (Sun 12- Av main course £11 **Restaurant** L served all week 12-2.15 D served Mon-Sat 6.30-9 Av 3 course à la carte £21 Greene King Greene King IPA, Morland Speckled Hen. 9 **Facilities** Children's licence Gard Dogs allowed Parking Play Area

LITTLETON MAP 05 SU

Pick of the Pubs

The Running Horse ★★★★ INN

88 Main Rd SO22 6QS
☎ 01962 880218 01962 886596
e-mail: runninghorse@btconnect.com
dir: *3m from Winchester, signed from Stockbridge Rd*

Built two hundred years ago, this pretty rural gastro-pub, bordere on both sides by stud farms, has been completely revamped; the modern décor, including leather tub chairs positioned around a roaring fire, has added to the attractive ambiance. Locally brewed real ales are well kept, but the focus here is undoubtedly on good eating – the competent chefs source seasonal produce of impeccable freshness. Choose between dining alfresco on the front or rear terrace, casually in the bar, or more formally in the stylish restaurant. Dinner could begin with timbale of smoked trout, salmon and spring onion; continue with crispy leg of lamb with dauphinoise potatoes; and round off with lemon and lime cheesecake. Sunday lunch is served in the traditional way, and the wine list is competitively priced.

Open 11-3 5.30-11 (Sun 12-7.30) **Bar Meals** L served all week 12-2 D served Mon-Sat 6.30-9.30 Sun 12-4 Av main course £16 **Restaurant** L served all week 12-2 D served Mon-sat 6.30-9.30 (Sun 12-3) Av 3 course à la carte £25.30 Ringwood Best, Itchen Valley Winchester Ale. 15 **Facilities** Garden Dogs allowed Parking **Rooms** 9 bedrooms en suite S£55 D£55

The Bugle

ıis historic Grade II listed waterside pub has recently been restored to its former glory, much the appreciation of local drinkers. It sparked a successful rescue campaign by villagers when using developers threatened to demolish the site.

e pub was subsequently bought local independent operators, der whose ownership it has en lovingly restored in close nsultation with English Heritage, ng traditional methods and terials. Features include exposed ams and brickwork, an oak : and a wood burning stove, is a heated terrace with lovely ws over the River Hamble. A ating list of locally brewed beers ke an ideal partner for one of appetising bar bites: perhaps eet and sour chicken wings; me-made fishcakes with chive urre blanc and a poached egg; n hock terrine with piccalilli, or ats' cheese and caramelised onion t. Sandwiches are also available lunchtime fare, all served with parsnip crisps! Diners might like to try bean and chickpea stew with herb dumplings; pot-roasted chicken with chive mash, baby onions and French beans; or English lamb shank with rosemary mash and braised onions. The classic chargrilled Angus steak burger and rib-eye steak, not to mention beer-battered fish and chips with minted mushy peas and tartare sauce, are also welcome options. Desserts, meanwhile, are really not to be missed. The tarte Tatin with butterscotch sauce and clotted cream, and vanilla crème brûlée with raspberry sorbet more than compensate in terms of flavour for what they may add to the waist. Keep an eye out for daily specials on the blackboard.

🍷

MAP 05 SU40
High St SO31 4HA
☎ 023 8045 3000
📠 023 8045 3051
e-mail:
manager@buglehamble.co.uk
dir: *M27 junct 8, follow signs to Hamble. In village centre turn right at mini-rdbt into one-way cobbled street, pub at end*

Open 11–11 (Fri–Sat 11–12)
Bar Meals L served all week 12–2.30 D served all week 6–9.30 (Fri 12–3, 6–10.30, Sat 12–10, Sun 12–9) Av main course £10
Restaurant L served all week 12–2.30 D served all week 6.30–9.30 (Fri–Sat 12–3, 6.30–10.30, Sun 12–9) Av 3 course à la carte £20
Rotating locally brewed beers, Courage Best. 🍷 8

PUB CYCLES

IBSLEY - HAMPSHIRE

The Old Beams

Cycle information

Distance: 12 miles/19.3km (2h)
Map: OS Explorer OL22 New Forest
Start/finish: Ashley Twinning (free) car park; grid ref: SU 139048
Trails/tracks: old railway cycleway, roads and forest tracks
Landscape: the tree-lined old railway leads into mixed woodland, heath and lakes
Public toilets: Moors Valley Country Park
Tourist information: Ringwood, tel: 01425 470896
Cycle hire: Moors Valley Country Park visitor centre, tel: 01425 470721
The pub: The Old Beams, Ibsley
Two main road crossings and slow-moving traffic on country park access road.

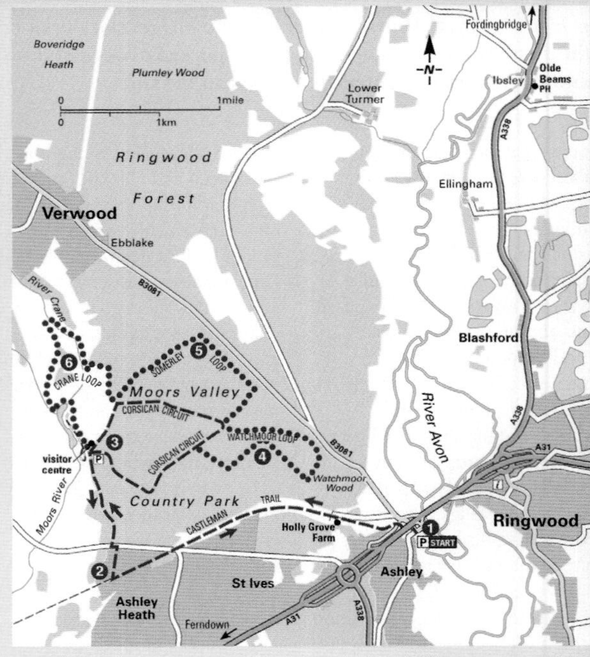

Cycle directions

❶ Leave the car park by the road entrance, zig-zag across Hurn Lane and join the combined cycleway/pavement under the A31. Bear left past the phone-box, then stop at the A31 slip road. Cross with care, then bear left on to the Castleman Trail towards Ashley Heath. The narrow gravel track bears to the right and pulls clear of the A31 through a tunnel of young oak trees. Soon the old line widens out into a 'dual carriageway' of narrow tracks separated by gorse and brambles. Watch out for cars as you cross the lane at Holly Grove Farm. You'll speed along the next section to the road crossing at Ashley Heath. Stop here, and cross Horton Road with care. There's a convenience shop on your right as you rejoin the Castleman Trail and continue along the tree-shaded cycleway. Very soon, pass a section of the former platform at Ashley Heath, complete with its railway name-board. Continue for 600yds (549m), then look out for the narrow exit into Forest Edge Drive on the right.

❷ Go through here and follow this residential road to the T-junction with Horton Road. Take care as you zig-zag left and right into the Moors Valley Country Park – it's only 50yds (46m), Follow the tarred entrance road for the last 0.5 mile (800m) to reach the visitor centre, with a restaurant, toilets and other facilities. Now follow one of the four waymarked cycle routes around the forest.

❸ The Corsican Circuit (2 miles/3.2km) is the basic ring at the heart of the park, which you can extend by adding one or more of the loops. It leads east from the visitor centre and loops anti-clockwise. The level route passes the Play Trail entrance, then circles back on good, gravelled forest rides.

❹ Take the Watchmoor Loop (1.5 miles/ 2.3km) off the Corsican Circuit. It follows sandy tracks and penetrates some of th quieter areas of the forest. You'll see a of open heathland, as well as plenty of light conifer woodland, before rejoinin the Corsican Circuit.

❺ Take the optional Somerley Loop (1 mile/1.6km). This weaves its way over gravel and dirt tracks through some of the denser parts of the forest, though there are still some wide heather verge in places. It is the most undulating trail ending with a steep downhill section.

❻ The Somerley Loop joins on to the Cra Loop (2 miles/3.2km), which on its ow is great for young families. This pretty route heads out beside the golf course and Crane Lake, before returning besic the miniature railway. Watch out for ca on the final section, which shares one the park roads.

)NGPARISH MAP 05 SU44

Pick of the Pubs

The Plough Inn

;P11 6PB ☎ 01264 720358
e-mail: eat@theploughinn.info
web: www.theploughinn.info
dir: *From M3 junct 8 take A303 towards Andover. In 6m take 33048 towards Longparish*

See Pick of the Pubs on page 274

)WER WIELD MAP 05 SU64

Pick of the Pubs

The Yew Tree

;O24 9RX ☎ 01256 389224 📠 01256 389224

Named after a nearby 650-year-old yew, this charming Hampshire ree house first served ale in 1845. In winter a crackling log fire)urns in the bar, but as the days lengthen attention turns to the adjacent cricket ground. Indeed, the Yew Tree's association with England's favourite summer sport has been immortalised in Elizabeth Gibson's book *Cricket and Ale*. The resident Cheriton Pots ale is backed up by a selection of guest beers from up to 15 ocal breweries, as well as a bi-annually changing wine list. The ocal reputation is for good fun and good food, and the hearty Mediterranean-influenced menu won't disappoint. Parma ham and mozzarella parcels could be followed by lamb and mint pudding with rosemary jus; oven-baked whole sea bass; or, for vegetarians, Moroccan butternut squash and vegetable stew. Apricot and white chocolate bread and butter pudding is one of several indulgent desserts.

Open 12-3 6-11 (all day Sun in Summer) **Bar Meals** L served Tue-Sat 12-2 D served Tue-Sat 6.30-9 (Sun 6.30-8.30) Av main course £9.95 Free House Cheriton Pots, Hidden Pint, Tripple ff Moondance, Hogsback Tea & Itchen Valley Hampshire Rose.. 13 **Facilities** Garden Dogs allowed Parking

YMINGTON MAP 05 SZ39

he Kings Arms

Thomas St SO41 9NB ☎ 01590 672594
r: *Approaching Lymington from N on A337, left onto St omas St. Pub 50yds on right*

ig Charles I is reputed to have patronised this historic coaching , which these days enjoys an enviable reputation for its cask ales, used on 150-year-old stillages. Local Ringwood ales as well as tional brews are served. It is a real community pub, with a dartboard d Sky TV, and the open brick fireplaces are used in winter.

The Kings Arms

Open 11-11 (Sun 12-10.30) **Bar Meals** L served all week 12-2.30 D served all week 6.30-9 Av main course £8 **Restaurant** L served all week 12-2.30 D served all week 6-8.30 Whitbread Weekly rotating guest ales. **Facilities** Garden **Notes**

Mayflower Inn

Kings Saltern Rd SO41 3QD
☎ 01590 672160 📠 01590 679180
e-mail: info@themayflower.uk.com
dir: *A337 towards New Milton, left at rdbt by White Hart, left to Rookes Ln, right at mini-rdbt, pub 0.75m*

A favourite with sailors and dog walkers, this solidly built mock-Tudor inn overlooks the Lymington River, with glorious views to the Isle of Wight. There's a magnificent garden with a purpose-built play area for children and an on-going summer barbecue in fine weather. Light bites and big bowl salads are backed up with heartier choices like traditional lamb and rosemary hotpot, pan-fried liver and bacon, and beer battered fish of the day.

Open 11-12 (Sun 12-10.30) **Bar Meals** L served all week 12-9.30 D served all week 6.30-9.30 Av main course £8.50 **Restaurant** L served all week 12-9.30 D served all week 6.30-9.30 Enterprise Inns Ringwood Best, Fuller's London Pride, 6X, Goddards Fuggle Dee Dum. 8 **Facilities** Garden Dogs allowed Parking Play Area

LYNDHURST MAP 05 SU30

New Forest Inn

Emery Down SO43 7DY ☎ 023 8028 4690

Delightfully situated in the scenic New Forest, this rambling inn lies on land claimed from the crown by use of squatters' rights in the early 18th-century. Ale was once sold from a caravan which now forms the front lounge porchway. Lovely summer garden and welcoming bars with open fires and an extensive menu.

Open 11-11 Rest: 3.30 - 6 Nov-Apr **Bar Meals** L served all week 12-2.30 D served all week 6-9.30 Av main course £10 **Restaurant** L served all week 11-2.30 D served all week 6-9.30 Enterprise Inns Ringwood Best, Fullers London Pride, Abbot Ale, Old Hooky. **Facilities** Children's licence Garden Dogs allowed Parking Play Area

The Plough Inn

Ramblers walking the Test Way – a route that follows one of southern England's finest chalk streams – will be delighted to stumble across this 400-year-old pub: the footpath cuts right through the inn's car-park.

The River Test itself runs only 100 yards away, and with two lake fishing courses within strolling distance, it's also popular with trout fishermen, not to mention the resident duck population. The inn is also an ideal meeting place for both family and business get-togethers. New owners Paul and Sarah Bingham took over the Plough recently, and have carried out extensive renovation to restore it to the same high standard as their previous venture – The Star Inn in East Tytherley. The short, simple menu provides a good balance between traditional and more inventive dishes. Starters range from a classic Caesar salad to chicken and rabbit spring rolls with celeriac remoulade; scallop, lobster and prawn risotto; or ham hock terrine with foie gras, lentils and Parma ham. Main courses are no less appetising: seared tuna with sweet pepper relish and tapenade mash; seafood ragout with saffron, cumin and mussel broth; steak and kidney pudding; battered fish of the day; or sausages and mash. Vegetarians can enjoy field mushrooms stuffed with curried lentils, tomato salsa and couscous, while many dishes can be adapted for a gluten-free diet. Round off with bread and butter pudding; or a Belgian chocolate torte with raspberries. In addition to a good value 32 bin wine list, a limited edition selection from Paul and Sarah's private cellar is also on offer.

🍷
MAP 05 SU44
SP11 6PB
☎ 01264 720358
e-mail: eat@theploughinn.info
web: www.theploughinn.info
dir: *From M3 junct 8 take A303 towards Andover. In 6m take B3048 towards Longparish.*

Open 11–2.30 6–11 Closed: 25 Dec
Bar Meals L served all week 12–2.30 D served all week
Restaurant L served all week 12–2 D served Mon–Sat 6.30–9 Av 3 course à la carte £25
Enterprise Inns
Ringwood, Fullers London Pride, Wadworth 6x, HSB. 🍷 10
Facilities Children's licence Garden Dogs allowed Parking

England

'NDHURST continued

ıe Oak Inn

ıkney Ln, Bank SO43 7FE ☎ 02380 284601

nail: oakinn@fullers.co.uk

: *From Lyndhurst signed A35 to Christchurch. After ·istchurch follow A35 1m, turn left at Bank sign*

ıies, pigs and deer graze outside this former ciderhouse. Behind bay windows are a traditional woodburner, antique pine and an ·ensive collection of bric-a-brac. There is also a large beer garden for ·se fine summer days. A wide selection of fresh seafood, including ·sey crab gratin, and seared tuna steak, features among an interesting ·ice of dishes, including the local wild boar sausages and daily pies.

en 11.30-3 6-11.30 (Sun 12-10.30) **Bar Meals** L served all week 2.30 D served all week 6-9.30 (Sun 6-9) **Restaurant** L served all k D served all week Fullers Ringwood Best, Hop Back Summer ·tening, London Pride, Gales HSB. 9 **Facilities** Garden Dogs allowed ·ing

ıe *Trusty Servant*

ıstead SO43 7FY ☎ 023 8081 2137

nail: enquiries@trustyservant.co.uk

·ular New Forest pub overlooking the village green and retaining ıy Victorian features. The famous sign is taken from a 16th-century chester scholar's painting portraying the qualities of an ideal ·ege servant. The menu prides itself on its real food, good value and ·erous portions. You might sample snacks, home-made pies, steaks ı the grill, venison or tenderloin of pork. There's also a good choice ·egetarian dishes, such as sizzling Thai vegetable stir-fry.

en 11-11 (Sun 12-10.30) **Bar Meals** L served all week 12-9 D served ·eek 7-10 **Restaurant** L served all week 12-2.30 D served all week 7- Enterprise Inns Ringwood Best, Fuller's London Pride, Wadworth ·Timothy Taylor Landlord. **Facilities** Garden Dogs allowed Parking

APLEDURWELL MAP 05 SU65

ıe Gamekeepers

ıworth Rd RG25 2LU

01256 322038 01256 322038

nail: costellophil@hotmail.com

: *Exit M3 junct 6, take A30 towards Hook. Turn right after The ·ch pub. The Gamekeepers signed*

·ry rural location for this 19th-century pub, which has a large ·ided garden and, unusually, a well inside the building. Settle back leather settee with a pint, and enjoy the cosy atmosphere of low ·den beams and flagstone floors. An extensive menu includes an impressive range of seafood: loin of cod wrapped in Serrano ham, crispy pan-fried sea bass fillets, red snapper, salmon and monkfish.

Open 12-3 5-1am **Bar Meals** L served all week 12-3 D served all week 6.30-9.30 (Sun 12-4) **Restaurant** L served all week 12-2.30 D served all week 5.30-9.30 (Sun 12-4) Free House Badgers First Gold, London Pride, Ringwood Best, Moondance. 12 **Facilities** Children's licence Garden Dogs allowed Parking

MICHELDEVER MAP 05 SU53

Half Moon & Spread Eagle

Winchester Rd SO21 3DG

☎ 01962 774339 01962 774339

e-mail: team@thehalfmoonandspreadeagle.co.uk

dir: *Take A33 from Winchester towards Basingstoke. After 5m turn left after petrol station. Pub 0.5m on right*

Old drovers' inn located in the heart of a pretty thatched and timbered Hampshire village, overlooking the cricket green. The pub, comprising three neatly furnished interconnecting rooms, has a real local feel, and a few years back reverted to its old name having been the Dever Arms for eight years. An extensive menu ranges through Sunday roasts, Moon burgers, honeyed salmon supreme with lime courgettes, fresh battered cod, and half shoulder of minted lamb.

Open 12-3 6-11 **Bar Meals** L served all week 12-2 D served all week 6-9 (Fri-Sat 6-9.30, Sun 6-8.30) Av main course £10.50 **Restaurant** L served all week 12-2 D served all week 6-9 (Fri-Sat 6-9.30, Sun 6-8.30) Av 3 course à la carte £20 Greene King Greene King IPA, Abbot Ale, Guest Ales. 9 **Facilities** Garden Dogs allowed Parking Play Area

MONXTON MAP 05 SU34

Pick of the Pubs

The Black Swan 🍷

High St SP11 8AW ☎ 01264 710260 📠 01264 710961

dir: *Exit A303, at rdbt follow signs for Monxton, pub on main road.*

Thatch and clay tiles characterise the roofs of Monxton's houses and cottages, some built in the 16th century. The Black Swan stands on the Portway, the Roman road that used to link Old Sarum, just north of Salisbury, and Winchester. It dates from 1662, possibly earlier, and was for a long time known as Ye Swan. Who blackened its name, and why, isn't known, although we do know that the change occurred in the 19th century, by which time it was a popular refreshment stop. Travellers heading for one or the other of the two cathedral cities would have their horses fed and watered in the stable block, now the restaurant. The culinary team has developed a menu combining French, English and New World ideas. Where possible all vegetables are locally grown, while all meat and fish is free range. Children are welcome in the courtyard and restaurant for lunch and early suppers.

Open 12–11 **Bar Meals** L served all week 12–2 D served all week 6–9.30 (Fri–Sat 12–2.30, 6–10 Sun 7–9.30) Av main course £12 **Restaurant** L served all week 12–2 D served all week 6–9.30 (Fri–Sun 12–2.30, 6–10) Av 3 course à la carte £25 Enterprise Inns Timothy Taylor Landlords, Ringwood Best Bitter, Summer Lightning, London Pride. 🍷 9 **Facilities** Children's licence Garden Dogs allowed Parking

NEW ALRESFORD MAP 05 SU53

Pick of the Pubs

The Globe on the Lake

The Soke, Broad St SO24 9DB

☎ 01962 732294 📠 01962 732221

e-mail: duveen-conway@supanet.com

dir: *Telephone for directions*

See Pick of the Pubs on opposite page

NORTH WALTHAM MAP 05 SU

Pick of the Pubs

The Fox 🍷

RG25 2BE ☎ 01256 397288 📠 01256 398564

e-mail: info@thefox.org

dir: *From M3 junct 7 take A30 towards Winchester. Village signed on right. Take 2nd signed road*

A peaceful village pub situated down a quiet country lane enjoyin splendid views across fields and farmland – an ideal stop if you're on the M3 just south of Basingstoke. Built as three farm cottages in 1624, the Fox can offer families three large level gardens, one of which is a dedicated children's play area, and superb flower borders and hanging baskets in summer. The husband and wife team of Rob and Izzy MacKenzie split their responsibilities between bar and kitchen. Amidst over a thousand miniatures on show Rob ensures that the beers are kept in top condition, while Izzy produces mouthwatering traditional dishes using seasonal produce as it becomes available; she prepares everything by hand from the mayonnaise upwards. Starters such as country game terrine may be followed by Hampshire venison with glazed shallots and field mushrooms; halibut fillet stuffed with salmon mousseline; or butternut squash and champagne risotto.

Open 10–12 (Sun 10–12.30) **Bar Meals** L served all week 12–2.30 D served all week 6–9.30 (Sun 6–9) **Restaurant** L served all week 12.30–2.30 D served all week 6.30–9.30 (Sun 6.30–9) Punch Taverns Ringwood Best Bitter, Adnams Broadside, Brakspear, Guest Beer. 🍷 11 **Facilities** Children's licence Garden Dogs allowed Parking Play Area

See advert on page 27

The Globe on the Lake

an outstanding setting on the banks of a reed-fringed lake and wildfowl sanctuary, The Globe a convivial hostelry facing a prime Hampshire waterscape. The lake was created by Bishop de cy in the 12th century as a fish pond, and the great weir remains to this day an outstanding ece of medieval engineering.

inn on the site since then was obably all but destroyed during resford's great fire of 1689. The obe was rebuilt as a coaching n, sitting at the bottom of the wn's superb Georgian main eet. Waterfowl frequent the rden, sunbathing between the nic benches or by the children's yhouse. Inside the bar, a log fire zes on cooler days, while a smart ning room and unusual garden om share the stunning outlook er the water. In summer freshly pared food can be enjoyed the garden and on the heated r terrace. The daily changing ckboard features several fish hes, like tiger prawns cooked th fresh lime and chilli; or sh fillet of hake in beer batter th home-made tartare sauce and chips. Other specialities may include Meon Valley pork and leek sausages; Alresford watercress flan with a hint of English mustard; oven-roasted partridge; or sautéed lambs' liver with crispy bacon. At least ten puddings, all at the same price, range from the typically English (bread and butter pudding, custard) to the exotic (citrus meringue crush with kumquat citrus sauce). A mailing list keeps regulars informed of special events, when the chef's team will prepare a menu to suit – such as the Hampshire Food Festival, a musical quiz, or Burns' Night. Real ales, of course, plenty of house wines including one from a Hampshire vineyard, and local apple juice all supplement the perfect views.

MAP 05 SU53
The Soke, Broad St SO24 9DB
☎ 01962 732294
01962 732221
e-mail:
duveen-conway@supanet.com
dir: *Telephone for directions*

Open 11-3 6-11 (Summer Sat-Sun all day) Closed: 25-26 Dec
Bar Meals L served all week 12-2 D served all week 6.30-9 (wknds 12-2.30) Av main course £9.50
Restaurant L served all week 12-2 D served all week 6.30-9 (wknds 12-2.30) Av 3 course à la carte £20
Unique Pub Co
Wadworth 6X, Ringwood, Henley Brakspear Bitter, Fuller's London Pride.
Facilities Garden Play Area

England

OLD BASING MAP 05 SU65

The Millstone

Bartons Ln RG24 8AE ☎ 01256 331153
e-mail: millstone@wadworth.co.uk
dir: *From M3 junct 6 follow brown signs to Basing House*

Basingstoke's techno-doorstep is only a DVD's flip away, which makes this attractive old building's rural location, beside the River Loddon, all the more delightfully surprising. Nearby are the extensive ruins of Old Basing House, one of Britain's most famous Civil War sites. Typical main dishes might include battered or grilled cod; creamy vegetable korma; and spinach, mushroom and brie filo parcel. Snacks include baguettes, bocottas and ciabattas, jacket potatoes and ploughman's.

Open 11.30–11 (Sun 12–10.30) **Bar Meals** L served all week 12–2.30 D served all week 6–9.30 (Sat–Sun 12–9.30) Wadworth Wadworth 6X, Wadworth JCB, Henrys Smooth & Henrys IPA. 9 **Facilities** Garden Dogs allowed Parking

OVINGTON MAP 05 SU53

Pick of the Pubs

The Bush

SO24 0RE ☎ 01962 732764 01962 735130
e-mail: thebushinn@wadworth.co.uk
dir: *A31 from Winchester, E to Alton & Farnham, approx 6m turn left off dual carriageway to Ovington. 0.5m to pub*

Once a refreshment stop on the Pilgrim's Way linking Winchester and Canterbury, The Bush is as delightful as it is hard to find. Tucked away just off a meandering lane, and overhung by trees, the rose-covered building is a vision of a bygone age. A gentle riverside stroll along the Itchen flowing past the pretty garden will set you up for a leisurely drink or lingering meal. The interior is dark and atmospheric; there's a central wooden bar, high backed seats and pews, stuffed animals on the wall and a real fire. The regularly-changing menu makes good use of local produce. Choices range from bar snacks such as sandwiches and ploughman's lunches through to satisfying gastro-pub meals such as organic smoked trout mousse with warm toast, followed by slow-roasted belly pork on braised Savoy cabbage with organic cider jus. Finish with Eton mess or rhubarb crumble. Film crews love this spot.

Open 11–3 6–11 (Sun 12–3, 7–10.30) Closed: 25 Dec **Bar Meals** L served all week 12–2.30 D served all week 6.30–9.30 (Sun 7–8.30) Wadworth Wadworth 6X, IPA & Farmers Glory, JCB, Summersault. 12 **Facilities** Garden Dogs allowed Parking

OWSLEBURY MAP 05 SU

The Ship Inn

Whites Hill SO21 1LT ☎ 01962 777358 01962 777458
dir: *M3 junct 11 take B3335. Follow Owslebury signs*

Situated on a windswept chalk ridge on the edge of a pretty village, Ship dates back more than 300 years. A quaint old bar with low bea and ship's timbers add to the appeal. From the pub there are strikin views towards the Solent and the South Downs. Daily menus might include grilled herbed lamb cutlets, fillet of hake, pot roast guinea fo and lobster and mixed seafood tagliatelle. Good choice of lunchtime meals and snacks.

Open 11–3 6–11 (Jul–Aug 11–11) **Bar Meals** L served all week 12–2 D served all week 6.30–9.30 (Sun 12–11) Av main course £10.95 **Restaurant** L served all week 12–2 D served all week 6.30–9.30 (Sun 12–8.30) Av 3 course à la carte £20.95 Greene King Greene King Morland Original, Ringwood, IPA. 12 **Facilities** Garden Dogs allowed Parking Play Area

PETERSFIELD MAP 05 SU

The Good Intent ★★★★ INN

40–46 College St GU31 4AF
☎ 01730 263838 01730 302239
e-mail: pstuart@goodintent.freeserve.co.uk

Candlelit tables, open fires and well-kept ales characterise this 16th-century pub, and in summer, flower tubs and hanging baskets festoon the front patio. Regular gourmet evenings are held and the is live music on Sunday evenings. Sausages are a speciality (up to 1 varieties) alongside a daily pie and the likes of seafood chowder an Thai fish curry. As members of the Campaign For Real Food they ha well-established links with the local junior school.

Open 11–3 5.30–11 **Bar Meals** L served all week 12–2.30 D served all week 6–9.30 **Restaurant** L served all week 12–2 D served all week 6–9 Fullers HSB, GB, Buster. **Facilities** Garden Dogs allowed Parkin **Rooms** 3 bedrooms 2 en suite S£45 D£60

Pick of the Pubs

The Trooper Inn

Alton Rd, Froxfield GU32 1BD
☎ 01730 827293 01730 827103
e-mail: info@trooperinn.com
dir: *From A3 take A272 Winchester exit towards Petersfield (NB do not take A272 to Petersfield). 1st exit at mini-rdbt for Steep. 3m, pub on right.*

There's a relaxed atmosphere throughout the pine-furnished interior of this isolated free house, which stands high on the downs west of Petersfield. The building has had a chequered history since its first bricks were laid at the start of the 17th century, and it's said that it was used as a recruiting centre at the outset of the First World War. More recently, the 'pub at the top of the hill' faced closure in the mid-1990s before it was rescued and given a new lease of life by the present owners. Winter log fires now warm the bar, and the charming restaurant features wooden settles and a vaulted ceiling. Here, the locally-sourced menu ranges from fresh fig, feta and Parma ham salad to wild boar steak with Calvados sauce. Other options include poached fresh mussels, home-made vegetable lasagne, and fisherman's pie.

Open 12-3 6-12 Closed: 25-26 Dec & 1 Jan **Bar Meals** L served all week 12-2 D served all week 6.30-9 (Sun12-2.30, Fri-Sat 6.30-9.30) **Restaurant** L served all week 12-2 D served all week 6.30-9 (Sun 12-2.30, Fri-Sat 6-9.30) Free House Ringwood Best, Ballards, Guest ales. **Facilities** Garden Parking **Rooms** 8 bedrooms en suite S£69 D£89 (★★★★ INN)

The White Horse Inn

Priors Dean GU32 1DA ☎ 01420 588387 01420 588387
e-mail: info@stuartinns.com
dir: *A3/A272 to Winchester/Petersfield. In Petersfield left to Steep, 5m then right at small x-rds to East Tisted, take 2nd drive on right.*

Also known as the 'Pub With No Name' as it has no sign, this splendid 17th-century farmhouse was originally used as a forge for passing coaches. The blacksmith sold beer to the travellers while their horses were attended to. Restaurant dishes include carrot and cashew nut roast, and Gressingham duck breast with fondant potato and spiced grape chutney. Special fresh fish dishes are available on Fridays and Saturdays.

Open 11-2.30 6-11 (Sat 12-11, Sun 12-10.30) **Bar Meals** L served all week 12-2.30 D served Mon-Sat 7-9.30 **Restaurant** L served all week 12-2.30 D served Mon-Sat 7-9.30 Fullers No Name Best, No Name Strong, Fullers London Pride, Bass. 7 **Facilities** Garden Dogs allowed Parking

PILLEY MAP 05 SZ39

The Fleur de Lys

Pilley St SO41 5QG ☎ 01590 672158

Built in 1014, the Fleur de Lys has been serving ales since 1498. The traditional thatched inn and has been sympathetically refurbished, with an open fire and two wood burning stoves. Outside there's a large landscaped garden with wooden tables and chairs. Dishes include oven-roasted halibut; glazed wild hare stuffed with prunes; or local wild mushroom and asparagus mille-feuille.

Open 11.30-3 6-11 (Sun 12-3, 7-10.30) **Bar Meals** L served all week 12-2.15 D served all week 6.30-9.30 (Sun 12-2.30) Av main course £10 **Restaurant** L served all week 12-2.15 D served all week 6.30-9.30 Av 3 course à la carte £24 Enterprise Inns Ringwood Best, plus Guest ales. 9 **Facilities** Garden Dogs allowed Parking

PORTSMOUTH & SOUTHSEA MAP 05 SZ69

The Wine Vaults

43-47 Albert Rd, Southsea PO5 2SF
☎ 023 92864712 023 92865544
e-mail: winevaults@freeuk.com

Originally several Victorian shops, now converted into a Victorian-style alehouse with wooden floors, panelled walls, and seating from old churches and schools. Partly due to the absence of a jukebox or fruit machine, the atmosphere here is relaxed, and there is a good range of real ales and good-value food. A typical menu includes beef stroganoff, Tuscan vegetable bean stew, grilled gammon steak, salads, sandwiches, and Mexican specialities. Look out for celebs appearing at the local theatre.

Open 12-11 (Fri-Sat 12-12, Sun 12-10.30) **Bar Meals** L served all week 12-9.30 D served all week **Restaurant** L served all week 12-9.30 D served all week Free House Fuller's London Pride, Gales Ales, Fullers Discovery, Guest ales. 20 **Facilities** Children's licence Garden Dogs allowed

ROCKBOURNE MAP 05 SU11

Pick of the Pubs

The Rose & Thistle

SP6 3NL ☎ 01725 518236
e-mail: enquiries@roseandthistle.co.uk
dir: *Follow Rockbourne signs from A354 or A338 at Fordingbridge*

See Pick of the Pubs on page 280

The Rose & Thistle

This is a picture postcard pub if ever there was one, with a stunning rose arch, flowers around the door and a delightful village setting. The 16th-century free house, which rubs shoulders with thatched cottages and period homes, is conveniently placed for visiting the New Forest, Salisbury, and Breamore House, as well as Rockbourne's very own Roman villa.

The pub was created almost 200 years ago from two cottages, and still retains many of its original features. The low-beamed bar and dining area are furnished with country house fabrics, polished oak tables and chairs, cushioned settles and carved benches, and homely touches include floral arrangements and a scatter of magazines. Open fires make this a cosy retreat in cold weather, whilst the summer sun encourages visitors to sit in the neat cottage garden and watch the birds in their traditional dovecote. For the last 15 years Tim Norfolk has maintained his tradition of serving fine fresh food, good ales and some very decent wines from Europe, South America, South Africa and the Antipodes. Fish dishes are particularly well represented on the blackboard: monkfish wrapped in pancetta with pesto; skate wing in black butter with prawns and capers; whole grilled Dover sole; grilled fresh sardines; sea bream fillet on creamy crab spaghetti; whole John Dory stuffed with lime and coriander; Cornish crab and crevette salad – and many more. For a simple lunchtime favourite, locally made pork and London Pride sausages are served with whole grain mustard mash. As well as the fish specials, the dinner menu offers a small but perfectly formed range of starters, and steaks with a choice of sauces. You'll also find roasted rump of lamb, Gressingham duck, and chargrilled chicken fillet on pappardelle pasta with a tomato and olive sauce. Desserts include pot au chocolat; lavender crème brûlée; and lemon tart with forest fruits.

MAP 05 SU11
SP6 3NL
☎ 01725 518236
e-mail: enquiries@roseandthistle.co.uk
dir: *Follow Rockbourne signs from A354, or from A338 at Fordingbridge*

Open 11–3 6–11 (Oct–Apr Sun 11–8)
Bar Meals L served all week 12–2.30 D served all week 6.30–9.30 (Sun seasonal variation) Av main course £10
Restaurant L served all week 12–2.30 D served all week 6.30–9.30 (Sun seasonal variation) Av 3 course à la carte £18
Free House
Fuller's London Pride, Adnams Broadside, Hop Back Summer Lightning, Strongs Best Bitter.
18
Facilities Children's licence Garden Parking

OCKFORD MAP 05 SU10

he Alice Lisle

ockford Green BH24 3NA

01425 474700 01425 483332

ell-known New Forest pub with landscaped gardens overlooking ake, popular with walkers and visitors to the region. It was named er the widow of one of Cromwell's supporters who gave shelter two fugitives from the Battle of Sedgemoor. Choose from a varied enu which might include salmon and crab cakes, honey minted lamb oulder, liver and bacon, and Mexican enchilada. There's a good nge of starters and children's dishes.

pen 11–3 5.30–11 (Sun all day) **Bar Meals** L served all week -2 D served all week 6–9 (Sun 12–8) Av main course £7.95 **staurant** L served all week 12–2 D served all week 6–9 (Sun 12–8) Fullers HSB, Ringwood, Winter Brew, 49er. 7 **Facilities** Children's ence Garden Dogs allowed Parking Play Area

OMSEY MAP 05 SU32

Pick of the Pubs

The Dukes Head

Greatbridge Rd SO51 0HB 01794 514450

See Pick of the Pubs on page 283

he Three Tuns

3 Middlebridge St SO51 8HL

01794 512639 01794 514524

mail: threetunsromsey@aol.co.uk

r: *On Romsey bypass, 0.5m from main entrance of Broadlands tate*

ound 400 years old, centrally placed in this old market town, with fine abbey, and a short walk from the front gates of Broadlands, untry seat of Earl Mountbatten. Quality local ingredients form the sis of all meals, though the new landlords have taken the emphasis 'gastropub', and are now offering decent, normal pub food. Game mes from the Broadlands estate.

pen 12–3 5–12 (Fri–Sun 12–12) **Bar Meals** L served all week 12–2 served Mon–Sat 7–9.30 Closed Sun evening Av main course £12 **staurant** L served all week 12–2 D served Mon–Sat 7–9.30 Av 3 urse à la carte £29 Ringwood Best, Gale's HSB, London Pride. 8 **cilities** Garden Dogs allowed Parking

ROWLAND'S CASTLE MAP 05 SU71

The Castle Inn

1 Finchdean Rd PO9 6DA

023 9241 2494 023 9241 2494

e-mail: rogerburrell@btconnect.com

dir: *N of Havant take B2149 to Rowland's Castle. Pass green, under rail bridge, pub 1st on left opposite Stansted Park*

A Victorian building directly opposite Stansted Park, part of the Forest of Bere. Richard the Lionheart supposedly hunted here, and the house and grounds are open to the public for part of the year. Traditional atmosphere is boosted by wooden floors and fires in both bars. Menu options include pies, lasagne, curry, steaks, local sausages, and chilli.

Open 10.30–12 (Fri–Sat 10.30–1am) **Bar Meals** L served all week 12–6 D served all week 6–9 (Sun 12–3) Av main course £7.95 **Restaurant** L served all week 12–6 D served all week 6–9 (Sun 12–3) Av 3 course à la carte £16 Fullers Gales Butser, HSB, London Pride & Guest beers. 8 **Facilities** Garden Dogs allowed Parking

The Fountain Inn ★★★ INN

34 The Green PO9 6AB

023 9241 2291 023 9241 2291

e-mail: fountaininn@amserve.com

Set by the village green in pretty Rowlands Castle, The Fountain is a lovingly refurbished Georgian inn complete with resident ghost. Food is served in Sienna's bistro, where dishes include hand rolled, stone baked pizzas, pasta dishes, and specials like flame-grilled chicken and Serrano ham salad, and crusted fillet steak with a roasted vegetable chutney.

Open 5–11 (Fri–Sat 12–12 Sun 12–11) **Bar Meals** L served 12–3 D served Tue–Sat 5–8 Av main course £9 **Restaurant** L served Fri–Sun 12–3 D served Tue–Sat 6.30–10 (Sun 12–4) Av 3 course à la carte £15 Av 3 course fixed price £19.95 Free House Ruddles IPA, Abbot, Ruddles Cask. **Facilities** Garden Dogs allowed Parking Play Area **Rooms** 4 bedrooms en suite S£25 D£50

ST MARY BOURNE MAP 05 SU45

The Bourne Valley Inn

SP11 6BT 01264 738361 01264 738126

e-mail: bournevalleyinn@btinternet.com

Located in the charming Bourne valley, this popular traditional inn is the ideal setting for conferences, exhibitions, weddings and other notable occasions. The riverside garden abounds with wildlife, and children can happily let off steam in the special play area. Typical menu includes deep fried brie or a cocktail of prawns, followed by rack of lamb with a redcurrant and port sauce, salmon and prawn tagliatelle, steak and mushroom pie, and warm duck salad.

Open 11–11 (Sun 12–10.30) **Bar Meals** L served all week 12–2 D served all week 7–9 **Restaurant** L served all week 12–2 D served all week 7–9 Free House Guest ales. 8 **Facilities** Children's licence Garden Dogs allowed Parking Play Area

England

SELBORNE MAP 05 SU73

The Selborne Arms

High St GU34 3JR ☎ 01420 511247 01420 511754
e-mail: info@selbournearms.co.uk
web: www.selbornearms.co.uk
dir: *From A3 follow B3006, pub on left in village centre*

A traditional village pub, 17th-century in origin, The Selborne Arms is known for its friendly atmosphere and good food. Owners Nick and Hayley Carter have a great commitment to the slow cooking movement and are proud to showcase Hampshire food and drink: slow-cooked mutton, braised belly pork, local Chateaubriand, home-cured meats and home-made bread and preserves. Local real ales, cider made in the village and wine from just a few miles away are also featured.

Open 11–3 6–11 (Fri 5.30–11, Sun all day) **Bar Meals** L served all week 12–2 D served all week 7–9 **Restaurant** L served all week 12–2 D served all week 7–9 Courage Best, Ringwood 49er, Suthwyk Bloomfields, local Guest ales. 10 **Facilities** Garden Dogs allowed Parking Play Area

SOUTHAMPTON MAP 05 SU41

The White Star Tavern & Dining Rooms

28 Oxford St SO14 3DJ
☎ 023 8082 1990 023 8090 4982
e-mail: manager@whitestartavern.co.uk
dir: *Exit M3 junct 13, A33 to Southampton, towards Ocean Village & Marina*

A former seafarers' hotel has been stylishly renovated to create this attractive establishment incorporating a good blend of old and new. The all-day menu could include starters like pressed ham hock terrine with home-made piccalilli, followed by roasted monkfish tail on smoked bacon risotto. Typical puddings are chocolate sabayon tart, and plum and cinnamon pudding. On sunny days you can take a pavement table and watch the world go by on Southampton's restaurant row.

Open 12–11 (Fri–Sat 12–12) Closed: 25–26 Dec, 1 Jan **Bar Meals** L serv all week 12–2.30 D served all week 6.30–9.30 (Fri–Sat 12–3, 6.30–10, Sun 12–9) Av main course £12.50 **Restaurant** L served all week 12–2.30 D served all week 6.30–9.30 (Fri 6.30–10.30 Sun 12–9) Av 3 course à la ca £25 Enterprise Inns London Pride. 8

SPARSHOLT MAP 05 SU4

Pick of the Pubs

The Plough Inn

Main Rd SO21 2NW
☎ 01962 776353 01962 776400
dir: *From Winchester take B3049 (A272) W, left to Sparsholt, Inn 1m*

See Pick of the Pubs on page 284

STEEP MAP 05 SU7

Pick of the Pubs

Harrow Inn

GU32 2DA ☎ 01730 262685
dir: *Off A3 to A272, left through Sheet, take road opposite church (School Lane) then over A3 by-pass bridge.*

Under the determined stewardship of landlady Ellen McCutcheon, The Harrow Inn resisted all incursions into the 21st century. It has no till, has kept the traditional two tiny bars, and even still serves a ham and pea soup first on the menu over fifty years ago. After Ellen's death in 2004, the pub was taken over by her two daughters, who have promised their loyal customers that everything will be kept exactly as that grand old lady would have liked. The tile-hung 500-year-old building is tucked away down a sleepy lane. The bars, each with scrubbed elm tables, boarded walls and a selection of stuffed Victorian animals, are the perfect environment for relaxing over a pint of local ale. All in all, it's an unmitigated delight – though mind you bring cash or chequebook, because the only other option is the washing up.

Open 12–2.30 6–11 Closed: 25 Dec eve **Bar Meals** L served all week 12–2 D served all week 7–9 Av main course £6.75 Free House Ringwood Best, Oakleaf Bitter, Hop Back GFB, Bowman Ales & Suthwyk Bloomfields Bitter. **Facilities** Garden Dogs allowed Parking **Notes**

The Dukes Head

long, whitewashed, 400-year-old pub a little way out of Romsey, and little more than a hefty ıst from the Test, England's leading trout river. There are large gardens at the front and rear, hile inside are the main bar, the snug and four other rooms, all themed.

rst is the Duke's Room, dedicated 'edictably enough to dukes, ɔt just the high-ranking peer pe – Wellington, Edinburgh, ımberland and co – but also the self-styled sort, like John 'ayne and Ellington. Next is the shing Room, full of antique reels ıd other angling equipment; then e Headlines Room, complete ıth large refectory table, and splays of dramatic newspaper ɔnt pages; and finally the History ɔom, where visitors can immerse emselves in information about e area's past. Since taking over e pub at the beginning of 2006, ıdy Cottingham and Suzie Russell ıve quickly made their mark, ɔt least by shifting the balance the menu more firmly towards ɪh and seafood. This means you can reliably expect dishes featuring turbot, halibut, oysters, mussels and scallops, and much more, but if you don't want fish there'll almost certainly be a succulent fillet steak, duck breast or local game, such as venison. Food is largely locally sourced, seasonally influenced as far as possible, and freshly prepared by noted New Forest chef, Eddy Blanchard, and his team. Andy is an acknowledged wine expert and is proud of his well-balanced wine list, particularly the house merlot and pinot grigio. Go on a Sunday for wonderful live jazz, most likely outside in the summer, and on a Tuesday night for blues and folk.

MAP 05 SU32
Greatbridge Rd SO51 0HB
☎ 01794 514450

Open 11–11
Bar Meals L served Mon–Sat 12–3 D served all week 7–10 (No lunch Sun) Av main course £8
Restaurant L served all week 12–3 D served all week 7–10 Av 3 course à la carte £28 Av 2 course fixed price £12.50
Free House
Fuller's London Pride, Ringwood Best Bitter, 49ers, Summer Lightning. 8
Facilities Garden Dogs allowed Parking

The Plough Inn

The Plough seems to have started life about 200 years ago as a coach house for Sparsholt Mano on the other side of the road, becoming an alehouse just 50 years later. It stands in beautiful countryside, close enough to Winchester to draw many of its well-heeled citizens out for a meal or just a drink – perhaps after a walk in nearby Farley Mount Country Park.

From the outside, you can see that it has been much extended but, once inside, the main bar and dining areas blend together very harmoniously, helped by judicious use of farmhouse-style pine tables, a mix of wooden and upholstered seats, collections of agricultural implements, stone jars, wooden wine box end-panels and dried hops. The dining tables to the left of the entrance have a view across open fields to wooded downland, and it's at this end you'll find a blackboard menu offering lighter dishes exemplified by seafood pasta and basil cream sauce with garlic bread; pork and chive sausages with parsley mash and red wine gravy; and beef, ale and mushroom pie. The menu board at the right-hand end of the bar offers meals of a slightly more serious nature – maybe game casserole with herb dumplings; lamb shank with braised red cabbage and rosemary jus; seabass fillets with lemon mash and buttered leeks; and tomato, olive and courgette tart with a roasted pepper coulis. Lunchtime regulars know that 'doorstep' is the most apt description for the tasty sandwiches, perhaps crab and mayonnaise, or beef and horseradish. Puddings include plum and almond tart, melon, mango and ginger parfait, and pecan pie with clotted cream. Wadworth of Devizes supplies the real ales and there's a good wine selection. Booking is definitely advised for any meal. There's a good-sized car park and a delightful garden.

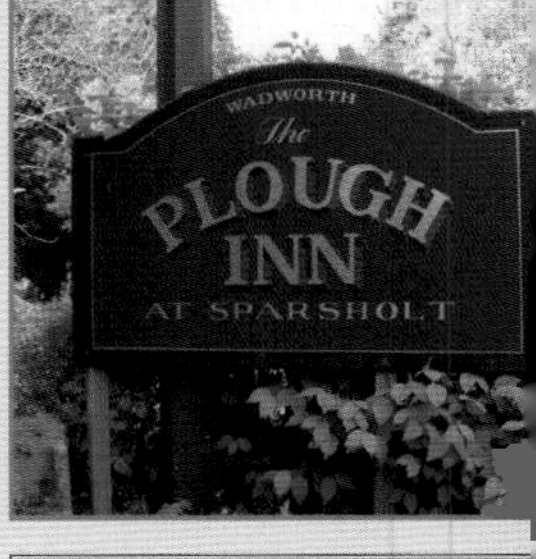

🍷
MAP 05 SU43
Main Rd SO21 2NW
☎ 01962 776353
📠 01962 776400
dir: *From Winchester take B3049 (A272) W, left to Sparsholt, Inn 1m.*

Open 11–3 6–11 (Sun 12–3, 6–10.30) Closed: 25 Dec
Bar Meals L served all week 12–2 D served all week 6–9
Restaurant L served all week 12–2 D served all week 6–9
Wadworth
Wadworth Henry's IPA, 6X, Old Timer & JCB. 🍷 14
Facilities Garden Dogs allowed Parking Play Area

TOCKBRIDGE MAP 05 SU33

layfly

stcombe SO20 6AZ ☎ 01264 860283 01264 861304
eb: www.themayfly.co.uk
r: *Between A303 & A30, on A3057*

e Mayfly has one of the prettiest locations in Hampshire, on an nd between the River Test and another smaller river to the rear. cess from the car park is via a small bridge. The current licensees ve been here 20 years, and they offer an all day buffet-style selection hot and cold meats, quiches and pies, along with hot and cold daily ecials. The pub is ideal for walkers and cyclists on the nearby Test y.

en 10–11 **Bar Meals** L served all week 11–9 D served all week Av main urse £9.50 Wadworth 6X, Ringwood 49er, Abbot Ale, Hobgoblin. 20 **cilities** Children's licence Garden Dogs allowed Parking

he Peat Spade

ngstock SO20 6DR ☎ 01264 810612
mail: info@peatspadeinn.co.uk

cked away in the Test Valley close to Hampshire's finest chalk stream his red-brick and gabled Victorian pub with unusual paned windows. ffers an informal atmosphere, a decent pint of Hampshire ale, and atisfying meal: perhaps salmon, haddock and scallop fish pie; local k medallions with hoi sin sauce; or baked goats' cheese with sweet tatoes and parsley oil dressing. Good use of local organic produce.

en 11.30–3 6.30–11 Closed: 25–26 Dec **Bar Meals** L served Mon–Sat -2.30 D served Mon–Sat 7–9.30 (Sun 12–3, 7–9) **Restaurant** L served n–Sun 12–2 D served Mon–Sun 7–9.30 Free House Ringwood st, Ringwood 49er & Guest ales. 10 **Facilities** Children's licence rden Dogs allowed Parking

TRATFIELD TURGIS MAP 05 SU65

he Wellington Arms ★★★ HL

327 0AS ☎ 01256 882214 01256 882934
mail: wellington.arms@virgin.net
r: *On A33 between Basingstoke & Reading*

oking at this Grade II listed hotel today, it is hard to believe it was ginally a farmhouse. The Wellington Arms is an ideal base for visiting nearby Stratfield Saye estate, formerly the home of the Duke of llington. Well-kept real ales complement a good selection of eating tions, including liver and bacon served with bubble and squeak; ak and kidney pudding; fanned avocado, cherry, tomato and bacon ad; and smoked salmon and prawn platter.

Open 11–11 (Sun 12–10.30) **Bar Meals** L served all week 12–10 D served all week 12–10 (Sun 12–9.30) **Restaurant** L served Sun–Fri 12–2 D served Mon–Sat 6.30–9.30 Av 3 course à la carte £24 Woodhouse Inns Badger Best Bitter & Tanglefoot. 12 **Facilities** Garden Dogs allowed Parking **Rooms** 28 bedrooms en suite S£95 D£120

TANGLEY MAP 05 SU35

The Fox Inn

SP11 0RU ☎ 01264 730276 01264 730478
e-mail: thefoxinntangley@hotmail.com
dir: *A343, 4m from Andover*

The 300-year-old brick and flint cottage that has been the Fox since 1830 stands on a small crossroads, miles, it seems, from anywhere. The blackboard menu offers reliably good lunchtime snacks and imaginative evening dishes. Enjoy a pint of Archers Village or Stonehenge Pigswill in the tiny, friendly bar, and perhaps a moules mariniere or sea bass fillets in the unpretentious restaurant.

Open 12–3 6–11 (Sun 7–10.30) **Bar Meals** L served all week 12–2 D served all week 6–9 (Fri–Sat 6–9.30, Sun 7–9) **Restaurant** L served all week 12–2 D served all week 6–9 Free House Flowers IPA, Archers Village, Stonehenge Pigswill. **Facilities** Garden Dogs allowed Parking

TICHBORNE MAP 05 SU53

Pick of the Pubs

The Tichborne Arms

SO24 0NA ☎ 01962 733760 01962 733760
e-mail: n.burt@btinternet.com
dir: *A31 towards Alresford, 200yds right for Tichborne*

A heavily thatched free house in the heart of the Itchen Valley, dating from 1423 but destroyed by fire and rebuilt three times; the present red-brick building was erected in 1939. An interesting history is attached to this idyllic rural hamlet, which was dramatised in the feature film *The Tichborne Claimant*. The pub displays much memorabilia connected with the film's subject, Tom Castro's impersonation and unsuccessful claim to the title and estates of Tichborne. Real ales straight from the cask are served in the comfortable atmospheric bars, and all food is home made. Traditional choices range from steak, ale and stilton pie; crab salad; pheasant casserole; chicken, tarragon and mushroom pie; and fish pie to toasted sandwiches and filled jacket potatoes. Expect hearty old-fashioned puddings. A large, well-stocked garden is ideal for summer eating and drinking, with a beer festival the first weekend in June.

Open 11.30–2.30 6–11 **Bar Meals** L served all week 11.30–2 D served all week 6.30–9.30 Free House Ringwood Best, Otter Ale, Guest Beers. 8 **Facilities** Garden Dogs allowed Parking

UPPER FROYLE MAP 05 SU74

The Hen & Chicken Inn

GU34 4JH ☎ 01420 22115 📠 01420 23021

e-mail: bookings@henandchicken.co.uk

dir: *2m from Alton, on A31 next to petrol station*

Highwaymen once haunted the vicinity of this 16th-century inn, which retains a traditional atmosphere enhanced by large open fires, panelling and beams. Close by is the delightful old Georgian town of Farnham, famous for its castle, Maltings arts complex and various listed buildings. The lengthy and sophisticated menu offers an appealing range of dishes. Start with butternut squash and rocket ravioli, followed by pan-roasted skate wing; or an organic Mill Farm hand-pressed beef burger.

Open 11–3 5.30–11 (Fri–Sat 11–11 Sun 12–10.30) **Bar Meals** L served all week 12–2.30 D served all week 6–9 (Sun 12–9) **Restaurant** L served all week 12–2.30 D served all week 6–9 (Sun 12–9) Hall & Woodhouse Badger Best, Tanglefoot, King & Barnes Sussex Ale. 8 **Facilities** Garden Dogs allowed Parking Play Area

WARSASH MAP 05 SU40

The Jolly Farmer Country Inn

29 Fleet End Rd SO31 9JH

☎ 01489 572500 📠 01489 885847

e-mail: mail@thejollyfarmeruk.com

dir: *Exit M27 junct 9 towards A27 Fareham, right onto Warsash Road. 2m, left onto Fleet End Road*

Multi-coloured classic cars are lined up outside this friendly pub close to the Hamble River, and boasting its own golf society and cricket team. The bars are furnished in a rustic style with farming equipment on the walls and ceilings. There's also a patio and a purpose-built children's play area. Grills, including 8oz gammon steaks, and house specialities such as shank of lamb, chicken stroganoff, and fresh fillet of plaice characterise the menu.

Open 11–11 **Bar Meals** L served all week 12–2.30 D served all week 6–10 (Sun all day) **Restaurant** L served all week 12–2.30 D served all week 6–10 Whitbread Gale's HSB, Fuller's London Pride, Interbrew Flowers IPA. **Facilities** Garden Dogs allowed Parking Play Area

WELL MAP 05 SU74

The Chequers Inn

RG29 1TL ☎ 01256 862605 📠 01256 861116

e-mail: roybwells@aol.com

dir: *From Odiham High St turn right into Long Ln for 3m, left at T-junct, pub 0.25m on top of hill*

Set deep in the heart of the Hampshire countryside, in the village of Well near Odiham, this 15th-century pub is full of charm and old world character, with a rustic, low-beamed bar, log fires, scrubbed tables and vine-covered front terrace. The menu offers good pub food such as steak and Tanglefoot pie, fishcakes, slow whole roast pheasant; and the chef's ultimate beefburger, served with home-made chips, new potatoes or creamy mash.

Open 12–3 6–11 (Sat 12–11, Sun 12–10.30) **Bar Meals** L served all week 12–2.30 (Sat–Sun 12–3) D served all week 6.30–9.30 (Sun 6.30–8.30) Av main course £9 **Restaurant** L served all week 12–2.30 (Sat–Sun 12–3) D served all week 6.30–9.30 (Sun 6.30–8.30) Hall & Woodhouse Fursty Ferret, Badger First Gold, Tanglefoot & Hopping Hare. 8 **Facilities** Garden Dogs allowed Parking

WHERWELL MAP 05 SU3

The White Lion

Fullerton Rd SP11 7JF ☎ 01264 860317 📠 01264 860317

dir: *M3 junct 8, A303, then take B3048 to Wherwell; or take A3057 (S of Andover) then B3420 to Wherwell*

The White Lion is a well-known, historic pub in the heart of the Test Valley. Parts of it date back to before the Civil War, during which one of Cromwell's cannon balls smashed the front door, while another shot down the chimney and is still on display today. Pub favourites include ploughman's lunch, crispy battered haddock, the pie of the day and a daily curry. Salad platters feature smoked Hampshire trout or local ham.

Open 11–2.30 6–11 (Mon–Wed 6–10.30, Sun 7–10.30) Closed: 25 Dec **Bar Meals** L served all week 12–2 D served all week 7–9 (Sun 7–8.30) Av main course £9.50 **Restaurant** L served all week 12–2 D served all week 7–9 (Sun 7–8.30) Av 3 course à la carte £19.75 Punch Taverns Ringwood Best Bitter, Tetley Smooth Flow, Bass Bitter. 12 **Facilities** Garden Dogs allowed Parking

WHITCHURCH MAP 05 SU4

Watership Down Inn

Freefolk Priors RG28 7NJ ☎ 01256 892254

e-mail: mark@watershipdowninn.co.uk

dir: *On B3400 between Basingstoke & Andover*

Enjoy an exhilarating walk on Watership Down before relaxing with a pint of well-kept local ale at this homely 19th-century inn named after Richard Adams' classic tale of rabbit life. The menu choices rang from sandwiches, jacket potatoes, salads and ploughman's through t liver and bacon casserole, sausage and mash, mushroom stroganoff, Somerset chicken, and braised lamb shank in a red wine gravy. Don' expect any rabbit dishes!

Open 11.30–3.30 6–11 **Bar Meals** L served all week 12–2.30 D served all week 6–9.30 (Sun 7–8.30) Free House Oakleaf Bitter, Butts Barbus Barbus, Triple FFF Pressed Rat & Warthog, Hogs Back TEA. 8 **Facilities** Garden Parking Play Area

WHITSBURY MAP 05 SU1

The Cartwheel Inn

Whitsbury Rd SP6 3PZ ☎ 01725 518362

dir: *A338 to Salisbury exit at Fordingbridge North & Whitsbury. Take 4th right (Alexandria Rd)*

Handy for exploring the New Forest, visiting Breamore House and discovering the remote Mizmaze on the nearby downs, this extendec turn-of-the-century one-time wheelwright's and shop has been a pub since the 1920s. Well-known for being Grand National winner Desert Orchid's local; the horse re-opened the Cartwheel after its 2004 renovation with a pint of Ringwood Best.

Open 11.30–3 5.30–11 (Sat all day, Sun 12–10.30) **Bar Meals** L served all week 12–2 D served all week 6–9 (Sun 12–2.30) **Restaurant** L served all week D served all week (Sun 12–2.30, 6–9) Av 3 course à la carte £19 Ringwood Ringwood 49er, Old Thumper, Ringwood Best, Ringwoo Seasonal. 20 **Facilities** Garden Dogs allowed Parking Play Area

'HITWAY MAP 05 SU45

arnarvon Arms NEW 🍷

nchester Rd RG20 9LE ☎ 01635 278222 📠 01635 278444
nail: info@carnarvonarms.com
': *M4 junct 13 onto A34 S to Winchester. Exit at Tothill Services Highclere Castle, pub on right*

ilt in the mid 18th-century as a coaching inn for travellers bound nearby Highclere Castle, there's a distinctly Egyptian influence his attractively refurbished pub. Motifs inspired by the 5th Earl Carnarvon's discoveries in the Valley of the Kings adorn the ls, creating a stylish, informal environment. An able kitchen team patch the modern British menu with aplomb: try white bean and ncetta soup, and sautéed breast of guinea fowl. **Bar Meals** L served n–Sat 12–3 (Sun 12–6.30) **Restaurant** L served all week 12–3 served all week 6.30–9.30 Av 3 course à la carte £25 Av 3 course d price £14.95 Merchant Inns Plc Rotating Guest Ales. 🍷 15 **ilities** Garden Dogs allowed Parking

'ICKHAM MAP 05 SU51

reens Restaurant & Pub 🍷

e Square PO17 5JQ ☎ 01329 833197
nail: duckworthgreens@aol.com
': *2m from M27, on corner of historic Wickham Square*

at Greens, on a corner of Wickham's picturesque square, is such a pular rendezvous is entirely down to Frank and Carol Duckworth, o have run it for 22 years. Modern European cooking includes, unchtime, cottage pie with red wine jus; and tagliatelle of wild ishrooms, spinach and toasted pine nuts. At dinner, slow-braised ail with red wine, herbs and horseradish mash; open omelette, ats' cheese and wild rocket; and lots of fresh fish.

en 11–3 6–11 **Bar Meals** L served Tue–Sun 12–2 D served Tue–Sat 0–9.30 (Sun 12–4) Av main course £15 **Restaurant** L served Tue–Sun -2 D served Tue–Sat 6.30–9.30 (Sun 12–4) Av 3 course à la carte £23 Av 3 irse fixed price £12.95 Free House Fullers London Pride, Hopback nmer Lightning, Youngs Special, Guinness & Timothy Taylor. 🍷 10 **cilities** Garden Parking

'INCHESTER MAP 05 SU42

he Westgate Inn ★★★ INN 🍷

Romsey Rd SO23 8TP
: 01962 820222 📠 01962 820222
mail: wghguy@yahoo.co.uk
r: *Pub on corner Romsey Rd & Upper High St*

is establishment stands at the top end of Winchester's main opping street, opposite the medieval West Gate and historic Great ill. The popular bar serves home-cooked meals by day. The inn also uses The Gourmet Rajah, an innovative Indian restaurant. Expect a ix of English, Indian and Bangladeshi: chicken anjali in lemongrass d lime sauce perhaps, or bhindi gosht (steamed lamb cooked with ra); and fish dishes such as salmon ka sula. Tempting desserts clude saffron and honey cheesecake.

pen 11–11 **Bar Meals** L served all week 12–2.30 D served all week 6.30– Av main course £8.50 **Restaurant** L served all week 12–2.30 D served week 6.30–10 Av 3 course à la carte £15 Marstons Jennings ımberland, Banks Original, Marstons Burton Bitter. 🍷 7 **Facilities** Dogs owed **Rooms** 6 bedrooms en suite D£70

Pick of the Pubs

The Wykeham Arms 🍷

75 Kingsgate St SO23 9PE
☎ 01962 853834 📠 01962 854411
e-mail: wykehamarms@accommodating-inns.co.uk
dir: *Near Winchester College & Cathedral*

When you open the curved, glazed doors into this pub's main bar you enter not just a local but an institution. Its two bars are nearly always full of people talking, laughing and warming themselves by the open fires. Photographs, paintings and ephemera fill most vertical surfaces. The 'Wyk' is located in Winchester's ancient back streets close to the cathedral. Old Winchester College desks are placed inkwell to inkwell (Willie Whitelaw carved 'Manners Makyth Man' on one), and a good choice of wines is kept, with up to 20 by the glass. Both bars lead to intimate dining areas, where the daily menu might offer Moroccan bean soup with a crème fraîche and herb garnish; followed by roast tenderloin of pork with grain mustard mash, Savoy cabbage and bacon and a honey and mustard jus. Finish with lime and stem ginger cheesecake. There is a small walled garden outside.

Open 11–11 Closed: 25 Dec **Bar Meals** L served all week 12–2.30 D served Mon–Sat 6.30–8.45 (Sun 12–1.30) Av main course £14.50 **Restaurant** L served all week 12–2.30 D served Mon–Sat 6.30–8.45 (Sun 12–2) Av 3 course à la carte £25 Butser Bitter, HSB, London Pride, Chiswick. 🍷 18 **Facilities** Garden Dogs allowed Parking **Rooms** 14 bedrooms en suite S£62 D£95 (★★★★ INN)

HEREFORDSHIRE

ASTON CREWS MAP 10 SO62

Pick of the Pubs

The Penny Farthing Inn

HR9 7LW ☎ 01989 750366 📠 01989 750922
dir: *5m E of Ross-on-Wye*

A whitewashed, 17th-century blacksmith's shop and later coaching inn high above the River Wye Valley. From its large, sloping garden you can also take in, depending on which way you look, views of the Malvern Hills, the Black Hills and the Forest of Dean. Inside, there are lots of nooks and crannies with oak beams, antiques, saddlery, and cheerful log fires. The extensive menu gives considerable prominence to fish. The frequently changing selection might well include kingklip in a white wine and mushroom sauce; halibut or barramundi steak served with ginger and coriander butter; Thai fishcakes with date and lime chutney; and seafood kebab, comprising tuna, monkfish, salmon, prawns and avocado. Fish is far from all there is though, and on the main carte you may find honey-glazed pork fillet with apricots and almonds; and spring chicken breast marinated in olive oil, cracked black pepper, coriander, fresh ginger, cherries and lime juice.

Open 12–3 6.30–11 (Fri–Sun all day May–Sept) **Bar Meals** L served all week 12–2 D served all week 6–9 Av main course £10 **Restaurant** L served all week 12–2 D served all week 6–9 Av 3 course à la carte £22.50 John Smiths, Abbott Ale, Wadworth 6X. **Facilities** Garden Dogs allowed Parking

England

England

AYMESTREY MAP 09 SO46

Pick of the Pubs

The Riverside Inn

HR6 9ST ☎ 01568 708440 01568 709058
e-mail: theriverside@btconnect.com
web: www.theriversideinn.org
dir: *On A4110 18m N of Hereford*

See Pick of the Pubs on opposite page

BODENHAM MAP 10 SO55

England's Gate Inn

HR1 3HU ☎ 01568 797286 01568 797768
dir: *Hereford A49 onto A417 at Bosey Dinmore, 2.5m on right*

A pretty black and white coaching inn dating from around 1540, with atmospheric beamed bars and blazing log fires in winter. A picturesque garden attracts a good summer following, and so does the food. The menu features such dishes as pan fried lamb steak with apricot and onion marmalade, roasted breast of duck with parsnip mash and spinach and wild rice cakes with peppers on a chilli and tomato salsa.

Open 11–11 (Sunday 12–10.30) **Bar Meals** L served all week 12–2.30 D served all week 6–9.30 Av main course £8.95 **Restaurant** L served all week 12–2.30 D served all week 6–9.30 Av 3 course à la carte £16.95 Free House Wye Valley Bitter, Butty Bach, Shropshire Lad, Guest Ales. 7 **Facilities** Garden Dogs allowed Parking

Railway Inn

Dinmore HR1 3JP ☎ 01568 797053
dir: *7m from Hereford on A49. Right on Dinmore Hill.*

This 17th-century inn was originally built for railway construction workers and enjoys a picturesque setting by the river, with wonderful views of the Herefordshire countryside from the large gardens. Light snacks are served at lunchtime, but in the evenings full meals are available: perhaps spicy Cornish crab cake with noodle salad and a sweet chilli sauce followed by pan-fried duck breast with braised red cabbage and a red wine and grape reduction.

Open 11.30–2.30 6.30–11 **Bar Meals** L served Wed–Sat 12–2 **Restaurant** L served Wed–Sun 12–2 (Sun 12–2.30) D served Tue–Sat 7–9 Av 3 course fixed price £25.50 Enterprise Inns Butty Bach, Wye Valley Bitter, & John Smith's. **Facilities** Children's licence Garden Parking

CANON PYON MAP 09 SO44

The Nags Head Inn

HR4 8NY ☎ 01432 830252
dir: *Telephone for directions*

More than four hundred years old, with flagstone floors, open fires and exposed beams to prove it. A comprehensive menu might entice you into starting with slices of smoked salmon drizzled with brandy, lemon and cracked pepper, then to follow with medallions of lamb in a sticky Cumberland sauce, breast of Gressingham duck in a rich morello cherry sauce, or butterflied sea bass on sauteed strips of carrot and chopped coriander. Vegetarian options include stuffed peppers and tagliatelle. Curry nights and Sunday carvery. The large garden featur a children's adventure playground.

Open 11–2.30 6–11 **Bar Meals** L served Tue–Sun 12–2.30 D served all week 6.30–9.30 Sun 12–9 Av main course £5.95 **Restaurant** L served Tue–Sun 12–2.30 D served all week 6.30–9.30 Sun 12–9 Av 2 course fixec price £8.95 Free House Fuller's London Pride, Boddingtons, Flowe Nags Ale. **Facilities** Garden Parking Play Area

CRASWALL MAP 09 SO

The Bulls Head NEW

HR2 0PN ☎ 01981 510616
e-mail: info@tehbullsheadpub.com
dir: *From A465 turn at Pandy. Village in 11m*

If you like your pubs unchanged, seek out this 400-year-old drovers inn at the foot of 640-metre Black Hill. You get flagstone floors, wood-burning fires, a serving hatch, and bare-topped tables in the t charming dining areas. Craswall Pie, made with gammon, beef and butty bach gravy; rabbit casserole, fillet of salmon, beef Wellington a Mediterranean stuffed peppers are long standing favourites. Wye Va brewery supplies the beers.

Open 11–3 7–11 (Sat 11–11, Sun 11–6) **Bar Meals** L served Tue–Sun 12–2.50 D served Tue–Sat 7–9 Av main course £9 **Restaurant** L served Tue–Sun 12–2.50 D served Tue–Sat 7–9 Free House Butty Bach, Organic Bitter, Old Bull Spinny Dog. 7 **Facilities** Garden Dogs allowe

DORSTONE MAP 09 SO

Pick of the Pubs

The Pandy Inn

HR3 6AN ☎ 01981 550273 01981 550277
e-mail: magdalena@pandyinn.wanadoo.co.uk
dir: *Off B4348 W of Hereford*

Richard de Brito was one of the four Norman knights who killed Thomas à Becket in Canterbury Cathedral in 1170. After 15 years in the Holy Land he returned to England to build a chapel at Dorstone as an act of atonement. He is believed to have built The Pandy to house the workers, later adapting it to become an inn, which is now one of the oldest in the county. Later, during the Civil War in the 17th century, Oliver Cromwell is known to have taken refuge here. The ancient hostelry is located opposite the village green, and part of it retains its original flagstone floors and beams. The large garden, which offers 19 tables and a children's playground, has views of Dorstone Hill. Food is freshly prepared daily and the seasonal menu includes Pandy pies and home-mad puddings. Farmhouse ciders are served alongside local cask ales.

Open 12–3 6–11 Closed: Mon Oct–Jun **Bar Meals** L served all week 12–3 D served all week 6–9.30 **Restaurant** L served all week 12–3 D served all week 6–11 Free House Wye Valley Bitter & Butty Bach. 14 **Facilities** Children's licence Garden Dogs allowed Parking Play Area

PICK OF THE PUBS

The Riverside Inn

ongside the lovely River Lugg, overlooking a fine old stone bridge, this delightful black-and-white inn set amongst the peaceful woodland and meadows of the Welsh Marches. Anglers certainly appreciate e mile of private fly fishing for brown trout and grayling, but it's great for walkers too, situated as it about halfway along the Mortimer Way and close to several circular routes in the vicinity.

ılking packages are offered by e inn, with transportation to and m start/finish points included the room price. The interior, h its wood panelling, low beams d log fires, engenders a relaxed nosphere reflecting 300 years hospitality. Owner Richard esko has a very focused approach food, and locally grown and red produce is used as much as ssible in his kitchen. Visitors are lcome to take a stroll round the b's extensive vegetable, herb and it gardens. Real ales and ciders locally sourced, and the menu inly consists of English-style sine. Popular dishes include me-made smooth chicken liver té with Riverside chutney; home-de steak and kidney pudding; sted haunch of local venison on sweet and sour red cabbage; seared lambs' liver and bacon; tenderloin of local pork with a cheese and mushroom crust on a bed of pea purée with a Dijon sauce; and supreme of chicken wrapped in smoked bacon, stuffed with apricot and pistachio and served with a creamy apricot sauce. As befits a Herefordshire location, locally bred fillet and sirloin of beef always feature, but so too do vegetarian dishes such as mint and pea fritters with roasted peppers, and aubergine with fresh tomato and basil sauce. Gluten and dairy-free dishes can also be prepared for allergy sufferers if booked ahead.

MAP 09 SO46
HR6 9ST
☎ 01568 708440
Fax 01568 709058
e-mail: theriverside@btconnect.com
web: www.theriversideinn.org
dir: *On A4110 18m N of Hereford*

Open 11-3 6-11 Open All day in summer
Bar Meals L served all week 12.30-2.15 D served all week 7-9.15 (Sun 6.30-8.30) Av main course £8.95
Restaurant L served all week 12-2.15 D served all week 7-9.15 (Sun 6.30-8.30) Av 3 course à la carte £23.95
Free House
Wye Valley Seasonal. 7
Facilities Garden Dogs allowed Parking

England

FOWNHOPE MAP 10 SO53

The Green Man Inn

HR1 4PE ☎ 01432 860243 01432 860207

e-mail: info@thegreenmaninn.co.uk

dir: *From M50 take A449 then B4224 to Fownhope*

This white-painted 15th-century coaching inn has a host of beams inside and out. Set in an attractive garden close to the River Wye, it's an ideal base for walking, touring and salmon fishing. The extensive menu has something for everyone, with a range of filling sandwiches, jacket potatoes, burgers and ciabatta melts. Then there are hand-made pies, gourmet grills, and main course favourites like sausages and mash. All this, and sticky puddings too!

Open 11–11 (Fri–Sat 11–12 Sun 11–10.30) **Bar Meals** L served all week 12 D served all week 9.30 Av main course £7.50 Free House John Smith's Smooth, Samuel Smith. **Facilities** Children's licence Garden Dogs allowed Parking

HAMPTON BISHOP MAP 10 SO53

The Bunch of Carrots

HR1 4JR ☎ 01432 870237 01432 870237

e-mail: bunchofcarrotts@buccaneer.co.uk

dir: *From Hereford take A4103, A438, then B4224*

The name has nothing to do with crunchy orange vegetables – it comes from a rock formation in the River Wye, which runs alongside this friendly pub. Inside, expect real fires, old beams and flagstones. There is an extensive menu plus a daily specials board, a carvery, salad buffet, and simple bar snacks – Thai fishcakes, perhaps. Real ale aficionados should certainly sample the local organic beer.

Open 11–3 6–11 (Sat 11–11, Sun 12–10.30) **Bar Meals** L served all week 12–9 D served all week Av main course £10 **Restaurant** L served all week 12–2.30 D served all week 6–10 (Sun 12–9) Free House Directors, Butcombe, Organic Bitter & Guest Beer. 11 **Facilities** Garden Dogs allowed Parking Play Area

HEREFORD MAP 10 SO53

The Crown & Anchor

Cotts Ln, Lugwardine HR1 4AB

☎ 01432 851303 01432 851637

e-mail: c_a@oz.co.uk

dir: *2m from Hereford city centre on A438. Left into Lugwardine down Cotts Lane*

Old Herefordshire-style black-and-white pub with quarry tile floors and a large log fire, just up from the bridge over the River Lugg. Among the many interesting specials you might find fillets of Torbay sole with mussels and white wine; mushrooms in filo pastry with wild mushroom and marsala sauce; seafood tagliolini; supreme of chicken stuffed with wild mushrooms and chestnuts with cranberry and white wine sauce; or Brother Geoffrey's pork sausages with juniper and red wine sauce and mash. A long lunchtime sandwich list is available.

Open 12–11 Closed: 25 Dec **Bar Meals** L served all week 12–2 D served all week 7–10 Av main course £9 Enterprise Inns Worthington Bitter, Timothy Taylors Landlord, Marstons Pedigree, Butcombe Ale. 8 **Facilities** Garden Dogs allowed Parking

KIMBOLTON MAP 10 SO

Pick of the Pubs

Stockton Cross Inn

HR6 0HD ☎ 01568 612509

e-mail: info@stocktoncrossinn.co.uk

dir: *On A4112, off A49 between Leominster & Ludlow*

A drovers' inn dating from the 17th century, the Stockton Cross Inn stands beside a crossroads where alleged witches, rounded up from the surrounding villages such as Ludlow, were hanged. This grisly past is at odds with the peace and beauty of the setting which includes a pretty country garden with umbrellas and trees for shade. The building itself is regularly photographed by tourists and featured on calendars and chocolate boxes. New owners Mike Bentley and Samantha Rosenberg, along with head chef Wil Hayward, have introduced a popular traditional Sunday roast, as well as establishing a good reputation with their appealing menu of pub favourites (gammon steak with egg, plum tomato, field mushroom and home-made chips) and contemporary dishes such as sweet potato lasagne with potato coulis, vegetables and new potatoes. All meals are prepared on the premises using organic produce wherever possible.

Open 12–3 7–11 (6.30–11 Summer) **Bar Meals** L served all week 12–2.15 D served Tue–Sat 7–9 (Sun 12–2.30) **Restaurant** L served all week 12–2.15 D served Tue–Sat 7–9 Free House Wye Valley Butty Bach, Teme Valley This, Hobson's Town Crier, Flowers Best Bitter **Facilities** Garden Dogs allowed Parking

KINGTON MAP 09 SO

Pick of the Pubs

The Stagg Inn and Restaurant

Titley HR5 3RL ☎ 01544 230221 01544 231390

e-mail: reservations@thestagg.co.uk

dir: *Between Kington & Presteigne on B4355*

The Reynolds are celebrating their 10th anniversary at The Stagg this year. A lot has changed over that period, but the locals are still the same chatty bunch. As Nicola Reynolds says, 'A pub is never really owned, but looked after.' The inn was once shut to prevent the railway workers from Titley Junction from getting drunk and insulting the squire. These days it is a bustling place sti surrounded by lovely countryside. The décor has an authentic fee with local stone, and furniture from the area's antique markets. Chef patron Steve Reynolds makes great use of locally sourced ingredients. The lunch/bar snack menu offers the likes of devilled

:idneys, scallops on parsnip purée with black pepper oil, and hree-cheese ploughman's. Restaurant dishes are along the lines of mallard breast with fig and port sauce, fillet of beef with field nushroom and potato dauphinoise, and sea bass fillet on crab isotto.

)pen 12-3 6.30-11 Closed: 1st 2wks Nov & 1wk Feb **ar Meals** L served Tue-Sat 12-2 D served Tue-Thu 6.30-10 Av main ourse £9 **Restaurant** L served Tue-Sat 12-2 D served Tue-Sat .30-10 Av 3 course à la carte £27.50 Free House Hobsons Town rier, Hobsons Old Henry, Hobsons Best Bitter, Black Sheep. 10 **acilities** Garden Dogs allowed Parking

:DBURY MAP 10 SO73

e Farmers Arms

rse Rd, Wellington Heath HR8 1LS ☎ 01531 632010

: *Through Ledbury, pass railway station, right into Wellington ath, first right for pub*

ndy for the breathtaking high ground of the Malvern Hills and the uctive charms of Ross and the Wye Valley, this refurbished country retains lots of character and charm. In addition to the changes de there is an outdoor decked seating area with a large heated opy perfect for alfresco eating. The bar menu includes lots of pub ourites – ploughman's, local sausages of the week, fish and chips, k and ale pudding plus a choice of grills. The restaurant serves likes of haddock and white crab cakes with chilli and mango malade followed by a seasonal dish of honey roasted confit of bary duck leg with mulled red cabbage, plum and blackberry jus.

en 12-3 6-11 **Bar Meals** L served all week 12-3 D served all k 6-10 **Restaurant** L served all week 12-3 D served all week 6-10 nterprise Inns Guest Ales. 8 **Facilities** Children's licence Garden s allowed Parking Play Area

Pick of the Pubs

he Feathers Hotel ★★★ HL

ligh St HR8 1DS ☎ 01531 635266 01531 638955

-mail: mary@feathers-ledbury.co.uk

ir: *S from Worcester A449, E from Hereford A438, N from loucester A417*

he higgledy-piggledy black and white exterior of the Feathers otel is a familiar landmark on Ledbury's main street. This fine old oaching inn dates back to 1564, and a few minutes' drive brings ou to some of the loveliest countryside in the Welsh Borders. nce inside the panelled oak interior, enjoy the house speciality f a Bloody Mary in front of a roaring fire, before perusing a nenu that makes the most of the region's fine produce. Start with autéed pigeon breast, smoked bacon and lambs lettuce; or ham ock, parsley and boiled egg terrine with home-made piccalilli; ollowed by grilled John Dory fillet with garlic mash, mussel eignets and caviar beurre blanc. Carnivores can tuck into roast ump of local lamb with potato galette, or fillet of Herefordshire eef, with celeriac purée, creamed savoy cabbage and bacon.

pen 11-11 (Sun 12-10.30) **Bar Meals** L served all week 12-2 **estaurant** L served all week 12-2 D served all week 7-9.30 Free ouse Coors Worthington's Bitter, Interbrew Bass, Fuller's London ide, Greene King Old Speckled Hen. 18 **Facilities** Garden Parking **ooms** 19 bedrooms en suite S£79 D£115

The Talbot

14 New St HR8 2DX ☎ 01531 632963 01531 633796

e-mail: talbot.ledbury@wadworth.co.uk

dir: *Follow Ledbury signs, turn into Bye St, 2nd left into Woodley Rd, over bridge to junct, left into New St. Pub on right*

It's easy to step back into the late 16th century at this historic black-and-white coaching inn. Dating from 1596, the oak-panelled dining room (appropriately called Panels), with fine carved overmantle, still displays musket-bullet holes left after a skirmish between Roundheads and Cavaliers. A good choice of local ales and wines by the glass is offered. The chef is 'passionate about fish' so expect the likes of home-made salmon fishcakes or crayfish risotto.

Open 11.30-3 5-11 (Fri-Sat 5-12) **Bar Meals** L served all week 12-2.15 D served Mon-Sat 6.30-9.15 (Sun 12-2.30) Av main course £7 **Restaurant** L served all week 12-2.15 (Sun 11.30-2.30) D served all week 6.15-9.15 Av 3 course à la carte £20 Wadworth Wadworth 6X & Henrys Original IPA, Wye Valley Butty Bach, Wadworth Guest Ales & Henry's Smooth. 15 **Facilities** Parking **Rooms** 6 bedrooms en suite S£32.50 D£60.75 (★★★ INN)

The Trumpet Inn

Trumpet HR8 2RA ☎ 01531 670277

dir: *4m from Ledbury, at junct of A438 & A417*

This traditional black and white free house dates back to the late 14th century. The former coaching inn and post house takes its name from the days when mail coaches blew their horns on approaching the crossroads. The cosy bars feature a wealth of exposed beams, with open fireplaces and a separate non-smoking dining area. Light sandwich lunches and salad platters complement main dishes like salmon fishcakes; kleftiko; or vegetable stroganoff.

Open 12-11 (Sun 12-10.30) **Bar Meals** L served all week 12-3 D served all week 6-9 (Sun 6-8.30) **Restaurant** L served all week 12-3 D served all week 6-9 (Sun 6-8.30) Free House Wadworth 6X, Henrys IPA, Old Father Time. **Facilities** Garden Dogs allowed Parking

The Verzon U

Trumpet HR8 2PZ ☎ 01531 670381 01531 670830

e-mail: info@theverzon.co.uk

dir: *2.5m W of Ledbury on A438 towards Hereford*

A former farmhouse, this Georgian country house hotel stands in over four acres of countryside with views of the Malvern Hills. Versatile facilities include a large function room, a popular deck terrace and a comfortable lounge with an open fire. The menu makes good reading with classics like pan-fried rib-eye of Herefordshire beef with grilled field mushrooms, roast plum tomatoes, sautéed potatoes and sauce béarnaise, or steamed mussels with white wine, cream and parsley.

Open 8-11 **Bar Meals** L served all week 12-2 (Sun 12-2.30) D served all week 7-9 **Restaurant** L served all week 12-2 (Sun 12-2.30) D served all week 7-9 Av 3 course à la carte £25 Wye Valley Bitter, Butty Bach, Tetley Smoothflow. 7 **Facilities** Children's licence Garden Parking **Rooms** 8 bedrooms en suite S£65 D£80

England

LEOMINSTER MAP 10 SO45

The Grape Vaults

Broad St HR4 8BS ☎ 01568 611404

e-mail: jusaxon@tiscali.co.uk

An unspoilt pub with a small, homely bar complete with real fire – in fact it's so authentic that it's Grade II-listed, even down to the fixed seating. Real ale is a popular feature, and includes microbrewery products. The good food includes turkey and ham pie, bubble and squeak with bacon and egg, steak and ale pie, and various fresh fish dishes using cod, plaice, salmon and whitebait. No music, gaming machines, or alcopops!

Open 11–11 **Bar Meals** L served Mon–Sat 12–2 D served Mon–Sat 5.30–9 Punch Taverns Banks Bitter, Pedigree, Banks Original & Guest Ales. 6 **Notes**

The Royal Oak Hotel

South St HR6 8JA ☎ 01568 612610 01568 612710

e-mail: reservations@theroyaloakhotel.net

dir: *Town centre, near A44/A49 junct*

Coaching inn dating from around 1733, with log fires, antiques and a minstrels' gallery in the original ballroom. The pub was once part of a now blocked-off tunnel system that linked the Leominster Priory with other buildings in the town. Good choice of wines by the glass and major ales, and a hearty menu offering traditional British food with a modern twist.

Open 10–3 6–11 (Sat 10–11, Sun 12–10.30) **Bar Meals** L served all week 12–2.30 D served all week 7–9 **Restaurant** L served Sun 12–2 D served all week 7–9.30 Free House Shepherd Neame Spitfire, Wye Valley Butty Bach. **Facilities** Garden Dogs allowed Parking

LITTLE COWARNE MAP 10 SO65

The Three Horseshoes Inn

HR7 4RQ ☎ 01885 400276 01885 400276

e-mail: janetwhittall@hotmail.com

dir: *Off A456. At Stokes Cross, take turning signed Little Cowarne/Pencombe*

They no longer shoe horses at the blacksmith's next door, but this old ale house's long drinking pedigree – 200 years and counting – looks secure. The hop-bedecked bar serves local ales and cider, while meals made extensively from fresh local ingredients can be enjoyed in the restaurant or garden room. Portuguese fish stew (cataplana); fillet steak au poivre; and pea, rocket and parmesan risotto are typical. There are some en suite rooms upstairs.

Open 11–3 6.30–11 Closed: 25 Dec **Bar Meals** L served all week 12–2 D served all week 6.30–9.30 (Sun 12–3, 7–9) **Restaurant** L served all week 12–2 D served all week 6.30–9.30 Free House Marston's Pedigree, Greene King Old Speckled Hen, Wye Valley Bitter, Scottish Courage John Smith's. 12 **Facilities** Garden Parking **Rooms** 2 bedrooms en suite S£35 D£60 (★★★ INN)

MADLEY MAP 09 SO

The Comet Inn

Stoney St HR2 9NJ ☎ 01981 250600

e-mail: stevewilson@thecometinn.co.uk

dir: *6m from Hereford on B4352*

Located on a prominent corner position and set in two and a half acres, this black and white 19th-century inn was originally three cottages, and retains many original features and a roaring open fire. simple, hearty menu includes steak and ale pie, shank of lamb, grille gammon, chicken curry, cod in crispy batter, mushroom stroganoff, and a variety of steaks, baguettes, and jacket potatoes.

Open 12–3 6–11 (Fri–Sun & BH's all day) **Bar Meals** L served all week 12–3 D served Mon–Sun 6–9 (Sat all day, Sun 12–4) Av main course £5 **Restaurant** L served all week 12–2 D served Mon–Sat 7–9.30 Av 3 cour à la carte £15 Free House Hook Norton Best Bitter, Wye Valley Bitter, Tetley Smooth Flow, Carlsberg Tetley. 22 **Facilities** Garden Do allowed Parking Play Area

MICHAELCHURCH ESCLEY MAP 09 SO

The Bridge Inn

HR2 0JW ☎ 01981 510646 01981 510646

e-mail: nickmaddy@aol.com

dir: *From Hereford take A465 towards Abergavenny, then B43 towards Peterchurch. Left at Vowchurch & on to village*

By Escley Brook, at the foot of the Black Mountains and close to Off Dyke, there are 14th-century parts to this oak-beamed family pub: t dining room overlooks the garden, abundant with rose and begonia and the river – an ideal area for walkers and nature lovers. On rainy days guests may prefer the games room. Speciality dishes include st and kidney with crispy dumplings.

Open 12–11 **Bar Meals** L served all week 12–6 D served all week 6–9 **Restaurant** L served all week 12–3 D served all week 6–9.30 (Sun 12–6) Free House Wye Valley Beers, John Smiths, Bridge Bitter. 20 **Facilities** Garden Dogs allowed Parking Play Area

MUCH MARCLE MAP 10 SO

The Slip Tavern

Watery Ln HR8 2NG ☎ 01531 660246 01531 660700

e-mail: thesliptavern@aol.com

dir: *Follow signs off A449 at Much Marcle junction*

Curiously named after a 1575 landslip which buried the local churc this country pub is delightfully surrounded by cider apple orchards.

n attractive conservatory overlooks the award-winning garden, where ımmer dining is popular, and there's also a cosy bar. It's next to /estons Cider Mill, and cider is a favourite in the bar.

pen 11.30–2.30 6–11 (Sun 12–3, 7–10.30) Closed: Mon lunch **ar Meals** L served Tues-Sun 12–2.30 D served Tues-Sat 6.30–9 Av main ourse £7 **Restaurant** L served Tues-Sun 11.30–2 D served Tues-Sat 30–9.30 Av 3 course à la carte £18 Free House John Smiths, Tetleys mooth Flow, Guest Ales. 8 **Facilities** Garden Parking Play Area

)RLETON MAP 09 SO46

he Boot Inn

Y8 4HN ☎ 01568 780228 01568 780228

-mail: thebootorleton@hotmail.com

ır: *Follow A49 S from Ludlow to B4362 (Woofferton), 1.5m off 4362 turn left. Inn in village centre*

black and white timbered inn, The Boot dates from the 16th century, d in winter a blazing fire in the inglenook warms the bar. A range snacks and a regular menu, including a generous mixed grill, roast ıck and a salad selection, are supplemented by specials such as pork op with apple and cider sauce, vegetable lasagne, and fish pie with a eesy mash topping.

pen 12–3 6–11 **Bar Meals** L served Tue–Sun 12–2 D served all week 9 Av main course £11 **Restaurant** L served Tue–Sun D served all week 9 Av 3 course à la carte £18 Free House Hobsons Best, Local al Ales, Woods, Wye Valley. **Facilities** Children's licence Garden Dogs owed Parking Play Area

EMBRIDGE MAP 09 SO35

lew Inn

arket Square HR6 9DZ

: 01544 388427 01544 388427

r: *From M5 junct 7 take A44 W through Leominster towards ındrindod Wells*

ɔrn flagstone floors and open fires characterise this unspoilt black d white timbered free house. Formerly a courthouse, the building tes from the early 14th century. In summer, customers spill out o the pub's outdoor seating area in the Old Market Square. Under e same ownership for over 20 years, it attracts locals and summer ırists with dishes like lamb and vegetable hotpot; cream cheese and inach lasagne; and trout fillets in lemon butter.

en 11–2.30 6–11 **Bar Meals** L served all week 12–2 D served all week 9.30 (Sun 12–3, 7–10.30) **Restaurant** 12–2 7–9.30 Free House Fuller's London Pride, Kingdom Bitter, Three Tuns from Bishops Castle, ıck Sheep Best. **Facilities** Garden Parking

PETERSTOW MAP 10 SO52

The Red Lion Inn NEW

HR9 6LH ☎ 01989 730202

dir: *On A49, 2m from Ross-on-Wye*

A traditional country pub with oak beams and log fires on the A49 between Ross-on-Wye and Hereford. Choice is what the Red Lion is all about – from the real ales to the extensive menu of pub favourites served in both bar and restaurant. Thai fishcakes and Marie Rose prawns are typical starters, with representative mains being bangers and mash and chargrilled steaks. Many dishes can be served as light bites suitable for children or the smaller appetite.

Open 12–3 5.30–11.30 (Sat all day, Sun 12–5) **Bar Meals** L served Mon–Sat 12–2.30 D served all week 6–9 (Sun 12–3) Av main course £12 **Restaurant** 12–2.30 6–9 Av 3 course à la carte £20 Enterprise Inns Otto Bitter, Timothy Taylor Landlord, Malvern Hills Black Pear, Dorothy Goodbody's Golden Ale. **Facilities** Children's licence Garden Parking Play Area

ROSS-ON-WYE MAP 10 SO52

Pick of the Pubs

The Moody Cow

Upton Bishop HR9 7TT ☎ 01989 780470

dir: *Accessed from M50 junct 3 or junct 4. Upton Bishop on B4221*

An old stone-built inn with a patio area offering plenty of shaded seating in summer, the Moody Cow includes a rustic bar with exposed stone walls and farmhouse seating. Here, local Wye Valley bitter figures among the real ales, alongside a good selection of wines by the glass. Beyond the bar are two further rooms: the Fresco is set up for informal eating at wooden tables with raffia chairs and cow-themed displays; and the Snug where you can relax with a drink on comfy sofas by the wood-burning fire. The restaurant, on two levels and forming one leg of an L, is a converted barn with blue glazing, exposed beams and carpeted floors. To ensure consistency it offers just one menu throughout.

Open 12–2.30 6.30–11 (Sun 12–3) **Bar Meals** L served Tue–Sun 12–2 D served Tue–Sat 7–9 **Restaurant** L served Tue–Sun 12–2 D served Tue–Sat 7–9 Free House Hook Norton Best, Wye Valley Best. 7 **Facilities** Garden Dogs allowed Parking

SELLACK MAP 10 SO52

Pick of the Pubs

The Lough Pool Inn at Sellack

HR9 6LX ☎ 01989 730236 01989 730548

dir: *A49 from Ross-on-Wye towards Hereford signed Sellack/Hoarwithy*

See Pick of the Pubs on page 294

The Lough Pool Inn at Sellac

First, the pronunciation – it's Luff Pool, although locals call it the Love Pool. Maybe they know something! In the 1870s this typical Herefordshire black and white, half-timbered pub doubled as both beerhouse and butcher's shop, then in 1880, when it was granted inn status, it could sta open as long as there was an empty bed.

There are flagstones on the floor, duck-or-grouse beams and, at the rear, a dining room with solid rustic tables and chairs. This is a true destination pub, with people travelling from as far away as Cardiff and Cheltenham for a meal. Meals are served in both the bar and the adjoining restaurant areas and no two days' menus are exactly the same. However, there's always a tasty home-made soup, such as cream of organic parsnip, pear and curry, to start with; or twice-baked Herefordshire Hop cheese soufflé with walnut and Weston's cider cream; or maybe seared Scottish scallops with avocado salsa and sauce Andalouse. And for a main course, try tournedos of hake with creamed polenta, herb purée, roasted button onions with red wine and aniseed sauce; grilled fillet of Devon line-caught wild sea bass with lyonnaise potatoes, green beans and a herb cream; roast breast of Madgett's Farm duck with creamed swede, fondant potato and spiced cherry sauce; or braised lamb with red onion, foie gras and basil faggots, ratatouille and olive jus. Glazed lemon tart with raspberry sorbet will freshen the palate nicely. Children are encouraged to eat smaller portions chosen from the main menu. Owners Jan and David Birch have planted a herb garden, and plan to start growing their own salad leaves and vegetables. There are beautiful walks to the nearby River Wye, and the garden is popular for alfresco dining.

MAP 10 SO52
HR9 6LX
☎ 01989 730236
01989 730548
dir: *A49 from Ross-on-Wye towards Hereford, signed Sellack/ Hoarwithy.*

Open 11.30–3 6.30–11 (Sun 11–3, 6.30–10.30) Closed: 25 Dec
Bar Meals L served all week 12–3 D served all week 7–9.15 Av main course £12.50
Restaurant L served all week 12–3 D served all week 7–9.15 Av 3 course à la carte £22
Free House
Wye Valley, Scottish Courage John Smiths, Butcombe Bitter, Old Speckled Hen, Best Bitter & Butty Bach plus Guest ales. 10
Facilities Garden Dogs allowed Parking

SHOBDON — MAP 09 SO46

The Bateman Arms NEW ★★★★ INN

HR6 9LX ☎ 01568 708374
e-mail: martin.batemanarms@hotmail.co.uk
dir: *On B4362 off A4110 NW of Leominster*

An 18th-century, three-storey building of striking appearance, with old cobbled paving lining its street frontage. There's character inside too, where you can sit in the bar beneath ancient oak beams on 400-year-old wooden settles and enjoy a baguette, sandwich or jacket potato. Seasonal choices in the restaurant include Tex-Mex chilli topped with cheese on rice; chicken curry; deep-fried cod in beer batter; and roasted courgettes filled with pea risotto. Bedrooms are furnished in traditional style.

Open 12-3 7-11 **Bar Meals** L served all week 12-2 D served all week 7-9 Av main course £8 **Restaurant** L served all week 12-2 D served all week 7-11 Av 3 course à la carte £20 Free House Wye Valley, Kronenbourg, Carlsberg Export, Stowford Press & Guinness. **Facilities** Garden Parking **Rooms** 9 bedrooms en suite S£55 D£85

SYMONDS YAT (EAST) — MAP 10 SO51

Pick of the Pubs

The Saracens Head Inn ★★★★ INN

Ross-on-Wye HR9 6JL
☎ 01600 890435 📠 01600 890034
e-mail: contact@saracensheadinn.co.uk
web: www.saracensheadinn.co.uk
dir: *From Ross-on-Wye take A40 to Monmouth. 4m, take Symonds Yat East turn. 1st right before bridge. Right after 0.5m, turn right again in 1m*

Formerly a cider mill, the Saracens Head lies on the east bank of the River Wye just over a mile from the Welsh border. Situated in an area of outstanding natural beauty on the edge of the Royal Forest of Dean, the inn's eleven en suite bedrooms make an ideal base for exploring the unspoiled local countryside. The area takes its name from Robert Symonds, a 17th-century Sheriff of Herefordshire, whilst Yat is the local name for a gate or pass. An ancient hand ferry still plies the river in front of the inn, and walking, cycling and canoeing are all available locally. The wide choice of popular bar and restaurant fare includes traditional home-made dishes, many with a modern twist. Expect home-smoked Gloucestershire venison; warm smoked haddock and quail egg tart; and risotto of golden chanterelles with basil pesto and parmesan.

Open 11-11 **Bar Meals** L served all week 12-2.30 D served all week 7-9.15 **Restaurant** L served all week 12-2.30 D served all week 6.30-9 Free House Scottish Courage Theakstons Best & Old Peculier, Old Speckled Hen, Wye Valley Hereford Pale Ale, Wye Valley Butty Bach. 7 **Facilities** Garden Dogs allowed Parking **Rooms** 11 bedrooms en suite S£50 D£74

TILLINGTON — MAP 09 SO44

The Bell

HR4 8LE ☎ 01432 760395 📠 01432 760580
e-mail: beltill@aol.com
dir: *NE Hereford, on road to Weabley via Burghill*

Run by the same family since 1988, The Bell offers something for everybody, with quiet gardens, a formal dining area and a traditional public bar complete with oak parquet flooring, an open fire and a dart board. The varied menus cover all dining requirements, from bar snacks to more elaborate meals: smoked salmon terrine, followed by roast Madgett's Farm duck breast, or venison, wild boar and pheasant casserole, perhaps.

Open 11-3 6-11 (Sat-Sun all) **Bar Meals** L served all week 12-2.15 D served Mon-Sat 6-9.15 Sun 12-2.30 **Restaurant** L served all week 12-2.15 D served Mon-Sat 6-9.15 Av 3 course à la carte £15 London Pride, Hereford Bitter. **Facilities** Garden Dogs allowed Parking Play Area

ULLINGSWICK — MAP 10 SO54

Pick of the Pubs

Three Crowns Inn

HR1 3JQ ☎ 01432 820279 📠 01432 820279
e-mail: info@threecrownsinn.com
dir: *From Burley Gate rdbt take A465 toward Bromyard, after 2m left to Ullingswick, left after 0.5m, pub 0.5m on right*

An unspoilt country pub in deepest rural Herefordshire, where food sources are so local their distance away is referred to in fields, rather than miles. A hand-written sign even offers to buy surplus garden fruit and veg from locals. Parterres in the garden give additional space for growing more varieties of herbs, fruit and vegetables that are not easy, or even possible, to buy commercially. There's even a pea whose provenance can be traced back to some that Lord Carnarvon found in a phial in Tutankhamun's tomb. The menus change daily, but there is always fish, such as line-caught poached monkfish and proscuito with celeriac mousse and haricot blanc. Soufflés often appear too. Meat dishes have included braised belly of Berkshire pork, marinated lamb rumb with kidney kebab, and confit of Gressingham duck. Tuesday tasting evenings feature a set four-course dinner that changes week by week, with wines normally sold only by the bottle, available by the glass.

Open 12-2.30 7-11 (May-Aug 12-3, 6-11) Closed: 2wks from Dec 25 **Bar Meals** L served all week 12-2.30 D served all week 7-10 (Summer 6-10) **Restaurant** L served all week 12-2 D served all week 7-9.30 Free House Hobsons Best, Wye Valley Butty Bach & Dorothy Goodbody's, Guest beers. 9 **Facilities** Garden Parking

England

WALTERSTONE MAP 09 SO32

Carpenters Arms

HR2 0DX ☎ 01873 890353

dir: *Off A465 between Hereford & Abergavenny at Pandy*

There's plenty of character in this 300-year-old free house located on the edge of the Black Mountains where the owner, Mrs Watkins, was born. Here you'll find beams, antique settles and a leaded range with open fires that burn all winter. Popular food options include beef and Guinness pie; beef lasagne; and thick lamb cutlets. Ask about the vegetarian selection, and large choice of home-made desserts.

Open 12-3 7-11 **Bar Meals** L served all week 12-3 D served all week 7-9.30 **Restaurant** L served all week 12-3 D served all week 7-9.30 Free House Wadworth 6X, Breconshire Golden Valley & Rambler's Ruin. **Facilities** Garden Parking Play Area **Notes**

WELLINGTON MAP 10 SO44

The Wellington

HR4 8AT ☎ 01432 830367

e-mail: thewellington@hotmail.com

dir: *Off A49 into village centre, 0.25m on left*

Owners Ross and Philippa Williams left London in order to follow their dream of creating one of Herefordshire's finest dining pub. Staying true to their ideals and dedicated to the use of good local produce, they are now seeing the accolades rolling in. Start with red pepper and Perroche cheese ravioli, followed by pot roast of Welsh white pork with chestnuts and chorizo. Puddings are equally delicious: try cinnamon rice pudding with fig compote.

Open 12-3 6-11 (Sun 7-10.30) **Bar Meals** L served Tue-Sun 12-2 D served Mon-Sat 7-9 Av main course £6 **Restaurant** L served Tue-Sun 12-2 D served Mon-Sat 7-9 Av 3 course à la carte £23.50 Free House Hobsons, Wye Valley Butty Bach, Timothy Taylor Landlord & Guest Ales. 7 **Facilities** Garden Dogs allowed Parking Play Area

WEOBLEY MAP 09 SO45

Pick of the Pubs

The Salutation Inn

Market Pitch HR4 8SJ

☎ 01544 318443 01544 318405

e-mail: salutationinn@btinternet.com

dir: *A44, then A4112 8m from Leominster*

A black and white timber-framed pub dating back more than 500 years and situated in a corner of the country renowned for its hops, cattle and apple orchards. The inn, sympathetically converted from an old ale house and adjoining cottage, is the perfect base for exploring the lovely Welsh Marches and enjoying a host of leisure activities, including fishing, horse riding, golf, walking, and clay shooting. The book capital of Hay-on-Wye and the cathedral city of Hereford are close by. The Salutation Inn's Oak Room Restaurant offers a range of award-winning dishes created with the use of locally sourced ingredients. Chef's specials are also served in the traditional lounge bar with its welcoming atmosphere and cosy inglenook fireplace. Starters include confit of duck and pan-seared Cornish scallops, while main courses range from roast rump of Welsh lamb, and oven-baked fillet of salmon, to whole roast breast of chicken, and medley of sea bass and oysters.

Open 11-11 (Sun 12-10.30) **Bar Meals** L served all week 12-2.30 D served all week 6.30-9.30 (Sun 6.30-8) Av main course £10 **Restaurant** L served all week 12-2.30 D served Mon-Sat 7-9 Av 3 course à la carte £25 Free House Hook Norton Best, Coors Worthington's Creamflow, Wye Valley Butty Bach, Flowers Best Bitter. **Facilities** Children's licence Garden Parking **Rooms** 4 bedrooms en suite S£53 D£80

WHITNEY-ON-WYE MAP 09 SO2

Pick of the Pubs

Rhydspence Inn ★★ SHL

HR3 6EU ☎ 01497 831262 01497 831751

e-mail: info@rhydspence-inn.co.uk

dir: *N side of A438 1m W of Whitney-on-Wye*

Once a manor house, the Rhydspence Inn was also a favourite watering hole for Welsh and Irish drovers taking cattle, sheep and geese to market in London. These days the pub is rather more elegant, with a cosy bar and spacious dining room giving way to stunning views over the Wye Valley. The pub also has literary connections, appearing in *On The Black Hill* by Bruce Chatwin, and apparently acting as a site of inspiration for Shakespeare while penning *Much Ado About Nothing*. Food options range from simple bar snacks such as steak and kidney pie or beef lasagna to more elaborate dining: perhaps honey-fried scallops with a lime, soy and ginger dressing, followed by roast monkfish on sweet pepper compote. The friendly ghost of a former landlady is said to frequent the inn, though only when young children are staying.

Open 11-2.30 7-11 **Bar Meals** L served all week 11-1.45 D served all week 7-8.45 (Sun 12-2) Av main course £8.50 **Restaurant** L served all week 11-1.45 D served all week 7-8.45 (Sun lunch 12-2) Av 3 course à la carte £26 Free House Robinsons Best, Interbrew Bass. **Facilities** Garden Parking **Rooms** 7 bedrooms en suite S£42.50 D£85

VOOLHOPE MAP 10 SO63

'he Crown Inn

IR1 4QP ☎ 01432 860468 📠 01432 860770
-mail: thecrowninn1382@aol.com
ir: *B4224 to Mordiford, left after Moon Inn, in village centre*

arts of this mainly 18th-century inn date back to about 1520 as ıdicated by a mounting block at the front of the original building earing this date. Located in a beautiful conservation area close to ereford, Ross-on-Wye and Ledbury. The owners offer an extensive ıenu which includes steak, stout and mushroom pie; chicken, leek nd stilton vol-au-vent; salmon and broccoli au gratin; and lamb and ranberry casserole. Various light bites and home-made desserts.

pen 12-3 6.30-11 (Sun 6.30-10.30 Winter Mon-Fri 7-11) Closed: 25 ec **Bar Meals** L served all week 12-2 D served all week 6.30-9.30 v main course £7.95 **Restaurant** L served all week 12-2 D served all week .30-9.30 Av 3 course à la carte £17 Free House Wye Valley Best, lack Sheep, Guest ales. 6 **Facilities** Garden Parking

HERTFORDSHIRE

ALDBURY MAP 06 SP91

The Greyhound Inn

9 Stocks Rd HP23 5RT ☎ 01442 851228 📠 01442 851495
-mail: tim@valianttrooper203.freeserve.co.uk

'his quintessentially English country pub looks out over the village uck pond and ancient stocks. Nestling beneath the Chiltern Hills and lose to the National Trust's renowned Ashridge Estate, the Greyhound s also ideal for local walks. Log fires warm the bar in winter, whilst ummer brings the option of an alfresco lunch. Hearty, traditional ishes could include free-range pork sausages with onion gravy; chilled almon salad; or butternut squash, sage and pine nut risotto.

pen 11-11 Closed: 25 Dec **Bar Meals** L served all week 12-2.30) served Mon-Sat 6.30-9.30 **Restaurant** L served all week 12-2.30) served Mon-Sat 7-10 Hall & Woodhouse Badger Best, Tanglefoot, ing & Barnes & Sussex. 10 **Facilities** Garden Dogs allowed Parking

Pick of the Pubs

The Valiant Trooper

Trooper Rd HP23 5RW
☎ 01442 851203 📠 01442 851071
dir: *A41 at Tring junct, follow rail station signs 0.5m, at village green turn right, 200yds on left*

Family-run free house in a pretty village whose ancient stocks and duckpond often feature in films. The deeds date back to 1752, when it was The Royal Oak; it became The Trooper Alehouse in 1803, allegedly because the Duke of Wellington once discussed tactics here with his troops. In the 1880s a landlord would remove his wooden leg and bang it on the counter – maybe his way of calling 'Time!' The old stable block, which has also served as scout hut and local bikers' club, is now a comfortable 40-seater restaurant offering daily blackboard specials such as duck breast with oriental stir-fry; pork loin steak with sage sauce; sausage and mash with onion gravy; and grilled mackerel stuffed with tomato and onion. Hikers and cyclists descend from the surrounding Chiltern Hills for a pint of Tring Brewery's Jack O' Legs, or regularly changing guest beers. Dogs are welcome too.

Open 11.30-11 (Sun 12-10.30) **Bar Meals** L served all week 12-2 D served Tue-Sat 6.30-9.15 (Sun 12-2.30) Av main course £10 **Restaurant** L served all week 12-2 D served Tue-Sun 6.30-9.15 (Sun 12-2.30) Av 3 course à la carte £17 Free House Fuller's London Pride, Oakham J.H.B, Tring Jack O'Legs & Guest Beers. 8 **Facilities** Garden Dogs allowed Parking Play Area

ARDELEY MAP 12 TL32

The Jolly Waggoner

SG2 7AH ☎ 01438 861350

Cream-washed 500-year-old pub with exposed beams, roaring fires, antique furniture and a popular cottage garden. The inn also benefits from a lovely village setting and a variety of local walks. All the food is home made from fresh ingredients, ranging from appetising sandwiches to à la carte dining. Fish is something of a speciality, like dressed crab salad, swordfish or sea bass. Alternatively, try loin of lamb, calves' liver or steak and kidney pie.

Open 12-3 6-11 **Bar Meals** L served all week 12-2 D served all week 6.30-9 (Sun 12-3) Av main course £12 **Restaurant** L served all week 12.30-2 D served all week 6.30-9 Greene King Greene King IPA & Abbot Ale. **Facilities** Garden Parking

ASHWELL MAP 12 TL23

The Three Tuns

High St SG7 5NL ☎ 01462 742107 📠 01462 743662
e-mail: claire@tuns.co.uk

Many original features survive at this centuries-old inn, helping to create an old-world atmosphere in the heart of the village – a place to sit and watch the world go by. The freshly prepared menu changes daily, and includes best end of roast rack of lamb; fillet of pork Normandy with a creamy Calvados and apple sauce; provençal pinto bean stew; and seafood kebabs with a spicy chilli dip and savoury rice. To follow, try home-made profiteroles with butterscotch sauce, or frangipane tart with redcurrant glaze.

Open 11-11.30 (Fri-Sat 11-12, Sun 12-10.30) **Bar Meals** L served all week 12-2.30 D served all week 6.30-9.30 **Restaurant** L served all week 12-2.30 D served all week 6.30-9.30 Greene King Greene King IPA, Abbot, Guest ale. 7 **Facilities** Garden Dogs allowed Parking Play Area

BARLEY MAP 12 TL43

The Fox & Hounds

High St SG8 8HU ☎ 01763 848459 📠 01763 849274
e-mail: jamesburn1972@aol.com
dir: *A505 onto B1368 at Flint Cross, pub 4m*

Set in a pretty village, this former 17th-century hunting lodge is notable for its pub sign which extends across the lane. It has real fires, a warm welcome and an attractive garden. The owners have made their mark with their home-cooked food, offering a menu with a good range of dependable choices, including sirloin steak with chips and onion rings; barbecued ribs; and chilli and lasagne.

Open 12-11 (Sun 12-10.30) (Winter Mon-Fri 12-3, Sat & Sun all day) **Bar Meals** L served all week 12-10 D served all week 12-10 (Sun 12-9) Av main course £8 **Restaurant** L served 12-10 Av 3 course à la carte £13.95 Punch Taverns IPA, 6X, Adnams Best, Old Speckled Hen & Guest Beers. **Facilities** Garden Dogs allowed Parking Play Area

BUNTINGFORD MAP 12 TL32

The Sword Inn Hand ★★★★ INN

Westmill SG9 9LQ ☎ 01763 271356
e-mail: theswordinnhand@btconnect.com
dir: *Off A10 1.5m S of Buntingford*

This delightful 14th-century free house is set in a peaceful village amid rolling Hertfordshire countryside. A wealth of oak beams, flagstone floors and an open fireplace welcomes visitors to the bar, with its excellent local ales and guest beers. Chef Peter Moor's menu uses fresh, local produce that is delivered daily. The specials board may include sausage and mash, rack of lamb, cod and chips, or stuffed red peppers.

Open 12-3 5-11 (Fri-Sun all day) **Bar Meals** L served Mon-Sun 12-2.30 D served Mon-Sun 6.30-9.30 (Sun winter 12-5 summer 12-7) Av main course £8 **Restaurant** L served all week 12-2.30 D served all week 7-9.30 (Sun 12-5) Av 3 course à la carte £22 Free House Greene King IPA, Young's Bitter, Shephard Neame Spitfire & Guest Ales. 8 **Facilities** Garden Dogs allowed Parking Play Area **Rooms** 4 bedrooms en suite S£70 D£80

COTTERED MAP 12 TL32

The Bull at Cottered

Cottered SG9 9QP ☎ 01763 281243
e-mail: cordell1139@btinternet.com
dir: *On A507 in Cottered between Buntingford & Baldock*

A traditional village local in a picturesque setting, with low-beamed ceilings, antique furniture, cosy fires and pub games. The menu offers only home-made food, including calves' liver with smoked bacon and butter sauce; fillet of chicken in cream, wine, garlic and mushroom sauce; and smoked haddock-filled Arnold Bennett omelette. Home-made burgers, jacket potatoes, open toasted sandwiches and ploughman's are also available. There are log fires in winter, and a well-kept garden in summer.

Open 12-2.30 6.30-11 (Sun 7-10.30) **Bar Meals** L served all week 12-2 D served all week 6.30-9 (Sun 12-3, 6.30-9) Av main course £8 **Restaurant** L served all week 12-2 D served all week 6.30-9.30 (Sun 12-3, 6.30-9) Av 3 course à la carte £26.65 Av fixed price £19 Greene King Greene King IPA & Abbot Ale. 7 **Facilities** Garden Parking

FLAUNDEN MAP 06 TL0

Pick of the Pubs

The Bricklayers Arms

Hogpits Bottom HP3 0PH
☎ 01442 833322 📠 01442 834841
e-mail: goodfood@bricklayersarms.com
web: www.bricklayersarms.com
dir: *M25 junct 18 onto A404 (Amersham road). Right at Chenies for Flaunden*

See Pick of the Pubs on opposite page

HEMEL HEMPSTEAD MAP 06 TL0

Pick of the Pubs

Alford Arms

Frithsden HP1 3DD ☎ 01442 864480 📠 01422 876893
e-mail: info@alfordarmsfrithsden.co.uk
dir: *From Hemel Hempstead on A4146 take 2nd left at Water End. After 1m left at T-junct, right after 0.75m. Pub 100yds on right*

The pretty Victorian Alford Arms stands in the unruffled hamlet of Frithsden surrounded by National Trust woodland. The flower-filled garden overlooks the village green, and historic Ashridge Forest is on the doorstep – perfect for a walk or a spot of wild mushroom foraging. Cross the threshold and you'll immediately pick up on the lively, warm atmosphere, derived partly from the customers, and partly from the rich colours and mix of furniture and pictures in the dining room and bar. The seasonal menu balances originality with more traditional fare; thus starters could include seared king prawns and calamari on Thai-spiced couscous; or pan-fried pigeon breast with creamed Savoy cabbage, bacon and blueberry reduction. Typical main courses are Moroccan bean tagine with tabouleh and minted yogurt; pork, cheddar and onion sausages on champ with sage gravy; and slow-cooked shin of beef bourguignon. Tempting puddings include chocolate brownie with clotted cream.

Open 11-11 (Sun 12-10.30) Closed: 25-26 Dec **Bar Meals** L served all week 12-2.30 D served all week 7-10 (Sun 12-4) Av main course £12.75 **Restaurant** L served all week 12-2.30 D served all week 7-10 (Sun 12-4) Av 3 course à la carte £23.50 Salisbury Pubs Ltd Marstons Pedigree, Brakspear, Flowers Original, Rebellion IPA. 18 **Facilities** Garden Dogs allowed Parking

The Bricklayers Arms

ı 1722, this award-winning pub was nothing more than a pair of brick and flint cottages on ɪn unnamed lane; these days it's a destination for foodies the country over. The secret of the ricklayers' success is a happy marriage between traditional British and classic French cooking.

ıcked away in deepest rural ertfordshire, it's a favourite with ·cals, walkers and all those who ·ek a sunny and secluded garden › linger in during the summer ıonths. The ivy-covered exterior ıves way to an immaculate interior, ɔmplete with the expected ·w beams, exposed brickwork, ındlelight and open fires. The rench influence comes from head ıef Claude Paillet, who trained in aris at the three-Michelin-starred ierre Gagnaire restaurant. Claude as great respect for the traditions f this old English pub, and has evised a menu that combines the eartiness of British cooking with distinctly Gallic sophistication. A ɔod place to start might be pan-ied foie gras with roasted apples and a sherry jus; eggs meurette (poached eggs on garlic crouton with red wine, smoked bacon and onions); or crab with home-smoked salmon. Continue with slow-cooked haunch of venison in red wine; salmon and bream fillets in saffron bouillon; confit of Barbary duck with chestnut and port jus; or risotto of saffron and grilled peppers with sun blushed tomatoes and a parmesan twill. But be sure to save space for dessert, as the pudding menu is justifiably famous. Look out for crèpe filled with mascarpone and Cointreau cream; apple, raisin and cinnamon bread and butter budding; Bourbon vanilla crème brûlée; or white and milk chocolate layered mousse.

🍷

MAP 06 TL00
Hogpits Bottom HP3 0PH
☎ 01442 833322
📠 01442 834841
e-mail: goodfood@bricklayersarms.com
web: www.bricklayersarms.com
dir: *M25 junct 18 onto A404 (Amersham road). Right at Chenies for Flaunden*

Open 12–11.30
Bar Meals L served all week 12–2.30 D served all week 6.30–9.30 (Sun 12–4, 6–9) Av main course £14
Restaurant L served all week 12–2.30 D served all week 6.30–9.30 (Sun 12–4, 6.30–9) Av 3 course à la carte £26
🏛 Free House
🍺 Old Speckled Hen, Greene King IPA, London Pride, Timothy Taylor. 🍷 12
Facilities Garden Dogs allowed Parking

England

HEXTON MAP 12 TL13

The Raven

SG5 3JB ☎ 01582 881209 01582 881610
e-mail: jack@ravenathexton.f9.co.uk
dir: *5m W of Hitchin. 5m N of Luton, just outside Barton-le-Clay*

This neat 1920s pub is named after Ravensburgh Castle in the neighbouring hills. It has comfortable bars and a large garden with a terrace and play area. Snacks include ploughman's and salad platters, plus tortilla wraps, filled baguettes and jacket potatoes. The main menu offers lots of steak options, and dishes like smoky American chicken, whole rack of barbecue ribs, Thai red vegetable curry and an all-day breakfast.

Open 11–3 6–11 (Sat 11–11, Sun 12–10.30) **Bar Meals** L served all week 12–2 D served all week 6–10 (Sat–Sun 12–9) Av main course £9.50 **Restaurant** L served all week 12–2 D served all week 6–10 (Sat–Sun 12–9) Enterprise Inns Greene King Old Speckled Hen, Fullers London Pride, Greene King IPA. 24 **Facilities** Garden Parking Play Area

HINXWORTH MAP 12 TL24

Three Horseshoes

High St SG7 5HQ ☎ 01462 742280
dir: *E of A1 between Biggleswade & Baldock*

Thatched 18th-century country pub with a dining extension into the garden. Parts of the building date back 500 years, and the walls are adorned with pictures and photos of the village's history. Samples from a typical menu include chicken of the wood, lamb cutlets with champ, rainbow trout with almonds, sea bass provençale, steak and Guinness pie, bacon and cheese pasta bake, and roasted Tuscan red peppers.

Open 11.30–2.30 6–11 (Sun 12–7) **Bar Meals** L served all week 12–2 D served Mon–Sat 6.30–9 Av main course £7.50 **Restaurant** L served all week 12–2 D served Mon–Sat 6.30–9 Av 3 course à la carte £18 Greene King Greene King IPA, Abbot Ale, Guest ales. 6 **Facilities** Garden Parking

HITCHIN MAP 12 TL12

The Greyhound ★★★ INN

London Rd, St Ippolyts SG4 7NL ☎ 01462 440989
e-mail: greyhound@freenet.co.uk

The Greyhound was rescued from dereliction by the present owner who previously worked for the London Fire Brigade. It is now a popular, family-run hostelry surrounded by pleasant countryside yet handy for the M1 and Luton Airport. The food is good, wholesome and unpretentious, offering the likes of fresh fish, rabbit pie, faggots, steak and ale pie and home-made lasagne.

The Greyhou

Open 7–2.30 5–12 **Bar Meals** L served all week 12–2 D served all week 6–9 Av main course £9 **Restaurant** L served all week 12–2 D served all week 6–9 Free House Adnams, Guest. 8 **Facilities** Parking **Rooms** 5 bedrooms en suite S£47.50 D£52.50

HUNSDON MAP 06 TL4

Pick of the Pubs

The Fox and Hounds

2 High St SG12 8NH
☎ 01279 843999 01279 841092
e-mail: info@foxandhounds-hunsdon.co.uk
dir: *From A414 between Ware & Harlow take B180 in Stanstead Abbotts N to Hunsdon*

Nestling in a sleepy village in the heart of the Hertfordshire countryside, this pub has a warm, welcoming atmosphere and a large pretty garden. The bar is stocked with a fine array of locally brewed real ales, and meals can be taken in the bar, the lounge and the large, homely dining room. Expect serious, inspired cooking that combines classics with modern touches. Lunch could begin with mussels, cider, leeks and cream; or sautéed squid, chorizo and butter beans, followed by roast skate wing, lentils and salsa verde; or perhaps calves' liver persillade and duck fat potato cake. For dinner, perhaps celeriac, chestnut and pancetta soup; or sliced breast of mallard with watercress salad, followed by whole roast partridge and braised lentils; or fillet of black bream, mussels and saffron. Clementine and Campari jelly is an elegant way to round matters off.

Open 12–4 6–11 Closed: Last wk Jan & 1st wk Feb
Bar Meals L served Tue–Sat 12–3 D served Tue–Sat 6–10.30 (Sun 12–4) Av main course £13 **Restaurant** L served Sun 12–3 D served Thu–Sat 7–10 Av 3 course à la carte £35 Av 2 course fixed price £13 Free House Adnams Bitter, Adnams Broadside, Budvar, Guinness. 10 **Facilities** Children's licence Garden Dogs allowed Parking Play Area

ITTLE HADHAM MAP 06 TL42

he Nags Head 🍷

ıe Ford SG11 2AX ☎ 01279 771555 📠 01279 771555
mail: robinsonmark2002@yahoo.co.uk
r: *M11 junct 8 take A120 towards Puckeridge & A10. Left at ·hts in Little Hadnam. Pub 1m on right*

ırmerly a coaching inn, this 16th-century pub has also been a ewery, a bakery and Home Guard arsenal in its time. The 1960s oup Fairport Convention once performed in concert opposite and e pub ran dry! Open brickwork and an old bakery oven are among e features. An extensive menu offers everything from braised lamb nt and roast spiced duck breast to pasta carbonara and vegetarian ıxed grill. Plenty of starters and more than 20 fish courses.

pen 11–3 6–11 (Sun 12–3.30 7–10.30) Rest: Dec 25–26 Closed eve **ır Meals** L served all week 12 –2 D served all week 6–9 (Fri–Sat 6–9.30 n 7–9) Av main course £6.75 **Restaurant** L served all week 12–2 served all week 6–9 (Fri–Sat 6–9.30, Sun 7–9) Av 3 course à la carte 8.50 Greene King Greene King Abbot Ale, IPA, Old Speckled Hen & ıddles County Ale, Marstons Pedigree. 🍷 6 **Facilities** Garden

LD KNEBWORTH MAP 06 TL22

he Lytton Arms 🍷

ark Ln SG3 6QB ☎ 01438 812312 📠 01438 817298
-mail: thelyttonarms@btinternet.com
ır: *From A1(M) take A602. At Knebworth turn right at rail ation. Follow Codicote signs. Pub 1.5m on right*

ıe pub was designed around 1877 by Lord Lytton's brother-in-law, ho happened to be the architect Sir Edwin Lutyens, replacing the evious inn, now a residence next door. Also next door, but in a much ander way, is the Lytton estate, the family home for centuries. On the mple but wide-ranging menu are Mrs O'Keefe's flavoured sausages; ıicken or vegetable balti; honeyroast ham; chargrilled lambs' liver and acon; and fisherman's pie.

pen 11–11 (Sun 12–10.30) Rest: Closed 25–26 Dec eve **ar Meals** L served Mon–Sat 12–2.30 D served Mon–Sat 6.30–9.30 (Sun 2–5) Av main course £8 **Restaurant** L served Mon–Sat 12–2.30 D served on–Sat 6.30–9.30 (Sun 12–5) Av 3 course à la carte £17.50 Free House Fuller's London Pride, Adnams Best Bitter, Broadside, Wherry. 🍷 30 **acilities** Children's licence Garden Dogs allowed Parking

POTTERS CROUCH MAP 06 TL10

The Hollybush 🍷

AL2 3NN ☎ 01727 851792 📠 01727 851792
dir: *Ragged Hall Ln off A405 or Bedmond Ln off A4147*

The Hollybush is a picturesque country pub with a quaint, white-painted exterior, attractively furnished interior and a large enclosed garden. An antique dresser, a large fireplace and various prints and paintings help to create a delightfully welcoming atmosphere. Traditional pub fare is offered: ploughman's, burgers, jacket potatoes, salads, platters and toasted sandwiches. The pub is close to St Albans with its Roman ruins and good local walks.

Open 11.30–2.30 6–11 (Sun 12–2.30, 7–10.30) **Bar Meals** L served Mon–Sat 12–2 Fullers Fullers Chiswick Bitter, Fullers London Pride, ESB & Seasonal Ales. 🍷 7 **Facilities** Garden Parking

RICKMANSWORTH MAP 06 TQ09

The Rose and Crown 🍷

Harefield Rd WD3 1PP ☎ 01923 897680
e-mail: roseandcrown@morethanjustapub.com
dir: *M25 junct 17/18, follow Northwood signs. Past Tesco, pub 1.5m on right*

This 17th-century former farmhouse hosts events ranging from wine tastings to a monthly farmers' market. Inside the wisteria-clad building you'll find low-beamed ceilings and real fires, whilst the large garden looks out across the lovely Colne Valley. There's a strong emphasis on varied home-cooked food, supplied locally wherever possible. Baked lemon pollock fillet with fennel and parsnip mash; chicken pot roast; and juniper, venison and pigeon pie are typical dishes.

Open 12–11 (Sun 12–10.30) **Bar Meals** L served all week 12–6 D served all week 6–10 (Sun 12–9.30) Av main course £10 **Restaurant** L served all week 12–6 D served all week 6–10 (Sun 12–9.30) Av 3 course fixed price £14.50 London Pride, & Deuchars IPA. 🍷 11 **Facilities** Garden Dogs allowed Parking Play Area

ROYSTON MAP 12 TL34

Pick of the Pubs

The Cabinet Free House and Restaurant 🍷

High St, Reed SG8 8AH
☎ 01763 848366 📠 01763 849407
e-mail: thecabinet@btconnect.com
dir: *2m S of Royston, just off A10*

See Pick of the Pubs on page 302

The Cabinet Free House & Restauran

The Cabinet, meaning small room or meeting place, is a 16th-century country inn and restaurai located in the little village of Reed just off the A10 London to Cambridge road, within easy striking distance of the capital.

Simon Smith runs it with Christian Shotler as head chef. The refurbished inn has a cosy and comfortable interior with low beamed ceilings and an open fire. The lovely surroundings lend themselves to special occasions, particularly weddings, and the premises are licensed for civil ceremonies. Food is prepared from the best local produce but draws inspiration from around the world to offer an interesting variety of dishes including traditional favourites. There is a good menu choice, with a seasonal carte, fixed-price lunch and dinner menus of two or three courses, and Cabinet snacks at the bar available Tuesday to Friday 12 noon till 2pm. Among the bar snacks are tian of crab with aïoli and horseradish dressing, and pan-fried steak and onion confit with salad and chips. A seasonal selection from the carte could begin with dill infused salmon gravadlax with a beetroot compote and dressed leaves, followed by dry aged fillet of beef with potato rôsti, baby carrots and wild mushrooms. For a fitting finale, try baked bitter chocolate fondant with raspberry ice cream. Abbot Ale and Speckled Hen are two of the real ales served.

MAP 12 TL34
High St, Reed SG8 8AH
☎ 01763 848366
01763 849407
e-mail:
thecabinet@btconnect.com
dir: *2m S of Royston, just off A10*

Open 12–3 5.30–12 Open all day Sat–Sun (summer) Closed: 1 Jan
Bar Meals L served Mon–Sat 12–2.30 D served Mon–Fri 7–9.30 Av main course £7.50
Restaurant L served Mon–Sun 12–2.30 D served Mon–Sat 7–9.30 Av 3 course à la carte £35 Av 3 course fixed price £18.50
Abbot, Greene King IPA, Speckled Hen. 8
Facilities Garden Dogs allowed Parking

T ALBANS — MAP 06 TL10

ose & Crown

) St Michael St AL3 4SG

: 01727 851903 01727 761775

mail: ruth.courtney@ntlworld.com

aditional 16th-century pub situated in a beautiful part of St Michael's llage', opposite the entrance to Verulanium Park and the Roman useum. It has a classic beamed bar with a huge inglenook, and a mmer patio filled with flowers. The pub offers a distinctive range of nerican deli-style sandwiches, which are served with potato salad, ettle crisps and pickled cucumber. The "Cotton Club", for example, is a roast beef, ham, Swiss cheese, mayo, tomato, onion, lettuce and orseradish mustard filling.

pen 11.30-3 5.30-11 (Sat-Sun all day) **Bar Meals** L served all week -2 D served Mon-Sat 6-9.30 (Sat-Sun 12.30-2.30) Av main course £8 **estaurant** L served Mon-Sat 12-2 6-9.30 (Sat-Sun 12-2.30) Punch verns Adnams Bitter, Carlsberg-Tetley Tetley Bitter, Fuller's London ide, Courage Directors. 20 **Facilities** Children's licence Garden Dogs owed Parking

TANDON — MAP 06 TL32

he Kick & Dicky ★★★★ INN

G11 1NL ☎ 01920 821424

-mail: kickanddicky@btinternet.com

his family-run free house stands in a sleepy hamlet amid rolling untryside, just half a mile from the A120 and 15 minutes from anstead. Food includes a set price menu, tapas every Wednesday ght, a changing carte (casserole of veal shank on couscous; pan-fried ackerel on bok choy) and light lunch choices such as roasted pepper id olive salad with grilled haloumi or sausages, mash and gravy. The n has attractive en suite bedrooms.

pen 12-2.30 6-11 Closed: 1st wk in Jan **Bar Meals** L served Tue-Sat 12- (Sun 1-2) D served Tue-Sat Av main course £8.50 **Restaurant** L served e-Sat 12-2 D served Tue-Sat 7-9.30 Av 3 course à la carte £26 Free ouse Greene King IPA, Ruddles County, Adnams & Adnams Broadside. 7 **Facilities** Garden Parking **Rooms** 5 bedrooms en suite S£50 D£70

TAPLEFORD — MAP 06 TL31

'apillon Woodhall Arms NEW ★★★ INN

7 High Rd SG14 3NW ☎ 01992 535123 01992 582772

-mail: papillonwoodhall@aol.com

1998 the Woodhall Arms was redeveloped to incorporate the apillon Restaurant; the result is this pink-washed, twin-gabled building ehind a neat white picket fence. English- and continental-style vourites include fresh seafood ploughman's; chicken, honey-roast am, roast beef and onion bake with white wine and cream sauce; umberland sausages and mash; and veal escalopes Israeli, which eans topped with avocado, tomatoes, cheddar and gruyère. Ten en uite bedrooms include doubles, twins and singles.

pen 11-2.30 6.30-11 **Bar Meals** L served all week 12-2.30 D served un-Fri 6.30 **Restaurant** L served all week 12-2 D served all week 6.30-10 Sun 12-2.30, 6.30-9.30) Av 3 course à la carte £20 Av 2 course fixed price 11.95 Free House Greene King IPA, Archers, Cottage, Nethergate. 10 **Facilities** Garden Dogs allowed Parking **Rooms** 10 bedrooms n suite

TEWIN — MAP 06 TL21

The Plume of Feathers

Upper Green Rd AL6 0LX

☎ 01438 717265 01438 712596

dir: *E from A1(M) junct 6 towards WGC, follow B1000 towards Hertford. Tewin signed on left*

Built in 1596, this historic inn, firstly an Elizabethan hunting lodge and later the haunt of highwaymen, boasts several ghosts including a 'lady in grey'. Interesting menus change daily, and include a tapas bar from noon till close. Other options available are Moroccan spiced baby shark with king prawns and couscous, honey-roast duck with sweet potato wontons, or slow-roasted belly pork with bacon and cabbage. Be sure to book in advance.

Open 11-11 **Bar Meals** L served all week 12-2.30 D served Mon-Sat 6-9.30 (all day Summer) Av main course £10 **Restaurant** L served all week 11 D served Mon-Sat 11 (Sun 12-4) Av 3 course à la carte £20 Greene King IPA, Abbot Ales. 30 **Facilities** Garden Dogs allowed Parking

WALKERN — MAP 12 TL22

The White Lion

31 The High St SG2 7PA ☎ 01438 861251

dir: *B1037 from Stevenage*

In rolling chalk downland, Walkern manages to keep a respectable distance from nearby Stevenage, Britain's first 'new town'. The bar in this 16th-century pub has oak beams, an inglenook, leather sofas, newspapers and a computer for those who still need to surf the net over a pint of Greene King or cup of hot chocolate. The informal restaurant offers a traditional pub menu, with ham, egg and chips, fillet of beef stroganoff, and succulent steaks.

Open 12-2.30 4.30-11.30 (Fri 12-2, 4.30 - 12 Sat 12-12, Sun 12-10.30) **Bar Meals** L served all week 12-2.30 D served Tue-Sat 6-9.30 (Sun 12-5) Av main course £8 **Restaurant** L served all week 12-2.30 D served Tue-Sat 6-9.30 (Sun 12-5) Av 3 course à la carte £21 Greene King Greene King IPA & Abbot Ale, Guinness. 8 **Facilities** Children's licence Garden Dogs allowed Parking Play Area

The Fox

Around 250 years old, the Fox is opposite the village pond and next to the parish church. Its previous names were several: it was the Orange Tree until 1867, then the Dinsdale Arms (after the family who owned the village), then the Willian Arms.

It became the Fox in 1902, perhaps because the hunt kennels were near by, and for 30 years it was managed by the People's Refreshment House Association in an effort to maintain its respectability. In 2004 businessman Cliff Nye took it over, his second venture in the hospitality trade after a very successful start in north Norfolk. The building was immaculately restyled with flair and creativity, the bar modern but laid back with local artists' work on display, and a glazed atrium ceiling on the restaurant extension. Outside are a Spanish-style courtyard and two beer gardens, a good indication that this gastro-pub is also a welcoming watering hole: the range of beers includes real ales and a weekly guest, supported by top-selling continental lagers also on tap. Young and friendly staff serve food from the daily-changing menu, which includes fish and shellfish introduced by the Norfolk connection: Brancaster Staithe oysters are served au naturel or poached with quince purée and chervil; hand-picked mussels are prepared in a coconut, lemon grass and chilli cream, or classically marinière; and brill is poached with sweet red peppers, crushed new potatoes and asparagus cream. A typical lunch offers starters like smoked haddock rarebit on a toasted muffin, with poached egg and dressed rocket; then main courses of Hertfordshire pork sausages with creamed mash, or the Fox lamb and rosemary burger with hand-cut chips. The dinner menu includes the same delicious seafood options, augmented by the likes of pan-roasted local venison or chargrilled rib-eye steak. Desserts are all home made, including sorbets and ice creams.

NEW ◎ 🍷
MAP 12 TL23
Baldock Ln SG6 2AE
☎ 01462 480233
🖷 01462 676966
e-mail:
restaurant@foxatwillian.co.uk
web: www.foxatwillian.co.uk
dir: *A1(M) junct 9 towards Letchworth, 1st left to Willian, 0.5m on left*

Open 12–11 (Fri–Sat 12–12, Sun 12–10.30)
Bar Meals L served Mon–Sat 12–2
Restaurant L served all week 12–2 D served Mon–Sat 6.45–9.15 (Sun 12–2.45) Av 3 course à la carte £25
Free House
Adnam Bitter, Woodfordes Wherry, Fullers London Pride Plus, Staroprame. 🍷 12
Facilities Garden Dogs allowed Parking

WESTON MAP 12 TL23

The Rising Sun

Halls Green SG4 7DR

01462 790487 01462 790846

e-mail: therisingsun@hotmail.co.uk

dir: *A1(M) junct 9, A6141 towards Baldock. Right towards Graveley. In 100yds 1st left.*

Set in picturesque Hertfordshire countryside, the Rising Sun offers a regularly changing menu. Starters include stilton mushrooms, and salmon fishcakes with dill sauce. Main courses include chargrilled steaks, salmon with dill and mustard sauce, or smoked fish crumble. A huge choice of sweets, and blackboard specials change daily. The owners say that their pub may be hard to find on your first visit, but that it's well worth the trouble.

Open 11-2.30 6-11 (Sat-Sun Apr-Sep all day) **Bar Meals** L served all week 12-1.45 D served all week 6-8.45 (Sun 12-7.45) **Restaurant** L served all week 12-1.45 D served all week 6-8.45 (Sun 12-7.45) McMullens McMullen Original AK Ale, Macs Country Best. **Facilities** Garden Dogs allowed Parking Play Area

WILLIAN MAP 12 TL23

Pick of the Pubs

The Fox NEW

Baldock Ln SG6 2AE

01462 480233 01462 676966

e-mail: restaurant@foxatwillian.co.uk

web: www.foxatwillian.co.uk

dir: *A1(M) junct 9 towards Letchworth, 1st left to Willian, 0.5m on left*

See Pick of the Pubs on opposite page

KENT

BIDDENDEN MAP 07 TQ83

Pick of the Pubs

The Three Chimneys

Biddenden Rd TN27 8LW 01580 291472

dir: *From A262 midway between Biddenden & Sissinghurst, follow Frittenden signs. Pub immediatley on left in village of Three Chimneys*

The name of this 15th-century pub/restaurant is supposedly derived from trois chemins, which is what French prisoners during the Seven Years War (1756–63) called a nearby three-way road junction. Beyond this point was out of bounds, but a friendly sentry would light the candelabra in the window by the pub door to indicate that no English officials were inside. The prisoners could then safely slip in for a swift pint. The pub retains its original small-room layout, with low beams, wood-panelling, flagstone floors, old settles and warming fires. Food is freshly cooked to order from a menu featuring starters of marinated anchovy salad; sautéed chicken livers, mushrooms and bacon on toast; and garlic and herb bruschetta with roasted aubergine and peppers; and main courses such as roast fillet of cod with Icelandic prawns; duck leg confit with creamed potato, braised Puy lentils, chorizo and bacon; and grilled fillet steak.

Open 11.30-3 6-11 (Sun 12-3, 7-10.30) Closed: 25 Dec **Bar Meals** L served all week 12-1.50 D served all week 6-9.45 (Sun 7-9) Av main course £15.95 **Restaurant** L served all week 12-1.50 D served all week 6.30-9.45 (Sun 12-2.30, 7-9) Av 3 course à la carte £25 Free House Adnams, Harveys Best, & Harveys Old. 10 **Facilities** Garden Dogs allowed Parking

BOSSINGHAM MAP 07 TR14

The Hop Pocket

The Street CT4 6DY 01227 709866 01227 709866

e-mail: forgan50@aol.com

Birds of prey and an animal corner for children are among the more unusual attractions at this family pub in the heart of Kent. Canterbury is only five miles away and the county's delightfully scenic coast and countryside are within easy reach. All meals are cooked to order, using fresh produce. Expect fish pie, supreme of chicken, spicy salmon, Cajun beef, chilli nachos and fish platter. Extensive range of sandwiches and omelettes.

Open 11-3 6.30-11 **Bar Meals** L served Tue-Sun 12-2.30 D served all week 7-9.15 (Sun 12-3, 6.30-9) **Restaurant** L served Tue-Sun 12-2 D served all week 7-9.15 London Pride, Shepherd Neame Admiral, Master Brew, Adnams. **Facilities** Garden Dogs allowed Parking

BOYDEN GATE MAP 07 TR26

Pick of the Pubs

The Gate Inn

North Stream CT3 4EB 01227 860498

dir: *From Canterbury on A28 turn left at Upstreet*

This rural retreat is surrounded by marshland and pasture, with a beautiful garden overlooking a stream populated by ducks and geese. On display is the Chislet Horse, which the locals will explain better than this guide! Inside, quarry-tiled floors and pine furniture feature in the family-friendly interconnecting bars. It might be a challenge to decide on what to eat, since the huge menu offers a wide range of snacks and sustaining meals. There are 17 sandwich fillings (from home-cooked ham or double Gloucester cheese to black pudding); 9 different 'ploughpersons'; jacket potatoes with 16 different fillings; and 'Gateburgers' filled with various delights. A similarly tempting range of side orders includes garlic bread, sausages on sticks and nachos. There is a selection of wines by the glass and local beers to accompany your meal.

CONTINUED

BOYDEN GATE continued

Open 11-2.30 6-11 (Sun 12-4, 7-10.30) **Bar Meals** L served all week 12-2 D served all week 6-9 Shepherd Neame Shepherd Neame Master Brew, Spitfire, Seasonal Beers. 11 **Facilities** Garden Dogs allowed Parking **Notes**

BRABOURNE MAP 07 TR14

The Five Bells

The Street TN25 5LP ☎ 01303 813334 01303 814667
e-mail: fivebells@aol.com
dir: *5m E of Ashford*

A 16th-century free house pub surrounded by rolling hills and orchards and the perfect pit stop for walkers and cyclists. Originally a poor house, the old stocks are located across the road, while inside are whitewashed walls and a huge inglenook fireplace. An extensive menu and a range of popular daily specials include traditional steak and kidney pie; liver and bacon with sage and onion gravy; and fillet of salmon with creamed leeks and smoked salmon mash.

Open 11.30-3 6.30-11 **Bar Meals** L served all week 12-2 D served all week 6.30-9.30 Av main course £8 **Restaurant** L served all week 12-2 (Sun 12-2.30) D served all week 6.30-9.30 Free House Shepherd Neame Master Brew, London Pride, Greene King IPA, Adnams. 12 **Facilities** Garden Dogs allowed Parking Play Area

BROOKLAND MAP 07 TQ92

Pick of the Pubs

The Royal Oak NEW

High St TN29 9QR ☎ 01797 344215
e-mail: dzrj@btinternet.com
web: www.royaloakbrookland.co.uk
dir: *A259, 5m E of Rye. In village by church*

See Pick of the Pubs on opposite page

Pick of the Pubs

Woolpack Inn

TN29 9TJ ☎ 01797 344321

Smugglers' tales abound at this remote 15th-century inn surrounded by dykes and reed beds: an old spinning wheel, used to divide up smuggling contraband, can still be seen mounted from the ceiling. The place oozes charm and character, with open beams and an inglenook fireplace adding to the atmosphere. Wholesome home-made pub food includes snacks and hearty meals such as whole partridge in a red wine and cream sauce; cod and chips; and home-made chilli.

Woolpack Inn

Open 11-3 6-11 (Sat 11-11, Sun 12-10.30) **Bar Meals** L served all week 12-2.30 D served all week 6-9 (Sat-Sun 12-9) Av main course £7.50 Shepherd Neame Shepherd Neame Spitfire Premium Ale, Master Brew Bitter, Orangeboom. **Facilities** Garden Dogs allowed Parking Play Area

BURHAM MAP 06 TQ7

The Golden Eagle

80 Church St ME1 3SD ☎ 01634 668975 01634 66897
e-mail: kathymay@btconnect.com
dir: *S from M2 junct 3 or N from M20 junct 6 on A229, signs to Burham*

This popular free house has every appearance of a traditional English inn, set on the North Downs with fine views of the Medway Valley. What sets it apart is its 20-year history of serving oriental food. The chef's specialities are spare ribs, mee goreng, king prawn sambal, wortip crispy chicken, and sweet and sour crispy pork. Banana split and chocolate fudge cake are among the more occidental puddings. Vegetarians are well catered for.

Open 11.30-3 6.30-11 Closed: 25-26 Dec **Bar Meals** L served Mon-Fri 12-2 D served all week 7-10 (Sun 12-2.30, 7-9.30) Av main course £7.95 **Restaurant** L served all week 12-2 D served all week 7-10 (Sun lunch 12-2.30 dinner 7-9.30) Free House Wadworth 6X, Boddingtons. **Facilities** Parking

The Royal Oak

he history of this marshland pub is well documented, right back to when it was built as a house ı 1570. A succession of parish clerks and sextons lived here until 1736 when Jacob Ferriss took ver on the death of his father.

›ung Ferriss, however, was ›viously a bit of an entrepreneur ıd, with his rector's consent, ıded the role of ale-keeper to his b description. His drinks licence cognised this non-secular calling / forbidding him to 'suffer ale to tippled during divine service'. ıe job-sharing soon died out ıd it has been a pub ever since. ıe bar serves classic pub fare, ɔng the lines of home-cooked ›ney-roast ham; steak and kidney ıdding; and triple-decker toasted ndwiches. In the restaurant, gularly changing dishes draw on cal, seasonal produce including ,h specials; available all-year und though are traditional roast ›ef (cooked rare) and, in weekly tation, loin of pork, leg of ›mney lamb or crown of turkey.

Typical starters include smoked fish salad, deep-fried squid and grilled goats' cheese, with further main course possibilities of pheasant breasts stuffed with mushroom duxelle wrapped in bacon; mixed seafood herb pancake; trio of handmade sausages; and Mediterranean vegetables with spicy couscous. Among the puddings might be crumble of the day, toffee crème brûlée, or honeycomb crunch ice cream. Roast lunches are served on Sunday. A well-kept and tranquil garden borders the churchyard of St Augustine, one of only four in England with a separate bell tower. Romney Marsh has several more remarkable medieval churches.

NEW 🍷
MAP 07 TQ92
High St TN29 9QR
☎ 01797 344215
e-mail: dzrj@btinternet.com
web: www.royaloakbrookland.co.uk
dir: *A259, 5m E of Rye. In village by church*

Open 12-3 6-11 Closed: Sun pm
Bar Meals L served Mon-Sat 12-2.30 D served Mon-Sat 6.30-9.30 Av main course £11.95
Restaurant L served all week 12-2.30 D served Mon-Sat 6.30-9.30 Av 3 course à la carte £22
Enterprise Inns
Harvey's Best Bitter, Adnams Best Bitter. 🍷 8
Facilities Garden Dogs allowed Parking

England

CANTERBURY MAP 07 TR15

The Chapter Arms 🍷

New Town St, Chartham Hatch CT4 7LT

☎ 01227 738340 📠 01227 732536

dir: *3m from Canterbury. Off A28 in Chartham Hatch*

A flower-bedecked free house on the Pilgrims' Way with a garden featuring fish ponds and fruit trees. The property was once three cottages owned by Canterbury Cathedral's Dean and Chapter – hence the name. Daily menus rely on plenty of excellent fresh fish. Other choices might be slow roast shoulder of local pork with apple sauce, pan-fried beef fillet strips on rosti with rose peppercorn sauce, or roast pepper, aubergine and cherry tomato tart, topped with goats' cheese. Lighter snacks, such as filled baps, are also available. The pub is due to change hands in 2007.

Open 11–3 6.30–11 (Sun 12–10.30) Closed: 25 Dec eve **Bar Meals** L served all week 12–2 D served all week 6.30–8.30 (Sun 12–2.30) **Restaurant** L served all week 12–2 D served all week 7–9 (Sun 6.30–8.30) Free House Shepherd Neame Master Brew, Guest ales. 🍷 8 **Facilities** Garden Dogs allowed Parking Play Area

Pick of the Pubs

The Dove Inn 🍷

Plum Pudding Ln, Dargate ME13 9HB

☎ 01227 751360 📠 01227 751360

e-mail: nigel@thedoveinn.fsnet.co.uk

Between Faversham and Whitstable, tucked away in a sleepy hamlet, the Dove is a splendid Victorian public house with a good reputation for food. The interior is simple and relaxed, with stripped wooden floors and scrubbed tables, while outside there is a large, formal garden with (appropriately) a dovecote and doves. There is an inspiring selection of snacks, which might include caramelised pork with stir fry vegetables; or salt cod with chorizo and flageolet bean sauce. The main menu has plenty to tempt everyone: starters might include Bayonne ham and oyster mushroom tart; risotto of spring onion and crab; or grilled sardines. For the main course it would be hard to choose between braised shank of lamb; roast breast of duck; or one of the many fish dishes, such as lemon sole; smoked haddock; scallops; crevettes or crab. There is an interesting wine list, and also fine Shepherd Neame ales.

Open 11–3 6–11 **Bar Meals** L served Tue–Sun 12–2 D served Wed–Sat 7–9 Av main course £8 **Restaurant** L served Tue–Sun 12–2 D served Wed–Sat 7–9 Av 3 course à la carte £25 Shepherd Neame Shepherd Neame Master Brew. 🍷 10 **Facilities** Garden Dogs allowed Parking

Pick of the Pubs

The Granville 🍷

St End, Lower Hardres CT4 7AL

☎ 01227 700402 📠 01227 700925

dir: *On B2068, 2m from Canterbury towards Hythe*

Named after the Tudor warship, the Granville is a handsome solid building firmly anchored in the ancient village of Lower Hardres, just a five-minute drive from Canterbury city centre. With ample parking, a patio and large beer garden at the rear where summer barbecues take place, this Shepherd Neame pub is an ideal family venue, and dogs too are made welcome. Nevertheless this is not a place for pub grub. The short but lively menu is designed for sophisticated tastebuds, offering for starters the likes of rock oysters with shallot vinegar, smoked local wigeon (a small wild duck) with mustard fruits, and antipasti. Main courses always comprise three meat and three fish dishes: slow-roast Waterham Farm chicken with truffle cream sauce, and Dungeness brill fillet braised in Macvin and morels are two examples. There is no children's menu as such, but portions from the main menu can be served where appropriate.

Open 12–3 6–11 (Sun 12–10.30) Closed: 25 Dec **Bar Meals** L served Tue–Sat 12–2 D served Tue–Sat 7–9 (Sun 12–2.30) **Restaurant** L served Tue–Sat 12–2 D served Tue–Sat 7–9 (Sun 12–2.30) Shepherd Neame Masterbrew and 1 seasonal ale. 🍷 7 **Facilities** Garden Dogs allowed Parking **Notes**

The Old Coach House 🍷

A2 Barnham Downs CT4 6SA

☎ 01227 831218 📠 01227 831932

e-mail: fairestltd@aol.com

dir: *7m S of Canterbury on A2. Turn at Jet petrol station.*

A former stop on the original London to Dover coaching route, and listed in the 1740 timetable, this inn stands some 300 metres from the Roman Way. Noteworthy gardens with home-grown herbs and vegetables, weekend spit-roasts, and unabashed continental cuisine mark it as an auberge in the finest Gallic tradition. Food options incluc seafood, venison and other game in season, plus perhaps rib of beef with rosemary, pot au feux, and grilled lobster with brandy sauce.

Open 4–11 **Bar Meals** D served all week 6.30–9 Av main course £7.50 **Restaurant** D served all week 6.30–9 Av 3 course à la carte £24 Av 2 cour fixed price £18.50 Free House Interbrew Whitbread Best Bitter. 🍷 5 **Facilities** Garden Parking **Rooms** 10 beds en suite S£58 D£58 (★★ HL

Pick of the Pubs

The Red Lion 🍷

High St, Stodmarsh CT3 4BA

☎ 01227 721339 📠 01227 721339

e-mail: tiptop-redlion@hotmail.com

dir: *From Canterbury take A257 towards Sandwich, left into Stodmarsh*

Known to locals as The Old Junk Shop because of its impressively cluttered interior, the Red Lion was built in 1475 and until relatively recently was surrounded by hop fields. Fresh flowers adorn the tables, along with bric-a-brac that ranges from an antique sewing machine to the stuffed head of a water buffalo. Lunches are served daily, with Sunday roasts alternating weekly between beef, pork and lamb. Among the fish dishes might be baked sea bass with fresh tarragon and lime; pan-fried scallops and baby leeks; or Bantry Bay mussels with roasted peppers and free-range chicken chunks. Dishes tend to be seasonal and locally sourced: Stodmarsh lamb perhaps, or casseroled rabbit. Desserts are equally hearty, along the lines of a pineapple and Malibu crumble. Or you could simply enjoy a pint of Old Speckled Hen by the fire.

Open 10.30–11.30 **Bar Meals** L served all week 12–2.15 D served Mon–Sat 7–9.15 Sun 2 sittings, 12 & 2 **Restaurant** L served all week 12–9.15 D served Mon–Sat 7–9.15 Av 3 course à la carte £25 Greene King IPA, Ruddles Country, Speckled Hen. 🍷 7 **Facilities** Garden Dogs allowed Parking Play Area

Castle Inn

he Castle has starred in all sorts of films, including Elizabeth R, Room with a View, The Life of ogarth and The Wicked Lady. Take one look at its mellow brick exterior and immediately you'll e why.

he interior is equally photogenic, l nooks and crannies, period rniture and curios. First entioned in 1420, when it was a ivate house, it started selling ale about 1730. One of its bestsellers day is Larkins Traditional, brewed p the road at Larkins Farm. The ine list is a wine lover's dream, inning to well over 100 bins, hile whisky lovers can (over me, naturally) work their way rough 30 malts from Aberlour to mintoul. In the heavily beamed loon bar try ham hock terrine, ome-made marinated brie, or cket potato with local sausages id cheese. The more sophisticated staurant menu starts with itterflied and roasted herring with essed roquette, to be followed y pot-roast local pigeon wrapped in bacon on rosemary mash, or roast rack of Kentish lamb and salsa verde. Round off with caramel parfait or a selection of local ice creams. Behind the inn is a vine-hung courtyard garden with its own bar. Beyond that, over a bridge, is a lawn with beautifully tended flowerbeds.

MAP 06 TQ54
TN8 7AH
☎ 01892 870247
01892 871420
e-mail: info@castleinn.co.uk
dir: *1.5m S of B2027 between Tonbridge & Edenbridge.*

Open 11–11
Bar Meals L served all week 11–6 D served all week 6.30–9.30 (Sun 12–6 & 6.30–9.30) Av main course £6.50
Restaurant L served Thu–Mon 12–2 D served Wed–Mon 7–9.30 Av 3 course à la carte £30 Av 3 course fixed price £17.50
Free House
Larkins Traditional, Harveys Sussex, Young's Ordinary, Larkins Porter. 10
Facilities Children's licence Garden Dogs allowed

England

CANTERBURY continued

Pick of the Pubs

The White Horse Inn

53 High St, Bridge CT4 5LA

01227 832814 01227 832814

dir: *3m S of Canterbury, just off A2.*

This medieval and Tudor building was originally a staging post close to a ford on the main Dover to Canterbury road, and still provides a stirling service to modern travellers. An enormous log fire burning in the beamed bar during the winter months provides a guaranteed warm welcome, whilst the extensive garden is popular for al fresco dining on warmer days. Fullers and Shepherd Neame are amongst the real ales served in the bar, with up to ten wines available by the glass. You'll find a strong emphasis on food, with seasonal dishes created from the best local ingredients. Choose between the relaxed blackboard bar menu, and more formal dining in the restaurant.

Open 11–3 6–11 (Sun 12–5) Closed: 25 Dec, 1 Jan **Bar Meals** L served all week 12–2 D served all week 6.30–9 **Restaurant** L served Tue–Sun 12–2 D served Tue–Sat 7–9 Shepherd Neame Masterbrew, Greene King Abbot Ale, Fullers London Pride, Greene King IPA. 10 **Facilities** Garden Parking

CHARING MAP 07 TQ94

The Bowl Inn

Egg Hill Rd TN27 0HG 01233 712256 01233 714705

e-mail: info@bowl-inn.co.uk

dir: *M20 junct 8/9, take A20 to Charing then take A252 towards Canterbury. Left at top of Charing Hill down Bowl Road, 1.25m*

Built as a farmhouse in 1512, the Bowl stands on top of the North Downs, high above Charing. The small but varied menu of mostly traditional country pub snacks includes Kent-cured ham, English cheddar ploughman's, and hot bacon and sausage sandwiches. Relax in front of the huge old inglenook fireplace and play pool on an unusual rotating hexagonal table. Even in summer, if necessary, the south-facing sun terrace is covered (and heated).

Open 12–11.30 (Winter 4–11.30) **Bar Meals** L served Fri–Sun 12–9.30 D served all week 12–9.30 Free House Fullers London Pride, Adnams Southwold, Harveys Sussex Best, Whitstable IPA. 8 **Facilities** Garden Dogs allowed Parking

CHIDDINGSTONE MAP 06 TQ54

Pick of the Pubs

Castle Inn

TN8 7AH 01892 870247 01892 871420

e-mail: info@castleinn.co.uk

dir: *1.5m S of B2027 between Tonbridge & Edenbridge.*

See Pick of the Pubs on page 309

CHILHAM MAP 07 TR0

The White Horse

The Square CT4 8BY 01227 730355

dir: *A28 from Canterbury then A252, 1m turn left*

One of the most photographed pubs in Britain, The White Horse stands next to St Mary's church facing onto the 15th-century village square, where the May Fair is an annual event. The pub offers a traditional atmosphere and modern cooking from a monthly-changin menu based on fresh local produce. Dishes include fillet steak poache in red wine, and cod and smoked haddock fishcakes served with a sweet chilli sauce.

Open 11–11 (breakfast 8.30–10) (Sun 12–10.30, Jan–Feb 12–3, 7–11) **Bar Meals** L served all week 12–3 D served Tue–Sat 5.30–9 Free Hous Flowers Original, Fullers London Pride, Greene King Abbot Ale, Adnams Best. **Facilities** Garden

CHILLENDEN MAP 07 TR2

Pick of the Pubs

Griffins Head

CT3 1PS 01304 840325 01304 841290

dir: *A2 from Canterbury towards Dover, then B2046. Village on right*

See Pick of the Pubs on opposite page

DARTFORD MAP 06 TQ5

The Rising Sun Inn ★★★ INN

Fawkham Green, Fawkham DA3 8NL

01474 872291 01474 872779

A pub since 1702, The Rising Sun stands on the green in a picturesqu village not far from Brands Hatch. Inside you will find an inglenook lo fire and a cosy restaurant. Starters include crispy soy duck; stilton and bacon field mushrooms; and tempura tiger prawns. Follow with pork loin with honey and herb crust; Portuguese chicken piri-piri; or sea bass fillets with mango and garlic beurre. There is also an extensive range of steaks.

Open 11.30–11 **Bar Meals** L served all week 12–6.30 D served all week 6.30–9.30 (Sun 12–9) **Restaurant** L served all week 12–2.15 D served all week 6.30–9.30 (Sun 12–9) Free House Scottish Courage Courage Best, Courage Directors, London Pride, Timothy Taylors Lanlords. 7 **Facilities** Garden Parking **Rooms** 5 bedrooms en suite

PICK OF THE PUBS

CHILLENDEN-KENT

Griffins Head

Kentish Wealden hall house, dating from 1286 when Edward I was on the throne. It was once ccupied by the monks of All Saints Church who farmed the surrounding land until 1539, when lenry VIII's dissolution of the monasteries brought their occupation to an end.

fter that it reverted to being a rm again, and remained so until e mid-18th-century. It was given full licence to sell alcohol to oincide with the arrival of coaches n the main Canterbury to Deal oad. Inside is evidence of its long istory, with inglenook fireplaces nd beamed bars among many riginal features. Fine Kentish ales nd home-made food have helped is old inn to make its mark with sitors as well as locals, among em Kent's cricketing fraternity. he menu is typically English, nd specialises in game from cal estates in season, and locally ught fish where possible. Typical shes include lamb stew, braised eak, onions and mash, mussels arinière, and prawn chowder. Varm salads are another house speciality, and these might range from steak and roasted vegetable to a lightweight summer meal like sautéed prawn, squid, or scallops in garlic butter, all with salad. Other traditional pub dishes include lasagna, cottage pie, and ham, egg and chips. Desserts are also well worth trying, and these might vary from apple crumble or fruit pie on cooler days to chocolate chiller thriller; chocolate nemesis; raspberry almond torte; or home-made ice creams like passionfruit, ginger, or raspberry and strawberry. Outside is a very pretty garden where drinkers and diners can linger at their leisure. A vintage car club meets here on the first Sunday of every month.

MAP 07 TR25
CT3 1PS
☎ 01304 840325
📠 01304 841290
dir: *A2 from Canterbury towards Dover, then B2046. Village on right*

Open 10.30–11
Bar Meals L served all week 12–2 D served Mon-Sat 7–9.30
Restaurant L served Sun–Fri 12–2 D served Mon-Sat 7–9.30
Shepherd Neame
Shepherd Neame. 10
Facilities Garden Parking

England

DEAL MAP 07 TR35

The King's Head

9 Beach St CT14 7AH ☎ 01304 368194 📠 01304 364182
e-mail: booking@kingsheaddeal.co.uk
dir: *A249 from Dover to Deal, on seafront*

Traditional 18th-century seaside pub, overlooking the seafront. Deal's famous Timeball Tower is a few yards away and the pub is within easy reach of Canterbury, Walmer Castle and the Channel Tunnel. Bar meals include steaks, sandwiches and seafood, and there is a daily-changing specials board.

Open 10–11 (Sun 12–10.30) **Bar Meals** L served all week 11–2.30 D served all week 6–9 (Summer 11–9) Av main course £5.95 Free House Shepherd Neame Master Brew, Spitfire, Fullers London Pride. **Facilities** Garden Dogs allowed Play Area **Rooms** 14 bedrooms en suite S£40 D£50 (★★★ INN)

DOVER MAP 07 TR34

The Clyffe Hotel 🍷

High St, St Margaret's at Cliffe CT15 6AT
☎ 01304 852400 📠 01304 851880
e-mail: stay@theclyffehotel.com
dir: *3m NE of Dover*

Quaint Kentish clapperboard building dating back to the late 16th century. In its time it has been a shoemaker's and an academy for young gentlemen. Just a stone's throw from the Saxon Shore Way and the renowned White Cliffs of Dover. The main bar and neatly furnished lounge lead out into the delightful walled rose garden. Seared fillet of tuna and lightly steamed halibut are among the seafood specialities; other options include pan-fried chicken breast and penne pasta.

Open 11–12 (Wknds 11–1) **Bar Meals** L served all week 12–2.30 D served Mon–Sat 6–9.30 Av main course £9 **Restaurant** L served all week 12–2.30 D served Mon–Sat 6–9.30 Av 3 course à la carte £22 Free House Interbrew Bass, Boddingtons, Fullers London Pride. 🍷 30 **Facilities** Children's licence Garden Dogs allowed Parking Play Area

FAVERSHAM MAP 07 TR06

Shipwrights Arms 🍷

Hollowshore ME13 7TU ☎ 01795 590088
dir: *A2 through Ospringe, right at rdbt. Right at T-junct, left opposite Davington School, follow signs*

A classic pub on the Kent marshes, first licensed in 1738, and once a haunt of pirates and smugglers. There are numerous nooks and crannies, and Kent-brewed real ales are served traditionally by gravity straight from the cask. The self-sufficient landlord generates his own electricity and draws water from a well. Home-cooked food includes locally caught fish in season and with an emphasis on English pies and puddings during the winter.

Open 12–3 6–11 (Sun 6–10.30) **Bar Meals** L served Tue–Sun 12–2.30 D served Tue–Sat 7–9 Av main course £7.95 Free House Local Beers. **Facilities** Garden Dogs allowed Parking

FOLKESTONE MAP 07 TR2

The Lighthouse Inn ★★★ INN 🍷

Old Dover Rd, Capel le Ferne CT18 7HT
☎ 01303 223300 📠 01303 842270

Perched on the edge of Dover's famous White Cliffs, with sweeping Channel views, the Lighthouse began as an ale house in 1840, later becoming, successively, a billiard hall, convalescent home, psychiatric hospital and country club, while more recently still Channel Tunnel builders headquartered here. Most food is home made, from traditional bar meals like chilli con carne, to items on the carte and specials board, both of which offer a good choice of fish dishes.

Open 11–11 (Sun 11–10.30) **Bar Meals** L served all week 12–2.30 D served all week 6–9 (Sun 12–8.30) **Restaurant** L served all week 12–2.30 D served all week 6–9 (Sun 12–8) Av 3 course à la carte £20 Av 3 course fixed price £9.95 Oxford Hotels Abbot Ale, IPA & Guest Ales. 🍷 8 **Facilities** Children's licence Garden Parking Play Area **Rooms** 8 bedrooms en suite S£45 D£55

FORDCOMBE MAP 06 TQ5

Chafford Arms 🍷

TN3 0SA ☎ 01892 740267 📠 01892 740703
e-mail: bazzer@chafford-arms.fsnet.co.uk
dir: *On B2188 (off A264) between Tunbridge Wells & East Grinstead*

Barrie Leppard has been the landlord of this lovely, mid-19th-century tile-hung village pub for over 40 years – some achievement. Demand never flags for starters of smoked Weald trout with horseradish, and deep-fried mushrooms with garlic dip, nor indeed does it for main courses such as steaks, chicken Kiev, and signature dishes like hot and cold seafood platter for two, grilled lemon sole, prawn provençale, and courgette and aubergine cannelloni.

Open 11.45–11 (Sat all day) **Bar Meals** L served all week 12.30–2.15 D served Tue–Sat 7.15–9.15 Av main course £6.95 **Restaurant** L served all week 12.30–2.15 D served Tue–Sat 7.15–9.15 Enterprise Inns Larkins Bitter, Wadworth 6X. 🍷 9 **Facilities** Garden Dogs allowed Parking

GOUDHURST MAP 06 TQ7

Green Cross Inn

TN17 1HA ☎ 01580 211200 📠 01580 212905
dir: *A21 from Tonbridge towards Hastings turn left onto A262 towards Ashford. 2m, Goudhurst on right*

Food orientated pub in an unspoiled corner of Kent, originally built to serve the Paddock Wood-Goudhurst railway line, which closed in 1968. The dining-room is decorated prettily with fresh flowers, and the whole pub has been upgraded. Main courses in the bar range from home-made steak, kidney and mushroom pie with shortcrust pastry, calves' liver and bacon Lyonnaise. Restaurant fish dishes might include fillet of turbot with spinach and a creamy cheese sauce.

Open 11–3 6–11 (Closed winter Sun eve) **Bar Meals** L served all week 12–2.30 D served Mon–Sat 7–9.45 Av main course £10 **Restaurant** L served all week 12–2.30 D served Mon–Sat 7–9.45 Av 3 course à la carte £22.50 Free House Harveys Sussex Best Bitter, Guinness. **Facilities** Garden Parking

The Star & Eagle

commanding position at 400 feet above sea level gives the 14th-century Star & Eagle utstanding views of the orchards and hop fields that helped earn Kent the accolade 'Garden of ngland'.

he vaulted stonework suggests that nis rambling, big-beamed building nay once have been a monastery, nd the tunnel from the cellars robably surfaces underneath the eighbouring parish church. During ne 18th century the inn became ne headquarters of The Hawkhurst Gang, ruthless smugglers who also obbed and terrorised the locals. hese days, it's a place to unwind nd enjoy fine traditional and ontinental food, prepared under the uidance of Spanish chef/proprietor nrique Martinez. To help achieve is objective of providing complete iner satisfaction, the Bar and efectory menu offers a wide hoice. A typical meal might be eld mushrooms stuffed with bacon nd stilton; smoked salmon pasta vith creamy dill sauce; and warm elgian chocolate pudding. From his restaurant menu, possibilities include soup de poisson laced with brandy and fresh cream; Scottish rope mussels with chilli; and smoked salmon pancakes. Follow with pot-roast shoulder of lamb baked Spanish style; or sautéed calves' livers; and to finish, crepe suzette with orange and choclate ice cream; or stilton, brie and goats' cheese with a glass of vintage port. The wine list offers three champagnes and a selection of reasonably priced European and New World bins. One of the ten centrally heated bedrooms has a splendidly renovated four-poster bed, while in another is an old-fashioned half tester, its slightly less imposing relative. Should the romance overwhelm you, it may be helpful to know they can also host civil wedding ceremonies.

★★★★ INN

MAP 06 TQ73
High St TN17 1AL
☎ 01580 211512
01580 212444
e-mail: starandeagle@btconnect.com
dir: *Just off A21 towards Hastings. Take A262 into Goudhurst. Pub at top of hill next to church*

Open 11–11
Bar Meals L served all week 12–2.30 D served all week 7–9.30 (Sun 7–9)
Restaurant L served all week 12–2.30 D served all week 7–9.30 (Sun 7–9)
Free House
Flowers Original & Grasshopper Bitter, Adnams Bitter. 24
Facilities Garden Parking
Rooms 8 bedrooms en suite S£50 D£70

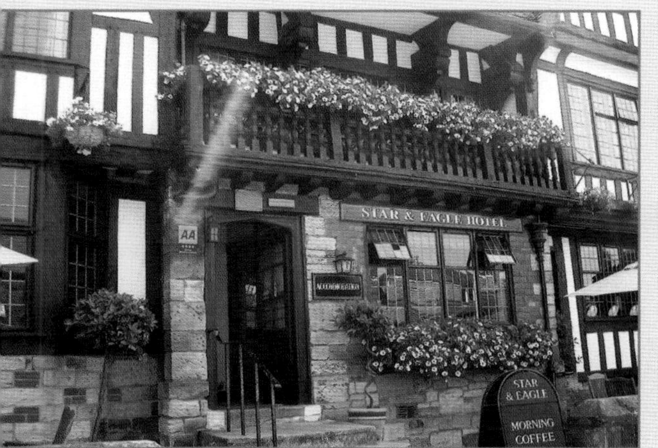

The Great House

The Great House is a wonderfully atmospheric 16th-century free house with lots of character and a lively history. It was once a haunt of smugglers who would struggle today to recognise the warm and comfortable ambience.

There are three dining areas to choose from, and the more recent addition of the Orangery, which is licensed for civil marriage ceremonies. This in turn opens onto a Mediterranean-style, stone-built terrace overlooking a pretty garden filled with mature trees and shrubs and featuring a Kentish lynch gate. An aromatic herb garden supplies the kitchen, whose informal brasserie menu is one of the main attractions, drawing discerning diners from some distance. Alongside the deli board selection (cheese, fish, antipasti, charcuterie), there are stone-baked pizzas, toasted paninis and salads (chicken Caesar, ocean, and roquefort). Starters include salmon and cod fishcake with sweet chilli sauce, and home-made pressé of foie gras with pear and orange chutney and toasted brioche. Mains range from The Great House lamb and mint burger with goats' cheese melt, beetroot salsa and chunky fries, to slow cooked venison casserole with fresh tagliatelle. For those on a meat-free diet there's a daily vegetarian fine tart as a starter – perhaps crispy vegetable basket with rocket and pesto dressing – and a main course such as pan-fried gnocchi with wild mushrooms, parmesan and peas. Part of the pub has recently been transformed into a deli/farmers' market. A wide selection of quality goods, fresh local fruits and vegetables and organic foods and meat produce are on offer here.

MAP 07 TQ73
Gills Green TN18 5EJ
☎ 01580 753119
01622 851881
e-mail: info@thegreathouse.net
dir: *Just off A229 between Cranbrook & Hawkhurst*

Open 11-11 (Sun 11–10.30)
Bar Meals L served all week 12–9.30 D served all week 12–9.30 (Sun 12–9.30) Av main course £10
Restaurant L served all week 12–9.30 D served all week 12–9.30 (Sun 12–9.30) Av 3 course à la carte £21 Av 2 course fixed price £11.50
Free House
Harveys, Guinness, Leffe, Youngs & St Miguel. 13
Facilities Children's licence Garden Parking

GOUDHURST continued

Pick of the Pubs

The Star & Eagle ★★★★ INN

High St TN17 1AL ☎ 01580 211512 01580 212444
e-mail: starandeagle@btconnect.com
dir: *Just off A21 towards Hastings. Take A262 into Goudhurst. Pub at top of hill next to church*

See Pick of the Pubs on page 313

GRAVESEND MAP 06 TQ67

The Cock Inn

Henley St, Luddesdowne DA13 0XB
☎ 01474 814208 01474 812850
e-mail: andrew.r.turner@btinternet.com
dir: *Telephone for directions*

There's a wonderful array of well-kept real bitters at this traditional English alehouse set in the beautiful Luddesdowne Valley. Woodburning stoves in the two bars with exposed beams set the warm ambience, with not a fruit machine, jukebox or child in sight. The good home-made food encompasses fresh sandwiches as well as dishes like cottage pie, beef madras curry and lamb hotpot. No table reservations.

Open 12–11 (Sun 12–10.30) **Bar Meals** L served all week 12–7 (Sun 12–8) Free House Adnams Southwold, Adnams Broadside Shepherd Neame Masterbrew, Goacher's Real Mild Ale, Harvey Best Bitter. **Facilities** Garden Dogs allowed Parking

HARRIETSHAM MAP 07 TQ85

The Pepper Box Inn

ME17 1LP ☎ 01622 842558 01622 844218
e-mail: pbox@nascr.net
dir: *Fairbourne Heath turn from A20 in Harrietsham. 2m to x-rds, straight over, 200yds, pub on left*

A delightful 15th-century country pub enjoys far-reaching views over the Weald of Kent from its terrace, high up on the Greensand Ridge. The pub takes its name from an early type of pistol, a replica of which hangs behind the bar. Typical dishes might include pot-roasted lamb shanks, local seasonal game, sea bass and Thai-style monkfish.

Open 11–3 6.30–11 **Bar Meals** L served all week 12–2.15 D served Tue-Sat 7–9.45 (Sun 12–3) Av main course £10.50 **Restaurant** L served Tue-Sat 12–2 D served Tue-Sat 7–9.45 Shepherd Neame Shepherd Neame Master Brew, Spitfire, Guest ales. 6 **Facilities** Garden Dogs allowed Parking

HAWKHURST MAP 07 TQ73

Pick of the Pubs

The Great House

Gills Green TN18 5EJ
☎ 01580 753119 01622 851881
e-mail: info@thegreathouse.net
dir: *Just off A229 between Cranbrook & Hawkhurst*

See Pick of the Pubs on opposite page

The Queens Inn

Rye Rd TN18 4EY ☎ 01580 753577 01580 754241
e-mail: info@thequeensinn.co.uk
dir: *In Hawkshurst, just off A21*

16th-century coaching inn with a wisteria-covered façade and an imposing entrance portico. Have a drink in the cosy reception area, the smart Wine Bar, the more cosmopolitan Piano Bar, the front garden, or heated courtyard. Seasonal menus offer snacks and salads, traditional English dishes, such as Guinness pie, and the more international pan-fried barramundi (Australia's favourite fish); mushroom, pinenut and coriander burrito; cannon of lamb en croûte; and tagliatelle carbonara.

Open 8.30–1 **Bar Meals** L served all week 12–10 D served all week 12–10 (Sun 12–8.30) Av main course £10 **Restaurant** L served all week 12–10 D served all week 12–10 (Sun 12.30–8.30) Av 3 course à la carte £22 Enterprise Inns Harveys Ale. 12 **Facilities** Children's licence Garden Parking

HERNHILL MAP 07 TR06

Pick of the Pubs

Red Lion

The Green ME13 9JR
☎ 01227 751207 01227 752990
e-mail: theredlion@lineone.net
dir: *S of A299 between Faversham & Whitstable*

Visitors to this historic inn will find a good range of local guest ales on tap, with a monthly changing menu and bar blackboards listing a choice of daily specials. Well-flavoured, robust dishes include Thai chicken; braised beef in ale and mushrooms; poached salmon with a creamy herb sauce; roast vegetable tartlet;

CONTINUED

England

HERNHILL continued

and seafood crumble. For dessert the options include waffles with ice cream and chocolate sauce; bread and butter pudding; and apple and fruit crumble. Meals are taken in the bar at rustic pine tables in front of roaring fires in winter and cooling draughts in the summer; all part of the charm of this handsome, half-timbered 14th-century hall house, which overlooks the village green towards the historic church. Master Brew is always on tap, along with guest ales like Speckled Hen and Spitfire.

Open 11.30–3 6–11 (Sun 12–3.30, 7–10.30) Closed: 25 Dec & 26 Dec, 1 Jan eves **Bar Meals** L served all week 12–2.30 D served all week 6–9.30 Av main course £8 **Restaurant** L served Sat & Sun 12–2.30 D served Fri–Sat 6–9.30 Free House Shepherd Neame Master Brew & Guest beers. 6 **Facilities** Garden Parking Play Area

HEVER MAP 06 TQ44

The Wheatsheaf

Hever Rd, Bough Beech TN8 7NU ☎ 01732 700254

dir: *M25 & A21 exit for Hever Castle. 1m past Castle on right*

The oldest part of this splendid creeper-clad inn was built as a hunting lodge for Henry V. Timbered ceilings and massive stone fireplaces set off various curios, such as the mounted jaw of a man-eating shark, and a collection of musical instruments. There's a light lunch menu Monday to Friday (pie and mash; fishcakes), and a carte supplemented by daily specials. Interesting options are wok-fried prawns with mini paella, and local pork and herb sausages.

Open 11 –11.30 **Bar Meals** L served all week 12–10 D served all week 12–10 **Restaurant** L served all week 12–10 D served all week 12–10 Free House Harveys Sussex Bitter, Shepherds Neame, Greene King Old Speckled Hen, Grasshopper. **Facilities** Garden Dogs allowed Parking

HODSOLL STREET MAP 06 TQ66

The Green Man

TN15 7LE ☎ 01732 823575

e-mail: the.greenman@btopenworld.com

dir: *On the North Downs between Brands Hatch & Gravesend on the A227*

A family-run 300-year-old pub located in the picturesque village of Hodsoll Street on the North Downs. An extensive menu is prepared to order using fresh local produce, and includes a wide variety of fish (especially on Wednesday, which is fish night) including mixed fish grill; haddock on Bombay potatoes, lamb shank, roast duck, and chicken stuffed with king prawns. Live music features every second Thursday night.

Open 11–2.30 6–11 (Fri & Sat 11–11, Sun 12–10.30) **Bar Meals** L served all week 12–2 D served all week 6.30–9.30 (Sun 6.30–9) Av main course £12 **Restaurant** L served all week 12–2 D served all week 6.30–9.30 (Sun 6.30–9) Av 2 course fixed price £10 Enterprise Inns Fuller's London Pride, Harveys, Old Speckled Hen, British Bulldog. **Facilities** Children's licence Garden Dogs allowed Parking Play Area

IDEN GREEN MAP 06 TQ7

The Peacock

Goudhurst Rd TN17 2PB ☎ 01580 211233

dir: *A21 onto A262, 1.5m past Goudhurst*

Grade II listed building dating from the 14th century with low beams, an inglenook fireplace, old oak doors, real ales on tap, and a wide range of traditional pub food. A large enclosed garden with fruit trees and picnic tables on one side of the building is popular in summer, and there's also a patio.

Open 12–11 (Sun 12–10.30) **Bar Meals** L served all week 12–2.45 D served Mon–Sat 6–8.45 (Sun 12–3) Av main course £6.95 **Restaurant** L served all week D served all week Shepherd Neame Shepherd Neame Master Brew, Spitfire and Guest ales. 12 **Facilities** Garden Dogs allowed Parking

IGHTHAM MAP 06 TQ5

Pick of the Pubs

The Harrow Inn

Common Rd TN15 9EB ☎ 01732 885912

dir: *1.5m from Borough Green on A25 to Sevenoaks, signed Ightham Common, left into Common Road, 0.25m on left.*

Within easy reach of both M20 and M26 motorways, yet tucked away down country lanes close to the National Trust's Knole Park and Igtham Mote, this Virginia creeper-hung stone inn dates back to the 17th century and beyond. The bar area comprises two rooms with a great brick fireplace, open to both sides and piled high with blazing logs in winter; meanwhile the restaurant boasts a vine-clad conservatory that opens to a terrace that's ideal for summer dining. Menus vary with the seasons, and seafood is a particular speciality: fish aficionados can enjoy dishes such as crab and ginger spring roll; swordfish with Cajun spice and salsa; or pan-fried fillets of sea bass with lobster cream and spinach. Other main courses have included Bishop's Finger (one of Shepherd Neame's fine beers) baked sausage with gammon, fennel, red onions and garlic; and tagliatelle with a wild mushroom, fresh herb, lemongrass and chilli ragoût. Look out for the grass floor!

Open 12–3 6–11 (Sun 12–3) Closed: 26 Dec, 1 Jan, BH Mon **Bar Meals** L served Tue–Sun 12–2 D served Tue–Sat 6–9 **Restaurant** L served Tue–Sun 12–2 D served Tue–Sat 6–9 Av 3 course à la carte £25 Free House Greene King Abbot Ale, IPA,. 8 **Facilities** Garden Parking

England

VY HATCH MAP 06 TQ55

Pick of the Pubs

The Plough at Ivy Hatch

High Cross Rd TN15 0NL ☎ 01732 810100

e-mail: enquiries@theploughpub.net

dir: *From M20 junct 2 take A20 then A227 through Ightham towards Tonbridge.*

When owner Michelle Booth took over the Plough in 2005, her aim was to showcase local produce and to reinstate the inn as 'an integral part of the local community'. Two years on, this cosy county pub is going from strength to strength. Set deep in Kent countryside, and just a quarter of a mile from the National Trust's 14th-century Ightham Mote, it's the perfect spot for a lingering lunch or supper. Food is sourced from nearby wherever possible, while wine, beer and bottled water alike derive from Kent. This eco-friendly attentiveness extends to the rubbish, which is all recycled. A typical menu might offer Kentish mussels in cider and cream, followed by roast local pheasant; casserole of wild rabbit; or slow roast pork belly with caramelised Hassleback apples and sage gravy. 2007 sees the opening of a new terrace and garden ideal for al fresco dining.

Open 12–3 6.30–11 (summer 10–3, 5.30–11) **Bar Meals** L served all week 12–2.30 D served all week 6–9.30 (Sun 12–8) Av main course £8.95 **Restaurant** L served all week 12–2.30 D served all week 7–9.30 (Sun 12–8, summer brunch 10–12 all week) Av 3 course à la carte £23 Av 3 course fixed price £15 Free House Harveys, Westerham & Larkins, Goachers. **Facilities** Garden Parking

LAMBERHURST MAP 06 TQ63

The Swan at the Vineyard

The Down TN3 8EU ☎ 01892 890170 01892 890401

web: www.theswan.org

With a large village green at the front and acres of Kentish vineyard to the rear, the Swan declares that it is 'not a traditional pub grub place', so don't expect jacket potatoes or chips. Instead choose from a comprehensive menu featuring Mediterranean vegetables with blue stilton creamed fondue; grilled sea-bass fillet with Cajun coriander prawns; and veal escalope poached in milk, garlic and nutmeg with dauphinoise potato. Award-winning English wines are attractively priced.

The Swan at the Vineyard

Open 12–3 6–11 (Sun 12–5) **Bar Meals** L served all week 12–2.15 D served all week 6–9.30 Av main course £7.50 **Restaurant** L served all week 12–2.15 D served all week 6–9.30 Av 3 course à la carte £20 Harveys Best, Adnams Broadside, Bombardier, Adnams Regatta. 7 **Facilities** Garden Dogs allowed Parking Play Area

LEIGH MAP 06 TQ54

The Greyhound NEW

Charcott TN11 8LG ☎ 01892 870275

e-mail: GHatcharcott@aol.com

dir: *B245 N towards Hildenborough. Left onto Leigh road, right onto Stocks Green road. Through Leigh, right then left at T-junct, right into Charcott*

The Greyhound's winter log fires and summer garden have been welcoming Charcott's locals for around 120 years, and visitors too – it was much favoured by pilots from Penshurst during the war. Tony French, who took it over three years ago, has maintained the traditional atmosphere in which music, pool table and fruit machine have no place. A well kept ale slips down while perusing the honest daily-changing menu based on local game and the county's succulent lamb and beef.

Open 12–3 5.30–12 (Sat & Sun all day) **Bar Meals** L served all week 12–2 D served all week 6.30–9.30 (Sun 12–3) Av main course £8.50 **Restaurant** L served all week 12–2 (Sun 12–3) D served all week 6.30–9.30 Av 3 course à la carte £18 Enterprise Inns Harvey, Black Sheep, Finchcocks. **Facilities** Garden Dogs allowed Parking

LINTON MAP 07 TQ75

The Bull Inn

Linton Hill ME17 4AW ☎ 01622 743612

e-mail: dominic@lintonbull.co.uk

dir: *S of Maidstone on A229 (Hastings road)*

A traditional 17th-century coaching inn in the heart of the Weald with stunning views from the glorious garden, and a large inglenook fireplace and wealth of beams inside. A tasty bar menu includes lasagna, spinach and ricotta tortellini, cod and chips, and bubble and squeak, as well as sandwiches, baguettes, and ploughman's. From the restaurant menu comes pan-fried venison steak wrapped in pancetta, served on sautéed oyster mushrooms.

Open 11–11 **Bar Meals** L served all week 12–3 D served Mon–Sat 7–10 (Sun 12–7) Av main course £8 **Restaurant** L served all week 12–3 D served all week 7–10 Av 3 course à la carte £8 Shepherd Neame Shepherd Neame Master Brew & Spitfire, Seasonal Ale. 7 **Facilities** Garden Dogs allowed Parking

England

LITTLEBOURNE MAP 07 TR25

King William IV

4 High St CT3 1UN ☎ 01227 721244 🖷 01227 721244
e-mail: sam@bowwindow.co.uk
dir: *From A2 follow signs past Howletts Zoo.*

Located just outside the city of Canterbury, the King William IV overlooks the village green and is well placed for Sandwich and Herne Bay. With open log fires and exposed oak beams, this friendly inn is a good place for visitors and locals.

Open 11-11 (Sun 12-10.30) **Bar Meals** L served all week 12-2.30 D served Tue-Sat 6-9 Av main course £10 **Restaurant** L served all week 12-2.30 D served all week 6-9 Free House Scottish Courage John Smith's, Sussex Harveys. **Facilities** Parking

MAIDSTONE MAP 07 TQ75

The Black Horse Inn NEW ★★★★ INN

Pilgrims Way, Thurnham ME14 3LD
☎ 01622 737185 🖷 01622 739170
e-mail: info@wellieboot.net
dir: *M20 junct 7, A249, right into Detling. Opposite Cock Horse Pub turn onto Pilgrims Way*

Tucked beneath the steep face of the North Downs on the Pilgrim's Way, this homely and welcoming free house has an open log fire in winter. The building is thought to have been a forge before its conversion to an inn during the middle years of the 18th century. The bar and restaurant menus range from traditional favourites like steak and ale pudding to sea trout on saffron rice with roasted red onions.

Open 11-11 **Bar Meals** L served all week 12-6 D served all week 6-10 Av main course £8 **Restaurant** L served all week 12-6 D served all week 6-10 Av 3 course à la carte £25 Av 3 course fixed price £12.25 Free House Kents Best, London Pride, Greene King IPA. 30 **Facilities** Garden Dogs allowed Parking **Rooms** 16 bedrooms en suite S£60 D£75

MARKBEECH MAP 06 TQ44

The Kentish Horse

Cow Ln TN8 5NT ☎ 01342 850493

Surrounded by Kent countryside, this pub is popular with ramblers, cyclists and families. The inn dates from 1340 and is said to have a smuggling history; it also boasts a curious street-bridging Kentish sign. The wide-ranging menu offers fresh starters such as Greek feta salad, or pint of shell-on prawns, followed by spinach and ricotta cannelloni; sausage and mash with onion gravy; and steak and Guinness pie. Regular folk festivals and other events.

Open 12-11 (Sun 12-10.30) **Bar Meals** L served all week 12-2.30 (Sun 12-3.30) D served Tue-Sat 7-9.30 Av main course £8.95 **Restaurant** L served all week 12-2.30 (Sun L 12-3.30) D served all week 7-9.30 Av 3 course à la carte £15.50 Harvey's Larkins, plus Guest ales. **Facilities** Garden Dogs allowed Parking Play Area

NEWNHAM MAP 07 TQ9

The George Inn

44 The Street ME9 0LL ☎ 01795 890237 🖷 01795 89072

The George is an attractive country inn with a large beer garden. Despite the passing of the centuries, the inn retains much of its histor character with beams, polished wooden floors, inglenook fireplaces and candlelit tables. In addition to the regular range of beers there's a changing winter/summer ale. Food is served in the bar and 50-seater restaurant. Bar snacks range from sandwiches to sausage and mash, while main meals could include pan-fried fillet of red snapper with crushed potatoes, baby fennel, fresh scampi and rosemary butter; or peppered duck breast with celeriac mash and cherry and port sauce. Regular events include live jazz, quizzes and murder mystery evening

Open 11-3 6.30-11 (Sun 12-4, 7-11) **Bar Meals** L served all week 12-2 D served all week 7-9.30 Av main course £12.50 **Restaurant** L served all week 12-2.30 D served all week 7-9.45 Av 3 course à la carte £25 Shepherd Neame Shepherds Neame Master Brew, Spitfire, Bishops Finger, Kent Best & Seasonal ale. 8 **Facilities** Garden Parking

PENSHURST MAP 06 TQ5

Pick of the Pubs

The Bottle House Inn

Coldharbour Rd TN11 8ET
☎ 01892 870306 🖷 01892 871094
e-mail: info@thebottlehouseinnpenshurst.co.uk
web: www.thebottlehouseinnpenshurst.co.uk
dir: *From Tunbridge Wells take A264 W, then B2188 N. After Fordcombe left towards Edenbridge & Hever. Pub 500yds after staggered x-rds*

See Pick of the Pubs on opposite page

The Bottle House Inn

well-regarded dining pub, The Bottle House has been run by Gordon and Val Meer and their ıughters for over 21 years. Built as a farmhouse in 1492, the building was later divided into vo properties.

ıomas Scraggs leased one of the ›ttages in 1806 and obtained a :ence to sell ales and ciders, but this time the pub didn't have a ıme. The building was completely furbished in 1938 and granted a ll licence. Today, low beams and copper-topped counter give the ır a warm, welcoming atmosphere ıd you'll find a good range of local ınd-pumped beers to accompany ȝht meals, ploughman's lunches, ıd filled baguettes. There's a milar feel to the dining room hile, on warmer days, diners can ıjoy the views from the pretty ırden with its pergola-covered ıtio. The daily-changing menu fers an extensive choice. As far as ›ssible, everything is made from cally supplied fresh produce, ıd a typical selection of dishes might begin with goose liver and Sauternes wine pâté with mixed leaves and toast, or potato wedges topped with chilli con carne, sour cream and melted mozzarella. Main course options follow with roasted wing of skate and lemon, caper and parsley butter, or minted Barnsley lamb chops with dauphinoise potatoes and port and redcurrant sauce. Puddings include some old favourites like rhubarb crumble and custard, or the classic crèpe Suzette with vanilla pod ice cream. A two-course menu and high chairs are also available for children.

MAP 06 TQ54
Coldharbour Rd TN11 8ET
☎ 01892 870306
Fax 01892 871094
e-mail: info@thebottlehouseinnpenshurst.co.uk
web: www.thebottlehouseinnpenshurst.co.uk
dir: *From Tunbridge Wells take A264 W, then B2188 N. After Fordcombe left towards Edenbridge & Hever. Pub 500yds after staggered x-rds*

Open 11–11 (Sun 11–10.30)
Closed: 25 Dec
Bar Meals L served Mon–Sat 12–10 D served Mon–Sat 12–10 (Sun 11.30–9) Av main course £11.50
Restaurant L served Mon–Sat 12–10 D served Mon–Sat 12–10 (Sun 11.30–9) Av 3 course à la carte £22
Free House
Larkins Ale, Harveys Sussex Best Bitter. 🍷 8
Facilities Children's licence Garden Dogs allowed Parking

The Dering Arms

The elegantly well-appointed Dering Arms was built in the 1840s as a hunting lodge serving the Dering Estate, once one of the largest of its kind. The impressive building with its curved Dutch gables and uniquely arched windows was built as a smaller replica of the main manor house.

Inside you'll find two traditional bars – complete with roaring fires in winter, a family room with a grand piano (customers are encouraged to try their hand) and an intimate restaurant. Chef/patron James Buss has run this distinctive inn with passion and flair since 1984. 'I run the kitchen personally', he explains, 'in order to maintain the high standards I feel are essential.' Everything is made on the premises, right down to the marmalade. Good use is also made of fresh vegetables from the family farm and herbs from the pub garden. The extensive menus reflect James's own love of fresh fish and seafood. Starters could include Provençale fish soup; Sussex smokies; grilled Cork oysters with chorizo; and sautéed chicken livers, while main courses feature the likes of grilled skate wing with capers; and pan-fried tuna steak, alongside blackboard specials of the day. The seafood special must be ordered 24hrs in advance, but expect the full *fruits de mer* dish of hot and cold seafood, served with fresh granary bread, for two people or more. Black tie 'Gourmet' evenings are held throughout the winter, giving diners a chance to sample a seven-course meal of unusual and intriguing dishes.

MAP 07 TQ94
Station Rd TN27 0RR
☎ 01233 840371
Fax 01233 840498
e-mail: jim@deringarms.com
dir: *M20 junct 8, A20 to Ashford. Right onto B2077 at Charing to Pluckley*

Open 11-3 6-11 Closed: 26-29 Dec
Bar Meals L served Tue-Sun 12-2 D served Tue-Sat 7-9.30
Restaurant L served Tue-Sun 12-2 D served Tue-Sat 7-9.30
Free House
Goacher's Dering Ale, Maidstone Dark, Gold Star, Old Ale. 7
Facilities Garden Dogs allowed Parking

:NSHURST continued

:he Leicester Arms

:h St TN11 8BT ☎ 01892 870551

: *From Tunbridge Wells take A26 towards Tonbridge. Left onto '765 towards Penshurst*

cturesque establishment with a large garden and meadow views, Leicester Arms was once part of the Penshurst Place estate and amed after Viscount De L'Isle, Earl of Leicester, grandson of the ner owner. Richard Burton and Elizabeth Taylor stayed here e filming *Anne of a Thousand Days*. Dishes range from croque ısieur, quiche, and battered cod from the bar menu to pan-fried ken supreme, and slow cooked lamb shank from the carte.

:n 11–11.30 **Bar Meals** L served all week 12–9.30 D served all week).30 **Restaurant** L served all week 12–9.30 D served all week 12–9.30 ıterprise Inns Old Speckled Hen, Shepherd Neame, Master Brew, :rs London Pride. **Facilities** Garden Dogs allowed Parking

Pick of the Pubs

:he Spotted Dog

marts Hill TN11 8EE

☎ 01892 870253 01892 870107

-mail: info@spotteddogpub.co.uk

:ir: *Off B2188 between Penshurst & Fordcombe*

'hen the trees are bare this 15th-century, typically Kentish :atherboarded pub enjoys fine views over the Weald from the ar terrace. In summer the trees are thick with foliage, but it's 'll a lovely spot for a drink or meal. The rambling interior cuts e mustard too, with beams, four open fireplaces, tiled and ık floors, and those little nooks and crannies that just seem to op up in old pubs. Deciding where and what to eat is simple, the single menu offers both traditional favourites and more ›phisticated fare, and applies throughout the pub at lunchtimes ıd evenings. There are staples like ham, eggs and chips, and ,h and chips, although some qualification might be necessary: e ham is honey-baked, the eggs free-range, and the fish is :er-battered cod. Otherwise there are starters like home-made icken liver parfait with plum chutney, and mains of Kentish usages with wholegrain mustard mash and red onion jus.

pen 11–3 6–11 (Seasonal times vary, ring for details) **ır Meals** L served all week 12–2.30 D served all week 6–9.30 (Sun –6) Av main course £8.95 **Restaurant** L served all week 12–2.30 served all week 6–9.30 (Sun 12–6) Free House Harveys Best, rkins Traditional, Guest ale. 9 **Facilities** Garden Dogs allowed rking

PLUCKLEY MAP 07 TQ94

Pick of the Pubs

The Dering Arms

Station Rd TN27 0RR

☎ 01233 840371 01233 840498

e-mail: jim@deringarms.com

dir: *M20 junct 8, A20 to Ashford. Right onto B2077 at Charing to Pluckley*

See Pick of the Pubs on opposite page

The Mundy Bois

Mundy Bois TN27 0ST ☎ 01233 840048 01233 840193

e-mail: helen@mundybois.com

An ale house since 1780 and formerly named the Rose and Crown, this creeper-clad pub is on the outskirts of Pluckley, considered to be the most haunted place in England. The bar menu offers home-made meals and snacks like Aberdeen Angus burgers or pork and cider gourmet sausage and mash. A patio dining area allows al fresco eating, and the garden has an adventure playground.

Open 11.30–3 6–11 (Fri–Sun 11.30–11) (May–Sep 10 Sat–Sun brunch) **Bar Meals** L served all week 12–2.30 D served all week 7–9.30 (May–Sep 10 Sat–Sun brunch) **Restaurant** L served all week 12–2.30 D served all week 7–9.30 Free House Master Brew, Wadworth 6X. 10 **Facilities** Garden Dogs allowed Parking Play Area

ST MARGARET'S AT CLIFFE MAP 07 TR34

Pick of the Pubs

The Coastguard

St Margaret's Bay CT15 6DY ☎ 01304 853176

e-mail: thecoastguard@talk21.com

dir: *2m off A258 between Dover & Deal, towards sea*

St Margaret's Bay is one of the most delightful spots on the Kentish coast, with breathtaking white cliffs and beach walks, not to mention The Coastguard's famed food and hospitality. The pub stands only a stone's throw from the water's edge and has spectacular views out to sea. Its menu includes award-winning fish dishes such as roast skate wing with samphire and cockles or fresh fish pie. The cooking is imaginative and makes excellent use of local produce – perhaps sirloin beef steak from a local farm,

CONTINUED

ST MARGARET'S AT CLIFFE continued

seared on sea salt with garlic butter and served with double-fried chips and the pub's 'garden of Kent' fresh salad. Other typical dishes include hot devilled crab; sea bass roasted on pebbles with a seaweed dressing; and chargrilled aubergine with a basil, pine nut and parmesan crust served with roast ratatouille and Kentish new potatoes. Excellent wines, whiskies, bottled beers and real ales.

Open 11-11 **Bar Meals** L served all week 12.30-2.45 D served all week 6.30-8.45 Av main course £12 **Restaurant** L served all week 12.30-2.45 D served all week 6.30-8.45 Free House Gadds of Ramsgate, Hop Daemon, Adnams, Caledonian. **Facilities** Garden Dogs allowed Parking Play Area

SANDWICH MAP 07 TR35

George & Dragon Inn

Fisher St CT13 9EJ ☎ 01304 613106 01304 621137

dir: *Between Dover & Canterbury*

An attractive, heavily beamed period pub/restaurant with plenty of character and close to the renowned Royal St Georges golf course, a favourite of James Bond creator Ian Fleming. A varied menu includes a good range of starters, followed by whole Dover sole, braised guinea fowl, smoked tuna steak, and lamb and potato vindaloo. Pizzas are prepared on the premises and cooked in a wood-burning oven, and there is a popular carvery on Sunday.

Open 11-3 6-11 (Sun 7-10.30) Closed: 26 Dec **Bar Meals** L served all week 12-2.15 D served all week 6-9.15 (Sun 7-9.15) **Restaurant** L served all week 12-2.15 D served all week 6-9.15 (Sun 7-9.15) Enterprise Inns Shepherd Neame Master Brew, Youngs Special, Harveys Sussex Best, Adnams Broadside. 7 **Facilities** Garden Dogs allowed

SELLING MAP 07 TR05

The Rose and Crown

Perry Wood ME13 9RY ☎ 01227 752214

e-mail: perrywoodrose@btinternet.co.uk

dir: *A28 right at Badgers Hill, left at end. 1st left signed Perry Wood. Pub at top*

Set amidst 150 peaceful acres of woodland, this 16th-century pub's beamed interior is decorated with hop garlands, corn dollies, horse brasses and brass cask taps. Outside, the perfumed summer garden includes a children's play area and bat and trap pitch. Expect a choice of four real ales including a guest, and a menu with a high comfort factor: cheesy cottage pie, cod and smoked haddock mornay, and steak and mushroom pudding are three examples.

Open 11-3 6.30-11 (Sun 12-6, 7-10.30) (Summer. Fri 11-4, 6-11, Sat all day) Rest: 25-26 Dec pm only, 1 Jan pm only **Bar Meals** L served all week 12-2 D served Tue-Sun 7-9.30 Av main course £8.95 **Restaurant** L served all week 12-2 D served Tue-Sat 7-9.30 Free House Adnams Southwold, Harveys Sussex Best Bitter, Goacher's Real Mild Ale. **Facilities** Garden Dogs allowed Parking Play Area

SEVENOAKS MAP 06 TQ

The White Hart Inn

Tonbridge Rd TN13 1SG ☎ 01732 452022

e-mail: sportingheros@btclick.com

A 16th-century inn close to Knole House, one of Kent's most famou and historic homes, noted for its glorious deer park. The pub's attractive garden, spacious terrace and traditional period interior dra customers from all corners of the county. The menu offers everythir from shank of lamb with garlic mash, and breast of chicken in artich sauce, to steak and kidney pudding, and beer-battered cod. Bloome sandwiches, ploughman's and baguettes make good snacks.

Open 11-3.30 6-12 **Bar Meals** L served all week 12-2.30 (Sun 12-4.3 D served Mon-Sat 6-9.30 Av main course £8.50 **Restaurant** L served week 12-2.30 (Sun 12-4.30) D served Mon-Sat 6-9 Av 3 course à la car £21 Harveys Sussex, Shepherd Neame Spitfire, Adnams Best, Guest beers. 8 **Facilities** Children's licence Garden Parking Play Area

SMARDEN MAP 07 TQ

The Bell

Bell Ln TN27 8PW ☎ 01233 770283

Built in the year 1536, the Bell was originally a farm building on a la estate. It was used as a blacksmiths forge right up until 1907, but it had also been an alehouse since 1630. A typical menu includes sea king scallops with spinach and crab sauce, chargrilled chicken breas with mozzarella, basil and wild mushroom sauce, gammon steak w beetroot mash and parsley sauce, and tournedos of monkfish Rossi

Open 12-3 5.30-11 (Fri-Sat 12-11 Sun 12-10.30) **Bar Meals** L served all week 12-2.30 D served Sun-Thur 6.30-9.30 (Fri-Sat 6.30-10) Av ma course £11 **Restaurant** L served all week 12-2.30 D served all week 6.30-9.30 (Fri-Sat 6.30-10) Free House Shepherd Neame Master Brew Spitfire, Interbrew Flowers IPA, Fuller's London Pride, Guest ales. **Facilities** Garden Dogs allowed Parking

Pick of the Pubs

The Chequers Inn ★★★★ INN

'he Street TN27 8QA

☎ 01233 770217 📠 01233 770623

:-mail: reception@thechequerssmarden.com

lir: *Through Leeds village, left to Sutton Valence/Headcorn 'hen left for Smarden. Pub in village centre*

ghost is said to haunt the bedrooms of the Chequers – an tmospheric 14th-century inn with a clapboard façade in the entre of one of Kent's prettiest villages. The inn has its own eautiful landscaped garden with large duck pond and attractive outh-facing courtyard. Real ales such as Speckled Hen are erved in the low beamed bars. Here the food ranges from club andwiches and jacket potatoes to smoked ham, eggs and chips, nd lambs' liver with bacon. For an à la carte meal two separate estaurants offer a choice of ambience: the Red Restaurant has n opulent and romantic setting, while the Gold Restaurant is less ormal in style and suitable for the whole family; both serve the ame menus. Typical starters are smoked duck salad, or lambs' idney croûte, while main courses may include apple roasted pork oin steak, Barbary duck breast, and saddle of rabbit.

pen 11–11 (Sun 12–10.30) **Bar Meals** L served all week 12–2.30) served all week 6–9.30 (Sun 12–3, 6–8.30) Av main course £9.95 **estaurant** L served all week 12–2.30 D served all week 6.30–9.30 Sun 12–3, 6–8.30) Av 3 course à la carte £22.50 Av 2 course fixed rice £9.95 Free House Harveys, IPA, Abbot, Speckled Hen. 9 **Facilities** Garden Dogs allowed Parking **Rooms** 4 bedrooms n suite S£40 D£70

'ELDHURST MAP 06 TQ54

Pick of the Pubs

George & Dragon

;peldhurst Hill TN3 0NN

☎ 01892 863125 📠 01892 863216

:-mail: julian@speldhurst.com

3uilt around 1500, the George and Dragon is a venerable imber-clad village hostelry. Some say its origins are earlier, when ;peldhurst would have seen archers departing for the Battle of Agincourt. At the beginning of the 17th century the curative oowers of the village's iron-rich waters were discovered, which put nearby Tunbridge Wells on the map. Today's customers enjoy a nodern gastro-pub, where refreshments include a range of local organic fruit juices. The menu offers half a dozen eclectic choices at each stage: you could start with local smoked eel on toast, and 'ollow with Ashdown Forest wild mushroom risotto; or lunch ightly on a plate of Kentish hop pork sausages. The fish selection s exceptional, with sea bass, sea bream, brill, turbot, skate, lobster, nussels and razor clams all making regular appearances. Food can be served in the two gardens – one a modern layout with bay trees and herbs, the other a Mediterranean garden with 200-year-old olive tree.

Open 11–11 **Bar Meals** L served all week 12–3 D served Mon–Sat 7–10.30 **Restaurant** L served all week 12–2.30 D served Mon–Sat 6–10 Av 3 course à la carte £20 Av 3 course fixed price £17 Free House Harveys Best, Sussex Pale, Larkins & Porter. 10 **Facilities** Children's licence Garden Dogs allowed Parking

TENTERDEN MAP 07 TQ83

White Lion Inn

57 High St TN30 6BD ☎ 01580 765077 📠 01580 764157

e-mail: whitelion.tenderden@marstonstaverns.co.uk

dir: *On A28 (Ashford to Hastings road)*

A 16th-century coaching inn on a tree-lined street of this old Cinque Port, with many original features retained. The area is known for its cricket connections, and the first recorded county match between Kent and London was played here in 1719. The menu offers plenty of choice, from calves' liver and bacon, shoulder of lamb, and Cumberland cottage pie to tuna pasta bake and various ploughman's.

Open 7–11 (Fri–Sat 7–12) **Bar Meals** L served all week 12 D served all week 9.30 (Sun 12–8.30) Av main course £8 **Restaurant** L served all week 12 D served all week 9.30 (Sun 12–8.30) Av 3 course à la carte £17 Lionheart Greene King IPA, Adnams Broadside, Banks, Marstons Pedigree. 10 **Facilities** Garden Dogs allowed Parking

TONBRIDGE

See **Penshurst**

TUNBRIDGE WELLS (ROYAL) MAP 06 TQ53

Pick of the Pubs

The Beacon ★★★★ INN

Tea Garden Ln, Rusthall TN3 9JH

☎ 01892 524252 📠 01892 534288

e-mail: beaconhotel@btopenworld.com

dir: *From Tunbridge Wells take A264 towards East Grinstead. Pub 1m on left*

See Pick of the Pubs on page 324

The Crown Inn

The Green, Groombridge TN3 9QH ☎ 01892 864742

e-mail: crowngroombridge@aol.com

dir: *Take A264 W of Tunbridge Wells, then B2110 S*

Dating back to 1585, this charming free house was a favourite haunt for Keira Knightley and the cast of *Pride and Prejudice* during filming at Groombridge Place in 2005. Low beams and an inglenook fireplace are the setting for the lunchtime bar menu, which features toasted ciabattas, jackets and hot pub favourites. Evening diners might choose grilled cod with prawn and parsley butter; chicken and home-made ratatouille; or sun-blushed tomato pasta with peppers and roquette.

Open 11–3 6–11 (Summer Fri–Sun all day) **Bar Meals** L served all week 12–3 (Sun 12–4) D served Mon–Sat 7–9 **Restaurant** L served all week 12–3 (Sun 12–4) D served Mon–Sat 7–9 Free House Harveys IPA, Greene King IPA & Abbot Ale, Larkins. 8 **Facilities** Garden Dogs allowed Parking Play Area

The Beacon

Located along the attractively wooded Tea Garden Lane, The Beacon stands high on a sandsto[ne] outcrop overlooking one of the best views in southeast England. It was built in 1895 by Sir Walter Harris, a lieutenant of the City of London, as his country home.

Sir Walter commissioned only the finest craftsmen, so the property has a host of impressive architectural features, including some fine stained glass windows, patterned ceilings and an oak-panelled bar. After Harris's death the house passed through various hands, including those of a Mayor of Tunbridge Wells, until the Second World War when it became a hostel for Jewish refugee girls. There are 17 acres of grounds to explore, with lakes, woodland walks and a chalybeate spring, which was first used in 1708, predating by 40 years its more famous counterpart in The Pantiles at Tunbridge Wells. You can enjoy a drink on the terrace in summer or by the log fire in the bar. Draught beers and a good selection of wines are offered, with plenty by the glass. Food is served in the main restaurant or one of three private dining rooms. A separate spacious function room is also available, with its own bar. The menus take full seasonal advantage of county-grown produce to which, as a member of Kentish Fare, the kitchen is committed. Seafood is purchased daily and served in dishes such as grilled halibut fillet with pea cream and salsa verde, or wild sea bass fillets with roast vine tomatoes on tagliatelle. Alternatively try braised oxtail with root vegetables, parsley mash and buttered cabbage. Three bedrooms are available (two doubles and a single): the Georgian Room, the Colonial Room and the Contemporary Room.

★★★★ INN ➪ 🍷
MAP 06 TQ53
Tea Garden Ln, Rusthall TN3 9JH
☎ 01892 524252
📠 01892 534288
e-mail: beaconhotel@btopenworld.com
dir: *From Tunbridge Wells take A264 towards East Grinstead. Pu[b] 1m on left*

Open 11–11 (Sun 12–10.30)
Bar Meals L served all week 12–2.30 D served all week 6.30–9.30
Restaurant L served all week 12–2.30 D served all week 6–9.30 (Fri–Sat 6.30–10, Sun 12–5, 6.30–9.30)
Free House
Harveys Best, Timothy Taylor Landlord, Larkins Traditional. 🍷 1[2]
Facilities Children's licence Garden Parking Play Area
Rooms 3 bedrooms en suite S£68.50 D£97

UNBRIDGE WELLS (ROYAL) continued

Pick of the Pubs

The Hare on Langton Green

angton Rd, Langton Green TN3 0JA
☎ 01892 862419 📠 01892 861275
e-mail: hare@brunningandprice.co.uk
dir: *From Tunbridge Wells follow A264 towards East Grinstead. Village on A264*

here has been an inn on this site since the 16th century, though e previous version was partially destroyed in a fire in 1900. hat remained was too dilapidated to restore, and the present ctorian-Tudor model was built a year later. In a spooky twist, a oman holding a child is said to haunt the main staircase and llar, though what era she dates back to nobody can say. On the mfortably comprehensive daily-changing menu starters and ain dishes might include rabbit rillettes; teriyaki chicken skewers; d baked figs with rocket and air-dried ham, to be followed by ıssic cassoulet; ham hock with mustard and cider sauce'; or noked haddock and mussel casserole topped with a poached g. Light bites and sandwiches are also available. In addition to eene King IPA and Abbot ales, there's an impressive range of alt whiskies and wines by the glass.

pen 12-11 (Fri-Sat 12-12, Sun 12-10.30) **Bar Meals** L served all eek 12-9.30 D served all week 12-9.30 (Fri-Sat 12-10, Sun 12-9) **estaurant** L served all week 12-9.30 D served all week (Fri-Sat -10, Sun 12-9) Greene King Greene King IPA & Abbot Ale. 16 **Facilities** Garden Dogs allowed Parking

ESTERHAM MAP 06 TQ45

e Fox & Hounds

s Hill TN16 1QG ☎ 01732 750328
ail: hickmott1@hotmail.com

up on Kent's Greensand Ridge, this late-18th-century ale house ins a large National Trust estate incorporating an old water r now protected as a home for hibernating bats. The pub has revamped to include a traditionally styled restaurant, where e-prepared starters include anchovy and balsamic onion tart, and -fried brie with cranberry sauce, while among the mains are skate with capers, lamb shank with garlic mash, and daily specials.

n 11.30-3 6-11 (Sat-Sun all day) Closed: Dec 25 **Bar Meals** L served eek 12-2 (Sat 12-2.30, Sun 12-3) D served Tue-Sat 6-9 **aurant** L served all week 12-2 D served Tue-Sat 6-9 Sun 12-3 eene King Greene King IPA, Abbot Ale, Ruddles County. 9 **ities** Garden Dogs allowed Parking

WEST MALLING MAP 06 TQ65

Pick of the Pubs

The Farmhouse

97 The High St ME19 6NA
☎ 01732 843257 📠 01622 851881
e-mail: info@thefarmhouse.biz
dir: *M20 junct 4, S on A228. Right to West Malling. Pub in village centre*

See Pick of the Pubs on page 326

WHITSTABLE MAP 07 TR16

Pick of the Pubs

The Sportsman

Faversham Rd CT5 4BP
☎ 01227 273370 📠 01227 262314
dir: *3.5m W of Whitstable*

Reached via a winding lane across open marshland from Whitstable, and tucked beneath the sea wall, the Sportsman may seem an unlikely place to find such good food. The rustic yet comfortable interior, with its wooden floors, stripped pine furniture and interesting collection of prints has a warm and welcoming feel. The full range of Shepherd Neame ales is served, including seasonal brews, and there is an excellent wine list. Remember that food is not served on Sunday evenings or Mondays, or you could be disappointed. The daily menu is based on local produce, with fish dishes steamed wild sea bass with a mussel pistou, or seared Thornback ray with cockles, sherry vinegar and brown butter. Starters also feature lots of seafood, typically rock oysters and hot chorizo. Amongst the mains is braised shoulder of Monkshill Farm lamb and mint sauce.

Open 12-3 6-11 Closed: 25 Dec **Bar Meals** L served Tue-Sat 12-2 (Sun 12-3) D served Tue-Sat 7-9 **Restaurant** L served Tue-Sat 12-2 (12-3 Sun) D served Tue-Sat 7-9 Av 3 course à la carte £26 Shepherd Neame Shepherd Neame Late Red, Spitfire, Master Brew, Porter. 8 **Facilities** Garden Dogs allowed Parking

WYE MAP 07 TR04

The New Flying Horse

Upper Bridge St TN25 5AN
☎ 01233 812297 📠 01233 813487
e-mail: newflyhorse@shepherd-neame.co.uk

This 17th-century posting house retains much of its original character after being refurbished. Winter log fires warm the bar and dining area, where you'll find a good selection of meals. In warmer weather, customers can wine and dine in the prize-winning garden, which was featured at the 2005 Chelsea Flower Show. Expect a wide range of seasonal specials, classic dishes and vegetarian options, produced from the finest local ingredients.

Open 11-11 (Closed pm on w/days Oct-May) **Bar Meals** L served all week 12-2 D served all week 6-9 Av main course £9.95 **Restaurant** L served all week 12-2.30 D served all week 6-9 Shepherd Neame Master Brew Spitfire, Plus guests. 8 **Facilities** Garden Dogs allowed Play Area **Rooms** 9 bedrooms en suite S£55 D£80 (♦♦♦♦ GA)

The Farmhouse

A modern gastro-pub, The Farmhouse occupies a handsome Elizabethan property at the heart of the village of West Malling. The pub has served travellers and locals alike for many a year, and has a relaxing atmosphere with a stylish bar and two dining areas: the first is warm and airy and the second has authentic high ceilings and distinctive décor.

These can also be made available for private dining and special occasions. Outside there is a spacious walled garden with an area of decking overlooking 15th-century stone-built barns. Speciality drinks, along with the real beers and a good selection of wines by the glass, include a good choice of organic fruit juices and malt whiskies. Menus are constantly changing and all the dishes are freshly cooked and based on locally sourced produce. Alongside the deli board selection (cheese, fish, antipasti, charcuterie), there are stone-baked pizzas, toasted paninis and salads (chicken Caesar, ocean, wood pigeon and roquefort). Starters range from home-made soup with crusty bread, to the chef's signature dish of fresh scallops. Main courses follow through with seared fillet of sea bass with sweet potato mash, leek fondue and saffron rice; or traditionally reared Kentish Limousin beef with black pepper, blue cheese or garlic butter sauce. Bar food is available all day, and themed evenings are a feature throughout the year. The 15th-century barn at the rear of the pub has recently been transformed into a deli/farmers' market. A wide selection of quality delicatessen goods, fresh local fruits and vegetables is offered along with organic foods and meat.

MAP 06 TQ65
97 The High St ME19 6NA
☎ 01732 843257
01622 851881
e-mail: info@thefarmhouse.biz
dir: *M20 junct 4, S on A228. Right to West Malling. Pub in village centre*

Open 11–11 (Sun 11–10.30)
Bar Meals L served all week 12–9.30 D served all week 12–9.30 (Sun 12–9.30) Av main course £10
Restaurant L served all week 12–9.30 D served all week 12–9.30 (Sun 12–9.30) Av 3 course à la carte £21 Av 2 course fixed price £11.50
Free House
Harveys, Guinness, Leffe, Youngs & St Miguel. 13
Facilities Children's licence Garden Parking

LANCASHIRE

ASHALL EAVES MAP 18 SD64

Pick of the Pubs

'he Red Pump Inn NEW

:litheroe Rd BB7 3DA

☎ 01254 826227 📠 01254 826750

-**mail:** info@theredpumpinn.co.uk

ir: *3m from Clitheroe, NW, follow 'Whitewell, Trough of owland & Bashall Eaves' signs.*

See Pick of the Pubs on page 329

LSBORROW MAP 18 SD53

vd Nell's Tavern

y's Thatched Hamlet, Canal Side PR3 0RS

01995 640010 📠 01995 640141

iail: info@guysthatchedhamlet.com

M6 junct 32 N on A6. 5m signs to Guy's Thatched Hamlet

Wilkinson family have owned and run Guy's Thatched Hamlet over twenty years, and this country-style tavern forms part of entertainment complex beside the Lancaster Canal, alongside ues for craft shopping, accommodation and dancing. All-day fare pified by steamed chicken, leek and mushroom pie; lamb cutlets; ion salad; and Caesar style smoked chicken baguette. 'Sweet tooth :ials' include apple pie and lemon crisp.

n 9–3am Closed: 25 Dec **Bar Meals** L served all week 11–9 D served eek 11–9 Av main course £6.50 **Restaurant** L served all week 12–2.30 rved all week 5.30–10.30 (Sat 12–1am, Sun 12–10.30) Av 3 course à la £10.50 Av 2 course fixed price £7.25 Free House Boddingtons r, Jennings Bitter, Copper Dragon, Black Sheep. 40 **Facilities** Garden allowed Parking Play Area

See advert on this page

BLACKBURN MAP 18 SD62

Pick of the Pubs

The Millstone at Mellor ★★ HL

Church Ln, Mellor BB2 7JR

☎ 01254 813333 📠 01254 812628

e-mail: info@millstonehotel.com

dir: *M6 junct 31, A59 towards Clitheroe, past British Aerospace. Right at rdbt signed Blackburn/Mellor. Next rdbt 2nd left, top of hill on right*

Set in the heart of the glorious Ribble Valley, the Millstone was once a 17th-century tithe barn. The name derives from the circular grinding stone incorporated in the façade. This old inn was the original flagship of Daniel Thwaites' Blackburn brewery, and from 1948 to 1971 the pumps were manned by former England cricket legend Big Jim Smith. Inside, the original oak beams and linenfold panelling set the scene for a range of good value bar and restaurant dishes. For lunch, try crispy duck spring rolls, followed by the Millstone fish pie. From the evening à la carte, tuck into chicken and pork rillette, with a main course of roast rack of Pendle spring lamb and fondant potatoes. Compote of new

CONTINUED

England

BLACKBURN continued

season rhubarb makes for an elegant finish, though there are 23 en suite bedrooms should you not feel inclined to stagger home.

The Millstone at Mellor

Open 11–11 (Fri–Sat 11–12, Sun 12–10.30) **Bar Meals** L served all week 12–9.30 D served all week 12–9.30 (Sun 12–9) **Restaurant** L served all week 12–2.15 D served all week 6.30–9.30 (Sun 12–9) Shire Hotels Warsteiner, Lancaster Bomber, Thwaites Original Cash Bitter. 12 **Facilities** Parking **Rooms** 23 bedrooms en suite S£71 D£99

BLACKO MAP 18 SD84

Moorcock Inn

Gisburn Rd BB9 6NG ☎ 01282 614186 01282 614186
e-mail: boo@patterson1047.freeserve.co.uk
dir: *M65 junct 13, A682 to Blacko*

Family-run country inn with traditional log fires and good views towards the Pendle Way, ideally placed for non-motorway travel to the Lakes and the Yorkshire Dales. Home-cooked meals are a speciality, with a wide choice including salads and sandwiches, and vegetarian and children's meals. Tasty starters like cheesy mushrooms, and garlic prawns are followed by lasagne, various steak choices, pork in orange and cider, and trout grilled with lemon and herb butter.

Open 12–2 6–9 (Sat all day, Sun 6–8) **Bar Meals** L served all week 12–2 D served Tue–Sun 6–9.30 (Sun 12–7.30) **Restaurant** L served all week 12–2.30 D served Tue–Sun 6–9 (Sun 12–6) Thwaites Thwaites, Best Bitter, Smooth, Warfsteiner. **Facilities** Garden Parking

CARNFORTH MAP 18 SD

Old Station Inn

Station Ln, Burton LA6 1HR
☎ 01524 781225 01524 782662
e-mail: willparks@hotmail.co.uk
dir: *M6 to A6 signed Milnthorpe (Kendal), 3m before Milntho turn right signed Burton/Holme*

Built in 1860 to serve the nearby mainline railway, this Victorian fre house was formerly the Station Hotel. Seafood is a speciality, and a single menu is served in the bar and non-smoking restaurant. Choi include grilled mackerel with garlic butter; and seared marlin with saffron rice and chargrilled peppers.

Open 12–11 **Bar Meals** L served all week 12–9 D served all week 12– (Sun 12–8) Av main course £10 **Restaurant** L served all week 12–9 D served all week 12–9 (Sun 12–8) Av 3 course à la carte £20 Av 2 cour fixed price £11.95 Free House Jennings, Lancaster Brewery & 4 G Ales. **Facilities** Garden Dogs allowed Parking Play Area

CATFORTH MAP 18 SI

The Running Pump NEW

Catforth Rd PR4 0HH ☎ 01772 690265
e-mail: twochefs@therunningpump.co.uk
dir: *M6 junct 32 onto A6 at Broughton B5269*

Taking its name from one of the many natural springs in the area, Running Pump was built as cottages for agricultural workers. In its long, beamed bar and adjacent snug, both with log fires, snacks ar available, while in the restaurant a modern British carte offers pan-turkey escalope on mash with cranberry sauce; fillet of beef on but mash with mushroom and brandy cream sauce; and grilled sea ba on prawn risotto.

Open 11–12 **Bar Meals** L served Tue–Sat 12–2.30 D served Tue–Sat 6–9.30 (Sun 12–9) **Restaurant** L served Tue–Sat 12–2 D served Tue–S 6–9.30 (Sun 12–8.30) Av 3 course à la carte £22.50 Av 4 course fixed pr £11.25 Robinsons Robinsons, Unicorn Best Bitter, Guest Ales, Old (at Christmas). **Facilities** Parking

CHIPPING MAP 18 SI

Dog & Partridge

Hesketh Ln PR3 2TH ☎ 01995 61201 01995 61446
dir: *M6 junct 31A, follow Longbridge signs. At Longbridge lef 1st rbdt, straight on at next 3 rdbts. At Alston Arms turn right. pub on right*

Dating back to 1515, this pleasantly modernised rural pub in the Ri Valley enjoys delightful views of the surrounding fells. The barn ha been transformed into a welcoming dining area, where home-mac food on the comprehensive bar snack menu is backed by a special board offering the likes of hot potted shrimps with toast; tiger praw in filo with sweet and sour dip; roast leg of baby lamb; and pan-fri cod with potato cake.

Open 11.45–3 6.45–11 (Sun 11.45–10.30) **Bar Meals** L served Tue–S 12–1.45 **Restaurant** L served Tue–Sun 12–1.30 D served Tue–Sun 7–9 (Sun 12–8.30) Av 3 course à la carte £22 Av 4 course fixed price £15.75 Free House Carlsberg-Tetley. **Facilities** Parking

The Red Pump Inn

hree miles from Clitheroe, a million miles from hectic' is the promise of this friendly old inn. ·t in the historic hamlet of Bashall Eaves and surrounded by working farms, there are superb ews of the glorious Ribble Valley in every direction.

ıe pub was originally built in '56, and has been lovingly stored by new owners Jon and artina Myerscough. They have t to meet the ghost that reputedly .ards an ancient stone protecting e inn from the Pendle witches. ıt such is their devotion to eating a warm and welcoming ıditional rural inn that in barely o years they have built a loyal .se of locals and returning visitors. rinking and eating areas divide to a bar, a snug with real fire, arge dining room and a rather ecial coach house with cafe and li. Local, regional and national sk-conditioned ales make this a ıe beer-lover's paradise; wines old d new suit every pocket and taste, ith more than ten served by the ass. The menu makes impressive se of local produce, including hare, pheasant, venison, and partridge. Extra-matured local beef comes into its own on weekly steak nights, and Fridays see a celebration of fish and seafood in dishes such as potted crayfish tails; calamari with aïoli; and fresh hake, seabass and snapper feature regularly. Bread and preserves are home made, herbs come from the garden, and a vegetable plot is underway that will eventually make the restaurant self-sufficient. Examples of the hearty country style include confit of rabbit with red onion marmalade; butter roasted partridge; and slow-roast pork belly with mustard mash and apple cabbage. Children's portions are equally nutritious, chosen from the adults' seasonal menu. Three en suite bedrooms are available if you fancy a spot of fishing on the well-stocked River Hodder.

NEW

MAP 18 SD64

Clitheroe Rd BB7 3DA

☎ 01254 826227

🖷 01254 826750

e-mail: info@theredpumpinn.co.uk

dir: *3m from Clitheroe, NW, follow 'Whitewell, Trough of Bowland & Bashall Eaves' signs.*

Open 12-2.30 6-11 (Sun 12-9.30, BH 12-5)

Bar Meals L served all week 12-2 D served all week 6-9 (Sun 12-7) Av main course £9

Restaurant L served all week 12-2 D served all week 6-9 (Sun 12-7) Av 3 course à la carte £17

Free House

Bowland Brewery, Red Pump Ale. 10

Facilities Garden Parking

Rooms 3 bedrooms en suite S£49 D£65 (★★★★ GA)

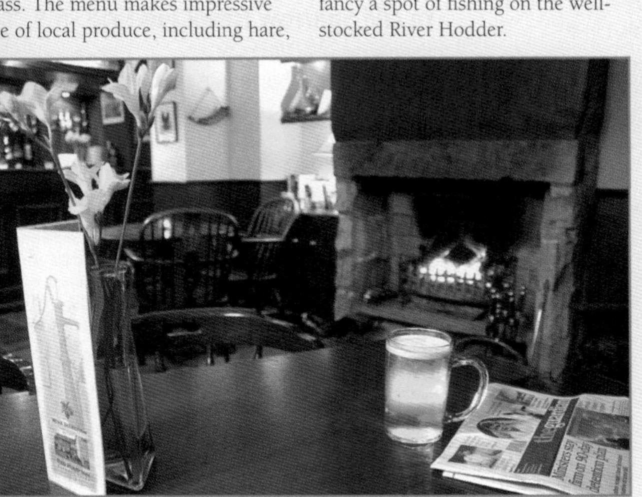

CLITHEROE MAP 18 SD74

Pick of the Pubs

The Assheton Arms

Downham BB7 4BJ ☎ 01200 441227 01200 440581
e-mail: asshetonarms@aol.com
dir: *From A59 to Chatburn, then follow Downham signs*

The inn is named after Lord Clitheroe's family (they own the whole village) though it may be better known to viewers of the BBC serial *Born and Bred* as The Signalman's Arms. The sign depicts an Assheton ancestor gripping a scythe in an ill-fated attempt to evade Royalist troops during the English Civil War. Present-day visitors will find the single bar and sectioned rooms furnished with solid oak tables, wingback settees, the original stone fireplace, and a large blackboard listing the range of daily food on offer. An interesting selection of small dishes includes deep-fried cheddar and brie with gooseberry sauce; or cold potted Morecambe Bay shrimp. Main course choices range from Pernod-fried scampi, or slow roasted lamb shank, to halibut steak mornay, or cauliflower and mushroom provençale. The pub is well placed for a moorland walk up Pendle Hill, which looms over the village.

Open 12-3 7-11 (Sun all day) **Bar Meals** L served all week 12-2 D served all week 7-10 (Sun 12-9) Av main course £9.50 Free House Lancaster Bomber, Thwaites bitter, Daniels Smooth. 18 **Facilities** Dogs allowed Parking

The Shireburn Arms ★★★ HL

Whalley Rd, Hurst Green BB7 9QJ
☎ 01254 826518 01254 826208
e-mail: sales@shireburnarmshotel.com
web: www.shireburnarmshotel.com
dir: *Telephone for directions*

A privately run, 17th-century inn with super views, in the heart of the Ribble Valley. *Lord of the Rings* author J R R Tolkien used to drink here when visiting his son at Stonyhurst College nearby. The menu ranges from sandwiches and salads to steak and kidney pudding; roast sirloin of beef with Yorkshire pudding; vegetable lasagne; and poached salmon supreme. A conservatory links the restaurant with the patio and gardens.

The Shireburn Ar

Open 11–11 **Bar Meals** L served all week 12–2 D served all week 5.30–9.30 (Sun 12–9) **Restaurant** L served all week 12–2 D served all week 5.30–9.30 (Sun 12–9) Free House Scottish Courage Theakst Best Bitter, Mild & Guest Ales. 10 **Facilities** Garden Dogs allowed Parking Play Area **Rooms** 22 bedrooms en suite S£50 D£75

FENCE MAP 18 SD

Fence Gate Inn

Wheatley Lane Rd BB12 9EE
☎ 01282 618101 01282 615432
e-mail: info@fencegate.co.uk
dir: *From M65 junct 13 towards Clayton-le-Moors, 1.5m, pub back on right opposite T-junct for Burnley*

An extensive property, the Fence Gate Inn was originally a collectior point for cotton delivered by barge and distributed to surrounding cottages to be spun into cloth. Food is served both in the bar and the Topiary Brasserie. Highlights are a selection of sausages starring Lancashire's champion leek and black pudding with a hint of sage. There is a good choice of pasta.

Open 12–11 (Fri 12–12, Sat 12–1) **Bar Meals** L served all week 12–2.30 D served all week 6.30–9.30 (Sat 6.30–8 Sun 6–8.30) **Restaurant** L serv all week 12–2.30 D served all week 6.30–9.30 Free House Theakst Directors, Deuchers. 16 **Facilities** Garden Parking

Ye Old Sparrow Hawk Inn NEW

Wheatley Lane Rd BB12 9QG
☎ 01282 603034 01282 603035
e-mail: mail@yeoldsparrowhawk.co.uk
dir: *M65 junct 13, A6068, at rdbt take 1st exit 0.25m. Turn righ onto Carr Hall Rd, at top turn left 0.25m, pub on right*

Sipping a pint outside the half-timbered Sparrowhawk on a summer evening is one of life's great pleasures. The pub stands at the gatew to Pendle Forest, famous for its witches, but here, you'll find friendly service and stylish surroundings. The classically trained chefs work w locally sourced fresh ingredients to create menus that include fish p with seasonal greens and bacon lardoons; sausages with bubble an squeak; and chargrilled tuna with roasted Mediterranean vegetables

Open 12–11 **Bar Meals** L served all week 12–2.30 D served all week 5–9.30 (Sat 12–9.30, Sun 12–8) Av main course £9.50
Restaurant L served all week 12–2.30 D served all week 5–9 (Sat 12–9. Sun 12–8) Thwaites Cask, Draight Bass, Moorhouses Blonde Witch, B Sheep Best. 13 **Facilities** Garden Dogs allowed Parking

)RTON MAP 18 SD45

Pick of the Pubs

ʈhe Bay Horse Inn

.A2 0HR ☎ 01524 791204 📠 01524 791204
ɛ-mail: bayhorseinfo@aol.com
dir: *1m S from M6 junct 33*

'he quirky history of this inn recounts how it gave its name in he 19th century to the local railway station and surrounding rea, even though no settlement actually existed. And how it was ot this inn, but another one which had been called the Rising un. Suffice to say that today the pub is beautifully situated and raditional in style, with a warm welcome, real cask beers and a ;ood selection of malt whiskies. It also specialises in simple, fresh nd imaginative dishes from an award-winning chef who is wholly elf-taught. Craig Wilkinson exercises his culinary skills on the very ɔest of local ingredients, including an excellent choice of fresh fish: he seafood platter may cover smoked salmon, herring, mussels, ɔrawns and anchovies; daily specials may feature sea bass fillet, ıalibut or monkfish. A typical three-course choice could be ;moked Lancashire duck Caesar salad, followed by braised shank ɔf Cumbrian lamb, and finishing with sticky toffee pudding.

Dpen 12-3 6.30-11 (Sun 12-11) **Bar Meals** L served Wed-Sat 2-1.45 D served Wed-Sat 7-9.15 (Sun 12-3, 6.30-8.30) Av main :ourse £14.95 **Restaurant** L served Wed-Sun 12-1.45 D served Ved-Sat 7-9.15 (Sun 12-3, 6.30-8.30) Av 3 course à la carte £25 Av 3 course fixed price £14.50 Thwaites Lancaster Bomber, Moorhouses Pendle Witch, Masham Brewery & Black Sheep. 11 **Facilities** Garden Parking

OOSNARGH MAP 18 SD53

he Bushell's Arms

ıurch Ln PR3 2BH ☎ 01772 865235 📠 01772 865235
r: *Take A6 N to Garstang, right onto Whittingham Lane, after ı left into Church Lane. Pub on right of village green*

Bushell was a philanthropic Georgian who built not just a hospital his villagers but this pub too, opposite the village green and church; eems that patients were entitled to a daily pint. Now under new ınagement, it has transmogrified to a Spanish bar and restaurant, :h a menu devoted entirely to reasonably-priced tapas. According to ur hunger, choose from a simple dish of olives to plates of fajitas or afood paella.

en 12-2 6-11 (Fri-Sat 6-1am, Sun 6-10.30) **Bar Meals** L served ın-Sun 12-2 **Restaurant** L served all week 12-2 D served all week 9.45 Enterprise Inns Black Sheep, Tetleys Extra Cold. 12 **cilities** Children's licence Garden Parking

ASLINGDEN MAP 15 SD72

armers Glory

ɔundhill Rd BB4 5TU ☎ 01706 215748 📠 01706 215748
r: *On A667, 8m from Blackburn, Burnley & Bury, 1.5m from 56*

ɔne-built 300-year-old pub situated high above Haslingden on the ge of the Pennines. Formerly a coaching inn on the ancient route to ıalley Abbey, it now offers locals and modern A667 travellers a wide-ıging traditional pub menu of steaks, roasts, seafood, pizzas, pasta, curries and sandwiches. Entertainment is held every Wednesday and Friday, and a large beer garden with ornamental fishpond.

Open 12-3 6.30-12.30 **Bar Meals** L served all week 12-2.30 D served all week 6.30-9.30 **Restaurant** L served all week 12-2.30 D served all week 6.30-9.30 Punch Taverns Carlsberg-Tetley Tetley Bitter, Lees Speckled hen, Jennings. **Facilities** Garden Parking

HESKIN GREEN MAP 15 SD51

Farmers Arms

85 Wood Ln PR7 5NP ☎ 01257 451276 📠 01257 453958
e-mail: andy@farmersarms.co.uk
dir: *On B5250 between M6 & Eccleston*

Long, creeper-covered country inn with two cosy bars decorated with old pictures and farming memorabilia. Once known as the Pleasant Retreat, this is a family-run pub proud to offer a warm welcome and a traditional theme. Typical dishes include steak pie, fresh salmon with prawns and mushroom, rack of lamb, and chicken curry.

Open 12-11 (Sun 12-10.30) **Bar Meals** L served all week 12-9.30 D served all week Av main course £6 **Restaurant** L served all week 12-9.30 D served all week Enterprise Inns Timothy Taylor Landlord, Pedigree, Black Sheep, Interbrew Boddingtons. 7 **Facilities** Garden Dogs allowed Parking Play Area

HEST BANK MAP 18 SD46

Hest Bank Hotel

2 Hest Bank Ln LA2 6DN
☎ 01524 824339 📠 01524 824948
e-mail: hestbankhotel@hotmail.com
dir: *From Lancaster take A6 N, after 2m left to Hest Bank*

Comedian Eric Morecambe used to drink at this canalside former coaching inn, first licensed in 1554. Awash with history and 'many happy ghosts', it now offers cask ales and a wide selection of meals all day, with local suppliers playing an important role in maintaining food quality. The good-value menu – only a couple of steak dishes break the £10 mark – may range from a large pot of Bantry Bay mussels to the pub's own lamb hotpot made to a traditional recipe.

Open 11.30-11 (Sun 11.30-10.30) Rest: 25 Dec no food **Bar Meals** L served all week 12-9 D served all week **Restaurant** L served all week 12-9 D served all week Av 3 course à la carte £12 Av 2 course fixed price £6.95 Punch Taverns Interbrew Boddingtons, Timothy Taylor Landlord, Deuchars IPA, Blacksheep Bitter & Guest beers. 7 **Facilities** Garden Parking

LANCASTER MAP 18 SD46

The Stork Inn

Conder Green LA2 0AN ☎ 01524 751234 📠 01524 752660
e-mail: the.stork@virgin.net
dir: *M6 junct 33 take A6. Left at Galgate & next left to Conder Green*

White-painted coaching inn spread along the banks of the Conder Estuary, with a colourful 300-year history that includes several name changes. The quaint sea port of Glasson Dock is a short walk along the Lancashire Coastal Way, and the Lake District is easily

CONTINUED

England

LANCASTER continued

accessible. Seasonal specialities join home-cooked food like steak pie, locally-smoked haddock, salmon fillet with bonne femme sauce, and Cumberland sausage with onion gravy and mashed potatoes.

Open 11–11 (Sun 12–10.30) **Bar Meals** L served all week 12–3 D served all week 6–9 Av main course £6.95 **Restaurant** L served all week 12–2.30 D served all week 6–9 Free House Boddingtons, Pedigree, Black Sheep, Guest ales. **Facilities** Garden Dogs allowed Parking Play Area

The Sun Hotel and Bar

LA1 1ET ☎ 01524 66006 01524 66397

e-mail: info@thesunhotelandbar.co.uk

dir: *6m from junct 33 of M6*

The original inn was built in the 1600s where the medieval Stoop Hall once stood. Now Lancaster's oldest licensed premises, the Sun's popular bar serves real ales from Lancaster Brewery, while its seasonal menu is backed up by daily specials. Ingredients are largely sourced locally, so you may know the provenance of your Gloucester Old Spot pork, your pan-fried salmon, and your wild mushroom, asparagus and blue cheese risotto. The cheese selection is truly extensive.

Open 10–1am **Bar Meals** L served all week 12.30–3.30 D served none Av main course £8 Thwaites Lancaster Bomber, Leifmans Frambozen, Lancaster Duchy, Lancaster Blonde. 24 **Facilities** Garden **Rooms** 15 bedrooms en suite S£60 D£60 (★★★★ GA)

Pick of the Pubs

The Waterwitch

The Tow Path, Aldcliffe Rd LA1 1SU

☎ 01524 63828 01524 34535

e-mail: thewaterwitch@mitchellsinns.co.uk

dir: *6m from junct 33 of M6*

The Waterwitch takes its name from three longboats that worked the adjacent Lancaster canal in the late 18th century. It occupies an old stables, tastefully converted to retain original features such as stone walls and interior slab floors. In just a few years the pub has acquired celebrity status and a clutch of awards, yet it still remains a genuine pub with the broad appeal of a wine bar and restaurant. It is noted for its ever-changing selection of fine cask-conditioned real ales, impressive wine list and guest cheeses. The talented team of chefs work with locally-sourced produce including fish that arrives daily from Fleetwood harbour. Traditional, classical and international influences combine on menus that might include king prawns with a Thai stir fry; Cumberland sausages on herb mash with red wine jus; or lamb steak with rosemary, mint and mustard on couscous.

Open 10–12 **Bar Meals** L served all week 12–3 D served all week 5–9 (Sun 12–5 6–9) Av main course £12.95 **Restaurant** L served all week 12–3 D served all week 5–9.30 (Sun 12–5, 6–9) Av 3 course à la carte £25 Thwaites Lancaster Bomber, Warsteiner, Moorhouse Ales, Lancaster Brewery Bitters. 27 **Facilities** Garden

Ye Olde John O'Gaunt NEW

53 Market St LA1 1JG ☎ 01524 65357 01524 65357

dir: *M6 junct 33 A6 towards Lancaster. Right at 7th set of lights Pub on right of Market St in 50yds*

Quaint, small and very old, this building was originally built for Lancaster's chief constable in 1725 but has been a pub since 1850. If you love live music, real ale or whisky this place is probably hard to beat, with its seven live music sessions a week, excellent selection of ales and up to 100 malts. Home-made food could include cullen skin chilli con carne; and tuna pasta.

Open 11–11 (Fri–Sat 11–11.30) **Bar Meals** L served Mon–Sat 11.30–2.30 Punch Taverns Boddingtons, Greene King Abbot, Timothy Taylor Landlord, Deuchars. 15 **Facilities** Children's licence Garden Dogs allowed **Notes**

PARBOLD MAP 15 SD4

Pick of the Pubs

The Eagle & Child

Maltkiln Ln L40 3SG ☎ 01257 462297 01257 464718

dir: *3m from M6 junct 27. Over Parbold Hill, follow signs for Bispham Green on right*

Many years ago, legend has it, the local landowner Lord Derby and his wife were childless, but he fathered a child following an illicit liaison with a girl from the village. The child was placed in an eagle's nest so that when the lord and his wife were out walking they happened to hear the child cry. The lady insisted that the little boy was a gift from God, so they took him home and reared him as their son. Hence the pub's name (known locally as the Bird and Bastard). The pub maintains its traditional atmosphere and offers five regularly changing guest ales and a beer festival every May. All the food is made on the premises with ingredients from local suppliers. A good choice of dishes includes grilled sea bass with crabmeat and oriental vegetables; medallions of beef fillet with pepper sauce, and a vegetarian five-bean chilli and rice.

Open 12–3 5.30–11 (Sun 12–10.30) **Bar Meals** L served all week 12–2 D served all week 6–8.30 (Sun 12–8.30, Fri–Sat 6–9) Av main course £12 **Restaurant** L served all week 12–2 D served all week 6–8.30 (Fri–Sat 6–9, Sun 12–8.30) Av 3 course à la carte £19 Free House Moorhouses Black Cat, Thwaites Bitter, 5 Guest beers. 6 **Facilities** Garden Dogs allowed Parking

artford Country Inn & Hotel

former farmhouse, definitely three and possibly even four hundred years old. Today it is a 'easantly rambling, three-storey inn standing sentinel by the 40p toll bridge over the tidal River 'yre, a few miles from its meeting with the Irish Sea.

ıis is the Fylde, a rich green plain ınning from the coast towards e foothills of the Pennines, and a orld apart from brash Blackpool mere 15 minutes' drive to the uth. In the capable hands of ndrew and Tracy Mellodew, the artford has won many awards. ndrew was running the pub when, 7 years ago, Tracy, then a young, ıpecunious student, got a job ehind the bar. On mentioning it to er father she discovered that her 'eat-grandfather had once been its ndlord. The beams in the main -shaped bar are decorated with olished horse brasses; leading f are table-filled alcoves, while ore tables are upstairs around ıe gallery. The pub's own Hart rewery out the back produces up) 30 different real ales, depending n the season, among them Dishie Debbie and what sounds like her complete antithesis, Ice Maiden. An all-embracing bar/restaurant menu includes sandwiches, hot baguettes, jacket potatoes, pizzas and salads, as well as lamb Henry; red snapper; rib-eye steak; turkey pie and pork pie platter; and mushroom and red pepper stroganoff. Check out the frequently updated specials board for curries, moussaka, sea bass, and lemon sole with prawns. Regular desserts include chocolate fudge cake, apple pie and pavlovas. Eat outside overlooking the river, along 1.5 miles of which the Cartford owns exclusive fishing rights. The ghost of George, a sheep-rustler allegedly hanged in the pub, has lain low for some years, but a former barmaid remembers how he used to nudge her, although she never saw him.

MAP 18 SD52
Little Eccleston PR3 0YP
☎ 01995 670166
🖷 01995 671785
e-mail: cartfordhotel@tiscali.co.uk

Open 12–3 6.30–11 Closed: Dec 25
Bar Meals L served Mon–Sat 12–2 D served all week 6.30–9.30 Av main course £5.50
Restaurant L served 12–2 D served 6.30–9.30
Free House
Hart Beers, Fullers London Pride, Moorhouse, Guest ales.
Facilities Dogs allowed Parking Play Area
Rooms 6 bedrooms en suite S£36.95 D£48.95 (★★★ INN)

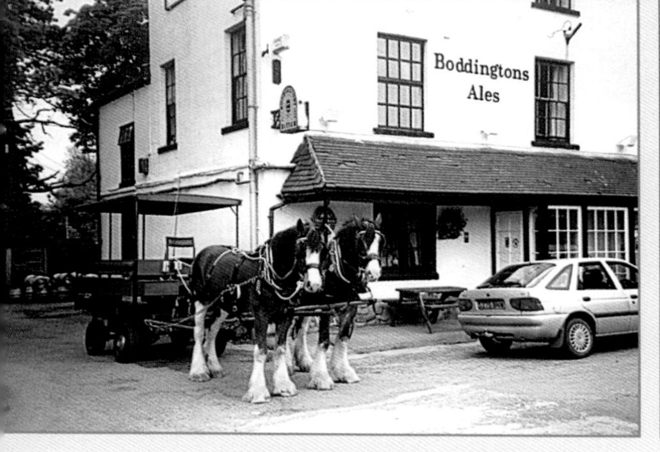

England

PRESTON MAP 18 SD52

Pick of the Pubs

Cartford Country Inn & Hotel 🍷

Little Eccleston PR3 0YP
☎ 01995 670166 📠 01995 671785
e-mail: cartfordhotel@tiscali.co.uk

See Pick of the Pubs on page 333

RAWTENSTALL MAP 15 SD82

The Boars Head NEW

69 Church St, Newchurch BB4 9EH ☎ 01706 214687

dir: *From Rawtenstall right at lights onto Newchurch Rd, past market 1.5m. Pub on right set back behind green*

Dating from 1674 and located on one of the oldest streets in Newchurch, The Boar's Head has been refurbished in a style befitting its venerable age. Expect open fires, real ales and magnificent views of the Rossendale valley from the beer garden. In summer you could use the pub's own bowling green – balls are kept behind the bar. Food-wise, don't miss the chunky home-made chips. Other treats might include Lancashire hotpot or home-made lamb curry.

Open 4–12 (Fri–Sun 12–1) **Bar Meals** L served Fri–Sun 12–2 D served all week 4–8 Av main course £6 Punch Taverns Black Sheep Best Bitter, Old Speckled Hen, Hoegarden White Beer, Tetleys Mild. **Facilities** Children's licence Garden Parking

RIBCHESTER MAP 18 SD63

The White Bull 🍷

Church St PR3 3XP ☎ 01254 878303
e-mail: wbribchester@btinternet.com

dir: *Exit M6 junct 29, A59 towards Clitheroe, left at lights onto B6245, 2nd left in Ribchester.*

Grade II listed courthouse in the Roman town of Ribchester, built in 1707 using four Roman columns as front porch pillars. The former Roman bathhouse can be seen from the beer garden. Cask beers in the lounge and bars accompany a comprehensive selection of traditional pub food supplemented by regularly changing specials, such as fillet steak Rossini, and supreme of chicken filled with chorizo sausage and candied apricot.

Open 12 –11 **Bar Meals** L served all week 12–9 D served all week 12–9 (Sun 12–8) Av main course £9.50 **Restaurant** L served all week 12–9 D served all week 12–9 (Sun 12–8) Av 3 course à la carte £15 Enterprise Inns Taylors Landlord, Boddingtons Bitter, Black Sheep Best, Abbots Ale. 🍷 10 **Facilities** Garden Parking

SAWLEY MAP 18 SD7

The Spread Eagle NEW 🍷

BB7 4NH ☎ 01200 441202 📠 01200 441973

dir: *Off A159 between Clitheroe & Skipton, N of Sawley*

Great food and beautiful views are just two good reasons to visit this whitewashed pub on the banks of the river Ribble. The 17th-century bar provides oak beams, a log fire and over 50 malt whiskies. The modern dining rooms offer perhaps pan-fried sea bass with a buttere pea stock and a gnocchi of broad beans; or roast fillet of pork with ar apple purée, pancetta and piccalilli velouté.

Open 12–2 6–9 Closed: 1st wk in Jan **Bar Meals** L served Tue–Sat 12–2 **Restaurant** L served Tue–Sun 12–2 D served Tue–Sat 6–8.45 Av 3 course à la carte £21 Av 3 course fixed price £18.50 Free House Sawley's Drunken Duck, Black Sheep, Hoegarrden. 🍷 16 **Facilities** Garden Parkir

SLAIDBURN MAP 18 SD7

Hark to Bounty Inn 🍷

Townend BB7 3EP ☎ 01200 446246 📠 01200 446361
e-mail: manager@hark-to-bounty.co.uk

dir: *From M6 junct 31 take A59 to Clitheroe then B6478, throug Waddington, Newton, onto Slaidburn*

A family-run 13th-century inn known as The Dog until 1875 when Bounty, the local squire's favourite hound, disturbed a post-hunt drinking session with its loud baying. The squire's vocal response obviously made a lasting impact. View the ancient courtroom, last used in 1937. The current family of landlords have been here some 25 years, and the kitchen offers the likes of black pudding with branc and stilton; local organic pork with mustard and brown sugar; Bowla lamb shoulder with root vegetable and redcurrant gravy; or smoked mackerel kedgeree.

Open 11–11 **Bar Meals** L served all week 12–2 D served all week 6–9 (S 12–8) Av main course £9 **Restaurant** L served Tue–Sun 12–2 D served Tue–Sat 6–9 (Sunday 12–9) Scottish Courage Theakston Old Pecul Theakstons Bitter, Archers Best, Moorhouses. 🍷 8 **Facilities** Children's licence Garden Dogs allowed Parking

Freemasons Arms

you're asking for directions to this unpretentious pub below Pendle Hill, you may be told that 's tucked away down a ginnel – for the benefit of outsiders, that's a passageway between the ɔuses.

ıring its two hundred years or ore of existence monks from :arby Whalley Abbey have lived :re, and freemasons used to meet secret here, hence the name. nce you've found it you'll be glad, :cause today it has a spacious ır area, a rather refined dining om upstairs and an enthusiastic :oprietor, Ian Martin, who insists ı carefully sourced, seasonal food probably the principal reason for ; good local reputation. Starters : lighter dishes can include risotto ıke with spiced tomato sauce and ɔrgonzola cream; large prawns ith pancetta and tomato and ɔdka dressing; chicken ravioli with ild mushroom sauce; and seared ng scallops with roast beetroot. ıain courses include chargrilled ɔwland pork chop; slow roast shoulder of lamb; and Goosnargh duck confit with sautéed artichokes. There's always a good choice of fish, perhaps seafood gratin; grilled salmon with creamed leeks and parsley sauce; brochette of monkfish and king scallops with potato purée; sea bass with sautéed pak choi and red wine and ginger sauce; or sole goujons with lemon, garlic and parsley mayonnaise. Beers are mainly locally brewed, including Bowland's Hen Harrier, Moorhouse's Best Bitter, and Bank Top's Flat Cap. Quite remarkable, however, is the wine list containing over 500 bins, and a large selection of vintage Armagnacs, Cognacs and malt whiskies. There is seating outside, but no garden as such, although the surrounding Ribble Valley scenery is superb and well worth exploring.

MAP 18 SD73
8 Vicarage Fold, Wiswell BB7 9DF
☎ 01254 822218
e-mail: freemasons@wiswell.co.uk
dir: *From A59, onto A671, Wiswell is 1st left*

Open 12-3 6-11 Closed: 25-26 Dec, 1-2 Jan
Bar Meals L served Wed-Sun 12-2 D served Wed-Sun 6-9.30 (Sun 12-8) Av main course £9
Restaurant L served Wed-Sun 12-2 D served Wed-Sun 6-9.30 (Sun 12-8) Av 3 course à la carte £25 Av 2 course fixed price £11.95
Free House
Bowland Brewery Hen Harrier, Black Sheep Bitter, Moorhouse Pride of Pendle, Guinness. 🍷 15

The Three Fishes

The Three Fishes, a public house throughout its 400 years of existence, was supposedly named after the 'three fishes pendant' in the coat of arms of John Paslew, last abbot of nearby Whalley Abbey. Look above the entrance to see them carved in stone.

They are said to represent the three rivers – Hodder, Calder and Ribble – that meet within the parish. The 21st-century interior very much respects the past (certainly no one was daft enough to strip out the big open fires). The strength of the menu of regional and British classics comes from using Lancashire and the North West's finest produce, supplied by 'local food heroes' whose contributions are honoured around the walls. Local names abound on the menu: among the starters, for instance, are Andrew Ireland's horseshoe black pudding with English mustard and onion relish; treacle-baked free range Middlewhite Garstang ribs with devilled black peas; and warm Morecambe Bay shrimps with blade mace butter and toasted muffin. The acknowledgements continue with main courses such as Fleetwood fish and seawater prawns baked with mashed potato, sprinkled with Mrs. Kirkham's Lancashire cheese; heather-reared Bowland lamb Lancashire hotpot; and Wallings Farm free range Gloucester Old Spot sausages, mash and onion gravy. Throughout the year the head chef works closely with his 'heroes' to showcase something special – Formby asparagus, Westmoreland damsons, or Lancashire cauliflowers, for example. Look for the house specialities – elm wood platters of home-cured meats, local and Scottish seafood, or vegetables. Desserts include chocolate and orange pudding with clotted cream; Lancashire curd tart with organic lemon cream; and a selection of ten Lancashire cheeses. Salads, lunchtime sandwiches and light meals are also available, while children have their own menu of proper food in smaller portions.

MAP 18 SD73
Mitton Rd, Mitton BB7 9PQ
☎ 01254 826888
01254 826026
e-mail: kaye@northcotemanor.com
dir: *3m from Whalley, signed to Stonyhurst*

Open 12–11 Closed: 25 Dec
Bar Meals L served all week 12–2 D served all week 6–9 (Sat 5.30–9, Sun 12–8.30)
Free House
Thwaites Traditional, Thwaites Bomber, Bowland Brewey Hen Harrier. 8
Facilities Children's licence Garden Dogs allowed Parking

UNSTALL MAP 18 SD67

Pick of the Pubs

The Lunesdale Arms

LA6 2QN ☎ 015242 74203 📠 015242 74229
e-mail: info@thelunesdale.co.uk
dir: *M6 junct 36. A65 Kirkby Lonsdale. A638 Lancaster. Pub 2m on right*

Presided over by an ever-popular landlady, this bright and cheery pub in a small village in the beautiful Lune Valley has established quite a reputation for high quality food, outstandingly different wines, and fine regional beers. Everything is prepared freshly, with meat supplied mainly by local farms, most of the salad leaves and vegetables grown organically, and all the bread baked in the pub's kitchens. Light meals at lunchtime include chicken Florentine; lambs' liver with bacon and mash; or just a bowl of parsnip, lime and ginger soup. Begin dinner with chicken liver paté and medlar jelly, or clams and mussels marinière, then consider following with slow-roasted shoulder of lamb on Vermont baked beans; fillets of plaice with salmon, sun-blushed tomato and langoustine sauce; or sirloin steak with béarnaise sauce. Puddings include rhubarb fool with a Grasmere gingerbread biscuit; chocolate brownie and ice cream; or mango and passionfruit parfait.

Open 11–3.30 6–1 Closed: 25–26 Dec **Bar Meals** L served Tue–Fri 12–2 (Sat–Sun 12–2.30) D served Tue–Sun 6–9 **Restaurant** L served Tue–Fri 12–2 (Sat–Sun 12–2.30) D served Tue–Sun 6–9 Free House Black Sheep, Dent Aviator, Guinness. **Facilities** Dogs allowed Parking

WHALLEY MAP 18 SD73

Pick of the Pubs

Freemasons Arms

8 Vicarage Fold, Wiswell BB7 9DF ☎ 01254 822218
e-mail: freemasons@wiswell.co.uk
dir: *From A59, onto A671, Wiswell is 1st left*

See Pick of the Pubs on page 335

Pick of the Pubs

The Three Fishes

Mitton Rd, Mitton BB7 9PQ
☎ 01254 826888 📠 01254 826026
e-mail: kaye@northcotemanor.com
dir: *3m from Whalley , signed to Stonyhurst*

See Pick of the Pubs on opposite page

WHITEWELL MAP 18 SD64

Pick of the Pubs

The Inn At Whitewell

★★★★★ INN

Forest of Bowland BB7 3AT
☎ 01200 448222 📠 01200 448298
e-mail: reception@innatwhitewell.com
dir: *From B6243 follow Whitewell signs*

Whitewell lies in the heart of the Forest of Bowland surrounded by magnificent fell country. This ancient inn, parts of which date from the 13th century, stands on the east bank of the River Hodder, and at one time was the forest-keeper's house. Its somewhat eccentric interior is packed with a random collection of bric-a-brac and furnishings. Outside are two acres of riverside grounds incorporating an extensive herb garden that supplies the kitchen. For lunch, try the signature dish, Whitewell fish pie, or roast breast of Goosnargh (a village not far away) cornfed chicken with stilton potato cake, roast pears and warm Cumberland sauce. At dinner, enjoy charred fillet of beef with parsley-crushed potatoes and soft cauliflower cream; roast loin of Bowland lamb with potato galette, soft onions, carrot and cumin seed purée; or the day's market fish.

Open 11–3 6–11 **Bar Meals** L served all week 12–2 D served all week 7.30–9.30 Av main course £12 **Restaurant** D served all week 7.30–9.30 Av 3 course à la carte £25 Free House Marston's Pedigree, Bowland Bitter, Copper Dragon, Boddingtons Bitter. 20 **Facilities** Garden Dogs allowed Parking **Rooms** 23 bedrooms en suite S£70 D£98

WRIGHTINGTON MAP 15 SD51

Pick of the Pubs

The Mulberry Tree

WN6 9SE ☎ 01257 451400 📠 01257 451400
dir: *M6 junct 27 into Mossy Lea Rd, 2m on right*

The building, dating from 1832, has been in its time a wheelwright's, a brewery, a blacksmith's and a pub, but is now a sought-after venue for discerning diners. The Mulberry Tree was set up by former Roux brothers' head chef Mark Prescott – ranked in Great Britain's top ten of contemporary chefs – and James Moore. Customers are at ease in its clean, airy space while choosing from a feast of options. The bar menu offers speciality sandwiches (lunchtime only) and an interesting range of dishes

CONTINUED

England

WRIGHTINGTON continued

from oysters or eggs Benedict to home-made burgers, fish and chips, or chargrilled cumin marinated lamb chops. At dinner the ingredients move upmarket with foie gras and lobster, along with slow roast belly pork served with buttered Savoy cabbage, rosemary scented parmentier potatoes and apple and sage sauce, or roast fillet of salmon with a chilli and spring onion teriyaki glaze, ginger and lime butter.

Open 12–2.30 6–9.30 (Fri–Sat 6–10) Closed: 26 Dec, 1 Jan **Bar Meals** L served all week 12–2.30 D served all week 6–9.30 (Fri 6–10, Sat–Sun all day) Av main course £14 **Restaurant** L served all week 12–2.30 (Sun 12–3) D served all week 6–10 Av 3 course à la carte £26 Free House Interbrew Flowers IPA. 8 **Facilities** Children's licence Parking

YEALAND CONYERS MAP 18 SD57

The New Inn

40 Yealand Rd LA5 9SJ ☎ 01524 732938
e-mail: charlottepinder@hotmail.com
dir: *M6 junct 35, for Kendal (A6) 3m, past Holmere Hall, next junct on left, up hill turn left at T-junct.*

Beneath the glorious red autumnal leaves of its all-enveloping façade of Virginia creeper lies this traditional 17th-century village inn. There's a warm and friendly atmosphere in the beamed bar, dominated by a large stone fireplace. Food served in the bar, restaurant and beer garden includes a full range of sandwiches, warm baguettes and light meals, beef in beer, fillet steaks, roast duck, salmon fillet, Whitby scampi, and vegetarian tagliatelle. Fish and chip Fridays are popular.

Open 11.30–11 (Sun 12–10.30) **Bar Meals** L served all week 11.30–9.30 D served all week 11.30–9.30 (Sun 12–9.30) Av main course £9.95 **Restaurant** L served all week 11.30–9.30 D served all week 11.30–9.30 (Sun 12–9.30) Av 3 course à la carte £16 Av 3 course fixed price £12.95 Frederic Robinson Hartleys XB, Robinson's Seasonal Bitter, Old Tom. **Facilities** Garden Dogs allowed Parking

LEICESTERSHIRE

BELTON MAP 11 SK4

Pick of the Pubs

The Queen's Head NEW

★★★★ RR

2 Long St LE12 9TP ☎ 01530 222359 01530 224860
e-mail: enquiries@thequeenshead.org
dir: *On B5324 between Coalville & Loughborough*

See Pick of the Pubs on opposite page

BIRSTALL MAP 11 SK5

Pick of the Pubs

The Mulberry Tree

White Horse Ln LE4 4EF
☎ 0116 267 1038 0116 267 1039
e-mail: will@mulberrypubco.com
dir: *M1 junct 21A, A46 towards Newark 5.5m. Exit A46 at Loughborough*

Set by Watermead Country Park in the heart of old Birstall, the Mulberry Tree offers peaceful waterside dining and a heated courtyard in addition to its bar and restaurant. The building, originally called the White Horse, dates from the 18th century when it was used for coal storage by the barges that plied the Grand Union canal. Today it's a sought-after gastro-pub whose executive head chef, Walter Blakemore, counts Claridges and Le Caprice among his previous kitchens. Expect well-sourced food of a high order, with starters such as black pudding and crispy bacon salad; and spiced crab cake on green onion risotto. The main courses, each with a helpful wine recommendation, follow classic lines varying from pan-fried beef fillet (hung for 21 days) to pot roasted free range chicken; fish may include grilled swordfish or roast scallops. Desserts are irresistible, with proven favourites such as warm Bakewell tart with raspberry ripple ice cream.

Open 12–3 5.30–11.30 (Sat–Sun 12–11) **Bar Meals** L served all week 12–2.30 D served Mon–Sat 6–9.30 Av main course £6 10 **Notes**

The Queen's Head

gastro-pub with six individually designed en suite bedrooms, converted from a traditional llage ale house. The Queen's Head opened in May 2004 after a six-month renovation ogramme by owners Henry and Ali Weldon.

s just a five-minute hop in the car om Nottingham East Midlands rport, the M1, or Donington rk Motor Racing Circuit. On hot mmer days the covered deck is eal for alfresco dining, while the rden is a great place for refreshing inks with friends. The bar is a ntemporary space with rustic ertones; here a pint of real ale and newspaper can be enjoyed from e comfort of a leather sofa. Head ef Marc Billings is winning hearts d minds with the precision of his odern European cooking, served both the bistro and the restaurant. ı eclectic bar menu is served at nchtime except on Sundays, and weekday evenings; it comprises choice of ciabattas, Queen's ead classics such as home-made rgers, or salad and pasta dishes. reasonably-priced daily changing set menu is a popular option, when customers can choose two or three courses from the likes of Parma ham and rocket bruschetta; braised pork with a herb mash; and chocolate bread and butter pudding. The seasonal à la carte menus offer a good array of fresh ingredients sourced locally whenever possible. Dinner menu dishes are noted for their added complexity, with half a dozen choices at each stage – ravioli of partridge with celeriac purée and bacon cream could be followed by poached turbot with crab brandade, saffron leeks, and a champagne and caviar sauce. Throughout the year the pub hosts cookery demonstrations and wine tastings, and quarterly jazz sessions promise good music with a glass of bubbly and a two-course dinner.

NEW ★★★★ RR ❀❀ 🍷
MAP 11 SK42
2 Long St LE12 9TP
☎ 01530 222359
🖷 01530 224860
e-mail:
enquiries@thequeenshead.org
dir: *On B5324 between Coalville & Loughborough*

Open 12–3 7–11 (Sun 12–4)
Closed: 25–26 Dec
Bar Meals L served Mon–Sat 12–2.30 D served Mon–Fri 7–9.30 Av main course £5
Restaurant L served all week 12–2.30 D served Mon–Sat 7–9.30 (Sun 12–4) Av 3 course à la carte £29 Av 3 course fixed price £16
Free House
Worthington, Fullers Discovery, Pedigree, Wicked Hathern & Carling. 🍷 14
Facilities Garden Dogs allowed Parking
Rooms 6 bedrooms en suite S£65 D£70–£100

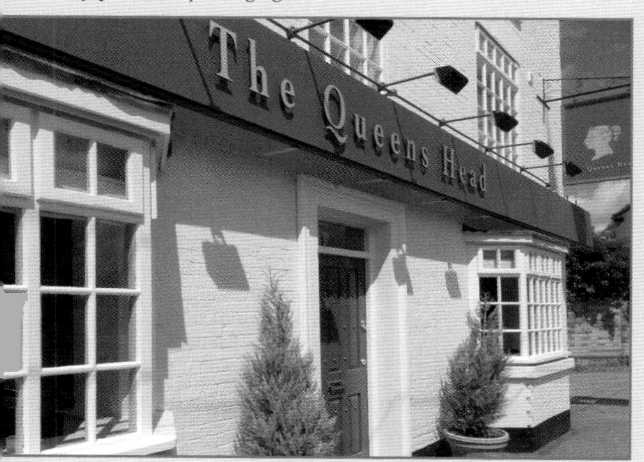

BREEDON ON THE HILL MAP 11 SK42

The Three Horseshoes

Main St DE73 8AN ☎ 01332 695129 📠 01332 695128
e-mail: Ian@Thehorseshoes.com
web: www.thehorseshoes.com
dir: *5m from M1 junct 23a. Pub in centre of village*

Originally a farrier's – the stables can still be seen outside in the courtyard – The Three Horseshoes is around 230 years old and Grade II listed. Opposite the pub is an original round house lockup, for the detention of felons. A hearty menu is served amid the warm wood, old beams and welcoming old pub atmosphere. Typical dishes are beef, mushroom and red wine casserole; venison with roast parsnips, and monkfish with stir-fried oriental vegetables.

Open 11.30–2.30 5.30–11 Closed: 25–26 Dec, 1 Jan **Bar Meals** L served Mon–Sat 12–2 (Sun 12–3) D served Mon–Sat 5.30–9.15 Av main course £6.95 **Restaurant** L served Mon–Sat 12–2 (Sun 12–3) D served Mon–Sat 6–9.15 Av 3 course à la carte £28 Free House Marstons Pedigree, Speckled Hen, Theakstons. **Facilities** Garden Dogs allowed Parking

BRUNTINGTHORPE MAP 11 SP68

Joiners Arms

Church Walk LE17 5QH ☎ 0116 247 8258
e-mail: stephen@thejoinersarms.co.uk
dir: *4m from Lutterworth*

More restaurant than village pub, with restored natural oak beams, tiled floor, pleasant décor, and lots of brassware and candles. Menus change constantly, although old favourites staying put include medallions of Scottish beef with dauphinoise potatoes and diane sauce; calves' liver, smoked bacon, mash and red wine jus; and grilled halibut with sautéed potatoes and petit pois, with specials boards offering additional choices. Maybe caramelised rice pudding or raspberry soufflé afterwards.

Open 12–1.45 6.30–11 **Bar Meals** L served Tue–Sun 12–1.45 D served Tue–Sat 6.30–9.30 **Restaurant** L served Tue–Sun 12–1.45 D served Tue–Sat Free House Greene King IPA, John Smiths, Guinness. 8 **Facilities** Parking

EAST LANGTON MAP 11 SP7

Pick of the Pubs

The Bell Inn

Main St LE16 7TW ☎ 01858 545278 📠 01858 545748
dir: *A6 N towards Leicester, follow The Langtons signs on B6047, 1.5m. Take 1st right signed East Langton*

A creeper-clad, 16th-century listed building tucked away in a quiet village with good country walks all around. The cosy inn has a pretty walled garden, low beams and an open log fire. Peter Faye and Joy Jesson are enthusiastic owners, proud to offer local meats, vegetables and cheeses as well as locally brewed ales. The Langton micro-brewery operates from outbuildings, and produces two regular brews as well as seasonal ales. The wine list is carefully chosen too, and there is always a selection of bin ends and special wines too. There's a wide range of food on menus in both the Long Bar and Green Room, from starters and light bites to more hearty fare. Starters include the likes of marinated wild wood pigeon breast on a beetroot and thyme purée, with a saffron beurre blanc. Main courses might offer choices like loin of lamb encased in a green herb and mixed peppercorn crust, on a purée of celeriac, parsnip and sweet basil leaves, complemented by a puy lentil and pancetta sauce.

Open 12–2.30 7–11 Closed: Dec 25 **Bar Meals** L served all week 12–2 (Sun 12–2.30) D served Mon–Sat 7–9.30 Av main course £10 **Restaurant** L served all week 12–2 D served Mon–Sat 7–9.30 Av 3 course à la carte £25 Free House Greene King IPA & Abbot Ale, Langton Bowler Ale & Caudle Bitter. 7 **Facilities** Children's licence Garden Parking

FLECKNEY MAP 11 SP

The Old Crown

High St LE8 8AJ ☎ 0116 240 2223
e-mail: old-crown-inn@fleckney7.freeserve.co.uk

Close to the Grand Union Canal and Saddington Tunnel, a traditiona village pub that is especially welcoming to hiking groups and familie Noted for good real ales and generous opening times (evening mea from 5pm) offering a wide choice of popular food. The garden has lovely views of fields and the canal, as well as a pétanque court.

Open 11–11 (Sun 12–10.30) **Bar Meals** L served all week 12–2 D serve Tue–Sat 5–9 Av main course £8 **Restaurant** L served all week 12–2 D served Tue–Sat 8–9 Everards Brewery Everards Tiger & Beacon, Scottish Courage Courage Directors, Adnams Bitter, Greene King Abbot A **Facilities** Garden Dogs allowed Parking Play Area **Notes**

England

RIMSTON MAP 11 SK62

ıe Black Horse

/lain St LE14 3BZ ☎ 01664 812358

ʼ: *Telephone for directions*

ʼaditional 16th-century coaching inn displaying much cricketing morabilia in a quiet village with views over the Vale of Belvoir. nty of opportunities for country walks, or perhaps a game of anque on the pub's floodlit pitch. Good home-cooked meals with ly specials, including lots of game and fish. Look out for the squirrel pot! Fish choices and specials include monkfish, lemon sole, whole led plaice, and Arctic char.

en 12-3 6-11 (Sun 12-7) **Bar Meals** L served all week 12-2 n 12-3) D served Mon, Sat-Sun 6-9 Av main course £8 **staurant** L served all week 12-2 (Sun 12-3) D served Mon-Sun 6-9 ree House Adnams, Marstons Pedigree, Archers, Belvoir Mild & Guest s. **Facilities** Children's licence Garden Dogs allowed

ALLATON MAP 11 SP79

Pick of the Pubs

The Bewicke Arms ★★★★ INN

1 Eastgate LE16 8UB

☎ 01858 555217 📠 01858 555598

dir: *S of A47 between Leicester & junct of A47/A6003*

On Easter Monday 1770, a local chatelaine was saved from being gored by a raging bull when a hare ran across the bull's path. In gratitude, she arranged for two hare pies and a generous supply of ale to be made available to the parish poor each succeeding Easter Monday. The Bewicke Arms is now famous for this annual hare pie event – with scrambling and bottle kicking thrown in for good measure. For the rest of the year, the 400-year-old thatched inn serves Grainstore Triple B amongst other real ales, and robust meals such as chilli con carne with real steak, and local gammon with home-made chips. The climbing frame and gardens are child friendly, as are the fish fingers offered on the junior menu. There is a tea shop and gift shop attached.

Open 12-3 6-11 (Sun all day, Winter 7-11) Closed: Easter Monday **Bar Meals** L served all week 12-2 D served Mon-Sat 7-9.30 (Sun May-Oct) Av main course £8.95 **Restaurant** L served all week 12-2 D served Mon-Sat 7-9.30 Av 3 course à la carte £17.50 Av 2 course fixed price £5.95 Free House Grain Store Brewery, Greene King IPA, Grainstore Triple B, Guest beers. 18 **Facilities** Garden Parking Play Area **Rooms** 3 bedrooms en suite S£40 D£55

HATHERN MAP 11 SK52

The Anchor Inn

Loughborough Rd LE12 5JB ☎ 01509 842309

e-mail: l.cdaytondevil@hotmail.com

dir: *M1 junct 24, A6 towards Leicester. Pub 4.5m on left*

The Anchor was once a coaching inn, with stables accessed through an archway off what is now the A6. Alongside a good range of real ales are snacks galore, a lengthy restaurant menu and plenty of vegetarian options. Rosemary and garlic coated brie wedges could be followed with Cajun chicken; fillet steak sizzler, or beef madras. Unquestionably family-friendly, there's a fenced-off children's play area in the garden.

Open 12-11.30 **Bar Meals** L served all week 12-3 D served all week 5-10 (12-9) Av main course £6.25 **Restaurant** L served all week 12-9.30 D served all week 12-9.30 Av 3 course à la carte £12.50 Everards Brewery Everards Tiger, Original, Pitch Black, Abbot Ale. 20 **Facilities** Children's licence Garden Parking Play Area

LONG CLAWSON MAP 11 SK72

The Crown & Plough

East End LE14 4NG ☎ 01664 822322 📠 01664 822322

e-mail: crownandplough@btconnect.com

Following an extensive programme of refurbishment, the pub retains the atmosphere of a village local but with a contemporary flavour. It has a good reputation for its food served from one menu throughout the bar, snug, restaurant and landscaped garden. There's a good choice of fish (pan-fried sea bass with home-made tagliatelle, mussels and clams), and the likes of whole roast partridge with gratin potatoes and Savoy cabbage.

Open 11.30-2 5.30-11 (Fri-Sat 5.30-1) **Bar Meals** L served Tue-Sun 12-2 (Sun 12-3) D served Tue-Sat 6.30-9.30 Av main course £14 **Restaurant** L served Tue-Sun 12-2 (Sun 12-3) D served Tue-Sat 6.30-9.30 Av 3 course à la carte £26 Shepherd Neame, Spitfire, Lancaster Bomber, Marstons Pedigree. **Facilities** Garden Parking

LOUGHBOROUGH MAP 11 SK51

The Swan in the Rushes

21 The Rushes LE11 5BE ☎ 01509 217014 📠 01509 217014

e-mail: tynemill@tynemill.co.uk

dir: *On A6 in front of Sainsbury's*

A 1930s tile-fronted real ale pub with two drinking rooms, a cosmopolitan atmosphere and no frills. The oldest of The Tynemill independent chain pubs (since 1986), it always offers ten ales, including six guests, and hosts two annual beer festivals, acoustic open-mic nights, folk club, and skittle alley. The simple menu lists dishes like Lincolnshire sausages, chilli, Kefalonian meat pie, and vegetables à la crème, with baguettes, jacket potatoes, and ploughman's also available.

Open 11-11 (Fri-Sat 11-12 Sun 12-11) **Bar Meals** L served all week 12-3 D served Mon-Fri 6-9 (Sun 12-5) Av main course £5.95 Tynemill Ltd Archers Golden, Castle Rock Gold, Castle Rock Harvest Pale, Adnams Bitter. 14 **Facilities** Dogs allowed Parking

England

MEDBOURNE MAP 11 SP89

The Nevill Arms

12 Waterfall Way LE16 8EE

☎ 01858 565288 📠 01858 565509

e-mail: nevillarms@hotmail.com

dir: *A508 from Northampton to Market Harborough, then B664 for 5m. Left for Medbourne*

Warm golden stone and mullioned windows make this traditional old coaching inn, in its riverside setting by the village green, truly picturesque. The popular pub garden has its own dovecote and is a great attraction for children who like to feed the ducks. A choice of appetising home-made soups, spicy lamb with apricots, smoked haddock and spinach bake, and pork in apple cream and cider are typical examples of the varied menu, though new owners in 2007 might change things. Reports please.

Open 12-2.30 6-11 (Sun 12-3, 7-10.30) Rest: 25 Dec, 31 Dec Closed eve **Bar Meals** L served all week 12-2 D served all week 7-9.45 (Sun 7-9.30) Free House Fuller's London Pride, Adnams Bitter, Greene King Abbot Ale, Guest Beers. **Facilities** Garden Parking

MOUNTSORREL MAP 11 SK51

The Swan Inn ★★★★ INN

10 Loughborough Rd LE12 7AT

☎ 0116 230 2340 📠 0116 237 6115

e-mail: swan@jvf.co.uk

dir: *On A6 between Leicester & Loughborough*

A Grade II-listed former coaching inn dating back to 1688, set on the banks of the River Soar. Granite walls, flagstone floors and exposed beams set the scene, with roaring log fires in winter and a secluded riverside garden. A good range of cask-conditioned beers is served alongside regularly changing guest ales. Nibbles like olives, or caviar with sour cream blinis, may precede freshly cooked courses such as steak and kidney pudding or pan-fried calves' liver.

Open 12-2.30 5.30-11 (Sat all day, Sun 12-3, 7-10.30) **Bar Meals** L served all week 12-2 D served Mon-Sat 6.30-9.30 Av main course £9 **Restaurant** L served all week 12-2 D served Mon-Sat 6.30-9.30 Av 3 course à la carte £17 Free House Black Sheep Bitter, Theakstons XB, Old Peculier, Ruddles County. **Facilities** Garden Dogs allowed Parking **Rooms** 1 bedroom en suite S£72 D£72

MOWSLEY MAP 11 SP68

The Staff of Life 🍷

Main St LE17 6NT ☎ 0116 240 2359

dir: *Exit M1 junct 20, A5199 to Market Harborough. Left in Husbands Bosworth onto old A50 (Leicester). Pub 3m turn right*

Once a private Edwardian home, this smartly turned-out pub retains many original features, including a wood-panelled ceiling and flagstone floors. The emphasis is on beautifully prepared and presented food, with some British and lots of international influences. Try pan-fried scallops and black pudding, followed by roast belly of pork on apple and raisin mash. Leave room for the handcrafted desserts: mint and honeycomb cheesecake, or white chocolate brûlée with port wine figs.

Open 12-3 6-11 (Sun 12-11) **Bar Meals** L served Tue-Sun 12-2.30 (Sun 12-3) D served Mon-Sat 6.30-9.15 Av main course £12.50 **Restaurant** L served Tue-Sun 12-2.30 D served Mon-Sat 6.30-9.15 Av 3 course à la carte £22.50 Av 3 course fixed price £14.50 Free House Marstons, Banks Original. 🍷 19 **Facilities** Garden Parking

NEWTOWN LINFORD MAP 11 SK5

Pick of the Pubs

The Bradgate 🍷

37 Main St LE6 0AE ☎ 01530 242239 📠 01530 249391

e-mail: lynne@mulberrypubco.com

dir: *M1 junct 22, A50 towards Leicester 1.5m. At 1st rdbt left towards Newton Linford 1.5m, at end of road turn right 0.25m. Pub on right*

Long a favourite with locals and walkers, both as a watering hole and for fine dining. A recent makeover has left the pub with a modern, natural look, partly owing to the extensive use of light wood bar, flooring and furniture, and off-white walls. The food is very much in keeping, meeting the demand for style and innovation on the plate. Start with spiced crab cake, green onion risotto and sweet chilli oil; follow with braised pork with fondant potato and summer cabbage and light apple and white wine sauce; or roast scallops with pak choi and sweet potato; and finish with warm pear galette and almond and Armagnac ice cream. The pub is family friendly with a children's menu and a large play area. Four-legged visitors on a lead are welcome in the beer garden.

Open 11.30-3 5.30-11 (Sat 11.30-11, Sun 12-10.30) **Bar Meals** L served all week 12-2.30 D served Mon-Sat 6-9 (Fri-Sat 6-9.30) **Restaurant** 6-9 (Sun 6-9.30) Carling, Tiger, Sunchaser. 🍷 10 **Facilities** Garden Parking Play Area

OADBY MAP 11 SK

Pick of the Pubs

Cow and Plough 🍷

Gartree Rd, Stoughton Farm LE2 2FB

☎ 0116 272 0852 📠 0116 272 0852

e-mail: enquiries@steaminbilly.co.uk

dir: *3m Leicester Station A6 to Oadby. Turn off to BUPA Hospital, pub 0.5m beyond*

This fascinating free house is housed in converted Victorian farm buildings and decorated with historic inn signs and brewing memorabilia. The pub dates back to 1989, when licensee Barry Lount approached the owners of Stoughton Grange Farm, who were then in the process of opening the farm to the public.

Although the farm park attraction has since closed, the Cow and Plough continues to prosper, hosting functions and events such as beer festivals in the former farm buildings. The pub also brews its own Steamin' Billy beers, named after the owners' Jack Russell terrier, and has won many awards for its hospitality and beers. Lunch might start with artichoke and chestnut soup; followed by roasted red snapper with coriander salsa verde on lamb's leaf and beetroot salad; or rib-eye steak on celeriac and smoked bacon mash with mustard and shallot sauce. Typical desserts include lemon and sultana cheesecake.

Open 12-3 5-11 (Open all day Sat-Sun) **Bar Meals** L served Tue-Sun 12-3 (Sun 12-5) D served Tue-Sun 6.30-9.30 **Restaurant** L served Tues-Sun 12-3 (Sun 12-5) D served Tues-Sat 6.30-9.30 Av 3 course à la carte £20 Av 2 course fixed price £12.95 Free House Steamin Billy Bitter, Steamin Billy Mild, Skydiver, London Pride & Abbeydale. 8 **Facilities** Garden Dogs allowed Parking

OLD DALBY — MAP 11 SK62

Pick of the Pubs

The Crown Inn

Debdale Hill LE14 3LF ☎ 01664 823134

e-mail: jack100harrison@aol.com

dir: *A46 turn for Willoughby/Broughton. Right into Nottingham Ln, then left to Old Dalby*

A classic creeper-covered, old-style pub dating from 1509, set in extensive gardens and orchards, with small rooms, all with open fires. The new owners place a strong emphasis on fresh seasonal produce: if the food doesn't come from Leicestershire, and admittedly the fish doesn't because it is landed in Brixham, the county's suppliers are otherwise wholeheartedly supported. There's a good choice of real ales to help wash down a meal, or to enjoy without food: Wells Bombardier, Hook Norton, and Harvest Pale are among the selection.

Open 12-3 6-11 (Winter 12-2.30, 6.30-11) Rest: 25-26 Dec, 1 Jan Closed in eve **Bar Meals** L served Tue-Sun 12-2 D served Mon-Sat 7-9.30 Av main course £12.50 **Restaurant** L served Tue-Sun 12-2 D served Tue-Sat 7-9.30 Av 3 course à la carte £20 Free House Wells Bombardier, Hook Norton, Scottish Courage Directors, Castle Rock Hemlock, Beaver. **Facilities** Garden Dogs allowed Parking

REDMILE — MAP 11 SK73

Peacock Inn

Church Corner, Main St NG13 0GA

☎ 01949 842554 📠 01949 843746

e-mail: reservations@thepeacockinnredmile.co.uk

dir: *From A1 take A52 towards Nottingham. Turn left, follow signs for Redmile & Belvoir Castle. In Redmile at x-rds turn right. Pub at end of village*

Set beside the Grantham Canal in the Vale of Belvoir, this 16th-century stone-built pub is only two miles from the picturesque castle. The inn has a local reputation for good quality food and real ales, and offers a relaxed setting for wining and dining. The menus are based on local seasonal produce; try smoked haddock with creamed spinach tagliatelle, or lamb Wellington with dauphinoise potatoes, followed by an eminently tempting raspberry and white chocolate cheesecake.

Open 12-2.30 6-9 (Fri-Sat 6-9.30, 6-9 Sun 12-4)) **Bar Meals** L served all week 12-2.30 D served all week 6-9 (Fri-Sat 6-9.30, Sun 12-4) Av main course £12.95 **Restaurant** L served Sun 12-4 D served all week 6-9 (Fri-Sat 6-9.30) Av 3 course à la carte £26 Av 2 course fixed price £11.95 Tradition Free House Plc Youngs Bitter, Bombardier. 8 **Facilities** Children's licence Garden Dogs allowed Parking **Rooms** 9 bedrooms en suite S£55 D£69.95

SADDINGTON — MAP 11 SP69

The Queens Head

Main St LE8 0QH ☎ 0116 2402536

dir: *Between A50 & A6 S of Leicester, NW of Market Harborough*

A traditional prize-winning English pub with terrific views from the restaurant and garden over the Saddington Reservoir. The inn specialises in real ale and good food, with four specials boards to supplement the evening menu. Foil-cooked cod fillet, roast Banbury duck, lamb shank with garlic mash, steak and ale pie, monkfish medallions with Parma ham, and pan-fried tuna steak with sweet pepper and oyster sauce guarantee something for everyone.

Open 12-3 5.30-11 **Bar Meals** L served all week 12-2 D served Mon-Sat 6.30-9.30 Sun lunch 12.30-3 Av main course £6.50 **Restaurant** L served all week 12-2 D served Mon-Sat 6.30-9.30 Av 3 course à la carte £20 Everards Brewery Everards Tiger Best & Beacon Bitter + Guests. **Facilities** Garden Parking

England

SILEBY MAP 11 SK61

The White Swan

Swan St LE12 7NW ☎ 01509 814832 01509 815995

The building dates from the 1930s and behind its unassuming exterior is a free house of some character, with a book-lined restaurant and a homely bar with an open fire. Food ranges from filled rolls, hot baguettes and home-made beef burgers, to the likes of baked chicken breast with leeks, bacon and stilton sauce; pan-fried sirloin steak; and fish pie from the weekly changing menu. Sunday roasts and pensioner lunches are popular options.

Open 12–2.30 7–11 Closed: 1–7 Jan **Bar Meals** L served Tue–Sun 12–1.30 D served Tue–Sat 7–9.30 **Restaurant** D served Tue–Sat 7–9.30 Free House Marston's Pedigree, Carlsberg-Tetley Ansells, Banks, Fuller's London Pride. **Facilities** Garden Parking

SOMERBY MAP 11 SK71

Stilton Cheese Inn

High St LE14 2QB ☎ 01664 454394

This attractive 17th-century inn enjoys a good reputation for its food, beer, wine and malt whiskies. Built from mellow local sandstone, it stands in the centre of the village of Somerby surrounded by beautiful countryside. An interesting range of food from the regularly-changing specials board includes fresh salmon and spinach wrapped in pastry; wild mushroom risotto with garlic bread; and rack of lamb in mint and redcurrant glaze.

Open 12–3 6–11 **Bar Meals** L served all week 12–2 D served all week 6–9 (Sun 7–9) **Restaurant** L served all week 12–2 D served all week 6–9 (Sun 7–9) Free House Grainstore Ten Fifty, Brewster's Hophead, Belvoir Star, Carlsberg-Tetley Tetley's Cask. 10 **Facilities** Garden Parking

STATHERN MAP 11 SK73

Pick of the Pubs

Red Lion Inn

Red Lion St LE14 4HS

☎ 01949 860868 01949 861579

e-mail: info@theredlioninn.co.uk

dir: *From A1 (Grantham), A607 towards Melton, turn right in Waltham, right at next x-rds then left to Stathern*

Traditional pub values underpin every aspect of this welcoming inn, whose menus offer an exuberant romp through the finest local produce. Relax in the stone-floored bar or the lounge with its sofa, magazines and newspapers. There's also an informal dining area and an elegant dining room. Besides the hand-pumped local beers, speciality beers and bottled ciders are also available. Seasonal highlights include roast chestnuts by the open fire in winter, and home-made lemonade to wash down summer barbecues in the enclosed rear garden. Meals combine traditional and international influences: start with duck ravioli with mushroom broth, or Thai-style steamed mussels; then follow with organic pork loin with green beans and sage and onion mash, or pan-fried sea bream with potato and chorizo parmentier. With a couple of day's notice you can take home breads, meats and sauces supplied by the Red Lion's sister pub, The Olive Branch at Clipsham.

Open 12–3 6–11 (Sat 12–11, Sun 12–5.30) Closed: 26 Dec, 1 Jan **Bar Meals** L served all week 12–2 D served Mon–Sat 7–9.30 (Sat 6–9.30 Sun 12–3) **Restaurant** L served all week 12–2 D served Mon–Sat 7–9.30 (Sun 12–3) Av 3 course à la carte £26 Av 3 course fixed price £16 Rutland Company Ltd Grainstore Olive Oil, Brewster's VPA, Exmoor Gold. London Pride, Leffe. 8 **Facilities** Garden Dogs allowed Parking Play Area

THORPE LANGTON MAP 11 SP7

The Bakers Arms

Main St LE16 7TS ☎ 01858 545201 01858 545924

dir: *Take A6 S from Leicester then left signed 'The Langtons'*

A thatched pub set in a pretty village, with plenty of period charm and an enthusiastic following. The modern pub food is one of the key attractions, though this remains an informal pub rather than a serious dining pub or restaurant. An intimate atmosphere is created with low beams, rug-strewn quarry-tiled floors, large pine tables, and open fires The area is popular with walkers, riders and mountain bikers.

Open 12–3 6.30–11 **Bar Meals** D served Tue–Sat 6.30–9.30 **Restaurant** L served Sat–Sun 12–2.15 D served Tue–Sat 6.30–9.30 Free House Langton Brewery, Bakers Dozen Bitter. **Facilities** Garden Parking **Notes**

WOODHOUSE EAVES MAP 11 SK5

The Wheatsheaf Inn

Brand Hill LE12 8SS ☎ 01509 890320

e-mail: richard@wheatsheafinn.net

dir: *M1 junct 22, follow Quorn signs*

Around the turn of the 19th century, when local quarrymen wanted somewhere to drink, they built themselves the Wheatsheaf. It's what locals call a Dim's Inn, a succession of pubs run by three generations of the Dimblebee family. Bistro-style menus include chargrilled prime eaks and vegetarian options like butternut squash and cashew nut ast. Fresh fish is a feature of the daily chalkboard – maybe monkfish nd scallops pan-fried in garlic butter with sweet chilli sauce.

pen 12–2.30 6–11 (All day wknds summer) **Bar Meals** L served on–Sat 12–2 (Sat–Sun 12–2.30) D served Mon–Sat 7–9.30 **estaurant** L served all week 12–2 (Sun 12–2.30, all day at wknds in mmer) D served Mon–Sat 7–9.30 Av 3 course à la carte £16.50 Free ouse Greene King Abbot Ale, Draught Burton Ale, Timothy Taylor ndlord, Adnams Broadside. 14 **Facilities** Garden Dogs allowed arking

VYMONDHAM — MAP 11 SK81

Pick of the Pubs

The Berkeley Arms

59 Main St LE14 2AG

01572 787587 01572 787587

e-mail: bturnbull@tiscali.co.uk

dir: *B676 out of Melton 7m. 2m from A1 - 5th Witham Junction. 6m from Oakham*

This award-winning 500-year-old stone built country inn is fast becoming a favoured dining destination. Rustic pine gives a clean, uncluttered look throughout, with open fires, slate floors and oak beams contributing to the atmosphere. In warmer weather the patio tables and lawned rear garden are popular with families and walkers. You'll find Marstons Pedigree and Greene King IPA at the bar, alongside a guest ale and specialist beers. Lunchtime brings ploughman's, filled ciabattas, salads and jacket potatoes, with a range of pub favourites like beer-battered cod, and lasagne. The evening menu might begin with duck liver parfait or home-made ravioli stuffed with chorizo and tomato, before moving on to fillet of salmon and tagliatelle with Thai dressing. Booking is advisable, especially in the evenings. Look out for the traditional pub games.

Open 12–3 6–11 **Bar Meals** L served all week 12–2 D served all week 6.30–9 Av main course £7 **Restaurant** L served all week 12–2 D served Mon–Sat 6.30–9 Av 3 course à la carte £20 Pubmaster Marstons Pedigree, Carling, Guinness, Greene King IPA & Guest Ale. **Facilities** Garden Parking

LINCOLNSHIRE

ALLINGTON — MAP 11 SK84

The Welby Arms ★★★★ INN

The Green NG32 2EA 01400 281361 01400 281361

dir: *From Grantham take either A1 N, or A52 W. Allington 1.5m*

With its views across the village green towards Allington Manor, this proper village pub provides a quiet retreat for travellers from the nearby A1, and lies within easy reach of south Lincolnshire's historic houses and market towns. The constantly changing menu might include halibut fillet with pesto and cheese crumb crust, slow braised lamb shank, and medallions of pork with a Dijon mustard sauce. There's also a tempting array of home-made sweets.

Open 12–2.30 6–11 (Sun 12–4, 6–10.30) **Bar Meals** L served all week 12–2 **Restaurant** L served all week 12–2 D served all week 6.30–9.30 (Sun 8.30–9) Free House Scottish Courage John Smith's, Interbrew Bass, Timothy Taylor Landlord, Greene King Abbot. 8 **Facilities** Garden Parking **Rooms** 3 bedrooms en suite S£48 D£60

ASWARBY — MAP 12 TF03

The Tally Ho Inn

NG34 8SA 01529 455205 01529 455773

e-mail: enquire@tally-ho-aswarby.co.uk

dir: *3m S of Sleaford on A15 towards Bourne/Peterborough*

Built from sturdy old pillars and beams and exposed stonework, this handsome inn is located on the Aswarby Estate and has strong connections with major hunts and other field sports. The old English garden, complete with fruit trees, overlooks estate parkland and grazing sheep. Favourite dishes at lunch and dinner include suet pudding with braised beef and mushrooms, and lamb and stilton casserole. Baguettes and toasted sandwiches are also served at lunchtime.

Open 11–11 (Sun 11–10.30) **Bar Meals** L served all week 12–2 D served all week 6–9.30 (Sun 7–9) Av main course £12 **Restaurant** L served Mon–Sun 12–2 D served Mon–Sat 6–9.30 (Sun 7–9) Av 3 course à la carte £21 Free House Tiger, Batermans XB & XXXB. 7 **Facilities** Garden Dogs allowed Parking

BARNOLDBY LE BECK — MAP 17 TA20

The Ship Inn

Main Rd DN37 0BG 01472 822308 01472 823706

e-mail: silgy386@aol.com

dir: *M180 junct 5, A18 past Humberside Airport. At Laceby Junction rdbt (A18 & A46) straight over follow Skegness/Boston signs. Approx 2m turn left signed Waltham & Barnoldby le Beck*

A pub since 1725, the Ship was named after the 'Mayflower', in which the Pilgrim Fathers set sail from nearby Immingham. The bar is filled with maritime bric-a-brac, and outside is a beautiful garden. Menus are likely to feature fillet, sirloin and gammon steaks; beef and ale pie; oven-baked chicken breast; and regularly changing specials, particularly fish. The Ship's own vessels use environmentally-friendly longlines to catch, among others, cod, turbot, plaice, skate and brill.

Open 12–3 6–11 **Bar Meals** L served all week 12–2 (Sun 12–2.30) D served all week 7–9.30 Av main course £12 **Restaurant** L served all week 12–2 D served all week 7–9.30 Av 3 course à la carte £22 Punch Taverns Black Sheep Best, Timothy Taylor Landlord, Carlsberg-Tetley Tetley's Smooth, Boddingtons. 7 **Facilities** Garden Parking

BELCHFORD — MAP 17 TF27

The Blue Bell Inn NEW

1 Main Rd LN9 6LQ 01507 533602

dir: *Off A153 between Horncastle & Louth*

Food is very much to the fore at this welcoming pub set in the heart of the Wolds. The secret of its success is husband and wife team Darren and Shona – he is the chef, she handles front-of-house. Expect comfortable armchairs and cask ales in the bar, and modern cooking – perhaps mussels with a Thai style sauce, followed by wild fallow venison with pumpkin, sage and bacon risotto and a beetroot jus.

Open 11.30–2.30 6.30–11 Closed: 2nd & 3rd wk in Jan **Bar Meals** L served Tue–Sat 11.30–2 D served Tue–Sat 6.30–9 **Restaurant** L served Tue–Sun 11.30–2 D served Tue–Sat 6.30–9 Free House Black Sheep, Timothy Taylor Landlord & Guest. **Facilities** Garden Parking

BOURNE MAP 12 TF02

The Wishing Well Inn

Main St, Dyke PE10 0AF ☎ 01778 422970 01778 394508

dir: *Take A15 towards Seaford. Inn in next village*

This village free house started life as a one-room pub 105 years ago, but the building itself is 300 years old. Inside there's a wealth of old oak beams, as well as two inglenook fireplaces in the bar and restaurant areas, the smaller of which also houses a wishing well. Outside, an attractive beer garden backs onto the children's play area. Dine on pub favourites such as steak and ale pie or a giant mixed grill.

Open 9–11 (Winter 9–3, 5–11) **Bar Meals** L served all week 12–9 D served all week **Restaurant** L served all week 12–2 D served all week 6.30–9 Free House Greene King Abbot Ale, Tiger Bitter, 3 Guest's. 7 **Facilities** Children's licence Garden Parking Play Area

See advert on opposite page

BRIGG MAP 17 TA00

The Jolly Miller

Brigg Rd, Wrawby DN20 8RH ☎ 01652 655658

e-mail: dandmigib@aol.com

dir: *1.5m E of Brigg on A18, on left*

Popular country inn a few miles south of the Humber Estuary. The pleasant bar and dining area are traditional in style, and there's a large beer garden. The menu offers a good range of food with most dishes under £5. Tuck into a chip butty; vegetable burger bap; home-made curry; or steak with onion rings. Puddings include hot chocolate fudge cake and banana split. Play area and children's menu. Coach parties accepted with advanced booking.

Open 12 -12 (Tue 3–11, Fri–Sat 12–1) **Bar Meals** L served all week 12–7.30 (Sun 12–3) D served all week 12–7.30 Av main course £6 **Restaurant** L served all week 12–7.30 (Sun 12–3) D served all week 5–7.30 Enterprise Inns Guinness, Carling, Carling Premier. **Facilities** Children's licence Garden Parking Play Area

COLEBY MAP 17 SK96

The Bell Inn

3 Far Ln LN5 0AH ☎ 01522 810240 01522 811800

dir: *8m S of Lincoln on A607. In Coleby village right at church*

One of the three original buildings that became today's rural Bell Inn actually was a pub, built in 1759. The dining area is also divisible by three – a brasserie, a restaurant, and a terrace room. Main courses may include braised shoulder of lamb on Greek-style potatoes; steamed steak and mushroom pudding; and smoked tofu and sweet potato strudel. A separate fish and seafood menu may offer grilled haddock on a sweet potato, goats' cheese and aubergine gateau.

Open 11.30–3 5.30–11 (Sun 11.30–10.30) Closed: 1 Jan–14 Jan **Bar Meals** L served all week 12–2.30 D served all week 5.30–9 (Sun 12–8 Av main course £12 **Restaurant** L served all week 12–2.30 D served all week 5.30–9.30 (Sun 12–3,5.30–8.30) Av 3 course à la carte £25 Av 3 cour fixed price £15.95 Pubmaster Carlsberg-Tetley Bitter, Batemans XB, Wadworths 6X, Jennings. 8 **Facilities** Garden Dogs allowed Parking

CONINGSBY MAP 17 TF2

The Lea Gate Inn

Leagate Rd LN4 4RS ☎ 01526 342370 01526 345468

e-mail: theleagateinn@hotmail.com

dir: *Off B1192 just outside Coningsby*

The oldest licensed premises in the county, dating from 1542, this was the last of the Fen Guide Houses that provided shelter before th treacherous marshes were drained. The oak-beamed pub has a pries hole and a very old inglenook fireplace among its features. The same family have been running the pub for nearly 25 years. Both the bar and restaurant serve food and offer seasonal menus with lots of loca produce (including game in season) and a good vegetarian choice.

Open 11.30–2.30 6.30–11 (Sun 12–2.30, 6.30–10.30) **Bar Meals** L serve all week 12–2 D served all week 6.30–9.30 Av main course £7.95 **Restaurant** D served all week 6.30–9.15 Free House Scottish Courage Theakstons XB, Bombardier. 7 **Facilities** Garden Parking Pla Area

DONINGTON ON BAIN MAP 17 TF2

The Black Horse Inn ★★★ INN

Main Rd LN11 9TJ ☎ 01507 343640 01507 343640

e-mail: mike@blackhorse-donington.co.uk

Ideal for walkers, this old-fashioned country pub is set in a small villa in the heart of the Lincolnshire Wolds on the Viking Way. A large grassed area surrounded by trees is ideal for enjoying a drink or dini alfresco on sunny days. Dining options include the non-smoking dini room, the Blue Room, and the Viking Snug.

Open 12–3 6–11 **Bar Meals** L served all week 12–2 D served all week 7–9 (Sat–Sun 7–9.30) **Restaurant** L served all week 12–2 D served all week 7–9 (Sat–Sun 7–9.30) Free House John Smiths, Greene King, Theakstons. **Facilities** Garden Dogs allowed Parking **Rooms** 8 bedroo en suite

WERBY MAP 12 TF14

'he Finch Hatton Arms

3 Main St NG34 9PH ☎ 01529 460363 🖷 01529 461703

r: *From A17 to Kirkby-la-Thorne, then 2m NE. 2m E of A153 :tween Sleaford & Anwick*

'iginally known as the Angel Inn, this 19th-century pub was given e family name of Lord Winchelsea, who bought it in 1875. After a equered history and a short period of closure, it reopened in the 80s and these days offers pub, restaurant and hotel facilities. It offers extensive and varied menu to suit all tastes and budgets, but with its ditional ale and regular customers it retains a 'local' atmosphere.

›en 11.30–2.30 6.30–11 Closed: 25–26 Dec **Bar Meals** L served all :ek 11.30–2 D served all week 6.30–10 (Sun 6.30–9.30) Av main course) **Restaurant** L served all week 11.30–2 D served all week 6.30–10 (Sun 30–9.30) Av 3 course à la carte £18 Free House Everards Tiger Best, xons Major, Guest beer. **Facilities** Children's licence Garden Parking

REISTON MAP 12 TF34

ings Head

ıurch Rd PE22 0NT ☎ 01205 760368

r: *From Boston towards Skegness on A52 follow signs for RSPB serve Freiston Shore*

is pub started life in the 15th century as two tied cottages and retains :nty of old world charm. Outside you'll find award-winning flower splays; inside there's a coal fire and, thankfully, no juke boxes or mes machines. Expect a warm welcome from Ann Brewster's partner l, who has won an award for his well-kept cellar. Ann's cooking es local produce and includes traditional delights such as steak and lney pie or casseroles with dumplings.

›en 11–2.30 7–11 (Sun 12–3 7.30–10.30) **Bar Meals** L served ɔn–Tue 12–2 D served Fri–Sat 7–9 (Sun 12–3) Av main course £7 **:staurant** L served Mon–Sun 12–2 D served Fri–Sat 7–9 (Sun 12–3) Av 3 urse à la carte £10 Av 2 course fixed price £7 Batemans Batemans & Dark Mild, Worthington Cream Flow & John Smiths, Guinness. **cilities** Parking **Notes**

ROGNALL MAP 12 TF11

he Goat 🍷

5 Spalding Rd PE6 8SA ☎ 01778 347629

mail: graysdebstokes@btconnect.com

r: *A1 to Peterborough, A15 to Market Deeping, old A16 to alding, pub about 1.5m from junct of A15 & A16*

milies are welcome at this cosy, friendly country free house, which s an open fire, large beer garden and plenty to amuse the children. ain courses include beef stroganoff; pork in sweet and sour sauce; :k and mushroom pie; warm bacon and stilton salad; and home- ıde prawn curry. Beer is taken seriously, with five different guest ales ch week and regular beer festivals throughout the year.

The Goat

Open 11.30–3 6–11 (Sun 12–10.30) Closed: 25 Dec **Bar Meals** L served all week 12–2 D served all week 6.30–9.30 (Sun 12–9) Av main course £8 **Restaurant** L served all week 12–2 D served all week 6.30–9.30 (Sun 12–9) Av 3 course à la carte £16 Free House Elgood, Batemans, Abbeydale, Nethergate Guest ale. 🍷 16 **Facilities** Garden Parking Play Area

England

England

GEDNEY DYKE MAP 12 TF42

The Chequers

PE12 0AJ ☎ 01406 362666 📠 01406 362666

dir: *King's Lynn A17, 1st rdbt after Long Sutton take B1359*

In a pretty village close to the Wash, this 18th-century country inn has a good selection of food. Local quails eggs with bacon; or bang bang chicken; and fish specials like marinaded loin of tuna with tomato salsa; or baked sea bass with lobster fish cake are popular. Lincolnshire pork and leek sausages; and wild mushroom gateau crêpe with parmesan shavings are non-fish options. Well-chosen ales, patio garden and outdoor eating in summer.

Open 12-2 7-11 (Fri-Sat 7-12, Sun 12-2 7-10.30) Closed: 26 Dec **Bar Meals** L served Tue-Sun 12-2 D served Tue-Sun 7-9 (Sun 12-2.30) **Restaurant** L served Tue-Sun 12-2 D served Tue-Sun 7-9 (Sun 12-2.30, 7-9) Free House Adnams Best, Greene King Abbot Ale, Speckled Hen, IPA. 10 **Facilities** Garden Parking

GRANTHAM MAP 11 SK93

The Beehive Inn

10/11 Castlegate NG31 6SE ☎ 01476 404554

dir: *A52 to town centre, left at Finkin St, pub at end*

Grantham's oldest inn (1550) is notable for having England's only living pub sign – a working beehive high up in a lime tree. Otherwise, this simple town hostelry offers a good pint of Newby Wyke and good-value, yet basic bar food. Kids will enjoy the bouncy castle that appears during the summer.

Open 12-11 (Fri-Sat 12-12) **Bar Meals** L served all week 12-2 Av main course £4 Free House Newby Wyke Real Ales, Everards. **Facilities** Garden

HECKINGTON MAP 12 TF14

The Nags Head

34 High St NG34 9QZ ☎ 01529 460218

dir: *5m E of Sleaford on A17*

Overlooking a village green boasting the only eight-sailed windmill in the country. This listed, white-painted coaching inn, built in 1645, was reputedly visited by highwayman Dick Turpin after stealing some horses. He was later captured in York. On the menu: home-made pies, including chicken and stilton, beef and ale, and homity; salmon, scampi, mussels, haddock and sea bass. Patio garden with lots of tables and play area.

Open 11-12.30 **Bar Meals** L served all week 12-2 D served all week 7-9 Punch Taverns 15 **Facilities** Garden Parking

HOUGH-ON-THE-HILL MAP 11 SK9

The Brownlow Arms NEW

★★★★★ INN

High Rd NG32 2AZ ☎ 01400 250234 📠 01400 251993

e-mail: armsinn@yahoo.co.uk

dir: *Take A607 Grantham to Sleaford Rd, Hough-on-the-Hill is signed from Barkston*

Set in a picturesque stone village, this 17th-century inn has the setting and atmosphere of a well-tended country house. Chef Paul Vidic has created a menu of classical dishes with modern influences. Start with potted brown shrimp and Avruga caviar Chantilly, followed by wild sea bass fillet with saffron and lovage mash, and rhubarb parfait. A landscaped terrace looks out over tree-lined fields. Take advantage of four double bedrooms to explore the region's antiquities.

Open 6.30-11 (Sun 12-3) Closed: 25-27 Dec, 1-20 Jan & 1 wk in Sep **Bar Meals** L served Sun 12-3 **Restaurant** L served Sun 12-2 D served Tue-Sat 6.30-9.30 Av 3 course à la carte £27.50 Free House Timothy Taylor Landlord, Marstons, Pedigree. **Facilities** Garden Parkir **Rooms** 4 en suite S£65 D£96

LINCOLN MAP 17 SK9

Pyewipe Inn

Fossebank, Saxilby Rd LN1 2BG

☎ 01522 528708 📠 01522 525009

e-mail: enquiries@pyewipeinn.co.uk

dir: *On A57 past Lincoln/A46 Bypass, signed in 0.5m*

First licensed in 1778, the Pyewipe (local dialect for lapwing) stands ir four acres alongside the Roman-built Fossedyke Navigation. From the grounds there's a great view of nearby Lincoln Cathedral. All food is bought locally and prepared by five qualified chefs. With up to eight menu boards to choose from, expect beef, mushroom and Guinness pie; fillet of lamb with onion mash and roasted garlic, thyme chicken on saffron risotto, and much more.

Open 11-11 (Sun 12-10.30) **Bar Meals** L served all week 12-9.30 D served all week Sun 12-9 Av main course £9 **Restaurant** L served all week 12-9.30 D served all week Sun 12-9 Av 3 course à la carte £19 Fr House Timothy Taylor Landlord, Greene King Abbot Ale, Interbrew Bas Bombardier. **Facilities** Garden Dogs allowed Parking

The Victoria

6 Union Rd LN1 3BJ ☎ 01522 536048

dir: *From city outskirts follow signs for Cathedral Quarter. Pub 2 mins' walk from all major up-hill car parks*

Situated right next to the Westgate entrance of the Castle and within a stone's throw of Lincoln Cathedral, a long-standing drinkers' pub with a range of real ales, including six changing guest beers, as well as two beer festivals a year. It also offers splendid meals made from exclusively home-prepared food including hot baguettes and filled bacon rolls, Saturday breakfast and Sunday lunches. House specials include sausage and mash, various pies, chilli con carne and home-made lasagne. Licensee due to change 2007.

Open 11-11 (Fri-Sat 11-11.30 Sun 12-11) **Bar Meals** L served Mon-Fri 12-2.30 (Sat 11-2.30, Sun 12-2) **Restaurant** L served Sun 12-2 Tynemill Ltd Timothy Taylor Landlord, Batemans XB, Castle Rock Harvest Pale, Guest Beers. **Facilities** Garden

England

Pick of the Pubs

Wig & Mitre

30/32 Steep Hill LN2 1TL
01522 535190 01522 532402
e-mail: email@wigandmitre.com
dir: *By cathedral, & castle car park, at top of Steep Hill*

The Wig and Mitre's many 14th-century timbers bear witness to its survival through numerous reincarnations. These days it's a peaceful haven, free of music, situated at the top of Steep Hill in the upper part of medieval Lincoln between the castle and the cathedral. The pub has continuous service from 8am to around midnight every day, all year round. The breakfast menu – which can include champagne – runs until 12 noon, while the sandwich and snacks menu is modern and interesting (toasted plum bread with jam; pan-fried chicken breast on ciabatta with tarragon mustard mayonnaise). A meal from the classically-inspired main menu could include salad of warm baby boudin, chorizo and croutons with Dijon dressing, followed by roasted fillet of halibut bourguignon, or perhaps pan-fried fillet of pork with black pudding and celeriac purée. An extensive wine list is supported by some great real ales.

Open 8-12 **Bar Meals** L served all week 8-11 D served all week 8-11 Av main course £13.95 **Restaurant** L served all week 8-11 D served all week 8-11 Av 3 course à la carte £26.50 Av 3 course fixed price £13.95 Free House Black Sheep Special, Batemans XB. 34 **Facilities** Dogs allowed

LOUTH — MAP 17 TF38

Masons Arms

Cornmarket LN11 9PY 01507 609525 0870 7066450
e-mail: info@themasons.co.uk
dir: *In the centre of Louth on the corn market*

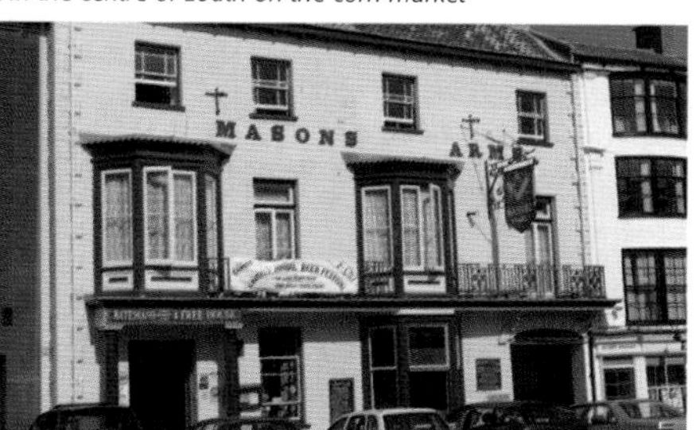

A Grade II listed building, located in the heart of Georgian Louth, dates back to 1725. In the days when it was known as the Bricklayers Arms, the local Masonic lodge met here. The downstairs Market Bar is for beer lovers, while the 'upstairs' restaurant offers an à la carte menu where you might find the likes of honey roast ham, fried egg and home-made chips; steak and kidney pie; and cauliflower cheese.

Open 10-11 (Fri-Sat 10-12, Sun 12-11) **Bar Meals** L served all week 12-2.30 D served Mon-Sat 6-8.30 (Sun 12-3) Av main course £6.95 **Restaurant** L served Sun 12-3 Free House Kelham Island Pale Rider, Marston's Pedigree, Batemans XB Bitter, XXXB & 2 Guest Beers. **Facilities** Children's licence **Rooms** 10 bedrooms 5 en suite S£30 D£45 (★★ INN)

NEWTON — MAP 12 TF03

The Red Lion

NG34 0EE 01529 497256
e-mail: theredlion@netbreeze.co.uk
dir: *10m E of Grantham on A52*

Dating from the 17th century, The Red Lion is particularly popular with walkers and cyclists, perhaps because the flat Lincolnshire countryside makes for easy exercise. Low beams, exposed stone walls and an open fire in the bar help to create a very atmospheric interior. Popular dishes include haddock in beer batter, lemon sole with parsley butter sauce, breadcrumbed scampi, and home-made steak and ale pie. The carvery serves cold buffets on weekdays, hot ones on Friday and Saturday evenings, and Sunday lunchtime.

Open 12-3 6-11 (Sun 12-4, 7-10.30) **Bar Meals** L served all week 12-2 D served Sun-Wed 7-9 (Thu-Sat 6-9) **Restaurant** L served Sun 12-2 D served Sun-Wed 7-9 (Thu-Sat 6-9) Free House Batemans, Everards, Guest ale. **Facilities** Garden Dogs allowed Parking

PARTNEY — MAP 17 TF46

Red Lion Inn

PE23 4PG 01790 752271 01790 753360
dir: *On A16 from Boston, or A158 from Horncastle*

Parts of this Lincolnshire inn date back 400 years, but reports of a ghost seem to be unsubstantiated. All the pub's food is home made and freshly cooked to order using local produce wherever possible. The comprehensive menu offers a selection for vegetarians, plus steaks, main courses and daily specials. Typical dishes are vegetable and cheese roast; lamb moussaka; and cod and prawns in cheese sauce, as well as traditional roasts for Sunday lunch.

Open 12-3 7-11 (Sun 12-2.30, 7-10.30) **Bar Meals** L served Wed-Sun 12-2 D served all week 7-9.30 Av main course £7 **Restaurant** L served Wed-Sun 12-2 D served Wed-Sun 7-9.30 Free House Batemans, Guinness, Tetleys & Guest Ales. **Facilities** Garden Parking

RAITHBY — MAP 17 TF36

Red Lion Inn

PE23 4DS 01790 753727
dir: *Take A158 from Horncastle, right at Sausthorpe, keep left into Raithby*

Traditional beamed black-and-white village pub, parts of which date back 300 years. Log fires provide a warm welcome in winter. A varied menu of home-made dishes includes seabass with lime stir fry vegetables, roast guinea fowl with tomato, garlic and bacon, and medallions of beef with peppercorn sauce.

Open 7-11 (Wknds & BHs 12-2.30) **Bar Meals** L served Sat-Sun 12-2.30 D served Wed-Mon 7-9.30 Av main course £9 **Restaurant** L served Sat-Sun 12-2.30 D served Wed-Mon 7-10 Av 3 course à la carte £14 Free House Raithby, Carlsberg, Pedigree, Adnams Broadside & Batemans XXX. **Facilities** Garden Dogs allowed Parking

SKEGNESS — MAP 17 TF56

Best Western Vine Hotel ★★★ HL

Vine Rd, Seacroft PE25 3DB
☎ 01754 763018 & 610611 📠 01754 769845
e-mail: info@thevinehotel.com
dir: *In Seacroft area of Skegness. S of town centre*

Substantially unchanged since 1770, the Vine is the second oldest building in Skegness. Set amid two acres of gardens, the ivy-covered hotel was bought by the brewer Harry Bateman in 1927. Now, this charming hostelry offers comfortable accommodation and a fine selection of Batemans ales. The bar menu ranges from soup or a simple sandwich to bistro-style salads and substantial mixed grills; there's a traditional Sunday carvery, too.

Open 11-11 (Sun 12-10.30) **Bar Meals** L served all week 12-2.15 D served all week 6-9.15 (Sat-Sun all day) Av main course £7 **Restaurant** L served all week 12.30-2 D served all week 6.30-9.15 (Sun 12-2.30) Av 3 course à la carte £20 Free House Batemans XB & XXXB, Valiant & Blacksheep. 8 **Facilities** Children's licence Garden Dogs allowed Parking **Rooms** 24 bedrooms en suite S£59 D£84

SOUTH WITHAM — MAP 11 SK91

Blue Cow Inn & Brewery

High St NG33 5QB ☎ 01572 768432 📠 01572 768432
e-mail: bookings@thebluecowinn.co.uk
dir: *Between Stamford & Grantham on A1*

Just in Lincolnshire, with the Rutland border a few hundred yards away, this once-derelict, 13th-century inn stands close to the source of the River Witham. Part-timbered outside, the interior has a wealth of beamed ceilings and walls, stone floors and open log fires when the easterly winds whip across the Fens from Siberia. Owner Simon Crathorn also, brews his own beers. The inn has a patio beer garden for warm evenings.

Open 12-11 **Bar Meals** L served all week 12-2.30 D served all week 6-9.30 Av main course £8 **Restaurant** L served all week 12-2.30 D served all week 6-9.30 Av 3 course à la carte £15 Free House **Facilities** Garden Dogs allowed Parking **Rooms** 6 beds en suite S£45 D£55 (★★ INN)

STAMFORD — MAP 11 TF00

The Bull & Swan Inn

24a High St, St Martin's PE9 2LJ
☎ 01780 763558 📠 01780 763558
e-mail: bullandswan@btconnect.com
dir: *B1081 towards Stamford, on right in outskirts of town*

A 17th-century coaching inn retaining many original features, close to historic Burghley House. There are two log fires in winter and a large patio garden for summer use. Live music is provided indoors every Sunday in winter and in the garden every Friday in summer. The menu ranges from sandwiches to steaks or moules marinière, while daily specials offer the likes of roasted smoked duck breast or medallions of pork.

Open 11.30-11 (Mon 5-11, Sun 12-11) **Bar Meals** L served Tues-Sun 12-2 (Sat Lunch 12-5) D served Mon-Sat 6.30-9 Av main course £10 **Restaurant** L served Tues-Sun 12-2 D served Mon-Sat 6.30-9 Av 3 course à la carte £16 Jennings Cumberland, Greene King Abbot Ale, Adnams Bitter, Guest ales. 12 **Facilities** Garden Dogs allowed Parking

Pick of the Pubs

The George of Stamford ★★★ HL

71 St Martins PE9 2LB
☎ 01780 750750 📠 01780 750701
e-mail: reservations@georgehotelofstamford.com
dir: *From Peterborough take A1 N. Onto B1081 for Stamford, down hill to lights. Hotel on left*

Forty coaches a day once stopped at this 16th-century inn – 20 going north and 20 going south. The two doors that admit customers to The George are marked respectively London and York, and the London Room and the York Bar were once waiting rooms used by passengers while horses were changed in the courtyard outside. It is a magnificent building, with its famous gallows sign spanning the road. Today's visitors will appreciate the welcoming log fires, oak-panelled restaurants, walled monastery garden and cobbled courtyard. The wine list is notable and the food is essentially traditional in style with bar snacks, a bistro-style restaurant carte, and informal meals in the Garden Lounge. Brittany seafood platter is a speciality of the house, and the old-style dessert and cheese trolleys are a feature. The hotel also has 47 bedrooms individually designed by Julia Vannocci, plus a business centre and a panelled conference room.

Open 11-11 (Sun 12-11) **Bar Meals** L served all week 11.30-2.30 Av main course £6.95 **Restaurant** L served all week 12.30-2.30 D served all week 7.30-10.30 Av 3 course à la carte £33.65 Av 2 course fixed price £18.95 Free House Adnams Broadside, Fuller's London Pride, Greene King Ruddles Bitter. 16 **Facilities** Garden Dogs allowed Parking **Rooms** 47 bedrooms en suite S£85 D£125

SURFLEET SEAS END — MAP 12 TF

The Ship Inn NEW

154 Reservoir Rd PE11 4DH
☎ 01775 680547 📠 01775 680541
e-mail: info@shipinnsurfleet.com
dir: *Off A16 towards Surfleet Reservoir*

A fenland pub by the lock gates controlling the Rivers Glen and Welland, and Vernatti's Drain. Dating from only 2003, it occupies the footprint of an earlier hostelry, which the drainage-fixated Vernatti b in 1642. The bar is panelled in hand-crafted oak, while upstairs is the restaurant overlooking the marshes. Locally sourced food includes Whitby scampi; home-made pies; roast rib of Lincolnshire beef; and pan-fried salmon in the restaurant.

en 11.30-3 6-11 (Fri-Sat 6-12) **Bar Meals** L served Tue-Sun 12-2 served Mon-Sat 6.30-9 Av main course £7.50 **Restaurant** L served 1 12-2 D served Fri-Sat 7-9 Av 3 course à la carte £22.50 Free House Adnams, Pedigree. **Facilities** Parking

'OODHALL SPA MAP 17 TF16

illage Limits Motel

xwould Rd LN10 6UJ ☎ 01526 353312 📠 01526 353312

mail: enquiries@villagelimits.com

r: *At rdbt on main street follow Petwood Hotel signs. Motel in 0yds*

e pub and restaurant are situated in the original part of the building, expect bare beams and old world charm. Typical meals include fillet ak with wild mushrooms and stilton; whole grilled rainbow trout; d gammon, egg and chips. There's a good choice of real ales to sh it all down. Just one mile away you'll find the village of Woodhall a, whose grand hotels grew up after iodine- and bromide-rich waters re discovered there in the 19th century.

en 12-2.30 6-11 **Bar Meals** L served all week 12-2 D served all week 9 **Restaurant** L served all week 12-2 D served all week 6.30-9 Free use Bateman XB, Black Sheep Best, Barnsley Bitter, Carlsberg-Tetley ley's Smooth Flow. **Facilities** Garden Parking **Rooms** 8 bedrooms suite S£40 D£60 (★★★★ GA)

'OOLSTHORPE MAP 11 SK83

Pick of the Pubs

The Chequers Inn ★★★★ INN

Main St NG32 1LU ☎ 01476 870701

e-mail: justinnabar@yahoo.co.uk

dir: *3m from A607. Follow heritage signs to Belvoir Castle*

Just a stone's throw from Belvoir Castle, The Chequers Inn mixes modern style with traditional features including five real fires. Drinkwise, there is an extensive range of continental lagers, real ales and fine wines plus fifty single malts. You can dine anywhere, from the traditional bar to the Bakehouse Restaurant (which contains the oven from the pub's previous incarnation as the village bakery, built in 1646) or the more intimate Red Room. There is a strong emphasis on home cooking and quality ingredients, including locally sourced steaks and sausages. Bar snacks include steaks, salad and interesting sandwiches. In the evenings things get more serious, perhaps with roast Gressingham duck breast with braised red cabbage, fondant potato and cider jus, or medallions of monkfish with chorizo and saffron risotto. There are further delights outside: the pub has a cricket pitch, a pétanque pitch, and castle views from the mature garden.

Open 12-3 5.30-11 **Bar Meals** L served all week 12-2.30 D served all week 6-9.30 (Sun 12-4, 6-8.30) Av main course £13 **Restaurant** L served all week 12-2.30 D served all week 6-9.30 (Sun 12-4, 6-8.30) Av 3 course à la carte £25 Av 3 course fixed price £15 Free House Olde Trip & Brewster's Marquis. 25 **Facilities** Children's licence Garden Dogs allowed Parking **Rooms** 4 bedrooms en suite S£49 D£59

LONDON

E1

Town of Ramsgate Plan 2 F4

62 Wapping High St E1W 2NP ☎ 020 7481 8000

dir: *0.3m from Wapping tube station & Tower of London*

A 500-year-old pub close to The City, decorated with bric-a-brac and old prints. Judge Jeffries was caught here while trying to flee the country and escape the kind of justice he dealt out. Press gangs used to work the area, imprisoning men overnight in the cellar. The owners continue to offer real ale and value for money bar food, which can be enjoyed on the decked terrace overlooking the river Thames.

Open 12-12 **Bar Meals** L served all week 12-9 D served all week 12-9 Av main course £7.50 Free House Adnams, Youngs, Fullers London Pride. 7 **Facilities** Garden Dogs allowed

E9

Pick of the Pubs

The Empress of India NEW Plan 2 F4

130 Lauriston Rd, Victoria Park E9 7LH

☎ 020 8533 5123 📠 020 8533 4483

e-mail: info@theempressofindia.com

dir: *Mile End Station right onto Grove Rd and Lauriston Rd*

This majestic Victorian pub is the latest addition to Tom and Ed Martin's gastro-pub empire, which also includes the acclaimed Gun in Docklands, The Well in Clerkenwell and The White Swan on Fetter Lane, EC4. The Martins have reinstated its original name, given in honour of Queen Victoria's additional role as Empress of India, and the beautifully styled interior takes its cue from these Victorian and colonial associations: mussel shell chandeliers, a mosaic tiled floor, Chesterfield-style banquette seating and an antique tiger's head all lend the place a singular appeal. The menu is full of bright and breezy modern British delights: for lunch perhaps dressed Dorset crab; Welsh rarebit or a warm salad of Arbroath smokie, dandelion and quail's egg. More substantial meals might include corn-fed chicken with pancetta, avocado and baby spinach on sourdough; or the 'mighty game pie' with Savoy cabbage and chestnuts.

Open Closed: 25-26 Dec **Restaurant** L served all week 12-3 D served all week 6-10 (Sun 12-4, 6.30-9.30) Av 3 course à la carte £28 Greenwich Meantime Helles Lager, Greenwich Meantime Indian Pale Ale, Paulaner Weiss Beer. 30

England

E14

Pick of the Pubs

The Grapes — Plan 2 G4

76 Narrow St, Limehouse E14 8BP

☎ 020 7987 4396 020 7987 3137

Charles Dickens once propped the bar up here, and so taken was he by its charms that the pub appears, thinly disguised, as The Six Jolly Fellowship Porters in his novel *Our Mutual Friend*. While the novelist might still recognise the interior, the surroundings have changed dramatically with the development of Canary Wharf and the Docklands Light Railway. However, the tradition of old-fashioned values is maintained by the provision of the best cask conditioned ales in the atmospheric bar downstairs, while in the tiny upstairs restaurant only the freshest fish is served. This is a fish lover's paradise with a menu that includes sea bass, monkfish, Dover sole and bream, all available with a range of different sauces. Meat eaters and vegetarians should not, however, be deterred from experiencing this evocative slice of old Limehouse; traditional roasts are served on Sundays, and sandwiches and salads are always available.

Open 12-3 5.30-11 (Sat 12-11, Sun 12-10.30) Closed: 25-26 Dec, 1 Jan **Bar Meals** L served all week 12-2 D served Mon-Sat 7-9 (Sat 12-2.30, Sun 12-3.30) Av main course £7.50 **Restaurant** L served Mon-Fri 12-2.15 D served Mon-Sat 7.30-9.15 (Sun 12-3.30) Punch Taverns Adnams, Marstons Pedigree, Carlsberg-Tetley Tetley's Bitter, Timothy Taylor's Landlord. 6 **Facilities** Dogs allowed

Pick of the Pubs

The Gun — Plan 2 G4

27 Coldharbour, Docklands E14 9NS

☎ 020 7515 5222 020 7515 4407

e-mail: info@thegundocklands.com

dir: *From South Quay DLR, east along Marsh Wall to mini rdbt. Left, over bridge 1st right.*

Destroyed by fire several years ago, this grade two listed 18th-century pub re-opened in 2004 following painstaking restoration works carried out in close consultation with English Heritage. It stands on the banks of the Thames directly across the water from the Millennium Dome and a stone's throw from Canary Wharf. The surrounding area was once home to the dockside iron foundries which produced guns for the Royal Navy fleets. The Gun itself used to shelter smugglers. There is still a spy hole on the secret circular staircase that was once used to look out for the 'revenue men'. Today the modern pub menu is a major attraction, with choices ranging from bar food (pint o' prawns with aioli; Irish rock oysters; beef shin burger with fat chips) to evening meals such as ham hock and confit foie gras terrine, followed by braised daube of beef with Alsace bacon and truffle mash.

Open 11-12 (Sat 11.30-12, Sun 11.30-10.30) Closed: 26 Dec **Bar Meals** L served all week 12-3.45 D served all week 6-10.30 (Sat-Sun 11-4 Sun 6-9.30) Av main course £9 **Restaurant** L served all week 12-3 D served all week 6-10.30 (Sat-Sun 11-4 Sun 6-9.30) Av 3 course à la carte £30 Lowenbrau, Guinness, San Miguel, Hoegaarden. 22 **Facilities** Children's licence Garden

EC1

Pick of the Pubs

The Bleeding Heart Tavern — Plan 1 E4

19 Greville St EC1N 8SQ

☎ 020 7242 8238 020 7831 1402

e-mail: bookings@bleedingheart.co.uk

dir: *Close to Farringdon tube station, at corner of Grenville St & Bleeding Heart Yard*

The first record of this old tavern off London's famous Leather Lane dates from 1746, a time when Holborn had a boozer for every five houses. It traded until 1946, was a grill for 52 years, then reopened as The Tavern Bar in 1998. The legend behind the name is too gruesome for a food review, particularly when referring to the free-range organic British meat, game and poultry dishes that can be found downstairs in the Dining Room. Here an open rotisserie and grill provides spit-roasted, ale-fed suckling pig, Suffolk lamb burger; grilled salmon with leeks and lemon confit; and Scottish rib-eye steak, all served with roast potatoes. Tavern Classics include poached haddock kedgeree; Lincolnshire rabbit casserole; and French bangers and mash. The Tavern is also open for 'full English' breakfast with freshly squeezed orange juice and home-baked croissants.

Open 7-11 Closed: BHs, 10 days at Xmas **Bar Meals** L served Mon-Fri 11 D served Mon-Fri 6-10.30 Av main course £10 **Restaurant** L served Mon-Fri 12-3 D served Mon-Fri 6-10.30 Av 3 course à la carte £20 Free House Adnams Southwold Bitter Broadside & Fisherman. 17

Pick of the Pubs

The Eagle — Plan 1 E4

159 Farringdon Rd EC1R 3AL ☎ 020 7837 1353

dir: *Angel/Farringdon tube N end of Farringdon Rd*

When it first opened in 1990, The Eagle was a front-runner of a new breed of stylish eating and drinking establishments we know now as the gastro pub. Back then London's hipsters would not have hung out in the drab Farringdon Road, but these days Clerkenwell is quite the trendy district. The Eagle has remained one of the neighbourhood's top establishments – no mean feat, given the competition today. The airy interior includes a wooden-floored bar and dining area, a random assortment of furniture, and an open-to-view kitchen that produces a modern, creative daily-changing menu with a Southern European/Pacific Rim/South American theme. Seen frequently are Romney Marsh lamb chops with cracked wheat, broad beans, mint and cucumber; Gloucester Old Spot and cockles; roast pollock with purple sprouting broccoli; and linguini with crab, coriander and lemon. Draught and bottled beers, and an international wine list are all well chosen.

Open 12–11 **Bar Meals** L served Mon–Fri 12.30–3 (Sat–Sun 12.30–3.30) D served Mon–Sat 6.30–10.30 Av main course £9.50 Free House Wells Eagle IPA & Bombardier. 14 **Facilities** Dogs allowed

Pick of the Pubs

The Jerusalem Tavern

Plan 1 F4

55 Britton St, Clerkenwell EC1M 5NA
☎ 020 7490 4281 020 7490 4281
e-mail: beers@stpetersbrewery.co.uk
dir: *100mtrs NE of Farringdon tube station; 300mtrs N of Smithfield*

Named after the Priory of St John of Jerusalem, this historic tavern has been in four different locations since it was established in the 14th century. The current building dates from 1720, when a merchant lived here, although the frontage dates from about 1810, by which time it was the premises of one of Clerkenwell's many watch and clockmaker's workshops. A fascinating and wonderfully vibrant corner of London that has only recently been 'rediscovered', centuries after Samuel Johnson, David Garrick and the young Handel used to drink in this tavern. Its dark, dimly-lit Dickensian bar, with bare boards, rustic wooden tables, old tiles, candles, open fires and cosy corners, is the perfect film set – and that is what is has been on many occasions. The Jerusalem Tavern, a classic pub in every sense of the description, is open every weekday and offers the full range of bottled beers from St Peter's Brewery (which owns it), as well as a familiar range of pub fare, including game pie, risotto, sausage and mash and various roasts.

Open Mon–Fri 11–11 Closed: 25 Dec **Bar Meals** L served Mon–Fri 12–3 D served Mon–Fri 5–10 Av main course £8.50 St Peters Brewery St Peters (complete range).

Pick of the Pubs

The Peasant

Plan 1 D3

240 St John St EC1V 4PH
☎ 020 7336 7726 020 7490 1089
e-mail: eat@thepeasant.co.uk
dir: *Exit Angel & Farringdon Rd tube station. Pub on corner of St John St & Percival St*

In the heart of the Clerkenwell, in a building dating back to 1860, this award-winning pub retains many original Victorian features including the lovingly restored mahogany horseshoe bar with its original inlaid mosaic floor, and a fabulous conservatory. The upstairs restaurant has had similar treatment and is beautifully lit by period chandeliers. The extensive range of pumped and bottled beers is supplemented by organic cider, rums, malt whiskeys and a good wine list. Light bites like mixed olives in garlic and herb brine or a pint of prawns are served in the bar, alongside sharing platters like vegetable mezze or Irish rock oysters, and mains like roast Toulouse sausages on swede, carrot and miso mash with bacon soffritto. The restaurant menu offers unusual cuisine like grilled kangaroo fillet with oyster mushrooms, bean sprouts and mint salad with vanilla-soy dressing to start, and wild boar spezzatino with baby fennel, turnip and shallot.

Open Mon–Fri 12–11 Closed: 24 Dec–2 Jan **Bar Meals** L served Sun–Fri 12–11 D served Mon–Sun 6–11 (Sun all day) Av main course £8.50 **Restaurant** L served all week 12–3.30 D served Mon–Sat 6–11 Av 3 course à la carte £30 Av 2 course fixed price £14 Free House Bombardier. 12 **Facilities** Garden Dogs allowed

The Well

Plan 1 F5

180 Saint John St, Clerkenwell EC1V 4JY
☎ 020 7251 9363 020 7404 2250
e-mail: drink@downthewell.co.uk
dir: *Farringdon tube station left to junction; left onto St John St*

A gastropub in trendy Clerkenwell offering a regularly changing, modern European lunch and dinner menu, an extensive wine selection, and lots of draught and bottled beers. The lower ground features a leather-panelled aquarium bar with exotic tropical fish in huge tanks. Start with twice-baked goats' cheese soufflé, or snails with Pernod and garlic butter; then Huntsman sausages with mashed potato and red onion jam; or pan-fried halibut with curly kale, cep purée and port jus.

Open 11–12 (Sun 11–11) **Bar Meals** L served Mon–Sun 12–3 D served Mon–Sun 6–10.30 **Restaurant** L served Mon–Sun 12–3 D served Mon–Sun 6–10.30 San Miguel, Paulaner, Red Stripe, Kronenbourg. 15 **Facilities** Children's licence

Ye Olde Mitre

Plan 1 E4

1 Ely Court, Ely Place, By 8 Hatton Garden EC1N 6SJ
☎ 020 7405 4751
web: www.pub-explorer.com
dir: *Chancery Lane tube station exit 3 to Holborn Circus, left into Hatton Garden. Pub in alley between 8 & 9 Hatton Garden*

A famous old establishment, hidden up an alleyway off Hatton Garden, Ye Olde Mitre dates from 1546. Queen Elizabeth once danced around the cherry tree in the corner of the bar. These days there's also a lounge and an outside beer barrel area. Three permanent real ales are served and a minimum of two changing guest ales weekly. The snack menu offers toasted sandwiches, pork pies, scotch eggs, sausages, pickled eggs and gherkins.

Open 11–11 (Wknds 11–12 Aug 12–5) Closed: 25 Dec, 1 Jan, BH **Bar Meals** L served Mon–Fri 11.30–9.30 Punch Taverns Adnams Bitter, Adnams Broadside, Duechars IPA, Roosters. 9 **Facilities** Garden

England

EC2

Old Dr Butler's Head Plan 1 F4

Mason's Av, Coleman St, Moorgate EC2V 5BT

☎ 020 7606 3504 📠 020 7600 0417

e-mail: olddrbutlershead@shepherdneame.co.uk

dir: *Telephone for directions*

Dr Butler sold 'medicinal ale' from taverns displaying his sign. This, the only survivor, was rebuilt after the Great Fire of London, while the frontage is probably Victorian. Pub lunches are served in the pleasantly Dickensian gas-lit bar, where Shepherd Neame real ales are on tap, and steak and suet pudding is a speciality. More intimate dining areas, including a carvery, are upstairs, where dinner is by arrangement. The City empties at weekends, so the pub closes.

Open Mon–Fri 11–11 **Bar Meals** L served Mon–Fri 12–3 D by arrangement only Av main course £7.95 **Restaurant** L served Mon–Fri Shepherd Neame Shepherd Neame Spitfire, Bishops Finger Master Brew, Shepherd Neame Best.

EC4

The Black Friar Plan 1 F3

174 Queen Victoria St EC4V 4EG ☎ 020 7236 5474

Located on the site of Blackfriar's monastery, where Henry VIII dissolved his marriage to Catherine of Aragon and separated from the Catholic church. The pub has made several TV appearances because of its wonderful Art Noveau interior. It is close to Blackfriars Bridge and gets very busy with after-work drinkers. A traditional-style menu includes the likes of steak and ale pie, sausage and mash, and sandwiches.

Open 11.30–11 (Sat 11.30–11, Sun 12–9.30) **Bar Meals** L served all week 12–9 D served all week 12–9 Six Continents Retail Fullers London Pride, Adnams, Timothy Taylor, Speckled Hen. **Facilities** Garden

The Old Bank of England 🍷 Plan 1 E4

194 Fleet St EC4A 2LT ☎ 020 7430 2255 📠 020 7242 3092

e-mail: oldbankofengland@fullers.co.uk

dir: *Pub by Courts of Justice*

Until its conversion in 1994, this magnificent building housed the Law Courts' branch of the Bank of England. Set between the site of Sweeney Todd's barbershop and his mistress's pie shop, the Old Bank stands above the original bank vaults and the tunnels in which Todd butchered his unfortunate victims. Bar meals range from soup, sandwiches and burgers to speciality pies and hot dishes like braised lamb shank in red wine jus.

Open 11–11 Closed: wknds & BHs **Bar Meals** L served Mon–Fri D served Mon–Thurs 9 (Fri 8) Av main course £8 Fullers London Pride, ESB, Chiswick, Discovery & Guest ales. 🍷 10 **Facilities** Garden

Pick of the Pubs

The White Swan 🍷 Plan 1 E4

108 Fetter Ln, Holborn EC4A 1ES

☎ 020 7242 9696 📠 020 7404 2250

e-mail: info@thewhiteswanlondon.com

dir: *From Chancery Lane station towards St Paul's Cathedral. At HSBC bank left into Fetter Lane.*

This pub has been restored into a handsome, traditional city pub downstairs, while the upper floor is now a beautiful dining room with a mirrored ceiling, cream wallpaper, fawn leather and pristine linen-clad tables. Regulars now flock here, either to enjoy its extensive selection of cocktails, spirits, wines and real ales or to savour the food, which is made with the very best available ingredients, including fresh fish hand selected each morning at Billingsgate market. The bar menus change regularly and might include a pint of prawns, fish and chips, pheasant pie or wild boar and apple sausages; while a meal in the dining room might begin with braised rabbit tortellini with cep foam, followed by red wine braised monkfish cheeks with gremolata mash and deep-fried leeks. Finish with desserts such as passion fruit pannacotta or pecan pie with home-made maple syrup ice cream.

Open 11–11 (Wed–Thu 11–12 Fri 11–1) **Bar Meals** L served Mon–Fri 12–3 D served Tue–Fri 6–10 **Restaurant** L served Mon–Fri 12–3 D served Mon–Fri 6–10 Av 3 course à la carte £30 Av 2 course fixed price £23 London Pride, Red Stripe, Greene King IPA, Guinness. 🍷 13

N1

Pick of the Pubs

The Barnsbury 🍷 Plan 2 F4

209–211 Liverpool Rd, Islington N1 1LX

☎ 020 7607 5519 📠 020 7607 3256

e-mail: info@thebarnsbury.co.uk

The Barnsbury, in the heart of Islington, is a welcome addition to the London scene as a gastropub that gets both the prices and food right. The recent addition of a walled garden has added a secluded and sought-after summer oasis for al fresco dining. The food is cooked from daily supplies of fresh produce which have been bought direct from the market, resulting in interesting menus with a slight nod to international cuisine. Starters include leek and smoked haddock chowder; Welsh rarebit crouton with scallops and tiger prawns, and Thai fragrant salad; and chargrilled halloumi, aubergine, parsley and harissa oil. Mains include choices like roast chicken breast with pappardelle and wild mushroom sauce; chargrilled rib-eye steak with béarnaise sauce, chips and salad; and goats' cheese and ricotta ravioli, artichokes and sun dried tomatoes. Desserts range through lemon mousse brûlée; French apple tart with butterscotch sauce and Calvados crème fraiche; and chocolate mousse with oranges in Grand Marnier.

Open 12–11 Closed: 24–26 Dec, 1 Jan **Bar Meals** L served all week 12–3 D served all week 6.30–10 (Sun 6.30–9.30) Av main course £12 **Restaurant** L served all week 12–3 D served all week 6.30–10 (Sun 6.30–9.30) Av 3 course à la carte £22 Free House Timothy Taylor Landlord, Fullers London Pride, Guest ale. 🍷 12 **Facilities** Garden

he Compton Arms 🍷 Plan 2 F4

Compton Av, Off Canonbury Rd N1 2XD
: 020 7359 6883
mail: thecomptonarms@ukonline.co.uk

e best kept secret in N1: a late 17th-century country pub in the ddle of town with a peaceful, rural feel, frequented by a mix of :als, actors and musicians. Real ales from the hand pump, and good ue steaks, mixed grill, big breakfast and Sunday roast. One local scribed the Compton Arms as "an island in a sea of gastro-pubs". pect a busy bar when Arsenal are at home.

pen 12–11 Closed: 25 Dec pm **Bar Meals** L served all week 12–2.30 served all week 6–8.30 (Sat–Sun 11–4) Av main course £6 Greene ng Greene King IPA, Abbot Ale, Morlands, plus Guest ale. 🍷 8 **cilities** Garden Dogs allowed

he Crown 🍷 Plan 2 F4

6 Cloudsley Rd, Islington N1 0EB
: 020 7837 7107 020 7833 1084
mail: crown.islington@fullers.co.uk

is Grade II listed Georgian building in the Barnsbury village nservation area of Islington boasts one of only two remaining barrel rs in London. It specialises in high quality gastro food, and has an usual range of branded rums. The daily changing menu typically atures starters to share like spare ribs or assorted platters with Turkish tbreads, and mains such as lamb burgers, a variety of sausages, hcakes, and steak and ale pie. Vegetarians are well catered for.

pen 12–11 Closed: 25 Dec **Bar Meals** L served all week 12–3 D served week 6–10 (Sat 12–10, Sun 12–9) Av main course £9.50 Fullers Fullers London Pride, Kirin, Fullers Discovery & Fullers Organic oneydew. 🍷 12 **Facilities** Garden Dogs allowed

Pick of the Pubs

The Drapers Arms 🍷 Plan 2 F4

44 Barnsbury St N1 1ER
☎ 020 7619 0348 020 7619 0413
e-mail: info@thedrapersarms.co.uk
dir: *Right from Highbury & Islington station, 10mins along Upper St. Barnsbury St on right opp Shell service station*

Smart Islington gastro-pub offering one menu throughout, though it is preferable to book the upstairs dining room which attracts a good crowd – celebrities from television, politics and the arts among others. The downstairs bar is open plan, with wooden floor boards, wooden tables and chairs, and a noisy buzz of conversation, especially at weekends. A wide choice of food includes a range of appetising starters, from roast portabello mushroom and caraway seed soup, to roast quail, puy lentil vinaigrette and quince. For a main course, try spaghetti with roast squash, sage, garlic and feta; calves' liver and bacon with celeriac mash and onion jus; or smoked haddock, pea and bacon risotto. To finish, savour the delights of sticky toffee pudding with custard and toffee sauce, or lime leaf and coconut crème brûlée.

Open 11–11 Closed: 24–27 Dec, 1 & 2 Jan **Bar Meals** L served all week 12–3 D served all week 7–10 (Sun 6.30–9.30) Av main course £12 **Restaurant** L served Sun 12–3 D served Mon–Sat 7–10.30 Av 3 course à la carte £25 Free House Old Speckled Hen, Courage. 🍷 18 **Facilities** Garden Dogs allowed

Pick of the Pubs

The Duke of Cambridge 🍷 Plan 2 F4

30 St Peter's St N1 8JT
☎ 020 7359 3066 020 7359 1877
e-mail: duke@dukeorganic.co.uk

The first organic pub in the UK, the Duke of Cambridge opened in December 1998 and was the first UK pub to receive Soil Association certification. Founder and MD Geetie Singh combines hers skills and passion for food and ethical business to create a value-driven company with minimal environmental impact. There is no music, TV or electronic machines. The company recycles and reuses wherever possible and operates a fish purchasing policy approved by the Marine Conservation Society. Even the electricity is wind and solar sourced, and with 100% organic wines and twice-daily changing blackboard menu you can really feel virtuous while tucking into a few courses and a glass or two of your favourite tipple. Try a delicious starter like wild duck, apple and celeriac salad with hazelnut dressing; followed perhaps by whole baked organic trout wrapped in Parma ham with spinach. The cheese plate looks like a tempting option afterwards, enjoy Cornish brie, Godminster cheddar and Welsh goats' cheese with hot onion relish and home-made oat cakes.

Open 12 –11 (Sun 12–10.30) Closed: Dec 25–26 **Bar Meals** L served Mon-Fri 12.30–3 (Sat–Sun 12.30–3.30) D served all week 6.30–10.30 (Sun 7–10) Av main course £12 **Restaurant** L served Mon–Fri 12.30–3 (Sat–Sun 12.30–3.30) D served all week 6.30–10.30 (Sun 7–10) Free House Eco Warrior, St Peter's Best Bitter, East Kent Golding. 🍷 12 **Facilities** Children's licence Dogs allowed

The House 🍷 Plan 2 F4

63–69 Canonbury Rd N1 2DG
☎ 020 7704 7410 020 7704 9388
e-mail: info@inthehouse.biz

This successful gastro-pub has featured in a celebrity cookbook and garnered plenty of praise since it opened its doors a few years ago. Expect a thoroughly modern menu delivering devilled kidneys and ceps on toasted brioche with smoked bacon; chargrilled rib of Buccleuch beef with a mustard and shallot crust, gratin dauphinoise, green beans and jus gras; traditional favourites like shepherd's pie, and smoked haddock with bubble and squeak.

Open 12–11 Closed: 24 Dec, 1 Jan **Bar Meals** L served Tue–Sat 12–2.30 (Sat–Sun 12–3.30) D served all week 5.30–10.30 (Sun 6.30–9.30) **Restaurant** L served Tue–Sat 12–2.30 (Sat–Sun 12–3.30) D served all week 5.30–10.30 (Sun 6.30–9.30) Adnams, Guinness. 🍷 8 **Facilities** Garden Dogs allowed

England

N1 continued

The Northgate 🍷 Plan 2 F4

113 Southgate Rd, Islington N1 3JS

☎ 020 7359 7392 📠 020 7359 7393

dir: *Nearest tube Old St, or Angel. 5 mins on Bus no. 38/73 from Angel. 7 mins from bus no. 21/76/141 from Old st.*

This popular pub was transformed from a run-down community local into a friendly modern establishment serving excellent food. There's a regular guest beer, two real ales, and a good mix of draught lagers and imported bottled beers. The menu changes daily, and might include smoked haddock fishcake, slow-roast tomatoes with lemon butter; roast confit duck leg, mustard mash and Savoy cabbage; and roast aubergine, goats' cheese and onion tart with mixed leaves.

Open 12–11 (Sat 12–12, Sun 12–10.30, Mon 5–11) Closed: 24–26 Dec, 1 Jan **Bar Meals** L served all week 12–10.30 D served all week 6.30–9.30 Av main course £12 **Restaurant** L served Sat–Sun 12–10.30 D served all week 6.30–9.30 Av 3 course à la carte £20 IPA, Fuller's London Pride & Guest ales. 🍷 18 **Facilities** Garden Dogs allowed

N6

Pick of the Pubs

The Flask 🍷 Plan 2 E5

Highgate West Hill N6 6BU ☎ 020 8348 7346

e-mail: info@theflaskhighgate.co.uk

A 17th-century former school in one of London's loveliest villages. Dick Turpin hid from his pursuers in the cellars, and TS Elliot and Sir John Betjeman enjoyed a glass or two here. The interior is listed and includes the original bar with sash windows which lift at opening time. Enjoy a glass of good real ale, a speciality bottled beer (choice of 15), or a hot toddy while you peruse the menu, which changes twice a day. Choices range through sandwiches and platters to chargrills and home-made puddings.

Open 12–11 **Bar Meals** L served all week 12–3 D served all week 6–10 (Sun 12–9.30) Av main course £8 Six Continents Retail Adnams, Timothy Taylor Landlord, Caledonian IPA, Harveys Sussex. 🍷 12 **Facilities** Garden Dogs allowed

N19

The Landseer 🍷 Plan 2 E5

37 Landseer Rd N19 4JU ☎ 020 7263 4658

e-mail: info@thelandseer.wanadoo.co.uk

dir: *Nearest tube stations: Archway & Tufnell Park*

Sunday roasts are a speciality at this unpretentious gastro pub. Well-kept beers like Marston's Pedigree, Courage Director's and Green King IPA are supported by a range of wines served by the glass. This is an ideal spot to relax with the weekend papers, or while away an evening with one of the pub's extensive library of board games. Weekend lunches and daily evening meals are served from separate bar and restaurant menus.

Open 5–11 (Sat–Sun 12–12) Closed: 25 Dec **Bar Meals** L served Sat–Sun 12–5 D served all week 6–10 (Sun 6–9.30) Av main course £9 **Restaurant** L served Sat–Sun 12–5 D served all week 6–10 (Sun 6–9.30) Free House Marston's Pedigree, Courage Directors, Greene King IPA. 🍷 11 **Facilities** Children's licence Garden Dogs allowed

NW1

The Chapel 🍷 Plan 1 B

48 Chapel St NW1 5DP

☎ 020 7402 9220 📠 020 7723 2337

e-mail: thechapel@btconnect.com

dir: *By A40 Marylebone Rd & Old Marylebone Rd junct. Off Edgware Rd by tube station*

There's an informal atmosphere at this bright and airy Marylebone gastro-pub with stripped floors and pine furniture. The open-plan building derives its name from nothing more than its Chapel Street location, but it enjoys one of the largest gardens in central London with seating for over 60 customers. Fresh produce delivered daily is served in starters like broccoli and watercress soup, and mains such a pan-roasted chicken breast with sautéed ratte potatoes.

Open 12–11 (Sun 12–10.30) Closed: Dec 25–26, Jan 1, Easter **Bar Meals** L served all week 12–2.30 (Sun 12.30–3) D served all week 7–10 **Restaurant** L served all week 12–2.30 (Sun 12.30–3) D served all week 7–10 Punch Taverns Greene King IPA & Adnams. 🍷 10 **Facilities** Garden Dogs allowed

Pick of the Pubs

The Engineer 🍷 Plan 2 E4

65 Gloucester Av, Primrose Hill NW1 8JH

☎ 020 7722 0950 📠 020 7483 0592

e-mail: info@the-engineer.com

Situated in a very residential part of Primrose Hill close to Camden Market, this unassuming corner street pub is worth seeking out. Built by Isambard Kingdom Brunel in 1841, it attracts a discerning dining crowd for imaginative and well-prepared food and a friendly, laid-back atmosphere. Inside it is fashionably rustic, with a spacious bar area, sturdy wooden tables with candles, simple decor and changing art exhibitions in the restaurant area. A walled, paved and heated garden to the rear is extremely popular in fine weather. The fortnightly-changing menu features an eclectic mix of inspired home-made dishes and uses organic or free-range meats. Typical examples could be miso-marinated cod with wasabi mash and soy sherry sauce; or chicken breast stuffed with pumpkin, ricotta and sage with warm pasta and asparagus. Side dishes include baker fries or rocket and parmesan salad, while desserts include tasty combinations like apple and blackberry chimichanga.

Open 9 –11 **Bar Meals** L served all week 12–3 D served all week 7–11 (Sat–Sun 12.30–4) Av main course £14 **Restaurant** L served all week 12–3 D served all week 7–11 (Sat–Sun 12.30–4) Av 3 course à la carte £50 Six Continents Ltd Erdinger, Leffe, Bombardier, Hook Norton. 🍷 10 **Facilities** Children's licence Garden Dogs allowed

The Globe 🍷 Plan 1 E

43–47 Marylebone Rd NW1 5JY

☎ 020 7935 6368 📠 020 7224 0154

dir: *Corner Marylebone Rd & Baker St, opposite Baker St tube station*

Built in 1735, the Globe Tavern is contemporaneous with the adjoinir Nash terraces and the Marylebone Road itself. The first omnibus service from Holborn stopped here, and the Metropolitan Railway ru

-neath the road outside. The pub retains much of its 18th-century -aracter, and the owners proudly serve traditional English fare. -mbardier and London Pride are amongst the ales that accompany -shes like sausages, mash and onion gravy, grilled tuna steak, scampi, -d fish and chips.

-pen 11–11 (Sun 12–10.30, Fri–Sat 11–11.30) Closed: 25 Dec, 1 Jan **-r Meals** L served all week 11–10 D served all week 11–10 (Sun 12–8, -on–Sat winter 11–9) Av main course £5.50 Punch Taverns Scottish -urage Directors, Bombardier, Youngs, IPA. 17

Pick of the Pubs

The Lansdowne

Plan 2 E4

90 Gloucester Av, Primrose Hill NW1 8HX
020 7483 0409 020 7586 1723
e-mail: thelansdownepub@thelandsdownepub.co.uk
dir: *Chalk Farm tube station cross Adelaide Road, left into Gloucester Ave for 500yds*

In 1992, Amanda Pritchett started The Lansdowne as one of the earliest dining pubs in Primrose Hill. Stripping the pub of its fruit machines, TVs and jukebox, she brought in solid wood furniture and back-to-basics décor; today, it blends a light, spacious bar and outdoor seating area with a slightly more formal upper dining room. All that apart, however, its success depends on the quality of its cooking. All food is freshly prepared on the premises, using organic or free-range ingredients wherever possible, and portions are invariably generous. The seasonal menu offers dishes like spiced red lentil soup with Greek yoghurt; home-cured bresaola with rocket, capers and parmesan; pan-fried sardines on toast with watercress; confit pork belly with prunes, potatoes and lardons; poached sea trout with crushed herb potatoes; polenta with roast pumpkin, buffalo mozzarella and walnut; hot chocolate fondant with double cream; and peached poached in saffron with yoghurt and nuts.

Open 12–11 (Sat–Sun 9.30–11) Closed: 26 Dec **Bar Meals** L served all week 12–3 D served all week 7–10 (Sun 12.30–3.30 & 7–9.30) Av main course £14 **Restaurant** L served Sat–Sun 1–3 D served Tue–Sun 7–10 Av 3 course à la carte £28 Bass Staropramen. 6 **Facilities** Dogs allowed

-he Queens

Plan 2 E4

-9 Regents Park Rd, Primrose Hill NW1 8XD
020 7586 0408 020 7586 5677
-mail: thequeens@geronimo-inns.wanadoo.co.uk
-ir: *Nearest tube - Chalk Farm*

- one of London's most affluent and personality-studded areas, this -ictorian pub looks up at 206ft-high Primrose Hill. Main courses may -clude seared calves' liver with bacon and sage mash, roast vegetable -orkshire pudding, smoked chicken with mango and mange-tout peas, -nd whole roasted plaice with prawns and pancetta. On Sundays -here's a selection of roasts, as well as fish, pasta and salad. Beers -clude Youngs and guests.

-pen 11–11 (Fri–Sat 11–12, Sun 12–10.30) **Bar Meals** L served all week -2–3 (Sat 12–5) D served all week 7–10 (Fri–Sat 7–10.30) Av main course -9.50 **Restaurant** L served all week 12–3 D served all week 7–10 (Sun -–9) Geronimo Inns Ltd 12 **Facilities** Dogs allowed

NW3

The Holly Bush

Plan 2 E5

Holly Mount, Hampstead NW3 6SG
020 7435 2892 020 7431 2292
e-mail: info@hollybushpub.com

The Holly Bush was once the home of English portraitist George Romney and became a pub after his death in 1802. The building has been investigated by 'ghost busters', but more tangible 21st-century media celebrities are easier to spot. Depending on your appetite, the menu offers snacks and starters; smaller plates (a pint of prawns; Adnams rarebit); bigger plates (organic 21-day hung rump steak, pan-roast chicken) and a choice of sausages and pies, including vegetarian versions.

Open 12–11 **Bar Meals** L served all week 12.30–4 D served all week 6.30–10 (Sat 12–10, Sun 12–9) **Restaurant** L served Mon–Fri 12.30–10 D served all week 6.30–10 (Sat 12–10, Sun 12.30–9) Av 3 course à la carte £25 Punch Retail Harveys Sussex Best, Adnams Bitter & Broadside, Lowenbrau, London Pride. 10 **Facilities** Dogs allowed

Spaniards Inn

Plan 2 E5

Spaniards Rd, Hampstead NW3 7JJ
020 8731 6571 020 8731 6572

Believed to be the birthplace of highwayman Dick Turpin, this former tollhouse is a famous landmark beside Hampstead Heath. Named after two brothers who fought a fatal duel in 1721, it was mentioned by Bram Stoker in *Dracula*, and is still much frequented by celebrities. Traditional British fare is on offer, such as fish and chips, sausage and mash, and steamed steak and kidney pudding. In summer the stone flagged courtyard provides a shady retreat.

Open 11–11 (Wknds 10–11, Summer Fri–Sat 11–12) **Bar Meals** L served all week 11–10 D served all week 11–10 (Sat–Sun 10–10) Av main course £7.50 **Restaurant** L served all week 12–10 D served all week (Sat–Sun 10–10) Av 3 course à la carte £15 Fullers London Pride, Adnams Best, Martson's Old Empire, Oakhams JHB & Guest ales. 16 **Facilities** Garden Dogs allowed Parking

Ye Olde White Bear

Plan 2 E5

Well Rd, Hampstead NW3 1LJ 020 7435 3758

Victorian family-run pub with a Hampstead village feel and varied clientele from dustmen to Hollywood stars. There has been a pub on this site since 1704. All day bar food includes steak and Guinness pie, home-made cheeseburger, vegetarian lasagne, cod in beer batter, and tuna steak. Look out for the theatrical memorabilia, and there's a patio at the rear.

Open 11–11 (Thu–Sat 11–11.30) **Bar Meals** L served all week 12–9 D served all week 12–9 **Restaurant** L served all week D served all week Punch Retail Fuller's London Pride, Youngs, Shepherd Neame Spitfire, Wychwood Hobgoblin. 12 **Facilities** Garden

England

NW5

Dartmouth Arms 🍷 Plan 2 E5

35 York Rise NW5 1SP ☎ 020 7485 3267
e-mail: info@darmoutharms.co.uk
dir: *5min walk from Hampstead Heath*

Comedy nights, regular quizzes and themed food nights (perhaps steak or mussels) are popular fixtures at this pub close to Hampstead Heath. Food choices include a brunch menu, 'posh' sandwiches, a selection from the grill and platters themed by country (Spanish, Greek, English). Alongside the specials board, there are always hearty meals like bangers and mash or burgers. English ciders are a speciality.

Open 11–11 (Sat 10–11 Sun 10–10.30) **Bar Meals** L served all week 11–3 D served all week 6–10 (Sat–Sun 10–10) Av main course £7.95 **Restaurant** 11–3 6–10 (Sat & Sun 10–10) Punch Taverns Adnams, Archers & London Pride. 🍷 7 **Facilities** Dogs allowed

Pick of the Pubs

The Junction Tavern 🍷 Plan 2 E5

101 Fortess Rd NW5 1AG
☎ 020 7485 9400 020 7485 9401
dir: *Between Kentish Town and Tufnell Park tube stations*

This friendly local, halfway between Kentish Town and Tufnell Park underground stations, is handy for Camden and the green spaces of Parliament Hill and Hampstead Heath. The pub specialises in real ales, holding regular beer festivals, where enthusiasts mingle in the conservatory or large heated garden choosing from a range of 40-plus ales served straight from the cask. The daily-changing seasonal menus offer an interesting choice at lunch and dinner, plus a good-value set Sunday lunch with two options per course. There's Tuscan bread and oil or marinated olives to get the juices flowing, or a starter of salt and pepper squid with preserved lemon and coriander couscous. Main courses range from a lunchtime chargrilled lamb burger to pan-fried skate wing with new potatoes and saffron aïoli in the evening. Finish with chilled cardamom and vanilla rice pudding with apricot compote, or chocolate brownie, coffee cream and rum raisins.

Open 12–11 (Sun 12–10.30) Closed: 24–26 Dec, 1 Jan **Bar Meals** L served all week 12–3 D served all week 6.30–10.30 (Sun 12–4, 6.30–9.30) Av main course £12 **Restaurant** L served all week 12–3 D served all week 6.30–10.30 (Sun 12–4, 6.30–9.30) Av 3 course à la carte £24 Av 2 course fixed price £15 Enterprise Inns Caledonian Deuchars IPA, Guest ales & 4 Real Ale pumps. 🍷 12 **Facilities** Garden Dogs allowed

The Lord Palmerston NEW 🍷 Plan 2 E5

33 Dartmouthhill Park NW5 1HU ☎ 020 7485 1578
e-mail: lordpalmerston@geronimo-inns.co.uk
dir: *From Tuffnel Park Station turn right and continue straight up Dartmouth Park Hill. Pub on right, corner of Chetwynd Rd*

Stylishly revamped London pub in the Dartmouth Park conservation area. It has two open fires in winter and fully opening windows in summer, plus a large front terrace and garden for dining at the rear. Food is taken seriously, with dishes ranging from vegetarian cassoulet to guinea fowl breast with bubble and squeak and roasted shallot and tarragon sauce. Four real ales and five continental lagers are always on tap.

Open 12–11 (Sun 12–10.30) **Bar Meals** L served all week 12–3 D served all week 7–10 (Sun 12–9) Av main course £12 **Restaurant** L served all week 12–3 D served all week 7–10 (Sun 12–9) Av 3 course à la carte £20 Geronimo Inns Ltd Adnams Best, Sharps Eden Ale. 🍷 25 **Facilities** Children's licence Garden Dogs allowed

Pick of the Pubs

The Vine Plan 2 E5

86 Highgate Rd NW5 1PB
☎ 020 7209 0038 020 7209 9001
e-mail: info@thevinelondon.co.uk
dir: *Nearest tube: Kentish Town*

What looks like an Edwardian London pub on the outside has a very contemporary feel on the inside, with its copper bar, wooden floors, huge mirrors and funky art. Comfy leather sofas and an open fire make for a relaxed atmosphere. The Vine is billed as a bar, restaurant and garden, and the latter is a great asset – fully covered for year round use and popular for wedding receptions. Two dramatically decorated rooms are also available upstairs for private meetings or dinner parties. Lunchtime dishes range from bruschetta, and free-range burgers to linguine dressed with fresh blue swimmer crab. In the evening you might choose between chargrilled tuna with pak choi and roasted sesame oil, oven baked whole sea bass with cherry tomatoes and mussels, pasta with wild boar ragu and truffle oil, or home-made free range beefburgers.

Open 12–11 Closed: 26 Dec **Bar Meals** L served all week 12.30–3 D served all week 6.30–10.30 **Restaurant** L served all week 12–3.30 D served all week 6–10.30 Punch Taverns Fullers London Pride, IPA. **Facilities** Garden Parking

NW6

The Salusbury Pub and Dining Room 🍷 Plan 2 D

50–52 Salusbury Rd NW6 6NN ☎ 020 7328 3286
e-mail: thesalusbury@aol.com
dir: *100mtrs left from Queens Park tube & train station*

Gastropub with a lively and vibrant atmosphere, offering a London restaurant-style menu without the associated prices. The award-winning wine list boasts more than a hundred wines including mature offerings from the cellar. The owners are appreciated by a strong local following for continuity of quality and service. Example dishes are roas sea bream with Roman artichokes, leg of duck confit with lentils and cotechino, and Angus rib-eye steak.

Open 12–11 Closed: 25–26 Dec & 1 Jan **Bar Meals** L served Tue-Sun 12.30–3.30 D served all week 7–10.15 (Sun 7–10) Av main course £12 **Restaurant** L served Tue–Sun 12.30–3.30 D served all week 7–10.15 (Sun 7–10) Av 3 course à la carte £25 Broadside, Guinness, Staropramen & Aspall Cider. 🍷 13 **Facilities** Dogs allowed

W8

Pick of the Pubs

The Salt House NEW Plan 2 D4

63 Abbey Rd, St John's Wood NW8 0AE
☎ 020 7328 6626 📠 020 7604 4084
e-mail: salthousemail@majol.co.uk
dir: *Turn right outside St Johns Wood tube. Left onto Marlborough Place, right onto Abbey Rd, pub on left*

Describing itself as a mere scuttle from the Beatles' famous Abbey Road zebra crossing, this 18th-century inn promises a two-fold commitment to good food: to source excellent ingredients and to home cook them. With the exception of the odd bottle of ketchup, everything, including bread, buns and pasta, is made on site. Meanwhile, meats are Rare Breed Survival Trust accredited and fish has been caught by Andy in Looe. Espeto of chicken livers, chorizo, smoked bacon with lemon and parsley farofa; or aromatic crispy duck with hoi sin sauce could be followed by glazed crispy pork with black pudding mash; Catalan-style chargrilled fillet of wild halibut; or rack of Elwy Valley lamb with dauphinoise potatoes. A function room is available for larger parties, while street-side heaters allow for al fresco dining even on inclement days.

Open 10-12 **Bar Meals** L served 10-5 D served 5-10 Av main course £8 **Restaurant** L served 12-5 D served 6-10.30 Av 3 course à la carte £30 Abbot Ale, Guinness. 14 **Facilities** Children's licence Dogs allowed

NW10

The Greyhound Plan 2 D4

64-66 Chamberlayne Rd NW10 3JJ
☎ 020 8969 8080 📠 020 8969 8081
e-mail: thegreyhound@needtoeat.co.uk
dir: *Corner of Chamberlayne Rd & Mortimer Rd*

This pub was created from a derelict building, much to the delight of the locals, who have been flocking in ever since. Customers range from a smattering of supermodels to young families and older couples, all clearly enjoying the friendly atmosphere. There's an eclectic wine list, and a menu each for the bar and dining room. Expect dishes such as pumpkin risotto, breaded calamari, roast duck breast with sweet potato puree and wild sea trout and baby leeks.

Open 12-11 (Mon 5-11, Fri-Sat 12-12) Closed: 25-26 Dec, 1 Jan **Bar Meals** L served Fri-Sun 12.30-3 D served all week 6.30-10.30 (Sun 12.30-6) Av main course £9.50 **Restaurant** L served Sat-Sun 12.30-3 D served all week 6.30-10.30 (Sun 12.30-7) Av 3 course à la carte £20 Free House Guinness, & Guest ales. 14 **Facilities** Garden Dogs allowed

William IV Bar & Restaurant Plan 2 D4

786 Harrow Rd NW10 5JX
☎ 020 8969 5944 📠 020 8964 9218
dir: *Telephone for directions*

The William IV enjoys a strong local following of people drawn to the revitalized interior including a music-orientated bar (Virgin Records around the corner), and modern European food. A very flexible array of dishes typically includes chargrilled sirloin steak with chips and beetroot pesto; baked plaice with green beans; and pea, broad bean and mint tart. Plenty of fish too.

Open 12-11 (Fri-Sat 12-1, Sun 12-10.30) Closed: Dec 25 & Jan 01 **Bar Meals** L served all week 12-3 (Sun 12-4.30) D served all week 6-10.30 Av main course £10 **Restaurant** L served all week 12-3 D served all week 6-10.30 Av 3 course à la carte £18 Free House Fuller's London Pride. 7 **Facilities** Garden

SE1

The Anchor Plan 1 F3

Bankside, 34 Park St SE1 9EF
☎ 020 7407 1577 & 7407 3003 📠 020 7407 7023
e-mail: anchor.0977@thespirit.group.com

In the shadow of the Globe Theatre, this historic pub lies on one of London's most famous tourist trails. Samuel Pepys supposedly watched the Great Fire of London from here in 1666, and Dr Johnson was a regular, with Oliver Goldsmith, David Garrick and Sir Joshua Reynolds. The river views are excellent, and inside are black beams, old faded plasterwork, and a maze of tiny rooms. A varied menu includes fish and chips, pan-fried halibut with olives, and cod in crispy bacon served on wilted spinach.

Open 11-11 (Thu-Sat 11-12) Closed: 25 Dec **Bar Meals** L served all week 12-8 D served all week **Restaurant** L served all week 12-2.30 D served all week 5-10 Spirt Group Courage Directors, Greene King IPA, Adnams Broadside, Bombardier & Guest Ales. 14 **Facilities** Garden

England

SE1 continued

Pick of the Pubs

The Anchor & Hope ◎◎ ♀ Plan 1 E2

36 The Cut SE1 8LP

☎ 020 7928 9898 📠 020 7928 4595

e-mail: anchorandhope@btconnect.com

dir: *Nearest tube: Southwark & Waterloo*

A gastro-pub which has picked up many accolades for its cooking. But the Anchor and Hope is nonetheless a down-to-earth and friendly place where children with parents and dogs with owners are all made welcome. If weather permits, pavement seating allows you to watch the world go by as you enjoy a pint or one of many wines sold by the glass. The wine list is notable for its straightforward approach to prices, which are mainly in whole pounds; at the lower end half a bottle can be bought for half the price of a full one – an honest approach appreciated by the pub's faithful diners. The short menu too is refreshingly unembroidered. Starters may include smoked sprats or grilled razor clams. Main courses are hearty and rustic: English boar cooked in cider and roast partridge are two examples. Four or five trusted desserts complete the uncomplicated picture.

Open 11–11 (Mon 5–11) Closed: Last 2 wks in Aug, BH, Xmas, New Year **Bar Meals** L served Tue-Sat 12–2.30 (Sun 12–2) D served Mon–Sat 6–10.30 Av main course £13 **Restaurant** L served Tue–Sat 12–2.30 (Sun 12–2) D served Mon–Sat 6–10.30 Av 3 course à la carte £23 Av 4 course fixed price £30 Bombardier, Youngs Ordinary, IPA, Erdinger. ♀ 18 **Facilities** Garden Dogs allowed

The Bridge House Bar & Dining Room ♀ Plan 1 G2

218 Tower Bridge Rd SE1 2UP

☎ 020 7407 5818 📠 020 7407 5828

e-mail: the-bridgehouse@tiscali.co.uk

dir: *5 min walk from London Bridge/Tower Hill tube stations*

The nearest bar to Tower Bridge, The Bridge House has great views of the river and city and is handy for London Dungeons, Borough Market, Tate Modern, London Eye, Globe Theatre and Southwark Cathedral. It comprises a bar, dining room and new café, plus facilities for private functions. Typical dishes are chargrilled steak, beer battered haddock, and calves' liver with black pudding, smoked bacon, parsley mash and red wine gravy.

Open 11.30–11 (Thu–Sat 11.30–12 Sun 12–10.30) Closed: 25–26 Dec **Bar Meals** L served all week 11.30–10.30 D served all week 5.30–10.30 **Restaurant** L served all week 11.30–2.30 D served all week 5.30–10.30 Adnams Adnams Best Bitter, Adnams Broadside, Adnams Explorer & Guest Ale. ♀ 32

Pick of the Pubs

The Fire Station ◎ ♀ Plan 1 D2

150 Waterloo Rd SE1 8SB

☎ 020 7620 2226 📠 020 7633 9161

e-mail: firestation.waterloo@pathfinderpubs.co.uk

dir: *Turn right at exit 2 of Waterloo Station*

Close to Waterloo Station, and handy for the Old Vic Theatre and the Imperial War Museum, this remarkable conversion of a genuine early-Edwardian fire station has kept many of its former trappings intact. The rear dining room faces the open kitchen. An interesting menu includes dishes such as Fire Station avocado Caesar salad, baked cod with cheese polenta and pimento and pesto dressing, roast spiced pork belly with sticky rice and pak choi. Alternatively try tandoori seared yellowfin tuna loin, calves' liver with bacon or mustard mash, or lemon sole with Jerusalem artichokes. There are also imaginative midweek and Sunday set-price lunches.

Open 11–11 (Mon–Tue 11–12, Wed–Thu 11–1) Closed: 25–26 Dec, 1 Jan **Bar Meals** L served all week 12–5.30 D served all week 5.30–10.30 Av main course £6.95 **Restaurant** L served all week 12–2.45 D served all week 5–11 (Sat 12–11, Sun 12–9.30) Av 3 course à la carte £14.50 Pathfinder Pubs Adnams Best Bitter, Fuller's London Pride, Young's Bitters, Shepherd Neame Spitfire. ♀ 8

Pick of the Pubs

The Garrison NEW ♀ Plan 1 G2

99–101 Bermondsey St SE1 3XB

☎ 020 7407 3347 📠 020 7407 1084

e-mail: info@thegarrison.co.uk

dir: *From London Bridge tube station, E towards Tower Bridge 200mtrs, right onto Bermondsey St. Pub in 100mtrs*

See Pick of the Pubs on opposite page

The George Inn Plan 1 G

77 Borough High St SE1 1NH

☎ 020 7407 2056 📠 020 7403 6956

e-mail: 7781@greeneking.co.uk

dir: *From London Bridge tube station, take Borough High St exi left. Pub 200yds on left*

The only remaining galleried inn in London, this striking black and white building dates back at least to 1542 when it numbered one William Shakespeare among its clientele. Dickens mentioned it in *Littl Dorrit*, and his original life assurance policy is displayed along with 18th-century rat traps. The George has fading plasterwork, black bean and a warren of tiny rooms. Food is a straightforward choice includin steak, mushroom and ale pie, roast sirloin of beef, and gammon stea

Open 11–11 (Fri–Sat 11–12, Sun 12–10.30) Closed: 25 Dec **Bar Meals** L served all week 12–5 D served Mon–Sat (Sun 5–10) Av mair course £5.45 **Restaurant** D served Mon–Sat 5–10 Av 3 course fixed price £8.45 Laurel Pub Partnership Greene King Abbot Ale, George Inn Al IPA, Wadworth's 6X. **Facilities** Children's licence Garden

The Garrison

his artfully restyled London pub looks ordinary enough from the outside but inside it sports a ·lightful hotch potch of decorative themes, from French brasserie chic to the type of limed-and-hitewashed look you might expect in a trendy seaside cafe.

ıtique odds and ends, including ismatched chairs and tables, ıd to the quirky charm. In the ree years since it opened the pub ıs established a solid following, sulting in a villagey, community oe. The menu is typical of the ·lightfully eclectic, modern-yet-ıditional cooking that typically rns the label 'gastropub': a ıy of inspired eating begins at eakfast, with everything from the ırrison 'full and proper' breakfast omelette; scrambled eggs with .red salmon; buttermilk Scotch .ncakes with clotted cream, aple syrup and fruit conserve; the house muesli with fruit d Greek yogurt. For lunch, try illed haloumi, tomato petal and bergine stack with bell pepper ıaigrette; organic Arbroath salmon tartare with avocado mousse and melba toast; or thyme caramelized shallot tarte Tatin with soft goats' cheese, followed perhaps by pot roast pheasant with bread sauce and pan gravy; Oxfordshire rump of beef with tomato, Portobello mushroom and pommes Pont Neuf; or line-caught sea bass with sage and butternut dumplings. Side dishes include buttered spinach, dauphinoise potatoes and various salads. Many of the same choices are available in the evening, while bar snacks include Japanese seaweed peanuts; cheese on toast; a 'fish finger sarni'; and feta, mint and pine nut rolls. The wine list is compact but fairly comprehensive; other drink choices range from St Peters Organic ale to Cidre Breton.

NEW 🍷
Plan 1 G2
99–101 Bermondsey St SE1 3XB
☎ 020 7407 3347
📠 020 7407 1084
e-mail: info@thegarrison.co.uk
dir: *From London Bridge tube station, E towards Tower Bridge 200mtrs, right onto Bermondsey St. Pub in 100mtrs*

Open 8–11 (Sat 9–11, Sun 9–10.30)
Bar Meals L served all week 12.30–4 D served all week 6–9.30 Av main course £11.50
Restaurant L served all week 12–3.30 D served all week 6.30–10 (Sun 12–4, 6–9.30) Av 3 course à la carte £22.50
Free House
St Peters Organic Ale, Paulaner, Celis White, Becks Vier. 🍷 12
Facilities Dogs allowed

England

SE1 continued

The Market Porter 🍷 Plan 1 F3

9 Stoney St, Borough Market, London Bridge SE1 9AA

☎ 020 7407 2495 📠 020 7403 7697

dir: *Close to London Bridge Station*

Traditional tavern serving a market community that has been flourishing for about 1,000 years. Excellent choice of real ales. Worth noting is an internal leaded bay window unique in London. The atmosphere is friendly, if rather rough and ready, and the pub has been used as a location in *Lock, Stock and Two Smoking Barrels*, *Only Fools and Horses*, and *Entrapment*. Menu includes bangers and mash, roasted lamb shank, beetroot and lemon marinated salmon, and a hearty plate of fish and chips. Early morning opening.

Open 6–8.30 (Sat 11–11 Sun 12–10.30) **Bar Meals** L served Mon–Sun 12–3 6–9 Av main course £5.50 **Restaurant** L served Mon–Fri 12–3 6–9 Av 3 course à la carte £17.50 Free House Harveys Best, Scottish Courage Courage Bests. 🍷 10

The Old Thameside 🍷 Plan 1 F3

Pickford's Wharf, Clink St SE1 9DG

☎ 020 7403 4243 📠 020 7407 2063

Just two minutes' walk from Tate Modern, the Millennium Bridge and Shakespeare's Globe, this former spice warehouse is also close to the site of England's first prison, the Clink. The pub features a large outdoor seating area that overhangs the River Thames, and the friendly staff are always happy to point bewildered tourists in the right direction! Traditional pub fare includes fish and chips, sausage and mash, curries and vegetarian pies.

Open 12–11 11–12 Closed: 25 Dec **Bar Meals** L served all week 12–10 Av main course £6.95 **Restaurant** L served All D served All Fuller's London Pride, Adnams Bitter, Landlords Ale. 🍷 10 **Facilities** Children's licence Garden

SE5

The Sun and Doves 🍷 Plan 2 F3

61–63 Coldharbour Ln, Camberwell SE5 9NS

☎ 020 7924 9950 📠 020 7924 9330

e-mail: mail@sunanddoves.co.uk

This attractive Camberwell venue survived bomb damage during the last war, and today it's recognized for good food, drink and art – the pub showcases local artists, many of whom are well known. For a London pub it has a decent sized garden, planted in Mediterranean style, and a paved patio offers fixed seating for the summer months. Drinks options, apart from real ales and wines, include a long list of cocktails and shooters, through to Fairtrade coffee and herbal infusions. The menu is stylishly simple, with snacks and an honestly priced lunch and dinner menu.

Open 11–12 Closed: 25–26 Dec **Bar Meals** L served all week 12–10.30 D served all week 12–10.30 (Sun 12–9) Av main course £10 **Restaurant** L served all week 11–11 D served all week 10.30 Av 3 course à la carte £18 Old Speckled Hen, San Miguel & Ruddles. 🍷 8 **Facilities** Garden Dogs allowed Play Area

SE10

The Cutty Sark Tavern 🍷 Plan 2 G

4–6 Ballast Quay, Greenwich SE10 9PD ☎ 020 8858 314

dir: *Nearest tube: Greenwich. From Cutty Sark ship follow river towards The Millennium Dome (10 min walk)*

Originally the Union Tavern, this 1695 waterside pub was renamed when the world famous tea-clipper was dry-docked upriver in 1954. Inside, low beams, creaking floorboards, dark panelling and from the large bow window in the upstairs bar, commanding views of the Thames, Canary Wharf and the Millennium Dome. Well-kept beers, wines by the glass and a wide selection of malts are all available alo with bangers and mash, seafood, vegetarian specials and Sunday roasts. Busy at weekends, especially on fine days.

Open 11–11 (Sun 12–10.30) **Bar Meals** L served all week 12 D served a week 9 (Sun 12–5) Av main course £9 Free House Fullers London Pride, St Austells Tribute, Adnams Broadside, Addlestones Cider. 🍷 8 **Facilities** Children's licence Garden

Pick of the Pubs

Greenwich Union Pub Plan 2 G

56 Royal Hill SE10 8RT

☎ 020 8692 6258 📠 020 8305 8625

e-mail: andy@meantimebrewing.com

dir: *From Greenwich DLR & main station exit by main ticket hall, turn left, 2nd right into Royal Hill. Pub 100yds on right*

Comfortable leather sofas and flagstone floors help to keep the original character of this refurbished pub intact. Interesting beers (including chocolate and raspberry!), lagers and even freshly-squeezed orange juice, along with a beer garden make thi a popular spot. Try a foccacia sandwich; pearl barley risotto with courgette and radicchio; or chicken with spicy broccoli and sweet shallots; or, if it's fish you're after, grilled fillet of sea bass with seasonal vegetable ratatouille, or sauté of fresh mussels in white wine, cream and chives. The Meantime Brewery Co, which brews the beers on offer, was the only UK brewery to win awards at the 2004 Beer World Cup.

Open 12–11 (Sat 11–11, Sun 11.30–10.30) **Bar Meals** L served Mon–Sun 12.30–10 D served Mon–Fri (Sat–Sun 10–9) Av main course £8 Free House Kolsch, Pilsener, Wheat Beer, Raspberry Beer & Chocolate Beer. **Facilities** Children's licence Garden Dogs allowed

Pick of the Pubs

North Pole Bar & Restaurant 🍷 Plan 2 G

131 Greenwich High Rd, Greenwich SE10 8JA

☎ 020 8853 3020 📠 020 8853 3501

e-mail: north-pole@btconnect.com

web: www.northpolegreenwich.com

dir: *From Greenwich rail station turn right, pass Novotel. Pu on right (2 min walk)*

See Pick of the Pubs on opposite pag

North Pole Bar & Restaurant

he North Pole prides itself on offering a night out under one roof: there's the stylish Piano Restaurant with resident ivory-tinkler from Thursday to Saturday evenings; then there's the funky cocktail bar where an expert hand mixes and shakes at your command; and finally there's the South Pole basement DJ bar, where you can dance the night away from Wednesday to Saturday.

There is also a terrace, which makes an ideal spot for a glass of Pimms on a summer evening. A few years ago the whole building was refurbished to a high standard, and it now includes a VIP bar for private parties. An extensive bar menu is available all day, every day from 12 until 10.30pm, with choices ranging from sandwiches with French fries and salad through to main meals such as fish and chips or mushroom ravioli. The cooking style in the Piano Restaurant is modern European with a French twist. Typical starters include crispy deep-fried squid with lime and chilli mayonnaise; pan-fried foie gras with toasted brioche, shiitake mushrooms, crispy leeks and veal jus; and a risotto of oven-roasted squash, baby spinach, fresh parmesan and sage butter. You could follow with grilled rib-eye steak with potato gratin, ratatouille, baby carrots and thyme jus; or oven-roasted monkfish tail on a tomato and pepper stew with a black olive salsa. For dessert, perhaps a hot apple and mixed berry crumble or a honey and pistachio iced parfait with berry compote. Sunday brings roast dinners in the bar and the restaurant. Look out for regular live music including funk, soul and Latin.

Plan 2 G3
131 Greenwich High Rd,
Greenwich SE10 8JA
☎ 020 8853 3020
020 8853 3501
e-mail: north-pole@btconnect.com
web: www.northpolegreenwich.com
dir: *From Greenwich rail station turn right, pass Novotel. Pub on right (2 min walk)*

Open 12–12 (Sun 12–11.30, Thu 12–1, Fri & Sat 12–2)
Bar Meals L served all week 12–10.30 D served all week
Restaurant L served Sun 12–4 D served all week 6–11 Av 3 course à la carte £25 Av 3 course fixed price £25
Free House
Stella Artois, Staropramen, Leffe, Carling. 20

England

SE16

The Mayflower 🍷 Plan 2 F3

117 Rotherhithe St, Rotherhithe SE16 4NF

☎ 020 7237 4088 📠 020 7064 4710

dir: *Exit A2 at Surrey Keys rdbt onto Brunel Rd, 3rd left onto Swan Rd, left at T-junct, pub 200mtrs on right*

From the patio here you can still see the renovated jetty from which the eponymous 'Mayflower' embarked on her historic voyage to the New World. Billed as 'London's riverside link with the birth of America' the pub has a collection of memorabilia, as well as an unusual licence to sell both British and American postage stamps. Pub fare includes stuffed pork loin; Cajun chicken supreme; and fresh pasta with smoked bacon, spinach and mushrooms, plus plenty of fish and seafood.

Open 11–3 5.15–11 (Sun 12–10.30, May–Oct 11–11) **Bar Meals** L served all week 12–2.30 D served all week 6.30–9.30 (Sat–Sun 12–9) **Restaurant** L served all week 12–2.30 D served all week 6.30–9.30 (Sun 12–9) Greene King Greene King Abbot Ale, IPA, Old Speckled Hen. 🍷 30 **Facilities** Garden Dogs allowed

SE21

The Crown & Greyhound 🍷 Plan 2 F2

73 Dulwich Village SE21 7BJ

☎ 020 8299 4976 📠 020 8693 8959

With a tradition of service and hospitality reaching back to the 18th century, the Crown and Greyhound counts Charles Dickens and John Ruskin amongst its celebrated patrons. Modern day customers will find three bars and a restaurant in the heart of peaceful Dulwich Village. The weekly-changing menu might feature bean cassoulet with couscous; or an 8oz Angus burger with cheddar cheese and potato wedges. There are daily salads, pasta and fish dishes, too.

Open 11–11 (Sun 12–10.30) **Bar Meals** L served all week 12–10 D served all week 12–10 (Sun 12–9) Av main course £7 **Restaurant** L served all week 12–10 D served all week 12–10 (Sun 12–9) Fuller's London Pride & Guest ales. 🍷 15 **Facilities** Garden Dogs allowed

SE22

Pick of the Pubs

Franklins 🍷 Plan 0

157 Lordship Ln, Dulwich SE22 8HX ☎ 020 8299 9598

e-mail: info@franklinsrestaurant.com

dir: *0.5m S from East Dulwich station along Dog Kennel Hill & Lordship Lane*

Franklins is as much pub as it is bar/restaurant, and there are real ales and lagers on tap here, including Young's, Kronenbourg and Guinness among them. The restaurant interior is stripped-back, modern and stylish with bare floors, exposed brick walls and smartly clothed tables, while the bar is more traditional. The upwardly mobile and appreciative clientele enjoy the no-frills short menu, which opens with the likes of sweetbread terrine, steamed mussels, and wet garlic soup. Main courses continue in the same unfussy vein, with choices such as mutton faggots and pease pudding, Old Spot belly with fennel and black pudding, and Glamorgan sausages, spinach and tomato. Bar snacks include Welsh rarebit, and there are comforting desserts like rhubarb and custard, and bread and butter pudding. From Monday to Friday the excellent value set lunch menus allow the option of two or three courses.

Open 12–12 Closed: 25–26 & 31 Dec, 1 Jan **Bar Meals** L served all week 12–6 D served all week 6–10.30 (Sun 1–10.30) Av main course £14 **Restaurant** L served all week 12–6 D served all week 6–10.30 (Sun 1–10.30) Av 3 course à la carte £25 Av 2 course fixed price £11 Free House Youngs, Estrella, Guinnesss. 🍷 11 **Facilities** Dogs allowed

SE23

The Dartmouth Arms 🍷 Plan 2 F

7 Dartmouth Rd, Forest Hill SE23 3HN

☎ 020 8488 3117 📠 020 7771 7230

e-mail: info@thedartmoutharms.com

dir: *800mtrs from Horniman Museum – South Circular Rd (Eas*

Transformed old pub, with two smart public bars and a restaurant in the former lounge bar. Along with the traditional pint, there's a choic of cocktails, coffees and teas, and an eclectic range of bar snacks taki in pork scratchings, pickled eggs and olives. Dishes from the dinner menu are braised lamb shank, pumpkin and butternut squash risottc and salmon with pea purée and crayfish cream.

Open 12–12 (Fri & Sat 12–1, Sun 12–11) Closed: 25–26 Dec & 1 Jan **Bar Meals** L served all week 12–3.30 D served all week 6.30–10.30 (Sun 12–9) **Restaurant** L served all week 12–3.30 D served all week 6.30–10.3 (Sun 12–9) Av 3 course à la carte £23 Enterprise Inns Old Speckled Hen, Staropramen, London Pride, Kronenbourg Blanc & Brakspears. 🍷 10 **Facilities** Garden Parking

SW1

The Albert 🍷 Plan 1 I

52 Victoria St SW1H 0NP

☎ 020 7222 5577 & 7222 7606 📠 020 7222 1044

e-mail: thealbert.westminster@thespiritgroup.com

dir: *Nearest tube - St James Park*

Built in 1854, this Grade II Victorian pub is named after Queen Victoria's husband, Prince Albert. The main staircase is decorated with portraits of British Prime Ministers, from Salisbury to Blair, and the pub is often frequented by MPs. To make sure they don't miss a vote, there's even a division bell in the restaurant. The pub was the only building in the area to survive the Blitz of WW2, with even its o cut-glass windows remaining intact. The traditional menu includes a carvery, buffet, a selection of light dishes and other classic fare.

Open 11–11 (Sun 12–10.30) Closed: 25 Dec, 1 Jan **Bar Meals** L served all week 11–10 D served all week **Restaurant** L served all week 12–9.30 D served all week 5.30–9.30 Spirit Group Bombardier, Courage Directors & Best, London Pride, John Smiths. 🍷 14

The Buckingham Arms 🍷 Plan 1 I

62 Petty France SW1H 9EU ☎ 020 7222 3386

e-mail: buckinghamarms@youngs.co.uk

dir: *Nearest tube: St James's Park*

Known as the Black Horse until 1903, this elegant, busy Young's pub is situated close to Buckingham Palace. Popular with tourists, busine people and real ale fans alike, it offers a good range of simple pub od, including the 'mighty' Buckingham burger, nachos with chilli, icken ciabatta and old favourites like ham, egg and chips in its long r with etched mirrors.

en 11–11 (Sat 11–5.30, Sun 12–5.30) **Bar Meals** L served all week 11 served Mon–Fri 9 (Sun 12–4) Young & Co Youngs Bitter, Special & nter Warmer & Bombardier. 11 **Facilities** Dogs allowed

he Clarence — Plan 1 D3

5 Whitehall SW1A 2HP
: 020 7930 4808 020 7321 0859
r: *Between Big Ben & Trafalgar Sq*

is apparently haunted pub, situated five minutes' walk from Big Ben, Houses of Parliament, Trafalgar Square and Buckingham Palace, s leaded windows and ancient ceiling beams from a Thames pier. ical of the menu choice are sausage and mash; pesto penne pasta th brie or chicken; and pie of the day. Daily specials are available. e pub has a friendly atmosphere and is handy for the bus and tube.

en 10–12 (Sun–Tue 10–11) Closed: 25 Dec **Bar Meals** L served all ek 10–12 D served all week Av main course £5 **Restaurant** L served all ek D served all week Av 3 course à la carte £15 Scottish & Newcastle ewery Bombardier, Fullers London Pride, Youngs, Adnams Broadside Guest ale. 17

he Grenadier — Plan 1 B2

Wilton Row, Belgravia SW1X 7NR
: 020 7235 3074 020 7235 3400
r: *From Hyde Park Corner along Knightsbridge, left into Old rracks Yd, pub on corner*

gularly used for films and television series, the ivy-clad Grenadier nds in a cobbled mews behind Hyde Park Corner, largely discovered by tourists. Famous patrons have included King George and Madonna! Outside is the remaining stone of the Duke's ounting block. Expect traditional favourites on the blackboard, and ep an eye out for the ghost of an officer accidentally flogged to ath for cheating at cards.

en 11–11 (Sun 11–10.30 and BHs 12–6) **Bar Meals** L served week 12–2.30 D served all week 6–9.30 Av main course £7.50 **staurant** L served all week 12–3 D served all week 6–9 Av 3 course à la te £30 Punch Taverns Timothy Taylor Landlord. Shepherd Neame itfire, Fuller's London Pride, Bombardier. 10

Pick of the Pubs

Nags Head — Plan 1 B2

53 Kinnerton St SW1X 8ED 020 7235 1135

s this London's smallest pub? The award-winning Nag's Head is certainly compact and bijou, with a frontage like a Dickens shop and an unspoilt interior. Located in a quiet mews near Harrods, its front and back bars, connected by a narrow stairway, boast wooden floors, panelled walls, and low ceilings. It was built in the early 19th-century to cater for the footmen and stable hands who ooked after the horses in these Belgravia mews. The full Adnams range is served, along with a good value menu: daily specials, a help yourself salad bar, and traditional favourites such as real ale sausages, mash and beans; steak and mushroom pie; and chilli con carne are all on offer. Typical salads include brie of stilton salad and smoked salmon salad. There are also ploughman's unches and sandwiches.

Open 11–11 (Sun 12–10.30) **Bar Meals** L served all week 11–9.30 D served all week Free House Adnams Best, Broadside, Fisherman & Regatta. **Notes**

The Orange Brewery — Plan 1 C1

37–39 Pimlico Rd SW1 W8NE 020 7730 5984
dir: *Nearest tube - Sloane Square or Victoria*

The name comes from local associations with Nell Gwynne, a 17th-century purveyor of oranges and a favourite of Charles II. The building dates from 1790, and fronts onto an appealing square. Beers are brewed in the cellar, including SW1, SW2 and Pimlico Porter, and regulars will find a different guest beer every month. Expect traditional pub food; steak, Guinness and suet pudding, chicken curry, or scampi and chips are favourites.

Open 11–11 (Sun 12–10.30) Rest: 24 Dec Close at 6 **Bar Meals** L served 12–3 5–8.30 (Sat–Sun 12–4) Av main course £6 Scottish & Newcastle Brewery Greene King IPA, Old Speckled Hen, Bombardier, London Pride. 18 **Facilities** Dogs allowed

The Wilton Arms — Plan 1 B2

71 Kinnerton St SW1X 8ED
020 7235 4854 020 7235 4895
e-mail: wilton@shepherd-neame.co.uk

Flower-filled baskets and window boxes adorn this early 19th-century pub, named after the 1st Earl of Wilton but known locally as 'The Village Pub'. High settles and bookcases create individual seating areas in the air-conditioned interior, whilst a conservatory now covers the old garden. Shepherd Neame ales accompany the selection of traditional pub favourites, which includes toasted sandwiches, chicken dishes and a range of ploughman's. Look out for daily blackboard specials, too.

Open 11–11 **Bar Meals** L served Mon–Sat 12–3.45 D served Mon–Sat 5.30–10 Shepherd Neame Spitfire, Holsten, Orangeboom, Bishops Finger.

SW3

The Admiral Codrington — Plan 1 B2

17 Mossop St SW3 2LY
020 7581 0005 020 7589 2452
e-mail: admiral.codrington@333holdingsltd.com
dir: *Telephone for directions*

The local nickname for this smart and friendly gastro-pub is, inevitably, The Cod. Although this old Chelsea boozer was given a complete makeover that resulted in a stylish new look when it re-opened, it still retains a relaxed and homely feel. The modern British menu runs to vodka-cured salmon; Wag Yu beef sausages; roast breast of Norfolk chicken; and porcini risotto. Virtually all the well-chosen wines are available by the glass.

Open 11.30–12 (Sun 12–10.30) **Bar Meals** L served all week 12–2.30 **Restaurant** L served all week 12–2.30 (Sun 12–4) D served all week 6.30–11 Stella, Heineken, Becks. 20 **Facilities** Garden

England

SW3 continued

Pick of the Pubs

The Builders Arms 🍷 Plan 1 B1

13 Britten St SW3 3TY ☎ 020 7349 9040

e-mail: buildersarms@geronimo-inns.co.uk

dir: *Sloane Square tube station down Kings Rd, right at Habitat onto Chelsea Manor St, at end right onto Britten St*

Just off Chelsea's famous Kings Road, a three-storey Georgian back-street pub built by the same crew that constructed St Luke's church over the way. Inside, leather sofas dot the spacious informal bar area, where a brief, daily changing menu offers a good choice of modern English food with a twist, but if further ideas are needed, consult the specials board. Starters on the main menu might include mackerel and dill fishcake with spicy tomato ketchup; mussels and clams with Magners Irish cider, red onion and cream sauce; and sautéed chicken livers with smoked Black Forest bacon and broad beans. Typical main courses are baked codling fillet with parmentier potatoes and mustard lentils; pan-fried sea bass with caramelised shallot and gremolata; and courgette, sun-blushed tomato and feta risotto. There are 30-plus bins, with French producers just about taking the lead. When the sun shines the outdoor terrace is highly popular.

Open 11–11 (Thu–Sat 11–12) Closed: 25–26 Dec **Bar Meals** L served all week 12-3 (Sat 12–3.30, Sun 12–4) D served all week 7–10 **Restaurant** L served all week (Sat 12–3.30, Sun 12–4) D served all week 7–10.15 7–9.15) Adnams, London Pride, Deuchars IPA. 🍷 16 **Facilities** Dogs allowed

Pick of the Pubs

The Coopers of Flood Street 🍷 Plan 1 B1

87 Flood St, Chelsea SW3 5TB

☎ 020 7376 3120 020 7352 9187

e-mail: Coopersarms@youngs.co.uk

dir: *Sloane Square tube station onto Kings Road. 1m W, opposite Waitrose, left. Pub half way down Flood St*

A quiet backstreet Chelsea pub close to the Kings Road and the river. Celebrities and the notorious rub shoulders with the aristocracy and the local road sweeper in the bright, vibrant atmosphere, while the stuffed brown bear, Canadian moose and boar bring a character of their own to the bar. Food is served here and in the quiet upstairs dining room, with a focus on meat from the pub's own organic farm. The fresh, adventurous menu also offers traditional favourites that change daily: seared king scallops and chorizo; grilled chicken, bacon, avocado and sunblushed tomato salad might precede chargrilled harissa lamb steak with Moroccan vegetable couscous; bangers and mash with onion gravy; and ricotta and spinach tortellini. Spotted dick with custard, and chocolate fudge cake with cream bring their own sweet pleasures. Good staff-customer repartee makes for an entertaining atmosphere.

Open 11–11 (Sun 12–10.30) **Bar Meals** L served all week 12.30–9.30 D served all week12.30–9.30 Av main course £9.95 Young & Co Youngs Special, Youngs Bitter, Wells Bombardier. 🍷 15 **Facilities** Garden Dogs allowed

The Cross Keys Plan 2 E

1 Lawrence St, Chelsea SW3 5NB

☎ 020 7349 9111 020 7349 9333

e-mail: xkeys.nicole@hotmail.co.uk

dir: *From Sloane Square walk down Kings Rd, left onto Old Church St, then left onto Justice Walk, then right*

A fine Chelsea pub close to the Thames and dating from 1765 that's been a famous bolthole for the rich and famous since the 1960s. The stylish interior includes the bar and conservatory restaurant, plus the Gallery and the Room at the Top – ideal for private parties. A set menu might offer porcini mushroom risotto, and smoked haddock and leek fishcake, while the carte goes for steamed mussels and clam marinière, and grilled swordfish steak with fennel and orange salad.

Open 12–12 (Sun 12–11) Closed: 23–29 Dec, 1–4 Jan & BH **Bar Meals** L served all week 12–3 D served Mon–Fri 6–8 Av main course £15 **Restaurant** L served all week 12–3 D served all week 6–11 (Sat 12–4 7–11 Sun 12–4, 7–10.30) Scottish & Newcastle Brewery Directors, Best, Guinness.

The Phene Arms 🍷 Plan 1 E

Phene St, Chelsea SW3 5NY

☎ 020 7352 3294 020 7352 7026

e-mail: info@thephenearms.com

dir: *200yds from Kings Rd*

Built in 1851 and named after a doctor who introduced tree planting to London's streets, the pub was once George Best's local. It has a bar, a restaurant area, and a roof terrace, great for basking in the summer. Co-owners Christian and Kerstin Sandefeldt offer a northern French/Scandinavian menu, thus Swedish meatballs with lingonberries appear alongside roasted halibut with white haricot beans. Fondue a raclette are served on Sundays and Mondays.

Open 11-12 (Sun 12–10.30) **Bar Meals** L served all week 12–4 D served all week 4–10 (Sun 4–9) Av main course £8 **Restaurant** L served only for large pre-booked groups 12–7 D served all week 7–10 (Sun 4–9) Av 3 course à la carte £23 Free House Adnams Bitter Broadside, Fullers London Pride. 🍷 12 **Facilities** Garden Dogs allowed

SW4

Pick of the Pubs

The Belle Vue 🍷 Plan 2 E3

1 Clapham Common Southside SW4 7AA

☎ 020 7498 9473 020 7627 0716

e-mail: sean@sabretoothgroup.com

An independently owned freehouse overlooking the 220 acres of Clapham Common, one of South London's largest green spaces. Free internet access makes it a great place to catch up on work or leisure pursuits, with a coffee, hot snack or some tapas-style nibbles close at hand. A daily changing bistro-style lunch and dinner menu specialises in fish and shellfish, such as pan-fried giant tiger prawns in Thai spices; grilled marlin steak with pepper sauce; dressed Cornish crab salad; and chef's special fish pie. Other possibilities are braised leg of rabbit; steak and kidney pie; Thai green chicken curry; and Mediterranean vegetarian lasagne. Sunday lunch is very popular, and in addition to all the regular roasts are fish and vegetarian dishes. The wine list features over

25 wines and champagnes by the glass, and Harvey's Sussex Bitter is the house real ale.

The Belle Vue

Open 11–11 (Sun & Thu 11–12, Fri–Sat 11–1) Closed: 25–26 Dec **Bar Meals** L served all week 12.30–3.30 D served Mon–Fri 6.30–10 (Sat–Sun 12.30–10) Av main course £6.50 Free House Harveys Sussex Bitter, Courage Directors. 35

he Coach & Horses

Plan 2 E3

3 Clapham Park Rd SW4 7EX

020 7622 3815 020 7622 3832

mail: info@barbeerian-inns.com

r: *5 mins walk from Clapham High Street & Clapham Common)e station*

spite its city location, this attractive coaching inn feels like a ıntry pub. It draws a wide clientele, from locals to trendy young)fessionals. As the owner says: "Fine wines and Guinness sold in ıal amounts." Good roast dinners make it particularly busy on ndays, while Saturday is barbeque day. Samples from a specials ard include chicken kebabs, marinated in lemon and fresh herbs h wild rice, warm pitta and coriander chutney; chunky vegetable w with herb dumplings and crusty bread; or hearty fish pie with a ff pastry lid.

en 12 –11 (Sun 12–10.30) **Bar Meals** L served all week 12.30–2.30 erved all week 6–9.30 Sat 12.30–3, 6–9; Sun 12.30–5, 7–9 main course £10 London Pride, Adnams, Kronenbourg. 8 **:ilities** Children's licence Garden Dogs allowed

he Royal Oak

Plan 2 E3

10 Clapham High St SW4 7UT 020 7720 5678

mail: savagecorp@mac.com

me to pubs, bars and restaurants galore, these days Clapham ;h Street has a real neighbourhood feel about it. Maybe this ditional London boozer doesn't look much from outside, but its ky gastropub interior admirably compensates. A typical menu ers rib of beef with horseradish; mushroom and tarragon sausage d-in-the-hole; and fresh fish, including oysters, and potted salmon. ıside-brewed Adnams real ales are very much at ease in this urban /ironment.

en 12 –11 (Sun 12–10.30) **Bar Meals** L served all week 12–6 D served week 6–10.30 Av main course £8.50 Enterprise Inns Adnams adside, Adnams Bitter & Guinness. 8 **Facilities** Children's licence ;s allowed

The Windmill on the Common

Plan 2 E2

Clapham Common South Side SW4 9DE

020 8673 4578 020 8675 1486

e-mail: windmillhotel@youngs.co.uk

dir: *5m from London, just off South Circular A205 at junct with A24 at Clapham*

The original part of this unusually-named pub was known as Holly Lodge and at one time was the property of the founder of Youngs Brewery. Having undergone a major refurbishment the Windmill offers a varied menu with something for all tastes and appetites – sandwiches, wraps, grills, salads and steaks. Vegetarian dishes include dishes such as home-made butternut squash ravioli and wild mushroom risotto.

Open 11–12 (Sun 12–11) **Bar Meals** L served all week 12–3 D served all week 6–10.30 (Sat 12–10, Sun 12–9) **Restaurant** L served all week 12–3 D served all week 6–10.30 (Sat 12–10, Sun 12–9) Young & Co Youngs Bitter, Guinness. 17 **Facilities** Children's licence Garden Parking

SW6

Pick of the Pubs

The Atlas

Plan 2 D3

16 Seagrave Rd, Fulham SW6 1RX

020 7385 9129 020 7386 9113

e-mail: theatlas@btconnect.com

dir: *2mins walk from West Brompton tube station*

Located in a fashionable part of London where a great many pubs have been reinvented to become trendy diners or restaurants, here is a traditional local that remains true to its cause. The spacious bar area – split into eating and drinking sections – attracts what in rural enclaves would be quaintly referred to as outsiders, but to be a local here you can even come from Chelsea, Hampstead or Hammersmith. Dinner menus might feature starters such as roast butternut squash risotto with sage, sweet peppers and parmesan, followed by a variety of tempting mains that may include grilled rib-eye steak with celeriac and parsnip mash and oregano, tomato and chilli jam; pan-roasted salmon fillet with baked fennel and leeks with cream and olives and salsa fresca; and roast duck leg with figs, dates, cinnamon, bay and white wine mashed potato with wholegrain mustard and salsa verde. One of only a handful of London pubs to have a walled garden.

Open 12–11 (Sun 12–10.30) Closed: 24 Dec–1 Jan, Easter **Bar Meals** L served all week 12.30–3 D served all week 7–10.30 (Sun 7–10) Av main course £12 Free House Fuller's London Pride, Adnams Broadside, London Pride, Caledonian IPA. 13 **Facilities** Garden

England

SW6 continued

The Imperial 🍷 Plan 1 B1

577 Kings Rd SW6 2EH

☎ 020 7736 8549 📠 020 7731 3874

dir: *Telephone for directions*

Mid 19th-century food pub in one of London's most famous and fashionable streets, with a paved terrace at the back. Vibrant and spacious inside, with wooden floors, striking features, and a lively and varied clientele. A selection of pizzas, sandwiches, salads, and burgers feature on the popular menu. Look out for the wild boar sausage with bubble and squeak.

Open 12–11 Closed: BHs **Bar Meals** L served Mon–Sat 12–2.30 D served Mon–Fri 7–9.30 Av main course £6 T.E.A, London pride. 🍷 7 **Facilities** Garden

The Salisbury Tavern 🍷 Plan 2 D3

21 Sherbrooke Rd SW6 7HX

☎ 020 7381 4005 📠 020 7381 1002

e-mail: thesalisburytavern@longshotplc.com

Since this sister pub to Chelsea's famous Admiral Codrington opened in 2003, it has quickly established itself as one of Fulham's most popular bar-restaurants. Its elegantly simple, triangular bar and dining area, fitted out with high-backed banquettes as well as individual chairs, is given a lofty sense of space by a huge skylight. Modern European menus offer a great selection of snacks, full, all-day English breakfast, and home-made dishes.

Open 11–11 Closed: 24–26 Dec **Bar Meals** L served all week 12–2.30 D served all week 7–11 Av main course £12.50 **Restaurant** L served all week 12–2.30 D served all week 7–11 Av 3 course à la carte £25 Av 3 course fixed price £17.50 Bombardier, Heineken, San Miguel. 🍷 27 **Facilities** Children's licence

Pick of the Pubs

The White Horse 🍷 Plan 1 A1

1–3 Parson's Green, Fulham SW6 4UL

☎ 020 7736 2115 📠 020 7610 6091

e-mail: whitehorsesw6@btconnect.com

dir: *140mtrs from Parson's Green tube*

This coaching inn has stood on this site since at least 1688, and has advanced impressively since then, with its polished mahogany bar and wall panels, open fires and contemporary art on the walls. A large modern kitchen is behind the imaginative, good value meals served in the bar and Coach House restaurant. For lunch, you might try basil-infused seared tuna with Greek salad, or pork sausages with mash, summer cabbage and beer onion gravy. In the evening there might be seared turbot with summer vegetable and black-eye bean broth, or chowder of gurnard, conga eel and smoked bacon. Every dish from the starters through to the desserts comes with a recommended beer or wine, and the choice of both is considerable. In fact the 2-day beer festival held annually in November with over 300 beers waiting to be sampled is a magnet for lovers of real ale and European beers.

Open 11–12 (Fri–Sat 11–1) **Bar Meals** L served all week 12–10.30 D served all week 12–10.30 Av main course £8.25 **Restaurant** L served all week 12–10.30 D served all week 12–10.30 Av 3 course à la carte £20 Adnams Broadside, Fullers ESB, Harveys Sussex Best Bitter, Oakam JHB. 🍷 20 **Facilities** Garden Dogs allowed

SW7

The Anglesea Arms 🍷 Plan 1 A

15 Selwood Ter, South Kensington SW7 3QG

☎ 020 7373 7960

e-mail: enquiries@angleseaarms.com

dir: *Telephone for directions*

The interior has barely changed since 1827, though the dining area has proved a popular addition with its panelled walls and leather-clad chairs. Lunch and dinner menus place an emphasis on quality ingredients, fresh preparation and traditional British cooking. Expect the likes of moules marinière, a pint of prawns, and crab, chilli, parsley linguine; rare roast beef with Yorkshire pudding, horseradish and roast potatoes; or steak and field mushroom pie.

Open 11–11 (Sun 12–10.30) Closed: 25–26 Dec **Bar Meals** L served all week 12–3, (Sat–Sun 12–5) D served all week 6.30–10 (Sat 6–10, Sun 6–9.30) Av main course £11 **Restaurant** L served all week 12–3, (Sat–Sun 12–5) D served all week 6.30–10 (Sat 6–10, Sun 6–9.30) Av 3 course à la carte £19 Free House Fuller's London Pride, Adnams Bitter, Broadside, Brakspear Special. 🍷 21 **Facilities** Garden Dogs allowed

Pick of the Pubs

Swag and Tails 🍷 Plan 1 B2

10/11 Fairholt St, Knightsbridge SW7 1EG

☎ 020 7584 6926 📠 020 7581 9935

e-mail: theswag@swagandtails.com

dir: *3–4mins walk form Harrods. Off Brompton Rd turn onto Montpelier St, 1st left onto Cheval Place, 2nd right onto Montpelier Walk, take 1st left .*

See Pick of the Pubs on opposite page

Swag and Tails

neighbourhood institution set in a quiet backstreet off Knightsbridge, this flower bedecked ictorian pub is just three or four minutes' walk from Harrods, Harvey Nichols, the V&A and yde Park.

ɔng established owners have built ɔ a successful and welcoming ıb-restaurant business with a scerning local trade. The clientele predominantly up-market – this an extremely wealthy area – with sidents and local business people well as ladies lunching or taking break from a shopping trip. ripped wooden floors, original ood panelling, large windows ıd mirrors create a light and ry feel, rather different from the pically sombre pub of this era. ıe atmosphere is relaxed and formal, made cosy in winter by a aring fire, and staff are friendly, ıowledgeable and well trained. ɔod is a priority, with an ever ıanging menu to keep the regulars ɔming back several times a week.

The choice of dishes reflects the variety of quality fresh produce available. Cooking encompasses traditional British fare as well as Thai, Mediterranean and other international options. Reflecting the range are pan-seared fillet of sea bass with wok-fried noodles, spring onion, chilli, steamed kai lan and a soy butter sauce; rocket tortelloni with roasted butternut squash and parmesan cream sauce; sirloin steak sandwich with salad, red onions and horseradish mayonnaise; and roast breast of duck with truffled Jerusalem artichokes, buttered green beans and a tomato and herb dressing.

Plan 1 B2
10/11 Fairholt St, Knightsbridge
SW7 1EG
☎ 020 7584 6926
020 7581 9935
e-mail:
theswag@swagandtails.com
dir: *3–4mins walk form Harrods. Off Brompton Rd turn onto Montpelier St, 1st left onto Cheval Place, 2nd right onto Montpelier Walk, take 1st left .*

Open 11–11 Closed: BH, Xmas & New Year
Bar Meals L served Mon–Fri 12–3 D served Mon–Fri 6–10 Av main course £13.75
Restaurant L served Mon–Fri 12–3 D served Mon–Fri 6–10 Av 3 course à la carte £27.75
Free House
Adnams Bitter, Wells Bombardier Premium Bitter. 13
Facilities Dogs allowed

England

SW8

The Masons Arms 🍷 Plan 2 E3

169 Battersea Park Rd SW8 4BT
☎ 020 7622 2007 📠 020 7622 4662
e-mail: themasonsarms@ukonline.co.uk
dir: *Opposite Battersea Park BR Station*

More a neighbourhood local with tempting food than a gastro-pub, the worn wooden floors and tables support refreshingly delightful staff and honest, modern cuisine. Here you'll find a warm and welcoming atmosphere, equally suited for a quiet romantic dinner, partying with friends, or a family outing. Open fires in winter and a summer dining terrace. Daily changing menus feature escobar fillet with paw paw and cucumber salad, pan-fried blackened tuna, and spinach and duck spring roll.

Open 12-11 (Sun 12.30-10.30) **Bar Meals** L served 12-3 (Sat 12-5, Sun 12.30-4) D served 6-10 (Sat 6-9, Sun 6.30-9) Av main course £19 **Restaurant** L served 12-3 (Sat 12-5, Sun 12.30-4) D served 6-10 (Sat 6-9, Sun 6.30-9) Av 3 course à la carte £19 Free House Star of Promise, London Pride. 🍷 12 **Facilities** Garden Dogs allowed

SW10

Pick of the Pubs

The Chelsea Ram 🍷 Plan 2 E3

32 Burnaby St SW10 0PL
☎ 020 7351 4008 📠 020 7351 5557
e-mail: bookings@chelsearam.co.uk

A popular neighbourhood gastro-pub, The Chelsea Ram is located close to Chelsea Harbour and Lots Road, a little off the beaten track. There is a distinct emphasis on fresh produce in the monthly-changing menu, which includes fish and meat from Smithfield Market. Start with a selection of bread, marinated olives and balsamic vinegar, or enjoy a mezze selection or crispy fried calamari to share. Among the main courses, a modern approach to some old favourites includes battered haddock with minted pea purée and hand cut chips, or pork and leek sausages with creamy mash and caramelised red onion gravy. Alternatives are the Ram burger with Apple Wood cheddar, or hand-made sun-dried tomato and mascarpone ravioli with rocket and toasted pine nuts. Finish with a nostalgic knickerbocker glory topped with hot fudge sauce or a selection of English cheeses, oat biscuits and home-made chutney.

Open 11-11 (Sun 12-10.30) **Bar Meals** L served all week 12-3 (Sun 12-3.30) D served all week 6.30-10 (Sun 7-9.30) Av main course £8.95 **Restaurant** L served all week 12-3 D served all week 6.30-10 (Sun 12-3.30, 7-9.30) Av 3 course à la carte £20 Young & Co Youngs Bitter, Bombardier, & Guinness. 🍷 16 **Facilities** Children's licence Dogs allowed

Pick of the Pubs

The Hollywood Arms 🍷 Plan 1 A1

45 Hollywood Rd SW10 9HX
☎ 020 7349 7840 📠 020 7349 7841
e-mail: hollywoodarms@youngs.co.uk
dir: *1min from Chelsea & Westminster Hospital, 200mtrs are from Fulham rd.*

Recently acquired by Young's brewery, this listed building is one of Chelsea's hidden treasures. The interior has been elegantly refurbished, augmenting its original charm with rich natural woods, pastel shades and modern fabrics. The large upstairs lounge has elegant mouldings around the ceiling and large open fires at each end, with the bar centred on its length; four huge picture windows make the ambience light and airy. The ground floor pub and restaurant retains much of its traditional atmosphere. Here the chefs lovingly create menus from scratch using high quality ingredients; some, such as cheeses and cured meats, have won national or international recognition. Small plates will produce Rannoch Smokery smoked goose breast, or salt and pepper squid, while main courses offer the home-made half-pound beefburger and chips, Welsh lamb cutlets, or Muffs of Bromborough Old English herb sausages. Award-winning Burtree House Farm puddings are among the desserts.

Open 11-11.30 (Thu-Sat 11-12, Sun 12-10) **Bar Meals** 12-4 D served all week 6-9 (Sun 12-10.30) Av main course £9.95 **Restaurant** L served Mon-Sun 11-3 D served all week 6-10 (Sun 12-10.30) Av 3 course à la carte £10 Youngs Guinness. 🍷 12 **Facilities** Children's licence Dogs allowed

Pick of the Pubs

Lots Road Pub and Dining Room 🍷 Plan 2 E3

114 Lots Rd, Chelsea SW10 0RJ ☎ 020 7352 6645
e-mail: lotsroad@thespiritgroup.com
dir: *5-10 mins walk from Fulham Broadway Station*

Situated in the heart of Chelsea's bustle, this is the kind of establishment the term gastro-pub was coined for – a smart, comfortable, well-designed space which segues smoothly between jaunty bar area and the more secluded and grown-up restaurant. Slate grey and cream walls and wooden tables create a light, pared-down feel, and attentive staff are set on making you feel comfortable. There's an excellent wine list, and cocktails both quirky and classic. The menu changes daily, and offers plenty of imaginative, modern dishes. Start with the likes of warm smoked chicken, chorizo and chick pea salad; or a spicy fish cake with tartare sauce; after that, perhaps Toulouse sausages with creamy mash and onion gravy; or a whole Scottish trout with spinach and parsley risotto. Puddings are delightfully rich – think sticky toffee pudding – and the more restrained will enjoy cheeses served with Bath Olivers.

Open 11-11 (Fri-Sat 11-12) **Bar Meals** L served all week 12-10.30 D served all week 12-10.30 (Sun 12-10) Av main course £9 **Restaurant** L served all week 12-3 D served all week 12-10.30 (Sun 12-10) Av 3 course à la carte £20 Wadworth 6X, London Pride, Adnams, Guinness. 🍷 33 **Facilities** Children's licence Dogs allowed

he Sporting Page 🍷 Plan 1 A1

Camera Place SW10 0BH
☎ 020 7349 0455 📠 020 7352 8162
mail: sportingpage@frontpagepubs.com
r: *Nearest tube - Sloane Square or South Kensington*

small whitewashed pub happily tucked away between the King's d Fulham Roads. Its rather smart interior of varnished pine and sewood, and sporting murals, undoubtedly appeals to Bolly-quaffing ty types unwinding here after a day's work. Its popular modern itish menu includes traditional comfort food such as bangers d mash, smoked haddock and salmon fishcakes, and spaghetti rbonara. Despite its side street location there's seating for 60 outside.

pen 11-11 Closed: 25-26 Dec **Bar Meals** L served all week -2.30 D served Mon-Fri 7-10 Av main course £8 Front Page bs Ltd Charles Wells Bombardier & Fuller's London Pride. 🍷 12 **cilities** Garden Dogs allowed

W11

he Castle 🍷 Plan 2 E3

5 Battersea High St SW11 3HS
☎ 020 7228 8181 📠 020 7924 5887
mail: thecastle@tiscali.co.uk
r: *Approx 10min walk from Clapham Junction*

uilt in the mid-1960s to replace an older coaching inn, this ivy-vered pub tucked away in 'Battersea Village', has rugs and rustic rnishings on bare boards inside, and an outside enclosed patio rden. A typical menu offers fresh salmon and dill fishcakes; Cajun icken sandwich; organic lamb steak; and fresh swordfish steak with ocado salsa.

pen 12-11 Closed: 25-26 Dec **Bar Meals** L served all week 12-3 served all week 7-9.45 (Sun 12.30-4.30, 6-9.30) Av main course £8.50 Young & Co Youngs Bitter & Special, Goddard's Winter Warmer. 🍷 14 **cilities** Garden Dogs allowed Parking

Pick of the Pubs

The Fox & Hounds 🍷 Plan 2 E3

66 Latchmere Rd, Battersea SW11 2JU
☎ 020 7924 5483 📠 020 7738 2678
e-mail: foxandhoundsbattersea@btopenworld.com
dir: *From Clapham Junction exit onto High St turn left, through lights into Lavender Hill. After post office, left at lights. Pub 200yds on left*

London still has hundreds of Victorian corner pubs (think Queen Vic in EastEnders), built to serve only a handful of nearby streets. Following a relatively recent makeover, the Fox & Hounds still retains the relaxed feel of a true neighbourhood local. The style is simple – bare wooden floors, an assortment of furniture, a walled garden, extensive patio planting and a covered and heated seating area. But in one particular respect – the food – it has changed immeasurably since the late 19th century. Fresh ingredients are delivered daily from London's markets, and the Mediterranean-style menu changes accordingly, with possible starters of antipasti, pan-roast rainbow trout, and ricotta and baby artichoke salad. For mains, think Spanish chicken casserole with chorizo, mushrooms, red wine, thyme and roast garlic mash; and grilled tuna steak, couscous salad and spring onion and chilli salsa.

Open 12-3 5-11 (Fri-Sat 12-11, Sun 12-10.30, Mon 5-11) Closed: Easter wknd & 24 Dec-1 Jan **Bar Meals** L served Fri-Sat 12.30-3 (Sun 12.30-4) D served all week 7-10.30 Av main course £12 Free House Deuchars IPA, Harveys Sussex Best Bitter, Fullers London Pride. 🍷 13 **Facilities** Garden

SW13

The Bull's Head 🍷 Plan 2 D3

373 Lonsdale Rd, Barnes SW13 9PY
☎ 020 8876 5241 📠 020 8876 1546
e-mail: jazz@thebullshead.com

Facing the Thames and established in 1684, the Bull's Head has become a major venue for mainstream modern jazz and blues. Nightly concerts draw music lovers from far and wide, helped in no small measure by some fine cask-conditioned ales, over 200 wines, and more than 80 malt whiskies. Traditional home-cooked meals are served in the bar, with dishes ranging from haddock and crab to a variety of roasts and pies. Popular home-made puddings. An important and intrinsic feature of the pub is the Thai menu, available throughout the pub in the evening.

Open 11-11.30 Closed: 25 Dec **Bar Meals** L served all week 12-3 D served all week 6-11 Av main course £5.50 **Restaurant** D served all week 6-11 Young & Co Young's Special, Bitter, Winter Warmer. 🍷 32 **Facilities** Garden Dogs allowed

Pick of the Pubs

The Idle Hour 🍷 Plan 2 D2

62 Railway Side, Barnes SW13 0PQ ☎ 020 8878 5555
e-mail: theidlehour@aol.com
dir: *Off White Hart Ln from rail crossing past school*

As the name suggests, this small organic gastro-pub is just the spot for whiling away an afternoon. The location – hidden away from the main drag – makes it a favourite with shy celebrities. The enclosed garden is stylishly designed, as is the interior with its roaring fire. The emphasis on organic produce extends from food to all the wines as well as many of the soft drinks. Sundays see all-day opening for an organic roast, or spit-roast pig in summer. The weekday menu changes regularly and features some traditional choices alongside more adventurous dishes. Typical starters include goats' cheese with roasted beetroot, or tomato and white bean soup. Main courses might include tuna Niçoise; home-made steak and Guinness pie; and pea and mint risotto with parmesan cheese. The dessert menu takes in such delight as rhubarb crumble, bread and butter pudding, and chocolate brownies.

Open 5-1am (Sun all day) **Bar Meals** L served Sun 1-9 D served all week 7-10 **Restaurant** L served Sun only D served all week Av 3 course à la carte £17.50 Free House Heineken, Red Stripe, Hoegaarden, Leffe & Adnams. 🍷 12 **Facilities** Children's licence Garden

England

SW15

Pick of the Pubs

The Spencer Arms NEW Plan 2 D3

237 Lower Richmond Rd, Putney SW15 1HJ

☎ 020 8788 0640

e-mail: info@thespencerarms.co.uk

dir: *Corner of Putney Common & Lower Richmond Rd, opposite Old Putney Hospital*

See Pick of the Pubs on opposite page

SW18

Pick of the Pubs

The Alma Tavern Plan 2 E3

499 Old York Rd, Wandsworth SW18 1TF

☎ 020 8870 2537

e-mail: alma@youngs.co.uk

dir: *Opposite Wandsworth town rail station*

Step off the train at Wandsworth Town and you can't (indeed, shouldn't) miss this pub/brasserie/restaurant standing imposingly on a corner. Built around 1900 and surmounted by a dome, at street level its shiny green wall tiles are punctuated only by the door. The bright and airy central bar can be all things to all people: a civilised place for a frothing cappuccino, a pint of Young's, or a bowl of marinated olives with bread and oils. Cheese, charcuterie and Greek deli boards are another attractive option, or a hot dish of beer battered cod, or Alma burger with bacon and brie topping and thick cut chips. At the back is a spacious restaurant opening onto the colourful courtyard. Here an all-day menu offers dishes such as chargrilled barramundi niçoise salad; and seared calves' liver with pancetta, sage and parsnip mash and port wine reduction.

Open 11–12 (Sun 12–11) **Bar Meals** L served Mon–Sat 12–10.30 D served Mon–Sat 12–10.30 Av main course £12 **Restaurant** L served all week 12–4 D served all week 6–10.30 (Sun 12–9.30) Av 3 course à la carte £22 Young & Co Youngs Bitter, Youngs Special, Youngs Winter Warmer, Youngs guest/seasonal ales. 17 **Facilities** Dogs allowed Parking

Pick of the Pubs

The Cat's Back NEW Plan 2 D3

86–88 Point Pleasant, Putney SW18 1NN

☎ 020 8877 0818 & 8874 2937

e-mail: info@thecatsback.com

dir: *2 min walk from Wandsworth Park, by river*

Built in 1865 for lightermen on the Thames and Wandle, this vestige of a once working riverside stands defiant, as new apartments advance from all sides. Its unique name is simply explained: when a regular's lost moggy turned up again after a month, they were the owner's words as he entered the bar. The character of this wonderfully idiosyncratic London boozer is evident, from the old globe-topped petrol pump out among the tables and chairs on the pavement, to the collection of dodgy Victorian photographs and other paraphernalia inside. Food is served all day in the first-floor dining room, where the chef uses his overseas experience to inspire home-cooked duck breast with berry jus; jumbo shrimps in coconut milk with rice; red tuna with black and white sesame, mash and teriyaki; and medallions of polenta with ratatouille and fried onion. Live music can break out at any time.

Open 11–12.30 (Fri–Sat 11–2) Closed: 24–31 Dec
Bar Meals L served all week 12–10.30 D served all week 12–10.30 (Sun 1–4 only) Av main course £13 **Restaurant** L served Mon–Fri 12–3 (Sun 1–4) D served Mon–Sat 6.30–10.30 Av 3 course à la carte £17 Free House Beck Vier, Red Stripe, Castlemaine, Stella & Guest Ales. **Facilities** Dogs allowed

Pick of the Pubs

The Earl Spencer Plan 2 D2

260–262 Merton Rd, Southfields SW18 5JL

☎ 020 8870 9244 020 8877 2828

e-mail: theearlspencer@hotmail.com

dir: *Southfields tube station Replingham Rd, left at junct with Merton Rd to junct with Kimber Rd*

This splendid, airy Edwardian pub has been renovated in true gastro-pub style but retains traditional features such as a log fire and polished wood furnishings. Situated just five minutes from Southfields tube, it offers a good selection of wines and beers at the bar, plus a high standard of cooking. The emphasis is on home-cooked food from a daily changing menu using only fresh, quality, seasonal ingredients. Bread is baked daily, and fish is home smoked. From the eclectic modern British menu starters could include ham and parsley terrine with dressed white beans, cornichons and toast; or spiced spinach and potato filo parcels with aubergine raita. Follow with pan-fried duck breast with root vegetable mash, green beans, red wine onion gravy and horseradish crème fraîche; or penne pasta with lamb shoulder, peas, basil, rocket and parmesan. For the true gourmet there are also special gastronomic evenings in the function room.

Open 11–11 (Sun 12–10.30) **Bar Meals** L served all week 12.30–2.30 D served all week 7–10 (Sun 12–3, 7–9.30) Guinness, Hook Norton 12 **Facilities** Garden Dogs allowed

The Freemasons Plan 2 I

2 Northside, Wandsworth Common SW18 2SS

☎ 020 7326 8580 020 7223 6186

e-mail: info@freemasonspub.com

The aim of this stylish, popular pub is to get back to basics: to provid excellent, affordable food while maintaining all the ambiance of the friendly local. The space has been considered well, and with details like a round, black walnut bar, an open kitchen, modern art on the walls and plenty of sofas to settle into. Both food and drink are taken seriously, and there's are daily changing menus.

Open 12–11 (Sun 12–10.30) Closed: 25–26 Dec, 1 Jan **Bar Meals** L serv all week 12–3 D served all week 6.30–10 (Sun 12.30–5, 6.30–9.30) Av ma course £10 **Restaurant** L served all week 12–3 D served all week 6.30–1 (Sun 12.30–5, 6.30–9.30) Av 3 course à la carte £20 Free House Timothy Taylor, Tiger Ale, Guinness. 20 **Facilities** Garden Dogs allowed

The Spencer Arms

he Spencer Arms was reopened in 2005 by Notting Hill restaurateur Jamie Sherriff, and Adrian nes, former head chef of Yorkshire's award-winning Shibden Mill Inn. They have transformed ı attractive and cosy Victorian tavern overlooking Putney Common's leafy woods and dog- alking trails into an equally attractive and cosy gastropub.

the process they have created arge sunlit bar area and dining om, and a relaxed fireside area with ather banquettes, all tricked out pastels and dark wood. Parents th children to park quietly while ey enjoy a drink should do so ar the bookshelves and games est. Two daily changing lunch d dinner menus incorporate e best ingredients sourced from and how unusual is this? – not cessarily local suppliers. For ample, meats come from a highly garded butchers in Coventry, fish landed by day-boats and trawlers to Falmouth, Plymouth and westoft, RSPCA-accredited salmon reared in Sutherland, Kentish rms produce the cheeses, and fruit d vegetables are delivered daily om London's New Covent Garden arket. Bar snacks include a wide selection of freshly prepared British-style tapas such as potted shrimps, mini-shepherd's pie and salt-cod fritters, as well as comforting classics like Welsh rarebit, eggy bread with grilled herrings, and steamed cockles with shallot vinegar. The main menus feature Loch Duart salmon with crayfish; corn-fed poussin with stuffing balls; venison chop with creamed cabbage; and the somewhat unexpected duck burger with goats' cheese and home-made beetroot pickle. But we're back in 'old favourite' territory with desserts like bread and butter pudding, stewed plums with soft meringue, lemon curd tart, and home-made apple crumble ice cream. The adventurous spirit kicks in again with sgroppino (vodka and lemon sorbet) and brandy parfait with mandarins. Car parking might be a bit tricky.

NEW ❀ 🍷
Plan 2 D3
237 Lower Richmond Rd, Putney
SW15 1HJ
☎ 020 8788 0640
e-mail:
info@thespencerarms.co.uk
dir: *Corner of Putney Common & Lower Richmond Rd, opposite Old Putney Hospital*

Open 10–12 Closed: 25 Dec & 1 Jan
Bar Meals L served all week 12.30–2.30 D served all week 6.30–10 (L Sat 12–3, Sun 12–4, D Sun 6.30–9.30) Av main course £12
Restaurant 12.30–2.30 6.30–10 (L Sat 12–3, Sun 12–4, D Sun 6.30–9.30) Av 3 course à la carte £22.50
Free House
Heineken, Bitburger, Guinness, Aspall Cyder. 🍷 14
Facilities Dogs allowed

England

SW18 continued

The Old Sergeant 🍷 Plan 2 D2

104 Garrett Ln, Wandsworth SW18 4DJ

☎ 020 8874 4099 📠 020 8874 4099

Traditional, friendly and oozing with character, The Old Sergeant enjoys a good reputation for its beers, but also offers some decent malt whiskies. It's a great place to enjoy home-cooked food too: the menu could include salmon fish cakes with a sweet chili sauce, duck and orange sausages with coriander mash and gravy, or Thai fishcakes. One of the first pubs bought by Young's in the 1830s.

Open 12–11 (Sun 12–10.30) **Bar Meals** L served all week 12–2.30 D served all week 6–9.30 (Sun 12–9) Av main course £7.50 **Restaurant** L served Mon–Fri D served Mon–Fri (Thu–Sat 7–9.30) Av 3 course à la carte £20 Youngs Youngs Ordinary, Youngs Special. 🍷 12 **Facilities** Garden Dogs allowed

The Ship Inn 🍷 Plan 2 E3

Jew's Row SW18 1TB ☎ 020 8870 9667 📠 020 8874 9055

e-mail: drinks@theship.co.uk

dir: *Wandsworth Town BR station nearby. On S side of Wandsworth Bridge*

Situated next to Wandsworth Bridge on the Thames, the Ship exudes a lively, bustling atmosphere. The saloon bar and extended conservatory area lead out to a large beer garden, and in the summer months an outside bar is open for business. There is a popular restaurant, and all-day food is chosen from a single menu, with the emphasis on free-range produce from the landlord's organic farm. Expect the likes of lamb cutlets, chargrilled marlin fillet, shepherds pie, and peppers stuffed with hazelnuts and goats' cheese.

Open 11–11 (Sun 11–10.30) **Bar Meals** L served all week 12–10 D served all week 7–10.30 (Sun 7–10) Av main course £9 **Restaurant** L served all week 12–10.30 D served all week 12–10.30 (Sun 12–10) Av 3 course à la carte £18 Young & Co Youngs: PA, SPA, Waggle Dance, Winter Warmer. 🍷 15 **Facilities** Garden Dogs allowed

SW19

The Brewery Tap 🍷 Plan 2 D2

68–69 High St, Wimbledon SW19 5EE ☎ 020 8947 9331

e-mail: thebrewerytap@hotmail.com

A small, cosy one room pub, big on sports like football, rugby and cricket. It is also the closest pub to the Wimbledon tennis championships. Breakfast is served till 12.30pm, and snacks take in wooden platters, sandwiches and salad bowls. More substantial lunches are hot salt beef, and bangers and mash (with veggie sausage alternative). The only evening food is tapas on Wednesday. Special events are held for Burns' Night, Bastille Day etc.

Open 11–11 (Fri–Sat 11–12am) (Sun 11–10.30, 25 Dec 12–2) **Bar Meals** L served all week 11–2.30 (Sun 12–5) D served Tue–Thu 6–8.45 Av main course £8.50 Enterprise Inns Fuller's London Pride, Adnams, Guest Beers. 🍷 13 **Facilities** Dogs allowed

W1

The Argyll Arms 🍷 Plan 1 C

18 Argyll St, Oxford Circus W1F 7TP ☎ 020 7734 6117

dir: *Nearest tube - Oxford Circus*

A tavern has stood on this site since 1740, but the present building is mid-Victorian and is notable for its stunning floral displays. There's a popular range of sandwiches and the hot food menu might offer vegetarian moussaka, beef and Guinness pie, chicken and leek pie, haddock and lasagne.

Open 11–11 (Sun 12–10.30) Closed: 25 Dec **Bar Meals** L served all week 11–10 D served all week (Sun 11–9) Av main course £6.95 **Restaurant** L served all week (Sun 12–9) Bass, Fullers London Pride, Greene King IPA & Guest Beers. 🍷 15

French House 🍷 Plan 1 D

49 Dean St, Soho W1D 5BG

☎ 020 7437 2477 📠 020 7287 9109

e-mail: fhrestaurant@aol.com

Historic pub used by the Free French during World War II, and Soho bohemians since the 1950s when the likes of Dylan Thomas, Francis Bacon and Brendan Behan were regulars. The bar is small – they do not serve pints – and the music is the conversation. There is a small restaurant on the first floor where the menu changes regularly, including dishes like braised lamb shank, fillet steak, and black bream fillet with citrus cannellini stew.

Open 12–12 **Bar Meals** L served Mon–Sat 12–3 Av main course £6 **Restaurant** L served Mon–Sat 12–3 D served Mon–Sat 5.30–11 Av 3 cour à la carte £30 Free House Budvar, Kronenbourg, Leffe, Guinness & Becks. 🍷 22

Red Lion 🐟 🍷 Plan 1 C

No 1 Waverton St, Mayfair W1J 5QN

☎ 020 7499 1307 📠 020 7409 7752

e-mail: gregpeck@globalnet.co.uk

dir: *Nearest tube - Green Park*

Built in 1752, The Red Lion is one of Mayfair's most historic pubs. Originally used mainly by 18th-century builders, the clientele is now more likely to be the rich and famous of Mayfair, yet the friendly welcome remains. The pub was used as a location in the 2001 Brad P and Robert Redford movie, *Spy Game*. The bar menu has a traditiona pub feel, offering the likes of steak and stilton pie, Cumberland sausage, chicken masala, rack of pork ribs, and steak sandwich. Piano music on Saturday nights.

Open 11.30–11.20 Closed: 25–26 Dec, 1 Jan **Bar Meals** L served Mon–Sa 12–2.30 D served all week 6–9.45 Av main course £7 **Restaurant** L serve Mon–Sat 12–2.30 D served all week 6–9.30 Av 3 course à la carte £23 Punch Taverns Greene King IPA, London Pride, Bombardier, Youngs Ordinary. 🍷 12

/2

he Cow

Plan 2 D4

Westbourne Park Rd W2 5QH
020 7221 5400 020 7727 8687
mail: thecow@btconnect.com
r: *Nearest tubes - Royal Oak & Westbourne Park*

ıce known as the Railway Tavern, the pub was reputedly renamed er a former landlady with attitude. An equally plausible explanation hat drovers and their livestock passed this way headed east to ndon's Smithfield Market. Whatever, 'eat heartily and give the house ood name' is the sound philosophy of the pub, which specialises oysters, Guinness and Cuban cigars. Seafood figures strongly, and re are meat dishes among the blackboard specials.

en 12–11 Closed: 25 Dec **Bar Meals** L served all week 12–4 D served week 6–10.30 Av main course £12 **Restaurant** L served Sat–Sun 12–4 erved all week 6–11 Free House London Pride, Guinness. 10

he Prince Bonaparte

Plan 2 D4

Chepstow Rd W2 5BE
020 7313 9491 020 7792 0911

irst-generation gastro pub where Johnny Vaughan filmed the ongbow ads. Renowned for its bloody Marys, good music and quick, ndly service, the pub proves popular with young professionals and DJ nights on Fridays and Saturdays. The building is Victorian, with airy and open plan interior. Typical meals include sausages and sh, tomato and mozzarella bruschetta, sea bass with spinach, and cy chicken gnocchi.

en 12–11 (Close 10.30 Sun) **Bar Meals** L served all week 30–10 D served all week 12.30–10 Fri–Sat 12–9 Av main course £8.50 **staurant** L served all week 12.30–3 D served all week 6.30–10 (Sun 0–9) Av 3 course à la carte £20 Bass Fullers London Pride, ropramen, Greene King IPA, guest. 13 **Facilities** Dogs allowed

he Westbourne

Plan 2 D4

1 Westbourne Park Villas W2 5ED
020 7221 1332 020 7243 8081
r: *On corner of Westbourne Park Rd & Westbourne Park Villas*

ssic Notting Hill pub/restaurant favoured by bohemian clientele, luding a sprinkling of celebrities. Sunny terrace is very popular in nmer. Tempting, twice-daily-changing menu is listed on a board hind the bar and might include baked filo roll with butternut squash, otta, sage and nutmeg; pot roasted pheasant with bacon, shallots, ter mushrooms, garlic mash and winter greens; or fillet of seabass ked with lentils, chicory, thyme, white wine and Vermouth.

en 12–11 (Mon 5–11, Sun 12–10.30) Closed: 24 Dec–2 Jan **r Meals** L served Tue–Sun 12.30–3 D served Mon–Fri 7–10 (Sat–Sun).30) Av main course £12 **Restaurant** L served Tues-Sun 12.30–3 erved Mon–Fri 7–10 (Sat–Sun 7–9.30) Av 3 course à la carte £22 Av 2 ırse fixed price £10.50 Free House Leffe, Warsteiner, Hoegaarden, l Speckled Hen. 9 **Facilities** Garden Dogs allowed

W4

MAP 06 TQ27

England

Pick of the Pubs

The Devonshire House

Plan 2 C3

126 Devonshire Rd, Chiswick W4 2JJ
☎ 020 8987 2626 020 8995 0152
e-mail: info@thedevonshire.co.uk
dir: *150yds off Chiswick High Rd. 100yds from Hogarth rdbt & A4*

A laid back and unpretentious gastro-pub located in a leafy district of Chiswick, the Devonshire House was formerly known as the Manor Tavern. Its transformation into an attractive, light and airy bar and restaurant happened a few years back. It serves an interesting mix of modern British and Mediterranean dishes, and changes daily depending on the fresh produce currently available. You can whet your appetite with some marinated olives, French farmhouse bread or oriental spiced crackers and nuts before launching in to the menu proper. A typical three courses might comprise salad of smoked eel and new potatoes with horseradish cream; roast saddle of new season lamb, farci, pea purée and caramelised pearl onions; and roast winter plums on toasted brioche and mascarpone ice cream. Children are made to feel welcome with a secure garden to play in, plus books, crayons and games to keep them entertained.

Open 12–11 Closed: 25–26 Dec **Bar Meals** L served Tue–Sun 12–3 D served Tue–Sun 7–11 **Restaurant** L served Tue–Sun 12–3 D served Tue–Sun 7–11 Unique London Pride, Guinness. 15 **Facilities** Children's licence Garden Dogs allowed

The Pilot

Plan 2 C3

56 Wellesley Rd W4 4BZ
☎ 020 8994 0828 020 8994 2785
e-mail: the.pilotpub@ukonline.co.uk
dir: *Telephone for directions*

A large garden makes this Chiswick pub a real winner, especially in summer, while indoors the atmosphere is always friendly and welcoming. An exciting menu includes pan-seared bison with sweet potato, spring onion hash and red wine jus; steamed barracuda on jasmine rice cooked in Asian crab broth with pak choi; and stuffed baby squid with wild rice and chorizo on tomato, anchovy and caper sauce.

Open 12–11 (Sun 12–10.30) Closed: 25 Dec Rest: 1 Jan close 5.30 **Bar Meals** L served Mon–Sun 12–3.30 D served Mon–Fri 4.30–10 Sat 12–10, Sun 12–9.30 Av main course £9.50 **Restaurant** L served all week 12–3.30 D served all week 6.30–10 Av 3 course à la carte £18.50 Staropramen, London Pride. 10 **Facilities** Garden

England

W4 continued

Pick of the Pubs

The Swan 🍷 Plan 2 C3

1 Evershed Walk, 119 Acton Ln W4 5HH

☎ 020 8994 8262 📠 020 8994 9160

e-mail: theswanpub@btconnect.com

dir: *Pub on right at end of Evershed Walk*

The Swan is a gastro-pub for all seasons, much appreciated by the locals for its international range of beers and multicultural atmosphere. The staff and cosy wood panelled interior are welcoming, and there's a large lawned garden or heated patio area for alfresco refreshment. Good food is at the heart of the operation. Expect modern, mostly European cooking with a strong Italian influence: perhaps a starter of cannellini bean and porcini mushroom soup; or a plate of antipasti – chicken liver and armagnac purée on crostini perhaps, poached cod and herb aioli, and goats' cheese with caponata and pesto. Main courses continue the south-European influence with the likes of caldeirada, a Portuguese fish stew containing mussels, squid, prawns, tomato, sage, green pepper, saffron, coriander and white wine; and grilled Tuscan sausages with braised Puy lentils, choricero and nora pepper. Finish with the likes of dark chocolate and almond cake, or gorgonzola and taleggio cheeses with shaved apple, grilled bread and rocket.

Open 5-11 (wknds 12-11) Closed: Estr & 23 Dec-2 Jan **Restaurant** L served Sat-Sun 12.30-3 D served Mon-Sat 7-10.30 (Sun 7-10) Av 3 course à la carte £20 London Pride, San Miguel, Deuchars IPA & Guinness. 🍷 12 **Facilities** Garden Dogs allowed

W5

The Red Lion 🍷 Plan 2 C3

13 St Mary's Rd, Ealing W5 5RA

☎ 020 8567 2541 📠 020 8840 1294

e-mail: red.lionealing@bt.click.com

dir: *Telephone for directions*

The pub opposite the old Ealing Studios, the Red Lion is affectionately known as the 'Stage Six' (the studios have five), and has a unique collection of film stills celebrating the Ealing comedies of the 50s. Sympathetic refurbishment has broadened the pub's appeal, and the location by Ealing Green has a leafy, almost rural feel, plus there's an award-winning walled garden. Pub food ranges through oysters, burgers, bangers and mash, and fillet steak.

Open 11-11 (Sun 12-11) **Bar Meals** L served all week 12-3 D served Mon-Sat 7-9.30 Fullers Fullers London Pride, Chiswick, ESB. 🍷 50 **Facilities** Garden Dogs allowed

The Wheatsheaf 🍷 Plan 2 C4

41 Haven Ln, Ealing W5 2HZ ☎ 020 8997 5240

dir: *1m from A40 junct with North Circular*

Just a few minutes from Ealing Broadway, this large Victorian pub has a rustic appearance inside. Ideal place to enjoy a big screen sporting event or a warm drink among wooden floors, panelled walls, beams from an old barn, and real fires in winter. Traditional pub grub includes cottage pie; beer battered cod and chips; steak, ale and mushroom pie; pork and leek sausage and mash; and vegetable lasagne.

Open 12-11 (Sat 11-11, Sun 12-10.30) **Bar Meals** L served all week 12-3 D served Mon-Sat 6-9 (Sat 12-8, Sun 12-5) Av main course £6.25 Fullers Fullers London Pride, ESB & Chiswick, Guest ales. 🍷 10 **Facilities** Garden Dogs allowed

W6

Pick of the Pubs

Anglesea Arms 🍷 Plan 2 D3

35 Wingate Rd W6 0UR

☎ 020 8749 1291 📠 020 8749 1254

e-mail: anglesea.events@gmail.com

Real fires and a relaxed atmosphere are all part of the attraction at this traditional corner pub. Behind the Georgian façade the decor is basic but welcoming, and the place positively hums with people eagerly seeking out the highly reputable food. A range of simple, robust dishes might include starters like pigeon, duck and foie gras terrine, Anglesea charcuterie platter, or butternut squash and goats' curd risotto. Among main courses could be slow-cooked belly of pork, wild sea bass, lentils, wild mushrooms and red wine, pot-roast stuffed saddle of lamb, and toasted sea bass with saffron potatoes. Puddings are also exemplary: expect poached pear, brandy snap and pear sorbet, chocolate, pecan and hazelnut 'brownie' cake with vanilla ice cream, or perhaps buttermilk pudding with pineapple and almond biscotti. A savoury alternative might be Cornish yarm with chutney and water biscuits.

Open 11-11 (Sun 12-10.30) Closed: 24-31 Dec **Bar Meals** L served all week 12.30-2.45 (Sun 12.30-3.30) D served all week 7-10.30 (Sun 7-10.15) Av main course £13.95 **Restaurant** L served all week 12.30-2.45 (Sun 12.30-3.30) D served all week 7-10.45 (Sun 7-10.15) Av 3 course à la carte £25 Free House Greene King, Old Speckled Hen, Fuller's London Pride, Timothy Taylors Landlord. 🍷 20

The Stonemasons Arms 🍷 Plan 2 I

54 Cambridge Grove W6 0LA

☎ 020 8748 1397 📠 020 8846 9636

e-mail: stonemasonsarms@london-gastros.co.uk

dir: *Hammersmith tube. Walk down King St, 2nd right up Cambridge Grove, pub at end*

This welcoming West London gastro-pub must boast some of the m unusual sausages in the capital, including kangaroo and crocodile. They're just one of the innovations on a punchy menu inspired by traditional British and continental dishes. If kangaroo doesn't appeal, how about smoked eel, chorizo and rocket salad; marinated tuna; ar a bowl of home-made damson ice cream? Look out also for the Krie beer jelly, a perfect accompaniment to chicken liver paté.

Open 12-11 (Sun 12-10.30) **Bar Meals** L served all week 12-3 D serve Mon-Fri 6-10 (Sat-Sun all day) Av main course £11 **Restaurant** L serve all week 12-3 D served all week 6-10 (Sat 12-10, Sun 12-9.30) Av 3 course à la carte £24 Fullers London Pride, Organic Honeydew, Kronenbourg, Staropramen. 🍷 16

/8

he Churchill Arms 🍷 Plan 2 D3

9 Kensington Church St W8 7LN ☎ 020 7727 4242

r: *Off A40 (Westway). Nearest tube-Notting Hill Gate*

ai food is the speciality at this traditional 200-year-old pub with ong emphasis on exotic chicken, beef, prawn and pork dishes. / Kaeng Panang curry with coconut milk and lime leaves, or Pad ew Wan stir-fry with sweet and sour tomato sauce. Oriental feasts twithstanding, the Churchill Arms has many traditional British ɔects including oak beams, log fires and an annual celebration of nston Churchill's birthday.

en 11–11 (Thu–Sat 11–12) **Bar Meals** L served all week 12–10 D served n–Sat 12–10 Av main course £5.85 **Restaurant** L served all week 12–10 served Mon–Sat 12–10 Av 3 course à la carte £10 Av 1 course fixed price 85 Fullers Fullers London Pride, ESB & Chiswick Bitter, Gales. 🍷 25 **cilities** Garden Dogs allowed

lall Tavern NEW 🍷 Plan 2 D4

–73 Palace Gardens Ter, Notting Hill, Kensington W8 :U ☎ 0207 727 3805 📠 0207 792 9620

mail: info@malltavern.co.uk

r: *E along Bayswater Rd, 2nd turn on left*

s 100-year-old pub in the heart of Notting Hill was taken over in 06 by two young chefs whose enthusiasm for cooking simply leaps m the pages of the menus. Their modern pubby offerings might lude slow-braised lamb shank with mash and honey glazed carrots; d fillet of sea bream with lemon thyme risotto and fennel jus. Drinks lude continental beers and an extensive wine list.

en 12–11.30 Closed: 25–26 Dec **Bar Meals** L served all week 12–11.30 erved all week 12–11.30 Av main course £9 **Restaurant** L served n–Fri 12–3 (Sat 11–4, Sun 12–4) D served all week 7–11 Av 3 course à la te £25 Av 3 course fixed price £16.50 Enterprise Inns Staropramen, fe Blond, & Tiger. 🍷 20 **Facilities** Garden Dogs allowed

he Scarsdale 🍷 Plan 2 D3

A Edwardes Square, Kensington W8 6HE

020 7937 1811 📠 020 7938 2984

r: *Exit Kensington High Street Station, left along High St. vards Sq is next left after Odeon Cinema.*

9th-century, free-standing local with a stone forecourt enclosed railings, just off Kensington High Street. The Frenchman who veloped the site was supposedly one of Bonaparte's secret agents. ere's so much about this place, not least its intriguing mix of tomers, that ensures you don't forget which part of London you in. The food is modern European and highly praised, but the pendous Bloody Marys are the real talking point.

en 12–11 (Sun 12–10.30) Closed: 25–26 Dec **Bar Meals** L served all ek 12–10 D served all week 12–10 (Sun 12–9) **Restaurant** L served all ek 12–2.30 D served all week 6–10 (Sun 12–3, 6–9) Punch Taverns London Pride, Old Speckled Hen, Youngs, Greene King IPA. 🍷 20 **ilities** Garden Dogs allowed

The Windsor Castle 🍷 Plan 2 D4

114 Campden Hill Rd W8 7AR ☎ 0207 243 9551

dir: *From Notting Hill Gate, S towards Holland Park, left opposite pharmacy*

Established in 1845, this pub takes its name from the royal castle, which could once be seen from the upper-floor windows. Unchanged for years, it boasts oak panelling and open fires, and is reputedly haunted by the ghost of Thomas Paine, author of *The Rights of Man*. A good variety of food is served in the bar, from speciality sausages and mash, to salads, sandwiches, snacks like half-a-dozen oysters, and lamb with roasted vegetables.

Open 12–11 (Sun 12–10.30) **Bar Meals** L served all week 12–3.30 D served all week 5–10 (Sat 12–10, Sun 12–9) Timothy Taylor Landlord, Fullers London Pride, Adnams Broadside. 🍷 10 **Facilities** Garden Dogs allowed

W9

The Waterway 🍷 Plan 2 D4

54 Formosa St W9 2JU

☎ 020 7266 3557 📠 020 7266 3547

e-mail: olly&tridge@theebury.co.uk

Trendy Maida Vale restaurant and bar in a canalside setting with a large decking area. The bar is also a great place to relax with its comfy sofas and open fires, and there is an interesting choice of drinks, including cocktails and champagne by the glass. The restaurant menu might offer Londoner sausage sandwich; red wine braised pork belly with herb gnocchi, shallots and turnips; or pan-fried gilt head bream.

Open 12–11 **Bar Meals** L served all week 12.30–10.15 D served all week 12.30–10.15 (Sun 12.30–9.45) **Restaurant** L served all week 12.30–3.30 (Sun 12.30–4) D served all week 6.30–10.15 (Sun 7–9.45) Guinness, Hoegaarden. 🍷 10 **Facilities** Garden Dogs allowed

W10

Golborne Grove 🍷 Plan 2 D4

36 Golborne Rd W10 5PR

☎ 020 8960 6260 📠 020 8960 6961

e-mail: golborne@groverestaurants.co.uk

dir: *From Ladbroke Grove into Portobello Rd, left to Golborne Res and right. From Westbourne Park tube station and left into Elkstone Rd towards Golbourne Rd.*

A popular dining destination, this award-winning gastro-pub is located at the north end of Notting Hill, with a ground floor bar area and function room upstairs. Local architectural photos, 1920's Venetian mirrors and squashy 1960's sofas contribute to the appealing interior. The drinks range encompasses beers, cocktails and a reasonable wine list. Fish features strongly in dishes like pan-fried red snapper fillet with roast vegetables and pine kernels, couscous and Greek salad.

Open 12–11 (Sat 12–12, Sun 12–11.30) **Bar Meals** L served all week 12.30–3.45 D served all week 6.30–10.15 Av main course £13 **Restaurant** L served all week 12.30–3.45 D served all week 6.30–10.15 Av 3 course à la carte £19.50 Enterprise Inns Fuller's London Pride, Guinness. 🍷 10 **Facilities** Garden Dogs allowed

England

W10 continued

The North Pole 🍷 Plan 2 D4

13–15 North Pole Rd W10 6QH
☎ 020 8964 9384 📠 020 8960 3774
e-mail: northpole@massivepub.com
dir: *Right from White City tube station, past BBC Worldwide, right at 2nd lights, 200yds on right. 10 mins walk*

A trendy modern gastro-pub with large windows and bright décor, formerly owned by Jade Jagger, and just five minutes' walk from BBC Worldwide. Expect leather sofas, armchairs, daily papers, a good range of wines by the glass, cocktails and a lively atmosphere in the bar. Separate bar and restaurant menus continue to show real interest, with simply described modern fusion dishes. Fish dishes feature haddock, prawns, whitebait, oysters and mussels.

Open 12–11 **Bar Meals** L served all week 12–3 D served all week 6–9.30 (Fri & Sun 12–4, 6–9.30) Av main course £10 **Restaurant** L served all week 12–3 D served all week 6–9.30 (Fri & Sun 12–4, 6–9.30) Free House Fosters, Kronenbourg, San Miguel, Guinness. 🍷 14 **Facilities** Children's licence Dogs allowed

W11

Portobello Gold 🍷 Plan 2 D4

95–97 Portobello Rd W11 2QB
☎ 020 7460 4900 📠 020 7229 2278
e-mail: reservations@portobellogold.com

This quirkily stylish Notting Hill pub has a thriving programme of live music, but that doesn't mean the food is an afterthought. Meals are served in the bar or in the lush tropical conservatory, close enough to hear the live music but not so close as to make conversation impossible. The 'funky', international menu could include oysters; Thai mussels; fajitas; aubergine and marrow parmigiana; or Cumberland pork sausages and mash. There are 16 beers and an extensive range of wines by the glass.

Open 10–12 Closed: 25 Dec–1 Jan **Bar Meals** L served all week 12–12 D served all week 12–12 Av main course £11 **Restaurant** L served all week 12–11 D served Mon–Sat 7–11 (Sun 1–8) Enterprise Inns Staropramen, Guinness, London Pride & Hoegaarden. 🍷 16 **Facilities** Dogs allowed

W14 MAP 02 XX00

Pick of the Pubs

The Cumberland Arms 🍷 Plan 2 D3

29 North End Rd, Hammersmith W14 8SZ
☎ 020 7371 6806 📠 020 7371 6848
e-mail: thecumberlandarmspub@btconnect.com
dir: *Kensington Olympia turn left, at Hammersmith Rd right, at T-jet (North End Rd) left, 100yds on left.*

Close to Olympia, the Cumberland is one of the most popular gastro-pubs in this neck of London. Its rich blue-painted façade with gold lettering is a welcoming sight, and mellow furniture and stripped floorboards characterise the interior; pavement benches and tables help alleviate the pressure inside. Friendly staff, an affordable wine list and well-kept ales are the draw for those seeking after-work refreshment. It's also a great place for tasty plates of unpretentious Mediterranean food, with a daily-changing selection of Italian, Spanish and North African dishes. Lunchtime sandwiches may include mozzarella with slow-roasted tomatoes and pesto, or grilled Italian sausage with tomato and chilli jam. Mixed antipasti could include marinated feta and chickpea salad, poached mackerel fillet on crostini with salsa verde, and pan-roasted pork ribs. Main courses are typified by rabbit and porcini risotto with parmesan; spaghetti with beef meatballs, tomato and oregano; and grilled red tuna with couscous salad and salsa fresca.

Open 12–11 Closed: 23 Dec–2 Jan **Bar Meals** L served all week 12.30–3 (Sun 12.30–3.30) D served all week 7–10.30 (Sun 7–10) Hoegaarden, London Pride, Deuchars Caledonian, Fosters Staropramen. 🍷 12 **Facilities** Garden

The Havelock Tavern 🍷 Plan 2 I

57 Masbro Rd, Brook Green W14 0LS
☎ 020 7603 5374 📠 020 7602 1163
dir: *Nearest tubes: Shepherd's Bush & Olympia*

The Havelock is still run very much as a boozer despite being a gastropub – but with the good food. It has been under the same ownership/management team since 1996, the year it re-opened in it current guise. It remains popular with lunchtime customers who wa a quick one-course meal before returning to work. In the evenings it offers more substantial food with a reasonably priced, ever-rolling two/three course menu. Maybe piri-piri chicken salad or smoked haddock kedgeree.

Open 11–11 (Sun 12–10.30) Closed: 5 days at Xmas & Etr Sun **Bar Meals** L served all week 12.30–2.30 D served all week 7–10 (Sun 12–3, 7–9.30) Free House Flowers Original Cask, Marston's Pedigr Fuller's London Pride. 🍷 11 **Facilities** Garden **Notes**

WC1

Pick of the Pubs

The Lamb 🍷 Plan 1 E

94 Lamb's Conduit St WC1N 3LZ ☎ 020 7405 0713
e-mail: lambwc1@youngs.co.uk
dir: *Russell Square, turn right, 1st right, 1st left, 1st right*

This building was first recorded in 1729, was 'heavily improved' between 1836–1876, and frequented by Charles Dickens when he lived nearby in Doughty Street (now housing the Dickens Museum). This really is a gem of a place, with its distinctive greer tiled façade, very rare glass snob screens, dark polished wood, and original sepia photographs of music hall stars who performec at the nearby Holborn Empire. The absence of television, piped music and fruit machines allows conversation to flow, although there is a working polyphon. Home-cooked bar food includes a vegetarian corner (vegetable curry, or burger), a fish choice including traditional fish and chips; and steaks from the griddle, plus pies and baked dishes from the stove. Favourites are steak and ale pie (called the Celebration 1729 pie); sausage and mash; liver and bacon; and fried egg and chips. For something lighter, t a ploughman's or a vegetable samosa with mango chutney.

Open 11–12 (Sun 12–4, 7–10.30) **Bar Meals** L served all week 12–3 D served Mon–Thu & Sat 6–9 Av main course £7 Young & Co Youngs (full range). 🍷 11 **Facilities** Garden

England

'C2

he Lamb and Flag 🍷 Plan 1 D3

Rose St, Covent Garden WC2E 9EB

· 020 7497 9504 📠 020 7379 7655

r: *Leicester Square, Cranbourne St exit, turn left into Garrick 2nd left*

ensed during the reign of Elizabeth 1, the Lamb and Flag exudes trong atmosphere, with low ceilings and high-backed settles both king feaures of the bar. In 1679 the poet Dryden was almost killed in earby alley. These days office workers and Covent Garden tourists ong the surrounding streets. Typical examples of the varied menu lude mince beef and onion pie with mash, cauliflower cheese, and d in the hole.

en Mon–Thur 11–11 (Fri–Sat 11–11.30, Sun 12–10.30) Closed: 25–26 c, Jan 1 **Bar Meals** L served all week 11–3 (Sat 11–5, Sun 12–5) main course £6.25 Courage Best & Directors, Young's PA & Special, arles Wells Bombardier, Greene King IPA. 🍷 10

Pick of the Pubs

The Seven Stars Plan 1 E4

53 Carey St WC2A 2JB ☎ 020 7242 8521

e-mail: ns@nathansilver.com

dir: *From Temple N via The Strand & Bell Yard to Carey St. From Holborn SE via Lincoln's Inn Fields & Searle St to Carey St.*

This is one of those all too rare examples of an old London public house that has escaped being tarted up. Somehow, probably because it stood alone, it survived the Great Fire of 1666, eventually to become a favourite with judges, barristers and litigants taking breathers from duty in the Royal Courts of Justice over the road, and pit musicians from West End shows. Its co-proprietor (with Nathan Silver) and chef is pub food cookbook writer and broadcaster, Roxy Beaujolais, on whose daily changing blackboard you will probably see oysters; corned beef hash and fried egg; roast guinea fowl in lemony jus; Napoli sausages with mash; cockles, mussels and razor clams marinière; and chargrilled sea bream. Even if you don't need the loo, pretend you do for the fun of navigating the ridiculously narrow Elizabethan stairs. Ms Beaujolais and Mr Silver also own The Bountiful Cow off High Holborn.

Open 11.30–11.30 Closed: BH **Bar Meals** L served all week 12–5 D served all week 5–9.30 Av main course £9 Free House Adnams Best, Broadside, Fuller's London Pride, Harveys & Dark Star Best. **Facilities** Dogs allowed

MERSEYSIDE

BARNSTON MAP 15 SJ28

Fox and Hounds 🍷

Barnston Rd CH61 1BW

☎ 0151 648 7685 📠 0151 648 0872

e-mail: ralphleech@hotmail.com

dir: *M53 junct 4 take A5137 to Heswell. Right to Barnston on B5138*

The pub, located in a conservation area, dates from 1911 and its Edwardian character has been preserved in the pitch pine woodwork and leaded windows. Collections of 1920s/1930s memorabilia (ashtrays, horse brasses and police helmets) also feature. Six real ales, five lagers, 60 whiskies and 12 wines by the glass are served alongside a range of bar snacks, notably a variety of platters, toasted ciabatas and jacket potatoes. Daily specials may include beef pie, lamb shank, fish of the day and seasonally inspired dishes.

Open 11–11 **Bar Meals** L served all week 12–2 Av main course £5.95 Free House Websters Yorkshire Bitter, Theakston, Best & Old Peculier & Guest beers. 🍷 12 **Facilities** Garden Dogs allowed Parking

LIVERPOOL MAP 15 SJ39

Everyman Bistro 🍷

9–11 Hope St L1 9BH ☎ 0151 708 9545 📠 0151 703 0290

e-mail: bistro@everyman.co.uk

dir: *In town centre, between 2 cathedrals. Bistro in basement of Everyman Theatre on Hope St*

In a cellar under the famous Everyman Theatre, this much-loved bar was dubbed Liverpool's 'most Bohemian venue' by the local paper. Regulars, including students, lecturers and media types, rate the food highly, not least because only prime local produce is used. Although the menu changes twice a day (and never repeats itself), typical dishes are sweet potato, mushroom and coconut curry; ricotta cheese lasagne; shepherds pie with leek mash; and a range of puds.

Open 12–12 (Thu–Fri 12–2, Sat 11–2) **Bar Meals** L served Mon–Sat 12–12 D served Mon–Sat 12–12 (Thu–Fri 12pm–2am, Sat 11am–2am) Av main course £8 **Restaurant** L served Mon–Sat 12–5 D served Mon–Sat 5–12 Av 3 course à la carte £14 Free House Cains Bitter, Black Sheep, Derwent Pale Ale, Copper Dragon. 🍷 8

England

SOUTHPORT MAP 15 SD31

The Berkeley Arms

19 Queens Rd PR9 9HN ☎ 01704 500811
e-mail: enquiries@berkeley-arms.com

Part of the Berkeley Arms Hotel, just off Southport's famous Lord Street. There are never fewer than eight real ales on sale at any one time here, which gives the pub a shrine-like status among beer drinkers. The pub does not serve food.

Open 12–11 Adnams Southwold, Banks Bitter, Hawkshead Bitter, Landlord. **Facilities** Garden Dogs allowed Parking

NORFOLK

BAWBURGH MAP 13 TG10

Pick of the Pubs

Kings Head

Harts Ln NR9 3LS ☎ 01603 744977 01603 744990
e-mail: info@kingshead-bawburgh.co.uk
dir: *From A47 W of Norwich take B1108 W*

See Pick of the Pubs on opposite page

BINHAM MAP 13 TF93

Chequers Inn

Front St NR21 0AL ☎ 01328 830297
e-mail: steve@binhamchequers.co.uk
dir: *On B1388 between Wells-next-the-Sea & Walsingham*

The Chequers is now home to the Front Street Brewery, but even though they brew their own beer they still have regular Norfolk/East Anglian guest ales. The pub has been owned by a village charity since the early 1600s and was originally a trade hall. Many stones from the nearby priory were used in its construction. The daily changing menu offers dishes such as Norfolk duck paté, fresh lobster thermidor, and plum crumble.

Open 11.30–2.30 6–11 (Sun 12–2.30, 7–10.30) **Bar Meals** L served all week 12–2 D served all week 6–9 Av main course £9.25 **Restaurant** L served all week 12–2 D served all week 6–9 Free House Varying range of East Anglian beers. **Facilities** Children's licence Garden Parking

BLAKENEY MAP 13 TG

The Kings Arms

Westgate St NR25 7NQ ☎ 01263 740341 01263 7403
e-mail: info@blakeneykingsarms.co.uk

This Grade II listed free house is located on the beautiful north Norf coast, close to the famous salt marshes, and is run by Marjorie and Howard Davies, who settled here after long and successful showbiz careers. The Kings Arms is an ideal centre for walking, or perhaps a ferry trip to the nearby seal colony and world-famous bird sanctuarie. Locally-caught fish and seasonal seafood feature on the menu, together with local game, home-made pies and pastas.

Open 11–11 **Bar Meals** L served Mon–Sat 12–9.30 D served Mon–Sat 12–9.30 (Sun 12–9) Av main course £7 Free House Greene King Speckled Hen, Woodfordes Wherry Best Bitter, Marston's Pedigree, Adnar Best Bitter. 12 **Facilities** Garden Dogs allowed Parking Play Area

Pick of the Pubs

White Horse Hotel

4 High St NR25 7AL ☎ 01263 740574 01263 741303
e-mail: enquiries@blakeneywhitehorse.co.uk
dir: *From A148 (Cromer to King's Lynn rd) turn onto A149 signed to Blakeney.*

See Pick of the Pubs on page 38

BLICKLING MAP 13 TG

Pick of the Pubs

The Buckinghamshire Arms

Blickling Rd NR11 6NF ☎ 01263 732133
dir: *From Cromer (A140) take exit at Aylsham onto B1354*

'The Bucks', a late 17th-century coaching inn by the gates of Blickling Hall (NT), is Norfolk's most beautiful inn, say its owners. Anne Boleyn's ghost is said to wander in the adjacent courtyard and charming garden. The lounge bar and restaurant, with their solid furniture and wood-burning stoves, are appealing too. Meals can be taken in either, with menus offering fresh local food servec in both traditional and modern ways, with starters such as brie wedge in beer batter; baked crab; and Waldorf salad. Sample main courses, all served with salad or vegetables, new potatoes or chips, include venison with port and blackberries; grilled whole lemon sole; home-made lasagne; sautéed lambs' kidneys with Marsala; and salmon and prawn tagliatelle. The Victorian cellar houses real ales from Norfolk, Suffolk and Kent.

Open 11.30–3 6–11 (Sun 12–3, 7–10.30) Closed: 25 Dec **Bar Meals** L served all week 12–2.30 D served all week 7–9 **Restaurant** L served all week 12–2 D served all week 7–9 Free House Adnams, Woodforde's, Yemans. 17 **Facilities** Garden Parking

Kings Head

he Kings Head has been sitting on the banks of the restful river Yare since the 17th century. 's a genuine village pub with heavy timbers and bulging walls – just the place to relax after an :hausting shopping spree in Norwich.

ith the village green opposite, the ıb is big on traditional charm in e form of wooden floors, log fires, mfy leather seating and pine dining rniture. The place to be on long mmer evenings is the south-facing tio or the secluded, landscaped rden. Seasonal menus offer a wide oice of modern British, European d Oriental dishes, all from the st quality local produce, including rbs and vegetables from the pub rden and flour-based products from arby Letheringsett Mill. Lunch can anything from the quick and easy, ch as a filled roll or ciabatta, to a ɔre leisurely three-courser, maybe turing as a main course Moroccan ırinated chicken supreme with bergine ragout, lemon couscous, ınach and crème fraîche; home-ıde steak and mushroom pudding robably the largest in Norfolk'), ney-roasted carrots, mashed swede and buttery spinach; or smoked haddock and prawn kedgeree, soft free range egg, chilli, coriander and crispy onions. From the evening carte a typical starter might be potted brown shrimps with mace butter, lemon and toasted ciabattas, followed by free range belly of pork slow cooked in local cider, with cauliflower purée, banana shallots, chorizo and purple sprouting broccoli, then steamed apricot sponge pudding and golden syrup. Too much? Then something lighter – a vanilla crème brûlée, perhaps? A £25 tasting menu includes native oysters, white onion soup, pan-seared scallops, fillet steak and a local cheese plate. The famed Sunday roast lunch menu offers a choice of four local meats, all sourced from within 15 miles of the pub. A long wine list has something for everyone.

🍷

MAP 13 TG10

Harts Ln NR9 3LS

☎ 01603 744977

📠 01603 744990

e-mail: info@kingshead-bawburgh.co.uk

dir: *From A47 W of Norwich take B1108 W*

Open 11.30–11 (Sun 12–10.30)
Closed: 25–27 Dec eve, 1 Jan eve
Bar Meals L served all week 12–2 D served all week 6.30–9 Av main course £9
Restaurant L served all week 12–2 D served all week 6.30–9 Av 3 course à la carte £25 Av 3 course fixed price £18
Free House
Adnams, Woodforde's Wherry, Green King IPA, Courage Directors. 🍷 15
Facilities Children's licence Garden Parking

White Horse Hotel

A short, steep stroll from Blakeney quayside stands the 17th-century White Horse, formerly a coaching inn. The same team has run it for fourteen years. Blakeney itself is a gem, with narro streets of flint-built fishermen's cottages winding down to a small tidal harbour.

The creeks and estuary beyond are surrounded by vast sea lavender marshes, and the mud flats are home to samphire and mussels, while skylarks, redshanks and oyster-catchers fill the skies. The shingle ridge of Blakeney Point dominates the horizon: a thousand acres of marram grass dunes and wide open spaces. A twice-yearly changing menu is based loosely around the shellfish seasons, thus expect simply cooked mussels through the winter and crab in spring and summer. As you might expect, all the shellfish and much of the fish comes from along this very stretch of coast, while local estates provide game, fruit and even asparagus. You may eat in the bustling bar, the light, airy conservatory, or the more formal Stables dining room. Apart from fish, the restaurant menu offers wild boar casserole with sweet and sour red cabbage; and grilled mustard breast of guinea fowl on curly kale. A blackboard of daily specials, again with the accent on fish, adds further choice. Begin with warmed salad of pigeon breast, bacon, pine kernels and a sharp raspberry dressing; then roast loin of English lamb, herb-crushed potatoes, redcurrant sauce; or grilled fillet of sea bass with crayfish butter, rocket salad and new potatoes. Desserts are limited to chocolate, strawberry or vanilla ice cream, and a selection of cheeses. A 50-bin wine list, a dozen of which are available by the glass, and four well-kept real ales complete the picture.

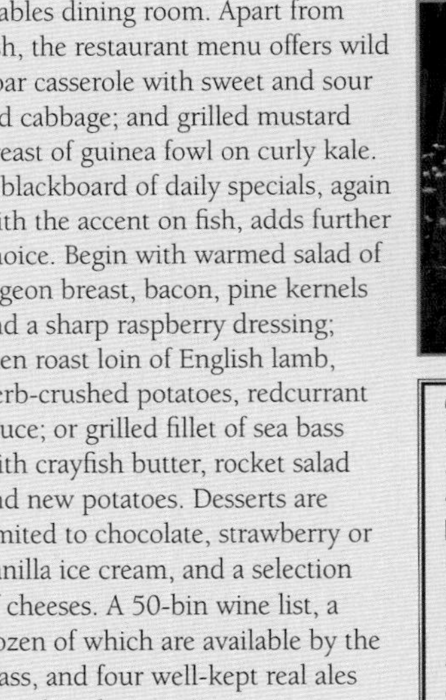

MAP 13 TG04
4 High St NR25 7AL
☎ 01263 740574
01263 741303
e-mail: enquiries@blakeneywhitehorse.co.uk
dir: *From A148 (Cromer to King's Lynn rd) turn onto A149 signed to Blakeney.*

Open 11-3 6-11
Bar Meals L served all week 12–2.15 D served all week 6–9 Av main course £10
Restaurant D served all week 7–9 Av 3 course à la carte £25
Free House
Adnams Bitter, Woodfordes Wherry, Greene King IPA & Abbott. 12
Facilities Garden Parking

England

RANCASTER STAITHE MAP 13 TF74

Pick of the Pubs

The White Horse ★★ HL

PE31 8BY ☎ 01485 210262 01485 210930

e-mail: reception@whitehorsebrancaster.co.uk

dir: *A149 (coast road), midway between Hunstanton & Wells-next-the-Sea*

Scrubbed pine tables, high-backed settles and painted walls all combine to create a bright, welcoming atmosphere at this gloriously situated dining pub. Here, North Norfolk's heritage coast forms the backdrop to well kept ales and local seafood. From the conservatory restaurant with its adjoining sun deck, diners can watch the sea retreating over the salt marsh, stranding a jumble of little boats under the wide East Anglian sky. The pub, which was extensively refurbished for 2007, enjoys a fine reputation for fresh local produce on its daily-changing menus. Filled lunchtime ciabattas come with parsnip crisps and dressed leaves, whilst the bar menu also includes hot dishes like slow-roast pork belly with caramelised apple; and Brancaster Staithe mussels in white wine and parsley sauce. And, if you just can't tear yourself away from the view, fifteen tastefully furnished bedrooms look out over the water towards Scolt Head Island.

Open 11–11 (Sun 12–10.30) **Bar Meals** L served all week 12–2 D served all week Av main course £9.25 **Restaurant** L served all week 12–2 D served all week 6.30–9 Av 3 course à la carte £25 Free House Adnams Best Bitter, Fullers London Pride, Woodfordes Wherry & Guest. 12 **Facilities** Garden Dogs allowed Parking **Rooms** 15 bedrooms en suite S£75 D£100

RISTON MAP 13 TG03

he John H Stracey ★★★ INN

est End NR24 2JA ☎ 01263 860891 01263 862984

mail: johnhstracey@btconnect.com

16th-century inn, renamed in the mid–1970s after the famous British lterweight champion who used to spar with the then owner's son. interior full of character, with log fire and knick-knacks. The wide oice of straightforward pub food includes ploughman's, sandwiches, e bites', steaks cooked in various styles, home-made steak and ale e, duck à l'orange, curries, pastas, scampi, lobster, Dover sole and ads. Vegetarian and children's selections too. Old Speckled Hen and ddles County in the bar.

pen 11–2.30 6.30–11 (Sun 7–10.30) **Bar Meals** L served all week –2 D served all week 6.30–9.30 **Restaurant** L served all week 12–2 served all week 6.30–9.30 Free House Greene King Old Speckled n & IPA, Greene King Ruddles County,. **Facilities** Garden Parking **ooms** 1 bedroom en suite S£28.50 D£64

BURNHAM MARKET MAP 13 TF84

Pick of the Pubs

The Hoste Arms ★★★ HL

The Green PE31 8HD

☎ 01328 738777 01328 730103

e-mail: reception@hostearms.co.uk

dir: *Signed off B1155, 5m W of Wells-next-the-Sea*

Built as a manor house in 1550, the Hoste Arms has been an inn since 1720. Over the centuries it has also been a courthouse and livestock market – not to mention a spell as a Victorian brothel. It was rescued in 1989 after 130 years of decline, and is now a beautifully presented hotel with striking interior design. The Hoste's owner Paul Whittome has recently 'dug deep' to create a cellar, additional private dining space and an orangery. The cellar is decked in marble with in-floor lighting; the loos also deserve mention, being perhaps among the most expensive in the country. Expect to dine on starters such as potted duck or local oysters, followed by seared collops of monkfish or tea-smoked breast of guinea fowl. Cheeses include local Binham Blue and neighbouring Suffolk Gold, and irresistible desserts entice with praline and milk chocolate fondant, or caramel parfait with vanilla cream.

Open 11–11 **Restaurant** L served all week 12–2 D served all week 7–9 (Fri 7–9.30) Free House Woodforde's Wherry Best, Greene King Abbot Ale & IPA, Adnams Best Bitter, Adnams Broadside. 11 **Facilities** Garden Dogs allowed Parking **Rooms** 36 bedrooms en suite S£88 D£117

BURNHAM THORPE MAP 13 TF84

Pick of the Pubs

The Lord Nelson

Walsingham Rd PE31 8HL

☎ 01328 738241 01328 738241

e-mail: simon@nelsonslocal.co.uk

dir: *B1355 (Burnham Market to Fakenham road), pub 9m from Fakenham & 1.75m from Burnham Market. Pub near church opposite playing fields*

See Pick of the Pubs on page 385

Please see walk on page 386

England

CLEY NEXT THE SEA — MAP 13 TG04

Pick of the Pubs

The George Hotel 🍷

High St NR25 7RN ☎ 01263 740652 📠 01263 741275
e-mail: thegeorge@cleynextthesea.com
dir: *On A149 through Cley next the Sea, approx 4m from Holt*

See Pick of the Pubs on page 388

COLTISHALL — MAP 13 TG21

Kings Head 🍷

26 Wroxham Rd NR12 7EA
☎ 01603 737426 📠 01603 736542
dir: *A47 (Norwich ring road) onto B1150 to North Walsham at Coltishall. Right at petrol station, right past church.*

This 17th-century free house stands on the banks of the River Bure, right in the heart of the Norfolk Broads. Hire cruisers are available at nearby Wroxham, and fishing boats can be hired at the pub. If you prefer to stay on dry land you'll find a warm welcome at the bar, with a range of real ales that includes Adnams Bitter, Directors and Marston's Pedigree. There's an inviting menu, too, served in both the bar and the restaurant.

Open 11-3 6-11 (Sun all day) Closed: 26 Dec **Bar Meals** L served all week 12-2 D served all week 7-9 Av main course £12.50 **Restaurant** L served all week 12-2 D served all week 7-9 Av 3 course à la carte £25 Free House Adnams Bitter, Directors, Marston's Pedigree. 🍷 10 **Facilities** Parking

DEREHAM — MAP 13 TF91

Yaxham Mill ★★★★ INN

Norwich Rd, Yaxham NR19 1RP
☎ 01362 851182 📠 01362 691482
e-mail: yaxhammill@btinternet.com

A converted windmill in the middle of open Norfolk countryside and dating back to 1810. The miller's house and chapel were transformed into a restaurant and bar. Menus cater for all tastes, with grilled lemon sole, minted lamb steak, sweet and sour chicken, and chilli con carne among other dishes. Home-made pies, including steak and kidney and cottage, are something of a speciality.

Open 12-3 6-11 (Sun 6-10.30) **Bar Meals** L served all week 12-2 D served all week 6.30-9 (Sun 12-8) Av main course £8.95 **Restaurant** L served all week 12-2 D served all week 6.30-9 Av 3 course à la carte £15 Free House Bombardier, Youngs & Guest Ales. **Facilities** Garden Parking **Rooms** 11 bedrooms en suite S£48 D£60

EAST RUSTON — MAP 13 TG

The Butchers Arms 🍷

Oak Ln NR12 9JG ☎ 01692 650237
dir: *Off School Road opposite East Ruston allotment*

A quintessential village pub, which is now the only commercial establishment here. You won't find a jukebox or pool table, but outsi is 'Mavis', a 1954 Comma fire engine. From fresh local produce landlady Julie Gollop prepares roast beef and Yorkshire pudding; liver and bacon casserole; home-cooked ham, egg and chips; grilled gammon, pineapple and chips; and salads. Between noon and 2pm on weekdays she also produces a single-choice, £3.00 lunch – amazi value.

Open 12-3 6.30-11 (Summer 6-11) **Bar Meals** L served all week 12-2 D served all week 7-8.30 (Summer 7-9) Av main course £6.50 **Restaurant** L served all week 12-2 D served all week 7-8.30 (Summer 6.30-9) Av 3 course à la carte £15 Free House Adnams, Woodford Old Speckled Hen, Greene King IPA. 🍷 7 **Facilities** Children's licence Garden Dogs allowed Parking **Notes**

EATON — MAP 13 TG

The Red Lion 🍷

50 Eaton St NR4 7LD ☎ 01603 454787 📠 01603 456939
e-mail: redlioneaton@hotmail.co.uk
dir: *Off A11, 2m S of Norwich city centre*

This heavily-beamed 17th-century coaching inn has bags of characte thanks to its Dutch gables, panelled walls and inglenook fireplaces. The covered terrace enables customers to enjoy one of the real ales sample the extensive wine list outside during the summer months. T extensive lunch menu offers everything from toasted paninis to wing of Lowestoft skate with prawns and capers; or roast Aylesbury duckli with sausage stuffing.

Open 11-3 6-11 (Sun 12-3, 7-10.30) **Bar Meals** L served all week 12-2.15 D served all week 7-9 **Restaurant** L served all week 12-2.15 D served all week 7-9 Av 3 course à la carte £21 Enterprise Inns C Speckled Hen, Courage Directors, Greene King IPA, Adnams Bitter. 🍷 10 **Facilities** Garden Parking

The Lord Nelson

ɔratio Nelson was born in Burnham Thorpe in 1758. The pub, originally called the Plough, ɪs already over 100 years old; in 1798 its name was changed to honour his victory over the ench in the Nile. Visitors today can soak up an atmosphere that has changed little since; you n even sit on Nelson's high-backed settle.

ere's no bar – drinks are served m the taproom, with real ales aight from the cask. When lson was without a ship, he spent any hours in the pub composing ters of protest to the Admiralty. n the declaration of war against ance in 1793, he celebrated being en a command by treating the ole village to a meal upstairs. er his death at Trafalgar in 1805, body was immersed in a barrel rum to preserve it for the long rney home. Sailors started taking s of this questionable marinade an effort to acquire his gifts. They led it 'Nelson's Blood'; its secret nd of 100 proof Navy rum and ces lives on, sold here in nips or ttles. Otherwise, the only 'change blood' is in the team running place. In 2006 Simon Alper and Peter De Groeve took over, Simon with long experience on the drinks side, and Peter importing a wealth of European food influences from his native Belgium. His aim is to provide a different eating experience based on traditional produce, in dishes such as duck in Norfolk lavender sauce; Waterzooi – chicken, potatoes and vegetables cooked in cream and wine; asparagus Flamande; and fillet of pork in a Leffe beer sauce. Desserts may include a white chocolate mousse with grapefruit and kumquats. Families are welcomed, and children will enjoy the huge garden. Dirty wellies and soggy doggies straight from the beach are no problem in 'Nelson's local'.

MAP 13 TF84
Walsingham Rd PE31 8HL
☎ 01328 738241
01328 738241
e-mail:
simon@nelsonslocal.co.uk
dir: *B1355 (Burnham Market to Fakenham road), pub 9m from Fakenham & 1.75m from Burnham Market. Pub near church opposite playing fields*

Open 12-3 6-11 (Sun 12-10.30)
Bar Meals L served all week 12-2 (Sat-Sun 12-2.30) D served Mon–Sat 6-7.30 (Sat/Sun 12-2.30, no food Sun eve) Av main course £7
Restaurant L served all week 12-2 D served Mon-Sat 7-9 Av 3 course à la carte £25.40
Greene King
Greene King Abbot Ale & IPA, Woodforde's Wherry, Nelson's Revenge. 13
Facilities Garden Dogs allowed Parking Play Area

Lord Nelson

Walk information

Distance: 4 miles (6.4km)
Map: OS Explorer 251 Norfolk Coast Central
Start/finish: on-street parking on main road in Burnham Overy Staithe; grid ref TF 844441
Ascent/gradient: 1
Paths: waymarked paths and some paved lanes; 1 stile
Landscape: wild salt marshes and mudflats, fields and meadows

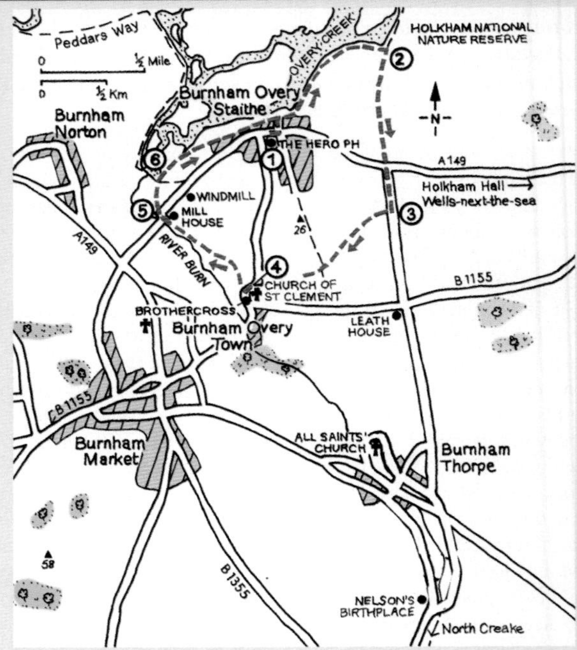

Walk directions

A Find the Hero pub, then turn right, then immediately left down East Harbour Way until you reach Overy Creek. Turn right next to the black-painted house, go through a gate and then bear left along the waterfront. The bank you are on was raised to protect the adjacent land from sudden incursions by the sea. Eventually, the path reaches a T-junction.

B At the junction, turn right, around the gate, into a marshy meadow of long grass. This area is part of Holkham National Nature Reserve and the sand dunes, salt marshes and mudflats. Cross a stile, then follow the grass track until you reach the A149. Cross to the track opposite, and follow this until you have passed two fields on your right.

C Go through the gap at the entrance to the third field, which may or may not be marked as a footpath. Keep to the right until you reach a waymarker pointing left, across the middle of the field. Keep going in a straight line, through gaps in hedges, until you reach a dirt lane. Cross this and go down the track opposite, towards the Norman tower of Burnham Overy's Church of St Clement, which is topped by a 17th-century bell turret.

D Turn left at the end of the track onto Mill Road, then right up the track called Marsh Lane. Go through the gate and into a field, so that the River Burn is off to your left, with the round Saxon tower of Burnham Norton in the distance to your left and Burnham Overy windmill straight ahead. Go through the gate by Mill House, which dates from 1820.

E Cross the A149, with the pond on your left, then take the public footpath into the next field. If the stile is too choked by brambles, use the main gate, but keep the hedge not too far from your right. In the distance you will see the sails of Burnham Overy windmill. Note: there's no fully passable direct route to Burnham Overy from this point.

F At the junction of paths, turn right and continue for 1/2 mile (0.4km) to reach the A149 main coast road. Turn left and follow this back into the centre of Burnham Overy Staithe.

While there

You can explore the seven Burnhams – Market, Overy, Overy Staithe, Overy Tow[n], Norton, Deepdale and Thorpe. Burnham Norton's church has a Saxon round tower, while Burnham Market has a handsome green, fringed by elegant 18th-century houses. Along the coast to the east is Holkham Hall with its Bygones Museum, while nearby Wells-next-the-Sea is famous [for] its whelks and sprats.

Look for

In the marshes look for sea aster and samphire. In the summer months, you will also see the purple bloom of sea lavender. Besides wading birds that inhabit the salt marshes and mudflats all year, you will als[o] see noisy Brent geese, with their characteris[tic] black heads and white rumps, in the winter

England

RPINGHAM MAP 13 TG13

Pick of the Pubs

The Saracen's Head

NR11 7LX ☎ 01263 768909 📠 01263 768993
e-mail: saracenshead@wolterton.freeserve.co.uk
dir: *A140, 2.5m N of Aylsham, left through Erpingham, pass Spread Eagle on left. Through Calthorpe follow to Aldborough, and on to pub*

Standing as it does in the middle of nowhere, the Saracen's Head is an ideal escape from the rat-race. This former coach house was built in 1806 and modelled on a Tuscan farmhouse. There's no piped music, no fruit machines, and no ordinary pub food – just daily-changing menus reflecting owner Robert Dawson-Smith's enduring passion for cooking up some of Norfolk's most delicious wild and tame treats. According to seasonal availability, these may include wok-sizzled sirloin strips with anchovy, or pot-roast leg of lamb with red and white beans. A good array of seafood could feature baked Cromer crab, or grilled bass with white wine. The delightful walled garden features the Shed, a small workshop run by Robert's daughter; this is the place to seek out that essential piece of retro furniture or modern artwork. Seven en suite bedrooms continue the arty and eclectic feel.

Open 12-3 6-11.30 (Sun 12-3, 7-10.30) Closed: 25 Dec **Bar Meals** L served all week 12.30-2 D served all week 7.30-9 Av main course £12.25 **Restaurant** L served all week 12.30-2 D served all week 7.30-9 Av 3 course à la carte £24 Av 2 course fixed price £8 Free House Adnams Best Bitter, Woodforde's Wherry. **Facilities** Garden Parking **Rooms** 6 bedrooms en suite S£45 D£90 (★★★★ RR)

AKENHAM MAP 13 TF92

he Wensum Lodge Hotel

ridge St NR21 9AY ☎ 01328 862100 📠 01328 863365
-mail: enquiries@wensumlodge.fsnet.co.uk
ir: *20m from Norwich, 20m from King's Lynn*

ensum Lodge is a converted mill dating from around 1700, idyllically cated by the River Wensum, for which the hotel has fishing rights. ome-cooked food is prepared from locally supplied ingredients, with guettes, jacket potatoes and an all-day breakfast on the light bite enu. The carte might have baby peeled prawns on dressed leaves ith chilli dip; and Wensum burger topped with bacon, cheese, salad id relish in a toasted bun served with fries.

Open 11-11 **Bar Meals** L served all week 11.30-3 (Sun 12-3) D served all week 6.30-9.30 **Restaurant** L served all week 11.30-3 (Sun 12-3) D served all week 6.30-9.30 (Sun 6.30-9) Free House Greene King Abbot Ale & IPA, Old Mill Bitter, Carling. **Facilities** Garden Parking

The White Horse Inn ★★★★ INN

Fakenham Rd, East Barsham NR21 0LH
☎ 01328 820645 📠 01328 820645
e-mail: subalpine19@whsmith.net.co.uk
dir: *1.5m N of Fakenham on minor road to Little Walsingham*

Ideally located for birdwatching, walking, cycling, fishing, golf and sandy beaches, this refurbished 17th-century inn offers en suite rooms and a characterful bar with log-burning inglenook. Good range of beers and malt whiskies. Fresh ingredients are assured in daily specials, with fish especially well represented. Typical choices include chicken breast stuffed with stilton, peppered mackerel fillets, sweet and sour pork, and venison steak. There is also a grill menu. Birdwatching tours can be arranged.

Open 11.30-3 6.30-11 **Bar Meals** L served all week 12-2 D served all week 7-9.30 Av main course £9.95 **Restaurant** L served all week 12-2 D served all week 7-9.30 Adnams Best, Adnams Broadside, Tetley, Wells Eagle IPA. **Facilities** Garden Parking **Rooms** 3 bedrooms en suite S£40 D£60

GREAT RYBURGH MAP 13 TF92

The Boar Inn

NR21 0DX ☎ 01328 829212 📠 01328 829421
dir: *Off A1067 4m S of Fakenham*

The village, deep in rural Norfolk, has one of the county's unusual round-towered Saxon churches. Opposite is the 300-year-old Boar, dispensing a good variety of food, including beef Madras with rice, sweet and sour chicken with noodles, plaice fillet with prawns in mornay sauce, scallops, lemon sole, and prime Norfolk steaks. Specials include skate wing with garlic and herb butter, and wild boar steak with cranberry and red wine jus. Bar/alfresco snacks and children's meals.

Open 12-2.30 5.30-12 (All day 1 May-30 Sep) **Bar Meals** L served all week 12-2 D served all week 7-9 **Restaurant** L served all week 12-2 D served all week 7-9 Av 3 course à la carte £15 Free House Courage Best & guest ale. **Facilities** Garden Parking

The George Hotel

Located near the sea and marshes, The George is hugely popular with bird watchers and even has its own 'bird bible' in which bird sightings are recorded by visitors to the pub. A rambling, characterful country property, it stands on historic Cley's winding High Street.

The beer garden backs onto the marshes, from where you can see Cley's famous mill, while the lovely oak-floored bar provides a year-round welcome for locals and visitors alike. The George is in many ways a classic Edwardian Norfolk inn, but there's a modern edge to both the décor and the cooking, which makes use of carefully selected local produce. You can snack in the lounge bar or dine in the light, airy, painting-filled restaurant. At lunchtime the menu runs from sandwiches (hot chicken, avocado, crispy bacon and red pesto mayonnaise; or brie, smoked ham and fresh mango) to starters and light meals such as warm pan-fried chicken liver, duck liver and rocket salad with balsamic dressing; or hearty main courses – perhaps home-made steak, kidney and suet pudding; or Tuscan chicken stew with white kidney beans, chorizo sausage and crusty baguette. Dinner brings starters of roast parsnip and honey soup laced with cream, followed by braised pork belly with spiced red cabbage, wilted spinach and honey glaze. More typically pubby options include Norfolk ham, egg and chips; and a home-made beef burger. Seafood is a real strength: look out for Morston oysters; moules marinière; or main courses such as whole black sea bream baked with fresh herbs and served with star anise beurre blanc. Finish with decadent pancakes or a honey and lavender crème brûlée. Now under the same ownership as the White Horse at Blakeney.

MAP 13 TG04
High St NR25 7RN
☎ 01263 740652
01263 741275
e-mail:
thegeorge@cleynextthesea.com
dir: *On A149 through Cley next the Sea, approx 4m from Holt*

Open 11–11 (Sun & BHs 11–10.30)
Bar Meals L served all week 12–2 D served all week 6.30–9 (Sun 12–2.30) Av main course £10.95
Restaurant L served all week 12–2 D served all week 6.30–9 (Sun 12–2.30) Av 3 course à la carte £20
Free House
Greene King IPA, Abbot Ale, Yetmans Beers & Leffe. 8
Facilities Garden Dogs allowed Parking

:APPISBURGH MAP 13 TG33

he Hill House

R12 0PW ☎ 01692 650004 📠 01692 650004
r: *5m from Stalham, 8m from North Walsham*

hen Sir Arthur Conan Doyle stayed in this 16th-century coaching inn was inspired to write a Sherlock Holmes story: *The Adventure of e Dancing Men*. Changing guest ales, good value bar food and a ge summer garden form the main appeal today, alongside an old orld friendliness. Look out for the summer solstice beer festival each ne for the chance to sample over forty real ales.

pen 12-3 7-11(Thu-Sun all day) (Summer all day) **Bar Meals** L served week 12-2.30 D served all week 7-9.30 (Sun 7-9) Av main course £7 **staurant** 12-2.30 D served all week 7-9.30 (Sun 7-9) Av 3 course à la rte £20 Free House Shepherd Neame Spitfire, Buffy's, Woodforde's herry, Adnams Bitter. 9 **Facilities** Garden Dogs allowed Parking

IEVINGHAM MAP 13 TG12

larsham Arms Freehouse

olt Rd NR10 5NP ☎ 01603 754268
mail: nigelbradley@marshamarms.co.uk
ir: *On B1149 N of Norwich airport, 2m through Horsford wards Holt*

uilt as a roadside hostel for poor farm labourers by Victorian nilanthropist and landowner Robert Marsham. Some original features main, including the large open fireplace. A spacious garden with aved patio is family-friendly, as is the dedicated family room. A goodly nge of fresh fish dishes includes cod, haddock, sea bass, herrings and ab. Specialities such as minted lamb casserole and the local butcher's usages are backed by a daily blackboard. Desserts like chocolate ownies are home made.

pen 11-11 **Bar Meals** L served all week 11.30-2.30 D served all week -9.30 (Sun 12-2.30, 6.30-9) **Restaurant** L served all week 12-2.30 served all week 6-9.30 (Sun 6.30-9) Free House Adnams est, Woodforde's Wherry Best Bitter, Mauldens, Worthington. 8 **acilities** Garden Parking Play Area **Rooms** 11 bedrooms en suite :54.50 D£85 (★★★★ INN)

See advertisement under NORWICH

HEYDON MAP 13 TG12

Earle Arms

The Street NR11 6AD ☎ 01263 587376
e-mail: haitchy@aol.com
dir: *Signed between Cawston & Corpusty on B1149 (Holt to Norwich road)*

Heydon is one of only thirteen privately owned villages in the country and is often used as a film location. It dates from the 16th century, and inside are log fires, attractive wallpapers, prints and a collection of bric-a-brac. One of the two rooms offers service through a hatch, and there are tables outside in the pretty back garden. Locally reared meat goes into dishes like braised lamb shank or fillet of beef marchand de vin. Fish choices include plaice goujons, crayfish omelette, and sea bass fillet with lemon butter.

Open 12-3 6-11 **Bar Meals** L served Tue-Sun 12-2 D served Tue-Sun 7-8.30 **Restaurant** L served all week 12-2 D served all week 7-8.30 Av 3 course à la carte £25 Free House Adnams, Woodfordes Wherry. **Facilities** Garden Parking

HOLKHAM MAP 13 TF84

Pick of the Pubs

Victoria at Holkham ★★ SHL

Park Rd NR23 1RG ☎ 01328 711008 📠 01328 711009
e-mail: victoria@holkham.co.uk
dir: *On A149, 3m W of Wells-next-the-sea*

The Victoria stands at the gates of landlord Tom Coke's Palladian ancestral home, Holkham Hall, just minutes from the golden sands of Holkham Beach. Its opulent, colonial-style interior is full of furniture and accessories from Rajahstan and other exotic places. Outside is a courtyard where summer barbecues are popular. Tom Coke would argue that the Victoria's main attraction is what he calls 'some of the most consistently good food in North Norfolk', which won them a second AA Rosette in 2006. Key words here are fresh, local and seasonal, whether it be shellfish, fish or samphire from the north Norfolk coast, beef from farms on the Holkham estate, organic chickens from a tenant farmer, venison from the herd of fallow deer or, in the winter, wild game from family shoots. An eclectic, yet sensibly priced, wine list proves popular, and there are always several real ales on tap.

Open 12-12 **Bar Meals** L served out of season only D served all week **Restaurant** L served all week 12-2.30 D served all week 7-9 Adnams Best, Woodfordes Wherry, Guest ale. 12 **Facilities** Children's licence Garden Dogs allowed Parking Play Area **Rooms** 10 bedrooms en suite

England

HORSEY MAP 13 TG42

Nelson Head 🍷

The Street NR29 4AD ☎ 01493 393378

dir: *On B1159 (coast road) between West Somerton & Sea Palling*

Located on a National Trust estate, which embraces nearby Horsey Mere, this 17th-century inn will, to many, epitomise the perfect country pub. It enjoys the tranquility of a particularly unspoilt part of the Norfolk coast – indeed, glorious beaches are only half an hour's walk away – and the sheltered gardens look out towards the dunes and water meadows. Fresh cod, plaice and home-made fish and prawn pie are usually available. Local beers are Woodforde's Wherry and Nelson's Revenge.

Open 11-3 6-11 (Winter hrs vary Etr–Oct open all day) **Bar Meals** L served all week 12-3 D served all week 6-8.30 Av main course £7.50 **Restaurant** L served all week 12-2 D served all week 6-8.30 Av 3 course à la carte £12 Free House Woodforde's Wherry & Nelson's Revenge. 🍷 7 **Facilities** Garden Dogs allowed Parking Play Area

HORSTEAD MAP 13 TG21

Recruiting Sergeant 🍷

Norwich Rd NR12 7EE ☎ 01603 737077 📠 01603 736905

dir: *On B1150 between Norwich & North Walsham*

The name of this inviting country pub comes from the tradition of recruiting servicemen by giving them the King or Queen's shilling in a pint of beer. It offers good food, ales and wines in homely surroundings with a patio and lawned garden for alfresco dining. The menu is ever changing, with inventive dishes such as fresh oysters with a tabasco, lime and red onion dressing, duck breast on an apple and potato rosti and chicken breast stuffed with mozzarella and chorizo. There is also a vast daily specials menu, including fish and vegetarian dishes.

Open 11-11 **Bar Meals** L served all week 12-2 D served all week 6.30-9 (Fri-Sat 6.30-9.30, Sun 12-9) Av main course £15 **Restaurant** L served all week 12-2 D served all week 6.30-9 (Sun 12-9) Av 3 course à la carte £20 Free House Adnams, Woodefordes, Greene King Abbot Ale, Scottish Courage. 🍷 13 **Facilities** Garden Dogs allowed Parking

ITTERINGHAM MAP 13 TG13

Pick of the Pubs

Walpole Arms 🍷

NR11 7AR ☎ 01263 587258 📠 01263 587074

e-mail: goodfood@thewalpolearms.co.uk

dir: *From Aylsham towards Blickling. After Blickling Hall take 1st right to Itteringham*

See Pick of the Pubs on opposite page

KING'S LYNN MAP 12 TF6

The Stuart House Hotel, Bar & Restaurant ★★ HL

35 Goodwins Rd PE30 5QX

☎ 01553 772169 📠 01553 774788

e-mail: reception@stuarthousehotel.co.uk

dir: *Follow signs to town centre, pass under Southgate Arch & take immediate right, after 100yds, turn right again.*

An oasis in the historic port of King's Lynn, only minutes from the town centre. It was built in 1860 as a private house for a wealthy local businessman, not becoming a hotel until a century or so later. Proprietor David Armes has decorated and furnished it throughout in an appropriately elegant style. From a changing menu come tourned Rossini, Norfolk chicken with stilton and wild mushrooms, and pan-fried fillet of cod with Norwegian prawns. Specials available dependin on season.

Open 6-11 **Bar Meals** D served all week 7-9.15 (Lunch available for pre-booked parties of 12 or more) Av main course £9 **Restaurant** D served all week 7-9.15 (Lunch available for pre-booked parties of 12 or more) Av 3 course à la carte £25.95 Free House Adnams, Woodfordes, Greene King, Oakham JHB. **Facilities** Children's licence Garden Parking Play Area **Rooms** 18 bedrooms en suite S£68 D£89

LARLING MAP 13 TL9

Angel Inn 🍷

NR16 2QU ☎ 01953 717963 📠 01953 718561

dir: *5m from Attleborough, 8m from Thetford. 1m from station.*

Wheel-back chairs, an oak-panelled settle, a wood-burning stove and huge collection of water jugs contribute to the homely atmosphere of this 17th-century former coaching inn on the Norwich to Thetford roa Food ranges from sandwiches and light bites such as Welsh rarebit or omelette, through to full meals – perhaps prawn cocktail followed by chicken and mushroom stroganoff, or whitebait followed by hot and spicy pork with noodles.

Open 10-11 **Bar Meals** L served all week 12-9.30 D served all week 12-9.30 (Fri-Sat 12-10) Av main course £8.50 **Restaurant** L served all week 12-9.30 D served all week 12-9.30 (Fri-Sat 12-10) Av 3 course à la carte £18 Free House Adnams Bitter, Wolf Bitter, Caledonian Deuchars IPA, Timothy Taylor Landlord & Mauldons. 🍷 7 **Facilities** Garde Parking Play Area

PICK OF THE PUBS

ITTERINGHAM-NORFOLK

Walpole Arms

ong-term Norfolk residents Richard Bryan and Keith Reeves, together with their respective amilies, combined their talents in 2001 when they took over this traditional village pub in the eautiful north Norfolk countryside.

ichard's lifetime passion for food as been partly channelled into roadcasting, notably as producer of BC TV's *Masterchef*, while Keith is highly respected wine merchant, upplying customers throughout East nglia. With the addition of chef ndy Parle, a veteran of Michelin-tarred restaurants in Norwich and ondon, the team seem to have every ase covered, and the success of his award-winning venture proves hat they have indeed got the recipe ight. The Walpole arms has been pub since 1836, although the ak-beamed bar suggests something lder. In fact, Robert Horace Walpole, direct descendant of Britain's first rime minister, once owned it. Today is both a real pub and a dining estination. Andy and his team use he best seasonal and local produce o create thoroughly modern and nspired pub food. Both restaurant and bar offer a daily changing three-course carte; on Saturdays a special brunch menu is served, and on Sundays there's a delicious roast. Typical starters include Moroccan style broad bean, feta and pomegranate salad; and ballotine of turkey, bacon and chestnut with cranberry relish. Follow with slow roast belly pork with saffron and chick pea stew and black kale; or Morston mussels with salsa rosso and crusty bread. Wash it down with wine from Keith's comprehensive wine list, and finish with desserts such as drop scones with quince compote, pistachio ice cream and crème fraîche. Outside are large grassy areas with tables and a vine-covered patio. There are magnificent walks through the Blickling and Mannington estates nearby.

MAP 13 TG13
NR11 7AR
☎ 01263 587258
Fax 01263 587074
e-mail:
goodfood@thewalpolearms.co.uk
dir: *From Aylsham towards Blickling. After Blickling take 1st right to Itteringham*

Open 12–3 6–11 (Sun 7–10.30)
Closed: 25 Dec
Bar Meals L served all week 12–2 (Sun 12.30–2.30) D served Mon–Sat 7–9.30 Av main course £12
Restaurant L served Sat–Sun 12–2 D served Mon–Sat 7–9.30 (Sun 12.30–2.30) Av 3 course à la carte £22.50
Noble Rot Associates
Adnams Broadside & Bitter, Woodfordes Wherry Best Bitter & Walpole. 🍷 12
Facilities Garden Dogs allowed Parking Play Area

England

LITTLE FRANSHAM MAP 13 TF91

The Canary and Linnet

Main Rd NR19 2JW ☎ 01362 687027

dir: *On A47 between Dereham & Swaffham*

A pretty, former blacksmith's cottage fulfilling the key requirements of a traditional English country pub – low ceilings, exposed beams and an inglenook fireplace. Its sign once showed footballers in Norwich City (Canaries) and Kings Lynn (Linnets) strips, but now features two birds in a cage. Food offered throughout the bar, conservatory restaurant and garden includes steak and ale pie, medallions of pork in stilton sauce, and seared Cajun spiced swordfish steak with lime and coriander dressing.

Open 12-3 6-11 (Sun 7-10) **Bar Meals** L served all week 12-2 D served all week 6-9 **Restaurant** L served all week 12-2 D served all week 6-9.30 Free House Greene King IPA, Tindall's Best, Adnams Bitter, Wolf. **Facilities** Garden Dogs allowed Parking

LITTLE WALSINGHAM MAP 13 TF93

The Black Lion Hotel

Friday Market Place NR22 6DB

☎ 01328 820235 01328 821407

e-mail: lionwalsingham@btinternet.com

dir: *From King's Lynn take A148 & B1105, or from Norwich take A1067 & B1105.*

A former coaching inn, dating in part from 1310, built to accommodate Edward III and Queen Philippa of Hainault when they visited the shrine at Walsingham (the hotel takes its name from her coat of arms). The friendly bar has a welcoming fire in winter, and in the restaurant the seasonal menu might offer scrumpy pork hock; rainbow trout Cleopatra; and spinach, cherry tomato and mozzarella herb pudding.

Open 11-3 6-1 (Sat-Sun 11am-1am) **Bar Meals** L served all week 12-2.30 (Sun 12-3) D served all week 7-9 **Restaurant** L served all week 12-2.30 (Sun 12-3) D served all week 7-9 Av 3 course à la carte £16 Enterprise Inns Woodforde's Wherry, Blacksheep Special, John Smiths Smooth, & Woodforde's Nelson's Revenge. 7 **Facilities** Garden Dogs allowed

MARSHAM MAP 13 TG12

The Plough Inn

Norwich Rd NR10 5PS ☎ 01263 735000 01263 735407

e-mail: enq@ploughinnmarsham.co.uk

dir: *On A140, 10m N of Norwich, 12m from Cromer, 7m from Norwich Airport & Norfolk Broads at Wroxham*

An attractive, traditional 18th-century country pub and restaurant, extended and modernised over the years. The menus are carefully annotated and chosen to provide a range of foods based on local seasonal produce. Lunchtime specials available Monday to Saturday offer choices like catch of the day or pan-fried sausages. Bar snacks are also served in the friendly bar.

The Plough Inn

Open 12-3 5-11 (Sat 6-11, Sun 12-10.30) **Bar Meals** L served all week 12-2.30 D served all week 6.30-9 (Sun 12-8) Av main course £10 **Restaurant** L served all week 12-2.30 D served all week 6.30-9 (Sun 12-8) Av 3 course à la carte £20 Free House IPA, Adnams. 9 **Facilities** Garden Parking **Rooms** 11 bedrooms en suite S£60 D£85 (★★★★ INN)

MUNDFORD MAP 13 TL8

Crown Hotel

Crown Rd IP26 5HQ ☎ 01842 878233 01842 878982

dir: *A11 to Barton Mills junct, then A1065 to Brandon & onto Mundford*

Built in 1652, the Crown has been many things – a famous hunting lodge; the local magistrates' court; even a doctors' waiting room. Its most unusual feature, in these pancake-flat parts, is that it is set into a hill! Traditional food is served in the bar, and a more elaborate menu is available in the restaurant; perhaps tian of Brixham crab followed by lamb rump with flageolet purée, fondant potato, garlic confit and mint jus.

Open 11-2am **Bar Meals** L served all week 12-3 D served all week 7-10 **Restaurant** L served all week 12-3 D served all week 7-10 Free House Courage Directors, Marston Pedigree, Archers, Greene King IPA & Guest ales. **Facilities** Garden Dogs allowed Parking

The Gin Trap Inn

he Gin Trap is a sprawling white-painted inn in the attractive village of Ringstead, just a few iles inland from the North Norfolk coast and Hunstanton. From the early 70s until just a few :ars ago it was packed with old gin traps and farm implements (hence the name).

few years ago the pub was ven a refit and most of the traps sappeared. Nowadays the 'gin' the title refers to the drink. od is taken very seriously, a big parture from the bar-only food rved until a few years ago. A : lunch menu might offer warm nfit duck and prune basket with uffle mayonnaise to start, then aised chicken and white wine t pot with winter vegetables, d to finish, bread and butter dding with vanilla custard. om the evening menu come rters like glazed clam and cockle gliatelle with chive and caviar h cream, and pressed cornfed icken, apricot and sage terrine th home-made piccalilli and ed bread. Main dishes might include line caught seared wild sea bass with pea mash, crispy onion rings and dill butter sauce, and braised beef bourguignon with pancetta lardoons, glazed baby onions, button mushrooms and mashed potato. Desserts are likely to be hard to resist, with the choice perhaps including rich chocolate and blood orange marquise with pistachio crème anglaise, and poached red wine pear with sable biscuit and Chantilly cream. Given the proximity of Ringstead to the coast, it is not surprising that fish is always served. Three smart en suite bedrooms add extra appeal for anyone wanting to stay in the area. A new 40-seater conservatory dining area has considerably widened the scope.

MAP 12 TF74
High St PE36 5JU
☎ 01485 525264
e-mail:
thegintrap@hotmail.co.uk
dir: *take A149 from King's Lynn towards Hunstanton. In 15m turn right at Heacham for Ringstead*

Open 11–3 (open all day summer) 6–11
Bar Meals L served all week 12–2 D served all week 6–9 Av main course £10
Restaurant L served all week 12–2 D served all week 6–9 Av 3 course à la carte £20
Free House
Adnams Best, Woodfordes Wherry, plus guest ales. 8
Facilities Garden Dogs allowed Parking

England

NORWICH MAP 13 TG20

Adam & Eve

Bishopsgate NR3 1RZ ☎ 01603 667423 01603 667438
e-mail: theadamandeve@hotmail.com

First recorded as an alehouse in 1249, the Adam & Eve was used by workmen constructing the nearby cathedral. Labour was cheap, as the men were paid in bread and ale! Centuries later the pub is acknowledged as one of the ten most haunted buildings in Norwich. The comprehensive menu offers everything from home-made cheese and ale soup, beef and mushroom pie, trawlerman's pie and spinach and feta goujons.

Open 11–11 (Sun 12–10.30) Closed: 25–26 Dec, 1 Jan **Bar Meals** L served all week 12–7 (Sun 12–2.30) Enterprise Inns Adnams Bitter, Scottish Courage Theakston Old Peculier, Greene King IPA, Wells Bombardier. 10 **Facilities** Parking

Pick of the Pubs

The Mad Moose Arms NEW

2 Warwick St NR2 3LB
☎ 01603 627687 01508 494946
e-mail: madmoose@animalinns.co.uk

After a complete refurbishment The Mad Moose now combines a decidedly stylish ground floor bar with an elegant upstairs restaurant. While the bar is a vibrant combination of red walls, exposed brickwork and gleaming wood, and comes complete with flat-screen televisions, the restaurant is rather more glamorous, with chandeliers, sea-green drapes and a feature wall depicting a fairytale forest. The bar menu might offer warm fig salad with mascarpone and Parma ham; and Cumberland sausages with thyme polenta, while regularly changing specials include pot roast chicken breast with braised Puy lentils. Upstairs, cooking is confident and ambitious. Start with chicken liver and Madeira parfait with saffron pickled courgettes, followed by breast of Gressingham duck with thyme fondant potatoes and a sticky fig tartlet. Desserts such as pistachio and almond tart, or freestanding crème brûlée with lemon shortbread and strawberry ice cream are as pleasing to the eye as the taste buds.

Open 12–12 (Fri–Sat 12–12.30) **Bar Meals** L served all week 12–2 D served all week 6–10 Av main course £7 **Restaurant** L served Sun 12–2 D served Mon–Sat 7–10 Av 3 course à la carte £25 Av 3 course fixed price £22.50 Free House Adnams Broadside & Greene King IPA. 9 **Facilities** Garden

Ribs of Beef

24 Wensum St NR3 1HY ☎ 01603 619517 01603 625446
e-mail: roger@cawdron.co.uk
dir: *From Tombland (in front of cathedral) turn left at Maids Head Hotel. Pub on right on bridge (200yds)*

Welcoming riverside pub incorporating remnants of the original 14th-century building destroyed in the Great Fire in 1507. Once used by the Norfolk wherry skippers, it is still popular among boat owners cruising the Broads. The menu offers a wide range of sandwiches, burgers and jacket potatoes, as well as Scottish salmon and dill fish cakes, Adnams' braised brisket of beef, vegetarian lasagne, and a choice of omelettes.

Open 11–11 (Fri–Sat 11am–12am) **Bar Meals** L served all week 12–2.30 (Sat–Sun 12–5) D served by arrangement Av main course £5.95 Free House Woodforde's Wherry, Adnams Bitter, Adnams Broadside, Marston's Pedigree & Elgoods Mild. 8

REEPHAM MAP 13 TG1

The Old Brewery House Hotel

Market Place NR10 4JJ ☎ 01603 870881 01603 87096
dir: *Off A1067 (Norwich to Fakenham road), B1145 signed Aylsham*

A grand staircase, highly polished floors and wooden panelling characterise this fine hotel, originally built as a private residence in 1729. It became a hotel in the 1970s, retaining many of its Georgian features. Alongside the real ales and fine wines, there's a bar menu o freshly produced dishes.

Open 11–11 (Sun 12–10.30) **Bar Meals** L served all week 12–2 D served all week 6.30–9.15 (Sun 12–2.15, 7–9) Av main course £7 **Restaurant** L served all week 12–2 D served all week 6.30–9.30 Av 3 cou à la carte £20 Free House IPA, Greene King Abbot Ale & Old Speck Hen. **Facilities** Garden Dogs allowed Parking **Rooms** 23 bedrooms en suite S£50 D£85

RINGSTEAD MAP 12 TF

Pick of the Pubs

The Gin Trap Inn

High St PE36 5JU ☎ 01485 525264
e-mail: thegintrap@hotmail.co.uk
dir: *take A149 from King's Lynn towards Hunstanton. In 15m turn right at Heacham for Ringstead*

See Pick of the Pubs on page 393

The Wildebeest Arms

/hat strikes the first-time visitor to this comfortable inn is the collection of African tribal art, 'hich seems to reference the pub's name, with its masks, primitive instruments, large carved ippos and a giraffe.

he extensive open-plan, oak-eamed bar and dining area with ark wooden furniture, sunny :llow rag-washed walls, allied to ›ft lighting, lend a homely feel. he invariably friendly and efficient :rvice is a notable plus; meals are :rved at substantially proportioned ee-trunk tables or, if preferred n brighter days, in the garden. If :putation is everything, then these ays The Wildebeest has it in spades: ooking from the open kitchen is iodern, and has both the quality ıd price to bring in customers om miles around East Anglia. he menus are exceptional, and articularly well compiled, blending classic base with French and ritish elements. There is a good-alue, fixed-price lunch menu du ›ur of two or three courses (smoked ıicken and watercress salad with crispy Alsace bacon; Binham Blue cheese and caramelised red onion risotto, and pannetone bread and butter pudding with pistachio crème anglaise). The dinner carte starts perhaps with Morston mussels, with white wine, onion, parsley and cream sauce. Main courses take in artichoke and red onion tartlet with creamed leeks, wild mushrooms and shaved parmesan; and grilled fillet of sea bass with thyme sautéed potatoes, etuvée leeks, fennel and mushroom duxelle, brown shrimp and lemon and caper beurre blanc. Finish with a dessert of hot dark chocolate fondant with caramel sauce and chocolate ice cream, or a selection of fine cheeses. The wines too, are eye-catchingly well priced. Because of its high regard locally, this is a pub where booking is essential, especially for dinner.

MAP 13 TG20
82–86 Norwich Rd NR14 8QJ
☎ 01508 492497
01508 494946
e-mail:
wildebeest@animalinns.co.uk

Open 12–3 6–11 (Sun 12–3 7–10.30) Closed: 25–26 Dec
Bar Meals L served All D served All
Restaurant L served all week 12–2 D served all week 7–10
Free House
Adnams. 12
Facilities Garden Parking

England

SALTHOUSE MAP 13 TG04

The Dun Cow

Coast Rd NR25 7XG ☎ 01263 740467

dir: *On A149 coast road, 3m E of Blakeney, 6m W of Sheringham*

Overlooking some of the country's finest freshwater marshes, the front garden of this attractive pub is inevitably popular with birdwatchers and walkers. The bar area was formerly a blacksmith's forge, and many original 17th-century beams have been retained. Children are welcome, but there's also a walled rear garden reserved for adults. The menu includes snacks, pub staples like burgers and jacket potatoes, and main courses like gammon steak, pasta and meatballs, plaice and chips, and lasagne.

Open 11-11 (Sun 12-10.30) **Bar Meals** L served all week 12-8.45 D served all week 12-8.45 Av main course £7 Pubmaster Greene King IPA & Abbot Ale, Adnams Broadside. **Facilities** Garden Dogs allowed Parking

SNETTISHAM MAP 12 TF63

Pick of the Pubs

The Rose & Crown ★★ HL

Old Church Rd PE31 7LX

☎ 01485 541382 01485 543172

e-mail: info@roseandcrownsnettisham.co.uk

dir: *10m N from King's Lynn on A149 signed Hunstanton. Inn in village centre between market square & church*

With its rose-covered façade, the Rose & Crown looks every inch the quintessential English village inn. The same is true inside, as from its 14th-century core it spreads out beneath low, beamed ceilings through twisting pamment-tile floored passages, past cosy corners into more contemporary areas. Each of the three convivial bars has its own character (and characters!). The menu partners traditional pub favourites with more exotic dishes, all prepared to a high standard and using, where possible, locally supplied produce. Beef, for example, comes from cattle that grazed nearby salt marshes, fishermen still in their waders deliver Branscaster mussels and Thornham oysters, and strawberries and asparagus grow all around. A regularly changing menu offers, for example, beef stew and dumplings; salmon and butterfish brochettes; braised knuckle of lamb; and roast pumpkin salad. The pretty walled garden was once the village bowling green. Bedrooms are individually decorated in fresh contemporary style.

Open 11-11 (Sun 12-10.30) **Bar Meals** L served all week 12-2 (Sat-Sun 12-2.30) D served all week 6.30-9 (Fri-Sat 6.30-9.30) Av main course £10 **Restaurant** L served all week 12-2 (Sat-Sun 12-2.30) D served all week 6.30-9 (Fri-Sat 6.30-9.30) Av 3 course à la carte £20 Free House Adnams Bitter & Broadside, Interbrew Bass, Fuller's London Pride, Greene King IPA. 20 **Facilities** Garden Dogs allowed Parking Play Area **Rooms** 16 bedrooms en suite S£60 D£85

STOKE HOLY CROSS MAP 13 TG2

Pick of the Pubs

The Wildebeest Arms

82-86 Norwich Rd NR14 8QJ

☎ 01508 492497 01508 494946

e-mail: wildebeest@animalinns.co.uk

See Pick of the Pubs on page 395

STOW BARDOLPH MAP 12 TF6

Pick of the Pubs

The Hare Arms

PE34 3HT ☎ 01366 382229 01366 385522

e-mail: trishmc@harearms222.wanadoo.co.uk

dir: *From King's Lynn take A10 to Downham Market. After 9m village signed on left*

This attractive ivy-clad pub, built during the Napoleonic wars, takes its name from the surrounding estate, ancestral home of the Hare family since 1553. In the care of Trish and David McManus since 1976, the Hare has preserved its appeal and become deservedly popular. Here farming folk can chat with business people uninterrupted by piped music, peacocks wander around outside, and the cat warms itself by the fire. The L-shaped bar and adjoining conservatory, packed with decades-worth of fascinating bygones, offer an extensive menu of regular pub food, supplemented by daily specials; the award-winning steak and peppercorn pie is now a permanent fixture. Upmarket fixed-price and à la carte menus are served in the evening. Plentiful fish dishes may include smoked haddock bake, or lemon sole cooked on or off the bone. There's even a standalone vegetarian menu with starters such as deep-fried courgette and feta cakes; and main courses like split jalapeno peppers stuffed with cream cheese.

Open 11-2.30 6-11 (Sun 7-10.30) Closed: 25-26 Dec **Bar Meals** L served all week 12-2 D served all week 7-10 **Restaurant** L served Sun 12-2 D served Mon-Sat 7-9.30 Av 3 course à la carte £35 Av 3 course fixed price £23.50 Greene King Greene King, Abbot Ale, IPA & Old Speckled Hen & Guest. 7 **Facilities** Garden Parking

Chequers Inn

he 16th-century Chequers, with its unusual low-slung thatched roof, is hidden among the trees ı the edge of Thompson village. Like its namesakes elsewhere, it takes its title from the use of chequered cloth to make calculations, often of wages, at least halfway intelligible to medieval gricultural workers.

anor courts, dealing with rents, ttings of land, and small crimes, ere held here in the 18th century; ter it became a doctor's surgery. riginal features inside include xposed beams and timbers, while d farming memorabilia hangs from e walls. Food may be chosen from e bar menu, carte or daily specials oard. Starters include devilled hitebait; prawns and smoked lmon; and chef's own chicken ver paté. There's plenty of main ourse choice, such as pan-fried eef medallions with shallots, leeks, arlic and double cream; Barnsley ops with mushroom and smoked eddar; breast of chicken with wild ushrooms and tarragon sauce; aked sea bass with thyme, sun-ushed tomatoes and lime; and a ood choice of fish, including baked sea bream with thyme, sun-blushed tomato and garlic. Nut roast, cheesy pancake and vegetable lasagne should satisfy vegetarian tastes. Among the specials look out for steak and kidney pudding; smoked duck breast with crisp leaf salad and orange and hazelnut dressing; and seafood linguine with garlic, wine and cream sauce. Finally, for dessert, there may well be home-made apple pie, treacle sponge and spotted dick. A climbing frame and swings in the garden will appeal to younger visitors, and the views extend over open land and woods. Nearby is the eight-mile Great Eastern Pingo Trail that navigates a succession of glacially formed swampy depressions in the ground known, as you will have guessed, as pingos.

MAP 13 TL99
Griston Rd IP24 1PX
☎ 01953 483360
Fax 01953 488092
e-mail: richard@chequers_inn.wanadoo.co.uk
dir: *Between Watton & Thetford off A1075*

Open 11.30–2.30 6.30–11 (Sun 12–3, 6.30–10.30)
Bar Meals L served all week 12–2 D served all week 6.30–9.30 Av main course £8.50
Restaurant L served all week 12–2 D served all week 6.30–9.30 Av 3 course à la carte £25
Free House
Fuller's London Pride, Adnams Best, Wolf Best, Greene King IPA. 7
Facilities Garden Dogs allowed Parking Play Area
Rooms 3 bedrooms en suite S£40 D£60 (★★★★ INN)

The Orange Tree

This refurbished country pub stands by the ancient Peddar's Way, opposite the church in one of North Norfolk's lovely coastal villages. Thornham is an excellent base for discovering the speci coastline around Brancaster Bay and the famous bird reserve of Titchwell, and it's just a few minutes' walk from Thornham's harbour and superb beach.

Two large beer gardens and a children's play area add to the Orange Tree's family appeal; roast Sunday lunch is particularly popular, served from midday through to 6pm. The bar and restaurant are very stylish, but the building still has that special feel of a traditional rural pub. Greene King and Adnams furnish the beers in the bar alongside stouts and continental lagers, while the short wine list easily meets demand with about ten served by the glass. Lunchtime snacks start with a range of sandwiches: perhaps honey and mustard ham; Norfolk brie and grape relish baguette with home-smoked nuts. Light lunches include home-made burger with streaky bacon and avocado salad, Monterey Jack cheese, hand-cut chips and red pepper ketchup; and tossed penne pasta with tallegio and basil velouté and asparagus spears. The cooking moves up several gears for the à la carte menu, which might open with grilled garlic sardines, tomato and basil bruschetta and preserved lomons. Fish features strongly at both levels, and might appear in such mains as chargrilled seabass with orange and anchovy gremolata potato salad, or sautéed barramundi with chorizo and squid tagliatelle and basil pesto. For meat lovers there could be steak sizzler with garlic king prawns, or maple roast duck breast, confit rhubarb and red wine jus. A healthy and nutritious menu for children is cooked freshly to order, including tossed linguini, chargrilled vegetables and pesto.

★★★ INN ◎ 🍷
MAP 12 TF74
High St PE36 6LY
☎ 01485 512213
📠 01485 512424
e-mail: email@theorangetreethornham.co.uk

Open 11–11 (Sun 12–10.30)
Closed: 25 Dec
Bar Meals L served all week 12–2 D served Mon–Sat 6–9 Av main course £9
Restaurant L served all week 12–2 D served Mon–Sat 6–9 Av 3 course à la carte £24
Punch Taverns
Greene King IPA, Adnams Bitter, Carling (extra cold), Guinness & Carlsberg. 🍷 10
Facilities Garden Dogs allowed Parking Play Area
Rooms 6 bedrooms en suite S£40 D£50

England

WANTON MORLEY MAP 13 TG01

arbys Freehouse

.2 Elsing Rd NR20 4NY
· 01362 637647 01362 637928
mail: louisedarby@hotmail.co.uk
r: *From A47 (Norwich to King's Lynn) take B1147 to Dereham*

ilt in the 1700s as a large country house, then divided into cottages the late 19th century. In 1987, after the village's last traditional pub sed, it was converted into the pub you see today, while retaining old beams and inglenooks. Traditional pub food includes steak and ıshroom pudding, braised lamb shank, chargrilled pork loin, scampi, er-battered haddock, steaks, curries and a vegetarian selection. ildren have their own menu and a play area.

en 11.30-3 6-11 (Sat 11.30-11, Sun 12-10.30) **Bar Meals** L served week 12-2.15 D served Mon-Fri 6.30-9.45 (Sat 12-9.45, Sun 12-8.45) **staurant** L served all week 12-2.15 D served all week 6.30-9.45 Free use Woodforde's Wherry, Badger Tanglefoot, Adnams Broadside, nams Best. **Facilities** Garden Dogs allowed Parking Play Area

HOMPSON MAP 13 TL99

Pick of the Pubs

Chequers Inn

Griston Rd IP24 1PX
☎ 01953 483360 01953 488092
e-mail: richard@chequers_inn.wanadoo.co.uk
dir: *Between Watton & Thetford off A1075*

See Pick of the Pubs on page 397

HORNHAM MAP 12 TF74

Pick of the Pubs

Lifeboat Inn ★★ HL

Ship Ln PE36 6LT ☎ 01485 512236 01485 512323
e-mail: reception@lifeboatinn.co.uk
dir: *A149 to Hunstanton, follow coast road to Thornham, pub 1st left*

The Lifeboat is a 16th-century inn overlooking Thornham Harbour and the salt marshes. Despite being extended, its original character has been retained. Inside, the warm glow of paraffin lamps enhances the welcoming atmosphere, while the adjoining conservatory is renowned for its ancient vine and adjacent walled patio garden. The best available fish and game feature on the frequently changing menus, in the form of Brancaster mussels – always a popular starter – steamed in chardonnay with lemon grass, ginger and double cream. For a satisfying main course try local partridge casserole with Guinness and mushrooms, bacon, herbs and creamy horseradish mash. If you want to stay and explore the area, 22 en suite bedrooms are available and numerous attractions lie within easy reach of the inn. These include Thornham beach, Blakeney, Cley, Sandringham and Nelson's birthplace at Burnham Thorpe.

Open 11-11 **Bar Meals** L served all week 12-2.30 D served all week 6.30-9.30 **Restaurant** D served all week 7-9.30 Free House Adnams, Woodforde's Wherry, Greene King Abbot Ale & IPA. 10 **Facilities** Garden Dogs allowed Parking Play Area **Rooms** 22 bedrooms en suite S£66 D£92

Pick of the Pubs

The Orange Tree NEW ★★★ INN

High St PE36 6LY ☎ 01485 512213 01485 512424
e-mail: email@theorangetreethornham.co.uk

See Pick of the Pubs on opposite page

THORPE MARKET MAP 13 TG23

Green Farm Restaurant & Hotel ★★ HL

North Walsham Rd NR11 8TH
☎ 01263 833602 01263 833163
e-mail: enquiries@greenfarmhotel.co.uk
web: www.greenfarmhotel.co.uk
dir: *On A149*

This 16th-century flint-faced former farmhouse overlooks the village green and features a pubby bar as well as a restaurant with an interesting menu. Typical dishes may include grilled marinated breast of duck served on a herbal ratatouille with a sage and balsamic jus, roasted pork cutlet with a sweet pepper crust and spicy garlic and okra sauce, or seabass on roasted fennel and lemon cream sauce.

Open 10-11 **Bar Meals** L served all week 12-2 D served Mon-Fri 6.30-8.30 (Fri-Sat 6.30-9) Av main course £9.50 **Restaurant** L served all week 12-2 D served Mon-Fri 6.30-8.30 (Fri-Sat 6.30-9) Av 3 course à la carte £30 Av 5 course fixed price £26 Free House Greene King IPA, Wolf Best Bitter. **Facilities** Garden Dogs allowed Parking **Rooms** 20 bedrooms en suite S£62.50 D£75

The Crown

A former coaching inn, The Crown overlooks the tree-lined green known as The Buttlands. Striking contemporary décor and furnishings work well with the old-world charm of the 17th-century building.

Food is served in the bar with its old beams and open fire, or the sunny coloured restaurant or vibrant conservatory, while on fine days you can sit outside on the sun deck. In style, the cooking brings together modern British and Pacific Rim flavours, along with traditional options for the more conservative of diners. One thing is certain though – you can be sure of ambitious and freshly prepared food made from the best ingredients. The bar menu is divided into three sections, from 'savoury little things' to sandwiches and more hearty options. Goats' cheese and rosemary brûlée with toast and tomato pickle, or smoked ham, butterbean and almond terrine on toasted brioche with onion marmalade might suit smaller appetites; hungrier folk will be satisfied by a more substantial confit of duck leg with chargrilled aubergine; paella with monkfish crab claws, squid, clams and chorizo, or baked fillet of cod with saffron mash and celeriac remoulade. The regularly changing restaurant menu might take in flash-fried squid, bacon and black pudding, or terrine of lamb shank and sweetbreads with sauerkraut, followed by Thai marinated duck breast with seared scallops and chilli jam, or feta, parmesan and basil risotto with roasted cherry tomatoes. Round off with such sophisticated sweet things as olive oil chocolate mousse or Mumma Coughbroughs apple and walnut pudding with clotted cream.

MAP 13 TF94
The Buttlands NR23 1EX
☎ 01328 710209
01328 711432
e-mail: reception@thecrownhotelwells.co.uk
dir: *10m from Fakenham on B1105*

Open 11–11
Bar Meals L served all week 12–2.30 D served all week 6.30–9.30
Restaurant D served all week 7–9
Free House
Adnams Bitter, Woodefordes Wherry, Guest Ale, Bitburger.
12
Facilities Children's licence Garden Dogs allowed Parking
Rooms 12 bedrooms en suite S£70 D£90

England

ITCHWELL MAP 13 TF74

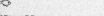

Pick of the Pubs

Titchwell Manor Hotel ★★★ HL

PE31 8BB ☎ 01485 210221 01485 210104
e-mail: margaret@titchwellmanor.com
dir: *A149 between Brancaster & Thornham*

In the same hands for nearly twenty years, this Victorian manor house has been tastefully updated with a light modern décor. The emphasis here is very much on food. Smart public rooms include a lounge, informal bar, and a delightful conservatory restaurant. From its pretty walled garden the sea views are glorious, and its proximity lends a major influence to the menus. Uncluttered menus are priced simply in whole pounds, the cooking is skilled and interesting, and the presentation is studied. Lunch options include sandwiches, starters such as Brancaster oysters, and light cooked meals of pan-fried lemon sole with new potatoes, or deep-fried haddock with minted mushy peas. For dinner you might find bream or halibut, with roast rack of lamb or seared Holkham venison if meat is preferred. Families are particularly welcome, and there is a colourful children's menu for under 12s with lots of choice.

Open 11–11 **Bar Meals** L served all week 12–2 D served all week 6.30–9.30 **Restaurant** L served all week 12–2 D served all week 6.30–9.30 Free House Greene King IPA. **Facilities** Garden Dogs allowed Parking **Rooms** 16 bedrooms en suite S£35 D£50

WARHAM ALL SAINTS MAP 13 TF94

Pick of the Pubs

Three Horseshoes

NR23 1NL ☎ 01328 710547
dir: *Wells A149 to Cromer, right onto B1105 to Warham*

Gaslights in the main bar, scrubbed wooden tables, a grandfather clock ticking away in the corner – this is a charming old gent of a pub that first opened its doors to locals in 1725. Real ales are served directly from the cask through a hole in the bar wall, and the largely original interior includes a curious green and red dial set into the ceiling: it's a rare surviving example of Norfolk twister, an ancient Norfolk pub game. Vintage posters, clay pipes, photographs and memorabilia adorn the walls, while down a step are old one-arm bandits. The traditional home-made food could come straight from Mrs Beeton's own kitchen, with Norfolk potted pork cheese; marinated local herrings; Norfolk beef and ale pie; steak and kidney pudding and lots of local fish and shellfish. Remain in Mrs B territory for puddings, especially sponges, tarts and crumbles.

Open 11.30–2.30 6–11 (Sun 6–10.30) **Bar Meals** L served all week 12–1.45 D served all week 6–8.30 Av main course £8.90 Free House Greene King IPA, Woodforde's Wherry. **Facilities** Garden Dogs allowed Parking **Notes**

WELLS-NEXT-THE-SEA MAP 13 TF94

Pick of the Pubs

The Crown

The Buttlands NR23 1EX
☎ 01328 710209 01328 711432
e-mail: reception@thecrownhotelwells.co.uk
dir: *10m from Fakenham on B1105*

See Pick of the Pubs on opposite page

WEST BECKHAM MAP 13 TG13

The Wheatsheaf

Manor Farm, Church Rd NR25 6NX ☎ 01263 822110
e-mail: danielclarejoe@tiscali.co.uk
dir: *2m from Sheringham on A148, opposite Sheringham Park.*

Former manor house converted to a pub over 20 years ago that retains many original features. Sample one of the real ales from Woodfordes Brewery and relax in the large garden. The extensive menu caters for all appetites, large or small, and may feature saddle of lamb stuffed with spinach and stilton with a brandy gravy, pork and oregano meatballs in a tomato sauce on tagliatelle with garlic bread, or chick pea, pepper and pineapple curry served with rice and home-made chapattis.

Open 11.30–3 6.30–11 (Winter 12–3, 6.30–11) (Sun 12–3, 7–10) **Bar Meals** L served all week 12–2 D served Mon–Sat 6.30–9 **Restaurant** L served all week 12–2 D served Mon–Sat 6.30–9 Free House Woodforde's Wherry Best Bitter, Nelson's Revenge, Norfolk Nog, Greene King IPA & Guest Ales. 7 **Facilities** Garden Dogs allowed Parking Play Area

WINTERTON-ON-SEA MAP 13 TG41

Fishermans Return

The Lane NR29 4BN ☎ 01493 393305 01493 393951
e-mail: fishermans_return@btopenworld.com
dir: *8m N of Great Yarmouth on B1159*

Long beaches and National Trust land are within walking distance of this 300-year-old brick and flint pub – ideal for a spot of bird or seal watching. Under the same ownership for over 30 years, the Fisherman's Return has a popular menu that, aptly, includes good fish and seafood options from the blackboard (moules marinière; whole grilled plaice) plus snacks and jacket potatoes.

Open 11–2.30 6–11 (Sat 11–11, Sun 12–10.30) **Bar Meals** L served all week 12–2 D served all week 6.30–9 Av main course £8.75 Free House Woodforde's Wherry & Norfolk Nog, Adnams Best Bitter & Broadside and Greene King IPA & Guest Ales. 10 **Facilities** Garden Dogs allowed Parking Play Area

England

WIVETON MAP 13 TG04

Wiveton Bell

Blakeney Rd NR25 7TL ☎ 01263 740101
e-mail: enquiries@wivetonbell.co.uk
dir: *1m from Blakeney*

The former port of Wiveton is now over two miles from the sea, but you can see ships' timbers in the pub and the old quay still survives behind the village church. In this picturesque free house you'll find Woodforde's Norfolk ales, and meals are served daily in the bar or restaurant. On warmer days you can eat in the garden, too.

Open 12–11 **Bar Meals** L served all week 12–3 D served all week 6–9.30 (Sun 12–6) **Restaurant** L served all week 12–3 D served all week 6–9.30 Av 3 course à la carte £22 Free House Woodforde's Nelson's Revenge & Wherry. 11 **Facilities** Garden Dogs allowed Parking

WOODBASTWICK MAP 13 TG31

The Fur & Feather Inn

Slad Ln NR13 6HQ ☎ 01603 720003 01603 722266
dir: *Leave Norwich on Salhouse/Wroxham road, follow brown signs for Woodfordes Brewery. Pub next door*

This idyllic country pub is ideal for real ale lovers: Woodforde's Brewery is next door, and of course the ales are offered here, straight from the cask. The pub was originally two farm cottages, and now boasts three cosy bar areas and a smart restaurant where you can enjoy steak and ale pie, home baked ham, and goats' cheese, pepper and tomato lasagne, for example, followed by pannacotta and Norfolk honey or a baked vanilla cheesecake maybe.

Open 11.30–3 6–11 (Summer Mon–Sat 11.30–11, Sun 12–10.30) **Bar Meals** L served all week 12–2 (Sun 12–2.30) D served all week 6–9 Av main course £9.50 **Restaurant** L served all week 12–2 D served all week 6–9 (Sun 12–2.30) Woodforde's Woodforde's Wherry, Sundew, Norfolk Nog, Nelson's Revenge. 8 **Facilities** Garden Parking

NORTHAMPTONSHIRE

ASHBY ST LEDGERS MAP 11 SP56

The Olde Coach House Inn

CV23 8UN ☎ 01788 890349 01788 891922
e-mail: oldcoachhouse@traditionalfreehouses.com
dir: *M1 junct 18 follow A361/Daventry signs. Village on left*

A late 19th-century farmhouse and outbuildings, skilfully converted into a pub with dining areas and meeting rooms, set in a village that dates way back to the Domesday Book of 1086. The village was home to Robert Catesby, one of the Gunpowder plotters. Beer is taken seriously here, with up to eight regularly changing real ales and legendary beer festivals. The pub also serves fresh, high quality food in comfortable surroundings, and summer barbecues.

Open 12–11 (Sun 12–10.30) **Bar Meals** L served all week 12–8.30 D served all week 12–8.30 Av main course £7 **Restaurant** L served all week D served all week Av 3 course à la carte £20 Free House Everards Original, Everards Tiger, Marstons Pedigree, Guest beer. **Facilities** Garden Parking Play Area

ASHTON MAP 11 SP7

The Old Crown

1 Stoke Rd NN7 2JN ☎ 01604 862268
dir: *M1 junct 15. 1m from A508 from Roade*

Attractive 17th-century inn with traditional beamed interior and walls decorated with many prints and mirrors. Outside there are two attractively-planted gardens for alfresco dining. Snacks such as soups, sandwiches and salads are available, along with main courses like seared fennel-crusted tuna on Mediterranean couscous; charred aubergine and coconut curry; five-herb roasted chicken breast with potato and celeriac mash; and steamed steak, mushroom, bacon, stilton and herb suet pudding.

Open 12–3 6–11 (Sat–Sun all day) **Bar Meals** L served Mon–Sat 12–2.30 (Sun lunch 12–4) D served Tue–Sun 6.30–9.30 Av main course £7.95 **Restaurant** L served Mon–Sun 12–2.30 Sun lunch 12–3 D served Mon–Sat 6.30–9 Charles Wells Bombardier, Fosters, Red Stripe. 7 **Facilities** Garden Parking

BADBY MAP 11 SP5

The Windmill Inn

Main St NN11 3AN ☎ 01327 702363 01327 311521
e-mail: info@windmillinn-badby.com
dir: *M1 junct 16 take A45 to Daventry then A361 S. Village in 2m*

Traditional thatched pub dating back to the 17th century, with beamed and flagstone bars and a friendly, relaxed atmosphere. Close by are Blenheim Palace and Warwick Castle, and a few hundred yards away is the only thatched youth hostel in England and Wales. A varied menu includes fish kebabs in a Thai marinade; steak and kidney pudding; Cajun-style chicken supreme; and baked fillet of cod with olive oil, garlic and herbs.

Open 11.30–3.30 5.30–12 **Bar Meals** L served all week 12–2 D served all week 7–9.30 **Restaurant** L served all week 12–2 D served all week 7–9.30 Free House Bass , Flowers, Wadworth 6X, Fullers London Pride. **Facilities** Garden Dogs allowed Parking

BULWICK MAP 11 SP9

Pick of the Pubs

The Queen's Head

Main St NN17 3DY ☎ 01780 450272
e-mail: queenshead-bulwick@tiscali.co.uk
dir: *Just off A43, between Corby & Stamford*

See Pick of the Pubs on opposite page

The Queen's Head

his charming old building is thought to have been a pub since the 17th century, although parts f it date back to 1400. The name comes from the Portuguese wife of Charles II, Katherine of raganza, who was well known for her very elaborate hair-dos.

verlooking the village church, is every inch the quintessential nglish pub, with exposed beams, ur open fireplaces, wooden eams and flagstone floors in a arren of small rooms. Relax by the re or on the patio with a pint of pitfire or a local Rockingham Ale, ıd some hearty pub food. Many ıgredients are sourced from the ırrounding area, and the pub is ell known for its use of local game ke teal, woodcock, partridge and heasant. Lunch brings sandwiches, ıteresting snacks (chorizo ıusages; toasted seeds) and full ıeals such as duck and chicken ver terrine with quince jelly ıllowed by Cornish crab, tomato, ennel and saffron risotto with basil. Iany of the dishes incorporate alian influences and ingredients.

The evening menu opens with the likes of Jerusalem artichoke soup with crisp pancetta and white truffle oil; or buffalo mozzarella with a salad of fresh figs, rocket, parmesan and spiced fig vinegar. Follow with roast saddle of rabbit with a pine nut, parsley, garlic and sage stuffing and a morel mushroom sauce; or poached potato gnocchi with spinach and leeks in a goats' cheese and sage sauce with white truffle oil. Typical desserts include almond and apricot tart with Devonshire cream; and warm lemon and almond polenta cake. The menu is backed by a comprehensive wine list, while ale lovers will find three guest ales sourced from microbreweries alongside the regular selection at the bar.

MAP 11 SP99
Main St NN17 3DY
☎ 01780 450272
e-mail: queenshead-bulwick@tiscali.co.uk
dir: *Just off A43, between Corby & Stamford*

Open 12-3 5-11
Bar Meals L served Tue-Sun 12-2.30 D served Tue-Sat 6-9.30 (Sun 12-3) Av main course £5.95
Restaurant L served Tue-Sun 12-2.30 D served Tue-Sat 6-9.30 (Sun 12-3) Av 3 course à la carte £25 Av fixed price £10.95
Free House
Shepherd Neame, Spitfire, Elland & Guest Ales, Rockingham Ales & Newby Wyke. 9
Facilities Garden Dogs allowed Parking

George and Dragon

An attractive, honey-stoned, 16th-century pub tucked away beside the church in a pretty village protected by Conservation Area status. Formerly a free house, the pub is now owned by the Everard brewery of Leicester.

There's a welcoming feel to the three comfortable bars, where the traditional atmosphere is upheld by an abundance of low beams, simple wooden chairs and settles, log fires (which really are lit), and warm terracotta decor. The blackboards list an interesting selection of food, from sandwiches and baked butternut squash or jacket potatoes (filled with flaked tuna and lemon mayonnaise, prawns with a lime dressing), to favourites and specials: you'll find fish pie at lunchtime, along with fish and chips; pork and apple burgers; root vegetable bake; smoked duck salad; and warm bacon and green leaf salad. In the evening the menu lists starters like goats' cheese and caramelized pears; stuffed mushrooms; rabbit and prune paté; smoked fish platter; and potted prawns, with such main dishes as smoked salmon and avocado salad; steak and Everard Tiger beer pie; wild mushroom risotto; lambs' liver and bacon; venison kebabs; and baked trout in butter sauce. Desserts come in the guise of marmalade bread and butter pudding; chocolate fondue; and ginger and orange pudding, and are seriously irresistible. The George and Dragon is well placed for M40 travellers and is also very popular with the business community in nearby Banbury. The Northamptonshire countryside is a delightful area to explore, and the inn is also well placed for visits to Oxfordshire.

MAP 11 SP44
Silver St OX17 2JR
☎ 01295 711500
01295 710516
e-mail:
thegeorgeanddragon@msn.com
dir: *M40 junct 11 Daventry road. Chacombe 1st right*

Open 12-11 (Sun 12-10.30)
Bar Meals L served all week 12-2.30 D served Mon-Sat 6.30-9.30 (Sun 12-3) Av main course £10
Restaurant L served all week 12-2.30 D served Mon-Sat 6-9.30 (Sun 12-3)
Free House
Everards Tiger, Everards Beacon & weekly Guest Ales.
Facilities Garden Dogs allowed Parking

HACOMBE MAP 11 SP44

Pick of the Pubs

George and Dragon

Silver St OX17 2JR ☎ 01295 711500 🖷 01295 710516
e-mail: thegeorgeanddragon@msn.com
dir: *M40 junct 11 take Daventry road. Chacombe 1st right*

See Pick of the Pubs on opposite page

LIPSTON MAP 11 SP78

he Bulls Head

ırborough Rd LE16 9RT ☎ 01858 525268
r: *On B4036 S of Market Harborough*

ıerican airmen once pushed coins between the beams as a good k charm before bombing raids, and the trend continues with foreign per money pinned all over the inn. In addition to its good choice real ales, the pub has an amazing collection of over 500 whiskies. e menu includes shark steaks, whole sea bass, hot toddy duck, and ak pie.

en 11.30–3 5.30–11 (Summer Sat–Sun all day) **Bar Meals** L served week 12–2.30 D served all week 6.30–9 **Restaurant** L served all week –2.30 D served all week 6.30–9 Free House Tiger, Beacon, Guest & asonal Beers. 14 **Facilities** Children's licence Garden Dogs allowed king

OLLYWESTON MAP 11 SK90

he Collyweston Slater NEW

–89 Main Rd PE9 3PQ ☎ 01780 444288
mail: info@collywestonslater.co.uk
r: *4m SW of Stamford, A43 2m off A1*

e area around Collyweston is famous for its slate, hence the usual name. An extremely sleek refit in 2006 combines the best of ntemporary and traditional furnishings, not to mention a floodlit tanque piste popular with visitors and villagers alike. Menus change equently to make the most of seasonal produce, backed by an tensive and well-constructed wine list and a good range of real ales.

pen 10.30–3 5–11 (Sat 10.30–11, Sun 12–4) Closed: 2–10 Jan **r Meals** L served all week 12–2.30 (Sun 12–3) D served all week 30–9.30 Av main course £12.50 **Restaurant** L served all week 12–2.30 ın 12–3) D served all week 6.30–9.30 Av 3 course à la carte £24 Slaters Ale, Tiger, Bitter, Original Bitter. 8 **Facilities** Garden Parking

CRICK MAP 11 SP57

The Red Lion Inn

52 Main Rd NN6 7TX ☎ 01788 822342 🖷 01788 822342
dir: *From M1 junct 18, 0.75m E on A428, follows signs for Crick from new rdbt*

A thatched, stone-built coaching inn dating from the 17th century, with beams and open fires. The Marks family, landlords here for over 25 years, give their regulars and visitors exactly what they want – a friendly atmosphere, real ales and traditional food. The daily home-made steak pie is a lunchtime favourite, while fillet and sirloin steaks are a speciality in the evening. Fish eaters will find trout, stuffed lemon sole, salmon and seafood platter.

Open 11–2.30 6.15–11 (Sun 12–3, 7–10.30) **Bar Meals** L served all week 12–2 D served Mon–Sat 6.30–9 Av main course £6.50 Wellington Pub Co Websters, Wells Bombardier, Greene King Old Speckled Hen & Guest Beer. **Facilities** Garden Dogs allowed Parking

FARTHINGSTONE MAP 11 SP65

Pick of the Pubs

The Kings Arms

Main St NN12 8EZ ☎ 01327 361604 🖷 01327 361604
e-mail: paul@kingsarms.fsbusiness.co.uk
dir: *M1 junct 16, A45 towards Daventry. At Weedon, A5 towards Towcester. Right signed Farthingstone*

You'll find this cosy 18th-century Grade II listed inn tucked away in unspoilt countryside near Canons Ashby (a National Trust property). With good walks nearby and real fires in winter, it's very much the traditional country pub, albeit it a highly distinctive one, with gargoyles peering from the stonework and a fascinating garden bursting with flowers, vegetables and herbs. The pub has a retail business specialising in regional British fish, meat and cheeses, and this passion is reflected on the short menu where dishes might include game casserole with parsley mash; Islay smoked venison with salad; Loch Fyne fish platter; Cumbrian wild boar sausages with mash; home-made steak and kidney-filled Yorkshire pudding; and a platter of British cheeses. Naturally the commitment to sourcing regional specialities extends to the excellent real ales.

Open 12–2.30 7–11 **Bar Meals** L served Sat–Sun 12–2 Free House Gt. Oakley, Thwaites Original, Adnams, Brakspear Bitter. **Facilities** Garden Dogs allowed Parking **Notes**

England

FOTHERINGHAY MAP 12 TL09

Pick of the Pubs

The Falcon Inn

PE8 5HZ ☎ 01832 226254 01832 226046

dir: *N of A605 between Peterborough & Oundle*

Fotheringhay is a perfect stone village with important historic connections. Overlooking the extraordinary church, which plays host to some serious concerts, is the attractive 18th-century, stone-built Falcon, set within gardens redesigned by award-winning landscape architect, Bunny Guinness. It's a true local, with a Tap Bar regularly used by the Adnams-fuelled village darts team. The highly praised classic Italian food from Chris Kippings and David Sims makes use of the latest season's olive oil and other fresh, seasonal ingredients. But there are British classics too on the bar snack board, like Lancashire hotpot, potted shrimps and bangers and mash. Diners in the smart restaurant and conservatory extension will find a truly Italian menu featuring dishes not normally encountered in your local trattoria. Starters include pea, parsley and mint risotto with chardonnay, crème fraîche and parmesan (risotto con piselle); and main dishes might be home-made pizza with ricotta, asparagus, roast garlic, oregano and pecorino, served with a rocket salad.

Open 11.30–3 6–11 (Sat 6–10, Sun 12–3, 7–10.30)
Bar Meals L served all week 12–2.15 D served all week 7–9.30
Restaurant L served all week 12–2.15 D served all week 6.15–9.30
Free House Adnams Bitter, Greene King IPA, Scottish Courage John Smith's, Nethergate. 20 **Facilities** Garden Parking

GRAFTON REGIS MAP 11 SP74

The White Hart

Northampton Rd NN12 7SR ☎ 01908 542123

e-mail: alan@pubgraftonregis.co.uk

dir: *M1 junct 15 on A508 between Northampton & Milton Keynes*

In 1464, Edward IV married Elizabeth Woodville in this historic village, where the stone-built thatched White Hart was first licensed in 1750. The restaurant menu might list salmon fillet with prawn sauce, or mature Welsh fillet steak topped with home-made chicken liver paté. From the lounge menu, you can choose from the likes of mustard and sugar-baked ham; steak, stilton and mushroom pie; or home-made lasagne. Round off with raspberry charlotte or banoffee pie.

Open 12–2.30 6–11 (Sun 7–10.30) **Bar Meals** L served Tue–Sun 12–2 D served Tue–Sat 6–9.30 (Sun 7–9) Av main course £8 **Restaurant** L served Tue–Sun 12–1.30 D served Tue–Sat 6.30–9 Av 3 course à la carte £22 Free House Greene King, Abbot Ale & IPA. 14 **Facilities** Garden Parking

GREAT OXENDON MAP 11 SP78

Pick of the Pubs

The George Inn

LE16 8NA ☎ 01858 465205 01858 465205

e-mail: info@thegeorgegreatoxenden.co.uk

A country dining pub on the A508, the George is 600 years old in parts; it reputedly accommodated soldiers after the battle of Naseby. In more recent times it belonged to heavyweight boxing champion Jack Gardiner. Original beams, a lovely log fire and old photographs lend stacks of charm. Today the George has a county-wide reputation for excellent food and service, but customers are welcome to call in for a pint or a glass of wine from the extensive list. Three dining areas comprise the cosy restaurant, a conservatory overlooking award-winning gardens, and a patio. In charge is David Dudley ably supported by his son Philip, previously a pastry chef for Raymond Blanc. The lunchtime choice includes 'Old Comforts' like grilled breaded haddock; and the 'Original George Grazing Boards' proffer perhaps smoked salmon, peppered mackerel and braden rost. The accent on quality continues throughout the impressive dinner menu.

Open 11.30–3 5.30–11 **Bar Meals** L served Mon–Sat 12–2 Av main course £12 **Restaurant** L served Mon–Sat 12–2 D served Mon–Sat 7–10 Av 3 course à la carte £25 Free House Batemans Guest Ale, Adnams Bitter, Youngs Special. 12 **Facilities** Garden Dogs allowed Parking

HARRINGTON MAP 11 SP7

Pick of the Pubs

The Tollemache Arms NEW

49 High St NN6 9NU ☎ 01536 710469

e-mail: joandmark.owen@tiscali.co.uk

dir: *6m from Kettering, off A14. Follow signs for Harrington*

This thatched and whitewashed pub stands in the lovely Northamptonshire village of Harrington, a popular retreat from the nearby towns of Northampton, Kettering and Market Harborough. There are open fires in the winter months and panoramic views from the large garden. Food and drink are served all day every day from midday. The menu combines modern, classic and traditional influences, so starters could include moules marinière; Brixworth paté with chutney and toast; and goats' cheese ravioli, while main courses range from Thai vegetable stir fry to pork medallions with black pudding, fondant potato and a brandy and tomato sauce. A good choice of real ales includes Charles Wells Bombardier and Eagle IPA, plus two guests. Real ale lovers should look out for the annual beer festival in August, while other events include a magical Christmas Fayre.

Open 12–11 (Sun 12–10.30) **Bar Meals** L served all week 12–9.30 D served all week 12–9.30 Av main course £12.50 **Restaurant** L served all week 12–6 D served all week 6–9.30 Av 3 course à la carte £20 Charles Wells Bombardier, Eagle IPA, Draught Red Stripe, & Guest Ales. 15 **Facilities** Garden Parking

The Red Lion

his friendly 300-year-old pub offers an appealing blend of contemporary and classic decor, ith oak beams, leather upholstery and a smartly turned out dining room. The quiet garden is a vourite with local walkers and cyclists, and in fine weather lunch can be taken on the patio or wns.

nildren are also made welcome, d can enjoy the outdoor play ea. Food options range from a nple ciabatta sandwich to an aginative modern European enu, as well as more traditional b fare. Among the dishes on fer are chorizo sausage and black dding with an apple and potato sti; pigeon and pomegranate th bacon and rocket salad; and easant with a duo of port and ngerbread sauces. Wine is taken riously here, and there is an tensive list of over 200 bins, cluding 20 available by the glass. oughtful drinking choices have so been selected to complement e food: perhaps a Troutmaster esling with a goats' cheese, tichoke and red onion tartlet; or a characterful South African Blaauwklippen Zinfandel with a hearty rib-eye steak. The pub owners are determined to create the best wine list in the country, and all wines are available at a take-home price. Desserts are equally mouthwatering, ranging from chocolate truffle and fig tart with white chocolate sauce, to a selection of speciality English and French cheeses served with celery, chutney, grapes and biscuits. Function facilities are provided for meetings and weddings, and regular themed evenings include a weekly curry night and monthly wine dinners, an excellent introduction to the impressive list.

MAP 11 SP68
43 Welland Rise LE16 9UD
01858 880011
e-mail: andrew@redlionwinepub.co.uk
web: www.redlionwinepub.co.uk
dir: *From Market Harborough take A4304, then A50. After 1m turn left*

Open 12–2 6–11 (Sun 12–5)
Bar Meals L served Wed–Sun 12–2 D served Mon–Sat 6.30–9.45 (Sun 12–3) Av main course £10
Restaurant L served Wed–Sun 12–2 D served all week 6.30–9.45 (Sun 12–3) Av 3 course à la carte £18.50 Av 2 course fixed price £10
Free House
Adnams, Youngs, Boddingtons, Timothy Taylor. 20
Facilities Garden Parking Play Area

England

KETTERING MAP 11 SP87

The Overstone Arms 🍷

Stringers Hill, Pytchley NN14 1EU
☎ 01536 790215 📠 01536 791098
dir: *1m from Kettering, 5m from Wellingborough*

The 18th-century coaching inn is at the heart of the village and has been home to the Pytchley Hunt, which over the years has attracted many royal visitors. Years ago guests would travel up from London, staying here or at Althorp Hall, mainly for the hunting. Despite its rural location, the pub is just a mile from the busy A14. Home-made pies, grilled trout, steaks, lasagne and curry are typical dishes.

Open 12-2.30 6.30-11 **Bar Meals** L served all week 12-2 D served all week 7-9.30 **Restaurant** L served all week 12-2 D served all week 7-9.30 Unique Greene King, Marston's Pedigree, Interbrew Bass, Adnams Bitter. 🍷 8 **Facilities** Garden Parking

LOWICK MAP 11 SP98

The Snooty Fox 🍷

NN14 3BH ☎ 01832 733434
e-mail: the.snooty.fox@btinternet.com
dir: *Off A14, 5m E of Kettering on A6116. Over 1st rdbt, left into Lowick*

Exquisite carved beams are among the more unusual features at this 16th-century building which has been a pub since 1700. Originally the manor house, it is supposedly haunted by a horse and its rider killed at the Battle of Naseby. The kitchen specialises in grill and rotisserie cooking, so check out the rack of Cornish lamb, Gloucester Old Spot pork belly, sirloin steaks, and others. Fresh Cornish fish is also a feature, as is a good wine list.

Open 12-12 Closed: 25 Dec Rest: 26 Dec & 1 Jan closed eve
Bar Meals L served all week 12-2.30 D served all week 6-9.30
Restaurant L served all week 12-2 D served all week 6.30-9.30 Av 2 course fixed price £12 Free House Jennings Cumberland, Greene King IPA, Fullers London Pride, Morland Old Speckled Hen & Morland Original. 🍷 7
Facilities Garden Parking

NORTHAMPTON MAP 11 SP76

The Fox & Hounds 🍷

Main St, Great Brington NN7 4JA
☎ 01604 770651 📠 01604 770164
e-mail: althorpcoachinn@aol.com
dir: *A428 past Althorp House gates, left before railway bridge. Great Brington 1m*

Flagstone floors, beams and open fires, not to mention a beautiful walled garden, are some of the charms of this 16th-century coaching inn, which stands on the Althorp Estate, ancestral home of the Spencer family. Equally praiseworthy are the numerous guest ales and reputation for quality food. Jacket potatoes and ciabatta sandwiches feature on the snack menu; other meals include chicken stuffed with haloumi cheese; tom yam tiger prawns, and grilled Scottish salmon.

The Fox & Houn

Open 11-11 (Sun 12-10.30) **Bar Meals** L served all week 12-2.30 D served all week 6.30-9.30 (Sun 6.30-8.30) Av main course £7.95 **Restaurant** L served all week 12-2.30 D served all week 6.30-9.30 (Sun 6.30-8.30) Av 3 course à la carte £21.95 Free House Greene King IPA, Speckled Hen, Fullers London Pride, Abbot Ale. 🍷 8 **Facilities** Garde Dogs allowed Parking

OUNDLE MAP 11 TLO

The Montagu Arms 🍷

Barnwell PE8 5PH ☎ 01832 273726 📠 01832 275555
e-mail: ianmsimmons@aol.com
dir: *Off A605 opposite Oundle slip road*

One of Northamptonshire's oldest inns, the Montagu Arms was originally three cottages dating from 1601, housing the workmen building the nearby manor house. The inn has a large garden, well equipped for children's play, and overlooks the brook and village gre of the royal village of Barnwell. An extensive menu serving the bar an restaurant ranges through snacks and sharing platters, and dishes suc as Rutland sausages and mash, stuffed chicken, and crispy fish pie.

Open 12-3 6-11 (Sat-Sun all day) **Bar Meals** L served all week 12-2.30 D served all week 7-10 Av main course £8 **Restaurant** L served all week 12-2.30 D served all week 7-10 Av 3 course à la carte £15 Free House Digfield Ales, Adnams Broadside, Hop Back Summer Lightning, Fullers London Pride. 🍷 14 **Facilities** Garden Parking Play Area

SIBBERTOFT MAP 11 SP6

Pick of the Pubs

The Red Lion 🍷

43 Welland Rise LE16 9UD 📠 01858 880011
e-mail: andrew@redlionwinepub.co.uk
web: www.redlionwinepub.co.uk
dir: *From Market Harborough take A4304, then A50. After 1m turn left*

See Pick of the Pubs on page 407

The Crown

'ama trekking and Lord Lucan are two of the unusual associations with this attractive 16th-ntury inn. The former is available in the village, while the latter was allegedly spotted having pint in the pub the night after his children's nanny was famously murdered.

ɔwever, the inn's history stretches .ck much further than that. It's en serving ales since the reign of izabeth I, with the first recorded vner being All Souls College, xford. A cross-country route .ting back to 1593 provides the st documented evidence of The ·own. The present owner, Robert ·over, acquired the freehold the inn in 2003, having long lieved in its potential as a dining stination. His policy has always en to use food prepared from :sh ingredients, complemented a 45 bin wine list. The result? ter a significant upswing in de, the pub has gained a central le in the local community. A pical menu might start with ef carpaccio rolled with roast getables and melted stilton; or salmon gravadlax, celeriac and fennel salad with horseradish crème fraîche. Mains might range from Italian-style chicken with red wine, olives, thyme and herb rice, or seafood pie made from smoked haddock, mussels, squid and salmon, to confit of pheasant with plum and red cabbage sauerkraut, or the ever welcome Cumberland sausages, bacon mash and onion gravy. To round off, consider sampling lemon curd and ginger sponge pudding; spiced apple pie and custard; or chocolate biscuit cake and vanilla ice cream. Nearby attractions include Sulgrave Manor, the ancestral home of George Washington, and Silverstone race circuit.

MAP 11 SP54
Helmdon Rd NN12 8PX
☎ 01295 760310
01295 760310
e-mail: thecrown-weston@tiscali.co.uk
web: www.thecrownweston.co.uk
dir: *Accessed from A43 or B4525*

Open 12-3 6-12 (Sun 6-11.30)
Closed: 25 Dec
Bar Meals L served Wed-Sun 12-2.30 D served Mon-Sat 6-9.30 Av main course £8.50
Free House
Greene King IPA , Hook Norton Best, Black Sheep, Landlord. 6
Facilities Garden Dogs allowed Parking

England

STOKE BRUERNE — MAP 11 SP74

The Boat Inn

NN12 7SB ☎ 01604 862428 01604 864314
e-mail: info@boatinn.co.uk
web: www.boatinn.co.uk
dir: *In village centre, just off A508 or A5*

Right on the waterside and just across the lock from a popular canal museum, this traditional thatched free house has been run by the same family since 1877. Here you'll find cosy bars, open fires and flagstone floors, as well as a traditional skittle alley. Home-made soups, burgers and baguettes support more substantial bar meals, including steak and ale pie; seafood platter; and root vegetable, cranberry and goats' cheese roast.

Open 9–11 (Mon–Thurs Winter closed 3–6) **Bar Meals** L served all week 9.30–9 D served all week Av main course £8.50 **Restaurant** L served Tue–Sun 12–2 D served all week 7–9 (Sun 6.30–8.30) Av 3 course fixed price £24 Free House Banks Bitter, Marstons Pedigree, Adnams Southwold, Frog Island Best. **Facilities** Children's licence Garden Dogs allowed Parking

SULGRAVE — MAP 11 SP54

The Star Inn

Manor Rd OX17 2SA ☎ 01295 760389 01295 760991
dir: *M1 junct 15A follow signs for Silverstone race circuit. M40 junct 11, A422 to Brackley. Signs for Sulgrave Manor*

A 17th-century inn with real ales (Hook Norton) served in the cosy bar area, with its flagstone floors and large inglenook fireplace; in summer there's a vine-covered patio. The menu offers the likes of Oathill Farm gammon steak, Bury black pudding hash with a poached egg and mustard sauce, and wild sea bass with tomato, fennel and potato salad.

Open 11–2.30 6–11 (Sun 12–5 only) Closed: 25–26 Dec Rest: Closed Mon Lunchtimes **Bar Meals** L served Tue–Sat 12–2 (Sun 12.30–3) D served Tue–Sat 6.30–9 Av main course £9.50 **Restaurant** L served Tue–Sat 12–2 (Sun 12.30–3) D served Tue–Sat 6.30–9.30 Av 3 course à la carte £1 Hook Norton Hook Norton Best, Old Hooky, Generation & Haymak **Facilities** Garden Parking

WADENHOE — MAP 11 TL

Pick of the Pubs

The King's Head

Church St PE8 5ST ☎ 01832 720024
e-mail: info@kingsheadwadenhoe.co.uk
dir: *From A605, 3m from Wadenhoe rdbt. 2m from Oundle*

The stone-built, partially thatched 16th-century inn lies at the end of a quiet country lane. What better to do on a warm afternoon than sit in its extensive gardens, with pint or spritzer in hand, and watch passing rivercraft on the slow-flowing Nene. The warm and welcoming interior has quarry-tiled and bare-boarded floors, heavy oak-beamed ceilings, pine furniture and open log fires. Vegetables and herbs come from the inn's own garden, and other local sources provide most of the remaining produce. Dishes include hearty home-made classics such as butcher's sausages, mash and onion gravy; beer-battered haddock, hand-cut chips and garden peas; and chicken, bacon and goats' cheese salad. Seafood and game in season are offered daily, while typical year-round dishes include tomato tarte Tatin; braised lamb shank; and pork chop. Nearly 20 wines are available by the glass. Challenge the locals to a game of Northamptonshire skittles – if you dare.

Open 11–3 5.30–11 (Sun 12–4) **Bar Meals** L served all week 12–2.15 D served Mon–Sat 7–9.15 (Sun 12–3.30) Av main course £10 **Restaurant** L served all week 12–2.15 D served Mon–Sat 6.30–9.15 (Sun 12–3.30) Free House 1 Kings Head Bitter, Barnwell Bitter, JHB, Tribute. 18 **Facilities** Garden Dogs allowed Parking

WESTON — MAP 11 SP

Pick of the Pubs

The Crown

Helmdon Rd NN12 8PX
☎ 01295 760310 01295 760310
e-mail: thecrown-weston@tiscali.co.uk
web: www.thecrownweston.co.uk
dir: *Accessed from A43 or B4525*

See Pick of the Pubs on page 40

WOODNEWTON — MAP 11 TL

The White Swan

22 Main St PE8 5EB ☎ 01780 470381
dir: *5m off A605/A47*

Welcoming village local comprising a simple, single oblong room, o end focusing on the bar and wood-burning stove, the other set up as a dining area. The regularly changing blackboard menu may offer home-made soup; parsnip and pancetta spaghetti; pan-fried pork fil medallions; lemon grass plaice with coriander salsa and coconut rice Finish with a traditional home-made sweet, like fruit crumble or stick toffee pudding.

en 12–2.30 6–11 (Sun 12–3.30) **Bar Meals** L served Wed–Sun 12–1.30 served Tue–Sat 6.30–8.30 (Sun 12–2.30) **Restaurant** L served Wed–Sun –1.30 D served Tue–Sat 6.30–8.30 (Sun 12–2.30) Free House Adnams, London Pride, Bass, Batemans. **Facilities** Garden Parking

NORTHUMBERLAND

LLENHEADS MAP 18 NY84

he Allenheads Inn

E47 9HJ ☎ 01434 685200 01434 685200
mail: philann@phomer.fsbusiness.co.uk
: *From Hexham take B6305, then B6295 to Allenheads*

18th-century free house with a lively atmosphere, the Allenheads is situated in the fabulous countryside of the North Pennines, fect for walking and exploring the nearby market towns and oying the many local attractions. Relax in the popular Antiques Bar, the unusually-named Forces Room, and enjoy pies, chilli, curry, gers, or one of the pub's seasonal specials.

en 12–4 7–11 (Fri–Sun 12–11) **Bar Meals** L served all week 12–2.30 erved all week 7–9 **Restaurant** L served all week 12–2.30 D served all ek 7–9 Free House Greene King Abbott Ale, Tetley Bitter, Timothy lor Landlord, Black Sheep Bitter and Guest Ales. **Facilities** Garden Dogs wed Parking

LNWICK MAP 21 NU11

asons Arms

mford, Nr Rennington NE66 3RX ☎ 01665 577275
nail: bookings@masonsarms.net
: *NE of Alnwick on B1340, 0.5m past Ronnington*

stefully modernised 200-year-old coaching inn, known by the l community as Stamford Cott. It is a useful staging post for ors to Hadrian's Wall, Lindisfarne and the large number of nearby courses. The substantial home-cooked food is available in the and the restaurant, and is made using the best of local produce. cal examples include lemon sole with prawns and parsley sauce; thumbrian game casserole; and curry.

en 12–2 6.30–11 (Sun 7–10.30) **Bar Meals** L served all week 12–2 rved all week 6–9 (Winter 6.30–8.30) **Restaurant** L served all week 2 D served all week 6–9 (Winter 6.30–8.30) Av 3 course à la carte £16 ee House Scottish Courage John Smith's, Theakston Best, Secret gdom, Gladiator. **Facilities** Children's licence Garden Dogs allowed ing

BAMBURGH MAP 21 NU13

Pick of the Pubs

Victoria Hotel ★★ HL

Front St NE69 7BP ☎ 01668 214431 01668 214404
e-mail: enquiries@victoriahotel.net
dir: *In centre of village green*

See Pick of the Pubs on page 413
Please see walk on page 414

BELFORD MAP 21 NU13

Blue Bell Hotel ★★ HL

Market Place NE70 7NE ☎ 01668 213543 01668 213787
e-mail: bluebell@globalnet.co.uk
dir: *Off A1 25m from Berwick, 15m from Alnwick*

Richard Burton and Elizabeth Taylor are among a host of illustrious movie stars and television celebrities who have stayed at this 17th-century coaching inn on the A1 London to Edinburgh route. Choices from the restaurant menu may include chicken liver paté with oatcakes as a starter, followed by grilled sirloin steak on roast asparagus with a stilton crust; and gingered rhubarb crumble with custard to finish.

Open 11–2.30 6.30–11 **Bar Meals** L served all week 11–2 D served all week 6.30–9 **Restaurant** L served all week 12–2 D served all week 7–9 Free House Interbrew Boddingtons Bitter, Northumbrian Smoothe, Calders, Tetleys Smooth. **Facilities** Garden Parking **Rooms** 17 bedrooms en suite

BERWICK-UPON-TWEED MAP 21 NT95

The Rob Roy

Dock Rd, Tweedmouth TD15 2BE
☎ 01289 306428 01289 303629
e-mail: therobroy@btinternet.com
web: www.therobroy.co.uk
dir: *Exit A1 2m S of Berwick at A1167 signed Scremerston, right at rdbt signed Spittal, 1m to Albion pub on left*

Ideally situated for exploring the coasts and castles of Northumberland and Berwickshire, the Rob Roy was built as a Tweed-side cottage 150 years ago. Today it's a privately-run hostelry with salmon fishing paraphernalia decorating the bar. Fresh fish is a speciality and the

CONTINUED

England

BERWICK-UPON-TWEED continued

seafood platter for two, with eight different varieties of fish and shellfish, is popular with locals and tourists alike. Alternatives on the bar menu could be deep-fried squid, or pork medallions sautéed in masala.

The Rob Roy

Open 12–2.30 7–11 Closed: 3wks Feb or Mar, 25 Dec & 1 Jan **Bar Meals** L served Thu–Mon 12–2 D served Wed–Mon 7–9 (Sun 7–8.30) Av main course £8.50 **Restaurant** L served Thu–Mon 12–1.45 D served Wed–Mon 7–9 (Sun 7–8.30) Av 3 course à la carte £30 Free House Tennants 70/-. 8 **Rooms** 5 bedrooms en suite S£40 D£60 (★★★ RR)

BLANCHLAND MAP 18 NY95

The Lord Crewe Arms

DH8 9SP ☎ 01434 675251 01434 675337

e-mail: lord@crewearms.freeserve.co.uk

dir: *10m S of Hexham via B6306*

Once the abbot's house of Blanchland Abbey, this is one of England's oldest inns. Antique furniture, blazing log fires and flagstone floors make for an atmospheric setting. Wide-ranging, good-value bar and restaurant menus with specials offer filled rolls, salads, savoury bean hot pot, and game pie. Watch out, there are lots of ghosts!

Open 11–11 **Bar Meals** L served all week 12–2 D served all week 7–9.15 Av main course £7 **Restaurant** D served all week 7–9.15 Free House Black Sheep, John Smiths, Guinness. **Facilities** Garden Dogs allowed Parking

CARTERWAY HEADS MAP 19 NZ05

Pick of the Pubs

The Manor House Inn

DH8 9LX ☎ 01207 255268

dir: *A69 W from Newcastle, left onto A68 then S for 8m. Inn on right*

Refurbished after a fire and looking better than ever, this free house enjoys spectacular views across open moorland and the Derwent Reservoir from its lonely position high on the A68. The cosy stone-walled bar, with its log fires, low-beamed ceiling and massive timber support, offers a good range of well-kept real ales and around 70 malt whiskies. Built circa 1760, the inn has a succession of dining areas, and a huge collection of mugs and jugs hangs from the beams in the cosy candlelit restaurant. Typical dishes include Cumberland sausage and mash; pan-fried scallops with chili jam; filo baskets of king prawns and mussels; roast duck breast; and various steaks. Home-made puddings are a feature, as is the choice of up to 16 local cheeses.

Open 11–11 **Bar Meals** L served all week 12–9.30 D served all week 12–9.30 (Sun 12–9) Av main course £11 **Restaurant** L served all week 12–2.30 D served all week 7–9.30 (Sun 7–9) Free House Theakstons Best, Mordue Workie Ticket, Greene King Ruddles County, Scottish Courage Courage Directors. 12 **Facilities** Children' licence Garden Dogs allowed Parking **Rooms** 4 bedrooms en suite S£38 D£60 (★★★★ INN)

CHATTON MAP 21 NU

The Percy Arms Hotel

Main Rd NE66 5PS ☎ 01668 215244 01668 215277

dir: *From Alnwick take A1 N, then B6348 to Chatton*

Traditional 19th-century forming coaching inn, situated in the heart c rural Northumberland. Expect a warm, traditional pub welcome, as well as a selection of fine beers, wines and tempting food. Bar menu includes Aberdeen Angus steaks, deep-fried haddock, steak and kidr pie and a wide selection of fish and seafood dishes. Bar games inclu snooker, pool and darts, but those who wish to can still enjoy a quie pint in comfort.

Open 11–11 (Sun12–10.30) **Bar Meals** L served all week 12–2 D served all week 6.30–9 **Restaurant** L served all week 12–1.30 D served all week 6.30–8.30 Jennings Jennings Cumberland Cream, Guest beers. **Facilities** Children's licence Garden Parking **Rooms** 8 bedrooms en su S£35 D£70 (★★ SHL)

CORBRIDGE MAP 21 NY

The Angel of Corbridge

Main St NE45 5LA ☎ 01434 632119 01434 633496

e-mail: info@theangelofcorbridge.co.uk

dir: *0.5m off A69, signed Corbridge*

Stylish 17th-century coaching inn overlooking the River Tyne. Relax with the daily papers in the wood-panelled lounge or attractive bars, or enjoy a home-made dish or two from the extensive menu choice Options include pan-fried chicken breast with spicy couscous, salmc and lemon fish cakes and risotto of asparagus and leek.

Open 10–11 (Sun 11–10.30) **Bar Meals** L served all week 12–3 D serve Mon–Sat 6–9 Av main course £9 **Restaurant** L served all week 12–3 D served Mon–Sat 6–9 Av 3 course à la carte £25 Free House Timothy Taylor Landlord & local beers. 10 **Facilities** Children's lice Garden Parking

Victoria Hotel

his exuberant stone-built Northumbrian hotel has been substantially refurbished and now ɔasts 29 bedrooms and an indoor children's play area. The modern brasserie with its stylish ɔmed glass ceiling serves up food of a similarly modern bent.

arters like Seahouses smoked ıddock fishcakes served with a lsa vierge, or tian of Farne Island ab with tiger prawns and black ıve tapenade open the menu. ain courses include Cajun-iced Gressingham duck breast ı a creamed leek and orange uce, or darn of wild salmon on by spinach with red wine and yme sauce. Glazed lemon tart th raspberries, dark chocolate ousse with creme Anglaise and ackcurrant sorbet, and a selection Northumbrian cheeses might chosen to round off the meal. rvice is friendly and attentive and e location – close to the famous stle and overlooking Bamburgh's historic village green – is very appealing. The building may be cool and modernised but the welcome is warm and traditional. The hotel is popular as a base for golfing breaks, as there are a lot of courses along this spectacular stretch of coastline. The nearest course is Bamburgh, in the heart of the village, which provides an 18-hole course for golfers of all standards. The area has also become popular with fans of Harry Potter, as nearby Alnwick Castle was used as a location in the recent films.

★★ HL 🍷
MAP 21 NU13
Front St NE69 7BP
☎ 01668 214431
📠 01668 214404
e-mail:
enquiries@victoriahotel.net
dir: *In centre of village green*

Open 11–11 (Fri–Sat 11–12)
Bar Meals L served all week 12–9 D served all week 7–9 Av main course £6
Restaurant L served Sun 12–2 D served all week 7–9 Av 3 course à la carte £22
Free House
John Smiths plus Guest ales. 🍷 6
Facilities Dogs allowed Parking
Rooms 29 bedrooms en suite S£44 D£78
(Please see walk on page 414)

BAMBURGH - NORTHUMBERLAND

Victoria Hotel

Walk information

Distance: 8.5 miles (13.7km)
Map: OS Explorer 340 Holy Island & Bamburgh
Start/finish: by Bamburgh Castle (pay-and-display); grid ref NU 183348
Ascent/gradient: 2
Paths: field paths, dunes and beach; 10 stiles
Landscape: coastal pasture and dunes

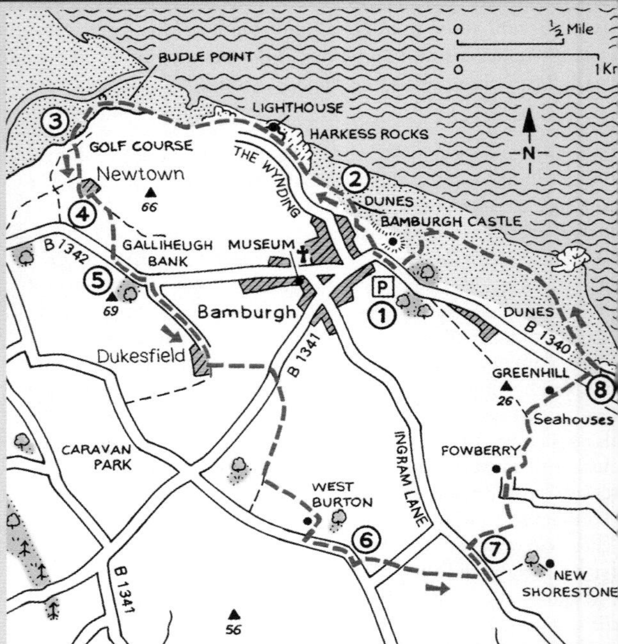

Walk directions

A Walk towards Bamburgh village, where you'll find the museum, the hotel and the church where Grace Darling is buried. Our route, however, continues along the beach, reached either across the green below the castle or by following the Wynding, just beyond, and then crossing the dunes behind.

B To the left, the sand soon gives way to Harkess Rocks. Pick your way round to the lighthouse at Blackrocks Point, which is more easily negotiated to the landward side. Continue below the dunes, soon regaining a sandy beach to pass around Budle Point.

C Shortly before a derelict pier, climb onto the dunes towards a World War II gun emplacement, behind which a waymarked path rises onto a golf course. Continue past markers to a gate, leaving along a track above a caravan park. At a bend, go through a gate on the left (marked 'Private') and carry on at the edge of the field to reach the cottages at Newtown.

D Beyond, follow a wall on the left to regain the golf course over a stile at the top field-corner. Bear right to pass left of a look-out, and continue on a grass track to the main road.

E Walk down Galliheugh Bank to a bend and turn off to Dukesfield. Approaching the lane's end, go left over a stile, walk past a house to the field's far corner and continue by a hedge to a road. Cross to follow a green lane opposite and eventually, just after a cottage, reach a stile on the left. Make for West Burton farm, turn right through the farmyard to a lane and then go left.

F Beyond a bend and over a stile on the left, signed 'New Shorestone', bear half-right across a field. Emerging on to a quiet lane, go over another stile opposite and continue in the same direction to Ingram Lane.

G Some 300 yards (274m) to the left, a gated track on the right leads away and then around to the left towards Fowberr Meeting a narrow lane, go left to the far then turn right immediately before the entrance onto a green track. In the next field, follow the left perimeter around th corner to reach a metal gate. Go throug that, and remain beside the right-hand wall to reach a double gate, there turnir right across a final field to Greenhill. Ke ahead to the main road.

H Continue across to the beach and head north to Bamburgh. Approaching the castle, turn inland, over the dunes, whe a cattle fence can be crossed by one of several gates or stiles. Work your way through to regain the road by the car park.

England

RASTER MAP 21 NU21

ottage Inn 🍷

ınstan Village NE66 2UD

• 01665 576658 📠 01665 576788

mail: enquiries@cottageinnhotel.co.uk

r: *NW of Howick to Embleton road*

: in six acres of woodland, in an area of outstanding natural beauty, s 18th-century inn lies in a hamlet close to the coast. Nearby Dunstanburgh Castle, one of Northumberland's great historic dmarks. Inside is a beamed bar, together with a restaurant, ıservatory and patio. One menu serves all and includes the ever-pular Craster kippers, steak and game pie, venison sausages, and getable risotto. Local ingredients are used wherever possible.

en 11–12 **Bar Meals** L served all week 12–2.30 D served all ek 6–9.30 Av main course £8.50 **Restaurant** L served all week -2.30 D served all week 6–9.30 Av 3 course à la carte £19 Free use Mordue, Tetley's, Farne Island, Black Sheep & Landlord. 🍷 7 **:ilities** Garden Parking Play Area

·lly Fisherman Inn

ıven Hill NE66 3TR ☎ 01665 576461

mail: muriel@silk8234.fsnet.co.uk

: first landlord, in 1847, was a fisherman – presumably a jovial ow. The pub stands right by the water in this tiny fishing village rld-renowned for its kippers. The menu is not extensive, but it kes full use of the sea's bounty with home-made kipper paté; bmeat soup with whisky and cream; and oak-smoked or fresh non sandwiches. For something different, try Geordie stottie cake za. Nearby Dunstanburgh Castle is worth a visit.

en 11–3 6.30–11 (Jun–Aug all day) **Bar Meals** L served all week -2.30 (Sun 12–2.30) Punch Taverns Black Sheep, John Smith's, ckled Hen. **Facilities** Garden Dogs allowed Parking **Notes**

GLINGHAM MAP 21 NU11

Pick of the Pubs

Tankerville Arms

NE66 2TX ☎ 01665 578444 📠 01665 578444

dir: *B6346 from Alnwick*

See Pick of the Pubs on page 417

TAL MAP 21 NT93

lack Bull

'12 4TL ☎ 01890 820200 📠 07092 367733

nail: blackbulletal@aol.com

: *10m N of Wooler right off A697, left at junct for 1m then left) Etal*

: only thatched pub in Northumberland, the Black Bull stands by the ıs of Etal Castle, not far from the River Till, with the grand walking ıntry of the Cheviots on the doorstep. Traditional pub food includes t bites such as sandwiches and hot baguettes, and hearty main ırses including chicken, leek and stilton pie; Cumberland sausage l mash; and steak and ale casserole with cheesy dumplings.

Open 11–3.30 5.30–11 (Summer all day, closed Mon in winter) **Bar Meals** L served all week 12–2 D served all week 6–9 (Summer all day) **Restaurant** L served all week 11.30–2.30 D served all week 6–9.30 (Summer all day) Pubmaster Jennings, Deuchers, John Smith Smooth. **Facilities** Children's licence Garden Parking

FALSTONE MAP 21 NY78

The Blackcock Inn ★★★ INN

NE48 1AA ☎ 01434 240200 📠 01434 240200

e-mail: dbdelboy@yahoo.co.uk

dir: *Exit A1 junct 43 to Hexham and follow A6079 to Bellingham, brown signs to Kielder & Falstone*

Stone walls, log fires and original beams reflect the 18th-century origins of this traditional family-run free house. Nestling close to Kielder Water, the Blackcock makes an ideal base for walking, boating and fishing; the inn is also handy for the Rievers cycle route. The menu includes grills and pub favourites, as well as dishes like lamb shank in red wine and rosemary; and mushroom, brie, rocket and redcurrant filo bundle.

Open 12–2 7–11 **Bar Meals** L served Wed–Sun 12–2 D served all week 7–8.30 **Restaurant** L served Wed–Sun 12–2 D served all week 7–8.30 Free House Blackcock Ale, John Smiths & Guest beer. **Facilities** Children's licence Garden Dogs allowed Parking Play Area **Rooms** 4 bedrooms en suite S£40 D£60

Pick of the Pubs

The Pheasant Inn ★★★★ INN

Stannersburn NE48 1DD

☎ 01434 240382 📠 01434 240382

e-mail: enquiries@thepheasantinn.com

dir: *A69, B6079, B6320, follow signs for Kielder Water*

See Pick of the Pubs on page 418

GREAT WHITTINGTON MAP 21 NZ07

Pick of the Pubs

Queens Head Inn

NE19 2HP ☎ 01434 672267

dir: *Off A68 & B6318 W of Newcastle upon Tyne*

At the heart of Hadrian's Wall country this old pub/restaurant, once a coaching inn, radiates a welcoming atmosphere in

CONTINUED

England

GREAT WHITTINGTON continued

comfortable surroundings of beamed rooms, oak settles and open fires. In addition to Black Sheep beers there are some three-dozen wines of choice and nearly as many malt whiskies. Menus combine the best of local and European ingredients, without losing touch with the classics. Expect starters like tempura of black pudding with a beetroot and red onion relish and crisp salad. Follow that with a main course such as pork tenderloin on an orange and onion marmalade with black pudding fritters and cider and sage jus. Traditional desserts include old favourites like sticky toffee pudding, bread and butter pudding, and baked vanilla cheesecake.

Open 12-3 6-11 **Bar Meals** L served Tue-Sun 12-2 D served Tues-Sun 6.30-9 **Restaurant** L served Tue-Sun 12-2 D served Tues-Sun 6.30-9 Av 3 course à la carte £22.50 Av 2 course fixed price £12.50 Free House Black Sheep, Queens Head & Hambleton. **Facilities** Garden Parking

HALTWHISTLE MAP 21 NY76

Milecastle Inn

Military Rd, Cawfields NE49 9NN ☎ 01434 321372
e-mail: clarehind@aol.com
dir: *Leave A69 into Haltwhistle. Pub 2m junct B6318*

Stand in the garden of this stone-built rural inn and you'll be rewarded with spectacular views towards Hadrian's Wall, a fine background to an afternoon's eating and drinking. The beamed bar has open fires and even a resident ghost. Separate bar and restaurant menus are supplemented by daily specials, and dishes range from home-made pies, steaks and curries to venison casserole and honey-roast duckling, with a good vegetarian selection.

Open 12-9 (Nov–Mar 12-3 6-11) **Bar Meals** L served all week 12-3 D served all week 6-9 (Summer all day) Av main course £8 **Restaurant** L served all week 12-3 D served all week 6-9 (Apr–Nov all day) Av 3 course à la carte £18 Free House Big Lamp, Prince Bishop, Carlsberg-Tetley. **Facilities** Garden Parking

HAYDON BRIDGE MAP 21 NY8

The General Havelock Inn

Ratcliffe Rd NE47 6ER ☎ 01434 684376 01434 68428
e-mail: generalhavelock@aol.com
dir: *On A69, 7m west of Hexham*

General Havelock was a hero of the Indian mutiny, while the inn tha bears his name was built from traditional Northumbrian stone in 1766. You can gaze down to the River Tyne from both the restaurant housed in a converted barn, and the tranquil south-facing patio. Locally sourced ingredients inspire fresh, modern dishes like breast Gressingham duck on apple mash. Desserts include bread and butte pudding with apricot compote.

Open 12-2.30 7-11 **Bar Meals** L served Tue–Sun 12-2 D served Tue–S 7-9 (Sun 8-11) **Restaurant** L served Tue–Sun 12-2 D served Tue–Sat 7 (Sun 8-11) Free House Hesket Newmarket, Wylam Magic, Helvell Gold, Matfen Brewery - Neil's Best. 9 **Facilities** Children's licence Garden Dogs allowed

HEDLEY ON THE HILL MAP 19 NZ

Pick of the Pubs

The Feathers Inn

NE43 7SW ☎ 01661 843607 01661 843607
e-mail: marina@thefeathersinn.com

From its hilltop position, this small stone-built free house overlooks the splendid adventure country of the Cheviots. The three-roomed pub is well patronised by the local community, but strangers too, are frequently charmed by its friendly and relaxed atmosphere. Families are welcome, and a small side room can be booked in advance if required. Old oak beams, coal fires and rustic settles set the scene and there's a good selection of traditional pub games like shove ha'penny and bar skittles. The stone walls are decorated with local photographs of rural life. Although the pub has no garden, food and drinks can be served a tables on the green in good weather. The menus change regularl and the imaginative home cooking includes an extensive choice of vegetarian meals. Expect spiced lentil and vegetable hotpot with naan bread, gingered salmon cakes with coriander salsa, pork casseroled with tarragon and Dijon mustard, and seafood pancake. An appetising range of puddings. Coach parties by arrangement.

Open 12-3 6-11 (Sun 7-10.30) Closed: 25 Dec **Bar Meals** L served Sat–Sun 12-2.30 D served Tue–Sun 7-9 Free House Mordue Workie Ticket, Big Lamp Bitter, Fuller's London Pride, Northumberland County. **Facilities** Children's licence Parking

PICK OF THE PUBS

EGLINGHAM-NORTHUMBERLAND

Tankerville Arms

he Tankerville Arms nestles in idyllic countryside about seven miles from Alnwick. Inside it is arm and welcoming, with traditional features that enhance its character. A hotchpotch of tables nd chairs and loads of bric-a-brac make it easy to feel at home here.

ne pub attracts everyone from andparents with children to milies and young people – all are elcome and equally well catered r. The secret weapon here is chef hn Blackmore who has travelled from the South to put his nique stamp on the food. Fresh cal produce is given careful but novative handling by a kitchen orking at the peak of its talents, d the results appear on the same enu throughout the pub. Look ut for starters like warm salad black pudding and bacon with Cumberland sauce, and main urses such as steak and ale pie, breast of corn-fed chicken on a rragon mash. Fish ranges from deep-fried scampi and chips to smoked haddock on a potato and cheese gratin. Smoked salmon comes from Craster, venison from the Duke of Northumberland's estate, and other game is from Burnside Farm. A great range of beers can be enjoyed on their own or with a meal, like Greene King Ruddles Best, Black Sheep Best, or Mordue Workie Ticket.

MAP 21 NU11
NE66 2TX
☎ 01665 578444
01665 578444
dir: *B6346 from Alnwick*

Open 12–2 7–11 (times may vary, ring for details) Closed: 25 Dec
Bar Meals L served all week 12–2 D served all week 6–9 Av main course £9.75
Restaurant L served all week 12–2 D served all week 6–9 Av 3 course à la carte £18
Free House
Greene King Ruddles Best, Scottish Courage Courage Directors, Black Sheep Best, Mordue Workie Ticket.
Facilities Garden Parking Play Area

The Pheasant Inn

This sprawling stone-walled pub was originally a large farmstead, but for over 250 years one room has always been used as a bar. It's been in the hands of the Kershaws since 1985 and they've succeeded in keeping the rustic atmosphere intact.

Around the walls old photos record local people engaged in long-abandoned trades and professions. Robin and Irene cook with relish, producing wholesome, traditionally English fare. Meals may be taken al fresco in the pretty grassed courtyard with a stream running through, or in the oak-beamed restaurant with its cottagey furnishings and warm terracotta walls. The bar menu changes daily according to season, but classic dishes like steak and kidney pie, home-made soups, lasagne, ploughman's and sandwiches are always available. Sample dishes from the blackboard might include cream of spiced lentil soup, or goats' cheese with caramelised red onion tartlet. Main courses, in addition to fish dishes such as grilled sea bass with lemon and parsley butter, include plenty of local meats: game and mushroom pie, perhaps, or cider-baked gammon with Cumberland sauce. Round off with bread and butter pudding, or apple with orange crumble. Traditional Sunday lunches such as roast sirloin of beef with Yorkshire pudding come with all the trimmings, and vegetarians are well looked after. Timothy Taylor and Wylam Gold are two of the brews in the bar, backed by a choice of 35 malt whiskies. Kielder Water, the largest artificial lake in Europe, is nearby, along with some of Northumberland's most unspoilt countryside. Guests tempted to stay overnight can book one of eight en suite bedrooms, with views over that same stunning landscape.

★★★★ INN
MAP 21 NY78
Stannersburn NE48 1DD
☎ 01434 240382
🖷 01434 240382
e-mail:
enquiries@thepheasantinn.com
dir: *A69, B6079, B6320, follow signs for Kielder Water*

Open 11-3 6-11 (times vary, ring for details) Closed: 25-26 Dec
Bar Meals L served all week 12-2.30 D served all week 7-9 Av main course £8.95
Restaurant L served Mon-Fri 12-2.30 D served all week 7-9 (Sun 12-2) Av 3 course à la carte £22
Free House
Theakston Best, Marstons Pedigree, Timothy Taylor Landlord, Wylam Gold.
Facilities Garden Dogs allowed Parking Play Area
Rooms 8 bedrooms en suite S£50 D£85

HEXHAM MAP 21 NY96

Pick of the Pubs

Battlesteads Hotel & Restaurant

Wark NE48 3LS ☎ 01434 230209 01434 230039
e-mail: info@battlesteads.com
dir: *10m N of Hexham on B6320 (Kielder road)*

Built as a farmhouse in 1747, this family-run hotel is close to Hadrian's Wall and Kielder Forest. There's a cosy fire in the bar, where cask and bottle-conditioned beers from neighbourhood micro-breweries are served. Freshly cooked meals make good use of local lamb, beef and pork, while fish comes from North Shields. Among the main courses are blackened salmon with sauté potatoes and sweet chilli sauce; Cajun-style chicken breast with prawns and bacon; and haloumi and mushroom stack with roast baby vine tomatoes. Or try a special, such as wild rabbit casserole with prunes in red wine; celeriac lasagne with fresh parmesan and fig balsamic; or beef Madras with rice and home-made chapatis. The Sunday carvery is very popular. Over a drink in the sunny walled beer garden ponder on how nearby Bellingham is pronounced (clue: not as you'd expect). Modernised en suite rooms include some for those with disabilities.

Open 11-11 (Winter closed Mon–Fri 3–6) **Bar Meals** L served all week 12–3 D served all week 6.30–9.30 Av main course £9.50 **Restaurant** L served all week 12–3 D served all week 6.30–9.30 Av 2 course fixed price £9.50 Free House Wylam Gold Tankard, Black Sheep Special, Durham White Velvet, Durham Magus. **Facilities** Children's licence Garden Dogs allowed Parking **Rooms** 14 bedrooms en suite S£45 D£80 (★★★★ INN)

Pick of the Pubs

Dipton Mill Inn

Dipton Mill Rd NE46 1YA ☎ 01434 606577
e-mail: ghb@hexhamshire.co.uk
dir: *2m S of Hexham on B6306*

The millstream runs right through the gardens of this quintessentially English country pub, once part of a farm. The rugged local countryside around Hadrian's Wall is something of a walker's dream, and there is an assortment of other Roman sites in the area to explore. Alternatively, you could play golf nearby or enjoy an afternoon at Hexham races just down the road.
The Dipton Mill is the home of the Hexhamshire Brewery ales, including Devil's Water and Old Humbug. Food is served evenings and lunchtimes with all dishes being freshly prepared and using local produce where possible. Perhaps sample haddock baked with tomato and basil; steak and kidney pie; dressed crab salad; or chicken in a sherry sauce. To follow, try syrup sponge and custard – perfect after a day of bracing Northumberland winds.

Open 12-2.30 6-11 (Sun 12-3) Closed: 25 Dec **Bar Meals** L served all week 12–2 D served Mon–Sat 6.30–8.30 Av main course £7 Free House Hexhamshire Shire Bitter, Old Humbug, Devil's Water, Devil's Elbow & Whapweasel. 17 **Facilities** Children's licence Garden **Notes**

Miners Arms Inn

Main St, Acomb NE46 4PW ☎ 01434 603909
dir: *17m W of Newcastle on A69, 2m W of Hexham.*

Close to Hadrian's Wall in a peaceful village, this charming 18th-century pub has stone walls, beamed ceilings and open fires. Real ales are a speciality, as is good home-cooked food. Good setting for cyclists and walkers, and the garden has an aviary.

Open 5-11 (Etr, Sum, Xmas Hols all wk 12-11) **Bar Meals** L served Sat 12–2.30 (Sun 12–3.30) D served all week 6–8.30 Av main course £6 **Restaurant** L served Sat & BHs 12–2.30 (Sun 12–3.30) D served all week 6–8.30 Free House Black Sheep Bitter, Yates, Durham White Velvet, Boddingtons. 7 **Facilities** Children's licence Garden Dogs allowed **Notes**

LONGFRAMLINGTON MAP 21 NU10

Pick of the Pubs

The Anglers Arms

Weldon Bridge NE65 8AX
☎ 01665 570271 & 570655 01665 570041
e-mail: johnyoung@anglersarms.fsnet.co.uk
dir: *From N, 9m S of Alnwick right Weldon Bridge sign. From S, A1 to by-pass Morpeth, left onto A697 for Wooler & Coldstream. 7m, left to Weldon Bridge*

See Pick of the Pubs on page 420

Granby Inn

Front St NE65 8DP ☎ 01665 570228 01665 570736
dir: *On A697, 11m N of Morpeth*

A friendly 200-year-old coaching inn that retains much of its original character, including fine old oak beams. Set in the heart of Northumberland, between the Cheviots and the coast, this family-run business specialises in good home-cooked food: grilled trout, glazed lamb cutlets, steak au poivre and grilled ham. These might be followed by toffee and pecan sponge pudding or sherry trifle. Lighter bites include sandwiches, pasta and omelettes.

Open 11-3 6-11 Closed: 25–26 Dec **Bar Meals** L served all week 11.30–2 D served all week 6–9.30 (Sun 12–3, 7–10.30) Av main course £8.35 **Restaurant** L served all week 11.30–2 D served all week 6–9.30 (Sun 12–3, 7–10.30) Free House Stones Best Bitter, Worthington E. 11 **Facilities** Parking

PICK OF THE PUBS

LONGFRAMLINGTON-NORTHUMBERLAND

The Anglers Arms

Deep in rural Northumberland, this former coaching inn dates from the 1760s, since when it has commanded the picturesque Weldon Bridge over the River Coquet. The interior reveals an abundance of bric-a-brac, antiques and fishing memorabilia, as well as attractive hand-painted wall tiles.

A carefully tended half-acre of garden contains a children's play park and plenty of general space to eat and drink. Bar meals, such as Whitby wholetail scampi, Northumbrian sausage casserole, and oriental sizzling platter are popular, but for more style and a different set of options you may dine in the main restaurant or even in the somewhat unusual surroundings of a converted railway carriage. In both you'll find starters such as scallop and bacon salad; black pudding with mashed potato, poached egg and cheese sauce; and smoked chicken and wild mushroom tartlet. Main courses include pork tenderloin wrapped in Parma ham with bubble and squeak and cognac sauce; cod and crab fishcakes with asparagus and tenderstem broccoli; roast halibut with king prawns and Greenland mussels in white wine sauce; and warm tomato and feta quiche with red onion chutney. Turn to the blackboard for daily changing desserts and selections of Continental and English cheeses, including one with nettles and herbs made locally at Otterburn. Sandwiches include baked ham, and brie and beef tomato, while duck and orange is a possibility from the list of salads. The Anglers is a good base for walking in the Cheviot Hills and visiting Northumberland's famous castles. Guests staying overnight may fish free of charge along the one mile of the inn's privately owned riverbank.

MAP 21 NU10
Weldon Bridge NE65 8AX
☎ 01665 570271 & 570655
📠 01665 570041
e-mail: johnyoung@anglersarms.fsnet.co.uk
dir: *From N, 9m S of Alnwick right Weldon Bridge sign. From S, A1 to by-pass Morpeth, left onto A697 for Wooler & Coldstream 7m, left to Weldon Bridge*

Open 11-11 (Sun 12-11)
Bar Meals L served all week 12-9.30 D served all week 12-9.30 (Sun 12-9)
Restaurant L served all week 12-2 D served all week 7-9
Free House
Worthington, Carling, Boddingtons & 3 Guest Ales.
Facilities Children's licence Garden Dogs allowed Parking Play Area

ONGHORSLEY MAP 21 NZ19

inden Tree ★★★★ HL

nden Hall NE65 8XF ☎ 01670 500033 01670 500001
mail: lindenhall@macdonald-hotels.co.uk
r: *Off A1 on A697, 1m N of Longhorsley*

iginally two large cattle byres, this popular bar takes its name from
 linden trees in the grounds of Linden Hall Hotel, an impressive
orgian mansion. Straightforward meals range from aubergine and
occoli bake, braised lamb shank, or medallions of pork, to grilled
mon, or poached smoked cod fillets.

en 11-11 (Sun 12-10.30) **Bar Meals** L served all week (Sun
-4) D served all week to 9.30 (Sun 6-9) Av main course £10
staurant L served all week (Sun 12-4) D served all week to 9.30 (Sun
9) Av 3 course à la carte £20 Free House Worthington 1744,
eene King IPA, Cafereys. **Facilities** Children's licence Garden Parking
oms 50 bedrooms en suite S£48 D£58

OW NEWTON BY THE SEA MAP 21 NU22

he Ship Inn

e Square NE66 3EL ☎ 01665 576262
mail: forsythchristine@hotmail.com
r: *NE from A1 at Alnwick*

e beach is only a stroll away from this pretty inn, which overlooks
 green. Low Newton was purpose-built as a fishing village in the
h century and remains wonderfully unspoilt. Bustling in summer
d a peaceful retreat in winter, The Ship offers a menu that includes
nty of fresh, locally caught fish and free-range meats. Try kipper
é, followed by Borders' sirloin steak with onion marmalade, with
al unpasteurised cheese to finish.

en 11-4 6.30-11 (School holidays all day) Closed: Winter Mon, Tue &
d eve. **Bar Meals** L served Tue-Sat 12-2.30 D served 7-8 Av main
urse £10 Free House Original Northumberland, Farm Island Local
wery, Guest beers. **Facilities** Garden Dogs allowed **Notes**

ETHERTON MAP 21 NT90

he Star Inn NEW

E65 7HD ☎ 01669 630238
r: *7m from Rothbury*

wned by the same family since 1917, this pub has also been in every
tion of the CAMRA real ale guide. No food is served, but cask ales
the peak of condition are the speciality.

en 7.30-10.30 (Fri 7.30-11) Free House Castle Eden Ale (Cask).
ilities Parking **Notes**

NEWTON ON THE MOOR MAP 21 NU10

Pick of the Pubs

The Cook and Barker Inn

★★★★ INN

NE65 9JY ☎ 01665 575234 01665 575234
dir: *0.5m from A1 S of Alnwick*

From its elevated position in the picturesque village of Newton on the Moor, this traditional inn commands outstanding views of the Cheviot Hills and the Northumbrian coast. An extensive, thoughtful menu makes excellent use of local produce, with fish from North Shields quay a particular speciality. Try sea fresh prawns with chilli squid, mussels, scallops and garlic butter; grilled halibut with pea purée; or pan-fried lemon sole with prawns and capers. For those less inclined to the fruits of the sea, there is organic pork and black pudding terrine wrapped in country bacon; or spinach and reggiano parmesan risotto with wild woodland mushrooms, followed by pan-fried local pheasant with creamed cabbage, or game casserole with cranberry dumplings. Real ales and a dozen wines by the glass are also on offer.

Open 11-3 6-11 **Bar Meals** L served all week 12-2 D served all week 6-9 **Restaurant** L served all week 12-2 D served all week 7-9 Av 3 course fixed price £25 Free House Timothy Taylor Landlord, Theakstons Best Bitter, Fuller's London Pride, Batemans XXXB. 12 **Facilities** Garden Parking **Rooms** 19 bedrooms en suite S£47 D£75

ROWFOOT MAP 21 NY66

The Wallace Arms

NE49 0JF ☎ 01434 321872 01434 321872
e-mail: www.thewallacearms@btconnect.com

The pub was rebuilt in 1850 as the Railway Hotel at Featherstone Park station, when the now long-closed Haltwhistle-Alston line (today's South Tyne Trail) was engineered. It changed to the Wallace Arms in 1885. Sample menu includes modestly-priced haddock fillet in beer batter, salmon fillet in lemon and tarragon sauce, steak and ale pie, grilled sirloin steak, and smoked haddock and prawn pasta. There are light snacks, burgers and sandwiches, if you prefer.

Open 11-3 4-12 (Opening times vary) **Bar Meals** L served all week 12-2.30 D served all week 6-9 **Restaurant** L served all week 12-2.30 D served all week 6-9 Free House Hook Norton Old Hooky, Young's Special, Greene King IPA, Greene King Abbot Ale. **Facilities** Garden Parking **Rooms** 2 bedrooms en suite (★★★★ INN)

The Olde Ship Hotel

Grain was once exported through the tiny port of Seahouses, which may explain why this forme farmhouse was built overlooking the harbour in 1745. But if it seems now a rather unusual plac for such a building, it's been the perfect location since 1812 for a pub. In fact, today it is a fully residential hotel, which has been managed by the same family for 90 years.

On the right sort of day you can enjoy a pint of Black Sheep in the garden while watching the local fishing boats bob up and down below. The main saloon bar and the snug, low-beamed Cabin Bar are full of character, with scrubbed pine floors made from ships' decking, unusual stained glass windows, and a fascinating array of seafaring mementoes such as diving helmets, oars, fish baskets, branding irons, lamps and the nameplate from the 'Forfarshire' of Grace Darling fame. Simple lunch, dinner and bar menus take full advantage of the sea, with starters of Craster kipper, rollmop herrings and crab soup; and stuffed whiting, Bosun's fish stew, and fillet of lemon sole just some of the probable main courses. Others include roast rib of beef and Yorkshire pudding, creamy lemon pork, chicken and mushroom casserole, and vegetable lasagne. Featuring in the desserts section could well be golden apricot crumble, fresh fruit salad, and Turkish delight ice cream. Bedrooms are neat and well appointed, some with views over to the bird and seal sanctuary on the Farne Islands. Boats will take you there from the nearby pier. In the garden try your hand at putting or a traditional game of quoits.

NEW ★★ HL
MAP 21 NU23
9 Main St NE68 7RD
☎ 01665 720200
01665 721383
e-mail:
theoldeship@seahouses.co.uk
dir: *Lower end of main street above harbour*

Open 11–11 (Sun 12–11)
Bar Meals L served all week 12–2 D served all week 7–8.30 Av main course £9.25
Restaurant L served Sun 12–2 D served all week 7–8.15 (no dinner end Nov–end Jan) Av 4 course fixed price £24
Free House
Black Sheep, Theakstones Best Scotch, Farne Island. 10
Facilities Children's licence Garden Parking
Rooms 18 bedrooms en suite S£50 D£100

EAHOUSES MAP 21 NU23

Pick of the Pubs

The Olde Ship Hotel NEW ★★ HL

9 Main St NE68 7RD

☎ 01665 720200 01665 721383

e-mail: theoldeship@seahouses.co.uk

dir: *Lower end of main street above harbour*

See Pick of the Pubs on opposite page

ARDEN MAP 21 NY96

he Boatside Inn

E46 4SQ ☎ 01434 602233 601061

r: *Just off A69 west of Hexham, follow signs to Warden wborough & Fourstones*

ractive stone-built inn situated where the North and South Tyne ers meet, beneath Warden Hill Iron Age fort. The name refers to rowing boat that ferried people across the river before the bridge s built. It is a popular destination for walkers, promising real ale d good food cooked from local produce. Dishes include seafood w, battered haddock, and slow roast lamb shoulder. There is also a rden with a lawn area and barbecue.

en 11–11 **Bar Meals** L served all week D served all week Av main ırse £8 **Restaurant** L served all week D served all week Av 3 course à la te £25 Free House Black Sheep. 15 **Facilities** Children's licence rden Dogs allowed Parking

ARENFORD MAP 21 NU12

Pick of the Pubs

The White Swan

NE70 7HY ☎ 01668 213453 01668 213453

dir: *100yds E of A1, 10m N of Alnwick*

This 200-year-old coaching inn stands near the original toll bridge over the Waren Burn. Formerly on the Great North Road, the building is now just a stone's throw from the A1. Inside, you'll find thick stone walls and an open fire for colder days; in summer, there's a small sheltered seating area, with further seats in the adjacent field. The Dukes of Northumberland once owned the pub, and its windows and plasterwork still bear the family crests. Visitors and locals alike enjoy the atmosphere and award-winning Northumbrian dishes: try Seahouses kippers with creamy horseradish sauce; venison pudding with lemon suet crust and fresh vegetables; or roast pork hock with wine and herbs. Vegetarians are well catered for, with interesting dishes like beetroot and potato gratin; artichoke and leek pancakes; and celeriac pan Haggarty with fresh tomato sauce. Book ahead to avoid disappointment.

Open 12–2 7–11 (Sun 7–10) **Bar Meals** L served Sun 12–2 D served Tues-Sun 7–9 Av main course £8.50 **Restaurant** L served 12–1.30 (Sun 12–4) D served 7–9.30 Av 3 course à la carte £16.50 Free House Scottish Courage John Smith's. 8 **Facilities** Garden Parking

WHALTON MAP 21 NZ18

Pick of the Pubs

Beresford Arms NEW

NE61 3UZ ☎ 01670 775225 01670 775351

e-mail: beresford.arms@btconnect.com

dir: *5m from Morpeth town centre on B6524*

The landlords at this ivy-covered coaching inn have worked hard to maintain the feel of a 'proper' country pub, while at the same time ensuring it conveys a modern feel. It lies in the picturesque village of Wharton, popular with cyclists and walkers enjoying the delights of nearby Kielder Forest and Northumberland National Park. Start a meal with home-made soup, or prawn and avocado salad with Marie Rose sauce; follow with grilled Wallington Hall rib-eye steak with tomato, mushrooms, onion rings and chips; or one of Stevie's Wonders, such as grilled fillet of sea bass on spiced couscous with an oriental sauce; and finish with a crumble, or something that's bound to involve fresh berries, whipped cream or chocolate sauce. 'Doorstop' sandwiches are served at lunchtime. 'Elves, leprechauns and kids under 4ft 9ins' can opt for chicken or crispy fish goujons, beefburger or sausages.

Open 11–3 5.30–11 (May–Sep all day) **Bar Meals** L served all week 12–2 (Sun 12–5) D served Mon–Sat 6–9 Av main course £11 **Restaurant** L served Sun 12–3 D served Fri–Sat 6–9 Av 3 course à la carte £25 Enterprise Inns Blacksheep, Timothy Taylor, Strongbow. **Facilities** Garden Parking

NOTTINGHAMSHIRE

BEESTON MAP 11 SK53

Victoria Hotel

Dovecote Ln NG9 1JG ☎ 0115 925 4049 0115 922 3537

e-mail: hopco.victoriabeeston@virgin.net

dir: *M1 junct 25, A52 E, right at Nurseryman PH, right opp Rockaway Hotel into Barton St, then 1st left*

The Victoria dates from 1899 when it was built next to Beeston Railway Station, and the large, heated patio garden is still handy for a touch of train-spotting. It offers an excellent range of traditional ales, continental beers and lagers, farm ciders, a good choice of wines by the glass and single malt whiskies. Dishes on the menu you may find Lincolnshire sausages, and smoked chicken and bacon pasta. Half the menu is meat-free or vegan.

Open 11–11 (Sun 12–11) Closed: 26 Dec **Bar Meals** L served all week 12–8.45 D served all week (Sun 12–7.45) **Restaurant** L served all week D served all week 12–8.45 (Sun 12–7.45) Free House Batemans XB, Castle Rock Harvest Pale, Castle Rock Hemlock, Everards Tiger & 6 Guest ales. 30 **Facilities** Garden Dogs allowed Parking

England

BINGHAM MAP 11 SK73

The Chesterfield NEW

Church St NG13 8AL ☎ 01949 837342
e-mail: eat@thechesterfield.co.uk
dir: *Off A52 & A46 junct. Pub off market square*

One of the earliest buildings in the centre of this small market town, the Chesterfield has recently been refurbished in contemporary style. The pub now features a stylish bar and gastro-style restaurant, as well as a private dining room and garden. Lunchtime brings snacks and sandwiches, plus a traditional Sunday roast. Typical restaurant choices include rack of lamb with apricots and cheese; seared fresh salmon salad; and grilled haloumi with couscous and curry sauce.

Open 12–11 (Wknds 12–12) **Bar Meals** L served Mon–Sat 12–2.30 D served all week 5–10 Av main course £10 **Restaurant** L served all week 12–2.30 D served all week 5–10 Av 3 course à la carte £20 Timothy Taylor Landlord, Marston Pedigree, Charles Wells Bombardier, Shepherd Neame Spitfire & London Pride. 12 **Facilities** Garden Parking

BLIDWORTH MAP 16 SK55

Fox & Hounds NEW

Blidworth Bottoms NG21 0NW ☎ 01623 792383
e-mail: info@foxandhounds-pub.com
dir: *Right off B6020 between Ravenshead & Blidworth*

A traditional country pub, extensively refurbished four years ago to create attractive surroundings in which to eat and drink. It was probably built as a farmhouse in the 19th century, when Blidworth Bottoms was a thriving community, with shops and a post office. A reputation for good pub food comes from dishes such as steak and ale pie; Mediterranean chicken; blackened salmon in Cajun spices; home-made vegetarian cottage pie; and hot chilli con carne.

Open 11.30–12am **Bar Meals** L served all week D served all week Av main course £7.95 **Restaurant** L served all week D served all week Greene King Hardy & Hanson Cask Bitter, Olde Speckled Hen, Olde Trip. 9 **Facilities** Children's licence Garden Dogs allowed Parking Play Area

CAUNTON MAP 17 SK76

Pick of the Pubs

Caunton Beck

NG23 6AB ☎ 01636 636793 01636 636828
e-mail: email@wigandmitre.com
dir: *6m NW of Newark on A616*

No ordinary free house, this highly civilised pub-restaurant opens for breakfast at 8am and carries on serving food until around midnight every day of the year. It is built around a 16th-century cottage in a country setting and is set amid herb gardens and a dazzling rose arbour. Behind the pub you'll see ducks on the banks of the beck beside the village church. Real ales complement an extensive international wine list, including an impressive choice by the glass. The main menu, served throughout the pub, offers dishes such as braised oxtail pieces with roast garlic, thyme potato and winter vegetable stew, and whole roast sea bass with sun-blushed tomato and olive compote, together with helpful suggestions for suitable wines. There are also breakfast and snack menus, plus a blackboard of daily specials: maybe sausages and mash, or seared calves' liver and back bacon with balsamic onions.

Open 8–12 **Bar Meals** L served all week 8–11 D served all week 8–11 Av main course £13.95 **Restaurant** L served all week 8–11 D served all week 8–11 Av 3 course à la carte £26.25 Av 3 course fixed price £13.95 Free House Batemans Valiant, Websters Yorkshire, Marstons Pedigree. 34 **Facilities** Garden Dogs allowed Parking

CAYTHORPE MAP 11 SK6

Black Horse Inn

NG14 7ED ☎ 0115 966 3520
dir: *12m from Nottingham off A612 to Southwell*

Three generations of the same family have run this small, beamed country pub where old-fashioned hospitality is guaranteed. It has its own small brewery, producing Caythorpe Dover Beck bitter, a coal fir in the bar, and delicious home-cooked food prepared from seasonal ingredients. Fresh fish is a speciality; other choices might include Chinese dim sum; king prawns in garlic and cream sauce; fillet steak; and omelettes with various fillings. Good local walks.

Open 12–3 5.30–11 (Sat 6–11, Sun 8–10.30) **Bar Meals** L served Tue–Sa 12–1.45 D served Tue–Fri 7–8.30 **Restaurant** L served Tue–Sat 12–1.45 D served Mon–Sat 7–8.30 Free House Interbrew Bass, Adnams Bitte Greene King Abbot Ale, Black Sheep. **Facilities** Garden Dogs allowed Parking **Notes**

COLSTON BASSETT MAP 11 SK7

Pick of the Pubs

The Martins Arms Inn

School Ln NG12 3FD ☎ 01949 81361 01949 81039
dir: *Off A46 between Leicester & Newark*

See Pick of the Pubs on opposite page

ELKESLEY MAP 17 SK6

Robin Hood Inn

High St DN22 8AJ ☎ 01777 838259
e-mail: robinhooda1@clara.co.uk
dir: *5m SE of Worksop off A1 towards Newark-on-Trent*

Parts of this unassuming village inn date back to the 14th century. Ceilings and floors are deep red, while the green walls are adorned with pictures of food. The comprehensive food choice is available in both the bar and restaurant, and includes a fixed price menu, carte and daily specials board. Grilled gammon steak with pineapple, vine tomato, chips and peas; and brie, pesto and cherry tomato filo tart ar possibilities.

Open 11.30–3 6–11 **Bar Meals** L served Tue–Sun 12–2 D served Mon–Sat 6–9.30 Av main course £10 **Restaurant** L served Tue–Sun 12–2 D served Mon–Sat 7–9.30 Av 3 course à la carte £18 Av 3 course fixed price £14 Enterprise Inns Marston's Pedigree & Tetley Bitter. 8 **Facilities** Garden Parking Play Area

The Martins Arms Inn

he Nottinghamshire village of Colston Basset, set in the stunning Vale of Belvoir, is renowned r its stilton cheese. This award-winning 18th-century inn stands right at the heart of the llage, next to a market cross that dates back to 1257.

ıe listed building has a real untry house feel to it, with riod furnishings, traditional inting prints and winter fires the Jacobean fireplace. Indeed, charming is the inn that it has ade regular appearances on both gional and national television. ıe acre of landscaped grounds backing on to National Trust land ncludes a herb garden and well-tablished lawns. The inn is a free use, with an impressive range of ıl ales, including Black Sheep Best, mothy Taylor Landlord, London ide and Marston's Pedigree. gional ingredients are a feature of e appetising and inventive menus, d even in the bar the fare is ıbitious and delicious. Try smoked ddock rarebit with plum tomato, cket and basil oil, or tartlet of me-dried tomato, pine kernels and parmesan with vanilla and basil cream sauce, to be followed by slow braised lamb shank with white bean purée and chorizo; or honey glazed duck, marinated in earl grey tea, with orange fondant potatoes and blackberry jus. Plainer tastes will be satisfied with the classic ploughman's lunch, comprising Melton Mowbray pork pie, Colston Bassett stilton or cheddar, home-cured ham, pickles and bread. Over in the restaurant, sample duck liver and foie gras parfait with banana and golden raisin compote, before moving on to roast cod with black olive and basil crust, or wild salmon filled with veal mousse and wrapped in Parma ham. Just make sure that space is left for dessert: a trio of chocolate cheesecake with mandarin coulis and home-made fudge is not to be missed.

MAP 11 SK73
School Ln NG12 3FD
☎ 01949 81361
01949 81039
dir: *Off A46 between Leicester & Newark*

Open 12–3 6–11 (Sun 7–10.30)
Closed: 25 Dec eve
Bar Meals L served all week 12–2 D served Mon–Sat 6–10
Av main course £10
Restaurant L served all week 12–2 D served Mon–Sat 7–9.30
Av fixed price £26.50
Free House
Marston's Pedigree, Interbrew Bass, Greene King Abbot Ale, Timothy Taylor Landlord, Wherry, IPA. 7
Facilities Garden Dogs allowed Parking

PICK OF THE PUBS

MORTON-NOTTINGHAMSHIRE

The Full Moon Inn

Tucked away in a remote hamlet close to the River Trent, this village inn boasts plenty of entertainment for all the family, including television, games machines, piped music, board game and a children's play area.

Wheelback chairs, roaring fires, fresh flowers and an unusual and colourful collection of Christmas plates around the walls add to the charming old world atmosphere. Two friendly resident cats may well be found curled up on a settle in the main beamed bar, where you can enjoy regularly changing guest ales alongside the likes of Dover Beck, Ruddles Best and Bombardier. A lengthy, thorough menu covers all the classic options. For lunch, try bangers and mash; lasagne verde; or a home-made steak and kidney pie. Evening diners could start with green lipped mussels topped with bacon and melted cheese; prawn and avocado timbale; or garlic and stilton mushrooms, before sampling Kashmir chicken; grilled haddock; crispy duck leg confit with port wine jus, or an impressive array of steaks and grills. Vegetarians certainly won't go hungry with a choice of parsnip and chestnut bake; hand-made Mediterranean vegetable pie; or the 'Full Moon combi', a sizeable platter of carrot and coriander fingers, breaded mushrooms, onion rings and spinach and feta goujons. The puddings also merit further inspection, particularly chocolate and raspberry decadence; hand-made fruit pie; and bread and butter pudding. The shady and peaceful back terrace makes a lovely spot for summer escapism. Don't miss the Early Doors special: a reduced rate two-course meal available Monday to Thursday between 6 and 7pm.

NEW 🍷
MAP 17 SK75
Main St NG25 0UT
☎ 01636 830251
Fax 01636 830554
e-mail:
sales@thefullmooninn.co.uk

Open 11-3 6-11 (Fri–Sat 6-12, Sun 12-3.30, 7-11) Closed: 26 Dec & 1 Jan
Bar Meals L served Mon-Sat 12-2 D served all week 6-9.30 (Sun 7-9.30) Av main course £8.95
Restaurant 12-2 6-9.30 (Sun 7-9.30) Av 3 course à la carte £16
Free House
Ruddles Best, Bombardier, Dover Beck, Guest Beers. 🍷 10
Facilities Garden Parking Play Area

England

ALAM — MAP 17 SK65

he Waggon and Horses 🍷

ıe Turnpike, Mansfield Rd NG22 8AE
☎ 01636 813109 📠 01636 816228

od-led pub serving Thwaites real ales. The award-winning menu ght typically include oriental-style duck pancakes; slow-roasted nb shoulder with redcurrant, garlic, rosemary and fresh mint sauce ve'd never consider taking this off the menu'); and calves' liver with amelised onion, crispy bacon and rich ale and thyme sauce. Fish is o a strength: choices might include seared scallops with pea purée d crisp pancetta; and langoustine broth with sweet potatoes and allots.

pen 11.30–3 5.30–11 (Sat–Sun all day) Closed: 25–26 Dec **r Meals** L served all week 12–2.15 (Sun 12–2.45) D served Mon–Sat 9.15 Av main course £13 **Restaurant** L served all week 12–2.15 un 12–2.45) D served Mon–Sat 6–9.15 Av 3 course à la carte £23 Thwaites Bomber, Thwaites Original, Warsteiner, Thwaites Smooth. 3 **Facilities** Garden Parking

IMBERLEY — MAP 11 SK44

he Nelson & Railway Inn

Station Rd NG16 2NR
☎ 0115 938 2177 📠 0115 938 2179
ir: *1m N of M1 junct 26*

e landlord of more than 30 years gives this 17th-century pub its stinctive personality. Next door is the Hardy & Hanson brewery that pplies many of the beers, but the two nearby railway stations that ıce made it a railway inn are now sadly derelict. A hearty menu of ıb favourites includes soup, ploughman's, and hot rolls, as well as ills, steak and kidney pie, and gammon steak.

pen 11–12 (Sun 12–11) **Bar Meals** L served all week 12–2.30 served all week 5.30–9 (Sat 12–9, Sun 12–6) **Restaurant** L served week 12–2.30 D served all week 5.30–9 (Sat 12–9, Sun 12–6) Hardy & Hansons Hardys & Hansons Best Bitter, Cool & Dark, de Trip. **Facilities** Children's licence Garden Dogs allowed Parking **ooms** 10 bedrooms en suite (★★ INN)

AXTON — MAP 17 SK76

he Dovecote Inn 🍷

loorhouse Rd NG22 0NU ☎ 01777 871586
-mail: dovecoteinn@yahoo.co.uk
ir: *Exit A1 at Tuxford through Egmanton to Laxton*

family-run, 18th-century pub, owned by the Crown Estates, in a llage where a rare example of the medieval open-field farming stem still survives. All food is freshly prepared, ranging from home-ade pies, steaks, roasts and various European dishes to daily fresh sh, such as sea bass stuffed with Atlantic prawns, and plaice with hite wine cream sauce. Two en suite rooms are in renovated listed rm buildings next to the inn.

pen 11.30–3 6.30–11.30 (Fri–Sat 6–11.30) **Bar Meals** L served all eek 12–2 D served all week 6.30–9 **Restaurant** L served all week 2–2 D served all week 6.30–9 Free House Mansfield Smooth, anks Smooth, Marston's Pedigree, Bombardier & Black Sheep. 🍷 10 **acilities** Garden Dogs allowed Parking **Rooms** 2 bedrooms en suite £40 D£60 (★★★★ INN)

MORTON — MAP 17 SK75

Pick of the Pubs

The Full Moon Inn NEW 🍷

Main St NG25 0UT ☎ 01636 830251 📠 01636 830554
e-mail: sales@thefullmooninn.co.uk

See Pick of the Pubs on opposite page

NEWARK-ON-TRENT — MAP 17 SK75

Willow Tree Inn NEW ★★★ INN

Front St, Barnby-in-the-Willows NG24 2SA
☎ 01636 626613 📠 01636 626060
e-mail: howard@willowinn.f9.co.uk
dir: *5m from Newark, follow signs A17 (Sleaford). From A1 1st right after Newark Golf Club, turn at Barnby sign 1m. Pub on left at T-junct*

The Willow Tree occupies a century-old Grade II listed building with lovely oak beams and low ceilings. What was once the landlord's living room is now a cosy restaurant complete with log fire. Typical dishes here might include chicken liver terrine, followed by venison casserole, and a dessert of home-made bread and butter pudding. The flower-filled courtyard is perfect for summer evenings.

Open 7–11 (Sat–Sun 12–3, 7–11) Closed: 25 Dec **Bar Meals** L served Sat–Sun 12–2 D served all week 7–9.30 (Sun 7–9) Av main course £7.95 **Restaurant** L served Sat–Sun 12–2 D served all week 7–9.30 (Sun 7–9) Av 3 course à la carte £18 Av 2 course fixed price £9.95 Free House John Smiths, Springhead, Timothy Taylor, Pedigree & Greene King IPA. **Facilities** Children's licence Garden Dogs allowed Parking **Rooms** 8 bedrooms en suite S£45 D£55

NOTTINGHAM — MAP 11 SK53

Cock & Hoop 🍷

25 High Pavement NG1 1HE
☎ 0115 852 3231 📠 0115 852 3236
e-mail: drink@cockandhoop.co.uk
dir: *Follow tourist signs for 'Galleries of Justice'. Pub opposite*

Tasteful antiques, a real fire, a cellar bar and some striking bespoke artwork characterize this traditional Victorian alehouse. It stands opposite the Galleries of Justice, where Lord Byron is said to have watched hangings from his lodgings above the pub. A new kitchen and new menus planned for 2007.

CONTINUED

England

NOTTINGHAM continued

Open 12–1am Closed: 25–26 Dec **Bar Meals** L served all week 12–10 D served all week Av main course £15 Free House Deuchars IPA, Cock & Hoop, London Pride, Timothy Taylors Landlord. 7 **Facilities** Children's licence Dogs allowed

Fellows Morton & Clayton

54 Canal St NG1 7EH ☎ 0115 950 6795 0115 953 9838
e-mail: info@fellowsmortonandclayton.co.uk

Surrounded by the impressive Castle Wharf complex, with a cobbled courtyard overlooking the Nottingham canal, 'Fellows' was converted from a former warehouse in 1979. The pub, which has been under the same tenancy since 1990, is a regular Nottingham in Bloom award winner. The varied menu includes chargrilled chicken and bacon salad; spicy bean burger on toasted ciabatta; and Spanish haddock with smoked salmon and seafood. Sandwiches and lighter lunches are also on offer.

Open 11–11 (Fri–Sat 11–12) **Bar Meals** L served all week 11–9 D served Mon–Sat 11–9 (Sun 12–6) **Restaurant** L served all week 11.30–2.30 (Sun 12–6) Enterprise Inns Timothy Taylor Landlord, Fuller's London Pride, Nottingham EPA, Duechers IPA. **Facilities** Garden Parking

Ye Olde Trip to Jerusalem

1 Brewhouse Yard, Castle Rd NG1 6AD
☎ 0115 947 3171 0115 950 1185
e-mail: 4925@greeneking.co.uk
dir: *Built into the rock on which Nottingham Castle sits*

Said to be Britain's oldest inn, the Trip is surely one of the most unusual. Parts of the building penetrate deep into the sandstone of Castle Rock, and customers are warned to look out for uneven steps, floors and low doorways. It also would be wise to avoid cleaning the Cursed Galleon. The menu caters for most tastes, ranging from burgers, wraps and jacket potatoes to main course dishes like stilton and vegetable crumble; smoked haddock fish pot; and hickory barbecue chicken.

Open 10.30–12 (Sun–Thu 10.30–11) **Bar Meals** L served all week 12–8 (Sat–Sun 12–6) Av main course £5.99 Greene King Ye Olde Trip Ale, Greene King IPA, Abbot Ale, Guest Beers. 11 **Facilities** Children's licence Garden

RUDDINGTON MAP 11 SK53

Three Crowns NEW

23 Easthorpe St NG11 6LB ☎ 0115 921 3226
e-mail: simon@nottinghamthai.co.uk
dir: *A60 towards Loughborough. Right at 1st lights into Ruddington Village, right & right again, pub 500yds on left*

A modern pub with an authentic Thai restaurant next door, where traditionally attired waitresses from the Land of Smiles glide between the tables. Lunchtime pub snacks include baguettes, omelettes, burgers, traditional pies and Thai stir-fries. The restaurant serves pork, chicken, beef, duck, fish and seafood curries of various strengths, and other Thai dishes, as well as steaks. Traditional roasts and other non-Thai meals are served on Sundays.

Open 12–3 5–11 (Sat–Sun all day) **Bar Meals** L served all week 12–2 D served Tue–Sat 6.30–10 Av main course £9.50 **Restaurant** D served Tue–Sat 6.30–10 Av 3 course à la carte £26 Av 3 course fixed price £20.95 Free House Adnams, Nottingham Brewery, Landlord, Cottage Brewery. 18 **Facilities** Dogs allowed

THURGARTON MAP 17 SK

The Red Lion

Southwell Rd NG14 7GP ☎ 01636 830351
dir: *On A612 between Nottingham & Southwell*

This 16th-century inn was once a monks' alehouse. Pub food can be enjoyed in the bar, restaurant or garden. Main courses include beef and Guinness casserole, chicken breast in garlic and mushroom sau or a variety of steaks. For a lighter option, try a salad with roast ham or poached salmon and prawn; or the cheese platter with local blue stilton. Look out for the 1936 newspaper cutting reporting the murd of a previous landlady by her niece!

Open 11.30–2.30 6.30–11 (Sat–Sun & BHs all day) **Bar Meals** L served all week 12–2 D served all week 7–9.30 (Sat–Sun 12–9.30) Av main cour £7.95 **Restaurant** L served all week 12–2 D served all week 7–10 Fre House Greene King Abbot Ale, Jenning Cumberland, Carlsberg-Tetley, Black Sheep. 7 **Facilities** Garden Parking

TUXFORD MAP 17 SK

The Mussel & Crab

NG22 0PJ ☎ 01777 870491 01777 872302
e-mail: musselandcrab1@hotmail.com
dir: *From Ollerton/Tuxford junct of A1& A57. N on B1164 to Sibthorpe Hill. Pub 800yds on right*

Fish and seafood dominate the menu at this quirky pub with a fabulous curved zinc bar and a multitude of eating areas. You can pl liar dice, admire the fish in the gents' toilets, and sit on large carved wooden hands in the bar. Up to 22 blackboards offer constantly changing dishes featuring snapper, sole, sea bass, crab, lobster, loca shot wild pigeon breast, cheese soufflé and much more.

Open 11–2.30 6–11 **Bar Meals** L served all week 11.30–2.30 D served week 6–10 **Restaurant** L served all week 12–2.30 D served all week 6– (Sun 12–2.45, 6–9) Free House Carlsberg-Tetley Tetley Smooth, Te Cask, Guinness. 16 **Facilities** Garden Dogs allowed Parking

OXFORDSHIRE

BINGDON MAP 05 SU49

he Merry Miller

thill OX13 6JW ☎ 01865 390390 📠 01865 390040
mail: rob@merrymiller.co.uk
: *1m from Marcham interchange on A34*

y inventory of the Merry Miller must include its wealth of risqué nts. Despite the beams, flagstones and stripped pine tables, the erior of this 17th-century former granary is more redolent of Tuscany which at least ensures that the pasta dishes feel at home! But lunch uld just as easily be a club sandwich or seafood salad bowl, whilst ening diners might choose roasted Gressingham duck; or tomato, ats' cheese and puy lentil tartlettes.

en 12–10.30 (Fri–Sat 12–11, Sun 12–10.30) **Bar Meals** L served all week -2.45 D served all week 6.30–9.45 (Sun all day) **Restaurant** L served week 12–2.45 D served all week 6.30–9.45 Av 3 course à la carte) Greene King Greene King IPA & Old Speckled Hen. 15 **cilities** Garden Dogs allowed Parking

DDERBURY MAP 11 SP43

ed Lion ★★ HL

e Green OX17 3LU ☎ 01295 810269 📠 01295 811906
r: *Off M40 3m from Banbury*

ine stone-built coaching inn on the Banbury to Oxford road, erlooking the village green. Established in 1669, the Red Lion was ce known as the King's Arms, and had a tunnel in the cellar used by yalists in hiding during the Civil War. Enter the rambling, beamed erior to find daily newspapers, real ales, good wines and a varied enu, with plenty of fish choices like home-made Thai salmon fish kes, chargrilled tuna steaks, and salmon steak parcels.

en 11–11 (Fri–Sat 11–11.30) **Bar Meals** L served all week 12–3 served all week 7–9.30 (Sat–Sun & BHs 12–9.30) **Restaurant** L served week 12–3 D served all week 7–9.30 (Sun 12–9.30) Greene King Greene King IPA, Abbot Ale, Old Speckled Hen. 11 **Facilities** Garden king **Rooms** 12 bedrooms en suite S£65 D£85

RDINGTON MAP 05 SU48

Pick of the Pubs

The Boar's Head ★★★★ INN

Church St OX12 8QA
☎ 01235 833254 📠 01235 833254
e-mail: info@boarsheadardington.co.uk
dir: *Off A417 E of Wantage*

See Pick of the Pubs on page 431

BAMPTON MAP 05 SP30

The Romany

Bridge St OX18 2HA ☎ 01993 850237 📠 01993 852133
e-mail: romany@barbox.net

A shop until 20 years ago, The Romany is housed in an 18th-century building of Cotswold stone with a beamed bar, log fires and intimate dining room. The choice of food ranges from bar snacks and bar meals to a full à la carte restaurant menu, with home-made specials like hotpot, Somerset pork, or steak and ale pie. There is a good range of vegetarian choices. Regional singers provide live entertainment a couple of times a month.

Open 11–11 **Bar Meals** L served all week 12–2 D served all week 6.30–9 Av main course £6 **Restaurant** L served all week 12–2 D served all week 6.30–9 Free House Archers Village, plus Guest ales. **Facilities** Garden Dogs allowed Parking Play Area

BANBURY MAP 11 SP44

The George Inn

Lower St, Barford St Michael OX15 0RH ☎ 01869 338226

Handy for both Banbury and Oxford, this 300-year-old thatched village pub features old beams, exposed stone walls and open fireplaces. It stands in a large garden, with a patio and orchard, overlooking open countryside. Live music is an established tradition, and the pub hosts a variety of rock, folk and solo artists. There's a good choice of real ales, and options from the single menu include baguettes, baked potatoes, pasta, pies, and fish and chips.

Open 12–3 7–11 (Sun 12–4) **Bar Meals** 7–9 Free House Timothy Taylor Landlord, IPA, Copper Ale, Greene King. **Facilities** Garden Dogs allowed Parking **Notes**

The Wykham Arms

Temple Mill Rd, Sibford Gower OX15 5RX
☎ 01295 788808
e-mail: info@wykhamarms.co.uk
web: www.wykhamarms.co.uk
dir: *Between Banbury & Shipston-on-Stour off B4035*

A centuries' old thatched inn built of mellow stone with stunning countryside views, and originally part of William of Wykham's estate. The bar menu is typified by Hooky braised beef pie with crisp pastry croute; and wild boar and apple sausages with beer mustard mash and caramelised onion gravy. Restaurant mains range from baked Cornish

CONTINUED

BANBURY continued

plaice with ratatouille and dill crushed potato, to confit of Gressingham duck with dauphinoise potato, roast shallots, garlic and mushroom.

Open 11-3 6-11.30 **Bar Meals** L served Tue-Sun 12-2.30 D served Tue-Sat 6.30-9.45 (Sun 12-3.30) Av main course £10 **Restaurant** L served Tue-Sun 12-2.30 D served Tue-Sat 7-9.45 (Sun 12-3) Av 3 course à la carte £25 Free House Hook Norton Best, Guinness, St Austell Tribute, Adnams Broadside. 17 **Facilities** Children's licence Garden Dogs allowed Parking

Ye Olde Reindeer Inn

47 Parsons St OX16 5NA

01295 264031 01295 264018

e-mail: tonypuddifoot@aol.com

dir: *1m from M40 junct 11, in town centre just off market square*

Oliver Cromwell stayed in the Reindeer during the Battle of Edge Hill in 1642, and royalty, as well as the merely plain rich, used the magnificent Globe Room on their way to and from the capital. The original panelling was removed from here before the First World War and stored in London, finally being returned in 1964. The menu comprises hot or toasted sandwiches, ploughman's, omelettes, salads and other snacks, with daily specials.

Open 11-11 (Sun 12-3.30) **Bar Meals** L served Mon-Sat 11-2.30 (Sun 12-3) D served Mon-Sat **Restaurant** L served all week 12-2 (Sun 12-3) D served all week Hook Norton Hook Norton Best, Hook Norton Haymaker, Old. **Facilities** Garden Parking

BARNARD GATE MAP 05 SP41

Pick of the Pubs

The Boot Inn

OX29 6XE 01865 881231

e-mail: info@theboot-inn.com

dir: *Off A40 between Witney & Eynsham*

A popular pub renowned for its collection of footwear given by a host of celebrities, politicians and sports personalities including the Bee Gees, George Best and Jeremy Irons. The Boot is set in beautiful countryside on the edge of the Cotswolds, near the ancient village of Eynsham, just a few miles west of Oxford. Run by Australian-born chef Craig Foster since 2003, the inn offers exposed beams, stone-flagged floors, a roaring log fire in winter, a pleasant garden in summer, a welcoming bar and secluded dining areas. Well-known and reliable brewers are on tap, while the wine list would satisfy the most cosmopolitan of oenophiles. The lunch menu offers sandwiches and salads, chargrilled lamb or chicken burgers, or light dishes such as tartiflette (bacon, potato and onion baked with reblochon cheese). For dinner, a starter of home-made salmon rillettes wrapped in Scottish smoked salmon could be followed by monkfish brochettes with a lime and ginger butter.

Open 11-3 6-11 (Summer all day) **Bar Meals** L served all week 12-2.30 D served all week 7-10 **Restaurant** 12-2.30 7-9.30 Av 3 course à la carte £25 Free House Hook Norton Best, Adnams Best, Fullers London Pride, Youngs Best. 7 **Facilities** Garden Parking

BECKLEY MAP 05 SP5

Pick of the Pubs

The Abingdon Arms

High St OX3 9UU 01865 351311

e-mail: chequers89@hotmail.com

dir: *M40 junct 8, signs at Headington rdbt for Beckley*

Expect a warm welcome at this cosy, traditional pub set in a pretty village to the north of Oxford. It has been smartly updated, and good food is also helping to put it on the map, backed by excellent beers from Brakspear's. A range of sandwiches and bar snacks is available at lunchtime, while a full meal could include marinated crab with chilli, coriander and rocket, followed by chargrilled medallions of lamb with spinach mash and mustard cream sauce. The atmosphere in the pub is always friendly, and there are roaring log fires in winter. In the summer you can sit on the patio and enjoy the spectacular views of Otmoor. Some years ago this area was popular with the writer Evelyn Waugh, and today it is just round the corner from an RSPB bird reserve. There are opportunities for many pleasant walks in the area.

Open 12-3 6-11 (Sat-Sun all day) **Bar Meals** L served all week 12-2.30 (Sun 12-3) D served Mon-Sat 7-9.30 (Summer 6.30-8.30) Av main course £10 **Restaurant** L served all week 12-2.30 (Sun 12-3) D served Mon-Sat 7-9.30 (Summer 6.30-8.30) Av 3 course à la carte £20 Brakspear Brakspears Bitter, Special & Guest. 8 **Facilities** Garden Parking

BLACK BOURTON MAP 05 SP2

Pick of the Pubs

The Vines

Burford Rd OX18 2PF

01993 843559 01993 840080

e-mail: info@vineshotel.com

web: www.vinesblackbourton.co.uk

dir: *From A40 Witney, take A4095 to Faringdon, then 1st right after Bampton to Black Bourton*

See Pick of the Pubs on page 432

BLOXHAM MAP 11 SP4

The Elephant & Castle

OX15 4LZ 0845 873 7358

e-mail: bloxhomelephant1@btconnect.com

dir: *Just off A361, in village centre*

The arch of this 15th-century Cotswold-stone coaching inn still straddles the former Banbury to Chipping Norton turnpike. Locals play darts or shove-ha'penny in the big wood-floored bar, whilst the two-roomed lounge boasts a bar-billiards table and a large inglenook fireplace. The reasonably priced menu offers a range of sandwiches and crusty filled baguettes, plus pub favourites like roast chicken breast with stuffing, crispy battered cod, and seafood platter.

Open 10-3 5-11 (Sat-Sun all day) **Bar Meals** L served Mon-Sat 12-2 **Restaurant** L served Mon-Sat 12-2 Hook Norton Hook Norton Best Bitter, Hook Norton Seasonal Ales, Guest Ales. **Facilities** Garden Parking Play Area

PICK OF THE PUBS

ARDINGTON-OXFORDSHIRE

The Boar's Head

he Boar's Head is situated within the decidedly magical village of Ardington, which forms part f the famous Lockinge Estate. The estate was laid out in the 19th century by Lord Wantage, and as remained entirely unspoilt.

ne inn itself has been serving the ill-flourishing local community r the past 150 years. As well as reerfully maintaining its role as e village local, the Boar's Head has rnered a reputation as a serious ning destination. Candles, fresh owers and blazing log fires create st the right romantic atmosphere, ith scrubbed pine tables giving a stic touch. Food, happily enough, the passion of the kitchen team, d everything from bread to ice eam, and pasta to pastries is ade on the premises. A typical eal could begin with seared foie as on a toasted brioche with ion marmalade, or an assiette Cornish scallops, followed by ast loin of suckling pig with uid chips; poached fillet of venison, or fillet of Newlyn sea bass with ratatouille and chorizo. Hot pistachio soufflé with iced chocolate cream makes for a spectacular finish. Should you feel inclined to take advantage of three pristine and very stylish en suite rooms, you could explore the region further. Ardington is an ideal base for walking or cycling, and footpaths wind down through nearby villages or run up to the ancient Ridgeway a few miles away. Golfers will be delighted by several excellent courses nearby, while fly-fishers can try their luck in the village's well-stocked trout lakes.

★★★★ INN 🏵🏵 🍷
MAP 05 SU48
Church St OX12 8QA
☎ 01235 833254
🖷 01235 833254
e-mail: info@boarsheadardington.co.uk
dir: *Off A417 E of Wantage*

Open 12–3 6.30–11
Bar Meals L served all week 12–2.30 D served all week 7–10
Restaurant L served all week 12–2.15 D served all week 7–10
Free House
Hook Norton Old Hooky, West Berkshire Brewery Dr. Hexter's, Warsteiner, Butts Brewery. 🍷 8
Facilities Garden Parking
Rooms 3 bedrooms en suite S£75 D£85

PICK OF THE PUBS

BLACK BOURTON-OXFORDSHIRE

The Vines

Long acclaimed for its fine dining in elegant surroundings, this stone-built Cotswold hotel is set in the beautiful village of Black Bourton, surrounded by its own delightful gardens. John Clegg & the BBC's Real Rooms team famously designed and decorated The Vines restaurant and bar.

The effect is stunning – very different from the more predictable styles favoured for a building of this character. Here you can enjoy lunch or dinner from the carte or special daily menus of modern British dishes with an international twist. Particularly popular are the likes of venison with chocolate sauce, honey soused pigeon, and rack of lamb, all created from fresh local produce. The good-value Let's Do Lunch menu goes down well with the locals, as does the traditional Sunday lunch, and there is also a special children's selection. To complement the food, the cellar offers a choice of over 36 Old and New World wines. The spacious lounge area with its leather sofas is a comfortable place to relax with a drink or light snack while enjoying a chat or a game of chess, particularly by a cosy log fire on a cold evening. On sunny days you can eat outside on the patio and play a nostalgic game of Aunt Sally. The Vines provides a superb setting for a wedding reception, anniversary or other special event, and owners Ahdy and Karen Gerges pride themselves on their professional planning expertise. The hotel is ideally placed for anyone on business in Oxford, Swindon, Witney or Brize Norton and makes an ideal base for exploring the Cotswolds. Burford is less than four miles away.

MAP 05 SP20
Burford Rd OX18 2PF
☎ 01993 843559
Fax 01993 840080
e-mail: info@vineshotel.com
web: www.vinesblackbourton.co.uk
dir: *From A40 Witney, take A4095 to Faringdon, then 1st right after Bampton to Black Bourton*

Open 12-3 6-11
Bar Meals L served Tue–Sun 12–2 D served Mon–Sun 6.30–9.30
Restaurant L served Tue–Sun 12–2 D served Tue–Sun 6.30–9.30
Free House
Old Hookey, Tetley Smooth, Carlsberg-Tetley. 7
Facilities Children's licence Garden Parking

RIGHTWELL BALDWIN MAP 05 SU69

Pick of the Pubs

The Lord Nelson Inn

OX49 5NP ☎ 01491 612497

dir: *Off B4009 between Watlington & Benson*

See Pick of the Pubs on page 434

ROADWELL MAP 05 SP20

hilli Pepper

L7 3QS ☎ 01367 860385

mail: info@chilli-pepper.net

r: *A361 from Lechlade to Burford, after 2m right to Kencot oadwell, right after 200mtrs. Right at x-rds*

ractive 16th-century Cotswold stone inn overlooking the manor d parish church. It used to be known as The Five Bells Broadwell, t the change of name has brought a hot new look. The bars are full character with beams and flagstones, and there are lots of places eat. The menu takes in starters like Caesar salad with chargrilled icken, and then pan-fried fillet of venison with a cream wild berry d brandy sauce.

en 12–2.30 6–12 (Summer opening varies) Closed: 25–26 Dec **r Meals** L served Tue–Sun 12–2.30 D served Tue–Sat 6–10 Av main ırse £9 **Restaurant** L served Tue–Sun 12–2.30 D served Tue–Sat 9.30 Av 3 course à la carte £25 Free House Kronenbourg, Becks, dweiser, Fosters. 12 **Facilities** Garden Dogs allowed Parking

BROUGHTON MAP 11 SP43

Saye and Sele Arms

Main Rd OX15 5ED ☎ 01295 263348 01295 272012

e-mail: mail@sayeandselearms.co.uk

dir: *3m from Banbury Cross*

The pretty, stone-built Saye & Sele is just five minutes' walk from Broughton Castle, a popular film location (*Shakespeare in Love, Edward VIII*). Licensed for 300 years, the pub is these days known for its food, and new chef/proprietor Danny McGeehan puts an emphasis on wholesome, carefully prepared dishes – perhaps parfait of chicken livers with apple and calvados chutney, followed by tournedos of pork fillet wrapped in smoked bacon, on apple mint mash.

Open 11.30–2.30 7–11 (Sun 12–5) Closed: 25 Dec **Bar Meals** L served all week 12–2 D served Mon–Sat 7–9.30 (Sun 12–3) **Restaurant** L served all week 12–2 D served Mon–Sat 7–9.30 (Sun 12–3) Free House Wadworth 6X, Adnams Southwold, 2 Guest beers. 8 **Facilities** Garden Dogs allowed Parking

BURCOT MAP 05 SU59

The Chequers

OX14 3DP ☎ 01865 407771 01865 407771

e-mail: enquiries@thechequers-burcot.co.uk

dir: *On A415 (Dorchester/Abingdon road)*

Once a staging post for barges on the Thames, the Chequers is a typical thatched country pub, now under new management. It dates back 400 years, while the beam over the large inglenook fireplace is even older. There is a snack and light meal menu available at lunchtime, while diners can sample such delights as Gloucester Old Spot grilled chop with apple mash; and local venison steak with a chocolate and red wine reduction.

Open 12–3 6–11 (Closed Sun eve) **Bar Meals** L served all week 12–2.30 (Sun 12–3) D served Mon–Sat 6–9.30 Av main course £12 **Restaurant** L served all week 12–2.30 (Sun 12–3) D served Mon–Sat 6–9.30 Av 3 course à la carte £20 Free House Hook Norton Bitter, Ridgway. 21 **Facilities** Garden Parking

The Lord Nelson Inn

In Nelson's day this 17th-century pub was known as the Admiral Nelson, but when, in 1797, our naval hero was elevated to the peerage, its name was elevated too. For more than a century after that, passing travellers and villagers slaked their thirst here.

In 1905, following complaints from the church and the local squire about over-indulgent estate workers, the inn was closed and it became a shop, a post office and then a private house. In 1971 a couple driving past liked the look of it, bought it, renewed its licence and restored it to its former glory, decorating the interior in traditional style, in keeping with its age. These days, it's always full of fresh flowers and lit candles. During the summer the pretty, weeping willow-draped garden, and the rear terrace, are popular places to eat and drink. All the food is freshly cooked, using local produce where possible. The lunch menu may offer stir-fry beef with hoi sin, plum sauce and noodles; or fillet of sea bass with sweet chilli dressing; while at dinner there may be local partridge with bacon and mixed vegetables; fresh oven-roasted poussin with lardons and Italian herbs; lamb cutlets with fresh rosemary; fillet of cod with a herb crust; and ratatouille feuilleté with tomato confit and basil. Typical weekly specials include fillet steak; fresh grilled John Dory with capers; and noisettes of English lamb with fresh rosemary. Real ales served in the beamed bar are supplied by Black Sheep, Brakspear, John Smiths, and West Berkshire Brewery, and the comprehensive wine list includes 20 by the glass. In the early 1990s the RSPB chose the nearby Chiltern escarpment to reintroduce the red kite – you'll be unlucky not to see at least one.

MAP 05 SU69
OX49 5NP
☎ 01491 612497
dir: *Off B4009 between Watlington & Benson*

Open 11-3 6-11 (Sun 7-11)
Bar Meals L served all week 12-2.30 D served all week 6-10.30 (Sun 7-10)
Restaurant L served all week 12-2.30 D served all week 6-10.30 (Sun 7-10) Av 3 course à la carte £25 Av 2 course fixed price £11.95
Free House
West Berkshire Brewery, Brakspear, John Smiths & Black Sheep. 20
Facilities Garden Parking

England

URFORD MAP 05 SP21

iolden Pheasant

High St OX18 4QA ☎ 01993 823223 01993 822621
mail: robrichardson@goldenpheasant-burford.co.uk
r: *M40 junct 8, follow A40/Cheltenham signs into Burford*

uilt of mellow Cotswold limestone, this 18th-century private hotel s a cheery stone-flagged and -walled bar, plus lounge and brasserie. ek out the gravadlax with lemon mayonnaise, antipasti, or deep-fried membert with warm cranberry sauce starters, then consider smoked ddock with spring onion mash and Welsh rarebit sauce; beef oganoff with mushrooms and rice; lamb and mint sausages with ustard mash and red wine gravy; or stir-fried vegetable curry.

pen 9–11 **Bar Meals** L served all week 12–3 D served all week 6.30–9.30 **staurant** L served all week 12–3 D served all week 6.30–9 Abbot, A. 7 **Facilities** Garden Dogs allowed Parking

Pick of the Pubs

The Inn for All Seasons ★★ HL

The Barringtons OX18 4TN
☎ 01451 844324 01451 844375
e-mail: sharp@innforallseasons.com
web: www.innforallseasons.com
dir: *3m W of Burford on A40*

See Pick of the Pubs on page 437

Pick of the Pubs

The Lamb Inn ★★★ HL

Sheep St OX18 4LR ☎ 01993 823155 01993 822228
e-mail: info@lambinn-burford.co.uk
web: www.cotswold-inns-hotels.co.uk/lamb
dir: *M40 junct 8, A40 & Burford signs, turning down the hill into Sheep St*

See Pick of the Pubs on page 438

CHADLINGTON MAP 10 SP32

The Tite Inn

Mill End OX7 3NY ☎ 01608 676475 0870 7059308
e-mail: willis@titeinn.com
dir: *3m S of Chipping Norton*

Sixteenth-century Cotswold-stone free house where, in 1642, Royalist troops sank a few stiffeners before the Battle of Edgehill nearby. The lunch menu features Thai coconut chicken curry with basmati rice; lambs' kidneys braised in red wine; and bobotie, a South African sweet and spicy meatloaf. At dinner try deep-fried goujons of plaice with tartare sauce; baked gammon with Dijon cream sauce; or vegetarian Brazil nut roast with fresh tomato sauce.

Open 12–2.30 6.30–11 (Sun 12–3, 7–10.30) Closed: 25–26 Dec **Bar Meals** L served Tue–Sun 12–2 D served Tue–Sun 7–9 (Sun 12–2.30) Av main course £9.95 **Restaurant** L served Tue–Sun 12–2 D served Tue–Sat 6.30–9 (Sun 12–2.30) Av 3 course à la carte £19 Free House Ramsbury, Sharps, Cotswold Premium Lager & 4 Guest beers. 8 **Facilities** Garden Dogs allowed Parking

CHALGROVE MAP 05 SU69

Pick of the Pubs

The Red Lion Inn

The High St OX44 7SS ☎ 01865 890625
e-mail: annie@redlionchalgrove.co.uk
dir: *B480 from Oxford Ring road, through Stadhampton, left then right at mini-rdbt, at Chalgrove Airfield right into village*

The Red Lion is an attractive cream-painted and beamed pub, parts of which date back to the 11th century. Later in its life, in 1637, it became the property of the church and provided free dining and carousing for the church wardens. Today the emphasis is on a warm welcome, a good pint of real ale, and a range of traditional and imaginative dishes from the lunchtime or evening menu. Among the starters from the dinner menu are pan-fried calves' liver with Parma ham, petit leaf and coarse grain mustard jus, or tortilla wrap with sautéed crayfish, crab and king prawns in a white wine cream. Main dishes take in half shoulder of lamb in redcurrant and rosemary sauce, and chicken wrapped in smoked bacon set on black pudding mash with sun-dried tomato sauce.

Open 12–3 6–11.30 (Winter 12–2.30, Sun 7–11) Closed: 1 Jan **Bar Meals** L served all week 12–2 D served Mon–Sat 6.30–9 **Restaurant** L served all week 12–2 D served Mon–Sat 6.30–9 Av 3 course à la carte £19.50 Free House Fuller's London Pride, Adnams Best, Timothy Taylors Landlord. 8 **Facilities** Garden Dogs allowed Play Area

CHARLBURY MAP 11 SP31

Pick of the Pubs

The Bull Inn

Sheep St OX7 3RR ☎ 01608 810689
e-mail: info@bullinn-charlbury.com
dir: *1.5m after Woodstock left on B4437 to Charlbury*

See Pick of the Pubs on page 441

CHECKENDON MAP 05 SU68

The Highwayman

Exlade St RG8 0UA ☎ 01491 682020 📠 01491 682229
e-mail: thehighwayman@skyeinns670.fsnet.co.uk
dir: *On A4074*

An early 17th-century listed inn which has undergone a major refurblishment programme. The emphasis in the character bar is on wooden floors and open fireplaces. The famous Maharajah's Well nearby is surrounded by numerous walks in the glorious Chiltern beechwoods. Seared salmon fillet, pan-fried calves' liver, and honey mustard and lemon chicken escalope are typical examples from the inviting menu.

Open 12–3 6–11 (Sat-Sun & BH all day) Closed 25 Dec **Bar Meals** L served all week 12–3 D served all week 7–9.30 **Restaurant** L served all week 12–2.30 D served all week 7–9.30 Free House Fuller's London Pride, Loddon Ferryman's Gold, Butlers Brewers & guest ale. **Facilities** Garden Dogs allowed Parking Play Area

CHINNOR MAP 05 SP70

Pick of the Pubs

The Sir Charles Napier

Spriggs Alley OX39 4BX
☎ 01494 483011 📠 01494 485311
dir: *M40 junct 6 to Chinnor. Right at rdbt, up hill to Spriggs Alley*

People tend to linger in this cosy, charming pub, tucked amongst the beech woods of the Chiltern Hills. Huge log fires, comfortable sofas and an eclectic jumble of old furnishings create a haven it's very hard to leave. In the summer, lunch is served on the vine- and wisteria-shaded terrace overlooking extensive lawns and herb gardens. Come winter, locals wander in bearing fungi, berries, pheasant and pigeon for the pot. From a summer menu try halibut with piperade, fennel and black olive tapenade; while in winter sample roast grouse with bubble and squeak and bread sauce. The blackboard might include skate wing with shrimps and capers. An extensive wine list balances Old and New Worlds well, with even Lebanon squeezing in. Inside and out are works in stone, marble and wood by local sculptor Michael Cooper. Sir Charles Napier, incidentally, was responsible for conquering Sind in India in 1843.

Open 12–3.30 6.30–12 Closed: 25–26 Dec **Bar Meals** L served Tue–Fri 12–2.30 D served Tue–Thu 7–9.30 Av main course £12.50 **Restaurant** L served Tue–Sun 12–2.30 (Sun 12–3.30) D served Tue–Sat 7–10 Av 3 course à la carte £35 Av 2 course fixed price £16.50 Free House Wadworth 6X, Wadwoth IPA. 15 **Facilities** Garden Parking

CHIPPING NORTON MAP 10 SP3

The Chequers

Goddards Ln OX7 5NP ☎ 01608 644717 📠 01608 64623
e-mail: enquiries@chequers-pub.co.uk
dir: *Town centre, next to theatre*

Log fires, low ceilings and soft lighting make for a cosy atmosphere in the bar of this popular 16th-century inn. By contrast, the courtyard restaurant is wonderfully bright and airy. Well-kept real ale, good wines and decent coffee are served along with freshly prepared contemporary dishes. Look for starters like wild mushroom risotto; ar mains including baked cod in Parma ham with sun-dried tomato and pine nut couscous; and chicken stir-fry with cashew nuts.

Open 11–11 (Sun 12–10.30) Closed: 25 Dec **Bar Meals** L served all week 12–2.30 D served Mon–Sat 6–9.30 (Sun 12–5) Av main course £9.50 **Restaurant** L served all week 12–2.30 D served Mon–Sat 6–9 (Sun 12–5) Av 3 course à la carte £17.50 Fullers Fuller's Chiswick Bitter, London Pride & ESB, Organic Honeydew. 18

CHISLEHAMPTON MAP 05 SU5

Pick of the Pubs

Coach & Horses Inn ★★★ INN

Watlington Rd OX44 7UX
☎ 01865 890255 📠 01865 891995
e-mail: enquiries@coachhorsesinn.co.uk

A young girl killed during the Civil War is believed to haunt this delightful 16th-century inn. Set in peaceful countryside on the old Roman road Icknield Street, the inn, as the name attests, once provided hospitality for the stage coaches travelling from Birmingham to London. Among the features inside are roaring log fires in winter, quaint beams and an old bread oven. Start with warm duck and home-cured bacon salad, before tucking into the likes of open steak and kidney pie, or pan-fried chicken with cider and mustard sauce. Vegetarians might like roasted butternut squash risotto; spinach, tomato and mushroom lasagne; or peppers stuffed with rice, sun-dried tomatoes, basil and coriander. The daily specials fish board could include mixed seafood grill; fresh fillet of sea bass; and red snapper. Grills, poultry and game are also perennial favourites.

Open 11.30–11 **Bar Meals** L served all week 12–2 D served Mon–Sat 7–10 **Restaurant** L served all week 12–2 D served Mon–Sat 7–10 Free House Hook Norton Best, London Pride, Old Hooky. 8 **Facilities** Garden Parking **Rooms** 9 bedrooms en suite

The Inn for All Seasons

its lifetime this 16th-century coaching inn has been a garage, a filling station and two quarry ·ttages whose occupants quarried the stone for St Paul's Cathedral. Within its solid Cotswold one walls is a treasure-trove of ancient oak beams, inglenooks and contemporary furniture.

ıere are several guest ales, among ɛm always a Wychwood from arby Witney, and a large selection wines by the glass. The Sharp nily has owned the Inn since 86; Matthew Sharp, the chef, s worked with the Roux Brothers d Anton Mosimann. Connections th the right people in Brixham arantee a wonderful supply of h for specials such as whole lled lemon sole with lemon d parsley butter; poached wing skate with a baby caper and allot butter sauce; and red Thai ı curry with chunky vegetables voured with lemon grass and lime ves. If you prefer land over sea, ›k to the main menu for starters ch as crispy duck and orange ad; or pressed Gloucester ham ck, vegetable and caper terrine with onion chutney, followed by lemon and tarragon roasted free-range chicken on garlic and chorizo risotto; or perhaps marinated local venison steak chargrilled and served on a parsnip purée with sticky red cabbage and game jus. Desserts might include William pear and red plum oat crumble; hot chocolate fondant with French vanilla ice cream; or a blackberry pancake with crème fraîche. For those seeking a lunchtime snack, there are grilled paninis, and mouthwatering snacks such as bubble and squeak with bacon and fried egg, or steamed Oxfordshire suet pudding with tangy sauce alongside the main à la carte menu. There is a good selection of wines by the glass.

★★ HL ➪ 🍷
MAP 05 SP21
The Barringtons OX18 4TN
☎ 01451 844324
📠 01451 844375
e-mail: sharp@innforallseasons.com
web: www.innforallseasons.com
dir: *3m W of Burford on A40*

Open 11–2.30 6–11 (Sun 12–3, 7–10.30)
Bar Meals L served all week 11.30–2.30 D served all week 6.30–9.30 (Sun 12–2.30, 7–9) Av main course £10.50
Restaurant L served all week 11.30–2.30 D served all week 6.30–9.30 (Sun 12–2.30, 7–9) Av 3 course à la carte £19
Free House
Wadworth 6X, Interbrew Bass, Wychwood, Badger. 🍷 15
Facilities Children's licence Garden Dogs allowed Parking Play Area
Rooms 10 bedrooms en suite S£68 D£90

PICK OF THE PUBS

BURFORD-OXFORDSHIRE

The Lamb Inn

A traditional English inn with stone flagged floors, real ale and log fires set at the heart of the Cotswolds – anyone hoping for a classic country pub will not be disappointed at the Lamb. With its 500 years of history, this honey-coloured stone-built coaching inn lies just off the centre of Burford, whilst still having easy access to the shops.

In summer you can visit the walled cottage garden, admire the herbaceous borders and perhaps take lunch on the lawn. A spacious restaurant with mullioned windows overlooks the lovely garden and courtyard, while the cheerful interior combines original features with modern fabrics, enhanced by flowers, candles and light jazz. There's nothing old-world about the menus, which present a delicious blend of English and international cooking. The chef uses locally produced meat, cheese and vegetables whenever possible, as well as organic meat and fish when available. Menus are changed regularly, and always include a fish board advertising the likes of pan-fried lemon sole with sautéed potatoes and parsley butter; and whole grilled sea bass with green salad and citrus dressing. From the main menu come lamb and date tagine with spicy bulgar wheat; game pie with chips and pickled onions; Cumberland sausage and lamb kidney casserole with horseradish and parsley mash; goats' cheese and red onion tart; crayfish and saffron risotto; and on Sundays, traditional roasts. If you can still manage a dessert, you could opt for chocolate tart with rum and raisin ice cream; sticky toffee pudding; or poached autumn fruits with rice pudding ice cream. There is also a Summer Bar and Garden Menu, serving interesting sandwiches (cold rare Aberdeen Angus beef with horseradish potato salad), and salads like poached pear and Oxford Blue, or classic Caesar salad with chargrilled chicken and anchovies.

★★★ HL @@ ₸
MAP 05 SP21
Sheep St OX18 4LR
☎ 01993 823155
🖷 01993 822228
e-mail: info@lambinn-burford.co.uk
web: www.cotswold-inns-hotels.co.uk/lamb
dir: *M40 junct 8, A40 & Burford signs, turning down the hill into Sheep St*

Open 11–11
Bar Meals L served all week 12–2.30 D served all week 6.30–9.30 Av main course £9.50
Restaurant L served all week 12–2.30 D served all week 7–9.30 Av 3 course fixed price £32.50
Free House
Hook Norton Best, Brakspear.
₸ 9
Facilities Garden Dogs allowed
Rooms 17 bedrooms en suite D£145

HRISTMAS COMMON MAP 05 SU79

Pick of the Pubs

The Fox and Hounds

OX49 5HL ☎ 01491 612599
e-mail: kiran.daniels@btconnect.com
dir: *M40 junct 5, 2.5m to Christmas Common (on road towards Henley)*

See Pick of the Pubs on page 442

HURCH ENSTONE MAP 11 SP32

Pick of the Pubs

The Crown Inn

Mill Ln OX7 4NN ☎ 01608 677262 📠 01608 677394
e-mail: crown_inn@btconnect.com
dir: *Off A44*

Award-winning chef Tony Warburton runs this stone-built 17th-century free house on the eastern edge of the Cotswolds with his wife Caroline. In the summer season you can while away the long evenings eating or drinking in the quiet and secluded rear garden, which is sheltered from the wind but enjoys the best of the late sunshine. Indoors, you'll find a traditional rustic bar with an open fire; a spacious, slate floored conservatory; and a richly decorated beamed dining room. All meals are prepared on the premises using fresh produce, including pork, beef and game from the local farms and estates. Starters including carrot soup, and smoked fish plate herald main course choices like breast of pheasant with bacon and cranberry sauce; and pasta with roast peppers, goats' cheese, pesto and cream. A home-made pudding or cheese plate will round things off nicely.

Open 12–3 6–11 (Sun 12–3) **Bar Meals** L served Tue–Sun 12–2 D served Tue–Sat 7–9 Av main course £10 **Restaurant** L served Tue–Sun 12–2 D served Tue–Sat 7–9 Av 3 course à la carte £20 Free House Hook Norton Best Bitter, Timothy Taylor Landlord & Hobgoblin. 8 **Facilities** Garden Dogs allowed Parking

LIFTON MAP 11 SP43

uke of Cumberland's Head

X15 0PE ☎ 01869 338534 📠 01869 338643
mail: info@dukeatclifton.com
r: *A4260 from Banbury, then B4031 from Deddington*

ilt in 1645, this thatched and beamed stone pub was named to nour the Duke whose forces fought for his uncle, Charles I, at e nearby Battle of Edge Hill; important strategic decisions were pposedly made around the pub's inglenook fireplace. Today it offers hoice of real ales, two dining rooms, and a wonderful garden in mmer. The menu may start with avocado and prawns, continue with ef braised in beer, and finish with tiramisu.

pen 12–2.30 6.30–11 (Closed Mon Lunch) Closed: 25 Dec **r Meals** L served Tue–Sun 12–2 D served Mon–Sat 6–9 Av main course 1 **Restaurant** L served Wed–Sun 12–2 D served Wed–Sat 7–9.30 Av 3 urse à la carte £21.50 Av 3 course fixed price £20 Clifton Public House anagement Ltd Hook Norton, Adnams, Deuchers & Black Sheep. **cilities** Garden Dogs allowed Parking

CRAY'S POND MAP 05 SU68

Pick of the Pubs

The White Lion

Goring Rd, Goring Heath RG8 7SH
☎ 01491 680471 📠 01491 684254
e-mail: reservations@thewhitelioncrayspond.com
dir: *From M4 junct 11 follow signs to Pangbourne, through toll bridge to Whitchurch. N for 3m into Crays Pond*

See Pick of the Pubs on page 445

CUMNOR MAP 05 SP40

Pick of the Pubs

Bear & Ragged Staff

28 Appleton Rd OX2 9QH
☎ 01865 862329 📠 01865 865947
dir: *A420 from Oxford, right to Cumnor on B4017*

A 700-year-old pub allegedly haunted by the mistress of the Earl of Warwick. With a tad more certainty it is believed that Oliver Cromwell's brother Richard chiselled out the royal crest above one of the two massive, original fireplaces, which with the wooden beams and floors, help to create a powerfully historic atmosphere. The pub caters for a wide cross-section of locals, as well as being popular with visitors from further afield, many drawn by the extensive menu. Starters include roasted garlic king prawn skewers; timbale of salmon, crab and prawns; and crispy duck spring rolls with vermicelli noodles. Mains to consider are roasted vegetable tagliatelle; chargrilled tuna steak with chorizo and sweet chilli sauce; medallions of oriental pork with fresh ginger, spring onions and egg noodles; home-made steak and kidney pudding; fillet of Appleton beef (hung for four weeks); and the locally renowned Cape bobotie.

Open 12–11 (Sun 12–10.30) **Bar Meals** L served all week 12–2.30 D served all week 6–9.30 **Restaurant** L served all week 12–3 D served all week 6–9 Morrells IPA, Old Speckled Hen, Abbot Ale, Old Hooky. **Facilities** Garden Parking Play Area

Please see walk on page 446

England

CUMNOR continued

The Vine Inn 🍷

11 Abingdon Rd OX2 9QN

☎ 01865 862567 📠 01865 862567

dir: *A420 from Oxford, right onto B4017*

An old village pub whose name, when you see the frontage, needs no explanation. In 1560, the suspicious death of an Earl's wife in Cumnor Place first had people asking 'Did she fall, or was she pushed?'. A typical menu here could include lamb shank with a red wine and mint sauce, pan-fried fillet steak with brandy and mushroom sauce, and the day's fresh fish. There's also a good range of snacks. Children love the huge garden.

Open 11–3 6–11 (Sun 12–10.30) **Bar Meals** L served Mon-Fri 12–2.15 (Sat 12–3, Sun 12–6) D served Mon–Sat 6–9.15 **Restaurant** L served Mon–Fri 12–2.15 (Sat 12–3, Sun 12–6) D served Mon–Sat 6.30–9.15 Punch Taverns Adnams Bitter, Carlsberg-Tetely Tetely Bitter, Hook Norton, guest beers. 🍷 7 **Facilities** Children's licence Garden Dogs allowed Parking Play Area

CUXHAM MAP 05 SU69

The Half Moon 🍷

OX49 5NF ☎ 01491 614151 📠 01491 614606

e-mail: info@thehalf-moon.com

dir: *M40 junct 6 follow Watlington signs. Right at T-junct, 2nd right to Cuxham. Pub in 1m on right, just past Cuxham sign*

New owners Andrew Hill and Eilidh Ferguson have taken over this 16th-century thatched village pub, handy for the M40, Oxford and Henley-On-Thames. There's a large beer garden (children and dogs welcome) and a thriving vegetable patch. Andrew, the chef, likes to use as much of an animal as possible, so you'll find dishes like duck hearts on toast, or ox tongue with confit carrot and salsa verde on the twice daily changing blackboard menu.

Open 12–2.30 5.30–11 Closed: Sun eve **Bar Meals** L served all week 12–2 (Sun 12–3) D served all week 6–9 Av main course £12.50 **Restaurant** L served all week 12–2 (Sun 12–3) D served all week 6–9 Av 3 course à la carte £23.50 Brakspear Brakspear Ordinary, 4 Seasonals. 🍷 10 **Facilities** Garden Dogs allowed Parking

DEDDINGTON MAP 11 SP4

Pick of the Pubs

Deddington Arms ★★★ HL 🍷

Horsefair OX15 0SH ☎ 01869 338364 📠 01869 337010

e-mail: deddarms@oxfordshire-hotels.co.uk

dir: *M40 junct 11 to Banbury. Follow signs for hospital, then towards Adderbury & Deddington, on A4260*

This historic old coaching inn has been welcoming travellers since the 16th century. It overlooks the picturesque market square in Deddington, one of the gateways to the Cotswolds, and offers innovative, freshly prepared food served in friendly surroundings. Good quality ales and an international wine list add to the experience. Settle in the oak beamed bar with its flagstone floors and cosy fireplace for a bar snack, or move to the elegant restaurant where a meal might begin with pan-fried pigeon breast with apple fritters and Irish cider jus, followed by roasted rump of lamb with basil mash, puy lentils and paysanne vegetables. A tempting dessert menu might offer espresso ice cream parfait with bitter chocolate sorbet, and there's also an enticing selection of traditional cheeses. Accommodation includes 27 en suite bedrooms with cottage suites and four-poster luxury.

Open 11–12 (Fri–Sat 11am–1am) **Bar Meals** L served all week 12–2 D served all week 6.30–9 Av main course £9.50 **Restaurant** L served all week 12–2 D served all week 6.30–10 (Sun 7–9) Av 3 course à la carte £27.50 Free House Tetleys Bitter, Green King IPA, Deuchar & Guest Ale. 🍷 8 **Facilities** Parking **Rooms** 27 bedrooms en suite S£90 D£99

The Unicorn 🍷

Market Place OX15 0SE ☎ 01869 338838 📠 01869 3385

e-mail: carol@putland.com

dir: *6m S of Banbury on A4260*

Exposed beams and an open fire characterise the bar of this 17th-century coaching inn, and for warmer days, there's a walled secret garden. Back indoors there are two restaurants and a snug. Fish dish are offered from a daily blackboard (fresh grilled sardines; whole baked sea bream stuffed with butter, lemon & fresh herbs), while th seasonal menu might include pot roasted pheasant, or lamb rump w aubergine fritters.

Open 12–11 (Fri–Sat 12–12) **Bar Meals** L served all week 12–2.30 (Sun 12–3) D served 6.30–9 (except Sun winter) **Restaurant** L served all week 12–2.30 (Sun 12–3) D served Mon–Sat 6–9.30 (except Sun winter) Av 3 course à la carte £19 Hook Norton, Fullers London Pride. 🍷 8 **Facilities** Garden

The Bull Inn

his fine 16th-century coaching inn with a smart stone exterior presides over the main street of harlbury (named Sheep Street – which gives an indication of the agricultural preoccupations at once held sway in these parts), a beautifully preserved Cotswold town surrounded by lovely untryside.

espite the proximity to the great itdoors, the inn is also close to oodstock and only 15 minutes om Oxford by train to Charlbury ation. The interior is full of period aracter, with exposed beams and glenook fireplaces, where log fires ırn in cooler weather. There's a aditional bar with wooden floors d a tastefully furnished lounge d dining room. Outside, the vine-vered terrace is a delightful spot sit and enjoy a drink or a meal summer weather. Food is served both the bar and restaurant, with tions ranging from lunchtime guettes in the bar, to more serious tions. Diners might like to start th roasted Tuscan red peppers ed with ratatouille, topped with chamel sauce and breadcrumbs, or perhaps home-made chicken liver paté on hot toast. Main courses range from such classic English fare as beef and Hook Norton ale pie with a puff pastry lid, to a more Mediterranean porcini stuffed ravioli with red pesto cream and parmesan. Pork Napoleon, chicken Napoli and a seafood pie bursting with cod, hoki, char and prawn, make further appetising options. Sunday lunch options are equally diverse, with rare roast sirloin of beef with home-made Yorkshire pudding offered alongside a vegetarian-friendly spinach and ricotta tortellini with fresh parmesan.

🍷
MAP 11 SP31
Sheep St OX7 3RR
☎ 01608 810689
e-mail: info@bullinn-charlbury.com
dir: *1.5m after Woodstock left on B4437 to Charlbury*

Open 11.30–2.30 6–11
Bar Meals L served Tue–Sun 12–2 D served Tue–Sat 7–9 Av main course £10.50
Restaurant L served Tue–Sun 12–2 D served Tue–Sat 7–9 (Sun 12–2.30) Av 3 course à la carte £25
Free House
Hook Norton Bitter, Brakspear Special, Stella Artois, Carling & Guest Ales. 🍷 8
Facilities Garden Parking

The Fox and Hounds

Renovations in recent years have transformed this charming 500-year-old inn into a stylish dining pub with an immaculate interior, a large restaurant complete with open-plan kitchen, and four cosy bar areas.

Run by Kieron Daniels, owner of the successful Three Tuns in Henley, the pub has a changing selection of special and seasonal beers and an imaginative menu that places a clear emphasis on quality ingredients, local where possible. If you have special dietary requirements, you are encouraged to ask for your meal to be adapted, and smaller portions are available for children. The lunch menu includes sandwiches (perhaps Welsh rarebit; Scottish smoked salmon with cucumber and cream cheese; or Woods Farm gammon with melted cheddar and a leaf salad), and excellent value hot dishes, many of which are available in two portion sizes. Typical choices include roast red onion, oven-dried tomato, butternut, rocket and three cheese tart; confit of Wood's Farm belly pork with barbeque sweet potatoes, green beans and orange gravy; and 'lunch for a fiver' deals such as Angus beef and celeriac hash with a fried free-range egg and walnut mustard. From the evening menu, choose starters such as chicken liver parfait with red onion marmalade and toast; or roast beetroot with green bean, parmesan, salsa verde and rocket salad. Follow with roast local partridge with colcannon and rosemary gravy; wild sea bass with winter vegetable minestrone and salsa verde; or Aberdeen Angus rib-eye steak with sautéed potatoes, roast vine tomatoes, Spanish onion and parsley butter. If you have room, the decadent desserts include rhubarb parfait; apricot and almond tart with Jersey cream; and panettone bread and butter pudding with vanilla custard.

🍷
MAP 05 SU79
OX49 5HL
☎ 01491 612599
e-mail:
kiran.daniels@btconnect.com
dir: *M40 junct 5, 2.5m to Christmas Common (on road towards Henley)*

Open 12-3 5.30-11 Closed: 25 Dec, 31 Dec eve
Bar Meals L served all week 12-2.30 D served all week 7-9.30
Restaurant L served all week 12-2.30 D served all week 7-9.30
Av 3 course à la carte £25 Av 1 course fixed price £5
Brakspear
Brakspear Bitter, Special & seasonal beers. 🍷 14
Facilities Garden Dogs allowed Parking

England

›ORCHESTER (ON THAMES) MAP 05 SU59

leur De Lys

High St OX10 7HH ☎ 01865 340502 📠 01865 340502
·mail: mail@fleurdorchester.co.uk

vely old pub in the High Street, with much character inside and out. ıas a cosy bar and dining room, and a pretty garden.

›en 11–11 (Sun 12–10.30) Closed: Winter 3–6 **Bar Meals** L served week 12–2 D served all week 6.30–9.30 Av main course £9.95 **·staurant** L served all week 12–2 D served all week 6.30–9.30 Av 3 course ı carte £22.50 Av 3 course fixed price £15 Free House Carsberg, nams, Brakspear, Hooky. 8 **Facilities** Garden Dogs allowed ·king **Rooms** 5 bedrooms en suite S£45 D£55

Pick of the Pubs

The George ★★★ HL

25 High St OX10 7HH
☎ 01865 340404 📠 01865 341620
e-mail: thegeorgehotel@fsmail.net
dir: *From M40 junct 7, A329 S to A4074 at Shillingford. Follow Dorchester signs. From M4 junct 13, A34 to Abingdon then A415 E to Dorchester*

DH Lawrence was a frequent visitor to this 15th-century coaching nn, believed to be one of the oldest public houses in Britain. The George, now under new management, stands at the centre of the picturesque village of Dorchester. Inside, oak beams and nglenook fireplaces help to create a welcoming atmosphere, while outside there is an attractive garden. The Potboys bar is a raditional taproom – just the spot to enjoy a pint of Brakspear while tucking into steak and Guinness pie; vegetable curry, or goats' cheese and pesto roasted peppers. The Carriages restaurant, with its secret garden, serves a full menu with, for example, chicken and wild mushroom terrine, or spiced sausage, black pudding and poached egg salad as starters. Main courses might be sea bass and mushroom risotto; pan-seared tuna steak, or tian of roast vegetables with rocket pesto.

Open 11–11 (Sun 12–10.30) Closed: 25 Dec & 1 Jan **Bar Meals** L served all week 12–2.30 D served all week 6.30–9.30 (Sun 6.30–10) **Restaurant** L served all week 12–2.30 D served all week 6.30–9.30 (Fri–Sat 6.30–10) Av 3 course à la carte £25 Brakspear & Wadworth 6X. **Facilities** Garden Parking **Rooms** 17 bedrooms en suite S£80 D£95

Pick of the Pubs

The White Hart ★★★ HL

High St OX10 7HN ☎ 01865 340074 📠 01865 341082
e-mail: whitehart@oxfordshire-hotels.co.uk
dir: *A4074 5m from M40 junct 7/ A329 to Wallingford*

The White Hart is located eight miles south of Oxford right at the centre of the High Street in the historic village of Dorchester-on-Thames. The inn has been providing hospitality to travellers for around 400 years, and the bars attract locals, residents and diners alike. Log fires and candlelight create an intimate atmosphere for the enjoyment of innovative dishes prepared from fresh ingredients. A good-value fixed-price lunch is available Monday to Saturday, with a choice of three starters, mains and desserts; perhaps Caesar salad, seared salmon on pomme purée and pepper coulis, and raspberry meringue tart with berry compote. The carte menu doubles your choice and includes imaginative dishes such as home-made gravadlax with dill, sweet potato salad and lemon oil, followed by glazed suckling pig with rosemary and apricots, dauphnoise potato and port sauce.

Open 11–11 **Bar Meals** L served all week 12–2.30 D served all week 6.30–9.30 **Restaurant** L served all week 12–2.30 D served all week 6.30–9.30 Free House Greene King, Marstons Pedigree, St Austell Tribute, Deuchars Caledeonian IPA. 12 **Facilities** Parking **Rooms** 28 bedrooms en suite D£60

EAST HENDRED MAP 05 SU48

The Wheatsheaf

Chapel Square OX12 8JN
☎ 01235 833229 📠 01235 821521
e-mail: info@thewheatsheaf.org.uk
dir: *2m from A34 Milton interchange*

In a pretty village close to the Ridgeway path, this 16th-century pub was formerly used as a courthouse. Spit-roasts and barbecues are popular summer features of the attractive front garden, which overlooks the village. In the bar and restaurant you'll find specials boards and a single menu that changes every month. Expect mushroom and pumpkin risotto, truffle oil and parmesan shavings; poached salmon, tarragon and white wine sauce with new potatoes; or belly of pork with bok-choi, apple and cider gravy and mashed potato.

Open 11.30–3 6–11 (Sat, Sun, BHs all day) **Bar Meals** L served all week 12–2.30 D served Mon–Sun 6.30–9 Av main course £7.95 **Restaurant** L served all week 12–2 (Sun 12–2.30) D served Mon–Sun 6.30–9.30 Av 3 course à la carte £23 Greene King IPA, Budvar, plus 2 Guest ales. 8 **Facilities** Garden Dogs allowed Parking

England

FARINGDON MAP 05 SU29

Pick of the Pubs

The Lamb at Buckland

Lamb Ln, Buckland SN7 8QN
☎ 01367 870484 01367 870675
e-mail: enquiries@thelambatbuckland.co.uk
dir: *Just off A420 3m E of Faringdon*

The 18th-century Lamb displays a fair few appropriately ovine artefacts. It has a village location on the fringe of the Cotswolds in the Vale of the White Horse and is renowned for its excellent food. A reliable menu, supplemented by daily specials, offers the likes of veal kidneys sautéed with shallots, smoked bacon, fresh herbs and mushrooms; and breast of Gressingham duck, roasted pink and served with apple and Calvados sauce. Items from the specials board might include brace of roast teal with sage and onion stuffing, or medallions of Scotch beef fillet with wild mushroom sauce. Friday night is fish night – a piscatorial extravaganza – with dishes like cullen skink, home-smoked sprats, monkfish and prawn ragout, and seared fillet of wild sea bass served with shrimp and saffron risotto. Special event catering is a speciality at the Lamb, for weddings, private parties and business lunches.

Open 10.30–3 5.30–11 Closed: 24 Dec–7 Jan **Bar Meals** L served Tue–Sun 12–2 D served Tue–Sat 6.30–9.30 Av main course £12 **Restaurant** L served Tue–Sun 12–2 (Sun 12–3) D served Tue–Sat 6.30–9.30 Av 3 course à la carte £25 Free House Hook Norton, Adnams Broadside, Arkells 3Bs. 12 **Facilities** Garden Parking

Pick of the Pubs

The Trout at Tadpole Bridge

Buckland Marsh SN7 8RF ☎ 01367 870382
e-mail: info@trout-inn.co.uk
dir: *Off A420 signed Bampton, pub 2m*

New owners took over this 17th-century pub in 2006, and then gave the whole place a thorough makeover. Lying deep in the countryside on the banks of the Thames, it was first a coal storage house, then cottages, before becoming an inn towards the end of the 19th century. If you just want a decent pint and a simple snack, you'll be as warmly welcomed as if you had chosen to dine more formally. Links with local growers, shoots and other suppliers have been extended, while fish comes daily from South Coast ports. From the seasonal menu or daily specials board a typical meal might be smoked haddock fishcake with lightly poached egg, hollandaise sauce and crispy pancetta, followed by fillet of venison with butter bean potato cake and spiced pear chutney, then crème brûlée with roasted bananas. The balanced wine list includes some great examples from the world's top vineyards.

Open 11.30–3 6–11 Closed: 25–31 Dec, 1 Jan & 1st wk in Feb **Bar Meals** L served all week 12–2 D served Mon–Sat 7–9 Av main course £13.50 **Restaurant** L served all week 12–2 D served Mon–Sat 7–9 Av 3 course à la carte £28 Free House Ramsbury Bitter, Youngs PA Bitter, Butts Barbus, West Berkshire Brewery Mr Chubbs Lunchtime Bitter. 10 **Facilities** Garden Dogs allowed Parking

FIFIELD MAP 10 SP2

Merrymouth Inn

Stow Rd OX7 6HR ☎ 01993 831652 01993 830840
e-mail: tim@merrymouthinn.fsnet.co.uk
web: www.hotelinthecotswolds.co.uk
dir: *On A424 between Burford & Stow-on-the-Wold*

A beautifully restored Cotswold inn dating back to the 13th century. At that time it was owned by the monks of nearby Bruern Abbey, to which hitherto undiscovered underground passages are said to lead. A blackboard of fresh fish, vegetarian and other daily specials include such dishes as a warm salad of scallops and bacon and gilt head sea bream with fennel and tomato. Home-made puddings include raspberry marshmallow meringue.

Open 12–2.30 6–10.30 **Bar Meals** L served all week 12–2 D served all week 6.30–9 (Sun 7–8.30) Av main course £10 **Restaurant** L served all week 12–2 D served all week 6.30–9 (Sun 7–9) Av 3 course à la carte £21 Free House Hook Norton Best Bitter, Adnams Broadside. 7 **Facilities** Garden Dogs allowed Parking

The White Lion

Jp in the Chilterns, in the hamlet of Crays Pond, stands the popular 250-year-old White Lion. nearby field is the home of the annual Woodcote Rally, the third largest steam, vintage and eteran transport fair in England.

.s you might expect, while 's on, the pub acts as the rganisers' unofficial headquarters. hotographs taken at rallies uring the last 40 or so years line ie deep terracotta walls. Also orth a browse is the collection f fascinating old menus from imous restaurants around the vorld. The beamed ceilings are ow, so be prepared to stoop. For everal reasons, the food is of a high tandard: partly through working losely with local producers, partly ecause each dish is prepared o order, and partly because the ienu is changed daily. New rench managers for 2007, Magali lagnein and Loïc Genestier, have rought a gastropub atmosphere nd thoroughly French menus vith them. From a daily choice of around eight starters and main courses, supplemented by some specials, you might find crab salad with asparagus and coriander and tomato mayonnaise; scallops with creamy lemon and coriander sauce; pork and prune terrine; half lobster casserole with baby vegetables and saffron jus; and fillet steak with wild mushrooms and red wine sauce. Desserts are likely to include warm gooey chocolate with coffee ice cream, and crème brûlée. A selection of farmhouse cheeses is kept in peak condition. There is always a good choice of Devon fish and seafood on the menu, and everything that is served is home made. The view from outside extends across the Thames Valley.

🍷
MAP 05 SU68
Goring Rd, Goring Heath
RG8 7SH
☎ 01491 680471
📠 01491 684254
e-mail: reservations@thewhitelioncrayspond.com
dir: *From M4 junct 11 follow signs to Pangbourne, through toll bridge to Whitchurch. N for 3m into Crays Pond*

Open 10-3 6-11 (Closed Sun eve, Mon) Closed: 25-26 Dec, 1 Jan
Bar Meals L served Tue-Sun 12-2 D served Tue-Sat 6.30-9 Av main course £13.95
Restaurant L served Tue-Sun 12-2 D served Tue-Sat 6.30-9 Av 3 course à la carte £28.40
Greene King
IPA, Abbot Ale, Guinness, Fosters. 🍷 11
Facilities Garden Dogs allowed Parking Play Area

CUMNOR - OXFORDSHIRE

Bear & Ragged Staff

Walk information

Distance: 6 miles (9.7km)
Map: OS Explorer 180 Oxford
Start/finish: parking spaces by village hall, Cumnor; grid ref SP 458044
Ascent/gradient: negligible
Paths: field paths, quiet lanes and tracks; 1 stile
Landscape: fields and pasture beside the River Thames

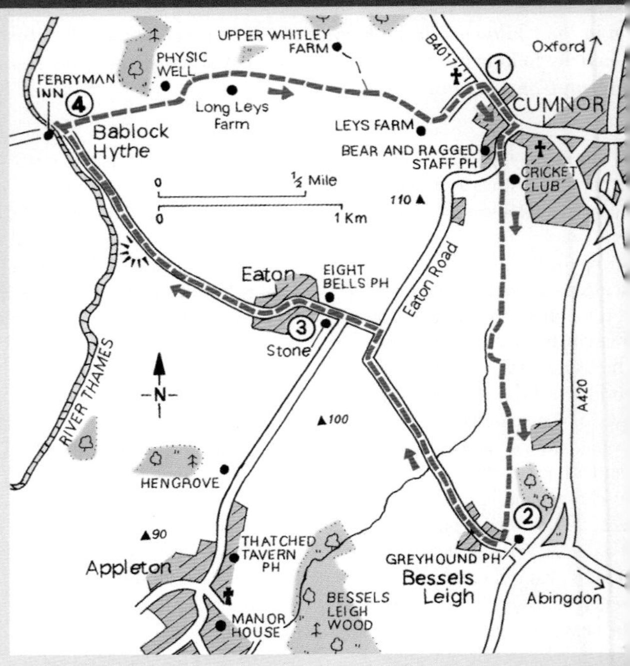

Walk directions

A Turn right from the parking area and walk along to the mini-roundabout. Turn right into Appleton Road and pass the Bear and Ragged Staff pub on the right. Veer half-left just a few paces beyond it and join a footpath signposted to Bessels Leigh. Pass the cricket club on the left and continue on the track. When it peters out continue ahead in the field, keeping a ditch on your right. Pass along a line of trees on the far side of the field, turn left, then turn right and make for an opening in the corner (may be concealed by vegetation in summer). Go straight on to a galvanised gate and keep some houses over to the left, beyond the pasture. Cross a footbridge to a galvanised gate, swing left and cross the field towards the road. Keep in line with telephone wires and make for a waymark in the field corner. Follow the drive to the road.

B Turn right to follow the road through Bessels Leigh and continue out in the countryside, cutting between farmland. On reaching a junction, keep left to the next junction. Go straight on into the village of Eaton and pass the Eight Bells pub.

C Follow the lane out of Eaton and through flat countryside. When it becomes enclosed by trees, look for a view of the Thames on the left. Continue to Bablock Hythe and look across the river to the Ferryman Inn. Walk back along the lane for a few paces and turn left at the bridleway signposted 'Cumnor'.

D Pass through a gate and when, some time later, the path curves to the left, look for the Physic Well in the trees to the left of your route. This is a muddy spring which was once greatly valued as a source of healing waters. Emerge from the trees and cut between fields towards pylons. Go through a gate, join a drive and walk ahead. Ignore the turning to Upper Whitley Farm and continue into Cumnor, passing Leys Farm on the right. Look for the United Reformed church and return to the village hall and the Bear and Ragged Staff.

While there

Pause and savour the peace and tranquillity of Bablock Hythe. The 19th-century poet Matthew Arnold knew this place well and made references to Bablock Hythe and the surrounding countryside in his work. It was his 'Scholar Gipsy' who 'oft was met crossin the stripling Thames at Bablock-hythe.' The Romans crossed the river here, and a ferry has operated for more than 1,000 year

Look for

As you enter Eaton by road from Bessels Leigh, look for a memorial stone by the entrance to West Farm. The stone recalls tha the trees here were given by staff and friend of A Howard Cornish MBE JP (1895–1964), County Alderman and lifelong farmer here.

ILKINS MAP 05 SP20

he Five Alls

L7 3JQ ☎ 01367 860306
-mail: info@thefivealls.co.uk
ir: *A40 exit Burford, Filkins 4m, A361 to Lechlade*

1 18th-century inn in a peaceful village on the edge of the Cotswolds. ne interior is all bare wood floors, terracotta walls and rustic furniture, th the odd leather sofa thrown in for good measure. Home-made re ranges from steak and chips to lobster with spaghetti in tomato nd cream sauce. Sandwiches and omelettes are also available at nch. The lawned garden has an over-sized chess set, quoits and a atio for summer snacks.

pen 11-3 5.30-11 (Sat-Sun all day) **Bar Meals** L served all week 12-30 D served all week 6.30-9 (Sun 12-7) **Restaurant** L served all week -2.30 D served all week 6.30-9 (Sun 12-7) Brakspear Brakspear tter, Special & Wychwood, Seasonal Ales. 8 **Facilities** Garden Dogs owed Parking

'RINGFORD MAP 11 SP62

'he Butchers Arms

X27 8EB ☎ 01869 277363
ir: *4m from Bicester on A4421 towards Buckingham*

ora Thompson mentioned this traditional village pub in her 1939 ovel *Lark Rise to Candleford* about life on the Northamptonshire/ xfordshire border. A good selection of fresh fish and other seafood, cluding mussels, crab and king prawns, is offered, as well as liver, acon and onions, peppered fillet steak, half a roast duck, and steak nd kidney pie. Pumps display Adnams Broadside and Marston's edigree labels. From the patio watch the cricket during the summer.

Open 12-1.30am **Bar Meals** L served all week 12-9.30 D served all week 12-9.30 Av main course £9.95 **Restaurant** L served all week 12-9.30 D served all week 12-9.30 (Sun 12-4) Av 3 course à la carte £25 Punch Taverns Deuchars IPA, Interbrew Bass, Marstons Pedigree, Adnams Broadside. **Facilities** Garden Dogs allowed Parking

FYFIELD MAP 05 SU49

Pick of the Pubs

The White Hart

Main Rd OX13 5LW ☎ 01865 390585
e-mail: info@whitehart-fyfield.com
dir: *6m S of Oxford just off A420*

See Pick of the Pubs on page 448

GORING MAP 05 SU68

Miller of Mansfield

High St RG8 9AW ☎ 01491 872829 01491 873100
e-mail: reservations@millerofmansfield.com
dir: *From Pangbourne take A329 to Streatley. Right on B4009, 0.5m to Goring*

This beautiful old building has been completely renovated. There is a full bar menu and a restaurant open for breakfast, lunch and dinner 365 days a year. Modern European menus might offer roast loin of venison or grilled fillet of sea bass in the restaurant, and fish and chips or steak sandwich in the bar. There is a marble paved area in the garden with plants and statues under a canopy with gas heating.

Open 8-11 **Bar Meals** L served Mon-Sat 11-10 (Sun 12-4) D served all week 11-10 (Sun 6.30-9.30) Av main course £11.95 **Restaurant** L served all week 12-3 D served all week 6-10 Av 3 course à la carte £22 Free House Good Old Boy, Rebellion IPA, Organic Jester. 15 **Facilities** Garden Dogs allowed Parking

The White Hart

It might not give too much away from the outside, but the interior of this former chantry house is breathtaking. It was built in 1442 to house two priests and five almsmen (poor men) whose sole duty was to pray for the soul of the lord of the manor, the chapel's founder.

Among the many original features is a tunnel – probably an escape route for priests during the Dissolution of the Monasteries – that runs from the corner of the bar to the manor house. In the cosy, low-ceilinged bar, centre stage is taken by a large inglenook fireplace, while in stark contrast is the main restaurant, a grand hall of a place with soaring eaves and beams, huge stone-flanked window surrounds and flagstone floors, overlooked by a minstrel's gallery. Menus change daily, depending on what is seasonal and available. Given that Mark and Kay Chandler are self-confessed 'passionate foodies', they know where everything comes from, and how it has been treated, and they make everything themselves, including bread and pasta with locally milled flour, cure their own gravadlax, and grow some of their own herbs, fruit and vegetables. Apart from starters that include carpaccio of tuna with niçoise salad, and fennel soup with baby clams, there are antipasti, mezze and fish sharing-boards for two. Typical main courses include pan-fried duck breast with rhubarb sauce and sweet potato fondant; Cape-style seafood curry with turmeric rice; and gnocchi with chilli-roasted pumpkin, nutmeg and sage butter. Don't ignore the good dessert list and wide-ranging wine list. Regular themed food evenings – French, Italian and seafood, for example – are popular. Two beer festivals are held every year (May Day and August bank holiday weekends) with at least 12 real ales, live jazz and hog roasts.

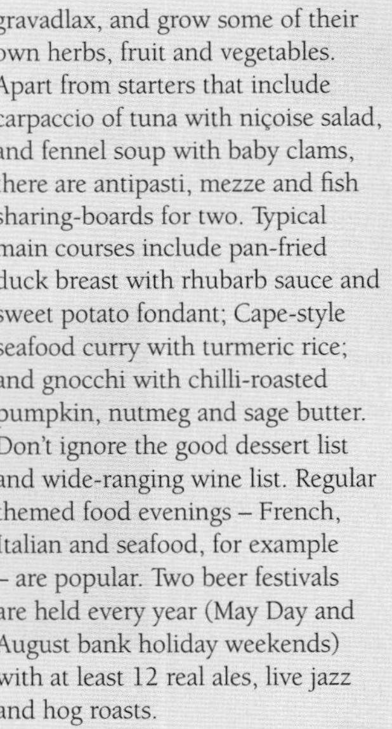

MAP 05 SU49
Main Rd OX13 5LW
☎ 01865 390585
e-mail:
info@whitehart-fyfield.com
dir: *6m S of Oxford just off A420*

Open 12-3 6-11 (Summer: Sat 11.30-11, Sun 12-10.30)
Bar Meals L served all week 12-2.30 D served Mon-Sat 6.30-9.30 (Sun 12-4) Av main course £13
Restaurant L served all week 12-2.30 D served Mon-Sat 6.30-9.30 (Sun 12-4) Av 3 course à la carte £26 Av 2 course fixed price £13.95
Free House
White Horse Ale, Carling, Old Hooky, Village Idiot & Guest Ales. 🍷 10
Facilities Garden Parking Play Area

England

GREAT TEW MAP 11 SP42

Pick of the Pubs

The Falkland Arms

OX7 4DB ☎ 01608 683653 01608 683656
e-mail: sjcourage@btconnect.com
dir: *Off A361, 1.25m, signed Great Tew*

This 500-year-old inn takes its name from Lucius Carey, 2nd Viscount Falkland, who inherited the manor of Great Tew in 1629. Nestling at the end of a charming row of Cotswold stone cottages, the Falkland Arms is a classic: flagstone floors, high-backed settles and an inglenook fireplace characterise the intimate bar, where a huge collection of beer and cider mugs hangs from the ceiling. Home-made specials such as beef and ale pie or salmon and broccoli fishcakes supplement the basic lunchtime menu, served in the bar or the pub garden. In the evening, booking is essential for dinner in the small dining room. Expect parsnip soup or grilled goats' cheese salad, followed by chicken breast with bacon and mushrooms in shallot sauce; salmon and prawns with lemon and dill sauce; or mushroom and herb stroganoff.

Open 11.30–2.30 6–11 (Sat 11.30–3, Sun 12–3, 7–10.30) Rest: 25–26 Dec & 1 Jan closed eve **Bar Meals** L served all week 12–2 Av main course £8 **Restaurant** L served all week 12–2 D served Mon–Sat 7–8 Av 3 course à la carte £20 Wadworth Wadworth 6X & Henry's IPA & Guest ales. 12 **Facilities** Garden Dogs allowed

HAILEY MAP 11 SP31

Bird in Hand

Whiteoak Green OX29 9XP
☎ 01993 868321 01993 868702
e-mail: welcome@birdinhandinn.co.uk
dir: *From Witney N onto B4022 through Hailey to Whiteoak Green for 5m. From Charlbury S onto B4022 for 5m*

Classic Cotswold stone inn set in the Oxfordshire countryside just outside the village of Hailey. Grade II listed dating from the 16th century, with a beamed interior and huge inglenook fireplaces. Log fires provide a warm welcome in winter. A popular choice from the carte might be Poffley End chicken with stilton and apricots, beef Wellington with roast parsnips, or steak and ale pie with sweet potato mash and baby spinach. Monthly themed special events.

Open 11–11 **Bar Meals** L served all week 12–3 D served Mon–Thur 6–9, Fri–Sat 6–10, Sun 12–6 Av main course £12 **Restaurant** L served all week 12–3 D served all week 6–9 (Fri–Sat 6–10, Sun 12–6) Av 3 course à la carte £25 Heavitree Old Speckled Hen, Brakspear, Hobgoblin & Old Hooky. 8 **Facilities** Garden Parking

HENLEY-ON-THAMES MAP 05 SU78

Pick of the Pubs

The Cherry Tree Inn ★★★★ RR

Stoke Row RG9 5QA
☎ 01491 680430 01491 682168
e-mail: info@thecherrytreeinn.com
dir: *B481 towards Reading & Sonning Common 2m, follow Stoke Row sign*

There's a confident blend of ancient and modern inside this 400-year-old listed building. Originally three flint cottages, the Cherry Tree has been comprehensively re-fitted, mixing the original flagstone floors, beamed ceilings and fireplaces with contemporary décor, strong colours and comfortable modern

CONTINUED

England

HENLEY-ON-THAMES continued

furnishings. The contemporary theme continues throughout the pub, which offers Brakspear real ales, fine malt whiskies and over 40 different wines, including 12 served by the glass. Service is informal, with a variety of classic European dishes prepared from fresh local ingredients. Lunchtime choices include grilled focaccia with goats' cheese, peppers and pesto; as well as more substantial dishes like belly of pork with black pudding and creamy mash. À la carte options range from chargrilled rib-eye steak, to grilled squid and chorizo salad. Outside, the large south-facing garden is perfect for alfresco summer dining.

Open 12–11 (Sun 12–10.30) Closed: 25–26 Dec & 1 Jan **Bar Meals** L served all week 12–4 D served all week 7–10 Av main course £10.95 **Restaurant** L served all week 12–3 D served all week 12–10 (Sun 12–4, 7–10) Av 3 course à la carte £25 Brakspear Brakspear Bitter, Brakspear Special, Douvel, Orval. 12 **Facilities** Garden Parking **Rooms** 4 bedrooms en suite D£95

Pick of the Pubs

The Five Horseshoes

Maidensgrove RG9 6EX

01491 641282 01491 641086

e-mail: admin@thefivehorseshoes.co.uk

dir: *From Henley-on-Thames A4130, after 1m B480 to right, signed Stonor. Left through woods, over common, pub on left*

See Pick of the Pubs on opposite page

The Golden Ball

Lower Assendon RG9 6AH

01491 574157 01491 574157

e-mail: thegoldenball@tiscali.co.uk

dir: *A4130 from Henley-on-Thames, right onto B480, pub 300yds on left*

Traditional country pub in the Chiltern Valley a mile from Henley-on-Thames. It is a listed brick and flint building, originally two 17th-century cottages. Dick Turpin frequented the place and hid from capture in a recess by the chimney upstairs. There's a large car park and a south facing beer garden for fine weather, while log fires keep things cosy in winter. Food includes sandwiches, pies, butcher's sausage of the day, and Brakspear beer-battered haddock.

Open 11–3 6–11 (Sun 7–10.30) **Bar Meals** L served all week 12–2.30 D served all week 6.30–9.30 Brakspear Brakspear Ordinary, Season Special. 11 **Facilities** Children's licence Garden Dogs allowed Parking Play Area

Pick of the Pubs

Three Tuns Foodhouse

5 The Market Place RG9 2AA 01491 573260

e-mail: thefoodhouse@aol.co.uk

dir: *In front of town hall*

Centuries-old hostelry and one of Oxfordshire's more distinctive pubs, the Three Tuns Foodhouse began life as a gallows mortuary where bodies were brought after public execution. The coffin drop lies behind what is now the bar. These days, the inn is an altogether different place, with the décor an eclectic mix of art deco, Chinese and 1950s and '60s retro furniture. There is also a courtyard garden covered by an old wisteria, and a bar decorated with a zinc bar, cow parsley wallpaper and a collection of rare French bedside clocks. Chef Michael Jones is responsible for the modern British cuisine in the restaurant and ensures the use of seasonal and local produce in the daily changing menu. Ingredients are sourced from local farms and markets, as well as Billingsgate, Borough and Smithfield markets. The tempting menu is characterised by confit Gressingham duck leg, whole lemon sole, and braised local rabbit.

Open 12–3 5.30–11 **Bar Meals** L served all week D served all week **Restaurant** L served all week 12–2.30 D served all week 6–10 Brakspear, Hoegaarden. 8 **Facilities** Garden Dogs allowed Parking

Pick of the Pubs

WhiteHartNettlebed ★★★ HL

High St, Nettlebed RG9 5DD

01491 641245 01491 649018

e-mail: info@whitehartnettlebed.com

dir: *On A4130 between Henley-on-Thames & Wallingford*

See Pick of the Pubs on page 452

The Five Horseshoes

his 17th-century pub prides itself on its traditional atmosphere with old pub games, log fires, ɛavy beams and brass and wrought iron features. The Five Horseshoes is located in an area of ıtstanding natural beauty, and its two gardens offer stunning views over the Chiltern Hills.

ıne of the gardens has a barbecue here hog roasts are held in ımmer; the other is available r bookings with a marquee for ecial occasions. Inside is a large staurant and two snug bar areas. akspear Ordinary, Special and asonal ales are served alongside ıe wines, with a good choice by e glass. There is a separate bar enu and "Room with a View" enu: from the former you can oose a light meal like potted ɔrnish crab; Barbary duck terrine; d wild mushroom risotto. Five ɔrseshoes classics include pork e, bangers and mash, and burger th suitable accompaniments. om the restaurant menu there ight be chicken liver parfait to start, roasted fillet of sea bream, and dark chocolate mousse. Hikers and mountain bikers are welcome, but are asked to leave muddy boots at the door. Dogs are permitted in the gardens and bar.

MAP 05 SU78
Maidensgrove RG9 6EX
☎ 01491 641282
01491 641086
e-mail:
admin@thefivehorseshoes.co.uk
dir: *From Henley-on-Thames take A4130, after 1m B480 to right, signed Stonor. Left through woods, over common, pub on left*

Open 12–3.30 6–11 (Sat 12–11, Sun 12–6)
Bar Meals L served all week 12–2.30 D served all week 6.30–9.30 (Sat 12–3, Sun 12–4) Av main course £8.50
Restaurant L served all week 12–2.30 D served all week 6.30–9.30 (Sat 12–3, Sun 12–4) Av 3 course à la carte £25
Brakspear
Brakspear Ordinary, Special & Seasonal. 9
Facilities Garden Dogs allowed Parking

WhiteHartNettlebed

Both Royalist and parliamentary soldiers made a habit of lodging in local taverns where possibl during the English Civil War, and this 15th-century inn was one such billeting house for troops loyal to the king.

During the 17th and 18th-century, the area was plagued by highwaymen, including the notorious Isaac Darkin, who was eventually caught, tried and hung at Oxford Gaol. These days, the beautifully restored hotel is favoured by a stylish crowd who appreciate the chic bar, restaurant and bistro, not to mention the welcoming atmosphere. Dining styles vary from doorstop Brakspear ham and whole grain mustard sandwiches in the bar, to an inviting à la carte restaurant menu. You could begin with rolled braised pigs' trotters with warm potato salad; or seared scallops with lobster sausages; and move on to local wood pigeon and foie gras with fondant potatoes and Sauternes juice; or provençal polenta tian, glazed goats' cheese and roast garlic. Keep an eye out for blackboard specials: the catch of the day could be gilthead bream with mussel ragout and Pernod jus; or sea bass fillet with crushed new potatoes. A lengthy wine list includes some extravagant options, or you could visit for afternoon tea and the delights of home-made muffins, scones and an excellent array of teas. Weddings, meetings and parties can be hosted, with the option of using the elegant red and orange rooms. Twelve luxurious en-suite bedrooms are named and decorated after different flavours: sample Blackcurrant, Caramel or Pistachio, each of which has an accompanying recipe.

★★★ HL ⇨ 🍷
MAP 05 SU78
High St, Nettlebed RG9 5DD
☎ 01491 641245
🖷 01491 649018
e-mail:
info@whitehartnettlebed.com
dir: *On A4130 between Henley-on-Thames & Wallingford*

Open 7am–11
Bar Meals L served all week 12–2.30 D served all week 6–10 (Sun 12–4)
Restaurant L served all week 12–2.30 D served all week 6–10 (Sun 12–4)
Brakspear, Guinness, & Strongbow. 🍷 12
Facilities Garden Parking Play Area
Rooms 12 bedrooms en suite S£85 D£95

IOOK NORTON MAP 11 SP33

Pick of the Pubs

The Gate Hangs High ★★★★ INN

Whichford Rd OX15 5DF
☎ 01608 737387 01608 737870
e-mail: gatehangshigh@aol
dir: *Off A361 SW of Banbury*

A charming country pub in beautiful countryside near the mystical Rollright Stones, and Hook Norton, from whose renowned brewery come its cask-conditioned, dry-hopped ales. The pub is on the old drovers' road from Wales to Banbury; a tollgate that once stood outside was said to hang high enough for small creatures to pass under, although owners of larger beasts had to pay. In the low-beamed bar, polished horse brasses reflect the glow from the candles, pretty wall lights and roaring log fire. The Gate is well known for dishes featuring black pudding; its rôsti version, topped with bacon and poached egg, is one. Also typical are salmon and prawn pie; roasted half-duck with leeks and marmalade; lambs' kidneys, bacon and onion; and fillet steak with stilton and bacon. The blackboard offers daily fish and other specials. Children have their own play area outside; dogs are welcome in the bar.

Open 12-3 6-11 (Sat all day, Sun 12-4, 7-10.30) Closed: 25 Dec Eve **Bar Meals** L served all week 12-2.30 D served all week 6-10 Av main course £8.95 **Restaurant** L served all week 12-2.30 D served all week 6-10 (Sat 12-11, Sun 12-10.30) Av 3 course à la carte £8.95 Av 3 course fixed price £11.50 Hook Norton Hook Norton - Best, Old Hooky, Haymaker & Generation. **Facilities** Garden Dogs allowed Parking **Rooms** 4 bedrooms en suite S£40 D£50

un Inn

igh St OX15 5NH ☎ 01608 737570 01608 737535
·mail: joyce@the-sun-inn.com
:r: *Just off A361*

traditional Cotswold stone inn with oak beams, flagstone floors and ı inglenook fireplace. The tasty bar snacks might include linguini of esh mussels with cream and white wine sauce, or Mexican tortilla raps, alongside the more usual baguettes and jackets. There is a ıily fish menu featuring fresh pacific oysters, perhaps, or red snapper. ıe main menu offers dishes like pan-fried pigeon breast with warm arinated wild mushroom salad and pancetta.

pen 11.30-3 6-11.30 **Bar Meals** L served all week 12-2 D served all eek 7-9.30 Av main course £8.50 **Restaurant** L served all week 12-2 served all week 7-9.30 Av 3 course à la carte £18.50 Hook Norton Hook Norton Best Bitter, Old Double Stout, Hooky Dark, 303 & Twelve ays. 8 **Facilities** Garden Parking

KELMSCOTT MAP 05 SU29

The Plough Inn

GL7 3HG ☎ 01367 253543 01367 252514
e-mail: plough@kelmscottgl7.fsnet.co.uk
dir: *From M4 onto A419 then A361 to Lechlade & A416 to Faringdon, signs to Kelmscot*

The Plough dates from 1631 and is set in the beautiful village of Kelmscott a short walk from Kelmscott Manor, once home to William Morris. The inn is on the Thames Path midway between Radcot and Lechlade, so is a haven for walkers and boaters. Cotswold stone walls and flagstone floors set the scene for real ales and an extensive menu. Dishes include tempura of seafood with sweet chilli sauce, and pot roasted whole partridge.

Open 11-12 (Fri-Sat 11-2am) **Bar Meals** L served all week 12-2.30 D served Mon-Sat 7-9 Av main course £14 **Restaurant** L served all week 12-2.30 D served Mon-Sat 7-9 Free House Hook Norton, Timothy Taylor, Wychwood. **Facilities** Garden Dogs allowed Parking

LEWKNOR MAP 05 SU79

The Leathern Bottel

1 High St OX49 5TW ☎ 01844 351482

Run by the same family for more than 25 years, this 16th-century coaching inn is set in the foothills of the Chilterns. Walkers with dogs, families with children, parties for meals or punters for a quick pint are all made equally welcome. In winter there's a wood-burning stove, a good drop of Brakspears ale, nourishing specials and a quiz on Sunday. Summer is the time for outdoor eating, the children's play area, Pimm's and Morris dancers.

Open 11-3 6-11 Closed: 25-26 Dec **Bar Meals** L served all week 12-2 D served all week 7-9.30 Av main course £7.95 Brakspear Brakspear Ordinary, & Special. 12 **Facilities** Garden Dogs allowed Parking Play Area

England

LOWER SHIPLAKE MAP 05 SU77

The Baskerville Arms ★★★★ INN

Station Rd RG9 3NY ☎ 0118 940 3332 ▤ 0118 940 7235
e-mail: enquiries@thebaskerville.com
dir: *Just off A4155, 1.5m from Henley*

This welcoming pub stands on the popular Thames Path just a few minutes from historic Henley-on-Thames. Brick-built on the outside, modern-rustic inside, it boasts an attractive garden where summer barbecues are a common fixture. Light meals are served in the bar, while the restaurant offers the likes of seared sea bass with shellfish bisque and saffron risotto; and chargrilled rib-eye steak with home-made chips. Booking is essential during Henley Regatta (early July).

Open 11.30–2.30 6–11 (Sun 11.30–2.30, 5.30–11) **Bar Meals** L served all week 12–2 (Sun 12–2.30) D served Mon–Sat 7–9.30 **Restaurant** L served Mon–Sun 12–2 D served Mon–Sat 7–9.30 Av 3 course fixed price £18.50 London Pride, Loddon Hoppit, Bass. 8 **Facilities** Garden Dogs allowed Parking Play Area **Rooms** 5 bedrooms en suite S£45 D£75

See advertisement under HENLEY-ON-THAMES

LOWER WOLVERCOTE MAP 05 SP40

Pick of the Pubs

The Trout Inn

195 Godstow Rd OX2 8PN
☎ 01865 302071 ▤ 01865 302072
dir: *From A40 at Wolvercote rdbt (N of Oxford) through village to pub*

See Pick of the Pubs on opposite page

MARSTON MAP 05 SP50

Victoria Arms

Mill Ln OX3 0PZ ☎ 01865 241382
e-mail: kyffinda@yahoo.co.uk
dir: *From A40 signs to Old Marston, sharp right into Mill Lane, pub in lane 500yds on left*

Friendly country pub situated on the banks of the River Cherwell, occupying the site of the old Marston Ferry that connected the north and south of the city. The old ferryman's bell is still behind the bar. Popular destinations for punters, and fans of TV sleuth Inspector Morse, as the last episode used this as a location. Typical menu includes lamb cobbler, steak and Guinness pie, spicy pasta bake, battered haddock, and ham off the bone.

Open 11.30–11 (Oct–Apr closed afternoons) **Bar Meals** L served all week 12–2.30 D served all week 6–9 (Sun 12–6) Av main course £5.95 Wadworth Henrys IPA, Wadworth 6X, JCB, Guest beers. 15 **Facilities** Garden Dogs allowed Parking

MIDDLETON STONEY MAP 11 SP5

Best Western Jersey Arms Hotel

★★ HL

OX25 4AD ☎ 01869 343234 ▤ 01869 343565
e-mail: jerseyarms@bestwestern.co.uk
dir: *3m from junct 9/10 of M4. 3m from A34 on B430*

This charming family-run free house was built as an ale house in the 13th century, on what used to be the estate of Lord Jersey. The cosy bar offers a good range of popular bar food with the extensive menu supplemented by daily blackboard specials. In the beamed and panelled Livingston's restaurant with its Mediterranean terracotta décor, the cosmopolitan brasserie-style menu features dishes like salad niçoise; spinach and cream cheese pancakes; and duck confit with cherry and cinnamon sauce.

Open 12–11 **Bar Meals** L served all week 12–2.15 D served all week 6.30–9.30 (Sun 6.30–9) Av main course £7.95 **Restaurant** L served all week 12–2.15 D served all week 6.30–9.30 Av 3 course à la carte £22 Free House Interbrew Flower, Bass. **Facilities** Garden Parking **Rooms** 20 bedrooms en suite S£79 D£99

MILTON MAP 11 SP4

The Black Boy Inn NEW

OX15 4HH ☎ 01295 722111
e-mail: info@blackboyinn.com
dir: *From Banbury A4260 to Adderbury, right signed Bloxham. In Milton, pub on right*

The name apparently refers to King Charles II, who was born with an unusually dark complexion. After an extensive programme of refurbishment in 2007, this 16th-century coaching inn is once again thriving as an integral part of the local community. Look out for classic dishes such as Mr Parson's pork and stilton sausages; tomato and basil shepherds' pie; and home-made burger with red onion marmalade.

Open 12–11 (Sun 12–10.30) **Bar Meals** L served Mon–Sat 12–2.30 Av main course £9 **Restaurant** L served all week 12–3 D served Mon–Sat 6.30–9.30 Av 3 course à la carte £20 Merchant Inns Plc Rotating Guest Ales. 8 **Facilities** Garden Dogs allowed Parking Play Area

The Trout Inn

n old riverside inn on the banks of the Isis, as the Thames is known here. It was built around 133 as a hospice to serve Godstow Nunnery, the ruins of which are on the opposite bank. ollowing the Dissolution of the Monasteries, some of the abbey's stones were removed and used rebuild the former hospice as a hostelry.

/ith stone walls, slate roof, leaded indows, great oak beams, flagged oors and ancient fireplaces lways lit in winter), it is arguably xford's most atmospheric inn. atthew Arnold and Lewis Carroll ertainly knew it, as did Colin exter's fictional Inspector Morse. single menu sets out to meet all stes. Start with a prawn cocktail, ish mussels, or maybe breaded at mushrooms. Then deliberate etween a chargrilled steak, or ake fillet in coriander and coconut umb; breaded wholetail scampi ith dressed mixed salad and asoned chips, or minted lamb irger with onion; or maybe beef, ushroom and ale pie. Listed pub classics are lemon and acked pepper glazed chicken; and chargrilled calves' liver and bacon. Freshly cut sandwiches (Gloucestershire ham and Wexford Cheddar; and salt beef with gherkins and English mustard, for example) are served with seasoned chips. A short but perfectly adequate wine list offers examples from Australasia, South America, South Africa, Italy and Spain. Mulled wine is served in winter; Pimm's in summer. A ghost, well known locally as The White Lady, visits the Trout regularly. She is Rosamund, the much-loved mistress of Henry II, who 'embowered' her here. Her feet are never seen, as the floor level is now higher than that of the old hospice. She also knocks bottles off tables and stands behind people in the bar (but never buys her round!).

MAP 05 SP40
195 Godstow Rd OX2 8PN
☎ 01865 302071
01865 302072
dir: *From A40 at Wolvercote rdbt (N of Oxford) through village to pub*

Open 11–11
Bar Meals L served all week
D served all week
Vintage Inns
Bass, Adnams, Stella, Carlsberg & Carling. 20
Facilities Garden Parking

England

MURCOTT MAP 11 SP51

The Nut Tree Inn

Main St OX5 2RE ☎ 01865 331253

dir: *Off B4027 NE of Oxford via Islip & Charlton-on-Moor*

Once three adjoining 15th-century cottages, this thatched inn is full of rustic charm, set in extensive hedged gardens with trees and lawns. Inside there are stripped oak beams, wood-burning stoves and unusual carvings. New owners have introduced new menus: start with pavé of home-smoked Orkney salmon with whipped horseradish cream, followed by roast best end of Oxfordshire lamb with butternut squash purée. The wine list is lengthy and well chosen.

Open 12-3 6.30-11 **Bar Meals** L served Tue-Sat 12-2.30 D served Tue-Thu 7-9 Av main course £9 **Restaurant** L served Tue-Sun 12-2.30 D served Tue-Sat 7-9 Av 3 course à la carte £27 Av 3 course fixed price £15 Free House Hook Norton, Wadworths 6X, Oxfordshire Ales. 10 **Facilities** Garden Dogs allowed Parking

OXFORD MAP 05 SP50

The Anchor NEW

2 Hayfield Rd, Walton Manor OX2 6TT

☎ 01865 510282 01865 510275

dir: *A34 ring road N, exit Peartree rdbt, 1.5m then right at Polstead Rd, follow road to bottom, pub on right*

Following a major refurbishment, the recent reopening of the art deco-styled, fire-warmed Anchor must have been a huge relief for North Oxford's well-heeled, discerning locals. Now very much back on the map for its well-kept ales, carefully chosen wines and good quality seasonal British food, including steak and kidney pudding, mash and greens; smoked haddock fishcakes with home-cut chips and salad; and, for the kids, boiled organic eggs with Marmite soldiers.

Open 11-11 (Sun 12-10.30) Closed: 25 Dec **Bar Meals** L served all week 12-2.30 (Sun 12-3.30) D served all week 6-9.30 (Sun 7-9) Av main course £10 **Restaurant** L served all week 12-2.30 (Sun 12-3.30) D served all week 6-9.30 (Sun 7-9) Av 3 course à la carte £22 Wadworth Wadworth 6X, Henrys IPA, Bishops Tipple, Heineken & Carlsberg. 11 **Facilities** Parking

Turf Tavern

4 Bath Place, off Holywell St OX1 3SU

☎ 01865 243235 01865 243838

e-mail: turftavern.oxford@laurelpubco.com

Situated in the heart of Oxford, approached through hidden alleyways and winding passages, this famous pub lies in the shadow of the city wall and the colleges. It is especially popular in the summer when customers can relax in the sheltered courtyards. Eleven real ales are served daily, from a choice of around 500 over a year, along with some typical pub fare. The pub has been featured in TV's *Inspector Morse*, and was frequented by JRR Tolkien.

Open 11-11 (Sun 12-10.30) **Bar Meals** L served all week 12-7.30 D served all week Greene King Traditional Ales, changing daily. 6 **Facilities** Garden Dogs allowed

PISHILL MAP 05 SU7

Pick of the Pubs

The Crown Inn

RG9 6HH ☎ 01491 638364 01491 638364

e-mail: jcapon@surfree.co.uk

dir: *On B480 off A4130, NW of Henley-on-Thames*

See Pick of the Pubs on opposite page

RAMSDEN MAP 11 SP3

Pick of the Pubs

The Royal Oak

High St OX7 3AU ☎ 01993 868213 01993 868864

dir: *From Witney B4022 towards Charlbury, right before Hailey, through Poffley End*

See Pick of the Pubs on page 458

ROKE MAP 05 SU6

Home Sweet Home

OX10 6JD ☎ 01491 838249 01491 835760

dir: *Just off the B4009 from Benson to Watlington, signed on B4009*

Long ago converted from adjoining cottages by a local brewer, this pretty 15th-century inn stands in a tiny hamlet surrounded by lovely countryside. Oak beams and the large inglenook fireplace dominate a friendly bar with an old-fashioned feel. Starters might include spicy nachos topped with cheese for two to share; while main courses run Cornish crab fishcakes with home-made tartare sauce; or calves' liver and bacon with an onion gravy. Extensive Sunday menu.

Open 11-2.30 6-11 (Sun 12-3) Closed: Dec 25-26 Rest: closed Sun eve **Bar Meals** L served all week 12-2 D served Mon-Sat 6-9 **Restaurant** L served Mon-Sun 12-2 D served Mon-Sat 7-9 Free House Black Sheep, Loddon Brewery Beers- Hoppit & Branoc. 10 **Facilities** Garden Dogs allowed Parking

PICK OF THE PUBS

PISHILL-OXFORDSHIRE

The Crown Inn

pretty, 15th-century brick and flint coaching inn, but with 11th-century origins as an alehouse. 's important to get the village name straight. The wags who separate the two syllables of Pishill 'e probably right, since old maps do show a second 's'.

uite simply, in days gone by aggon drivers would stop at the n for a swift half after the stiff mb from Henley-on-Thames, hile their waiting horses would lieve themselves (an explanation en Great Aunt Maude can ndle). Eight or nine centuries o there was a thriving monastic mmunity here; later, when Henry II was persecuting Catholics, any priests were smuggled up the l from the big house at nearby onor and hidden in the Crown's iest's hole (reputably the largest the country). One such priest, ther Dominique, met a sticky end hilst hiding out at The Crown and s ghost still haunts the pub on the niversary of his death, although body is quite sure when that is.

Fast forward to the 1960s when it became a favourite music venue for fans of George Harrison, Ringo Starr, Dusty Springfield and other live performers in the old barn. Nowadays there is live music in the barn on the last Wednesday of the month. Menus change seasonally, and there is a selection of daily specials. Start with prawn, avocado and smoked salmon cocktail, and move on to braised lamb shank on a vegetable and potato rosti with redcurrant sauce. Mouthwatering puddings include banana pancakes with maple syrup and vanilla ice cream. On a fine day sit in the extensive gardens overlooking the valley.

MAP 05 SU78
RG9 6HH
☎ 01491 638364
01491 638364
e-mail: jcapon@surfree.co.uk
dir: *On B480 off A4130, NW of Henley-on-Thames*

Open 11.30–2.30 6–11 (Sun 12–3, 7–10.30) Closed: 25–26 Dec
Bar Meals L served all week 12–2.30 D served all week 7–9.30 (Sun 12–3, 7–9) Av main course £6
Restaurant L served all week 12–2.30 D served all week 7–9.30 (Sun 12–3, 7–9) Av 3 course à la carte £22
Free House
Brakspears, West Berkshire Brewery. 8
Facilities Garden Parking

The Royal Oak

This 17th-century former coaching inn is set opposite the church in the pretty Cotswold village of Ramsden. Once upon a time a stopping point for the London to Hereford stagecoach, these days the inn is more popular with walkers eager to explore the lovely surrounding countryside.

Whether walking or not, however, the inn makes a fine place to stop for refreshment, and its old beams, warm fires and stone walls provide a very cosy welcome. It is a free house with beers sourced from local breweries, such as Hook Norton. The wine list has over 200 wines, specialising in those from Bordeaux and Languedoc, many of them available by the glass. The bar menu regularly features a pie of the week, and there are also favourites such as real Italian meatballs; home-made beef burgers; and wild mushroom pasta with shitake and porcini. Every Thursday evening there is a special offer of steak with wine and dessert. The main menu features such treats as, for starters, moules marinière with Hebridean mussels; chicken liver parfait with cognac and raisins; or baked avocado, cheese and prawn gratin. Main courses include roast half shoulder of new season Westwell lamb with rosemary and garlic jus; smoked haddock cooked with whisky, cream and cheese; confit of duck leg with quince sauce and Puy lentils; and pan-fried calves' liver with wild mushroom sauce. Several fish dishes are always on offer, such as seared yellow fin tuna; roast fillet of Atlantic cod with tapenade crust; and salmon with whisky and horseradish.

MAP 11 SP31
High St OX7 3AU
☎ 01993 868213
01993 868864
dir: *From Witney take B4022 towards Charlbury, then right before Hailey, through Poffley End*

Open 11.30–3 6.30–11 Closed: 25 Dec
Bar Meals L served all week 12–2 D served all week 7–10 Av main course £10.50
Restaurant L served all week 12–2 D served all week 7–10 Av 3 course à la carte £25
Free House
Hook Norton Old Hooky, Best, Adnams Broadside, Youngs Special. 🍷 30
Facilities Garden Dogs allowed Parking

HENINGTON MAP 11 SP34

he Bell

<15 6NQ ☎ 01295 670274
mail: the_bellshenington@hotmail.com
r: *A422 through Wroxton. Shenington signed on left*

erlooking a picturesque village green surrounded by mellow ne houses, this attractive and comfortable 300-year-old pub is nveniently located for exploring much of the nearby Oxfordshire untryside as well as the Cotswolds. The pub offers home-cooked d prepared in-house, and the blackboard menu changes frequently. ecialities include lamb and mint casserole; chicken wrapped in con with stilton sauce; and duck with port and black cherries. Expect acle tart or fruit pavlova to follow.

en 12–2.30 7–11 **Bar Meals** L served Tue–Sun 12–2 D served all ek 7–11 Av main course £8.95 **Restaurant** L served Tues-Sun 12–2 erved all week 7–10 Free House Hook Norton, Flowers. 8 **ilities** Garden Dogs allowed

HIPTON-UNDER-YCHWOOD MAP 10 SP21

Pick of the Pubs

The Shaven Crown Hotel

High St OX7 6BA ☎ 01993 830330 01993 832136
e-mail: relax@theshavencrown.co.uk
dir: *On A361, opposite village green & church*

See Pick of the Pubs on page 461

OUTH MORETON MAP 05 SU58

he Crown Inn

gh St OX11 9AG ☎ 01235 812262
mail: sallyandjohn@tesco.net
r: *Village on right of A4130*

endly village pub located midway between Wallingford and lcot. It prides itself on its home-prepared food, and has real ale tap. Families are welcome and customers come from far and le. During the summer the garden is very popular. Dishes include aks, shoulder of lamb, fresh battered haddock, and salmon fillet landaise.

Open 11–3 5.30–11 (Sun 12–3, 7–10.30) Closed: Dec 25–26 **Bar Meals** L served all week 12–2 D served all week 7–9.30 Av main course £9.50 **Restaurant** L served all week 12–2 D served all week 7–9.30 Wadworth Wadworth 6X & Henrys IPA, Guest beers. 8 **Facilities** Garden Dogs allowed Parking

SOUTH STOKE MAP 03 SU58

The Perch and Pike

RG8 0JS ☎ 01491 872415 01491 871001
dir: *On the Ridgeway Hiking Trail 1.5m N of Goring*

The Perch and Pike, just two minutes' walk from the River Thames, was the village's foremost beer house back in the 17th century. There is plenty of atmosphere in the original pub and in the adjoining barn conversion, which houses the 42-seater restaurant. Food ranges from a selection of sandwiches to the likes of smoked haddock and salmon fish cakes, and venison with celeriac mash and Madeira jus. New owners recently took over.

Open 12–3 6–11 (Fri–Sat 11–11, Sun 12–10.30) **Bar Meals** L served 12–3 D served Mon–Sat 6.30–9.30 (Sun 12–5) Av main course £7.50 **Restaurant** L served all week 12–3 D served Mon–Sat 7–9.30 (Sun 12–5) Av 3 course à la carte £24 Brakspear Brakspear beers. 7 **Facilities** Children's licence Garden Dogs allowed Parking Play Area

STADHAMPTON MAP 05 SU69

Pick of the Pubs

The Crazy Bear ★★★★★ RR

Bear Ln OX44 7UR ☎ 01865 890714 01865 400481
e-mail: enquiries@crazybear-oxford.co.uk
dir: *M40 junct 7 onto A329 for 4m, left after petrol station, 2nd left into Bear Lane*

From the outside it looks like a traditional 16th-century pub, but The Crazy Bear's interior is utterly distinctive, combining contemporary and art deco influences. The bar is quite traditional, except that it serves champagne and oysters as well as more conventional bar snacks. There are two award-winning restaurants, one serving Thai food, and the other modern British, as well as some stylish bedrooms and a wonderful garden with a waterfall and statues. The extensive food choices should please everyone: 'all day' breakfasts are served from 7am to 10am and from noon until 10pm, and include such tantalising offerings as duck eggs Benedict or farm-smoked haddock kedgeree. Lunch options include sandwiches and a good value set menu during the week. The main menu, available all day, might feature sautéed foie gras with chives and aged balsamic, followed by fillet of venison with fondant potato, braised red cabbage and juniper sauce.

Open 11–11 **Bar Meals** L served all week 12–10 D served all week 12–10 Av main course £15 **Restaurant** L served all week 12–6 D served all week 6–10 (Sun 12–10) Av 3 course à la carte £35 Av 3 course fixed price £19.50 Free House Old Speckled Hen, Greene King IPA, Ruddles County. 15 **Facilities** Garden Parking **Rooms** 17 bedrooms en suite S£95 D£115

England

STANTON ST JOHN MAP 05 SP50

Star Inn

Middle Rd OX33 1EX ☎ 01865 351277 01865 351006
e-mail: murwin@aol.com
dir: *B4027 Stanton exit, 3rd left Middle Rd, pub 200yds*

Although the Star is only a short drive from the centre of Oxford, this popular pub still retains a definite 'village' feel. The oldest part dates from the early 17th century, and in the past, the building has been used as a butcher's shop and an abattoir. The garden is peaceful and secluded. A varied menu features shoulder of lamb in redcurrant and rosemary, spinach and mushroom strudel, or roast vegetable and goats' cheese tart.

Open 11–2.30 6.30–11 **Bar Meals** L served all week 12–2 D served Mon–Sat 6.30–9.30 (Sun 12–2, 7–9.30) Av main course £8.50 Wadworth Wadworth 6X, Henrys IPA & JCB. 7 **Facilities** Garden Dogs allowed Parking Play Area

The Talkhouse

Wheatley Rd OX33 1EX ☎ 01865 351648 01865 351085
e-mail: talkhouse@fullers.co.uk
dir: *Village signed from Oxford ring road*

First recorded as a pub in 1783, the Talkhouse comprises three bar and dining areas, all with a Gothic look and a welcoming atmosphere. Recently taken over by Fuller, Smith & Turner, new menus have been introduced, accommodation is being refurbished and a wider range of drinks is available. Reports on the new set-up are welcome.

Open 12–11 **Bar Meals** L served all week 12–3 D served all week 6–9 Av main course £12 **Restaurant** L served all week 12–3 D served all week 6–9.30 Av 3 course à la carte £20 Av 2 course fixed price £15.50 Fullers London Pride, ESB, Discovery. 6 **Facilities** Garden Dogs allowed Parking

STOKE ROW MAP 05 SU68

Pick of the Pubs

Crooked Billet

RG9 5PU ☎ 01491 681048 01491 682231
dir: *From Henley to Oxford on A4130. Left at Nettlebed for Stoke Row*

See Pick of the Pubs on page 462

SUTTON COURTENAY MAP 05 SU

Pick of the Pubs

The Fish

4 Appleford Rd OX14 4NQ
☎ 01235 848242 01235 848014
e-mail: info@thefish.uk.com
dir: *From A415 in Abingdon, B4017, left onto B4016 to village*

Around 1890 the original Fish, a thatched 16th-century building, succumbed to a fire and was replaced by today's brick and tile version. The River Thames is only a short stroll away in this attractive and historic village where early 20th-century Prime Minister Herbert Asquith, and writer George Orwell are both buried. The emphasis is very much on food, although drinkers should not be put off. Steve and Marilyn England serve good value bistro lunches in the all-purpose front bar, and outside in the attractive garden in fine weather. Starters typifying their style are duck confit with hoi sin or sweet chilli sauce; mozzarella salad with tomatoes and pesto; and pan-seared Cornish scallops flambéed in pastis. Main dishes include pollock with mussel sauce sizzling prawns in chilli and lime sauce; rack of English lamb with minted gravy; and rich tomato gratinée with pasta and parmesan shavings.

Open 12–3 6–11 **Bar Meals** L served all week 12–2 D served Mon–Sat **Restaurant** L served all week 12–2 (Sun 12–2.30) D served Mon–Fri 7–9 (Sat 7–9.30) Greene King Greeen King IPA, Guest Beer. 10 **Facilities** Garden Dogs allowed Parking

The Shaven Crown Hotel

lieved to be one of the ten oldest inns in England, The Shaven Crown is steeped in history, ving been built as a hospice to the neighbouring Bruern Monastery. Built of honey-coloured tswold stone around a medieval courtyard, parts of it, including the gateway, are up to 700 ars old.

llowing the Dissolution of the nasteries, Queen Elizabeth I ed it as a hunting lodge before ing it to the village in 1580, en it became the Crown Inn. It s not until 1930 that a brewery h a touch of humour changed name to reflect the tonsorial rstyles adopted by monks. e leader of the British Union of scists, Oswald Mosley, was held der house arrest here during rld War II. Not surprisingly ne of the rooms are named after n, whereas the small and cosy nking area with a log fire is, as u might expect, called the Monks r (and it serves Oxfordshire real s). Bar food includes salads d pastas, steak and kidney pie, sausage and mash, and chicken curry. The carte offers starters of deep-fried brie with raspberry coulis; and roast carrot and parsnip salad with walnut dressing. Popular main courses are pheasant casserole with winter vegetables; venison steak with wild mushroom and chive sauce; fresh fish is delivered daily; and, for vegetarians, goats' cheese tart with red pepper coulis. Pre-dinner drinks can be taken in the impressive Great Hall, and in the intimate candlelit dining room. Outside, apart from the enclosed courtyard, is a tree-dotted lawned area.

MAP 10 SP21
High St OX7 6BA
☎ 01993 830330
01993 832136
e-mail:
relax@theshavencrown.co.uk
dir: *On A361, halfway between Burford & Chipping Norton opposite village green & church*

Open 12-2.30 5-11 (Sat-Sun all day)
Bar Meals L served all week 12-2 D served all week 6-9.30 (Sat-Sun all day) Av main course £9.50
Restaurant L served Sat-Sun 12-2 D served all week 7-9 Av 3 course à la carte £20
Free House
Hook Norton Best, Old Hooky & Archers Wychwood, Hobgoblin, Arkells. 10
Facilities Garden Dogs allowed Parking

Crooked Billet

It seems a shame to spoil the secret, but this charmingly rustic pub, tucked away down a single track lane in deepest Oxfordshire, is a popular hideaway for the well-heeled and the well-known. It dates back to 1642 and was once the haunt of highwayman Dick Turpin; forced to hide here fro local law enforcers, he whiled away the hours by courting the landlord's pretty daughter, Bess.

Many of its finest features are unchanged, including the low beams, tiled floors and open fires that are so integral to its character. Famous customers, several of whom were introduced to the pub by the late George Harrison, have included Kate Winslet, who famously held her first wedding reception here; Eastenders cast members; and Jeremy Paxman. Menus are the work of award-winning chef/proprietor Paul Clerehugh. Local produce and organic fare are the mainstays of his kitchen, to the extent that he will even exchange a lunch or dinner for the locals' excess veg. Begin perhaps with seared partridge breasts with creamed cabbage, lardons, chestnuts and juniper jus; or crispy duck salad, frisée, spring onions, cucumber and chilli dressing. To follow, there's a good range of fish mains, including seared tuna with soba noodles and bok choy; lemon sole, hollandaise sauce and sugarsnaps; halibut with prawns and mussels, sautée potatoes and baby spinach; seared scallops with artichoke, confit tomato and herb salad; and whole prepared lobster with lemon butter and chipped potatoes. Alternatives might include roast rack of the pub's own lamb, dauphinoise potatoes and baby summer vegetables; or pan-fried English calves' liver with bacon crisps, carrot and parsnip rôsti. Notwithstanding the occasional famous face, the pub hosts music nights, free wine tastings and other events, and contributes some of its profit to the daily meals it provides for a local primary school.

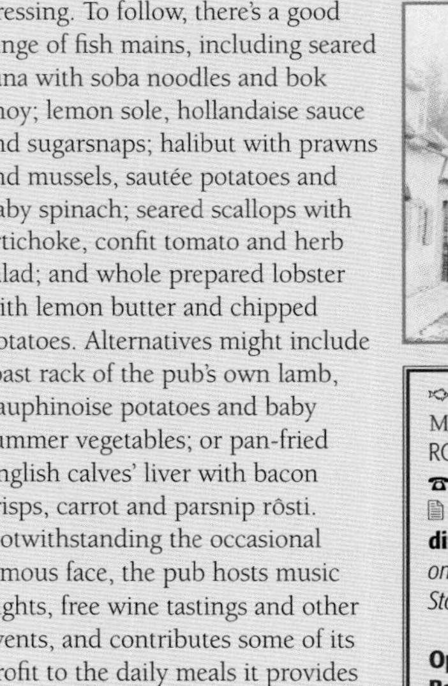

MAP 05 SU68
RG9 5PU
☎ 01491 681048
01491 682231
dir: *From Henley to Oxford on A4130. Left at Nettlebed for Stoke Row*

Open 12–11 (Sun 12–10.30)
Bar Meals L served all week 12–2.30 D served all week 7–10
Restaurant L served all week 12–2.30 D served all week 7–10 (Sun all day)
Brakspear
Brakspear Bitter. 12
Facilities Garden Parking

England

VALCLIFFE — MAP 11 SP33

ag's Head 🍷

:15 5EJ ☎ 01295 780232 📠 01295 788977

: *6m W of Banbury on B4035*

; friendly, 600 year-old thatched village inn enjoys picture postcard ‹s and a pretty village setting. It seems that Shakespeare used to ‹k here, until he was barred! Blending a traditional pub feel with a ily-friendly environment, the Stag also offers a beautiful terraced den and play area. Freshly prepared dishes include goats' cheese with chips or salad; moules marinière with chorizo and crusty ad; and Oxfordshire liver and bacon with red wine and onion gravy. k out for the landlord's own paintings of local scenes.

en 12–2.30 Mon–Sat 6–11 **Bar Meals** L served Tue–Sat 12–2 1 12–3) D served Tue–Sat 6.30–9.30 Av main course £7.95 **taurant** L served Tue–Sat 12–2 (Sun 12–3) D served Tue–Sat 6.30–9.30 ree House Adnams Bitter, Deuchars IPA, Wye Valley IPA, Badgers d. 🍷 8 **Facilities** Garden Dogs allowed Play Area

VERFORD — MAP 11 SP33

Pick of the Pubs

The Mason's Arms 🍷

anbury Rd OX7 4AP

☎ 01608 683212 📠 01608 683105

-mail: themasonschef@hotmail.com

ir: *Between Banbury & Chipping Norton on A361*

his award-winning three hundred-year-old pub was once ındown and empty, until proprietor Bill Leadbeater and his wife, harmaine, arrived some years ago. Items on the main menu are eaded 'Bill's Food', which leaves no doubt over who's in charge ı the kitchen. Start with grilled pigeon breast, hazelnut mash and ed wine jus. To follow try pan-fried skate wing with brown shrimp utter; chickpea and mushroom jalfrezi; or roast breast of free ange chicken, cured ham and bread sauce. On the lunch menu ou'll find light bites like smoked salmon, and more substantial ems such as polenta-fried fillet of hake. For dessert, in addition ɔ a good selection of farmhouse cheeses, there's iced Ceylon ea parfait or glazed lemon tart. The Mason's Arms is a mere eer mat's flick from Hook Norton Brewery, whose Best Bitter is vailable in the bar.

pen 10–3 6–11 (Jul–Aug all day) Closed: 25–26 Dec **ar Meals** L served Mon–Sat 12–2.15 (Sun lunch 12–3) D served l week 7–9.15 Av main course £7 **Restaurant** L served all week 2–2.15 D served all week 7–9.15 Av 3 course à la carte £23 Av 3 course ked price £15.95 Free House Hook Norton Best & Brakspear pecial. 🍷 7 **Facilities** Children's licence Garden Parking

SYDENHAM — MAP 05 SP70

Pick of the Pubs

The Crown Inn

Sydenham Rd OX39 4NB ☎ 01844 351634

e-mail: haydn.hughes3@btinternet.com

dir: *B4009 towards Chinnor. Left at Kingston Blount. Or off B4445 4m from Thame*

This pretty 17th-century inn lies in a picturesque village opposite its 900-year-old church. Refurbished to incorporate both traditional and modern styles, old photographs hang harmoniously on the walls alongside contemporary paintings. Croque monsieur, filled baguettes and jacket potatoes appear on the lunchtime snacks menu, while the regular carte offers a selection of British, French and Mediterranean-style food, with fish featuring regularly: perhaps monkfish with Parma ham, escalope of salmon, or fillets of sea bass. A Thai menu broadens the geographical purview even further.

Open 12–2.30 6–11 (Oct–Mar 6–10, Mon & Tue May–Sep 12–5 Sun) **Bar Meals** L served Sun–Fri 12–2 D served Mon–Thur 6.30–9 (Fri–Sat 7–9.30) Av main course £9.50 Greene King IPA, Ruddles County, Guinness. **Facilities** Garden Parking

TADMARTON — MAP 11 SP33

The Lampet Arms ★★★ GA

Main St OX15 5TB ☎ 01295 780070 📠 01295 788066

dir: *Take B4035 from Banbury to Tadmarton, 5m*

Victorian-style free house offering well-kept ales and hearty home cooking. The pub is named after Captain Lampet, the local landowner who built it and mistakenly believed he could persuade the council to have the local railway line directed through the village, thereby increasing trade. Typical menu choices include steaks; chicken kiev; steak and ale pie; chilli con carne; and a selection of sandwiches and baguettes.

Open 12–12 (Sun 12–11.30) Rest: Winter wkday 4–12 **Bar Meals** L served all week 12–3 D served all week 7–9 Av main course £7.50 **Restaurant** L served all week 12–3 D served all week 7–9 Free House Hook Norton, Theakstons, Fosters, Guinness. **Facilities** Children's licence Garden Dogs allowed Parking **Rooms** 4 bedrooms en suite S£45 D£65

TETSWORTH — MAP 05 SP60

The Old Red Lion NEW 🍷

40 High St OX9 7AS ☎ 01844 281274 📠 01844 281863

e-mail: fitz@the-red-lion-tetsworth.co.uk

dir: *Oxford Service area, turn right onto A40. At junct turn left then right onto A40 signed Stokenchurch*

The village green fronts the pub affording great views of summer cricket and winter football matches. Refurbishment in recent years has doubled the size of the bar and created two new eating areas. The menu has some Afro-Caribbean influences with dishes of salted cod and ackees fritter with spicy mango salsa, and jerk chicken with rice and peas, island sauce and fried plantain garnish. Live jazz and blues nights are a feature.

CONTINUED

England

TETSWORTH continued

Open 11.30-3 6.30-11 (Sat-Sun 11.30-11) **Bar Meals** L served Mon-Sat 12-2.30 Av main course £8.95 **Restaurant** L served all week 12-2.30 D served Mon-Sat 6.30-9.30 (Mon 6.30-9) Av 3 course à la carte £19.95 Free House 9 **Facilities** Garden Parking

THAME MAP 05 SP70

The Swan Hotel

9 Upper Hight St OX9 3ER

☎ 01844 261211 01844 261954

dir: *Hotel in town centre*

Dating from the 16th century, this former coaching inn overlooks the market square at Thame. The Tudor-painted ceiling is a feature of the upstairs restaurant, where you can enjoy freshly cooked Thai food. Downstairs in the cosy bar you'll find an open fire, bar snacks and a good selection of beers such as Hook Norton, Brakspears and Shepherd Neame.

Open 11-11 (Thu 11-12, Fri-Sat 11-1am, Sun 12-11) **Bar Meals** L served all week 12-3 D served Mon-Sat 6-10.30 (Sun 12-4) Av main course £9 **Restaurant** L served all week 12-3 D served Mon-Sat 6-10.30 (Sun 12-5) Av 3 course à la carte £20 Av 2 course fixed price £18 Free House Hook Norton, London Pride, Brakspears, Shepherd Neame Spitfire & Otter. 10 **Facilities** Dogs allowed Parking

TOOT BALDON MAP 05 SP50

Pick of the Pubs

The Mole Inn

OX44 9NG ☎ 01865 340001 01865 343011

e-mail: info@themoleinn.com

dir: *5m SE from Oxford city centre off B480*

This stone-built, Grade II listed pub has been the subject of an extensive renovation programme in recent years. The top-notch makeover has earned it a glowing and well-deserved reputation, due in no small measure to the efforts of award-winning chef/host Gary Witchalls. Inside, a great deal of care and attention has been lavished on this classic old local, and now customers can relax in black leather sofas amid stripped beams and solid white walls. The dining areas are equally striking with their intimate lighting and terracotta floors. Gary's inspired menu draws plenty of foodies from nearby Oxford and further afield, tempted by dishes such as loin of Old Spot pork with Toulouse Savoy cabbage and mustard mash; sea scallops, crayfish and crab risotto; or squab pigeon with bubble and squeak, celeriac fondant and smoked bacon velouté.

Open 12-11 Closed: 25 Dec, 1 Jan **Bar Meals** L served all week 12-2.30 D served all week 7-9.30 (Sun 12-10) Av main course £13 **Restaurant** L served all week 12-2.30 D served all week 7-9.30 (Sun 12-4, 6-9) Av 3 course à la carte £25 Free House Hook Norton, London Pride, Spitfire, Guinness. 11 **Facilities** Garden Parking

WANTAGE MAP 05 SU

The Hare

Reading Rd, West Hendred OX12 8RH

☎ 01235 833249 01235 833268

dir: *At West Hendred on A417*

A late 19th-century inn mid-way between Wantage and Didcot, modernised in the 1930s by local brewers, Morland, and featuring a colonial-style verandah and colonnade. Inside it retains the more original wooden floors, beams and open fire.

Open 12-3 6-12 (Fri-Sun 11.30-11) **Bar Meals** L served all week 12-2 D served 7-9 Av main course £7 **Restaurant** L served all week 12-2 D served all week 7-9 Av 3 course à la carte £16 Greene King Gre King Abbot Ale, IPA, Morland Original. 8 **Facilities** Garden Dogs allowed Parking

WHEATLEY MAP 05 SP

Bat & Ball Inn

28 High St OX44 9HJ ☎ 01865 874379 01865 873363

e-mail: bb@traditionalvillageinns.co.uk

dir: *Through Wheatley towards Garsington, left signed Cuddesdon*

Do not be surprised to discover that the bar of this former coaching inn is packed to the gunnels with cricketing memorabilia. The owner claim that their collection puts to shame even that of Lords cricket ground! The comprehensive menu, supplemented by daily specials, likely to feature steaks, fresh-baked pie of the day, herb-battered fres cod, and maybe chargrilled Toulouse sausages. Lighter meals include lamb Peshwari, and warm spinach and pancetta salad.

Open 11-11 **Bar Meals** L served all week 12-2.45 D served all week 6.30-9.45 (Sun 12-9.30) **Restaurant** L served all week 12-2.30 D served all week 6.30-9.30 (Sun 12-9.30) Free House Marston's Pedigree, House LBW Bitter, Guinness. 10 **Facilities** Garden Dogs allowed Parking

WITNEY MAP 05 SP3

The Bell Inn

Standlake Rd, Ducklington OX29 7UP

☎ 01993 702514 01993 706822

e-mail: danny@dpatching4.wanadoo.co.uk

dir: *1m S of Witney in Ducklington, off A415*

Nearly 700 years have passed since the men building the adjacent church also erected their own living accommodation. Their hostel eventually became the Bell, and much extended over the years, it even embraces William Shepheard's former brewery, which closed in 1886. Today it is a popular, traditional village local, with many original features – and a collection of some 500 bells. Home-made pies, stew and burgers are a speciality.

Open 12-3 5-11 (Fri-Sun 12-11) Closed: 25-26 Dec & 1 Jan **Bar Meals** L served all week 12-2 D served Mon-Sat 6-9 **Restaurant** L served all week 12-2 D served Mon-Sat 6-9 Greene King Greene King, IPA & Old Speckled Hen, Morland Original, Guinness **Facilities** Garden Parking Play Area

White Hart

ucked away in the quiet village of Wytham, close to the A34, is this smart gastropub, concealed ithin a traditional Cotswold stone inn. If it looks familiar, it may be because it has featured in ome of the Inspector Morse television programmes.

serves real ale, but is redominantly a place to eat, and oasts an extensive wine list. There re a number of rooms inside, all ith warming fires, as well as a plendid conservatory. When it is arm enough to sit outside, the lediterranean-style terrace is a harming and comfortable place to lax. The proprietor sources eggs, hicken, pork and bacon from a cal farm less than a mile away, nd all the meat is either free range r organic. The well presented enu is supplemented by the pecials boards with fresh fish and ame dishes always featured in eason. Among the many starters e carpaccio of beef with wild ocket; asparagus spears wrapped in pancetta with lemon hollandaise; smoked haddock fishcakes; or a selection of all of them to share as an antipasti plate. Main courses include pork fillet with white bean, tomato and spinach broth with crispy Parma ham; mussels, clams and prawn linguini with coriander and chilli oil; chicken breast wrapped in pancetta with sun-dried tomato tagliatelle; pink duck breast with potato fondant and parsnip purée; local sausages with cannellini bean and belly pork stew; or one of the dishes from the specials board. For those who are still hungry, there are some tasty desserts, such as raspberry panacotta with lemon and vanilla syrup; or pears poached in red wine with mascarpone cheese.

MAP 05 SP40
OX2 8QA
☎ 01865 244372
e-mail: whitehartwytham@aol.com
web: www.whitehartoxford.co.uk
dir: *Just off A34 NW of Oxford*

Open 12–10
Bar Meals L served all week 12–3 D served Mon–Sun 6.30–10 Av main course £13.50
Restaurant L served 12–3 all week D served Mon–Sun 6.30–10
Hook Norton, Leffe & Landlord. 60
Facilities Garden Parking

England

WITNEY continued

The Three Horseshoes NEW

78 Corner St OX28 6BS ☎ 01993 703086

dir: *From Oxford on A40 towards Cheltenham take 2nd turn to Witney. At rdbt take 5th exiti to Witney. Over flyover, through lights. At next rdbt take 5th exit into Corn St. Pub on left*

Built of Cotswold stone, this historic Grade II-listed pub is situated in Witney's original main street. Inside, the stone walls add to the charm of the part wooden, part flagged floors and low ceilings; two large log fires blaze in winter. Traditional pub lunches serve home-made cottage pie or chilli con carne, while evening menus may proffer cured calves' tongue or slow-roast belly pork. Visit on the last Friday of the month (excluding December) for a complete fish menu.

Open 12–3 6.30–11 (Sun 12–4.30) **Bar Meals** L served all week 12–2 D served Mon-Thu 6.30–9 (Sun 12–3) Av main course £9.50 **Restaurant** L served all week 12–2 (Sun 12–3) D served Mon–Sat 6.30–9 Av 3 course à la carte £25 Admiral Taverns Harveys Sussex Ale, Marstons Pedigree, Greene King Abbot & Guiness. **Facilities** Garden **Notes**

WOODSTOCK MAP 11 SP41

Pick of the Pubs

The Kings Head Inn ★★★★ GA

Chapel Hill, Wootton OX20 1DX ☎ 01993 811340

e-mail: t.fay@kings-head.co.uk

dir: *1.5m N of Woodstock off A44. In village centre near church*

Originally a shop, the pub has been sensitively modernised to offer a perfect blend of old world character and 21st-century comfort. Winter brings cosy log fires, and in summer you can enjoy peaceful meals in the garden. The pub has a growing reputation for offering excellent cuisine. The bar menu ranges from sandwiches to the likes of warm Gressingham duck salad with spicy plum sauce; or chargrilled fillet of seabass on roasted tomatoes with caramelised shallots. The restaurant menu opens with perhaps Szechuan seared pigeon breast with shallots caramelised in sesame oil; or toasted goats' cheese on a rotunda of roasted plum, beef and cherry tomatoes drizzled with basil pesto. Follow with chargrilled medallions of local Appleton pork fillet on a bed of red onion marmalade with a delicate orange and juniper berry sauce; or Cantonese braised leg and pink-roasted breast of Gressingham duck with a duck sherry gravy. For dessert, perhaps sticky gingerbread pudding with brandy and ginger wine; or caramelised citrus tart with a raspberry coulis and Anglaise sauce. Almost all the menu is gluten free.

Open 11–2 6.30–11 (Sun 12–2.30) Closed: Dec 25–26 **Bar Meals** L served Tue–Sat 12–2 D served Tue–Sat 7–9 Av main course £8.95 **Restaurant** L served Tue–Sun 12–2 D served Tue–Sat 7–9 Av 3 course à la carte £24 Free House Hook Norton Old Hooky, Hooky Bitter & Guest Beers. 7 **Facilities** Garden Parking **Rooms** 3 bedrooms en suite S£60 D£75

WOOLSTONE MAP 05 SU2

The White Horse NEW ★★★ INN

SN7 7QL ☎ 01367 820726 01367 820566

e-mail: whitehorse@btconnect.com

dir: *Off A420 at Watchfield onto B4508 towards Longcot signed for Woolstone*

Unusual windows add to the appeal of this black-and-white-timbered, thatched, Elizabethan village pub. Upholstered stools line the traditiona bar, where a fireplace conceals two priest holes, visible to those who don't mind getting their knees dirty. Lunchtime bar snacks include fajit burgers and fish and chips. An extensive menu of freshly prepared English and international dishes in the oak-beamed restaurant includes steak and ale pie, curries, steaks, fish pie and mushroom stroganoff.

Open 11.30–3 5.30–11 (Sat in summer 11.30–11) **Bar Meals** L served Mon Sat D served Mon–Sat Av main course £10 **Restaurant** L served all week 1 2.30 D served Mon–Sat 6–9 Av 3 course à la carte £22 Arkells Arkells, Carling, Guinness, Stowford & Press Cider. **Facilities** Garden Dogs allowed Parking **Rooms** 6 bedrooms en suite S£50 D£65

WYTHAM MAP 05 SP4

Pick of the Pubs

White Hart

OX2 8QA ☎ 01865 244372

e-mail: whitehartwytham@aol.com

dir: *Just off A34 NW of Oxford*

See Pick of the Pubs on page 465

RUTLAND

BARROWDEN MAP 11 SK9

Pick of the Pubs

Exeter Arms

LE15 8EQ ☎ 01572 747247 01572 747247

e-mail: info@exeterarms.com

dir: *From A47 turn at landmark windmill, village 0.75m S*

Barrowden is an attractive stone village in the Welland Valley, not far from Rutland Water, and in the centre, overlooking the village green and duck pond, is the Exeter Arms. It is a 17th-century inn that in the past has been a smithy, dairy and postal collection point. Now it is a welcoming pub and restaurant, serving home-made beers. These are made in the barn next door and rejoice in names such as Beach Boys, Bevin Boys and Fun Boy Four. The food is exceptional, being locally sourced from organic producers where possible. From the main menu (which changes regularly), choose starters such as maple smoked duck breast; confit of free range rabbit; or razor clam chowder. Main courses could include lobster tail and spider crab gumbo; roast suckling pig; fillet of beef en croute; or wild mushroom and cashew nut tartlet. The desserts are equally imaginative with, for example, date and lime rock cake served with hot butterscotch sauce.

Open 12–2.30 6–11 (Sun & BHs 7–10.30) **Bar Meals** L served Tue–Sat 12–2 D served Tue–Sat 9 **Restaurant** L served Tue–Sun 12–2 D served Tue–Sat 7–9 Own Beers: Beach Boys, Bevin Boys, Farmers Boy, Boys With Attitude. 10 **Facilities** Garden Dogs allowed Parking Play Area

Fox & Hounds

his imposing 17th-century building stands opposite the green in the centre of Exton, a charming illage with its many stone and thatched cottages. Barnsdale Gardens and the amenities of utland Water are not far away. At the rear of the pub is a large walled garden, which makes a erfect setting for an al fresco meal or a marquee reception.

ne pub has a reputation for good od and hospitality, and is an ideal opping-off point for those making e most of the many good walks the surrounding area. Its menu is e work of Italian chef/proprietor alter Floris and his team, and mbines the best of traditional nglish and Italian cuisine. There an impressive list of over 25 thentic, thin-crust pizzas (for enings only), which are certainly ot on the small side. The 'casual nch' menu features panini, salads, aditional sandwiches and filled abattas, while the main menu ens with the likes of Scottish lmon with red onions, capers d cream cheese; asparagus and uyere tart on a bed of salad izzled with extra virgin olive oil; and paté with chutney. Main dishes are pan-fried lambs' liver and bacon with onion gravy and creamy mashed potato; or perhaps linguini with jumbo prawns and Scottish smoked salmon in a garlic cream sauce. There is also a regularly changing menu of desserts such as sticky ginger sponge with ginger wine sauce, or baked cheesecake. This is a very popular inn, especially when village events, such as the spring bank holiday street market, are taking place.

MAP 11 SK91
19, The Green LE15 8AP
☎ 01572 812403
01572 812403
e-mail: sandra@foxandhoundsrutland.co.uk
dir: *Take A606 from Oakham towards Stamford, at Barnsdale turn left, after 1.5m turn right towards Exton. Pub in village centre*

Open 11–3 6–11
Bar Meals L served all week 12–2 D served Mon–Sat 6.30–9 Av main course £10
Restaurant L served all week 12–2 D served all week 6.30–9 Av 3 course à la carte £20
Free House
Greene King IPA, Grainstore Real Ales, John Smiths Smooth, Timothy Taylor. 🍷 8
Facilities Garden Dogs allowed Parking Play Area

England

CLIPSHAM — MAP 11 SK91

Pick of the Pubs

The Olive Branch

Main St LE15 7SH ☎ 01780 410355 01780 410000

e-mail: info@theolivebranchpub.com

dir: *2m off A1 at B664 junct, N of Stamford*

This 19th-century pub was saved from closure nine years ago by three young men with the help of local villagers, friends and family. It is now a highly successful business that has expanded to include a second pub, the Red Lion Inn at Stathern. It has an attractive front garden and terrace, and a beautifully refurbished interior with open fires, shelves of books and furniture from local antique fairs (all for sale). In the bar is a rare 'nurdling chair', one of only three in the country. Look out for the interesting range of bottled beers, with suggestions on beer and food pairings. The menu combines traditional, classic and modern influences: typical dishes include Lincolnshire sausages with mustard mash and onion gravy; pumpkin risotto with toasted pumpkin seeds; and pan-fried foie gras with sweet potato rôsti and caramelised baby onions. A range of Olive Branch produce is available to buy.

Open 12–3.30 6–11 (Sun 12–10.30, Summer Sat 12–11) Closed: 26 Dec–1 Jan **Bar Meals** L served all week 12–2 D served all week 7–9.30 (Sun 12–3, 7–9) Av main course £15.50 **Restaurant** L served all week 12–2 D served all week 7–9.30 (Sun 12–3, 7–9) Av 3 course à la carte £27.50 Av 3 course fixed price £13.95 Rutland Inn Co Ltd Grainstore 1050 & Olive Oil, Fenland, Brewster's, VPA. 15 **Facilities** Garden Dogs allowed Parking

COTTESMORE — MAP 11 SK91

The Sun Inn

25 Main St LE15 7DH ☎ 01572 812321

e-mail: cheviotinns@hotmail.co.uk

dir: *3m from Oakham on B668*

Dating back to 1610, this whitewashed thatched pub boasts oak beams and a cosy fire in the bar. A well-priced menu supplemented by specials is on offer: chicken, leek and ham pie, steaks and grills, and plenty of fish choices like whole sea bass, swordfish steak and red snapper fillet are served. Lunchtime snacks include baguettes; ham, eggs and chips; and ploughman's. Apparently the ghost of a young girl is sometimes seen behind the bar.

Open 11.30–2.30 5–11 (Fri 11–3, Sat 11.30–11.30, Sun 12–11) **Bar Meals** L served Mon–Sat 12–2.15 (Sun 12–8.30) D served Mon–Thu 6–9 (Fri–Sat 5.30–9.30, Sun 12–8.30) Av main course £9 **Restaurant** L served all week 12–2.15 D served Mon–Thu 6–9 (Fri–Sat 5.30–9.30, Sun 12–8.30) Av 3 course à la carte £16 Everards Brewery Adnams Bitter, Everards Tiger, Carling, Kronenbourg. 9 **Facilities** Garden Dogs allowed Parking

EMPINGHAM — MAP 11 SK9

The White Horse Inn ★★ HL

Main St LE15 8PS ☎ 01780 460221 01780 460521

e-mail: info@whitehorserutland.co.uk

dir: *From A1 take A606 signed Oakham & Rutland Water. From Oakham take A606 to Stamford*

This 17th-century village courthouse close to Rutland Water has lost none of its period charm. If you're pedalling around the lake – and it' a popular activity – there's no better place to finish the day. The warm welcome, open fire, beamed bar and comfortable restaurant add up a recipe for total relaxation. The beers are well kept, and the reasonab priced menus include several fish choices such as moules marinières and home-made seafood crumble.

Open 8–11 Closed: 25 Dec **Bar Meals** L served all week 12–2.15 D serve all week 7–9.30 (Sun 12–9) Av main course £10 **Restaurant** L served all week 12–2.15 D served all week 7–9.30 (Sun 12–9) Enterprise Inns John Smith's, Grainstore Triple B, Ruddles Best, Abbot Ale. 9 **Facilities** Garden Dogs allowed Parking **Rooms** 13 bedrooms en suite S£50 D£65

EXTON — MAP 11 SK9

Pick of the Pubs

Fox & Hounds

19, The Green LE15 8AP

☎ 01572 812403 01572 812403

e-mail: sandra@foxandhoundsrutland.co.uk

dir: *A606 from Oakham, left at Barnsdale after 1.5m right towards Exton. Pub in village centre*

See Pick of the Pubs on page 467

The Old Plough

his genteel and very popular country pub dates back to 1783. Its village location makes it andy for visiting the lovely Georgian town of Oakham, as well as touring the rest of the old ounty of Rutland. Braunston itself is one of Rutland's finest villages.

he pub enjoys a picturesque cation just a short distance om Rutland Water. An old red rick coaching inn that has kept s traditional identity despite eing tastefully modernised, The ld Plough's interior includes a aditional tiled floor, a real fire id mellow yellow walls in the ar; and a bright, airy conservatory ining room with a black and hite tiled floor and modern pine rniture. The large, landscaped eer garden has a very popular oodlit pétanque pitch. If you're ot sure how to play, just ask, id one of the locals should be eased to help you. Expect lots speciality evenings and various eekend entertainments, plus an enthusiasm for good food which extends to candle-lit dinners in the picturesque conservatory, as well as light lunches on the terrace. The menu typically delivers favourites such as liver, bacon and onions, and Cajun chicken, as well as steak and kidney pudding, Braunston chicken stuffed with creamy cheese, trio of sausages with mustard mash and Calvados sauce, mushroom stroganoff, salmon en croûte, and beer-battered cod fillet. Regular guest ales are always available, plus beers from Grainstore Brewery and a good selection of speciality European beers, including fruit beers, Orval, Duvel, Gulden Draak and Triple Karmeliet.

MAP 11 SK80
2 Church St, Braunston LE15 8QT
☎ 01572 722714
01572 770382
e-mail:
info@oldploughrutland.com
dir: *A606 to Oakham, at 1st mini-rdbt right onto High St, to rail crossing. Left then 2nd left signed Braunston.*

Open 11–11 (Fri–Sat 11–12)
Bar Meals L served all week 12–2.30 D served all week 6–9.30 (Sun 12–9) Av main course £9.95
Restaurant L served all week 12–2.30 D served all week 6–9.30 (Sun 12–9) Av 3 course à la carte £19
Free House
Boddingtons, Bass Cask, Greene King IPA, Grainstore. 9
Facilities Garden Dogs allowed Parking Play Area

GLASTON MAP 11 SK80

The Old Pheasant NEW

Main Rd LE15 9BP ☎ 01572 822326 01572 823316

e-mail: info@theoldpheasant.co.uk

dir: *On A47 just outside Uppingham*

The stuffed head of a wild boar presides over the bar of this picture-perfect inn, which also features a smart stone-walled restaurant complete with evocative relics of farming history. Menus are constructed around quality produce, locally sourced where possible. Seasonal game from shoots is regularly featured, alongside trout from nearby rivers. Try home-cured gravadlax, honey glazed duck breast, and chocolate marquise, or an excellent range of cheeses.

Open 8–11 Closed: 2–7 Jan **Bar Meals** L served all week 12–2 D served Mon–Sat 6.30–9 Av main course £12 **Restaurant** L served all week 12–2 D served Mon–Sat 6.30–9 Av 3 course à la carte £23 Free House Pheasant Ale, Timothy Taylors Landlord, Fullers London Pride, Everards Original & Greene King Abbot Ale. 8 **Facilities** Children's licence Garden Parking

LYDDINGTON MAP 11 SP89

Old White Hart

51 Main St LE15 9LR ☎ 01572 821703 01572 821965

e-mail: mail@oldwhitehart.co.uk

dir: *From A6003 between Uppingham & Corby take B672*

Set amongst the sandstone cottages of rural Lyddington, this honey-coloured stone free house close to Rutland Water has retained its original beamed ceilings, stone walls and open fires, and is surrounded by well-stocked gardens. Greene King and Timothy Taylor are amongst the beers on offer, along with interesting, freshly prepared food. The menu includes English mustard toad in the hole, and there are fish and vegetarian choices plus daily specials.

Open 12–3 6.30–11 Closed: 25 Dec **Bar Meals** L served all week 12–2 (Sun 12–2.30) D served Mon–Sat 6.30–9 Av main course £10 **Restaurant** L served all week 12–2 (Sun 12–2.30) D served Mon–Sat 6.30–9 Av 3 course à la carte £23 Free House Greene King IPA & Abbot Ale, Timothy Taylor Landlord, Fullers London Pride. 7 **Facilities** Garden Parking Play Area

OAKHAM MAP 11 SK80

Barnsdale Lodge Hotel ★★★ HL

The Avenue, Rutland Water, North Shore LE15 8AH

☎ 01572 724678 01572 724961

e-mail: enquiries@barnsdalelodge.co.uk

dir: *Off A1 onto A606. Hotel 5m on right, 2m E of Oakham*

A former farmhouse, Barnsdale Lodge has been in the proprietor's family since 1760 as part of the adjoining Exton Estate. It stands overlooking Rutland Water in the heart of this picturesque little county. There's a cosy bar with comfortable chairs and a courtyard with outdoor seating. The bistro-style menu draws on local produce and offers dishes such as lobster bisque and individual Wellington of lamb fillet. There is also an attractive summer lunch menu.

Open 7–11 **Bar Meals** L served all week 12.15–2.15 D served all week 7–9.30 **Restaurant** L served all week 12–2.15 D served all week 7–9.30 Av 3 course à la carte £25 Free House Rutland Grainstore, Courage Directors, John Smith's. 10 **Facilities** Garden Dogs allowed Parking Play Area **Rooms** 44 bedrooms en suite S£65 D£80

The Blue Ball

6 Cedar St, Braunston-in-Rutland LE15 8QS

☎ 01572 722135

e-mail: blueball@rutlandpubco.net

dir: *From A1 take A606 to Oakham. Village SW of Oakham. Pu next to church.*

A 17th-century thatched inn with open log fires and a cosy bar area, reputedly Rutland's oldest pub. There are five dining areas under low beamed ceilings, where typical dishes include pork fillet served with a brandy, cream and peppercorn sauce with caramelised apples; chicke breast with a mushroom and tarragon sauce; and spinach and ricotta tortellini in a tomato sauce with shavings of gran padano cheese.

Open 12–3 6–11 (Sat–Sun all day) **Bar Meals** L served Mon–Fri 12–2 (Sat–Sun 12–3) D served Mon–Sat 6.30–9 Av main course £10.95 **Restaurant** L served Mon-Fri 12–2 (Sat–Sun 12–3) D served Mon–Sat 6.30–9 Av 3 course à la carte £22 Free House Old Speckled Hen, Sa Miguel, Greene King IPA. 13 **Facilities** Children's licence Garden Dog allowed Parking

The Grainstore Brewery

Station Approach LE15 6RE

☎ 01572 770065 01572 770068

e-mail: grainstorebry@aol.com

web: www.grainstorebrewery.com

dir: *Next to Oakham rail station*

Founded in 1995, Davis's Brewing Company is housed in the three-storey Victorian grain store next to Oakham railway station. Finest quality ingredients and hops are used to make the beers that can be sampled in the pub's Tap Room. Filled baguettes, and stilton and po pie ploughman's are of secondary importance, but very tasty all the same. Go for the brewery tours and blind tastings; or attend the ann beer festival during the August Bank Holiday.

Open 11–11 (Fri–Sat 11–12) **Bar Meals** L served all week 11–2.30 Fr House Rutlands Panther, Triple B, Ten Fifty, Steaming Billy Bitter. **Facilities** Garden Dogs allowed Parking

Kings Arms

he Kings Arms is a family-run, 17th-century inn situated in the quaint village of Wing, close to utland Water. It is popular for its good food, beer and ambiance. All the food is freshly prepared nd produced in-house, even the sauces, relishes, bread, ice creams and sorbets.

ne regular menu offers an tensive choice of dishes and atures Aberdeen Angus beef oast rib and fillet steak), and esh lobster (platter, cold dressed, r-fried). Daily specials include esh fish options like sea bream grilled vine tomatoes with baby inach, mange-tout, three-grain e and Noilly Prat sorrel sauce. pical of the bar meal selection e the Wing burger, steak and ale e, lamb tagine, and cod in beer tter. Finish with a Kings Arms eese slate, or a chef's vanilla affle with your choice of three me-made ice creams. Good value t lunches are offered between esday and Saturday. Eight en ite letting rooms are available, t away from the pub with their vn private entrance. Four rooms are located on the ground floor and four on the first floor. Family rooms accommodate up to four people and are ideal for those participating in outdoor activities in and around Rutland Water: fishing, walking, cycling and sailing. The large off-road car park is also convenient for light boats and motorised campers. There is a function room suitable for seminars, meetings and private celebrations, and the inn provides an ideal base from which to explore the market towns of Oakham, Uppingham and Stamford, as well as the nearby attractions of Burleigh House, Barnsdale Gardens, Rockingham Speedway and the historic Wing Maze.

★★★★ INN
MAP 11 SK80
Top St LE15 8SE
☎ 01572 737634
01572 737255
e-mail: info@thekingsarms-wing.co.uk
dir: *1m off B6003 between Uppingham & Oakham*

Open 12–3 6.30–11
Bar Meals L served Tue–Sun 12–2 D served Tue–Sun 6.30–9 (Sun 6.30–8) Av main course £13
Restaurant L served Tue–Sun 12–2 D served Tue–Sun 6.30–9 (Sun 6.30–8) Av 3 course à la carte £25
Free House
Timothy Taylor Landlord, Marstons Pedigree, Shepherd Neame Spitfire. 20
Facilities Parking
Rooms 8 bedrooms en suite S£65 D£75

OAKHAM continued

Pick of the Pubs

The Old Plough 🍷

2 Church St, Braunston LE15 8QT

☎ 01572 722714 📠 01572 770382

e-mail: info@oldploughrutland.com

dir: *A606 to Oakham, at 1st mini-rdbt right onto High St, to rail crossing. Left then 2nd left signed Braunston*

See Pick of the Pubs on page 469

SOUTH LUFFENHAM — MAP 11 SK90

The Coach House Inn NEW

3 Stamford Rd LE15 8NT

☎ 01780 720166 📠 01780 720866

e-mail: thecoachhouse123@aol.com

dir: *On A6121, off A47 between Ayston & Duddington*

Horses were once stabled here while weary travellers enjoyed a drink in what is now a private house next door. An extensive refurbishment in 2001 created a comfortable and elegant inn, with a 40-seater dining room, cosy bar and six en suite bedrooms. A short, appealing menu in the Ostler's Restaurant might feature goats' cheese, poached pear and walnut tart, followed by fillet of beef with chicken liver paté and rôsti potato.

Open 12–2.30 5–11 Closed: 25 Dec & 1 Jan **Bar Meals** L served Tue–Sun 12–2 D served Mon–Sat 6.30–9 Av main course £9 **Restaurant** L served Tue–Sun 12–2 D served Mon–Sat 6.30–9 Av 3 course à la carte £20 Free House IPA, Adnams, JHB, Kronenbourg & Guinness. **Facilities** Dogs allowed Parking **Rooms** 6 bedrooms en suite S£45 D£65 (★★★★ INN)

STRETTON — MAP 11 SK91

Pick of the Pubs

The Jackson Stops Inn 🍷

Rookery Rd LE15 7RA

☎ 01780 410237 📠 01780 410280

e-mail: james@jacksonstops-inn.fsnet.co.uk

For those keen on tracking down uniquely named pubs, this is a winner. You can guarantee nowhere else will have acquired its name by virtue of an estate agent sign that once hung outside for so long that locals dispensed with the original moniker of The White Horse Inn! The thatched stone inn actually dates from the 17th century, and has plenty of appealing features: log fires, scrubbed wood tables and no fewer than four dining rooms, as well as a 90-bin wine list. The cooking itself is distinctive and memorable. Home-cured salmon with blinis and crème fraîche could be followed up with a melting osso buco Milanaise (braised shin of veal with saffron risotto); then an iced mocha parfait with hot doughnuts. Cheeses are not only hand crafted but come direct from the Paris Cheese Market, while the truffles with your coffee are all home made.

Open 12–2.30 6.30–11 Closed: 26 Dec–1 Jan **Bar Meals** L served Tue–Sun 12–2 D served Tue–Sat 7–10 Av main course £11 **Restaurant** L served Tue–Sun 12–2 D served Tue–Sat 7–10 Av 3 course à la carte £26 Free House Oakham Ales JHB, Aldershaws Old Boy, Adnams Broadside, Timothy Taylor Landlord. 🍷 10 **Facilities** Garden Parking

Ram Jam Inn 🍷

The Great North Rd LE15 7QX

☎ 01780 410776 📠 01780 410361

dir: *On A1 N'bound carriageway past B668, through service station into car park*

The inn is thought to have got its current name some time during the 18th century when the pub sign advertised 'Fine Ram Jam', though few people, if indeed anyone, are sure what that might have been. These days, the informal café-bar and bistro exude warmth. The patio overlooks the orchard and paddock, and in fine summer weather is set for alfresco dining from the comprehensive all-day menu.

Open 7–11 **Bar Meals** L served all week 12–9.30 D served all week Av main course £8.95 **Restaurant** L served all week 12–9.30 D served all week Av 3 course à la carte £16 Free House Scottish Courage John Smith's Cask and Smooth, Marstons Pedigree, Greene King IPA. 🍷 8 **Facilities** Garden Parking Play Area

WING — MAP 11 SK8

Pick of the Pubs

Kings Arms ★★★★ INN 🍷

Top St LE15 8SE ☎ 01572 737634 📠 01572 737255

e-mail: info@thekingsarms-wing.co.uk

dir: *1m off B6003 between Uppingham & Oakham*

See Pick of the Pubs on page 471

SHROPSHIRE

BISHOP'S CASTLE — MAP 15 SO3

Boars Head 🍷

Church St SY9 5AE ☎ 01588 638521 📠 01588 630126

e-mail: sales@boarsheadhotel.co.uk

dir: *In town centre*

One of Bishop's Castle's earliest surviving buildings, this former coaching inn was granted its first full licence in 1642. According to legend, it escaped being destroyed by fire during the Civil War becau many of the Royalists were drinking here at the time. The integrity of the pub remains intact, with exposed beams, log fires and a chimney containing a priest hole. An appetising menu offers the likes of Spanis paella and chicken in cream and sherry sauce.

Open 11.30–11 (Sun 12–10.30) **Bar Meals** L served all week 12–3 D served all week 6.30–9 (Sun 12–9.30) Av main course £8 **Restaurant** L served all week 12–3 D served all week 6.30–9 Av 3 course à la carte £20 Free House Scottish Courage Courage Best & Courage Directors & regular guests. 🍷 8 **Facilities** Children's licence Parking

he Three Tuns Inn 🍷

'op St SY9 5BW ☎ 01588 638797

': *22m SW of Shrewsbury*

aditional timber-framed town centre inn established in 1625, and rewery since 1642 – so expect a wondrous choice of real ales. No ed music or fruit machine either; instead you may find live jazz, Morris dancing in summer. A recent refurbishment has preserved public bar, snug, and lounge while adding a classy oak-framed ss-sided dining room. Here a modern eclectic menu may start with ken liver parfait, and follow with pork and apple sausages.

en 12–11 (Sun 12–10.30) **Bar Meals** L served all week 12–3 D served veek 7–9 Av main course £9 **Restaurant** L served all week 12–3 erved all week 7–9 Av 3 course à la carte £18 Free House Three s XXX, Steamer, Scrooge, Clerics Cure (all by Three Tuns). 🍷 10 **ilities** Garden Dogs allowed

RIDGNORTH MAP 10 SO79

alfway House Inn NEW ★★★ INN 🍷

obury Rd, Eardington WV16 5LS

01746 762670 01746 768063

nail: info@halfwayhouseinn.co.uk

: *A458 towards Shrewsbury. Follow brown tourist signs to pub*

5th-century coaching inn previously called the Red Lion. The name nged in 1823 when a young princess Victoria rested here en route n Pitchford Hall to Great Witley Court; when she asked where she , she was told 'Half way there'. The hospitably-run inn is known both the quality and quantity of its pub grub, which ranges from a ble ploughman's to a rainbow trout cooked in herb butter.

en 5–12 (Sat–Sun all day) Closed: Sun eve (exc BH wknds) **Meals** L served Sat–Sun 12.30–2.30 D served Mon–Sat 5.30–8.30 nain course £10 **Restaurant** L served Sat–Sun 12.30–2.30 D served –Sat 5.30–8.30 Av 3 course fixed price £22.50 Free House oldens Golden Glow, Woods Shropshire Lad, Hobson's Town Crier, nness & Weston's Export Cider. 🍷 10 **Facilities** Garden Parking Play **Rooms** 10 bedrooms en suite S£45 D£55

Pheasant Inn NEW

Linley Brook WV16 4TA ☎ 01746 762260

e-mail: pheasant-inn@tiscali.co.uk

dir: *From Bridgnorth take B4373. Pub 400yds up lane signed from B4373. 2.5m from Broseley*

A quiet, rural and traditionally run free house, the perfect country pub. Open fires and woodburners heat its two rooms, where locals play bar billiards, dominoes and card games. Pub food includes excellent gammon and beefsteaks, from a prize-winning local butcher; battered plaice and scampi; home-made lasagne verde; beef curry and chilli; and ploughman's and toasted sandwiches. Local walks include one leading down to the River Severn.

Open 12–2.30 6.30–11 (Sat–Sun 12–3, Sun 6.30–10.30) (Summer 6–11) **Bar Meals** L served all week 12–2 D served all week 6.30–9 Av main course £6.50 Free House Hobson Bitter, Hobson Town Crier, Wye Valley HPA, Salopian Shropshire Gold. **Facilities** Garden Parking **Notes**

BURLTON MAP 15 SJ42

Pick of the Pubs

The Burlton Inn 🍷

SY4 5TB ☎ 01939 270284 01939 270204

e-mail: robertlesterrce@yahoo.co.uk

dir: *On A528 towards Ellesmere*

This pretty old building has been transformed into a classy, contemporary interpretation of an 18th-century inn, with a fresh looking dining area, a soft furnished space for relaxation, and a traditional bar – the perfect place for a pint of Robinson Unicorn or Oldham Best among other real ales. A good choice of food is offered, including a list of starters doubling as light meals – maybe venison terrine or Thai style mussels. Among the main courses is a choice of steaks; pan-fried glazed belly pork with flavours of soy, coriander, celery, leek and onion, served with parsnip mash and fresh vegetables; and grilled sea bass fillets on pea, goats' cheese and pancetta risotto. Don't miss the home-made desserts. Outside there is a lovely patio area, carefully planted to provide a blaze of colour in summer.

Open 11–3 6–11 (Sun 12–4, 7–10.30) Closed: 25 Dec, 1 Jan **Bar Meals** L served all week 12–2 D served all week 6.30–9.45 (Sun 7–9.30) Av main course £8 **Restaurant** L served all week 12–2 D served all week 6.30–9.45 (Sun 7–9.30) Av 3 course à la carte £20 Robinsons Robinsons Unicorn, Double Hop, Old Stockport, Smooth. 🍷 12 **Facilities** Garden Parking

England

CHURCH STRETTON MAP 15 SO49

The Royal Oak

Cardington SY6 7JZ ☎ 01694 771266

Reputedly the oldest pub in Shropshire, dating from 1462, this Grade II listed pub is all atmosphere and character. Nestling in the out-of-the-way village of Cardington, the pub, with its low beams, massive walls and striking inglenook, is a great place to seek out on cold winter days. In the summer it is equally delightful with its peaceful garden and patio. Packed lunches are available on request, and there's a free walkers' guide to the area.

Open 12–3 7–12 (Fri 6–1am, Sat 7–1am, Sun 7–12am) **Bar Meals** L served Tue–Sun 12–2 D served Tue–Sat 7–9 Av main course £7.50 **Restaurant** L served Tue–Sun 12–2 D served Tue–Sat 7.30–9 Free House Hobsons Best Bitter, Duck, Hopsons, Three Tuns XXX. **Facilities** Garden Parking Play Area **Notes**

CLEOBURY MORTIMER MAP 10 SO67

Pick of the Pubs

The Crown Inn ★★★★ INN

Hopton Wafers DY14 0NB

☎ 01299 270372 01299 271127

dir: *On A4117 8m E of Ludlow, 2m W of Cleobury Mortimer*

See Pick of the Pubs on opposite page

CLUN MAP 09 SO38

The Sun Inn

10 High St SY7 8JB ☎ 01588 640559 01588 640277

e-mail: marieboul@hotmail.com

dir: *On A498 N of Knighton*

A 15th-century inn of cruck frame construction set in a pretty Shropshire village. There are two bars, the stone-flagged snug and carpeted lounge furnished with settles and featuring a piece of 17th-century wallpaper. Freshly prepared home-cooked food is served, including a good choice of fish, such as whole grilled halibut with horseradish sauce, and favourites like beef and Guinness pie. In fine weather food and drinks can be enjoyed outside on the patio area.

Open 12–12 (Sat–Sun 12pm–1am) **Bar Meals** L served Thu–Tue 12–2 D served all week 6–9 Av main course £10.95 **Restaurant** L served all week 12–2 D served all week 6–9 (Sun 7–8.30) Av 3 course à la carte £17.50 Jennings Cockerhoop, Camerons Creamy Bitter, Banks Original & Guest Beers. **Facilities** Children's licence Garden Dogs allowed Parking

COCKSHUTT MAP 15 SJ42

The Leaking Tap

Shrewsbury Rd SY12 0JQ

☎ 01939 270636 01939 270746

e-mail: nicklaw@btconnect.com

This friendly pub in the centre of Cockshutt village features beamed bars and log fires, and serves a selection of guest ales and food cooked from local produce. Lunchtime or evening menus are available, including a vegetarian selection, might include oven-baked salmon with roasted fennel; almond crusted fish cakes; and baked cod with herbs and stilton.

Open 12–3 6–11 Rest: 25 Dec closed pm **Bar Meals** L served all week 12–2 D served Mon–Sat 6–9.30 Sun Av main course £9.50 **Restaurant** L served all week 12–2 D served Mon–Sat 6–9.30 Av 3 course à la carte £17 Banks Bitter, Banks Original, Guest Beers. 12 **Facilities** Parking

CRAVEN ARMS MAP 09 SO4

The Sun Inn

Corfton SY7 9DF ☎ 01584 861239 & 861503

e-mail: normanspride@aol.com

dir: *On B4368 7m N of Ludlow*

Landlady Teresa Pearce uses local produce in a delicious array of traditional dishes, while husband Norman brews the Corvedale ales on site, using local borehole water. First licensed in 1613, this historica pub in beautiful Corvedale is popular with walkers, who can be foun tucking into the likes of faggots and mushy peas; lamb hotpot; or vegetarian casserole and dumplings. Keep an eye out for regular sma beer festivals.

Open 12–2.30 6–12 (Fri–Sat 6–1am) **Bar Meals** L served all week 12–2 D served all week 6–9 (Sun 12–3, 7–9) Av main course £8 **Restaurant** L served all week 12–2 D served all week 6–9.30 (Sun 12–3, 7–9) Free House Corvedale Normans Pride, Secret Hop, Dark & Delicious, Julie's Ale. 14 **Facilities** Children's licence Garden Dogs allowed Parking Play Area

CRESSAGE MAP 10 SJ

The Riverside Inn

Cound SY5 6AF ☎ 01952 510900 01952 510926

dir: *On A458 7m from Shrewsbury, 1m from Cressage*

In three acres of garden alongside the River Severn, this extensively refurbished coaching inn offers river view dining both outdoors and a modern conservatory. The same menu is served throughout, with traditional and exotic pub dishes: perhaps Peking duck pancakes wit hoisin sauce, or 'Pee-kai' chicken breasts with satay sauce, and spina sorrel and mozzarella parcels.

Open 12–3 6–11 Summer Sat–Sun all day **Bar Meals** L served all week 12–2.30 D served all week 6.30–9.30 **Restaurant** L served all week 12–2 D served all week 7–9.30 Free House Shropshire Gold, Worthingtc Guest beers. **Facilities** Garden Dogs allowed Parking

HODNET MAP 15 SJ

The Bear Hotel

TF9 3NH ☎ 01630 685214 01630 685787

e-mail: info@bearhotel.org.uk

dir: *Junct A53 & A442 right at rdbt. Hotel in village centre*

An illuminated cellar garden, once a priest hole, is one of the more unusual attractions at this 16th-century coaching inn. There was also a bear pit in the car park until 1970. Hodnet Hall Gardens are close by. An extensive menu includes bar snacks and restaurant meals, wi steak options featuring prominently as well as dishes like Caesar sal or deep-fried brie to start, and baked pheasant or salmon en croute mains. Renowned locally for medieval banquets in the baronial hall.

Open 10.30am–1am (Sun 12–10.30) **Bar Meals** L served all week 12–2 (S to 2.45–9) D served all week 6–9 Av main course £8.50 **Restaurant** L ser all week 12–2 D served all week 6–9.30 Free House Theakston, Worthers, Guest Ales. **Facilities** Garden Parking

The Crown Inn

quick glance at this 16th-century, one-time coaching inn suggests that it is constructed from irginia creeper, so densely does its foliage cover every square inch of the façade, except the indows.

rrounded by tumbling streams, sh farmland and wooded valleys, e Crown was once estate owned d its informal Rent Room bar was here local tenants paid whatever ey owed. In the full service à carte restaurant you can dine neath exposed beams warmed, if cessary, by fires blazing in the large glenooks. Fresh local produce lies hind the seasonal menus featuring t just traditional dishes, but also ore adventurous house specialities. e daily blackboards offer a dizzying oice, with starters such as trio of eadcrumbed deep-fried local cheeses th Burgundy and redcurrant sauce; sh crab and mussel chowder; and occoli and goats' cheese pancakes th parmesan crust. The Crown is rticularly well known for its fish hes, nailing its colours to the st in a big way with a particularly nerous selection, including whole roast silver bream with charred corn, avocado and coriander salsa; medallions of monkfish on dauphinoise potatoes with chervil cream; and sautéed king scallops on courgette spaghetti with cucumber and chilli oil. But fish is not the whole story, of course, and the boards continue with roast breast of Barbary duck with orange and Armagnac glaze; traditional faggots with mushy peas, onion gravy and golden chips; pork tenderloin with mushrooms, cream and white wine; and breast of chicken filled with banana, wrapped in bacon and melted smoked cheese on a light mustard sauce. The thoughtful wine list, put together by local merchants, includes a wide range of fine ports, Armagnacs and Cognacs. Bedrooms are individually furnished and all offer en suite facilities. There's a duck pond in the surrounding immaculately kept gardens.

★★★★ INN 🍷
MAP 10 SO67
Hopton Wafers DY14 0NB
☎ 01299 270372
🖷 01299 271127
dir: *On A4117 8m E of Ludlow, 2m W of Cleobury Mortimer*

Open 12-3 6-12
Bar Meals L served all week 12-2.30 D served all week 6-9.30 (Sun 12-9) Av main course £9.50
Restaurant L served all week 12-2.30 D served all week 7-9.30 Av 3 course à la carte £25.50 Av 2 course fixed price £13.95
Free House
Ludlow Gold, Hobsons Best + Guest beers. 🍷 10
Facilities Garden Parking Play Area
Rooms 18 bedrooms en suite S£59.50 D£95

IRONBRIDGE MAP 10 SJ60

The Malthouse

The Wharfage TF8 7NH ☎ 01952 433712 01952 433298

e-mail: enquiries@themalthouseironbridge.com

An inn since the 1800s, the Malthouse is located in the village of Ironbridge, now a designated UNESCO World Heritage Site famous for its natural beauty and award-winning museums. Party menus are available for both the popular jazz bar and the restaurant, while the main menu offers dishes ranging from lasagne or faggots to monkfish and pancetta baked and served with sweet chorizo, mussel and tomato cassoulet.

Open 11-11 (Sun 12-3 6-10.30) **Bar Meals** L served all week 12-2.30 D served all week 6-9.30 Av main course £8 **Restaurant** L served all week 12-2 D served all week 6.30-9.45 Av 0 course fixed price £23 Punch Taverns Directors, greene King IPA, Badger. 10 **Facilities** Children's licence Garden Parking

LLANFAIR WATERDINE MAP 09 SO27

Pick of the Pubs

The Waterdine ★★★★★ RR

LD7 1TU ☎ 01547 528214

e-mail: info@waterdine.com

dir: *4.5m W of Knighton off B4355, right opposite Lloyney Inn, 2m into village, opp church*

The River Teme runs through the bottom of the garden of this beautiful old inn, marking the border between England and Wales. The Waterdine has been supplying scrumpy to sheep drovers and farmers for hundreds of years, and is proud to continue the tradition of refreshing weary travellers and meeting their every need. There are two dining rooms, the Garden Room looking out over the lovely Teme, and the Taproom, tucked away in the oldest part of the building with heavy beams and a stone floor. Chef owner Ken Adams has a highly productive garden, and his menus are based on home-grown and locally supplied organic produce, so dishes are appropriately seasonal. Typical examples are baked black pudding with apple purée and Hereford cider sauce; and rack of Kerry lamb with lamb and kidney brochette.

Open 12-3 7-11 Closed: 1 wk Winter, 1wk Spring
Bar Meals L served Tue-Sun (bookings only) 12-1.45
Restaurant L served Tue-Sun 12-1.45 D served Tue-Sat 7-9 Av 3 course fixed price £30 Free House Wood Shropshire Legends, Parish Bitter & Shropshire Lad. 8 **Facilities** Garden Parking
Rooms 3 bedrooms en suite

LUDLOW MAP 10 SO57

The Church Inn ★★★★ INN

Buttercross SY8 1AW ☎ 01584 872174 01584 877146

web: www.thechurchinn.com

dir: *Town centre*

The inn stands on one of the oldest sites in Ludlow, dating back some seven centuries, and through the ages has been occupied by a blacksmith, saddler, druggist and barber-surgeon. These days it enjoys a good reputation for decent beer and traditional pub food – cod in beer batter, locally made faggots, and three cheese pasta and broccoli bake. A new 34-seat function room is available, and nine en suite bedrooms with televisions and tea-making facilities.

Open 11-11 **Bar Meals** L served Mon-Fri 12-2.30 (Sat 12-3.30, Sun 12-3) D served all week 6.30-9 **Restaurant** L served Mon-Fri 12-2.30 (Sat 12-3.30, Sun 12-3) D served all week 6.30-9 Free House Hobsons Town Crier, Old Hooky, Weetwood, Wye Valley Bitter. 14 **Facilities** Dogs allowed **Rooms** 9 bedrooms en suite S£35 D£60

The Clive Bar & Restaurant with Rooms

★★★★★ RR

Bromfield SY8 2JR

☎ 01584 856565 & 856665 01584 856661

e-mail: info@theclive.co.uk

dir: *2m N of Ludlow on A49, between Hereford & Shrewsbury*

The Cookhouse Café Bar is part of a complex, which includes the Clive Restaurant with rooms, and function facilities in a former farmhouse and outbuildings. The name reflects the building's association with Robert Clive, who laid the foundations of British rule in India. There's a café bar menu featuring starters, salads, lunch dishes like bangers and mash or cod and chips, and substantial mains like breast of pheasant and game mousse with port sauce. A separate menu covers baguettes, sandwiches and buns.

Open 11-11 (Sun 11-10) Closed: 25-26 Dec **Bar Meals** L served all week 12-3 D served all week 6-10 (Sat-Sun 12-10) Av main course £9.9 **Restaurant** L served all week 12-3 D served all week 6-10 (Sat-Sun 12-10) Av 3 course à la carte £25 Free House Hobsons Best Bitter, Interbrew Worthington Cream Flow, Caffreys. 10 **Facilities** Garden Parking **Rooms** 15 bedrooms en suite S£50 D£75

The Roebuck Inn

Brimfield SY8 4NE ☎ 01584 711230 01584 711654

dir: *Just off A49 between Ludlow & Leominster*

This country inn dating back to the 15th century offers cosy bars with inglenooks and wood panelling, a bright, airy dining room and comfortable bedrooms. Imaginative food includes lemon spiced gravadlax; pan-seared scallops; goats' cheese fritters; or smoked chicken ravioli to start, and main courses ranging from roast rack of lamb or chicken breast to glazed chilli and ginger salmon or steamed fillets of sole. New owners 2007.

Open 11.30-3.30 6.30-11 **Bar Meals** L served Mon-Sat 12-2.30 (Sun 12-3.30) D served all week 7-9 **Restaurant** L served Mon-Sat 12-2.30 (Sun 12-3.30) D served all week 7-9.30 Free House Bank's Bitter, Camerons Strongarm, Marstons Pedigree plus Guests. **Facilities** Garden Dogs allowed Parking

England

Pick of the Pubs

Unicorn Inn

Corve St SY8 1DU ☎ 01584 873555 🖷 01584 876268

dir: *A49 to Ludlow*

Dating from the early 17th century, this low, attractive timber-framed building backs on to the once flood-prone River Corve. During the great flood of 1885 a photograph was taken of men sitting drinking around a table in the bar while water lapped the doorway. Apparently it wasn't unusual for empty beer barrels to float out of the cellar and down the river. Log fires in winter and the sunny riverside terrace in summer prove very appealing. Both bar and restaurant menus are served at lunch and dinner 364 days per year. The candlelit restaurant dining room offers good British and European dishes with fillet of beef, mixed peppers and onion souvlaki; roulade of chicken and apricots with cambozala cheese sauce; and lamb Shrewsbury. In the bar you could try duck Koresh with chelo – an Iranian dish served with basmati rice – or the more prosaic battered cod, salad and chips.

Open 12–3 6–11 (Sun 12–3.30, 6.30–10.30) Closed: Dec 25 **Bar Meals** L served all week 12–2.15 D served all week 6–9.15 (Sun 6.30–9.15) Av main course £7 **Restaurant** L served all week 12–2.15 D served all week 6–9.15 (Sun 6.30–9.30) Av 3 course à la carte £22.50 Free House Timothy Taylor's Landlord, Fuller's London Pride, Thwaites Original, Guest ales. 8 **Facilities** Garden Dogs allowed Parking

MADELEY MAP 10 SJ60

The New Inn

Blists Hill Victorian Town, Legges Way TF7 5DU

☎ 01952 601018 🖷 01785 252247

e-mail: sales@jenkinsonscaterers.co.uk

dir: *Between Telford & Broseley*

Here's something different – a Victorian pub that was moved brick by brick from the Black Country and re-erected at the Ironbridge Gorge Open Air Museum. The building remains basically as it was in 1890, and customers can buy traditionally brewed beer at five-pence farthing a pint – roughly £2.10 in today's terms – using pre-decimal currency bought from the bank. The mainly traditional menu includes home-made soup, steak and kidney pudding, and ham and leek pie.

Open 11–4 Closed: 24–25 Dec, 1 Jan **Bar Meals** L served all week 12–3 Av main course £7.50 **Restaurant** L served all week 12–3 Banks Bitter, Banks Original, Pedigree. **Facilities** Garden Parking Play Area

MARTON MAP 15 SJ20

The Sun Inn

SY21 8JP ☎ 01938 561211

e-mail: info@suninn.biz

dir: *On B4386 in centre of Marton opposite village shop*

This classic stone free house dates back to 1760 and is surrounded by glorious Shropshire countryside. Both bar and restaurant have been attractively refurbished, with the contemporary restaurant offering a modern English and Mediterranean menu and an impressive selection of fresh fish dishes. A typical meal might include a starter of asparagus and quail's egg salad with parmesan cracknels, followed by breast of duckling with pomegranate, molasses and sherry, served with okra.

Open 12–2 7–11 **Bar Meals** L served Wed–Sun 12–2 D served Tue–Sat 7–9.30 Av main course £8.95 **Restaurant** L served Wed–Sun 12–2 D served Tue–Sat 7–9.30 Av 3 course à la carte £25.30 Av 2 course fixed price £12.95 Free House Hobsons Best Bitter, Worthington Creamflow & Guest Ales. 9 **Facilities** Parking

MUCH WENLOCK MAP 10 SO69

The George & Dragon

2 High St TF13 6AA ☎ 01952 727312

e-mail: miltonmonk@btconnect.com

dir: *On A458 halfway between Shrewsbury & Bridgnorth*

500 water jugs hanging from the ceiling are part of an astonishing collection of brewery memorabilia in this historic, allegedly haunted Grade II listed pub. Next door to the market square, Guildhall and ruined priory, the inn's welcoming atmosphere draws both locals and visitors from further afield. Expect a good range of popular dishes, with snacks at lunchtime, and the likes of roasted duck breast in plum sauce, and smoked haddock among the evening specials.

Open 12–11 **Bar Meals** L served all week 12–2 D served Mon–Tue, Thu–Sat 6–9 **Restaurant** L served all week 12–2 D served Mon–Tue, Thu–Sat 6.30–9 Punch Retail Greene King Abbot Ale, IPA, Hobsons Town Crier, Timothy Taylors Landlord. 8

Longville Arms

Longville in the Dale TF13 6DT

☎ 01694 771206 🖷 01694 771742

dir: *A49 to Church Stretton, then B4371 to Longville*

Prettily situated in a scenic corner of Shropshire, ideally placed for walking and touring, this welcoming country inn has been carefully restored. Solid elm or cast-iron-framed tables, oak panelling and wood-burning stoves are among the features that help to generate a warm, friendly ambience. Favourite main courses on the bar menu and specials board include steak and ale pie, chicken wrapped in bacon and stuffed with paté, smoked haddock, mixed fish platter, and a range of steaks.

Open 12–3 6.30–11 **Bar Meals** L served all week 12–2.15 D served all week 6.30–9.15 Av main course £9.95 **Restaurant** L served Sun 12–2.15 D served Fri–Sat 7–9.15 Av 3 course à la carte £20 Av 3 course fixed price £12.95 Free House Stella, Becks & local Guest beers. **Facilities** Garden Dogs allowed Parking Play Area

England

MUCH WENLOCK continued

The Talbot Inn

High St TF13 6AA ☎ 01952 727077 📠 01952 728436
e-mail: the_talbot_inn@hotmail.com
dir: *M54 junct 4, follow Ironbridge Gorge Museum signs, then Much Wenlock signs*

Dating from 1360, the Talbot was once a hostel for travellers and a centre for alms giving. The delightful courtyard was used in the 1949 Powell and Pressburger film *Gone to Earth*. Daily specials highlighted on the varied menu may include steak and kidney pie, baked seabass, Shropshire pie and cod mornay.

Open 11-3 6-11 (Sun 12-3, 7-10.30, Summer, Sat-Sun 11-11) Closed: 25 Dec **Bar Meals** L served all week 12-2.30 D served all week 7-9.30 **Restaurant** L served all week 12-2.30 D served all week 7-9.30 Free House Bass. 7 **Facilities** Garden Parking

Pick of the Pubs

Wenlock Edge Inn

Hilltop, Wenlock Edge TF13 6DJ
☎ 01746 785678 📠 01746 785285
e-mail: info@wenlockedgeinn.co.uk
dir: *4.5m from Much Wenlock on B4371*

This inn perches at one of the highest points of Wenlock Edge's dramatic wooded ledge. Originally a row of 17th-century quarrymen's cottages, the cosy interior contains a small country-style dining room and several bars, one with a wood-burning stove. Outside, a furnished patio takes full advantage of the views stretching across Apedale to Caer Caradoc and the Long Mynd. Start your meal with Bantry Bay mussels; home-made chicken liver paté; or oak smoked salmon, followed by a hearty main course like steak and ale pie or roast vegetable and blue stilton wellington. Puddings include warm chocolate brioche pudding with rich chocolate sauce; and the pub favourite sticky toffee pudding with toffee sauce. The lunchtime menu offers freshly baked baguette sandwiches as well as a range of hot dishes.

Open 12-3 7-11 **Bar Meals** L served Wed-Sat 12-2 (Sun 12-3) D served Wed-Sat 7-9 Av main course £8.50 **Restaurant** L served Wed-Sat 12-2 (Sun 12-3) D served Wed-Sat 7-9 Free House Hobsons Best & Town Crier, Salopian Shropshire Gold, Three Tuns Brewery Edge Ale exclusive to Wenlock Edge Inn. **Facilities** Garden Dogs allowed Parking

MUNSLOW MAP 10 SO5

Pick of the Pubs

The Crown Country Inn ★★★★ INN

SY7 9ET ☎ 01584 841205 📠 01584 841255
e-mail: info@crowncountryinn.co.uk
dir: *On B4368 between Craven Arms & Much Wenlock*

See Pick of the Pubs on opposite page

NORTON MAP 10 SJ7

Pick of the Pubs

The Hundred House Hotel ★★ HL

Bridgnorth Rd TF11 9EE
☎ 01952 730353 📠 01952 730355
e-mail: reservations@hundredhouse.co.uk
dir: *On A442, 6m N of Bridgnorth, 5m S of Telford centre*

See Pick of the Pubs on page 480

PICKLESCOTT MAP 15 SO4

Bottle & Glass Inn NEW

SY6 6NR ☎ 01694 751345
e-mail: masonsarmsinn@aol.om
dir: *Turn off A49 at Dorrington*

The hamlet of Pickelscott lies in the northern foothills of the Long Mynd, or Mountain. The landlord of this 16th-century pub, who has been here for 30-odd years, occasionally hears the ghost of a wooden-legged predecessor tap-tapping around, somehow upsetting the pub's electrics. A typical starter is roquefort-stuffed pear with gre[illegible] mayonnaise. Homity pie; game and red wine casserole; and haddock with cheese sauce on spinach are among the main courses.

Open 12-3 6-12 **Bar Meals** L served Tue-Sun 12-2 D served Tue-Sat 7-9 Av main course £11.50 **Restaurant** L served Tue-Sun 12-2 D serve[illegible] Tue-Sat 7-9 Av 3 course à la carte £19.50 Free House Hobsons, Three Tuns XXX, Woods. **Facilities** Dogs allowed Parking

The Crown Country Inn

he Crown has a lovely setting, below the rolling hills of Wenlock Edge in the Vale of the River orve. It is a three-storey, Grade II listed Tudor building retaining many original features, such s the sturdy oak beams, flagstone floors and prominent inglenook fireplace in the main bar rea.

ne inn was once a Hundred ouse, where courts sat and passed dgement on local villains. It oesn't take much to imagine how must have felt to be on trial, and erhaps the black-clothed Charlotte metimes seen in the pub was ntenced here. Meals are served in e main bar, the Bay dining area, id the Corvedale Restaurant at ecified times. Owners Richard id Jane Arnold have a strong mmitment to warm hospitality, aditional ales and good food. chard is head chef and has been Master Chef of Great Britain for ore than a decade. He has been oking professionally for over 20 ars. Top quality local produce is quired from trusted sources and featured strongly in dishes such as fishcake of the house's own alder wood smoked salmon and herbs with pea purée and caper butter sauce; and griddled loin of pork with sweet potato purée, chorizo sausage and red onion cream. An impressive cheeseboard lists a dozen English and Welsh cheeses in order of strength, but for something sweet how about iced vanilla parfait with compote of prunes and shortbread biscuit. The restaurant is also available for private parties. Three large bedrooms are located in a converted Georgian stable block.

★★★★ INN

MAP 10 SO58

SY7 9ET

☎ 01584 841205

01584 841255

e-mail:
info@crowncountryinn.co.uk

dir: *On B4368 between Craven Arms & Much Wenlock*

Open 12–2 6.30–11 Closed: 25 Dec

Bar Meals L served Tue–Sun 12–2 D served Tue–Sat 6.30–9

Restaurant L served Tue–Sun 12–2 D served Tue–Sat 6.30–9 Av 3 course à la carte £25

Free House

Holden's Black Country Bitter, Black Country Mild, Holden's Golden Glow, Holden's Special Bitter & Three Tuns Brewery 3X. 7

Facilities Children's licence Garden Parking Play Area

Rooms 3 bedrooms en suite S£50 D£70

The Hundred House Hotel

This fine, creeper-clad building has been run lovingly by the Phillips family for the past 21 year The main part is Georgian, but the half-timbered, thatched barn in the courtyard is 14th centur and was used as a courthouse in medieval times.

Downstairs there's a complex warren of lavishly decorated bars and dining rooms with exposed brickwork, beamed ceilings, quarry-tiled floors and oak panelling and, everywhere you look, aromatic bunches of drying herbs and flowers. Mellow brick, stained glass, Jacobean panelling, open log fires and cast-iron cooking pots from Ironbridge create, to quote a guest, 'A haven of kindness, comfort and service'. The words 'Temperance Hall' on the Art Nouveau stained-glass doors set the tone for an experience that is unique, sometimes witty and always delightful. The quirky charm extends to the bedrooms and to the beautiful herb and flower gardens. Food is in the modern English/ Continental style, with seasonality a particular virtue. Stocks, pies and pasta are all home made. In the bar/brasserie, among many other dishes, you can order pan-fried potato cakes; Greek salad; and a mezze of houmous, tomato, fennel and smoked aubergine salads. From the à la carte you might try tea-smoked duck breast with sesame, orange and ginger dressing followed by roast Apley partridge stuffed with mushroom and cotechino. Don't miss the specials menu though, or you'll go without such treats as venison terrine with fig, pear and hazelnut salad; chicken gumbo, or monkfish, salmon and scallop casserole with lobster and tarragon bisque. A long and lovely dessert menu offers raspberry and meringue ice cream terrine; tiramisu; crème brûlée, and a selection of home-made ice creams and sorbets. Keep an eye out for the special 'posh nosh' gourmet evenings too.

★★ HL ◎◎ 🍷
MAP 10 SJ70
Bridgnorth Rd TF11 9EE
☎ 01952 730353
Fax 01952 730355
e-mail:
reservations@hundredhouse.co.uk
dir: *On A442, 6m N of Bridgnorth, 5m S of Telford centre*

Open 11–2.30 6–11 (Sun 11–10.30) Closed: 25–26 Dec eve
Bar Meals L served Mon–Sat 12–2.15 D served Mon–Sat 6–9 (Sun 7–9) Av main course £8.95
Restaurant L served all week 12–2.15 D served Mon–Sat 6–9 Av 3 course fixed price £19.95
Free House
Heritage Bitter, Highgate Saddlers Bitter, Highgate Dark Mild, Everards Tiger. 🍷 16
Facilities Garden Parking
Rooms 10 bedrooms en suite S£69 D£99

HIFNAL MAP 10 SJ70

dfellows Wine Bar

arket Place TF11 9AU ☎ 01952 461517 01952 463855

mail: reservations@odley.co.uk

r: *M54 junct 4, 3rd exit at rdbt, at next rdbt take 3rd exit, past trol station, round bend under rail bridge. Bar on left*

uirky, much-loved wine bar with an elevated dining area leading o an attractive conservatory, and live music every Sunday. Owner att Jones is on a mission to serve only the real and traceable: drinks clude at least four real ales and real cider, as well as organic herbal as. All meat and game is sourced from Shropshire rare breed farms, icken is free-range, and vegetables are organic if possible; even the ffees are fairly traded.

pen 12–12 Closed: 25–26 Dec, 1 Jan **Bar Meals** L served all week –2.30 D served all week 5–9.30 (Sun 12–9) Av main course £7 **staurant** L served all week 12–2.30 D served all week 5–9.30 (Sun 12–9) 3 course à la carte £18 Free House Salopian, Wye Valley, Holdens, dlow Gold & Three Tuns. 12 **Facilities** Parking **Rooms** 7 bedrooms suite S£42.50 D£52.50 (★★★ INN)

HREWSBURY MAP 15 SJ41

he Armoury

ctoria Quay, Victoria Av SY1 1HH

01743 340525 01743 340526

mail: armoury@brunningandprice.co.uk

e original armoury building, abandoned in 1882, was 'moved' here om the Armoury Gardens in 1922, owing to the scarcity of building aterials after World War I. It was a bakery until 1974 and thereafter a arehouse. In 1995 it was renovated, opened as a pub and renamed e Armoury. With its riverside location and large warehouse windows, makes an impressive pub. Recent alterations have seen the place ened out into a combined restaurant and bar area, and the same enu is served throughout. Real ales include Shropshire Lad and ree Tuns Steamer.

pen 12–11 (Mon-Sat 12–11, Sun 12–10.30) Closed: 25–26 Dec **ar Meals** L served all week 12–9.30 D served all week 6–9.30 (Sun –9) **Restaurant** L served all week D served all week Brunning & ice Roosters APA, Salopian Shropshire Gold, Deuchars IPA, Woods ropshire Lad. 16

The Mytton & Mermaid Hotel ★★★ HL

Atcham SY5 6QG ☎ 01743 761220 01743 761292

e-mail: admin@myttonandmermaid.co.uk

dir: *From M54 junct 7 signed Shrewsbury, at 2nd rdbt take 1st left signed Ironbridge/Atcham & follow for 1.5m, hotel on right after bridge*

Idyllically set overlooking the Severn, this stylish, 1735-built country house hotel was once owned by Clough Williams-Ellis, creator of Portmeirion in North Wales. Named after a profligate local squire, Mad Jack's Bar has log fires and comfy sofas, while in the candlelit restaurant the seasonal menu might, for example, permit a three-course dinner of baked crab and ginger tartlet; braised shoulder of lamb with root vegetables and rosemary and mustard mash; and orange and lemon tart.

Open 11am–12am Closed: 25 Dec **Bar Meals** L served all week 12–2.30 D served all week 6.30–10 (Sun 12–3) Av main course £11 **Restaurant** L served all week 12–2.30 D served all week 7–10 (Sun 12–3) Av 3 course à la carte £27.50 Free House Shropshire Lad, Ruddles, Salopian Icon, Courage Directors. 12 **Facilities** Garden Parking **Rooms** 20 bedrooms en suite S£70 D£95

The Plume of Feathers ★★★ INN

Harley SY5 6LP ☎ 01952 727360 01952 728542

e-mail: feathersatharley@aol.com

Nestling under Wenlock Edge, this 17th-century inn has stunning views across the valley. Look for the Charles I oak bedhead, full size cider press and inglenook fireplace. Food reflects the seasons, with a changing fish menu; bar meals such as Shropshire baked ham with egg and chips; and restaurant dishes such as lamb en croûte stuffed with wild mushroom and leek gratin, with oxtail gravy; or pan-fried duck breast with black cherry sauce.

Open 12–3 5–11 (Sat 12–11.30, Sun 12–10.30) **Bar Meals** L served all week 12–2 D served all week 6.30–9 (Sun 12–9) **Restaurant** L served all week 12–2 D served all week 6.30–9 (Sun 12–9) Free House Worthingtons, Guinness, Directors, Carling & Guest beers. **Facilities** Children's licence Garden Parking Play Area **Rooms** 9 bedrooms en suite S£49.95 D£65

England

STOTTESDON MAP 10 SO68

Fighting Cocks NEW

1 High St DY14 8TZ ☎ 01746 718270 📠 01746 718270
e-mail: sandrafc-5@hotmail.com
dir: *11m from Bridgnorth off B4376*

This 17th-century coaching inn once brewed ale for the monks in the church opposite. It remains a very traditional pub, with old-fashioned games such as quoits, darts and dominoes. Evening meals are served from Tuesday to Saturday, with lunch available on Saturdays and Sundays. The food is all home made on the premises and combines traditional European and occasional Asian influences. Real ales are a strength; choices typically include Hobson's Best and Wye Valley Bitter.

Open 6–12 (Fri 5–12, Sat–Sun 12–12) **Bar Meals** L served Sat–Sun 12–2.30 D served Tue–Sat 7–9 Av main course £8.95 **Restaurant** L served Sat–Sun 12–2.30 D served Tue–Sat 7–9 Av 3 course à la carte £15 Free House Hobsons Best, Hobsons Town Crier, Hobsons Mild, Wye Valley HPA. **Facilities** Garden Dogs allowed Parking

UPPER AFFCOT MAP 09 SO48

The Travellers Rest Inn 🍷

SY6 6RL ☎ 01694 781275 📠 01694 781555
e-mail: reception@travellersrestinn.co.uk
dir: *On A49, 5m S of Church Stretton*

Locals and passing trade enjoy the friendly atmosphere, great range of real ales and good pub grub at this traditional south Shropshire inn on the A49 between Church Stretton and Craven Arms. Food to suit the appetite and the pocket is served all day until 9pm. Expect to see starters of smoked mackerel or prawn cocktail, traditional mains like steak or chilli con carne, and puddings such as spotted Dick.

Open 11–11 **Bar Meals** L served all week 11.30–8.30 D served all week 11.30–8.30 (Sun 12–8.30) Wood Shropshire Lad, Hobsons Best Bitter, Bass, Guinness. 🍷 14 **Facilities** Children's licence Garden Dogs allowed Parking

WENTNOR MAP 15 SO39

The Crown Inn

SY9 5EE ☎ 01588 650613 📠 01588 650436
e-mail: crowninn@wentnor.com
dir: *From Shrewsbury A49 to Church Stretton, follow signs over Long Mynd to Asterton, right to Wentnor*

Outdoor enthusiasts of all persuasions will appreciate the location of this 17th-century coaching inn below the Long Mynd. Its homely atmosphere, which owes much to log fires, beams and horse brasses, makes eating and drinking here a pleasure. Meals are served in the bar or separate restaurant. Typical daily changing, traditional home-made dishes include pork tenderloin filled with marinated fruits; pan-fried breast of duck with a burnt orange sauce; and grilled sea bass with couscous.

Open 12–3 6–11 (Sat 12–11, Sun 12–10.30) Closed: 25 Dec
Bar Meals L served all week 12–2 D served all week 6–9 (Sat–Sun 12–9) Av main course £6 **Restaurant** L served all week 12–2 D served all week 6–9 (Sat–Sun 12–9) Free House Hobsons, Old Speckled Hen, Three Tuns, Wye Valley. **Facilities** Garden Parking Play Area

WESTON HEATH MAP 10 SJ7

Pick of the Pubs

The Countess's Arms 🍷

TF11 8RY ☎ 01952 691123 📠 01952 691660
e-mail: countesssarms@countessarms.co.uk
dir: *1.5m from Weston Park. Turn off A5 onto A41 towards Newport*

Described as a large contemporary eatery in a refurbished traditional pub, the interior of the Countess's Arms spectacularly belies its outside appearance, as all the internal walls and floors have been removed and an extension has been added. The internal structure now comprises a spacious gallery bar from where customers can look down on the blue glass mosaic-tiled bar below. The establishment is owned by restaurateur and food critic the Earl of Bradford, whose family seat is just down the road. Bar snacks include chilli nachos, seafood dim sum, sausage with bubble and squeak, and Countess burger with hand-cut chips. Full meals, served in the Gallery Bar or Garden Room Restaurant, offer imaginative combinations like roast pork fillet, haggis and field mushroom 'Wellington' with roasted vegetables, or chargrilled teriyaki halloumi with sesame noodle salad and sweet chilli dressing. The place is particularly popular for its jazz night on Fridays.

Open 12–11 (Sun 12–10.30) **Bar Meals** L served all week 12–6 D served all week 6–9.30 (Sun 12–8.30) **Restaurant** L served all week 12–6 D served all week 6–9.30 (Sun 12–8.30) Free House Woods, Shropshire Lad, Salopian, Shropshire Gold. 🍷 10 **Facilities** Garden Parking

WHITCHURCH MAP 15 SJ5

Willeymoor Lock Tavern 🍷

Tarporley Rd SY13 4HF ☎ 01948 663274
dir: *2m N of Whitchurch on A49 (Warrington/Tarporley)*

A former lock keeper's cottage idyllically situated beside the Llangollen Canal. Mrs Elsie Gilkes has been licensee here for around 30 years. Low-beamed rooms are hung with a novel teapot collection; there are open log fires and a range of real ales. Deep-fried fish and a choice of grills rub shoulders with traditional steak pie, chicken curry and vegetable chilli. Other options include salad platters, children's choice and gold rush pie for dessert.

Open 12–3 6–11 (Sun 12–2.30 7–10.30) Closed: 25 Dec & 1 Jan
Bar Meals L served all week 12–2 D served all week 6–9 (Winter Sun 7–9)
Restaurant L served all week 12–2 D served all week 6–9 Free House Guest Ales, Abbeydale, Moonshine, Weetwood. 🍷 8 **Facilities** Garden Parking Play Area **Notes**

/OORE MAP 15 SJ74

wan at Woore 🍷

antwich Rd CW3 9SA ☎ 01630 647220

r: *A51 (Stone to Nantwich road). 10m from Nantwich*

furbished 19th-century dining inn by the A51 near Stapley Water ardens. Four separate eating areas lead off from a central servery. aily specials boards supplement the menu, which might include spy confit of duck, slow roast knuckle of lamb, roasted salmon vegetable linguine, or red onion and garlic tarte Tatin. There's a parate fish menu, offering grilled red mullet fillets, perhaps, or seared na on roasted sweet peppers.

pen 12–12 **Bar Meals** L served Mon–Sat 12–6 D served Mon–Sat 6–9 at 9.30) Av main course £8 Inn Partnership Wells Bombardier, ddingtons. 🍷 6 **Facilities** Garden Dogs allowed Parking

SOMERSET

.PPLEY MAP 03 ST02

he Globe Inn

\21 0HJ ☎ 01823 672327

ir: *A38 towards Exeter. Village signed in 5m*

is quirky 500-year-old pub on the Somerset-Devon border is dden in maze of lanes, and is known for its large collection of Corgi d Dinky cars, Titanic memorabilia, and old advertising posters and amel signs from the 20s, 30s and 40s. As far as the food goes, you ight be offered duck in Madeira sauce; venison pie with bacon; ushrooms and shallots; Moroccan lamb; or sea bass with chive and ne butter.

pen 11–3 6.30–12 **Bar Meals** L served Tue–Sun 12–2 D served Tue–Sun -9.30 Av main course £10 **Restaurant** L served Tue–Sun D served e–Sun 7–9.30 Av 3 course à la carte £20 Free House Palmers opper Ale, Palmers 200, Exmoor Ales, Appleys Ale. **Facilities** Garden arking Play Area

.SHCOTT MAP 04 ST43

he Ashcott Inn 🍷

0 Bath Rd TA7 9QQ ☎ 01458 210282 📠 01458 210282

ir: *M5 junct 23 follow signs for A39 to Glastonbury*

ating back to the 16th century, this former coaching inn has an tractive bar with beams and stripped stone walls, as well as quaint d seats and an assortment of oak and elm tables. Outside is a opular terrace and a delightful walled garden. A straightforward enu offers 'Home Favourites' such as Cumberland sausages, pasta carbonara, Spanish omelette and steak baguette, while poultry and seafood choices include chicken provençal, tuna steak with salad, or chicken tikka masala. Vegetarians may enjoy mushroom stroganoff with gherkins and capers, or stilton and walnut salad.

Open 11–11 **Bar Meals** L served all week D served all week Av main course £7 **Restaurant** L served all week 12 D served all week 9.30 (Sun 12–8.30) Av 3 course à la carte £17 Heavitree Otter. 🍷 12 **Facilities** Garden Dogs allowed Parking Play Area

Ring O'Bells 🍷

High St TA7 9PZ ☎ 01458 210232

e-mail: info@ringobells.com

dir: *From M5 junct 23 follow signs A39 & Glastonbury. Turn left off A39, at post office follow signs to church & village hall*

This free house has been run by the same family for 19 years, during which it has stacked up many awards for its ales, food and service. Parts of the building date from 1750, and it looks every inch the traditional village pub, with beams, an old fireplace and a collection of bells and horse brasses. All dishes are made on the premises, with meals ranging from traditional pub favourites to Moroccan lamb with couscous.

Open 12–3 7–11 (Sun 7–10.30) Closed: 25 Dec **Bar Meals** L served all week 12–2 D served all week 7–10 Av main course £9 **Restaurant** L served all week 12–2 D served all week 7–10 Av 3 course à la carte £15 Free House Guest beers. 🍷 8 **Facilities** Garden Parking Play Area

ASHILL MAP 04 ST31

Square & Compass

Windmill Hill TA19 9NX ☎ 01823 480467

dir: *Turn off A358 at Stewley Cross service station (Windmill Hill) 1m along Wood Road, behind service station*

There's a warm, friendly atmosphere at this traditional free house, beautifully located overlooking the Blackdown Hills in the heart of rural Somerset. Lovely gardens make the most of the views, and the refurbished bar area features hand-made settles and tables. There is a good choice of home-cooked food, including beef casserole with cheesy dumplings; tasty shortcrust game pie; and duck breast with port and orange sauce. The barn next door was built by the current owners from reclaimed materials for use as a music venue.

Open 12–2.30 6.30-late Closed: 25–26 Dec **Bar Meals** L served all week 12–2 D served all week 7–10 Av main course £7 Free House Exmoor Ale & Gold Moor Withy Cutter, Wadworth 6X, Branscombe Bitter, Exmoor Ale. **Facilities** Garden Dogs allowed Parking

AXBRIDGE MAP 04 ST45

Lamb Inn

The Square BS26 2AP ☎ 01934 732253 📠 01934 733821

Parts of this rambling 15th-century free house were once the guildhall, but it was licensed in 1830 when the new town hall was built. Standing across the medieval square from King John's hunting lodge, the pub's comfortable bars have log fires; there's also a skittle alley and large terraced garden. Snacks and pub favourites support contemporary home-made dishes like pan-fried salmon in cheese and chive coating; and Mediterranean roasted vegetable pancakes in stilton sauce.

Open 11.30–11 (Mon–Wed, 11.30–3, 6–11) **Bar Meals** L served all week 12–2.30 D served Mon–Sat 6.30–9.30 Butcombe Brewery Butcombe Gold, Guest Beers. **Facilities** Garden Dogs allowed

England

BATH MAP 04 ST76

Pick of the Pubs

The Hop Pole

7 Albion Buildings, Upper Bristol Rd BA1 3AR
☎ 01225 446327 🖷 01225 471876
e-mail: hoppole@bathales.co.uk
dir: *20 min walk from Bath on A4 towards Bristol. Pub located opposite Victoria Park*

Opposite the Royal Victoria Gardens and just off the canal path, this is a great spot for quaffing summer ales. One of just six pubs belonging to Bath Ales, a fresh young micro brewery, The Hop Pole has a stripped-down, stylish interior and a garden to the rear complete with patio heaters and pétanque pitch. The atmospheric old skittle alley has been transformed into a restaurant, where the home-cooked food ranges from imaginative bar snacks and sandwiches (Cornish crab mayonnaise, for example, or home-made houmous) through to full meals. You could start with chicken liver parfait or carpaccio of beef, before moving on to honey roast breast of Barbary duck, or medallions of monkfish with chargrilled Mediterranean vegetables, sun-dried tomatoes and pesto. For dessert, perhaps bread and butter pudding with clotted cream, or cheeses with Bath Oliver biscuits.

Open 12-11 (Fri-Sat 12-12) **Bar Meals** L served all week 12-2 (Sun 12-2.30) D served Mon-Sat 7-9 Av main course £8.95 **Restaurant** L served Sun 12-2.30 D served Mon-Sat 7-9 Bath Ale Ltd Bath Ales: Gem, Spa, Barnstormer, Festivity & Wild Hare. **Facilities** Garden

Pick of the Pubs

King William

36 Thomas St BA1 5NN ☎ 01225 428096
e-mail: info@kingwilliampub.com
dir: *At junct of Thomas St & A4 (London Rd), on left leaving Bath towards London. 15 mins walk from Bath Spa*

Since buying this 19th-century city tavern in 2004, Charlie and Amanda Digney have transformed the run-down old boozer into a stylish and sophisticated gastropub. Now, the friendly and unpretentious free house offers the best of everything: real ales from local brewers, Westons' organic cider, and up to fifteen wines served by the glass. Standing on a corner site just off the London Road, the King William boasts a cosy snug in the cellar and a chic upstairs restaurant to showcase the couple's passion for good, locally-sourced food and drink. Lunchtime diners might chose cauliflower cheese and greens; or mussel and smoked haddock chowder from the short, regularly changing menu. In the evening, celeriac and walnut salad might precede venison and kidney pudding with horseradish mash, followed by poached plums in mulled wine. You're strongly advised to book.

Open 12-3 5-12 (Wknds 12-12) Closed: 25-26 Dec **Bar Meals** L served all week 12-2.30 D served Mon-Sat 6.30-10 Av main course £12 **Restaurant** L served Sun (or prior booking) D served Wed-Sat 6.30-10 Av 3 course à la carte £24 Av 2 course fixed price £22.50 Free House Copper Ale, Peroni, Danish Dynamite, Staropramen & Amarillo. 15 **Facilities** Dogs allowed

The Old Green Tree

12 Green St BA1 2JZ ☎ 01225 448259
dir: *Town centre*

Loved for its faded splendour, this 18th-century, three-roomed, oak-panelled pub has a dim and atmospheric interior and a front room decorated with World War II Spitfires. Food ranges from pub basics like soup and bangers and mash ('probably the best sausages in Bat[h]') through to smoked duck and poached apple salad; or mussels in wh[ite] wine and cream sauce. Great for real ales, German lager, malt whiski[es] and real coffee.

Open 11-11 (Sun 12-10.30) Closed: 25 Dec **Bar Meals** L served all wee[k] 12-3 Av main course £8.50 Free House Spire Ale, Brand Oak Bitte[r], Pitchfork, Mr Perrretts Stout & Summer Lightning. 12 **Notes**

Pack Horse Inn

Hods Hill, South Stoke BA2 7DU
☎ 01225 832060 🖷 01225 830075
e-mail: info@packhorseinn.com
dir: *2.5m from Bath city centre, A367(A37), then B3110 toward[s] Frome. South Stoke turn on right*

This country inn maintains a tradition of hospitality that dates back to the 15th century. It was built by monks to provide shelter for pilgrims and travellers, and still has the original bar and inglenook fireplace. Outside an extensive garden overlooks the surrounding countryside. All the meals are home made, from sandwiches and snacks to main courses of spinach, pea and forest mushroom risotto; Normandy chicken, or pepper smoked mackerel fillet with horseradish sauce.

Open 11.30-2.30 6-11 (Sat 11-11, Sun 12-10) **Bar Meals** L served all week 12-2 D served Tue-Sun 6-9 Av main course £8 Innspired Butcombe Bitter, 6X, London Pride & Real Ciders. 6 **Facilities** Children's licence Garden Dogs allowed

England

he Raven NEW

Queen St BA1 1HE ☎ 01225 425045
mail: enquiries@theravenofbath.co.uk
r: *Between Queen Sq & Milsom St*

al ale lovers flock to this traditional, family-owned free house, set two Georgian townhouses on a quiet cobbled street in the centre Bath. 200 ales have been served in the past year alone, including exclusively brewed Raven and Raven's Gold. And what better companiment for your pint than a home-made pie with mash and avy? Or you could try chicken of Aragon, lamb, or mushroom and paragus.

en 11.30–11.30 (Fri–Sat 11.30–12) Closed: 25–26 Dec **r Meals** L served all week 12–2.30 (Sun 12.30–4) D served Mon–Sat 3.30 (Sat all day) Av main course £7.25 Free House Raven & ven's Gold. 7

he Star Inn

Vineyards BA1 5NA ☎ 01225 425072
mail: landlord@star-inn-bath.co.uk
r: *On A4*

en described as a rare and unspoilt pub of outstanding historic erest, and listed on the National Inventory of Heritage Pubs, this pressive building stands amid Bath's glorious Georgian architecture, d was first licensed in 1760. Famous for its pints of Bass served from jug and including many original features such as 19th-century skell and Chambers bar fittings and a lift to transport barrels from cellar. Large selection of rolls at lunchtime.

en 12–2.30 5.30–12 (Sat–Sun all day) Punch Taverns Bellringer, ss, Timothy Taylor Landlord, Bath Star. 6

ECKINGTON MAP 04 ST85

Voolpack Inn

11 6SP ☎ 01373 831244 01373 831223
mail: 6534@grenneking.co.uk
r: *Just off A36 near junction with A361*

nding on a corner in the middle of the village, this charming, ne-built coaching inn dates back to the 1500s. Inside there's an active, flagstoned bar and outside at the back, a delightful terraced den. The lunch menu offers soup and sandwich platters, and larger hes such as home-made sausages and mash; fresh herb and tomato elette; steak and ale pie; and beer-battered cod and chips. Some of se are also listed on the evening bar menu.

en 11–11 (Sun 12–10.30) **Bar Meals** L served all week 12–2.30 served all week 6.30–9.30 (Sun 11–3, 6.30–9) **Restaurant** L served all ek 12–2.30 (Sun 12–3) D served all week 6.30–9.30 Av 3 course à la carte Old English Inns Greene King IPA, Abbot Ale, Guest beer. 8 **cilities** Garden Dogs allowed Parking

BICKNOLLER MAP 03 ST13

The Bicknoller Inn

32 Church Ln TA4 4EL ☎ 01984 656234
e-mail: info@bicknollerinn.co.uk

A 16th-century thatched country inn set around a courtyard with a large garden under the Quantock Hills. Inside you'll find traditional inglenook fireplaces, flagstone floors and oak beams, as well as a new theatre-style kitchen and restaurant. Meals range from sandwiches and pub favourites like hake in beer batter (priced for an 'adequate' or 'generous' portion), to the full three courses with maybe smoked salmon; chicken supreme cooked in red wine, and warm treacle tart.

Open 12–3.30 6–12 (Summer 11.30–11) **Bar Meals** L served all week 12–3 D served all week 6–9.30 Av main course £7.50 **Restaurant** L served all week 12–3 D served all week 6–9.30 Av 3 course à la carte £25 Palmers Copper, Palmers IPA, Guest beers. **Facilities** Garden Dogs allowed Parking Play Area

BLAGDON MAP 04 ST55

The New Inn

Church St BS40 7SB ☎ 01761 462475 01761 463523
e-mail: the.new-inn@virgin.net
dir: *From Bristol take A38 S then A368 towards Bath*

Open fires, traditional home-cooked food, and magnificent views across fields to Blagdon Lake are among the attractions at this welcoming 17th-century inn, tucked away near the church. A hearty pub food menu offers lamb chops, Mexican chilli, battered cod and chips, grilled rainbow trout, beef and Butcombes pie, and a selection of filled rolls, jacket potatoes, ploughman's; and basket meals.

Open 11.30–2.30 7–10.30 (times vary, contact for details) **Bar Meals** L served all week 12–2 D served all week 7–9 Av main course £6.95 Wadworth Wadworth 6X, Henry's IPA. 8 **Facilities** Garden Parking

BLUE ANCHOR MAP 03 ST04

The Smugglers

TA24 6JS ☎ 01984 640385 01984 641697
e-mail: simonandsuzie@aol.com
dir: *Off A3191, midway between Minehead & Watchet*

'Fresh food, cooked well' is the simple philosophy at this friendly 300-year-old inn, standing just yards from Blue Anchor's sandy bay. The Cellar Bar menu features a range of sandwiches, baguettes, filled baked potatoes, pizzas, pastas, grills, salads and speciality sausages, as well as plenty of fish and seafood. Honey-roast ham, chicken tikka korma, and minted lamb cutlets are listed among the 'comfort food' selection. In fine weather diners eat in the large walled garden.

Open 12–11 (Open all wknd Nov–Etr) Closed: (Nov–Etr 12–3, 6–11, 11–11 wkends) **Bar Meals** L served all week 12–10 D served all week 12–10 Av main course £7 **Restaurant** L served Sun 12–3 D served Thu–Sun 7–10 Av 4 course fixed price £24.95 Free House Smuggled Otter, Otter Ale, Alderstones Cider. 6 **Facilities** Children's licence Garden Dogs allowed Parking Play Area

The Black Horse

Down a little lane behind a stone wall is the pretty, whitewashed Black Horse, a true country inn with a façade (water supplies permitting) dripping with flowers in baskets. It was built in the 14th century and at one time what is now the small Snug Bar was the village lock up, as the surviving bars on one of the windows testify.

The impression that it has failed to enter the 21st century (and possibly the 20th too) – and its many regulars and visitors are very grateful for this – is largely created in the traditional bar by the low beams, the jugs and pint pots hanging from them, the flagstone floors, the wooden settles and the old guns above the big open fireplace. Excellent traditional ales and Thatcher's and Black Rat ciders are served straight from their jacketed casks. At one time, the late Adge Cutler, lead singer of Somerset band, The Wurzels, and avowed scrumpy-drinking legend, used to drink here. The kitchen in this listed building is tiny, which limits its output to traditional pub food served lunchtimes only (and not at all on Sundays), but very tasty it is too. The repertoire includes hot filled baguettes and baps, moussaka, cottage pie, beef stew, chilli and lasagne. Run by friendly hosts Nick and Jane Evans for the past 14 years, this delightful pub attracts a good crowd of locals, walkers, cyclists and horse-riders. The large rear garden includes a children's play area, and there's a separate family room. On Monday nights someone usually turns up with a guitar. Outside there's a large beer garden and children's play area.

MAP 04 ST47
Clevedon Ln BS20 7RH
☎ 01275 842105
e-mail:
theblack.horse@tiscali.co.uk
dir: *3m from junct 19 off M5.10m from Bristol, 2m outside Portishead*

Open 11–11
Bar Meals L served Mon–Sat 12–2
Enterprise Inns
Scottish Courage Courage Best, Wadworth 6X, Sharps Eden Ale, Shepherd Neame Spitfire.
7
Facilities Garden Dogs allowed Parking Play Area
Notes

RADFORD-ON-TONE MAP 04 ST12

ʼhite Horse Inn

gent St TA4 1HF ☎ 01823 461239
mail: donna@pmccann1.wanadoo.co.uk
ːb: www.whitehorseinnbradford.co.uk
r: *N of A38 between Taunton & Wellington*

ɜ stone-built inn dates back more than 300 years and stands posite the church in the heart of a delightful thatched village. Sit :he restaurant or separate bar area, or out on the garden patio in nmer. Home-cooked dishes are prepared from seasonal ingredients. ʒetarians have a good choice, and dishes range from burgers, salads d curry in the bar to steaks and pork chops in the restaurant.

en 11.30–3 5.30–12 **Bar Meals** L served all week 12–2 D served week 6.30–9 **Restaurant** L served all week 12–2 D served all week 0–9 Enterprise Inns Cotleigh Tawney, John Smith's, London Pride, ectors. 7 **Facilities** Garden Dogs allowed Parking

UTLEIGH MAP 04 ST53

he Rose & Portcullis

b Rd BA6 8TQ ☎ 01458 850287 01458 850120

s stone built 16th-century free house takes its name from the coat arms granted to the local lord of the manor. Thatched bars and an ·lenook fireplace are prominent features of the cosy interior; there's o a skittle alley, garden, and children's play area. Grills and pub ·ourites like ham, egg and chips rub shoulders on the menu with ›re adventurous fare: oriental duck with ginger and honey; and lentil)ussaka are typical choices.

en 12–3 6–11 **Bar Meals** L served all week 12–2 D served all week 9 **Restaurant** L served all week 12–2 D served all week 7–9 Free use Interbrew Flowers IPA, Butcombe Bitter, Archers Best. 7 **cilities** Garden Dogs allowed Parking Play Area

HEW MAGNA MAP 04 ST56

Pick of the Pubs

The Bear and Swan

South Pde BS40 8SL ☎ 01275 331100 01275 331204
e-mail: enquiries@bearandswan.co.uk
dir: *A37 from Bristol. Turn right signed Chew Magna onto B3130. Or from A38 turn left on B3130*

The Bear and Swan is a light and airy, oak-beamed gastro-pub with a large open fire, comfy chairs and tables, real ales, and a good selection of fine wines and beers in the bar. A big screen shows requested sports games. The restaurant offers a daily changing menu made from the finest locally sourced produce, along with an à la carte menu with a large range of fish, game, seafood, local meats and vegetarian dishes. A lunchtime menu at the bar highlights filled baguettes, soups and old favourites like locally made sausages, mash and mustard gravy; and gammon, free range eggs and chips. This list changes daily, too, to ensure that only the freshest produce is used. Fish aficionados will find different surprises everyday – from smoked haddock on wilted spinach with poached egg; and baked salmon en croute on chive butter sauce; to fresh scallops on risotto with pea purée; and pan-fried skate wing on caper salad.

Open 11–12 (Sun 11–7) **Bar Meals** L served all week 12–2 D served Mon–Sat 7–9.30 Av main course £6.50 **Restaurant** L served all week 12–2 (Sun 12–3) D served Mon–Sat 7–9.30 Av 3 course à la carte £25 Free House Butcombe Bitter, Courage Best. 10 **Facilities** Garden Dogs allowed Parking

CHISELBOROUGH MAP 04 ST41

The Cat Head Inn NEW

Cat St TA14 6TT ☎ 01935 881231
e-mail: info@thecatheadinn.co.uk
dir: *1m off A303 to Crewkerne A356*

Converted from an old farmhouse in 1897, this creeper-clad honey-gold hamstone pub with award-winning beer garden is close to good walking paths. 'More than just a pub' is the motto here, and flagstone floors, open fires and contemporary artefacts create a unique atmosphere. Choose from several real ales and local ciders while browsing the menu – the lunchtime range includes a trio of deep-fried monkfish, haddock and plaice; and dinner could start with mouthwatering tapas for two.

Open 12–3 6–12 Closed 25 Dec eve **Bar Meals** L served all week 12–2 D served all week 7–9.30 **Restaurant** L served all week 12–2 D served all week 7–9.30 Av 3 course à la carte £25 Enterprise Inns Butcombe, Otter, Speckled Hen, Tribute. 8 **Facilities** Garden Children's Licence Play Area **Notes**

CHURCHILL MAP 04 ST45

The Crown Inn

The Batch BS25 5PP ☎ 01934 852995
dir: *Right at Churchill lights, after 200mtrs left and up the hill*

Totally unspoilt gem of a stone-built pub situated at the base of the Mendip Hills and close to invigorating local walks. Originally a coaching stop on the old Bristol to Exeter route, it once housed the village grocer's and butcher's shop before real ale became its main commodity. Today, an ever-changing range of local brews are tapped straight from the barrel in the two rustic stone-walled and flagstone-floored bars. Freshly prepared food is served at lunchtime only, the blackboard listing rare beef sandwiches, filled jacket potatoes, cauliflower cheeses, locally-caught trout and popular casseroles. Peaceful front terrace for summer alfresco sipping.

Open 11–11 **Bar Meals** L served all week 12–2.30 (Sun 12–3) Av main course £5 Free House Palmers IPA, Draught Bass, P G Steam, Butcombe. 7 **Facilities** Children's licence Garden Dogs allowed Parking **Notes**

CLAPTON-IN-GORDANO MAP 04 ST47

Pick of the Pubs

The Black Horse

Clevedon Ln BS20 7RH ☎ 01275 842105
e-mail: theblack.horse@tiscali.co.uk
dir: *3m from junct 19 off M5. 10m from Bristol*

See Pick of the Pubs on opposite page

England

CLUTTON MAP 04 ST65

Pick of the Pubs

The Hunters Rest ★★★★ INN 🍷

King Ln, Clutton Hill BS39 5QL

☎ 01761 452303 📠 01761 453308

e-mail: info@huntersrest.co.uk

dir: *Follow signs for Wells A37 through Pensford, at large rdbt left towards Bath, 100mtrs right into country lane, 1m*

See Pick of the Pubs on opposite page

COMBE HAY MAP 04 ST75

Pick of the Pubs

The Wheatsheaf Inn 🍷

BA2 7EG ☎ 01225 833504 📠 01225 833504

e-mail: info@wheatsheafcombehay.com

dir: *From Bath A369 to Odd Down, left at park towards Combe Hay. 2m to thatched cottage & turn left*

This pretty black and white timbered free house nestles on a peaceful hillside close to the route of the former Somerset Coal Canal, just four miles south of Bath off the A367. The 17th-century building is decorated with flowers in summer, and the gorgeous south-facing garden is an ideal spot for summer dining. The rambling, unspoilt bar is stylishly decorated, with massive wooden tables and sporting prints, and boasts an open log fire in cold weather. An integral part of the local community, this picturesque setting has also featured as a BBC TV documentary location. The daily menus feature ploughman's lunches, and an impressive selection of freshly-cooked hot dishes. Terrine of home-smoked partridge with green tea jelly and apple chutney; and crisp belly pork with south coast scallops and pork juices are typical choices. Don't miss the fresh artisan breads, or desserts such as hot raspberry soufflé or baked Alaska.

Open 10.30–3 6–11 (Fri–Sat 11–11, Sun 12–6) Closed: 25–26 Dec and 1st 2 wks January **Bar Meals** L served Tue–Sat 12–2.30 D served Fri–Sat 12–10 Av main course £8.50 **Restaurant** L served all week 12–2 D served all week 6.30–9.30 (Fri–Sat 6.30–10) Av 3 course à la carte £28 Free House Butcombe Bitter, Butcombe Brunel, Cheddar Valley Cider. 🍷 13 **Facilities** Garden Dogs allowed Parking

Please see walk on page 490

CORTON DENHAM MAP 04 ST

Pick of the Pubs

The Queens Arms 🍷

DT9 4LR ☎ 01963 220317

e-mail: relax@thequeensarms.com

dir: *From A30, B3145 signed Wincanton. 1.5m left at red sign to Corton Denham. 1.5m, left down hill, right into village.*

Enjoy a pint of ale and a pork pie by the open fire at this late 18th-century free house. The Queens Arms nestles at the heart of the ancient village of Corton Denham, just north of Sherborne on the Somerset/Dorset border. Drink is taken seriously here; choose from an exciting range of international beers, and a number of locally brewed ales and Somerset ciders. Earthy British dishes using the freshest local and seasonal produce are served. Sandwiches and fishy platters support lunchtime dishes like sausage and mash with onion marmalade, whilst the evening might bring grilled lime chicken with spicy lentils; or roasted vegetable stack with cherry tomatoes and pesto potatoes.

Open 11–3 6–11 (Sat–Sun & BHs all day) **Bar Meals** L served all week 12–3 D served all week 6–10 (Sun 12–3.30, 6–9.30) Av main course £10.70 **Restaurant** L served all week 12–3 D served all week 6–10 (Sun 12–3.30, 6–9.30) Av 3 course à la carte £20 Free House Butcombe, Timothy Taylor, Bath Spa & Bath Organic Lager. 🍷 16 **Facilities** Garden Dogs allowed Parking

CRANMORE MAP 04 ST

Strode Arms 🍷

BA4 4QJ ☎ 01749 880450 📠 01749 880823

dir: *S of A361, 3.5m E of Shepton Mallet, 7.5m W of Frome*

Rambling, mostly 15th-century building, formerly a farmhouse and coaching inn, with a splendid front terrace overlooking the village du pond. Spacious bar areas are neatly laid-out with comfortable countr furnishings and warmed by open log fires. The food draws local din and visitors to the nearby East Somerset Railway.

Open 11.30–2.30 6–11 **Bar Meals** L served all week 12–2 D served Mon–Sat 6.30–9 Av main course £8 **Restaurant** L served all week 12–2 D served Mon–Sat 6.30–9 Wadworth Henry's IPA, Wadworth 6X, 🍷 7 **Facilities** Garden Dogs allowed Parking

CREWKERNE MAP 04 ST

The Manor Arms ★★★ INN 🍷

North Perrott TA18 7SG ☎ 01460 72901 📠 01460 74055

e-mail: bookings@manorarmshotel.co.uk

dir: *From A30 take A3066 towards Bridport for 1.5m*

On the Dorset-Somerset border, this 16th-century Grade II listed pub and its neighbouring hamstone cottages overlook the village green. Th popular River Parrett trail runs by the door. The inn has been lovingly restored and an inglenook fireplace, flagstone floors and oak beams are among the charming features inside. Bar food includes fillet steak medallions, pan-fried whole plaice, shank of lamb, and chicken suprer

Open 11–11 (Sun 12–10.30) **Bar Meals** L served all week 12–2.30 D served all week 7–9 Av main course £6 **Restaurant** L served all week 12–2.30 D served all week 7–9 Free House Butcombe, Otter, Fullers London Pride, 5 Guest ales. 🍷 8 **Facilities** Garden Parking **Rooms** 8 bedrooms en suite S£50 D£60

The Hunters Rest

ul Thomas has been running this popular free house for 20 years, and has established a great putation for its warm welcome and good home-made food. The views from over the Cam Valley the Mendip Hills and across the Chew Valley to Bristol are breathtaking and well worth a visit their own account.

e Hunters Rest was originally ilt around 1750 for the Earl of arwick as a hunting lodge, and en the Earl sold his estate in 72 it became a tavern serving growing number of coal miners rking in the area. Mining has ished now and the inn has been nsformed into an attractive place eat and stay, with its five well- pointed bedrooms, including ne four poster suites. A range real beers and a reasonably ced wine list are offered, with ood choice by the glass. The nu includes filled rolls; oggies ant filled pastries); grills using at from local farms and a iety of vegetarian dishes (stilton d broccoli oggie, and roasted vegetable lasagne). Dishes among the blackboard specials might include smoked cod fishcakes with dill mayonnaise, rabbit casserole with crusty bread, or Barnsley lamb chops with redcurrant and rosemary gravy. There are some real old favourites among the desserts, such as apple crumble and treacle pudding, and banoffee meringue roulade and chocolate indulgence. In the summer you can sit out in the landscaped garden and watch the miniature railway take customers on rides, while in winter you can cosy up to the crackling log fires.

★★★★ INN 🍷
MAP 04 ST65
King Ln, Clutton Hill BS39 5QL
☎ 01761 452303
📠 01761 453308
e-mail: info@huntersrest.co.uk
web: www.huntersrest.co.uk
dir: *Follow signs for Wells A37 through Pensford, at large rdbt left towards Bath, 100mtrs right, pub 1m*

Open 11.30-3 6-11 (Fri-Sun all day)
Bar Meals L served all week 12-2 D served all week 6.30-9.45 (Sat-Sun 12-10)
Restaurant L served all week 12-2 D served all week 6.30-9.45 (Sat-Sun 12-10)
Free House
Interbrew Bass, Otter Ale, Sharp's Own, Hidden Quest & Butcombe. 🍷 14
Facilities Garden Dogs allowed Parking Play Area
Rooms 5 bedrooms en suite S£62.50 D£87.50

Wheatsheaf

Walk information

Walk details
Distance: 6.5 miles (10.4km)
Map: OS Explorer 142 Shepton Mallet
Start/finish: street parking in village centre, or car park below Peasedown Rd; grid ref ST 739583
Ascent/gradient: 2
Paths: byways, stream sides and some field paths; 12 stiles
Landscape: grassy hillsides and valleys
Note: a torch is useful to explore the long barrow

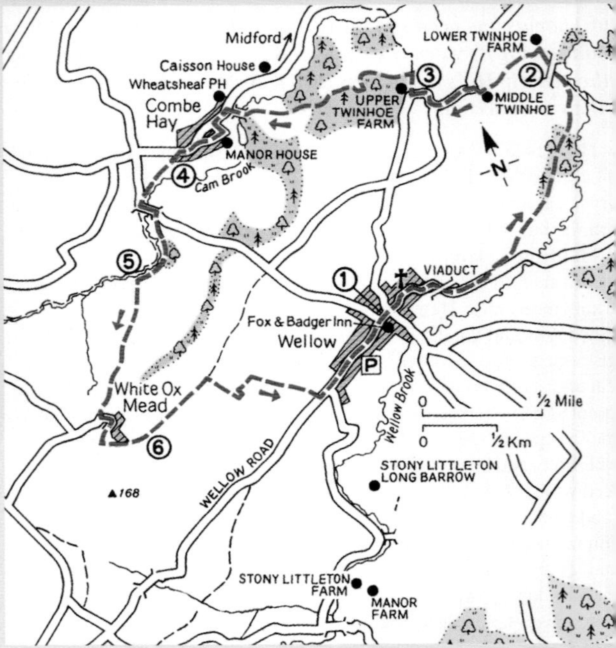

Walk directions

A Head out past the church and under a viaduct. Immediately after Wellow Trekking a track starts just above the road. Where it becomes unclear, cross to the hedge opposite and continue above it. A new track runs through a wood, then down to the valley floor. Where a bridleway sign points right, turn left to pass under a railway bridge.

B Just before Lower Twinhoe Farm turn left into a signposted green track. At the hilltop the track fades into thistly ground. Bear right, before Middle Twinhoe, to a small gate. Turn right along the farm's driveway to a lane. Turn left, then to the right around farm buildings and bend left towards Upper Twinhoe. Just before this farm a signed track descends to the right.

C After 130 yards (118m) turn left through a double gate and along a field top. The path then slants down through scrubby woodland towards Combe Hay. From the wood edge follow the lower edge of a field to a stone bridge into the village, with the Wheatsheaf pub ahead to your right. Follow the main road left, to pass the Manor House.

D After the last house of Combe Hay, find a gap in the wall on the left. Bear right, down to the Cam Brook, and follow it to a road bridge. Cross it and continue with the stream down on your right through a field and a wood. Follow the stream along another field to a stile, then along the foot of a short field to a gateway.

E Don't go through this gateway, but turn up the field edge to a stile on the right instead. Slant up left across the next field to a nettly way between high thorns. At the top of this bear right in a rutted track to a lane. Turn uphill to White Ox Mead, and follow the lane for another 60 yards (55m) to a stile. Slant up to another stile, and turn up a tarred track to where it divides near a shed without walls.

F Keep ahead on a rutted track along the hill crest. Ignore a waymarked stile to pass under low- and high-voltage electr cables. Here a small metal gate on the right leads to a hoof-printed path down beside a fence. At the foot of the field turn left, then left again (uphill), round a corner to a gate. Turn left across the field top and down its edge to the stree leading into Wellow.

While there

Radstock Museum gives much of its space the coal industry. It has a reconstructed mi tunnel and items from that most attractive of ages (to look at afterwards if not to live through!), the industrial 18th century.

England

ROSCOMBE MAP 04 ST54

he Bull Terrier ★★★ INN

ng St BA5 3QJ ☎ 01749 343658
mail: barry.vidler@bullterrierpub.co.uk
r: *Half way between Wells & Shepton Mallet on A371*

rmerly known as the 'Rose and Crown', the name of this unspoiled age free house was changed in 1976. First licensed in 1612, this is e of Somerset's oldest pubs. The building itself dates from the late th century, though the fireplace and ceiling in the inglenook bar later additions. One menu is offered throughout, including ginger icken; bacon, mushroom and tomato pasta special; hot smoked ackerel with horseradish; and vegan tomato crumble.

en 12–2.30 7–11.30 **Bar Meals** L served all week 12–2 D served all ek 7–9 (Sun 12–1.45) Av main course £7 **Restaurant** L served all week -2 D served all week 7–9 (Sun 12–1.45) Av 3 course à la carte £16 Free use Butcombe, Courage Directors, Marston's Pedigree, Greene King d Speckled Hen & Ruddles County. **Facilities** Garden Dogs allowed rking **Rooms** 2 bedrooms en suite S£30 D£52

DINNINGTON MAP 04 ST41

Dinnington Docks

TA17 8SX ☎ 01460 52397 📠 01460 52397
e-mail: hilary@dinningtondocks.co.uk
dir: *On A303 between South of Petherton & Ilminster*

This welcoming and traditional village pub on the old Fosse Way has been licensed for over 250 years. Rail or maritime enthusiasts will enjoy the large collection of memorabilia, and it's an ideal location for cycling and walking. The pub is well known for the quality of its cask ales, and farmhouse cider is also available. You won't find any pool tables, loud music or fruit machines, but instead good conversation and a varied selection of freshly prepared food available every lunchtime and evening, made using local produce wherever possible.

Open 11.30–3.30 6–12 **Bar Meals** L served all week 12–2.30 D served all week 6–9.30 (Sun 7–9.30) Av main course £5.50 **Restaurant** L served all week 12–2.30 D served all week 6–9.30 (Sun 7–9.30) Av 3 course à la carte £15 Free House Butcombe Bitter, Wadworth 6X, Guest Ales. **Facilities** Garden Dogs allowed Parking Play Area

ROWCOMBE MAP 03 ST13

Pick of the Pubs

Carew Arms 🍷

TA4 4AD ☎ 01984 618631 📠 01984 618428
e-mail: info@thecarewarms.co.uk
dir: *10m from both Taunton & Minehead, off A358*

Set in The Quantock Hills, England's first designated Area of Outstanding Natural Beauty, the Carew Arms has been welcoming travellers since the 16th century. It was originally known as The Three Lions, and owes its name to the Carew family, who became lords of the manor in Queen Elizabeth I's reign. The traditional front bar remains unaltered and retains its original flagstone floor and deep inglenook fireplace. At lunchtime butcher's pork sausages, bubble and squeak and onion gravy, and chef's steak and ale pie are possibilities. In the evening starters might be Brixham king scallops with hot garlic butter, while mains include baked chicken breast with spinach and stilton cheese sauce; rack of lamb with bubble and squeak and red wine jus; and garlic-roasted vegetables with red pepper jus. The Ambroses have created a peaceful south-facing garden for that quiet drink or light lunch. Local beers are much in demand.

Open 11–3 6–11 (Apr–Sep phone for details) **Bar Meals** L served all week 12–2 D served all week 7–9.30 Av main course £10 **Restaurant** L served all week 12–2.30 D served Mon–Sat 7–10 Av 3 course à la carte £22 Free House Exmoor Ale, Otter Ale, Cotleigh Ales. 🍷 8 **Facilities** Garden Dogs allowed Parking

DITCHEAT MAP 04 ST63

Pick of the Pubs

The Manor House Inn 🍷

BA4 6RB ☎ 01749 860276 📠 0870 286 3379
e-mail: giles@themanoratditcheat.co.uk
dir: *From Shepton Mallet take A371 towards Castle Cary, in 3m turn right to Ditcheat*

Tucked away in a charming Mendip village offering easy access to the Bath and West showground and the East Somerset steam railway, this delightful brick-built free house with its flagstone floors was originally known as the White Hart. Here you'll find Butcombe Bitter, John Smith's and regular guest ales, as well as local brandies and up to 19 wines served by the glass. Starters include pan-fried pigeon breast with bacon on mixed leaves; and smoked salmon on risotto with roasted beetroot and dill dressing. Main course dishes range from rack of lamb with herb crust, parsnip purée and red wine sauce; to sea bass fillets on stir-fry vegetables with spring onion and beetroot sauce. Round off with plum tart and lemon zest sorbet; or Bakewell tart with clotted cream.

Open 12–3 7–11 **Bar Meals** L served all week 12–2.30 D served Mon–Sat 6–10 (Sun 7–9) Av main course £12.50 **Restaurant** L served all week 12–2 D served all week 7–9.30 (Sun 7–9) Free House Butcombe, Scottish Courage John Smith's & Guest Ales. 🍷 19 **Facilities** Garden Dogs allowed Parking

PICK OF THE PUBS

EXFORD-SOMERSET

The Crown Hotel

The Crown Hotel dates from the 17th century and was the first purpose built coaching inn on Exmoor. The venerable establishment is located in a pretty village amid three acres of gardens and woodland, with a fast flowing trout stream running through, and is surrounded by beautiful countryside and moorland.

Outdoor pursuits are very popular with the patrons here, including walking, hunting, horse-riding and shooting. The cosy country bar remains very much at the heart of village life. Welcoming log fires are lit in the lounge and bar in winter, and there are lovely water and terrace gardens for summer use. Real ales, fine wines and good food are permanent fixtures along with the relaxing and homely atmosphere. Bar food ranges through lunchtime sandwiches, baguettes and baked potatoes, to the likes of butternut squash risotto, steak and chips, or marinated chicken breast with vegetable noodles and sweet and sour sauce. Further choice is offered from the blackboard menu with its pasta of the day or daily seafood special. Quality ingredients are sourced locally where possible and cooked to order. In the smart dining room you might anticipate a meal of pan-fried Cornish scallops with celeriac remoulade, vanilla dressing and parsnip crisps, followed by loin of fallow venison with caramelised figs, chestnut purée, dauphinoise potatoes and cranberry and port sauce. A fitting finish could be cherry clafoutis with chilled cherry purée and pear sorbet. If you fancy staying over and exploring the delights of this lovely area, accommodation is available in 17 en suite bedrooms.

★★★ HL 🏵🏵 🍷
MAP 03 SS83
TA24 7PP
☎ 01643 831554
📠 01643 831665
e-mail:
info@crownhotelexmoor.co.uk
dir: *From M5 junct 25 follow Taunton signs. Take A358 then B3224 via Wheddon Cross to Exford*

Open 11-3 6-11 (Apr-Sep 11-11, wknd all year)
Bar Meals L served all week 12-2 D served all week 6.30-9.30 Av main course £8.50
Restaurant D served all week 7-9 Av 3 course à la carte £30
Free House
Exmoor Ale, Ansells, Worthingtons, Wild Cat & Exmoor Gold. 🍷 8
Facilities Garden Dogs allowed Parking
Rooms 17 bedrooms en suite S£65 D£99

England

DUNSTER — MAP 03 SS94

Pick of the Pubs

The Luttrell Arms NEW ★★★ HL ◎

High St TA24 6SG ☎ 01643 821555 📠 01643 821567

dir: *A39 Bridgewater to Minehead, A396 Dunster. 2m before Minehead*

Built in the 15th-century as a guesthouse for the Abbots of Cleeve, this beguiling hotel has retained all its atmospheric charms. Open fires and oak beams make the bar a welcoming place in winter, while the bedrooms are period pieces complete with leather armchairs and four-poster beds. A rib-sticking wild venison casserole with ale and horseradish sauce is just the thing for a chilly day, while in the more formal restaurant you could tuck into smoked haddock fishcakes, followed by wild pigeon and mushroom parcels with cider jus. Desserts include sticky ginger parkin with vanilla-steeped pineapple and ginger ice cream in the restaurant, and clotted cream rice pudding in the bar. Locally brewed beers and a good value wine list make staying the night an appealing option, especially since the murmuring of ghostly monks is rumoured to cure even the most stubborn insomnia.

Open 10-11 **Bar Meals** L served all week 12-3 D served all week 7-10 Av main course £10.95 **Restaurant** L served all week 12-3 D served all week 7-10 Av 3 course fixed price £28.50 Free House Exmoor Gold Fox, Cottleigh, Cheddar Valley Cider & Guest Ale. **Facilities** Garden Dogs allowed **Rooms** 28 bedrooms en suite

EAST COKER — MAP 04 ST51

Pick of the Pubs

The Helyar Arms ★★★★ INN ◎

Moor Ln BA22 9JR ☎ 01935 862332 📠 01935 864129

e-mail: info@helyar-arms.co.uk

dir: *3m from Yeovil. Take A57 or A30, signs for East Coker*

Log fires warm the old world bar in this charmingly traditional 15th-century inn, reputedly named after Archdeacon Helyar, a chaplain to Queen Elizabeth I. A Grade II listed building, it dates back in part to 1468 and its separate restaurant occupies an original apple loft. The kitchen makes full use of local produce, especially cheeses, beef and bread. Bar snacks include ploughman's lunches; the Helyar chargrilled pizza; and speciality sandwiches such as bacon, Somerset brie and cranberry ciabatta. A main meal could begin with warm, crusty bread with olive tapenade followed by a starter of sautéed lamb's kidneys with roasted red onion and deep-fried sage leaves. Main courses range from traditional favourites such as shepherd's pie (made with hogget lamb mince and served with glazed carrots) to a spicy Thai red chicken curry with jasmine rice. You could finish with profiteroles or rhubarb crème brûlée.

Open 11-3 6-11 (Sun 12-10.30) **Bar Meals** L served all week 12-2.30 D served all week 6.30-9.30 (Sun 6.30-9) Av main course £11 **Restaurant** L served all week 12-2.30 D served all week 6.30-9.30 (Sun 6.30-9) Av 3 course à la carte £22 Punch Taverns Butcombe Bitter, Greene King IPA, Flowers Original, Carlsberg. 30 **Facilities** Garden Dogs allowed Parking **Rooms** 6 bedrooms en suite S£59 D£79

EXFORD — MAP 03 SS83

Pick of the Pubs

The Crown Hotel ★★★ HL ◎◎

TA24 7PP ☎ 01643 831554 📠 01643 831665

e-mail: info@crownhotelexmoor.co.uk

dir: *From M5 junct 25 follow Taunton signs. Take A358 then B3224 via Wheddon Cross to Exford*

See Pick of the Pubs on opposite page

FAULKLAND — MAP 04 ST75

Tuckers Grave

Faulkland BA3 5XF ☎ 01373 834230

Tapped ales and farm cider are served at Somerset's smallest pub, a tiny atmospheric bar with old settles. Lunchtime sandwiches and ploughman's lunches are available, and a large lawn with flower borders makes an attractive outdoor seating area. The grave in the pub's name is the unmarked one of Edward Tucker, who hung himself here in 1747.

Open 11-3 6-11 Closed: 25 Dec Free House Interbrew Bass, Butcombe Bitter. **Facilities** Garden Dogs allowed Parking **Notes**

FRESHFORD — MAP 04 ST76

The Inn at Freshford

BA2 7WG ☎ 01225 722250 📠 01225 723887

dir: *1m from A36 between Beckington & Limpley Stoke*

With its 15th-century origins, and log fires adding to its warm and friendly atmosphere, this popular inn in the Limpley Valley is an ideal base for walking, especially along the Kennet & Avon Canal. Extensive gardens. The à la carte menu changes weekly to show the range of food available, and a daily specials board and large children's menu complete the variety. Typical home-made dishes are patés, steak and ale pie, lasagne and desserts; a nice selection of fish dishes includes fresh local trout.

Open 11-3 6-11 (Sun 7-11) **Bar Meals** L served all week 12-2 D served all week 6-9 Av main course £10 **Restaurant** L served all week 12-2 D served all week 6-9 Av 3 course à la carte £20 Latona Leisure Butcombe Bitter, Courage Best & Guest ale. 12 **Facilities** Garden Dogs allowed Parking

FROME — MAP 04 ST74

Pick of the Pubs

The Horse & Groom

East Woodlands BA11 5LY

☎ 01373 462802 📠 01373 462802

e-mail: kathybarrett@btconnect.com

dir: *A361 towards Trowbridge, over B3092 rdbt, take immediate right towards East Woodlands, pub 1m on right*

Located at the end of a single track lane, this attractive 17th-century building is adorned with colourful hanging baskets in

CONTINUED

England

FROME continued

summer and surrounded by lawns fronted by severely pollarded lime trees. The bar, furnished with pine pews and settles on a flagstone floor and a large inglenook fireplace, offers shove ha'penny, cribbage, dominoes and a selection of daily newspapers for your diversion. There's also a carpeted lounge, including three dining tables in addition to the conservatory-style garden room with 32 covers. A great choice of drinks includes smoothies and milkshakes, and designated drivers are provided with free soft drinks. The lunch and bar menu is offered at lunchtime along with baguettes, salads and daily specials. In the evening, the bar and baguette menus are complemented by a full carte served in all areas. Typical dishes are smoked salmon roulade followed by peppered venison with Cumberland sauce.

The Horse & Groom

Open 11.30–2.30 6.30–11 (Sun 12–3, 7–10) **Bar Meals** L served Tue–Sat 12–2 (Sun 12–2.30) D served Tue–Sat 6.30–9 Av main course £9 **Restaurant** L served Tue–Sat 12–2 (Sun 12–2.30) D served Tue–Sat 6.30–9 Av 3 course à la carte £25 Av 2 course fixed price £10 Wadworth 6X, Butcombe Bitter, Branscombe Branoc, Timothy Taylor Landlord. 9 **Facilities** Garden Dogs allowed Parking

Pick of the Pubs

The Talbot 15th Century Coaching Inn

★★★ INN

Selwood St, Mells BA11 3PN

01373 812254 01373 813599

e-mail: roger@talbotinn.com

dir: *A362 towards Radstock, left for Mells*

In the beautiful medieval village of Mells, this rambling 400-year-old coaching inn is reputedly the home of the nursery rhyme Little Jack Horner; the manor estate certainly once belonged to a Thomas Horner, but the truth will never be known. Through an archway with huge double doors is a sunny cobbled courtyard incorporating a vine-covered pergola with Provençal-style tables and chairs. Across the courtyard, the tastefully restored tithe barn now houses the public bar, where cask-conditioned real ales are drawn straight from the barrel. To the left of the courtyard amongst a warren of stone-floored corners and passageways is the restaurant with low oak-beamed ceilings and stripped pews, as well as fresh flowers and candles on the tables. The menus encapsulate typically British cooking, and as head chef Mark Jones is also a fresh fish specialist, expect an excellent choice of seafood, such as whole Brixham lemon sole or grilled Devon scallops.

Open 12–2.30 6.30–11 **Restaurant** L served all week 12–2 D served all week 6.30–9.15 (Sun 12–2.30, 7–9) Av 3 course à la carte £23 Free House Butcombe & London Pride. **Facilities** Garden Dogs allowed Parking **Rooms** 7 bedrooms en suite S£75 D£95

HASELBURY PLUCKNETT MAP 04 ST4

Pick of the Pubs

The White Horse at Haselbury

North St TA18 7RJ 01460 78873

e-mail: haselbury@btconnect.com

dir: *Just off A30 between Crewkerne & Yeovil on B3066*

Patrick and Jan Howard have run this inn for over nine years, but during recent renovations they decided to change its name from The Haselbury Inn back to its original name, The White Horse. Set in the peaceful village of Haselbury Plucknett, the building started life as a rope works and flax store, later becoming a cider house. Its interior feels fresh and warm but retains the original character of exposed stone and open fires. The eclectic menu is founded on locally-sourced ingredients. There's an excellent selection of fish specials – perhaps lemon-baked fillet of salmon with a lobster sauce; or grilled red mullet stuffed with feta, sun-dried tomatoes, shallots and garlic. Other choices might include pork, spinach and herb terrine with home-made spicy apple chutney and toast followed by roast Gressingham duck with a plum sauce. Early bird dinners are served until 8pm; booking is recommended at busy times.

Open 11.45–2.30 6–11 **Bar Meals** L served all week 12–2 (Sun 12–3) D served all week 6.30–9.30 **Restaurant** L served all week 12–2 (Sun 12–3) D served all week 6.30–9.30 Av 3 course à la carte £20 Av 3 course fixed price £12.95 Free House Palmers IPA, Otter Ale. 10 **Facilities** Garden Parking

HINTON BLEWETT MAP 04 ST5

Ring O'Bells

BS39 5AN 01761 452239 01761 451245

e-mail: jonjenssen@btinternet.com

dir: *On A37 toward Wells, small road signed in Clutton & Temp Cloud*

On the edge of the Mendips, this 200-year-old pub offers good views of the Chew Valley. An all-year-round cosy atmosphere is boosted by log fire in winter, and a wide choice of real ales. The bar-loving shove ha'penny players attract a loyal following. Good value dishes include beef in Guinness served in a giant Yorkshire pudding, and chicken reast with stilton and bacon. Baguettes, sandwiches and ploughman's lso available.

Open 11-3.30 5-11 (Sat 11-4, 6-11 Sun 12-4, 7-10.30)
Bar Meals L served all week 12-2 D served all week 6.30-10
Restaurant L served all week 12-2 (Sat 12-2.30, 12-2.30) D served all week 7-10 Free House Butcombe, Fuller's London Pride, Badger Tanglefoot, Gem. **Facilities** Garden Dogs allowed Parking Play Area

HINTON ST GEORGE — MAP 04 ST41

Pick of the Pubs

The Lord Poulett Arms ★★★★ INN

High St TA17 8SE ☎ 01460 73149
e-mail: steveandmichelle@lordpoulettarms.com
dir: *2m N of Crewkerne, 1.5m S of A303*

See Pick of the Pubs on page 496

HOLCOMBE — MAP 04 ST64

The Ring O' Roses ★★ HL

Stratton Rd BA3 5EB ☎ 01761 232478 📠 01761 233737
e-mail: info@ringoroses.co.uk
dir: *On A367 to Stratton-on-the-Fosse, concealed left opposite Downside Abbey signed Holcombe, next right, pub 1.5m on left*

This country inn boasts a large garden with views of nearby Downside Abbey and the Somerset countryside. The lunch menu runs to various sandwiches and wraps, while the evening choice is supplemented by a specials board: start with crispy squid with sweet chilli dip; or asparagus tips with tomato and basil hollandaise sauce, and move on to grilled Scottish salmon with cucumber and prawn cream; pork stroganoff; or spinach and ricotta ravioli.

Open 11.30-11 (Sat 11.30-2.30, 6.30-11 Sun 12-2.30, 7-10.30)
Bar Meals L served all week 12-2 D served all week 7-9 (Sun 12-1.30, 7-8.30) **Restaurant** L served all week 12-2 D served all week 7-9 (Sun 12-1.30, 7-8.30) Free House Otter Ale, Otter Bitter, Guinness. 7
Facilities Garden Dogs allowed Parking **Rooms** 8 bedrooms en suite S£65 D£85

ILCHESTER — MAP 04 ST52

Ilchester Arms

The Square BA22 8LN ☎ 01935 840220 📠 01935 841353
e-mail: ilchester@yahoo.co.uk
dir: *A37 to Ilchester/Yeovil, left towards Ilchester at 2nd sign. Hotel 100yds on right*

First licensed in 1686, this elegant Georgian building was owned between 1962 and 1985 by the man who developed Ilchester cheese. Brendan McGee, the head chef, and his wife Lucy are well settled in now, enabling Brendan to create an extensive bistro menu offering pan-fried fillet of red snapper, rich lamb casserole, and vegetable moussaka. Sandwiches, paninis, salads, the house burger, and beef and ale pie are available at the bar.

Open 11-11 Closed: 26 Dec **Bar Meals** L served all week 12-2.30 D served Mon-Sat 7-9.30 Av main course £11.50 **Restaurant** L served all week 12-2.30 D served Mon-Sat 7-9.30 Av 3 course à la carte £21.50 Free House Butcombe, Flowers IPA. 12 **Facilities** Children's licence Garden Parking Play Area

ILMINSTER — MAP 04 ST31

New Inn

Dowlish Wake TA19 0NZ ☎ 01460 52413
dir: *From Ilminster signs for Kingstone and Perry's Cider museum, follow pub signs in Dowlish Wake*

A 350-year-old stone-built pub tucked away in a quiet village close to Perry's thatched cider mill. There are two bars with woodburning stoves, and a games room with bar billiards and a dart board. In the garden is a water feature, with shady trees and a skittle alley. The menu features local produce and West Country specialities, including plenty of fish, steaks and home-made pies. There's a good vegetarian choice, along with ploughman's and light bites.

Open 11.30-3 6-11 **Bar Meals** L served all week 12-2.30 (Sun 12-3) D served all week 6-9 Av main course £6 **Restaurant** L served all week 12-2.30 (Sun 12-3) D served all week 6-9 Av 3 course à la carte £15 Enterprise Inns Butcombe Bitter, Otter, Perry's Cider, Poachers Bitter. 10 **Facilities** Children's licence Garden Dogs allowed Parking

KILVE — MAP 03 ST14

The Hood Arms

TA5 1EA ☎ 01278 741210 📠 01278 741477
e-mail: easonhood@aol.com
dir: *A39 to Kilve*

This traditional, friendly 17th-century coaching inn is set among the Quantock Hills and provides thirsty walkers among other visitors with traditional ales. A good range of fresh fish includes grilled loin of swordfish with pink peppercorn sauce or fresh fillet of halibut stuffed with smoked salmon with a mushroom sauce. Non-fish choices might include home-made beef and Guinness pie, Mississippi chicken goujons with sweet chilli salsa, or Somerset pork loin with caramelised onion, cider and apple gravy.

Open 11-3 6-11 (Sun 12-2, Winter all week 12-2, 6-10)
Bar Meals L served all week 12-2.30 D served all week 6.15-9 (Winter Sun-Tue 7-8.30) Av main course £9.95 **Restaurant** L served all week 12-2 D served all week 7-9 (Winter Sun-Tue 7-8.30) Av 3 course à la carte £23 Free House Sharps Doom Bar, Cotleigh Tawney Ale, Tribute, St Austell. 8 **Facilities** Garden Dogs allowed Parking Play Area

The Lord Poulett Arms

Fronting the street in one of Somerset's loveliest and most peaceful villages is this stone-built, thatched pub. Built in 1680, it has been superbly restored by its owners Michelle Paynton and Steve Hill, to include a pale green bar with bare flagstones and boarded floors, a pleasing mix of old oak and elm tables, and ladderback, spindleback and Windsor chairs.

Helping to make the darker green dining room a delightful place to eat are real fires, including one with a huge bressemer beam across the top, more wooden floors, a big old settle, and yet more harmoniously mixed chairs and tables. Here a meal might start with baby spinach and pea soup with crispy pancetta garnish; braised ox tongue, baby onion confit and thyme gravy; Dorset mackerel, bacon and new potato terrine with caper and shallot vinaigrette; or mozzarella, peach and beetroot salad with crème fraîche dressing. Main courses are particularly inventive, with sweet soy glazed bacon loin, faggot and champ; seared turbot, summer vegetable and black-eyed bean broth; gurnard, conger eel and smoked bacon chowder; braised scrag end of lamb, turnip mash and port reduction; and mixed mushrooms and wild rocket tagliatelle in a cheddar cream sauce. For dessert, try vanilla crème brûlée with a rhubarb compote and shortbread; or gooseberry cheesecake with an elderflower and mint jelly; alternatively Lovington's Somerset ice creams come in half a dozen flavours, including vanilla clotted cream, and hive honeycomb. The bedrooms have exposed hamstone walls, antique beds and, providing a nostalgic touch, slipper baths. Dine in the wild flower meadow under a mistletoe-covered apple tree, admire the ancient fives wall while swaying in the big stripey hammock, or play boules on the lavender-edged piste. Somerset ales are served straight from the barrel, and ciders direct from the jug.

★★★★ INN 🍷
MAP 04 ST41
High St TA17 8SE
☎ 01460 73149
e-mail: steveandmichelle@lordpoulettarms.com
dir: *2m N of Crewkerne, 1.5m S of A303*

Open 12-3 6.30-11
Bar Meals L served all week 12-2 D served all week 7-9
Restaurant L served all week 12-2 D served all week 7-9 Av 3 course à la carte £22
Free House
Hopback, Branscombe, Cotleigh, Archers. 🍷 7
Facilities Garden Dogs allowed Parking
Rooms 4 bedrooms en suite S£59 D£88

England

KINGSDON MAP 04 ST52

Kingsdon Inn NEW

TA11 7LG ☎ 01935 840543

dir: *From A303 take A372 then turn right onto B3151, right into village then right at post office*

The three charmingly decorated, saggy-beamed rooms in this pretty thatched pub give off a relaxed and friendly feel. Stripped pine tables and cushioned farmhouse chairs are judiciously placed throughout, and there are enough open fires to keep everywhere well warmed. Traditional country cooking includes pheasant, venison and other game in season; pork fillets with apricot and almonds; roast half duck with local scrumpy cider sauce; and seared sea bass with fennel and cream.

Open 12-3 5-11.30 (25 Dec & 1 Jan - phone for times) **Bar Meals** L served all week 12-2 D served all week 6.30 (Sun 7-9) Av main course £7.95 **Restaurant** L served all week 12-2 D served all week 6.30 (Sun 7-9) Free House Butcombe Cask, Otter Cask, Guest ale. 10 **Facilities** Children's licence Garden Dogs allowed Parking

LANGLEY MARSH MAP 03 ST02

The Three Horseshoes

TA4 2UL ☎ 01984 623763 01984 623763

e-mail: marellahopkins@hotmail.com

dir: *B3227 to Wiveliscombe. Turn right up hill at lights. From square, turn right, follow Langley Marsh signs for 1m*

This handsome 17th-century red sandstone pub has had only four landlords during the last century. It remains a free house, with traditional opening hours, child-free bars and a good choice of ales straight from the barrel. The landlord's wife prepares home-cooked meals, incorporating local ingredients and vegetables from the pub garden. Typical specials include halibut steak baked with tomatoes and wine; and pheasant breast with smoked bacon and cranberries. There's an enclosed garden with outdoor seating.

Open 12-2.30 7-11 (Sun 7-9 Winter) Closed: Early July **Bar Meals** L served Tues-Sun 12-1.45 D served Tues-Sun 7-9 Av main course £7.25 **Restaurant** L served all week 12-1.45 (Sun 12-2.30) D served all week 7-9 Free House Palmer IPA, Otter Ale, Fuller's London Pride, Adnams Southwold. **Facilities** Garden Parking

LANGPORT MAP 04 ST42

The Old Pound Inn ★★★ INN

Aller TA10 0RA ☎ 01458 250469 01458 250469

Built as a cider house, the Old Pound Inn dates from 1571 and retains plenty of historic character with oak beams, open fires and a garden that used to be the village pound. It's a friendly pub with a good reputation for its real ale and home-cooked food, but also provides function facilities for 200 with its own bar. Whimsically named dishes include portly venison, horsy wild boar, and fruit 'n' nut trout.

Open 11-11 **Bar Meals** L served all week 12-1.45 D served all week 6-9.45 **Restaurant** L served all week 12-1.45 D served all week 6-9.45 Butcombe,Butcombe Gold, Yorkshire Bitter, Courage Best. **Facilities** Garden Dogs allowed Parking **Rooms** 6 bedrooms en suite

Rose & Crown

Huish Episcopi TA10 9QT ☎ 01458 250494

dir: *M5 junct 25, A358 towards Ilminster. Left onto A378. Village in 14m (1m from Langport). Pub near church in village*

In the same family for four generation, this traditional inn has flagstone floors, Gothic windows, a thatched roof and no bar – just as it was in 1640. Folk evenings, Irish music and storytelling nights are a regular feature, and home-made food is served using local produce wherever possible. Choose from sandwiches, soup, steak and ale pie, and chicken breast in tarragon sauce. Vegetarian meals are always available, along with home-made puddings like apple crumble or chocolate torte.

Open 11.30-2.30 5.30-11 (Fri-Sat 11.30-11, Sun 12-10.30) **Bar Meals** L served all week 12-2 D served Mon-Sat 6-7.30 Free House Teignworthy Reel Ale, Mystery Tor, Hop Back Summer Lightning, Butcombe Bitter. **Facilities** Garden Dogs allowed Parking Play Area **Notes**

LEIGH UPON MENDIP MAP 04 ST64

The Bell Inn

BA3 5QQ ☎ 01373 812316 01373 812434

e-mail: rodcambourne@aol.com

dir: *From Frome take A37 towards Shepton Mallet. Turn right, through Mells, on to Leigh upon Mendip*

The Bell was built in the early 16th century to house workers constructing the village church, and Pilgrims used to stop here en route to Glastonbury. There is a bar with two inglenook fireplaces, a 30-seat restaurant, a skittle alley/function room and a large garden with children's play equipment. Snacks and meals are served (mussels with Thai curry, lamb stew and dumplings). A three-mile walk around the lanes starts and finishes at the pub.

Open 12-3 6-12 (Sun 12-12) **Bar Meals** L served all week 12-2 D served all week 6.30-9.30 (Sun 12-2.30) **Restaurant** L served all week 12-2 D served all week 6.30-9.30 (Sun 12-2.30) Av 3 course à la carte £16 Wadworth Wadworth 6X, Butcombe Bitter, Wadworths JCB, Henrys IPA. 12 **Facilities** Garden Dogs allowed Parking Play Area

LONG SUTTON MAP 04 ST42

Pick of the Pubs

The Devonshire Arms ★★★ INN

TA10 9LP ☎ 01458 241271 01458 241037

e-mail: mail@thedevonshirearms.com

dir: *Exit A303 at Podimore rdbt onto A372. Continue for 4m, left onto B3165.*

A fine-looking stone-built former hunting lodge set on a pretty village green. Step through its imposing portico, decorated with the Devonshire family coat of arms, to discover unexpectedly contemporary styling that successfully complements original features, such as a large open fire. The pub is renowned locally for its food, which, wherever possible, is made with the best local produce. For lunch try slow-cooked pork hock with roasted vegetables and cider sauce, or Mediterranean fish stew with new potatoes, tomato and basil. Alternatively, just settle for a ploughman's with Keen's cheddar, Somerset brie, honey roast ham and chutney. At dinner, give thought to hand-picked crab créme brûlée with fennel salad; pan-fried breast of pheasant with roasted bacon and caramelised button onions; fillet of West Country beef, with red onion potato cake and cep sauce; or gratinated goats' cheese with puy lentils, roasted vegetables and pomegranate.

Open 12-3 6-11 Closed: 25 Dec **Bar Meals** L served all week 12-2.30 D served Mon-Sat 7-9.30 Av main course £8.95 **Restaurant** 12-2.30 D served Mon-Sat 7-9.30 Free House Teignworthy 'Real Ale', Hopback 'Crop Circle'. 8 **Facilities** Children's licence Garden Parking Play Area **Rooms** 8 bedrooms en suite S£60 D£75

LOVINGTON MAP 04 ST53

Pick of the Pubs

The Pilgrims

BA7 7PT ☎ 01963 240597

e-mail: thejools@btinternet.com

dir: *From A303 take A37 to Lyford, right at lights, 1.5m to The Pilgrims on B3153.*

See Pick of the Pubs on opposite page

LOWER VOBSTER MAP 04 ST74

Pick of the Pubs

Vobster Inn

BA3 5RJ ☎ 01373 812920 01373 812920

e-mail: info@vobsterinn.co.uk

dir: *4m W of Frome*

See Pick of the Pubs on page 500

LUXBOROUGH MAP 03 SS9

Pick of the Pubs

The Royal Oak Inn

TA23 0SH ☎ 01984 640319 01984 641561

e-mail: info@theroyaloakinnluxborough.co.uk

dir: *From A38 at Washford take minor road S through Roadwater*

See Pick of the Pubs on page 503

MARTOCK MAP 04 ST4

The Nag's Head Inn

East St TA12 6NF ☎ 01935 823432

dir: *Telephone for directions*

Expect a warm welcome at this 200-year-old former cider house set in a picturesque village in rural south Somerset. Alfresco eating and drinking is encouraged in the landscaped garden and a huge orchard area, with the home-made food being much sought after locally. Lamb shanks, venison casserole, various Thai and other oriental dishes, and delicious steaks are also available in the bar and restaurant.

Open 12-2.30 6-11 (Fri-Sun all day) **Bar Meals** L served Tue-Sun 12-2 D served Mon-Sat 6-9 **Restaurant** L served Tue-Sun 12-2 D served Mon-Sat 6-8.30 Av 3 course à la carte £13 Free House Guinness, Worthington. **Facilities** Garden Dogs allowed Parking

MONKSILVER MAP 03 ST0

Pick of the Pubs

The Notley Arms

TA4 4JB ☎ 01984 656217

dir: *Village on B3227 N of Wiveliscombe*

See Pick of the Pubs on page 504

MONTACUTE MAP 04 ST4

The Kings Arms Inn NEW

49 Bishopston TA15 6UU ☎ 01935 822513

e-mail: kingsarmsmont@aol.com

dir: *From A303 onto A3088 at rdbt signed Montacute. Hotel in village centre*

Mons Acutus (thus Montacute) is the steep hill at whose foot the hamstone-built Kings Arms has stood since 1632. Have a snack in the fire-warmed bar, or something more substantial chosen from the daily changing restaurant menu, such as fillet of beef in oyster sauce; baked salmon fillet with hollandaise; or baked tomatoes stuffed with olives, spring onions and feta.

Open 7-11 **Bar Meals** L served all week 12 D served all week 9 (Sun carvery) Av main course £11.95 **Restaurant** L served all week 12-2.30 D served all week 7-9 Greene King Ruddles County, Abbot Ale, Old Speckled Hen. 10 **Facilities** Garden Dogs allowed Parking

The Pilgrims

)wners Sally and Jools Mitchington appealingly declare, 'we work on the basis that you are ere to enjoy yourself, and we are here to help.' With such an attitude, it's unsurprising that this ıformal pub with its restaurant quality food has won so many awards.

he emphasis is on local produce ɔoked at home, so the fish is elivered from Bridport, all the ıeat comes from local farms, ıe cheeses derive from the West :ountry and the bread is home ıade using locally milled organic our. Even the beer is made round ıe corner. An interesting variety f inexpensive dishes is available : lunchtime, including Cornish ıussels cooked in cider with leeks ıd garlic; mutton kofta kebab; and ɔcal wild boar and herb sausages ith mustard mash. The à la carte ıenu features such delicacies as ɔt potted haddock in cheese sauce ith tomato salsa; goats' cheese aked in filo pastry; or teriyaki beef. lain courses make imaginative use f Somerset flora and fauna: try reast of free-range local chicken poached in Burrow Hill cider with Dorset bacon lardons; or perhaps a line-caught wild Dorset sea bass, pan-fried with fennel mash and Pernod sauce. The cheeses are unusual local varieties, and the desserts are all home made (except the ice cream, which is made in the village). Some examples are risotto rice pudding with Seville orange compote; or a retro Black Forest sundae, made with Lovington's Double Choc Chunk ice cream, kirsch-marinated black cherries and clotted cream. Wisely, the team observe that children tend to prefer small portions of adult food to their own menu. All dishes can be produced in smaller quantities for a lower price, and that goes for less peckish adults too.

MAP 04 ST53
BA7 7PT
01963 240597
e-mail: thejools@btinternet.com
dir: *From A303 take A37 to Lyford, right at lights, 1.5m to The Pilgrims on B3153.*

Open 12-3 7-11 Closed: Oct
Bar Meals L served all week 12-2 D served all week 7-9 Av main course £10
Restaurant L served all week 12-2 D served all week 7-9 Av 3 course à la carte £29
Free House
Cottage Brewing Champflower, Budvar & Erdinger, Stowford Press Cider. 12
Facilities Children's licence Garden Dogs allowed Parking

Vobster Inn

After more than a year of searching for the right business and home, the Davila family finally took up residence in the Vobster Inn in September 2005. Acknowledging the warm support from regulars and neighbours, they have been putting their stamp on it ever since.

The original part of the building, which stands in four acres of grounds and mature gardens, dates back to the 17th century, although there has probably been an inn here for even longer. Surrounded by stunning countryside, it is a popular destination for walkers. Both bar and restaurant menus feature seafood and West Country meats, but there's a distinctive Spanish bias, reflecting Raf Davila's birthplace on the rugged Galician coast. Seafood choices may include Spanish onion soup with Manchego cheese crouton; and Galician Marisco paella with mussels, prawns, clams and crevettes as starters. Among the main courses might be baby wild turbot; whole gilt-head bream wrapped in bacon; and roast Nile perch with kumquat confit. Other options could include Dutch calves' liver with parsley mash and red wine gravy; braised featherblade of beef with garlic and chive risotto; and Catalan butterbean and chickpea stew. All desserts, such as pistachio parfait, and lemon posset with warm red berries, are home-made. Lighter options include bread and home-marinated olives, rare beef or smoked mackerel and vine tomato sandwiches, and grilled Somerset brie, bacon and cranberry ciabatta. Children are particularly welcome and have their own menu as well, although they are also encouraged to try smaller portions from the main menus. Smokers are welcome to inhale in the grounds 'so long as they don't breathe out', to quote the pub's website.

MAP 04 ST74
BA3 5RJ
☎ 01373 812920
01373 812920
e-mail: info@vobsterinn.co.uk
dir: *4m W of Frome*

Open 12-3 6.30-11
Bar Meals L served all week 12-2 D served all week 7-9 (Fri-Sat 9.30) Av main course £12.50
Restaurant L served all week 12-2 D served Mon-Sat 7-11
Free House
Butcombe Blonde, Butcombe & Ashton Press Cider. 8
Facilities Garden Parking

ıONTACUTE continued

ʼhe Phelips Arms

he Borough TA15 6XB ☎ 01935 822557 📠 01935 822557
-mail: infophelipsarms@aol.com
ir: *From Cartgate rdbt on A303 follow signs for Montacute*

17th-century listed ham stone building overlooking the village square ıd close to historic Montacute House (NT). The emphasis is on the uality of the food, and everything is prepared on the premises using ıe best local and West Country produce. The menu features an clectic selection of dishes cooked in a robust style, and there is a small ut delicious pudding menu, and an extensive wine list.

ıpen 11.30–2.30 6–11 Closed: 25 Dec **Bar Meals** L served all week 2–2 D served Tue–Sat 7–9 Av main course £12 **Restaurant** L served l week 12–2 (Sun 12–2.30) D served Tue–Sat 6–9 Av 3 course à la carte 21 Palmers Palmers IPA & 200 Premium Ale, Copper Ale. 35 **acilities** Garden Dogs allowed Parking

ıORTH CURRY MAP 04 ST32

ʼhe Bird in Hand

Queen Square TA3 6LT ☎ 01823 490248

friendly 300-year-old village inn, with large stone inglenook ʼreplaces, flagstone floors, exposed beams and studwork. Cheerful ʼaff provide a friendly welcome, and the place is atmospheric at night y candlelight. A recent addition to the excellent range of real ales Red Heron, from a new brewery in the village. Blackboard menus ʼature local produce, and the constantly changing seafood – from kate wing and monkfish tail to scallops and crabmeat – is all supplied y a Plymouth fishmonger.

ıpen 12–3 6–11 (Fri–Sat 6–12) Rest: 25–26 Dec Closed eve **ar Meals** L served all week 12–2 D served all week 7–9 (Fri–Sat 7–9.30) v main course £7.50 **Restaurant** L served all week 12–2 D served all week -9.30 Av 3 course à la carte £23 Free House Badger Tanglefoot, xmoor Gold, Otter Ale, Cotleigh Barn Owl. 8 **Facilities** Dogs allowed arking

ıORTON ST PHILIP MAP 04 ST75

Pick of the Pubs

George Inn

High St BA2 7LH ☎ 01373 834224 📠 01373 834861
e-mail: georgeinnnsp@aol.com
dir: *From Bath take A36 to Warminster, after 6m take A366 on right to Radstock, village 1m*

See Pick of the Pubs on page 506

NUNNEY MAP 04 ST74

The George at Nunney ★★ HL

Church St BA11 4LW ☎ 01373 836458 📠 01373 836565
e-mail: enquiries@georgeatnunneyhotel.wanadoo.co.uk
dir: *0.5m N off A361*

The garden was used in the Middle Ages as a place of execution, but this rambling old coaching inn is deservedly popular these days. Set in a historic conservation village, it serves a wide choice of food. Big steaks, mixed grill, steak and ale pie, and double chicken breasts with choice of sauces, plus a separate fish menu including brill, sea bass, hake, red mullet and fresh dressed crabs.

Open 12–3 5–11 **Bar Meals** L served all week 12–2 D served all week 7–9 Av main course £8 **Restaurant** L served all week 12–2 D served all week 7–9 Av 3 course à la carte £18 Av 3 course fixed price £12 Free House Highgate Brewery Saddlers Best Bitter, Wadworth 6X, Interbrew Bass and Guest Ales. 8 **Facilities** Garden Parking **Rooms** 10 bedrooms 9 en suite S£56 D£75

OVER STRATTON MAP 04 ST41

The Royal Oak

TA13 5LQ ☎ 01460 240906 📠 01460 242421
e-mail: info@the-royal-oak.net
dir: *A3088 from Yeovil left onto A303. Over Stratton on right after South Petherton*

Blackened beams, flagstones, log fires, pews and settles set the scene in this welcoming old thatched inn built from warm Hamstone, which has the added attraction of a garden, children's play area and barbecue. Expect real ales, including Tanglefoot from the Badger brewery in Blandford Forum, and dishes ranging from beer battered haddock and chips with home-made tartare sauce to supreme of chicken in an apricot, ginger and white wine sauce.

Open 11–11 (Sat–Sun 11–3, 6.30–11) **Bar Meals** L served all week 12–2.30 D served all week 6.30–9.30 **Restaurant** L served all week 12–2.30 D served all week 6.30–9.30 Woodhouse Inns Badger Best, Tanglefoot, Sussex Best Bitter. **Facilities** Garden Dogs allowed Parking Play Area

PITNEY MAP 04 ST42

The Halfway House

TA10 9AB ☎ 01458 252513
dir: *On B3153, 2m from Langport & Somerton*

This pub is largely dedicated to the promotion of real ale, and there are always six to ten available in tip-top condition, shown on a blackboard. This delightfully old-fashioned rural pub has three homely rooms boasting open fires, books and games, but no music or electronic games. Home-cooked meals (except Sundays when it is too busy with drinkers) include soups, local sausages, sandwiches and a good selection of curries and casseroles in the evening.

Open 11.30–3 5.30–11 (Sun 12–3, 7–10.30) Closed: 25 Dec **Bar Meals** L served Mon–Sat 12–2.30 D served Mon–Sat 7–9.30 Av main course £6.95 Free House Butcombe Bitter, Teignworthy, Otter Ale, Cotleigh Tawny Ale. 8 **Facilities** Garden Dogs allowed Parking Play Area

England

PORLOCK MAP 03 SS84

The Ship Inn

High St TA24 8QD ☎ 01643 862507 📠 01643 863224
e-mail: mail@shipinnporlock.co.uk
dir: *A358 to Williton, then A39 to Porlock*

Many travellers have been welcomed to this 13th-century inn, including Wordsworth, Coleridge and even Nelson's press gang. Nestling at the foot of Porlock's notorious hill, where Exmoor tumbles into the sea, its thatched roof and traditional interior provide an evocative setting for a meal, drink or overnight stay. Regularly changing menus include ploughman's, light bites and dishes such as supreme of salmon on horseradish mash with parsley and lemon crème. A new beer garden with children's play area have now been added.

Open 11–12 (Sun 12–11) **Bar Meals** L served all week 12–2 (Sun 12.30–2.30) D served all week 6.30–9 (Sun 7–9) Av main course £8 **Restaurant** L served Sun 12–2 (Sun 12.30–2.30) D served all week 7–9 Av 3 course à la carte £17 Free House Tribute, Exmoor Ale, Butcombe, Otter. **Facilities** Garden Dogs allowed Parking Play Area

The Anchor Hotel & Ship Inn NEW

Porlock Weir TA24 8PB ☎ 01643 862753 📠 01643 862843
e-mail: info@theanchorhotelandshipinn.co.uk

A three-star hotel restaurant and 16th-century inn all in one, right on the harbour front at the point where the road ends. Just offshore is an ancient submarine forest, visible during only the lowest tides. Traditional pub food in Mariners Bar includes smoked mackerel; hot and fruity chicken curry; home-made steak and kidney pie; and four-cheese and roast onion quiche. Among dinner choices in the Harbourside Restaurant are rack of lamb; lobster thermidor; and cannelloni verde.

Open 11–11 **Bar Meals** L served all week 12–3 D served all week 6.30–8.30 Av main course £7.50 **Restaurant** L served all week 12–2.30 D served all week 7–9.30 Av 3 course à la carte £34.20 Free House Exmoor Ale, Exmoor Fox, Cotleigh Barn Owl, Cotleigh 25 & Taunton. **Facilities** Children's licence Garden Dogs allowed Parking

PRIDDY MAP 04 ST55

New Inn

Priddy Green BA5 3BB ☎ 01749 676465
dir: *A39 3m before Wells*

Overlooking the village green high up in the Mendip Hills, this old, former farmhouse is popular with walkers, riders and cavers, and once served beer to the local lead miners. A typical dinner menu features liver and bacon, chargrilled steaks, Brixham plaice, and fillet of pork with braised red cabbage. Priddy hosts the 'friendliest folk festival in England' every July, and there's a skittle alley.

Open 12–3 7–11 **Bar Meals** L served all week 12–2 D served all week 7–9.30 Av main course £6.50 **Restaurant** L served all week 12–2 D served all week 7–9.30 Av 3 course à la carte £12 Free House Interbrew Bass, Fuller's London Pride, Wadworth 6X, New Inn Priddy. **Facilities** Garden Dogs allowed Parking Play Area

RODE MAP 04 ST8

The Mill at Rode 🍷

BA11 6AG ☎ 01373 831100 📠 01373 831144
e-mail: info@themillatrode.co.uk
dir: *6m S of Bath*

A sympathetically modernised, former grist mill with an original waterwheel that the River Frome, which runs through the beautiful gardens, still coaxes into turning. According to the menu, the owners are 'making a huge effort' to provide the best local ingredients – judge for yourself with Wiltshire pheasant breast on celeriac mash with gin and juniper sauce; savoury ragout of Bath blue cheese, celery and sweet potato; or Springleaze fillet steak with wholegrain mustard sauce.

Open 12–11 **Bar Meals** L served all week 12–10 D served all week 12–10 **Restaurant** L served all week 12–10 D served all week 12–10 Free House Butcombe Bitter, Erdinger, Guinness, Guest beers. 🍷 8 **Facilities** Garden Parking Play Area

RUDGE MAP 04 ST8

The Full Moon at Rudge ★★★★ INN 🍷

BA11 2QF ☎ 01373 830936 📠 01373 831366
e-mail: enquiries@thefullmoon.co.uk
dir: *From A36 follow signs for Rudge*

This venerable 16th-century free house still retains its small, stone-floored rooms furnished with scrubbed tables. Strategically placed at the crossing of two old drove roads, the inn enjoys great views of Westbury White Horse. Modern British cooking is the watchword: characteristic dishes include roasted lamb hock with white bean purée and rosemary red wine sauce; and vegetarian pancake gateau. Look out for the home-made pie and sausage board.

Open 11–11 **Bar Meals** L served all week 12–2.30 D served all week 6.30–9.30 **Restaurant** L served all week 12–2.30 D served all week 6.30–9.30 Free House Butcombe Bitter, Wadworth 6X, Timothy Taylor, Worthington Cream Flow. 🍷 7 **Facilities** Garden Dogs allowed Parking **Rooms** 17 bedrooms en suite S£57.50 D£74.50

The Royal Oak Inn

'or as long as anyone can remember, this 14th-century building within the unspoilt surroundings ·f Exmoor National Park has been an inn and the focal point of the village. At some point, hough, the back bar was an abattoir, as the hooks in the ceiling beams testify, and it has also erved as a tailor's shop and post office.

'here is no piped music, no fruit 1achine and mobile phones can't :ceive a signal here, which many 'ill find a huge blessing. Until 996, drinkers in the Blazing tump bar (so called after a stingy)rmer landlord who put only ne log on the fire at a time) held 1eir breath as the ceiling sagged)ur inches when someone walked verhead. Renovation has resolved 1at problem, while leaving its ıstic character intact, although uring a downpour you still might eed Wellington boots when an nstoppable torrent rushes down 1e hill, through the front door nd out the back, without even :opping to buy a pint of Exmoor 'old. Tastefully decorated dining :eas include the Green Room, ideal for intimate candlelit dinners, the Red Room for family gatherings or parties, and the Old Dining Room, just off the bar. The fine food, ranging from lunchtime snacks to classic country fare, makes full use of high quality local fare and has a well-deserved reputation. Selected from an autumn menu are grilled fillet of red snapper with garlic, chilli and olive oil spaghetti; seared pigeon breasts with smoked pancetta, peas and savoy cabbage; and enoki and oyster mushroom risotto with tempura aubergine. A specials board of daily fish and other seasonal dishes is offered in addition to the regular menu. The suntrap courtyard patio makes a delightful setting for a meal or peaceful drink.

MAP 03 SS93
TA23 0SH
01984 640319
01984 641561
e-mail: info@theroyaloakinnluxborough.co.uk
dir: *From A38 at Washford take minor road S through Roadwater*

Open 12–2.30 6–11 Closed: 25 Dec
Bar Meals L served all week 12–2 D served all week
Restaurant L served all week 12–2 D served all week 7–9 Av 3 course à la carte £25
Free House
Tawney, Palmers 200, Exmoor Gold, Palmers IPA.
Facilities Garden Dogs allowed Parking

The Notley Arms

An English country drinking and dining pub in a hamlet on the edge of Exmoor, built in the 1860s and named after a prominent local family. The stream that runs through the village and alongside the pub garden is called the Silver, derived from silva, which is Latin for wooded area.

When monks from Monmouthshire arrived at nearby Cleeve Abbey, the village became known as Silva Monachorum, which over the centuries has mutated to Monksilver. Jane and Russell Deary prepare and cook everything themselves, with a distinct bias towards traditional but imaginative British dishes, using fresh produce from the south west of England. That said, you'll soon spot ostrich steaks, biltong, droewors and bobotie, southern African specialities that reflect the Dearys' Zimbabwean origins. Menus also offer pork and three-mustard stroganoff; Exmoor sirloin steak; Somerset lamb shank braised in red wine and redcurrant jus; 'deerstalker' venison pie; chicken teriyaki with stir-fry vegetables and egg noodles; and Thai-style butternut and pineapple curry. Depending on fish catches delivered fresh from St Mawes in Cornwall, there may be baked red mullet, chunky cod fillet, sea bass en papillote, and much more. Smaller portions of most dishes are available for children. Puddings include Somerset apple and hazelnut cake with toffee sauce and clotted cream, and raspberry yoghurt meringue with raspberry coulis and toasted almonds. Well-tended flower borders make the garden look very pretty, and there's a selection of outdoor toys to keep children happy. The pub stands on the 36-mile Coleridge Way, which runs from Nether Stowey, the poet's one-time home, to Porlock.

🍷
MAP 03 ST03
TA4 4JB
☎ 01984 656217
dir: *Village on B3227 N of Wiveliscombe towards Watchet & Minehead*

Open 12–2.30 6.30–11 (Fri 12–2, 6.30–9)
Bar Meals L served Tue–Sun 12–2 D served all week 7–9 (Wkdys in winter 7–9) Av main course £7.50
Enterprise Inns
Exmoor Ale, Wadworth 6X & Bath Ales. 🍷 10
Facilities Garden Dogs allowed Parking Play Area

HEPTON MALLET MAP 04 ST64

Pick of the Pubs

The Three Horseshoes Inn

★★★★ INN

Batcombe BA4 6HE ☎ 01749 850359 01749 850615

dir: *A359 to Bruton. Batcombe signed, pub by church*

Formerly an inn with its own smithy, the 17th-century building of honey-coloured stone has been transformed into a popular dining pub. The lovely rear garden overlooks the 15th-century tower of the parish church. The atmosphere is cosy and relaxed, with attentive service from the owners and their small team of staff. Exposed beams, terracotta walls and an inglenook fireplace are features of the long, low main bar, where real ales are served from hand pumps. Cooking is traditionally based, including home-cured hams, home-made sausages and dishes prepared from local organic and Soil Association certified growers or farmers' markets. Daily specials might include Fowey mussels marinières with crusty bread and a large pot of fries, and home-made bangers and mash with onion gravy from the carte. Gourmand quiz dinners are a regular feature. There are three stylishly decorated letting bedrooms, two with en suite facilities and one with a private bathroom.

Open 12-3 6.30-11 **Bar Meals** L served all week 12-2 D served all week 7-9 Av main course £12.50 **Restaurant** L served all week 12-2 D served all week 7-9 Av 3 course à la carte £23.50 Free House Butcombe Bitter, Bats in the Belfry & Adnams Broadside. 8 **Facilities** Garden Dogs allowed Parking **Rooms** 2 bedrooms en suite S£50 D£70

Pick of the Pubs

The Waggon and Horses

Frome Rd, Doulting Beacon BA4 4LA

☎ 01749 880302 01749 880602

e-mail: portsmouthpnni@hotmail.com

dir: *1.5m N of Shepton Mallet at x-rds with Old Wells-Frome road, 1m off A37*

This rural coaching inn has views over Glastonbury, and is very much at the heart of artistic life in the local community. A pretty, whitewashed building with leaded windows and a large garden, it has a flower-filled paddock and an upstairs skittle alley that doubles as a concert hall and gallery, with regular exhibitions and monthly jazz sessions. Food choices typically include sandwiches, filled baguettes, and pub classics such as locally sourced ham with eggs laid by the resident chickens; and steak with all the trimmings. Starters from the main menu might include a hearty pheasant and lentil soup, followed by lamb navarin, or grilled fillet of cod with béarnaise sauce. If you have room, finish the meal with comforting treats like sticky toffee pudding or treacle tart. The bar offers a varying range of real beers, a good choice of wines by the glass, local Somerset Royal cider brandy, and an interesting selection of cocktails.

Open 11.30-3 6-11 (All day Fri-Sun in summer) **Bar Meals** L served all week 11.30-2.30 D served all week 6-9.30 (Sat-Sun all day in summer) **Restaurant** L served all week 11.30-2.30 D served all week 6-9.30 (Sat-Sun all day in summer) Av fixed price £10 Innspired Wadworth 6X, Greene King IPA, Butcombe. 12 **Facilities** Children's licence Garden Dogs allowed Parking

SHEPTON MONTAGUE MAP 04 ST63

The Montague Inn

BA9 8JW ☎ 01749 813213 01749 813213

e-mail: themontagueinn@aol.com

dir: *From Wincanton & Castle Cary turn right off A371*

This comfortably refurbished, stone-built village inn nestles in rolling unspoilt Somerset countryside on the edge of sleepy Shepton Montague. Tastefully decorated throughout, with the homely bar featuring old dark pine and an open log fire, and a cosy, yellow-painted dining room. Menu choices include bacon and brie ciabatta, Scottish venison steak, home-made pies, mushroom lasagne, and organic lamb. Local beers and ciders are served directly from the cask. The attractive summer terrace with rural views is perfect for summer sipping.

Open 12-3 6-11 **Bar Meals** L served Tue-Sun 12-2 D served Tue-Sat 7-9 **Restaurant** L served Tue-Sun 11-2 D served Tue-Sat 7-9 Free House Bath Ale, Butcombe Gold, Abbot Ale & Guest Beer. 7 **Facilities** Garden Parking

George Inn

Originally a monastic guest house built by Carthusian monks, this 14th-century building's fame as an historic inn has seen it immortalised in countless watercolours, engravings and photographs.

Its early history is linked to the success of the monks' cloth fairs, started in Norton St Philip in 1345, which eventually required the hostelry's living rooms to be emptied of furniture to make storage space for bales. By the late 17th century the George had room for 35 beds and stabling for 90 horses. Norton's prosperity then declined, but the inn's position on a busy coaching crossroads (Bath to Salisbury and Wells to London) ensured its survival. In more recent years it has been used as a film location – Albert Finney leapt from the gallery here in *Tom Jones* and the Italian director Pasolini used the top floor for scenes from *Canterbury Tales*. The fact that its historical charm remains intact is thanks in no small part to a loving and sympathetic restoration carried out in the 1990s by Wadworth Brewery, who worked closely with conservation groups and skilled craftsmen to restore full hotel status to these ancient buildings with as little impact as possible on the medieval structure. The Monmouth bar still boasts an inglenook open fire and a 700-year old writing table once used by the monks. Food is served here and in the main dining room; expect plenty of reliable dishes that complement the age-old surroundings. Begin, perhaps, with farmhouse paté, before moving on to a home-made steak, mushroom and 6X pie; but if you fancy something less traditional, you could try chilli Thai fishcakes, followed by lamb tagine. The menu also includes some good vegetarian choices such as a goats' cheese and caramelised red onion tartlet, followed by a main course of

MAP 04 ST75
High St BA2 7LH
☎ 01373 834224
01373 834861
e-mail: georgeinnnsp@aol.com
dir: *From Bath take A36 to Warminster, after 6m take A366 on right to Radstock, village 1m*

Open 11–2.30 5.30–11 (all day wknds summer)
Bar Meals L served all week 12–2 D served all week 7–9.30 (Sun all day from Mar) Av main course £7.95
Restaurant L served all week 12–2 D served all week 7–9.30 (Sun all day from Mar)
Wadworth
Wadworth 6X, Henrys IPA, Wadworth Bishops Tipple, J.C.B.
15
Facilities Garden Dogs allowed Parking

LOUGH GREEN MAP 04 ST21

Pick of the Pubs

Farmers Inn NEW

TA3 5RS ☎ 01823 480480 01823 481177
e-mail: letsgostay@farmersinnwesthatch.co.uk
dir: *A358 S. At Nags Head pub left for RSPCA at top of hill*

An exceedingly glamorous refurbishment has transformed this 300-year-old malt house into a chic bar and restaurant. The Cotswold stone exterior gives way inside to a luxurious expanse of pale wood, accented with ruby-red feature walls and bar. Paintings of stags and bulls adorn the walls, while the real things might be found in the form of loin of Highland venison with Savoy cabbage and bacon in the restaurant; or roast Scotch beef sandwich with creamed horseradish in the bar. A short, elegant menu of modern British dishes could start with carpaccio of tuna and celeriac remoulade, or gateau of white crab, smoked salmon, avocado and caviar; followed by stuffed saddle of Cotswold rabbit, sun blushed tomatoes and garlic mash. Cheltenham, Newbury and Warwick racecourses are all nearby, and the inn attracts jockeys, trainers and owners, not least for the trainer and jockey quiz night.

Open 12-2.30 6-11 **Bar Meals** L served all week 12-2.30 D served all week 7-9.30 Av main course £10 **Restaurant** L served all week 12-2.30 D served all week 7-9.30 Av 3 course à la carte £25 Free House Otter Ale, Exmoor Ale. 14 **Facilities** Garden Dogs allowed Parking **Rooms** 5 bedrooms en suite S£60 D£80 (★★★★★ INN)

PARKFORD MAP 04 ST62

he Sparkford Inn

gh St BA22 7JH ☎ 01963 440218 01963 440358
mail: sparkfordinn@sparkford.fsbusiness.co.uk
r: *Just off A303, 400yds from rdbt at Sparkford*

5th-century former coaching inn with beamed bars and a cinating display of old prints and photographs. It is set in an ractive garden just off the A303 between Wincanton and Yeovil. The staurant offers a popular lunchtime carvery, light meals and a full ening menu, featuring steaks from the grill. Dishes include marinated jun chicken breast; smoked haddock and bacon au gratin; and bean, ery and coriander chilli.

en 11-3 5.30-11 (Summer 11-11) **Bar Meals** L served all week 12-2 served all week 7-9.30 **Restaurant** L served all week 12-2 D served all ek 7-9.30 Free House Marstons Pedigree, Banks Bitter & Guest s. **Facilities** Garden Dogs allowed Parking Play Area

STANTON WICK MAP 04 ST66

Pick of the Pubs

The Carpenters Arms

BS39 4BX ☎ 01761 490202 01761 490763
e-mail: carpenters@buccaneer.co.uk
dir: *A37 to Chelwood rdbt, then A368*

In the tranquil hamlet of Stanton Wick overlooking the Chew Valley, just 20 minutes from Bath and Bristol, this charming stone-built free house was formerly a row of miners' cottages. Flower-bedecked and with oodles of cottagey style, a spacious terrace beckons for an alfresco drink. Behind the pretty façade is a comfortable bar with low beams, a chatty, music-free atmosphere, and real ales. The light lunchtime menu served Monday to Saturday may offer south coast mussels; smoked salmon and chive omelette; and Thai-style chicken with mixed salad. The Carpenters' reputation for serving seasonal and local produce means that dinner menus and daily specials change regularly. You may find starters such as salmon and cod fishcake with lemon and caper mayonnaise, or sauté of king prawns on wilted spinach; main courses like grilled fillet of trout, or pan-roasted pork tenderloin; and puddings such as chocolate brownie, or Italian bread and butter pudding.

Open 11-11 Closed: 25-26 Dec **Bar Meals** L served all week 12-2 D served all week 7-10 (Sun 7-9) Av main course £12.95 **Restaurant** L served all week 12-2 D served all week 7-10 (Sun 7-9) Av 3 course à la carte £23 Buccaneer Holdings Butcombe Bitter, Scottish Courage Courage Best, Wadworth 6X. 12 **Facilities** Garden Parking **Rooms** 12 bedrooms en suite S£67 D£95 (★★★★ INN)

England

STAPLE FITZPAINE MAP 04 ST21

Pick of the Pubs

The Greyhound Inn ★★★★ INN

TA3 5SP ☎ 01823 480227 01823 480773

e-mail: thegreyhound-inn@btconnect.com

dir: *From M5 take A358 E, signed Yeovil, in 1m turn right, signed Staple Fitzpaine, left at T-junct, pub on right at x-rds.*

There's a warm welcome for everyone at this attractive and award-winning 16th-century free house with its flagstone bars and open winter fires. The inn takes its name from the men on horseback who dispatched news before the days of Royal Mail. As well as a good choice of real ales like Otter Ale, King & Barnes Sussex and Badger First Gold, traditional Somerset cider is also available on hand pump. The comprehensive menu features a variety of dishes using the finest local Somerset ingredients, including local cheeses, pork, beef and lamb. Specials are carefully chosen to take advantage of the changing seasons, and fish is freshly delivered each morning from Brixham. Typical seafood dishes include smoked haddock and mussel chowder; salmon gravlax timbale; and crab farcie with citrus dressing. In the summer months you can enjoy the large split level beer garden that surrounds the building.

Open 12-3 5.30-11 **Bar Meals** L served Mon-Sat 12-2 D served Mon-Fri 6.45-9 Av main course £8 **Restaurant** L served 12-3 D served 6.45-9 Av 3 course à la carte £19 Free House Badgers First Gold, King & Barnes Sussex, Otter Ale. 7 **Facilities** Garden Dogs allowed Parking Play Area **Rooms** 4 bedrooms en suite S£55 D£80

STOGUMBER MAP 03 ST03

The White Horse

High St TA4 3TA ☎ 01984 656277 01984 656873

dir: *Off A358 to Stogumber, 2m into village centre. Right at T-junct & right again, opposite church*

A mile down a pretty country lane from the West Somerset Steam Railway station, this traditional village free house incorporates the historic village Market Hall. The extensive menu includes local fish and steaks, washed down with Cotleigh Tawny Bitter, Greene King and local guest beers. Like other local pubs, the White Horse once brewed Stogumber ale, which could allegedly 'cure anything from leprosy to flatulence'.

Open 11-11 (Sun 12-11) **Bar Meals** L served all week 12-2 D served all week 7-9 Av main course £10 **Restaurant** L served all week 12-2 D served all week 7-9 Av 3 course à la carte £20 Free House Cotleigh Tawny Bitter, Marstons Pedigree, Greene King, Abbot Ale. **Facilities** Garden Dogs allowed Parking **Rooms** 3 bedrooms en suite S£35 D£70 (★★★ INN)

STOKE ST GREGORY MAP 04 ST3

Rose & Crown

Woodhill TA3 6EW ☎ 01823 490296 01823 490996

e-mail: info@browningpubs.com

dir: *A358 towards Langport, left at Thornfalcon, left again, signs to Stoke St Gregory*

The pub has been in the same family for over 25 years and is proud c its reputation for good food, local produce and a warm reception. Bui in the 18th century, it became a pub in 1867, and is set in the Somers Levels at the heart of the willow industry. The interior is cluttered and cosy, full of nooks and crannies with a well in the middle of the bar. Lots of fish appears on menus – expect perhaps pan-fried gurnard wi honey, orange and almonds, and Brixham crab salad.

Open 11-3 7-11 **Bar Meals** L served all week 12.30-2 D served all week 7-9.30 (Sun 12-2, 7-9) Av main course £9.70 **Restaurant** L served all week 12.30-2 D served all week 7-9.30 (Sun 12-2, 7-9) Av 3 course à la carte £22 Free House Exmoor Fox, Stag, Guest Ales, Butcombe. 8 **Facilities** Children's licence Garden Parking

TAUNTON MAP 04 ST2

Pick of the Pubs

Queens Arms

Pitminster TA3 7AZ ☎ 01823 421529 01823 451068

e-mail: theqa@btconnect.com

dir: *In Corfe, right signed Pitminster for 0.75m*

Situated in the heart of Pitminster, the Queens Arms even gets a mention in the Domesday Book of 1086, recording that this ancient building was then a mill. Today, the pub combines the traditional welcome of a classic country inn with a touch of continental influence. Oak and slate floors and roaring log fires in winter add to the appeal, while in summer the patio garden is the perfect spot for a cold drink or after-dinner coffee. The chef uses only the finest locally produced ingredients, with fish delivered daily from Brixham. Meat and game are produced in Somerset, and the vegetables are grown locally. Starters include smoked salmon, moules marinière, and mushroom and blue cheese bouchee. Among the main courses are beef and otter pie, fish and chips, traditional Irish stew, liver and bacon, Somerset lamb shank, and home-made fishcakes. Extensive and impresive wine list.

Open 12-3 6-11 (Sun 7-10.30) **Bar Meals** L served Tue-Sun 12-2.15 D served Mon-Sun 7-9.15 Av main course £8.45 **Restaurant** L served Tue-Sun 12-2.15 D served Mon-Sun 7-9.15 Av 3 course à la carte £18 Enterprise Inns Otter Ale, Otter Bitter & London Pride. 8 **Facilities** Garden Dogs allowed Parking

TRISCOMBE MAP 04 ST13

Pick of the Pubs

The Blue Ball

TA4 3HE ☎ 01984 618242 01984 618371
e-mail: info@blueballinn.co.uk
dir: *A358 past Bishops Lydeard towards Minehead*

Hidden away down a narrow lane in the Quantock Hills, this 'old pub' is actually a converted 18th-century thatched barn. Inside are A-frame wood ceilings, solid beech furniture, lavish carpets and furnishings, log fires and, from the windows, breathtaking views south to the Blackdown Hills. A team of talented chefs makes absolutely everything except butters and oil, using ingredients from mostly local suppliers, all of whom are chosen with considerable care. For a three-course lunch try crab tian with Thai dressing; venison sausages with spring onion mash and mustard sauce; or cinnamon pannacotta with blackberry compote. Alternatively, in the evening, there may be hand-dived seared scallops with black pudding and chorizo dressing; pot-roasted rack of lamb with roasted swede, quince and sage aioli; or nougatine parfait with mango and mint salsa. Meals are also served in the garden and on the patio. West Country real ales are available.

Open 12-3 7-11 **Bar Meals** L served all week 12-1.45 D served all week 7-8.45 (Sun 7-9 Apr-Dec) **Restaurant** L served all week 12-2 D served all week 7-8.45 (Sun dinner 7-9 Apr-Dec) Av 3 course à la carte £26 Free House Cotleigh Tawny, Exmoor Gold & Stag, Butcombe, Sharps. 100 **Facilities** Garden Dogs allowed Parking

WATERROW MAP 03 ST02

Pick of the Pubs

The Rock Inn ★★★★ INN

TA4 2AX ☎ 01984 623293 01984 623293
e-mail: lnp@rockinn.co.uk
dir: *From Taunton take B3227. Waterrow approx 14m W*

The name derives from the rock face a third of this former smithy was once carved out of. Indeed, part of its still visible behind the bar, next to a cheerfully roaring fire. The inn dates back over 400 years and is set in a lovely green valley beside the River Tone. Award-winning ales and home-made food are served, including fresh fish daily from Brixham, and Aberdeen Angus beef from their own farm two miles away. Start with double-baked jubilee soufflé, followed by local pan-fried pork fillet; free-range chicken and ham pie; Exmoor venison steak; or, for the vegetarians, red onion and goats' cheese tart. Miles of wonderful walking and fishing country make this region much cherished by outdoor types. Stop off for a night or two in one of eight cosy rooms: the promise is that your dog will be made as welcome as you!

Open 12-3 6-11 **Bar Meals** L served all week 12-2.30 D served all week 6.30-9.30 (Sun 7-9) Av main course £9.50 **Restaurant** L served all week 12-2.30 D served all week 6.30-9.30 (Sun 7-9) Av 3 course à la carte £19.50 Free House Cotleigh Tawny, Exmoor Gold, Otter Ale, London Pride. 11 **Facilities** Children's licence Dogs allowed Parking **Rooms** 8 bedrooms en suite S£40 D£70

WASHFORD MAP 03 ST04

The Washford Inn

TA23 0PP ☎ 01984 640256
e-mail: washfordinn@freedomnames.co.uk

A pleasant family inn located beside Washford Station, a stop on the West Somerset Railway between Minehead and Bishop's Lydeard – the longest privately-owned line in Britain. A service runs all year, using both diesel and nostalgic old steam locos. A good range of beers and a simple menu of proven pub favourites such as omelette and chips, grilled steaks, and all-day breakfast. Chicken nuggets, sausages or pizzas for young trainspotters.

Open 12-11 **Bar Meals** L served all week 12-8.30 D served all week Av main course £7.50 **Restaurant** L served all week 12-2.30 D served all week 5-9 Scottish & Newcastle Adnams Broadside, Theakstons Best Mild, Ringwood. **Facilities** Garden Dogs allowed Parking Play Area

WELLS MAP 04 ST54

The City Arms

69 High St BA5 2AG ☎ 01749 673916 01749 672901
e-mail: query@thecityarmsatwells.co.uk

One of the historic sights of Wells, by 1591 this early 16th-century building had become a jail, hence the small barred windows. On the menu expect to find dishes like smoked haddock, spinach and cream bake; stuffed field mushrooms; chargrilled chicken Caesar; and fine Aberdeen Angus steaks. Weekly changing specials include cottage pie, and macaroni and broccoli cheese bake. As one of only two free houses in the city it serves seven real ales.

Open 8-11 (Fri-Sat 8am-12am, Sun 9am-11pm) **Bar Meals** L served all week 9 D served all week 10 (Winter 9) **Restaurant** L served all week 12 D served all week 6-9 Butcombe, Greene King, Sharps. 16 **Facilities** Children's licence Garden Dogs allowed

England

WELLS continued

Pick of the Pubs

The Fountain Inn & Boxer's Restaurant 🍷

1 Saint Thomas St BA5 2UU

☎ 01749 672317 📠 01749 670825

e-mail: eat@fountaininn.co.uk

dir: *City centre. Follow The Harringtons signs to junct of Tor St & St Thomas St*

Dating back to the 16th century and built to house builders working on nearby Wells Cathedral, the award-winning Fountain Inn & Boxer's Restaurant has a well-earned reputation for good food. Chef manager Julie Pearce uses the finest local produce to create an impressive selection of quality home-cooked food served in both the bar and the restaurant. Old favourites on the bar specials board may include lasagne bolognaise with dressed side salad; fresh cod in beer batter with chips and home-made tartare sauce; and Butcombe, beef and mushroom pie with new potatoes and fresh vegetables. Among the restaurant mains are fillet steak stuffed with haggis and wrapped in smoked bacon, blackberry and red wine jus, gratin dauphinoise and fresh vegetables; oven-baked wild salmon escalope topped with fresh asparagus, balsamic, bell pepper and red onion dressing, new potatoes and fresh vegetables; and roasted rump of lamb with an orange, redcurrant and red wine jus.

Open 10.30–2.30 6–11 (Sun 12–3, 7–10.30) Closed: 25–26 Dec **Bar Meals** L served all week 12–2 D served all week 6–10 (Sun 12–2.30, 7–9.30) **Restaurant** L served all week 12–2.30 D served all week 6–10 (Sun 7–9.30) 🏠 Innspired 🍺 Butcombe Bitter, Interbrew Bass, Scottish Courage Courage Best. 🍷 23 **Facilities** Parking

The Pheasant Inn 🍷

Worth, Wookey BA5 1LQ ☎ 01749 672355

e-mail: pheasant@dsl.pipex.com

dir: *W of Wells on the B3139 towards Wedmore*

Popular country pub at the foot of the Mendips, where you can enjoy some impressive views and relax with a pint of real ale beside a welcoming log fire. The menu ranges through light bites, a pasta and pizza section, and dishes such as slow roast lamb shank with minty Somerset sauce, and escalope of pork with cider and sage cream sauce. Friday night is fish night, and there are some great puddings.

Open 11.30–2.30 6–11 (Sat 11.30–11, Sun 12–10.30) **Bar Meals** L served all week 12–2 D served all week 6.30–9.30 (Sun 7–9) **Restaurant** L serve all week 12–2 D served all week 6.30–9.30 (Sun 7–9) 🏠 Enterprise Inns 🍺 Butcombe, Greene King Old Speckled Hen, Pedigree, Butcombe Blond. 🍷 6 **Facilities** Children's licence Garden Dogs allowed Parking

WEST CAMEL MAP 04 ST5

The Walnut Tree ★★ HL ❁

Fore St BA22 7QW ☎ 01935 851292 📠 01935 851292

e-mail: info@thewalnuttreehotel.com

dir: *Off A303 between Sparkford & Yeovilton Air Base*

Close to the border between Dorset and Somerset, this well-kept inn in a quiet village. The Leyland Trail passes close by and brings plenty walkers. The cosily carpeted lounge bar and two restaurants entice the hungry with smoked duck breast with caramelised onions in an apple and brandy sauce; venison fillet on dauphinoise potatoes in a port an redcurrant sauce; and roasted beef fillet with a wild mushroom farci wrapped in bacon.

Open 11–3 6.30–11.30 Closed: 25–26 Dec **Bar Meals** L served all week 12–2 D served all week 6–9.30 **Restaurant** L served All 12–2 D served All 7–9.30 🏠 Free House 🍺 Butcombe Bitter, Otter Ale & Bitter. **Facilities** Garden Parking **Rooms** 13 bedrooms en suite S£72 D£98

WEST HUNTSPILL MAP 04 ST3

Crossways Inn 🍷

Withy Rd TA9 3RA ☎ 01278 783756 📠 01278 781899

e-mail: crossways.inn@virgin.net

dir: *On A38 3.5m from M5*

Run by Mike and Anna Ronca since 1973, this 17th-century coaching inn is an integral part of village life. The interior is warmly furnished and free of piped music, although live jazz, blues, Gaelic music and ven opera get the green light some evenings. Blackboards display ıe day's temptations, from snacks to traditional pies, various curries nd a selection from the grill. There's a family room, skittle alley and ecluded garden.

pen 12–3 5.30–11 (Sun 12–4.30, 7–10.30) Closed: 25 Dec **ar Meals** L served all week 12–2 D served all week 6.30–9 (Sun 2–2.30, 7–9) Av main course £7.50 **Restaurant** L served all week 12–2 served all week 6.30–9 Av 3 course à la carte £14.50 Free House Interbrew Bass, Flowers IPA, Fuller's London Pride, Exmoor Stag. 8 **acilities** Garden Dogs allowed Parking

VHEDDON CROSS — MAP 03 SS93

'he Rest and Be Thankful Inn ★★★ INN

A24 7DR ☎ 01643 841222 01643 841813
-mail: stay@restandbethankful.co.uk
ir: *5m S of Dunster*

ears ago, travellers were grateful for a break at this coaching inn, early 1,000 feet up in Exmoor's highest village. Old world charm ends with friendly hospitality in the bar and spacious restaurant, here log fires burn in winter and home-cooked food is served. In ddition to the restaurant menu there is a weekly specials board, a light nch menu and a traditional Sunday carvery. The pub also has a skittle ley and pool table.

pen 10–2.30 6.30–12 **Bar Meals** L served all week 12–2 D served week 7–9 Av main course £8.50 **Restaurant** L served all week 12–2 served all week 7–9 Free House Exmoor Ale, Proper Job, Tribute, arlsberg. **Facilities** Garden Parking **Rooms** 5 bedrooms en suite S£37 £70

VITHYPOOL — MAP 03 SS83

Pick of the Pubs

The Royal Oak Inn ★★ HL

TA24 7QP ☎ 01643 831506 01643 831659
e-mail: roy.bookings@ccinns.com
dir: *Through Taunton on B3224, then B3223 to Withypool*

Bang in the middle of Exmoor's breathtaking walking country is this 300-year-old inn with a colourful history. Down the ages it has played host to a number of well-known names – like, R D Blackmore and Eisenhower, and it was once owned by spymaster Maxwell Knight. You can dine in the bar or in the strikingly decorated dining room, where local produce freshly turned into tasty meals. Start, perhaps, with deep-fried camembert coated in a crispy coconut and almond crumb with grape and apple chutney, go on to confit of lamb with creamed leeks, fondant potatoes and a rosemary jus, and finish with apricot and brandy bread and butter pudding served with crème Anglaise. Stay over in one of the eight comfortable bedrooms and bring a copy of Blackmore's *Lorna Doone* with you: the beamed ceilings, log fires and friendly staff contribute to a wonderful atmosphere that is sure to work its magic on you.

Open 11–2.30 6–11 **Bar Meals** L served all week 12–2 D served all week 6.30–9.30 **Restaurant** L served all week 12–2 D served all week 7–9.30 Av 3 course à la carte £2 Free House Courage Directors, Exmoor Ale, John Smiths. 16 **Facilities** Dogs allowed Parking **Rooms** 8 bedrooms 7 en suite S£50 D£65

WOOKEY — MAP 04 ST54

The Burcott Inn

Wells Rd BA5 1NJ ☎ 01749 673874
dir: *3m from Wells on B3139*

Set on the edge of a charming village, this 300-year-old stone-built inn features low beamed ceilings, a flagstone floor, log fires and a copper top bar. The range of real ales changes frequently as does the blackboard menu, featuring seafood specialities and locally sourced beef and lamb. Options range through lunchtime snacks, steak and ale pie, slow roasted lamb rump, and vegetable and cashew nut bake. The large garden affords views of the Mendip Hills.

Open 11.30–2.30 6–11 Closed: 25–26 Dec, 1 Jan **Bar Meals** L served all week 12–2.30 D served Tue–Sat 6.30–9.30 **Restaurant** L served all week 12–2 D served Tue–Sat 6.30–9.30 Av 3 course à la carte £18 Free House Teignworthy Old Moggie, Cotleigh Barn Owl Bitter, RCH Pitchfork, Branscombe BVB. **Facilities** Garden Parking

YARLINGTON — MAP 04 ST62

The Stags Head Inn

Pound Ln BA9 8DG ☎ 01963 440393 01963 440393
e-mail: mrandall1960@tiscali.co.uk
dir: *A37 signed Castle Carey 3m, left signed Yarlington, 2nd right into village*

Halfway between Wincanton and Castle Cary lies this completely unspoilt country inn with flagstones, real fires and no electronic intrusions. A sample menu includes slow-roasted lamb shank on creamed mash with redcurrant and rosemary; haddock fillet in beer batter; or chargrilled rump steak with chips, onion rings and mushrooms. Burgers and light bites also available.

Open 12–2.30 6–11 (Sat–Sun 12–3) Closed: 25 Dec **Bar Meals** L served Tue–Sun 12–2 D served Tue–Sat 7–9 Free House Greene King, IPA, Bass. **Facilities** Children's licence Garden Dogs allowed Parking

England

STAFFORDSHIRE

ALREWAS MAP 10 SK11

The Old Boat

DE13 7DB ☎ 01283 791468 01283 792886

Standing on the Trent and Mersey Canal, the pub was originally used by canal construction workers and bargemen. The snug at the end of the bar was once the cellar, where casks of ale were rolled off the barges and kept cool in up to two feet of water. Typical dishes include roast Packington pork belly with sage and apple mash; roast lamb with braised red onions; and grilled turbot with sautéed cabbage and chorizo.

Open 12–2 6–11 (Sun 12–3) **Restaurant** L served all week 12–2 D served all week 6–9 (Sun 12–3) Av 3 course à la carte £21.95 Marston's Pedigree & John Smith's. 8 **Facilities** Garden Parking

ALSAGERS BANK MAP 15 SJ74

The Gresley Arms

High St ST7 8BQ ☎ 01782 720297 01782 720297

A 200-year-old pub in a semi-rural location set between two country parks, making it a popular stopping off point for walkers and cyclists. It is a friendly local, with a traditional bar, separate lounge and large family room, serving real ale and real food at a reasonable price. The menu encompasses basket meals (chicken, scampi, beefburger), steaks with sauces, light bites, main meals and daily specials, such as braised lamb shank, and tagliatelle nicoise.

Open 12–3 6–11 (Fri–Sun all day) **Bar Meals** L served all week 12–2.30 D served all week 6–9.30 (Sat–Sun 12–9.30) Av main course £6 **Restaurant** L served all week 12–3 D served all week 6–9.30 (Sat–Sun 12–9.30) 6 guest beers. **Facilities** Garden Dogs allowed Parking **Notes**

ALSTONEFIELD MAP 16 SK15

Pick of the Pubs

The George NEW

DE6 2FX ☎ 01335 310205

e-mail: emily@thegeorgeatalstonefield.com

dir: *7m N of Ashbourne, sidned Milldale/Alstonefield*

Situated right at the heart of Alstonefield, this 18th-century coaching inn has been run by three generations of the same family since the 1960s. Since landlady Emily Hammond followed in her parents' footsteps, a sympathetic restoration of the dining room has taken place, revealing original windows and a Georgian fireplace hidden for over a century. She has also been busy building on an impressive local reputation for excellent home-cooked food. The focus is on seasonal, regional and traditional dishes, with plenty of hearty options for the walkers and fishermen who flock to the pub by day, including meat and potato pie; smoked mackerel fishcakes; and an appealing range of sandwiches. By night, sample the likes of gin and juniper cured salmon with apple and fennel cream; roast partridge and pear with bacon and shallot gravy; and raspberry crème brûlée.

Open 11–3 6–11 (Sat–Sun 11–11) **Bar Meals** L served all week 12–2.30 D served Mon–Sat 7–9 Av main course £8.50 **Restaurant** L served all week 12–2.30 D served Mon–Sat 7–9 Marstons Marston's Bitter, Marston's Pedigree, Jennings, Cumberland Ale. **Facilities** Children's licence Garden Dogs allowed Parking

ALTON MAP 10 SK0

Bulls Head Inn

High St ST10 4AQ ☎ 01538 702307 01538 702065

e-mail: janet@thebullshead.freeserve.co.uk

dir: *M6 junct 14, A518 to Uttoxeter (Alton Towers signs). Onto B5030 to Rocester, then B5032 to Alton village centre*

Traditional beers, home cooking and well-equipped accommodation are provided in the heart of Alton, less than a mile from Alton Towers theme park. Oak beams and an inglenook fireplace set the scene for the old world bar, the cosy snug and the country-style restaurant. Menus offer the likes of sirloin steak, deep-fried breaded plaice, lasagne verde, steak, ale and mushroom pie, and hunter's chicken.

Bar Meals L served all week 12–2 (Sat 12–2.30, Sun 12–3) D served all week 6–9.30 Av main course £8 **Restaurant** L served all week 12–2 D served all week 6.30–9.30 Av 3 course à la carte £15 Free House Cask Ale, Guest beers. **Facilities** Parking **Rooms** 7 bedrooms en suite S£45 D£60 (★★★ GA)

ANSLOW MAP 10 SK2

The Burnt Gate Inn

Hopley Rd DE13 9PY ☎ 01283 563664

e-mail: theburntgateinn@aol.com

dir: *From Burton B5017 towards Abbots Bromley. At top of Henhurst Hill turn right Inn on Hopley Rd, 2m from town centre*

Originally two cottages and a farmhouse, parts of the inn are 300 and 125 years old respectively, and it has been more recently extended. The name relates to a tollgate opposite the pub by a wood, both burnt down to make way for arable land. Cask ales and real food are served along with traditional steaks, vegetarian dishes and game in season, plus fresh fish from the daily specials board. A gluten free menu is also available.

Open 12–2.30 6–11 (Sun 12–3, 7–10.30) **Bar Meals** L served all week 12–2.15 D served Mon–Sat Av main course £7.95 **Restaurant** L served all week 12–2 (Sun 12–3) D served Mon–Sat 6.30–9 Av 3 course à la carte £20 Av 3 course fixed price £14.50 Free House Pedigree (Cask ales), Guest beers. 8 **Facilities** Parking

BURTON UPON TRENT MAP 10 SK2

Burton Bridge Inn

24 Bridge St DE14 1SY ☎ 01283 536596

dir: *Telephone for directions*

With its own brewery at the back, this is one of the oldest pubs in the area. The unspoilt old-fashioned interior has oak panelling, feature fireplaces, and a distinct lack of electronic entertainment. A full range of Burton Bridge ales is on tap, and the menu includes straightforward meals like roast pork, jacket potatoes, or beef cobs, as well as traditional filled Yorkshire puddings. Long alley skittles upstairs.

Open 11.30–2.30 5–11 **Bar Meals** L served Mon–Sat Burton Bridge Brewery Burton Bridge Gold Medal Ale, Burton Bridge Festival Ale, Burton Bridge Golden Delicious & Bridge Bitter. 15 **Facilities** Garden Dogs allowed **Notes**

The Holly Bush Inn

Aside from the quality of its food and welcome, the charming Holly Bush boasts two notable distinctions. It is generally recognised as the second pub in the country to have been licensed. This event took place during Charles II's reign (1660–1685), though the building itself is far older, possibly dating back to 1190.

econdly, when landlord Geoff Iolland's son became a joint licensee t the age of 18 years and 6 days, he vas the youngest person ever to be ;ranted a licence. In the Domesday ook the village of Salt was recorded s Selte, which in Old English neant a salt pit, even though there's o written evidence of workings vithin the parish. The comfortably ld-fashioned interior contains all he vital ingredients: heavy carved eams, open fires, attractive prints nd cosy alcoves. The team are nore enthusiastic than ever in heir attempts to reduce food miles nd support local producers. This ommitment to the environment ven extends to the waste food, vhich goes into the pub's wormery o create compost. Beef, pork, hicken and dairy products all ome from known and trusted local farmers, with animal transportation reduced to a minimum. Seasonal starters could include pan-fried Cornish brie with redcurrant sauce; or farmhouse paté on toast. Move on to 'civet' of venison, a traditional slow-cooked casserole with home-cured bacon; grilled Staffordshire pork chops; or braised lamb and apples. A particular favourite on the menu is the champagne banger, a sausage made on the premises using local free-range pork and sparkling wine from Staffordshire's Halfpenny Green vineyard. A lengthy seafood menu attests to the excellent relationships developed with Torbay's fishermen: try roast monkfish and saffron mash; or sautéed scallops, clams, prawn and home-smoked bacon with cream and tagliatelle. While wines aren't local, they're certainly well chosen.

MAP 10 SJ92
Salt ST18 0BX
☎ 01889 508234
Fax 01889 508058
e-mail:
geoff@hollybushinn.co.uk

Open 12-11
Bar Meals L served all week 12–9.30 D served all week 12–9.30
Free House
Adnams, Pedigree & Guest Ales. 12
Facilities Garden Dogs allowed Parking

England

BUTTERTON MAP 16 SK05

The Black Lion Inn 🍷

ST13 7SP ☎ 01538 304232
e-mail: blacklioninn@hotmail.com
dir: *From A52 take B5053*

This charming, 18th-century village inn lies on the edge of the Manifold valley, in the heart of the Peak District's walking and cycling country. Winter fires add to the pleasure of a well-kept pint. The popular bar menu includes pies and steaks, as well as lamb casserole, spinach and ricotta cannelloni, and plenty of interesting fish dishes.

Open 12–3 7–11 Rest: Mon Closed lunch **Bar Meals** L served Wed–Sun 12–1.45 D served all week 7–8.45 **Restaurant** L served Tues-Sun 12–2 D served all week 7–9.30 Free House Scottish Courage Theakston Best, Greene King, Titanic. 🍷 10 **Facilities** Garden Parking

CAULDON MAP 16 SK04

Yew Tree Inn

ST10 3EJ ☎ 01538 308348 01782 212064
dir: *Between A52 & A523. 4.5m from Alton Towers*

The Yew Tree is so well known that people come from all over the world to see it. The pub dates back 300 years and has plenty of character and lots of fascinating artefacts, including Victorian music boxes, pianolas, grandfather clocks, a crank handle telephone, a pub lantern and an award-winning landlord who's been here for over forty years. A varied snack menu offers locally made, hand-raised pork pies, sandwiches, baps, quiche and sweets.

Open 10–2.30 6–11 (Sun 12–3) Free House Burton Bridge, Grays Mild, Bass. **Facilities** Dogs allowed Parking **Notes**

CHEADLE MAP 10 SK04

The Queens At Freehay

Counslow Rd, Freehay ST10 1RF
☎ 01538 722383 01538 723748
dir: *4m from Alton Towers*

Parts of this cheerful pub date from 1800. It was taken over by the present owner's parents in 1999 and is the forerunner of a number of successful food pubs run by the family. An extensive food choice includes lunchtime light bites, and popular dishes like vegetable tikka masala; chicken and broccoli bake; and poached breast of chicken. Alton Park is a mere four miles away.

Open 12–2.30 6–11 (Sun 6.30–11) Closed: 25–26, 31 Dec & 1 Jan **Bar Meals** L served all week 12–2 D served all week 6–9.30 (Sun 12–2.30, 6.30–9.30) Av main course £10.45 **Restaurant** L served all week 12–2 D served all week 6–9.30 (Sun 12–2.30, 6.30–9.30) Free House Draught Bass, Draught Worthington Bitter. **Facilities** Garden Parking

ECCLESHALL MAP 15 SJ82

The George 🍷

Castle St ST21 6DF ☎ 01785 850300 01785 851452
e-mail: information@thegeorgeinn.freeserve.co.uk
dir: *6m from M6 junct 14*

A family-run, 16th-century former coaching inn with its own micro-brewery, where the owners' son produces award-winning Slater's ales. Occasional beer festivals are held, and the menu features a wide variety of dishes, including spicy chilli tortillas; roast salmon with hoi sin sauce, chive mash and stir-fry veg; and cod in Slater's ale batter. A selection of salads, baked potatoes and sandwiches is also available.

Open 11–11 (Sun 12–10.30) Closed: 25 Dec **Bar Meals** L served all week 12–9.30 D served all week 6–9.30 (Sun 12–8.30) Av main course £9.50 **Restaurant** L served all week 12–2.30 D served all week 6–9.45 Free House Slaters Ales. **Facilities** Dogs allowed Parking

KING'S BROMLEY MAP 10 SK1

Royal Oak NEW 🍷

Manor Rd DE13 7HZ ☎ 01543 472 289
e-mail: shropshall@btinternet.com
dir: *Off A515*

The Royal Oak looks and feels like a quaint village local but award-winning chef and licensee Mathew Shropshall offers cooking of seriou intent alongside more familiar pub grub. There are lunchtime wraps, melts and sandwiches, and comfort food such as steak and ale pie or beer battered cod and chips. The serious stuff might include Barbary duck with a Seville orange and mustard sauce; or braised oxtails with sauce bourguignon and parsnip mash.

Open 11.45–3 6–11 **Bar Meals** L served all week 12–2.30 D served all week 6–9 Av main course £9.95 **Restaurant** L served all week 12–2.30 D served all week 6–9 Marstons Pedigree Bitter, Banks Bitter, Sneck Lifter, Cocker Hoop. 🍷 10 **Facilities** Garden Dogs allowed Parking

PUB CYCLES

WATERHOUSES - STAFFORDSHIRE

Ye Olde Crown Hotel

Cycle information

Distance: 17 miles/27.4km (4h30)
Map: OS Explorer OL24 White Peak
Start/finish: Waterhouses Old Station, grid ref SK 085503
Trails/tracks: the entire route is tarred, some of it badly pitted, about 3 miles (4.8km) is shared with light road traffic, one tunnel
Landscape: limestone gorges, ash woods and good views towards the moorlands
Public toilets: Waterhouses and Hulme End stations
Tourist information: Leek, tel 01538 483741
Cycle hire: Waterhouses Old Station, tel 01538 308609; also Brown End Farm, tel 01538 308313
The pub: Ye Olde Crown Hotel, Waterhouses, near Point 1 on route

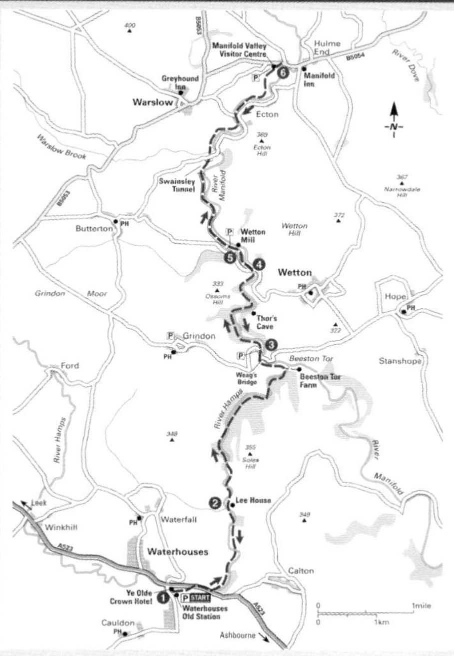

Cycle directions

1 The signal box at the old station is the starting point. This was an interchange between the standard gauge line to Leek and the narrow gauge Leek and Manifold Light Railway. It meandered through these remote valleys between 1904 and 1934, and we follow this route. The ride soon joins a wide cycle-pavement beside the main road. At the crossing point, carefully cross into the 'No Traffic' lane opposite. You'll immediately cross a bridge over the River Hamps, one of many such crossings in the next few miles. It's an easy trip along the tarred way towards the enclosing valley sides.

2 Soon after Lee House Farm (teas and meals here in season) the ash woods close in and the route becomes tunnel-like beneath these bird-rich boughs. In 2 miles (3.2km) the route curves gradually left to reveal Beeston Tor. Here, the Hamps meets with the River Manifold, flowing south beneath the Tor towards the distant River Dove. The route runs parallel to an access road before reaching a gateway and a lane at Weag's Bridge.

3 Carefully cross straight over and ride through the car park to and through the gate at the end, regaining a non-trafficked stretch. The view is spectacular, the river gyrating between immensely steep cliffs cloaked in some of England's finest ash woods. As the route leaves the trees around a left-hand curve, look back to see the awesome Thor's Cave, high above the valley. An interpretation board tells its history; a steep path leads up to it.

4 The tortuous road between Wetton and Grindon is soon reached at a gated bridge. Beyond here, and for the next 3 miles (4.8km), you will share the road with other traffic, so care is needed. It's Continue ahead along the flatter route marking the old railway to reach the popular tea rooms at Wetton Mill. Beware of traffic here at another minor junction. This is a good place to turn around if you are taking the shorter alternative route (9 miles/14.5km round trip).

5 Continuing north, the road keeps company with the river to reach Swainsley Tunnel. This is shared with vehicles, but is wide enough for bike and car and also well lit. At the far end go back on to a segregated track, cycling north to pass beneath bald Ecton Hill and its sombre mining remains. Crossing another road here, the valley sides gradually pull back for the final approach to journey's end, the station at Hulme End.

6 Turn around here and retrace your route back to the start. Take care at Weag's Bridge to take the gated lane rather than the access road to the caravan site at Beeston Tor Farm.

LEEK MAP 16 SJ95

Ye Olde Royal Oak

Wetton DE6 2AF ☎ 01335 310287
e-mail: brian@rosehose.wanadoo.co.uk
dir: *A515 towards Buxton, left in 4m to Manifold Valley-Alstonfield, follow signs to Wetton*

Formerly part of the Chatsworth estate, this stone-built inn dates back over 400 years and has wooden beams recovered from oak ships at Liverpool Docks. The Tissington walking and cycling trail is close by, and the pub's moorland garden includes a camper's croft. Tuck into steak and Guinness pie, wild mushroom lasagne, mixed grill, or filled Staffordshire oatcakes.

Open 12-3 7-11 (Sat-Sun all day Etr-Sep) Rest: Closed Mon in Winter **Bar Meals** L served Wed-Mon (Wed-Sun Winter) 12-2 D served Wed-Mon (Wed-Sun Winter) 7-9 Av main course £6 Free House Theakstons Best Bitter, Greene King Abbot, Guest Beers. **Facilities** Garden Dogs allowed Parking

Three Horseshoes Inn ★★★ HL

Buxton Rd, Blackshaw Moor ST13 8TW
☎ 01538 300296 01538 300320
e-mail: enquiries@threeshoesinn.co.uk
dir: *On A53, 3m N of Leek*

There are great views from the attractive gardens of this sprawling, creeper-covered inn. Inside, the main bar features wood fires in the winter, with a good selection of real ales and guest beers. Visitors can choose roast meats in the bar carvery, the relaxed atmosphere of the brasserie (one rosette), or the more formal restaurant. Choices include eggs Benedict with smoked haddock and spinach; and roasted vegetable, rosemary and goats' cheese tarte Tatin.

Open 12-3 6-11 **Bar Meals** L served all week 12-2 D served all week 6.30-9 (Sun 12-3, 6-8.30 Summer all day) Av main course £8 **Restaurant** L served Wed-Sat (Sun 12.15-1.30) D served Sat 6.30-9 Av 3 course à la carte £25 Free House Theakstons XB Courage Directors, Morland Old Speckled Hen, John Smiths. 12 **Facilities** Garden Parking Play Area **Rooms** 27 bedrooms 26 en suite S£68 D£76

NORBURY JUNCTION MAP 15 SJ72

The Junction Inn

ST20 0PN ☎ 01785 284288 01785 284288
dir: *From M6 take road for Eccleshall, left at Gt Bridgeford towards Woodseaves, left towards Newport, left for Norbury Junction*

Not a railway junction, but a beautiful stretch of waterway where the Shropshire Union Canal meets the disused Newport arm. The inn offers fabulous views and a great stop off point for canal walkers. Food ranges from baguettes, burgers and basket meals to grills and home-made pies. Popular options are sizzling chicken fajitas, giant battered cod and a gargantuan mixed grill. Caravans are welcome and canal boat hire is available.

Open 11-11 **Bar Meals** L served all week 11-9 D served all week 11-9 Av main course £6 **Restaurant** L served all week 12-9 D served all week 12-9 Free House Banks Mild, Banks Bitter, Junction Ale and Guest ales. **Facilities** Garden Dogs allowed Parking Play Area

STAFFORD MAP 10 SJ9

Pick of the Pubs

The Holly Bush Inn

Salt ST18 0BX ☎ 01889 508234 01889 508058
e-mail: geoff@hollybushinn.co.uk

See Pick of the Pubs on page 513

Pick of the Pubs

The Moat House ★★★★ HL

Lower Penkridge Rd, Acton Trussell ST17 0RJ
☎ 01785 712217 01785 715344
e-mail: info@moathouse.co.uk
dir: *M6 junct 13 towards Stafford, 1st right to Acton Trussell*

Grade II listed mansion dating back to the 15th century and situated behind its original moat. Quality bedrooms, conference facilities and corporate events are big attractions, and with four honeymoon suites, the Moat House is a popular venue for weddings. Inside are oak beams and an inglenook fireplace, and the bar and food trade bring in both the hungry and the curious who like to savour the charm and atmosphere of the place. Major refurbishments have contributed a stylish lounge area serving brasserie-style food. Among the more popular dishes are rocket and goats' cheese soup or tuna spring roll, followed by braised shank of lamb with bubble and squeak and a rosemary jus; seared seabass with fennel, baby spinach and a mussel nage; or plaice fillets with crab mousse, asparagus and saffron broth. If there's room afterwards, try bread and butter pudding, steamed treacle sponge or chocolate fudge brownie.

Open 10-11 Closed: 25-26 Dec, 1-2 Jan **Bar Meals** L served Mon-Sat 12-2.15 D served Sun-Fri 6-9.30 Av main course £12.50 **Restaurant** L served all week 12-2 D served all week 7-9.30 Av 3 course à la carte £34.50 Av 3 course fixed price £29.50 Free House Bank's Bitter, Marston's Pedigree, Murphys. 13 **Facilities** Children's licence Garden Parking **Rooms** 32 bedrooms en suite S£125 D£135

STOURTON MAP 10 SO8

The Fox Inn

Bridgnorth Rd DY7 5BL
☎ 01384 872614 & 872123 01384 877771
e-mail: fox-inn-stourton@dial.pipex.com
dir: *5m from Stourbridge town centre, on A458*

Late 18th-century pub set amid beautiful countryside near Kinver village. Walkers from many nearby rambling areas are attracted by its warm atmosphere and historic surroundings, with many original features still in place. There's also a large garden to enjoy, complete with weeping willow, gazebo and an attractive patio area. Fish features on the menu, and the Batham and Enville ales are very appealing.

Open 11.30-3 5-11 (Sat-Sun 11-11) **Bar Meals** L served all week 12.30-2.15 D served Tue-Sat 7-9.30 (Sun 3-5.30) **Restaurant** L served Tue-Sun 12-9.30 D served Tue-Sat 7-9.30 (Sun 12.30-5.15) Free House Bathams Ale, Enville Ale, Murphy's, Boddingtons & Stella. 8 **Facilities** Garden Parking

The Crown Inn

This 19th-century former coaching inn is very much a family affair. Charles and Sue Davenhill have owned it for 30 years, and in 2001 were joined by their daughter and son-in-law, Anna and Mark Condliffe.

Charles is now reputedly the longest-serving licensee in all of North Staffordshire. Food is a major part of the pub's success, and it's famed locally not just for the vastness of the portions, but also the consistently good quality. An appealingly organised menu offers a wide range of dishes for varying appetites. Possibilities include medallions of pork in creamy apple, mustard and cider sauce; hickory chicken baked with Monterey Jack cheese; haddock fillet with green pesto; rainbow trout fillets oven baked with julienne of vegetables; or steak, ale and mushroom pie. Vegetarians have some excellent options, including kofta kebabs made not with the customary lamb, but ground aduki beans, coriander and cumin, on a bed of bulgur wheat and mint, as well as Moroccan tagine, and aubergine parmigiana. For the less than ravenous a soft floury bap may well suffice. They come with a variety of fillings, such as Cajun chicken or French brie, and are all served open with crispy salad garnish and home-made coleslaw. From the sweet menu, try hot chocolate pudding with chocolate orange sauce, or a selection of local and French cheeses. At the bar there's always a choice of six traditional real ales, one of which is a regularly changing guest. The wine list is limited to a choice of eleven, of which seven may be drunk by the glass. And don't expect any jukeboxes: they're strictly barred in an attempt to preserve the charming rural atmosphere.

MAP 15 SJ74
Den Ln CW3 9BT
☎ 01270 820472
Fax 01270 820547
e-mail:
mark_condliffe@hotmail.com
dir: *Village on A531, 1m S of Betley*

Open 12-3 6-11 (Sun 6-10.30)
Closed: 26 Dec
Bar Meals L served Tue-Sun 12-2 D served all week 6.30-9.30 (Sat 6-10, Sun 12-3, 6-9)
Av main course £9.50
Free House
Marston's Pedigree, Marston's Bitter, Adnam's Bitter, Sneck Lifter, & Timothy Taylor Landlord. 7
Facilities Garden Parking

England

TATENHILL MAP 10 SK22

Horseshoe Inn 🍷

Main St DE13 9SD ☎ 01283 564913 📠 01283 511314

dir: *From A38 at Branston follow signs for Tatenhill*

Probably five to six hundred years old, this historic pub retains much original character, including evidence of a priest's hiding hole. In winter, log fires warm the bar and family area. In addition to home-made snacks like chilli con carne, and Horseshoe brunch, there are sizzling rumps and sirloins, chicken curry, moussaka, battered cod with chips and mushy peas, and a pasta dish of the week. And specials too – beef bourguignon, or steak and kidney pudding, for instance.

Open 11–11 **Bar Meals** L served all week 12–9.30 D served all week 12–9.30 (Sun 12–9) Av main course £7.50 **Restaurant** L served all week 12–9.30 D served all week 12–9.30 Av 3 course à la carte £14 W'hampton & Dudley Marstons Pedigree. 🍷 14 **Facilities** Garden Dogs allowed Parking Play Area

TUTBURY MAP 10 SK22

Ye Olde Dog & Partridge Inn

High St DE13 9LS ☎ 01283 813030 📠 01283 813178

e-mail: info@dogandpartridge.net

dir: *On A50 NW of Burton-on-Trent (signed from A50 & A511)*

A beautiful period building resplendent in its timbers and whitewashed walls, with abundant flower displays beneath the windows. The inn has stood in this charming village since the 15th century when Henry IV was on the throne. Five hundred years of offering hospitality has resulted in a well-deserved reputation for good food, served in two smart eating outlets.

Open 11–11 Rest: 25–26 Dec Closed eve **Bar Meals** L served all week 11.30–11 D served all week 11.30–11 Free House Marston's Pedigree, Courage Director's. **Facilities** Garden Parking

WATERHOUSES MAP 16 SK05

Ye Olde Crown

Leek Rd ST10 3HL ☎ 01538 308204 📠 01538 308204

e-mail: kerryhinton@hotmail.co.uk

dir: *From Ashbourne take A52 then A523 towards Leek*

A traditional village local, Ye Olde Crown dates from around 1647 when it was built as a coaching inn. Sitting on the bank of the River Hamps, and on the edge of the Peak District National Park and the Staffordshire moorlands, it's ideal for walkers. Inside are original stonework and interior beams, and open fires are lit in cooler weather.

Open 12–2.30 6–11 (Sat–Sun all day) **Bar Meals** L served all week 12–2.30 D served all week 6.30–8.30 (Sun 12–6) Av main course £7 **Restaurant** L served Tue–Sun 12–2.30 D served Tue–Sat 6–8.30 (Sun 12–6) Marstons Marstons, Burton Bitter, Guest Ale. **Facilities** Children's licence Parking

Please see cycle ride on page 515

WOODSEAVES MAP 15 SJ7

The Plough Inn 🍷

Newport Rd ST20 0NP ☎ 01785 284210

dir: *Woodseaves at junct with A519, 5m from Eccleshall on A519 towards Newport*

Built in the mid-18th century for workers constructing the nearby canal, the Plough is a traditional country pub with winter fires and hanging baskets for the summer. There's a good selection of real ales, and the bar menu features favourites like sausages, mash and red wine gravy. The restaurant menu offers more adventurous options like deep-fried goats' cheese with ratatouille and chargrilled potatoes; or pan-fried duck with cranberry and orange sauce.

Open 12–2 6–11 **Bar Meals** L served Wed–Sun 12–2.30 D served Tue–Sat 6–9.30 (Sun 12–4, Summer 6–8.30) Av main course £9.95 **Restaurant** L served 12–2 D served Tue–Sat 6–9 (Sun 12–8 Summer) Av 3 course à la carte £16.95 Av 2 course fixed price £7.50 Free House Spitfire, 6X, Grumpy Chef, Titanic Full Kiln Ale. 🍷 2 **Facilities** Garden Parking

WRINEHILL MAP 15 SJ7

Pick of the Pubs

The Crown Inn 🍷

Den Ln CW3 9BT ☎ 01270 820472 📠 01270 820547

e-mail: mark_condliffe@hotmail.com

dir: *Village on A531, 1m S of Bentley*

See Pick of the Pubs on page 517

SUFFOLK

ALDEBURGH MAP 13 TM4

The Mill Inn ★★★ INN

Market Cross Place IP15 5BJ

☎ 01728 452563 📠 01728 451923

e-mail: peeldennisp@aol.com

dir: *Follow Aldeburgh signs from A12 on A1094. Pub last building on left before sea*

A genuine fisherman's inn located less than 100 metres from the seafront, and a short walk from the town and bird sanctuaries. Seafood bought fresh from the fishermen on the beach is a speciality here, with Dover sole, mussels, crab, herrings and sea bass all part of the tchen's repertoire. Well-kept Adnams Bitter, Broadside, Regatta nd Fisherman can all be enjoyed at this favourite haunt of the local eboat crew.

pen 11–3 6–11 (11–11 Summer) **Bar Meals** L served all week 12–2 served Tue–Sat 7–9 **Restaurant** L served Tue–Sun 12–2 D served ie–Sat 7–9 Adnams Adnams Bitter, Broadside, Regatta & Fisherman, LD. **Facilities** Dogs allowed **Rooms** 4 bedrooms S£50 D£55

ALDRINGHAM — MAP 13 TM46

The Parrot and Punchbowl Inn & Restaurant

ldringham Ln IP16 4PY ☎ 01728 830221

-mail: paul@parrotandpunchbowl.fsnet.co.uk

ir: *On B1122 1m from Leiston, 3m from Aldeburgh, on x-rds to horpeness*

)riginally called The Case is Altered, it became the Parrot in 1604 and s such enjoyed considerable notoriety, particularly during the 17th entury, as the haunt of Aldringham's smuggling gangs. Don't ask if nere's any contraband gin on offer; just study the menu and try and ecide between medallions of pork fillet, whole baked sea bass, deep-ied cod in Adnam's beer batter, or an Aberdeen Angus fillet steak. Parrot sandwiches' are generously overfilled.

)pen 12–3 5.30–12 (Sun 12–3) Rest: Winter 12–3 all week **ar Meals** L served all week 12–2.30 D served all week 6.30–9.30 Av main ourse £5 **Restaurant** L served all week 12–2.30 D served all week .30–9.30 Av 3 course à la carte £20 Enterprise Inns Adnams, Guest eer. 10 **Facilities** Garden Parking Play Area

BARNBY — MAP 13 TM49

Pick of the Pubs

The Swan Inn

Swan Ln NR34 7QF ☎ 01502 476646 01502 562513

dir: *Just off A146 between Lowestoft & Beccles*

See Pick of the Pubs on page 521

BRANDESTON — MAP 13 TM26

The Queens Head

The Street IP13 7AD ☎ 01728 685307

e-mail: thequeensheadinn@btconnect.com

dir: *From A14 take A1120 to Earl Soham, then S to Brandeston*

Once four cottages, The Queens Head has been serving ale to the villagers of Brandeston since 1811. A large open bar allows drinkers and diners to mix, while a huge garden has plenty of potential in summer months. The menu might offer such dishes as goats' cheese, red onion and pesto tart; home-cooked ham and eggs with bubble and squeak; or pan-fried sea bass with seared scallop and cherry tomato mash.

Open 12–3 6–11 **Bar Meals** L served all week 12–2 D served all week 6.30–9 Av main course £10 **Restaurant** L served all week D served all week Adnams Adnams Broadside & Bitter + Guest ales. 8 **Facilities** Garden Dogs allowed Parking

BROCKLEY GREEN — MAP 12 TL74

The Plough Inn

CO10 8DT ☎ 01440 786789 01440 786710

e-mail: info@theploughhundon.co.uk

dir: *Take B1061 from A143, approx 1.5m beyond Kedington*

Originally a small alehouse providing local farmers with liquid refreshments, this friendly inn has been skilfully renovated to create a rustic interior featuring oak beams and soft red brickwork. Its seafood is a major reason for visiting, but look out for the 'Simply Wild' blackboard during the game season. The garden offers glorious views over the Suffolk countryside, and guests who wish to explore the area further can stay in one of eight en suite bedrooms.

Open 12–3 6–11 **Bar Meals** L served all week 12–2.30 D served all week 6–9 (Sun 12–7) Av main course £6.50 **Restaurant** L served all week 12–2.30 D served all week 6–9 (Sun 12–7) Av 3 course à la carte £20 Free House Greene King IPA, Woodforde's Wherry Best Bitter, Theakstons XB, Abbot Ale. 12 **Facilities** Garden Parking **Rooms** 8 bedrooms en suite S£60 D£85 (U)

BROME — MAP 13 TM17

Pick of the Pubs

The Cornwallis Hotel

IP23 8AJ ☎ 01379 870326 01379 870051

e-mail: info@thecornwallis.com

dir: *Just off A140 at Brome, follow B1077 to Eye. Pub is 30 metres on the left*

A handsome looking building, dating from 1561, the one-time Dower House to Brome Hall. Within its 20 peaceful acres are an avenue of limes, some impressive yew topiary and a pretty water garden, while inside many of the original beams, panels and oak

CONTINUED

England

BROME continued

and mahogany settles remain from earliest times. In the log-fired Tudor Bar look into the murky depths of a 60-foot well. Virtually everything emanating from the kitchen uses fresh, mostly locally supplied ingredients, whether it's roasted cod with chorizo mash, wilted spinach and cockles; winter warmer sausages with braised vegetables; or cannelloni of butternut squash and Amaretto with ginger and onion marmalade, salsify and crispy leeks. The same applies to steak, kidney and Adnam's ale pudding; mussels with Thai curry broth and seaweed focaccia; and open ravioli of chicken with baby leeks, marinated peppers and pesto cream. Refreshing desserts include strawberry and vanilla pannacotta with lavender sorbet, and a selection of Scottish cheeses and biscuits.

Open 11–11 **Bar Meals** L served all week 12–2.30 D served all week 6–9.30 Av main course £10 **Restaurant** L served all week 12–2.30 D served all week 6–9.30 Av 3 course fixed price £27 Free House Adnams, Greene King IPA, St Peters Best. 16 **Facilities** Garden Parking

BURY ST EDMUNDS MAP 13 TL86

The Linden Tree

7 Out Northgate IP33 1JQ ☎ 01284 754600

dir: *Opposite railway station*

Built to serve the railway station, this is a big, friendly Victorian pub, with stripped pine bar, dining area, non-smoking conservatory and charming garden. The family-orientated menu ranges from beef curry, home-made pies, and liver and bacon, to crab thermidor, fresh sea bass, and mushroom and lentil moussaka. Youngsters will go for the burgers, scampi, or pork chipolatas. Freshly filled ciabattas at lunchtime.

Open 11–3 5–11 (Fri–Sat 11–11, Sun 12–4, 5.30–10.30) Closed: 26 Dec **Bar Meals** L served all week 12–2 D served all week 6–9.30 (Sun & BH 12–3 & 5.30–9) Av main course £8.99 **Restaurant** L served all week 12–2 D served all week 6–9.30 (Sun 12–3 & 5.30–9) Greene King Greene King, IPA & Old Speckled Hen & Guest. **Facilities** Garden Dogs allowed Play Area

The Nutshell

17 The Traverse IP33 1BJ ☎ 01284 764867

Unique pub measuring 15ft by 7ft, and said to be Britain's smallest. Somehow more than 100 people and a dog managed to fit inside in the 1980s. The bar's ceiling is covered with paper money, and there have been regular sightings of ghosts around the building, including a nun and a monk who apparently weren't praying! No food is available, though the pub jokes about its dining area for parties of two or fewer.

Open 12–11 (Sun 12–10.30) Greene King Greene King IPA & Abbot Ale, Guest Ales. **Facilities** Dogs allowed **Notes**

The Old Cannon Brewery ★★★ INN

86 Cannon St IP33 1JR ☎ 01284 768769 01284 701137

e-mail: info@oldcannonbrewery.co.uk

dir: *A14 to Bury St Edmunds town centre, at 1st rdbt left onto Northgate St, right onto Cadney Ln, left at end onto Cannon St, pub 100yds on left*

This solid and spacious former beer house and brewery was built in 1845 and is affectionately known as 'The Old Can'. It boasts a unique conversation piece in the bar – a mirror-polished, stainless steel mash tun and boiler, the source of some terrific real ales. The innovative menu might offer crayfish, pawpaw and feta salad with chil vinaigrette, followed by ale and beef stew with a herb dumpling. Lunc also brings filled baguettes.

Open 12–3 5–11 (Sun 7–10.30) Closed: 25 Dec, 1 Jan **Bar Meals** L serve Tue–Sun 12–2 D served Tue–Sat 6.30–9.30 Av main course £7 Free House Old Cannon Best Bitter, Old Cannon Gunner's Daughter, Old Cannon Blonde Bombshell, Adnams Bitter. 7 **Facilities** Garden Parking **Rooms** 5 bedrooms en suite S£55 D£69

The Three Kings ★★★★ INN

Hengrave Rd, Fornham All Saints IP28 6LA

☎ 01284 766979

e-mail: thethreekings@keme.co.uk

dir: *Bury St Edmunds (2m), A14 junct 42 (1m)*

A traditional 17th-century coaching inn situated in the pretty village of Fornham All Saints, the Three Kings features wood panelled bars and nine comfortable en suite bedrooms in its converted outbuildings. Traditional favourites on the bar menu include ham, egg and chips, as well as more contemporary dishes like warm bacon and chorizo salad and slow roasted duck confit. There are daily fish specials, and meals can also be served in the conservatory, restaurant and courtyard.

Open 12–11 **Bar Meals** L served all week 12–2 (Sat–Sun 12–2.30) D served all week 5.30–9 (Sun–Mon 6–8) Av main course £6 **Restaurant** L served Sun 12–2 D served Sat 7–9 (Sun 12–2.30) Greene King Greene King IPA, Abbot & Ridleys Rumps. 14 **Facilities** Children's licence Garden Parking **Rooms** 9 bedrooms en suit S£57.50 D£75

CAVENDISH MAP 13 TL8

Bull Inn

High St CO10 8AX ☎ 01787 280245

dir: *A134, then right at green, pub 3m on right*

A Victorian pub set in one of Suffolk's most beautiful villages, with an unassuming façade hiding a splendid 15th-century beamed interior. Expect a good atmosphere and decent food, with the daily-changing blackboard menu listing perhaps curries, shank of lamb, fresh fish and shellfish, and a roast on Sundays. There's a pleasant terraced garden.

Open 11–3 6–11 (Sun 12–4) **Bar Meals** L served Mon–Sat 12–2 (Sun 12–2.30) D served Tue–Sat 6.30–9 Av main course £9 **Restaurant** L served Sun–Sat 12–2 (Sun 12–2.30) D served Mon–Sat 6.30–9 Av 3 course à la carte £16 Adnams Adnams Bitter & Broadside, Nethergate Suffolk County. **Facilities** Dogs allowed Parking

The Swan Inn

vo windows upstairs, two down and a central door – the classic front elevation of buildings 'erywhere. Behind the distinctive pink-painted façade of this warm and friendly gem in the iffolk countryside is one of Suffolk's foremost fish restaurants.

is, after all, owned by Donald .d Michael Cole, whose family ve been fish wholesalers in westoft since grandfather set the business in 1936. With ep-sea trawling in deep decline the mid–1980s, Donald thought prudent to diversify and bought e run-down Swan. It was during e refurbishment that he had a nghy installed up in the rafters .though he might try and kid u there's just been a particularly gh tide!). The property dates m 1690, and in the rustic sherman's Cove restaurant you'll .d the original low beams and a llection of nautical memorabilia, cluding trawlers' bells, wheels d a binnacle, all placed on show 'a tribute to the brave people ıo bring ashore the fruits of the sea'. The menu, which lists some 80 different seafood dishes, is very much aimed at fish-lovers, with starters including smoked sprats, smoked trout paté and Italian seafood salad, and main dishes such as whole grilled wild sea bass; whole grilled turbot; whole grilled Dover sole; monkfish tails in garlic butter; and crab gratin. The Swan has its own smokehouse, one of just three remaining out of 200 in what was once one of Britain's busiest fishing ports. Anyone preferring meat to fish has a choice of fillet, rump and gammon steaks.

MAP 13 TM49
Swan Ln NR34 7QF
☎ 01502 476646
01502 562513
dir: *Just off A146 between Lowestoft & Beccles*

Open 11–3 6–12
Bar Meals L served all week 12–2 D served all week 7–9.30
Restaurant L served all week 12–2 D served all week 7–9.30
Free House
Interbrew Bass, Adnams Best, Broadside, Greene King Abbot Ale.
Facilities Garden Parking Play Area

England

CHILLESFORD MAP 13 TM35

The Froize Inn

The Street IP12 3PU ☎ 01394 450282

e-mail: dine@froize.co.uk

dir: *On B1084 between Woodbridge (8m) & Orford (3m)*

This former gamekeeper's cottage, built on the site of Chillesford Friary, is a distinctive red-brick building that dates back to around 1490. Inside is a thoroughly traditional English pub with a modern dining room. The menu emphasises rustic English and continental dishes, using locally-sourced ingredients. Choices might include baked Scottish salmon, devilled kidneys, local dressed crab salad, venison pie or lobster salad. The pub stands on the popular Suffolk Coastal Path.

Open 11.30–2.30 6.30–11 **Bar Meals** L served Tue–Sun 12–2 D served Thu–Sat 7–8.30 **Restaurant** L served Tue–Sun 12–2 D served Thu–Sat 7–8.30 Free House Adnams. 11 **Facilities** Garden Parking

COCKFIELD MAP 13 TL95

Three Horseshoes

Stow's Hill IP30 0JB ☎ 01284 828177 01284 828177

e-mail: john@threehorseshoespub.co.uk

dir: *A134 towards Sudbury, left onto A1141 towards Lavenham*

Originally a thatched long hall, The Three Horseshoes was built around 1350 and still has an oak kingpost supporting its massive beams and vaulted ceilings. Eat amid the old world charm of the restaurant and bar, or in the conservatory with views over rolling countryside. There are over 100 dishes to choose from, including steak and Abbot Ale pie; fresh cod poached in brandy and lobster sauce; stilton and vegetable crumble; and numerous steaks.

Open 10–3 6–11 (Sun 6–10.30) **Bar Meals** L served Wed–Mon 12–2 D served Wed–Mon 6–9.30 (Sun 12–3, 6–9) Av main course £7.50 **Restaurant** L served Wed–Mon 12–2.30 D served Wed–Mon 7–9.30 (Sun 12–2.30, 6–9) Av 3 course à la carte £16 Free House Adnams, Horseshoes Bitter, Directors, Theakstons XB & Websters Yorkshire. 13 **Facilities** Garden Dogs allowed Parking Play Area

COTTON MAP 13 TM

Pick of the Pubs

The Trowel & Hammer Inn

Mill Rd IP14 4QL ☎ 01449 781234 01449 781765

e-mail: sallyselvage@tiscali.co.uk

dir: *A14 signs to Haughley, then Bacton, then turn left for Cotton*

A herd of nine carved teak elephants trekking through the main hall way to the outdoor swimming pool gives you a clue that this is no ordinary pub. At first sight the well maintained, wisteria-clad building belies its 16th-century origins; but, once inside, the old oak timbers and traditional fireplace give a better idea of its age. Nevertheless contemporary needs haven't been forgotten, and licensee Sally Burrows has created secluded areas within the main bars to cater for all age groups. In the summer months the garden, with its tropical theme and thatched poolside umbrellas, is a relaxing place for a drink and a bite to eat. The menus are a blend of traditional farmhouse cooking and international cuisine, so expect to find the regular Sunday roast rubbing shoulders with more exotic dishes that include crocodile and kangaroo.

Open 12–11 (Fri–Sat 12–1am) **Bar Meals** L served all week 12–3 D served all week 6–9.30 (Sun all day) Av main course £9.45 **Restaurant** L served all week 12–3 D served Mon–Sat 6–9.30 Free House Adnams Bitter & Broadside, Greene King IPA & Old Speckled Hen. **Facilities** Garden Parking

DENNINGTON MAP 13 TM

The Queens Head

The Square IP13 8AB ☎ 01728 638241 01728 638037

e-mail: denningtonqueen1@btinternet.com

dir: *Ipswich A14 to A12. Framlingham B1116, then signs to Dennington.*

A 500-year-old inn with a resident ghost, a bricked-up tunnel to the neighbouring church, and a coffin hatch. Locally brewed cider is available alongside the real ales. On the extensive main menu, which changes every six months, might be duck with port and raspberry sauce; cottage pie; Irish hotpot with dumplings; and fillet of plaice parcels. Daily specials, sandwiches, griddles and children's meals, vegetarian and gluten-free dishes add to the choice.

Open 9–3 6.30–11 (Sun–Fri 9–10, Summer 6–11) Closed: 25–26 Dec **Bar Meals** L served all week 12–2 D served all week 6.30–9 Av main cou £8.50 **Restaurant** L served all week 12–2 D served all week 6.30–9 Av 3 course à la carte £16 Free House Adnams, St Peters, Woodfordes & Mauldons. **Facilities** Garden Parking Play Area

UNWICH MAP 13 TM47

he Ship Inn

James St IP17 3DT ☎ 01728 648219 🖷 01728 648675
mail: shipinn@tiscali.co.uk
: *N on A12 through Yoxford, right signed Dunwich*

s old smugglers' haunt exudes great warmth and character, and is ed for traditional food and local ales. As one would expect, fresh al fish features prominently on the menu, including cod, mackerel, wns, scampi, and fishcakes. The specials board may supplement se with sole, haddock, sardines and crab according to availability, d in fine weather the Dunwich fish can be eaten in the garden.

en 11-11 (Sun 12-10.30) **Bar Meals** L served all week 12-3 D served week 6-9 (Sat-Sun 12-6 6-9) **Restaurant** L served all week 12-3 erved all week 6-9 (Sat-Sun 12-6 6-9) Free House Adnams, uldons. **Facilities** Garden Dogs allowed Parking

ARL SOHAM MAP 13 TM26

ictoria

e Street IP13 7RL ☎ 01728 685758
: *From A14 at Stowmarket take A1120 towards Yoxford*

s friendly, down to earth free house is a showcase for Earl Soham ers, which for many years were produced from a micro-brewery ind the pub. In 2001 the brewery moved to the Old Forge building posite the village green, where production still continues. The toria offers traditional pub fare, including ploughman's, jacket atoes, macaroni cheese, and smoked salmon salad. Heartier meals ude casseroles and curries, and home-made desserts.

en 11.30-3 6-11 (Sun 12-3, 7-10.30) **Bar Meals** L served all week 0-2 D served all week 6-10 (Sun 12-2, 7-10) Free House Earl am-Victoria Bitter, Albert Ale, & Gannet Mild, Earl Soham Porter, Edward **Facilities** Garden Dogs allowed Parking

RWARTON MAP 13 TM23

e Queens Head

e Street IP9 1LN ☎ 01473 787550
: *From Ipswich B1456 to Shotley*

s handsome 16th-century Suffolk free house provides an ospheric stop for a pint of locally-brewed Adnams or Greene King . There's a relaxed atmosphere in the bar with its bowed black oak ms, low ceilings and cosy coal fires, and magnificent views over the ds to the Stour estuary. The wide-ranging menu offers traditional dishes and snacks, while daily specials include pheasant casserole, nach and red lentil curry, Guinness-battered cod and chips, and ne-made fishcakes. Booking is advised at weekends.

en 11-3 6.30-11 (Sun 12-3, 7-10.30) Closed: 25 Dec **Meals** L served all week 12-1.45 D served all week 7-9 **taurant** L served all week 12-2 D served all week 7-9.30 Free House Adnams Bitter & Broadside, Greene King IPA, Aspall Cider, Guinness & ngbow. **Facilities** Garden Parking

EYE MAP 13 TM17

The White Horse Inn ★★★★ INN

Stoke Ash IP23 7ET ☎ 01379 678222 🖷 01379 678800
e-mail: mail@whitehorse-suffolk.co.uk
dir: *On A140 between Ipswich & Norwich*

A 17th-century coaching inn set amid lovely Suffolk countryside. The heavily-timbered interior accommodates an inglenook fireplace, two bars and a restaurant. There are seven spacious motel bedrooms in the grounds, as well as a patio and secluded grassy area. An extensive menu is supplemented by lunchtime snacks, grills and daily specials from the blackboard. Try grilled butterflied breast of chicken, Lincolnshire sausages and mash, lasagne, or salmon and haddock tagliatelle.

Open 8-11 (Sun 8-10.30) **Bar Meals** L served all week 11-9.30 D served all week 11-9.30 **Restaurant** L served all week 11-9.30 D served all week 11-9.30 Free House Adnams, Greene King Abbot, IPA Smooth. **Facilities** Children's licence Garden Parking **Rooms** 11 bedrooms en suite S£49.50 D£59.50

FRAMLINGHAM MAP 13 TM26

The Station Hotel

Station Rd IP13 9EE ☎ 01728 723455
e-mail: framstation@btinternet.com
dir: *Bypass Ipswich towards Lowestoft on A12 6m left onto B1116 towards Framlingham*

The buildings of the former station hotel have been put to good use since Framlingham's railway closed in 1962. There's an antique bed showroom and a motorcycle repair shop, whilst the hotel has established a fine reputation for its seafood and locally brewed beers. Expect Orford lobster salad; smoked haddock with creamed leeks and poached egg; slow-roast pork belly with mash and root vegetables; and butternut squash and sage risotto.

Open 12-2.30 5-11 Closed: 25-27 Dec **Bar Meals** L served all week 12-2 D served all week 7-9 (Fri-Sat 7-9.30) Av main course £6.50 **Restaurant** L served all week 12-2 D served all week 7-9 (Fri-Sat 7-9.30) Av 3 course à la carte £20 Free House Earl Soham Victoria, Albert & Mild, Veltins, Nusto. **Facilities** Garden Dogs allowed Parking

FRAMSDEN MAP 13 TM15

The Dobermann Inn

The Street IP14 6HG ☎ 01473 890461
dir: *S off A1120 (Stowmarket/Yoxford)*

Previously The Greyhound, the pub was renamed by its current proprietor, a prominent breeder and judge of Dobermanns. The thatched roofing, gnarled beams, open fire and assorted furniture reflect its 16th-century origins. Food ranges from sandwiches and salads to main courses featuring game from a local estate in season, and plenty of fish choices. Reliable favourites include steak and mushroom pie, Dover sole, and sirloin steak. Vegetarians can feast on mushroom stroganoff or spicy nut loaf.

Open 12-3 7-11 Closed: 25-26 Dec **Bar Meals** L served Tue-Sun 12-2 D served Tue-Sat 7-10 Free House Adnams Bitter & Broadside, Mauldons Moletrap Bitter, Adnams Old WA. **Facilities** Garden Parking **Notes**

GREAT GLEMHAM MAP 13 TM36

The Crown Inn 🍷

IP17 2DA ☎ 01728 663693

dir: *A12 Ipswich to Lowestoft, in Stratford-St-Andrew left at Shell garage. Crown 1.5m*

Cosy 17th-century village pub overlooking the Great Glemham Estate and within easy reach of the Suffolk Heritage Coast. You can eat in the extensively renovated bars and large flower-filled garden, where moussaka, carbonnade of beef, Somerset lamb casserole, roasted vegetables with pasta, and spinach and feta cheese tart from the specials menu might be followed by fresh fruit pavlova or traditional sherry trifle.

Open 11.30–2.30 6.30–11 (Closed Mon) **Bar Meals** L served Tue–Sun 11.30–2.30 D served Tue–Sun 6.30–10 Free House Adnams Bitter & Broadside. 🍷 7 **Facilities** Garden Dogs allowed Parking Play Area

HALESWORTH MAP 13 TM37

Pick of the Pubs

The Queen's Head 🍷

The Street, Bramfield IP19 9HT

☎ 01986 784214 📠 01986 784797

e-mail: qhbfield@aol.com

dir: *2m from A12 on the A144 towards Halesworth*

The owners of the Queen's Head are enthusiastic supporters of the 'local and organic' movement – reflected by the pub's daily changing menu which proudly names the farms and suppliers from which the carefully chosen ingredients are sourced. The pub is a lovely old building in the centre of Bramfield village on the edge of the Suffolk Heritage Coast, just 15 minutes from Southwold. The enclosed pub garden, ideal for children, is overlooked by the thatched village church with its unusual separate round bell tower. The pub interior welcomes with scrubbed pine tables, exposed beams, a vaulted ceiling in the bar and enormous fireplaces. As well as baguettes and ploughman's written on boards, there is often an inexpensive weekday lunch special, such as beef and vegetable casserole served with home-made crusty bread. A full meal may comprise grilled dates wrapped in bacon followed by whole mackerel with piperade, and a dessert like warm Bakewell tart to finish.

Open 11.45–2.30 6.30–11 (Sun 12–3, 7–10.30) Closed: 26 Dec **Bar Meals** L served all week 12–2 D served all week 6.30–10 (Sun 7–9) Av main course £9.95 Adnams Adnams Bitter & Broadside. 🍷 7 **Facilities** Garden Dogs allowed Parking

HITCHAM MAP 13 TL95

The White Horse Inn

The Street IP7 7NQ ☎ 01449 740981 📠 01449 740981

e-mail: lewis@thewhitehorse.wanadoo.co.uk

dir: *13m from Ipswich & Bury St Edmunds*

This semi-detached Grade II listed building in two storeys is the only pub in Hitcham, and estimated in parts to be around 400 years old. The family run inn has a welcoming atmosphere where you can relax and enjoy home-cooked food washed down by one of the large selection of wines. Please note that from November to the end of March this pub is closed on Mondays and Tuesdays.

Open 12–3 6–11 Closed: Mon–Tue from Nov to Mar **Bar Meals** L served all week 12–2 D served all week 6–9 **Restaurant** L served all week 12–2 D served all week 6–9 (Fri–Sat 6–9.30) IPA, Adnams Best Bitter, Rattlesden Best, Stowmarket Porter & Adnams Fisherman. **Facilities** Garden Dogs allowed Parking

HOLBROOK MAP 13 TM

The Compasses

Ipswich Rd IP9 2QR ☎ 01473 328332 📠 01473 327403

e-mail: rickandjayne@tiscali.co.uk

dir: *From A137 S of Ipswich, take B1456/B1080 to Holbrook*

Holbrook is bordered by the rivers Orwell and Stour, and this traditional country pub, which dates back to the 17th century, is on the Shotley peninsula. The menu is varied and appetizing, and always features a good seafood selection on the specials board, including seafood lasagna, fish pie, and grilled salmon with bonne femme sauce.

Open 12–2.30 6–11 (Sun 12–3, 6–10.30) Closed: 25–26 Dec, 1 Jan **Bar Meals** L served all week 12–2.15 D served all week 6–9.15 **Restaurant** L served all week 12–2.15 D served all week 6–9.15 Punch Taverns Greene King IPA, Adnams Bitter, Carlsberg Export & Guest Ale **Facilities** Garden Parking Play Area

HONEY TYE MAP 13 TL

The Lion 🍷

CO6 4NX ☎ 01206 263434 📠 01206 263434

e-mail: enquiries@lionhoneytye.co.uk

dir: *On A134 midway between Colchester & Sudbury*

Located in an Area of Outstanding Natural Beauty this traditional country dining pub has low-beamed ceilings and an open log fire inside, and a patio with tables and umbrellas for outside eating and drinking. The menu offers a good choice of daily fresh fish (oven baked red snapper supreme with tomato and prawn confit), pub favourites (home-made steak and ale pie), and main dishes such as braised lamb shank with rosemary, garlic and red wine jus.

Open 11–3 5.30–11 (Sun 12–10.30) **Bar Meals** L served all week 12–2 D served all week 6–9.30 (Sun 12–9.30) Av main course £8 **Restaurant** L served all week 12–2 D served all week 6–9.30 (Sun 12–9.30) Av 3 course à la carte £17 Free House Greene King IPA, Adnams Bitter, Guest ale. 🍷 7 **Facilities** Garden Parking

ORRINGER MAP 13 TL86

eehive

e Street IP29 5SN ☎ 01284 735260 📄 01284 735523

r: *From A14 1st turn for Bury St Edmunds, sign for Westley & worth Park*

the High Street in Horringer, near Bury St Edmunds and the ional Trust's Ickworth Park. The Victorian flint and stone cottage ull of period features, with lots of small rooms and antique tables ssed with white linen napkins. In summer visitors head for the patio d the picnic benches in the walled beer garden. On the chalk board ect two or three fish dishes, such as salmon with fresh tarragon or oked haddock Florentine.

en 11.30–2.30 7–11 Closed: Dec 25–26 **Bar Meals** L served veek 12–2 D served Mon–Sat 7–9.45 Av main course £10.95 **staurant** L served all week 12–2 D served all week 7–9.45 Av 3 course carte £20 Greene King Greene King IPA & Abbot Ale, Guest rs. 8 **Facilities** Garden Parking

OXNE MAP 13 TM17

he Swan

w St IP21 5AS ☎ 01379 668275

mail: info@hoxneswan.co.uk

s 15th-century Grade II listed lodge, reputedly built for the Bishop Norwich, has large gardens running down to the River Dove, with ast willow tree. Inside, the restaurant and front bar boast a 10ft lenook fireplace, ornate beamed ceilings and old planked floors. d ranges from lunchtime snacks like golden whitebait or soup of day, to a weekly changing lunch and dinner menu. Traditional nes include venison and wild mushroom pie, with innovative ions like sweet potato and saffron fricassée.

en 11.30–3 6–11 (Sun 12–10.30) **Bar Meals** L served all week 2.30 D served all week 7–9.30 (Sun 12–4, 7–9) Av main course £10 **staurant** L served all week 12–2.30 D served all week 7–9.30 (Sun 12–4,) Enterprise Inns Adnams Best Bitter & 4 other real ales. 10 **ilities** Garden Dogs allowed Parking

ICKLINGHAM MAP 13 TL77

The Plough Inn NEW

The Street IP28 6PL ☎ 01638 711770 📄 01638 583885

e-mail: info@ploughpubinn.co.uk

This old, flint-built village pub is part of the Iveagh Estate, which revamped it in 2004, enlarging the restaurant in the process. Among the numerous fish dishes are grilled red snapper with rougail sauce; and pan-fried skate wing in rosemary and caper butter. Other main courses include beef fillet pie; cottage pie; pork and herb sausages; lemon basil chicken; and poacher's pot, which contains wild boar, rabbit, pheasant and venison in real ale and red wine.

Open 11–2.30 6–12 **Bar Meals** L served Mon–Sat 12–2.30 D served all week 6–8.45 (Sun 7–8.45) Av main course £9.95 **Restaurant** L served all week 11.30–2 D served all week 6–8.45 (Sun 7–8.45) Av 3 course à la carte £18.50 Free House IPA, Wherry, London Pride, Adnams. 26 **Facilities** Garden Parking

Pick of the Pubs

The Red Lion

The Street IP28 6PS ☎ 01638 711698

dir: *A1101 from Bury St Edmunds 8m. In Icklingham on main street*

A sympathetically restored, 16th-century thatched country inn set back from the road behind a grassed area with flower beds and outdoor furniture. The interior, glowing by candlelight in the evening, features exposed beams, a large inglenook fireplace, wooden floors, and antique furniture. The pub backs onto the River Lark, and was formerly the site of a coal yard and a maltings. It is particularly well known for game, and for fresh fish and seafood, delivered daily from Lowestoft. Among the 15–20 varieties of fish on offer, depending on the season, are mussels, oysters, red snapper, scallops, plaice, zander, and sea bass.

Open 12–3 6.30–11 (Sun 7–10.30) Closed: 25 Dec **Bar Meals** L served all week 12–2.30 D served all week 6.30–10 (Sun 7–9) Av main course £9 **Restaurant** L served all week 12–2.30 D served all week 6.30–10 (Sun 7–9) Greene King Greene King Abbot Ale & IPA, Norlands Speckled Hen. 15 **Facilities** Garden Parking

IXWORTH MAP 13 TL97

Pykkerell Inn

38 High St IP31 2HH ☎ 01359 230398 📄 01359 230398

dir: *On A143 from Bury St Edmunds towards Diss*

This former coaching inn dates from 1530 and still retains most of its original beams, inglenook fireplace and other features. The wood-panelled library is just off the lounge, and the 14th-century barn now encloses a patio and barbecue. The extensive menu includes vegetarian options and children's meals, as well as traditional Sunday roast lunch. Menu boards highlight a variety of fresh fish, and may include red snapper, monkfish and Dover sole.

Open 12–3 6–11 **Bar Meals** L served all week 12–2.30 D served all week 7–10 Av main course £9.50 **Restaurant** L served all week 12–2.30 D served all week 6–10 Av 3 course à la carte £15.95 Greene King Greene King IPA & Abbot Ale. **Facilities** Garden Dogs allowed Parking

England

KETTLEBURGH MAP 13 TM26

The Chequers Inn

IP13 7JT ☎ 01728 723760 & 724369 📠 01728 723760

e-mail: info@thechequers.net

dir: *From Ipswich A12 onto B1116, left onto B1078 then right through Easton*

The Chequers is set in beautiful countryside on the banks of the River Deben. The landlord serves a wide range of cask ales, including two guests. In addition to snack and restaurant meals, the menu in the bar includes local sausages and ham with home-produced free-range eggs. The riverside garden covers two acres and seats a hundred people.

Open 12–2.30 6–11 **Bar Meals** L served all week 12–2 D served all week 7–9.30 Sun 12–2 7–9 Av main course £5.50 **Restaurant** L served all week 12–2 D served all week 7–9.30 Sun 7–9 Av 3 course à la carte £16.50 Free House Greene King IPA, Black Dog Mild & 3 Guest Ales. **Facilities** Garden Dogs allowed Parking Play Area

LAVENHAM MAP 13 TL94

Pick of the Pubs

Angel Hotel ★★★★ RR

Market Place CO10 9QZ

☎ 01787 247388 📠 01787 248344

e-mail: angellav@aol.com

dir: *7m from Sudbury on A1141*

See Pick of the Pubs on opposite page

LAXFIELD MAP 13 TM27

Pick of the Pubs

The Kings Head

Gorams Mill Ln IP13 8DW ☎ 01986 798395

Beautifully situated overlooking the river, the garden of this thatched 16th-century alehouse was formerly the village bowling green. Beer is still served straight from the cask in the original tap room, whilst high-backed settles and wooden seats add to the charming atmosphere. Traditional home-cooked dishes complement the à la carte menu and chef's specials and, on warmer evenings, the rose gardens and arbour are perfect for al fresco dining.

Open 12–3 6–11 (Sun 7–11, Summer wkends all day) **Bar Meals** L served all week 12–2 D served all week 7–9 Av main course £7 **Restaurant** L served all week 12–2 D served all week 7–9 (Sun 12–3) Av 3 course à la carte £19.50 Av 3 course fixed price £25 Adnams Adnams Best & Broadside, Adnams Seasonal Ales & Guest ale. **Facilities** Garden Dogs allowed Parking Play Area

LEVINGTON MAP 13 TM2

Pick of the Pubs

The Ship Inn

Church Ln IP10 0LQ ☎ 01473 659573

dir: *Off A14 towards Felixstowe. Nr Levington Marina*

See Pick of the Pubs on page 528

LIDGATE MAP 12 TL

Pick of the Pubs

The Star Inn

The Street CB8 9PP ☎ 01638 500275 📠 01638 500275

e-mail: tereaxon@aol.com

dir: *From Newmarket clocktower in High St follow signs towards Clare on B1063. Lidgate 7m*

It may look like a traditional English pub, but The Star also houses a much-loved Spanish restaurant which is particularly popular with trainers on Newmarket race days, and with dealers and agents from all over the world during bloodstock sales. The star of the Star is undoubtedly the owner, a Catalan landlady who has made her mark with Spanish dishes plus some imaginative international and British choices. The pretty pink-painted Elizabethan building is made up of two cottages with gardens front and rear; inside, two traditionally furnished bars with heavy oak and pine furniture lead into a fairly simple dining room. The menu offers appealingly hearty food, just the thing after a day at the races: perhaps paella Vanelciana; cod in garlic mousseline; home-made lasagne; parrillada of fish; and venison with port. Friendly staff are on hand if any translation is required.

Open 11–3 6–11 Closed: 25–26 Dec, 1 Jan **Bar Meals** L served all week 12–2 (Sun 12–2.30) D served Mon–Sat 7–10 (Sun 7–11) Av main course £15.50 **Restaurant** L served all week 12–2 (Sun 12–2.30) D served Mon–Sat 7–10 Av 3 course à la carte £26.50 Av 2 course fixed price £12 Greene King Greene King IPA, Ruddles County & Abbot Ale. **Facilities** Garden Parking

Angel Hotel

ne attractive, bustling Angel Hotel stands in the market place of beautiful Lavenham, a storical village whose streets are lined with crooked timber-framed houses. First licensed in 420, it was originally a 'high hall' house: smoke from a central fire would drift out through roof nts.

ound 1500, ventilation proved when two wings with ick chimneys were added to the ilding, along with a first-floor lar room. Now the residents' ting room, it contains a rare rgetted ceiling, in which patterns re applied to the wet plaster. the cellar is a huge Elizabethan ick arch supporting the chimney ove. There is no real division tween the bar and restaurant eas, both of which have historic tures including exposed timbers, arge inglenook fireplace, and a dor shuttered shop window. The igel does its best to source all its oduce from local suppliers; the enu changes daily, with everything epared on the premises. There always home-made soups, pies d casseroles, fresh fish, game in season and vegetarian dishes. Typical starters from a dinner menu include chicken, apricot and sun-dried tomato terrine; haddock, crab and chilli fishcakes with spicy tomato sauce; and tomato, butternut squash and sweet potato soup. Main courses might be steak and ale pie; chargrilled tuna with lemon and thyme risotto; lamb, chick pea and butternut squash casserole; or Gressingham duck breast with sweet potato and chestnut rôsti. You could finish with a selection of English cheeses, or perhaps steamed syrup sponge pudding with custard. Eight en suite bedrooms enable excellent dinner, bed and breakfast packages to be offered, and the chance to linger.

★★★★ RR

MAP 13 TL94
Market Place CO10 9QZ
☎ 01787 247388
01787 248344
e-mail: angellav@aol.com
dir: *7m from Sudbury on A1141*

Open 11–11 (Sun 12–10.30)
Closed: 25–26 Dec
Bar Meals L served all week 12–2.15 D served all week 6.45–9.15 Av main course £12
Restaurant L served all week 12–2.15 D served all week 6.45–9.15 Av 3 course à la carte £22
Free House
Adnams Bitter, Nethergate, Greene King IPA, & Broadside.
10
Facilities Children's licence Garden Parking
Rooms 8 bedrooms en suite S£60 D£80

The Ship Inn

The timbers of this part–14th-century thatched inn are impregnated with the salt of the sea. It stands within sight of the Orwell estuary and the Suffolk marshes, where old sailing vessels were beached and their hulks broken up for their precious beams.

Attractive front and rear patios are adorned with hanging and potted plants. Walls and flat surfaces inside are full of seafaring pictures, curiosities and keepsakes, and it may seem a bit too ordered and cosy ever to have been the smugglers' haunt it once was. But wait, read the old newspaper cuttings on the wall and you'll be in no doubt that excise men and contraband often ended up here, though ideally not at the same time. In summer, when shellfish comes into season, the kitchen buys huge quantities of lobster, crab, mussels, clams and oysters in addition to haddock, hake, salmon, mackerel and snapper from around the coast. This means a good choice of fish and seafood starters and main courses from the daily changing blackboard menu – perhaps something griddled in herb, lemon and garlic oil, or accompanied by a light sauce. Local game includes pigeon, pheasant, partridge, rabbit, hare and estate-reared venison, although the kitchen is also noted for its meats, including chargrilled chicken brochettes; fillet of pork or beef; and liver and bacon, served with black pudding and Madeira sauce. Home-made desserts range from crème brûlée to baked chocolate and pecan tart. Alternatively, there is a good selection of British cheeses. Finish your meal with coffee (again, a good selection available) and home-made almond biscuits. Regional ales include Adnams and Greene King, and there's a range of Scottish and Irish malts and wines by the glass, including champagne. Everything is served by smiling, attentive staff.

MAP 13 TM23
Church Ln IP10 0LQ
☎ 01473 659573
dir: *Off A14 towards Felixstowe. Nr Levington Marina*

Open 11.30–3 6.30–11 (Sat–Sun 11.30–11) Closed: 25–26 Dec, 1 Jan
Bar Meals L served all week 12–2 (Sun 12–3) D served all week 6.30–9.30 Av main course £9.95
Restaurant L served all week 12–2 D served all week 6.30–9.30 (Sun 12–3, 6.30–9)
Punch Taverns
Greene King IPA, Adnams Best & Broadside. 11
Facilities Garden Parking

IELTON MAP 13 TM25

Vilford Bridge

ilford Bridge Rd IP12 2PA
: 01394 386141 01394 386141
mail: wilfordbridge@yahoo.com
r: *A12 signs to Bawdsey & Orford, cross rail lines, pub on left*

t down the road from the famous Sutton Hoo treasure ship, Mike d Anne Lomas have been running the free house at Wilford Bridge the last 17 years. As a former West End chef, Mike specialises in food dishes; look out for mussels and sprats in season, as well as g prawns, cod, salmon, trout, sea bass and others as available. At bar, guest ales supplement the regular choice of beers.

en 11–11 Closed: 25–26 Dec **Bar Meals** L served all week 11.30–9.30 erved all week 11.30–9.30 Av main course £10 **Restaurant** L served all ek 11.30–9.30 D served all week 11.30–9.30 Av 3 course à la carte £19.25 Free House Adnams Best, Broadside, Scottish Courage John Smith's & est Ales. **Facilities** Garden Parking

ONKS ELEIGH MAP 13 TL94

Pick of the Pubs

The Swan Inn

The Street IP7 7AU ☎ 01449 741391
e-mail: carol@monkseleigh.com
dir: *On B1115 between Sudbury & Hadleigh*

Vattle and daub discovered during renovation work is displayed behind glass in this 14th-century thatched free house. In those days, the interior would have been open to the roof, and evidence of the former smokehole still exists. The main restaurant, with its magnificent open fireplace, may once have been used as the manorial court. Menus change almost daily to make the most of locally available ingredients, and autumn sees a steady stream of rabbit, hare, partridge and pheasant delivered to the door from local shoots. Lunchtime starters could be salad of grilled pigeon breast, crispy smoked bacon and walnut salad; and chilled Suffolk asparagus with parmesan flakes. Main courses might well include grilled turbot fillet, lobster and crayfish sauce and crushed celeriac; pan-fried saddle of venison with braised red cabbage; or spicy Moroccan chicken breast with cucumber and mint yoghurt.

Open 12–3 7–11 Closed: 25–26 Dec **Bar Meals** L served Wed–Sun 12–2 D served Wed–Sun 7–9.30 **Restaurant** L served Wed–Sun 12–2 D served Wed–Sun 7–9.30 Free House Greene King IPA, Adnams Bitter & Broadside. 20 **Facilities** Garden Parking

NAYLAND MAP 13 TL93

Pick of the Pubs

Anchor Inn

26 Court St CO6 4JL ☎ 01206 262313 01206 264166
e-mail: enquiries@anchornayland.co.uk
dir: *From Colchester take A134 towards Sudbury, right towards Nayland signed Horkesley Rd. Pass bridge, pub on right*

The Anchor is the only pub in this picturesque Suffolk village and is believed to be the last remaining place from where press gangs recruited their 'volunteers'. The 15th-century building stands by the River Stour, and over the last few years the adjoining Anchor Inn Heritage Farm and kitchen garden have been established. Produce grown here is crucial to the quality of the food, and many customers combine a visit to the pub with a wander around the farm, where they can see Suffolk Punch horses at work. The bar serves Adnams Ales and good food in a warm and lively atmosphere. The inn has its own smokery, and home-smoked fish and cheeses are a feature of the menu, as is the selection of home-made pickled products: eggs, samphire and onions. Other options range from huffer sandwiches, through lemon battered east coast haddock, to grilled fillet of longhorn beef.

Open 11–3 5–11 (Sat 11–11, Sun 11–10.30) **Bar Meals** L served all week 12–2.30 D served all week 6.30–9 (Fri–Sat 6.30–9.30 Sun 10–3, 4.30–8.30) Av main course £9 **Restaurant** L served all week 12–2.30 D served all week 6.30–9 (Fri–Sat 6.30–9.30 Sun 10–3, 4.30–8.30) Av 3 course à la carte £18.50 Free House Adnams, IPA, Mild, Fosters. **Facilities** Garden Parking

ORFORD MAP 13 TM45

Jolly Sailor Inn

Quay St IP12 2NU ☎ 01394 450243 0870 128 7874
e-mail: jacquie@jollysailor.f9.co.uk
dir: *On B1084 E of Woodbridge, Orford signed from A12*

Until the 16th century, Orford was a bustling coastal port. This ancient, timber-framed smugglers' inn stood on the quayside – but, as Orford Ness grew longer, the harbour silted up and fell out of use. Nevertheless, the pub still serves visiting yachtsmen, and local fishermen supply fresh fish to the kitchen. There's also a daily roast, and other dishes might include seasonal local pheasant in red wine; or fresh pasta with a choice of sauces.

Open 11.30–2.30 7–11 **Bar Meals** L served all week 12–2 D served all week 7.15–8.45 Av main course £6.50 Adnams Adnams Bitter & Broadside. **Facilities** Garden Dogs allowed **Notes**

ORFORD continued

King's Head

Front St IP12 2LW ☎ 01394 450271

e-mail: ian_thornton@talk21.com

dir: *From Woodbridge follow signs for Orford Castle on B1084. Through Butley & Chillesford on to Orford*

An inn with a smuggling history, The King's Head stands on the old market square, a short walk from the quay. The atmospheric interior includes a beamed bar serving Adnams ales, and a wood-floored restaurant offering plenty of local produce. Typical starters include garlic mushrooms; whitebait; and smoked mackerel, followed perhaps by 'boozy beef' (made with Adnams ale); cod in beer batter; or vegetable stir fry. Bar snacks include sandwiches, burgers and things with chips.

Open 11.30-3 6-11 **Bar Meals** L served all week 12-2 (Sun 12-2.45) D served all week 6-9 (Sun 7-9) Av main course £7.25 **Restaurant** L served all week 12-2 (Sun 12-2.30) D served all week 6-9 (Sun 7-9) Av 3 course à la carte £14 Adnams Adnams Bitter, Adnams Broadside, Adnams Regatta, Adnams Tally Ho & Adnams Explorer. **Facilities** Garden Dogs allowed Parking

POLSTEAD MAP 13 TL93

Pick of the Pubs

The Cock Inn

The Green CO6 5AL ☎ 01206 263150 01206 263150

e-mail: mail@cockinn.info

dir: *Colchester/A134 towards Sudbury then right, follow signs to Polstead*

Originally a 17th-century farmhouse, the pub has oak beams, quarry-tiled floors and a Victorian restaurant extension. It overlooks the green in a lovely village at the heart of Constable country, and with some of Suffolk's prettiest landscapes right on the doorstep, it's not surprising that the pub attracts its fair share of cyclists and ramblers. The menu changes frequently and there's always a great choice. A Suffolk huffer might suffice: these large, soft white baps come with a myriad choice of fillings. The list of starters may feature king prawns in filo pastry with tomato and chilli relish, minted lamb pieces, or devilled whitebait with a tartare dip. Mains may include salmon fillet in orange butter sauce, spinach and ricotta nutty bake, garlic and herb tagliatelle with stir fried vegetables, or beer-marinated turkey escalope. Families are especially welcome – there's a children's menu, a play area and an award-winning garden with a water feature and hanging baskets.

Open 11-3 6-11 (Sat-Sun all day Winter, Sun & BHs 12-3, 6-10.30) **Bar Meals** L served Tues-Sun 11.30-2.30 D served Tues-Sun 6.30-9.30 (Sun 12-2.30, 6.30-9) Av main course £8 **Restaurant** L served Tue-Sat 11.30-2.30 (Sun 12-2.30) D served Tue-Sat 6.30-9.30 (Sun 6.30-9) Av 3 course à la carte £17 Free House Greene King IPA, Adnams, Ansels Mild, Carlsberg & Guinness. **Facilities** Garden Dogs allowed Parking Play Area

REDE MAP 13 TL8

The Plough

IP29 4BE ☎ 01284 789208

dir: *On A143 between Bury St Edmunds & Haverhill*

Picture-postcard half-thatched 16th-century pub, with an old plough outside. A recent revamp has given the building a cream exterior and restored the beams to their original colour, promoting a fresher, mor open feel inside. An adventurous array of blackboard-listed dishes m include fish dishes such as poached sea trout with samphire, grilled skate, or whole plaice topped with wild mushrooms and prawns. Otherwise, traditional country recipes feature partridge, venison, or Gloucester Old Spot served in a cider sauce.

Open 11-3 6.30-11 **Bar Meals** L served all week 12-2 D served Mon-S 7-9 **Restaurant** L served all week 12-2 D served Mon-Sat 7-9 Admi Taverns Greene King IPA, Abbot Ale, London Pride & Ruddles County. **Facilities** Garden Parking

ST PETER SOUTH ELMHAM MAP 13 TM

Pick of the Pubs

St Peter's Hall

NR35 1NQ ☎ 01986 782288 01986 782505

dir: *From A143/A144 brown signs to St Peter's Brewery*

A pub and brewery in a magnificent moated hall that originally dates from 1280. In 1539 it was enlarged using stones salvaged from nearby Flixton Priory, destroyed during the Dissolution. Look for the chapel above the porch, the carvings on the façade, and the tombstone in the entrance, not to mention the stone floors, lofty ceilings, and period furnishings. The brewery, which you can visit, produces seventeen (yes, seventeen) different beers, and is housed in what until 1996 were long-derelict former agricultural buildings. Starters may include home-made game pâté with spiced ale chutney; and stilton, grape and spicy olive salad with wholegrain mustard dressing. There are usually six to eight main courses, among them St Peter's steak and ale pie; pork fillet in sage and white wine cream sauce; and plaice fillet with lemon and dill cream sauce. For vegetarians, there's wild mushroom risotto with truffle oil, lemon and thyme.

Open 11-3 6-11 (Wknds and BH all day) **Bar Meals** L served all week 12-2 D served all week 7-9 Av main course £10.25 **Restaurant** L served all week 12-2 D served all week 7-9 Av 3 course à la carte £25 St Peters Brewery Golden Ale, Organic Ale, Grapefruit Beer, Cream Stout. 7 **Facilities** Garden Parking

NAPE MAP 13 TM35

Pick of the Pubs

The Crown Inn

Bridge Rd IP17 1SL ☎ 01728 688324

dir: *A12 N to Lowestoft, right to Aldeburgh, then right again in Snape at x-rds by church, pub at bottom hill.*

Visitors to Snape Maltings, home of the Aldeburugh Music Festival, will be delighted to stumble across this 15th-century former smugglers' inn, a mere 400 yards away. Set close to the River Alde, the pub is highly atmospheric, with abundant old beams, brick floors and, around the large inglenook, probably the finest double Suffolk settle in existence. Install yourselves cosily here, and remember how evocative burning logs sound when there are no gaming machines or piped music to drown the crackles. Daily changing menus and specials are always on offer, including starters of home-made pork and pigeon terrine; and goats' cheese cheesecake with mixed leaves. Main courses might range from lamb tagine with couscous to turbot fillet on lemon risotto, or battered local cod and chips. Puddings, all home made, include such classics as spotted dick and custard, while 15 of the 40 wines are available by the glass.

Open 12-3 6-11 (Sun 7-11) Closed: 25-26 Dec eve
Bar Meals L served all week 12-2 D served all week 7-9 Av main course £10.25 **Restaurant** L served all week 12-2 D served all week 7-9 Av 3 course à la carte £20 Adnams Adnams Best, Broadside, Old Ale, Regatta. 15 **Facilities** Garden Parking

'he Golden Key

'iory Ln IP17 1SQ ☎ 01728 688510

-mail: snapegoldenkey@aol.com

ating from around 1480, this extended, cottage-style pub still ouses three large open fireplaces. Landlord Alan Booth used to be a assical music record producer, and orchestras often eat here before erforming down the road at the famous Snape Maltings. The menu cludes roasts every day; chicken tikka masala; cod in Adnam's batter ith hand-cut chips; and Moroccan lamb tagine.

pen 12-3 6-11 Closed Sun eve Nov-Etr Closed: 25 Dec
ar Meals L served all week 11.30-2 D served all week 5.30-9 Av main ourse £5.95 **Restaurant** L served all week 11.30-2 D served Mon-Sat 30-9 Av 3 course à la carte £17.95 Adnams Adnams Best, Broadside Regatta, Tally Ho, Oyster Ale. 12 **Facilities** Garden Parking

Plough & Sail

Snape Maltings IP17 1SR

☎ 01728 688413 01728 688930

e-mail: enquiries@snapemaltings.co.uk

dir: *Snape Maltings on B1069 S of Snape. Signed from A12*

An enjoyable and popular part of any visit to Snape Maltings, the Plough and Sail rubs shoulders with the famous concert hall, art gallery and shops. The rambling interior includes a restaurant, and the large terrace provides summer seating. Sweet potato moussaka or wild boar sausages with green pea mash are typical light lunches, whilst evening diners might expect a slow braised lamb shank, or baked cod with Welsh rarebit and creamed leeks. New tenants were due to take over in Spring 2007.

Open 11-3 5.30-11 **Bar Meals** L served Mon-Fri 12-2.30 **Restaurant** L served all week 12-2.30 D served Mon-Fri 7-9 (Sat-Sun 7-9.30) Free House Adnams Broadside, Adnams Bitter, Explorer, Fishermans. 10 **Facilities** Garden Dogs allowed Parking

SOUTHWOLD MAP 13 TM57

Pick of the Pubs

The Crown Hotel ★★ HL

The High St IP18 6DP

☎ 01502 722275 01502 727263

e-mail: crown.hotel@adnams.co.uk

dir: *From A12 take A1095 to Southwold. Into town centre, Pub on left*

As the flagship operation for Adnams' brewery, the Crown fulfils the roles of pub, wine bar, eatery and small hotel. Originally a posting inn dating from 1750, it offers a wide selection of Adnams' ales, with some 20 wines by the glass. Alternatively you can visit the cellar and kitchen store in the hotel yard for a full selection of wines and bottled beers. The bar area has been expanded, so the whole place buzzes with lively informality as blue-shirted waiting staff attend to customers installed on green leather cushioned settles or at the green-washed oak-panelled bar. It's a popular place, especially in summer when customers are queueing at the door. The seaside location means seafood is well represented, with roasted fillet of hake or seared sea bass. Land-based options may include braised lamb sweetbreads or roast local partridge, Norfolk smoked eel, or confit of rabbit ravioli. Excellent puddings include warm treacle tart with clotted cream.

Open 8-3 6-11 (all day peak times) **Bar Meals** L served all week 12-2.30 D served all week 6.30-9.30 Av main course £14.50 Adnams Adnams Ales. 20 **Facilities** Children's licence Parking **Rooms** 13 bedrooms en suite S£83 D£126

The Randolph

41 Wangford Rd, Reydon IP18 6PZ

☎ 01502 723603 01502 722194

e-mail: reception@therandolph.co.uk

dir: *A1095 from A12 at Blythburgh 4m, Southwold 1m from Darsham Train Station*

This grand late-Victorian pile in large gardens was built by Adnams, the ubiquitous local brewers, who named it after Lord Randolph Churchill,

CONTINUED

England

SOUTHWOLD continued

Sir Winston's father. Standing just out of town, it successfully combines its functions as pub, restaurant and hotel; more accurately perhaps, this happy state of affairs is all down to owners David and Donna Smith. Their menus are full of interesting twists.

Open 11-12 **Bar Meals** L served all week 12-2 D served all week 6.30-9 Av main course £10 **Restaurant** L served all week 12-2 D served all week 6.30-9 Av 3 course à la carte £18 Av 3 course fixed price £17.50 Adnams Bitter, Adnams Broadside, Guest ale. 6 **Facilities** Garden Parking

STANTON MAP 13 TL97

The Rose & Crown NEW

Bury Rd IP31 2BZ ☎ 01359 250236

dir: *On A413 from Bury St Edmunds towards Diss*

Three acres of landscaped grounds surround this 16th-century coaching inn. Curl up on one of the comfy sofas in the split-level bar for a pint of locally brewed Adnam's Broadside, before perusing a menu that offers the likes of seared scallop, chorizo and black pudding salad; glazed pork loin chops; and sea bass with crayfish and saffron risotto. The adjoining Cobbled Barn is a popular spot for weddings and parties.

Bar Meals L served Mon-Sat 12-3 D served all week 6-10 Av main course £9.95 **Restaurant** L served all week 12-3 D served all week 6-10 Av 3 course à la carte £18 Punch Taverns Greene King IPA, Adnams Broadside. **Facilities** Garden Parking Play Area

STOKE-BY-NAYLAND MAP 13 TL93

Pick of the Pubs

The Angel Inn ★★★★ INN

CO6 4SA ☎ 01206 263245 01206 263373

e-mail: the.angel@tiscali.co.uk

dir: *From A12 take Colchester right turn, then A134, 5m to Nayland. From A12 S take B1068*

Set in a landscape immortalised in the paintings of local artist, John Constable, the Angel is a 16th-century inn with beamed bars, log fires and a long tradition of hospitality now continued under the Horizon Inns umbrella. The relaxed, modern feel extends to the air-conditioned conservatory, the patio and sun terrace. Tables for lunch and dinner may be reserved in The Well Room, which has a high ceiling open to the rafters, a gallery leading to the pub's accommodation, rough brick and timber studded walls, and the well itself, fully 52 feet deep. Eating in the bar, by comparison, is on a strictly first-come, first-served basis but the same menu is served throughout. Starters might feature baked goats' cheese with roasted field mushroom, beefsteak tomato and red onion confit for example. Main courses offer a range of meat, seafood and vegetarian options, typically including griddled whole plaice served with salad and French fries. There is an extensive wine list.

Open 11-11 **Bar Meals** L served all week 12-2 D served all week 6.30-9.30 (Sun 12-5, 5.30-9.30) **Restaurant** L served all week 12-2 D served all week 6.30-9.30 (Sun 12-5, 5.30-9.30) Free House Greene King IPA & Abbot Ale, Adnams Best. 9 **Facilities** Garden Parking **Rooms** 6 bedrooms en suite S£60 D£65

Pick of the Pubs

The Crown

CO6 4SE ☎ 01206 262001 01206 264026

e-mail: thecrown@eoinns.co.uk

dir: *Exit A12 signed Stratford St Mary/Dedham. Through Stratford St Mary 0.5m, left follow signs to Higham. At village green turn left, left again 2m, pub on right*

A modernised and extended village inn, dating from 1560, with glorious views over the Box Valley, in one of the most beautiful parts of Suffolk. Wherever possible, local produce is the basis for a regularly evolving Modern British menu, typically containing braised oxtail in rich red wine sauce with celeriac and parsley mash; chicken breast with creamed savoy cabbage, crispy bacon and sautéed potatoes; and butternut squash with rocket, goats' cheese and sage risotto. The fish board reflects seasonality, daily availability, price and weather; nothing is frozen. Look out for pan-fried Mersea skate wing with smoked bacon and caper butter; Adnams beer-battered haddock with home-made tartare sauce; and Scottish rope-grown mussels in garlic, white wine, shallot and cream sauce. The owner's passion for wine is reflected in his wine shop, where diners may buy bottles to accompany their meal or to take away.

Open 11-11 (Sun 12-10.30) Closed: 25-26 Dec **Bar Meals** L served all week 12-2.30 D served all week 6-9.30 (Fri-Sat 12-10, Sun 12-9) Av main course £10.50 **Restaurant** L served all week 12-2.30 D served all week 6-9.30 (Fri-Sat 12-10, Sun & BH 12-9) Av 3 course à la carte £20 Free House Adnams Best Bitter, Greene King IPA, Guinness, Guest beers. 28 **Facilities** Garden Dogs allowed Parking

STOWMARKET MAP 13 TM(

Pick of the Pubs

The Buxhall Crown

Mill Rd, Buxhall IP14 3DW

☎ 01449 736521 01449 736528

e-mail: trevor@buxhallcrown.fsnet.co.uk

When Trevor Golton and Cathy Clarke bought the Buxhall Crown in 1999, their aim was to create their own 'dream pub', serving good food in a relaxed, sociable environment. Together, they've transformed the 17th-century building from just another rundown village local into one of East Anglia's most welcoming and applauded gastro-pubs. Hand-pumped real ales and an extensive wine list complement an interesting and varied menu that changes every few weeks. Fire up your palate with shredded duck and hoi sin sauce pancake rolls; or a simple, warm smoked chicken Caesar salad. Main courses range from the ever-popular haddock in beer batter with home-cut chips to more adventurous fare: try chestnut potato cakes with rarebit topping and port sauce; roasted lambs' hearts with apricot stuffing, mashed potato and red wine gravy; or suet crust game pie with juniper gravy and seasonal vegetables.

Open 12-3 6.30-11 Closed: 25-26 Dec **Bar Meals** L served Tue-Sun 12-2 D served Tue-Sat 6.30-9.30 Av main course £25 **Restaurant** L served Tue-Sun 12-2 D served Tue-Sat 6.30-9.30 Greene King Greene King IPA, Woodforde's Wherry, Tindals Best Bitter, Cox & Holbrook. 30 **Facilities** Garden Dogs allowed Parking

Bell Inn

'he inn dates back 600 years and is located at the heart of the lovely coastal village of Valberswick, near the green, beach and the ancient fishing harbour on the River Blyth. The ırge garden enjoys lovely beach and sea views.

ıside, the building's great age evident from the low beams, one-flagged floors, high wooden ttles and open fires. Food is all ome cooked with local produce aturing strongly, particularly fresh sh. Specialities include starters of cally smoked sprats or Suffolk nokies – flaked smoked haddock a creamy cheese sauce – both rved with granary toast and a lad garnish. Among the main ourses are grilled skate wing with per and almond butter, new otatoes and mixed leaf salad, Walberswick fish pie, which ntains cod, smoked haddock, awns and hard-boiled egg in rich white sauce topped with ashed potato and cheese. The fish ıd chips are excellent, and are so available on a takeaway basis during normal service hours. The comprehensive menu offers just as many non-fishy dishes, with the likes of baked Suffolk ham, lamb burger in toasted ciabatta, hot and spicy chilli, and chargrilled sirloin steak. For vegetarians there might be sweet potato, spinach and cumin curry, or red onion, mushroom and blue cheese tartlets. Breakfast is served 9–9.30am, including the normal choice of cooked breakfasts, fruit, cereal, toast, teas and coffees, and snack lunches are also offered: farmer's, butcher's and fisherman's platters, sandwiches and ploughman's. A further treat is afternoon tea in the bar, with a choice of teas, coffees and pastries.

MAP 13 TM47
Ferry Rd IP18 6TN
☎ 01502 723109
01502 722728
e-mail: bellinn@btinternet.com
dir: *From A12 take B1387, follow to beyond village green, right down track*

Open 11–3 6–11 (Sun 12–10.30, Fri–Sat 6–12)
Bar Meals L served all week 12–2 D served all week 6–9 (Sun 12–2.30, Winter 7–9) Av main course £8.50
Restaurant D served Fri–Sat 7–9 Av 3 course à la carte £25
Adnams
Adnams Best, Broadside, Regatta, Old Ale. 15
Facilities Garden Dogs allowed Parking

The Westleton Crown

Nestled in a quiet village close to Norfolk's wild salt marshes, the coast and RSPB bird reserves, is this atmospheric and hospitable inn. Its origins go back to the 12th century, but the building itself dates from the 17th.

The original buildings belonged to nearby Sibton Abbey, and the Crown has succeeded in combining the rustic charm of its heritage with the comforts of contemporary living. Inside you will find crackling log fires, real ales, good wines and an astonishing range of malt whiskies. The team at the Crown are passionate about cooking, and have achieved two Rosettes from the AA. Meals are made from fresh, locally-sourced ingredients, and can be taken in the parlour, the dining room or the conservatory. Start with baked goats' cheese with red onion crumble, or spicy pumpkin tart, before moving on to roast loin of venison with griottine cherries and root vegetable creamed potatoes; the Crown's own cod and chips; or breast of Suffolk chicken filled with a chestnut and sun-blush tomato stuffing. Leave some space for dessert, which may take the form of pear tarte Tatin with blackberry ice cream, home-made arctic roll, or marmalade and orange steamed sponge pudding with English egg custard sauce. If you get too full up to move, or you want to take advantage of the wonders of the Norfolk Heritage Coast, there are 25 comfortable, individually styled and recently refurbished bedrooms complete with flat screen TVs and internet access. Dogs are welcome to stay with their owners for a small charge of £5 a night.

★★★ HL ◎◎ 🍷
MAP 13 TM46
The Street IP17 3AD
☎ 01728 648777
📠 01728 648239
e-mail:
reception@westletoncrown.co.uk
dir: *Turn off A12 just past Yoxford N'bound, follow signs for Westleton 2m*

Open 7.30 –11 (Sun 7.30–10.30)
Bar Meals L served all week 12–2.30 D served all week 7–9.30 Av main course £14
Restaurant L served all week 12–2.30 D served all week 7–9.30 Av 3 course à la carte £20
Free House
Adnams, Green Jack, St Peters, Woodfordes. 🍷 9
Facilities Garden Dogs allowed Parking
Rooms 25 bedrooms en suite S£85 D£110

TRADBROKE MAP 13 TM27

'he Ivy House

/ilby Rd IP21 5JN ☎ 01379 384634
-mail: stensethhome@aol.com

grade two listed thatched pub just off the main street in Stradbroke. ıe separate restaurant has been refurbished recently to include beech bles and chairs and white china. There's an extensive wine list plus ı impressive, daily changing menu that makes good use of local 'oduce. Typical dishes include crayfish salad with lemon dressing llowed by roast Gressingham duck breast with stir-fried vegetables, ›odles and plum sauce. Outside is a lawn and pond.

pen 12–2.30 6–11 **Restaurant** L served all week 12–2 D served all week 30–9 Av 3 course à la carte £22 Free House Adnams, Woodfords, ıffy's, Carlsberg. 7 **Facilities** Garden Dogs allowed Parking

WILLAND MAP 13 TM15

1oon & Mushroom Inn

igh Rd IP6 9LR ☎ 01473 785320 01473 785320
-mail: nikki@ecocleen.fsnet.co.uk
ır: *6m N of Ipswich on Westerfield road*

ıis 300-year-old free house has a reputation as 'the pub that time ıssed by', and the owners intend to keep it that way. Winter fires and ›od company still prevail, and East Anglian ales flow straight from the rrel. Locally sourced ingredients are the foundation of good home oking; maybe deep-fried tempura prawns or home-made duck pâté llowed by ale-cooked beef with dumplings or lamb in red wine, then ›acle sponge or crème brûlée.

›en 11.30–2.30 6–11 (Mon 6–11 only, Sun 12–3 & 7–10.30) **ır Meals** L served Tue–Sat 12–2 (Sun 12–3) D served all week 6.30–9 main course £8.95 **Restaurant** L served Tues–Sun 12–2 D served all ›ek 6.30–9 Free House Nethergate Umbel, Woodfords Wherry, ıffy's Hopleaf, Brewers Gold. 10 **Facilities** Garden Dogs allowed rking

HORPENESS MAP 13 TM45

he Dolphin Inn

›ace Place IP16 4NA ☎ 01728 454994
mail: info@thorpenessdolphin.com
r: *A12 onto A1094 & follow Thorpeness signs*

the heart of Thorpeness, this traditional village inn offers good food, d alfresco dining in the summer. Pan-fried pigeon breasts are served a starter with red pepper dressing; lamb kleftiko is marinated in red ne and served the Cypriot way with onions, herbs, rice and Greek 'ad; and there's a fish selection too.

›en 11–3 6–11 Restricted hours in winter **Bar Meals** L served all week -2 D served all week 6.30–9 Av main course £9 **Restaurant** L served all ›ek 12–2 D served all week 6.30–9 Av 3 course à la carte £18 Adnams st, Adnams Broadside. 8 **Facilities** Garden Dogs allowed Parking

TOSTOCK MAP 13 TL96

Gardeners Arms

IP30 9PA ☎ 01359 270460
e-mail: robert.richards@btconnect.co.uk
dir: *A14 follow signs to Tostock, turn at slip road through Beyton. Left at T-junct over A14, left into Tostock. 1st right to end of road*

Parts of this charming pub, at the end of the village green, date back 600 years. The basic bar menu – salads, grills, ploughman's, sandwiches, toasties, etc – is supplemented by specials boards that offer six starters and 12 main courses in the evening. Look out for lamb balti, Thai king prawn green curry, steak and kidney pie, and chicken and stilton roulade. There's a large grassy garden.

Open 11.30–3 6.30–11 (Sun 12–3.30, 7–10.30) **Bar Meals** L served all week 12–2.30 D served Mon–Sat 7–9 **Restaurant** L served all week 12–2.30 D served Mon–Sat 7–9 Greene King Greene King IPA, Greene King Abbot, Greene King seasonal beers. **Facilities** Garden Parking

WALBERSWICK MAP 13 TM47

Pick of the Pubs

Bell Inn

Ferry Rd IP18 6TN ☎ 01502 723109 01502 722728
e-mail: bellinn@btinternet.com
dir: *From A12 take B1387, follow to beyond village green, bear right down track*

See Pick of the Pubs on page 533

WESTLETON MAP 13 TM46

Pick of the Pubs

The Westleton Crown ★★★ HL

The Street IP17 3AD ☎ 01728 648777 01728 648239
e-mail: reception@westletoncrown.co.uk
dir: *Turn off A12 just past Yoxford N'bound, follow signs for Westleton for 2m*

See Pick of the Pubs on opposite page

England

England

SURREY

ABINGER MAP 06 TQ14

The Volunteer 🍷

Water Ln, Sutton RH5 6PR

☎ 01306 730798 📠 01306 731621

dir: *Between Guildford & Dorking, 1m S of A25*

Enjoying a delightful rural setting with views over the River Mole, this popular village pub was originally farm cottages and first licensed about 1870. An ideal watering hole for walkers who want to relax over a pint in the attractive pub garden. Typical fish dishes include lobster thermidor, Mediterranean squid pasta and fillet of sea bass, while Thai coconut chicken, partridge with red wine and junipers and fillet of braised beef on fennel feature among the meat dishes.

Open 11.30 –11 (Sun 12–10.30) **Bar Meals** L served all week 12–2.30 D served all week 6–9.30 (Sat 12–9.30, Sun 12–8) **Restaurant** L served all week 12–2.30 D served all week 6–9.30 (Sat 12–9.30, Sun 12–8) Woodhouse Inns Badger Tanglefoot, King & Barns Sussex, plus Guest ales. 🍷 9 **Facilities** Garden Parking

ALBURY MAP 06 TQ04

The Drummond Arms Inn ★★★ INN

🍷

The Street GU5 9AG ☎ 01483 202039 📠 01483 205361

e-mail: info@thedrummondarms.co.uk

dir: *6m from Guildford*

Triple gables at the second-floor level add an interesting architectural twist to this village pub, set in an attractive garden overlooking the River Tillingbourne. The menu offers sandwiches, old favourites (fish and chips; sausage and mash), and regular main courses such as braised lamb shank, or chicken New Yorker (with barbecue sauce and mozzarella cheese); fish dishes feature strongly. There is also a choice of daily specials.

Open 11–11 **Bar Meals** L served all week 12–2.30 D served Mon–Sat 6.30–9.30 (Sun 12–6, Summer 12–9) Av main course £10 **Restaurant** L served all week 12–2.30 D served Mon–Sat 7–9.30 (Sun 12– Summer 12–9) Av 3 course à la carte £20 Merlin Inns Ltd Courage Best, Gales HSB, Old Speckled Hen & Shere Drop. 🍷 8 **Facilities** Garden Parking **Rooms** 11 bedrooms en suite S£65 D£80

Villiam IV

ttle London GU5 9DG ☎ 01483 202685

r: *Just off A25 between Guildford & Dorking. Near Shere*

is quaint country pub is only a stone's throw from Guildford, yet ep in the heart of the Surrey countryside. The area is great for hiking d the pub is popular with walkers, partly due to its attractive garden, ich is ideal for post-ramble relaxation. A choice of real ales and lackboard menu that changes daily is also part of the attraction. pect steak and kidney pie, pot-roast lamb shank, battered cod and ps, and Sunday roasts.

en 11–3 5.30–11 (Sun 12–3, 7–10.30) Closed: 25 Dec **r Meals** L served all week 12–2 D served Mon–Sat 7–9 Av main course 50 **Restaurant** L served Sun 12–2 D served Mon–Sat 7–9 Free use Flowers IPA, Hogs Back, Surrey Hills Brewery. **Facilities** Garden gs allowed Parking

ETCHWORTH MAP 06 TQ25

he Red Lion ★★ INN

d Reigate Rd RH3 7DS

01737 843336 01737 845242

mail: info@redlion-betchworth.com

in 18 acres with a cricket ground and rolling countryside views, this ard-winning, 200-year-old pub offers an extensive menu. Beyond guettes and ploughman's lunches the choice includes sole and oked salmon, Barbary duck breast, aubergine and broccoli fritters, ep-fried plaice and chips, Toulouse sausage and mash, and steak d ale pie. The area is ideal for walkers.

en 12–11.30 (Sun 12–11) **Bar Meals** L served all week 12–3 D served week 6–10 (Sun 12–9.30) Av main course £9 **Restaurant** L served week 12–3 D served all week 6–10 (Sun 12–9.30) Punch Taverns Fullers London Pride, Greene King, IPA, Adnams Broadside. 6 **ilities** Garden Parking **Rooms** 6 bedrooms en suite S£40 D£50

LACKBROOK MAP 06 TQ14

he Plough at Blackbrook

15 4DS ☎ 01306 886603 01306 886603

: *A24 to Dorking, then toward Horsham, 0.75m from epdene rdbt left to Blackbrook*

ce a coaching inn and a popular haunt of highwaymen, this pub ers outstanding views and a charming cottage garden. The ever-nging menu may include rabbit and bacon pie; roast herb crusted k of lamb with a red wine jus; and baked spinach and potato uphinoise. Alternatively, try moussaka, chilli and rice, sirloin steak or deep-fried battered cod and chips. Jacket potatoes, ploughman's and toasted deli bagels round off the appetising menu.

Open 11–3 6–11 (Sun 12–10.30) Closed: 25–26 Dec, 1 Jan **Bar Meals** L served all week 12–2 D served Tue–Sat 7–9 **Restaurant** L served all week 12–2 D served Tue–Sat 7–9 (Sun 12–4) Av 3 course à la carte £25 Hall & Woodhouse Badger King & Barnes Sussex, Tanglefoot, Badger Best, Fursty Ferret & Festive Feasant. 18 **Facilities** Children's licence Garden Dogs allowed Parking Play Area

BLACKHEATH MAP 06 TQ04

The Villagers Inn

Blackheath Ln GU4 8RB ☎ 01483 893152

e-mail: kbrampton@ringstead.co.uk

More than a hundred years old, this free house stands on the edge of Blackheath, a natural woodland area of several square miles in the heart of Surrey. A menu of traditional pub food includes steak and kidney pie, chicken pie, and fillet steak. A covered patio extends the opportunity for alfresco dining. Real ales are represented by London Pride, Hair of the Dog and Youngers Special.

Open 12–3 6–11 (Fri–Sat 12–11, Sun 12–10.30) **Bar Meals** L served all week 12–2.30 D served all week 6–9 (Sun all day) Av main course £7 **Restaurant** L served all week 12–2.30 D served all week 6–9 Av 3 course à la carte £16 T.E.A, London Pride, Youngs Special, Teardrop. **Facilities** Garden Dogs allowed Parking Play Area

BRAMLEY MAP 06 TQ04

Jolly Farmer Inn

High St GU5 0HB ☎ 01483 893355 01483 890484

e-mail: enquiries@jollyfarmer.co.uk

dir: *From Guildford take A281. Bramley 3.5m S of Guildford*

The family that own this friendly 16th-century free house have a passion for cask ales, and you'll always find up to eight real ales and six lagers, as well as an impressive range of Belgian bottled beers. All meals are freshly cooked to order: expect the likes of slow-roast chicken supreme; seafood tagliatelle; and wild boar steak with foie gras on the specials board, alongside burgers and grills.

Open 11–12.30 (Sun 12–12) **Bar Meals** L served all week 12–2.30 D served all week 6.30–10 (Sun 7–9.30) **Restaurant** L served all week 12–2.15 D served all week 6.30–10 (Sun 7–9.30) Av 3 course à la carte £20 Free House 8 continually changing Cask Beers. 16 **Facilities** Garden Dogs allowed Parking

England

CHIDDINGFOLD MAP 06 SU93

The Crown Inn

The Green GU8 4TX ☎ 01428 682255 01428 685736

dir: *On A283 between Milford & Petworth*

Historic inn, dating back over 700 years, with lots of charming features, including ancient panelling, open fires, distinctive carvings and huge beams. Reliable food ranges from sausage and mash with onion gravy, chicken tagliatelle, freshly battered fish and chips, and decent sandwiches, warm salads and ploughman's at lunchtime, to Torbay sole, monkfish and tiger prawns pan-fried with ginger and lime cream sauce and served on tagliatelle, and roast duck with sweet plum sauce on the evening menu.

Open 11–11 (Sun 12–10.30) **Bar Meals** L served all week 12–3 D served Mon–Sat 6.30–9.30 (Sun 12–9) Av main course £9.95 **Restaurant** L served all week 12–3 D served Wed–Sun 6.30–9.30 Hall & Woodhouse London Pride, Moon Dance, Crown Bitter, Summer Lightning. 9 **Facilities** Garden Dogs allowed

The Swan Inn & Restaurant ★★★★ INN

Petworth Rd GU8 4TY ☎ 01428 682073 01428 683259

e-mail: the-swan-inn@btconnect.com

dir: *Between Petworth & Godalming on A283*

This appealing 14th-century village pub successfully manages to balance the traditional and contemporary, with bare floors, wooden furniture and big leather sofas giving a relaxed, stylish feel. The chef makes impressive use of seafood, fish and local game: look out for crayfish, feta and pink grapefruit salad with crème fraîche and chive dressing; followed by smoked haddock on lentils with saffron stew; and cherry crème brûlée.

Open 11–11 (Sun 12–10.30) **Bar Meals** L served all week 12–2.30 D served all week 6.30–10 Av main course £12.95 **Restaurant** L served Mon–Fri 12–2.30 (Sat–Sun 12–3) D served all week 6.30–10 Free House Hogs Back TEA, Ringwood Best, Fuller's London Pride. 15 **Facilities** Garden Parking **Rooms** 11 bedrooms en suite S£70 D£70

CHURT MAP 05 SU83

Pick of the Pubs

Pride of the Valley ★★★★ BB

Tilford Rd GU10 2LH

☎ 01428 605799 01428 605875

e-mail: reservations@prideofthevalleyhotel.com

dir: *4m from Farnham on outskirts of Churt Valley*

Charming and traditional, the Pride of the Valley is in the heart of the beautiful Surrey countryside and sits within its own idyllic country garden. Built in 1868, this award-winning inn is a great place for all occasions, and once enjoyed the regular patronage of former Prime Minister, David Lloyd George. The menu is extensive and international in its flavours. Catering for all tastes, ages and appetites in both the restaurant and the bistro, the well-prepared food is available everyday for lunch and dinner. At the bars you will discover a selection of fine wines, spirits and local ales.

Open 10.30–11 **Bar Meals** L served all week 12–2.30 D served all week 6.30–9.30 **Restaurant** L served all week 12–2.30 D served all week 6.30–9.30 Free House Doom Bar, Hogs Back brewery beers. 8 **Facilities** Garden Dogs allowed Parking **Rooms** 14 bedrooms en suite

CLAYGATE MAP 06 TQ1

Swan Inn & Lodge

2 Hare Ln KT10 9BS ☎ 01372 462582 01372 467089

e-mail: info@theswanlodge.co.uk

dir: *At Esher/Oxshott junct of A3 take A244 towards Esher. Right at 1st lights, pub 300yds on right*

Rebuilt in 1905 overlooking the village green and cricket pitch, yet barely 15 miles from Charing Cross. There's an attractively furnished continental-style bar and a Thai restaurant offering nearly 75 starters, soups, curries, stir-fries, and seafoods. The Thai menu is available at lunchtime and in the evenings, as are calamari, Cajun chicken burgers scampi, roast beef and lamb, and paninis. Dishes of the day appear o the specials board.

Open 11–11.30 **Bar Meals** L served Mon–Sat 12–2.30 (Sun 12–4) D served Mon–Sat 6–10.30 Av main course £5 **Restaurant** L served all week 12–2.30 (Sun 12–4) D served Mon–Sat 6–10.30 Av 3 course à la carte £13.50 Wellington Pub Co London Pride, Adnams, Brakspear. 8 **Facilities** Children's licence Garden Dogs allowed Parking Play Area

COBHAM MAP 06 TQ1

The Cricketers

Downside KT11 3NX ☎ 01932 862105 01932 868186

e-mail: info@thecricketersdownside.co.uk

dir: *Off A3 signed Cobham. Straight over 1st rdbt, right at 2nd. 1m right opp Waitrose into Downside Bridge Road*

Traditional, family-run pub, parts of which date back to 1540, with beamed ceilings and log fires. The inn's charming rural setting makes it popular with walkers, and the pretty River Mole is close by. There is a salad and light meals menu, with dishes like fishcakes and Barnsley chops. The main menu offers pan-fried cod fillet with saffron mash, steamed mussels and creamy sorrel sauce, or lamb shank cooked in aromatics and red wine sauce.

Open 11–11 (Sun 12–10.30) **Bar Meals** L served all week 12–3 D served Mon–Sat 6.30–10 (Sun 12–8) **Restaurant** L served Sun 12–4 D served Thu–Sat 10 Enterprise Inns Speckled Hen, London Pride, IPA. 9 **Facilities** Children's licence Garden Dogs allowed Parking Play Area

Stephan Langton

Walk information

Distance: 4 miles (8.4km)
Map: OS Explorer 146 Dorking, Box Hill & Reigate
Start/finish: woodland parking at Starveall Corner; grid ref TQ 130432
Ascent/gradient: 2
Paths: easy woodland tracks, but poor waymarking; many stiles
Landscape: thickly wooded sandstone heaths

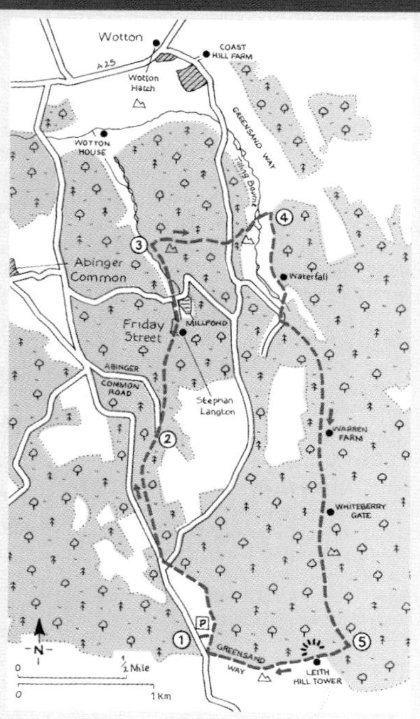

Walk directions

Leave the car park at the gate near the top left-hand corner. After 45 yards (41m), turn left onto a woodland path and follow it to a crossroads. Turn left and drop down to a road junction. Take the road towards Abinger Common and Wotton; then, 90 yards (82m) further on, turn onto the narrow, unsignposted path on your right. Cross a tarmac drive, and continue as it widens into a woodland ride.

Leave the woods and continue briefly along Abinger Common Road. When you reach a house called St John's, fork right onto the bridleway and follow it through to Friday Street. Pass the Stephan Langton pub and the millpond, and drop down past the letter box at Pond Cottage. Follow the rough track towards Wotton, bear left past Yew Tree Cottage, and continue to a gate.

Turn right over the stile, and climb the sandy track into the woods. Soon it levels off, bears left past a young plantation, then veers right at the far end. Two stiles carry you across Sheephouse Lane, and soon you're dropping to another stile. Nip over, and follow the fence across the Tilling Bourne until you reach two steps up to a stile.

Cross the stile, and turn right onto the Greensand Way. It brushes the road at the Triple Bar Riding Centre then turns left onto a public bridleway. Keep right at the National Trust's Henman Base Camp, and right again at Warren Farm, where the forest road ends. Here the waymarked Greensand Way forks right again, along the narrow woodland track. Keep ahead when you come to the bench and three-way signpost at Whiteberry Gate, climbing steadily at first, then more steeply, until you come to a barrier and five-way junction.

E The way ahead dives steeply down; turn right, still following the waymarked Greensand Way as it pushes up towards Leith Hill Tower. Pass the tower, taking the left-hand fork towards Starveall Corner. Follow the broad track back to the barrier at Leith Hill Road, then swing right onto the signposted bridleway. After 140yds (128m), turn left for the last little stretch back to the car park.

While there

In return for climbing the 75 spiral steps of Leith Hill Tower you'll get a view that stretches from the London Eye to the coast. Built in 1766 by Richard Hull of Leith Hill Place, it's popularly believed he wanted to raise the 967-foot (295-m) hill to exactly 1,000 feet (305m). After his death in 1772, he was buried beneath its floor. During the next hundred years the tower was raised to its present height of 1,029 feet (329m). The National Trust took over in 1923.

Look for

Shortly after you join the Greensand Way you'll see an impressive waterfall on your left, cascading 65 feet (20m) into a pool. It's fed by a leat from Brookmill Pond and was built around 1738 as part of an ambitious landscaping project.

England

COLDHARBOUR MAP 06 TQ14

Pick of the Pubs

The Plough Inn ★★★★ INN

Coldharbour Ln RH5 6HD

01306 711793 01306 710055

e-mail: ploughinn@btinternet.com

dir: *M25 junct 9 onto A24 to Dorking. A25 towards Guildford. Coldharbour signed from one-way system*

For fifteen years, the husband-and-wife owners of this 17th-century pub have been slowly rebuilding, refurbishing and upgrading it to create a warm, welcoming hostelry with excellent accommodation, superb food, and – since 1996 – its own real ales. A well-worn smugglers' route from the coast to London once passed its door, which probably explains why the resident ghost is a matelot. The surrounding North Downs draw customers in the shape of walkers, horseback riders, cyclists, and Londoners simply anxious to escape the city and relax in convivial surroundings. Three real fires in winter and candlelight in the evenings create a suitable ambience. Fish dishes are always plentiful, and could feature pan-fried baby squid, grilled sardines, and monkfish. Other representative dishes are confit of duck; braised beef with onions in home-brewed porter; and pork fillet with fresh asparagus roulade. Desserts like apple and red fruit crumble with custard are irresistible; and the collection of fine wines completes a thoroughly agreeable experience.

Open 11.30–11 Closed: 25 Dec **Bar Meals** L served all week 12–2.30 D served all week 6.30–9.30 (Sun 6–9) Av main course £9.50 **Restaurant** L served all week 12–2.30 D served all week 6.30–9.30 (Sun 6.30–9) Av 3 course à la carte £21.50 Free House Crooked Furrow, Leith Hill Tallywhacker, Ringwood Old Thumper, Timothy Taylor Landlord. 8 **Facilities** Children's licence Garden Dogs allowed Parking **Rooms** 6 bedrooms en suite S£59.50 D£69.50

COMPTON MAP 06 SU94

The Withies Inn

Withies Ln GU3 1JA 01483 421158 01483 425904

An unobtrusively modernised 16th-century pub with attractive low beams standing in unspoiled country on Compton Common, just below the Hog's Back. Proprietor Brian Thomas presents a varied menu with a good choice of bar snacks and, in the restaurant, beef Wellington, chicken Kiev, and poached halibut with prawns. Seasonal specialities include shellfish, game, and suckling pig. The splendid garden is one of the pub's chief attractions.

Open 11–3 6–11 **Bar Meals** L served all week 12–2.30 D served all week 7–10.30 Av main course £5.75 **Restaurant** L served all week 12–2.30 D served Mon–Sat 7–10 Av 3 course à la carte £28 Free House Greene King IPA, Tea, Fullers London Pride, Sussex. 8 **Facilities** Garden Dogs allowed Parking

DORKING MAP 06 TQ1

The Stephan Langton

Friday St, Abinger Common RH5 6JR 01306 730775

dir: *Leave A25 at Hollow Lane, W of Wootton. S for 1.5m then left into Friday Street*

A lovely brick and timber inn named after the 13th-century archbisho of Canterbury and local boy who was instrumental in drawing up the Magna Carta. Although it looks much older, and was built on the site of another inn, this secluded hostelry only dates back to 1930. Some of Surrey's loveliest walks are found nearby, including the challenging Leith Hill, and walkers find this a perfect place to recover. The pub is being gradually refurbished to match Jonathan Coomb's upmarket food. The bar choice includes Moroccan-style braised lamb, while the dinner menu offers chargrilled squid with chilli and rocket, and seare marlin niçoise.

Open 11–3 5–11 (wknd all day Summer) **Bar Meals** L served Tues-Sun 12.30–2.30 D served Tues-Sat 7–10 Av main course £12 **Restaurant** D served Tues-Sat 7–10 Av 3 course à la carte £25 Free House Fuller's London Pride, Adnams, Hogsback Tea. **Facilities** Gard Dogs allowed Parking

Please see walk on page 5

DUNSFOLD MAP 06 TQ0

The Sun Inn

The Common GU8 4LE 01483 200242 01483 20114

e-mail: suninn@dunsfold.net

dir: *A281 through Shalford & Bramley, take B2130 to Godalmin Dunsfold on left after 2m*

This 500-year-old family-run inn overlooks the village cricket green ar offers a warm welcome, blazing fires and a broad selection of food. Typical starters include deep-fried brie with cranberry sauce, prawn and avacado salad, and Sun Inn special nachos. Follow with a choice popular favourites such as steak and kidney pudding, Italian meatball creamy fish pie, trio of speciality sausages and mash, or salmon fishcakes with lime and mango salsa.

Open 11–3 5–11 (Fri–Sat 11–1am, Sun 12–10.30) **Bar Meals** L served all week 12–2.30 D served all week 7–9.15 (Sun 7–8.30) Av main course £7.95 **Restaurant** L served all week 12–2.30 D served all week 7–9.15 (Su 7–8.30) Av 3 course à la carte £16 Punch Taverns Harveys Sussex, Adnams, Guest ales. 9 **Facilities** Garden Dogs allowed Parking

EFFINGHAM MAP 06 TQ1

The Plough

Orestan Ln KT24 5SW 01372 458121 01372 458121

dir: *Between Guildford & Leatherhead on A246*

A modern pub with a traditional feel, The Plough provides a peaceful retreat in a rural setting close to Polesden Lacy National Trust proper Home-cooked dishes include the likes of wild boar with mushroom sauce, bangers with spring onion mash and gravy, rib-eye steak, and pan-fried sea bass with saffron broth and green beans. Once owned Jimmy Hanley and used in the 1960s TV series *Jim's Inn*, it also boas a popular beer garden.

England

pen 11.30–3 5.30–11 (Sun 12–3, 7–10.30) Closed: 25, 26 Dec, 1 Jan ve) **Bar Meals** L served all week 12–2.30 D served all week 7–10 **staurant** L served all week 12–2.30 D served all week 7–10 Young Co Youngs IPA, Special, Winter Warmer. 12 **Facilities** Garden rking

GHAM MAP 06 TQ07

he Fox and Hounds

shopgate Rd, Englefield Green TW20 0XU
: 01784 433098 01784 438775
mail: thefoxandhounds@4cinns.co.uk
r: *From village green left into Castle Hill Rd, then right into shopsgate Rd*

e Surrey border once ran through the centre of this pub on the edge Windsor Great Park, convenient for walkers and riders. Features clude a large garden, handsome conservatory and weekly jazz nights. enus offer a range of daily-changing fish specials as well as dishes e orange and sesame chicken fillets on coriander and lime noodles, roast pork with grain mustard glaze and parmesan crisps.

en 11–11 (Fri–Sat all day, Sun 12–10.30) **Bar Meals** L served week 12–2.30 D served all week 6.30–9.30 Av main course £7 **staurant** L served all week 12–2.30 D served all week 6.30–10 Hogsback Brewery Traditional English Ale, Brakspears Bitter. 8 **cilities** Garden Dogs allowed Parking

LSTEAD MAP 06 SU94

Pick of the Pubs

The Woolpack

The Green GU8 6HD
01252 703106 01252 705914
e-mail: woolpack.country.inn@hotmail.co.uk
dir: *A3 S, take Milford exit, follw signs for Elstead on B3001*

See Pick of the Pubs on page 542

ARNHAM MAP 05 SU84

he Bat & Ball Freehouse

Bat & Ball Ln, Boundstone GU10 4SA
01252 792108 01252 794564
mail: info@thebatandball.co.uk
eb: www.thebatandball.co.uk
: *From A31 Farnham bypass follow signs for Birdworld. Left at ngal Lounge into School Hill. At top over staggered x-rds into ndrock Hill Road. After 0.25m left into Viler Bourne Lane*

well worth the effort of finding this 150-year-old inn, tucked away he end of a lane in a wooded valley to the south of Farnham. Not prisingly, cricketing memorabilia features, and there are six hand mps serving a constantly changing selection of cask conditioned s. A varied menu includes home-made puff pastry pies, and fresh is usually offered from the daily blackboard, maybe whole baked bass drizzled with pesto olive oil.

The Bat & Ball Freehouse

Open 11–11 (Sun 12–10.30) **Bar Meals** L served all week 12–2.15 D served all week 7–9.30 (Sun 12–3, 6–8.30) Av main course £8.95 **Restaurant** L served all week 12–2.15 D served all week 7–9.30 (Sun 12–3, 6–8.30) Av 3 course à la carte £17.95 Free House Youngs Bitter, Hogs Back TEA, Bat & Ball Bitter, Archers Ales. 8 **Facilities** Garden Dogs allowed Parking Play Area

See advertisement under ABINGER

FOREST GREEN MAP 06 TQ14

Pick of the Pubs

The Parrot Inn

RH5 5RZ 01306 621339 01306 621255
e-mail: drinks@theparrot.co.uk
dir: *B2126 from A29 at Ockley, signed Forest Green*

This attractive 17th-century inn stands opposite the village green and cricket pitch in a rural hamlet. As well as having the expected oak beams and huge fire, it has its own butchery, charcuterie and farm shop. Owners Charles and Linda Gotto have a farm just a couple of miles away, where they raise shorthorn cattle, saddleback pigs, Suffolk sheep and Black Rock hens. The pub makes its own sausages, preserves and chutneys, and much of the menu uses home-grown or home-made produce. The cooking style blends modern, traditional and European influences. You could begin with a pancetta and avocado bruschetta with roast peppers, followed by poached shoulder of mutton with celeriac mash, braised cabbage and caper sauce. Not to be forgotten is a good range of real ales, which can be enjoyed in the bar or one of the four pub gardens.

Open 11–11 (Fri–Sat 11–12) **Bar Meals** L served all week 12–3 D served Mon–Sat 6–10 (Sun 12–6) Av main course £10.50 **Restaurant** L served all week 12–3 D served Mon–Sat 6–9.30 (Sun 12–6) Free House Ringwood Best, Youngs PA, Timothy Taylor Landlord, Sharp's Doom Bar. 14 **Facilities** Garden Dogs allowed Parking

PICK OF THE PUBS

The Woolpack

Sheep were so plentiful round here in the 17th century that the area needed a wool exchange. Once in possession of this simple fact, it shouldn't take much to deduce from its name that this quaint old pub once performed that very function.

Times change, of course, and over the years the building has also been a butcher's shop, a bicycle repairer's and even the local Co-op, before becoming the popular pub it is today. The surrounding hundreds of acres of common land attract ramblers galore, especially at lunchtime, and their arrival in the bar is often heralded by the rustle of protective plastic shopping bags over their muddy boots. In the carpeted bar, weaving shuttles and other remnants of the wool industry make appealing features, as do the open log fires, low beams, high-backed settles, window seats and spindle-backed chairs. A good range of cask-conditioned beers is offered, and large blackboards display frequently changing main meals, sandwiches, ploughman's and burgers. The new owners

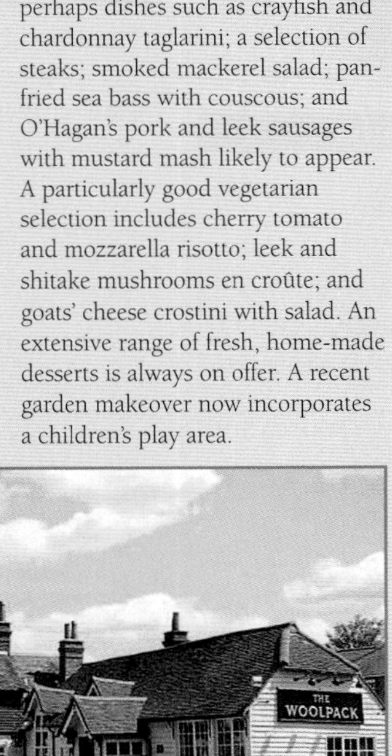

have installed a new team of chefs in the kitchen, and are planning their menus around the best of local produce, taking account of the seasons. Lunchtime brings an extensive menu with a broad appeal, whilst in the evening a range of traditional pub food is served: perhaps dishes such as crayfish and chardonnay taglarini; a selection of steaks; smoked mackerel salad; pan-fried sea bass with couscous; and O'Hagan's pork and leek sausages with mustard mash likely to appear. A particularly good vegetarian selection includes cherry tomato and mozzarella risotto; leek and shitake mushrooms en croûte; and goats' cheese crostini with salad. An extensive range of fresh, home-made desserts is always on offer. A recent garden makeover now incorporates a children's play area.

MAP 06 SU94
The Green GU8 6HD
☎ 01252 703106
🖷 01252 705914
e-mail: woolpack.country.inn@hotmail.co.uk
dir: *A3 S, take Milford exit, signs for Elstead on B3001*

Open 12-3 5.30-11 (Sat 12-11, Sun 12-10.30)
Bar Meals L served all week 12-2.30 D served all week 6-9.30 (Sun 12-3, 7-9)
Restaurant L served all week 12-2.30 D served all week 7-9.30 (Sun 12-3, 7-9)
Punch Taverns
Greene King Abbot Ale, Brakspears, Spitfire, London Pride. 🍷 13
Facilities Garden Dogs allowed Parking Play Area

England

GUILDFORD MAP 06 SU94

The Keystone 🍷

Portsmouth Rd GU2 4BL ☎ 01483 575089
e-mail: drink@thekeystone.co.uk
dir: *0.5m from Guildford train station. Right out of station. Cross pedestrian crossing & follow road downhill. Past Indian restaurant, 200yds on left*

A smart town bar with parquet flooring, leather sofas, pub games, a book swap facility, and live music most Saturday nights. Adherence to traditional pub values ensures the provision of fairly priced, home-made modern British food. Select from the menu's tapas section to start, then browse among the salads, burgers and main courses, such as mushroom and aubergine cassoulet; lime and coriander chicken breast salad with herby couscous; and cider and leek fish pie.

Open 12–11 (Fri–Sat 12–12, Sun 12–7) **Bar Meals** L served Mon-Fri 12–3 (Sat–Sun 12–5) D served Mon–Thu 5–9 Av main course £7.50 Black Sheep, 6X, Carlsberg. 🍷 10 **Facilities** Garden

Red Lion 🍷

Shamley Green GU5 0UB
☎ 01483 892202 01483 894055

Attractive old village pub with large front and rear gardens, ideal for whiling away summer afternoons watching the local cricket team play on the green opposite. In the cosy bar or large comfortable restaurant, there's plenty of choice from a variety of menus.

Open 7.30–11.30 (all day in Summer; closed 4–6pm Winter) **Bar Meals** L served all week 12–3 D served all week 7–10 Av main course £12 **Restaurant** L served all week 12–3 D served all week 7–10 Punch Taverns Youngs Pedigree, Adnams Broadside. 🍷 6 **Facilities** Children's licence Garden Parking

HASCOMBE MAP 06 TQ03

The White Horse 🍷

The Street GU8 4JA ☎ 01483 208258 01483 208200
dir: *B2130 from Godalming, on left 0.5m after Hascombe*

A friendly 16th-century pub situated in picturesque countryside that is good for walking. The pub is particularly noted in summer for its colourful garden, with hanging baskets and flowers. Restaurant menu and extensive blackboard specials in the bar may offer Thai style salmon and prawn fishcakes, steak burger, pies, and calves' liver and bacon. Fresh fish is delivered daily.

Open 11–3.30 5.30–11 (Sat 12–11, Sun 12–10.30) **Bar Meals** L served all week 12–2.30 D served all week 7–10 Av main course £9 **Restaurant** L served all week 12–2 D served Mon–Sat 7–10 Av 3 course à la carte £25 Punch Taverns Adnams, Harveys Flowers. 🍷 6 **Facilities** Garden Dogs allowed Parking

HASLEMERE MAP 06 SU93

The Wheatsheaf Inn ★★★ INN 🍷

Grayswood Rd, Grayswood GU27 2DE
☎ 01428 644440 01428 641285
e-mail: thewheatsheaf@aol.com
dir: *Leave A3 at Milford, A286 to Haslemere. Grayswood 1.5m N*

A stunning display of hanging baskets adorns this Edwardian village inn at the start of one of Surrey's lovliest walks. Award-winning chefs provide a high standard of cuisine, showcased in themed evenings that include special dessert or gourmet fish nights, when you might encounter poached plaice and scampi roulade; or grilled sea bass on sautéed leeks with chervil sauce. The magnificent viewpoint at Black Down, beloved of Alfred, Lord Tennyson, is nearby.

Open 11–3 6–11 **Bar Meals** L served all week 12–2 D served all week 7–10 (Sun 12–2.30, 7–9.45) Av main course £9.95 **Restaurant** L served all week 12–2 D served all week 7–10 Av 3 course à la carte £21 Free House Badger 1st Gold, Ringwood Best, Ringwood 49er & Greene King IPA. 🍷 8 **Facilities** Garden Parking **Rooms** 7 bedrooms en suite S£55 D£75

HINDHEAD MAP 06 SU83

Devil's Punchbowl Inn 🍷

London Rd GU26 6AG ☎ 01428 606565 01428 605713
e-mail: devilspunchbowl@ep-ltd.com
dir: *M25 take A3 to Hindhead*

The hotel, which dates from the early 1800s, stands 900ft above sea level with wonderful views as far as London on a clear day. The 'punchbowl' is a large natural bowl in the ground across the road. The menu, while not large, has something for everybody with deep-fried camembert with cranberry sauce, whitebait, and smoked haddock fishcakes as starters; main courses include steaks, grilled sea bass and Cumberland sausages. There is a separate snack menu.

Open 11–11 **Bar Meals** L served all week 12–6 D served all week 6–10 (Sun 12–9) Av main course £7.95 **Restaurant** L served all week 12–3 D served all week 6–10 Av 3 course à la carte £15 Eldridge Pope Bass, 6X, Tetleys, Bombardier. 🍷 10 **Facilities** Children's licence Garden Dogs allowed Parking

England

LEIGH MAP 06 TQ24

The Plough 🍷

Church Rd, LEIGH RH2 8NJ

☎ 01306 611348 📠 01306 611299

dir: *Telephone for directions*

A welcoming country pub overlooking the village green and situated opposite St Bartholomew's Church. Varied clientele, good atmosphere and quaint low beams which are conveniently padded! A hearty bar menu offers steak sandwiches, burgers, melts, salads, ploughmans' and jacket potatoes, while the restaurant area menu features tomato and artichoke pasta, smoked haddock fillet mornay, or Mexican style tortilla wraps.

Open 11-11 (Sun 12-10.30) **Bar Meals** L served all week all day D served all week all day Av main course £8.95 **Restaurant** L served all week all day D served all week all day ⊕ Hall & Woodhouse ◀ Badger Best, Tanglefoot, Sussex Bitter. 🍷 15 **Facilities** Garden Dogs allowed Parking

LINGFIELD MAP 06 TQ34

Pick of the Pubs

Hare and Hounds 🍷

Common Rd RH7 6BZ

☎ 01342 832351 📠 01342 832351

e-mail: hare.hounds@tiscali.co.uk

dir: *A22 signs for Lingfield Racecourse into Common Rd*

An 18th-century country pub close to Lingfield Park racecourse, the Hare and Hounds has a good name for its innovative modern English and European food. The menus provide early clues to the original approach taken by the kitchen – for a start, there's 'Something soup' rather than the more conventional 'Soup of the day'. Start with aubergine caviar blinis with oven-dried plum tomatoes and mushroom salad; or seared scallops with pea purée, orange and vanilla sauce. Then, how about swordfish loin with truffle mash, pak choi and cannelloni bean relish? Or even roast veal chop with spinach and sage gnocchi, Parma ham and garlic jus; or risotto primavera, available as a large or small portion? The Sunday menu goes beyond traditional roasts with Cumberland sausages, chargrilled gammon steak, and pan-fried fillet of John Dory with clam chowder. Head for the split-level decked garden for a drink in the sun.

Open 11.30-11 Closed: 1 Jan **Bar Meals** L served all week 12-2.30 D served Mon-Sat 7-9.30 (Sun 12-3.30) **Restaurant** L served all week 12-2.30 D served Mon-Sat 7-9.30 (Sun 12-3.30) ⊕ Punch Taverns ◀ Greene King IPA, Flowers Original, Old Speckled Hen, Guinness. 🍷 8 **Facilities** Children's licence Garden Dogs allowed Parking

MICKLEHAM MAP 06 TQ1

Pick of the Pubs

King William IV

Byttom Hill RH5 6EL ☎ 01372 372590

dir: *From M25 junct 9, A24 signed to Dorking, pub just before Mickleham*

Former ale house for Lord Beaverbrook's staff at his nearby Cherkley estate, the building dates from 1790 and has a terraced garden with fine country views. There's a panelled snug and larger back bar with an open fire, cast iron tables and grandfather clock. The chef proprietor serves good food alongside real ales including vegetarian specialities. Expect fisherman's pie, calves' liver and smoked bacon, baked tagliatelle with wild mushroom sauce, and the weekly Sunday roast.

Open 11-3 6-11 (Sun 12-10.30) Closed: 25 Dec **Bar Meals** L served all week 12-2 D served Mon-Sat 7-9.30 (Sun 12-5) Av main course £9.75 **Restaurant** L served all week 12-2 D served Mon-Sat 7-9.30 (Sun 12-5) ⊕ Free House ◀ Hogs Back TEA & Hop Garden Gold, Badger Best, Adnams Best, Guest Beers. **Facilities** Garden

The Running Horses 🍷

Old London Rd RH5 6DU

☎ 01372 372279 📠 01372 363004

e-mail: info@therunninghorses.co.uk

web: www.therunninghorses.co.uk

dir: *Off A24 between Leatherhead & Dorking*

This pub has a history of sheltering highwaymen; a secret ladder-way leading to the roof once helped them evade capture. Its interior may resonate with history, right down to its bare beams and real fires, but the menus have a modern edge. Bar food ranges from sandwiches to shank of lamb braised in balsamic and burgundy; restaurant choices include honey and soya-glazed pork fillet on beetroot and rocket risotto with Calvados cream sauce.

Open 11.30-11 (Sun 12-10.30) Closed: 25-26 Dec, 31 Dec eve & 1 Jan eve **Bar Meals** L served all week 12-2.30 (Sat-Sun 12-3) D served all week 7-9.30 Av main course £10 **Restaurant** L served all week 12-2.30 (Sat-Sun 12-3, 6-9) D served all week 7-9.30 Av 3 course à la carte £27 ⊕ Punch Taverns ◀ Fuller's London Pride, Young's Bitter, Abbot, Adnams Bitter. 🍷 9 **Facilities** Garden Dogs allowed

England

ЕWDIGATE MAP 06 TQ14

he Surrey Oaks

arkgate Rd RH5 5DZ ☎ 01306 631200 01306 631200
-mail: ken@surreyoaks.co.uk
/eb: www.surreyoaks.co.uk
ir: *A24 signs to Newdigate, at T-junct left, 1m on left*

cturesque oak-beamed pub located one mile outside the village of ewdigate. Parts of the building date back to 1570, and it became an n around the middle of the 19th century. There are two bars, one ith an inglenook fireplace, as well as a restaurant area, patio and beer ırden with boules pitch. A typical specials board features Barnsley mb chop with minted gravy, chicken and ham pie, and grilled plaice ith parsley butter.

pen 11.30–2.30 (Sat 11.30–3, 6–11) 5.30–11 (Sun 12–10.30)
ar Meals L served all week 12–2 D served Tue–Sat 7–9 Av main course .50 **Restaurant** L served all week 12–2 D served Tue–Sat 7–9
3 course à la carte £15 Harveys Sussex Best, Surrey Hills Ranmore e and Guest beers. 8 **Facilities** Garden Dogs allowed Parking Play ea

)CKLEY MAP 06 TQ14

Pick of the Pubs

Bryce's at The Old School House

RH5 5TH ☎ 01306 627430 01306 628274
e-mail: bryces.fish@virgin.net
dir: *8m S of Dorking on A29*

Formerly a boarding school, this Grade II listed building dates back to 1750 and was bought by Bill Bryce in 1982. He's passionate about fresh fish and offers a huge range, despite the location in rural Surrey. It's more of a restaurant than a pub, although there is a bar with its own interesting bar menu (open sandwiches; white Portland crab risotto, battered cod and chips). The restaurant offers seven starters and seven main courses – all fish – with some non-fish daily specials. Options to start include a soufflé of Arbroath smokie, Avruga caviar and parsley, or tartar of swordfish with lime, ginger and cinnamon. Mains take in fillet of sea bream on a porridge of mussels, chorizo and Parma ham with plum tomatoes and thyme fish cream; and pan-seared king scallops and calves' liver served with cauliflower and red wine and rosemary jus. Private parties are a speciality.

Open 11–3 6–11 Closed: 25–26 Dec & 1 Jan **Bar Meals** L served all week 12–2.30 D served Mon–Sat 6.30–9.30 **Restaurant** L served all week 12–2.30 D served Mon–Sat 7–9.30 Free House London Pride, Youngs IPA, Scottish Courage John Smith's Smooth. 15 **Facilities** Dogs allowed Parking

The Kings Arms Inn ★★★★ INN

Stane St RH5 5TS ☎ 01306 711224 01306 711224
e-mail: enquiries@thekingsarmsockley.co.uk
dir: *From M25 junct 9 take A24 through Dorking towards Horsham, A29 to Ockley*

The many charms of this heavily-beamed 16th-century inn include welcoming log fires, a priest hole, a friendly ghost, an award-winning garden and six attractively furnished bedrooms. Set in the picturesque village of Ockley and overlooked by the tower of Leith Hill, it's an ideal setting in which to enjoy home-cooked food such as honey-glazed pork belly with roast onions and mashed potato; coq au Riesling; or rabbit and winter vegetable casserole.

Open 11–2.30 6–11 (Sat 11–3, Sun 12–3, 7–10.30) **Bar Meals** L served all week 12–2 D served all week 7–9 (Fri–Sat 7–10) Av main course £12 **Restaurant** L served all week 12–2 D served all week 7–9 (Fri–Sat 7–10) Free House Flowers IPA, Old Speckled Hen, Castlemaine 4X, & Murphy's. 15 **Facilities** Garden Parking **Rooms** 6 bedrooms en suite S£55 D£80

PIRBRIGHT MAP 06 SU95

The Royal Oak 🍷

Aldershot Rd GU24 0DQ ☎ 01483 232466

dir: *M3 junct 3, A322 towards Guildford, then A324 towards Aldershot*

A genuine old world pub specialising in real ales (up to nine at any time), and well known for its glorious prize-winning garden. The Tudor cottage pub has an oak church door, stained glass windows and pew seating, and in winter there are welcoming log fires in the rambling bars. The menu may include smoked salmon and pesto, braised lamb shoulder, steak and ale pie, and penne pasta Alfredo, along with various specials.

Open 11–11 (Sun 11–10.30) **Bar Meals** L served all week 12–6 D served all week 6–10 Sat–Sun 12–9.30 Av main course £7 Laurel Pub Partnership Flowers IPA, Hogsback Traditional English Ale, Bass Ringwood Ale, Abbots Ales. 🍷 18 **Facilities** Garden Dogs allowed Parking

REDHILL MAP 06 TQ25

William IV Country Pub 🍷

Little Common Ln, Bletchingly RH1 4QF ☎ 01883 743278

Tucked away down a leafy lane close to the Pilgrims' Way, this early Victorian hostelry has been completely refurbished. The building, which was formerly a pair of cottages, now has a lovely family atmosphere with a few reminders of William IV decorating the walls. The chef specialises in freshly prepared dishes that include coq au vin; rib-eye steaks; leek and potato bake; and roasted stuffed peppers.

Open 12–3 6–11 Closed: 25–26 Dec eve **Bar Meals** L served all week 12–2.30 (Sun 12–3) D served Mon–Sun 6.45–9.30 Av main course £9 **Restaurant** L served all week 12–2.30 (Sun 12–4) D served all week 7–9.30 Av 3 course à la carte £20 Punch Taverns Harveys Sussex Best, Fullers London Pride, Greene King IPA, San Miguel Lager & Carling extra cold. 🍷 7 **Facilities** Garden Dogs allowed Parking Play Area

SOUTH GODSTONE MAP 06 TQ34

Fox & Hounds 🍷

Tilburstow Hill Rd RH9 8LY ☎ 01342 893474

It is said that pirate-turned-smuggler John Trenchman haunts this inn. He died in the pub's cellar when set upon by the king's men; his grave (complete with skull and crossbones) is in the nearby churchyard. Despite its gruesome past, this is a cosily traditional inn, parts of which date from 1368. The menu includes good seafood specials: perhaps whole baked seabass or fresh tuna niçoise. Outside is a large garden with pleasant rural views.

Open 12–11 (Sun 12–3.30, 7–11) **Bar Meals** L served all week 12–3 D served all week 6–9 (Fri–Sun 12–9) Av main course £9.95 **Restaurant** L served all week 12–3 D served all week 6–9 (Fri–Sun 12–9) Greene King All Greene King. 🍷 12 **Facilities** Garden Dogs allowed Parking

STAINES MAP 06 TQ0

The Swan Hotel 🍷

The Hythe TW18 3JB ☎ 01784 452494 📠 01784 461593

e-mail: swan.hotel@fullers.co.uk

dir: *Just off A308, S of Staines Bridge. 5m from Heathrow*

This 18th-century inn stands just south of Staines Bridge and was once the haunt of river bargemen who were paid in tokens which could be exchanged at the pub for food and drink. It has a spacious, comfortable bar, and a menu based on traditional home-cooked food Examples range from sausage and mash; pot-roast lamb shank; and steak and ale pie, to seafood risotto or vegetarian noodle bowl.

Open 12–11 **Bar Meals** L served all week 12–6 D served all week 6–9.30 (Sun 12–8) **Restaurant** L served all week 12–6 D served all week 6–9.30 Fullers Fuller's London Pride, ESB. 🍷 10 **Facilities** Garden Dogs allowed

VIRGINIA WATER MAP 06 TQ0

The Wheatsheaf Hotel 🍷

London Rd GU25 4QF ☎ 01344 842057 📠 01344 842932

e-mail: wheatsheaf.hotel.4306@thespiritgroup.com

dir: *From M25 junct 13, take A30 towards Bracknell*

The Wheatsheaf dates back to the second half of the 18th century and is beautifully situated overlooking Virginia Water on the edge of Windsor Great Park. Chalkboard menus offer a good range of freshly prepared dishes with fresh fish as a speciality. Popular options are bee battered cod and chips, roast queen fish with pesto crust, and braised lamb shank on mustard mash.

Open 11–10 (Sun 12–10) **Bar Meals** L served all week 12–10 D served all week 12–10 (Sun 12–9.30) Av main course £8 **Restaurant** L served all week 12–10 D served all week Chef & Brewer Guest Ales. 🍷 6 **Facilities** Garden Parking

The Inn @ West End

\ regular at the Inn is on record as saying that it isn't a restaurant and it isn't a pub – more a ort of community centre that serves great food and wine and has lots of fun. Owners Gerry and \nn Price fully agree, since they clearly put a lot of effort into everything.

'he food, the wine, the beer and he service are all highly rated, ut so are the share club, the oules, the golf society, the clay igeon competitions, the wine astings, the film and quiz nights, nd much more. A team of five hefs is responsible for a modern ritish menu based on the freshest ngredients – in fact, the only ought-in product is ice cream. ierry and Ann grow their own erbs and whatever else they can hoehorn into their vegetable patch; ey supplement their harvest vith produce from a local grower vhose smallholding they pass n their weekly fish-buying trips) Portsmouth Harbour, and the roduct of these buying jaunts are nany and varied. Game usually omes straight from the farm for processing – the Inn even has its own plucking machine to cope with the large numbers of wild mallard, teal and pigeon. At lunchtime try English crumpet with hot smoked Scottish salmon, scrambled egg and chives; for a main course at lunch or dinner, Cumberland sausages with mash, spinach and onion gravy; black bream fillet with lemon butter; or roasted Moroccan spiced vegetables with apricot couscous and mint and coriander yoghurt, are among the choices. The wine list is exceptional.

MAP 06 SU96
42 Guildford Rd GU24 9PW
01276 858652
01276 485842
e-mail: greatfood@the-inn.co.uk
dir: *On A322 towards Guildford 3m from M3 junct 3, past Gordon Boys rdbt*

Open 12–3 5–11
Bar Meals L served all week 12–2.30 D served all week 6–9.30 (Sun 12–3, 6–9) Av main course £14
Restaurant L served all week 12–2.30 D served all week 6–9.30 (Sun 12–3, 6–9) Av 3 course à la carte £25 Av 2 course fixed price £11.75
Free House
Youngs Bitter, Fuller's London Pride. 12
Facilities Garden Dogs allowed Parking

England

WARLINGHAM MAP 06 TQ35

The White Lion

CR6 9EG ☎ 01883 629011

This listed 15th-century inn on Warlingham Green has low ceilings, oak beams and inglenook fireplace, along with an extension that carefully combines the old and the new. Four real ales and five lagers are always available, and there's a varied menu offering sandwiches, light bites and dishes of Thai green chicken; lamb shank with rosemary and stilton; and roquefort tortellini among a good choice of vegetarian dishes.

Open 12–11 (Sun 12–10.30) **Bar Meals** L served all week 12–9 D served all week 12–9 Av main course £6 Bass Fullers London Pride, Bass, Youngs, Pedigree. 18 **Facilities** Garden Parking

WEST CLANDON MAP 06 TQ05

Onslow Arms

The Street GU4 7TE ☎ 01483 222447 01483 211126

e-mail: onslowarms@massivepub.com

dir: *A3 then A247*

Although it dates from 1623 and retains some historic features, this pub certainly moves with the times – customers may land on the helipad when flying in for live music every Wednesday. The Cromwell Bar has a good choice of real ales, and the beamed interior provides a contrast to the contemporary restaurant alongside. L'Auberge serves classic French cuisine (particularly good value at lunch time), while La Rotisserie offers a range of soups, salads, omelettes and baguettes.

Open 11–11 (Sun 12–10.30) **Bar Meals** L served all week 12–2.30 D served all week 7–9.30 (Fri–Sat 7–10, Sun 12–9) **Restaurant** L served all week 12.30–2.30 D served all week 7–10 (Sun 7–9) Massive Ltd Scottish Courage Courage Best & Directors, Bitter, Bombardier Premium, Hogs Back TEA & Pedigree. 11 **Facilities** Children's licence Garden Dogs allowed Parking

WEST END MAP 06 SU96

Pick of the Pubs

The Inn @ West End

42 Guildford Rd GU24 9PW

☎ 01276 858652 01276 485842

e-mail: greatfood@the-inn.co.uk

dir: *On A322 towards Guildford 3m from M3 junct 3, just beyond the Gordon Boys rdbt*

See Pick of the Pubs on page 547

WEST HORSLEY MAP 06 TQ05

Pick of the Pubs

The King William IV

83 The Street KT24 6BG

☎ 01483 282318 01483 282318

e-mail: kingbilly4th@aol.com

dir: *On The Street off A246 (Epsom to Guildford)*

When laws limiting the consumption of gin were passed in the 1830s, the King William IV began a swift trade in ale through its street-level windows. Fortunately, many of the original Georgian features have been preserved, giving this traditional countryside local a warm and welcoming atmosphere, augmented by open fires in winter and a light and airy conservatory restaurant. Today it's popular with walkers, not least for the large garden and terrace to the rear, with colourful tubs and floral baskets. Beers include several lagers, while the generously proportioned wine list proffers a good selection by the glass. The well-priced menu ranges over reliable starters such as deep-fried French brie or crispy garlic mushrooms, and leads on to equally popular mains like seared tuna, or marinated minty lamb rumps. Children can tuck into home-made lasagne and a shot of sugar-free 'safari juice'. Under new ownership – any reports?

Open 11.30–11 (Fri 11.30–12) **Bar Meals** L served all week 12–3 D served all week 6.30–9.30 Av main course £8 **Restaurant** L served all week 12–3 D served all week 6.30–9.30 Av 3 course à la carte £19 Enterprise Inns Fosters, Stella, Kronenbourg, Sheerdrop. 12 **Facilities** Children's licence Garden Dogs allowed Parking

WITLEY MAP 06 SU9

The White Hart

Petworth Rd GU8 5PH ☎ 01428 683695

dir: *A3 signs to Milford, then A283 towards Petworth. 2m on left*

A delightfully warm and welcoming pub, built in 1380 as a hunting lodge for Richard II; it became licensed in 1700. Richard's personal emblem was the white hart, here associated with this pub. Open fires, oak beams, Shepherd Neame ales and hearty portions of good value home-cooked food complete the picture: hunter's chicken, pig and poultry pie, and the master's cod piece perhaps. To the rear is an orchard with large garden, terrace and swings for children.

Open 11–3 5.30–11 (Sun 12–5) **Bar Meals** L served all week 12–2.30 D served Mon–Sat 6.30–9.30 **Restaurant** L served all week 12–2.30 D served Tue–Sat 6.30–9.30 Shepherd Neame Shepherd Neame Master Brew, Spitfire, Holsten Export, Seasonal Ale. 7 **Facilities** Garden Dogs allowed Parking Play Area

England

SUSSEX, EAST

ALCISTON MAP 06 TQ50

Pick of the Pubs

Rose Cottage Inn

BN26 6UW ☎ 01323 870377 01323 871440
e-mail: ian@alciston.freeserve.co.uk
dir: *Off A27 between Eastbourne & Lewes*

A traditional Sussex pub with roses round the door in a cul-de-sac village at the foot of the South Downs. It is an ideal base for long walks in unspoilt countryside, especially along the old coach road to the south which is closed to motorised traffic. The pub, in the same family for more than 40 years, has established a reputation for good home-cooked food served in peaceful surroundings (no children under 10). Lunchtime eating is primarily casual, either in the bar or the patio garden, with booking necessary only on Sundays; in the evening, the rambling cosy dining rooms are ideal for a special occasion. A 'fresh daily' philosophy applies here, with locally supplied Sussex beef, free-range lamb and pork, and seasonal fish, game and organic vegetables. In addition to the more traditional dishes, the chef creates authentic curries using fresh spices, and his 'jolly posh' fish pie continues to satisfy the cognoscente.

Open 11.30-3 6.30-11 (Sun 12-3, 7-10.30) Closed: 25-26 Dec **Bar Meals** L served all week 12-2 D served all week 7-9.30 (Sun 7-9) **Restaurant** L served all week 12-2 D served Mon-Sat 7-9 Av 3 course à la carte £18 Free House Harveys Best, King & Co Horsham best. 9 **Facilities** Garden Dogs allowed Parking

ALFRISTON MAP 06 TQ50

George Inn

High St BN26 5SY ☎ 01323 870319 01323 871384
e-mail: info@thegeorge-alfriston.com
dir: *Telephone for directions*

Splendid 14th-century, Grade II-listed flint and half-timbered inn set in magical South Downs village. The George boasts heavy oak beams, ancient inglenook fireplace and a network of smugglers' tunnels leading from its cellars. The three chefs create delights such as flat mushrooms sautéed in garlic with smoked bacon and goats' cheese; skate wings in black butter and capers; and monkfish wrapped in Parma ham on a mixed bean cassoulet. Good puddings too.

Open 12-11 (Fri-Sat 12-12, Sun 12-10.30) Closed: 25-26 Dec **Bar Meals** L served all week 12-2.30 D served all week 7-10 **Restaurant** L served all week 12-2.30 D served all week 7-10 Greene King Greene King Old Speckled Hen, Abbot Ale, 2 Guests. 12 **Facilities** Garden Dogs allowed

The Sussex Ox

Milton St BN26 5RL ☎ 01323 870840 01323 870715
e-mail: mail@thesussexox.co.uk
dir: *Off A27 between Polegate and Lewes. Signs to Milton Street*

Idyllically situated pub, tucked away down a meandering country lane and set in almost two acres of gardens. In recent years, improvements and adjustments have been made, but the friendly welcome and cosy atmosphere of a country pub have been retained. You can eat in the bar, or the Garden Room, or the more formal Dining Room. A typical menu includes shoulder of lamb roasted in honey and mustard, chargrilled venison steak with red onion and juniper reduction and steak chips, or corn-fed chicken supreme on a shallot, butterbean and tomato cassolette. Bar snacks, sandwiches and ploughman's are also available.

Open 11.30-3 6-11 (Winter Sun 12-5) **Bar Meals** L served all week 12-2 (Winter Sun 12-3) D served all week 6-9 Av main course £9 **Restaurant** L served all week 12-2 D served all week 6-9 Av 3 course à la carte £19 Free House Harveys Best, Dark Star Hophead, Golden Gate, Hop Back Summer Lightning. **Facilities** Garden Parking

ASHBURNHAM PLACE MAP 06 TQ61

Ash Tree Inn

Brownbread St TN33 9NX ☎ 01424 892104

The Ash Tree is a friendly old pub with three open fires, plenty of exposed beams and a traditional local atmosphere. Bar food includes ploughman's, salads and sandwiches, while the restaurant serves steaks, local lamb, steak and ale pie, and salmon in various sauces.

Open 12-3 7-11 (Summer 6.30-11) **Bar Meals** L served all week 12-2 D served Tue-Sat 7-9 **Restaurant** L served all week 12-2 D served Tue-Sun 7-9 Free House Harveys Best, Greene King Old Speckled Hen, Brakspear Bitter + Guest ales. **Facilities** Garden Dogs allowed Parking

BERWICK MAP 06 TQ50

Pick of the Pubs

The Cricketers Arms

BN26 6SP ☎ 01323 870469 01323 871411
e-mail: pbthecricketers@aol.com
dir: *Off A27 between Polegate & Lewes (signs for Berwick Church)*

A wonderful country pub in an unspoilt setting close to many popular walks, including the South Downs Way that runs atop the chalk scarp just to the south. It was formerly two 16th-century flint farmworkers' cottages, which then became an alehouse for 200 years before Harvey's of Lewes bought it around 50 years ago and turned it into a fully fledged pub. Three rooms with beams, stone floors and open fires are simply furnished with old pine furniture. In them, anything electronic that produces music is banned. The simple but perfectly adequate bar menu kicks off with pan-fried king Thai prawns, hot creamy garlic mushrooms, and coarse country paté, and continues with chargrilled barbecue chicken breast, 6oz fillet and 8oz sirloin steaks, and golden scampi, salad and chips. Nearby is Charleston Farmhouse, the country rendezvous of the London writers, painters and intellectuals known as the Bloomsbury Group.

Open 11-3 6-11 (Open all day at w/ends) (July-August all week 11-11) Closed: 25-Dec **Bar Meals** L served all week 12-2.15 D served all week 6.30-9 (Sat-Sun all day) Av main course £7 Harveys of Lewes Harveys Best Bitter, Pale & Armada, Kronenburg & Stowford Press Cider. 11 **Facilities** Garden Dogs allowed Parking

England

BLACKBOYS MAP 06 TQ52

The Blackboys Inn 🍷

Lewes Rd TN22 5LG ☎ 01825 890283 📠 01825 890283
e-mail: blackboys-inn@btconnect.com
dir: *A267 at Esso in Cross Hands take B2102 towards Uckfield. Village in 1.5m at junct of B2102 & B2192*

Set in 12 acres of beautiful countryside, the rambling, black-weatherboarded Blackboys Inn was first recorded as an ale house as long ago as 1349; parts of the building date from even earlier. It has a large garden overlooking a pond and a splendid beamed interior, complete with resident ghost. A meal might include mussels marinière, followed by half a pheasant slow roasted in red wine and brandy.

Open 11-11 Closed: Jan 1 **Bar Meals** L served all week 12 (Sun 3-6) D served all week 10 Av main course £10 **Restaurant** L served all week 10 D served all week 10 Av 3 course à la carte £20 Harveys of Lewes Harveys Sussex Best Bitter, Sussex Halow, Sussex XXXX Old Ale & Guest ales. 🍷 8 **Facilities** Garden Dogs allowed Parking

BODIAM MAP 07 TQ72

Pick of the Pubs

The Curlew at Bodiam 🍷

Junction Rd TN32 5UY ☎ 01580 861394
e-mail: enquiries@thecurlewatbodiam.co.uk
dir: *3m S of Hawkshurst on B2244 x-rds to Bodiam and Hurst Green*

See Pick of the Pubs on opposite page

BRIGHTON MAP 06 TQ30

The Basketmakers Arms

12 Gloucester Rd BN1 4AD
☎ 01273 689006 📠 01273 682300
dir: *From Brighton station main entrance 1st left (Gloucester Rd) bottom of hill*

Built in 1855, this is a traditional back-street pub, just off Brighton's Grand Parade, offering good real ales from seven handpumps, and home cooking using locally sourced, seasonal and organic ingredients. Among the specials are steak and ale pie; fish chowder; Irish stew; and Mexican chilli. Lighter meals include jacket potatoes with a choice of eight different fillings, home-made beef and vegetarian burgers, and sandwiches. Go on a Sunday for a delicious roast.

Open 11-11 (Thu-Sat 11-12, Sun 12-11) Closed: 26 Dec **Bar Meals** L served all week 12-3 (Sun 12-4) D served Mon-Sat 5.30-8.30 Av main course £6.50 Fullers HSB, Butser Bitter, GB, Festival Mild. **Facilities** Dogs allowed

The Chimney House NEW 🍷

28 Upper Hamilton Rd BN1 5DF
☎ 01273 556708 📠 01273 556708
e-mail: info@chimneyhouse.co.uk

The Chimney House has an open-plan kitchen where you can watch chefs prepare such delights as sautéed calves' sweetbread tartlet; or salt cod brandade with home-made aioli. Dishes like roast rack of hill-reared Blackface lamb are sourced from owner Jackie Nairn's fami farm in northwest Scotland. Finish up with chocolate brownie mousse and don't forget the wine list, compiled with the help of Hamish Anderson, award-winning buyer for Tate Britain.

Open 12-3 5-11 (Sun 5-7) **Bar Meals** L served all week 12-2.30 (Sun 12-3.30) D served Tue-Sat 6-9.30 Av main course £10 Harvey's Susse Best Bitter, Guinness. 🍷 10 **Facilities** Children's licence Dogs allowed

Pick of the Pubs

The Greys

105 Southover St BN2 9UA
☎ 01273 680734 & 606475
e-mail: chris@greyspub.com
dir: *0.5m from St. Peters Church in Hanover area of Brighton*

The Greys is something of an institution in Brighton, being renowned for its high quality food, Belgian beers and live country/folk music. Chris Beaumont and Gill Perkins are the driving force behind the dynamic little back-street pub in Brighton's Hanover district, though some of the credit is clearly due to chef 'Spats' Thomson Picken, a Maitrise Escoffier with 40 years in the business. This and other accolades explain the cooking and the language of the menu, both mostly French. There's a speedy menu for lunch and early evening, the carte, a special set three-course menu and a speciality themed eight-course menu available at two day's notice for a minimum of two people. Main courses, which come with a full supporting programme, include oxtail Alderton with all sorts of tasty vegetables, grilled river trout with Serrano ham, and a vegetarian tarte à l'oignon aux pistaches.

Open 12-11 (Mon 5.30-11, Fri-Sat 12-12) **Bar Meals** L served Tue-Sun 12-2 (Sun 12-3) D served Tue-Thur, Sat 6-9 Av main course £11 **Restaurant** L served Tue-Sun 12-2 (Sun 12-3) D served Tue-Thur, Sat 6-9 Enterprise Inns Timothy Taylor Landlord, Harveys, Leffe Blonde, Hoegaarden. **Facilities** Dogs allowed Parking

The Curlew at Bodiam

classic white weather-boarded, Grade II-listed pub, retaining many quaint and charming riginal features. Owing to its position at Bodiam Castle crossroads it was formerly known as he Junction Inn, the name being changed when the current proprietors moved here from London.

here are two air-conditioned estaurants, where tables are laid vith silver cutlery and Villeroy nd Boch china, and where Reidel lassware, and mirrors, original vatercolours and limited edition rints hang on the walls. The 1editerranean-influenced modern ritish food on the main carte hanges five times a year. Starters nay include beetroot gravadlax with ressed leaves; Spanish meats with asil; cherry tomato bruschetta; nd grilled goats' cheese on garlic roûtons. Fresh fish dishes may nclude pot au feu of fish with baby egetables, potatoes and saffron; oasted sea bream on Spanish otatoes with niçoise vinaigrette; or ea bass baked in salt. Alternatives re Moroccan vegetable tagine with piced couscous; fillet of pork with haggis mash, wilted spinach and red wine sauce; and pan-fried foie gras with oranges on potato terrine and top quality Serrano ham and olives. Desserts favour chocolate, fruits and citrus, while older favourites, such as crème brûlée, sticky toffee pudding and steamed syrup sponge (on Sundays) are never far away. Plates of miniature desserts for sharing is an ever-popular idea. The wine list runs to more than 200 bins, including house wines from France, Italy and Australia. Those feeling flush may spend up to £2,000 on a rare old Bordeaux or Burgundy. Adjoining the car park is a pretty garden and York stone terrace with a pond and bronze fountain surrounded by terracotta pots of jasmine.

MAP 07 TQ72
Junction Rd TN32 5UY
☎ 01580 861394
e-mail: enquiries@thecurlewatbodiam.co.uk
dir: *3m S of Hawkshurst on B2244 x-rds to Bodiam and Hurst Green*

Open 11.30–4 6–11 (Apr–Oct 11.30–11)
Bar Meals L served all week 12–2 D served Tue–Sat Av main course £7.95
Restaurant L served all week 12–2 D served Tue–Sat 7–9 Av 3 course à la carte £27.50
Free House
Badger Best, Fursty Ferret.
13
Facilities Garden Parking

England

BRIGHTON continued

The Market Inn ★★ INN 🍷

1 Market St BN1 1HH ☎ 01273 329483 📠 01273 777227

e-mail: marketinn@reallondonpubs.com

dir: *In Lanes area, 50mtrs from junct of North St & East St*

In the heart of Brighton's historic Lanes, this classic pub is within easy reach of the Royal Pavilion and seafront. The building was used by George IV for romantic liaisons, and now features two en suite bedrooms. Daily blackboard specials supplement the inexpensive pub menu which features salmon and dill fishcakes, jacket potatoes, and home-cooked curry. Seafood, vegetarian or spicy platters are available for sharing over a pint of Harveys or Bombardier ale.

Open 11–11 (Fri–Sat 11–1am, Sun 12–10.30) **Bar Meals** L served all week 11.30–3.30 D served Sat–Sun 6–8.30 (Sat–Sun 12–6) Av main course £6 Scottish Courage Harveys, Charles Wells Bombardier, Youngs Bitter. 🍷 7 **Facilities** Dogs allowed **Rooms** 2 bedrooms en suite

CHAILEY MAP 06 TQ31

The Five Bells Restaurant and Bar 🍷

East Grinstead Rd BN8 4DA

☎ 01825 722259 📠 01825 723368

e-mail: enq@fivebells-chailey.co.uk

dir: *5m N of Lewes on A275*

Handy for Sheffield Park, the Bluebell Railway, Plumpton racecourse and walks around Chailey. With origins in the 15th century and serving ale since the 17th, this country pub cum wine bar cum smart restaurant has many original features, including a large inglenook fireplace. The highly qualified kitchen team create modern European dishes rooted in English tradition from fresh, organic and free-range ingredients. Friday evenings host live jazz, and in summer the large bar terrace and secluded restaurant garden come into their own.

Open 12–3 6–11 **Bar Meals** L served all week 12–2.30 D served Tue–Sun 6.30–9.30 (Sun 16.30–8.30) Av main course £10 **Restaurant** L served all week 12–2.30 D served Tue–Sun 7–9.30 Av 3 course à la carte £23 Enterprise Inns Harvey's Best, Old Speckled Hen, Youngs Special, Hoegaarden. 🍷 9 **Facilities** Children's licence Garden Dogs allowed Parking

CHIDDINGLY MAP 06 TQ5

The Six Bells

BN8 6HE ☎ 01825 872227

dir: *E of A22 between Hailsham & Uckfield opposite Golden Cross PH*

Inglenook fireplaces and plenty of bric-a-brac are to be found at this large characterful free house which is where various veteran car and motorbike enthusiasts meet on club nights. The jury in the famous Onion Pie Murder trial sat and deliberated in the bar before finding the defendant guilty. Live music at weekends. Exceptionally good valu bar food includes stilton and walnut pie, lemon peppered haddock, Six Bells Yorkshire pudding with beef or sausage, vegetarian lasagne, cannelloni, and shepherd's pie.

Open 11–3 6–11 (Sat–Sun all day) **Bar Meals** L served all week 11–2.30 D served all week 6–10.30 (Sat–Sun 12–9) Free House Courage Directors, John Smiths, Harveys Best. **Facilities** Garden Dogs allowed Parking

COWBEECH MAP 06 TQ6

Pick of the Pubs

The Merrie Harriers 🍷

BN27 4JQ ☎ 01323 833108 📠 01323 833108

e-mail: rmcotton@btopenworld.com

dir: *Off A271, between Hailsham & Herstmonceux*

A Grade II listed, 17th-century, white clapboard building at the centre of the village with great country views. The beamed bar has a large inglenook fireplace, and there is another open fire in the lounge bar/dining room, which leads into the restaurant. The latter opens on to a pretty terrace with garden tables among the flowering tubs. A good choice of real ales (Timothy Taylor and Harveys among them) and nine wines by the glass is served, and all the food is prepared on the premises using local suppliers and produce – free range and organic wherever possible. Dishes might include slow roasted lamb shank with parsnip purée, Sussex steak and kidney pie with shortcrust pastry, and pan-fried fillet of sea bass with roast Mediterranean vegetables. Starters like wild mushroom risotto can double as mains.

Open 11.30–3 6–11 **Bar Meals** L served all week 12–2 D served all week 7–9 Av main course £20 **Restaurant** L served all week 12–2 D served all week 7–9 Free House Harveys, Timothy Taylor. 🍷 9 **Facilities** Garden Dogs allowed Parking

The Bull

)ating back to 1563, the Bull is one of the oldest buildings in this famously pretty Sussex ·illage. First used as an overnight resting place for travelling monks, the inn has also served as a ourthouse and staging post for the London-Brighton coach.

)wner Dominic Worrall took over ı 2003, and locals claim the inn ıas never been so popular. Real ale ɔvers will be delighted by the four ask conditioned ales, including ıe local Harvey's Best, while wine ırinkers can enjoy 13 regularly hanging wines by the glass. The ıodern British menu also changes ·equently (up to four times a week) ɔ make the most of the freshest ɔcal supplies, be it game from the alcombe Estate, South Downs ımb from village farms or fish from ıe nearby coast. These show up in ıch dishes as seared venison loin ıarinated in raspberry vinegar with ·alnut salad; and smoked mackerel ıd horseradish rillette with melba ɔast. Sample mains could range ·om pork tenderloin stuffed with red onion marmalade; or roasted duck breast with courgette spaghetti and Marsala jus; to poached fillet of salmon with tiger prawn gateaux; or stuffed aubergine with feta, pine nut and spinach au gratin. No one should miss the rare opportunity to sample Sussex pond pudding, a local speciality made with an alarming amount of butter, and here served with lemon and lime crème anglaise. Strawberry and mint crème brûlée, and rich chocolate and fudge brownie are equally alluring. Families are made very welcome, and half-sized portions are generally available for children. A huge garden commands stunning views over the South Downs.

NEW 🍷
MAP 06 TQ31
2 High St BN6 8TA
☎ 01273 843147
📠 01273 843147
e-mail:
info@thebullditchling.com
dir: *S on M23/A23 5m. N of Brighton, follow signs to Pyecombe/Hassocks then signed to Ditchling 3m*

Open 11–11 (Sun 11.30–10.30)
Bar Meals L served all week 12–2.30 D served Mon–Sat 7–9.30 (Sun 12–6) Av main course £10
Free House
Harveys Best, Timothy Taylors Landlord, Hop Back Summer Lightning, Gribble Plucking Pheasant. 🍷 13
Facilities Children's licence Garden Dogs allowed Parking Play Area

England

DANEHILL MAP 06 TQ42

Pick of the Pubs

The Coach and Horses

RH17 7JF ☎ 01825 740369 01825 740369

dir: *A22, right on A275, 2m to Danehill, left onto School Lane, 0.5m, pub on left*

In an age when the traditional village local is coming under increasing threat, the Coach and Horses proves that some classic hostelries can still survive. It was built in 1847 as an ale house with stabling and a courtyard between two large country estates. These days the stables form part of the comfortable country-style restaurant. Open fires and neatly tended gardens add colour to a setting that is full of character, with half-panelled walls, highly polished wooden floorboards and vaulted beamed ceilings. Food plays a key role in its success, with a good selection of lunchtime sandwiches and a constantly changing evening menu. Fish is well represented with the likes of spicy crab and seared scallop risotto. Alternatives might include casserole of Ashdown venison; chargrilled loin of pork with black pudding; or rib-eye steak with tarragon butter.

Open 11.30–3 6–11 **Bar Meals** L served all week 12–2 D served Mon–Sat 7–9 Av main course £11.50 **Restaurant** L served all week 12–2 D served Mon–Sat 7–9 Av 3 course à la carte £21 Free House Harveys Best & Old Ale, Brakspear, Wadsworth IPA, Archers Golden. 10 **Facilities** Garden Dogs allowed Parking Play Area

DITCHLING MAP 06 TQ31

Pick of the Pubs

The Bull NEW

2 High St BN6 8TA ☎ 01273 843147 01273 843147

e-mail: info@thebullditchling.com

dir: *S on M23/A23 5m. N of Brighton, follow signs to Pyecombe/Hassocks then signed to Ditchling 3m*

See Pick of the Pubs on page 553

EAST CHILTINGTON MAP 06 TQ31

The Jolly Sportsman

Chapel Ln BN7 3BA ☎ 01273 890400 01273 890400

e-mail: thejollysportsman@mistral.co.uk

dir: *From Lewes take A275, left at Offham onto B2166 towards Plumpton, take Novington Ln, after approx 1m left into Chapel Ln*

This characterful and sympathetically upgraded Victorian-style dining inn is the work of respected restaurateur Bruce Wass from Thackerays in Tunbridge Wells. Tucked down a quiet no-through road surrounded by downland, it feels isolated and romantic. Begin your meal with seared scallops, chilli and garlic linguini, followed by roast Sussex pork loin with caramelised garlic and seed mustard sauce, or perhaps poached skate wing with lemon, chive and butter sauce. Lovely garden.

Open 12–2.30 6–11 (Sun 12–4) Closed: 25–26 Dec **Bar Meals** L served Tue–Sat 12.30–2.15 (Sun 12–3) D served Tue–Thur 7–9 (Fri–Sat 7–10) Av main course £12 **Restaurant** L served Tue–Sun 12.30–2.15 (Sun 12–3) D served Tue–Thur 7–9.15 (Fri–Sat 7–10) Av 3 course à la carte £28 Av 3 course fixed price £15.75 Free House Guest beers. 9 **Facilities** Children's licence Garden Dogs allowed Parking Play Area

EXCEAT MAP 06 TV5

The Golden Galleon

Exceat Bridge BN25 4AB

☎ 01323 892555 01323 896238

dir: *On A259, 1.5m E of Seaford*

Once this was just a shepherd's bothy, but it has grown enough to comfortably accommodate TV crews making an episode of EastEnders, a Gary Rhodes commercial, and a Dickens costume drama. The pub overlooks Cuckmere Haven, and the Seven Sisters Country Park. A sample menu includes lemon chicken, fish and chips, Mediterranean vegetable and brie open pie, chicken carbonara linguine, traditional mixed grill, and beef, mushroom and ale pie.

Open 10.30–11 (Sun 11.30–10.30) **Bar Meals** L served all week 12–10 D served all week (Sun 12–9.30) Av main course £6.95 Free House 2 **Facilities** Garden Dogs allowed Parking

FLETCHING MAP 06 TQ4

Pick of the Pubs

The Griffin Inn

TN22 3SS ☎ 01825 722890 01825 722810

e-mail: info@thegriffininn.co.uk

dir: *M23 junct 10 to East Grinstead, A22, A275. Village signed on left*

'Just about anyone who walks into our bar with muddy boots' is made welcome at this Grade II-listed pub, reputedly the oldest licensed building in Sussex. Set in an unspoilt village just a stone's throw from the Ashdown Forest and overlooking the lovely Ouse Valley, it's handy for visiting Bateman's – the home of Rudyard Kipling – Glyndebourne, and the Bluebell Railway. The two-acre, west-facing garden offers glorious views, while inside old beams, wainscoting, open fires and pews enhance the character of the main bar. Menus change daily, with organic, locally sourced ingredients wherever possible. The emphasis is on modern British food with Mediterranean influences. A typical restaurant meal might start with seared scallops, pickled fennel and blood orange salad, before moving on to roast rump of Romney Marsh lamb, Swiss chard and lentil jus. Most of the 13 bedrooms boast four-poster beds.

Open 12–3 6–11 (Summer wknds all day) Closed: 25 Dec **Bar Meals** L served all week 12–2.30 D served all week 7–9.30 (Sun 7–9) Av main course £10 **Restaurant** L served all week 12.15–2.30 D served Mon–Sat 7.15–9.30 Av 3 course fixed price £30 Free House Harvey Best, Kings of Horsham, Hepworths. 15 **Facilities** Garden Parking Play Area

GUN HILL MAP 06 TQ51

Pick of the Pubs

The Gun Inn

TN21 0JU ☎ 01825 872361 📠 01622 851881

e-mail: info@thegunhouse.net

dir: *5m S of Heathfield, 1m off A267 towards Gun Hill. 4m off A22 between Uckfield & Hailsham*

A lovely 17th-century building and former courthouse set in delightful East Sussex countryside, with extensive views from a pretty terrace and garden. Wood dominates the interior, with beams, a beautiful wooden floor, and lots of hideaway places to drink and eat. A separate panelled dining room with a stunning fireplace is ideal for private parties. From a spring menu come starters of Sussex haddock smokie, garlic mushroom tart and antipasti, and main dishes of Chiddingly spring lamb hotpot, breaded scampi tail, and fresh market vegetable lasagne. Menu fixtures include stone-baked pizzas with a choice of toppings, and home-made beef, steak, lamb and fish pies. The Old Coach House behind the Gun has been transformed into a farmer's market offering a wide selection of fresh local fruits and vegetables, and organic foods, fish and meats.

Open 11–11 (Sun 11–10.30) **Bar Meals** L served all week 12–9.30 D served all week 12–9.30 Av main course £10 **Restaurant** L served all week 12–9.30 D served all week 12–9.30 Av 3 course à la carte £21 Av 2 course fixed price £11.50 Free House Harveys, Guinness, Leffe, Youngs. 13 **Facilities** Children's licence Garden Parking

HARTFIELD MAP 06 TQ43

Anchor Inn

Church St TN7 4AG ☎ 01892 770424

dir: *On B2110*

A 14th-century inn at the heart of Winnie the Pooh country, deep within the scenic Ashdown Forest. Inside are stone floors enhanced by a large inglenook fireplace. Sandwiches and salads are among the bar snacks, while for something more substantial you could try whole Dover sole; grilled pork loin on a bed of spaghetti; or medallions of beef fillet. Puddings include crème brûlée, ice cream gateau, and orange marmalade bread and butter pudding.

Open 11–11 **Bar Meals** L served all week 12–2 D served all week 6–10 **Restaurant** L served all week 12–2 D served Tue–Sat 7–9.30 Av 3 course à la carte £20 Free House Fuller's London Pride, Harveys Sussex Best Bitter, Interbrew Flowers IPA, Flowers Original Bitter & Bass. **Facilities** Garden Dogs allowed Parking

Pick of the Pubs

The Hatch Inn

Coleman's Hatch TN7 4EJ

☎ 01342 822363 📠 01342 822363

e-mail: Nickad@bigfoot.com

dir: *A22, 14m, left at Forest Row rdbt, 3m to Colemans Hatch, right by church. Straight on at next junct, pub on right*

See Pick of the Pubs on page 556

ICKLESHAM MAP 07 TQ81

The Queen's Head

Parsonage Ln TN36 4BL ☎ 01424 814552 📠 01424 814766

dir: *Between Hastings & Rye on A259, near church*

Though this distinctive tile-hung building dates from 1632, it's only been an alehouse since the 19th century. The traditional atmosphere has been preserved, with high-beamed ceilings, large inglenook fireplaces, church pews and a clutter of old farm implements. Hearty home-cooked food might include pork, sage, apple and cider pie; soft herrings' roe with toast; and a roast half shoulder of lamb.

Open 11–11 (Sun 12–10.30) **Bar Meals** L served all week 12–2.45 D served all week 6.15–9.30 (Sat–Sun 12–9.30) Av main course £8.95 **Restaurant** L served all week D served all week Free House Rother Valley Level Best, Greene King Abbot Ale, Whites 1066, Harveys Best. 10 **Facilities** Garden Parking Play Area

KINGSTON (NEAR LEWES) MAP 06 TQ30

The Juggs

The Street BN7 3NT ☎ 01273 472523 📠 01273 483274

e-mail: juggs@shepherd-neame.co.uk

dir: *E of Brighton on A27*

Named after the women who walked from Brighton with baskets of fish for sale, this rambling, tile-hung 15th-century cottage, tucked beneath the South Downs, offers an interesting selection of freshly-cooked food. The area is ideal for walkers, and families are very welcome.

Open 11–11 (Sun 12–10.30) **Bar Meals** L served all week 12–2.30 D served Mon–Sat 6–9 (Sun 12–3.30) Av main course £7.50 **Restaurant** L served all week 12–2.30 D served Mon–Sat 6–9 (Sun 12–3.30) Av 3 course à la carte £15.50 Shepherd Neame Shepherd Neame Spitfire, Best. 7 **Facilities** Garden Dogs allowed Parking

The Hatch Inn

Classically picturesque and reputedly dating from 1430, the Hatch Inn was converted from three cottages thought to have housed workers for the local water-driven hammer mill. It may also have been a smugglers' haunt, and is named after the coalmen's gate at the nearby entrance to Ashdown Forest.

The pub is superbly placed for a country walk (dogs are welcome), it features in a number of 'top ten pubs' lists, and has often served as a filming location for television dramas and advertisements. Only minutes away is the restored Poohsticks Bridge, immortalised in A.A. Milne's 'Winnie the Pooh' stories. There are two large beer gardens for al fresco summer dining, one of which enjoys views out over the forest. Cooking by the owner Nicholas Drillsma, who trained as a chef in both the UK and the US, combined with the customer service skills of his partner Sandra, have created a recipe for success; even a pair of original British Airways Concorde seats are proving popular! Quality ingredients and imaginative techniques produce an exciting menu, which includes a good selection of light bites and traditional dishes. These might include home-cured gravadlax of tuna loin; and oven-roasted Mediterranean vegetables with grilled goats' cheese. Fish dishes are well represented, with smoked haddock and leek risotto, Cajun salmon, pan-fried scallops, oven-roasted halibut, and Shetland mussels all making appearances. Lunchtime reservations are not taken, but evening booking is essential. This is when to look out for a starter of hot duck salad, served pink with fresh mango and field mushrooms; or poached pears with roquefort and balsamic syrup. Main courses might include locally-reared beef fillet with pont-neuf potatoes and béarnaise sauce; or pan-fried fillet of brill with salsa verde. For dessert, try the double crunch rhubarb and apple crumble, or sticky toffee pudding.

MAP 06 TQ43
Coleman's Hatch TN7 4EJ
☎ 01342 822363
01342 822363
e-mail: Nickad@bigfoot.com
dir: *A22, 14m, left at Forest Row rdbt, 3m to Colemans Hatch, right by church. Straight on at next junct, pub on right*

Open 11.30–3 5.30–11 (Sat–Sun all day Summer & BHs) Closed: 25 Dec
Bar Meals L served all week 12–2.30 D served Tue–Sun 7–9.15 (Fri–Sat 7–9.30 Sun 12–3, 6.30–8.30) Av main course £8.95
Restaurant L served all week 12–2.30 D served Tue–Sun 7–9.15 (Sun 12–3, 7–8.30) Av 3 course à la carte £28
Free House
Harveys, Fuller's London Pride, Larkins & Harvey's Old. 10
Facilities Garden Dogs allowed Play Area

LEWES MAP 06 TQ41

The Snowdrop

119 South St BN7 2BU ☎ 01273 471018

In 1836 Britain's biggest ever avalanche fell from the cliff above this pub, hence its deceptively gentle name. The owners provide good-value fresh food (all meat is free range), including doorstep sandwiches like Sussex cheese and home-made chutney, pizzas, home-made vegetable burger, and wild boar sausages. Vegetarians are well catered-for. Beer garden with a waterfall and palm tree!

Open 11-11 (Sun 12-10.30) **Bar Meals** L served all week 12-9 D served all week 12-9 Av main course £7 **Restaurant** L served all week 12-9 D served all week 12-9 Free House Harveys Best, Adnams Broadside plus Guests. **Facilities** Garden Dogs allowed

MAYFIELD MAP 06 TQ52

Pick of the Pubs

The Middle House

High St TN20 6AB ☎ 01435 872146 01435 873423

e-mail: kirsty@middle-house.com

dir: *E of A267, S of Tunbridge Wells*

See Pick of the Pubs on page 558

OFFHAM MAP 06 TQ41

The Blacksmiths Arms ★★★★ INN

London Rd BN7 3QD ☎ 01273 472971

e-mail: blacksmithsarms@tiscali.co.uk

web: www.theblacksmithsarms-offham.co.uk

dir: *2m N of Lewes on A275*

This attractive free house dates from about 1750 and is popular with walkers and cyclists on the nearby South Downs Way. Harvey's Sussex ales are served in the bar, where winter log fires burn in the inglenook fireplace. Owners Bernard and Sylvia Booker use excellent local produce in dishes like organic goats' cheese with mixed leaves and balsamic dressing; or wild sea bass fillets on a seafood risotto with lobster velouté.

Open 12-2.30 6.30-10.30 **Bar Meals** L served Tue-Sun 12-2 D served Tue-Sat 7-9 Av main course £11.50 **Restaurant** L served Tue-Sun 12-2 D served Tue-Sat 7-9 Av 3 course à la carte £22 Av 2 course fixed price £10.50 Free House Harveys Ales. 7 **Facilities** Garden Parking **Rooms** 4 bedrooms en suite S£40 D£60

RINGMER MAP 06 TQ41

The Cock

Uckfield Rd BN8 5RX ☎ 01273 812040 01273 812040

e-mail: matt@cockpub.co.uk

web: www.cockpub.co.uk

dir: *On A26 approx 2m N of Lewes (just outside Ringmer)*

Expect a friendly welcome at this family-run 16th-century free house. Original oak beams, flagstone floors and a blazing fire set a cosy scene. Harvey's ales and guest beers accompany the extensive menu, where typical choices include pork Dijonnaise; sea bass in white wine, cream and mustard sauce; and traditional favourites like steak and kidney pudding. The west-facing restaurant and garden have splendid views to the South Downs, with wonderful sunsets on clear evenings.

Open 11-3 6-12.30 (Sun 11-11.30) **Bar Meals** L served all week 12-2 D served all week 6-9.30 (Sun 12-9.30) Av main course £9 **Restaurant** L served all week 12-2 D served all week 6-9.30 (Sun 12-9.30) Av 3 course à la carte £18 Free House Harveys Sussex Best Bitter, Sussex XXXX Old Ale & Sussex XX Mild Ale, Fuller's London Pride, Harvey's Olympia. 8 **Facilities** Garden Dogs allowed Parking Play Area

RUSHLAKE GREEN MAP 06 TQ61

Pick of the Pubs

Horse & Groom

TN21 9QE ☎ 01435 830320 01435 830310

e-mail: chappellhatpeg@aol.com

Just across the road from the village green, this whitewashed inn dates from around 1650. The building was first licensed in 1775, and two years later it was listed as the Horse and Groom. Today you'll find a welcoming atmosphere surrounded by old beams, with Shepherd Neame ales dispensed from a row of hand pumps in the bar. Antique shotguns decorate the walls of the Gun Room restaurant, where you can choose an entirely fishy flavour for your meal: monkfish and organic salmon baked in parchment vanilla and vermouth; scallops sautéed with smoked bacon, spring onions, white wine and a butter oyster sauce; wild seabass fillets pan-fried and served with crushed olive, potato and white wine sauce; and mussels steamed in leeks, onions, white wine and pink peppercorns. On warmer days, meals are served in the garden, with fantastic views of the Sussex countryside.

Open 11.30-3 5.30-11 Closed: 25 Dec **Bar Meals** L served all week 12-2.15 D served all week 7-9.30 (Sun 7-9) **Restaurant** L served all week 12-2.30 D served all week 7-9.30 Shepherd Neame Master Brew, Shepherd Neame Spitfire, Shepherd Neame Kent Best. 7 **Facilities** Garden Dogs allowed Parking

The Middle House

This Grade I listed 16th-century village inn is a superb specimen of Elizabethan architecture, described as 'one of the finest examples of a timber framed building in Sussex'. The timber, wattle and daub structure has survived since 1575, when it was built for Sir Thomas Gresham, Elizabeth I's Keeper of the Privy Purse, and founder of the London Stock Exchange.

A private residence until the 1920s, still incorporating a private chapel, it retains a fireplace by master carver Grinling Gibbons, and a splendid oak-panelled restaurant. Occupying a dominant position in the High Street of this 1000-year-old village, the inn is typical of the many black-and-white properties in this part of the country, with its heavily beamed frontage incorporating ornate timber patterning. A truly family-run business from start to finish, the Middle House is owned by Monica and Bryan Blundell; their son Darren is general manager, and daughter Kirsty manages the restaurant, while son-in-law Mark is the head chef. An impressive selection of imaginative dishes is served, ranging from blackboard choices in the bar to more than 40 options on the more formal restaurant carte. Expect starters here like honey roast scallops served with chestnut purée and crispy bacon, or smoked haddock and vegetable terrine with a lemon vinaigrette. Main courses make good use of local produce in delicious dishes like roast lamb cutlets topped with black olive and rosemary risotto. Another traditional choice would be fanned marinated duck breast with a caramelised plum and ginger sauce. Vegetarians might try beetroot, red onion marmalade and goats' cheese tart with a balsamic glaze.

🍷
MAP 06 TQ52
High St TN20 6AB
☎ 01435 872146
📠 01435 873423
e-mail: kirsty@middle-house.com
dir: *E of A267, S of Tunbridge Wells*

Open 11–11 (Sun 12–10.30)
Bar Meals L served all week 12–2 D served all week 7–9.30 (Sun 12–2.30, 7–9) Av main course £11.95
Restaurant L served all week 12–2 D served Tue–Sat 7–9 Av 3 course à la carte £27
Free House
Harveys Best, Greene King Abbott Ale, Black Sheep Best, Theakston Best. 🍷 9
Facilities Garden Parking Play Area

England

RYE MAP 07 TQ92

The Globe Inn NEW

10 Military Rd TN31 7NX ☎ 01797 227918
e-mail: info@theglobe-inn.com
dir: *M20 junct 11 onto A2080*

A small, informal free house just outside the ancient town walls. An absence of gaming machines, jukeboxes and TV screens encourages even husbands and wives to talk to each other over their drinks, or while they enjoy their contemporary British food in the modern, wood-floored bar and restaurant area. Fresh fish comes from a local fisherman, organic meat from a National Trust farm at Winchelsea, and fruit and vegetables from Kent, the Garden of England.

Open 12–11 Closed: 2wks in Jan **Bar Meals** L served Tue–Sat 12–3 (Sun 12–4) **Restaurant** L served Tue–Sun 12–3 D served Tue–Sat 7–9.30 Av 3 course à la carte £25 Free House ESB, Harveys. 20 **Facilities** Children's licence Garden Dogs allowed Parking

Pick of the Pubs

Mermaid Inn ★★★ HL

Mermaid St TN31 7EY
☎ 01797 223065 01797 225069
e-mail: info@mermaidinn.com
dir: *A259, signs to town centre, then Mermaid Street*

Even the street is cobbled, as if to prepare the senses for the interior of an inn whose doors first opened in 1156. As a Cinque Port, the now silted-up harbour was once England's premier point of embarkation for France. Smugglers congregated here, and one or two of them may yet haunt the Mermaid's corridors and secret passages. The public rooms have huge beams, some recycled from ships' timbers, and fireplaces carved from French stone ballast rescued from the harbour. Popular at the bar are seafood platter, and moules marinière, while in the restaurant, famous for its linenfold panelling, English and French cooking holds sway. Only the freshest local ingredients are used for dishes such as grilled sirloin with horseradish mash, spinach, roast salsify and bordelaise sauce; and halibut with braised leeks, celeriac fondant and crab, artichoke and sundried tomato tortellini. Many of the characterful bedrooms have four-posters.

Open 11–11 **Bar Meals** L served all week 12–2.30 D served Sun–Fri 7–9.30 Av main course £8 **Restaurant** L served all week 12–2.15 D served all week 7–9.15 Av 3 course à la carte £30 Free House Greene King Old Speckled Hen, Scottish Courage Courage Best. 11 **Facilities** Garden Parking **Rooms** 31 bedrooms en suite S£90 D£160

Pick of the Pubs

The Ypres Castle Inn

Gun Garden TN31 7HH ☎ 01797 223248
e-mail: info@yprescastleinn.co.uk
dir: *Behind parish church by medieval Ypres Tower*

'The Wipers', as locals call it, was once the haunt of smugglers. Built in 1640 in weather-boarded style and added to in Victorian times, it's the only pub in the citadel area of Rye. Another plus is its garden – the roses, shrubs and views to the 13th-century Ypres Tower and River Rother make it an ideal spot for a pint from the range of tapped ales. Colourful art and furnishings help give the interior a warm and friendly atmosphere. The seasonally changing menu is largely sourced locally. A good range of lunchtime snacks includes ploughman's, jacket potatoes, and sandwiches backed by half a dozen daily specials. The evening menu may propose fishy starters like moules marinières or cracked Dungeness crab, a theme which could be continued with grilled Rye Bay plaice or pan-fried fillets of lemon sole. Meaty options are no less appealing: grilled rack of Romney salt-marsh lamb, or the pub's home-made prime beefburger with relish.

Open 11.30–3.30 6.30–11 (Fri–Sat 11.30–12, Sun 12–4) Closed: 2 wks mid Jan **Bar Meals** L served all week 12–2.30 Av main course £7 **Restaurant** L served all week 12–2.30 (12–3 Summer) D served Mon–Sat 7–9 Av 3 course à la carte £22 Free House Harveys Best, Adnams Broadside, Wells Bombardier, Timothy Taylor Landlord. 11 **Facilities** Garden Dogs allowed

SHORTBRIDGE MAP 06 TQ42

Pick of the Pubs

The Peacock Inn

TN22 3XA ☎ 01825 762463 01825 762463
e-mail: enquiries@peacock-inn.co.uk
dir: *Just off A272 & A26*

Mentioned in Samuel Pepys' diary, this traditional inn dates from 1567 and is full of old world charm, both inside and out. Today it is renowned for its food (created by no fewer than three chefs), and also the resident ghost of Mrs Fuller. The large rear patio garden is a delightful spot in summer. Food choices include toasted ciabatta and toasted foccacia with a variety of fillings. For the hungry there are starters such as chicken and duck liver pâté, or crayfish tails and smoked salmon, followed by seafood crepe, pan-fried sea bass fillets; steak, Guinness and mushroom

CONTINUED

SHORTBRIDGE continued

pie or fillet steak with garlic and stilton butter. For the non-meat eaters there's Mediterranean vegetable and mozzarella tartlet, or vegetarian tagine. The chefs' specials are interesting too.

The Peacock Inn

Open 11-3 6-11 Closed: 25-26 Dec **Bar Meals** L served all week 12-2.30 D served all week 6-9.30 (Sun 6-9) **Restaurant** L served all week 12-2.30 D served all week 7-10 (Sun 6-9) Av 3 course à la carte £21 Free House Abbott's Ale, Harveys Best Bitter, Fullers London Pride. 8 **Facilities** Garden Dogs allowed Parking

THREE LEG CROSS MAP 06 TQ63

The Bull

Dunster Mill Ln TN5 7HH

01580 200586 01580 201289

e-mail: enquiries@thebullinn.co.uk

dir: *From M25 exit at Sevenoaks toward Hastings, right at x-rds onto B2087, right onto B2099 through Ticehurst, right for Three Legged Cross*

Based around a 14th-century Wealden hall house and set in a peaceful hamlet close to Bewl Water, the Bull features oak beams, inglenook fireplaces and quarry tiled floors. There's a duck pond in the garden, together with a pétanque court and children's play area. Food is an important part of life at the Bull, with delicious home-cooked dishes that range from freshly baked baguettes to a full à la carte selection in the restaurant.

Open 12-11 Closed: 25-26 Dec eve **Bar Meals** L served all week 12-2.30 D served all week 6.30-9.30 (Sat-Sun 12-3, Summer all day) **Restaurant** L served all week 12-2.30 D served all week 6.30-9.30 Free House Harveys, Spitfire, Speckled Hen. **Facilities** Children's licence Garden Dogs allowed Parking Play Area

UPPER DICKER MAP 06 TQ5(

The Plough

Coldharbour Rd BN27 3QJ 01323 844859

dir: *Off A22, W of Hailsham*

17th-century former farmhouse which has been a pub for over 200 years, and now comprises two bars and two restaurants. Excellent wheelchair facilities, a large beer garden and a children's play area add to the appeal, and the Plough is also a handy stop for walkers. Expect such fish dishes as Sussex smokie or prawn, brie and broccoli bake, while other options include duck breast in spicy plum sauce, veal in lemon cream, and lamb cutlets in redcurrant and rosemary sauce.

Open 11-11 (Sun 12-3, 7-10.30, Summer wknd 11-11) **Bar Meals** L served all week 12-2.30 D served all week 6-9 (Sat-Sun all day) **Restaurant** L served all week 12-2.30 D served all week 6-9 Shepherd Neame Shepherd Neame Spitfire Premium Ale, Best & Bishop's Finger. 6 **Facilities** Garden Dogs allowed Parking Play Area

WADHURST MAP 06 TQ63

Pick of the Pubs

The Best Beech Inn

Mayfield Ln TN5 6JH

01892 782046 01982 782046

dir: *A26 onto A267, left then right onto B2100. At Mark Cross signed Wadhurst, 3m on right*

Under new management, the unusually-named Best Beech Inn is going from strength to strength. The inn dates back to 1680, and has been sympathetically refurbished in recent years to preserve the essentially Victorian character of its heyday. The result is a place bursting with personality, characterised by comfy chairs, exposed brickwork and open fireplaces. Ideally situated near the Kent and Sussex border, in an area of outstanding natural beauty, the inn includes a fine à la carte restaurant offering excellent European cuisine with a French influence. For those who prefer a more informal atmosphere, there is the bar bistro with a comprehensive menu available from the blackboard. Dinner could begin with pork rillette and apricot chutney, move on to bouillabaisse with saffron new potatoes, and finish with tarte au chocolate, marmalade syrup and vanilla ice cream.

Open 11-11 **Bar Meals** L served all week 12-2.30 D served all week 6-9.30 Av main course £10 **Restaurant** L served all week 12-2.30 D served all week 6-9 Av 3 course à la carte £20 Free House Harveys, Level Best, Youngs, London Pride. 7 **Facilities** Garden Dogs allowed Parking

The Lamb Inn

This family-run white-painted inn was built in 1526, but did not begin dispensing ales until 1640. It's popular with locals and walkers enjoying the tiny hamlet and lovely surrounding countryside of East Sussex.

Settle down in one of the comfortable cream sofas drawn up to the fire and enjoy a thoughtful selection of real ales and wines by the glass. Aside from the liquid refreshments, the pub is well known for its food, a mixture of traditional and modern cuisine. Everything is home made, including bread, and top quality produce is locally sourced as much as possible, including Limousin beef from a farm two miles away. Fish is a house speciality, offered daily on the specials board at lunch and dinner in dishes such as smoked mackerel, prawn and crayfish terrine with horseradish mayonnaise; salmon fillet on fresh pea and asparagus fricassée; or loin of local cod with olive tapenade and pesto mash. Alternatively, you could start with baked eggs en cocotte with mushrooms, gruyère and cream, or salad of fresh figs, roast beetroot, pancetta and local goats' cheese, before tucking into breast of Suffolk chicken on parmesan and onion mash; rump of local lamb with pistachio crust; or confit of duck leg with black cherry and orange. Non-carnivores could try the likes of home-made vegetarian Wellington, or pancake cannelloni. Desserts include blackcurrant and vanilla crème brûlée, and lemon and lime cheesecake with clotted cream.

A very pretty garden, including a terrace covered with flowers, is the perfect scented spot to while away a summer evening.

🍷

MAP 06 TQ60
BN27 1RY
☎ 01323 832116
web: www.lambinnwartling.co.uk
dir: *A259 from Polegate to Pevensey rdbt. Take 1st left to Wartling & Herstmonceux Castle. Pub 3m on right*

Open 11–3 6–11
Bar Meals L served all week 11.45–2.15 D served all week 6.45–9 (Sun 12–2.30)
Restaurant L served all week 11.45–2.15 D served all week 6.45–9 (Sun 12–2.30)
Harveys, Red River, Horsham Best, Toff's. 🍷 8
Facilities Garden Parking

The Dorset Arms

Back in the 15th century this white, weather-boarded building was an open-halled farmhouse with earthen floors. It has been an inn since the 18th century, and the name derives from the arms of the local Sackville family of Buckhurst Park, who were once the Dukes of Dorset.

Set on the borders of Kent and Sussex, the inn is ideally situated for explorations of nearby Ashdown Forest, home to everybody's favourite bear, Winnie the Pooh. It has many interesting features, including the massive wall and ceiling beams in the restaurant, the oak-floored bar, the huge open fireplace, and an old ice house buried in the hillside at the back. The prize-winning beers come from Harveys of Lewes, and a good number of wines from the extensive wine list are available by the glass. Bar snacks and daily specials are among the food choices, and the à la carte menu lists starters such as home-made chicken liver paté and toast; crispy coated camembert with port and redcurrant jelly; and deep-fried tempura battered king prawns with chilli dip. Main courses can include pan-fried loin of venison in Cumberland sauce; large tiger prawns sautéed in garlic, white wine and cream; half roast duckling with cherry and Amaretto sauce; and sliced boneless breast of chicken with bacon, leeks, cream and cider. Where possible the owners source all their ingredients locally. Blackboard specials might feature cheese-topped ratatouille bake; salmon fishcakes; or griddled whole plaice. The pub is a popular venue for the fishing and cricket teams, and holds regular quiz nights and music evenings.

MAP 06 TQ43
TN7 4BD
☎ 01892 770278
01892 770195
e-mail: pete@dorset-arms.co.uk
dir: *4m W of Tunbridge Wells on B2110 between Groombridge & Hartfield*

Open 11–3 6–11 (Sun 12–3, 7–10.30)
Bar Meals L served all week 12–2 D served Tue–Sat 7–9 Av main course £7.50
Restaurant L served all week 12–2 D served Tue–Sat 7–9 Av 3 course à la carte £20
Harveys of Lewes
Harveys Sussex Best & seasonal beers. 7
Facilities Garden Dogs allowed Parking

England

WARBLETON MAP 06 TQ61

The War-Bill-in-Tun Inn

Church Hill TN21 9BD ☎ 01435 830636 🖷 01435 830636
e-mail: whitton@thewarbillintun.wanadoo.co.uk

A 400-year-old smugglers' haunt, visited by The Beatles when they came to see their manager, Brian Epstein, who lived half a mile away. Locals still recall meeting Lennon and McCartney, as well as the resident ghost. Family run, the owners aim to offer good food and friendly service. Representative dishes include Gressingham duck, grilled trout with an almond and wine sauce, and light lunch dishes like jacket potatoes and scampi.

Open 12–3 7–11 **Bar Meals** L served all week 12–1.45 D served all week 7–9.30 **Restaurant** L served all week 12–1.45 D served all week 7–9.30 Free House Harveys Best, Bishop's Finger, Tanglefoot & Spitfire Smooth. **Facilities** Garden Dogs allowed Parking

WARTLING MAP 06 TQ60

Pick of the Pubs

The Lamb Inn 🍷

BN27 1RY ☎ 01323 832116
web: www.lambinnwartling.co.uk
dir: *A259 from Polegate to Pevensey rdbt. Take 1st left to Wartling & Herstmonceux Castle. Pub 3m on right.*

See Pick of the Pubs on page 561

WILMINGTON MAP 06 TQ50

The Giants Rest 🍷

The Street BN26 5SQ ☎ 01323 870207 🖷 01323 870207
e-mail: abecjane@aol.com
dir: *2m outside Polegate on A27 towards Brighton*

Tucked beneath the vast chalk figure of the Long Man of Wilmington, this family-owned, Victorian free house has an admirable commitment to home-prepared, seasonal food. Sit at a pine table, play a game or puzzle, and order ham, bubble and squeak and home-made chutney; rabbit and bacon pie; African spinach, peanut and sweet potato stew; or trout fillet with crème fraîche, horseradish and walnut sauce, washed down with a pint of Summer Lightning.

Open 11.30–3 6–11 (Sat–Sun 11.30–11) **Bar Meals** L served all week 12–2 (Sun 12–2.30) D served all week 7–9 Av main course £8 **Restaurant** L served all week 12–2 (Sun 12–2.30) D served all week 7–9 Free House Harveys Best, Timothy Taylor Landlord, Summer Lightning, Harveys Old. 🍷 7 **Facilities** Garden Dogs allowed Parking

WINCHELSEA MAP 07 TQ91

The New Inn 🍷

German St TN36 4EN ☎ 01797 226252

Elegant Winchelsea has seen much change over the centuries, not least the sea's retreat that ended its days as a thriving seaport. The 18th-century New Inn has witnessed change of a far more beneficial nature and is known today for its comfort, hospitality and excellent cuisine. Chalkboard specials include lobster tails with chips and salad, Rye Bay lemon sole, and chicken Kiev. The lovely walled garden is a delight on a sunny day.

Open 11.30am–12 **Bar Meals** L served all week 12–3 D served all week 6.30–9.30 (Sun 12–9) **Restaurant** L served all week 12–2.30 D served all week 6.30–9.30 (Sun 12–9) Greene King Morlands Original, Abbots Ale, Greene King IPA, Fosters. 🍷 10 **Facilities** Garden Dogs allowed Parking

WITHYHAM MAP 06 TQ43

Pick of the Pubs

The Dorset Arms 🍷

TN7 4BD ☎ 01892 770278 🖷 01892 770195
e-mail: pete@dorset-arms.co.uk
dir: *4m W of Tunbridge Wells on B2110 between Groombridge & Hartfield*

See Pick of the Pubs on opposite page

SUSSEX, WEST

AMBERLEY MAP 06 TQ01

Black Horse

High St BN18 9NL ☎ 01798 831552
e-mail: theblackhorse@btconnect.com

A traditional 17th-century tavern with a lively atmosphere, in a beautiful South Downs village. Look out for the display of sheep bells donated by the last shepherd to have a flock on the local hills. Food is served in the large restaurant and bar, including extensive vegetarian choice and children's menu. Lovely gardens, good local walks, and nice views of the South Downs and Wild Brookes. Dogs are welcome in the bar.

Open 11–11 (Sun 12–10.30) **Bar Meals** L served all week 12–3 D served all week 6–9 Av main course £9.45 **Restaurant** L served all week 12–3 D served 6–9 Punch Taverns Bombardier, Greene King IPA. **Facilities** Garden Dogs allowed

The Bridge Inn 🍷

Houghton Bridge BN18 9LR ☎ 01798 831619
e-mail: bridgeamberley@aol.com
dir: *5m N of Arundel on B2139. Next to Amberley station*

The Bridge Inn dates from 1650, and is Grade II listed. The following year Charles II stopped here to take ale after the Battle of Worcester, and nowadays cyclists and walkers enjoy exploring this delightful part of Sussex. Picturesque Amberley, Arundel Castle and Bignor Roman Villa are all close by.

Open 12–11 (Sun 12–10.30) **Bar Meals** L served all week 12–2.30 D served all week 6–9 (Sat 12–4, 6–9 Sun 12–8) Av main course £8.50 **Restaurant** L served all week 12–2.30 D served all week 6–9 (Sun 12–8) Av 3 course à la carte £16.50 Free House Harveys Sussex, Abbot Ale, Youngs, Timothy Taylor. 🍷 7 **Facilities** Garden Dogs allowed Parking

George & Dragon

An old smuggling inn down what is essentially a two and a half mile cul-de-sac in peaceful Burf'm (although next-door Wepham is Wep'm!). The Arun cuts through the chalk downs here, with mighty Arundel Castle guarding the gap.

The riverside and other local walks are lovely, but be ready to remove muddy footwear in the pub porch. Inside this lovely old inn are beamed ceilings and modern prints on the walls, and worn stone flags on the floor. The original old rooms have been opened out into one huge space that catches the afternoon and evening light. One alcove is hidden away up a few steps, with a couple of tables tucked away for an intimate drink or meal, and there's another nook with more tables. A small bar is accessed around a corner. It's very much a dining pub, attracting visitors from far and wide. The à la carte menu and specials board offer a good choice of dishes between them: for starters you could try prawn and crab cake on seasonal leaves; deep-fried whitebait with lemon and dill mayonnaise; or smoked chicken and duck terrine with orange chutney and melba toast; main courses might include walnut-crusted cod loin with parsnip purée and new minted potatoes; roasted duck breast with redcurrant and black cherry sauce and dauphinoise potatoes; pan-seared scallops with a lobster risotto and white wine sauce; slow-cooked lamb shank in a red wine and rosemary sauce, and favourites like battered fillet of haddock with fries. There are tables outside, ideal for whiling away an afternoon or evening in summer, listening to the cricket being played on the green a few steps away.

MAP 06 TQ00
BN18 9RR
☎ 01903 883131
dir: *Off A27 1m E of Arundel, signed Burpham, 2.5m pub on left*

Open 11–2.30 6–12 Closed: 25 Dec
Bar Meals L served all week 12–2 D served Mon–Sat 7–9 (Sun 12–2.30)
Restaurant L served all week 12–2 D served Mon–Sat 7–9 Av 3 course à la carte £25
Free House
Harvey Best, Brewery-on-Sea Spinnaker Bitter, Fuller's London Pride, King Brewery Red River.
Facilities Parking

ASHURST MAP 06 TQ11

Pick of the Pubs

The Fountain Inn 🍷

BN44 3AP ☎ 01403 710219

dir: *On B2135 N of Steyning*

This 16th-century free house is located just north of Steyning in a picturesque setting in the historic village of Ashurst. The interior features flagstone floors, low beams and a fantastic inglenook fireplace. There are two large garden areas in a delightfully tranquil setting by the large duck pond with seating for 200 people. The inn offers an extensive selection of home-made dishes to delight your taste buds, including its renowned burgers and steak and ale pies, and the regular range of well-kept real ales is supplemented by a weekly guest ale from local breweries. At lunchtime there is a choice of ploughman's, salads, freshly cut sandwiches, and Sussex smokie – smoked haddock and prawns in a cheese sauce. In the evening there is a good choice from the chargrill, notably steaks, and dishes like chicken breast with a sunblush tomato and pesto dressing. A fishy option might be sea bass, or a choice from the specials board.

Open 11.30–11 (Sun 12–10.30) **Bar Meals** L served all week 11.30–2 (Sun 12–3) D served Mon–Sat 6–9.30 Av main course £9.95 **Restaurant** L served all week 11.30–2 (Sun 12–3) D served Mon–Sat 6–9.30 Free House Harveys Sussex, Fuller's London, Adnams Broadside and Guest ales. 🍷 10 **Facilities** Garden Dogs allowed Parking

BARNHAM MAP 06 SU90

The Murrell Arms 🍷

Yapton Rd PO22 0AS ☎ 01243 553320

dir: *A27 through Arundel for 2m, left at The Oaks, follow road to end. Turn right at The Olive Branch*

Attractive white-painted inn distinguished by lavish window boxes and hanging baskets that add a wonderful splash of colour in summer. Built in 1750 as a farmhouse, it became a pub shortly after the railway station opened over 100 years later. A straightforward menu offers bacon hock, curries, belly pork with parsley sauce, bacon and onion suet pudding, and liver and bacon casserole with jacket potato. Various ales on tap.

Open 11–2.30 6–11 (Sat 11–11, Sun 12–10.30) **Bar Meals** L served all week 12–2 D served Fri–Wed 6–9 **Restaurant** L served all week D served all week Fullers Fullers London Pride, E.S.B, Butser Best, Horndean Special Brew. 🍷 28 **Facilities** Garden Dogs allowed Parking Play Area **Notes**

BURPHAM MAP 06 TQ00

Pick of the Pubs

George & Dragon

BN18 9RR ☎ 01903 883131

dir: *Off A27 1m E of Arundel, signed Burpham, 2.5m pub on left*

See Pick of the Pubs on opposite page

BURY MAP 06 TQ01

The Squire & Horse 🍷

Bury Common RH20 1NS

☎ 01798 831343 📠 01798 831343

dir: *On A29, 4m S of Pulbrough, 4m N of Arundel*

The original 16th-century building was extended a few years ago, with old wooden beams and country fireplaces throughout. All the food is freshly cooked to order. The fish specials change daily and main courses are served with a selection of vegetables. These could include barbequed barracuda fillet on a bed of prawn risotto, or calves' liver with bacon and red wine glaze. Thai food is a speciality, and the pub is renowned for its desserts.

Open 11.30–3 6–11 (Sun 12–3 6–10.30) (May–Sep Sat 11.30–11, Sun 12–10.30) **Bar Meals** L served all week 12–2 D served all week Av main course £14 **Restaurant** L served all week 12–2 D served all week 6–9 Av 3 course à la carte £20 Greene King IPA, Harveys Sussex, Guest ales. 🍷 8 **Facilities** Garden Parking

CHARLTON MAP 06 SU81

Pick of the Pubs

The Fox Goes Free 🍷

PO18 0HU ☎ 01243 811461 📠 01243 811712

e-mail: thefoxgoesfree.always@virgin.net

dir: *A286 towards Midhurst*

Once a favoured hunting lodge of William III, this 16th-century pub went on to host the first Women's Institute meeting in 1915. The lovely old brick and flint building nestles in unspoilt countryside, and with its two huge fireplaces, old pews and brick floors, it exudes charm and character. There are five places to eat:

CONTINUED

England

CHARLTON continued

the main bar, the main restaurant, the Snug, the Bakery and the Stable. Traditional favourites and classic recipes mingle on a menu of home-made food that includes starters of chicken liver parfait with apple chutney and toast; and rillette of poached and smoked salmon with soured cream. Typical main courses range from lasagne with chips and salad through to pan-fried chicken breast wrapped in Parma ham with creamed leeks and a red wine jus. There is also a good selection of real ales.

Open 11–11 (Sun 12–10.30) **Bar Meals** L served all week 12–2.30 D served all week 6.30–10 (Sat–Sun 12–10) **Restaurant** L served all week 12–2.30 D served all week 6–10 (Sat–Sun 12–10.30) Av 3 course à la carte £21 Free House Hampshire Special, Arundel Gauntlet, Ballards Best, Ringwood Special. 8 **Facilities** Garden Dogs allowed Parking **Rooms** 5 bedrooms en suite S£55 D£80 (★★★ INN)

CHICHESTER — MAP 05 SU80

Crown and Anchor

Dell Quay Rd PO20 7EE ☎ 01243 781712
e-mail: crown&anchor@thespiritgroup.com
dir: *A286 Chichester towards West Wittering, right for Dell Quay*

Nestling at the foot of the Sussex Downs with panoramic views of Chichester harbour, this unique hostelry dates in parts to the early 18th century when it also served as a custom house for the old port. It has a superb terrace for al fresco dining and enjoys a fine reputation for its fresh fish, which is delivered daily. Menu choices include fish (battered to order) and chips, grilled steaks, and steak and ale pie.

Open 11–11 (Sun 12–10.30) **Bar Meals** L served all week 12–3 D served all week 6–9 (Sun 12–9) Av main course £10 **Restaurant** L served all week 12–3 D served all week 6–9 (Sun 12–9) Av 3 course à la carte £40 Av 3 course fixed price £10 Punch Taverns Bombardier, Theakstons, & Guinness. 17 **Facilities** Children's licence Garden Dogs allowed Parking

Pick of the Pubs

Royal Oak Inn ★★★★★ INN

Pook Ln, East Lavant PO18 0AX
☎ 01243 527434 01243 775062
e-mail: nickroyaloak@aol.com
dir: *A286 from Chichester signed Midhurst, 2m then right at mini-rdbt, pub is over bridge on left*

Situated just two miles north of the Georgian streets of Chichester, this coaching inn is tucked away in a pretty Downland village within easy reach of the rolling hills of Sussex. The Royal Oak was a pub for many years, but has been exceptionally well converted to offer not only an elegant restaurant, but also stylish, sleekly furnished accommodation complete with state of the art entertainment systems. The brick-lined restaurant and bar achieve a crisp, rustic chic: details include fresh flowers, candles, and wine attractively displayed in alcoves set into the walls. The same attention to detail can be seen in the simple, contemporary menu: yellow-fin tuna loin, artichoke and sweet pepper salad; twice-cooked confit of duck leg, with red wine and puy lentil sauce; and chocolate and pistachio slice with elderflower ice cream. A lengthy wine list will be the delight of any connoisseur.

Open 12–11 Closed: 25 Dec **Bar Meals** L served all week 12–2 D served all week 6–9.30 **Restaurant** L served all week 12–2 D served all week 6–9.30 Av 3 course à la carte £25 Ballards, HSB, Sussex, Arundel. 12 **Facilities** Garden Parking **Rooms** 5 bedrooms en suite S£75 D£85

CHILGROVE — MAP 05 SU81

The Chilgrove White Horse ★★★★ RR

High St PO18 9HX ☎ 01243 535219 01243 535301
e-mail: info@whitehorsechilgrove.co.uk
dir: *On B2141 between Chichester & Petersfield*

Built in 1756, this long wisteria-covered hostelry is tucked right into the South Downs. Charmingly, owner Charles Burton worked here as a waiter in the 1970s, and vowed he would return to buy the place, a feat accomplished in 1998. The diverse menu features local and organic produce, complemented by a lengthy global wine list. Start with warm haddock tart, poached egg and hollandaise, follow it with organic fillet of beef, and finish perhaps with a raspberry soufflé.

Open 11–3 6–11 Closed: Mon **Bar Meals** L served Tue–Sun 11–3 D served Tue–Sat 6–11 Av main course £15 **Restaurant** L served Tue–Sun 11–3 D served Tue–Sat 6–11 Av 3 course à la carte £15 Free House Ballard's. 10 **Facilities** Garden Dogs allowed Parking **Rooms** 9 bedrooms en suite S£65 D£95

COMPTON MAP 05 SU71

Coach & Horses

The Square PO18 9HA ☎ 02392 631228

dir: *On B2146 S of Petersfield, to Emsworth, in centre of Compton*

The pub stands beside the square of this prettiest of downland villages. The original timber-framed 16th-century dining room and the pine-clad Victorian extension have an evocative ambience enjoyed by villagers and visitors alike. Well known locally for its rib-eye steaks with multifarious sauces, the menu also includes a good fresh fish selection. Also expect dishes such as chicken, mushroom and tarragon pie; sliced pigeon breast on tossed salad with bacon and mushrooms; salmon fishcakes; and bacon hock with mustard mash. Hearty bar snacks can accompany a good choice of real ales. There is also a skittle alley and sheltered rear garden.

Open 12-3 6-11 **Bar Meals** L served all week 12-2 D served all week 6-9 Av main course £9.95 **Restaurant** L served Tues-Sun 12-2 D served Tue-Sat 6-9 Av 3 course à la carte £40 Free House Fuller's ESB, Ballard's Best, Cheriton Diggers Gold, Dark Star Golden Gate. **Facilities** Dogs allowed **Notes**

DUNCTON MAP 06 SU91

The Cricketers

GU28 0LB ☎ 01798 342473 01799 344753

e-mail: info@thecricketersinn.com

Attractive white-painted pub situated in spectacular walking country at the western end of the South Downs. It has a delightful and very popular garden with extensive deck seating and weekend barbecues. Rumoured to be haunted, the inn has changed little over the years. Regularly changing menus feature, sometimes four a day! Look out for good hearty meals like beer-battered haddock or rib-eye steak, both with hand-cut chips. Ideal stop-off point for coach parties visiting Goodwood.

Open 11-3 6-11 (Fri-Sat all day Summer all day all wk) Rest: Sun Closed D **Bar Meals** L served all week 12-2.30 (Sun 12-3.30) D served Mon-Sat 7-9.30 Av main course £10 **Restaurant** L served all week 12-2.30 (Sun 12-3.30) D served Mon-Sat 7-9.30 Av 3 course à la carte £21 Free House Youngs Bitter, Archers Golden, Harvey Sussex, Ballards. 10 **Facilities** Garden Dogs allowed Parking Play Area

EAST ASHLING MAP 05 SU80

Horse and Groom ★★★★ INN

East Ashling PO18 9AX ☎ 01243 575339 01243 575560

e-mail: info@thehorseandgroomchichester.co.uk

web: www.thehorseandgroomchichester.com

dir: *3m from Chichester on B1278 2m off A27 at Fishbourne*

A substantially renovated 17th-century inn located at the foot of the South Downs. This is good walking country, and top tourist attractions lie within easy reach. The flagstoned and beamed bar is cosy, with a working range at one end and an open fire at the other. The underground cellar keeps ales at a constant temperature, and there are bar snack, blackboard and full à la carte menus.

Horse and Groom

Open 12-3 6-11 (Sun 12-6) **Bar Meals** L served all week 12-2.15 (Sun 12-2.30) D served Mon-Sat 6.30-9.15 Av main course £9.95 **Restaurant** L served all week 12-2.15 (Sun 12-2.30) D served Mon-Sat 6.30-9.15 Av 3 course à la carte £20 Free House Youngs, Harveys, Summer Lightning, Hop Head. 6 **Facilities** Garden Dogs allowed Parking **Rooms** 11 bedrooms en suite S£40 D£65

EAST DEAN MAP 06 SU91

Pick of the Pubs

The Star & Garter

PO18 0JG ☎ 01243 811318 01243 811826

e-mail: thestarandgarter@hotmail.com

dir: *A286 between Chichester & Midhurst. Turn off at Singleton for 2m*

East Dean is one of the county's prettiest villages, and the Star and Garter has been a pub there since 1740. There are bar snacks, of course, and the beer from the cellar comes from Ballards and other guest breweries. Seafood is the speciality, and the Shellfish Bar serves crab and lobster from Selsey as well as most other kinds of crustacea. Fish does not monopolise the menu, though. It is also possible to have the likes of grilled Buche Ruffec goats' cheese with baby beetroot; chicken breast wrapped in Parma ham with a white wine and tarragon sauce; and herb-crusted rack of lamb with rosemary jus from the daily-changing menu. Visitors to the races at nearby Goodwood will be pleased to learn that there are three attractively furnished bedrooms, one of which features a four-poster bed.

Open 11-3 (Fri 11.30-3, 5.30-11) 6-11 (Sat 11-11 Sun 12-10.30) **Bar Meals** L served all week 12-2.30 D served all week 6.30-10.30 (Sun 12-9.30) Av main course £12 **Restaurant** L served all week 12-2.30 D served all week 6.30-10.30 (Sat 12-10, Sun 12-9.30) Av 3 course à la carte £25 Free House Ballards Best, Nyewood Gold, Trotton Ale, Arundel Gauntlet & Leffe. 10 **Facilities** Garden Parking **Rooms** 3 bedrooms en suite S£40 D£60 (♦♦♦♦ GA)

Unicorn Inn

This cosy village pub dates from 1750, although it was not granted its first licence until 1839. This was the same year that the Anti-Corn Law League was formed by John Bright and Heyshott-born Richard Cobden, who might possibly have drunk here.

Set within the South Downs Area of Outstanding Natural Beauty (there's a good view of the Downs from the beautiful, south-facing rear gardens), the Unicorn is popular not just with locals, but with walkers and cyclists detouring from the South Downs Way. The bar, with beams and large log fire, is part of the original building, and very atmospheric it is too. The subtly lit, cream-painted restaurant, with matching table linen, is equally inviting. Locally sourced food is important, although some of the meats come from Smithfield, while fish arrives daily from Selsey a few miles away, and Portsmouth. Dishes available at both lunch and dinner include home-made chicken liver terrine; home-cured, home-cooked ham; pan-fried tiger prawns; traditional fish and chips; fisherman's pie; beef bourguignon and beef stroganoff; pan-fried English lamb filets with redcurrant jus; and twice-baked emmental and leek soufflé with tomato and olive dressing. Crab thermidor, and fillet of beef Wellington, may appear as specials, while the bar menu offers baguettes, and ploughman's. Three of the desserts on offer are fresh strawberries and Eton mess; pancake with banana and toffee sauce; and rich chocolate torte.

🍷
MAP 06 SU81
GU29 0DL
☎ 01730 813486
📠 01730 814896

Open 11.30–3 6.30–11 (Sun 12–4 closed Mon)
Bar Meals L served Tue–Sat 12–2 (Mon Summer, Sun 12–3) D served Mon–Sat 7–9 Av main course £8.95
Restaurant L served all week 12–2 6.30–9 (Sun 12–2.30)
Timothy Taylor Landlord, Horsham Best Bitter, Unicorn Best Bitter. 🍷 10
Facilities Garden Dogs allowed Parking

ELSTED MAP 05 SU81

Pick of the Pubs

The Three Horseshoes

GU29 0JY ☎ 01730 825746

dir: *A272 from Midhurst to Petersfield, after 2m left to Harting & Elsted, after 3m pub on left*

Tucked below the steep scarp slope of the South Downs is the peaceful village of Elsted, and this 16th-century former drovers' ale house. It's one of those quintessential English country pubs that Sussex specialises in, full of rustic charm, with unspoilt cottagey bars, worn tiled floors, low beams, latch doors, a vast inglenook, and a motley mix of furniture. On fine days the extensive rear garden, with roaming chickens and stunning southerly views, is hugely popular. Tip-top real ales, including Cheriton Pots from across the Hampshire border, are drawn from the cask, and a daily-changing blackboard menu offers good old country cooking. Main courses are likely to include steak, kidney and Murphy's pie; pheasant breast in cider with shallot and prune sauce; and in summer, crab and lobster. Excellent ploughman's are served with unusual cheeses. Puddings include treacle tart and raspberry and hazelnut meringue.

Open 11–2.30 6–11 (Sun 12–3, 7–10.30) **Bar Meals** L served all week 12–2 D served all week 7–9 (Sun 7–8.30) **Restaurant** L served all week 12–2 D served all week 7–9 Free House Flowerpots Ale, Ballard's Best, Fuller's London Pride, Timothy Taylors Landlord. **Facilities** Garden Dogs allowed Parking

FERNHURST MAP 06 SU82

Pick of the Pubs

The King's Arms

Midhurst Rd GU27 3HA

☎ 01428 652005 01428 658970

dir: *On A286 between Haslemere & Midhurst, 1m S of Fernhurst*

A Grade II-listed, 17th-century free house and restaurant set amidst rolling Sussex farmland. The pub and its outbuildings are built from Sussex stone and decorated with hanging baskets, flowering tubs, vines and creepers. The L-shaped interior is very cosy, with beams, lowish ceilings, and a large inglenook fireplace, with the bar one side and restaurant and small dining room the other. Everything is home made, from salad dressings to sorbets. Fishy offerings might be goujons of plaice with tartare sauce; monkfish loin in Parma ham with courgette ribbons, prawn and saffron sauce; or perhaps seared scallops with bacon and pea risotto. Alternatives to fish usually include Barbary duck breast with Savoy cabbage, baby roast potatoes and orange and port sauce; rack of English lamb with redcurrant and rosemary mash with lightly minted gravy; and fillet steak with dauphinoise potatoes, wild mushrooms and rich red wine jus. No food is served in the bar in the evenings. The large garden has some lovely trees, and a wisteria-clad barn is used for the pub's annual three-day beer festival at the end of August.

Open 11.30–3 5.30–11 Closed: 25 Dec **Bar Meals** L served all week 12–2.30 D served Mon–Sat 7–9.30 Av main course £12.50 **Restaurant** L served all week 12–2.30 D served Mon–Sat 7–9.30 Av 3 course à la carte £24 Free House W J King Brewery Horsham Best Bitter, Ringwood Brewery 49er, Hogsback TEA, Caledonian IPA. 10 **Facilities** Garden Dogs allowed Parking

The Red Lion

The Green GU27 3HY ☎ 01428 643112 01428 643939

dir: *Off A286 between Haslemere & Midhurst*

Built in the 16th-century, this pretty village inn is popular with walkers. Traditional features include beams and open fires, as well as well-kept gardens back and front. The varied menu of freshly cooked dishes is supplemented by blackboard specials. Typical are slow-cooked lamb shank; deep-fried Selsey cod in beer batter; and profiteroles. Seasonal guest ales accompany the likes of Fuller's ESB and London Pride.

Open 11–11.30 (Mon–Wed closed 3–5) **Bar Meals** L served all week 12–2.30 D served all week 6–9.30 **Restaurant** L served all week 12–2.30 D served all week 6–9.30 Fullers Fuller's ESB, Chiswick, London Pride, and Seasonal Guest. 8 **Facilities** Garden Dogs allowed Parking

HALNAKER MAP 06 SU90

Pick of the Pubs

The Anglesey Arms at Halnaker

PO18 0NQ ☎ 01243 773474 01243 530034

e-mail: angleseyarms@aol.com

dir: *4m E from centre of Chichester on A285 (Petworth road)*

This charmingly old-fashioned Georgian inn stands in two acres of landscaped grounds on the Goodwood estate. The famous Boxgrove archaeological site is only a mile away – home to the 500,000-year-old remains of the Boxgrove Man. There's a traditional atmosphere in the wood-floored bar with its winter fires and real ales. Ethical produce is taken seriously, and the kitchen team makes skilful use of meat from the fully traceable and organic estate herds, as well as locally-caught fish from sustainable stocks – a stipulation that even applies to the cod. Lunchtime visitors can tuck into the likes of O'Hagan's Oxford sausages with chive mash and onion gravy. After a flutter at the nearby Goodwood Races, call in for dinner. You could start with rillettes of duck and pork with pepper chutney; followed by braised lamb shank with Italian sauce and polenta. The extensive wine list features organic and biodynamic options.

Open 11–3 5.30–12 (Sat–Sun all day) **Bar Meals** L served all week 12–2.30 (Sun 12–3) D served all week 7–9.30 Av main course £8.95 **Restaurant** L served all week 12–2 (Sun 12–3) D served all week 7.30–9.30 Av 3 course à la carte £20 Punch Taverns Young's Bitter, Adnams Bitter, Hop Back Summer Lightning & Black Sheep Bitter. 10 **Facilities** Garden Dogs allowed Parking

HEYSHOTT MAP 06 SU81

Pick of the Pubs

Unicorn Inn 🍷

GU29 0DL ☎ 01730 813486 📠 01730 814896

See Pick of the Pubs on page 568

HORSHAM MAP 06 TQ13

The Black Jug 🍷

31 North St RH12 1RJ ☎ 01403 253526 📠 01403 217821

e-mail: black.jug@brunningandprice.co.uk

This busy town centre pub is close to the railway station and popular with Horsham's professional classes. Here you'll find a congenial atmosphere with friendly staff, an open fire, large conservatory and courtyard garden. Meals are freshly prepared using local ingredients wherever possible; light bites include chilli beef with cheese topping and crusty bread, whilst larger appetites might go for roasted vegetable Wellington; or pan-fried mackerel with horseradish mash.

Open 12–11 (Fri–Sat 12–12, Sun 12–10.30) **Bar Meals** L served all week 12 D served all week 10 **Restaurant** L served all week 12 D served all week 10 ⊕ Brunning & Price ◾ Weltons, Adnams Broadside, Greene King IPA & Guest Ales. 🍷 25 **Facilities** Garden Dogs allowed

Boars Head 🍷

Worthing Rd RH13 0AD ☎ 01403 254353 📠 01403 218114

e-mail: tazzrail@hotmail.com

dir: *On B2237, 1m from Horsham town centre, follow signs for Christs Hospital*

Built in 1761 as a farm, although late-Victorian additions have substantially altered the original structure. It's known locally as a friendly, traditional bar and restaurant with lots going on, from music evenings to beer festivals. Main dishes in the restaurant include grills; chicken, beef or vegetable fajitas; bangers and mash; fisherman's pie; and a weekly fish special. There's an extensive bar food menu as well. Look out for speciality food weeks, as well as a self-serve deli counter in the summer.

Open 11.30–3 5–11 (Fri–Sun all day) **Bar Meals** L served all week 12–2.30 D served Mon–Sat 6–9.30 (Sun 12–6) **Restaurant** L served all week 12–2.15 (Sun 12–4) D served all week 6.30–9 ◾ Badger, Sussex, Tanglefoot, Hofbrau. 🍷 10 **Facilities** Children's licence Garden Dogs allowed Parking

KINGSFOLD MAP 06 TQ13

The Dog and Duck

Dorking Rd RH12 3SA ☎ 01306 627295

e-mail: info@thedogandduck.fsnet.co.uk

dir: *On A24, 3m N of Horsham*

A warm, welcoming country pub on the main A24, the Dog and Duck might be small, but it has a very large garden. Children's play equipment and an ice cream bar are a hit in summer, and a golf driving range is planned. The pub has a growing reputation for its home-cooked food, and hosts many events: quizzes, darts evenings, a big beer festival and fundraising activities for St George's Hospital.

Open 12–3 6–11 (Fri–Sun & BHs 12–11) **Bar Meals** L served all week 12–2.30 (Sun 12–5) D served all week 6–9 **Restaurant** L served all week 12–2.30 (Sun 12–5) D served all week 6–9 Av 3 course à la carte £16 ⊕ Hall & Woodhouse ◾ King & Barnes Sussex, Badger Best, Guest ales. **Facilities** Garden Dogs allowed Parking

KIRDFORD MAP 06 TQ02

Pick of the Pubs

The Half Moon Inn

RH14 0LT ☎ 01403 820223 📠 01403 820224

e-mail: halfmooninn.kirdford@virgin.net

dir: *Off A272 between Billingshurst & Petworth. At Wisborough Green follow Kirdford signs*

See Pick of the Pubs on opposite page

LAMBS GREEN MAP 06 TQ23

The Lamb Inn 🍷

RH12 4RG ☎ 01293 871336 & 871933 📠 01293 871933

e-mail: ben@benbokoringram.wanadoo.co.uk

dir: *6m from Horsham between Rusper & Faygate*

Brewer W.J. King's first tenanted pub reopened in 2003 after extensive renovation. With stone flags underfoot, ancient beams overhead, and a double-sided open fire somewhere in between – yes, it's a real English pub. Everything is home made and freshly prepared. Try Cajun spiced catfish fillet with cucumber and onion salsa; or from a crammed specials board, pan-fried Barnsley chop glazed with honey, mint and grain mustard. In good weather there is plenty of seating outside.

Open 11–3 5.30–11 (Sun 12–4, 7–10.30) Closed: 25–26 Dec **Bar Meals** L served all week 12–2 (Sun 12–2.30) D served all week 7–9.30 (Sun 7–9) Av main course £8.95 ◾ WJ King & Co beers - Horsham Best Bitter, Red River, Kings Old Ale, Summer Ale. 🍷 12 **Facilities** Dogs allowed Parking

The Half Moon Inn

Officially one of the prettiest pubs in Southern England, this red-tiled 16th-century village inn is covered in climbing rose bushes, and sits directly opposite the church in this unspoilt Sussex village near the River Arun.

Although drinkers are welcome, the Half Moon is mainly a dining pub. The interior, with its low beams and log fires, has been fully redecorated. Well-presented cask ales and lagers are on offer, as well as a varied wine list featuring four house choices available by the glass. A talented young team specialises in 'British food with a twist', and there is plenty of variety. Lunch choices from the bistro menu might include starters twice-cooked blue cheese soufflé; chicken liver paté, and medalllions of lobster, followed by mains such as pan-fried venison with black pudding mash; pan-fried medallions of pork; fillet of salmon on a bed of buttered pasta; and pork and leek sausages with apple mash. Lunchtime snacks in the form of battered haddock with chips, Caesar salad, vegetarian pasta, and lamb curry with coriander rice, are also going down well. Home-made desserts take in the likes of ginger crème brûlée, rhubarb crumble and custard, and lemon tart with clotted cream, while the cheeseboard is impressive. At dinner, the menu is broadly similar, although the atmosphere changes, with candlelight, tablecloths and polished glassware. Well-tended gardens are an added draw in the summer, while for the more energetic, a pamphlet featuring local country walks is available.

MAP 06 TQ02
RH14 0LT
☎ 01403 820223
01403 820224
e-mail:
halfmooninn.kirdford@virgin.net
dir: *Off A272 between Billingshurst & Petworth. At Wisborough Green follow Kirdford signs*

Open 11–3 6–11 Closed: Sun eve
Bar Meals L served all week 12–2.30 D served Mon–Sat 6–9.30 Av main course £10
Restaurant L served all week 12–2.30 D served Mon–Sat 6–9.30
Laurel Pub Partnerships
Fuller's London Pride.
Facilities Garden Parking Play Area

England

LICKFOLD MAP 06 SU92

Pick of the Pubs

The Lickfold Inn

GU28 9EY ☎ 01798 861285
e-mail: thelickfoldinn@aol.com
dir: *From A3 take A283, through Chiddingfold, 2m on right signed 'Lurgashall Winery', pub in 1m*

See Pick of the Pubs on opposite page

LODSWORTH MAP 06 SU92

Pick of the Pubs

The Halfway Bridge Inn

Halfway Bridge GU28 9BP ☎ 01798 861281
e-mail: enquiries@halfwaybridge.co.uk
dir: *Between Petworth & Midhurst, next to Cowdray Estate & Golf Club on A272*

See Pick of the Pubs on page 574

Pick of the Pubs

The Hollist Arms

The Street GU28 9BZ ☎ 01798 861310
e-mail: george@thehollistarms.co.uk
dir: *1m N of A272, adjacent to Country Park*

A 15th-century building, roaring open fires, leather sofas and no fruit machines – the Hollist Arms, a pub since 1823, is as traditional as you could wish for. You'll probably need to book to enjoy dishes such as tiger prawns and leek gratin with fresh bread; home-made steak, Guinness and mushroom pie; or hoi sin duck in soy sauce with ginger, mushrooms and spring onions. Bar snacks range from toasties or sausages and mash.

Open 11–3 6–12 **Bar Meals** L served all week 12–2 (Sun 12–2.30) D served all week 7–9 Av main course £11 **Restaurant** L served all week 12–2 D served all week 7–9 Free House Youngs, Timothy Taylors Landlord, Horsham Best. 7 **Facilities** Children's licence Garden Dogs allowed Parking

LURGASHALL MAP 06 SU9

The Noah's Ark

The Green GU28 9ET ☎ 01428 707346 01428 707742
e-mail: amy@noahsarkinn.co.uk
dir: *Off A283 N of Petworth*

Thanks to its new owners – young and full of enthusiasm – the pub has undergone a sympathetic refurbishment, which maintains both modern standards and the charming character of the 16th-century village pub. Foodwise the focus is on fresh local produce sourced from butchers, greengrocers and other suppliers in West Sussex, and the menus are going down very well with the clientele. The place gets particularly busy in summer when there are cricket matches right outside the pub.

Open 11–3.30 6–11 (Fri–Sat 11–11.30, Sun 12–4, all day Summer) **Bar Meals** L served Mon–Sat 12–2.30 D served Mon–Sat 7–9.30 Av main course £11.50 **Restaurant** L served all week 12–2.30 D served all week 7–9.30 Av 3 course à la carte £23 Greene King Greene King IPA, Abbot & Guest Ale. 8 **Facilities** Children's licence Garden Dogs allowed Parking Play Area

MAPLEHURST MAP 06 TQ1

The White Horse

Park Ln RH13 6LL ☎ 01403 891208
dir: *5m SE of Horsham, between A281& A272*

In the tiny Sussex hamlet of Maplehurst, this traditional pub offers a break from modern life: no music, no fruit machines, no cigarette machines, just hearty, home-cooked pub food and an enticing range of ales. Sip Harvey's Best, Welton's Pride & Joy, or Dark Star Espresso Stout in the bar or whilst admiring the rolling countryside from the quiet, south-facing garden. Village-brewed cider is a speciality.

Open 12–2.30 6–11 (Sun 12–3, 7–10.30) **Bar Meals** L served Tue–Sun 12–2 (Sun 12–2.30, 7–9) D served Tue–Sun 6–9 Free House Harvey's Best, Welton's Pride & Joy, Dark Star Espresso Stout, King's Red River. **Facilities** Children's licence Garden Dogs allowed Parking Play Area **Notes**

The Lickfold Inn

'illages everywhere are losing their shop, post office and bus service, but heaven forbid that 'ie local pub should close. The hamlet of Lickfold may not have a shop or post office, but a bus ccasionally turns up, and it does have this delightful free house, dating back to 1460.

urthermore, it's thriving, in the ıpable hands of James and Andrea 'ickey. Period features include an ıcient timber frame containing tractive herringbone-patterned ricks, and a huge central chimney. ıside are two restaurant areas with ak beamed ceilings, and a cosy ar dominated by a large inglenook replace with a spit – the reason r the chimney's size – Georgian ttles, more beams and moulded anelling. Look for the recurring ırlic motif, which picks up on e village's Anglo-Saxon name, eac fauld', meaning an enclosure here garlic grows. The pub is eavily food oriented, offering asonal dishes cooked to order, omplemented by a choice of well-ept real ales and a comprehensive lection of wines. Start lunch or dinner with hot smoked Barbary duck with a truffled celeriac; or home-cured salmon with potato bread, pickled cucumber and a dill mascarpone. Typical main courses include seafood linguini; oven-baked Barbary duck with braised savoy cabbage and a broccoli purée, finished with braised a port and thyme jus; and tart of vine tomato and pesto. To finish, try classic bittersweet lemon tart with raspberry coulis. The menu changes every 10 to 12 weeks to take advantage of seasonal availability. The large courtyard and rambling terraced gardens are suitable for outdoor eating.

MAP 06 SU92
GU28 9EY
☎ 01798 861285
e-mail: thelickfoldinn@aol.com
dir: *From A3 take A283, through Chiddingfold, 2m on right signed 'Lurgashall Winery', pub in 1m*

Open 11–3.30 6–11.30 (BH Mon 12–2.30) Closed: 25–26 Dec
Bar Meals L served Tue–Sun 12–2.30 D served Tue–Sat 7–9.30 Av main course £10.75
Restaurant L served Tue–Sun 12–2.30 D served Tue–Sat 7–9.30 Av 3 course à la carte £26
Free House
Harveys Best Bitter, Youngs, 49er, Hogsback TEA. 12
Facilities Children's licence Garden Dogs allowed Parking

The Halfway Bridge Inn

This charming 17th-century brick-and-flint coaching inn stands in lovely countryside midway between Midhurst and Petworth, making it ideal for antique hunters drawn to Petworth's fabled shops, as well as the polo crowd heading for nearby Cowdray Park.

Locally it is very popular, not least because the new owners, Paul and Sue Carter, have made the inn an attractive destination for diners. Winter cosiness is guaranteed: the inn boasts two open fires, while in summer the sheltered patio and lawn come into their own. An intimate and casual atmosphere pervades the numerous dining rooms, where the emphasis is on local produce along with fresh meats, fish and vegetables from the London markets. Daily specials are chalked up on the blackboards, and the lunchtime bar menu includes the likes of seafood bisque, roast beef and horseradish sandwiches, and a choice of appetizer from the main menu. These include herb-crusted sardines with garlic focaccia; ricotta gnocchi with creamed peas and leeks; and seared foie gras on a sweetcorn pancake. Typical main courses are roast quail stuffed with chicken and wild mushroom mousse; West Sussex rack of lamb with redcurrant mint jus; fresh trout fillets with parsnip and horseradish purée; and home-made steak and kidney suet pudding with creamed potatoes. For dessert, perhaps baked rice pudding and butterscotch sauce; strawberry and raspberry mille feuille with blueberry coulis; or a baked mini camembert with home-made sultana and almond bread.

🍷
MAP 06 SU92
Halfway Bridge GU28 9BP
☎ 01798 861281
e-mail:
enquiries@halfwaybridge.co.uk
dir: *Between Petworth & Midhurst, next to Cowdray Estate & Golf Club on A272*

Open 11–11 Closed: 25 Dec
Bar Meals L served all week 12–2.30 D served all week 6.30–9.15 (Sun 12–2.30, 6.30–8.30)
Restaurant L served all week 12–2.30 D served all week 6.30–9.15 (Sun 12–2.30, 6.30–8.30) Av 3 course à la carte £25
Free House
Skinners Betty Stogs, Ballards Best Bitter, Ringwood Best Bitter.
🍷 14
Facilities Garden Dogs allowed Parking

ɪIDHURST MAP 06 SU82

ʼhe Angel Hotel

orth St GU29 9DN ☎ 01730 812421 01730 815928

ı imposing and well-proportioned, late-Georgian façade hides the ɹe Tudor origins of this former coaching inn. Its frontage overlooks e town's main street, while at the rear attractive gardens give way to eadowland and the ruins of Cowdray Castle. Bright yellow paintwork ı local cottages means they are Cowdray Estate-owned. Gabriel's the main restaurant, or try The Halo Bar where dishes range from acks and pasta to sizzlers and steaks, with additional specials.

ɔen 11–11 **Bar Meals** L served all week 12–2.30 D served all ɜek 6–9.30 Av main course £8 Free House HSB & Best. 6 **cilities** Children's licence Garden Dogs allowed Parking

ɪUTHURST MAP 06 TQ12

Pick of the Pubs

Black Horse Inn

Nuthurst St RH13 6LH

☎ 01403 891272 01403 891272

e-mail: clive.henwood@btinternet.com

dir: *4m S of Horsham, off A281 & A24.*

Built of clay tiles and mellow brick, this one-time smugglers' hideout is still appropriately secluded in a quiet backwater. It is a lovely old building, half masked by impressive window boxes in summer, forming part of what was originally a row of workers' cottages on the Sedgwick Park estate. The building was first recorded as an inn in 1817, and plenty of its history remains. Inside you'll find stone-flagged floors, an inglenook fireplace and an exposed wattle and daub wall. The place is spotlessly maintained with a warm and cosy atmosphere that's perfect for dining or just enjoying a drink. The pub has a reputation for good beers, including Harvey's, London Pride, Timothy Taylor Landlord and numerous guest beers. On sunny days, visitors can sit out on the terraces at the front and rear, or take their drinks across the stone bridge over a stream into the delightful back garden.

Open 12–3 6–11 (Sat–Sun, BH's all day) **Bar Meals** L served all week 12–2.30 D served all week 6–9.30 (wknds & BH's all day) **Restaurant** L served all week 12–2.30 D served all week 6–9.30 (wknds & BH's all day) Free House Harveys Sussex, W J King, Timothy Taylor Landlord, London Pride and Guest ales. 7 **Facilities** Children's licence Garden Dogs allowed Parking

OVING MAP 06 SU90

The Gribble Inn

PO20 2BP ☎ 01243 786893 01243 788841

e-mail: dave@thegribble.co.uk

dir: *From A27 take A259. After 1m left at rdbt, 1st right to Oving, 1st left in village*

Named after local schoolmistress Rose Gribble, the inn retains all of its 16th-century charm. Large open fireplaces, wood burners and low beams set the tone. There's no background music at this peaceful hideaway, which is the ideal spot to enjoy any of the half dozen real ales from the on-site micro-brewery. Liver and bacon; spinach lasagne with red peppers; and special fish dishes are all prepared and cooked on the premises.

Open 11–3 5.30–11 (Sat 11–11, Sun 12–10.30) **Bar Meals** L served all week 12–2.30 D served all week 6–9.30 Av main course £8.95 **Restaurant** L served all week 12–2.30 D served all week 6–9.30 Woodhouse Inns Gribble Ale, Reg's Tipple, Fursty Ferret, Badger First Gold & Pigs Ear. 10 **Facilities** Garden Dogs allowed Parking

PARTRIDGE GREEN MAP 06 TQ11

Pick of the Pubs

The Green Man Inn and Restaurant

Church Rd RH13 8JT ☎ 01403 710250 01403 713212

e-mail: info@thegreenman.org

dir: *Between A24 & A281, S of A272. Pub on B2135*

A stylish and attractive gastropub with a pretty garden, and decorated in a clean-looking, unfussy way that accentuates the late-Victorian interior. Seasonal menus with daily specials use only fresh, mostly locally sourced, ingredients. Examples of the range are pan-roasted breast of Barbary duckling with sweet

CONTINUED

England

PARTRIDGE GREEN continued

potato purée; pan-fried calves' liver with streaky bacon and bubble and squeak; supreme of salmon with red pepper and courgette linguine; and cheese and sage croquettes with creamed caraway Savoy cabbage. From the specials board come monkfish fillet with Chinese spices; smoked haddock with Welsh rarebit; and chateaubriand with béarnaise sauce. Tapas, bar snacks, light meals and sandwiches are also available at lunchtime. A short list of puddings could well feature crème brûlée, and pears and blackberries poached in red wine. Seating in the restaurant is supplemented by al fresco dining on the terrace.

Open 11.30–3.30 6.30–12 **Bar Meals** L served Tues-Sun 12–2.15 D served Tues-Sat Av main course £12 **Restaurant** L served Tues-Sun 12–2.15 (Sun 12–2.30) D served Tues-Sat 7–9.30 Av 3 course à la carte £25 Harveys Sussex Best, Guinness. **Facilities** Children's licence Garden Dogs allowed Parking

PETWORTH MAP 06 SU92

The Black Horse

Byworth GU28 0HL ☎ 01798 342424 01798 342868

e-mail: blackhorsebyworth@btconnect.com

dir: *A285 from Petworth town centre 2m, turn right signed for Byworth, 50yds on right*

Flagstone floors, scrubbed wooden tables and open fires set the scene at this 16th-century free house, once part of the old tanneries. The former kitchen has been transformed into a snug dining area complete with original Aga, whilst the large sloping garden offers views to the South Downs. Expect a range of home-made fresh pizza, light bites and daily specials; main meals include hand-made Thai fishcakes; and lamb shoulder in mint gravy.

Open 11.30–11 (Sun 12–10.30) **Bar Meals** L served all week 12–9 D served all week Av main course £8.95 **Restaurant** L served all week 12–9 D served all week 12–9 (Fri–Sat 12–9.30) Av 3 course à la carte £17.50 Arundel Gold, Youngs Bitter, Hogs Back Brew, London Pride. **Facilities** Garden Dogs allowed Parking

POYNINGS MAP 06 TQ21

Pick of the Pubs

Royal Oak Inn

The Street BN45 7AQ

☎ 01273 857389 01273 857202

e-mail: ropoynings@aol.com

dir: *Brighton A281 (signed for Henfield & Poynings), then signs into Poynings*

See Pick of the Pubs on opposite page

ROWHOOK MAP 06 TQ1

Neals Restaurant at The Chequers Inn

RH12 3PY ☎ 01403 790480 01403 790480

e-mail: thechequers1@aol.com

dir: *Off A29 NW of Horsham*

A 15th-century building of great character with original beams, flagstones and open fires. The landlord is a member of the Master Chefs of Great Britain, and emphasises fresh produce, locally-sourced where possible. Expect aromatic duck confit with mustard mash and red wine jus; local pheasant with honey-roasted vegetables, pancetta and thyme jus; and Thai fish cakes on pak choi. Tempting puddings include brioche and apricot butter pudding.

Open 11.30–3.30 6–11.30 **Bar Meals** L served all week 12–2 D served Mon–Sat 7–9.30 (Sun 12–2.30) Av main course £13.95 **Restaurant** L served all week 12–2 D served Mon–Sat 7–9.30 (Sun 12–2.30) Av 3 course à la carte £30 Av 3 course fixed price £27.50 Punch Taverns Harvey's Sussex Ale, Young's, Fuller's London Pride, plus Guest ale. 7 **Facilities** Garden Dogs allowed Parking

RUDGWICK MAP 06 TQ0

The Fox Inn

Guildford Rd, Bucks Green RH12 3JP

☎ 01403 822386 01403 823950

e-mail: seafood@foxinn.co.uk

dir: *On A281 midway between Horsham & Guildford*

'Famous for Fish!' is the claim of this attractive 16th-century inn, a message borne out by the extensive menu. Food offered includes all-day breakfast and afternoon tea, while the bar menu focuses on seafood, from fish and chips to the huge fruits de mer platter. Dishes include Foxy's famous fish pie; roasted cod loin with chorizo; and hand-made Cumberland sausage on stilton mash. A horse is apparently walked through the pub each Christmas day!

Open 11–11 **Bar Meals** L served all week 12–10 D served all week 12–10 **Restaurant** L served all week 12–10 D served all week 12–10 Av 3 course à la carte £25.28 Hall & Woodhouse King & Barnes Sussex, Badger Tanglefoot, Fursty Ferret. 8 **Facilities** Garden Dogs allowed Parking Play Area

SHIPLEY MAP 06 TQ1

Pick of the Pubs

The Countryman Inn

Countryman Ln RH13 8PZ

☎ 01403 741383 01403 741115

e-mail: countrymaninn@btopenworld.com

dir: *From A272 at Coulham into Smithers Hill Lane. 1m to junct with Countryman Lane*

See Pick of the Pubs on page 578

Royal Oak Inn

Tucked away in a fold of the South Downs below the Devil's Dyke, the recently refurbished Royal Oak was built as a small hotel in the 1880s. From the eye-catching window blinds and cream-painted exterior to the roaring winter fires within, this is a destination gastro-pub that's well worth seeking out.

Solid oak floors and old beams hung with hop bines blend effortlessly with contemporary décor and comfy sofas. It's been a free house under the ownership of Paul Day and Lewis Robinson for over a decade, and the relaxed and friendly atmosphere is due in no small part to their strong emphasis on team-building and staff training; the pub won 'Investor in People' status in 2005, and the plaque is proudly displayed at the entrance. In the bar Sussex-bred Harveys real ales rub shoulders with offerings from Greene King and Morland, and a decent wine list includes a red and a white from a Sussex vineyard; at least a dozen wines are served by the glass. Head chef David Wharton has led the busy kitchen team since 2001, and combines local and seasonal produce with sometimes ambitious international twists. Starters and light meals include sandwiches and ciabattas, or more elaborate preparations such as goats' cheese stuffed with basil and sun-blush tomatoes on a warm chick pea and capsicum salad. For the main course you may find pan-fried milk-fed calves' liver with pancetta and black pudding, roasted leek and mustard mash and a red wine jus. Puddings are ordered at the bar – chocolate and Amaretto terrine, and warm rhubarb and honey crumble are two examples; or choose, perhaps, a plate of fine local and English cheeses. In summer, the attractive garden with splendid views is the backdrop for award-winning barbecues. The place is popular with walkers, and dogs on leads are welcome.

MAP 06 TQ21
The Street BN45 7AQ
☎ 01273 857389
01273 857202
e-mail: ropoynings@aol.com
dir: *Brighton A281 (signed for Henfield & Poynings), then signs into Poynings*

Open 11–11 (Sun 12–10.30)
Bar Meals L served all week 12–9.30 D served all week 12–9.30 Av main course £11
Free House
Harveys Sussex, Abbot Ale, Greene King Morland Old Speckled Hen. 12
Facilities Garden Dogs allowed Parking Play Area

SHIPLEY-SUSSEX, WEST

The Countryman Inn

A rural hostelry in the traditional style, The Countryman is set in open countryside close to the small village of Shipley, surrounded by 3,500 acres of farmland owned by the Knepp Castle Estate.

The estate is in the process of being turned back into a more natural state, with the introduction of fallow deer, free roaming Tamworth pigs, Exmoor ponies and longhorn cattle. Many wild birds have also been encouraged to return to the area, as the new growth of wild grasses and plant life provide a welcoming habitat. You can even do a bit of bird spotting from the inn's garden in fine weather. Inside you'll find warming log fires, and cask conditioned Harvey's and Brakspear ales in the cosy bar, together with over 30 wines from around the world. Free-range meat and vegetables from local farms make their appearance on the menu alongside fresh fish from Shoreham and Newhaven and local game in season. Menus are frequently changing, but some popular dishes include Auntie Betty's lamb stew with fillet of lamb; monkfish thermidor; and mushroom ravioli with four cheese sauce. These might be preceded by Tuscan bean soup, home-made chicken liver pâté, or scallop and noodle salad. Shipley's historic eight-sided smock mill is worth a visit, and is just a mile's walk along a woodland bridle path from The Countryman. The mill is so called because of its likeness to the farm labourer's traditional cotton smock.

MAP 06 TQ12
Countryman Ln RH13 8PZ
☎ 01403 741383
01403 741115
e-mail: countrymaninn@btopenworld.com
dir: *From A272 at Coulham into Smithers Hill Lane. 1m to junct with Countryman Lane*

Open 11–3 6.30–11
Bar Meals L served all week 12–3 D served all week 7–9.30 Av main course £10
Restaurant L served all week 12–2.30 D served all week 7–9.30 Av 3 course à la carte £22
Harverys, Kings, Brakspear, Lowenbrau. 20
Facilities Garden Parking

SHIPLEY continued

George & Dragon

Dragons Green RH13 7JE ☎ 01403 741320

dir: *Signed from A272 between Coolham & A24*

A 17th-century, tile-hung cottage that provides welcome peace and quiet, especially on balmy summer evenings when the peaceful garden is a welcome retreat. Its interior is all head-banging beams and character inglenook fireplaces where a pint of Badger or Tanglefoot will not come amiss. The food is home made using fresh vegetables and 'real' chips and offers dishes such as roasts of lamb and crispy coated chicken breast with sweet-and-sour sauce. Shipley is famous for its smock mill.

Open 12-3 6-11 (Sat-Sun, BHs & summer all day) **Bar Meals** L served all week 12-2 (Sun 12-2.30) D served Mon-Sat 6.30-9 Av main course £8.50 **Restaurant** L served all week 12-2 6.30-9 Hall & Woodhouse Badger Best, Sussex Best, Firsty Ferret, Guest beer. **Facilities** Garden Dogs allowed Parking

SINGLETON MAP 05 SU81

The Partridge Inn

PO18 0EY ☎ 01243 811251 0870 804 4566

dir: *Telephone for directions*

The building probably dates from the 16th century, when it would have been part of a huge hunting park owned by the Fitzalan family, Earls of Arundel. Today, it is popular with walkers enjoying the rolling Sussex countryside and visitors to Goodwood for motor and horse-racing. A menu of typical pub fare includes liver and bacon, steak and ale pie, Goodwood gammon, salmon fishcakes, fish and chips, and home-made puddings. Formerly the Fox and Hounds.

Open 11.30-3 6-11 (Sat-Sun 11-11) **Bar Meals** L served all week 12-2 D served all week 6.30-9 (Sat-Sun 12-9) Av main course £9.50 **Restaurant** L served all week 12-2 D served all week 6.30-9 Enterprise Inns Gales Best, London Pride, Ringwood Best Bitter, Hopworths Sussex. **Facilities** Garden Dogs allowed Parking

SLINDON MAP 06 SU90

The Spur

BN18 0NE ☎ 01243 814216 01243 814707

dir: *Off A27 on A29 outside village of Slindon*

Nestling on top of the South Downs, just outside the village of Slindon, sits this 17th-century pub. Inside are an open plan bar and restaurant, warmed by log fires that create a friendly atmosphere. If you book in advance you can use the skittle alley, or enjoy a game of pool.

Open 11-3 6-11 **Bar Meals** L served all week 12-2 D served all week 7-9.30 (Sun-Tue 7-9) Av main course £10.95 **Restaurant** L served all week 12-2 D served all week 7-9.30 (Sun-Tues 7-9) Av 3 course à la carte £25 Free House Abbott, Greene King IPA, Courage Directors. 7 **Facilities** Garden Dogs allowed Parking

SOUTH HARTING MAP 05 SU71

The Ship Inn

GU31 5PZ ☎ 01730 825302

dir: *From Petersfield take B2146 towards Chichester*

17th-century inn made from a ship's timbers, hence the name. Home-made pies are a feature, and other popular dishes include fish pie, mussel chowder, calves' liver, rack of lamb, ham and asparagus mornay, and hot beef Hungarian goulash. A range of vegetarian dishes and bar snacks is also available.

Open 11-11 **Bar Meals** 12-2.30 D served Mon-Sat 7-9 **Restaurant** L served Mon-Sat 12-2.30 7-9.30 Free House Palmer IPA, Darkstar Brewery Hophead, Ballards Wassail & Palmers Copper Ale. **Facilities** Garden Dogs allowed Parking

STEDHAM MAP 05 SU82

Hamilton Arms/Nava Thai Restaurant

Hamilton Arms School Ln GU29 0NZ

☎ 01730 812555 01730 817459

e-mail: hamiltonarms@hotmail.com

web: www.thehamiltonarms.co.uk

dir: *Off A272 between Midhurst & Petersfield*

Colourful parasols on the front patio spill over onto the common opposite at this popular free house in a picturesque village setting. The pub is renowned for its authentic Thai cuisine, offered from a huge menu of soups, curries, salads and speciality meat, seafood and vegetarian dishes, also available to takeaway. Oriental beers, too, are served alongside local real ales. The pub has set up a charitable trust to help prevent child prostitution in Thailand.

Open 11-3 6-11 (Sun 12-4, 7-11, Fri-Sat 11-12) **Bar Meals** L served Tue-Sun 12-2.30 D served Tue-Sat 6-10.30 (Sun 7-9.30) Av main course £8 **Restaurant** L served Tue-Sun 12-2.30 D served Tue-Sat 6-10.30 (Sun 7-9.30) Av 3 course à la carte £20 Av 4 course fixed price £19.50 Free House Ballard's Best, Fuller's London Pride, Everards Tiger Best, HSB. 8 **Facilities** Garden Dogs allowed Parking Play Area

England

STEYNING MAP 06 TQ11

The White Horse Inn

23 High St BN44 3YE ☎ 01903 812347 01903 814084
e-mail: TheWhiteHorseInn@vwood.wanadoo.co.uk
dir: *9m NW of Brighton*

A 17th-century inn prominently positioned in a pretty village a mile from the South Downs Way. The main part of the inn burned down in 1949 (the night the fire brigade held their annual supper here!) and was re-housed in the kitchen, stables and coach house. Food is served in the bar or Woods restaurant.

Open 11–2.30 5.30–11 (Sun 12–3) Closed Sun eve **Bar Meals** L served all week 12–2.15 (Sun 12–3) D served Mon–Sat 6.30–9.15 Av main course £8 **Restaurant** L served all week 12–2.15 D served Mon–Sat 6.30–9.15 (Sun 12–3) Av 3 course à la carte £16 Av 3 course fixed price £15.90 Greene King IPA, Abbott Ale, Old Speckled Hen. 8 **Facilities** Children's licence Garden Parking

TROTTON MAP 05 SU82

Pick of the Pubs

The Keepers Arms NEW

GU31 5ER ☎ 01730 813724
e-mail: enquiries@keepersarms.co.uk
dir: *5m from Petersfield on A272, on right after narrow bridge*

The setting of this 17th-century free house is more than matched by the charm of the interior. Nestling amidst spectacular countryside, the inn backs onto Terwick Common, an area of outstanding natural beauty. A roaring fire keeps the place warm as toast for winter walkers, with battered sofas arranged invitingly by the hearth. The beamed dining room is also a treat, with solid oak floors, masses of candles and a woodburner. Food is taken seriously here, with real efforts made to source local and seasonal produce. Start with a warm salad of wood pigeon and black pudding; followed by chump of lamb with fondant potatoes and aubergine caviar; or seared sea bass, ratatouille and goats' cheese fritter. Hot chocolate fondant and pistachio ice cream could round things off, while a global wine list in matched by a thoughtful selection of real ales and ciders from the surrounding counties.

Open 12–3 6–11 (Sun 11.30–5, 7–10.30) **Bar Meals** L served all week 12–2 D served all week 7–10 (Sun 11.30–4.30) Av main course £14 **Restaurant** L served all week 12–2 D served Mon–Sat 7–10 (Sun 11.30–4.30) Av 3 course à la carte £27 Free House Dark Star Hophead, Ringwood Best, Ballards Best, Ringwood 49'er & Triple fff Moondance. 8 **Facilities** Children's licence Garden Dogs allowed Parking

WALDERTON MAP 05 SU71

The Barley Mow

PO18 9ED ☎ 023 9263 1321 023 9263 1403
e-mail: mowbarley@aol.co.uk
dir: *B2146 from Chichester towards Petersfield. Right signed Walderton, 100yds on left*

A pretty, ivy-clad, 18th-century pub in the rolling Sussex Downs, famous locally for its skittle alley, and used by the local Home Guard as its HQ in World War II. A value-for-money menu offers succulent chargrilled steaks; home-made meat pies and burgers; trout, tuna and jumbo cod; and vegetarian hot bake. Less filling options include ploughman's and sandwiches. The secluded, stream-bordered garden is a real sun-trap – perfect for a pint of Ringwood Old Thumper.

Open 11–3 6–11.30 (Sun 12–3, 6–10.30) **Bar Meals** L served all week 12–2 (Sun 12–2.30) D served all week 6–9.30 **Restaurant** L served all week 12–2.15 (Sun 12–2.30) D served all week 6–9.30 Free House Ringwood Old Thumper & Fortyniner, Fuller's London Pride, Itchen Valley Godfathers, Scottish Courage John Smith's & Brakspear. 8 **Facilities** Garden Dogs allowed Parking

WARNHAM MAP 06 TQ13

The Greets Inn

47 Friday St RH12 3QY ☎ 01403 265047 01403 265047
dir: *Off A24 N of Horsham*

A fine Sussex hall house dating from about 1350 and built for Elias Greet, a local merchant. A magnificent inglenook fireplace and low beams will be discovered in the flagstone-floored bar. There is a rambling series of dining areas where diners can sample the wares of the kitchen team. Look out for some good pasta and fish dishes.

Open 11–2.30 6–11 (Sun 12–2, 7–10.30) **Bar Meals** L served all week 12–2 D served all week 7–9.30 **Restaurant** L served all week 12–2 D served all week 7–9.30 Laurel Pub Partnerships Interbrew, Greene King IPA, Fuller's London Pride, Abbot Ale. **Facilities** Garden Dogs allowed Parking

WARNINGLID MAP 06 TQ22

The Half Moon

The Street RH17 5TR ☎ 01444 461227
e-mail: Info@thehalfmoonwarninglid.co.uk
dir: *1m from Warninglid/Cuckfield junct of A23*

Improvements by dedicated owners and staff continue at the Half Moon, while the 19th-century pub's natural character is carefully retained. The food-led business is growing all the time offering a good choice of dishes, with specials such as belly pork with shallot and sage jus, and whole grilled sea bass with dill and cucumber sauce. Intriguing puddings include coconut battered pineapple fritter served with toffee sauce, and almond brittle parfait with espresso shot.

Open 11.30–2.30 5.30–11 (Sun all day) **Bar Meals** L served all week 12–2 (Sun 12–4) D served Mon–Sat 6–9.30 Free House Harveys Sussex, Black Sheep, Spitfire, Wadworth 6X. 8 **Facilities** Garden Dogs allowed Parking

England

VINEHAM MAP 06 TQ22

The Royal Oak

N5 9AY ☎ 01444 881252 01444 881530

ir: *Wineham Lane runs between A272 (Cowfold-Bolney) & 2116 (Hurst-Henfield)*

fter dispensing ale for more than two centuries, this delightful 4th-century half-timbered cottage still retains its traditional, unspoilt naracter. Under the same management for over 30 years, it's a ue rural alehouse – so expect traditional, rustic furnishings, real ale raight from the cask and a limited menu of home-made soup, decent andwiches and ploughman's. Outside, the extensive gardens are ideal or summer drinking.

pen 11–2.30 5.30–11 (Sun 12–3, 7–10.30) **Bar Meals** L served all week –2.30 Punch Taverns Harveys Sussex Best Bitter. **Facilities** Garden ogs allowed Parking **Notes**

VISBOROUGH GREEN MAP 06 TQ02

Cricketers Arms

oxwood Rd RH14 0DG ☎ 01403 700369

-mail: craig@cricketersarms.com

ir: *On A272 between Billingshurst & Petworth. Turn at junct next village green, 100yds on right*

traditional village pub dating from the 16th century with oak beams, ooden floors and open fires. Fans of extreme sports should be aware at the Cricketers is the home of the British Lawn Mower Racing ssociation. A full bar menu ranges from snacks to three course meals nd Sunday roasts, with a large selection of specials. Typical dishes clude steak pie, sea bass in a prawn and oyster sauce, game dishes in eason, and 'mega' salads.

pen 12–11 **Bar Meals** L served all week 12–2 D served all week 30–9.30 (Thu–Sun 6.30–9) **Restaurant** L served all week 12–2 D served l week 6.30–9.30 (Thu–Sun 6.30–9) Enterprise Inns Adnams, arveys Sussex, Fullers London Pride. 34 **Facilities** Garden Dogs lowed Parking

TYNE & WEAR

NEWCASTLE UPON TYNE MAP 21 NZ26

Shiremoor House Farm

Middle Engine Ln, New York NE29 8DZ

☎ 0191 257 6302 0191 257 8602

swift pint of Jarrow River Catcher in New York? Since that's the name the village, it's eminently feasible at this popular North Tyneside ub, brilliantly converted from an old farm. Particularly appealing is the azed former granary where a wide range of traditional pub food is erved, including steak, ale and mushroom casserole; fillet of salmon ith prawn and dill sauce; and sizzling strips of chicken with sweet nilli sauce.

Shiremoor House Farm

Open 11–11 **Bar Meals** L served all week 12 D served all week 10 Free House Timothy Taylor's Landlord, Mordue Workie Ticket, Theakston BB, John Smiths. 12 **Facilities** Children's licence Garden Parking

NORTH SHIELDS MAP 11 NZ36

Magnesia Bank

1 Camden St NE30 1NH

☎ 0191 257 4831 0191 258 6847

e-mail: info@magnesiabank.com

dir: *2m E of Tyne Tunnel (N entrance)*

Set high up on the banks of the River Tyne above North Shields fish quay is this lively pub located in a converted bank. Its reputation for real ales is based on a local micro brewery's produce, with seven cask ales always on tap. The menu takes in starters of grilled field mushrooms topped with houmous, garlic and chilli tapenade, and mains of fish pie with salad and crusty bread. Several themed evenings are a special feature here.

Open 11–11.30 (Fri 11–12, Sat 10–12, Sun 11–11) **Bar Meals** L served all week 11–9.45 D served all week 11–9.45 (Sun 11.30–8.45) Av main course £10 **Restaurant** L served all week 12–9.45 D served all week 12–9.45 (Sun 11.30–8.45) Av 3 course à la carte £18.50 Free House Durham Brewery Magus, Mordue Brewery Workie Ticket, Black Sheep Bitter, Mordue 5 Bridges. 7 **Facilities** Children's licence

TYNEMOUTH MAP 21 NZ36

Copperfields ★★★ HL

Grand Hotel, Hotspur St NE30 4ER

☎ 0191 293 6666 0191 293 6665

e-mail: info@grandhotel-uk.com

dir: *On NE coast, 10m from Newcastle upon Tyne*

Copperfields bar is part of the Grand Hotel at Tynemouth, and is set on a cliff top commanding some of the most stunning views of natural coastline in the country. It was a frequent haunt of local boy Stan Laurel of Laurel and Hardy fame. Traditional home-cooked meals served in the bar include North Shields cod and chips, steak and mushroom pie and popular roast dinners.

Open 12–11 (Sun 12–10.30) **Bar Meals** L served all week 12–3 D served all week 3–8 **Restaurant** L served all week 12–3 D served Mon–Sat 6.30–9.45 Durham Magus, Bass '9', London Pride, Black Sheep. **Facilities** Children's licence Parking **Rooms** 44 bedrooms en suite S£65 D£75

WHITLEY BAY MAP 21 NZ37

The Waterford Arms

Collywell Bay Rd, Seaton Sluice NE26 4QZ

☎ 0191 237 0450 📠 0191 237 7760

dir: *A19 at Seaton Burn, signs for A190 to Seaton Sluice*

The building dates back to 1899 and is located close to the small local fishing harbour, overlooking the North Sea. Splendid beaches and sand dunes are within easy reach, and the pub is very popular with walkers. Seafood dishes are the speciality, including a jumbo cod, seared swordfish, lemon sole, halibut, and crab-stuffed plaice.

Open 12–11 (Sun 12–10.30) **Bar Meals** L served all week 12–4 D served all week 12–4 Av main course £5.95 **Restaurant** L served all week 12–9 D served all week 12–9 (Sun 12–4) Av 3 course à la carte £7.25 Pubmaster Tetleys, John Smiths, Scotch, Carling. **Facilities** Parking

WARWICKSHIRE

ALDERMINSTER MAP 10 SP24

Pick of the Pubs

The Bell ★★★★ INN

CV37 8NY ☎ 01789 450414 📠 01789 450998

e-mail: info@thebellald.co.uk

dir: *On A3400 3.5m S of Stratford-upon-Avon*

An 18th-century coaching inn, whose interior blends modern touches with traditional charms. The spacious conservatory restaurant overlooks a delightful old courtyard with views of the Stour Valley beyond. A good selection of starters and 'little dishes' could include avocado and crayfish tails with tomato vinaigrette on mixed leaves; pan-fried duck livers with Grand Marnier, spiced apple and toasted brioche; and a platter of mixed hors d'oeuvre. Follow with pork fillet filled with apricots and lemongrass, wrapped in Parma ham and served with Madeira jus and vegetables; or fillet of beef mignon with green beans, cherry tomatoes and a Jack Daniels and gorgonzola sauce. If you prefer a snack, there is also a selection of baguettes and light bites including hot cheese and bacon bruschetta; smoked salmon and cream cheese baguette with mixed leaves; and bacon, lettuce and tomato baguette. Those fond of fresh fish should keep an eye on the blackboard menu. New owners for Spring 2007.

Open 11.30–2.30 6.30–11 **Bar Meals** L served all week 12–2 D served all week 7–9.30 **Restaurant** L served all week 12–2 D served all week 7–9.30 Free House Greene King IPA, Abbot Ale, Hook Norton. 11 **Facilities** Garden Dogs allowed Parking **Rooms** 7 bedrooms 5 en suite S£27 D£45

ALVESTON MAP 10 SP2

Pick of the Pubs

The Baraset Barn NEW

1 Pimlico Ln CV37 7RF

☎ 01789 295510 📠 01789 292961

e-mail: barasetbarn@lovelypubs.co.uk

See Pick of the Pubs on opposite page

ARDENS GRAFTON MAP 10 SP1

Pick of the Pubs

The Golden Cross

B50 4LG ☎ 01789 772420 📠 01789 773697

e-mail: steve@thegoldencross.net

The Golden Cross offers a mellow, rug-strewn bar with a flagstone floor, massive beams and roaring fires, and a spacious dining room with restful décor and beautifully laid tables. On warmer days the patio is every bit as inviting. Well kept cask ales and good food at sensible prices are served, with dishes such as pheasant, chestnut and apricot terrine, followed by pan-fried fillet of brill with colcannon, purple sprouting broccoli and citrus butter.

Open 12–3 5–11 (Sat–Sun all day) **Bar Meals** L served all week 12–2.30 D served all week 6–9 (Sun 12–8) Av main course £12.50 **Restaurant** L served all week 12–2.30 D served all week 5.30–9.30 (Sun 12–8) Av 3 course à la carte £25 Charles Wells Tetley Cask, Hook Norton, UBU Purity Brewing & monthly Guest Ales. 8 **Facilities** Garden Parking

ASTON CANTLOW MAP 10 SP1

Pick of the Pubs

King's Head

21 Bearley Rd B95 6HY

☎ 01789 488242 📠 01789 488137

See Pick of the Pubs on page 584

The Baraset Barn

urrounded by Warwickshire countryside, the Baraset Barn is a much favoured destination astro-pub, with a dramatic interior styled from granite, pewter and oak. The original flagstones mind customers of the barn's 200-year history, but the glass-fronted kitchen introduces an up- -the-minute visual appeal.

opular draught beers reflect in-European tastes, as does e continental-style patio. A xurious lounge area with deep fas is perfect for coffee or a e-dinner aperitif. From the bar, one steps lead to the main dining ea with high oak beams and alls of London brick, and the pen mezzanine level makes for a rfect vantage point. The menu ings together eclectic flavours om around the globe, but fresh oducts are sourced locally when ssible from the Vale of Evesham. ood mileage from field to plate as been reduced, and hence the avours are sweeter and crispier, cording to head chef Ian. Menus hange weekly and might feature a and pancetta risotto; Baraset arn eggs Benedict; or pave of honey roast ham bubble and squeak, parsley sauce and truffle oil. The excellent fish choice features the Baraset fruits de mer for two, or oak smoked salmon. Carnivores will relish classic duck supper; spit-roast chicken; and roast rack of Shropshire lamb served with a mutton pie, while vegetarians could tuck into roast butternut, basil mascarponi and new potato tart with charred fennel and tomato sauce. A well-organised wine list adds to the package.

NEW 🍷
MAP 10 SP25
1 Pimlico Ln CV37 7RF
☎ 01789 295510
📠 01789 292961
e-mail:
barasetbarn@lovelypubs.co.uk

Closed 25 Dec, 1 Jan
Bar Meals L served Mon–Sat 12–2 Av main course £15
Restaurant L served all week 12–2.30 (Sun 12–4) D served Mon–Sat 6.30–9.30 Av 3 course à la carte £35
🍷 51
Facilities Garden Dogs allowed Parking
Notes

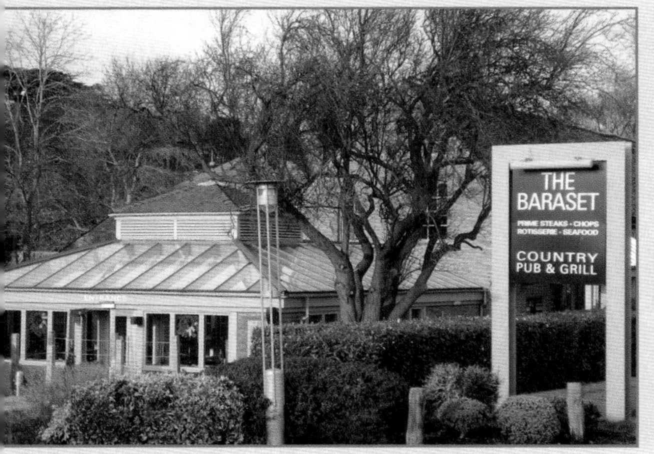

King's Head

It is reputed that William Shakespeare's parents held their wedding reception at the King's Head after they were married next door in the village church in 1557. These days, the colourful hanging baskets and wisteria-clad exterior of this lovingly restored Tudor hostelry invite further exploration.

Inside, you'll discover a comfortable village bar with wooden settles, a massive inglenook fireplace and an old-fashioned snug. There's also a quarry-tiled main room with attractive window seats and oak tables. Visitors can expect well-kept real ales and an excellent wine list. A single menu serves all areas, and the duck supper on beetroot and lentil ragout is still the pub's signature dish. A lunchtime sandwich could be filled with smoked mackerel paté or roast beef and aubergine tapenade. Other dishes from the award-winning modern British menu that might tickle the taste-buds include ham hock and honey glazed parsnip terrine with balsamic shallot jus; smoked mackerel and chicory salad with red onion and lemon mayonnaise, or green salad with asparagus, hard-boiled egg and walnut dressing. Main courses are similarly articulate and ambitious. Try saddle of rabbit with braised cabbage and juniper sauce, or venison casserole with calvados sauce and salsify purée. From the specials board, grilled halibut on truffle oil fettuccine makes an alluring option, as does roast monkfish fillet on artichokes, spinach and sun blushed cherry tomatoes. In summer, food is also served in the large and pretty garden, perhaps under the shadow of the inn's pride and joy – a huge chestnut tree.

🍷

MAP 10 SP16
21 Bearley Rd B95 6HY
☎ 01789 488242
📠 01789 488137
web: www.thekh.co.uk

Open 11–3 5.30–11 (Winter Sun 5.30–8.30)
Bar Meals L served all week 12–2.30 D served all week 6.30–9.30 (Sun 12–3)
Restaurant L served all week 12–2.30 D served all week 6.30–9.30 (Sun 12–3) Av 3 course à la carte £25 Av 3 course fixed price £15
Greene King Abbot Ale, Purity Gold & Mitchell and Butler Brew XI. 🍷 8
Facilities Garden Parking

3ROOM MAP 10 SP05

3room Tavern

ligh St B50 4HL ☎ 01789 773656 📠 01789 773656
-mail: webmaster@broomtavern.co.uk
lir: *N of B439 W of Stratford-upon-Avon*

)nce a haunt of William Shakespeare, this 16th-century brick and mber inn is smartly furnished, with a large beer garden where arbecues are held in summer. Very much at the heart of village life, is home to the Broom Tavern Golf Society, and fun days, charity vents and outings are a feature. The menu offers a large selection of egetarian dishes and seafood specials.

pen 12-3 6-11 (Fri-Sat 12-11, Sun 12-3) **Bar Meals** L served all eek 12-2 D served Mon-Sat 6-9 (Fri-Sat 6-9.30) Av main course £8 **estaurant** L served all week 12-2 D served all week 6.30-9 (Fri-Sat -9.30) Punch Taverns Green King IPA, Black Sheep & Timothy aylors Landlord. 20 **Facilities** Garden Dogs allowed Parking

:DGEHILL MAP 11 SP34

'he Castle Inn

)X15 6DJ ☎ 01295 670255 📠 01295 670521
-mail: castleedgehill@btopenworld.com
ir: *M40 then A422. 6m to Upton House, next right 1.5m*

fascinating property, the inn was built as a copy of Warwick Castle 1742 to commemorate the centenary of the Battle of Edgehill, and ands on the summit of Edgehill, 700 feet above sea level. It opened the anniversary of Cromwell's death in 1750, was first licensed in 322, and acquired by Hook Norton a hundred years later. Bar snacks, ndwiches, hot platters and steaks are served.

pen 12-3 6-11 (Summer wknds all day) **Bar Meals** L served all eek 12-2.30 D served all week 6.30-9 **Restaurant** L served all week -2 D served all week 6.30-9 (Summer extended hrs) Hook Norton Hook Norton Best, Old Hooky & Generation, Hooky Dark, Guest Ales. **cilities** Children's licence Garden Parking

TTINGTON MAP 10 SP24

'he Houndshill

anbury Rd CV37 7NS ☎ 01789 740267 📠 01789 740075
r: *On A422 SE of Stratford-upon-Avon*

mily-run inn situated at the heart of England, making it a perfect se for exploring popular tourist attractions such as Oxford, Blenheim, atford and the Cotswolds. The pleasant tree-lined garden is pecially popular with families. Typical dishes range from poached fillet of salmon, and faggots, mash and minted peas, to supreme of chicken and ham and mushroom tagliatelle. Alternatively, try cold ham off the bone or home-made steak and kidney pie.

Open 12-3 6-11 (Sun 7-10.30) Closed: Dec 25-28 **Bar Meals** L served all week 12-2 D served all week 7-9.30 Av main course £8.50 **Restaurant** L served all week 12-2 D served all week 9.30 Av 3 course à la carte £16.50 Free House Hook Norton Best, Spitfire. 7 **Facilities** Garden Dogs allowed Parking Play Area

FARNBOROUGH MAP 11 SP44

Pick of the Pubs

The Inn at Farnborough

OX17 1DZ ☎ 01295 690615
e-mail: enquiries@innatfarnborough.co.uk
dir: *A423 signed Southam. 4m, left onto single track road signed Farnborough, 1m right into village*

Formerly the butcher's house on the Farnborough Estate, once known as the Butcher's Arms, the inn is a Grade II listed free house in a picturesque village setting. Parts of the building date back 400 years, and include an original inglenook fireplace. A good range of real ales and 14 wines by the glass are served alongside dishes based on high-quality Heart of England produce. Typical dishes from the fixed price menu are Oxfordshire Cropredy Dexter meatballs with grain mustard sauce, and Dorset crab with salmon and scallop risotto and saffron sauce. Carte dishes include salmon fish cakes with baby spinach and hollandaise sauce; and specials such as rocket and Kenyan bean salad and salsa verde. Families are welcome, with smaller portions for children available, and there is a funky private dining room with claret walls and a zebra print ceiling.

Open 12-3 6-11 (Sat-Sun 6-12) Closed: 25 Dec **Bar Meals** L served all week 12-3 D served all week 6-11 (Sat-Sun all day) Av main course £13 **Restaurant** L served all week 12-3 D served all week 6-11 (Sat-Sun all day) Av 3 course à la carte £25 Av 3 course fixed price £12.95 Free House Leffe, Old Speckled Hen, Greene King IPA, Guinness. 16 **Facilities** Children's licence Garden Dogs allowed Parking

GREAT WOLFORD MAP 10 SP23

Pick of the Pubs

The Fox & Hounds Inn ★★★★ INN

CV36 5NQ ☎ 01608 674220 📠 01608 674160
e-mail: info@thefoxandhoundsinn.com
dir: *Off A44 NE of Moreton-in-Marsh*

An unspoilt village hostelry nestling in glorious countryside on the edge of the Cotswolds. Good food, good beer and exceptional whiskies are all on offer, along with an inviting ambience enhanced by old settles, Tudor inglenook fireplaces and solid ceiling beams adorned with jugs or festooned with hops. The bar entrance is a double-hinged 'coffin door' which once allowed coffins to be brought in and laid out prior to the funeral service. Allegedly, a secret tunnel, along which bodies were sometimes carried, linked the cellar with the nearby church, and obviously, there have been many ghostly sightings. The famously

CONTINUED

England

GREAT WOLFORD continued

controversial pub sign features Tony Blair and a number of foxes and foxhounds. As well as a range of traditional ales, the bar offers a staggering selection of almost 200 fine whiskies. On the menu, look for home-made salmon fishcakes, oven-roasted guinea fowl, grilled Dover sole, and rib-eye steak.

The Fox & Hounds Inn

Open 12–2.30 6–11 Closed: !st wk Jan **Bar Meals** L served Tue–Sat 12–2 D served Tue–Sat 7–9 Av main course £11.50 **Restaurant** L served Tue–Sun 12–2 D served Tue–Sat 7–9 (Wknds 7–9.30) Av 3 course à la carte £25 Free House Hook Norton Best, Guest beers. 7 **Facilities** Garden Dogs allowed Parking **Rooms** 3 bedrooms en suite S£45 D£70

HATTON — MAP 10 SP26

The Case is Altered

Case Ln, Five Ways CV35 7JD ☎ 01926 484206

This traditional free house proudly carries the standard for the old style of pub. It serves no food and does not accept children or dogs. That aside, it's a thoroughly welcoming spot for adults who appreciate the pleasures of a quiet pint. Hook Norton beers have a strong presence, and there is always a local and national guest ale to sup while enjoying lively conversation or just appreciating the atmosphere.

Open 12–2.30 6–11 (Sun 12–2, 7–10.30) Hook Norton Old Hooky, Greene King IPA, Guest beers. **Facilities** Parking **Notes**

ILMINGTON — MAP 10 SP24

Pick of the Pubs

The Howard Arms

Lower Green CV36 4LT

☎ 01608 682226 01608 682226

e-mail: info@howardarms.com

dir: *Off A429 or A3400*

The village of Ilmington is set in a crook of the Cotswold Hills, and on the picturesque village green you'll find the Howard Arms, a 400-year-old Cotswold stone inn. Established owners with many years experience in the business create a relaxed atmosphere for customers who enjoy the range of real ales and a good choice of wines by the glass. The weekly changing menu offers plenty of variety, with starters like parsnip fritters with stilton and walnut mayo dip, or deep-fried squid with parsley, garlic and smoked pancetta stuffing. Main courses range from beef, ale and mustard pie to pan-fried sea bass with herbed couscous, sunblush tomato and black olive dressing. Desserts offer just as much variety, whether you fancy a steamed marmalade pudding with Drambuie sauce, or gingered pannacotta with spiced rhubarb.

The Howard Arms

Open 11–3 6–11 (Sun 6–10.30) Closed: 25 Dec **Bar Meals** L served all week 12–2 D served all week 7–9 (Fri–Sat 7–9.30 Sun 12–2.30, 6–10.30) Av main course £11.50 **Restaurant** L served all week 12–2 D served all week 7–9 (Fri–Sat 7–9.30 Sun 12–2.30, 6–10.30) Av 3 course à la carte £27.50 Av 3 course fixed price £22.50 Free House Everards Tiger Best, Hook Norton Gold, Prurity Brewing 'Ubu', Bard's Brewery Nobel Fool. 15 **Facilities** Garden Parking **Rooms** 3 bedrooms en suite S£87.50 D£120 (★★★★★ INN)

LAPWORTH — MAP 10 SP1

Pick of the Pubs

The Boot Inn

Old Warwick Rd B94 6JU

☎ 01564 782464 01564 784989

e-mail: the bootinn@lovelypubs.co.uk

Beside the Grand Union Canal in the unspoilt village of Lapworth, this lively and convivial 16th-century former coaching inn is well worth seeking out. Apart from its smartly refurbished interior, the attractive garden is a great place to relax on warm days, while a canopy and patio heaters make it a comfortable place to sit even on cooler evenings. But the main draw is the modern brasserie-style food, with wide-ranging menus that deliver home-produced dishes. A selection from the menu might include prawn, smoked haddock and spring onion fishcake, served with lemon gremolata and herb aioli; haddock in tempura batter with pea purée, sauce gribiche and frites; and fillet steak with smoked roast garlic, spinach and mascarpone mash.

Open 11–12 Closed: Dec 25 **Bar Meals** L served all week 12–2.30 D served all week 7–10 Av main course £9 **Restaurant** L served all week 12–2.30 D served all week 7–10 Av 3 course à la carte £19 Av 4 course fixed price £27.50 Laurel Pub Partnerships Greene King Old Speckled Hen, Wadworth 6X, Scottish Courage John Smith's, Brew XI. 8 **Facilities** Garden Dogs allowed Parking

Please see cycle ride on opposite page

The Boot Inn

Cycle information

Distance: 9.75 miles/15.7km (2h)
Map: OS Explorer 220 Birmingham & Explorer 221 Coventry & Warwick
Start/finish: Kingswood; car park in Brome Hall lane; grid ref: SP 185710
Trails/tracks: quiet lanes, canal tow paths with mainly gravel surfaces
Landscape: hedged lanes, canals, rolling agricultural countryside
Public toilets: at the start
Tourist information: Solihull, tel 0121 704 6130
Cycle hire: Clarkes Cycle Shop, Henley Street and Guild Street, Stratford-upon-Avon, tel 01789 205057, www.cycling-tours.org.uk
The pub: The Boot Inn, Lapworth
Traffic on country lanes, one awkward right-hand turn, low bridges and overhanging branches along tow path

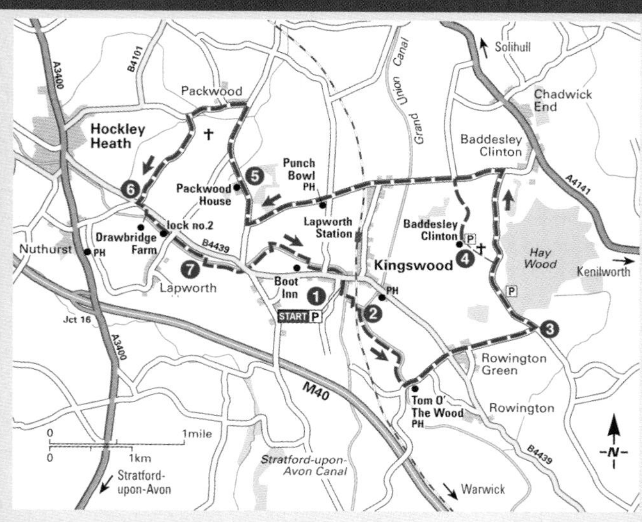

ycle directions

1 Join the Stratford-upon-Avon Canal behind the car park, turn right past a lock to a bridge where the canal splits. Cross to the spur, which drops through a second lock to another bridge, there dismounting to descend four steps on the far side. Follow the tow path away from the junction, going beneath a railway bridge to meet the Grand Union Canal.

2 Cycle along the tow path to the right for some 0.75 mile (1.2km) to the second bridge (No. 63), leaving immediately beyond it for the lane above. Over the bridge, climb away past the Tom O' The Wood pub. At a 'Give Way' crossroads, keep ahead over the B4439 for just over 0.5 mile (800m) to the end of the lane.

3 To the left, the way leads past Hay Wood, eventually meeting another junction. Go left again towards Lapworth and Baddesley Clinton, the lane shortly falling to pass the entrance of Baddesley Clinton, which lies opposite Netherwood Lane.

4 Turn left towards Hockley Heath, soon dropping to a blind humpback bridge spanning the Grand Union Canal. Keep going over a railway bridge and later, ahead at a crossroads beside the Punch Bowl. About 0.5 mile (800m) further on, the road turns sharply left. Exercising caution, turn off right onto a narrow lane leading past Packwood House.

5 Carry on for almost another 0.75 mile (1.2km) to the second lane signed to Packwood and Hockley Heath. After 0.5 mile (800m) turn left at an unsigned junction, then past Packwood's church, St Giles, to a main road, the B4439.

6 Turn left towards Lapworth and Warwick, but after 200 yards (182m) and just before some white cottages, swing off right onto a gravel track, the entrance to Drawbridge Farm. Meeting the canal a few yards/metres along, follow the tow path left to the first of a long series of locks (No 2) heralding the canal's descent to Kingswood. Prudent cyclists will then dismount to negotiate the sharp dip and low ridge immediately beyond the lock.

7 The path crosses to the opposite bank over a bridge below lock No 4, remaining on that side to pass beneath a road bridge and shortly reaching lock No 6. Beyond, locks form a staircase that drops the canal some 70ft (21m) in little over 0.5 mile (800m). The tow path reverts to the north bank below lock No 7, recrossing once more after lock No 14, where The Boot Inn lies, just along a track south of the canal. The final stretch continues along the tow path beneath a road bridge, bending past four more locks and under a final bridge to return you to the car park.

The Duck on the Pond

Children will be delighted to discover that the name of this attractive village inn does indeed indicate the presence of a pond replete with drakes and mallards. Adults, meanwhile, will be comforted to learn that the inn's appearance, which is reminiscent of a French bistro, is entirely substantiated by the food.

Winter fires light an entirely intriguing interior, crammed with French artwork, road signs and bottles, not to mention an unusual willow baton ceiling. Service is friendly and attentive, and you'll never be left without a drink for long. Food miles are also kept to a minimum, with the vast majority of produce sourced from within walking distance. And as far as the food goes, owners Andrew and Wendy Parry explain that it's quite simple – 'This is the food we love to eat and food we love to cook.' Their passion is evident in an appealing and well thought out menu that mixes traditional dishes with more innovative selections. Start with an impressive tower of prawns and filo pastry; fresh Scottish mussels steamed with chorizo, garlic and tomato sauce; or home-made chicken liver paté with focaccia and red onion marmalade. Follow on with breast of chicken stuffed with spinach and brie; roast pork with nettle stuffing on apple mash with cider cream; and grilled salmon with braised fennel and a caramelised lime, mango and pineapple salsa. Specials might include seared king scallops with sautéed black pudding, or Thai-marinated red snapper stir fry. Should you be feeling decadent, the lengthy wine list includes 12 different vintage Dom Perignons.

NEW 🍷
MAP 11 SP46
The Green CV47 9QJ
☎ 01926 815876
📠 01926 815766
e-mail:
duckonthepond@aol.com
dir: *On A423 in middle of Long Itchington, 1m N of Southam*

Open 12–3 5–11 (Sat 12–11, Sun 12–10.30)
Bar Meals L served Tue–Sun 12–2 D served Tue–Sun 6.30–10 (Sat–Sun 12–10) Av main course £12
Restaurant L served Tue–Sun 12–2.30 D served Tue–Sun 6.30–10 (Sat 12–10, Sun 12–9) Av 3 course à la carte £20
Charles Wells
Charles Wells Bombardier, Young's Winter Warmer, Carling, Red Stripe & Guinness. 🍷 10
Facilities Garden Parking

England

ONG ITCHINGTON MAP 11 SP46

Pick of the Pubs

The Duck on the Pond NEW

The Green CV47 9QJ
01926 815876 01926 815766
e-mail: duckonthepond@aol.com
dir: *On A423 in middle of Long Itchington, 1m N of Southam*

See Pick of the Pubs on opposite page

IONKS KIRBY MAP 11 SP48

'he Bell Inn

ell Ln CV23 0QY 01788 832352 01788 832352
-mail: belindagb@aol.com
ir: *Off The Fosseway junct with B4455*

he Spanish owners of this quaint, timbered inn, once a Benedictine riory gatehouse and then a brewhouse cottage, describe it as "a orner of Spain in the heart of England". Mediterranean and traditional uisine play an important role on the menu. Red snapper gallega, addle of lamb, fillet Catalan, chicken piri piri, and Mexican hot pot are opular favourites. Extensive range of starters and speciality dishes.

pen 12-2.30 7-11 Closed: 26 Dec, 1 Jan **Bar Meals** L served Tue-Sun 2-2.30 D served all week 7-10.30 **Restaurant** L served Tue-Sun 12-2.30 served all week 7-10.30 Free House Boddingtons, IPA & Ruddles. **acilities** Garden Parking

NAPTON ON THE HILL MAP 11 SP46

The Bridge at Napton

outham Rd CV47 8NQ 01926 812466
-mail: info@thebridgeatnapton.co.uk
ir: *At Bridge 111 on Oxford Canal on A425, 2m from Southam*

Vith a restaurant, three bars and a large garden this is an ideal place to noor the narrow boat, park the car or lean the bike against a wall. Built s a stabling inn at bridge 111 on the Oxford canal, the pub even has s own turning point for barges. There are some excellent ales, and he menu offers everything from gammon, egg and chips, through to almon in champagne and pink peppercorn sauce.

pen 12-3 6-11 (Apr-Nov: Sat-Sun all day) **Bar Meals** L served all week 2-2 **Restaurant** L served all week 12-2 D served all week 6-9 Punch averns Cask Marque acredited & 3 Guest ales. **Facilities** Garden Dogs llowed Parking Play Area

PRESTON BAGOT MAP 10 SP16

The Crabmill

B95 5EE 01926 843342 01926 843989
e-mail: thecrabmill@lovelypubs.co.uk
dir: *A4189 Henley-in-Arden lights. Left, 1.5m on left*

The name is a reminder that crab apple cider was once made at this 15th-century hostelry, which is set in beautiful rural surroundings. Restored to create an upmarket venue, the pub has a light, open feel. Even the menu seems fresh and stylish, with dishes ranging from a lunchtime croque monsieur or panini, to evening dishes such as Moroccan chicken with spiced potatoes and cucumber yogurt relish, and crab, crayfish and saffron risotto.

Open 11-11 (Sun 12-6) Closed: 25 Dec **Bar Meals** L served all week 12-2.30 (Sun 12.30-3.30) D served Mon-Sat 6.30-9.30 Av main course £12 **Restaurant** L served all week 12-2.30 (Sun 12.30-3.30) D served Mon-Sat 6.30-9.30 Av 3 course à la carte £23 Wadworth 6X, Tetleys, Greene King Abbot Ale. 8 **Facilities** Garden Dogs allowed Parking

PRIORS MARSTON MAP 11 SP45

Pick of the Pubs

The Hollybush Inn NEW

Hollybush Ln CV47 7RW
01327 260934 01327 262507
dir: *From Southam A425, off bypass and 1st right, 6m to Priors' Marston. Left after War memorial, next left 150 yds, left again*

Many pubs are central to their communities, but this one goes a step further – it provides lunches for the local school and is committed to supporting the village sports club. With its large fireplace burning brightly, it's a warm hub of village social activity with a very relaxed atmosphere; people can eat and/or drink wherever they choose. The bar menu ranges from baguettes to steak, Guinness and mushroom pie; and a dish of charcuterie is served with olives, spicy cornichons and bread. A three-course dinner could comprise pan-fried pigeon breast with beetroot salad; medallions of pork fillet; and blackberry and apple crumble – with custard of course!

Open 12-2 5.30-11 (Fri 5.30-12, Sat-Sun 12-3, Sat 6-12, Sun 7-10.30) **Bar Meals** L served all week 12-2 (Sun 12-2.30) D served all week 6.30-9.30 (Wed 6.30-9, Sun 7-9) Av main course £7.50 **Restaurant** L served all week 12-2 D served all week 6.30-9.30 Av 3 course à la carte £20 Free House Hook Norton, London Pride. 8 **Facilities** Garden Dogs allowed Parking **Notes**

The Red Lion

Originally built as a coaching inn in 1748, this grade II listed stone free house is located in an area of outstanding natural beauty. Though it is ideally situated for such major attractions as Stratford upon Avon, Warwick, Oxford and the Cotswold Wildlife Park, tales of witches in the village and a nearby prehistoric stone circle mean there is as much to interest the historian as the tourist.

The inside retains an old world atmosphere with oak beams, log fires, gleaming wood and comfy leather chairs. The bar is full of atmosphere, and visitors can eat there or in the restaurant area, choosing food from one long menu and specials from the blackboard. All tastes are catered for, from interesting sandwiches (hand-carved ham and wholegrain mustard on granary bread; buffalo mozzarella and beef tomato on ciabatta) to a lightly battered cod fillet, served on a sheet of 'The Red Lion Times'. Look out otherwise for such adventurous starters as home-made ham hock, leek and Parma ham terrine with grape chutney; or celeriac remoulade on a salad of roasted beetroot, apples and walnuts. Mains might include herb-crusted rack of lamb; steak and Hook Norton pie, or grilled sea bass with wilted garlic spinach and ratatouille. Round off with a warm pear and almond flan and mascarpone cheese, or an iced lime and ginger parfait. Those who choose to dine in the well-kept garden may be lucky enough to be joined by Cocoa, the pub's glamorous chocolate Labrador. Five elegant en suite bedrooms all feature such modern luxuries as Egyptian cotton bed linen and flat screen televisions.

★★★★ INN 🍷
MAP 10 SP24
Main St, Long Compton CV37 5JS
☎ 01608 684221
📠 01608 684968
e-mail:
info@redlion-longcompton.co.uk
web: www.redlion-longcompton.co.uk
dir: *On A3400 between Shipston on Stour & Chipping Norton*

Open 11–2.30 6–11 (Fri–Sun 11–11)
Bar Meals L served all week 12–2.30 D served all week 6–9.30 (Fri–Sun 12–9.30) Av main course £9.95
Free House
Hook Norton Best, Adnams, Timothy Taylor. 🍷 7
Facilities Garden Dogs allowed Parking Play Area
Rooms 5 bedrooms en suite S£50 D£80

RATLEY MAP 11 SP34

The Rose and Crown

OX15 6DS ☎ 01295 678148

dir: *Follow Edgehill signs, 7m N of Banbury on A422*

Following the Battle of Edgehill in 1642, a Roundhead was discovered in the chimney of this 11th (or 12th)-century pub and beheaded in the hearth. His ghost reputedly haunts the building. Enjoy the peaceful village location and the traditional pub food, perhaps including beef and ale pie, scampi and chips, chicken curry and the Sunday roast.

Open 12–2 7–11 (Fri–Sat 12–3, 6.30–12, Sun 12–4, 7–11) **Bar Meals** L served all week 12–2 D served all week 7–9 Av main course £10.50 **Restaurant** L served Tue–Sun 12–2 D served Tue–Sat 7–9 Av 3 course à la carte £18 Free House Wells Bombardier & Eagle IPA, Greene King Old Speckled Hen & Guest ale. **Facilities** Garden Dogs allowed Parking

RUGBY MAP 11 SP57

Pick of the Pubs

Golden Lion Hotel ★★★ HL

Easenhall CV23 0JA ☎ 01788 832265 01788 832878

dir: *Signs for Nuneaton. Through Newbold, then brown sign*

A charming 16th-century free house with low oak-beamed ceilings and narrow doorways. James and Claudia are the third generation of the Austin family at the Golden Lion, where you'll find traditional ales, roaring winter fires and an extensive wine list. Choose between home-cooked bar food such as red Thai chicken curry, or breast of chicken wrapped in bacon with tomato sauce, and melted cheese on spaghetti. For gourmet dining in the candlelit restaurant, start perhaps with tian of avocado and Marie Rose prawns, or a continental mixed meat platter with olives and crusty bread. Continue with oven-roasted loin of monkfish wrapped in Parma ham; whole grilled lemon sole; or lambs' liver, bacon, black pudding, mash, red wine and onion gravy. The pub is set amidst idyllic countryside in one of Warwickshire's best-kept villages, and its 21 en suite bedrooms, some with four-poster beds, offer outstanding accommodation.

Open 11–11 **Bar Meals** L served all week 12–3 D served all week 6–9.30 (Sun 12–9) Av main course £9.85 **Restaurant** L served Mon–Sat 12–2 (Sun 12–3) D served Mon–Sun 6–9.30 Av 3 course à la carte £19 Free House 7 **Facilities** Garden Parking **Rooms** 21 bedrooms en suite S£50 D£69

SHIPSTON ON STOUR MAP 10 SP24

The Cherington Arms

Cherington CV36 5HS ☎ 01608 686233

e-mail: thecheringtonarms@hooknorton.tablesir.com

An attractive 17th-century inn with exposed beams and Cotswold stone walls, stripped wood furniture and roaring log inglenook fire. The ever-changing chalkboard menus might announce crab fishcakes with mango and chilli salsa; home-made beef and Hooky (ie Hook Norton beer, as sold in the bar) pie; breast of chicken stuffed with sun-dried tomato and cream pesto; and risotto of chargrilled artichoke, asparagus and green beans. Outside are large riverside gardens with a mill race.

Open 12–3 6.30–11.30 (Summer wknds all day) **Bar Meals** L served Tue–Sun 12–2 (Sun 12–3) D served Tue–Sun 7–9 Av main course £9.75 **Restaurant** L served Tue–Fri 12–2 (Sat 12–2.30, Sun 12–3) D served Tue–Thur 7–9 (Fri–Sat 7–9.30) Av 3 course à la carte £18.75 Av 3 course fixed price £16.50 Hook Norton Hook Norton Best Bitter, Generation, Old Hooky, guest ales. 11 **Facilities** Garden Dogs allowed Parking

Pick of the Pubs

The Red Lion ★★★★ INN

Main St, Long Compton CV37 5JS

☎ 01608 684221 01608 684968

e-mail: info@redlion-longcompton.co.uk

web: www.redlion-longcompton.co.uk

dir: *On A3400 between Shipston on Stour & Chipping Norton*

See Pick of the Pubs on opposite page

White Bear Hotel

High St CV36 4AJ ☎ 01608 661558 01608 662612

e-mail: info@whitebearhotel.co.uk

dir: *A3400 to Shipston-on-Stour*

Open fires and wooden settles give the bars of this Georgian hotel a comfortable, timeless appeal. You'll find a range of real ales and keg beers, with up to eight wines available by the glass. The refurbished restaurant with its crisp white tablecloths makes dining a delicious experience: starters like pan-fried kidneys with black pudding precede main course options that include rack of lamb; and haddock with spinach and Welsh rarebit.

Open 11-12 (Sun 11–11) **Bar Meals** L served all week 12–2 D served Mon–Sat 6.30–9.30 Av main course £10 **Restaurant** L served all week 12–2 D served Mon–Sat 6.30–9.30 Av 3 course à la carte £18 Punch Taverns Adnams Old Hooky, Bass & Guest Ales. 8 **Facilities** Children's licence Garden Parking

England

SHREWLEY MAP 10 SP26

Pick of the Pubs

The Durham Ox Restaurant and Country Pub ♀

Shrewley Common CV35 7AY

☎ 01926 842283 📠 0121 705 9315

e-mail: reservations@durham-ox.com

dir: *After Hatton Country World A4177 signed 1.5m*

An award-winning pub/restaurant in a peaceful village just four miles from Warwick and Leamington. Warm and inviting, its old beams, roaring fire and traditional hospitality combine with a city chic that give it a competitive edge. Success is in no small measure due to the restaurant, where Master Chef Simon Diprose prepares impressive, seasonally changing classic and contemporary dishes. A meal might consist of deep-fried Boursin with ratatouille and basil sorbet; roast fillet of five-spice salmon with sweet corn, pak choi and coriander dressing; and hot chocolate and Snickers fondant with vanilla ice cream. For more examples of his style, consider roast vegetables with North African spices, couscous and yoghurt dressing; and fresh plaice fillet in crispy Cajun coating with buttered peas and chunky chips. Children are offered penne pasta, and home-made fishcakes from their own menu. Extensive gardens incorporate a safe children's play area.

Open 12-11 **Bar Meals** L served all week 12-3 D served all week 6-10 (Sun 12-9) Av main course £13.50 **Restaurant** L served all week 12-3 D served all week 6-10 (Sun 12-9) Av 3 course à la carte £24 Greene King IPA, Old Speckled Hen, Guinness & Abbot Ale. ♀21 **Facilities** Garden Parking Play Area

STRATFORD-UPON-AVON MAP 10 SP25

The Dirty Duck

Waterside CV37 6BA ☎ 01789 297312 📠 01789 293441

Frequented by members of the Royal Shakespeare Company from the nearby theatre, this traditional, partly Elizabethan inn has a splendid raised terrace overlooking the River Avon. In addition to the interesting range of real ales, a comprehensive choice of food is offered. Light bites, pastas, salads and mains at lunchtime, plus pub classics and 'make it special' dishes at night, from rustic sharing bread with herbs, garlic and olives to roast rack of lamb.

Open 11-12 (Sun 12-10.30) **Bar Meals** L served all week 12-5 D served Mon-Sat 5-10 Av main course £6 **Restaurant** D served Mon-Sat 5-10 Av 3 course à la carte £15 Whitbread Flowers Original, Morland Old Speckled Hen. **Facilities** Garden Dogs allowed

Pick of the Pubs

The Fox & Goose Inn ★★ INN ♀

CV37 8DD ☎ 01608 682293 📠 01608 682293

e-mail: mail@foxandgoose.co.uk

dir: *1m off A3400, between Shipston-on-Stour and Stratford-upon-Avon*

See Pick of the Pubs on opposite page

The One Elm ♀

1 Guild St CV37 6QZ ☎ 01789 404919

dir: *In town centre*

Standing on its own in the heart of town, the One Elm has two dining rooms: downstairs is intimate, even with the buzzy bar close by, while upstairs feels grander. The menu features chargrilled côte de boeuf for two, Aberdeen Angus rump steak, and tuna, as well as other main courses. The deli board offers all-day nuts and seeds, cheeses, charcuterie and antipasti. The secluded terrace induces in some a feeling of being abroad.

Open 11.30-11 Closed: 25 Dec **Bar Meals** L served all week 12-2.30 D served all week 6.30-10 (Sun all day) Av main course £10.50 **Restaurant** L served all week 12-2.30 D served all week 6.30-10 (Sun all day) London Pride, Old Speckled Hen, Timothy Taylor Landlord. ♀9 **Facilities** Garden Dogs allowed Parking

STRETTON ON FOSSE MAP 10 SP2

The Plough Inn

GL56 9QX ☎ 01608 661053

e-mail: saravol@aol.com

Family-run, 17th-century village pub, built from Cotswold stone, its traditional charms include bare beams and a real fire. Starters of home made soup with crusty bread or a goats' cheese crouton with smoked bacon on salad could be followed by beer-battered cod with chips and salad. There's a spit roast over a log fire on Sundays (September-May) and in addition the French chef prepares traditional dishes from his homeland for the specials board.

Open 11.30-3 6-11 (Sun 12-3, 7-10.30) Rest: no food Mon, 25 Dec **Bar Meals** L served Tue-Sun 12-2 D served Tue-Sat 7-9 Av main course £11.95 **Restaurant** L served Tue-Sun 12-2 D served Tue-Sat 7-9 Free House Hook Norton Best, Purity Gold Archers & Guest Ale. **Facilities** Garden Parking Play Area

The Fox & Goose Inn

\ busy, privately owned inn, formerly two cottages and a blacksmith's forge. It is located in \rmscote, a beautiful village eight miles south of Stratford-upon-Avon, set in lovely countryside ind within easy reach of Warwick and several Cotswold villages.

'he inn was given the total refurb reatment a few years ago, and he result is stylish and utterly istinctive. It includes a smart ining room, a cosy bar and four elightfully eccentric, luxury en uite bedrooms named after Cluedo haracters – Professor Plum, that ort of thing. Expect a king size ed, Egyptian cotton sheets and clawfoot bath. The bar, with its valls painted Eating Room Red, as lots of squishy velvet cushions, n open fire, flagstone floors and iles of reading matter to enjoy while supping a pint of Old Hooky r Shepherd Neame Spitfire. If you refer wine (or even champagne) here is a selection by the glass or ottle, and for further refreshments here is a menu of light meals and nibbles. The dining room offers a menu created from fresh produce and much imagination: you can expect to find goats' cheese parcel, or crab and salt cod tian with curry and vanilla oil, followed by rump of Lighthorne lamb with dauphinoise potatoes and Nicoise salad; cod pea linguini with caviar cream; and fillet steak with fondant potatoes and foie gras. Round off with home-made Eccles cake with vanilla ice cream and maple syrup, or pot au chocolat with espresso granite. Out in the garden there's a large grassy area, a decked space and 20 seats for dining under the vines and enjoying some lovely country views.

★★ INN 🍷
MAP 10 SP25
CV37 8DD
☎ 01608 682293
📠 01608 682293
e-mail: mail@foxandgoose.co.uk
dir: *1m off A3400, between Shipston-on-Stour and Stratford-upon-Avon*

Open 12–3 6–11
Bar Meals L served all week 12–2.30 D served all week 7–9.30 Av main course £11.95
Restaurant L served all week 12–2.30 D served all week 7–9.30 Av 3 course à la carte £23.50
Free House
Hook Norton Old Hooky, Spitfire, Tetley Smooth & Guinness. 🍷 8
Facilities Garden Parking
Rooms 4 bedrooms en suite S£55 D£85

TEMPLE GRAFTON MAP 10 SP15

The Blue Boar Inn

B49 6NR ☎ 01789 750010 📠 01789 750635
e-mail: blueboar@rutlandpubco.net
dir: *Left to Temple Grafton off A46 to 1st x-rds*

The oldest part of the inn dates from the early 1600s, and the restaurant features a 35-foot glass-covered well, home to a family of koi carp, from which water was formerly drawn for brewing. There are four open fires in the bar and restaurant areas, and a patio garden with views of the Cotswold Hills. A menu of traditional dishes is served, with variety provided by daily specials prepared from local produce, game in particular.

Open 11–12 **Bar Meals** L served all week 12–3 D served all week 6–10 (Sat 12–10, Sun 12–9) Av main course £9.95 **Restaurant** L served all week 12–3 D served all week 6–10 Rutland Inn Co. Ltd Morland Old Speckled Hen, Best, Deuchars IPA, Guest beer. 18 **Facilities** Children's licence Garden Parking

WARWICK MAP 10 SP26

The Rose & Crown

30 Market Place CV34 4SH
☎ 01926 411117 📠 01926 492117
e-mail: roseandcrown@peachpubs.com
dir: *5mins from A46 & M40*

Stylish gastropub located in the centre of Warwick with large leather sofas in the bar, a good choice of real ales and wines by the glass. Breakfast, lunch and dinner are served in the vibrant red restaurant. The deli board is a popular feature, with nuts and seeds, cheese, charcuterie, antipasti, fish and bread. Mains take in free range coq au vin, porterhouse steak, roast hake, and sausage of the week.

Open 8–11 8–12 **Bar Meals** L served all week 12–10 D served all week (Sun 12–9.30) **Restaurant** L served all week 12–2.30 D served all week 6.30–10 (Sun 12–3, 6.30–9.30) Speckled Hen, Black Sheep, Hoegaarden, & London Pride. 8 **Facilities** Dogs allowed

WELFORD-ON-AVON MAP 10 SP15

Pick of the Pubs

The Bell Inn NEW

Binton Rd CV37 8EB
☎ 01789 750353 📠 01789 750893
e-mail: info@thebellwelford.co.uk

Rumour has it that William Shakespeare contracted fatal pneumonia after stumbling home from a drink at the Bell in the pouring rain. Set deep in the heart of Warwickshire countryside, this is an outstanding 17th-century inn, complete with all those classic touches – open fires, flagstone floors, exposed beams, oak furniture – that make country pubs so charming. Food is taken seriously here, as the daily specials menus attest. Look out for the likes of roast chicken, fig and pear salad; Parma ham and celeriac remoulade, or smoked haddock kedgeree. Mains might take in Cajun swordfish steak on lime and coriander tabouleh; pan-roasted pork loin with olive oil mash; or blue stilton and leek quiche. Impressively, the inn's staff have also established an initiative – 'the future of food is fun' – designed to introduce local school children to the world of professional cooking.

Open 11.30–3 6.30–11 (Sat 11.30–11, Sun 12–11) **Bar Meals** L served all week 11.30–2.30 D served all week 6.45–9.30 (Fri–Sat 6.45–10, Sun 12–9.30) Av main course £11.50 **Restaurant** L served all week 11.30–2.30 D served all week 6.45–9.30 (Fri–Sat 6.45–10, Sun 12–9.30) Av 3 course à la carte £21.95 Enterprise Inns Hook Norton (various), Flowers Original, Hobsons Best, Wadsworth 6X. 13 **Facilities** Garden Parking

The Four Alls

Binton Bridges CV37 8PW
☎ 01789 750228 📠 01789 750262
e-mail: andrew@thefouralls.co.uk
dir: *B439 from Stratford-upon-Avon then left*

Contemporary art and modern furnishings give a continental feel to th striking interior of this centuries-old inn, set in the heart of Shakespear country. Outside, you'll find a riverside garden and patio as well as a front garden and play area. The menus also have a continental flavour lime marinated prawns with tomato salsa; chorizo, vine tomato and black olive pizza; chargrilled swordfish, wild mushroom linguini; and iced praline and coconut parfait with chocolate sauce.

Open 11–3 6–11 (Wknds & BHs all day) **Bar Meals** L served all week 12–2.30 D served all week 7–10 **Restaurant** L served all week 12–2 D served all week 7–10 Av 3 course à la carte £22 Enterprise Inns Black Sheep, Wadworth 6X, Spitfire. 10 **Facilities** Children's licence Garden Parking Play Area

The Bulls Head

ince changing hands in 2006, the Bull's Head has developed into a serious dining destination.)riginally two separate 16th-century cottages, the extensively refurbished Bulls Head is set in he ancient village of Wootton Wawen, and is ideally placed for touring and exploring the lovely andscapes of Warwickshire and the Cotswolds.

.ow beams, leather sofas, open fires nd old church pews set the scene 1 the bar and snug areas, and the ame tone and style are maintained 1 the magnificent 'great hall' estaurant, with its vaulted ceiling nd exposed beams. Outside, you'll nd a lawned garden and paved atio surrounded by mature trees.)wners Andrew and Wendy Parry escribe their cooking style quite imply as 'food we love to eat nd food we love to cook.' Local uppliers are personally visited in rder to ensure the very best of the ounty's produce finds its way to ne kitchen. Start with herb-baked vhole camembert with tomato nd sweet chilli chutney; home-ured Sambuca and lemongrass salmon with citrus potato salad; or a tower of prawns and filo pastry with rocket mayonnaise. Mains might take in pan-fried duck breast with leeks and bacon; Lighthorne shoulder of lamb stuffed with apricot, prune, pistachio and mint, or pea and lemon risotto served on roasted butternut squash with truffle oil. Keep an eye out for the daily specials, which could include smoked halibut; grilled mahi mahi with niçoise salad and a poached egg; and pork fillet stuffed with black pudding. What's more, service is taken seriously here, promising to be attentive without being overbearing.

MAP 10 SP16
Stratford Rd B95 6BD
☎ 01564 792511
dir: *On main rd B3400 4m N of Stratford upon Avon, 1m S of Henley-in-Arden*

Open 12–3 5–11 (Sun 12–10.30)
Bar Meals L served all week 12–9 D served all week 2–9 Av main course £12
Restaurant L served all week 12–2.30 D served all week 6–9.30 (Sat & Sun all day) Av 3 course à la carte £19
W'hampton & Dudley
Marston's Pedigree, Banks Bitter, Banks Original plus Guest ales. 10
Facilities Garden Parking

England

WITHYBROOK MAP 11 SP48

The Pheasant

Main St CV7 9LT ☎ 01455 220480 📠 01455 221296
e-mail: thepheasant01@hotmail.com
dir: *7m from Coventry*

This charming 17th-century free house has been in the same ownership since 1981. The pub stands beside the brook where withies were once cut for fencing. An inglenook fireplace, farm implements and horse-racing photographs characterise the interior, where daily blackboard specials supplement an extensive menu. Typical options include braised pheasant in Madeira sauce; cheesy fisherman's pie; and broccoli and walnut lasagne. Outside tables overlook the Withy Brook itself.

Open 11–1am (Sun 12–11) Closed: 25–26 Dec **Bar Meals** L served all week 12–2 D served all week 6.15–10 (Sun 12–9) Free House Courage Directors, Theakstons Best, John Smiths Smooth. 9 **Facilities** Garden Dogs allowed Parking

WOOTTON WAWEN MAP 10 SP16

Pick of the Pubs

The Bulls Head

Stratford Rd B95 6BD ☎ 01564 792511
dir: *On main rd B3400 4m N of Stratford upon Avon, 1m S of Henley-in-Arden*

See Pick of the Pubs on page 595

WEST MIDLANDS

BARSTON MAP 10 SP27

Pick of the Pubs

The Malt Shovel at Barston

Barston Ln B92 0JP ☎ 01675 443223 📠 01675 443223
web: www.themaltshovelatbarston.com

Heralded as a country pub and restaurant with a difference, the Malt Shovel certainly does not disappoint. It has been converted from an early 20th-century mill and stylishly decorated with modern soft furnishings and interesting art and artifacts. There is also a pretty garden for summer use. The bar is cosy and relaxed with log fires in winter, and the restaurant is housed in a converted barn next door. Fresh local produce is cooked to order, with some imaginative dishes making the best of seasonal ingredients. Seafood is a particular strength, and dishes include seared scallops on braised honey and vanilla potato fondant; and roasted fillet of wild marlin with red pepper risotto, rocket and white truffle oil. An alternative might be slow braised Royal Balmoral venison with sweet red cabbage, followed by an intriguing dessert: warm stack of kirsch blinis with plum and apricot chutney and caramelita ice cream.

The Malt Shovel at Barston

Open 12–3.30 5.30–11 (Sun & BHs 12–7) **Bar Meals** L served all week 12–2.30 (Sun 12–3.30) D served Mon–Sat 6.30–9.45 **Restaurant** L served all week 12–2.30 (Sun 12–3.30) D served Mon–Sat 7–9.45 Av 3 course à la carte £25 Free House Tribute, Brew XI, Old Speckled Hen. 8 **Facilities** Children's licence Garden Parking

BIRMINGHAM MAP 10 SP0

The Peacock

Icknield St, Forhill, nr King's Norton B38 0EH
☎ 01564 823232 📠 01564 829593

Despite its out of the way location, at Forhill just outside Birmingham, the Peacock keeps very busy serving traditional ales and a varied men (booking essential). Chalkboards display the daily specials, among which you might find braised partridge on a bed of pheasant sausage and mash, whole sea bass with crab, grilled shark steak with light curr butter, pan-fried sirloin steak with mild mushroom and pepper sauce, or lamb fillet with apricot and walnut stuffing. Several friendly ghosts are in residence, and one of their tricks is to disconnect the taps from the barrels. Large gardens with two patios.

Open 11–11 (Sun 12–10.30) **Bar Meals** L served all week 11 D served all week 10 Av main course £7.95 **Restaurant** L served all week 12–10 D served all week 6–10 Chef & Brewer Hobsons Best Bitter, Theakstons Old Peculier, Enville Ale. 20 **Facilities** Garden Parking

CHADWICK END MAP 10 SP27

Pick of the Pubs

The Orange Tree

Warwick Rd B93 0BN ☎ 01564 785364

A pub/restaurant in beautiful and peaceful countryside, yet only minutes from the National Exhibition Centre, Solihull and Warwick. Visitors will find a relaxed Italian influence, reflected in the furnishings and the food, not least the deli counter from which breads, cheeses and olive oils are served. Start with a plate of antipasti, perhaps, or chilli-crusted squid with pineapple and red onion salsa. A small section of the menu is devoted to dishes featuring salad leaves, of which chicory with gorgonzola and pear is an example. There are several pastas, including orechiette with tomatoes, garlic broad beans and goats' cheese; fired pizzas; and a range of stove-cooked, grilled or spit-roasted meats and fish. Comfortable seating and ambient music in the bar makes it great for just mingling and relaxing, while the sunny lounge area, all sumptuous leather sofas and rustic décor, opens up though oversized French doors to the patio.

Open 11–11 **Bar Meals** L served all week 12–2.30 (Sun 12–4.30) D served all week 6–9.30 Av main course £10 **Restaurant** L served all week 12–2.30 D served all week 6.30–9.30 Av 3 course à la carte £17.50 IPA, Tetleys. 8 **Facilities** Garden Dogs allowed Parking

HAMPTON IN ARDEN MAP 10 SP28

Pick of the Pubs

The White Lion

10 High St B92 0AA ☎ 01675 442833 01675 443168
e-mail: info@thewhitelioninn.com
dir: *Opposite church*

Locals gather in the Front Bar of this 400-year-old timber-framed village pub and, just as their counterparts do across the land, recount tales of times past. A listed building, it was originally a farmhouse, although licensed since at least 1836. The Lounge Bar has the more comfortable furniture and open fires, and provides an appealing range of traditional bar food. In the attractively designed and furnished restaurant you'll find modern English cuisine based on local, seasonal produce, including fresh fish on daily specials boards. For dinner, try a starter of spicy lamb koftas with Greek salad, followed by pan-fried duck breast with braised red cabbage, orange and blackberry and port jus; chargilled chicken supreme and confit chicken leg with red wine, bacon and mushroom sauce; or salmon and prawn fishcakes with fine green beans and hollandaise sauce. Plenty of choice for children, and roasts on Sundays.

The White Lion

Open 12–11 **Bar Meals** L served all week 12–2.30 (Sun 12–3) D served Mon–Fri 6.30–8.30 Av main course £10 **Restaurant** L served all week 12–2.30 D served all week 6.30–10 Av 3 course à la carte £21 Punch Taverns Brew XI, Black Sheep, Adnams, Old Hooky. **Facilities** Garden Parking

OLDBURY MAP 10 SO98

Waggon & Horses

17a Church St B69 3AD ☎ 0121 552 5467
e-mail: andrewgale@sabrain.com
dir: *Telephone for directions*

A listed back-bar, high copper-panelled ceiling and original tilework are among the character features to be found at this real ale pub in the remnants of the old town centre. Traditional pub food includes faggots and mash, pork and leek sausages, lasagne, chilli, and fish and chips. Beers from Brains of Cardiff and guests.

Open 12 -11 (Sun 12–10.30) **Bar Meals** L served Mon–Sat 12–3 D served Mon–Sat 5.30–8.30 S A Brain Enville White, Brains IPA, Oakham JHB, 3 Guest beers. 9 **Facilities** Parking

SEDGLEY MAP 10 SO99

Beacon Hotel & Sarah Hughes Brewery

129 Bilston St DY3 1JE ☎ 01902 883380 01902 884020
e-mail: andrew.brough@tiscali.co.uk

Little has changed in 150 years at this traditional brewery tap, which still retains its Victorian atmosphere. The rare snob-screened island bar serves a taproom, snug, large smoke-room and veranda. Proprietor John Hughes reopened the adjoining Sarah Hughes Brewery in 1987, 66 years after his grandmother became the licensee. Flagship beers are Sarah Hughes Dark Ruby, Surprise and Pale Amber, with guest bitters also available.

Open 12–2.30 5.30–10.45 (Fri 5.30–11, Sat 12–3 6–11, Sun 12–3 7–10.30) Sarah Hughes Brewery Sarah Hughes Dark Ruby, Surprise & Pale Amber, Guest Beers and seasonal products. 8 **Facilities** Children's licence Garden Dogs allowed Parking Play Area **Notes**

England

SOLIHULL MAP 10 SP17

The Boat Inn 🍷

222 Hampton Ln, Catherine-de-Barnes B91 2TJ
☎ 0121 705 0474 📠 0121 704 0600
e-mail: steven-hickson@hotmail.com

Village pub with a small, enclosed garden located right next to the canal in Solihull. Real ales are taken seriously and there are two frequently changing guest ales in addition to the regulars. There is also a choice of 14 wines available by the glass. Fresh fish is a daily option, and other favourite fare includes chicken cropper, Wexford steak, and beef and ale pie.

Open 11–11 (Sun 12–10.30) **Bar Meals** L served all week 12–10 D served all week 12–10 Av main course £7.95 Bombardier, Greene King IPA, 2 Guest ales. 🍷 14 **Facilities** Children's licence Garden Dogs allowed Parking

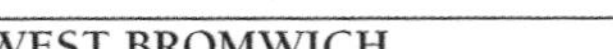

WEST BROMWICH MAP 10 SP09

The Vine

Roebuck St B70 6RD ☎ 0121 553 2866 📠 0121 500 0700
e-mail: bharat@thevine.co.uk
dir: *0.5m from junct 1 of M5. 2m from West Bromwich*

Well-known, family-run business renowned for its good curries and cheap drinks. Since 1978 the typically Victorian alehouse has provided the setting for Suresh "Suki" Patel's eclectic menu. Choose from a comprehensive range of Indian dishes (chicken tikka masala, goat curry, lamb saag), a barbecue menu and Thursday spit roast, offered alongside traditional pub meals like sausage and chips, chicken and ham pie, and toasted sandwiches. The Vine boasts the Midlands' only indoor barbeque.

Open 11.30–2.30 5–11 (Fri–Sun all day) **Bar Meals** L served all week 12–2 D served all week 5–10.30 (Sun 1–10.30) **Restaurant** L served all week D served all week 5–10.30 (Sat–Sun 1–10.30) Free House Banks, Brew XI, John Smiths. **Facilities** Garden

WIGHT, ISLE OF

ARRETON MAP 05 SZ58

The White Lion

PO30 3AA ☎ 01983 528479
e-mail: chrisandkatelou@hotmail.co.uk
dir: *B3056 (Newport to Sandown road)*

Oak beams, polished brass and open fires set a cosy tone in this 300-year-old former coaching inn, known for its well-priced bar food, and even for having a ghost, nicknamed George. Visitors can stoke up on traditional favourites such as steak, mushroom and ale pie; simple snacks such as filled baguettes and seasonal salads; or specials such as venison with a stilton glaze and fruits of the forest sauce. 'All-you-can-eat' curry night on Wednesdays (booking advised) .

The White Lic

Open 11–11 (Sun 12–11) **Bar Meals** L served all week 12–9 D served all week 12–9 Av main course £7 Enterprise Inns Badger Best, Fuller's London Pride, Timothy Taylor Landlord, John Smiths Smooth & Flowers Be

Facilities Garden Dogs allowed Parking Play Area

BEMBRIDGE MAP 05 SZ6

The Crab & Lobster Inn 🍷

32 Foreland Field Rd PO35 5TR
☎ 01983 872244 📠 01983 873495
e-mail: allancrab@aol.com

Refurbished, award-winning 19th-century pub just yards from the popular 65-mile coastal path, and including a raised deck and patio area offering superb sea views. Originally a fisherman's cottage built of island stone. Locally caught seafood is one of the pub's great attractions, with lemon sole, sea bass and fresh tuna among the dishe

Open 11–3 6–11 (Summer 11–11) **Bar Meals** L served all week 12–2.30 D served all week 6.00–9.30 Av main course £8.95 **Restaurant** L served all week 12–2.30 D served all week 7–9.30 Av 3 course à la carte £25 Enterprise Inns Interbrew Flowers Original, Goddards Fuggle-Dee-Dum, Greene King IPA, John Smiths. 🍷 10 **Facilities** Children's licence Garden Dogs allowed Parking

The Pilot Boat Inn

;tation Rd PO35 5NN ☎ 01983 872077 & 874101

-mail: michelle@pilotboatinn.com

lir: *On corner of harbour at bottom of Kings Rd*

ust a stone's throw from Bembridge harbour, this strikingly designed ee house enjoys a strong local following, whilst being handy for achtsmen and holidaymakers. Owners Nick and Michelle Jude offer n attractive menu of traditional favourites, including cod in beer atter with chips and peas; and bangers and mash with red wine and nion gravy. There's also a children's menu, together with specials like egetable balti with rice; and chunky lamb stew and mash.

pen 11–11 **Bar Meals** L served all week 12–2.30 D served all week 6–9 Ned 6–8.30) Av main course £7.95 **Restaurant** L served all week 12–2.30) served all week 6–9 Free House London Pride, Guinness, & IPA. **acilities** Dogs allowed Parking

3ONCHURCH MAP 05 SZ57

The Bonchurch Inn

onchurch Shute PO38 1NU

☎ 01983 852611 01983 856657

-mail: bonchurchinn@aol.com

lir: *Off A3055 in Bonchurch*

harles Dickens wrote part of *David Copperfield* while staying in this illage. The pub itself is a splendidly preserved former coaching inn nd stables, tucked away in a secluded continental-style courtyard. The ıenu focuses on Italian specialities, fish dishes and a range of ways vith meat. Try risotto Milanese; scampi Portofino with Pernod and ream; or chicken provençale with rice and vegetables. Ventnor and onchurch beaches are a mere stroll away.

pen 12–3.30 6.30–11 (Summer 11–11) Closed: 25 Dec **ar Meals** L served all week 11–2.15 D served all week 6.30–9 Av main ourse £8.50 **Restaurant** D served all week 6.30–8.45 Av 3 course à la arte £17 Free House Scottish Courage Courage Directors & Courage est. **Facilities** Garden Dogs allowed Parking

COWES MAP 05 SZ49

The Folly

olly Ln PO32 6NB ☎ 01983 297171

eached by land and water, and very popular with the boating aternity, the Folly is one of the island's more unusual pubs. Timber om an old sea-going French barge was used in the construction, nd wood from the hull can be found in the bar. The menus are vide ranging with something for everyone. House specialities include enison wellington, prime British beef ribs and slow cooked lamb.

pen 9–11 **Bar Meals** L served all week 12–9.30 D served all week 2–9.30 (Sun 12–9) Av main course £8 Greene King Greene King A, Old Speckled Hen & Goddards Best Bitter. 10 **Facilities** Garden ogs allowed Parking

FRESHWATER MAP 05 SZ38

Pick of the Pubs

The Red Lion

Church Place PO40 9BP

☎ 01983 754925 01983 754925

dir: *In Freshwater follow signs for parish church*

An unashamedly English pub where 'tradition and care' is the motto of owners Michael and Lorna Mence. The origins go back to the 11th century, although today's climber-clad building is clearly more recent. A garden at the rear is well furnished with hardwood chairs and tables, and a canvas dome comes into its own for candlelit alfresco dinners. The bar is comfortable with settles and chairs around scrubbed pine tables, the log fire burns throughout the winter, and pop music is definitely not played. Lorna is the talented head chef who prepares a mix of favourites for lunch and dinner seven days a week. Apart from their daily-changing blackboard, which includes a lot of English Channel seafood, there are light lunches of tortilla wraps, baguettes, ploughman's, bangers and mash, scampi, or ham, egg and chips. In the evening options range from asparagus in smoked salmon, to tagine of lamb with apricots.

Open 11.30–3 5.30–11 (Sun 12–3, 7–10.30) **Bar Meals** L served all week 12–2 D served all week 6.30–9 (Sun 7–9) Av main course £10.50 Enterprise Inns Interbrew Flowers Original, Fuller's London Pride, Goddards, Wadworth 6X. 16 **Facilities** Garden Dogs allowed Parking

NITON MAP 05 SZ57

Buddle Inn

St Catherines Rd PO38 2NE ☎ 01983 730243

e-mail: buddleinn@aol.com

dir: *In Niton take 1st L signed 'to the lighthouse'*

A spit away from the English Channel one way and the Coastal Path the other, this 16th-century, former cliff-top farmhouse can claim to be one of the island's oldest hostelries. Popular with hikers and ramblers (and their muddy boots and dogs), the interior has the full traditional complement – stone flags, oak beams and large open fire. Simple but well prepared food, including local crab (summer only), and grilled fresh sardines is served.

Open 11–12 **Bar Meals** L served all week 12–2.45 D served all week 6–9 Enterprise Inns Wight Spirit, Buddle Best, London Pride, Greene King. 9 **Facilities** Garden Dogs allowed Parking

NORTHWOOD MAP 05 SZ49

Travellers Joy

85 Pallance Rd PO31 8LS ☎ 01983 298024

e-mail: tjoy@globalnet.co.uk

Ruth and Derek Smith are heading for 20 years in charge of this 300-year-old alehouse, just a little way inland from Cowes. Don't expect dishes described on the menu as 'drizzled' or 'pan-roasted' here because the food is, well, uncomplicated – grilled gammon steak, double sausage with egg, chips and beans, honey-roast ham,

CONTINUED

England

NORTHWOOD continued

home-made steak and kidney pie, burgers and children's meals. Outside is a pétanque terrain, pets' corner and play area.

Open 11–3 5–12 (Sun 7–12) **Bar Meals** L served all week 12–2 D served all week 6–9 (Sun 7–9) Free House Goddards Special Bitter, Courage Directors, Ventnor Golden Bitter, Deuchars IPA. **Facilities** Garden Dogs allowed Parking Play Area

ROOKLEY MAP 05 SZ58

The Chequers

Niton Rd PO38 3NZ ☎ 01983 840314 01983 840820
e-mail: richard@chequersinn-iow.co.uk

Horses in the neighbouring riding school keep a watchful eye on comings and goings at this 250-year-old family-friendly free house. In the centre of the island, surrounded by farms, the pub has a reputation for good food at reasonable prices. Fish, naturally, features well, with sea bass, mussels, plaice, salmon and cod usually available. Other favourites are mixed grill, pork medallions, T-bone steak, and chicken supreme with BBQ sauce and cheese.

Open 11–11 **Bar Meals** L served all week 12–10 D served all week 12–10 (Sun 12–9.30) Av main course £7.95 **Restaurant** L served all week 12–10 D served all week (Sun 12–9.30) Free House Scottish Courage John Smiths, Courage Directors, Best, Wadsworth 6X. **Facilities** Children's licence Garden Dogs allowed Parking Play Area

SEAVIEW MAP 05 SZ69

Pick of the Pubs

The Seaview Hotel & Restaurant

★★★ HL

High St PO34 5EX ☎ 01983 612711 01983 613729
e-mail: reception@seaviewhotel.co.uk
dir: *B3330 (Ryde-Seaview rd), turn left via Puckpool along seafront road, hotel on left adjacent to sea*

Directly facing the sea, this is a smart, small hotel bulging with nautical associations. There are ships' wheels, oars, ship models, old pictures, and lots of polished wood and brass, particularly in the two bars. The one at the front is ideal in summer when you can look out at the passing crowds and the yachts at sea. The bar at the back, the Pump Bar, is crowded with the trophies of local sailors. Snacks in the bar include many fish dishes, but also venison sausage from Carisbrooke, as well as a range of doorstep sandwiches. A smart brasserie restaurant can be found in the Regatta Room, where dishes such as hot crab ramekin may be served. For those seeking a more substantial meal, the hotel's main restaurant at the front offers a civilised, relaxed experience.

Open 11–2.30 6–11 **Bar Meals** L served all week 12–2 D served all week 7–9.30 **Restaurant** L served all week 12–1.30 D served all week 7.30–9.30 Free House Goddards, Greene King Abbot Ale, Adnams Ale. **Facilities** Garden Dogs allowed Parking **Rooms** 17 bedrooms en suite

SHALFLEET MAP 05 SZ48

Pick of the Pubs

The New Inn

Mill Ln PO30 4NS ☎ 01983 531314 01983 531314
e-mail: info@thenew-inn.co.uk
dir: *6m from Newport to Yarmouth on A3054*

This is one of Wight's best-known dining pubs and, owing to its location on the National Trust-owned Newtown River estuary, an absolute mecca for yachties. Its name reflects how it rose phoenix-like from the charred remains of an older inn, which burnt down in 1743, and its original inglenook fireplaces, flagstone floors and low-beamed ceilings give it bags of character. The waterside location helps to explain its reputation for excellent fish and seafood dishes, such as grilled fillets of sole with lime, ginger and rocket; whole cracked-crab salad; prawn platter with garlic mayo; and seafood royale, a mammoth plate of fresh fish and crustaceans for two people. Other favourites include hot cooked baguettes; prime steaks with chips, onion rings and mushrooms; gammon, egg and chips; lamb steak with Moroccan-style bean salad; and home-made lasagne. With over 60 worldwide wines, the New Inn offers one of the island's most extensive selections.

Open 12–3 6–11 **Bar Meals** L served all week 12–2.30 D served all week 6–9.30 **Restaurant** L served all week 12–2.30 D served all week 6–9.30 Enterprise Inns Interbrew Bass, Goddards Special Bitter, Greene King IPA, Marston's Pedigree. 6 **Facilities** Garden Dogs allowed Parking

SHANKLIN MAP 05 SZ58

Fisherman's Cottage

Shanklin Chine PO37 6BN
☎ 01983 863882 01983 866145
e-mail: jill@shanklinchine.co.uk

At the foot of a deep ravine known as Shanklin Chine, the cottage was built about 1817 by William Colenutt, who also excavated the path through the Chine. Always on offer are stilton and vegetable crumble, lasagne, gammon and egg, salads, jacket potatoes, ploughman's and sandwiches, as well as a children's selection. Wider choice at dinner includes fisherman's pie, salmon mornay, Thai green curried chicken, and various specials. Sit outside and you're virtually on the beach.

Open 11–3 7–11 (Mar–Oct all wk) Closed: Nov–Feb **Bar Meals** L served all week 11–2 D served all week 7–9 Free House Scottish Courage Courage Directors & John Smiths Smooth. **Facilities** Garden Dogs allowed
Notes

SHORWELL MAP 05 SZ48

Pick of the Pubs

The Crown Inn

Walkers Ln PO30 3JZ

☎ 01983 740293 📠 01983 740293

e-mail: info@crownshorwell.com

dir: *Left at top of Carrsbrooke High Street Shorwell 6m*

Set in a pretty village in picturesque West Wight, with thatched cottages, a small shop, three manor houses, and the church opposite. In summer arum lilies decorate the garden stream, and a Wendy house, slide and swings keep youngsters amused. The building dates in parts from the 17th century, and different floor levels attest to many alterations. Log fires, antique furniture, and a friendly female ghost who disapproves of card playing complete the picture of this traditional family-run pub. Beers on tap include an island brew, and food consists of home-made favourites based on locally sourced lamb and beef, game in winter and fish in summer. The award-winning specials board usually features ten dishes, which may include steak and kidney pie, cottage pie, crown of pheasant, or lamb tagine. If fish is favoured, you may find a seafood platter, fish pie, crab and prawn gratin, or sea bass with red onion and sweet pepper salsa.

Open 10.30-3 6-11 (Sun eve 6-10:30, Summer hols all day) **Bar Meals** L served all week 12-2.30 D served all week 6-9 (6-9.30 wknds, Summer) **Restaurant** L served all week 12-2.30 D served all week 6-9 Enterprise Inns Interbrew, Flowers Original, Badger Tanglefoot, Wadworth 6X. **Facilities** Garden Dogs allowed Parking Play Area

VENTNOR MAP 05 SZ57

The Spyglass Inn

The Esplanade PO38 1JX

☎ 01983 855338 📠 01983 855220

e-mail: info@thespyglass.com

For centuries this area was a haunt of smugglers, and echoes of these activities can be seen in the huge collection of nautical memorabilia on the walls of this famous 19th-century inn. It has a superb position, right at the end of Ventnor Esplanade. Much of the food here is, naturally, fishy, with home-made fish chowder, Ventnor crab and lobster, but other dishes might include several varieties of pie; local sausages; or ham and leek bake.

The Spyglass Inn

Open 10.30-11 **Bar Meals** L served all week 12-9.30 D served all week 12-9.30 Free House Badger Best & Tanglefoot, Ventnor Golden, Goddards Fuggle-Dee-Dom, Yates Undercliff Experience. 8 **Facilities** Garden Dogs allowed Parking

YARMOUTH MAP 05 SZ38

Bugle Coaching Inn NEW ★★★ INN

The Square PO41 0NS ☎ 01983 760272 📠 01983 760883

e-mail: buglecoachinginn@btconnect.com

The 17th-century inn stands in Yarmouth's market square, close to the sea and the yachting harbour. Food is served in the bar, the heated and stone-flagged courtyard garden, and the more recently added Brasserie at the Inn. The oak-panelled bar, with its beams and log fires, opens into an attractive conservatory area. Sandwiches, ploughman's, and hot and cold dishes are served in the bar, while the brasserie specialises in locally landed fish and island produce.

Open 11-11 (Sun 12-10.30) **Bar Meals** L served all week 12-3 D served all week 6-9.30 (Sun 6-9) Av main course £8.95 Greene King IPA, London Pride, Flowers Original **Facilities** Garden Dogs allowed Parking **Rooms** 7 bedrooms en suite S£55 D£90 **Notes**

WILTSHIRE

ALDERBURY MAP 05 SU12

The Green Dragon

Old Rd SP5 3AR ☎ 01722 710263

dir: *1m off A36*

There are fine views of Salisbury Cathedral from this 15th-century pub, which is probably named after the heroic deeds of Sir Maurice Berkeley, the Mayor of Alderbury, who slew a green dragon in the 15th century. Dickens wrote *Martin Chuzzlewit* here, and called the pub the Blue Dragon. An interesting and daily changing menu features home-made meat and vegetarian dishes using locally sourced produce.

Open 11.30-3 6-11 (Sun 12-3, 7-11) **Bar Meals** L served all week 12-2.30 D served Mon-Sat 6.30-9.30 Av main course £6.50 **Restaurant** 12-2.30 D served all week 7-9 Av 3 course à la carte £16 Hall & Woodhouse Badger First Gold & Tanglefoot, Ferret. 14 **Facilities** Garden Dogs allowed Parking

England

ALVEDISTON MAP 04 ST92

Pick of the Pubs

The Crown

SP5 5JY ☎ 01722 780335 🖷 01722 780836

dir: *2.5m off A30 between Salisbury and Shaftesbury*

See Pick of the Pubs on opposite page

AXFORD MAP 05 SU27

Red Lion Inn 🍷

SN8 2HA ☎ 01672 520271 🖷 01672 521011

e-mail: info@redlionaxford.com

dir: *Marlborough centre follow Ramsbury signs 3m*

A pretty, 17th-century brick and flint pub with fine views over the Kennet Valley. In the bar there's a large inglenook, and a pleasing mix of sofas and more solid seating, while the restaurant is attractively laid out with white linen-covered tables and upholstered ladderback chairs. In addition to bar snacks, the menus offer plenty of choice, including chargrilled prime Aberdeen Angus steak; baked Barbary duck breast; grilled Brixham brill; and bean and mixed pulse casserole.

Open 12–2.30 6.30–11 (Sun 7–10.30) **Bar Meals** L served all week 12–2 D served all week 7–9 (Sat 7–9.30) Av main course £10 **Restaurant** L served all week 12–2 D served all week 7–9 (Sat 7–9.30) Av 3 course à la carte £25 Free House Ashford Ale, Ramsbury Gold & Guest Beers. 🍷 16 **Facilities** Garden Parking

BARFORD ST MARTIN MAP 05 SU03

Barford Inn 🍷

SP3 4AB ☎ 01722 742242 🖷 01722 743606

e-mail: thebarfordinn@btconnect.com

web: www.thebarfordinn.co.uk

dir: *On A30 5m W of Salisbury*

Customer satisfaction and service are the keynotes in this 16th-century former coaching inn five miles outside Salisbury. A welcoming lounge, lower bar area and intimate snug have greeted visitors for generations – during World War II the Wiltshire Yeomanry dedicated a tank to the pub, known then as The Green Dragon. The varied menu includes freshly cut ciabattas, chargrilled medallions of beef, seafood linguini, or vegetarian stuffed Creole-style aubergine, and there's a range of exotic coffees to finish.

Open 11–3 6–11 Closed: Xmas wk **Bar Meals** L served all week 12–2.30 D served Mon–Sat 7–9.30 **Restaurant** L served all week 12–2.30 D served Mon–Sat 7–9.30 Hall & Woodhouse Badger Dorset Best & Fursty Ferrett, Festive. 🍷 6 **Facilities** Garden Parking **Rooms** 4 bedrooms en suite (★★★ INN)

BERWICK ST JAMES MAP 05 SU03

Pick of the Pubs

The Boot Inn

High St SP3 4TN ☎ 01722 790243 🖷 01722 790243

e-mail: kathieduval@aol.com

dir: *Telephone for directions*

Half of this attractive 16th-century stone and flint inn was once a cobbler's workshop. Tucked away in picturesque countryside, the ivy-covered building is decorated with hanging baskets and surrounded by award-winning gardens, complete with flower borders and a summerhouse. The interior is traditional in style, and the atmosphere warm and friendly. Real ales are served, together with a menu of quality home-cooked food from Monday evening through to Sunday lunch. Fresh local produce, including herbs and vegetables from the garden, appear in daily changing dishes such as a crock of garlic mushrooms with crusty bread; whole roasted partridge with port and pink peppercorn jus; and red Thai chicken curry served with basmati rice and poppadom. A trio of fish options rounds off the menu, with home-made trout fishcakes, salad of warm scallops and crispy bacon, and a fish of the day according to availability.

Open 12–3 6–11 (Sun 7–10.30) Closed: 25–26 Dec **Bar Meals** L served Tue–Sun 12–2.30 D served Tue–Sat 6.30–9.30 Av main course £9.95 Wadworth Wadworth 6X, Henrys IPA, Guest beers. **Facilities** Garden Dogs allowed Parking

BOX MAP 04 ST8

The Northey NEW 🍷

Bath Rd SN13 8AE ☎ 01225 742333

e-mail: office@ohhcompany.co.uk

dir: *4m from Bath on A4 towards Chippenham.*

Once the station hotel, now a delightfully refreshing open plan bar and restaurant. Owner Sally Warburton's interior design makes good use of wooden and flagstone flooring, high-back oak chairs, leather loungers and handcrafted tables. Head chef Marco Appel masterminds classic French cooking with English influences, such as Aberdeen Angus with a choice of sauces; rack of lamb, rosemary and garlic mash and redcurrant jus; and grilled red mullet fillets with dill and crab couscous.

Open 10.30–3 6.30–12 **Bar Meals** L served all week 11–2 D served all week 6.30–9.30 Av main course £13 **Restaurant** L served all week 11–2 D served all week 6.30–9.30 Av 3 course à la carte £23 Wadworth Wadworth 6X, IPA, Malt 'n' Hops & Old Father Timer. 🍷 10 **Facilities** Garden Parking

The Crown

Tucked away in the Ebble Valley between Salisbury and Shaftesbury, the Crown is a well-known landmark with its pink-washed walls, thatched roof, clinging creepers and colourful window boxes.

Its old world setting is characterised by head-cracking low beams, two inglenook fireplaces that burn invitingly on cooler days, and comfortable furnishings. The inn serves entirely home-made food, with particular emphasis on fresh local produce whenever possible. The cosy bar sets the scene for anything from a simple sandwich to fresh fish and rib-eye steaks. Listed weekly on the specials board, expect to find a wide range of starters from a hearty leek and potato soup, through deep-fried camembert with redcurrant jelly; field mushrooms stuffed with garlic, parsley, bacon, breadcrumbs and cashew nuts; and filo-wrapped king prawns with a sweet chilli dip; to Chinese spring rolls with a hoisin dip. Main choices are just as appetizing, with pub favourites like chilli con carne with garlic bread; scampi, chips and salad; beef lasagna; and steak and kidney pie with a rich shortcrust pastry; and imaginative dishes like roast rump of lamb with a minted pea veloute; smoked haddock and spinach gratin topped with breadcrumbs and cheese; pan-fried duck breast with a plum sauce; and fresh whole lemon sole with herb butter. The pub makes a handy stopover for splendid local walks and visits to Salisbury Cathedral and Stonehenge. Outside there's a beer garden where food is also served.

MAP 04 ST92
SP5 5JY
☎ 01722 780335
📠 01722 780836
dir: *2.5m off A30 between Salisbury and Shaftesbury*

Open 12-3 6.30-11 (Sun 7-10.30)
Bar Meals L served all week 12-2.30 D served all week 6.30-9 Av main course £9.75
Restaurant L served all week 12-2 D served all week 6.30-9.30 Sun 12-2.30 Av 3 course à la carte £18
Free House
Ringwood Best, Timothy Taylor Landlord, Youngs Special Bitter.
Facilities Garden Dogs allowed Parking Play Area

The Tollgate Inn

Built in the 16th century, The Tollgate used to be a cider house known as The White Hart – and a right den of iniquity it allegedly was. As with many old buildings, it has a chequered history, having over the years been part weaving mill, part Baptist chapel, and even the village school.

When the nearby Kennet & Avon Canal was cut, some of the building was knocked down to make way for an approach road. The bar serves an excellent selection of real ales, mostly from West Country breweries, and you can eat in a small adjoining room with a woodburning stove, and decorated in country style. The restaurant proper is up wooden stairs in what was originally the chapel for the weavers working below – and cosy it is too, with its open fire, candles and antiques. Regular customers are attracted by modern British cooking with Mediterranean influences, locally sourced or supplied whenever possible. For example, hand-reared beef comes from the lush pastures of nearby Broughton Gifford and Corsham; the pub produces its own lamb; village shoots provide game; vegetables are grown in the surrounding fertile soils; and a specialist in town supplies the cheeses. Lunchtime light bites (Tuesday to Saturday only) include brie and grape quesadilla (a sort of tortilla); Tollgate potato cake; and Church Farm Gloucester Old Spot sausages with Dijon mustard mash. Daily deliveries from Brixham guarantee fresh fish, such as John Dory, grilled and served with smoked haddock in a fishcake with basil crème fraîche; and black bream and Cornish gurnard with lemon and tarragon risotto. Additional possibilities are fillet of beef Wellington, roasted local pheasant, and crusted cassoulet. The well-established garden and terrace is a tranquil and delightful place to eat. No children under 12 after 7pm.

★★★★ INN
MAP 04 ST86
Holt BA14 6PX
01225 782326
01225 782805
e-mail: alison@tollgateholt.co.uk
dir: *B3107 towards Melksham, pub on right*

Open 11-2.30 6-11
Bar Meals L served Tue-Sun 12-2 D served Tue-Sat 7-9.30
Restaurant L served Tue-Sun 12-2 D served Tue-Sat 7-9.30
Free House
Exmoor Gold, Glastonbury Ales Mystery Tor, York Ales, Sharp's Doom Bar. 9
Facilities Garden Dogs allowed Parking
Rooms 4 bedrooms en suite S£50 D£75

England

BOX continued

The Quarrymans Arms

Box Hill SN13 8HN ☎ 01225 743569 01225 742610

e-mail: john@quarrymans-arms.co.uk

dir: *Please phone pub for accurate directions*

Set high above the Box Valley, this 300-year-old miners' pub has fabulous country views and is packed with mining memorabilia. As well as being a focal point for the community the inn also attracts the many walkers, cavers, potholers, cyclists, mountain bikers and horse-riders visiting the area. There's a substantial snack menu, plus daily-changing blackboards; typical choices are seafood pasta, pork dijonnaise, or prime beef fillet with red wine and mushroom sauce.

Open 11–3.30 6–11 (Fri–Sun all day) **Bar Meals** L served all week 11–3 D served all week 6.30–10.30 **Restaurant** L served all week 11–3 D served all week 6.30–10.30 Av 3 course à la carte £18 Free House Butcombe Bitter, Wadworth 6X, Moles Best & local Guest Ales. 10 **Facilities** Garden Dogs allowed Parking

BRADFORD-ON-AVON MAP 04 ST86

The Dandy Lion

35 Market St BA15 1LL ☎ 01225 863433 01225 869169

e-mail: dandylion35@aol.com

New owners have refurbished this 17th-century town centre pub. But the spirit of the original Dandy Lion lives on through its well-kept ales and continental lagers, together with a mix of traditional English and rustic European food. The café-bar menu offers tasty grazing boards, hot-filled flatbreads, and thick-cut sandwiches alongside old comforts. Dinner in the air-conditioned restaurant could start with rich Tuscan pâté, and continue with poached chicken supreme. Home-made desserts include New York baked cheesecake.

Open 10.30–11 **Bar Meals** L served all week 12–3 D served all week Sun 12–8.30 Av main course £8.95 **Restaurant** L served Sun 12–2.30 D served all week 6–9.30 (Sun 12–8.30) Av 3 course à la carte £23 Wadworth Butcombe, Wadworth 6X, Henrys IPA, Hoegarden. 11

Pick of the Pubs

The Kings Arms

Monkton Farleigh BA15 2QH

☎ 01225 858705 01225 858999

e-mail: enquiries@kingsarms-bath.co.uk

dir: *Off A363, follow brown tourist signs to pub*

Dating back to the 11th century, this historic Bath stone building is situated in an attractive village just outside Bradford-on-Avon. Conversion into an alehouse took place in the 17th century, but original features remain, including the mullioned windows, flagged floors and a vast inglenook – said to be the largest in Wiltshire – in the medieval-style Chancel restaurant, which is hung with tapestries and pewter plates. The Bar and Garden menu offers light lunches such as Bath sausages, spring onion and smoked bacon mash; steak frites; three-egg omelette (with various fillings) and chips; and wild mushroom, spinach and asparagus lasagne. From the à la carte menu come main dishes such as duck breast with balsamic glaze, mascarpone and almond dauphinoise; game casserole with herb dumplings; brochette of sirloin steak and tiger prawns (known as the 'Trawler and Tractor'), while specials may include roast poussin with smoked bacon, parsley mash and cheddar cheese sauce; pork schnitzel with sesame-fried potatoes and dolcelatte cheese sauce; and chicken piri piri sizzle with white and wild rice.

The Kings Arms

Open 12 –11 (Sun 12–10.30) **Bar Meals** L served all week 12 D served all week 10.30 Av main course £10 Inspired Wadworth 6X, Buttcombe Bitter, Wychwood Hobgoblin, Shepherd Neame Spitfire. 8 **Facilities** Garden Dogs allowed Parking

Pick of the Pubs

The Tollgate Inn ★★★★ INN

Holt BA14 6PX ☎ 01225 782326 01225 782805

e-mail: alison@tollgateholt.co.uk

dir: *B3107 towards Melksham, pub on right*

See Pick of the Pubs on opposite page

BRINKWORTH MAP 04 SU08

Pick of the Pubs

The Three Crowns

SN15 5AF ☎ 01666 510366

dir: *A3102 to Wootton Bassett, then B4042, 5m to Brinkworth*

Run by the same landlord and landlady for 20 years, The Three Crowns stands on the village green facing the church in the longest village in England. The building extends into a large, bright conservatory and garden room, and then out onto a heated patio and garden, which has extensive views of the Dauntsey Vale. In winter, an open log fire provides a warm welcome in the bars, which are decorated with farming memorabilia donated by customers. Settle there for a pint of Archers Village or Camerons Castle Eden Ale, and perhaps a game of drafts, cribbage or chess. All the dishes are home made; the imaginative but traditionally-inspired food might include veal and mushroom pie, or wild boar with a sauce of shallots and apricots flamed with port and finished with a hint of cream and stilton cheese. There is an impressive selection of fish dishes.

Open 11–3 6–11 Closed: 25–26 Dec **Bar Meals** L served all week 12–2 (Sun 12–3) D served all week 6–9.30 (Sun 6–9) Av main course £15.20 **Restaurant** L served all week 12–2 D served all week 6–9.30 Av 3 course à la carte £22.50 Enterprise Inns Wadworth 6X, Archers Village Ale, Castle Eden, Fullers London Pride. 20 **Facilities** Garden Dogs allowed Parking Play Area

England

BROAD CHALKE MAP 05 SU02

The Queens Head Inn

1 North St SP5 5EN
01722 780344 & 0870 770 6634
0870 770 6635 & 01722 781322
dir: *A354 to Coombe Bissett right towards Bishopstone, 4m*

Attractive 15th-century-inn with friendly atmosphere and low-beamed bars, once the village bakehouse. On sunny days, enjoy the flower-bordered courtyard, whilst in colder weather the low beams and wood burner in the bar provide a cosy refuge. Menus include light snacks such as sandwiches, ploughman's lunches and home-made soups, as well as more substantial main courses: perhaps grilled trout with almonds, sirloin steak, or wild game casserole.

Open 11-3 6-11 (Sun 12-3, 7-11) **Bar Meals** L served all week 12-2 D served all week 7-9 **Restaurant** L served all week 12-2 D served all week 7-9 Free House Greene King IPA & Old Speckled Hen, Wadworth 6X, Ruddles County & Morlands Best. 7 **Facilities** Garden Parking

BURCOMBE MAP 05 SU03

The Ship Inn

Burcombe Ln SP2 0EJ 01722 743182 01722 743182
e-mail: theshipburcombe@mail.com
dir: *In Burcombe, off A30, 1m from Wilton*

This 17th-century Nadder Valley pub has a lovely riverside location and a beautiful garden, perfect for summer dining. Low beams characterise the interior, and winter fires provide a traditional background for the seasonal menus and daily changing specials. Sandwiches and light bites are available at weekday lunchtimes, while options from the main menu might include roast root vegetable and cheese bake, lamb gigot, fishcakes, and free-range rib-eye steak.

Open 11-3 6-11 (Sun 11-3, 6.30-10.30) Closed: 1st 2 wks in Jan **Bar Meals** L served all week 12-2.30 D served all week 6.30-9 (Sun 7-9) Av main course £12 **Restaurant** L served all week 12-2.30 D served all week 6.30-9 (Sun 7-9) Av 3 course à la carte £22 Flowers IPA, Wadworth 6X, Courage Best, Guinness & Kronenbourg. 8 **Facilities** Children's licence Garden Dogs allowed Parking

BURTON MAP 04 ST8

The Old House at Home

SN14 7LT 01454 218227 01454 218227
e-mail: ohhcompany@aol.com
dir: *On B4039 NW of Chippenham*

A stone, ivy-clad pub with beautiful landscaped gardens and a waterfall, and inside, low beams and an open fire. Overseen by the same landlord for some twenty years, the crew here are serious about food. The kitchen offers a good fish choice, vegetarian and pasta dishes, and traditional pub meals. Favourites include lamb cutlets with champ; salmon and crab cakes; Woodland duck breast with stuffing; butterfly red mullet; and king scallops in Cointreau.

Open 7-12 (Sun 11.30-3, 7-10.30) Closed: 25 & 26 Dec **Bar Meals** L served all week 12-2 D served Mon-Sat 7-10 (Sun 7-9.30) Free House Wadworth 6X, Butcombe Gold. 40 **Facilities** Garden Parking

CASTLE COMBE MAP 04 ST8

Pick of the Pubs

Castle Inn

SN14 7HN 01249 783030 01249 782315
e-mail: enquiries@castle-inn.info
dir: *A420, right into Castle Combe*

All the properties in drop-dead gorgeous Castle Combe are listed. The inn takes its name from a Norman castle, now almost vanished thanks to stone-filching villagers. The inn has faced the market place since the 13th century, but recent careful and considerate restoration has conserved its ancient charm, not least in the beamed bar with its large stone fireplaces. The bar menu follows the well-trodden path of baguettes and ploughman's; sausage, mash and onion gravy; fresh cod in beer batter; and chicken, bacon and avocado salad. In Oliver's Restaurant main courses include chargrilled rib-eye steak with pepper and shallot sauce; roast breast of duck with rôsti potato and plum sauce; Cajun salmon with mash and roasted cherry tomatoes; and pavé of tomato and mozzarella risotto on buttered spinach. A conservatory leads out to a pleasant courtyard.

Open 9.30-11 Closed: 25 Dec **Bar Meals** L served all week 11-3 D served Sun-Thu 6-9.30 (Fri-Sat 11-3, 6-10) Av main course £8.50 **Restaurant** L served Mon-Sat 11-3 D served Mon-Thu 6-9.30 (Sun 12-9.30, Fri-Sat 11-3, 6-10) Av 3 course à la carte £25 Free House Stella, Fosters, Guinness, Tunnel Vision. 7 **Facilities** Garden

CHRISTIAN MALFORD MAP 04 ST9

The Rising Sun

Station Rd SN15 4BL 01249 721571
dir: *From M4 junct 17 take B4122 towards Sutton Benger, left onto B4069, 1m to Christian Malford. Pub last building on left*

Built in 1832, the pub is set in the picturesque village of Christian Malford, and used to have a blacksmith's attached to it. Bi-monthly themed evenings, quiz nights and sports' club events are regular features, and the pub is one of the hosts of the Malford Challenge, eve

May, when the men of the village compete with their counterparts in Foxham in 10 events over a day. Seafood figures strongly on the menu.

Open 12-2.30 6.30-11 **Bar Meals** L served Thu-Sun 12-2 D served Mon-Sun 6.30-9.30 Av main course £6 **Restaurant** L served Thu-Sun 12-2 D served all week 6.30-9.30 Av 3 course à la carte £22 Free House Sussex, Rucking Mole. **Facilities** Garden Dogs allowed Parking

COLLINGBOURNE DUCIS — MAP 05 SU25

The Shears Inn & Country Hotel

The Cadley Rd SN8 3ED
01264 850304 01264 850301
e-mail: info@theshears-inn.co.uk
dir: *On A338 NW of Andover & Ludgershall*

As the name attests, this thatched 16th-century building was formerly a shearing shed for market-bound sheep. Now a thriving country inn, the daily chalkboard menus round up all the usual suspects as well as more unusual dishes such as poached chicken, spinach and Parma ham roulade; roasted goose breast and sweet cherry gravy; or oxtail in red wine.

Open 11-11 **Bar Meals** L served all week 12-2.30 D served all week 6.30-10 Av main course £10 **Restaurant** L served all week 12-2.30 D served all week 6-9.30 Av 3 course à la carte £15.20 Brakspear Brakspear Bitter, Hobgoblin & Guest Ales. 12 **Facilities** Children's licence Garden Dogs allowed Parking

CORSHAM — MAP 04 ST87

Pick of the Pubs

The Flemish Weaver NEW

63 High St SN13 0EZ 01249 701929
e-mail: nibags@blueyonder.co.uk
dir: *Next to Town hall on Cobham High St*

Historic Corsham Court is just a stone's throw away, as is a row of Flemish weavers' cottages in original condition. Previously called the Packhorse, the pub was closed for several months before being taken over by the current team in 2002. Work to restore the interiors followed, when original beams and fittings were carefully preserved. 'A breath of fresh air' is the ethos of the place, reflected in its well-kept real ales and the traceability of its food – a full list of suppliers is displayed in the bar, together with dates of local farmers' markets. Menus change daily, so specials are eschewed. At lunchtime choose from baguettes, salads, or larger plates such as diced venison in red wine, or free-range gammon steak and pineapple. For dinner choose from the likes of organic rump steak with stilton sauce, or five fish crumble with leeks; leave space for puddings which are all home made.

Open 10.30-3 5.30-11 (Sun 12-3 7-10.30) **Bar Meals** L served all week 12-2.30 D served Mon-Sat 7-9.30 Av main course £11.50 **Restaurant** L served all week 12-2.30 D served Mon-Sat 7-9.30 Av 3 course à la carte £21 Unique Bath Spa, Doom Bar, Banks, Speckled Hen & Bath Gem. 10 **Facilities** Garden Dogs allowed **Notes**

CORTON — MAP 04 ST94

Pick of the Pubs

The Dove Inn ★★★ INN

BA12 0SZ 01985 850109 01985 851041
e-mail: info@thedove.co.uk
dir: *A36 N of Salisbury signed for Corton and Boyton. Cross railway line, right at junct 1m, right into village.*

A thriving traditional pub tucked away in a lovely Wiltshire village near the River Wylye. A striking central fireplace is a feature of the refurbished bar, and the spacious garden is the venue for barbecues, and the perfect spot for a drink on long summer days. Award-winning menu is based firmly on West Country produce, with many ingredients coming from within just a few miles. Popular lunchtime bar snacks give way to a full evening carte, featuring starters like pan-fried pigeon breast with a redcurrant jus, or garlic king prawns with a sweet chilli dip, followed by oven-baked sea bass stuffed with fresh herbs; beef and ale pie served with mashed potato or fries; spicy chicken curry with basmatic rice; and pan-fried venison steak with a juniper berry and red wine sauce. Five en suite bedrooms arranged around a courtyard make The Dove an ideal touring base. Bath, Salisbury and Stonehenge are all close by.

Open 12-2.30 6-11 (Sun 7-10.30) **Bar Meals** L served all week 12-2 D served all week 7-9 (Sat 12-3, 7-9.30 Sun 12-3, 7-9) Av main course £9 **Restaurant** L served all week 12-2 D served all week 7-9 (Sun 12-3, 7-10.30) Av 3 course à la carte £18 Free House Spitfire, Youngs, Butcombe & Hop Back GFB. 10 **Facilities** Children's licence Garden Dogs allowed Parking **Rooms** 5 bedrooms en suite S£55 D£75

DEVIZES — MAP 04 SU06

The Bear Hotel ★★★ HL

The Market Place SN10 1HS
0845 456 5334 01380 722450
e-mail: info@thebearhotel.net
dir: *Pub is located in the market place*

Right in the centre of Devizes, home of Wadworth's Brewery, this old coaching inn dates from at least 1559 and lists Judge Jeffreys, George III, and Harold Macmillan amongst its notable former guests. You'll find old beams, log fires, fresh flowers, three bars and two restaurants. The menu offers pot-roasted partridge perhaps, and broccoli and mushroom strudel. Check out the weekly jazz sessions in the cellar.

CONTINUED

DEVIZES continued

Open 9.30–11 Closed: 25–26 Dec **Bar Meals** L served all week 11.30–2.30 D served all week 7–9.30 (Sun 7–9) **Restaurant** L served Sun 12.15–1.45 D served Mon–Sat 7–9.30 Av 2 course fixed price £22 Wadworth Wadworth 6X, IPA, JCB, Old Timer. 18 **Facilities** Garden Dogs allowed Parking **Rooms** 25 bedrooms en suite S£75 D£100

The Raven Inn

Poulshot Rd SN10 1RW ☎ 01380 828271 01380 828271

dir: *A361 Devizes towards Trowbridge, left for Poulshot*

A characterful half-timbered, 18th-century pub in an attractive village, from where you can easily walk to the Kennet & Avon Canal and along the towpath by the famous Caen Hill flight of locks. An extensive menu of home-cooked food includes light bites such as prawn curry and rice, and devilled whitebait. Pork stroganoff, herby salmon and special vegetable bake main courses compete for consumption with filled ciabattas, steaks and ham, eggs and french fries.

Open 11–2.30 6.30–11 (Sun 12–3, 7–10.30) **Bar Meals** L served Tue–Sun 12–2 D served Tue–Sun 7–9.30 (Sun 7–9) Av main course £9.25 **Restaurant** L served Tue–Sun 12–2 D served Tue–Sun 7–9.30 Wadworth Wadworth 6X, IPA, Summersault, Old Timer. 8 **Facilities** Garden Parking

DONHEAD ST ANDREW MAP 04 ST92

Pick of the Pubs

The Forester Inn

Lower St SP7 9EE ☎ 01747 828038 01747 828714

e-mail: possums1@btinternet.com

dir: *4.5m from Shaftsbury on A30 towards Salisbury.*

A traditional 16th-century inn close to the Dorset and Wiltshire border, the Forester has warm stone walls, a thatched roof, original beams and an inglenook fireplace. In recent years the inn has been extended to include a restaurant and a restaurant/ meeting room, which has double doors opening on to the lower patio area. The garden and large patio area are pleasant for eating and drinking outside. The restaurant has a growing reputation for its freshly cooked food and interesting choice of dishes including many seafood dishes as there are deliveries from Cornwall five times a week. Starters such as Gran Reserva Parma ham with fresh figs, gorgonzola and honey dressing, or crab tian with lamb's lettuce, tarragon and ginger dressing. Mains take in poussin, poached and chargrilled with black-eye bean cassoulet, and broucette of lambs' kidney with black pudding, mashed swede and a sherry and shallot vinegar. The dessert menu might include warm blueberry tart with home-made almond ice cream, or sticky toffee pudding with local clotted cream. The wine list has been painstakingly compiled by the landlord and reflects his passion for the subject.

Open 12–3 6.30–11 (Sun 7–10.30) **Bar Meals** L served all week 12–2 (Sun 12–3) D served all week 6–9 (Sun 7–9, Fri–Sat 6–9.30) **Restaurant** L served all week 12–2 (Sun 12–3) D served all week 7–9 (Fri–Sat 6–9.30) Av 3 course à la carte £20 Free House 6X, Ringwood, Butcombe. 17 **Facilities** Garden Dogs allowed Parking

EAST KNOYLE MAP 04 ST83

Pick of the Pubs

The Fox and Hounds

The Green SP3 6BN ☎ 01747 830573 01747 830865

e-mail: fox.hounds@virgin.net

dir: *1.5m off A303/A350 junc, follow brown signs*

See Pick of the Pubs on opposite page

EBBESBOURNE WAKE MAP 04 ST92

Pick of the Pubs

The Horseshoe

Handley St SP5 5JF ☎ 01722 780474

A gem of a 17th-century village inn that was possibly – and nobody's sure about this – a former farm building. Nothing very much has changed for at least 50 years, not counting the very necessary grafting on of a conservatory to accommodate more diners. The village is not that easy to find, but a good navigator and perseverance pay dividends. Beyond the climbing roses are two rooms filled with simple furniture, old farming implements and country bygones, linked to a central servery dispensing cask-conditioned ales straight from their barrels. Good value bar food is freshly prepared from local produce, with steak and kidney and pheasant and cranberry pies; fresh fish bake; lamb shank with rosemary and redcurrant sauce; honey roasted duckling; lambs' liver and bacon casserole; and pork and leek sausages in leek and onion gravy. All meals are accompanied by plenty of vegetables. Children are welcome, dogs are allowed, and there's a pretty, flower-filled garden.

Open 12–3 6.30–11 Closed: 26 Dec **Bar Meals** L served Tue–Sun 12–2 D served Tue–Sat 7–9.30 **Restaurant** 12–2 D served Tue–Sat 7–9.30 Free House Ringwood Best Bitter, Keystone & other bitters. **Facilities** Children's licence Garden Parking Play Area

FONTHILL GIFFORD MAP 04 ST93

Pick of the Pubs

The Beckford Arms

SP3 6PX ☎ 01747 870385 01747 870385

e-mail: beck.ford@ukonline.co.uk

dir: *2m off A303 (Fonthill Bishop turning) at x-rds by Beckford Estate*

See Pick of the Pubs on page 610

The Fox and Hounds

A traditional, late 15th-century thatched and beamed free house, built originally as three cottages. East Knoyle itself is situated on a greensand ridge and is surrounded by excellent walking country with views to the west of the delightful Blackmore Vale.

As well as once being home to the family of Jane Seymour, Henry VIII's second wife, it was the village where Sir Christopher Wren grew up, his father being the local vicar. A stone alongside the main road records that Wren was an 'Architect, Mathematician, Patriot'. The pub's interior is quaint and cosy, with wooden flooring, natural stone walls, flagstones and sofas within toasting distance of a winter fire. The conservatory has a New England feel – calm, light and comfortable. Snacks and main meals include ploughman's, ciabatta melts and pizzas (from the clay oven) and good old favourites like steamed steak and kidney pudding, bangers and mash, lasagne and smoked haddock, cod and salmon fishcakes. The specials menu, which points out that all meat, chicken and game is sourced from local farms and suppliers, is extensive. Starters include mussels in red Thai curry sauce; braised capsicums, chorizo and smoked paprika on garlic toast; and pork rillette, onion marmalade and pickles on toasted brioche. For a main dish there may be a 21-day old fillet or sirloin steak with a choice of sauces; venison medallions with port and cranberry sauce; beer-battered catch of the day with tartare sauce and chunky chips; Asian-style duck on noodles with hoi sin; or caramelised onion and leek tart with watercress and walnut salad. Pavlova with passion fruit coulis and cream, or warm chocolate fudge cake number among the desserts.

MAP 04 ST83
The Green SP3 6BN
☎ 01747 830573
Fax 01747 830865
e-mail: fox.hounds@virgin.net
dir: *1.5m off A303/A350 junc, follow brown signs*

Open 12–2.30 6–11
Bar Meals L served all week 12–2.30 D served all week 6.30–9.30
Restaurant L served all week 12–2.30 D served all week 6.30–9.30
Free House
Hidden, Wessex, Dorset Brewing Co, Youngs Bitter. 10
Facilities Garden Dogs allowed Parking

The Beckford Arms

Substantial 18th-century stone-built inn peacefully situated opposite the Fonthill Estate and providing a good base from which to explore the unspoilt Nadder Valley. Eddie and Karen Costello have transformed this rural retreat since arriving here a few years ago.

Beyond the basic locals' bar, you will find a rambling main bar, adjoining dining area and an airy garden room all decorated in a tastefully rustic style, complete with scrubbed plank tables topped with huge candles, and warm terracotta-painted walls. Expect a roaring log fire in winter, a relaxed, laid-back atmosphere, and interesting modern pub menus. From petit pain baguettes, hearty soups, salads, Asian-style fishcakes with sweet chilli dip, or a Thai curry at lunchtime, the choice of well presented dishes extends, perhaps, to rack of lamb with tomatoes, wine and Italian herbs, sautéed medallions of Wiltshire pork with caramelised apple, Calvados and cider, and salmon with Vermouth glaze in the evening. Generous bowls of fresh vegetables, colourful plates and friendly service all add to the dining experience here. Sun-trap patio and a delightful garden – perfect for summer sipping.

MAP 04 ST93
SP3 6PX
☎ 01747 870385
🖷 01747 870385
e-mail:
beck.ford@ukonline.co.uk
dir: *2m A303 (Fonthill Bishop turning) at x-rds by Beckford Estate*

Open 12–11 (Sun 12–10.30)
Closed: 25 Dec
Bar Meals L served all week 12–2.15 D served all week 7–9
Av main course £10.95
Restaurant L served all week 12–2.15 D served all week 7–9
Free House
Timothy Taylor Landlord, Abbot, Hopback Summer Lightning.
Facilities Garden Dogs allowed Parking

FORD — MAP 04 ST87

Pick of the Pubs

The White Hart 🍷

SN14 8RP ☎ 01249 782213 📠 01249 783075
e-mail: whitehart.ford@eldridge-pope.co.uk
dir: *From M4 junct 17 take A429 then A420 to Ford*

A rambling 15th-century coaching inn, the White Hart is located by a trout stream deep in the Wyvern Valley. Parts of the musical version of *Dr Doolittle* with Rex Harrison were filmed here in the late 1960s, and the site has also been used for a Carlsberg advert. It's a stone building with old beams and log fires, including a traditional bar and candlelit dining rooms, and the atmosphere is relaxed and informal. Dishes might include stuffed plaice fillets, rib-eye steak with pepper sauce, and venison medallions. In summer drinks can be taken out onto the grass area to the rear of the pub, and meals on the patio or pub front. There is also a picnic area, but drinks must be purchased in the pub.

Open 11–11 (Sun 12–10.30) **Bar Meals** L served all week 12–3 D served all week 6–9 (Sat–Sun all day) Av main course £10.50 **Restaurant** L served all week 12–2.30 D served all week 7–9.30 Eldridge Pope Wadworth 6X, Courage Best, Guest beer. 🍷 8 **Facilities** Garden Dogs allowed Parking

GREAT BEDWYN — MAP 05 SU26

Pick of the Pubs

The Three Tuns NEW

High St SN8 3NU ☎ 01672 870280 📠 01672 870890
e-mail: jan.carr2@btinternet.com

See Pick of the Pubs on page 612

GREAT CHEVERELL — MAP 04 ST95

Pick of the Pubs

The Bell Inn 🍷

High St SN10 5TH ☎ 01380 813277
e-mail: gillc@clara.co.uk
dir: *A360 from Salisbury through West Lavington, 1st left after black & yellow striped bridge to Great Cheverell*

A family friendly former coaching inn located on the northern edge of Salisbury Plain, run by mother and daughter team Gill and Sara Currie. The Curries were helped to find the premises in 2005 by the Channel 4 programme *Relocation, Relocation*. It's an 18th-century building, Grade II listed, with an L-shaped bar and an oak beamed restaurant. A further 40 people can be seated in the 200-foot garden, where popular barbecues are held in the summer months. There is also a function room available for receptions, private parties and meetings, which can accommodate up to 120 people. The menu is flexible enough to provide anything from a casual lunch to a special occasion dinner, with dishes based on local produce. Choose from steaks from the grill, sizzling stir-fries, and the likes of cod bourguignon, medallions of chicken with prunes and Calvados, and liver and bacon with a twist.

Open 12–3 6–11 (6pm–1am Fri–Sat) Closed: 26 Dec, 1 Jan **Bar Meals** L served Tue–Sun 12–2 D served Tue–Sun 7–9 Av main course £8.50 **Restaurant** L served Tue–Sun 12–2 D served Tue–Sun 7–9 Av 3 course à la carte £16 Av 2 course fixed price £6.75 Free House 6X, IPA, Guest Beer. 🍷 9 **Facilities** Garden Dogs allowed Parking

GREAT HINTON — MAP 04 ST95

Pick of the Pubs

The Linnet 🍷

BA14 6BU ☎ 01380 870354 📠 01380 870354
dir: *Just off A361*

Originally a woollen mill, the building was converted into a village local circa 1905. Chef/landlord Jonathan Furby has transformed it these days into a pub restaurant with a great reputation for food. Everything is prepared on the premises – bread, ice cream, pasta and sausages – with fresh, locally produced ingredients to the fore. There is a light lunch menu, and more substantial dinner menu. You might start with cod and shrimp fishcake with chive and garlic mayonnaise, moving on to the award-winning baked tenderloin of pork, filled with prunes and spinach, wrapped in smoked bacon and served with a wild mushroom sauce. Desserts include new variations of old favourites, like banoffee bread and butter pudding with almond cream. In summer there are seats in the large patio area in front of the pub.

Open 11–2.30 6.30–11 (Sun12–3, 7–10.30) Closed: 1 Jan **Bar Meals** L served Tue–Sun 12–2 D served Tue–Sun 6.30–9.30 **Restaurant** L served Tue–Sun 12–2 D served Tue–Sun 6.30–9.30 Wadworth Wadworth 6X & Henrys IPA. 🍷 8 **Facilities** Garden Parking

GRITTLETON — MAP 04 ST88

The Neeld Arms

The Street SN14 6AP ☎ 01249 782470 📠 01249 782168
e-mail: neeldarms@zeronet.co.uk
dir: *Telephone for directions*

This 17th-century Cotswold stone pub stands at the centre of a pretty village in lush Wiltshire countryside. Quality real ales and freshly prepared food are an equal draw to diners who will eagerly tuck in to lamb shanks, homemade steak and kidney pie or sausage and mash. Children are welcome and the small garden is especially popular for al fresco eating in fine weather.

Open 12–3 5.30–11 **Bar Meals** L served all week 12–2 D served all week 7–9.30 Av main course £5 **Restaurant** L served all week 12–2 D served all week 7–9.30 Av 3 course à la carte £19 Free House Wadworth 6X, Buckleys Best, Brakspear Bitter & IPA. **Facilities** Garden Dogs allowed Parking **Rooms** 6 bedrooms en suite S£40 D£60 (★★★ INN)

The Three Tuns

You'll find this popular country inn in the centre of the village, close to the Ridgeway Path and the Kennet and Avon Canal. It began trading in 1756 as the village bakery, and its bread oven is now a historic feature in this lovely, cluttered old building, while the cellar is said to have once been the local morgue.

Landlord Alan Carr, a retired TV actor-turned-chef, is responsible for a team producing each day's imaginative menu and food freshly prepared to order. He and his wife Jan took over in 2000 and completely refurbished the premises to create the cosy, traditional yet delightfully quirky (for example, life-size models of the Blues Brothers at separate tables) pub you see today. A roaring winter fire in the inglenook and lovely beer garden in summer attract a healthy year-round trade. Food is served at candlelit tables in the open plan bar area and there is a choice of lunch dishes, traditional bar food and a full evening carte menu. Local meat and game, augmented by twice-weekly deliveries of fresh Devon fish, feature in such dishes as slow-roasted lamb shank with cinnamon and red wine sauce; chicken, chorizo, belly pork and mixed sausage cassoulet; Spanish-style rabbit with peppers, tomatoes, white wine, onions and garlic; and tagliatelle with clams, slightly spicy tomato sauce and basil sauce. Chargrills are available every day except Sunday, which is the day Alan takes centre stage (ie the bar), blows a horn, Roly, the pub dog, barks and mine host raffles about 40 joints of meat, with the proceeds going towards the following week's consignment. Out back is a pleasant raised garden.

NEW
MAP 05 SU26
High St SN8 3NU
☎ 01672 870280
📠 01672 870890
e-mail: jan.carr2@btinternet.com

Open 11.30–3 6–11.30
Bar Meals L served all week 12–2 (Sun 12–2.30) D served all week 7–9 Av main course £10
Restaurant L served all week 12–2 (Sun 2–2.30) D served Mon–Sat 7–9 Av 3 course à la carte £20
Punch Taverns
Wadworth 6X, Fullers London Pride, Flowers IPA, Theakstons Black Sheep 🍷 9
Facilities Garden Dogs allowed Parking
Notes

HANNINGTON MAP 05 SU19

The Jolly Tar

Queens Rd SN6 7RP ☎ 01793 762245 📠 01793 765159
e-mail: jolly.ajc@btinternet.com
dir: *A419 towards Cirencester. At Bunsdon/Highworth sign follow B4109 towards Highworth, left at Freke Arms, follow Hannington & Jolly Tar pub signs. Pub in village*

Although it's a fair old trek to the sea, there is a connection – the marriage of a lady from a local land-owning family to a 19th-century battleship captain. Inside are old timbers, a log fire and locally brewed Arkells ales. On the menu, chicken, olive and prosciutto ribbon pasta; home-made lamb burger; Gloucester Old Spot sausages; and Jolly Fantastic fish pie. Specials may include tuna, prawn and red pepper chowder; and shepherds pie.

Open 12–3 6–11 **Bar Meals** L served all week 12–2.30 D served all week 6–9.30 (Sun 7–9.30) Av main course £9 **Restaurant** L served all week 12–2.30 D served all week 6–9.30 (Sun 7–9.30) Av 3 course à la carte £17.50 Arkells 3B, Noel Ale & Kingsdown. 9 **Facilities** Children's licence Garden Dogs allowed Parking Play Area

HEYTESBURY MAP 04 ST94

Pick of the Pubs

The Angel Coaching Inn

High St BA12 0ED ☎ 01985 840330 📠 01985 840931
e-mail: admin@theangelheytesbury.co.uk
dir: *From A303 take A36 toward Bath, 8m Heytesbury on left*

See Pick of the Pubs on page 614

HINDON MAP 04 ST93

Pick of the Pubs

Angel Inn

High St SP3 6DJ ☎ 01747 820696 📠 01747 820054
e-mail: info@theangelathindon.com
dir: *1.5m from A303, on B3089 towards Salisbury*

Elegant gastro pub where rustic charm meets urbane sophistication in a Georgian coaching inn with a brasserie menu. The interior is characterised by wooden floors, beams, large stone fireplaces and comfortable leather seating. Owner John Harrington maintains a relaxed, convivial pub atmosphere where excellent food and hospitality can be relied on. Lunch provides an extensive choice, with rolled shoulder of lamb stuffed with chicken and tarragon mousse, served with Madeira sauce; cold poached salmon with smoked trout mousse; open sandwich filled with prawn salad and smoked salmon; and Wiltshire ham, eggs and chips offering something for everyone. The main menu extends to confit of duck leg and slices of breast; grilled whole sole with lemon and caper butter; noisettes of lamb on pureed fennel with a lime and Pernod sauce; and seared calves' liver with smoked bacon on creamed potato. Outside is an attractive paved courtyard with garden furniture, where food is also served in fine weather.

Open 11–3 5–11 **Bar Meals** L served all week 12–2.30 D served all week 7–9.30 Av main course £8.50 **Restaurant** L served all week 12–2.30 D served Mon–Sat 7–9.30 Av 3 course à la carte £23.50 Free House Wadworth 6X, Buttcombe, Ringwood, Hidden Brewery. 14 **Facilities** Garden Dogs allowed Parking

Pick of the Pubs

The Lamb at Hindon ★★★★ INN

High St SP3 6DP ☎ 01747 820573 📠 01747 820605
e-mail: info@lambathindon.co.uk
dir: *From A303 follow signs to Hindon. At Fonthill Bishop right onto B3089 to Hindon. Pub on left*

Set in the heart of this charming Wiltshire village just 20 minutes from Salisbury, The Lamb began trading as a public house as long ago as the 12th century. By 1870 it supplied 300 horses for coaches going to and from London and the West Country. Today, the building retains plenty of its original character, with inglenook fireplaces, flagstone floors and heavy wooden beams. It also has 14 individually furnished bedrooms. In addition to a good selection of real ales there are extensive wine and whisky lists. The modern menu makes use of the best ingredients: you could start with a parfait of foie gras with Glenmorangie 10 year old malt whisky, red onion marmalade and olive oil crostini; then move on to red Thai chicken curry, or perhaps Macsween haggis with swede and potato gratin, buttered savory cabbage and thyme jus.

Open all day, incl breakfast **Bar Meals** L served all week 12–2.30 D served all week 6.30–9.30 (Sun 7–9) **Restaurant** L served all week 12–2.30 D served all week 6.30–9.30 (Sun 7–9) Youngs Bitter, Youngs Special & 2 Guest Beers. **Facilities** Garden Dogs allowed Parking **Rooms** 14 bedrooms en suite

HORTON MAP 05 SU06

The Bridge Inn

Horton Rd SN10 2JS ☎ 01380 860273 📠 01380 860273
e-mail: manager@thebridgeinnhorton.fsnet.co.uk
dir: *A361 from Devizes, right at 3rd rdbt*

The buildings that are now the Bridge Inn were originally a family-run farm, built around 1800, and then a flour mill and bakery. One of the grinding wheels is now a part of the patio. It makes a perfect place for boat watching, as narrowboats cruise past on the Kennet and Avon Canal. The menu takes in snacks, pub grub (sausage/fish and chips), grills, a vegetarian selection, and mains such as mixed fish crumble, and slow roast shoulder of lamb.

Open 11.30–3 6.30–11 (Sun 12–3, 7–10.30) **Bar Meals** L served all week 12–2.15 D served all week 7–9.15 (Sun 7–9) **Restaurant** L served all week 12–2.15 D served all week 7–9.15 (Sun 7–9) Wadworth Wadworth Henry's original IPA, 6X, Old Father Timer. 8 **Facilities** Garden Dogs allowed Parking

The Angel Coaching Inn

This 16th-century inn is surrounded by stunning countryside so if you have the time, take one of the walks which start and end there. The Angel itself has been transformed by a complete refurbishment into a striking blend of original features and contemporary comfort.

The beamed bar has scrubbed pine tables, warmly decorated walls and an attractive fireplace with a wood-burning stove. In summer, the secluded courtyard garden is very popular. Although very much a dining pub, it has not forsaken the traditional charm and character of its coaching inn past. You can eat in the restaurant, the bar, or, during the summer months, alfresco in the secluded courtyard garden which leads off the restaurant. Steaks are a speciality and are hung for 35 days in the pub's ageing rooms for the best possible quality and taste. Lunch might take in a starter of home-cured gravadlax with a lemon and caper dressing and wild rocket, followed by roast haunch of venison with peppercorn sauce, sautéed Savoy cabbage and mashed potato. If you fancy something simpler, plump for an aged steak, mushroom and Guinness pie; eggs Benedict; or sandwiches. The dinner menu is divided into starters (grilled goats' cheese, roasted vegetables and pesto; chicken liver parfait with fig chutney); 'simple classics' (perhaps classic fish pie with cod, haddock, salmon and prawns); and main courses such as wild mushroom gnocchi with blue cheese and rocket; or seared calves' liver with Lyonaise potatoes and bacon.

MAP 04 ST94
High St BA12 0ED
☎ 01985 840330
01985 840931
e-mail:
admin@theangelheytesbury.co.uk
dir: *From A303 take A36 toward Bath, 8m Heytesbury on left*

Open 12–12 Rest: 25 Dec 12–2
Bar Meals L served all week 12–2.30 (Sun 12–3) D served all week 7–9.30
Restaurant L served all week 12–2.30 D served all week 7–9.30
Greene King
Moorlands, Greene King IPA, 6X. 10
Facilities Garden Dogs allowed Parking

KILMINGTON MAP 04 ST73

The Red Lion Inn

BA12 6RP ☎ 01985 844263

dir: *B3092 off A303 N towards Frome. Pub 2.5m from A303 on right on B3092 just after turning to Stourhead Gardens*

This 14th-century coaching inn once provided spare horses to assist coaches in the climb up nearby White Sheet Hill. The interior, unchanged over decades, features flagstone floors, low beamed ceilings, antique settles and blazing log fires. The landlord has been here for over 25 years, and his typical menu includes meat or vegetable lasagne, chicken casserole and game pie, as well as a selection of pasties, baked potatoes and toasted sandwiches, at lunchtimes only.

Open 11.30–2.30 6.30–11 (Sun 12–3, 7–10.30) Closed: 25–26 Dec & 1 Jan **Bar Meals** L served all week 12–1.50 D served none Free House Butcombe Bitter, Jester, Guest Ale. 7 **Facilities** Garden Dogs allowed Parking **Notes**

LACOCK MAP 04 ST96

The George Inn

4 West St SN15 2LH ☎ 01249 730263 01249 730186

dir: *M4 junct 17 take A350, S*

Steeped in history and much used as a film and television location, this beautiful National Trust village includes an atmospheric inn. The George dates from 1361 and boasts a medieval fireplace, a low-beamed ceiling, mullioned windows, flagstone floors and an old tread wheel by which a dog would drive the spit. Wide selection of steaks and tasty pies, and fish options include specials in summer; finish with the home-made bread and butter pud.

Open 10–2.30 5–11 (Sat–Sun all day) **Bar Meals** L served all week 12–2 D served all week 6–9.30 **Restaurant** L served all week 12–2 D served all week 6–9.30 (vary in winter) Wadworth Wadworth 6X, Henrys IPA, J.C.B & Henrys Smooth. 13 **Facilities** Garden Dogs allowed Parking Play Area

Red Lion Inn

1 High St SN15 2LQ ☎ 01249 730456 01249 730766

e-mail: redlionlacock@wadworth.co.uk

dir: *Just off A350 between Chippenham & Melksham*

This historic 18th-century inn has kept its original features intact, from the large open fireplace to the flagstone floors and Georgian interior. Wadworth ales and a varied wine list accompany the home-cooked meals and daily specials. Fresh lunchtime sandwiches are accompanied by a portion of chips, whilst more substantial evening dishes include home-made spinach and mushroom lasagne; caramelised red onion and balsamic tart; or venison steak in red wine sauce.

Open 11.30–11 **Bar Meals** L served all week 12–2.30 D served all week 6–9 Av main course £8.50 **Restaurant** L served all week 12–2.30 D served all week 6–9 Wadworth Wadworth Henry's IPA & 6X, Seasonal & mild. 14 **Facilities** Garden Dogs allowed Parking

The Rising Sun

32 Bowden Hill SN15 2PP ☎ 01249 730363

The pub is located close to the National Trust village of Lacock, on a steep hill, providing spectacular views over Wiltshire from the large garden. Live music and quiz nights are a regular feature, and games and reading material are provided in the bar. Thai curries and stir-fries are popular options, alongside traditional liver, bacon and onions; steaks; and beef, ale and Stilton pie.

Open 12–3 6–11 (Sun all day, Summer Fri–Sun all day) **Bar Meals** L served all week 12–2 (Sun 12–3) D served all week 6–9 **Restaurant** L served all week 12–2 (Sun 12–2.30) D served all week 6–9 Moles Best, Molecatcher, Tap Bitter, Rucking Mole. 10 **Facilities** Garden Dogs allowed Parking Play Area

LIMPLEY STOKE MAP 04 ST76

The Hop Pole Inn

Woods Hill, Lower Limpley Stoke BA2 7FS

☎ 01225 723134 01225 723199

e-mail: latonahop@aol.com

Set in the beautiful Limpley Stoke valley, the Hop Pole dates from 1580 and takes its name from the hop plant that still grows outside the pub. Eagle-eyed film fans may recognise it as the hostelry in the 1992 film *Remains of the Day*. A hearty menu includes Thai vegetable curry; home-made pies; fresh local trout; and steaks. Giant filled baps and other light bites are available too.

Open 11–2.30 6–11 Closed: 25 Dec **Bar Meals** L served all week 12–2 D served all week 6.30–9 Av main course £8.50 **Restaurant** L served all week 12–2.15 D served all week 6.30–9.15 (Sun 7–9) Av 3 course à la carte £17 Free House Scottish Courage Courage Best, Butcombe Bitter, Marstons Pedigree, Guest Beers. 8 **Facilities** Garden Dogs allowed Parking

LITTLE CHEVERELL MAP 04 ST95

The Owl

Low Rd SN10 4JS ☎ 01380 812263 01380 812263

dir: *A360, after 10m left onto B3098, right after 0.5m.*

Sit in the pretty garden after dark and you'll discover that this pub is aptly named. As well as the hoot of owls, woodpeckers can be heard in summer. A brook runs at the bottom of the garden and there are views of Salisbury Plain. The pub itself is a cosy hideaway with oak beams and a fire in winter. Typical dishes include lasagna; Thai chicken curry; sizzling beef Szechwan; and stilton and mushroom pork.

Open all day **Bar Meals** L served all week 12–9 D served all week 12–9 Av main course £8.99 **Restaurant** L served all week 12–9 D served all week 12–9 Enterprise Inns Wadworth 6X, Hook Norton Best, Cotleigh Tawney Owl, Scottish Courage Courage Directors. **Facilities** Children's licence Garden Dogs allowed Parking Play Area

LOWER CHICKSGROVE MAP 04 ST92

Pick of the Pubs

Compasses Inn ★★★★ INN

SP3 6NB ☎ 01722 714318 01722 714318

e-mail: thecompasses@aol.com

dir: *A30 (1.5m W of Fovant) 3rd right to Lower Chicksgrove. In 1.5m left into Lagpond Lane 1m*

See Pick of the Pubs on page 617

England

LUDWELL MAP 04 ST92

The Grove Arms NEW ★★★ INN

SP7 9ND ☎ 01747 828328 01747 828960
e-mail: info@grovearms.com
dir: *On A30 3m from Shaftesbury*

This friendly 17th-century village inn was once owned by the aristocratic Grove family. The smartly turned out restaurant features the family coat of arms in pride of place, alongside a menu that makes good use of British produce. If you've ever dreamed of running a pub, look out for the sample days, designed to give you a taste of the realities of life behind the bar.

Open 12–12 **Bar Meals** L served all week 12–2.15 D served all week 6.15–9 Av main course £10 **Restaurant** L served all week 12–2.15 D served all week 6.15–9 Hall & Woodhouse Badger Gold, Festive Feasant & Hopping Hare. **Facilities** Dogs allowed Parking

MALMESBURY MAP 04 ST98

Pick of the Pubs

Horse & Groom NEW

The Street, Charlton SN16 9DL ☎ 01666 823904
e-mail: info@horseandgroominn.com
dir: *M4 junct 17 follow signs to Cirencester on A429. Through Corston & Malmesbury. Straight on at Priory rdbt, at next rdbt take 3rd exit to Cricklade, then to Charlton*

See Pick of the Pubs on page 618

The Smoking Dog

62 The High St SN16 9AT
☎ 01666 825823 01666 826513
e-mail: smokindog@sabrain.com

Log fires, solid wooden floors and a relaxed atmosphere greet visitors to this refined 18th-century stone-built pub, right in the heart of Malmesbury. There's an expanding range of real ales that features continually changing guest beers, and the pub has a good reputation for interesting, freshly-cooked food. Each May the thirsty and hungry can enjoy a popular beer and sausage festival.

Open 12–11 (Sun 12–10.30) (Fri & Sat 12–12) **Bar Meals** L served all week 12–2.30 D served Sun–Thu 6.30–9.30 (Sun 12–3, 6.30–9) **Restaurant** L served all week 12–3 D served all week 6.30–9.30 (Sun 12–3, 6.30–9) Av 3 course à la carte £17.50 Archers Best, Buckleys Best, Reverend James plus 3 guest bitters. 9 **Facilities** Garden Dogs allowed

Pick of the Pubs

The Vine Tree

Foxley Rd, Norton SN16 0JP
☎ 01666 837654 01666 838003
e-mail: tiggi@thevinetree.co.uk
dir: *5 mins junct 17 M4*

See Pick of the Pubs on page 621
Please see cycle ride on page 622

MARDEN MAP 05 SU05

The Millstream

SN10 3RH ☎ 01380 848308 01380 848337
e-mail: mail@the-millstream.net
dir: *Signed from A342*

The Millstream sits in lovely countryside in the Vale of Pewsey, within sight of both Salisbury Plain and the Marlborough Downs. It was tastefully refurbished a few years ago without losing its traditional feel: wooden floors, beamed ceilings, log fires and pretty muted colours create a cosy, welcoming interior. Books, games and comfy sofas add their own homely touch. A good choice of hand-pulled beers and an impressive wine list are an ideal accompaniment for the contemporary menu, where locally sourced seasonal produce, plus fish from Cornwall, hold sway. Look out for braised lamb shank, and spatchcock poussin, with all the trimmings.

Open 11.30–12 Closed: 25 Dec **Bar Meals** L served all week 12–3 (Sun 12–4) D served all week 6.30–9.30 Av main course £10.95 **Restaurant** L served Tue–Sat 12–3 (Sun 12–5) D served Tue–Sun Av 3 course à la carte £25 Av 2 course fixed price £11.95 Wadworth 6X, Henry's IPA, JCB, Bishops Tipple. 16 **Facilities** Children's licence Garden Dogs allowed Parking Play Area

Compasses Inn

'his immensely characterful 14th-century thatched inn stands in a tiny hamlet on the old 'rovers' track from Poole to Birmingham – a route that can still be traced today. The rolling ountryside that unfolds around it is part of a designated Area of Outstanding Natural Beauty.

nside the latched door, there's long, low-beamed bar with igh-backed stools, stone walls, vorn flagstone floors and a large nglenook fireplace in which a vood-burning stove blazes in older months. The adjacent dining oom is perfect for private parties.)ishes are written up on a regularly hanging blackboard menu and verything is freshly made from easonally available produce. wo chefs, Toby Hughes and Ian 'halmers, oversee operations. ypical starters could include duck, heasant and pigeon terrine with port and onion chutney; goats' heese and roasted red pepper oufflé; and mussels in a bacon, vhite wine and onion cream sauce. ollow with the likes of goose breast on roasted baby vegetables with a grape compote; chicken breast filled with goats' cheese, wrapped in bacon and served with a red onion confit; or slow-roasted shoulder of lamb with a red wine and mint jus. An impressive selection of fish and seafood dishes might include lemon sole fillets stuffed with salmon mousse; poached smoked haddock with black pudding and tomato concasse; and West Country lobster thermidor. The garden has a large grassed area with some lovely views and seats for 40 people. Four bedrooms are available, providing an ideal base for an exploration of the area.

★★★★ INN

MAP 04 ST92
SP3 6NB
☎ 01722 714318
01722 714318
e-mail: thecompasses@aol.com
dir: *A30 (1.5m W of Fovant) 3rd right to Lower Chicksgrove. In 1.5m left into Lagpond Lane, 1m*

Open 12-3 6-11 Closed: 25-26 Dec
Bar Meals L served all week 12-2 D served all week 7-9 Av main course £13
Restaurant L served all week 12-2 D served all week 7-9 Av 3 course à la carte £24
Free House
Interbrew Bass, Wadworth 6X, Ringwood Best, Chicksgrove Churl. 7
Facilities Garden Dogs allowed Parking
Rooms 4 bedrooms en suite S£65 D£85

Horse & Groom

Wiltshire's only outdoor bar is to be found in the walled gardens of this charming 16th-century coaching inn, which received a substantial refurbishment in 2007. The golden Cotswold stone exterior gives way inside to stone flags and roaring fires – the epitome of the rural pub. In the cosy, dog-friendly bar, weekly-changing guest ales include Cotswold Way and London Pride.

Though the drinks side of things is an integral part of the inn, don't expect any old pub grub to appear from the kitchens. Under the watchful eye of executive chef Rob Clayton, the team serve up an array of imaginative modern British dishes. In the bar, alongside an appetising range of nibbles you could tuck into Somerset brie, grilled bacon and cranberry ciabatta, or an array of classic dishes that takes in tomato and basil shepherd's pie; Mr Parson's pork and stilton sausages with mash and shallot sauce; and beer-battered fish of the day with crushed peas. In the restaurant, the à la carte menu might offer braised Gressingham duck leg with red wine and puy lentils, or saffron and roasted artichoke risotto to start. Mains range from double cooked shoulder of lamb with honey roast root vegetables, to grilled fillet of sea bream with a basil cream sauce, or pan-fried turbot with fennel confit and sauté potatoes. Warm dark chocolate and walnut fondant with vanilla ice cream; white chocolate and lime parfait; and red wine poached pears with spiced gingerbread ice cream will leave the sweet toothed spoiled for choice.

NEW 🍷
MAP 04 ST98
The Street, Charlton SN16 9DL
☎ 01666 823904
e-mail:
info@horseandgroominn.com
dir: *M4 junct 17 follow signs to Cirencester on A429. Through Corston & Malmesbury. Straight on at Priory rdbt, at next rdbt take 3rd exit to Cricklade, then to Charlton*

Open 12–11
Bar Meals L served Mon–Sat 12–2.30 Av main course £9.95
Restaurant L served all week 12–2.30 D served all week 6.30–9.30 Av 3 course à la carte £25 Av 3 course fixed price £14.95
Merchant Inns PLC
Archers, 6X, London Pride & Guest Ales. 🍷 8
Facilities Garden Dogs allowed Parking Play Area

MINETY

Pick of the Pubs

Vale of the White Horse Inn

SN16 9QY ☎ 01666 860175 📠 01666 860175
e-mail: info@vwhi.net
dir: *On B4040 (3m W of Cricklade 6m E of Malmesbury)*

This handsome and beautifully restored inn overlooks its own lake and in summer, sitting out on the large raised terrace surrounded by rose beds, it's hard to think of a better spot. The lower ground floor originally provided stabling for horses, and nowadays the village bar still serves the local community well. Here you'll find a good selection of real ales and a range of sandwiches and simple bar meals. Upstairs, lunch and dinner are served in the stone-walled restaurant with its polished tables and bentwood chairs. The menus offer something for most tastes, with starters including stilton, onion and sweet pepper quiche; and home-cured Bresaola beef salad. Main course options range from beer-battered cod and chips to roast chicken breast wrapped in smoked bacon and stuffed with brie, with daily specials featuring the likes of aubergine risotto, or baked salmon fillet with a black olive crust.

Open 11-11.30 **Bar Meals** L served all week 12-9.30 D served all week 12-9.30 (Sun 12-9) Av main course £9.50 **Restaurant** L served all week 12-9.30 D served all week 12-9.30 (Fri-Sat 12-10, Sun 12-9) Av 3 course à la carte £20 Free House Wadworth 6X, Three Castle Vale Ale, Grolsch, San Miguel & Adnams Broadside. 12 **Facilities** Children's licence Garden Parking

NEWTON TONY — MAP 05 SU24

Pick of the Pubs

The Malet Arms

SP4 0HF ☎ 01980 629279 📠 01980 629459
e-mail: maletarms@hotmail.com
dir: *8m N of Salisbury on A338, 2m from A303*

A 17th-century inn on the River Bourne in a quiet village. It was originally built as a dwelling house, much later becoming The Three Horseshoes, named after a nearby smithy. An earlier Malet Arms, owned by lord of the manor Sir Henry Malet, closed in the 1890s and its name was transferred. It's not just the village that's quiet: the pub is too, as fruit machines and piped music are banned. All food on the ever-changing blackboard menus is home cooked. Game is plentiful in season, often courtesy of the landlord who shoots pheasant and deer. Other choices might include roasted duck legs and Toulouse sausages on puy lentils braised in white wine; and chargrilled pork chop with scrumpy-soused shallots and grain mustard. The landlady makes all the puddings, often sourced from obscure old English recipes. There's a good range of real ales and ciders.

Open 11-3 6-11 (Sun 12-3, 7-10.30) Closed: 25-26 Dec, 1 Jan **Bar Meals** L served all week 12-2.30 D served all week 6.30-10 (Sun 7-9.30) Free House Ramsbury, Stonehenge, Tripple fff, Palmers & Archers. **Facilities** Garden Dogs allowed Parking Play Area

NUNTON — MAP 05 SU12

The Radnor Arms

SP5 4HS ☎ 01722 329722
dir: *A338 to Ringwood. Nunton signed on right*

A popular pub in the centre of the village dating from around 1750. In 1855 it was owned by the local multi-talented brewer/baker/grocer, and bought by Lord Radnor in 1919. Bar snacks are supplemented by an extensive fish choice and daily specials, which might include braised lamb shank, wild mushroom risotto, tuna with noodles, turbot with spinach or Scotch rib-eye fillet, all freshly prepared. Fine summer garden with rural views. Hosts an annual local pumpkin competition.

Open 11-3 6-11 (Sun 12-3, Sun 7-10.30) **Bar Meals** L served all week 12-2.30 D served Mon-Sat 7-9.30 **Restaurant** L served all week 12-2.30 D served all week 7-9.30 Hall & Woodhouse Badger Tanglefoot, Best & Golden Champion. **Facilities** Garden Dogs allowed Parking Play Area

OAKSEY — MAP 04 ST99

The Wheatsheaf Inn

Wheatsheaf Ln SN16 9TB ☎ 01666 577348
e-mail: info@thecompletechef.co.uk
dir: *Off A419, 6m S of Cirencester*

A village inn built in the 14th century from mellow Cotswold stone, the Wheatsheaf has one rather bizarre feature: an 18th-century 'royal' coffin lid displayed above the open fireplace. All the food is made on the premises from fresh local produce, and Sharp's Doom Bar, Hook Norton, and Wychwood Hobgoblin are some of the real ales kept in good condition behind the bar.

Open 11.30-2.30 6-11 (Sun 12-10.30) **Bar Meals** L served Tue-Sun 12-2 D served Tue-Sun 6.30-9.30 Av main course £7 **Restaurant** L served Tue-Sun 12-2 D served Tue-Sun 6.30-9.30 Av 3 course à la carte £21 Sharp's Doom Bar, London Pride, Hook Norton, Wychwood Hobgoblin. 9 **Facilities** Children's licence Garden Dogs allowed Parking

PEWSEY MAP 05 SU16

The Seven Stars

Bottlesford SN9 6LU ☎ 01672 851325 📠 01672 851583
e-mail: sevenstarsinn@hotmail.com
dir: *Off A345*

Set in a splendid seven acre garden, the front door of this creeper-clad 16th-century free house opens straight onto the low-beamed, oak-panelled bar. Meals are served both here and in the restaurant; at lunchtime, expect filled baguettes, ploughman's, and hot dishes like home-made Mexican chilli with rice. In the evening, typical choices include calves' liver with bacon and red wine sauce; and pan-fried monkfish with tiger prawns and leek sauce.

Open 11.30-3 6-11 **Bar Meals** L served all week 12-2.30 D served all week 6-9.30 Av main course £8 **Restaurant** L served all week 12-2.30 D served all week 6-9.30 Av 3 course à la carte £22 Free House Wadworth 6X, Badger Dorset Best, London Pride & Guest Ales. 9 **Facilities** Garden Dogs allowed Parking

PITTON MAP 05 SU23

Pick of the Pubs

The Silver Plough

White Hill SP5 1DU ☎ 01722 712266 📠 01722 712266
dir: *Salisbury A30 towards Andover, Pitton signed*

Surrounded by rolling countryside and with a peaceful garden, this popular pub is at the heart of a village full of thatched houses. Converted from a farmstead around 60 years ago, inside you will find beams strung with antique glass rolling pins – said to bring good luck – along with bootwarmers, Toby jugs and various other artefacts. It also features a skittle alley adjacent to the snug bar and there are darts and board games available. It is within easy reach of many lovely downland and woodland walks. Hughen and Joyce Riley offer a range of dishes at both lunchtime and evening, including children's meals. House specialities include half a roast shoulder of lamb with mint and garlic gravy, and red bream fillet with caramelised onions, prosciutto and pesto sauce.

Open 11-3 6-11 (Sun 12-3, 6-10.30) Rest: 25-26 Dec, 1 Jan Closed eve **Bar Meals** L served all week 12-2.15 D served all week 6-9 (Sat 6-9.30, Sun 6-8.30) **Restaurant** L served all week 12-2.15 D served all week 6-9 (Sat 6-9.30, Sun 6-8.30) Hall & Woodhouse Badger Tanglefoot, Badger Gold, King Barnes Sussex, Thirsty Ferrett. 32 **Facilities** Garden Dogs allowed Parking

ROWDE MAP 04 ST96

Pick of the Pubs

The George & Dragon

High St SN10 2PN ☎ 01380 723053
e-mail: thegandd@tiscali.co.uk

Winter log fires warm the panelled bars and dining room of this free house, not far from the Caen Hill lock flight on the Kennet and Avon Canal. The building dates from the 15th century, and has a Tudor rose carved on one of the restaurant beams. The pub specialises in seafood from Cornwall, so take your pick from the latest catch – whatever is available is chalked up on the blackboard. From the menu, you could try tomato and basil soup, or carpaccio of beef with light mustard dressing as a starter. Main course dishes might include oven-roasted chicken breast with dauphinoise potatoes, or an 8oz fillet steak with herb and blue cheese crust. Some starters are also available as a main course: try king prawn tagliatelle with pesto, rocket and chilli sauce, or double-baked cheese soufflé. Puddings include treacle tart with clotted cream, and chocolate bread and butter pudding.

Open 12-3 7-11 (Sat-Sun 12-4) Closed Mon morning Closed: 1-8 Jan **Bar Meals** L served Tue-Sun 12-3 (Sat-Sun 12-4) D served Tue-Fri 7-10 (Sat 7-11) Av main course £12.50 **Restaurant** L served Tues-Fri 12-3 (Sat-Sun 12-4) D served Tues-Fri 7-10 (Sat 7-11) Av 3 course à la carte £25.50 Av 3 course fixed price £15.50 Free House Butcombe Bitter, Milk Street Brewery Ales, Bath Ales Gem, ESB. 11 **Facilities** Garden Dogs allowed Parking

SALISBURY MAP 05 SU12

Pick of the Pubs

The Haunch of Venison

1-5 Minster St SP1 1TB
☎ 01722 411313 📠 01722 341774
e-mail: info@haunchofvenisonsalisbury.co.uk
dir: *In city centre adjacent to market place*

Probably the oldest hostelry in Salisbury, the earliest records for this heavily beamed and reputedly haunted inn date from 1320, when it housed craftsmen working on the cathedral spire. Charming details include what is believed to be the country's only surviving complete pewter bar top, as well as original gravity-fed spirit taps. With such a past, ghosts are inevitable. The one-handed Demented Whist Player is a favourite; his missing hand, severed in a card game as punishment for cheating, was found mummified in the 19th century, and it remains to this day, despite attempts on the part of thieves to remove it. The eclectic restaurant features modern and classic dishes with an upbeat slant. Try venison toad in the hole, bubble and squeak, or haddock chowder, and keep an eye out for local game and fish on the specials board. A thoughtfully coded menu offers plenty of scope for vegetarians and dairy-free diners.

Open 11-11 Closed: 25 Dec Eve **Bar Meals** L served all week 12-2 D served all week Av main course £10 **Restaurant** L served all week 12-2.30 D served all week 6-10 (Sun 6-9.30) Av 3 course à la carte £18 Av 3 course fixed price £9.90 Enterprise Inns Courage Best, Wadworth 6X, Summer Lightning. 6

The Vine Tree

In a former life co-owner Tiggi Wood organised the catering at Glyndebourne and Formula One events; she even trained chefs in Paris. Meanwhile, her partner Charlie Walker travelled internationally for Rothman's, and now handles the pub's finances and marketing.

Although it used to be a mill, workers apparently passed beverages out through front windows to passing carriages – an early drive-through it would seem. These days, the Vine Tree is well worth seeking out for its interesting modern pub food and memorable outdoor summer dining. In today's central bar a large open fireplace burns wood all winter, and there's a wealth of old beams, flagstone and oak floors. The building dates back to the 16th century and houses two resident ghosts; one of them, a small boy in polo kit, is apparently still hoping for chukkas in the neighbouring field - the site of England's earliest polo pitches. The region is still a sporty one, with polo, hunting, eventing and point-to-points all taking place locally. Ramblers and cyclists exploring Wiltshire's charms are frequent visitors, and the inn is situated on the official county cycle route. Cooking is modern British in style, with menus changing daily in response to local produce availability. Tiggi and Charlie are proud not to belong to the 'bought in, fake it' brigade, and so everything on the menus is produced in-house, including bread. Dishes include light bites and vegetarian options, local game and well-sourced fish and meats. There's also a terrific stock of wines. In addition to the suntrap terrace, there's a two-acre garden with two boules pitches. Most people arrive by foot or car, but horses, helicopters and hot air balloons have also been successfully catered for!

MAP 04 ST98
Foxley Rd, Norton SN16 0JP
01666 837654
01666 838003
e-mail: tiggi@thevinetree.co.uk
dir: *5 mins junct 17 M4*

Open 12-3 6-12 (Sun 12-12)
Bar Meals L served all week 12-2 D served all week 6-9.30 (Fri 6-10, Sat 12-2.30, 6-10 Sun 12-3.30, 7-9.30)
Restaurant L served all week 12-2 D served all week 6-9.30 (Fri 6-10, Sat 12-2.30, 6-10 Sun 12-3.30, 7-9.30)
Free House
Staropramen, Tinners, Becks Vier, Bath Ales. 30
Facilities Garden Dogs allowed Parking Play Area

The Vine Tree

Cycle information

Distance: 9.75 miles/15.7km (2h)
Map: OS Explorer 168 Stroud, Tetbury & Malmesbury
Start/finish: The Vine Tree, Norton (ask permission first); grid ref: ST 887846
Trails/tracks: country lanes and gravel tracks, a short town section at Malmesbury
Landscape: undulating hill farmland
Public toilets: in Malmesbury behind the town square
Tourist information: Malmesbury; tel: 01666 823748
Cycle hire: C H White & Son, 51 High Street, Malmesbury, tel 01666 822330 (prior bookings only)
The pub: The Vine Tree, Norton
Take great care through Malmesbury; steep descent and climb at Roman Bridge on the Fosse Way

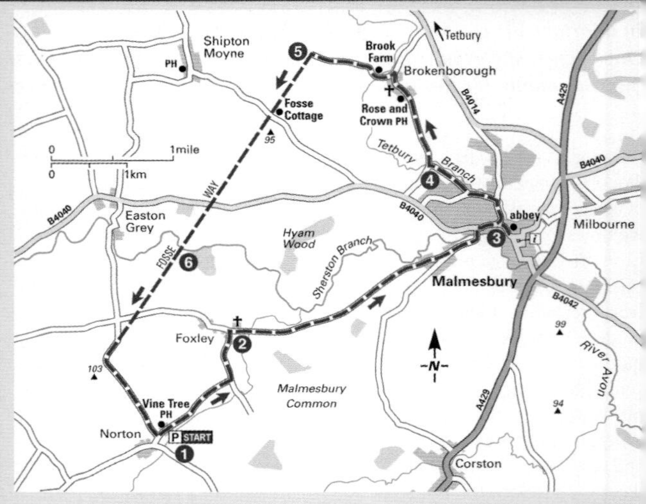

Cycle directions

1 Out of The Vine Tree car park, pedal easily away along the lane to the left, reaching a junction after 0.75 mile (1.2km). Keep left with the main lane, before long arriving at Foxley. Go right, passing the community's tiny church.

2 Continue along the lane for 2 miles (3.2km) to the outskirts of Malmesbury, where Common Road joins from the right. Keep going as the road shortly winds down to cross the Sherston branch of the River Avon, where there is a view right to the abbey church. Climb away, remaining with the main road as it bends right to a T-junction.

3 Go right, and then at the next junction, in front of The Triangle and war memorial, cross over into Gloucester Road, passing through the town to a mini-roundabout. There, bear left into Park Road, signed to Park Road Industrial Estate. Fork off right after 300yds (274m) to remain with Park Road. After passing a few more houses, the route abruptly leaves the town, and continues beside the Avon's Tetbury Branch along a narrow hedged lane.

4 Reaching a T-junction, go right, crossing the river towards Brokenborough. The lane climbs easily to the village, passing the Rose and Crown and then falling to the church and Church Lane. After 100yds (91m), turn off left into a lane marked as a cul-de-sac. After dropping to re-cross the river, the narrow lane climbs past Brook Farm, initially steeply, but soon levelling to continue between the fields.

5 The track ends at a T-junction with a broad, straight track, the Fosse Way. Go left. Very soon, the tarmac gives way to coarse gravel and stone, and although the way is firm, the surface is loose in places and there is a risk of skidding if you travel at speed. After 0.5 mile (800m), cross a lane by Fosse Cottage and carry on past a water-pumping station for another mile (1.6km) to the B4040. Keep an eye open for fast-moving traffic as you cross and continue, the track, before long, starting a steepening descent. It bends at the bottom to a bridge over the Sherston Branch.

6 The climb away on the far bank is very steep, and you may have to get off and push. Beyond, the way runs easily again for 0.5 mile (800m) to another road crossing. Keep ahead with the byway, the surface now of earth and a little rutted, shortly emerging onto another lane. Go ahead, staying with it as it soon bends left away from the line of the Roman road. Eventually dropping to a T-junction at the edge of Norton, go left to The Vine Tree.

SEEND MAP 04 ST96

Bell Inn

Bell Hill SN12 6SA ☎ 01380 828338

e-mail: bellseend@aol.com

According to local tradition, Oliver Cromwell and his troops enjoyed breakfast at this inn, quite possibly on 18 September 1645 when he was advancing from Trowbridge to attack Devizes Castle. The extensive menu runs to poached salmon with a prawn and cream sauce; spicy bean burgers; and barbecue pork ribs, while the specials board highlights liver and bacon casserole; chicken balti; and Highland sausages in whisky. The two-floor restaurant has lovely valley views.

Open 11.15–3 6-12 **Bar Meals** L served all week 11.45–2.15 (Sun 12–2.15) D served all week 6.15–9.30 Av main course £7.50 **Restaurant** L served all week 11.45–2.15 (Sun 12–2.15) D served all week 6.15–9.30 Av fixed price £7.50 Wadworth Wadworth 6X, Henry's IPA & Henrys Smooth. **Facilities** Garden Dogs allowed Parking Play Area

SEMINGTON MAP 04 ST86

The Lamb on the Strand

99 The Strand BA14 6LL

☎ 01380 870263 & 870815 01380 871203

dir: *1.5m E on A361 from junct with A350*

An 18th-century brick farmhouse that later became a beer and cider house. Today's popular dining pub provides what the owner describes as an 'eclectic cuisine de campagne', which translates as salmon fishcakes with dill mayonnaise; smoked haddock with Welsh rarebit topping; Wiltshire ham salad; cauliflower cheese with crispy bacon and French bread; and local sausages of the day with bubble and squeak.

Open 11.30–3 6.30–11 Closed Sun eve Closed: 25–26 Dec, 1 Jan **Bar Meals** L served all week 12–2 D served Mon–Sat 6.30–9 Av main course £9.25 Free House Butcombe Bitter, Ringwood Bitter, Shepherd Neame Spitfire, Guinness. 12 **Facilities** Garden Dogs allowed Parking

SHERSTON MAP 04 ST88

Carpenters Arms

SN16 0LS ☎ 01666 840665

dir: *On B4040 W of Malmesbury*

A 17th-century traditional village inn offering a warm welcome to families, dogs and walkers in wellies. The inn has four interconnecting rooms, with low, beamed ceilings, a wood-burner and a cosy old-world atmosphere. The sunny conservatory restaurant overlooks a beautiful garden. The menu offers a choice of starters like home-made soup, then a selection of meat dishes, curries, fish dishes, vegetarian options and blackboard specials. BBQs and hog roasts in summer.

Open 12–3 5.30–12 (All day wknds) **Bar Meals** L served all week 12–2 D served all week 7–9 (Fri–Sat 6.30–9.30) **Restaurant** L served all week 12–2 D served all week 7–9 (Fri–Sat 6.30–9.30) Enterprise Inns Whitbread Best, Bath Gem, Wickwar Bob & Guest Ale. **Facilities** Garden Dogs allowed Parking Play Area

STOFORD MAP 05 SU03

The Swan Inn ★★★ INN

Warminster Rd SP2 0PR ☎ 01722 790236

e-mail: info@theswanatstoford.co.uk

dir: *From Salisbury take A36 towards Warminster. Stoford on right 4m from Wilton*

A landmark former coaching inn overlooking the River Wylye, meadows and farmland. Family-owned since 1993, it offers good value, mostly locally sourced meals, such as mozzarella and beef tomato salad, followed perhaps by home-made beef chilli, or grilled whole rainbow trout, then tangy lemon meringue pie. Other facilities include a skittle alley and two gardens, one at the rear of the property, the other on the river bank. Guest rooms are comfortable and homely.

Open 11–3 6–11 **Bar Meals** L served all week 12–2 D served all week 6.30–9.15 (Sun 7–9) Av main course £9 **Restaurant** L served all week 12–2.15 D served all week 6.30–9.15 (Sun 7–9) Av 3 course à la carte £18 Free House Ringwood Best, Fuller's London Pride, Odyssey Best Bitter, Old Speckled Hen. 7 **Facilities** Garden Parking **Rooms** 9 bedrooms en suite S£45 D£55

STOURTON MAP 04 ST73

Pick of the Pubs

Spread Eagle Inn ★★★★ INN

BA12 6QE ☎ 01747 840587 01747 840954

e-mail: enquiries@spreadeagleinn.com

dir: *N of A303 off B3092*

Built at the beginning of the 19th century, this charming inn stands in the heart of the 2,650-acre Stourhead Estate, one of the country's most-visited National Trust properties. Before or after a walk through the magnificent gardens and landscapes there is plenty on offer here, including locally produced beers and traditional food. Expect perhaps Wiltshire pasty with onion gravy and chips; lamb casserole and roasted root vegetables; and Old Spot sausages with bubble and squeak mash and sweet mustard sauce. The restaurant menu shifts things up a gear with breast of Gressingham duck with parsnip purée and apple sauce; escalope of cod with lentils and bacon; and chump of Cotswold lamb with spiced apricots and rosemary. Finish with treacle tart with clotted cream; hot sticky toffee pudding; or chocolate roulade. The interior is smartly traditional.

Open 9–11 (Sun 9–10.30) **Bar Meals** L served all week 12–3 D served all week 7–9 Av main course £9 **Restaurant** L served all week 12–3 D served all week 7–9 Av 3 course à la carte £25 Free House Kilmington, Butcombe, San Migel, Fosters & Wadworth 6X. 8 **Facilities** Garden Parking **Rooms** 5 bedrooms en suite S£90 D£110

SWINDON MAP 05 SU18

The Sun Inn

Lydiard Millicent SN5 3LU ☎ 01793 770425
e-mail: thesuninnlm@yahoo.co.uk
dir: *3m W of Swindon, 1.5m from M4 junct 16*

This 18th-century free house is set in a conservation area, near Lydiard House and Park. The walls display an eclectic mix of artwork from local artists. There's an emphasis on real ale, and traditional food with a bistro touch is being continued by new owners. It would be a mistake to miss the smoked haddock and king prawns fish pot, while monkfish wrapped in bacon with as green bean and mussel sauce is also an appetising option.

Open 11.30–3 5.30–11 (Sun 6.30–10.30, Mar–Sep Sun all day) **Bar Meals** L served all week 12–2.30 D served all week 6.30–9.30 (Sun 6.30–9) Av main course £8.95 **Restaurant** L served all week 12–2.30 D served all week 6.30–9.30 (Sun 6.30 –9) Av 3 course à la carte £17.95 Free House Sharp's Doom Bar, West Berkshire, Wadsworth 6X, Wye Valley Brewery. 8 **Facilities** Garden Dogs allowed Parking

TOLLARD ROYAL MAP 04 ST91

King John Inn

SP5 5PS ☎ 01725 516207
dir: *On B3081 (7m E of Shaftesbury)*

Named after one of King John's hunting lodges, this Victorian building was opened in 1859. A friendly and relaxing place, it is today perhaps better known as Madonna's local after she and husband Guy Ritchie moved in close by. Also nearby is a 13th-century church, and the area is excellent rambling country. A typical menu offers old English favourites like bangers and apple mash; bacon, liver and kidney casserole; Dorset lamb cutlets; and Wiltshire gammon with peaches.

Open 11–3 6–12 (Sun 12–10.30) **Bar Meals** L served all week 12–2 D served all week 7–9 (All day Sun summer) **Restaurant** L served all week 12–2 (Sun 12–2.30) D served all week 7–9 Free House Courage Best, John Smith's, Wadworth 6X, Ringwood. **Facilities** Garden Dogs allowed Parking

UPTON LOVELL MAP 04 ST94

Prince Leopold Inn

BA12 0JP ☎ 01985 850460 01985 850737
e-mail: Princeleopold@Lineone.net
dir: *From Warminster A36 4.5m, left into Upper Lovell*

Built in 1887 as the local shop, post office and store to service the then prosperous woollen industry, the inn's name was chosen to honour Prince Leopold who lived nearby. Possibly unique in England, the Mediterranean-style restaurant has an eye-level fireplace with a charcoal barbecue grill. Seafood features strongly on a wide ranging menu, offering brill fillet on champ mash with hollandaise sauce and thyme scented onions alongside Thai green chicken curry.

Open 12–3 7–11 **Bar Meals** L served all week 12–2.30 D served all week 7–10 **Restaurant** L served all week 12–2.30 D served all week 7–10 Free House Ringwood Best, Scottish Courage John Smith's & San Miguel. 8 **Facilities** Garden Parking **Rooms** 6 bedrooms en suite S£45 D£65 (★★ INN)

WARMINSTER MAP 04 ST84

Pick of the Pubs

The Angel Inn

Upton Scudamore BA12 0AG
☎ 01985 213225 01985 218182
e-mail: mail@theangelinn.co.uk
dir: *From Warminster take A350 towards Trowbridge*

The Angel is a restored 16th-century coaching inn located in a small village close to Warminster. Access to the pub is via a walled garden and terrace, where meals and drinks can be taken in fine weather. Inside, the open fires and natural wood flooring create a relaxed atmosphere. Meals open a selection of home-made breads and flavoured olive oil. Chef's specials from the chalk board feature fresh sea fish from Brixham, which might include gilthead bream, barramundi or sea bass. Dishes from the menu might include steamed River Fowey mussels cooked in white wine, garlic and herbs, and roast rump of lamb with slow roast potato, confit tomatoes and sweet onion jus. For a vegetarian alternative, perhaps fresh linguine with baby bell peppers, cashew nuts, baby spinach and goats' cheese, finished with pesto dressing. Desserts range from iced white chocolate parfait with mango sorbet to sticky toffee pudding with butterscotch sauce.

Open 11-3 6-11 Closed: 25-26 Dec, 1 Jan **Bar Meals** L served all week 12-2 D served all week 7-9.30 Av main course £9.95 **Restaurant** L served all week 12-2 D served all week 7-9.30 Av 3 course à la carte £24 Free House Wadworth 6X, Butcombe, John Smith's Smooth, Guest Ales. 8 **Facilities** Garden Parking

The Bath Arms

Clay St, Crockerton BA12 8AJ

01985 212262 01985 218670

e-mail: batharms@hotmail.co.uk

dir: *From Warminster on A36 take A350 towards Shaftesbury then left to Crockerton, follow signs for Shear Water*

Well known free house on the Longleat Estate, where villagers are joined by walkers and tourists and regularly returning visitors from Bath, Salisbury and Shaftsbury. In recent years the kitchen and restaurant have been remodelled by chef proprietor Dean Carr, and the garden, formerly a wasteland, has been landscaped to provide a pleasant spot for outdoor dining. Dishes might be monkfish with pea and ham broth, and roast loin of pork, plus snacks and grills.

Open 11-3 6-11 (Summer all day) **Bar Meals** L served all week 12-2.30 D served all week 6-9.30 Av main course £13 **Restaurant** L served all week 12-2.30 D served all week 6-9.30 Av 3 course à la carte £20 Free House Crockerton Classic, Naughty Ferrit & Guest Ales. 10 **Facilities** Garden Dogs allowed Parking Play Area

The George Inn ★★★★ INN

BA12 7DG 01985 840396 01985 841333

A 17th-century coaching inn at the heart of the pretty village of Longbridge Deverill. Customers can enjoy a pint of real ale by the fire in the oak-beamed Longbridge bar, or sit outside in the two-acre garden on the banks of the River Wylye. Food is served in a choice of two restaurants, and there is a Sunday carvery in the Wylye Suite. Function facilities are available, plus accommodation in 11 en suite bedrooms.

Open 11-11 (Fri 11am-2am, Sun 12-10.30) Closed: 25-Dec from 3pm **Bar Meals** L served all week 12-2.30 D served all week 6-9.30 (Sun 6-9) **Restaurant** L served all week 12-2.30 D served all week 6-9.30 (Sun 6-9) Free House Scottish Courage John Smith's, Wadworth 6X, Hobdens Doverills Advocat. 11 **Facilities** Garden Parking Play Area **Rooms** 11 bedrooms en suite S£55 D£75

WESTBURY — MAP 04 ST85

The Duke at Bratton

Melbourne St, Bratton BA13 4RW

01380 830242 01380 831239

dir: *From Westbury follow B3098 for Whitehorse & Bratton*

Tucked away at the foot of the Westbury White Horse, this award-winning free house features a whalebone archway leading into the pub garden. The Duke is a good refreshment stop on the way to nearby Bratton Castle and Edington Priory church. Fresh local ingredients underpin the extensive menu, which ranges from omelettes and salads to grills and roasts. Applewood smoked trout with horseradish, vegetarian tagliatelle, and roast Wiltshire chicken are typical choices.

Open 12-3 6-11 (Fri-Sun 12-11) **Bar Meals** L served all week 12-2 D served all week 6-9 Av main course £6 **Restaurant** L served all week 12-2 D served all week 7-9 Av 3 course à la carte £17.50 Free House Moles Best, John Smiths Bitter, Moles Special, Guest beers. **Facilities** Garden Parking

WEST LAVINGTON — MAP 04 SU05

Pick of the Pubs

The Bridge Inn

26 Church St SN10 4LD

01380 813213 01380 813213

e-mail: portier@btopenworld.com

dir: *A360 towards Salisbury 7m. S of village past church*

The Bridge is a small but perfectly formed pub and restaurant in a village setting on the edge of Salisbury Plain. Inside there is a beamed bar and log fire with displays of local paintings for sale. Outside there's a large garden with a boule pitch. Cyrille Portier caters for most appetites, offering light lunch options of baguettes and salads alongside the carte, from which you can choose a starter as a snack if you wish. Pub favourites are offered on the specials board – fresh haddock in beer batter, salmon, cod and dill fishcakes, and Wiltshire ham with free-range eggs and pomme frites – and there's a distinctly French flavour to the main menu

CONTINUED

England

WEST LAVINGTON continued

with coq au vin, moules marinières, and confit de canard. Regular events include the Rook Supper in May, Harvest Festival in September and the Charity Beer Festival over the August Bank Holiday weekend.

Open 12–3 6.30–11 Closed: 2 wks in Feb **Bar Meals** L served Tue–Sun 12–2 D served Tue–Sat 6.30–9 Av main course £10 **Restaurant** L served Tue–Sun 12–2 (Sun 12–2.30) D served Tue–Sat 6.30–9 Av 3 course à la carte £25 Enterprise Inns Brakspear, Spitfire, Hobgoblin, Old Speckled Hen. 11 **Facilities** Garden Parking

WHADDON MAP 05 SU12

The Three Crowns

Southampton Rd SP5 3HB
01722 710211 01722 711537
e-mail: pubstuff@thethreecrowns.com
dir: *4m from Salisbury on A27*

Standing on the old Salisbury-Southampton road, this mid-18th-century pub is left in peace as traffic hurtles along the by-pass. According to legend, Edward III and his two royal prisoners, David of Scotland and John of France, visited an earlier hostelry in 1356 – thus the name. Warm and welcoming, with inglenook fireplaces, leather sofa and a miscellany of chairs. Blackboards offer a good choice, including steaks, red snapper, wild mushroom stroganoff, sandwiches, and Sunday roasts.

Open 12–2.30 5–11 (Sun all day) **Bar Meals** L served all week 12–2 D served all week 6–9 (Sun 12–8) **Restaurant** L served all week 12–2 D served all week 6–9 (Sun 12–8) Greene King Greene King IPA, Abbot Ale & Guest ale. 8 **Facilities** Garden Dogs allowed Parking **Rooms** 2 bedrooms en suite (★★★ INN) **Notes**

WHITLEY MAP 04 ST86

Pick of the Pubs

The Pear Tree Inn ★★★★★ RR

Top Ln SN12 8QX 01225 709131 01225 702276
e-mail: enquiries@thepeartreeinn.com
dir: *A365 from Melksham toward Bath, at Shaw right on B3353 into Whitley, 1st left in lane, pub is at end of lane*

The agricultural antiques that adorn this pub's interior are a testament to its past life as a farmstead. It has a lived-in, comfortable feel, with flagstone floors, two log fires and three or four real ales always on tap. While it also features a restaurant and luxury accommodation, drinkers are still very much welcome. Outside there is a large boules piste, an extensive patio area and a cottage garden. The surrounding acres of wooded farmland make it feel as though you are in the heart of a big estate. The menu delivers a modern take on hearty, traditional British food. There might be Middle White pork and liver paté with bacon, red onion marmalade and toast, followed by home-made venison sausages with swede and carrot purée, cabbage and bacon and onion gravy; finish with a dark chocolate brownie with clotted cream. There are also lunchtime sandwiches. Good wine list.

Open 11–3 6–11 Closed: 25–26 Dec, 1 Jan **Bar Meals** L served all week 12–2.30 D served all week 6.30–9.30 **Restaurant** L served all week 12–2.30 D served all week 6.30–9.30 Free House Wadworth 6X, Bath Ales Gem, Stonehenge Ales, Pigswill. 12 **Facilities** Garden Parking **Rooms** 8 bedrooms en suite S£75 D£105

WINTERBOURNE BASSETT MAP 05 SU07

The White Horse Inn

SN4 9QB 01793 731257 01793 739030
e-mail: ckstone@btinternet.com
web: www.whitehorsewinterbournebassett.co.uk
dir: *5m S of Swindon on A4361*

Lying just two miles north of the mysterious Avebury stone circle, the White Horse is an ideal base for walks on the historic Ridgeway path. Food is served in the bar and conservatory restaurant, as well as in the safe, lawned garden. Budget lunches and snacks are supported by a full menu and daily specials: look out for baked cod topped with tomato, herbs and mozzarella; mushroom stroganoff; and beef, ale and mushroom pie.

The White Horse Inn

Open 11-3 6-11 **Bar Meals** L served all week 12-2.30 D served all week 6-10 (Sun 7-10) **Restaurant** L served all week 12-2.30 D served all week 6-10 (Sun 7-10) Wadworth Wadworth 6X, IPA, Hophouse Brews & Heineken. 11 **Facilities** Garden Parking

WOODFALLS MAP 05 SU12

The Woodfalls Inn

The Ridge SP5 2LN 01725 513222 01725 513220
e-mail: enquiries@woodfallsinn.co.uk
dir: *B3080 to Woodfalls*

Located on an old coaching route on the northern edge of the New Forest, the Woodfalls Inn has provided hospitality to travellers since the early Victorian era. A more recent extension accommodates a purpose built function suite, in addition to the bar areas, conservatory, lounge and restaurant. Home-made dishes include chicken curry, beef or vegetable lasagne, and steak and ale pie. There is also a comprehensive selection of grills.

Open 11-11 **Bar Meals** L served all week 12-2.15 D served all week 6.30-9.30 Av main course £6.95 **Restaurant** L served all week 12-2.15 D served all week 6.30-9 Av 3 course à la carte £20 Free House Courage Directors & Best, Hopback's GFB, John Smiths, Ringwood 49er. 9 **Facilities** Garden Dogs allowed Parking

WOOTTON RIVERS MAP 05 SU16

Pick of the Pubs

Royal Oak

SN8 4NQ 01672 810322 01672 811168
e-mail: royaloak35@hotmail.com
dir: *3m S from Marlborough*

This 16th-century thatched and timbered inn is situated just 100 yards from the Kennet and Avon Canal. It's also very handy for exploring the 2600 ancient oaks of Savernake Forest, as well as visiting Stonehenge, Avebury, Bath and Marlborough. The interior is as charming as the setting, a cosy combination of low-beamed ceilings, exposed brickwork and open fires. Menus tend to be flexible, with an array of starters, main courses and fish dishes. Typical examples include foie gras with toasted brioche; Moroccan lamb with preserved lemons and coriander; scallops pan fried with bacon and mushrooms; and whole sea bass baked with lime leaves. The Royal Oak has 20 years experience in hosting weddings, and holds a licence for civil ceremonies. Discos, parties, film screenings and meetings can also be accommodated.

Open 10.30-3.30 6-11 (Sun 6-10.30) **Bar Meals** L served all week 12-2.30 D served all week 6.30-9.30 (Sun 12-3, 6.30-9) Av main course £13.25 **Restaurant** L served all week 12-2.30 D served all week 6.30-9.30 (Sun 12-3, 6.30-9) Av 3 course à la carte £22.50 Av 3 course fixed price £13.50 Free House Wadworth 6X, Guest ales inc local Ramsbury Bitter. 7 **Facilities** Garden Dogs allowed Parking **Rooms** 3 bedrooms en suite S£30 D£50 (★★★ INN)

WYLYE MAP 04 SU03

The Bell Inn ★★★ INN

High St, Wylye BA12 0QP
01985 248338 01985 248491
e-mail: thebellatwyle@hotmail.co.uk
dir: *From Salisbury take A36 N'bound to Warminster, then Wylye & A303 Honiton signed off A36. Follow signs for Wylye*

There's a wealth of old oak beams, log fires and an inglenook fireplace at this 14th-century coaching inn, situated in the pretty Wylye valley. In 2005 the Bell was taken over by the Hidden Brewery (located just two miles away in Dinton), and so Hidden beers are available, but thankfully, not too well hidden. Lunch and dinner menus feature mainly local ingredients.

Open 11.30-2.30 6-11 (Sun 12-3, 6-10.30) **Bar Meals** L served all week 12-2.30 D served all week 6.30-9.30 (Mon, Thu & Sun 6.30-9) Av main course £9 **Restaurant** L served all week 12-2 D served all week 6-9.30 (Mon, Thu & Sun 6.30-9) Free House Hidden Pint, Hidden Quest, Hidden Oldsarum, Hidden Fantasy. 10 **Facilities** Garden Dogs allowed Parking **Rooms** 3 bedrooms en suite S£51 D£65

WORCESTERSHIRE

ABBERLEY MAP 10 SO76

The Manor Arms at Abberley ★★★ INN

WR6 6BN 01299 896507 01299 896723
e-mail: themanorarms@btconnect.com
dir: *Signed from A443, Abberley B4202 toward Crofts Toft*

Set just across the lane from the Norman church of St Michael, the interior of this 300-year-old inn is enhanced by original oak beams and a log-burning fire. For food, expect a wide choice of grills and roasts, plus alternatives such as poached haddock with a poached egg and chive and butter sauce, or cheese and lentil terrine on a smooth tomato coulis. Good choice of real ales.

Open 12-3 6-11 (Winter closed Mon lunchtime) **Bar Meals** L served all week 12-2.30 D served all week 6-9 (Sat-Sun 12-3.30, Sun 6-8) Av main course £9 **Restaurant** D served all week 6-9 Enterprise Inns Timothy Taylor, Hookey Bitter, Hereford HPA, Flowers IPA. 11 **Facilities** Garden Dogs allowed Parking **Rooms** 10 bedrooms 8 en suite S£55 D£70

BEWDLEY MAP 10 SO77

Little Pack Horse

31 High St DY12 2DH ☎ 01299 403762 📠 01299 403762

e-mail: enquires@littlepackhorse.co.uk

dir: *From Kidderminster, ring road & Safari Park signs. Signs for Bewdley over bridge, left then right*

The interior of this historic timber-framed inn is warmed by cosy log fires and lit by candles at night. There are low beams, an elm bar, and a small outside patio for alfresco summer dining. Fresh fish and an extensive wine list are the house specialities. Expect trout with lemon butter; swordfish with caper and herb crust; lobster thermidore; and an impressive range of vegetarian and vegan dishes: aubergine, leek and parsnip crumble, perhaps.

Open 12-3 6-11 (Thu-Sat 6-12) **Bar Meals** L served all week 12-2.15 D served all week 6-9.30 (Sat 12-9.30, Sun 12-8) Av main course £7.50 **Restaurant** L served all week 12-3 D served all week 6-9.30 (Sat 12-9.30, Sun 12-8) Av 3 course à la carte £20 Punch Taverns Theakstons Best Wye valley HPA, Dorothy Goodbodies Golden Ale, Black Sheep Bitter, Shepherd Neame Spitfire. 16 **Facilities** Garden Dogs allowed

The Mug House Inn & Angry Chef Restaurant ★★★★ INN

12 Severnside North DY12 2EE

☎ 01299 402543 📠 01299 402543

e-mail: drew@mughousebewdley.co.uk

Nestling beside the River Severn in picturesque Bewdley, the inn's riverside seating area is popular on warmer days. The unusual name dates back to the 17th century, when 'mug house' was a popular term for an alehouse. Nowadays, visitors will find an extensive lunchtime bar menu, with à la carte options in the restaurant. Typical choices include rack of lamb with ratatouille and mash; butternut squash crumble; roast pollock, and grilled lobster in garlic butter.

Open 12 -11 **Bar Meals** L served all week 12-2.30 (Sun 12-5) D served Mon-Sat **Restaurant** L served all week 12-2.30 (Sun 12-5) D served Mon-Sat 7-9 Av 3 course à la carte £25 Punch Taverns Timothy Taylor's Landlord, Wye Valley, Hereford Pale Ale plus Guest beers. 7 **Facilities** Children's licence Garden Dogs allowed **Rooms** 7 bedrooms en suite S£60 D£75

BRANSFORD MAP 10 SO75

The Bear & Ragged Staff

Station Rd WR6 5JH ☎ 01886 833399 📠 01886 833106

e-mail: mail@bear.uk.com

dir: *signed from A4103*

Built in 1861 as an estate rent office, this lovely old pub has a good reputation for its food. Wide choices are available: in the bar, fillet of beef stroganoff with braised rice, for example, and in the restaurant, pan-fried saddle of wild rabbit in mushroom and white wine sauce, honey-roast garlic and shallots; shallow-fried pollock, capers and toasted pine kernels; and chargrilled polenta, stir-fried savoy cabbage and pak choi. Look out for ghostly Maude.

Open 11.30-2.30 6-11 (Sat 6.30-11, Sun 7-10.30) **Bar Meals** L served all week 12-2 D served Fri 6.30-9 (Sun 7-8.30) Av main course £10 **Restaurant** L served all week 12-2 D served all week 7-9 (Sun 7-8.30) Av 3 course à la carte £26.50 Free House St Georges Best & Shepherd Neame Spitfire. 10 **Facilities** Garden Parking

BRETFORTON MAP 10 SP04

Pick of the Pubs

The Fleece Inn

The Cross WR11 7JE ☎ 01386 831173

e-mail: nigel@thefleeceinn.co.uk

dir: *From Evesham follow signs for B4035 towards Chipping Campden. Through Badsey into Bretforton. Right at village hall, past church, pub in open parking area.*

The Fleece, or The Ark as it is known locally, has been part of Cotswold history for the six centuries since it was built as a longhouse. Amazingly, its last private owner, Lola Taplin, who died in front of the fire in the snug in 1977, was a direct descendant of the man who built it. Before departing for premises celestial she bequeathed it to the National Trust, its first licensed property. In February 2004 it caught fire and a massive restoration programme followed, but it looks as good as ever. Main courses include grilled meats and fish; traditional faggots with mash, mushy peas and gravy; Mexican beef chilli and rice; Whitby scampi with chips; and baked field mushrooms with spinach and cream cheese topping. To follow there's bread and butter pudding, apple crumble, and chocolate brandy cake with raspberry purée.

Open 11-11 (Sun 12-10.30) (Winter Mon-Fri 11-3, 6-11) **Bar Meals** L served all week 12-2.30 D served Mon-Sat 6.30-9 Av main course £6.50 Free House Hook Norton Best Bitter, Pigs Ear, Goff's White Knight, Slaters Supreme & Purity Ubu. 12 **Facilities** Children's licence Garden Play Area

BROMSGROVE MAP 10 SO97

Epic' Bar Brasserie

68 Hanbury Rd, Stoke Prior B60 4DN

01527 871929 01527 575647

e-mail: bromsgrove@epicbrasseries.co.uk

dir: *A38 from Bromsgrove towards Worcester, at x-rds take B4091 towards Hanbury, pub on right.*

Bar-cum-brasserie with a sleek contemporary look which accurately reflects the style of cooking. Produce is carefully sourced for excellence and ethical acceptability, and there's a predominantly organic menu for children. Otherwise, the cooking is thoroughly grown up, with a menu ranging through salads, pasta, risotto, meat and fish, including brodetta (Italian fish and shellfish stew), smoked salmon risotto, and slow-braised lamb shank. Outside there's a large patio and terrace area with an olive tree.

Open 11–11 (Sun 12–6) **Restaurant** L served all week 12–2.30 D served Mon–Sat 6.30–9.30 (Sun 12.30–3.30, Fri–Sat 6.30–10) Av 3 course à la carte £25 Av 3 course fixed price £12.95 Boddingtons, Guinness, Guest ale. 9 **Facilities** Children's licence Garden Parking

CLENT MAP 10 SO97

The Bell & Cross

Holy Cross DY9 9QL 01562 730319 01562 731733

At the foot of the Clent Hills, this award-winning pub/restaurant serves modern-style food in a traditional setting. The pub dates from the early 19th-century and today is owned by Roger Narbett, chef to the England football team. Several rooms make up the pub, and real ales are served along with an interesting wine list, twelve of which are available by the glass; in warmer weather the covered patio makes for pleasant al fresco dining.

Open 12–3 6–11 Closed: 25 Dec **Bar Meals** L served all week 12–2 D served all week 6.30–9.15 (Sun 12–2.30, 7–9) Av main course £6.95 **Restaurant** L served all week 12–2 D served all week 6.30–9.15 (Sun 12–2.30, 7–9) Av 3 course à la carte £21.50 Enterprise Inns Pedigree, Mild, Bitter & Guest Beers. 14 **Facilities** Children's licence Garden Dogs allowed Parking

CLOWS TOP MAP 10 SO77

The Colliers Arms

Tenbury Rd DY14 9HA 01299 832242

e-mail: colliersarms@aol.com

dir: *On A456 4m from Bewdley*

This popular pub-restaurant is family owned and run. All the food is home cooked, and plenty of fish is on offer, for example, smoked haddock and crab tart; or monkfish in a light curry sauce. Among the more traditional dishes might be home-made lasagne; liver and bacon. Do not leave without sampling one of the delicious home-made puddings.

Open 11–3 5.30–11 (Sat all day, Sun 11–6) **Bar Meals** L served all week 12–2 (Sun 11–3) D served Mon–Sat 6.30–9 Av main course £11 **Restaurant** L served all week 12–2 (Sun 11–3) D served all week 6.30–9 Av 3 course à la carte £20 Free House Hobsons Best, Town Crier, Guinness. 8 **Facilities** Garden Parking

DROITWICH MAP 10 SO86

Pick of the Pubs

The Chequers

Cutnall Green WR9 0PJ

01299 851292 01299 851744

A display of football memorabilia in the bar reveals that this is the home of Roger Narbett, chef of the England football team. Just five miles from Droitwich, The Chequers remains a charming and traditional village pub, with an open fire, panelled bar and richly coloured furnishings. Meanwhile sandblasted beams, a tiled and wooden floor and comfortable sofas give the dining room a more contemporary feel. Lunchtime brings baguettes, pasta and toasted paninis, plus a range of light hot dishes and desserts. The à la carte menu begins with choices like roasted squash, tomato and vegetable soup; and smoked duck parfait with caramelised plums, bacon salad and rustic bread. Main courses might include roasted Cornish cod with leeks, cheddar mash, prawns and parsley butter; or Warwickshire belly pork with white bean cassoulet and griddled apple. Finish, perhaps, with warm treacle tart and thick custard.

Open 12–3 6–11 Closed: 25 Dec & 1 Jan **Bar Meals** L served all week 12–2 D served all week 6.30–9.15 (Sun 12–2.30, 7–9) Av main course £10.35 **Restaurant** L served all week 12–2 D served all week 6.30–9.15 (Sun 12–2.30, 7–9) Av 3 course à la carte £17.50 Enterprise Inns Timothy Taylors, Enville Ale, Banks Bitter, Banks Mild. 11 **Facilities** Children's licence Garden Dogs allowed Parking

The Old Cock Inn

Friar St WR9 8EQ 01905 774233

This charming old pub has three stained-glass windows rescued from the local church after it was destroyed during the Civil War. The stone carving above the front entrance is believed to be of Judge Jeffreys who presided over the local magistrates' court. Various snacks and light meals feature on the menu, while more substantial fare includes rump steak, steak and Guinness pie, grilled cod with stilton and mushroom, and fillet of lamb with artichoke, wild mushrooms, mint, peppercorns and wine sauce.

Open 11.30–3 5.30–11 Closed: Sun evening **Bar Meals** L served all week 12–2.30 D served Mon–Sat 5.30–9.30 **Restaurant** L served all week 12–2.30 D served Mon–Sat 5.30–9.30 Bank's Brewery Marston's Pedigree & Bitter, Guest. **Facilities** Garden

England

FLADBURY MAP 10 SO94

Chequers Inn

Chequers Ln WR10 2PZ ☎ 01386 860276 01386 861286
e-mail: fretwelljohn.fretwell4@btinternet.com
dir: *Off A4538 between Evesham and Pershore*

The Chequers is a 14th-century inn with plenty of beams and an open fire, tucked away in a pretty village with views of the glorious Bredon Hills. Local produce from the Vale of Evesham provides the basis for home-cooked dishes offered from the monthly-changing menu, plus a choice of daily specials. There is also a traditional Sunday carvery. The pretty walled garden enjoys outstanding views, and the nearby River Avon is ideal for walking.

Open 11-3 5.30-11 **Bar Meals** L served all week 12-2 D served Tue-Sat 6-10 **Restaurant** L served all week 12-2 D served Mon-Sat 6-9 Free House Hook Norton Best, Fuller's London Pride, Black Sheep, plus Guests. **Facilities** Garden Parking

FLYFORD FLAVELL MAP 10 SO95

The Boot Inn ★★★★ INN

Radford Rd WR7 4BS ☎ 01386 462658 01386 462547
e-mail: enquiries@thebootinn.com
dir: *Worcester A422 towards Alcester. Right to village*

Parts of this family-run coaching inn date back to the 13th century, as the heavy beams, slanting doorways and genial resident ghost attest. There are gardens front and back, with a heated patio for those less clement days. Home-cooked food, from the menu and specials board, includes trout and apple salad, followed by baked cod and Welsh rarebit. There are five charming bedrooms in the converted coach house and, unusually, the restaurant features a well.

Open 12-12 **Bar Meals** L served all week 12-2 D served all week 6.30-10 (Sun 12-5.30, 7-9.30) Av main course £6 **Restaurant** L served all week 12-2 D served all week 6.30-10 (Sat 6-10, Sun 12-5.30, 7-9.30) Av 3 course à la carte £20 Old Speckled Hen, Worthingtons, Greene King IPA, London Pride & Adnams. 8 **Facilities** Garden Dogs allowed Parking **Rooms** 5 bedrooms en suite S£50 D£60

KEMPSEY MAP 10 SO84

Pick of the Pubs

Walter de Cantelupe Inn ★★★ INN

Main Rd WR5 3NA ☎ 01905 820572
dir: *4m S of Worcester city centre on A38.*

See Pick of the Pubs on opposite page

KINGTON MAP 10 SO95

Pick of the Pubs

The Red Hart

Stratford Rd WR7 4DD
☎ 01386 792559 01386 793748
e-mail: enquiries@redhart.co.uk
dir: *On A422 nr Flyford Flavell*

From a derelict shell in 2001, this beautiful, easy-going country pub and restaurant has been completely restored by a team of local craftsmen. The interior has been stripped to reveal its original looks, while some stunning contemporary touches have been added. The aim is to make everyone's dining experience, whether in bar or restaurant, utterly memorable. You could go for local game casserole with suet dumplings; beer-battered fish and chips with minted mushy peas; or rustic bean casserole with red onions, peppers and tomato. From the short lunch menu come specials like bangers and mash; black pudding and bacon salad; and smoked salmon and prawn risotto, while the evening might yield pan-seared scallops followed by crispy belly of pork, or pan-fried duck breast. Puddings could range from the sticky toffee classic to spiced winter fruit bread and butter pudding. Heated log burners are dotted strategically around the outside decking.

Open 12-3 5-11 (Fri-Sat 12-12, Sun 12-11) **Bar Meals** L served all week 12-2.30 D served all week 6-10 (Sat-Sun 12-10) **Restaurant** L served all week 12-2.30 D served all week 6-10 (Sun 12-10) Av 3 course à la carte £25 Marstons Banks, Pedigree. 10 **Facilities** Children's licence Garden Dogs allowed Parking

Walter de Cantelupe Inn

With its whitewashed walls bedecked with flowers, this authentic and charming little inn is a magnet for passing motorists and knowing locals alike. Outside, a walled and paved garden has been fragrantly planted with clematis, roses and honeysuckle, and its south-facing position is a sun-trap on hot days. A gas heater has extended its use into the cooler months.

The inn is named after the mid–13th-century Bishop of Worcester, Walter de Cantelupe, who was strongly against his parishioners' habit of brewing and selling of ales as a way to raise church funds. The pub was formed out of a row of cottages three centuries later, and its naming is presumably ironic! The food is written up each day on a blackboard, with choices to please both traditionalists and those seeking hearty, modern cooking. You could begin with celery and almond soup served with crusty granary bread; or perhaps deep-fried whitebait with a home-made tartar sauce. Main courses have a similar scope; there might be beef and local ale pie; plate-sized gammon steak with a fried free range egg; thick grilled pork chop with a cider, onion and cream sauce; seared tuna steak with chilli and lime butter; and a glazed chicory and butternut squash pancake. You could finish with hot marmalade bread and butter pudding; or local farmhouse ice creams. Look out for food-themed events such as the Balti Bonanza or the Outdoor Paella Fiesta. Other events include malt whiskey tastings and cookery demonstrations by Martin Lloyd-Morris who trained as a chef in France and worked at the London Hilton before bringing his talents to the Walter de Cantalupe. The pub's en suite accommodation is popular with visitors to historic Worcester, the Malvern Hills and Severn Vale.

★★★ INN
MAP 10 SO84
Main Rd WR5 3NA
☎ 01905 820572
dir: *4m S of Worcester city centre on A38*

Open 12–2 6–11 (Sun 12–3, 7–10.30, Summer 11.30–2.30)
Closed: Dec 25–26, Jan 1
Bar Meals L served Tue–Sat 12–2 (Sun 12–2.30) D served Tue–Thu 6.30–9 (Fri–Sat 6.30–10) Av main course £8
Restaurant L served Tue–Sun 12–2 D served Tue–Thu 7–9 (Fri–Sat 7–10) Av 3 course à la carte £17
Free House
Timothy Taylors Landlord, Cannon Royal, Kings Shilling, Hobsons Best Bitter.
Facilities Garden Dogs allowed Parking
Rooms 3 bedrooms en suite S£44.50 D£55

England

KNIGHTWICK MAP 10 SO75

Pick of the Pubs

The Talbot 🍷

WR6 5PH ☎ 01886 821235 📠 01886 821060

e-mail: admin@the-talbot.co.uk

dir: *A44 through Worcester, 8m right onto B4197 (at River Teme bridge)*

A late-14th-century traditional coaching inn run for 22 years by the Clift family, and managed today by sisters Annie and Wiz. They place huge importance on organic and locally produced ingredients, growing their own chemical-free vegetables, herbs and salad leaves in the garden. They also gather wild food from the fields and hedgerows, and even make their own preserves, breads, black pudding and raised pies. Most ingredients, if not home grown, are sourced from named suppliers within a five-mile radius, the only exceptions being fish from Cornwall and Wales. The Talbot is the home of the Teme Valley Brewery, which was started in 1997 using hops grown in the parish. The cask-conditioned ales, all on hand pump in the bar, are called This, That, T'other and Wot, while the care and attention devoted to them is reflected in the Talbot's and restaurant. Chef Jamie Tarbox prepares distinctive menus of flavoursome dishes using traditional and seasonal recipes.

Open 11-11 (Sun 12-10.30) Closed: 25 Dec pm **Bar Meals** L served all week 12-2 D served all week 6.30-9.30 (Sun 7-9) **Restaurant** L served all week 12-2 D served all week 6.30-9.30 (Sun 7-9) Av 3 course à la carte £35 Av 3 course fixed price £30 Free House Teme Valley This, That, T'Other & Wot, Hobsons Best Bitter Choice. 🍷 9 **Facilities** Garden Dogs allowed Parking

MALVERN MAP 10 SO74

The Anchor Inn NEW 🍷

Drake St, Welland WR13 6LN ☎ 01684 592317

e-mail: theanchor13@hotmail.com

dir: *M50 follow signs to Upton upon Severn. Turn left onto A4104 through town 2.5m. Pub on right*

The Anchor is an attractive pub with views of the Malvern Hills from its patio. There's a garden where children can play, and a welcoming fire in the dining room. Light bites and main meals are marked up on the chalkboard, with dishes such as pork loin stuffed with apple in stilton sauce, steak and kidney pie, and shank of lamb simmered in mint and rosemary gravy. Themed menus and quiz nights feature regularly.

Open 11.30-3 6.45-11 **Bar Meals** L served all week 12-2.50 D served Mon-Sat Av main course £9.99 Free House Black Sheep, Woods, Hook Norton, Greene King. 🍷 20 **Facilities** Garden Dogs allowed Parking

The Red Lion

4 St Ann's Rd WR14 4RG ☎ 01684 564787

dir: *In town centre*

One of the main walking routes in the Malvern Hills runs right by this thriving pub. Expect plenty of ramblers, not to mention locals intent on sampling the home-made food of Steve Hickman and his kitchen brigade's. Marston's Pedigree and weekly guest ales accompany a wide choice of snacks, starters and main course dishes and all freshly cooked to order. Seafood is a particular speciality: try pan-fried king prawns, or a hearty paella.

Open 12-3 5.30-11 (Sat-Sun 12-11) **Bar Meals** L served all week 12-2.45 D served all week 6-9.30 (Sat-Sun all day) **Restaurant** L served all week 12-2.45 D served all week 6-9.30 (Sat-Sun all day) Marstons Marstons Bitter, 4 Guest ales. **Facilities** Children's licence Garden

MARTLEY MAP 10 SO76

Admiral Rodney Inn ★★★★ INN

Berrow Green WR6 6PL ☎ 01886 821375 📠 01886 822048

e-mail: rodney@admiral.fslife.co.uk

dir: *At Knightwick right onto B4197. Inn 2m on left at Berrow Green*

This early 17th-century farmhouse-cum-alehouse stands in the heart of the countryside on the Worcester Way footpath. The stylishly traditional interior includes a split-level restaurant housed in an old barn, where dishes could include roast duck with juniper and red wine sauce or roasted pancetta-wrapped poussin with a honey and mustard dressing. Fish – freshly delivered from Cornwall – features strongly. In the bar, expect home-made pies, fish and chips, and perhaps Malaysian lamb curry. New owners for 2007.

Open 11-3 5-11 (Mon 5-11, Sat-Sun all day) **Bar Meals** L served Tue-Sat 12-2 (Sun 12-2.30) D served all week 6.30-9 (Sat 6.30-9.30) **Restaurant** L served Sun 12-2.30 D served Mon-Sun 7-9 (Sat 7-9.30) Free House Wye Valley Bitter, local Guest beers eg. Black Pear, Malvern Hills Brewery, Muzzle Loader & Cannon Royal. **Facilities** Children's licence Garden Dogs allowed Parking **Rooms** 3 bedrooms en suite S£35 D£55

)MBERSLEY MAP 10 SO86

Pick of the Pubs

Crown & Sandys Arms

Main Rd WR9 0EW ☎ 01905 620252 📄 01905 620769
e-mail: enquiries@crownandsandys.co.uk
dir: *3m from Droitwich, off A449*

A classy establishment run by Richard Everton who also owns the village deli and wine shop, so you can expect an ample range of wines by the glass and a good selection of real ales. The décor is bang up-to-date, yet the original beams and fireplaces seem to blend effortlessly with the trendy furnishings. Regular 'wine dinners' and themed evenings complement the modern menus, which burst with the latest flavours. Freshly-made sandwiches, paninis and baguettes are supplemented on weekdays by home-made pizzas prepared to order, with different topping requests usually accommodated. Choose from dishes such as beef carpaccio marinated with wasabi and herbs, sushi ginger, noodle and scallion salad; and pan-fried breast of chicken wrapped in Parma ham, porcini mushroom and blue cheese risotto. If seafood is your preference, exotic options (barramundi, mahi-mahi) may vie with the likes of red mullet, gurnard and mackerel in daily changing specials.

Open 11-3 5-11 **Bar Meals** L served all week 12-2.30 D served all week 6-10 (Sun 12-9) Av main course £7 **Restaurant** L served all week 12-2.30 D served all week 6-10 (Sun 12-9) Av 3 course à la carte £22 Free House Sadlers Ale, Marstons, Cumberland, Woods Shropshire Lad. 14 **Facilities** Garden Parking

?OWICK MAP 10 SO85

The Halfway House Inn

3astonford WR2 4SL ☎ 01905 831098 📄 01905 831704
lir: *From A15 junct 7 take A4440 then A449*

ituated on the A449 between Worcester and Malvern, this delightful ub is just a few minutes' drive from the picturesque spa town of Aalvern, a popular centre for exploring the Malvern Hills. The menu hoice ranges from Herefordshire fillet steak or roasted Gressingham luck breast to baked fillet of Scottish salmon and spinach, ricotta and eef tomato lasagne.

pen 12-3 6-11 **Bar Meals** L served all week 12-2 D served all week 6-9 **Restaurant** L served all week 12-2 D served all week 6-9 Free House Abbot Ale, St Georges Bitter, Fuller's London Pride, Timothy Taylor. **acilities** Garden Parking Play Area

STONEHALL MAP 10 SO84

The Fruiterer's Arms

Stonehall Common WR5 3QG
☎ 01905 820462 📄 01905 820501
e-mail: thefruiterersarms@btopenworld.com
dir: *Stonehall Common is 1.5m from St Peters Garden Centre Norton*

Pub on Stonehall Common, once frequented by the area's fruit pickers. Four guest ales are rotated weekly, and there's a main menu, specials menu and Sunday menu offered in the bar, restaurant, garden pavilion and garden. Favourite dishes include Swiss chicken with Alpine cheese, fillet of lamb with Madeira and rosemary, and the fresh fish of the day. The garden is large and has a purpose-built play area for children.

Open 12-3 6-11 (Summer Sat-Sun all day) **Bar Meals** L served all week 12-2 D served all week 6-9.15 Av main course £6.50 **Restaurant** L served all week 12-2.30 D served all week 6-9.15 (Sun all day) Av 3 course à la carte £28 Bombardier, St Austell Tribute, Guest ales. **Facilities** Children's licence Garden Parking Play Area

TENBURY WELLS MAP 10 SO56

Pick of the Pubs

The Fountain Hotel

Oldwood, St Michaels WR15 8TB
☎ 01584 810701 📄 01584 819030
e-mail: enquiries@fountain-hotel.co.uk
dir: *1m out of Tenbury Wells on the A4112 Leominster Road*

See Pick of the Pubs on page 634

Pick of the Pubs

The Peacock Inn

WR15 8LL ☎ 01584 810506 📄 01584 811236
e-mail: thepeacockinn001@aol.com
dir: *A443 to Tenbury Wells, 0.75m on right*

A 14th-century coaching inn overlooking the River Teme, with a sympathetic extension and pleasant patio eating area. The relaxing bars and oak-panelled restaurant are enhanced by oak beams, dried hops and open log fires, while upstairs the ghost of Mrs Brown, a former landlady, does its best to enliven the place. Local market produce features on the menus, specialities being fresh fish and game. Starters might include millefeuilles of black pudding and apple with wholegrain mustard dressing. For a main course try green Thai curry of chicken and tiger prawns served with jasmine rice, or a more traditional option like home-made steak pie with herb dumplings. Desserts include classics like sticky toffee pudding, alongside innovative options like pineapple mousse served with passion fruits.

Open 11.30-3.30 5.30-12 **Bar Meals** L served all week 12-2 D served all week 6.30-9 Av main course £10.50 **Restaurant** L served all week 12-2 D served all week 6.30-9 Av 3 course à la carte £17.50 Free House Hobsons Best Bitter, Spitfire, Tetley Cask. **Facilities** Children's licence Garden Dogs allowed Parking

The Fountain Hotel

A fine example of the black and white timbered inns that are common in these parts, the Fountain comes complete with all the hoped-for welcoming country atmosphere. In 1855 this former farmhouse began selling beer and cider to Welsh drovers herding their sheep to English markets; at that time it was known as the Hippodrome, after the horse-racing that used to take place on the common outside.

The hotel has been providing rest and sustenance for travellers ever since, as its motto suggests: 'Weary and thin they stagger in; happy and stout they waddle out'. The Fountain's oldest resident is its mischievous but friendly ghost, a landlord who died in 1958 while saving his dogs from a fire. Now run by Russell Allen, a well-travelled big-game fisherman, and his chef wife Michaela, the inn has been winning plaudits for its quality food and real ales. The theme in the restaurant is nautical, and its carefully prepared fish dishes are a real strength: they may include line-caught wild salmon from the river Tay, or local rainbow trout; among more exotic species you may find roast blue-fin tuna; barracuda cooked in home-made organic herb butter; red snapper sushi; and porbeagle shark. To complete the theme, book a table near the 1,000-gallon aquarium for a grandstand view of many unusual fish. Non-aquatic starters could include melon and sorbet, or garlic bruschetta. For a main course, try Berrington chicken in leek and stilton sauce; or oven-roasted duck with honey, ginger and soy sauce. Outside is a large secluded garden which includes the plot where organic herbs and vegetables are grown for the kitchen, a children's play area with a trampoline, and a heated patio. The hotel is open all day, and also serves food throughout the day.

MAP 10 SO56
Oldwood, St Michaels WR15 8TB
☎ 01584 810701
01584 819030
e-mail:
enquiries@fountain-hotel.co.uk
dir: *1m out of Tenbury Wells on the A4112 Leominster Road*

Open 9–11
Bar Meals L served all week 12–9 D served all week 12–9
Restaurant L served all week 12–10 D served all week 12–10
Free House
Fountain Ale, Old Speckled Hen, Greene King IPA, Wye Valley Bitter. 20
Facilities Children's licence Garden Parking Play Area
Rooms 11 bedrooms en suite S£49.95 D£49.95 (★★★★ INN)

~~T~~IBBERTON MAP 10 SO95

~~T~~he Bridge Inn

~~P~~lough Rd WR9 7NQ ☎ 01905 345874
~~e~~-mail: dlmagor@yahoo.com
~~d~~ir: *M5 junct 6, cross rdbt towards Evesham, 1st left to Crowle/ ~~T~~ibberton, through Tibberton to bridge/canal*

~~T~~he pub dates from 1820, when the Worcester/Birmingham canal was ~~c~~ut through, and is situated beside it. It provides a popular watering ~~h~~ole for boaters, ramblers and walkers, and has a canalside beer ~~g~~arden. One menu is served throughout, with dishes like mussels with ~~w~~hite wine, garlic and cream or chicken liver and port pâté to start, and ~~m~~ain courses of thick cut ham and eggs, or sausages and mash with ~~c~~aramelised onion gravy.

~~O~~**pen** 11.30–3 5–11 (Summer 11.30–11) **Bar Meals** L served all week ~~1~~2–2 D served all week 6–9 Av main course £6.50 **Restaurant** L served all ~~w~~eek 12–2 D served all week 6–9 Banks Bitter, Banks Original, Pedigree, ~~G~~uest ale. **Facilities** Children's licence Garden Dogs allowed Parking ~~P~~lay Area

~~U~~PTON SNODSBURY MAP 10 SO95

Bants NEW ★★★★ INN

~~W~~orcester Rd WR7 4NN ☎ 01905 381282 01905 381173
~~e~~-mail: info@bants.co.uk
~~d~~ir: *Exit M5 junct 6 and follow signs for Evesham. At 2nd rdbt ~~t~~urn left onto A422 towards Stratford. Bants 2m on left*

~~A~~ few years ago Sue and Steve Bant changed the pub's name (from ~~t~~he Coventry Arms) to celebrate twenty years of ownership. It's a ~~1~~6th-century free house serving traditional ales, with real fires in winter ~~w~~arming an eclectic mix of ancient beams and modern furnishings. ~~F~~ood served in three lounge bars and the dedicated conservatory ~~r~~estaurant has a high comfort factor: you may find fantastic faggots ~~w~~ith garlic mash, or corned beef hash on bubble and squeak with ~~f~~ried egg.

~~O~~**pen** 12–3 5.30–11.30 **Bar Meals** L served all week 12–2 D served all ~~w~~eek 6–9.30 Av main course £6.95 **Restaurant** L served all week 12–2 ~~D~~ served all week 6–9.30 Av 3 course à la carte £25 Guinness, London ~~P~~ride, Cats Whiskas. **Facilities** Garden Parking **Rooms** 7 bedrooms ~~e~~n suite S£45 D£55

YORKSHIRE, EAST RIDING OF

BEVERLEY MAP 17 TA03

White Horse Inn

22 Hengate HU17 8BN ☎ 01482 861973 01482 861973
e-mail: anna@nellies.co.uk
dir: *A1079 from York to Beverley*

Gas lighting, open fires, old cartoons and high-backed settles add to the charm of this classic 16th-century local. John Wesley preached in the back yard in the mid–18th century, and the pub's atmospheric little rooms arranged around the central bar are probably much as they were back then. Traditional bar food might include pasta dishes, fresh jumbo haddock, bangers and mash, and steak and ale pie. Toasted and plain sandwiches and daily specials also feature.

Open 11–11 (Sun 12–10.30) **Bar Meals** L served Mon–Sat 11–2.45 D served Mon–Sat Samuel Smith Samuel Smith Old Brewery Bitter & Sovereign Bitter. **Facilities** Garden Parking Play Area **Notes**

DRIFFIELD MAP 17 TA05

Best Western The Bell ★★★ HL

46 Market Place YO25 6AN
☎ 01377 256661 01377 253228
e-mail: bell@bestwestern.co.uk
dir: *Enter town from A164, right at lights. Car park 50yds on left behind black railings*

A delightful 18th-century coaching inn furnished with antiques, with an oak-panelled bar serving a good range of cask beers and 300 whiskies. Food ranges through broiled salmon fillet cooked with red peppers, lemon, garlic and capers; roasted whole pork fillet coated with honey and Dijon mustard; and oven roasted breast of English duckling with spicy plum sauce. Fresh coffee is served in the mornings 9.30–11.30 with scones, jam and cream.

Open 10 –11 Closed: 25 Dec, 1 Jan **Bar Meals** L served Mon–Sat 12–1.30 D served Mon–Sat 7–9.30 **Restaurant** L served Mon–Sat 12–1.30 D served all week 7–9.30 Av 4 course fixed price £19.50 Free House World Top, Falling Stones, Mars Magic, Hambleton Stallion & Stud. **Facilities** Parking **Rooms** 16 bedrooms en suite S£84 D£104

England

FLAMBOROUGH — MAP 17 TA27

The Seabirds Inn

Tower St YO15 1PD ☎ 01262 850242 01262 851874

dir: *On B1255 E of Bridlington*

Head west from famous Flamborough Head and you'll swiftly arrive at this 200-year-old village pub. A wide range of well prepared dishes includes so many regularly changing specials that questions will need to be answered – will it be pan-seared king scallops with home-made chilli butter? Lamb shanks with crushed rosemary potatoes in rich red wine sauce? Then again, from the regular menu, haddock fillet mornay, fillet steak Rossini, or roast vegetable lasagne? Decisions might be hard to reach.

Open 12–3 6.30–11 (Sun 7–10.30) Rest: Closed Mon eve in winter **Bar Meals** L served all week 12–2 D served all week 6.30–9 (Sat 6.30–9.30, Sun 7–9) Av main course £5.95 **Restaurant** L served all week 12–2 D served all week 6.30–9 (Sat 6.30–9.30, Sun 7–9) Av 3 course à la carte £22 Free House Scottish Courage John Smith's, Interbrew Boddingtons Bitter, Tetleys Creamflow. 9 **Facilities** Garden Dogs allowed Parking

HOLME UPON SPALDING MOOR — MAP 17 SE83

Ye Olde Red Lion Hotel

Old Rd YO43 4AD ☎ 01430 860220 01430 861471

dir: *Off A1079. At Market Weighton take A614*

A historic 17th-century coaching inn that once provided hospitality for weary travellers who were helped across the marshes by monks. It's still a great refuge, with a friendly atmosphere, oak beams and a cosy fire. The inspiring menu could include oven-baked duck breast with star anise sauce, corn fed chicken coq-au-vin or pan-seared sea bass with wilted greens and vierge sauce.

Open 11.30–2.30 5.30–11 (Sun 12–11) **Bar Meals** L served all week 12–2 D served all week 5.30–9 **Restaurant** L served all week 12–2 D served all week 5.30–9 Free House John Smiths, Black Sheep, Guinness. 7 **Facilities** Garden Parking

HUGGATE — MAP 19 SE85

The Wolds Inn ★★★ GA

YO42 1YH ☎ 01377 288217

e-mail: huggate@woldsinn.freeserve.co.uk

dir: *S off A166 between York & Driffield*

Probably the highest inn on the Yorkshire Wolds, 16th century in origin, with tiled roofs and white-painted chimneys, and a wood-panelled interior with open fires and gleaming brassware. Its elevation explains why the Wolds Topper, 'the mixed grill to remember', is so named; other main courses include steaks with a variety of sauces, rack of lamb, loin of pork, roast duckling, and Scottish salmon fillet, while vegetarians may consult their own blackboard.

Open 12–2 6.30–11 (May–Sep 6–11) **Bar Meals** L served Tue–Thu, Sat–Sun 12–2 D served Tue–Sun 6.30–9 (May–Sep 6–9) **Restaurant** L served Tue–Thu, Sat–Sun 12–2 D served Tue–Sun 6.30–9 (May–Sep Sun 6–9) Free House Carlsberg-Tetley Tetley Bitter, Timothy Taylor Landlord, Black Sheep. 7 **Facilities** Garden Parking **Rooms** 3 bedrooms en suite S£37 D£48

KILHAM — MAP 17 TA0

The Old Star Inn

Church St YO25 4RG ☎ 01262 420619 01262 420619

dir: *A164, 6m from Driffield*

Situated in the historic village of Kilham, with easy access to Bridlington, Scarborough and the Yorkshire Wolds, this quaint pub offers home-cooked food, real ale and a warm welcome. Food is sourced from local suppliers, with particular attention to reducing the travelling time of ingredients. Special diets are catered for, and children have half price portions for half price. John Smiths is the resident beer the three other pumps operating a rotation of guest ales.

Open 12–3 5.30–11 Rest: Oct and Etr school holidays **Bar Meals** L served Fri–Sun 12–6 D served Tue–Sun (Fri–Sun 12–9) **Restaurant** L served Sat–Sun 12–2 D served Tue–Sun 6–9.30 (12–6) Free House Scottish Courage John Smiths Cask, Deuchars, Theakstons, Black Sheep. 15 **Facilities** Garden Dogs allowed Parking Play Area

KINGSTON UPON HULL — MAP 17 TA0

The Minerva Hotel

Nelson St, Victoria Pier HU1 1XE

☎ 01482 326909 01482 617434

dir: *M62 onto A63, then Castle St, turn right at sign for fruit market into Queens St. At top of Queens St on right of pier*

The Minerva boasts old-fashioned rooms and cosy snugs at its riverside location with its ferry port, marina, and fishing fleet. It has a reputation for hospitality and delicious home-cooked food, and a good range of guest ales. Part of the Tattershall Castle Group.

Open 11–11 (Sun 12–10.30) **Bar Meals** L served all week 12–9.45 D served all week Sun 12–8.45 Av main course £5.95 **Restaurant** L served all week 12–9.45 D served all week Sun 12–8.45 Spirit Group Tetley Bitter, usually 4 Guest beers. 7 **Facilities** Children's licence

The Pipe & Glass Inn

)ating back to the 15th century, this acclaimed inn stands on the site of the original gatehouse o Dalton Park. A cosy, traditional bar with leather sofas and polished floors gives way to an xtensive dining room, complete with bespoke wooden tables and a large conservatory.

ın interesting array of real ales, ıcluding Copper Dragon, Wold ›op and Black Sheep, is matched y a wine list entirely sourced from mall producers. Ten are available y the glass, and each bin has a tory – just ask the knowledgeable taff. The thoughtful, elegant menu s a tribute to owner and head hef James Mackenzie's passion for ɔcally sourced food. You could start ff with potted Gloucester Old Spot ork with mulled pear and port hutney; a cold terrine of hare, ham ock and foie gras with cranberry nd satsuma relish; or cumin ɔasted monkfish, wilted samphire, moked eel and caper butter. Mains night include hay-baked chicken vith parsnip and smoky bacon itters; or braised Burdass lamb with pot of mutton and kidney Turbigo casserole. For those with simpler tastes, try the inn's stylish take on the classics – perhaps chicken Kiev with wild garlic butter, or dry-cured gammon steak with braised peas. Vegetarians are equally well catered for, and could select risotto of fairy-ring mushrooms and spiced crispy quail egg, followed by cheddar and chive omelette with scallion salad, from a short but appealing menu. Puddings are equally alluring: Brambly apple and bramble steamed sponge with cinnamon custard and green apple sorbet; or prune and Armagnac ice cream with walnut brittle.

NEW
MAP 17 SE94
West End HU17 7PN
☎ 01430 810246
e-mail:
email@pipeandglass.co.uk
dir: *Just off B1248. 7m from Beverley*

Open 12–3 6.30–11 (Sun 12–10.30) Closed: 2 wks in Jan
Bar Meals L served Tue–Sun 12–2 (Sun 12–4) D served Tue–Sat 6.30–9.30 Av main course £10
Restaurant L served Tue–Sun 12–2 (Sun 12–4) D served Tue–Sat 6.30–9.30 Av 3 course à la carte £25
Free House
John Smiths Cask, Wold Top, Copper Dragon, Black Sheep.
10
Facilities Garden Parking

England

LOW CATTON — MAP 17 SE75

The Gold Cup Inn

YO41 1EA ☎ 01759 371354 📠 01759 373833

dir: *1m S of A166 or 1m N of A1079, E of York*

Solid oak tables and pews – reputedly made from a single oak tree -set the scene in the restaurant of this 300 year-old family-run free house. There's a large beer garden, and the adjoining paddock drops down to the River Derwent. The appetising menu includes grills and salads, as well as main course dishes like mushroom and ricotta crêpes with gruyere cheese; baked cod with herb and breadcrumb crust; and duckling with port and blackcurrant sauce.

Open 12-2.30 6–11.30 (Sat -Sun all day) **Bar Meals** L served Tue–Sat 12–2 D served all week 6–9 (Sat–Sun 12–9) Av main course £7.50 **Restaurant** L served Sun 12–5.30 D served all week 6.30–9.30 Av 3 course à la carte £20 Av 3 course fixed price £15 Free House John Smiths, Black Sheep. 15 **Facilities** Garden Dogs allowed Parking Play Area **Notes**

LUND — MAP 17 SE94

The Wellington Inn

19 The Green YO25 9TE ☎ 01377 217294 📠 01377 217192

dir: *On B1248 NE of Beverley*

Nicely situated opposite the picture-postcard village green, the Wellington Inn is popular with locals and visitors alike, whether for a pint of real ale, a glass of house wine, or a plate of decent food. You can choose to eat from the bar menu or a la carte, and there's an extensive wine list. Expect king scallops with bacon and garlic risotto; or perhaps beef, mushroom and red onion suet pudding.

Open 12–3 6.30–11 **Bar Meals** L served Tue–Sun 12–2 D served Tue–Sat 6.30–9.30 Av main course £12.95 **Restaurant** D served Tue–Sat 7–9.30 Av 3 course à la carte £26 Free House Timothy Taylor Landlord, Black Sheep Best, John Smiths, Regular Guest. 8 **Facilities** Garden Parking

SOUTH CAVE — MAP 17 SE93

The Fox and Coney Inn

52 Market Place HU15 2AT

☎ 01430 422275 📠 01430 421552

e-mail: foxandconey@aol.com

dir: *4m E of M62 on A63. 4m N of Brough mainline railway*

Right in the heart of South Cave, this family run pub dates from 1739 and is probably the oldest building in the village. The inn, which is handy for walkers on the nearby Wolds Way, was known simply as The Fox until William Goodlad added the Coney (rabbit) in 1788. Jacket potatoes, salads and baguettes supplement varied hot dishes like steak in ale pie, chicken curry, seafood platter and mushroom Stroganoff.

Open 11.30–2.30 4.30–11 **Bar Meals** L served all week 11.30–2 D served all week 5.30–9.30 (Sun 12–3.30, 5.30–9) Av main course £7.95 **Restaurant** L served all week 11.30–2 D served all week 5.30–9.30 (Sun 12-9) Av 3 course à la carte £13.50 Enterprise Inns Timothy Taylors Landlord, Scottish Courage John Smith's & Theakston Cool Cask, Deuchers IPA, Guest Beers. 15 **Facilities** Garden Parking

SOUTH DALTON — MAP 17 SE9

Pick of the Pubs

The Pipe & Glass Inn NEW

West End HU17 7PN ☎ 01430 810246

e-mail: email@pipeandglass.co.uk

dir: *Just off B1248 7m from Beverley*

See Pick of the Pubs on page 637

SUTTON UPON DERWENT — MAP 17 SE7

St Vincent Arms

Main St YO41 4BN ☎ 01904 608349

e-mail: enquiries@stvincentarms.co.uk

dir: *Signs for Elvington on B1228, and on to Sutton upon Derwent*

The name comes from John Jervis, created the first Earl of St Vincent in the 18th century, and mentor to Admiral Lord Nelson. This is a warm family-run pub with an old-fashioned welcoming atmosphere, minus music or gaming machines but plus great food and beer. Food options include sandwiches, ciabatta, salads and full meals such as curried crab mayonnaise followed by chicken and ginger stir fry.

Open 11.30–3 6–11 **Bar Meals** L served all week 12–2 D served all week 7–9.30 Av main course £10 **Restaurant** L served all week 12–2 D served all week 7–9.30 Av 3 course à la carte £20 Timothy Taylor Landlord, Fullers ESB, Yorkshire Terrier, Charles Wells Bombardier. 8 **Facilities** Garden Parking

YORKSHIRE, NORTH

AKEBAR — MAP 19 SE1

The Friar's Head

Akebar Park DL8 5LY

☎ 01677 450201 & 450591 📠 01677 450046

e-mail: info@akebarpark.com

dir: *From A1 at Leeming Bar onto A684, 7m towards Leyburn. Entrance at Akebar Park*

The Friar's Head is a traditional stone-built Yorkshire Dales hostelry with a terrace overlooking lower Wensleydale. The wow factor comes from the large south-facing conservatory dining room, called The Cloister, with its stone flags, lush planting and fruiting vines. At night, by candlelight, the effect is quite magical. The blackboard menu offers daily changing fish, meat and vegetarian dishes, and from the carte comes stuffed breast of local pheasant, steaks, and Thai-style beef stir fry.

Open 10–2.30 6–11.30 (Sun 7–10.30) **Bar Meals** L served all week 12–2 D served all week 6–9.30 (Sun 7–9.30) Av main course £8 **Restaurant** L served all week 12–2 D served all week 6–9.30 (Sat 6–10, Sun 7–9.30) Av 3 course à la carte £20 Free House Scottish Courage John Smith's & Theakston Best Bitter, Black Sheep Best. 14 **Facilities** Garden Parking

See advert on this page

APPLETON-LE-MOORS MAP 19 SE78

Pick of the Pubs

The Moors Inn

YO62 6TF ☎ 01751 417435

e-mail: enquiries@moorsinn.co.uk

dir: *On A170 between Pickering & Kirbymoorside*

Whether you're interested in walking or sightseeing by car, this inn is a good choice for its location and good home-cooked food. Set in a small moors village with lovely scenery in every direction, in summer you can sit in the large garden and enjoy the splendid views. Dishes include pheasant casserole and fish pie, and in addition to hand-pumped Black Bull and Black Sheep, there is a selection of 50 malt whiskies.

Open 12–3 7–11 (lunch Sat–Sun only) **Bar Meals** L served Sat & Sun 12–2 D served Tue–Sun 7–9 **Restaurant** L served Sun 12–2 D served Tue–Sun 7–9 Free House Black Sheep, Black Bull. **Facilities** Garden Dogs allowed Parking **Notes**

APPLETREEWICK MAP 19 SE06

The Craven Arms

BD23 6DA ☎ 01756 720270

e-mail: thecravenarms@ukonline.co.uk

dir: *From Skipton take A59 towards Harrogate, B6160 N. Village signed on right. Pub just outside village.*

Originally a farm built for Sir William Craven (a Lord Mayor of London) in the mid-16th century, and later used as a weaving shed and courthouse, this historic building retains its original beams, flagstone floors and magnificent fireplace. The village stocks are still outside, with spectacular views of the River Wharfe and Simon's Seat. Food options range through sandwiches, home-made kids' food, jacket potatoes and dishes such as ratatouille bake and steak and mushroom pie.

Open 11.30–3 6.30–11 **Bar Meals** L served all week 12–2 D served all week 6.30–9 (Sun 12–2, 6.30–8.30) Av main course £8 **Restaurant** L served 12–2 D served 6.30–8.45 (Sun 6.30–8.30) Free House Tetley, Folly Ale, Timothy Taylors Landlord & Golden Best. 8 **Facilities** Garden Dogs allowed Parking

ASENBY MAP 19 SE37

Pick of the Pubs

Crab & Lobster

Dishforth Rd YO7 3QL

☎ 01845 577286 01845 577109

e-mail: reservations@crabandlobster.co.uk

dir: *A168 towards Thirsk, signs for Asenby*

Amid seven acres of garden, lake and streams stands this unique 17th-century thatched pub and adjacent small hotel. It is an Aladdin's cave of antiques and artefacts from around the world. Equally famous for its innovative cuisine and special gourmet extravaganzas, the menus show influences from France and Italy,

CONTINUED

ASENBY continued

with some oriental dishes too. The famous fish club sandwich (lunch only); and starters like chunky fish soup; mussels with Yorkshire ale, cabbage and bacon; or perhaps Thai green fish curry or fish pie, scallops and capers. Meat eaters are not ignored with main dishes like pan-fried Dutch calves' liver alongside an array of fish dishes including roast local cod chunk with slow-roasted belly pork, honey and capers and duck fat roastie. Alfresco eating and summer barbecues are on offer. There are good real ales and an extensive wine list, plus a pavilion open all day for food, drinks and coffees.

Open 11.30–11 **Bar Meals** L served all week 12–2.30 D served all week 7–9.30 (Sat 6.30–9.30) **Restaurant** L served all week 12–2 D served all week 7–9.30 (Sat 6.30–9.30) John Smiths, Scots 1816, Golden Pippin. 16 **Facilities** Garden Dogs allowed Parking

ASKRIGG — MAP 18 SD99

Kings Arms

Market Place DL8 3HQ ☎ 01969 650817 01969 650856
e-mail: kingsarms@askrigg.fsnet.co.uk
dir: *N off A684 between Hawes & Leyburn*

At the heart of the Yorkshire Dales, Askrigg's pub was known as The Drovers in the TV series *All Creatures Great and Small*. Built in 1762 as racing stables and converted to a pub in 1860, today it boasts a good range of real ales and an extensive menu and wine list. Favourites are roasted rack of Dales lamb with a mustard and herb crust, beer-battered haddock fillet with chips, chicken breast with linguini, seared sea bass on fresh pasta with a shellfish nage, or grilled gammon steak with eggs or pineapple rings. Spectacular inglenook fireplace.

Open 11–3 6–11 (Sat 11–11, Sun 12–10.30) **Bar Meals** L served all week 12–2 D served all week 6.30–9 Av main course £12 **Restaurant** 12–2 D served all week 7–9 Av 3 course à la carte £20.25 Free House Scottish Courage John Smiths, Black Sheep, Theakstons Best Bitter, Theakstons Old Peculier. 6 **Facilities** Garden Dogs allowed

AUSTWICK — MAP 18 SD76

The Game Cock Inn

The Green LA2 8BB ☎ 015242 51226
e-mail: richardlord495@hotmail.com

Richard and Trish Lord offer a warm welcome to this award-winning pub, set in the limestone village of Austwick. There's a large garden and children's play area, with winter log fires in the cosy bar. Expect real ale, a range of malt whiskies, and an imaginative menu. Typical dishes include giant ham shank with mash and pickled red cabbage, whilst one of the regular French evenings might feature fresh Toulouse sausage on provençale couscous.

Open 11.30–3 6–1am (Sun all day) **Bar Meals** L served all week 11.30–2 D served all week 6–9 (Sun 12–9) Av main course £6 **Restaurant** L served all week 11.30–2 D served all week 6–9 (Sun 12–9) Av 3 course à la carte £10 Thwaites Best Bitter & Smooth, Warfsteiner. **Facilities** Garden Parking Play Area

AYSGARTH — MAP 19 SE08

Pick of the Pubs

The George & Dragon Inn ★★ HL

DL8 3AD ☎ 01969 663358 01969 663773
e-mail: info@georgeanddragonaysgarth.co.uk
dir: *On A684 between Leyburn & Hawes, in village centre*

See Pick of the Pubs on opposite page

BAINBRIDGE — MAP 18 SD99

Rose & Crown Hotel ★★ HL

DL8 3EE ☎ 01969 650225 01969 650735
e-mail: stay@theprideofwensleydale.co.uk
dir: *On A684 in centre of village*

A 500-year-old coaching inn surrounded by spectacular scenery, whose cosy interior is home to the forest horn. Blown each evening from Holy Rood (September 27th) to Shrovetide, it would guide travellers safely to the village. The chef offers such delights as salmon and dill dumplings with caviar sauce, while a main course from the specials menu might consist of whole black bream baked in a sea salt crust and served with mint hollandaise. Other dishes could include haunch of rabbit studded with garlic or breast of chicken filled with crayfish.

Open 11–11 (Sun 12–10.30) **Bar Meals** L served all week 12–2.15 D served all week 6–9.15 Av main course £9.50 **Restaurant** L served Sun 12–2.15 D served all week 7–9.15 Av 3 course à la carte £20 Free House Websters Bitter, Black Sheep Best, Scottish Courage John Smith's, Old Peculier. **Facilities** Garden Dogs allowed Parking Play Area **Rooms** 11 bedrooms en suite S£40 D£74

BILBROUGH — MAP 16 SE54

Pick of the Pubs

The Three Hares Country Inn

Main St YO23 3PH ☎ 01937 832128 01937 834626
e-mail: info@thethreehares.co.uk
dir: *Off A64 between A659 and A1237 junctions*

See Pick of the Pubs on page 642

BOROUGHBRIDGE — MAP 19 SE36

Pick of the Pubs

The Black Bull Inn

6 St James Square YO51 9AR
☎ 01423 322413 01423 323915
dir: *From A1(M) junct 48 take B6265 E 1m*

See Pick of the Pubs on page 647

The George & Dragon Inn

The George & Dragon Inn is a 17th-century Grade II listed building in a superb location in the Yorkshire Dales National Park, near the beautiful Aysgarth Falls. This is Herriot country, of All Creatures Great and Small fame, and where Robin Hood Prince of Thieves was filmed.

The area is perfect for walking, touring and visiting local attractions, including Forbidden Corner, the cheese factory and the Wensleydale Railway. The owners are proud to continue a centuries-long tradition of Yorkshire hospitality at the inn, with visitors returning again and again to stay in the seven comfortable en suite bedrooms. In winter you can keep cosy by the fireside and in summer there is a flower-filled patio with tables and chairs where meals and drinks can be taken outside. A good choice of well-kept real ales is available and 16 wines are served by the glass. The inn has a great reputation for its food. Only the best, freshest produce is used, local wherever possible. The regular menu is supplemented by daily specials, including a good fresh fish element in dishes such as home-made Thai fishcakes with saffron rouille, and monkfish wrapped in Parma ham with a mango and pumpkin seed salsa. Alternative options are smooth chicken liver parfait with red onion marmalade, and local fillet of beef with Lyonnaise potatoes, sunblush tomatoes and Madeira wine sauce. Desserts range from traditional apple crumble with ice cream to the more exotic vanilla cheesecake with fruits of the forest and mulled wine.

★★ HL 🍷
MAP 19 SE08
DL8 3AD
☎ 01969 663358
📠 01969 663773
e-mail: info@georgeanddragonaysgarth.co.uk
dir: *On A684 between Leyburn & Hawes, in village centre*

Open 11–11 Closed: 2 wks in Jan
Bar Meals L served all week 12–2 D served all week 6–9 Av main course £12
Restaurant L served all week 12–2 (Sun 12–3) D served all week 6–9 Av 3 course fixed price £25
Free House
Black Sheep Best, John Smith's Cask, Smooth, Theakstons Bitter.
🍷 16
Facilities Garden Dogs allowed Parking
Rooms 7 bedrooms en suite S£40 D£72

The Three Hares Country Inn

Race-goers, foodies and locals alike flock to this 18th-century country pub, which is renowned for the quality of its food. A light and smartly turned-out brick-walled dining room provides an elegant setting for the culinary delights in store.

Local, seasonal produce, a menu that wisely balances tradition with simplicity, and assured cooking techniques combine to create an award-winning kitchen output. For lunch, tuck into chicken liver parfait; goats' cheese ravioli, or ham and pea risotto with crispy leeks, to be followed by confit duck leg with parmesan mash and red wine jus; baked Whitby fish pie topped with cheese; or pan-fried salmon with dressed spinach. The dinner menu might well open with the likes of smoked mackerel fillets, toasted brioche, concasse, capers and shallot rings. Follow with open lasagne of wild mushrooms, white wine, cream and herbs; oven-baked pork loin, crispy black pudding and caramelised Bramley apples; pan-fried sea bass fillet with saffron potatoes, or duck breast with buttered cabbage and bacon. Desserts such as apple and pear tarte Tatin with cinnamon ice cream, or chocolate brownie and griottine cherries maintain the momentum, and the selection of Yorkshire cheeses is excellent. Race-goers should look out for the racing brunch, which includes such trencherman fare as Yorkshire ploughman's; a 'Full Monty' breakfast; fillet steak sandwich with home-made chips; and roast ham sandwiches. In combination with a pint of Black Sheep bitter, it's just the thing to toast a win or console oneself after a loss. A heated terrace completes the package.

MAP 16 SE54
Main St YO23 3PH
☎ 01937 832128
01937 834626
e-mail:
info@thethreehares.co.uk
dir: *Off A64 between A659 and A1237 York junctions*

Open 12pm–12.30am
Bar Meals L served Tue–Sun 12–3
Restaurant L served Tue–Sun 12–3 D served Tue–Sat 7–9 Av 3 course à la carte £21.50
Free House
Timothy Taylors Landlord, Black Sheep, Farmers Blond, Guest ales each week. 10
Facilities Garden Parking

England

BREARTON MAP 19 SE36

Pick of the Pubs

Malt Shovel Inn

HG3 3BX ☎ 01423 862929

e-mail: malt-shovel@btconnect.com

dir: *A61 take B6165 towards Knaresborough. Left following signs to Brearton for 1m*

A 16th-century beamed free house, the Malt Shovel is the oldest building in a very old village. The rural setting has some good examples of ancient strip farming, and although the pub is surrounded by rolling farmland, it's just 15 minutes from Harrogate and within easy reach of both Knaresborough and Ripon. Open fires in winter, beer mugs, horse brasses and hunting scenes help to give the place both atmosphere and character, and you can enjoy a quiet game of dominoes or shove ha'penny without any intrusions beyond those of the two friendly resident ghosts. Home-cooked food includes the likes of haddock, beef lasagne, seafood gratin, chargrilled liver, haggis, smoked salmon salad, asparagus tart, lamb curry, rib-eye steak, and a range of sandwiches.

Open 12-3 6.45-11 (Sun 12-3, 7-10.30) **Bar Meals** L served Tue-Sun 12-2 D served Tue-Sat 7-9 Av main course £6.95 Free House Daleside Nightjar, Durham Magus, Black Sheep Best, Theakston Masham. **Facilities** Dogs allowed Parking

BROUGHTON MAP 18 SD95

The Bull

BD23 3AE ☎ 01756 792065

e-mail: janeneil@thebullatbroughton.co.uk

dir: *On A59 3m from Skipton on A59*

Like the village itself, the pub is part of the 3,000-acre Broughton Hall Estate, owned by the Tempest family for 900 years. Chef-cum-manager Neil Butterworth's compact, thoughtful menu offers Goosnargh duck breast with spring onion and coriander mash, chargrilled fillet steak, and goats' cheese on toast. The locally brewed Bull Bitter and guest ales are features, and twice a month a mystery meal is held on Guinea Pig Night.

Open 12-3 5.30-11 (Sat 12-11, Sun & BH 12-8) **Bar Meals** L served all week 12-2 D served Mon-Sat 6-9 (Sun 12-6) Av main course £10 **Restaurant** L served all week 12-2 D served Mon-Sat 6-9 (Sun & BHs 12-6) Av 3 course à la carte £20 Free House Scottish Courage, John Smith's Smooth, Bull Bitter, Guest Ales. 12 **Facilities** Garden Dogs allowed Parking

BURNSALL MAP 19 SE06

Pick of the Pubs

The Red Lion ★★ HL

By the Bridge BD23 6BU

☎ 01756 720204 01756 720292

e-mail: redlion@daelnet.co.uk

dir: *B6160 towards Bolton Abbey, Burnsall 7m*

See Pick of the Pubs on page 648

BYLAND ABBEY MAP 19 SE57

Pick of the Pubs

Abbey Inn

YO61 4BD ☎ 01347 868204 01347 868678

e-mail: abbeyinn@english-heritage.org.uk

dir: *From A19 signs to Byland Abbey/Coxwold*

See Pick of the Pubs on page 651

CARTHORPE MAP 19 SE38

Pick of the Pubs

The Fox & Hounds

DL8 2LG ☎ 01845 567433 01845 567155

dir: *Off A1, signed on both carriageways*

The Fox and Hounds has been standing in the sleepy village of Carthorpe for over 200 years. The restaurant was once the village smithy, and the old anvil and other tools of the trade are still on display, giving the place a nice sense of history. The pub has an excellent reputation for its food, which might include starters of honey roast ham hock terrine with home-made piccalilli; caramelised onion and goats' cheese tart; or Loch Fyne smoked salmon. Typical main courses include half roasted Gressingham duckling; or chicken breast with Yorkshire blue cheese and leeks. Vegetarians won't go hungry – there's a dedicated menu of five dishes, each available as a starter or main course. Leave room for award-winning desserts such as meringue with lemon curd ice cream served with seasonal fruit. All wines are available by the glass.

Open 12-3 7-11 Closed: 25-26 Dec eve & 1st wk in Jan **Bar Meals** L served Tue-Sun 12-2 D served Tue-Sun 7-9.30 Av main course £12.95 **Restaurant** L served Tue-Sun 12-2 D served Tue-Sun 7-9.30 Av 3 course à la carte £24 Av 3 course fixed price £15.95 Free House Black Sheep Best, Worthington's Bitter. **Facilities** Parking

New Inn Hotel

'Jewel of the Dales'

Clapham LA2 8HH

Yorkshire Dales National Park

Tel: 015242 51203

Email: www.info@newinn-clapham.co.uk

Website: www.newinn-clapham.co.uk

Contact us now for details of our special offers

Nestling beneath Ingleborough mountain, the beautiful old dales village straggles on either side of Clapham Beck, one half linked to the other by three bridges – the church is at the top, the New Inn at the bottom.

This family run Inn is set amidst a geological wonderland of limestone, cavern and fell country.

Being a true Village Inn, experience the warmth and friendliness that the Mannion family give to the New Inn, an 18th Century Coaching Inn, that they have lovingly and carefully refurbished over the past 18 years. Now being a finely appointed 18-bedroomed Inn with antique, 4-posters and kingsize beds, 2 bars with open

fires, restaurant and residents lounge, a wonderful blend of old and new, to retain the ambience of a true Dales village Inn run by Yorkshire folk.

Walk from our doorstep or tour the Dales or Lakes, Windermere being only 40 minutes drive away.

Pets welcome.

CHAPEL LE DALE MAP 18 SD77

The Old Hill Inn NEW

LA6 3A4 ☎ 015242 41256

dir: *From Ingleton take B6255 4m, on the right*

Built in 1615 as a farm, and later serving as a stopping place for drovers, this characterful inn specializes in delicious home-cooked food. The Old Hill is owned and run by a family of chefs: look out for Colin Martin's award-winning sugar sculptures on display. Sample dishes include beef casserole; pan-fried sea bass; and sautéed duck breast, while vegetarians can tuck into mushroom stuffed with ratatouille, chickpeas and Wensleydale cheese.

Open (telephone for details) Closed: 24–25 Dec **Bar Meals** L served Sat–Sun 12–2.30 D served Tue–Sun 6.30–8.45 Av main course £12 Free House Black Sheep Best, Black Sheep Emmerdale, Theakstons Best & Dent Aviator. **Facilities** Garden Parking

CLAPHAM MAP 18 SD76

New Inn

LA2 8HH ☎ 01524 251203 01524 251496

e-mail: info@newinn-clapham.co.uk

dir: *On A65 in Yorkshire Dale National Park*

There's a warm and friendly welcome at this 18th-century free house, nestling beneath the famous summit of Ingleborough. Outdoor enthusiasts Keith and Barbara Mannion have run the former coaching inn since 1987, and walkers and visitors to the Yorkshire Dales certainly appreciate the honest, wholesome food served in their dining room. Typical dishes include ricotta and spinach tortellini; poached salmon on mustard mash; and venison steak with redcurrant sauce.

Open 11–11 **Bar Meals** L served all week 12–2 D served all week 6.30–8.30 (Sun 6.30–8) Av main course £8.95 **Restaurant** L served all week 12–2 D served all week 6.30–8.30 (Sun 6.30–8) Av 3 course à la carte £22 Av 5 course fixed price £24 Free House Black Sheep Best, Tetley Bitter, Copper Dragon Pippin, Thwaites Best & Thwaites Bomber. 18 **Facilities** Children's licence Garden Dogs allowed Parking

See advert on opposite page

COLTON MAP 16 SE54

Ye Old Sun Inn

Main St LS24 8EP ☎ 01904 744261 01904 744261

e-mail: ashleyandkelly@yeoldsuninn.co.uk

dir: *4m from York, off A64*

Dating from the 18th century, this whitewashed local is set in the heart of the village. It began life as a coaching inn and still boasts open winter fires and beams throughout. There are tables and chairs in the large lawned garden for warmer days, and rolling countryside beyond. Menu choices include lime cured swordfish with fresh chillies; watercress and cream cheese roulade; and pork loin steak with a cheese and herb crumb.

Open 12–2.30 6–11 Closed: 1–26 Jan **Bar Meals** L served Tue–Sun 12–2 D served Tue–Sun 6.30–9.30 (Sun 12–4) **Restaurant** L served Tue–Sun 12–2 D served Tue–Sun 6–9.30 (Sun 12–7) Enterprise Inns John Smith, Timothy Taylors, Black Sheep, Guest Ale. 18 **Facilities** Garden Parking

CRAY MAP 18 SD97

Pick of the Pubs

The White Lion Inn

Cray BD23 5JB ☎ 01756 760262

e-mail: admin@whitelioncray.com

dir: *B6265 from Skipton, then B6160 towards Aysgarth. Cray 10m*

See Pick of the Pubs on page 652

England

CRAYKE MAP 19 SE57

Pick of the Pubs

AA PUB OF THE YEAR FOR ENGLAND 2007-8

The Durham Ox

Westway YO61 4TE ☎ 01347 821506 01347 823326

e-mail: enquiries@thedurhamox.com

dir: *Off A19 from York to Thirsk, then to Easingwold. From market place to Crayke, turn left up hill, pub on right*

Notes on the inn's menu tell us the eponymous ox was born around 1796 and grew to enormous proportions – five feet six inches tall, 11 feet from nose to tail, the same around its girth, and weighing 171 stones. No wonder the animal created such a sensation that over 2,000 prints of it were sold, one of which hangs in the bottom bar. Another claim to fame for this delightful country pub is that the hill outside is reputedly the one up which the Grand Old Duke of York marched his men. Today the Durham Ox prides itself on serving good pub food properly, and uses the best ingredients sourced locally when possible. The cosy oak-panelled bar with roaring fires and award-winning restaurant are equally acceptable venues for indulging in the justifiably revered menus. Expect the likes of baked queen scallops with garlic and gruyère cream, or braised lamb shank.

Open 12-3 6-11 (Sat-Sun 12-11) Closed: 25 Dec **Bar Meals** L served all week 12-3 D served all week 6-9.30 (Sun 6-8.30, Sat 6-10) Av main course £12.95 **Restaurant** L served all week 12-2.30 D served all week 6-9.30 (Sun 12-3, 6-8.30 Sat 6-10) Av 3 course à la carte £24.95 Free House John Smiths, Theakstons, Black Bull, Theakstons Old Peculier. 9 **Facilities** Garden Dogs allowed Parking **Rooms** 8 bedrooms en suite S£60 D£80

CROPTON MAP 19 SE78

The New Inn

YO18 8HH ☎ 01751 417330 01751 417582

e-mail: info@croptonbrewery.co.uk

Home of the award-winning Cropton micro-brewery, this family-run free house on the edge of the North York Moors National Park is popular with locals and visitors alike. Meals are served in the restored village bar and in the elegant Victorian restaurant: choices could include Whitby cod with mushy peas and home-made chips; three cheese and roasted vegetable frittata; an extensive range from the grill; plus lunchtime sandwiches and ciabatta rolls.

Open 11-11 **Bar Meals** L served all week 12-2 D served all week 6-9 Av main course £9 **Restaurant** L served all week 12-2 D served all week 6-9 Av 3 course à la carte £16 Free House Cropton Two Pints, Monkmans Slaughter, Yorkshire Moors Bitter, Honey Gold Bitter & Theakstons Best Bitter. 7 **Facilities** Garden Dogs allowed Parking Play Area **Rooms** 11 bedrooms en suite S£40 D£54 (★★★ INN)

EAST WITTON MAP 19 SE18

Pick of the Pubs

The Blue Lion

DL8 4SN ☎ 01969 624273 01969 624189

e-mail: bluelion@breathemail.net

dir: *From Ripon take A6108 towards Leyburn*

A coaching inn built towards the end of the 18th century, the Blue Lion has been sought out by tourists and hikers from far and wide since cattle drovers rested here on their journey through glorious Wensleydale. The pub's stone facade can hardly have changed since it first opened, while inside an extensive but sympathetic renovation programme has created rural chic interiors with stacks of atmosphere and charm. The bar, with its open fire and flagstone floor, is a beer drinker's haven; a blackboard displays imaginative but unpretentious bar meals. Diners in the candlelit restaurant can expect award-winning culinary treats which incorporate a wide variety of mainly Yorkshire ingredients. These may include terrine of pigeon and grouse with a beetroot salad; whole roast partridge with sautéed cabbage and bacon; and raspberry crème brûlée. The picture is completed by the wine list, which is extensive but not prohibitively expensive.

Open 11-11 **Bar Meals** L served all week 12-2.15 D served all week 7-9.30 **Restaurant** L served Sun 12-2.15 D served all week 7-9.30 Av 3 course à la carte £30 Free House Black Sheep Bitter, Theakston Best Bitter, Black Sheep Riggwetter, Worthingtons. 12 **Facilities** Garden Dogs allowed Parking

The Black Bull Inn

Built in 1258, The Black Bull was one of the main watering holes for coaches travelling what is now the A1. Back then it had stables and a blacksmith's shop attached. These days, it retains plenty of original features, including old beams, low ceilings and roaring open fires, not to mention the supposed ghost of a monk.

Plenty of traditional pub fare is the order of the day here, with extensive menus covering all the options. Starters such as chicken liver paté with Cumberland sauce; king prawn tails and queen scallops; and Scottish smoked salmon are sure to whet the appetite. The main courses that follow might include rump of English lamb with rosemary and olive mashed potato; duck breast with orange and Grand Marnier jus; pork tenderloin with pink peppercorn sauce; chicken breast wrapped in Parma ham with pan-fried wild mushroom; and a selection of very substantial steak dishes. Several fish options are also available, including the likes of salmon, halibut, sea bass, tuna and Dover sole. Some of the wicked desserts for the sweet-toothed are banoffee meringue roulade with toffee sauce; dark chocolate truffle torte; apple pie with custard; and mixed ice creams encased in brandy snap with fruit purées. Sizeable bar snacks range from pork and chive sausage with onion gravy, and deep-fried prawns, to Thai beef strips with egg noodles and stir-fry vegetables. Among the mouth-watering array of sandwiches are hot roast pork and applesauce; and cold smoked salmon with dill mayonnaise. Yorkshire beers are well represented in the bar, and there is a splendid selection of 17 malts to choose from.

MAP 19 SE36
6 St James Square YO51 9AR
☎ 01423 322413
01423 323915
dir: *From A1(M) junct 48 take B6265 E 1m*

Open 11–11 (Sun 12–10.30)
Bar Meals L served all week 12–2 (Sun 12–2.30) D served all week 6–9 (Fri–Sat 6–9.30)
Restaurant L served all week 12–2 (Sun 12–2.30) D served all week 6–9 (Fri–Sat 6–9.30)
Free House
Black Sheep, Scottish Courage John Smiths, Timothy Taylor Landlord, Cottage Brewing. 10
Facilities Dogs allowed Parking

The Red Lion

An old ferryman's inn with large gardens and terraces, standing by a five-arched bridge on the banks of the River Wharfe. Hospitality has been dispensed from here for centuries. The 900-year-old cellars are inhabited by a mischievous ghost who finds it amusing to turn off the beer taps and icemaker.

The original 'one-up, one-down' structure, now the main bar, dates from the 16th century. The Grayshon family, who purchased the hotel in 1991, have sympathetically upgraded The Lion, retaining of course its beamed ceilings, oak floors and panelling, and creaky sloping floors – in short, its historic character. A horse-trough that stood outside the front door now resides under the stone steps leading to the bedrooms – it was easier to build around it than move it! The Grayshons like to mention Jim, the head chef, in despatches; but then, he's not just good, he's their son-in-law. The menu features game in season from the nearby estates, beef from another son-in-law, Robert, and lamb from the Daggett family, both of whom farm just across the river. Fresh fish is delivered daily, cheeses are local, and other produce comes from Cumbria. The extensive brasserie menu features pheasant, partridge and venison terrine; roasted asparagus wrapped in Parma ham with parmesan shavings and mango chutney; seared calves' liver, bubble and squeak, fresh sage and roast garlic sauce; steak and kidney braised in Theakston's ale with fluffy suet pastry; and locally smoked haddock fishcakes. Regular specials are 10-oz rib-eye steak with peppercorn or béarnaise sauce; and fresh tuna steak with ginger and spring onion, egg noodles and soy dressing. From the lunchtime bar selection try loin of suckling pig, rôsti potato and shallots; or fish soup with aioli and gruyère cheese.

★★ HL ⊛ 🍷
MAP 19 SE06
By the Bridge BD23 6BU
☎ 01756 720204
🖷 01756 720292
e-mail: redlion@daelnet.co.uk
dir: *B6160 towards Bolton Abbey, Burnsall 7m.*

Open 8–11.30
Bar Meals L served all week 12–2.30 D served all week 6–9.30 Av main course £11
Restaurant L served all week 12–2.30 D served all week 7–9.30 Av 3 course à la carte £26.95 Av 3 course fixed price £26.95
Free House
Theakston Black Bull, Greene King Old Speckled Hen, Timothy Taylor Landlord, Scottish Courage John Smith's. 🍷 14
Facilities Garden Dogs allowed Parking
Notes
Rooms 14 bedrooms en suite S£62.50 D£125

England

EGTON MAP 19 NZ80

Pick of the Pubs

The Wheatsheaf Inn

YO21 1TZ ☎ 01947 895271 01947 895391

dir: *Off A169 NW of Grosmont*

This unassuming old pub sits back from the wide main road, so be careful not to miss it. The main bar is cosy and traditional, with low beams, dark green walls and comfy settles. There's a locals' bar too, but it only holds about twelve, so get there early. The pub is very popular with fishermen, as the River Esk runs along at the foot of the hill, and is a big draw for fly-fishers in particular. A warming menu of hearty grub includes a good choice of fresh fish dishes such as mussel and garlic soup; fish stew; fresh crab thermidor; and cullen skink. Other choices include chicken and bacon puff pie; lamb shank braised with redcurrant and Madeira gravy; fillet steak with béarnaise sauce; and fish stew with smoked cod, salmon, clams, mussels, and white prawns in saffron sauce.

Open 11.30-3 5.30-11.30 **Bar Meals** L served Tue-Sun 12-2 D served Tue-Sat 6-9 **Restaurant** L served Tue-Sun 12-2 D served Tue-Sat 6-9 Free House Black Sheep Bitter, Black Sheep Special, John Smith, Adnams. **Facilities** Garden Dogs allowed Parking

EGTON BRIDGE MAP 19 NZ80

Horseshoe Hotel

YO21 1XE ☎ 01947 895245

dir: *From Whitby take A171 towards Middlesborough. Village signed in 5m.*

An 18th-century country inn by the River Esk, handy for visiting the North Yorkshire Moors Railway. Inside are oak settles and tables, local artists' paintings and, depending on the weather, an open fire. Lunchtime bar food consists of sandwiches in granary bread and hot baguettes. The main menu includes starters like crab cakes with a sweet chilli dip, and then lasagne, scampi, or pie of the day. There is also a specials board.

Open 11.30-3 6.30-11 (Sat, Sun & BH's all day summer) Closed: 25 Dec **Bar Meals** L served all week 12-2 D served all week 7-9 **Restaurant** L served all week 12-2 D served all week 7-9 Free House Copper Dragon & John Smiths, Durham, Black Sheep & Archers. 7 **Facilities** Garden Dogs allowed Parking

ELSLACK MAP 18 SD94

Pick of the Pubs

The Tempest Arms

BD23 3AY ☎ 01282 842450 01282 843331

e-mail: info@tempestarms.co.uk

dir: *Skipton A59 towards Gisburn. Elslack signed on A56*

See Pick of the Pubs on page 655

ESCRICK MAP 16 SE64

Black Bull Inn ★★★★ INN

Main St YO19 6JP ☎ 01904 728245 01904 728154

e-mail: bookings@yorkblackbullinn.com

dir: *A64 take A19 for 5m. In Escrick 2nd left into main street*

A traditional village inn, the Black Bull enjoys a pretty setting conveniently located between York and Selby. Harrogate and the North Yorkshire Moors are also within easy striking distance. Dishes are prepared to order and might include lamb shanks with tomato and butter bean sauce, battered haddock, plus a range of steaks and grills. Function facilities are available, and the all en suite rooms have internet access and tea and coffee making facilities.

Open 12-3 5-11 (Sat-Sun all day) **Bar Meals** L served all week 12-2.30 D served all week 6-9.30 (Sun 11-8.30) Av main course £10 **Restaurant** L served all week 12-2.30 D served all week 6-9.30 (Sun 6-8.30) Av 3 course à la carte £17.50 Av 3 course fixed price £17.50 Enterprise Inns John Smiths, Theakstons. 7 **Facilities** Garden Parking **Rooms** 10 bedrooms en suite S£49 D£69

FADMOOR MAP 19 SE68

Pick of the Pubs

The Plough Inn

Main St YO62 7HY ☎ 01751 431515 01751 432492

dir: *1m N of Kirkbymoorside on A170*

See Pick of the Pubs on page 656

England

FELIXKIRK — MAP 19 SE48

Pick of the Pubs

The Carpenters Arms

YO7 2DP ☎ 01845 537369 🖷 01845 537889

dir: *2m from Thirsk on A170*

Set in the pretty hamlet of Felixkirk, this 18th-century inn is a mere skip from the market town of Thirsk, where the much-loved writer and vet James Herriott once practised. The inn has been in the capable hands of mother and daughter team Linda and Karen Bumby since 2000, and very welcoming they've made it, too. The Bistro bar is a cosy spot, with soft seating and big cushions, oil lamps, coloured checked tablecloths, carpenters' tools, old-fashioned toy balloons and various other knick-knacks on display. Tuck into local bangers and mash; home-made steak, Black Sheep Ale and mushroom pie, or Whitby breaded scampi. In the slightly more formal restaurant, with its white linen cloths and napkins, crystal glasses and locally made furniture, the menu also moves up a notch. Try pan-fried venison loin; whole roast sea bass; or butternut squash and yellow pepper strudel, one of several vegetarian dishes.

Open 11.30–3 6.30–11 (Sun 12–8) Closed: 1wk in Jan or Feb, 25 Dec **Bar Meals** L served Tue–Sun 12–2 D served Tue–Sat 6.30–9 Av main course £10.70 **Restaurant** L served Tue–Sun 12–2 D served Tue–Sat 6.30–9 Av 3 course à la carte £25 Free House Black Sheep Bitter, Timothy Taylor Landlord, Greene King Old Speckled Hen, John Smiths Cask. 12 **Facilities** Parking

GIGGLESWICK — MAP 18 SD86

Black Horse Hotel

32 Church St BD24 0BE ☎ 01729 822506

Set in the 17th-century main street, this traditional free house stands next to the church and behind the market cross. In the warm and friendly bar you'll find a range of hand-pulled ales. The menu of freshly-prepared pub favourites ranges from hot sandwiches or giant filled Yorkshire puddings to main course dishes like steak and ale pie; broccoli and sweetcorn vol-au-vent; and crispy battered haddock.

Open 12–2.30 5.30–11 (Sun 5.30–10.30) **Bar Meals** L served Tue–Sun 12–1.45 D served all week 7–8.45 **Restaurant** L served Tue–Sun 12–1.45 D served all week 7–8.45 Free House Carlsberg-Tetley Bitter, Timothy Taylor Landlord, Scottish Courage John Smiths, Timothy Taylor Golden Best. **Facilities** Garden Parking

GOATHLAND — MAP 19 NZ80

Birch Hall Inn

Beckhole YO22 5LE ☎ 01947 896245

e-mail: glenys@birchhallinn.fsnet.co.uk

dir: *9m from Whitby on A169*

This delightful little free house, tucked away in a remote valley close to the North York Moors steam railway, has been in the same ownership for 25 years. With just two tiny rooms separated by a sweet shop, it offers an open fire in the main bar, well-kept local ales and a large garden with tempting views of the local walks. The simple menu features locally-baked pies, butties, home-made scones and buttered beer cake.

Open 11–3 7.30–11 (Summer & Sun 11–11) **Bar Meals** L served all week 11–3 D served all week 7.30–11 Free House Black Sheep Best, Theakstons Black Bull, Cropton Yorkshire Moors Bitter, Daleside Brewery Legover. **Facilities** Garden Dogs allowed **Notes**

GREAT AYTON — MAP 19 NZ51

The Royal Oak ★★★ INN

123 High St TS9 6BW ☎ 01642 722361 🖷 01642 724047

e-mail: info@royaloak-hotel.co.uk

Real fires and a relaxed atmosphere are part of the attraction at this traditional corner pub, run by the Monaghan family since 1978. A range of robust starters like pigeon, duck and foie gras terrine, Anglesea charcuterie platter, and butternut squash and goats' curd risotto might be followed by slow-cooked belly of pork, Brittany 'Cotriade' fish stew, pot-roast stuffed saddle of lamb, and toasted sea bass with saffron potatoes.

Open 11–11 (Sun 12–10.30) Closed: Dec 25 **Bar Meals** L served all week 12–2 D served all week 6.30–9.30 Av main course £7 **Restaurant** L served all week 12–2 D served all week 6.30–9.30 Av 3 course à la carte £15.75 Scottish & Newcastle Brewery Theakstons, John Smiths Smooth, Directors. 10 **Facilities** Children's licence Garden **Rooms** 4 bedrooms en suite S£30 D£70

GREAT OUSEBURN — MAP 19 SE46

Pick of the Pubs

The Crown Inn

Main St YO26 9RF ☎ 01423 330430 🖷 01423 331095

The Crown remembers the days when regular visitors were cattle drovers and large parties of fishermen on coach outings from the coast. Barrett's Great Canadian Circus would winter in the village; the circus band was under the direction of Ambrose Tiller who went on to found the world-renowned dancing troupe the 'Tiller Girls'. The Crown prides itself on offering a wide choice of imaginative dishes prepared from the finest, mostly local fish, seafood, meat and game. The brasserie offers competitively priced two or three course meals including a half bottle of wine, while the bar offers its good value two course menu. Be prepared for a leisurely browse through the various menus and weekly changing specials board as the range of dishes, too numerous to single out, need careful consideration. In keeping with the range and standard of the cuisine there is an extensive wine list personally selected by the owners.

Open 12–2 5–11 (Sat–Sun 12–11, BHs all day) Closed: 25 Dec Rest: Mon–Fri Closed lunch **Bar Meals** L served Thurs–Fri 12–2 D served Mon–Fri 5–9 (Sat 12–5, Sun 12–9) Av main course £6 **Restaurant** L served Sun 12–9 D served Mon–Sat 5–9 (Sat 12–9.30) Free House Black Sheep Best, Scottish Courage, John Smith's, Hambeltons Best Bitter. 10 **Facilities** Garden Parking Play Area

Abbey Inn

Byland Abbey, a Cistercian monastery built almost 1,000 years ago, was probably Europe's largest ecclesiastical building at the time; at its zenith it housed over 200 monks and lay brothers. Thanks to Henry VIII it is now a ruin, albeit a beautiful one.

Over the road is the ivy-clad Abbey Inn, built in 1845 as a farmhouse by Fr John Molyneux and a team of monks, using some of the old abbey stones. In 2005 the whole site was taken over by English Heritage, and many Abbey Inn patrons are comforted in the knowledge that some of its profits are invested in preserving the historic ruins for future generations. Refurbishment has been sympathetic, and rug-strewn stone-flagged floors, large open fires, Jacobean furniture, fine tapestries and stuffed birds remain. Unusual objets d'art lurking in corners may take some noticing, as a pint of the inn's own real ale slips down. Two dining rooms at the front overlook the haunting profile of the abbey itself; a third is known, commemoratively, as the Piggery. The award-winning gastro-pub uses only fresh seasonal Yorkshire produce, and is booked up to four weeks ahead for its renowned Sunday lunch. A daily changing midday menu might offer starters and light bites of Abbey Inn seafood platter, or hickory-smoked chicken Caesar salad; and main dishes of honey and mustard roasted local ham, or griddled Barnsley chop – Lancashire hotpot style. The short but ample evening menu features half a dozen courses at each stage, with the same accent on fresh and seasonal ingredients: Whitby mackerel and confit potato terrine could be followed by the Abbey Inn poacher's casserole with sage and rosemary dumplings. Children are offered the same healthy food but in half-size portions, while early-bird diners benefit from a discounted menu.

MAP 19 SE57
YO61 4BD
☎ 01347 868204
01347 868678
e-mail: abbeyinn@english-heritage.org.uk
dir: *From A19 signs to Byland Abbey/Coxwold*

Open 11.30–3 6.30–11 Closed: 24–25 Dec
Bar Meals L served Tue–Sun 12–2 (Sun 12–3) D served Mon–Sat 6.30–9 Av main course £12
Restaurant L served Tue–Sun 12–2 (Sun 12–3) D served Mon–Sat 6.30–9 Av 3 course à la carte £25
Free House
Black Sheep Best, Byland Brew
20
Facilities Garden Parking

The White Lion Inn

Nestling beneath Buckden Pike, The White Lion is Wharfedale's highest inn. It also boasts some spectacular scenery, since it's set right at the heart of the Yorkshire Dales. Indeed, the celebrated fell-walker Wainwright once described this former drovers' hostelry as a 'tiny oasis', a claim that's just as accurate today.

All the qualities of a traditional Yorkshire inn have been maintained here, from warm hospitality to oak beams, log fire and flagstone floors. The age-old game of bull'ook is still played here alongside the more contemporary Giant Jenga. A good choice of hand-pulled real ales is offered and 20-plus malt whiskies. You can eat and drink in the bar or dining room, though the sight of the cascading Cray Gill, which runs past the inn, is sure to lure children out to the garden. Before or after a meal, you can also make your way across the stepping-stones in the gill to the open fells and many locally recognised walks, long and short. In the bar, wholesome food is cooked to order and served in generous portions. Lunchtime options include filled baguettes, ploughman's, and plate-sized Yorkshire puddings with a choice of fillings like Cumberland sausage or three-bean chilli. Also available, lunchtime and evenings, is a variety of substantial dishes such as pork fillet in a honey and mustard cream sauce; whole steamed Kilnsey trout, or steak and mushroom casserole cooked with root vegetables and beer gravy. A children's menu is also on offer. Ten en suite bedrooms are available if you want to linger, with well-behaved dogs welcome in ground floor rooms.

🍷
MAP 18 SD97
Cray BD23 5JB
☎ 01756 760262
e-mail:
admin@whitelioncray.com
dir: *B6265 from Skipton, then B6160 towards Aysgarth. Cray 10m*

Open 11–11 Closed: 25 Dec
Bar Meals L served all week 12–2 D served all week 5.45–8.30 Av main course £10
Free House
Timothy Taylor Golden Best, Copper Dragon Golden Pippin, Copper Dragon 1816, Wensleydale brewery Semerwater. 🍷 9
Facilities Garden Dogs allowed Parking
Rooms 10 bedrooms en suite S£55 D£70 (★★★ INN)

GREEN HAMMERTON MAP 19 SE45

The Bay Horse Inn

York Rd YO26 8BN ☎ 01423 330338 📠 01423 331279
e-mail: info@bayhorseinn.uk.com

A 200-year-old coaching inn located in a small village near the A1 and close to both York and Harrogate. Food is served in the bar and restaurant, and there is further seating outside, sheltered by the boundary hedge. Dishes might include bangers and mash, fish and chips, chicken and stilton, and a home-made pie of the day. Various steaks and grills are also a key feature of the menu.

Open 12-3) 6-12 (Summer 12-12 **Bar Meals** L served Mon-Thu 12-2 (Fri-Sat 12-2.30, Sun 12-3) D served Mon-Sat 6-9 **Restaurant** L served Mon-Sun 12-2 (Fri-Sat 12-2.30, Sun 12-3) D served Mon-Sat 6-9 New Century Inns Worthington, Timothy Taylor, Black Sheep & Guest. **Facilities** Garden Dogs allowed Parking

GRINTON MAP 19 SE09

The Bridge Inn NEW 🍷

DL11 6HH ☎ 01748 884224
e-mail: atkinbridge@btinternet.com
dir: *At Richmond take A6108 towards Reeth, 10m*

Set on the banks of the River Swale in the heart of the Yorkshire Dales National Park, this former coaching inn is well known for its friendliness and excellent real ales. The bar and restaurant menus are extensive, and range from such simple classics as steak and ale pie to Grinton lamb and barley casserole with minted dumplings; and Chinese gingered duck with spiced noodles. An extensive wine list is also on offer.

Open 12-11 **Bar Meals** L served all week 12-3 D served all week 12-9 (Sun 3-9) Av main course £10 **Restaurant** L served all week 12-5 (Sun 12-3) D served all week 5-9 Av 3 course à la carte £20 Jennings Cumberland Ale, Cocker Hoop, Deuchars IPA, Adnams. 🍷 7 **Facilities** Garden Dogs allowed Parking **Rooms** 5 bedrooms en suite S£42 D£64 (★★★ INN)

HAROME MAP 19 SE68

Pick of the Pubs

The Star Inn 🍷

YO62 5JE ☎ 01439 770397 📠 01439 771833
dir: *From Helmsley A170 towards Kirkbymoorside 0.5m. Turn right for Harome*

This award-winning gastro-pub is housed in a fine example of a 14th-century cruck-framed longhouse, with the former monks' dormitory converted into a distinctive coffee loft. A byre houses the dining room, while the bar is full of Mousey Thompson hand-carved oak furniture. Private dining is available in an enchanting room decorated with fairies and witches on broomsticks. In summer you can enjoy supper alfresco, surrounded by the heady scents of the herb garden. The home-grown herbs and seasonal produce from local suppliers are put to good use in the cooking: terrine of pressed ham knuckle with fried quail egg could be followed by pan-fried Middle Baxton fillet steak with bone marrow butter. Even the sandwiches are a cut above: butter-roast turkey with chestnut stuffing, Pickering watercress and cranberry, perhaps. Another offshoot of the pub is the Corner Shop, a delicatessen packed full of home-made delicacies and quality produce.

Open 11.30-3 6.30-11 Closed: 2 wks Spring **Bar Meals** L served Tue-Sat 11.30-2 D served Tue-Sat 6.30-9.15 (Sun 12-6) **Restaurant** L served Tue-Sat 11.30-2 D served Tue-Sat 6.30-9.15 (Sun 12-6) Free House Black Sheep Special, Copper Dragon, Hambleton Ales, John Smith's & Theakston Best. 🍷 10 **Facilities** Garden Parking

HARROGATE MAP 19 SE35

Pick of the Pubs

The Boars Head Hotel ★★★ HL 🍷

Ripley Castle Estate HG3 3AY
☎ 01423 771888 📠 01423 771509
e-mail: reservations@boarsheadripley.co.uk
dir: *On A61 in village centre*

See Pick of the Pubs on page 659

HAWES MAP 18 SD88

The Moorcock Inn 🍷

Garsdale Head LA10 5PU ☎ 01969 667488
e-mail: admin@moorcockinn.com
dir: *On A684 5m from Hawes*

Candles glow in the windows of this weathered free house, while inside fairy lights pick out a cosy blend of original stonework and bright colours, furnished with comfy sofas and traditional wooden chairs. In winter, locals savour the pub's home-brewed ales around the wood-burning stove, whilst on warmer days there are spectacular views from the garden. Typical fare takes in such traditional favourites as black pudding, chicken Wensleydale and gammon steak with eggs.

Open 11-11 **Bar Meals** L served all week 12-3 D served all week 6.30-9 Av main course £7.50 Free House Black Sheep, Tetleys Cask, Guest Ales. 🍷 7 **Facilities** Garden Dogs allowed Parking

HETTON MAP 18 SD95

Pick of the Pubs

The Angel 🍷

BD23 6LT ☎ 01756 730263 📠 01756 730363
e-mail: info@angelhetton.co.uk
dir: *A59 then B6265 towards Grassington/Skipton. Rylstone Pond signed*

A 600-year-old, ivy-clad Dales inn that probably started brewing beer for cattle drovers in the early 1800s. The interior is all nooks, crannies, oak beams and, in the winter, log fires; in summer you can eat or drink on the flagged forecourt and look up at Cracoe Fell. The Angel's modern British food, influenced particularly by France and Italy, is locally famous. Fresh fish arrives daily from Fleetwood and, depending on the catch, the restaurant menu or brasserie blackboard might offer wild sea bass with mussels, coriander and seafood broth; pan-seared brill fillet with braised fennel; or grilled silver mullet with sorrel velouté. Locally sourced

CONTINUED

England

HETTON continued

seasonal meats include Dales-bred lamb, beef and game. The more informal brasserie also offers nibbles, such as olives, to the more substantial haunch of venison with beetroot fondant and celeriac purée. Seasonal local ales include Wharfedale Folly, and there's a jolly good wine cellar.

Open 12–3 6–10.30 Closed: 25 Dec & 1wk in Jan **Bar Meals** L served all week 12–2 D served all week 6–9 (Sat 6–10) Av main course £8.95 **Restaurant** L served Sun 12–2 D served Mon–Sat 6–9 Av 3 course à la carte £22 Free House Blacksheep Bitter, Taylor Landlord, Wharfedale Folly, Copper Dragon Bitter. 24 **Facilities** Garden Parking **Rooms** 5 bedrooms en suite D£130

HOVINGHAM MAP 19 SE67

The Malt Shovel

Main St YO62 4LF 01653 628264 01653 628264

dir: *18m NE of York, 5 miles from Castle Howard*

Tucked away amid the Howardian Hills, in the Duchess of Kent's home village, the stone-built 18th-century Malt Shovel offers a friendly and traditional atmosphere with good-value food prepared from quality local ingredients. Popular options include pork and leeks, beef stroganoff, sirloin steak garni, chicken Stilton, and supreme of salmon. Fresh vegetables, hand-crafted chips and daily specials board featuring speciality game dishes complete the picture.

Open 11.30–2.30 6–11 (Fri–Sat 5–11, Sun all day) **Bar Meals** L served all week 12–2 D served all week 6–9 Sun 6–8 Av main course £6 **Restaurant** L served all week 12–2 D served all week 6–9 (Sun 6–8) Av 3 course à la carte £20 Punch Taverns Carlsberg-Tetleys Tetley's, Greene King IPA. **Facilities** Garden Parking

Pick of the Pubs

The Worsley Arms Hotel ★★★ HL

Main St YO62 4LA 01653 628234 01653 628130

e-mail: worsleyarms@aol.com

dir: *On B1257 between Malton & Helmsley*

In 1841 Sir William Worsley thought he would turn the village of Worsley into a spa to rival Bath, and built a spa house and a hotel. However, he reckoned without the delicate nature of his guests who disliked the muddy track between the two. Inevitably the spa failed, but the hotel survived and, together with the separate pub, forms part of the Worsley family's historic Hovingham Hall estate, birthplace of the Duchess of Kent, and currently home to her nephew. You can eat in the restaurant or the Cricketer's Bar (the local team has played on the village green for over 150 years). Hambleton Stallion beer from nearby Thirsk is on tap, and food choices include speciality ciabatta sandwiches, and dishes such as trio of local sausages with creamy leek mash and sweet shallot gravy, and pan-fried sea bass with Whitby crab risotto and bloody Mary dressing.

Open 12–2.30 7–11 **Bar Meals** L served all week 12–2 D served all week 7–10 **Restaurant** L served Sun 12–2 D served all week 7–10 Av 3 course à la carte £27.50 Free House Scottish Courage John Smith's, Hambleton Stallion. 20 **Facilities** Garden Dogs allowed Parking **Rooms** 20 bedrooms en suite

HUBBERHOLME MAP 18 SD97

The George Inn

BD23 5JE 01756 760223

dir: *B6265 to Threshfield then B6160 to Buckden. Follow signs for Hubbleholme.*

To check if the bar is open, look for a lighted candle in the window – a tradition that harks back to this building's former life as a vicarage, when a candle announced that the vicar was at home. Stunningly located beside the River Wharfe, this pub has flagstone floors, an open fire and an inviting summer terrace. Lunches include cheese melts and burgers; evening choices range from Thai fishcakes to Dales lamb chops with gravy.

Open 12–3 6–11 Closed: 1st 2 wks in Dec **Bar Meals** L served all week 12–2 D served all week 6.30–8.30 Av main course £8.50 Free House Black Sheep Best, Black Sheep Special, Skipton Brewery. **Facilities** Garden Parking

KILBURN MAP 19 SE57

The Forresters Arms

YO61 4AH 01347 868386 & 868550 01347 868386

e-mail: paulcussons@forrestersarms.fsnet.co.uk

dir: *6m from Thirsk*

Sturdy stone former coaching inn for travellers passing close by the famous White Horse of Kilburn on the North York Moors. The cosy lower bar has some of the earliest oak furniture by Robert Thompson, with his distinctive mouse symbol on every piece. Evidence of the inn's former stables can be seen in the upper bar. Steak and ale pie, pheasant casserole, home-made lasagne and lamb chops are popular dishes.

Open 11–11 **Bar Meals** L served all week 12–2.30 D served all week 6.30–9 Av main course £8 **Restaurant** L served all week 12–2.30 D served all week 6.30–9 Free House Scottish Courage John Smiths, Carlsberg-Tetley Tetley's, Hambleton. **Facilities** Dogs allowed Parking

KIRBY HILL MAP 19 NZ10

The Shoulder of Mutton Inn

DL11 7JH 01748 822772 01325 718936

e-mail: info@shoulderofmutton.net

dir: *4m N of Richmond*

A traditional 18th-century inn with panoramic views over Holmedale and beyond. Open log fires burn in the bar area and dining room, where stone walls and original beams provide just the right kind of backdrop for renowned daily-changing home-cooked dishes such as scallops with black pudding, and seafood sausage with lobster and crayfish sauce.

Open 6–11 12–3 **Bar Meals** L served Sat–Sun 12–2 D served Wed–Sun 7–9 Av main course £12 **Restaurant** L served Sun 12–2 D served Wed–Sun 7–9 Av 3 course à la carte £22 Free House Daleside, Black Sheep, Copper Dragon, Deuchars. **Facilities** Garden Parking **Rooms** 5 bedrooms en suite S£35 D£55 (★★★ INN)

The Tempest Arms

he stone-built houses and glorious vistas of this region of the Yorkshire Dales have remained irtually unchanged since Saxon times, and this welcoming inn itself dates back to 1690. The earby market town of Skipton is known as the gateway to the Dales.

he tiny hamlet of Elslack boasts s very own Roman Fort, as well s this spacious pub. The Tempest rms has two dining areas suitable or large groups: the Pickhill Barn, uilt in 1786, is a romantic setting ften used for civil weddings, amily gatherings, meetings and onferences, while the Tempest oom is a club-style room also uitable for small parties or private ining. Inside the main pub you an tuck up in a cosy corner by a rackling log fire and enjoy a fine vine or one of the hand-pulled orkshire ales on offer. There are wo dining styles available, either in he simple bar or the more formal estaurant. The seasonal specials nd vegetarian menu is jauntily known as the 'hymn sheet'. Here you'll find dishes like smoked haddock rarebit; or lobster bisque with prawn toast to start, followed by roast Bolton Abbey topside of beef with Yorkshire pudding. Other options range from spicy bean masala, to salmon fillet, potato rôsti and queenies. The bar menu is served throughout and features starters like seafood pancake, or shredded smoked duck with a warm brie salad. Main courses include Mr Bell's Cumberland sausages or lamb 'thingy me bob' (a local dish with a justifiable reputation). Sandwiches and side orders are also on offer.

MAP 18 SD94
BD23 3AY
01282 842450
01282 843331
e-mail: info@tempestarms.co.uk
dir: *Skipton A59 towards Gisburn. Elslack signed on A56*

Open 7–11 Closed: 25 & 26 Dec, 1 Jan in eve
Bar Meals L served all week 12–2.30 D served all week 6–9 (Sun 12–7.30) Av main course £10
Restaurant L served all week 12–2.30 D served all week 6–9 (Sun 12–7.30) Av 3 course à la carte £20
Free House
Black Sheep Best, Elslack Ale, Theakston Best, Timothy Taylor Best & Landlord. 10
Facilities Garden Parking

The Plough Inn

Ramblers sampling the delights of the North Yorkshire Moors National Park will be pleased to find this stylishly well-appointed country pub and restaurant in the pretty village of Fadmoor. The setting overlooking the village green could not be more idyllic, and the inn boasts dramatic views over the Vale of Pickering and the Wolds.

Inside it is cosy, snug and welcoming with log fires, beams and brasses in the bar: the ideal spot to enjoy a pint of Black Sheep Best while plotting further hikes. The food is an undoubted attraction, with meals available in the bar or in the attractively furnished rustic-style restaurant. A good value, two-course meal is available at lunchtime and early evening. Options include smoked salmon and asparagus terrine, followed by medallions of pork tenderloin with blue stilton and white wine sauce; or home-made steak and ale pie. The à la carte menu features such dishes as deep-fried duck and mango spring rolls; seafood paella with Italian sausage; and pan-seared king scallops with a fricassee of spring onion, garlic and bacon as starters, followed by, for example, basil and parmesan crusted cod; slow roasted boneless half Gressingham duckling with orange and brandy sauce; or fillet of beef Wellington topped with liver paté and Madeira sauce. A dedicated menu for vegetarians has a thoughtful range of options, including avocado and brie crumble; pear and stilton puff pastry parcels; and wild mushroom stroganoff. If you've room, round off with a decadent smooth dark chocolate and Malibu terrine, or peach and raspberry tiramisu.

MAP 19 SE68
Main St YO62 7HY
☎ 01751 431515
01751 432492
dir: *1m N of Kirkbymoorside on A170*

Open 12–2.30 6.30–11 Closed: 25–26 Dec, 1 Jan
Bar Meals L served Mon–Sun 12–1.45 D served Mon–Sat 6.30–8.45 (Sun 7–8.30)
Restaurant D served Mon–Sat 6.30–8.45 (Sun 7–8.30) Av 3 course à la carte £22 Av 2 course fixed price £12.95
Free House
Black Sheep Best, Scottish Courage John Smith's, Tetley Cask + Guest beers. 6
Facilities Patio Parking

England

KIRKBYMOORSIDE MAP 19 SE68

Pick of the Pubs

George & Dragon Hotel

17 Market Place YO62 6AA
01751 433334 01751 432933
dir: *Just off A170 in town centre*

This 17th-century former coaching inn has seen dramatic changes over the years: the restaurant used to be the brewhouse, and the garden room is the former rectory. Despite all this, centuries on, the inn is still providing a haven of hospitality in the heart of Kirkbymoorside. In the beamed interior visitors can sit by the log fire and sample hand-pulled real ales, wines by the glass and a choice of 30 malt whiskies. A good variety of food is served, from snacks and blackboard specials in the bar to candlelit dinners in the Knights' Restaurant (themed around George and the dragon). There's also a bistro, which opens partially onto the bar lounge.

Bar Meals L served all week D served all week 9.30 **Restaurant** L served all week 12–2.30 D served all week 6.30–9.30 (Sun 12–3.30, 6.30–9.30) Av 3 course à la carte £20 Av 3 course fixed price £18.50 Free House Black Sheep Best, Tetley, Timothy Taylors Landlord, Creamflow. 10 **Facilities** Garden Dogs allowed Parking

KIRK DEIGHTON MAP 16 SE35

The Bay Horse Inn NEW

Main St LS22 4DZ 01937 580058 01937 582443
dir: *1m N of Wetherby on the Knaresborough road*

The aim of this country inn is to source food locally, supporting Yorkshire farmers and fishermen. To this end, Charolais lamb and Limousin beef come from the lush green pastures of the Nidderdale Valley, bred by a farmer who has worked the land all his life. A simple menu makes the most of such quality produce, offering steak with onion rings; corn fed chicken, and roast loan of Harrogate venison.

Open 12–2.15 6–9.30 **Bar Meals** L served all week 12–2.30 **Restaurant** L served Tue–Sun 12–2.15 D served Mon–Sat 6–9.30 Av 3 course à la carte £22 Av 2 course fixed price £13.95 Free House Copper Dragon, Timothy Taylors Landlord, Black Sheep Bitter, John Smiths Cask & Deuchars IPA. 12 **Facilities** Dogs allowed Parking

KIRKHAM MAP 19 SE76

Pick of the Pubs

Stone Trough Inn

Kirkham Abbey YO60 7JS
01653 618713 01653 618819
e-mail: info@stonetroughinn.co.uk
dir: *1.5m off A64, between York & Malton*

This free house has a great reputation for its friendliness, fine food and real ales. It stands high above Kirkham Priory and the River Derwent, and was sympathetically converted into licensed premises in the early 1980s from Stone Trough Cottage. The cottage took its name from the base of a cross erected by a 12th-century French knight to commemorate a son killed in a riding accident. The cross has long since disappeared, but its hollowed-out base now stands at the entrance to the car park. A real fire, bare beams and wooden settles make for a pleasingly traditional interior. Food-wise there's a menu of serious intent that includes roast breast of guinea fowl with confit leg and a chanterelle sauce; whole grilled lemon sole with a shrimp beurre noisette dressing; and fillet of turbot with a basil and ginger sauce.

Stone Trough Inn

Open 12–2.30 6–11 (Sat 12–11, Sun 11.45–10.30) Closed: 25 Dec & 2–5 Jan **Bar Meals** L served Tue–Sun 12–2 D served Tue–Sun 6.30–8.30 Av main course £9.50 **Restaurant** L served Sun 12–2.15 D served Tue–Sat 6.45–9.30 Av 3 course à la carte £25 Free House Tetley Cask, Timothy Taylor Landlord, Black Sheep Best, Malton Brewery Golden Chance. 14 **Facilities** Garden Parking

KNARESBOROUGH MAP 19 SE35

Pick of the Pubs

The General Tarleton Inn

★★★★★ RR

Boroughbridge Rd, Ferrensby HG5 0PZ
01423 340284 01423 340288
e-mail: gti@generaltarleton.co.uk
dir: *A6055 to Knaresborough. Inn 4m on right*

An 18th-century coaching inn with contemporary comforts, unstuffy atmosphere, and top-class dining. Sir Banastre Tarleton distinguished himself during the American War of Independence, and the inn was probably opened by a member of his platoon in his honour. The low-beamed bar area is warm and welcoming, with log fires and cosy corners, and the restaurant offers the best of Yorkshire's larder. The covered courtyard is a light, modern setting, while the garden offers another option for summertime

CONTINUED

KNARESBOROUGH continued

refreshment. Real ales and an extensive wine list support an all-pleasing brasserie menu, which ranges from open sandwiches at lunchtime, to small dishes such as terrine of Yorkshire ham knuckle and foie gras, and main courses like confit of Dales lamb. For fish lovers, the seafood thermidor will be irresistible – monkfish, salmon, queenie scallops, sole, cod and tiger prawns in a mushroom and mustard sauce glazed with cheese.

Open 12-3 6-11 **Bar Meals** L served all week 12-2.15 D served all week 6-9.30 (Sun 6-8.30) Av main course £12.95 **Restaurant** L served Sun 12-2 D served Mon-Sat 6-9.30 Av 3 course à la carte £30 Av 3 course fixed price £32.50 Free House Black Sheep Best, Timothy Taylors Landlord, Guest beer. 10 **Facilities** Garden Parking **Rooms** 14 bedrooms en suite S£85 D£97

LANGTHWAITE MAP 19 NZ00

The Red Lion Inn NEW

DL11 6RE ☎ 01748 884218 01748 884133

e-mail: rlionlangthwaite@aol.com

dir: *Through Reeth into Arkengarthdale*

The unusually photogenic Red Lion Inn has appeared in several feature films as well as starring in the long running BBC serial *All Creatures Great and Small*. Owned by the same family for 43 years, it's also very much a traditional pub, hosting the local darts and quoits teams, and providing Black Sheep bitter and bar snacks for the hundreds of visitors attracted to this unspoiled stretch of the Yorkshire Dales.

Open 11-3 7-11 Free House 8 **Facilities** Garden Parking

LASTINGHAM MAP 19 SE79

Blacksmiths Arms

YO62 6TL ☎ 01751 417247 01751 417247

e-mail: blacksmithslastingham@hotmail.com

dir: *A170 towards Lastingham & Appleton-le-Moors signs*

Right opposite St Mary's church, this 17th-century stone-built free house stands in an idyllic North York Moors National Park setting. The inn boasts low-beamed ceilings and an open fire within the restaurant and bar area; outside, there's a cottage garden and decked seating area. Home-cooked dishes include Yorkshire hotpot; lamb and mint pie; crispy cod in beer batter; and broccoli pancake mornay. Snacks, sandwiches and daily specials are also available.

Open 12-2.30 6-11 **Bar Meals** L served all week 12-2 D served all week 7-9 **Restaurant** L served all week 12-2 D served all week 7-9 Free House Theakstons Best Bitter, 2 Guest ales e.g. Pheonix, Roosters. 10 **Facilities** Garden

LEYBURN MAP 19 SE19

The Old Horn Inn

Spennithorne DL8 5PR ☎ 01969 622370

e-mail: desmond@furlong1706.fsbusiness.co.uk

dir: *On A684 signed Spennithorne*

Low beams and open log fires characterise this traditional 17th-century free house. The former farmhouse, which has been a pub for at least 100 years, is named after the horn that summoned the farmer's workers to lunch. Today's customers enjoy good food in the dining room. Expect local hog and hop sausages with mash and red onion marmalade; baked salmon with prawns and basil sauce; and roasted vegetable lasagne with garlic ciabatta bread.

Open 12-3 6-11 (Sat & BHs all day during Jul-Aug) **Bar Meals** L served Tue-Sun 12-2 (12-3 in summer) D served Tue-Sun 6.30-9 Av main course £9 **Restaurant** L served Tue-Sun 12-2 (12-3 in summer) D served Tue-Sun 7-9 Black Sheep Bitter & Special, Scottish Courage John Smith's Cask, Coors Worthington's Cream Flow. **Facilities** Garden Dogs allowed **Notes**

Pick of the Pubs

Sandpiper Inn

Market Place DL8 5AT

☎ 01969 622206 01969 625367

e-mail: hsandpiper@aol.com

dir: *From A1 take A684 to Leyburn*

Although it has been a pub for only 30 years, the building that houses the Sandpiper Inn in is the oldest in Leyburn, dating back to around 1640. It has a beautiful summer garden, and inside, a bar, snug and dining room where an exciting and varied mix of traditional and more unusual dishes is served. Lunch brings sandwiches (prawn and rocket, avocado and bacon); and omelette Arnold Bennett. An evening meal could take in black pudding with caramelised apple and foie gras; and Moroccan spiced chicken with couscous; or roasted vegetable risotto with parmesan curls. Sunday lunch ranges from roasted rib-eye of Dales beef with onion gravy and Yorkshire pudding, to Masham sausage with mash and onion gravy.

Open 11.30-3 6.30-11 (Sun 12-3, 6.30-10.30) **Bar Meals** L served Tue-Sun 12-2.30 D served Tue-Sun 6.30-9 (Fri-Sat 6.30-9.30, Sun 7-9) Av main course £8 **Restaurant** L served Tue-Sun 12-2.30 (Sun 12-2) D served Tue-Sun 6.30-9 (Fri-Sat 6.30-9.30, Sun 7-9) Av 3 course à la carte £27 Free House Black Sheep Best, Black Sheep Special, Daleside, Copperdragon. 8 **Facilities** Garden Dogs allowed

The Boars Head Hotel

Sir Thomas and Lady Ingilby have transformed this delightful old coaching inn into an impressive hotel with luxurious furnishings, right at the heart of the Ripley Castle Estate. Originally known as the Star Inn, this was once the breakfast stop for the crowded charabancs that linked Leeds with Edinburgh.

Sir William Ingilby closed all three of Ripley's inns when he inherited the Estate soon after the First World War, and Ripley remained dry until the Star was re-opened as the Boar's Head Hotel in 1990. The new name recalls an incident during the 14th century when a former Thomas Ingilby earned his knighthood by killing a wild boar that had attacked King Edward III. Coming back to the present day, stable partitions in the bar and bistro add intimacy to the relaxed, candlelit atmosphere. Starters from the bistro menu range from rollmops with beetroot chutney and crusty French bread, to sauté of chicken liver with raspberry vinegar and dressed salad leaves. Among the mains you might find roast rump of lamb with grain mustard and mint crushed new potatoes, or spicy Spanish sausage with creamy chive mash. Finish with dessert – maybe dark chocolate mousse with red fruit compote – or your choice from a fine board of British farmhouse cheeses. Innovative modern British cooking is the trademark of the restaurant menu, where an all-in price permits permutations of seven choices at each of three courses: perhaps crab and langoustine pannacotta; slow cooked porchetta loin with creamed wild mushrooms and a bourbon and vanilla sauce; and baked apricot frangipane tart with cinnamon ice cream.

★★★ HL ❀❀ 🍷
MAP 19 SE35
Ripley Castle Estate HG3 3AY
☎ 01423 771888
01423 771509
e-mail: reservations@boarsheadripley.co.uk
dir: *On A61 in village centre*

Open 11–11 (Winter 12–3, 5–10.30)
Bar Meals L served all week 12–2.30 D served all week 6.30–9.30 (Winter 12–2, Sun–Wed 6.30–9)
Restaurant L served all week 12–2 D served all week 7–9
Free House
Theakston Best & Old Peculier, Daleside Crackshot, Hambleton White Boar, Black Sheep Best.
🍷 10
Facilities Garden Parking
Rooms 25 bedrooms en suite S£105 D£125

England

LINTON MAP 19 SD96

The Fountaine Inn 🍷

BD23 5HJ ☎ 01756 752210 📠 01756 753717
e-mail: fountaineinn1@tiscali.co.uk
dir: *10m from Skipton take B6265. Right after Quarry*

Within the magnificent Yorkshire Dales National Park, in a sleepy hamlet beside the River Beck, this 16th-century inn is named after a local man who made his fortune in the Great Plague of London in 1665 – burying the bodies! On a more cheerful note, the menu offers grilled king scallops with pumpkin seeds, chilli and coriander sauce; smoked fish platter; or Irish stew and baby vegetables.

Open 11–11 (Sun 12–10.30) **Bar Meals** L served all week 12–9 D served all week 12–9 Av main course £7 **Restaurant** L served Mon–Sun 12–3 D served Mon–Sun 6–9 Av 3 course à la carte £16 Free House Black Sheep Best, Carlsberg-Tetley Tetley Bitter, Scottish Courage John Smith's. 🍷 10 **Facilities** Garden Dogs allowed

LONG PRESTON MAP 18 SD85

Maypole Inn 🍷

Maypole Green BD23 4PH
☎ 01729 840219 📠 01729 840727
e-mail: landlord@maypole.co.uk
dir: *On A65 between Settle & Skipton*

This inn has been welcoming visitors since 1695, when Ambrose Wigglesworth welcomed his first customers. Hand-drawn ales and traditional home cooking underpin the operation. Located at the edge of the Yorkshire Dales National Park, it's a good base for walking and cycling. Relax in the beamed dining room or cosy bar over a pint and a simple snack, sandwich, steak or salad; or try a 'special' like beef in ale pie, braised shoulder of lamb, or pork in Pernod.

Open 11–3 6–11 (Sat 11–11 Sun 12–10.30) **Bar Meals** L served all week 12–2 D served all week 6.30–9 (Sun 12–11) Av main course £8 **Restaurant** L served all week 12–2 D served all week 6.30–9 (Sat 12–9.30 Sun 12–9) Enterprise Inns Timothy Taylor Landlord, Moorhouses Premier, Jennings, Cumberland. 🍷 10 **Facilities** Garden Dogs allowed Parking **Rooms** 39 bedrooms en suite S£29 D£39 (★★★ INN)

MARTON MAP 19 SE78

Pick of the Pubs

The Appletree 🍷

YO62 6RD ☎ 01751 431457 📠 01751 430190
e-mail: appletreeinn@supanet.com
dir: *From Kirkby Moorside on A170 then right after 1m*

100 years ago, the Appletree was a working farm, with the farmer's wife serving beer from her living room in earthenware jugs. The present owners have been here since 2001 and last year carried out a major refurbishment to restore the inn to its original size. Warm, rich colours, a huge fire in the cosy lounge and hundreds of candles at night add to the cosy feel. Today the local farmers are still regulars at the bar and their produce is used in the kitchen. Booking is essential for lunch and dinner, with lunches only served in the bar. Menus change daily: you could start with Whitby crab fishcakes, before moving on to smoked haddock, lemon and pea risotto, or caramelised shallot tarte Tatin; finish with either Yorkshire treacle tart with lemon curd ice cream; or an array of Yorkshire cheeses. Please note that The Appletree is closed on Monday and Tuesday.

Open 12–2.30 6–11 (Sun 12–3, 7–10.30) Closed: 2 weeks Jan **Bar Meals** L served Wed–Sun booking essential 12–2 (Sun 7–9) **Restaurant** L served Wed–Sun booking essential 12–2 D served Wed–Sat (6–9.30) booking essential (Sun 7–9) Free House Scottish Courage John Smiths Cask, Guest ales; Malton, York, Archers & Wychwood. 🍷 14 **Facilities** Garden Parking

MASHAM MAP 19 SE28

The Black Sheep Brewery

HG4 4EN ☎ 01765 689227 & 680100 📠 01765 689746
e-mail: sue.dempsey@blacksheep.co.uk
web: www.blacksheep.co.uk
dir: *Off A6108*

Paul Theakston, of Masham's famous brewing family, founded the Black Sheep brewery in the early nineties according to traditional brewing principles. The complex boasts a visitor centre where you can enjoy a 'shepherded' tour of the brewhouse and fermenting room, before popping into the cosy bistro and 'baa..r' to sample the five house ales. The brews also find their way into a range of hearty dishes, including lamb shank in Emmerdale Ale.

Open (Please phone for details) **Bar Meals** L served all week D served Wed–Sat Black Sheep Brewery Black Sheep Best Bitter, Emmerdale, Riggwelter & Black Sheep Ale. **Facilities** Garden Parking

See advert on opposite page

Kings Head Hotel ★★ HL 🍷

Market Place HG4 4EF ☎ 01765 689295 📠 01765 689070

dir: *B6267 towards Masham*

Overlooking Masham's large market square with its cross and maypole, this tastefully renovated Georgian inn boasts open fires in the public rooms and a pleasant terrace for summer dining. Unwind over a pint of Theakston's in the bar, or sample a range of traditional and contemporary dishes in the wood panelled restaurant. Options might include minted lamb shoulder with creamy mash; chicken with thyme dumplings and Savoy cabbage; and smoked salmon penne pasta.

Open 10.30–1am **Bar Meals** L served all week 12–2.45 D served all week 6–9.45 Av main course £8.95 **Restaurant** L served all week 12–2.45 D served all week 6–9.45 Spirit Group Theakstons Best Bitter, Black Bull & Old Peculier, Theakstons XB, Black Sheep. 🍷 14 **Facilities** Garden **Rooms** 23 bedrooms en suite S£55 D£70

MIDDLEHAM MAP 19 SE18

Black Swan Hotel 🍷

Market Place DL8 4NP ☎ 01969 622221 📠 01969 622221

e-mail: blackswanmiddleham@breathe.com

web: www.blackswan-middleham.co.uk

Dating back to the 17th century and backing onto Middleham Castle, home of Richard III, this historic pub is at the heart of Yorkshire's racing country. Horses can be seen passing outside every morning on their way to the gallops. The emphasis here is on good food, with an appealing choice including Black Swan grill, chicken curry, bangers and mash, lasagne, and Kilnsey trout roasted with parsley and thyme dressing. There's also a good vegetarian choice.

Open 10–3.30 6–12 (Sun 12–11.30) **Bar Meals** L served all week 12–2 D served all week 6.30–9 Av main course £7 **Restaurant** L served all week 12–2 D served all week 6.30–9 Av 3 course à la carte £18 Free House Scottish Courage John Smiths, Theakstons Best Bitter, Black Bull, Old Peculier & Guest Beers. 🍷 7 **Facilities** Garden Dogs allowed

MIDDLESMOOR MAP 19 SE07

Crown Hotel 🍷

HG3 5ST ☎ 01423 755204

dir: *Telephone for directions*

The original building dates back to the 17th century; today it offers the chance to enjoy a good pint of local beer by a cosy, roaring winter log fire, or in a sunny pub garden. Stands on a breezy 900ft hilltop with good views towards Gouthwaite Reservoir. Ideal for those potholing or following the popular Nidderdale Way.

Open 12–3 7–11 (Closed Mon Lunch Winter, BHs) **Bar Meals** L served Mon–Sun 12–2 D served all week 7–8.30 Av main course £7.50 **Restaurant** L served all week 12–2 D served all week 7–8.30 Free House Black Sheep Best, Worthingtons Smooth, Carling, Guinness. 🍷 20 **Facilities** Garden Dogs allowed Parking

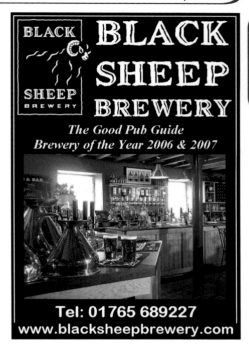

MIDDLETON (NEAR PICKERING) MAP 19 SE78

The Middleton Arms 🍷

Church Ln YO18 8PB ☎ 01751 475444

e-mail: themiddletonarms@aol.com

dir: *1m W of Pickering on A170*

Formerly known as The New Inn, the pub dates from the 17th century and retains much of its traditional charm. Menus draw on the best local produce and food is prepared to order by chef proprietor Andy Green. Seasonal fish and meat dishes are featured on the daily specials board, while regulars might include roasted Nidderdale chicken breast with creamy risotto, or pan-fried fillet of sea bass with watercress, orange and pine nut salad.

Open 6–11 **Bar Meals** D served Tue–Sun 6–9 (Sun 12–2, 6–10.30) Av main course £9.95 **Restaurant** L served 12–2 D served Tue–Sat 6–9 Av 3 course à la carte £20 Free House Timothy Taylor Landlord, Tetleys Smooth, Nick Stafford Hambleton Ales, Black Sheep. **Facilities** Parking

MOULTON — MAP 19 NZ20

Black Bull Inn NEW

DL10 6QJ ☎ 01325 377289 01325 377422
e-mail: Blackbullinn1@btconnect.com
dir: *1m S of Scotch Corner off A1*

Under new ownership after 43 years in one family's hands, but still impressing visitors, not least because you can dine in a 1932 Brighton Belle Pullman carriage. It specialises in fresh fish and seafood in a big way, with starters including Craster smoked salmon, and baked mussels in brie fondue. Main courses – offering plenty more fish, of course – include sautéed loin of venison, peppered fillet steak and rack of lamb, as well as specials.

Open 12–2 6.30–10.15 Closed: 24–26 Dec Rest: Sun **Bar Meals** L served Mon–Sat 12–2 Av main course £7 **Restaurant** L served Mon–Fri 12–2 D served Mon–Sat 6.45–10.15 Av 3 course à la carte £35 Av 3 course fixed price £18.95 Free House Theakstons Best, John Smiths Smooth. **Facilities** Garden Parking

MUKER — MAP 18 SD99

The Farmers Arms

DL11 6QG ☎ 01748 886297 01748 886375
dir: *From Richmond A6108 towards Leyburn, right onto B6270*

The last remaining pub – of three – in this old lead-mining village at the head of beautiful Swaledale, and a popular resting place for walkers on the Pennine Way and Coast-to-Coast route. With several miles under the belt, refuel with home-made steak pie; chicken alla Romana; deep-fried cod; liver and onions; or vegetable tandoori masala, aided and abetted by a pint of Castle Eden's Nimmos XXXX. Children's and smaller meals are also available.

Open 11–11 (Sun 11.30–11) **Bar Meals** L served all week 12–2.30 D served all week 6–8.45 Av main course £7.50 Free House Theakston Best & Old Peculier, John Smith's, Black Sheep, Guest Ales. 10 **Facilities** Garden Dogs allowed Parking

NORTH RIGTON — MAP 19 SE24

Pick of the Pubs

The Square and Compass

LS17 0DJ ☎ 01423 734228
e-mail: l13hud@aol.com
dir: *Just off A658, in village centre*

The Square and Compass was originally part of the Harewood estate and probably got its name by being used, many years ago, as a Mason's lodge. Today this pub, set in the beautiful Yorkshire village of North Rigton, is the ideal setting for celebrating special occasions, corporate dinners or simply enjoying a meal or drink with friends. You can relax and soak up the atmosphere while enjoying a light bar meal in the oak beamed bar and lounge, or go for a gourmet meal with fine wines in the tastefully restored restaurant. Both lunchtime and evening à la carte menus use only the freshest of local ingredients: starters could include a large Yorkshire pudding with onion gravy; and smooth pâté of chicken liver, brandy, garlic and orange. Mains dishes of rib-eye steak with garnish; chicken breast with smoked Wensleydale cheese wrapped in dry cured bacon; crispy haddock in beer batter; and chef's luxury fish pie provide a good variety.

Open 12–3 5–11 **Bar Meals** L served all week 12–2.30 D served all week 6–9.30 (Sun 12–6) Av main course £9.50 **Restaurant** L served Sun 12–6 D served Fri–Sat 6–9.30 Av 3 course à la carte £22.50 Black Sheep, Timothy Taylors Landlord, Hoegaarden. 46 **Facilities** Garden Parking

NUNNINGTON — MAP 19 SE67

The Royal Oak Inn

Church St YO62 5US ☎ 01439 748271 01439 748271
dir: *Opposite end of the village to Nunnington hall*

A solid stone pub in this sleepy rural backwater in the Howardian Hills, a short drive from the North Yorkshire Moors. The immaculate open-plan bar is furnished with scrubbed pine and decorated with farming memorabilia, just the place for a pint of Theakstons and a bite to eat. A typical menu features pork fillet in barbecue sauce, ham and mushroom tagliatelle, crispy roast duckling, and steak and kidney casserole.

Open 12–2.30 6.30–11 **Bar Meals** L served Tue–Sun 12–2 D served Tue–Sun 6.30–9 **Restaurant** L served Tue–Sun 12–2 D served Tue–Sun 6.30–9 Free House Scottish Courage Theakston Best & Old Peculier, Carlsberg-Tetley Tetley Bitter. 8 **Facilities** Parking

OSMOTHERLEY — MAP 19 SE49

Pick of the Pubs

The Golden Lion

6 West End DL6 3AA ☎ 01609 883526

The Golden Lion is a cosy sandstone building of some 250 years standing. The atmosphere is warm and welcoming, with open fires and wooden flooring on one side of the downstairs area. Furnishings are simple with a wooden bar, bench seating and tables, whitewashed walls, mirrors and fresh flowers. The extensive menu ranges through basic pub grub to more refined dishes. The starters are divided between fish, soups, vegetarian, pastas and risottos, meat and salads, and might include smoked salmon; buffalo mozzarella with tomato and basil; spicy pork ribs; and avocado and king prawn salad. Mains are along the lines of grilled seabass with new potatoes and peas; coq au vin; calves' liver with fried onions and mash; home-made beef burger with Mexican salsa; and spicy chilladas with fresh tomato sauce. Also interesting specials like pork stroganoff and rice, or lamb and feta lasagne. Sherry trifle, and bread and butter pudding with cream, are popular desserts.

Open 12–3 6–11 (Sat–Sun all day) Closed: 25 Dec **Bar Meals** L served all week 12–2.30 D served all week 6–9.15 Food all day when busy Av main course £9.95 **Restaurant** L served all week 12–2.30 D served all week 6–9.15 Av 3 course à la carte £18 Timothy Taylors Landlord, Hambleton Bitter, Jennings Bitter, Caledonian IPA. **Facilities** Garden Dogs allowed

Queen Catherine ★★ INN

7 West End DL6 3AG ☎ 01609 883209

e-mail: queencatherine@yahoo.co.uk

Named after Henry VIII's wife, Catherine of Aragon, who left her horse and carriage here while sheltering from her husband with nearby monks. There's no sense of menace around this friendly hotel nowadays, believed to be the only one in Britain bearing its name, and visitors can enjoy a well-cooked meal: monkfish tails, crab-stuffed chicken breast, lamb shank with minted gravy, Icelandic cod, and Whitby breaded scampi are all on the menu.

Open 12 –11 **Bar Meals** L served all week 12–2 D served all week 6–9 (Sun 12–9) **Restaurant** L served all week 12–2 D served all week 6–9 Free House Hambleton Ales-Stud, Stallion, Bitter, Goldfield. **Facilities** Dogs allowed **Rooms** 5 bedrooms en suite S£30 D£60

PATELEY BRIDGE — MAP 19 SE16

Pick of the Pubs

The Sportsmans Arms Hotel

Wath-in-Nidderdale HG3 5PP

☎ 01423 711306 01423 712524

dir: *A59/B6451, hotel 2m N of Pateley Bridge*

See Pick of the Pubs on page 665

PICKERING — MAP 19 SE78

Pick of the Pubs

Fox & Hounds Country Inn ★★ HL

Sinnington YO62 6SQ

☎ 01751 431577 01751 432791

e-mail: foxhoundsinn@easynet.co.uk

dir: *3m W of town, off A170*

A by-pass built in the late 1930s leaves the village of Sinnington, midway between the market towns of Kirkbymoorside and Pickering, a peaceful, unspoilt backwater. The village green has a maypole and the attractive little River Seven (no, not the Severn) supports a thriving duck population. This handsome 18th-century coaching inn has oak-beamed ceilings, old wood panelling and, when blue turns to grey, open fires. For those wanting a light lunch the menu offers cherry vine tomato and melted cheese tartlet, rocket and watercress salad; while for something more substantial there's grilled chicken and smoked bacon with plum tomatoes, lettuce and mayonnaise; and pan-fried salmon fillet, crushed potatoes and vegetable ribbons. A typical evening meal could be Peking pancakes with crispy duck, chilli jam and dipping sauce; pan-fried calves' liver with pancetta, mustard mash and shallot jus; and lemon tart with local clotted cream and raspberry coulis. A fresh fish menu changes every Friday.

Open 12–2 6–11 (Sun 6–10.30) **Bar Meals** L served all week 12–2 D served all week 6.30–9 (Sun 6.30–8.30) Av main course £10.85 **Restaurant** L served all week 12–2 D served all week 6.30–9 (Sun 6.30–8.30) Av 3 course à la carte £22 Free House Theakston Best, Black Sheep Special, Worthingtons Creamflow. 7 **Facilities** Garden Dogs allowed Parking **Rooms** 10 bedrooms en suite S£59 D£80

Horseshoe Inn

Main St, Levisham YO18 7NL

☎ 01751 460240 01751 460347

e-mail: info@horseshoelevisham.co.uk

web: www.horseshoelevisham.co.uk

dir: *A169 5m from Pickering*

A passionately run, family-owned 16th-century inn in a peaceful village in the North York Moors National Park. Using only the best local produce, it offers a varied blackboard menu of traditional, seasonal country and classic dishes, among which might be pan-flashed lambs' liver with crispy bacon and mash; Grandma Elsworth's steak and flatcap mushroom pie; and fresh Whitby halibut with hollandaise sauce. Sandwiches and baguettes are also available.

Open 11–3 6–11 **Bar Meals** L served all week 12–2 D served all week 6.30–9 **Restaurant** L served all week 12–2 D served all week 6.30–9 Free House Theakstons Best Bitter, Scottish Courage John Smiths, Old Peculier. **Facilities** Garden Parking

Pick of the Pubs

The White Swan Inn ★★★ HL

Market Place YO18 7AA

☎ 01751 472288 01751 475554

e-mail: welcome@white-swan.co.uk

dir: *A170 to Pickering, left at lights, 1st right onto Market Place, halfway up on left*

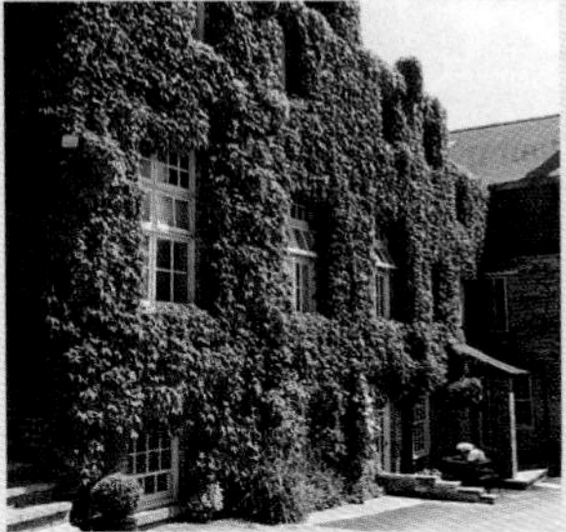

Owned and run by the Buchanan family for two decades, the White Swan stands just off the market place in this thriving Yorkshire town. Originally built in 1532 as a four-room cottage, the building was

CONTINUED

England

PICKERING continued

soon extended and pressed into service as a coaching inn for the York to Whitby stagecoach. Nowadays the inn blends traditional simplicity with understated style and luxury; the owners and staff take great pride in their service, with careful attention to every detail. There are comfy sofas to relax in, whilst the restaurant has stone flagged floors and a roaring winter fire. Lunchtime might bring sandwiches of Levisham beef with pesto and rocket; or dressed Whitby crab with celeriac; later on, the dinner menu could range from wild sea trout with minted peas and grilled new potatoes, to Swaledale lamb with tomato stew and chargrilled courgettes.

Open 10-3 6-11 **Bar Meals** L served all week 12-2 D served all week 6.45-9 Av main course £14 **Restaurant** L served all week 12-2 D served all week 6.45-9 Av 3 course à la carte £25 Av 3 course fixed price £12.95 Free House Black Sheep Best & Special, Yorkshire Moors Cropton Brewery, Timothy Taylors Landord. 12 **Facilities** Dogs allowed Parking **Rooms** 21 bedrooms en suite S£89 D£129

PICKHILL MAP 19 SE38

Pick of the Pubs

Nags Head Country Inn ★★ HL

YO7 4JG ☎ 01845 567391 01845 567212
e-mail: enquiries@nagsheadpickhill.co.uk
dir: *1m E of A1 (4m N of A1/A61 junct)*

This region of Yorkshire is known as 'Herriot country', after the books by the famous country vet. A direct descendant of the coaching inn tradition, the Nag's Head is a 200-year-old free house, set in the village of Pickhill. It's perfectly situated for exploring the local fells, playing a round of golf, fishing or having a flutter at nearby Thirsk, Ripon and Catterick races. Once you've worked up an appetite head inside, where beamed ceilings, stone-flagged floors and winter fires make for a most welcoming atmosphere. A lengthy, thoughtful menu is equally appealing. Starters like queenie scallops glazed with gruyere cheese precede main course options that include locally smoked Whitby haddock on a Welsh rarebit muffin; casserole of local game topped with suet pastry, or duo of pork loin and belly on root vegetable mash. On sunny days, meals can be taken in the secluded walled garden.

Open 11-11 **Bar Meals** L served all week 12-2 D served all week 6-9.30 (Sun 12-2.30, 6-9) Av main course £10.95 **Restaurant** L served Mon-Sun 12-2 D served Mon-Sat 7-9.30 (Sun 7-9) Av 3 course à la carte £22.50 Free House Hambleton Bitter & Goldfield, Black Sheep Best & Special, Old Peculier, Theakstons Best Bitter. 8 **Facilities** Garden Dogs allowed Parking **Rooms** 16 bedrooms en suite S£55 D£75

PICTON MAP 19 NZ40

The Station Pub NEW

TS15 0AE ☎ 01642 700067
dir: *1.5m from A19*

A family-run and family-friendly village pub, offering real food at reasonable prices. Just about everything is home made, with one menu serving both bar and dining room. While the children enjoy the outdoor play area, Mum and Dad can relax in front of the open fire and scan the extensive specials board. If fish is the order of the day, you may find oven-roasted cod with Wensleydale cheese, lime and ginger crumb; or sea bass fillets with stirfry.

Open 6-12 (Sat-Sun 12-3) **Bar Meals** L served Sat-Sun 12-2 D served all week 6.30-9 Av main course £9.90 **Restaurant** L served Sat-Sun 12-2 D served all week 6.30-9 Free House John Smiths Cask, John Smiths Smooth, Guinness, Kronenbourg 1664 & Fosters. 8 **Facilities** Garden Parking Play Area

REETH MAP 19 SE09

Pick of the Pubs

Charles Bathurst Inn ★★★★ INN

Arkengarthdale DL11 6EN
☎ 01748 884567 01748 884599
e-mail: info@cbinn.co.uk

See Pick of the Pubs on page 666

ROBIN HOOD'S BAY MAP 19 NZ90

Laurel Inn

New Rd YO22 4SE ☎ 01947 880400

Picturesque Robin Hood's Bay is the setting for this small, traditional pub which retains lots of character features, including beams and an open fire. The bar is decorated with old photographs, and an international collection of lager bottles. This coastal fishing village was once the haunt of smugglers who used a network of underground tunnels and secret passages to bring the booty ashore. Straightforward simple menu offers wholesome sandwiches and soups.

Open 12-11 (Sun 12-10.30) (Nov-Feb Mon-Fri 2-11) Free House Old Peculier, Theakstons Best & Deuchars IPA. **Facilities** Dogs allowed **Notes**

The Sportsmans Arms Hotel

Wath-in-Nidderdale is a conservation village, and one of the most picturesque and unspoilt settlements in the Yorkshire Dales National Park. Ray and Jane Carter have been running this unpretentious hotel for nearly 30 years, although son Jamie and daughter Sarah have leading roles too these days.

Dating from the 17th century, the sandstone-built Sportsmans Arms stands on the 53-mile, circular Nidderdale Way, hard by the dam over the River Nidd (some fishing rights belong to the hotel) that creates Gouthwaite Reservoir. Approach via an old pack-horse bridge, enter the hallway and find open log fires, comfortable chairs, a warm and welcoming bar and a charming restaurant. As much of the food as possible is locally sourced, but Ray has no qualms about occasionally buying foreign produce if he thinks it better. Always good, though, are the Nidderdale lamb, pork, beef, trout and game (season permitting) that can always be found on the menu. Fish arriving daily from Whitby and Redcar on the east coast, typically appears on the plate as turbot with spinach and mousseline; seared tuna with rocket salsa and Greek salad; or maybe lightly-cooked halibut with beurre blanc glazed with fresh parmesan. Best end of Nidderdale lamb is perfectly accompanied by creamy garlic mash, natural jus and tomato concassée; and chestnuts, cranberries and pancetta go well with saddle of venison. The wine list offers a wide selection of styles and prices. The annual Lobster Festival at the end of May is hugely popular.

MAP 19 SE16
Wath-in-Nidderdale HG3 5PP
☎ 01423 711306
Fax 01423 712524
dir: *A59/B6451, 2m N of Pateley Bridge*

Open 12-2 7-11 (Sun 7-10.30)
Closed: 25 Dec
Bar Meals L served all week 12-2 D served all week 7-9
Av main course £11.50
Restaurant L served all week 12-2 D served all week 7-9.30
Av 3 course à la carte £28
Free House
Black Sheep, Worthingtons, Folly Ale. 12
Facilities Garden Parking

Charles Bathurst Inn

As it is located about halfway along the coast-to-coast walk, this 18th-century inn is popular with ramblers, and in addition to the real ales and real food it offers 19 bedrooms for the weary of limb.

Set in remote and beautiful Arkengarthdale, the CB (as regulars call it) was a bunkhouse for lead miners employed by Charles Bathurst, an 18th-century lord of the manor and son of Oliver Cromwell's physician. The bar, once a barn and stable, now welcomes customers with its antique pine furniture, cosy fires and Theakstons ales. Charles and Stacy Cody bought the CB in 1996 and extensively renovated and extended the property to provide larger kitchens, spacious accommodation and the Terrace Room for private parties, weddings and conferences; the latter is furnished with Robert 'the mouse man' Thompson tables and chairs. They have also recently renovated and re-opened the Punch Bowl Inn at Low Row, a 17th-century listed building with spectacular views of Swaledale, which had been closed for three years. The CB's local suppliers are proudly acknowledged, and the menu features naturally reared Swaledale lamb and beef, fresh fish delivered daily from Hartlepool, and locally shot game according to season. This prime produce appears in dishes such as seared halibut fillet with smoked salmon and prawn risotto; and Swale Hall rump of lamb with spicy ratatouille, couscous and lamb jus. An interesting starter is rabbit toad in the hole made with home-made rabbit sausage and apple compote, and a popular dessert to round off your meal is sticky toffee pudding with caramel sauce and ice cream.

★★★★ INN 🍷
MAP 19 SE09
Arkengarthdale DL11 6EN
☎ 01748 884567
📠 01748 884599
e-mail: info@cbinn.co.uk

Open 11–12 Closed: Dec 25
Bar Meals L served all week 12–2 D served all week 6.30–9
Av main course £11
Restaurant L served all week 12–2 D served all week 6.30–9
Av 3 course à la carte £20
Free House
Theakstons, John Smiths Bitter & Smooth, Black Sheep Best & Riggwelter. 🍷 9
Facilities Garden Parking Play Area
Rooms 19 bedrooms en suite
S£70 D£92.50

ROSEDALE ABBEY MAP 19 SE79

Pick of the Pubs

The Milburn Arms Hotel ★★ HL 🍷

YO18 8RA ☎ 01751 417312 📠 01751 417541

e-mail: info@millburnarms.co.uk

dir: *A170 W from Pickering 3m, right at sign to Rosedale then 7m N*

In the heart of the Yorkshire Moors lies the picturesque village of Rosedale Abbey. Opposite the village green you will find this charming country house hotel dating back to 1776, and a perfect rural retreat. The family-run hotel offers 13 beautifully furnished en suite bedrooms, with a welcoming bar and log fires in the public rooms. Rosedale, once a centre for ironstone mining, is great for walking and you can quite literally begin a local hike at the front door of the hotel. Also close by are some of Yorkshire's best-loved attractions, including Castle Howard, Rievaulx Abbey and the region's famous steam railway. The Priory Restaurant is known for its quality cuisine: lobster and crab bisque, or a slice of pink melon and Parma ham sharpen the appetite for chicken breast with apricot and pork; pan-fried calves' liver with red wine shallot; or poached fillet of plaice filled with fresh prawns.

Open 11.30–3 6–11 Closed: 25 Dec **Bar Meals** L served all week 12–2.15 (Sun 12–3) D served all week 6–9 Av main course £15 **Restaurant** L served Sun 12–2.30 D served all week 6–9.15 Av 3 course à la carte £22.50 Av fixed price £10 Free House Black Sheep Best, Carlsberg-Tetley Tetely Bitter, John Smith's. 🍷 8 **Facilities** Garden Dogs allowed Parking **Rooms** 13 bedrooms en suite S£47.50 D£40

SAWDON MAP 17 SE98

The Anvil Inn NEW 🍷

Main St YO13 9DY ☎ 01723 859896

e-mail: theanvilinnsawdon@btinternet.com

dir: *1.5m N of Brompton-by-Sawdon, on A170*

A working forge until 1985, and deeds on a visiting American's laptop proved it was a smithy back in 1756! Tools, bellows and many horseshoes remain; the bar has the original furnace, a high pitched roof, exposed stone and wooden floors. It's a great real-ale local, sponsoring the village netball team and fielding two thirsty darts teams. Eating here scores a bullseye too – specials like potted calves' tongue followed by lamb Henry braised in Rioja are seriously good.

Open 12–2.30 6.30–11 (Summer 6–11) Closed: 26 Dec & 1 Jan **Bar Meals** L served Tue–Sat 12–2 (Sun 12–3) **Restaurant** L served Tue–Sat 12–2 (Sun 12–3 D served Tue–Sat 6.30–9) Free House Black Sheep Best, Daleside Blonde, Carling Lager, Hobgoblin Ale. 🍷 9 **Facilities** Children's licence Garden Dogs allowed Parking

SAWLEY MAP 19 SE26

The Sawley Arms 🍷

HG4 3EQ ☎ 01765 620642

dir: *B6265 to Pateley Bridge*

Run by the same owners for 37 years, this delightful 200-year-old pub was a frequent haunt of the late author and vet James Herriot. Additional dining space is provided in the conservatory, and dishes are prepared from local produce. Fish features strongly, for example as smoked haddock with cheese glaze on a bed of spinach. The pub is handy for the nearby attractions of Fountains Abbey and Ripon Cathedral. There's a wheelchair available for customers' use.

Open 11.30–3 6.30–10.30 Closed: 25 Dec **Bar Meals** L served all week 12–2.15 D served Tue–Sat 6.30–9 (Sun 6–8 in summer) Av main course £12 **Restaurant** L served all week 12–2.15 D served Tue–Sat 6.30–9 (Sun 6–8 in summer) Free House Theakston Best, Scottish Courage John Smith's. 🍷 8 **Facilities** Garden Parking

SCAWTON MAP 19 SE58

Pick of the Pubs

The Hare Inn 🍷

YO7 2HG ☎ 01845 597524

Mentioned in the Domesday Book, and once frequented by the abbots and monks of Rievaulx Abbey. In the 17th century ale was brewed here for local iron workers. Inside, as you might expect, are low-beamed ceilings and flagstone floors, a wood-burning stove providing a warm welcome in the bar, and an old-fashioned kitchen range in the dining area. Diners may find baked Whitby haddock with a minted pea crust, Aberdeen Angus sirloin steak and caramelized red onion sandwich, crab and king scallop thermidor with a crunchy parmesan topping, tagliatelle in crab and salmon cream sauce, and poached lemon sole with crisp pancetta and pimientos.

Open 12–3 6.30–11 (Sun 12–3.30, 6.30–11, Summer varies) **Bar Meals** L served Tue–Sat 12–2.30 (Sun 12–3) D served Tue–Sat 6.30–8.45 **Restaurant** L served Tue–Sun 12–2.30 D served Tue–Sat 6.30–8.45 Free House Black Sheep, Scottish Courage John Smiths, Guest Beers. 🍷 14 **Facilities** Garden Parking

SETTLE MAP 18 SD86

Golden Lion ★★★★ INN

Duke St BD24 9DU ☎ 01729 822203 01729 824103

e-mail: info@goldenlion.yorks.net

This traditional Dales coaching inn has been the silent witness to incalculable comings and goings in Settle's market place since around 1640. Its cosy bars, open fire, commodious restaurant and comfy bedrooms often meet the needs of travellers on the spectacular Settle-Carlisle railway line. There is a good choice of beers and a strong emphasis on food prepared from fresh ingredients, with specials such as moules marinière, Moroccan lamb curry and vegetable stirfry.

Open 11-11 **Bar Meals** L served all week 12-2.30 D served all week 6-10 Av main course £7.50 **Restaurant** L served all week 12-2.30 D served all week 6-10 Av 3 course à la carte £18 Thwaites Thwaites Bitter, Bomber, Thoroughbred, Smooth & Guest beers. 9 **Facilities** Children's licence Parking **Rooms** 12 bedrooms 10 en suite S£34 D£60

SKIPTON MAP 18 SD95

Devonshire Arms

Grassington Rd, Cracoe BD23 6LA

☎ 01756 730237 01756 730142

A convivial 17th-century inn convenient for the Three Peaks, and original setting for the Rhylstone Ladies WI calendar. There are excellent views of Rhylstone Fell. A wide range of cask ales plus extensive wine list will wash down a menu that includes steak and mushroom pie cooked in Jennings Sneckligter ale, lamb Jennings, chicken Diane, and haddock and chips.

Open 12-3 6-12 (Sat 12-1am, Sun 12-12) **Bar Meals** L served all week 12-2 (Sun 12-4) D served all week 6.30-9 **Restaurant** L served all week 12-2 D served all week 6.30-8.30 (Fri-Sat 6.30-9, Sun 12-4) W'hampton & Dudley Jennings, Jennings Cumberland, Snecklifter, Tetley's. 7 **Facilities** Garden Parking

SNAINTON MAP 17 SE98

Coachman Inn

Pickering Rd West YO13 9PL

☎ 01723 859231 01723 850008

e-mail: james@coachmaninn.co.uk

dir: *5m from Pickering, off A170 on B1258*

The Coachman is an imposing Grade II listed Georgian coaching inn, run by James and Rita Osborne. Main courses include asparagus, spinach and wild mushroom puff pastry tartlet with poached egg and hollandaise; slow-roast belly of pork with cider, celeriac, apples and crackling; wild salmon with casserole of summer vegetables; and roast fillet of Scarborough halibut with mushrooms, and pea and bacon risotto. Outside is a large lawned area with flowers, trees and seating.

Open 12-2 6-11 (Summer 5-11) **Bar Meals** L served Wed-Sun 12-2 D served Tue-Sat 7-9 (Sat-Sun 12-2.30, Fri-Sat 7-9.30) Av main course £9.50 **Restaurant** L served pre booking only 12-2 D served Tue-Sat 7-9 (Sat-Sun 12-2.30, Fri-Sat 7-9.30) Av 3 course à la carte £28 Free House John Smiths, Black Sheep, Wold Top, & Guinness. 7 **Facilities** Children's licence Garden Parking

STARBOTTON MAP 18 SD97

Fox & Hounds Inn

BD23 5HY ☎ 01756 760269 & 760367

Situated in a picturesque limestone village in Upper Wharfedale, this ancient pub was originally built as a private house, but has been a pub for more than 160 years. Make for the cosy bar, with its solid furnishings and flagstones, and enjoy a pint of Black Sheep or one of the guest ales. The menu offers steak and ale pie, lamb shank, pork medallions in brandy and mustard sauce, and a selection of steaks.

Open 11.30-3 6-11 (BHs open lunch only) Closed: 01Jan-22 Jan **Bar Meals** L served all week 12-2.30 D served all week 6-9 (Sun 12-8.15) Av main course £7 **Restaurant** 12-2.30 5.30-9 (Sun 12-8) Free House Black Sheep, Timothy Taylor Landlord, Boddingtons White Horse & Guest Beers. 8 **Facilities** Garden Parking **Rooms** 3 bedrooms en suite S£45 D£65

SUTTON-ON-THE-FOREST MAP 19 SE56

Pick of the Pubs

The Blackwell Ox Inn NEW ★★★★ INN

Huby Rd YO61 1DT ☎ 01347 810328 01347 812738

e-mail: enquiries@blackwelloxinn.co.uk

dir: *A1237 then B1363, left at t-junct*

Built as a house in the early 1820s, the Blackwell Ox takes its name from a shorthorn Teeswater ox that was slaughtered in 1779. Today, it's a friendly village pub, with open winter fires in the cosy bar and lounge, hand-pulled cask ales and summer dining in the garden. Five individually designed en suite bedrooms make this an inviting base for touring the Yorkshire countryside or visiting the nearby city of York. Head chef Steven Holding draws inspiration from the robust flavours of French and Spanish regional cookery, and sources his ingredients from local producers named on the menus. Dinner might begin with seared sea bass, crab bisque and dumplings, followed by braised Dexter beef, Jerusalem artichoke and potato gratin; or parsnip tarte Tatin with beetroot, crème fraiche and baby leaf salad. Leave room for warm chocolate pudding with salted caramel and clotted cream.

Open 12-2 5-11 **Bar Meals** L served all week 12-2 D served all week 6-9.30 (Sun 12-2.30, 6.30-9) Av main course £12 **Restaurant** L served Sun 12-2.30 D served all week 6-9.30 (Sun 6.30-9) Av 3 course à la carte £22 Av 3 course fixed price £13.50 Free House Black Sheep, John Smiths Cask, John Smiths Smooth, Guinness. 9 **Facilities** Garden Parking

Rose & Crown

Main St YO61 1DP ☎ 01347 811333 01347 811444

e-mail: mail@rosecrown.co.uk

dir: *On B1363 N of York*

Located in a picturesque village 10 miles north of York, the Rose & Crown has an informal, almost homely feel though the décor and food style is modern in its approach. The garden and patio at the back are well used during summer months. A choice of menus is usually available with a generous choice. Ballotine of chicken, foie gras and rabbit, roast halibut with Bombay potatoes, or pot roast pheasant are fine examples of the imaginative food.

Open 12-3 5.30-11 Closed: 1st wk Jan **Bar Meals** L served Tue-Sat 12-2 (Sunday 12-4) D served Tue-Fri 6-7 **Restaurant** L served Tue-Sun 12-2 D served Sun-Thu 6-9 (Fri-Sat 6-9.30) Free House Timothy Taylors Landlord, Black Sheep Bitter, Hoegaargen. 11 **Facilities** Garden Parking

PUB CYCLES

THORNTON LE DALE - NORTH YORKSHIRE

New Inn

Cycle information

Distance: 6 miles/9.7km (2h)
Map: OS Explorer OL27 North York Moors Eastern Area
Start/finish: car park at Adderstone Field, Dalby Forest; grid ref: SE 883897
Trails/tracks: forestry roads and a few narrow paths, mostly well graded
Landscape: conifer forest
Public toilets: Visitor Centre, Lower Dalby (not on route)
Tourist information: Dalby Forest Visitor Centre, tel 01751 460295
Cycle hire: Purple Mountain Bike Hire, Old Visitor Centre, Low Dalby, tel 01751 460011
The pub: New Inn, Thornton le Dale, off the route
There's a short, rough and slightly downhill section of track at the start. The forest drive road needs to be crossed with care twice

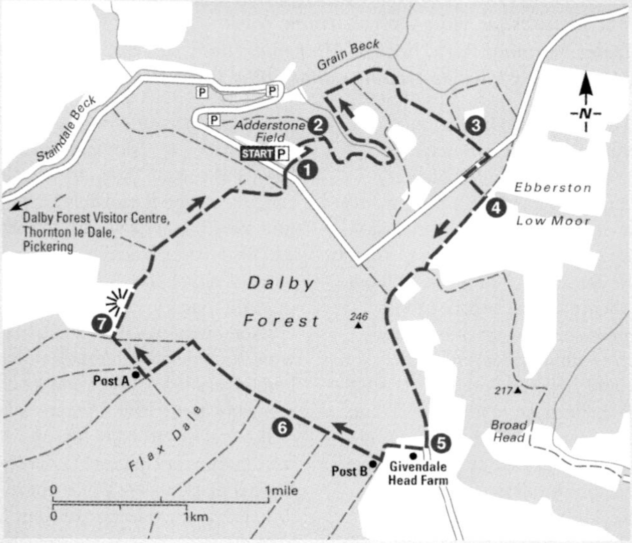

Cycle directions

❶ The green cycle route begins beyond the trees at the south east end of the large Adderstone Field (the furthest from the visitor centre). Here you turn left along a narrow slightly downhill track. Though still easy, it's the most difficult section of the route – use gentle braking if you're a little unsure. Ignore two lesser, unsigned left fork tracks.

❷ Turn right along a much wider forestry track which takes a winding course round the afforested valley of Worry Gill. Where the more demanding red route goes off on a rough track to the right, your green route goes straight on, still using a well-graded track.

❸ Where a track doubles back, go straight on up a steady hill before meeting the forest drive again. Cross this with care – it can be quite busy on summer weekends – before turning right along it for 200yds (183m). Turn left along a narrow path signed with red and green waymarkers and just before a 30 mph speed limit sign.

❹ The path reaches a flinted road at the south east edge of the forest. Turn right along this then left at the next junction. Looking left, you'll see the rougher high pastures of Ebberston Low Moor decline to the greener, more fertile fields of the Vale of Pickering.

❺ Turn right just before reaching Givendale Head Farm along a rutted farm track with a grassy island in the middle. Turn right at the next junction (Post B) on a downhill section, followed by an uphill one where you're joined by a farm track from the left.

❻ A long hill follows to a wide junction where you go straight on along a tarred lane. A sign tells you that you're now at the head of Flaxdale. Stay with the tarred lane at the next bend and junction. Turn right at the crossroads along a long sandy track (Post A), then right again at the next junction. Note the linear earthwork to both left and right – nobody seems to know the exact origins of these.

❼ Go straight on at the next junction past a stand of Scots pines, and fine views of High Rigg to Levisham Moor. There's another downhill section followed by an uphill one. Take a right fork at Newclose Rigg. Where the red route goes straight on, your green route veers right along the main track. There's a downhill left curve beyond which you take the upper right fork back to the forest drive opposite Adderstone Field.

The Buck Inn

The picturesque village of Thornton Watlass is where Wensleydale, gateway to the Yorkshire Dales National Park, begins. After more than 20 years as the Buck's landlords, Margaret and Michael Fox have no trouble maintaining its welcoming, relaxing atmosphere.

The pub overlooks the triangular village green, incorporating a cricket pitch whose boundary is actually the pub wall. Special breaks are offered for fishing enthusiasts, for lovers of racing, for golfers, and for those just wanting to chill out. There are three separate dining areas – the bar for informality, the restaurant for dining by candlelight, and on busy days the large function room is opened up. The menu ranges from traditional, freshly prepared pub fare to more exciting modern cuisine with weekly changing blackboard specials. Typical bar favourites are fish and chips; gammon steak with peas, egg and chips; steak and kidney pie; Masham rarebit topped with Wensleydale cheese; and cricketer's platter incorporating home-made paté and home-cooked ham; and lasagne. From the a la carte menu you ll probably find seared tuna steak with rocket and fusili pasta; baked parmigianna layers of aubergine and courgette in a rich tomato sauce; stuffed chicken breast in a light white wine sauce; and lamb shank with herbed mashed potatoes and a rich vegetable broth. Beer drinkers have a choice of five real ales served from hand pumps, including Masham-brewed Black Sheep, while whisky drinkers have a selection of some forty different malts to try, though perhaps not all at one sitting!

★★★ INN 🍷
MAP 19 SE28
HG4 4AH
☎ 01677 422461
🖷 01677 422447
e-mail:
inwatlass1@btconnect.com
dir: *A684 to Bedale, then B6268 towards Masham. Village 2m on right, hotel by cricket green*

Open 11–11 Closed: 25 Dec eve
Bar Meals L served all week 12–2 D served all week 6–9.30 (Sun 12–3, 6.30–9.30) Av main course £10
Restaurant L served all week 12–2 (Sun 12–3) D served all week 6.30–9.30 Av 3 course à la carte £18.50 Av 3 course fixed price £16.50
Free House
Theakston Best, Black Sheep Best, John Smith's & Guest beers. 🍷 7
Facilities Garden Dogs allowed Parking Play Area
Rooms 5 bedrooms en suite S£50 D£65

THORNTON LE DALE — MAP 19 SE88

The New Inn ★★★ INN

Maltongate YO18 7LF ☎ 01751 474226
e-mail: terryandjo1@btconnect.com

This Georgian coaching inn stands at the heart of a picturesque village complete with stocks and a market cross. The old world charm of the surroundings is echoed inside the pub, which has real fires, hand-pulled ales, and freshly cooked food. Typical examples include ham hock on a wholegrain mustard mash; poached salmon in a lemon and prawn sauce; fillet of turbot in a rose and crayfish sauce; and lamb with minted gravy.

Open 12-3 5-11 (Summer Mon-Sat 11-11, Sun 12-10.30) **Bar Meals** L served all week 12-2 D served all week 6.30-9 Av main course £7.50 **Restaurant** L served all week 12-2 D served all week 6.30-9 Av 3 course à la carte £19 Scottish & Newcastle Theakston Best, Bombardier, Black Sheep & Guest. **Facilities** Garden Dogs allowed Parking **Rooms** 6 bedrooms en suite S£43 D£66

Please see cycle ride on page 669

THORNTON WATLASS — MAP 19 SE28

Pick of the Pubs

The Buck Inn ★★★ INN

HG4 4AH ☎ 01677 422461 01677 422447
e-mail: inwatlass1@btconnect.com
dir: *A684 to Bedale, then B6268 towards Masham. Village 2m on right, hotel by cricket green*

See Pick of the Pubs on opposite page

TOPCLIFFE — MAP 19 SE37

The Angel Inn ★★ HL

YO7 3RW ☎ 01845 577237 01845 578000
e-mail: mail@angelinn.co.uk
dir: *A168(M) 3m from the A1*

A recent major refurbishment has given this old country inn a more contemporary feel, but with more than a nod to tradition. The restaurant has a good local reputation for creative dishes such as fillet of red mullet with warm potato, celeriac and beetroot salad; pheasant pot au feu; and, for two, seafood casserole under puff pastry. Most of the 15 bedrooms are in a new wing.

Open 11-11 **Bar Meals** L served all week 12-9 D served all week 12-9 Av main course £8.95 **Restaurant** L served all week D served all week John Smith, Black Sheep, Timothy Taylors. 8 **Facilities** Children's licence Garden Dogs allowed Parking **Rooms** 15 bedrooms en suite S£55 D£85

WASS — MAP 19 SE57

Pick of the Pubs

Wombwell Arms

YO61 4BE ☎ 01347 868280
e-mail: wykes@wombwellarms.wanadoo.co.uk
dir: *A168/A19 junct, York exit, left after 2.5m, left at Coxwold to Ampleforth. Wass 2m*

The building was constructed around 1620 as a granary, probably using stone from nearby Byland Abbey, and it became an ale house in about 1645. A series of stylishly decorated rooms provide the setting for bistro-style cooking. Local suppliers have been established for all the produce used: at least three vegetarian dishes are offered daily along with a good choice of fresh fish, including Whitby cod. Popular options are steak, Guinness and mushroom pie, country rabbit, and game casserole. Great location for those walking the North Yorks National Park.

Open 11-3 6.15-11 Closed Sun pm in low season **Bar Meals** L served all week 12-2.30 (Sun 12-3) D served all week Av main course £12 **Restaurant** L served all week 12-2.30 (Sun 12-3) D served all week 6.30-8.30 Av 3 course à la carte £20 Free House Black Sheep Best, Timothy Taylor Landlord, Tetley Extra Smooth. 7 **Facilities** Children's licence Garden Parking

WEAVERTHORPE — MAP 17 SE97

Pick of the Pubs

The Star Country Inn

YO17 8EY ☎ 01944 738273 01944 738273
e-mail: starweaverthorpe@aol.com
dir: *A64 towards Scarborough. 12m, at Sherborn right at lights . Weaverthorpe 4m, inn opoosite junct*

This brightly-shining Star has expanded over the years to incorporate adjoining cottages housing an extended dining area and comfortable accommodation for overnight guests. Situated in the heart of the Yorkshire Wolds, it makes a handy base for exploring the area and visiting such attractions as Nunnington Hall, Sledmere House, and Castle Howard, which was used extensively in the classic television series *Brideshead Revisited*. The area is

CONTINUED

WEAVERTHORPE continued

also popular with bird watchers and cyclists. The rustic facilities of bar and dining room, with large winter fires and a welcoming, convivial atmosphere, complement food cooked to traditional family recipes using fresh local produce. Typical dishes include pigeon in horseradish sauce; pheasant in red wine sauce; chicken and ribs; and a good number of fish dishes, ranging from fish pie; trout in lemon butter; and trio of fish in white wine, through to more exotic offerings such as mia mia from Hawaii.

Open 12-3 7-11 **Bar Meals** L served Wed-Mon 12-2 D served Wed-Mon 7-9.30 (Sun 12-3, 7-8.30) Av main course £7.50 **Restaurant** L served Wed-Mon 12-2 D served Wed-Mon 7-9.30 (Sun 12-3, 7-8.30) Av 3 course à la carte £15 Free House Carlsberg-Tetley Tetley Bitter, Scottish Courage John Smith's, Wold Top. **Facilities** Parking

WEST BURTON MAP 19 SE08

Fox & Hounds

DL8 4JY ☎ 01969 663111 01969 663279

e-mail: foxandhounds.westburton@virgin.net

dir: *A468 between Hawes & Leyburn, 0.5m E of Aysgarth*

Overlooking the village green in the unspoilt village of West Burton, this inn offers log fires and home cooking. Hand-pulled ales on offer at the bar include Black Sheep and Copper Dragon. Traditional pub food is provided to accompany your pint: dishes such as steak and kidney pie, curry, and lasagne will fortify you for country walks or visits to nearby waterfalls, castles or cheese-tasting at the Wensleydale Creamery.

Open 11am-12am Rest: Winter closed 3-6 **Bar Meals** L served all week 12-2 D served all week 6-8.30 Av main course £6.95 **Restaurant** L served all week 12-2 D served all week 6-8.30 Av 3 course à la carte £15 Free House Black Sheep, John Smiths, Tetleys, Copper Dragon. **Facilities** Dogs allowed Parking

WESTOW MAP 19 SE76

Pick of the Pubs

The Blacksmiths Inn NEW

Main St YO60 7NE ☎ 01653 618365

e-mail: info@blacksmithsinn.co.uk

dir: *From A64, Westow signed from top of Whitwell Hill. Turn right and onto T-junct. Pub on right on Main St*

Since Gary and Sarah Marshall took over The Blacksmiths Arms in 2005 they have transformed this 19th-century free house into a popular and award-winning gastro-pub. The house philosophy is to source excellent local produce and cook each dish from scratch – this goes for everything from stock to ice cream. Classic English dishes benefit from loving attention: try 21-day aged steak, home-made béarnaise sauce and triple cooked chips; or pan-fried free range pork sausages with crab apple sauce. A sample dinner might start with sautéed woodland mushrooms on toast with poached quail eggs, followed by pork loin and duck fat roasted potatoes. The attention to detail extends right down to the tables, which are elegantly dressed with linen and crystal. The wine list is something of a labour of love, extending to over 60 bins, with a particularly impressive range of good value Burgundies.

Open 6-11 (Sat 12-2 6-11, Sun 12-4) **Bar Meals** L served Sat 12-2 D served Wed-Sat 6-9 Av main course £11.50 **Restaurant** L served Sat 12-2 (Sun 12-3.30) D served Wed-Sat 6-9 Av 3 course à la carte £23 Av 3 course fixed price £11.95 Free House Blacksheep, Landord, John Smiths Cask. 13 **Facilities** Garden Dogs allowed Parking

WEST TANFIELD MAP 19 SE27

Pick of the Pubs

The Bruce Arms

Main St HG4 5JJ ☎ 01677 470325 01677 470796

e-mail: info@bruce-arms.co.uk

dir: *On A6108 Ripon/Masham Rd, close to A1*

The Bruce Arms is styled as a bistro, in a stone built, ivy-clad house dating from 1820, with traditional exposed beams, log fires and candles on the tables. A good wine list and real ales such as Black Sheep Best guarantee a decent accompaniment to starters like French onion soup, seared King scallops with potato and mushroom salad; and carpaccio of beef with fried quails' eggs and crispy onion rings. Main courses might be roast saddle of Holme Farm venison, or lamb shank with casserole of vegetables. A variety of fish dishes is also available, perhaps roasted fillets of wild sea bass with pancetta risotto will be on the menu.

Open 12-11 **Bar Meals** L served all week 12-9.30 D served Tue-Sat 12-9.30 Av main course £12 **Restaurant** L served Tue-Sun 12-2 D served Tue-Sun 6.30-9.30 Av 3 course à la carte £25 Free House Black Sheep Best, Black Sheep Ale & Worthington Smooth. 10 **Facilities** Garden Dogs allowed Parking

The Wensleydale Heifer Inn

Despite its inland location in the heart of Wensleydale, fish features strongly at the Wensleydale Heifer and it is the winner of the AA Seafish Pub of the Year for England 2007. The inn has its own restaurant and fish bar, both with a uniquely chic look.

The restaurant provides a lovely setting for a 'special occasion' meal, with chocolate brown leather chairs, linen clothed tables and original Doug Hyde pictures. Alternatively, the fish bar and snug are less formal in style with sea grass flooring, rattan chairs and wooden tables, perfect for a light meal in relaxing surroundings. For sitting comfortably with a coffee, pint, or a glass of the finest malt, there's the Whisky Club Lounge, where an open fire burns in cooler weather. The 17th-century former coaching inn has a whitewashed stone exterior with a sculptured garden and an attractive area of decking for sitting outside. Overnight accommodation is provided in nine en suite bedrooms, some with four-posters. The menu has something to appeal to all tastes, from traditional fish and chips to warm salad of maple roasted lobster. Ingredients include locally produced farmed meats, and there are hand-made after dinner chocolates. At lunchtime, the house speciality is hot fish ciabatta with Marie Rose sauce and frites, or for something more substantial choose from the two or three-course fixed-price lunch. From the carte you might try cured fish platter, famous fish pie with fennel and capers, or roast organic pork chop with black pudding mash, apple sauce and cider braised Savoy cabbage.

★★ HL ◎ ☞ 🍷
MAP 19 SE08
DL8 4LS
☎ 01969 622322
📠 01969 624183
e-mail:
info@wensleydaleheifer.co.uk
dir: *A684, at W of village*

Open 11–11
Bar Meals L served all week 12–2 D served all week 6–9
Av main course £6.95
Restaurant L served all week 12–2 D served all week 6.30–9
Free House
Burst Beer, Scottish Courage John Smith's, Black Sheep Best.
🍷 7
Facilities Garden Parking
Rooms 9 bedrooms en suite D£90

England

WEST WITTON MAP 19 SE08

Pick of the Pubs

The Wensleydale Heifer Inn ★★ HL

DL8 4LS ☎ 01969 622322 01969 624183

e-mail: info@wensleydaleheifer.co.uk

dir: *A684, at west end of village*

See Pick of the Pubs on page 673

WHASHTON MAP 19 NZ10

Hack & Spade NEW

DL11 7JL ☎ 01748 823721

dir: *A66 Penrith for 5m. Left towards Ravensworth for 2m. Left at x-rds for Whashton*

This unusually titled free house stands opposite the former quarry from which its name is derived. Nowadays, however, the quarry has been filled in to form part of the village green. Starters such as four cheese focaccia bites precede main course dishes like lamb shank in red wine and rosemary gravy; vegetarian Glamorgan sausage with tomatoes, and bubble and squeak; and salmon with breadcrumbs, lemon and parsley. Finish, perhaps, with organic country fruit crumble.

Open 11-11 Tue-Sat (Sun 12-3) **Bar Meals** L served Tue-Sun 12-2.30 D served Tue-Sat 7-9 Av main course £9.95 **Restaurant** L served Tue-Sun 12-2.30 D served Tue-Sat 7-9 Free House Boddingtons, Becks, John Smiths Smooth, Theakstons Original. **Facilities** Parking

WHITBY MAP 19 NZ81

The Magpie Café

14 Pier Rd YO21 3PU ☎ 01947 602058 01947 601801

e-mail: ian@magpiecafe.co.uk

More a licensed restaurant than a pub, the award-winning Magpie has been the home of North Yorkshire's best-ever fish and chips since the late 1930s when it moved to its present site in Pier Road. The dining rooms command excellent views of the harbour, the Abbey and St Mary's Church. Fresh Whitby fish, with up to 10 daily choices, and shellfish feature on the menu, as well as an extensive range of salads and over 20 home-made puddings.

Open 11.30-9 (11.30-6.30 Sun Nov-Mar) Closed: 5 Jan-6 Feb **Restaurant** L served all week 11.30-9 D served all week Av 3 course à la carte £25 Free House Crompton, Scoresby Bitter, Carlsberg-Tetley Tetley Bitter. 11

WIGGLESWORTH MAP 18 SD85

The Plough Inn

BD23 4RJ ☎ 01729 840243 01729 840638

e-mail: sue@ploughinn.info

dir: *From A65 take B6478 to Wigglesworth*

Dating back to 1720, the bar of this traditional country free house features oak beams and an open fire. There are fine views of the surrounding hills from the conservatory restaurant, where the pub's precarious position on the Yorkshire/Lancashire border is reflected in a culinary 'War of the Roses'. Yorkshire pudding with beef casserole challenges Lancashire hotpot and pickled red cabbage – the latest score is published beside the daily blackboard specials!

Open 11-3 6-11 Closed: 8-24 Jan & Mon Nov-Mar **Bar Meals** L served all week 12-2 D served all week 6.30-9 Av main course £9 **Restaurant** L served all week 12-2 D served all week 7-9 Av 3 course à la carte £21.50 Free House Carlsberg-Tetley Tetley Bitter, Black Sheep Best. 6 **Facilities** Garden Parking **Rooms** 9 bedrooms en suite S£54 D£84 (★★★ INN)

YORK MAP 16 SE65

Pick of the Pubs

Blue Bell

53 Fossgate YO1 9TF ☎ 01904 654904

e-mail: robsonhardie@aol.com

It's easy to do, but don't walk past the narrow frontage of York's smallest pub, which has been serving customers in the ancient heart of the city for 200 years. In 1903 it was given a typical Edwardian makeover, since when hardly anything has changed, and this includes the varnished wall and ceiling panelling, the two cast-iron tiled fireplaces, and the old settles. The layout is original too, with the taproom at the front and the snug down a long corridor at the rear, both with servery hatches. Quite fittingly, the whole interior is now Grade II-listed. The only slight drawback is that the pub's size leaves no room for a kitchen, so although sandwiches are available, don't go expecting anything more complicated. No fewer than six real ales are usually on tap, including rotating guests.

Open 11-11 **Bar Meals** L served All 11-6.30 Punch Taverns Deuchars IPA, Timothy Taylors Landlord, Adnams Bitter, Abbot Greene King. 10 **Facilities** Dogs allowed **Notes**

Lysander Arms 🍷

Manor Ln, Shipton Rd YO30 5TZ

☎ 01904 640845 📠 01904 624422

The Lysander Arms is a recently constructed pub built on the site of an old RAF airfield. The contemporary feel of the pub's interior includes a long, fully air-conditioned bar with modern furnishings, brick-built fireplace and large-screen TV. The lunch menu features a choice of ciabatta, melted bloomer and poppy bagel sandwiches; specialities such as blackened Cajun chicken with chargrilled peppers; and in the evening, beef from the chargrill, accompanied by thick chips.

Open 11–11 (Sat 11–12.30, Sun 12–10.30) **Bar Meals** L served Tue–Sun 12–2 (Sun 12–3) D served Tue–Sat 5.30–9 Av main course £7.50 **Restaurant** L served Tue–Sun 12–2 (Sun 12–3) D served Tue–Sat 5.30–9 Av 3 course à la carte £15 John Smiths Cask, Deuchars IPA. 🍷 18 **Facilities** Garden Dogs allowed Parking Play Area

YORKSHIRE, SOUTH

BRADFIELD — MAP 16 SK29

The Strines Inn

Bradfield Dale S6 6JE ☎ 0114 2851247

dir: *Off A57 toward Manchester*

A world away from nearby Sheffield, this popular Peak District free house nestles in breathtaking scenery opposite Strines Reservoir. Originally built for the Worrall family in 1275, most of the present building is 16th century; two of the three bars have open winter fires. Traditional home-made fare ranges from sandwiches, salads and daily fresh fish to substantial Yorkshire puddings with a choice of beef, pork or vegetarian fillings.

Open 10.30–3 5.30–11 (Mar–Sep & wknds all day) Closed: 25 Dec **Bar Meals** L served all week 12–2.30 D served all week 5.30–9 (wknds all day) Free House Marston's Pedigree, Kelham Island, Mansfield Cask, Bradfield Bitter & Old Speckled Hen. **Facilities** Garden Dogs allowed Parking Play Area

CADEBY — MAP 16 SE50

Pick of the Pubs

Cadeby Inn 🍷

Main St DN5 7SW ☎ 01709 864009

e-mail: cadebyinn@bpcmail.co.uk

Formerly a working farm before being converted into a pub, the Cadeby Inn is convenient for Conisbrough Castle, the Doncaster racecourse and the Earth Centre. The pub has recently added the Old Granary conference suite, an attractive venue with stone walls, mellow wood flooring and a rustic vaulted ceiling. John Smith's Cask and Black Sheep Bitter are mainstays at the bar, supported by Guinness, lagers and six wines served by the glass. The large front garden is enclosed by sandstone walls, with a patio area and a small back garden. Lunchtime brings an appealing range of sandwiches, as well as starters and light bites such as home-made soup or barbecued chicken wings. Larger appetites might consider butternut squash bake with sweet potato fries and vegetable jus; pork and leek sausages with cheddar mash and apple gravy; or blackened Cajun tuna with straw potatoes and sweet chilli sauce.

Open 11–11 **Bar Meals** L served all week 12–5 D served all week 6.30–9 Av main course £21 **Restaurant** L served all week 12–5 D served all week 6.30–9 Av 3 course à la carte £30 John Smiths Cask, Black Sheep Best Bitter, Guinness, Fosters. 🍷 6 **Facilities** Children's licence Garden Parking

DONCASTER — MAP 16 SE50

Waterfront Inn 🍷

Canal Ln, West Stockwith DN10 4ET ☎ 01427 891223

Built in the 1830s overlooking the Trent Canal basin and the canal towpath, the pub is now popular with walkers and visitors to the nearby marina. Real ales and good value food are the order of the day, including pasta with home-made ratatouille, broccoli and cheese bake, deep-fried scampi, half honey-roasted chicken, and home-made lasagne.

Open 11.30–11 **Bar Meals** L served all week 12–2 (Sun 12–3) D served all week 6.30–8.30 **Restaurant** L served all week 12–2 (Sun 12–3) D served all week 6.30–8.30 Enterprise Inns Scottish Courage John Smith Cask, Timothy Taylors, Greene King Old Speckled Hen, Deuchars IPA. 🍷 9 **Facilities** Garden Dogs allowed Parking Play Area

PENISTONE — MAP 16 SE20

Pick of the Pubs

Cubley Hall 🍷

Mortimer Rd, Cubley S36 9DF

☎ 01226 766086 📠 01226 767335

e-mail: cubley.hall@ukonline.co.uk

dir: *A628 towards Stalybridge, or A616 south of Penistone*

Over the centuries, Cubley Hall has seen service as everything from a gentleman's residence to a children's home. Despite those years of youthful battering, many original features such as mosaic floors, ornate plasterwork, oak panelling and stained glass survived, ready for the conversion in 1983 to a free house. Another seven years passed before the massive hewn-stone barn was converted into Cubley Hall's renowned restaurant, with its imaginative cuisine and all day Sunday carvery. There's also a simple bar menu, featuring such popular choices as chicken and ricotta pasta; bangers with cheddar and chive mash; vegetarian pizza with mountain goats' cheese; jumbo cod, chips and mushy peas; and fresh seasonal salads. Children have their own menu, and the best of local produce often finds its way into the blackboard specials.

CONTINUED

PENISTONE continued

Open 11–11 **Bar Meals** L served all week 12–9.30 D served all week 12–9.30 Av main course £8 **Restaurant** L served Sun 12–9.30 D served Wknds Av 3 course à la carte £16 Free House Carlsberg-Tetley Tetley Bitter, Burton Ale, Greene King Abbot Ale, Young's Special. 7 **Facilities** Garden Parking Play Area

The Fountain Inn

Wellthorne Ln, Ingbirchworth S36 7GJ

01226 763125 01226 761336

e-mail: enquiries@fountain-Ingbirchworth.co.uk

dir: *A629 to Huddersfield*

Parts of this former coaching inn date from the 17th century, and it is attractively located by Ingbirchworth Reservoir in the foothills of the southern Pennines. The interior is cosy and stylish, and the Rendezvous Suite is licensed for civil wedding ceremonies. The food is known for its quality based on fresh produce. Tuesday night is fish night with at least eight fish dishes. Quizzes, murder mystery, casino and races nights are a regular feature.

Open 11.45–11 **Bar Meals** L served all week 12–9.30 D served all week 12–9.30 (Sun 12–8) Av main course £9 **Restaurant** L served all week 12–9.30 D served all week 12–9.30 (Sun 12–8) Enterprise Inns Tetleys Cask, Theakstons Best, Black Sheep, John Smith Smooth. 8 **Facilities** Children's licence Garden Parking Play Area

SHEFFIELD MAP 16 SK38

Pick of the Pubs

The Fat Cat

23 Alma St S3 8SA 0114 249 4801 0114 249 4803

e-mail: info@thefatcat.co.uk

This reputedly haunted back-street pub was built in 1832, and is Grade II-listed. Beer-wise, it's hard to imagine anywhere better: there is a constantly changing list of guest beers from across the country, especially from micro-breweries. Traditional scrumpy and unusual bottled beers are also sold, while the Kelham Island Brewery, owned by the pub, accounts for at least four of the ten traditional draught real ales sold. The smart interior is very much that of a traditional, welcoming city pub; outside there's an attractive walled garden complete with Victorian-style lanterns, bench seating and shrubbery. Real fires in winter complete the cosy feel. Home-cooked food is offered at lunch and in the evening from a simple weekly menu that might feature steak pie with potatoes, peas and gravy; ploughman's lunch; and sausage and bacon casserole with rice. Look out for special events such as a beer and food evening.

Open 12–12 Closed: 25 Dec **Bar Meals** L served all week 12–2.30 D served Mon–Sat 6–7.30 Av main course £5 Free House Timothy Taylor Landlord, Kelham Island Bitter, Pale Rider, Pride of Sheffield. **Facilities** Garden Dogs allowed Parking **Notes**

Lions Lair

31 Burgess St S1 2HF 0114 263 4264 0114 263 4265

e-mail: info@lionslair.co.uk

dir: *On Burges Street next to John Lewis, between City Hall & Peace Gardens*

A modern café bar offering a friendly welcome from your hosts. It makes an intimate retreat, situated at the heart of the city with a small terrace outside. The menu is limited but there is a popular Sunday social where you're invited to come and chill out every Sunday and enjoy lunch, served from 1–5pm along with cheap cocktails.

Open 12–12 **Bar Meals** L served all week 12–3 D served all week 5–7 (Sun 12–5) Av main course £4.95 Punch Taverns Black Sheep, Tetley, Carlsberg, Redstripe. **Facilities** Garden

TOTLEY MAP 16 SK37

Pick of the Pubs

The Cricket NEW

Penny Ln, Totley Bents S17 3AZ 0114 236 5256

e-mail: enquiries@the-cricket.com

dir: *A621 from Sheffield 8m. Right onto Hillfoot Rd, 1st left onto Penny Ln*

The Cricket was originally a farmhouse, and started selling beer to navvies building the 5.6km Totley Tunnel on the railway line between Sheffield and Manchester. Today its south-facing garden overlooks Totley cricket pitch, while inside it successfully combines the old and new: the former is represented by the bar, with two large log fires, real ales and an extensive wine list, the latter by the smart dining area where you can enjoy traditional English or French food. The main menu offers roast guinea fowl with creamed savoy cabbage and smoky bacon; herb crust cod fillet with butterbean mash; beer-battered cod and chips; chicken, bacon and mushroom pie; and stilton, leek and walnut bake. A short early bird menu is available 6–7pm, Tuesday to Friday, and focuses on dishes like Cumberland sausage and mash with onion gravy, and penne pasta with goats' cheese, olives and cherry tomatoes. There's a particularly good choice on Sundays.

Open 12–3 5–11.30 (Sat–Sun 12–11.30) **Bar Meals** L served Tue–Sun 12–2.30 D served Tue–Sat 6–9.30 Av main course £10 **Restaurant** L served Sun 12–6 D served Tue–Sat 6–9.30 Av 3 course à la carte £22 Av 3 course fixed price £18 Black Sheep, Stonies. **Facilities** Children's licence Garden Dogs allowed Parking

YORKSHIRE, WEST

ADDINGHAM

MAP 19 SE04

Pick of the Pubs

The Fleece NEW

154 Main St LS29 0LY ☎ 01943 830491

dir: *Between Ilkley & Skipton*

This 17th-century coaching inn is popular with walkers, situated as it is at the intersection of several well-tramped footpaths. The stone-flagged interior boasts an enormous fireplace, wooden settles and a friendly bunch of locals. A pint of Black Sheep might be all you want, but if you feel peckish, be sure to consult the daily chalkboard. Much of the produce is local and organic, with beef and lamb coming from a nearby farm, allotment holders bringing surplus vegetables, and seasonal game delivered straight to the door. Simple flavoursome dishes are the speciality here. Favourites include meat and potato pie, and whole roast chicken, while fish is also a big draw. Try the likes of naturally smoked haddock and leek gratin; line-caught sea bass with celeriac fondant; or hand-dived king scallops with mint and pea purée.

Open 12–11 (Sun 12–10.30) **Bar Meals** L served all week 12–2.15 D served all week 6–9.15 (Sun & BH 12–8) Av main course £10 Punch Taverns Black Sheep, Copper Dragon, TImothy Taylor's Landlord, Tetleys. 25 **Facilities** Dogs allowed Parking

BRADFORD

MAP 19 SE13

New Beehive Inn

171 Westgate BD1 3AA ☎ 01274 721784 01274 735092

e-mail: newbeehiveinn@talk21.com

dir: *A606 into Bradford, A6161 200yds B6144, left after lights, pub on left.*

Classic Edwardian inn, dating from 1901 and retaining its period atmosphere with separate bars and gas lighting. Outside, with a complete change of mood, you can relax in the Mediterranean-style courtyard. The pub offers a good range of unusual real ales and a selection of over 100 malt whiskies, served alongside some simple bar snacks.

Open 12–11 (Sun 12–10.30) **Bar Meals** L served Mon–Sat 12–2 Av main course £5 Free House Timothy Taylor Landlord, Kelham Island Bitter, Hop Back Summer Lightning, Abbeydale Moonshine. **Facilities** Garden Parking

CLIFTON

MAP 16 SE12

The Black Horse Inn

HD6 4HJ ☎ 01484 713862 01484 400582

e-mail: mail@blackhorseclifton.co.uk

web: www.blackhorseclifton.co.uk

dir: *1m from Bridgehouse town centre. 0.5m from M62 junct 25*

The loom-wrecking Luddites used to meet at this 17th-century coaching inn, and in the 60s and 70s it was a regular haunt of those playing at the nearby Batley Variety Club. Stars like Roy Orbison, Showaddywaddy and Shirley Bassey stayed or drank here. The oak-beamed rooms with their open coal fires are just the place to sample the good, home-cooked food that's been served here for over half a century: fish dishes like Black Horse fish stew; and baked salmon and spinach in puff pastry are a particular speciality.

Open 11–12 **Bar Meals** L served all week 12–5.30 D served all week 5.30–9.30 (Sun 12–8.30) Av main course £13.50 **Restaurant** L served all week 12–2.30 D served all week 5.30–9.30 (Sun 12–8.30) Av 3 course à la carte £25 Enterprise Inns Black Sheep, Timothy Taylor Landlord, Old Speckled Hen,. 18 **Facilities** Garden Dogs allowed Parking

See advert on page 679

DEWSBURY

MAP 16 SE22

West Riding Licensed Refreshment Rooms

Dewsbury Railway Station, Wellington Rd WF13 1HF

☎ 01924 459193 01924 450404

e-mail: info@imissedthetrain.com

A converted Grade II listed railway station built in 1848 and located on the Trans-Pennine route between Leeds and Manchester. The pub supports northern micro-breweries and is linked to an Anglo-Dutch

CONTINUED

DEWSBURY continued

brewery in Dewsbury, providing guests with a regular choice of guest ales. A daily-changing menu offers such dishes as steak and kidney pie, stewed steak with horseradish dumplings, and sausage with bacon parcels and roast tomatoes.

Open 11–11 (Mon 12–11, Thu–Sat 11–12) Closed: 25 Dec **Bar Meals** L served Mon–Fri 12–3 D served Tue–Wed 6–9 Av main course £5 Free House Timothy Taylor Dark Mild & Landlord, Black Sheep Best, Anglo Dutch. 8 **Facilities** Garden Dogs allowed Parking **Notes**

HALIFAX MAP 19 SE02

The Rock Inn Hotel

Holywell Green HX4 9BS ☎ 01422 379721 01422 379110
e-mail: reservations@rockinnhotel.com
dir: *M62 junct 24, Blackley signs, left at x-rds, 0.5m on left*

Substantial modern extensions have transformed this attractive 17th-century wayside inn into a thriving hotel and conference venue in the scenic valley of Holywell Green. All-day dining in the brasserie-style conservatory is truly cosmopolitan; kick off with freshly prepared parsnip and apple soup or crispy duck and seaweed, followed by liver and bacon, Thai-style steamed halibut, chicken piri piri or vegetables jalfrezi.

Open 12 –11 **Bar Meals** L served all week 12–2.30 D served all week 5–9 Av main course £6 **Restaurant** L served all week 12–2.30 D served all week 5–9 Av 3 course fixed price £14.95 Free House Black Sheep, Taylor Landlord, John Smiths. **Facilities** Garden Dogs allowed Parking

Pick of the Pubs

Shibden Mill Inn ★★★★ INN

Shibden Mill Fold HX3 7UL
☎ 01422 365840 01422 362971
e-mail: shibdenmillinn@zoom.co.uk

This 17th-century free house nestles in a fold of the Shibden Valley overlooking Red Beck. It was once both a mill and a farm, and a sympathetic renovation has retained its original charm and character. The cosy, friendly bar with its oak beams and open fires, and the intimate candlelit restaurant, both bear witness to the inn's long history. Real ales, usually a choice of four, include a couple of regularly changing guest beers. The menus offer plenty of options, with starters including roast Shetland cod clam, and Lincolnshire pigeon faggot. Half a dozen fish dishes may feature grilled tuna steak niçoise; and red mullet and freshwater crayfish stew. Grills may offer lambs' liver or fillet of Yorkshire-reared beef. And traditionalists will welcome lamb casserole with roast vegetables, apple and mint dumplings; or cold Nidderdale ham hock with fried eggs, chips and green tomato chutney.

Open 12–2.30 5.30–11 **Bar Meals** L served Mon–Sat 12–2 D served Mon–Sat 6–9.30 (Sun 12–7.30) **Restaurant** L served all week 12–2 D served all week 6–9.30 (Sun 12–7.30) Av 2 course fixed price £9.95 Free House John Smiths, Theakston XB, Shibden Mill & 2 Guest Beers. 14 **Facilities** Garden Parking **Rooms** 11 bedrooms en suite S£75 D£90

HAWORTH MAP 19 SE03

The Old White Lion Hotel ★★ HL

Main St BD22 8DU ☎ 01535 642313 01535 646222
e-mail: enquiries@oldwhitelionhotel.com
dir: *A629 onto B6142, hotel 0.5m past Haworth Station*

This traditional 300-year-old coaching inn is set in the famous Brontë village of Haworth. In the charming bar the ceiling beams are held up by what look for all the world like pit props. From the carte in the candlelit restaurant choose smoked haddock rarebit; fillet of sea bass with roast feta and olives; or asparagus and wild mushroom crêpe.

Open 11–11 **Bar Meals** L served all week 11.30–2.30 D served all week 5.30–9.30 (Sat–Sun 12–9.30) Av main course £7 **Restaurant** L served Sun 12–2.30 D served all week 7–9.30 Av 3 course à la carte £21.65 Av 3 course fixed price £15 Free House Theakstons Best (Green Label), Carlsberg-Tetley Tetley Bitter, Scottish Courage John Smith's, Websters. **Facilities** Parking **Rooms** 14 bedrooms en suite S£54.60 D£76

HORBURY MAP 16 SE21

The Quarry Inn

70 Quarry Hill WF4 5NF ☎ 01924 272523
dir: *On A642 2.5m from Wakefield*

In the hollow of a disused quarry, this creeper-clad pub is built with stone actually quarried here, as are the bar fronts. Just beyond the main road outside are the River Calder and the Calder and Hebble Navigation. A good range of simple but appetising dishes in the bar and restaurant includes cottage pie, steaks, gammon, fish and chips, liver and onions, and Yorkshire puddings with various fillings.

Open 12–11 **Bar Meals** L served all week 12–2 Av main course £3.99 **Restaurant** L served all week 12–2 Av 3 course fixed price £5 Marstons Marston's Pedigree, Mansfield Smooth. **Facilities** Parking **Notes**

The Three Acres Inn

In the more than 30 years that Neil Truelove and Brian Orme have owned this award-winning country inn, it has long been locally famous for good quality food and a welcoming atmosphere. In a sense, perhaps, nothing changes for it was once a favourite with drovers bringing their sheep to market from their Pennine pastures.

The spacious interior is lavishly traditional (or perhaps traditionally lavish) in style – all rich reds, greens and yellows, exposed beams and large fireplaces. On summer evenings, sit out on the Champagne Bar's decked area, or in the bar, to enjoy a pint of Timothy Taylor Landlord, or one of the selection of wines by the glass. The food, available in both the bar and restaurant, is a successful fusion of traditional English and international influences, including plenty of fresh fish prepared as you watch. Dishes include hot seafood platter with aioli and 'proper' chips; Arbroath smokie fishcake on mixed greens with poached egg, hollandaise and horseradish; and grilled whole fresh lobster with thermidor sauce. Running an eye down a winter menu would reveal starters such as Breton fish soup with rouille, and gruyère croûtons; crispy Peking duck with pancakes, hoi sin and shredded greens; and Serrano ham with chorizo, Manchego cheese, and fig and port relish. Typical main dishes would include steamed game suet pudding; slow-cooked chicken curry; roast half of Lunesdale duck; and steak, kidney, mushroom and Black Sheep ale pie. The Saturday lunch menu offers some fine sounding sandwiches, such as Rannoch-smoked chicken with dry-cured bacon, roast vine tomato, rocket and poached free range egg. Ten of the twenty tastefully decorated bedrooms are in 'The Cottages', set in their own gardens. Within the pub is The Grocer delicatessen, where you can buy handpicked speciality foods and gifts, including ready-made meals based on Three Acres recipes.

MAP 19 SE08
HD8 4LR
☎ 01484 602606
01484 608411
e-mail: 3acres@globalnet.co.uk
dir: *A629 then B6116, left for village*

Open 12-3 7-11
Closed: 25-26 & 31 Dec, 1 Jan
Bar Meals L served all week 12-2 D served all week 7-9.45
Restaurant L served Sun-Fri 12-2 D served all week 7-9.45
Av 3 course à la carte £35
Av 3 course fixed price £21.95
Free House
Timothy Taylor Landlord, Black Sheep, Tetley Smooth, Tetley Bitter. 16
Facilities Garden Parking
Rooms 20 bedrooms en suite S£65 D£90 (★★★★ RR)

KIRKBURTON MAP 16 SE11

The Woodman Inn ★★★★ INN

Thunderbridge HD8 0PX

01484 605778 01484 604110

e-mail: thewoodman@connectfree.co.uk

dir: *5m S of Huddersfield, off A629*

Lovely old stone-built inn set in the wooded hamlet of Thunderbridge. One menu is offered throughout, but customers can eat in the bar downstairs or the more sophisticated ambience of the restaurant upstairs. Dishes include daily fresh fish (grilled brill with chilli), and the likes of wild boar and apple sausages. Wine is selected by the owners, whose family has been in the licensed trade since 1817. Accommodation is provided in adjacent converted weavers' cottages.

Open 12–11 (Fri–Sat 12.30–11) **Bar Meals** L served all week 12–6.30 D served all week 6.30–9 (Sun 12–8) Av main course £12 **Restaurant** L served all week 12–2 D served all week 6.30–9 (Sun 12–8) Free House Taylors Best Bitter, Tetleys Bitter. 13 **Facilities** Parking **Rooms** 12 bedrooms en suite S£45 D£55

LEDSHAM MAP 16 SE42

The Chequers Inn NEW

Claypit Ln LS25 5LP 01977 683135 01977 680791

e-mail: cjwrath@btconnect.com

dir: *Between A1 & A656 above Castleford*

Quaint creeper-clad inn located in an old estate village, with low beams, wooden settles, and a history traceable to 1540. Unusually the pub has been closed on Sundays ever since the lady of the manor was offended by the over-indulgence of her farm workers more than 160 years ago. Still owned by the same family, it serves a wonderful selection of real ales from Monday to Saturday, along with short menus of interesting choices that cannot fail to please.

Open 11–11 **Bar Meals** L served Mon–Sat 12–9.15 D served Mon–Sat 12–9.15 **Restaurant** D served Mon–Sat 7–9.15 Free House Theakston, John Smiths, Timothy Taylor Landlord, Brown Cow. **Facilities** Garden Dogs allowed Parking

LEEDS MAP 19 SE23

Whitelocks

Turks Head Yard, Briggate LS1 6HB

0113 245 3950 0113 242 3368

dir: *Next to Marks & Spencer in Briggate*

First licensed in 1715 as the Turks Head, this is Leeds' oldest pub. Classic features include a long bar with polychrome tiles, stained-glass windows and advertising mirrors, and there's a Dickensian-style bar at the end of the yard. New owners for 2007 planning a different approach to food and menus. Reports please.

Open 11–11 (Sun 12–10.30) **Bar Meals** L served all week 12–7 D served all week (Sun 12–6) Av main course £6 **Restaurant** L served all week 12–7 (Sun 4) D served all week Scottish Courage Theakston Best, Old Peculier & John Smiths, Deuchars, Guest Ales. 13 **Facilities** Garden

LINTHWAITE MAP 16 SE11

The Sair Inn NEW

Hoyle Ing HD7 5SG 01484 842370

The Sair belongs in a class of its own, because it offers no modern comforts and no food. It is just four rooms warmed by Yorkshire ranges, serving great ales brewed by Ron Crabtree who's been working on them for over 25 years and is still striving for perfection. Ron won't see his sixties again, but he says he'll keep going until he's created a unique English pub. Wonderful.

Free House **Notes**

LINTON MAP 16 SE34

The Windmill Inn

Main St LS22 4HT 01937 582209 01937 587518

dir: *From A1 exit at Tadcaster/Otley junction, follow Otley signs. In Collingham follow Linton signs*

A coaching inn since the 18th century, the building actually dates back to the 14th century, and originally housed the owner of the long-disappeared windmill. Stone walls, antique settles, log fires, oak beams and lots of brass set the scene in which to enjoy good bar food prepared by enthusiastic licensees. Expect the likes of chicken breast on mustard mash with onion jus, sea bass on pepper mash with tomato and basil sauce, baked salmon on Italian risotto, or king prawns in lime and chilli butter. While you're there, ask to take a look at the local history scrapbook.

Open 11.30–3 5–11 (Sat–Sun all day) **Bar Meals** L served all week 12–2 D served Mon–Sat 5.30–9 (Sun 12–6.30) **Restaurant** L served all week 12–2 D served Mon–Sat 5.30–9 (Sun 12–6.30) Scottish Courage Scottish Courage John Smith's & Theakston Best, Daleside, Greene King Ruddles County. 12 **Facilities** Garden Dogs allowed Parking

MARSDEN MAP 16 SE01

The Olive Branch NEW ★★★★ RR

Manchester Rd HD7 6LU 01484 844487

e-mail: mail@olivebranch.uk.com

dir: *On A62 between Marsden & Slaithwaite*

The landlord of this old moorland inn on the pack-horse route has a one great passion in life – to cook. The brasserie-style menus change daily to reflect his seasonal inspirations and available ingredients. Parfait of foie gras and chicken livers on toasted babky bread; roast monkfish tail with curried mussels; and rib-eye steak with snail, parsley

CONTINUED

MARSDEN continued

and garlic butter set the trend. Local hand-pulled beers are always available.

Open 12–2 6.30–9.30 (Closed Mon–Tue & Sat lunch times) Closed: 1st 2 wks Jan **Restaurant** L served Wed–Fri & Sun 12–2 D served all week 6.30–9.30 (Sun 1–8.30) Av 3 course à la carte £30 Av 3 course fixed price £18.95 Free House Dogcross Bitter, Greenfield Red Ale, Boddingtons, Becks Vier & Stella Artois. 16 **Facilities** Garden Parking **Rooms** 3 bedrooms en suite S£55 D£70

MYTHOLMROYD MAP 19 SE02

Shoulder of Mutton

New Rd HX7 5DZ ☎ 01422 883165

dir: *A646 Halifax to Todmorden, in Mytholmroyd on B6138, opposite rail station*

Award-winning Pennines' pub situated by a trout stream in the village where Poet Laureate Ted Hughes was born. Popular with walkers, cyclists, families and visitors to the area, the pub's reputation for real ales and hearty fare using locally sourced ingredients remains intact after 30 years of ownership. The menu ranges from snacks and sandwiches to vegetarian quiche; filled giant Yorkshire pudding; Cumberland sausages; and beef in ale.

Open 11.30–3 7–11 (Sat 11.30–11, Sun 12–10.30) **Bar Meals** L served Wed–Mon 11.3–2 D served Wed–Mon 7–8.15 (Sun 12–10.30) Av main course £4 **Restaurant** L served Wed–Mon 11.30–2 D served Wed–Mon 7–8.15 Av 1 course fixed price £3.99 Enterprise Inns Black Sheep, Copper Dragon, Greene King IPA, Taylor Landlord. 10 **Facilities** Garden Dogs allowed Parking Play Area **Notes**

NEWALL MAP 19 SE14

The Spite Inn

LS21 2EY ☎ 01943 463063

'There's nowt but malice and spite at these pubs', said a local who one day did the unthinkable – drank in both village hostelries, renowned for their feuding landlords. The Traveller's Rest, which became The Malice, is long closed, but the Roebuck has survived as The Spite. Salmon mornay, haddock, scampi, steak and ale pie, ostrich fillet and speciality sausages are likely to be on offer.

Open 12–3 6–11 (Thu–Sat 12–11, Sun 12–10.30) **Bar Meals** L served all week 12–2 (Sun 12–5) D served Tue–Thu 6–8.30 (Fri–Sat 6–9 6–9) Av main course £7.50 **Restaurant** L served all week 11.30–2 (Sun 12–5) D served Tue–Thu 6–8.30 (Sat 6–9) Unique Pub Co John Smiths Smooth, Tetleys, Copper Dragon, plus Guest ales. 10 **Facilities** Garden Dogs allowed Parking

RIPPONDEN MAP 16 SE01

Old Bridge Inn

Priest Ln HX6 4DF ☎ 01422 822595

dir: *5m from Halifax in village centre by church*

An award-winning pub prettily situated on the banks of the River Ryburn and set in a lovely Pennine conservation village. It boasts a fine cruck frame, wattle and daub, and remnants of an old bread oven. The imaginative menu offers such appetising dishes as shoulder of lamb slow roasted with red wine; meat and potato pie with mushy peas or pickled red cabbage; and chargrilled Mediterranean vegetable wraps. Impressive wine list and cosy real fires in winter.

Open 12–3 5.30–11 **Bar Meals** L served Mon–Sun 12–2 D served Mon–Fri 6.30–9.30 Free House Timothy Taylor Landlord, Golden Best, & Best Bitter, Black Sheep Best. 12 **Facilities** Garden Parking

SHELLEY MAP 16 SE21

Pick of the Pubs

The Three Acres Inn

HD8 8LR ☎ 01484 602606 01484 608411

e-mail: 3acres@globalnet.co.uk

dir: *A629 then B6116, left for village*

See Pick of the Pubs on page 680

SOWERBY MAP 16 SE02

Pick of the Pubs

The Travellers Rest

Steep Ln HX6 1PE ☎ 01422 832124 01422 831365

See Pick of the Pubs on opposite page

The Travellers Rest

The Travellers Rest is not your average pub restaurant. Stone built in 1730 and fully renovated in 2001 by Caroline Lumley, it sits high on a steep hillside with glorious views, a dining terrace, duck pond, huge car park and helipad.

A glass of champagne is as appropriate as a pint of Timothy Taylor in the cosy stone-flagged bar, where fresh flowers add glamour and the pub's dogs, Simba and Ruby, stretch out by the open fire. In the restaurant, beams, animal print sofas, more warmth from a wood-burning stove, and exposed stonework continue the emphasis on comfort and relaxation, with pine and mahogany tables set with giant wine glasses, candles and crisp linen. Dishes cooked to order from local produce are rooted in Yorkshire tradition yet refined with French flair, yielding an immaculate and happy mix of classic and contemporary cooking. Bar meals start with sandwiches on muffins or granary rolls, including a special chip buttie with cherry tomatoes, rocket and aïoli; and continue with plates high in comfort factor: corned beef hash with pickled red cabbage and mashed swede; chicken, mushroom and tarragon pie; fish and chips with pea purée; and sirloin steak on fried onion mash. Sample blackboard specials include a seafood medley (red mullet, salmon, mussels, lemon sole and crevettes); fillet steak with béarnaise and chips; tempura scampi over Caesar salad with white anchovies; and baked field mushrooms with melted goats' cheese. In the restaurant you'll find starters like pan-seared breast of wood pigeon with spiced apple, cranberry and red cabbage with a port reduction; and main courses such as slow-cooked lamb shank with bubble and squeak and gravy made with roasting juices and redcurrant jelly. Leave space for a pud – syrup sponge with custard, perhaps, or apple and sultana crumble.

MAP 16 SE02
Steep Ln HX6 1PE
☎ 01422 832124
Fax 01422 831365

Open 5-late (Sat 12–3, 5.30-late, Sun 12-late)
Bar Meals L served Sat–Sun 12–2.30 (Sun 12–3.30) D served Wed–Sun 5–9.30 (Sat 5–10, Sun 5.30–8.30) Av main course £9.95
Restaurant L served Sat–Sun 12–2.30 (Sun 12–3.30) D served Wed–Sun 5–9.30 (Sat 5–10, Sun 5.30–8.30) Av 3 course à la carte £28
Timothy Taylor Landlord, Timothy Taylor Best Bitter. 8
Facilities Garden Dogs allowed Parking

SOWERBY BRIDGE — MAP 16 SE02

Pick of the Pubs

The Millbank

HX6 3DY ☎ 01422 825588

e-mail: eat@themillbank.com

dir: *A58 Sowerby Bridge to Ripponden, right at Triangle*

A contemporary dining pub that still retains the function and traditional feel of the village free house it's always been, The Millbank stands in the Pennine conservation village of Mill Bank, home since 1971 to writer and poet, Glyn Hughes. Go into the churchyard and read one of his sonnets, The Rock Rose, engraved on a slate slab in the wall. Back in the pub, head for the cosy stone-flagged Tap Room for a real ale, or the main wooden-floored drinking area for more of a wine bar feel and stunning views of the gardens and valley. The dining room chairs are recycled mill and chapel seats, complete with prayer-book racks. The main menu has a modern, continental feel; you could start with sautéed foie gras with caramelized pear, duck leg and lentil stew, then move on to roast Goosnargh duck breast with cottage pie of the leg and orange sauce.

Open 12-3 5.30-11 (Sun 12-10.30) Closed: 1st 2 wks Oct & 1st wk Jan **Bar Meals** L served Tue-Sun 12-2.30 D served all week 6-9.30 (Fri-Sat 6-10 Sun 12-4.30, 6-8) Av main course £11.95 **Restaurant** L served Tue-Sun 12-2.30 D served Mon-Sun 6-9.30 (Fri-Sat 6-10, Sun 12-4.30, 6-8) Av 3 course à la carte £24 Av 2 course fixed price £11.95 Free House Timothy Taylor Landlord, Tetley Bitter, Lowenbrau, Erdinger & Carlsberg. 20 **Facilities** Garden

THORNTON — MAP 19 SE03

Pick of the Pubs

Ring O'Bells Country Pub & Restaurant

212 Hilltop Rd BD13 3QL

☎ 01274 832296 01274 831707

e-mail: enquiries@theringobells.com

dir: *A644. 4.5m follow Denholme signs, onto Well Head Rd into Hilltop Rd.*

See Pick of the Pubs on opposite page

WAKEFIELD — MAP 16 SE32

Pick of the Pubs

Kaye Arms Inn & Brasserie

29 Wakefield Rd, Grange Moor WF4 4BG

☎ 01924 848385 01924 848977

e-mail: kayearms@hotmail.co.uk

dir: *On A642 between Huddersfield & Wakefield*

This family-run dining pub stands alone on the Huddersfield to Wakefield road. Its bar menu offers the likes of cold rare roast beef with celeriac remoulade; braised veal and mushroom pasta; and honey-baked ham sandwiches. Over in the brasserie, try crab tart or chicken liver parfait; then confit of duck leg with French-style peas and dauphinoise potatoes; smoked haddock and poached egg with beetroot and spinach; or mature cheddar cheese soufflé with roquefort salad. Specials might take in braised shin beef or grilled fillet of John Dory with Greek salad. Raspberry soufflé is the house speciality, though bread and butter pudding with whisky and honey cream; and almond tart with vanilla crème anglaise are equally appealing. An extensive wine list comprehensively roams the world. The popular National Coal Mining Museum is close by.

Open 11.30-3 7-11 Closed: 25 Dec-2 Jan **Bar Meals** L served Tue-Sun 12-2 D served 7.15-9.30 (Sat 6.30-10) Av main course £7 **Restaurant** L served Tue-Sun 12-2 D served Tue-Sun 7.15-9.30 (Sat 6.30-10) Av 3 course à la carte £25 Free House Scottish Courage John Smiths, Theakstons Best, Guinness. 15 **Facilities** Parking

WIDDOP — MAP 18 SD93

Pack Horse Inn

HX7 7AT ☎ 01422 842803 01422 842803

dir: *Off A646 & A6033*

The Pack Horse is a converted Laithe farmhouse dating from the 1600s, complete with welcoming open fires. A beautiful location just 300 yards from the Pennine Way makes it popular with walkers, but equally attractive are the home-cooked meals, good range of real ales and fabulous choice of 130 single malt whiskies. Please note that from October to Easter the pub is only open in the evening.

Open 12-3 7-11 **Bar Meals** L served Tue-Sun (Summer only) 12-2 D served Tue-Sun 7-10 Av main course £7.95 Free House Thwaites, Theakston XB, Morland Old Speckled Hen, Black Sheep Bitter. 8 **Facilities** Dogs allowed Parking

Ring O'Bells Country Pub & Restaurant

On a clear day the views from the Ring O'Bells stretch across 20 to 30 miles of rugged Pennine moorland. The pub stands at the western end of the village of Thornton, birthplace of the Brontë sisters and where their father was curate.

Later, of course, Anne, Charlotte and Emily became inextricably associated with Haworth, which is a few miles away towards Keighley. The pub was converted from a Wesleyan chapel, so perhaps the ghost rumoured to haunt it is a former priest. The old-world bar serves Black Sheep cask-conditioned ale and a decent selection of malt whiskies, speciality liqueurs and wines by the glass. Local artists hang their work for sale in the airy Brontë Restaurant, originally two mill workers' cottages. The conservatory, which overlooks the valley and runs the whole length of the restaurant, is a popular place for a drink before or after dinner. Well regarded locally for 'quality, traditional and innovative dishes', the Ring O'Bells has a definite flair for the unusual, offering starters like coarse mixed game terrine with pickled pears; roast belly pork on haggis mash with red wine sauce; and tandoori-marinated chicken strips and Thai lamb samosa with chilli dressing and minted yogurt. And for main courses it can offer poached prime fresh haddock gratinated with prawn mornay sauce; roast breast of pheasant with mustard stuffing wrapped in bacon on beer-braised cabbage and apple; and medallions of fillet steak with corned-beef hash topped with fried egg. More traditional dishes include pastas, sausages, pies (with a choice of herb suet, shortcrust or puff pastry lid) and vegetarian dishes of the day. Desserts, made to order, range from crème brûlée with shortbread biscuits to sticky toffee Guinness cake with Tia Maria ice cream.

🍷
MAP 19 SE03
212 Hilltop Rd BD13 3QL
☎ 01274 832296
📠 01274 831707
e-mail:
enquiries@theringobells.com
dir: *4.5m follow Denholme signs, onto Well Head Rd into Hilltop Rd.*

Open 11.30–3.30 5.30–11 (Sun 12–4.30, 6.15–10.30) Closed: 25 Dec
Bar Meals L served all week 12–2 D served all week 5.30–9.30 (Sat–Sun 6.15–8.45) Av main course £10.95
Restaurant L served all week 12–2 D served all week 7–9.30 (Sun 6.15–8.45) Av 3 course à la carte £19.95
Free House
Scottish Courage John Smiths & Courage Directors, & Black Sheep Ale. 🍷 10
Facilities Parking

England

CHANNEL ISLANDS

GUERNSEY

CASTEL MAP 24

Pick of the Pubs

Fleur du Jardin NEW

Kings Mills GY5 7JT ☎ 01481 257996 📠 01481 256834

e-mail: info@fleurdujardin.com

dir: *2.5m from town centre*

Kings Mill is a quiet, picturesque village, home to some of Guernsey's finest farmhouses, as well as this friendly 15th-century hotel, renowned for its hospitality and homely atmosphere. All the charm of the old building has been kept intact, with granite walls, solid wood beams and real fireplaces in abundance. Those taller than the average Tudor might have to stoop in the bar, but that needn't prevent enjoyment of a pint of Guernsey Special. Imaginative use of local produce is what sets the award-winning restaurant apart. Start with timbale of Guernsey crab and guacamole; or pan-seared local scallops with sweet pepper salsa. Move on to game, mushroom and juniper berry pudding; local veal sausages with red onion mash; or linguini tossed with asparagus and rocket.

Open 12–12.45 **Bar Meals** L served all week 12–2 D served all week 6–9 Av main course £10.50 **Restaurant** L served all week 12–2 D served all week 6–9 Av 3 course à la carte £19 Sunbeam, Guernsey Special, London Pride. **Facilities** Children's licence Garden Dogs allowed Parking

Hotel Hougue du Pommier ★★ HL 🍷

Hougue du Pommier Rd GY5 7FQ

☎ 01481 256531 📠 01481 256260

e-mail: hotel@houguedupommier.guernsey.net

Old Guernsey farmhouse with the only feu du bois (literally 'cooking on the fire') in the Channel Islands. Fish, steaks, chicken and vegetarian dishes are offered along with a selection of bar meals. Play 'get the hook on the nose of the large black bull', again, the only one left in Guernsey. The 10-acre gardens have a swimming pool, barbecue and medieval area, where banquets are held the first Saturday of the month.

Open 10.30–11.45 **Bar Meals** L served all week 12–2.15 D served all week 6.30–9 **Restaurant** L served Sun 12–2.30 D served all week 6.30–9 Av 3 course à la carte £25 Av 5 course fixed price £21.95 John Smith's, Extra Smooth, Guernsey Best Bitter. 🍷 8 **Facilities** Children's licence Garden Dogs allowed Parking **Rooms** 43 bedrooms en suite

JERSEY

GOREY MAP 24

Castle Green Gastropub 🍷

La Route de la Cote JE3 6DR

☎ 01534 840218 📠 01534 840229

e-mail: enquiries@jerseypottery.com

dir: *Opposite main entrance of Gorey Castle*

A superbly located pub overlooking Gorey harbour and, in turn, overlooked by dramatic Mont Orgueil Castle. The views from the wooden sun terrace are breathtaking. An imaginative menu offers pan-Pacific-style dishes like Moroccan spiced lamb shoulder; Thai chicken burger; sushi and sashimi plate with pickled ginger and wasabi; along with fresh fillets of the day's catch , and summer seafood platter.

Open 11–11 (Open 7 days Jun–Sep) Closed: 2 weeks early Jan **Bar Meals** L served all week 12–2.30 D served all week 6–9 Winter no dinner Sun & Mon evening **Restaurant** L served all week 12–2.30 D served all week 6–9 Directors, John Smith Extra Smooth. 🍷 8 **Facilities** Parking

ST AUBIN MAP 24

Old Court House Inn

St Aubin's Harbour JE3 8AB

☎ 01534 746433 📠 01534 745103

e-mail: ochstaubins@jerseymail.co.uk

Dating from 1450, the original Courthouse at the rear of the property was first restored in 1611. Beneath the front part are enormous cellars where privateers stored their plunder alongside legitimate cargoes. Three bars offer food, and there are two restaurants, the Granite, and the Mizzen, with terrific views over the harbour, plus the courtyard, a real suntrap and ideal for alfresco eating. There's lots of locally caught fish on the menus of course. The wine list incorporates a worthy Director's Bin.

Open 11–11.30 **Bar Meals** L served Mon–Sun 12.30–2.15 D served Mon–Sun 7.30–10 **Restaurant** L served all week 12.30–2.30 D served all week 7.30–10 Free House Directors, Theakstons, John Smith, Jersey Brewery.

ST BRELADE MAP 24

La Pulente Hotel 🍷

La Route de la Pulente JE3 8HG

☎ 01534 744487 📠 01534 498846

dir: *West side of the Island, 5m from St Helier*

Amazing sea views, open fires on cold winter days and an inviting atmosphere are promised at this welcoming pub. The artistic bar and rustic restaurant are complemented in summer by a balcony and terrace, where freshly-caught fish can be enjoyed along with choices from the specials menu. Thai vegetable curry, pan-fried chicken supreme, home-made steak and ale pie, lobster and prawn salad, and braised lamb shank are typical.

Open 11–11 **Bar Meals** L served all week 12–2.15 (Sun 12–2.45) D served Mon–Sat 6–9 Av main course £7.50 **Restaurant** L served all week 12–2.15 (Sun 12–2.45) D served Mon–Sat 6–9 Av 3 course à la carte £15 Randalls Brewery Bass Bitter, Theakstons Best, Breda. 🍷 11 **Facilities** Parking

ST MARTIN MAP 24

Royal Hotel 🍷

La Grande Route de Faldouet JE3 6UG

☎ 01534 856289 📠 01534 857298

e-mail: johnbarker@jerseymail.co.uk

dir: *2m from Five Oaks rdbt towards St Martyn. Pub on right next to St Martin's Church*

A friendly atmosphere, value for money, and great food and drink are the hallmarks of this friendly local in the heart of St Martin. Roaring log fires welcome winter visitors, and there's a sunny beer garden to relax in during the summer months. Among the traditional home-made favourites are steak and ale pie, fresh grilled trout, monkfish and prawn Thai curry, and vegetarian lasagne. Ploughman's lunches, filled jacket potatoes, grills and children's choices are also on offer.

Open 9.30 –11.30 (Sun 11–11.30) **Bar Meals** L served all week 12–2.15 D served Mon–Sat 6–8.30 (Sun 12–2.30 Winter, 6–8.30 Summer) Av main course £8 **Restaurant** L served all week 12–2.15 D served Mon–Sat 6–8.30 Av 3 course à la carte £15 John Smiths Smooth, Theakstons, Guinness. 🍷 9 **Facilities** Garden Parking Play Area

ISLE OF MAN

PEEL MAP 24 SC28

The Creek Inn 🍷

Station Place IM5 1AT ☎ 01624 842216 📠 01624 843359

e-mail: jeanmcaleer@manx.net

dir: *Situated on the quayside opposite the House of Mannanan Museum overlooking Peel Castle and the Harbour*

Ideal for walkers, wildlife lovers and yachting enthusiasts, this family-run free house overlooks the harbour at Peel. Expect live music on Friday and Saturday nights, and a good selection of beers including locally brewed Okells ales. Fish and seafood dominate the menu, with the following available on any given day: Manx kippers, crab, lobster, seafood lasagne, salmon and broccoli bake, and king prawn thermidore.

Open 10–12 (Fri–Sat 10–1) **Bar Meals** L served all week 10–9.30 D served all week Av main course £6.95 **Restaurant** 10 Free House Okells Bitter, Okells Seasonal, Bushy's Bitter, 4 Guest Ales. 🍷 9 **Facilities** Children's licence Garden Parking

PORT ERIN MAP 24 SC26

Falcon's Nest Hotel ★★ HL

The Promenade, Station Rd IM9 6AF

☎ 01624 834077 📠 01624 835370

e-mail: falconsnest@enterprise.net

A popular hotel overlooking a beautiful, sheltered harbour and beach. In 1865 Gladstone, then prime minister, was responsible while staying here with his son for what he called 'an amusing incident' involving a teapot. The lounge and saloon bars serve local beers, over 150 whiskies, snacks and meals, although there is also a restaurant with carvery option. Fish include local crab, prawns, sea bass, lobster and local scallops known as queenies.

Open 10.30–12 **Bar Meals** L served all week 12–2 D served all week 6–9 Av main course £8 **Restaurant** L served all week 12–2 D served all week 6–9 Av 3 course à la carte £15.95 Free House Manx Guest Ale, Guinness, Carling & John Smith. **Facilities** Children's licence Dogs allowed Parking **Rooms** 35 bedrooms en suite S£35 D£60

Scotland

Tobermory, Isle of Mull

Scotland

CITY OF ABERDEEN

ABERDEEN MAP 23 NJ90

Old Blackfriars 🍷

52 Castle St AB11 5BB ☎ 01224 581922 📠 01224 582153

Stunning stained glass and a warm, welcoming atmosphere are features of this traditional city centre pub, situated in Aberdeen's historic Castlegate. It is built on the site of property owned by Blackfriars Dominican monks, hence the name. The menu runs from sandwiches and filled potatoes through to hearty dishes such as bangers and mash; chicken tikka masala; and beef au poivre. Finish with sticky toffee pudding or pancakes in maple syrup.

Open 11–12 (Sun 12.30–11, Fri–Sat 10–1am) Closed: 25 Dec **Bar Meals** L served all week 12–8.45 D served all week (Fri–Sat 12–7.45, Sun 12.30–8.45) Belhaven Abbot Ale, Deuchars IPA, Caledonian 80/-, Inveralmond. 🍷 12 **Facilities** Children's licence

ABERDEENSHIRE

BALMEDIE MAP 23 NJ91

The Cock & Bull Bar & Restaurant 🍷

Ellon Rd, Blairton AB23 8XY

☎ 01358 743249 📠 01358 742466

e-mail: info@thecockandbull.co.uk

dir: *A90 between Balmedie junct & Foveran*

What was once a coaching inn has been developed into a cosy gastro-pub. The bar area, warmed by a cast-iron range, has big sofas and a gallimaufry of hanging junk, from a ship's lifebelt to a trombone. The menu ranges from bar dishes of fish and chips, and cheese and bacon burger to restaurant fare like loin of monkfish wrapped in Parma ham with tarragon and chilli couscous and roasted red pepper reduction.

Open 10–1am (Sun 12–9) **Bar Meals** L served all week 12–5.30 D served 5.30–9 (Sun 12–7) Av main course £10 **Restaurant** L served all week 12–5.30 D served Mon–Sat 5.30–9 (Sun 12–7) Av 3 course à la carte £28 Free House Directors Ale, Guinness, & Guest Ale. 🍷 7 **Facilities** Children's licence Garden Parking Play Area

MARYCULTER MAP 23 NO89

Old Mill Inn

South Deeside Rd AB12 5FX

☎ 01224 733212 📠 01224 732884

e-mail: Info@oldmillinn.co.uk

dir: *5m W of Aberdeen on B9077*

This delightful family-run country inn stands on the edge of the River Dee, just over five miles from Aberdeen city centre. A former mill house, the 18th-century granite building has been tastefully modernised to include a restaurant where the finest Scottish ingredients feature on the menu: dishes like venison stovies, peppered carpaccio of beef, cullen skink, and chicken and venison terrine are typical.

Open 11–11 **Bar Meals** L served all week 12–2 D served all week 5.30–9.30 **Restaurant** L served all week 12–2 D served all week 5.30–9.30 Free House Interbrew Bass, Caledonian Deuchers IPA, Timothy Taylor, Landlord. **Facilities** Garden Parking **Rooms** 7 bedrooms en suite S£259 D£269 (★★★ SH)

NETHERLEY MAP 23 NO89

Pick of the Pubs

The Lairhillock Inn 🍷

AB39 3QS ☎ 01569 730001 📠 01569 731175

e-mail: lairhillock@breathemail.net

dir: *From Aberdeen take A90. Right at Durris turn.*

This award-winning 200-year-old former coaching inn stands in beautiful rural Deeside, only 15 minutes drive from Aberdeen. Real ales in the bar and real fires in the lounge keep out the winter chill, as do the bar lunches and suppers served daily. Dishes are robust and use fresh, quality, local produce. A typical meal from the pub menu includes traditional cullen skink, followed by grilled venison escalopes with a wild mushroom, red wine and juniper sauce. There is an impressive children's menu which offers a free ice cream to those who finish their main course! For a more formal dining option head for the atmospheric Crynoch restaurant where the menu might feature quail, roasted red pepper and pesto terrine, followed by corn fed chicken breast stuffed with a cep mushroom and chive mousse and served with a white burgundy sauce. Finish with crème brûlée or sticky toffee pudding.

Open 11–2 5–11 (Fri 11–2 5–12, Sat 11–12, Sun 11–11) Closed: 25–26 Dec, 1–2 Jan **Bar Meals** L served all week 12–2 D served all week 6–9.30 (Fri–Sat 6–10, Sun 5.30–9) Av main course £9.50 **Restaurant** L served Sun 12–1.30 D served Wed–Mon 7–9.30 Av 2 course fixed price £19.95 Free House Timothy Taylor Landlord, Courage Directors, Cairngorm, Tradewinds. 🍷 7 **Facilities** Garden Dogs allowed Parking

Crinan Hotel

The Crinan Hotel dates back some 200 years and has been run by owners Nick and Frances Ryan for over 36 years, making it a very long-standing place of welcome at the heart of community life in this tiny fishing village.

From its location at the northern end of the Crinan Canal, it enjoys fabulous views across the sound of Jura to the islands of Mull and Scarba. You can eat in the ground floor Panther Arms and Mainbrace Bar or in the Westward restaurant with its views over Loch Crinan to Jura, Scarba and the mountains of Mull. Whatever you choose, you can be sure of the freshest seafood – landed daily just 50 metres from the hotel! Typical choices from the Mainbrace menu include Loch Fyne princess clams with organic salad leaves, beurre blanc and French fries; and authentic Hungarian goulash with fresh bread. In the Westward restaurant you could enjoy crab ravioli with roast courgettes and shellfish cream, followed by pan-seared Scottish salmon with crushed potatoes, green beans and caper lemon butter; or perhaps roast loin of Duntrune venison with gratin potatoes, savoy cabbage, leeks and redcurrant jus lie. Finish, perhaps, with clafoutis of Scottish berries; or a selection of fine cheeses with hand crafted oat cakes and quince jelly. The hotel has 20 artistically decorated bedrooms, some with private balconies and all with breathtaking views of Loch Crinan or the Isles of Scarba, Jura and the whirlpool of the Corryvreckan. Boat trips can be arranged to the islands, and there is a classic boats regatta in the summer.

MAP 20 NR79
PA31 8SR
☎ 01546 830261
01546 830292
e-mail:
reservations@crinanhotel.com
dir: *From M8 Junc 30, cross Erskine bridge 2 take A8, N to Tarbet, continue onto A83. Take through Inverary to Lochgilphead. Take A816 to Oban for 2m, left onto A841 at Cairnbaan and follows signs to Crinan on B841*

Open 11–11
Bar Meals L served all week 12–2.30 D served all week 6–8.30 Av main course £10.50
Restaurant D served all week 7–8.30 Av 5 course fixed price £45
Free House
Argyll Fyne Ales, Belhaven, Interbrew Worthington Bitter, Tennents Velvet, Boddingtons.
Facilities Children's licence Garden Dogs allowed Parking
Rooms 20 bedrooms en suite S£105 D£190 (prices include dinner) (★★★★ SHL)

OLDMELDRUM MAP 23 NJ82

The Redgarth

Kirk Brae AB51 0DJ ☎ 01651 872353 📠 01651 873763
e-mail: redgarth1@aol.com
dir: *On A947*

A family-run inn, The Redgarth was built as a house in 1928 and has an attractive garden offering magnificent views of Bennachie and the surrounding countryside. Cask-conditioned ales and fine wines are served along with dishes prepared on the premises using fresh local produce. A typical selection might be honey and ginger prawns on a bed of salad leaves; roast Aberdeen Angus beef in a rich gravy with Yorkshire pudding; and raspberry white chocolate cheesecake.

Open 11-3 5-11 (Fri-Sat -11.45) Closed: Dec 25-26 Jan 1-3
Bar Meals L served all week 12-2 D served all week 5-9 (Fri-Sat 9.30)
Restaurant L served all week 12-2 D served all week 5-9 (Fri-Sat 5-9.30) Free House Inveralmond Thrappledouser, Caledonian Deuchers IPA, Taylor Landlord, Isle of Skye Red Cullin. 6 **Facilities** Children's licence Garden Parking

ARGYLL & BUTE

ARDUAINE MAP 20 NM71

Pick of the Pubs

Loch Melfort Hotel ★★★ HL

PA34 4XG ☎ 01852 200233 📠 01852 200214
e-mail: reception@lochmelfort.co.uk
dir: *On A816, 20m south of Oban*

One of the finest locations on the west coast of Scotland awaits visitors to this award-winning hotel and restaurant – the perfect place for a relaxing holiday or short break at any time of the year. The hotel stands in 26 acres of grounds next to the National Trust's Arduaine Gardens, and its lochside location gives spectacular views across Asknish Bay and the Sound of Jura. To the rear, the hotel is framed by woodlands and the magnificent mountains of Argyll. The restaurant offers superb dining with fresh local produce including meats, cheeses and locally caught fish and seafood. Meanwhile, the Skerry Bar/Bistro is very popular with both guests and locals for light lunches, teas and suppers. Here, the menu ranges from sandwiches, baguettes and toasties to dishes like warm Cajun chicken salad; tomato and basil pasta with mushrooms, spinach and crème fraiche; and venison sausages with champ mash and onion gravy.

Open 10.30-10.30 (Fri-Sat 10.30-11) Closed: Early Jan & Feb
Bar Meals L served all week 12-2.30 D served all week 6-9
Restaurant D served all week 7-9 Av 3 course à la carte £26 Free House 80/-, Theakstons, Guinness, Miller. **Facilities** Garden Dogs allowed Parking **Rooms** 25 bedrooms en suite S£54 D£85

CLACHAN-SEIL MAP 20 NM71

Pick of the Pubs

Tigh an Truish Inn

PA34 4QZ ☎ 01852 300242
dir: *14m S of Oban take A816. 12m, onto B844 towards Atlantic Bridge*

Following the Battle of Culloden in 1746, kilts were outlawed on pain of death. In defiance of this edict the islanders wore their kilts at home; but, on excursions to the mainland, they would stop at the Tigh an Truish – the 'house of trousers' – and change into the hated trews. Now popular with tourists and members of the yachting fraternity, the Tigh an Truish is handy for good walks and lovely gardens. It offers an appetising menu based on the best local produce, with a range of starters like sweet pickled herring with brown bread and salad; and home-made pâté with toast. Main course dishes include home-made vegetable lasagne with garlic bread; smoked haddock mornay with cheese crumble topping; home-made steak and ale pie; and locally caught prawns with garlic mayonnaise and salad. Watch out for the summer daily specials of locally caught seafood.

Open 11-3 5-11 (May-Sept all day) Closed: 25 Dec & Jan 1
Bar Meals L served all week 12-2 D served all week 6-8.30 Av main course £7.50 **Restaurant** L served all week 12-2 D served all week 6-8.30 Free House Local guest ales changing regularly.
Facilities Garden Dogs allowed Parking

CRINAN MAP 20 NR79

Pick of the Pubs

Crinan Hotel

PA31 8SR ☎ 01546 830261 📠 01546 830292
e-mail: reservations@crinanhotel.com
dir: *From M8, at end of bridge take A82, at Tarbert left onto A83. At Inverary follow Campbeltown signs to Lochgilphead, follow signs for A816 to Oban. 2m, left to Crinan on B841*

See Pick of the Pubs on page 691

Cairnbaan Hotel

Once upon a time, this late 18th-century coaching inn was frequented by fishermen on the Crinan Canal in flat-bottomed boats called puffers, but today's waterborne clientele is almost entirely sailing the waterway for pleasure.

The hotel offers high standards of hospitality and smart accommodation in en suite bedrooms, so there is no excuse for speeding away after a meal or drink. It's owned by ex-QE2 catering officer Darren Dobson, ashore now for some 20 years, and wife Christine, a former teacher, who plans the menus and does all the baking. Enjoy a meal in the serene restaurant, where the carte specialises in the use of fresh local produce, notably seafood and game. On the menu, look out for starters of moules marinière using secretly sourced large local mussels; deep-fried haggis balls with whisky gravy and neeps; and smoked lamb with gooseberry and mint jelly and fresh pear. Mains might include seared scallops with sauce vièrge, creamed potatoes and prosciutto crisp; Thai-spiced butternut squash risotto with vegetable crisps and red onion and coriander sambal; and confit of duck with redcurrant glaze, potatoes and vegetables. From the dessert menu come Mississippi mud pie; or fruit crumble with cream and custard. For a lunchtime snack, opt for ciabatta rolls with fillings such as smoked chicken with sun-blushed tomatoes and mayonnaise; or sausage, red onion and leaves. From nearby Oban there are sailings to Mull, Tiree, and Colonsay among other islands, and Inveraray Castle is well worth a visit, as is Dunadd Fort where the ancient kings of Scotland were crowned.

★★★ HL ® ♀
MAP 20 NR88
Cairnbaan PA31 8SJ
☎ 01546 603668
📠 01546 606045
e-mail: info@carinbaan.com
dir: *2m N, take A816 from Lochgilphead, hotel off B841*

Open 11-11
Bar Meals L served all week 12–2.30 D served all week 6–9.30
Restaurant D served all week 6–9.30 Av 3 course à la carte £24
Free House
Local Ales. ♀ 8
Facilities Garden Parking
Notes
Rooms 12 bedrooms en suite S£72.50 D£92.50

The Pierhouse Hotel & Seafood Restauran

The Pierhouse has the most spectacular setting on the shores of Loch Linnhe with views of the islands of Lismore and Shuna, and Ben Nevis and Glencoe. You can reach it by a picturesque road from Appin, or by sea, when you can tie up to one of the hotel's ten moorings in the harbour.

Originally the home of the Pier Master at Port Appin, who was responsible for overseeing the steam packets plying up and down the loch, the building is now a renowned small hotel with a good seafood restaurant. There is a popular bar with a terrace leading down to the private beach and shore. Lunch and dinner are served in both the bar and restaurant. Produce is locally sourced and seafood from Lismore, Loch Etive, Loch Linnhe, Mull and Inverawe plays a starring role so, not surprisingly, the Pierhouse received the AA Seafish Pub of Year Award for Scotland 2007. Favourite dishes are lobster served in a half shell fresh from the Pierhouse creel; a sumptuous seafood platter; beer battered fillets of fresh local haddock served with French fries and salad; and a mountain of giant langoustine with a cucumber mayonnaise dip. Fresh local meat, wild game and vegetarian dishes provide tempting alternatives and there is an extensive wine list. Twelve individually designed bedrooms include two with four-poster beds and loch views. All are en suite, with either bath or shower, and are equipped with internet access, colour televisions, direct dial telephones, hairdryers and tea and coffee making facilities. A traditional Finnish sauna for guests' use is a more unusual feature.

★★★ SHL
MAP 20 NM94
PA38 4DE
☎ 01631 730302
01631 730400
e-mail:
pierhouseads@btconnect.com

Open 8.00–11.30 (Sun 12–11.30)
Closed: 25 Dec
Bar Meals L served all week 12.30–2.30 D served all week 6.30–9.30 Av main course £5.79
Restaurant L served all week 12.30–2.30 D served all week 6.30–9.30 Av 3 course à la carte £25
Free House
Calders Cream, Calders 70/-, Carlsberg-Tetley Tetley Bitter.
Facilities Children's licence Garden Dogs allowed Parking
Rooms 12 bedrooms en suite D£40

DUNOON — MAP 20 NS17

Coylet Inn ★★★★ INN

Loch Eck PA23 8SG ☎ 01369 840426
e-mail: reservations@coylet-locheck.co.uk
dir: *9m N of Dunoon on A815*

Overlooking the shores of Loch Eck, this beautifully refurbished 17th-century coaching inn is a blissful hideaway with no television or games machines to disturb the peace. The inn is famous for its ghost, the Blue Boy; a film was even made of the story, starring Emma Thompson. Unwind by one of three log fires or plunder the impressive menus, where choices range from venison burger and chips to grilled sole with mussel cream.

Open 11–12 Closed: 25 Dec **Bar Meals** L served all week 12–2 D served all week 6–8.45 **Restaurant** L served all week 12–2 D served all week 6–8.45 Free House Caledonian Deuchars IPA, Highlander. **Facilities** Garden Parking **Rooms** 4 bedrooms en suite S£40 D£70

KILFINAN — MAP 20 NR97

Kilfinan Hotel Bar

PA21 2EP ☎ 01700 821201 01700 821205
e-mail: kilfinanhotel@btconnect.com
dir: *8m N of Tighnabruaich on B8000*

The hotel, on the eastern shore of Loch Fyne set amid spectacular Highland scenery, has been welcoming travellers since the 1760s. The bars are cosy with log fires in winter, and offer a fine selection of malts. There are two intimate dining rooms, with the Lamont room for larger parties. Menus change daily and offer the best of local produce: Loch Fyne oysters, of course, and langoustine grilled in garlic butter; cullen skink soup; and moules marinière, plus game, Aberdeen Angus beef and a variety of Scottish sweets and cheeses.

Bar Meals L served all week 12.30–2.30 D served all week 6.30–10 Av main course £6.95 **Restaurant** 12.30–2.30 D served all week 6.30–10.30 Av 3 course à la carte £25 Free House McEwens 70/-, McEwens 80/-, Fosters & Kronenbourg. **Facilities** Garden Parking

LOCHGILPHEAD — MAP 20 NR88

Pick of the Pubs

Cairnbaan Hotel ★★★ HL

Cairnbaan PA31 8SJ
☎ 01546 603668 01546 606045
e-mail: info@carinbaan.com
dir: *2m N, take A816 from Lochgilphead, hotel off B841*

See Pick of the Pubs on page 693

PORT APPIN — MAP 20 NM94

Pick of the Pubs

The Pierhouse Hotel & Seafood Restaurant ★★★ SHL

PA38 4DE ☎ 01631 730302 01631 730400
e-mail: pierhouseads@btconnect.com

See Pick of the Pubs on opposite page

STRACHUR — MAP 20 NN00

Pick of the Pubs

Creggans Inn ★★★ HL

PA27 8BX ☎ 01369 860279 01369 860637
e-mail: info@creggans-inn.co.uk
web: www.creggans-inn.co.uk
dir: *A815 down coast to Strachur*

From the hills above this informal family-friendly free house on the edge of Loch Fyne, you can gaze across the Mull of Kintyre to the Western Isles beyond. It has been a coaching inn since Mary Queen of Scots' day. Owned and run by the Robertson family for the last seven years, it maintains a good selection of real ales, wines by the glass and malt whiskies. There's a formal terraced garden and patio for alfresco summer drinking, and regional produce plays a key role in the seasonal menus: the famed Loch Fyne oysters of course, but also mussels from the same waters, cooked with Guinness and black pepper cream; and smoked salmon served with cucumber and dill crème fraîche. Robust main courses may feature venison sausages, steak and ale pie, and pan-fried rump of beef. Choose from the selection of home-made puddings and Scottish cheeses to finish.

Open 11–11 **Bar Meals** L served all week 12–2.45 D served all week 6–8.45 Av main course £10 **Restaurant** D served all week 7–9 Av 4 course fixed price £32 Free House Coniston Bluebird Bitter, Fyne Ales Highlander, Atlas Latitude, Deuchars IPA. 7 **Facilities** Garden Parking **Rooms** 14 bedrooms en suite S£65 D£110

Scotland

TAYVALLICH — MAP 20 NR78

Pick of the Pubs

Tayvallich Inn

PA31 8PL ☎ 01546 870282 📠 01546 870333
e-mail: rfhanderson@aol.com
dir: *From Lochgilphead take A816 then B841/B8025*

This 'house in the pass', as it translates, was converted from an old bus garage in 1976 and stands by a natural harbour at the head of Loch Sween with stunning views over the anchorage, especially from the picnic tables that front the inn in summer. The cosy bar with its yachting theme and the more formal dining-room feature original works by local artists and large picture windows from which to gaze out over the village and Tayvallich Bay. Those interested in the works of 19th-century engineer Thomas Telford will find plenty of bridges and piers in the area. Expect a lot of seafood, including Loch Etive mussels steamed in white wine, garlic and cream; seared scallops on pea purée and black pudding; and the Tayvallich Seafood Platter. Other options could include prime Scottish rib-eye with onion rings and tomatoes; and beer-battered haddock and chips.

Open 11–2.30 5.30–12 (Fri -Sat 5–1am, Sun 5–12) Closed: 25 Dec **Bar Meals** L served all week 12–2 D served all week 6–9 Av main course £12 **Restaurant** L served all week 12–2 D served all week 6–9 Free House Tennents, Guinness, Loch Fynk Ales. **Facilities** Garden Dogs allowed Parking

CLACKMANNANSHIRE

DOLLAR — MAP 21 NS99

Castle Campbell Hotel NEW ★★ SHL

11 Bridge St FK14 7DE ☎ 01259 742519 📠 01259 743742
e-mail: bookings@castle-campbell.co.uk
dir: *A91 (Stirling to St Andrews road). In centre of Dollar by bridge overlooking Dollar Barn & clock tower*

After exploring Dollar Glen's spectacular gorges, find a taste of real Scotland at this fine 1822 coaching inn. A local ale is always on tap, the wine list runs to several pages, and there are nearly 70 malts to choose from. The lunchtime bar menu and a broader dinner selection both benefit from carefully sourced regional produce – a ploughman's with Isle of Mull cheddar, Loch Fyne oysters followed by Loch Duart salmon, or a simple chargrilled Aberdeen Angus steak.

Open 12–11.30 (Fri 12–1am, Sun 12–11) **Bar Meals** L served all week 12–2 D served all week 5.30–8.45 (Sun 12–3, 5–8.45) Av main course £10 **Restaurant** L served all week 12–2 D served all week 5.30–8.45 (Sun 12–3, 5–8.45) Av 3 course à la carte £20 Free House Harviestoun Bitter & Twisted, Deuchars IPA (Guest), McEwans 70', Fosters & Kronenbourg. 7 **Facilities** Children's licence Dogs allowed Parking **Rooms** 9 bedrooms en suite S£40 D£65

DUMFRIES & GALLOWAY

ISLE OF WHITHORN — MAP 20 NX43

Pick of the Pubs

The Steam Packet Inn

Harbour Row DG8 8LL
☎ 01988 500334 📠 01988 500627
e-mail: steampacketinn@btconnect.com
dir: *A746 to Whithorn, then Isle of Whithorn*

This lively quayside pub stands in a picturesque village at the tip of the Machars peninsula. Sit by the picture windows and watch the fishermen at work, then look to the menu for a chance to sample the fruits of their labours. Extensive seafood choices – perhaps local lobster thermidor or a kettle of fish with Vermouth crème fraîche – are supported by the likes of steak and baby onion suet pudding or Thai pork ciabatta.

Open 11–11 (Winter Tue–Thu closed 2.30–6) Closed: 25 Dec **Bar Meals** L served all week 12–2 D served all week 6.30–9 Av main course £7.50 **Restaurant** L served all week 12–2 D served all week 6.30–9 Free House Scottish Courage Theakston XB, Caledonian Deuchars IPA, Black Sheep Best Bitter, Houston Killellan. 9 **Facilities** Children's licence Garden Dogs allowed Parking **Rooms** 7 bedrooms en suite S£30 D£60 (★★ INN)

KIRKCUDBRIGHT — MAP 20 NX65

Selkirk Arms Hotel

Old High St DG6 4JG ☎ 01557 330402 📠 01557 331639
e-mail: reception@selkirkarmshotel.co.uk
dir: *A75 between Dumfries & Stranraer*

A traditional white-painted pub on the street corner, with nice gardens to the rear. It has associations with the Scottish poet Robert Burns, and T. E. Lawrence (of Arabia), who lived nearby. Good choice of beers, including Youngers Tartan. Typical menu offers lamb or vegetable Madras, fresh Scottish haddock in crispy beer batter, steak and mushroom pie, spinach and cream cheese roulade, and haggis, neeps and tatties.

Open 11–12 **Bar Meals** L served all week 12–2 D served all week 6–9.30 **Restaurant** L served all week 12–2 D served all week 7–9.30 Free House Youngers Tartan, John Smiths Bitter, Criffel, Old Speckled Hen. 8 **Facilities** Children's licence Garden Dogs allowed Parking **Rooms** 16 bedrooms en suite S£40 D£85 (★★★ SH)

MOFFAT MAP 21 NT00

Black Bull Hotel

Churchgate DG10 9EG ☎ 01683 220206 01683 220483
e-mail: hotel@blackbullmoffat.co.uk

This historic pub was the headquarters of Graham of Claverhouse during the 17th-century Scottish rebellion, and was frequented by Robert Burns around 1790. The Railway Bar, in former stables across the courtyard, houses a collection of railway memorabilia and traditional pub games. Food is served in the lounge, Burns Room or restaurant. Dishes include Black Bull sizzlers (steak, chicken fillets, gammon) served on a cast iron platter; the daily roast, and deep-fried breaded haddock fillet.

Open 11–11 (Thu–Sat 11–12) **Bar Meals** L served all week 11.30–9.15 D served all week 11.30–9.15 **Restaurant** L served all week 11.30–3 D served all week 6–9.15 Free House McEwans, Scottish Courage Theakston. 10 **Facilities** Garden Parking **Rooms** 13 bedrooms en suite S£49 D£72 (★★★ SH)

NEW ABBEY MAP 21 NX96

Criffel Inn

2 The Square DG2 8BX
☎ 01387 850305 & 850244 01387 850305
e-mail: enquiries@criffelinn.com
dir: *A710 to New Abbey*

A former 18th-century coaching inn set on the Solway Coast in the historic conservation village of New Abbey close to the ruins of the 13th-century Sweetheart Abbey. The Graham family ensures a warm welcome and excellent home-cooked food using local produce. Dishes include chicken wrapped in smoked Ayrshire bacon served with Loch Arthur mature creamy cheese sauce; fish dishes feature sea trout and sea bass among several others. Lawned beer garden overlooking corn-mill and square; ideal for touring Dumfries and Galloway.

Open 12–2.30 5–11 (Sat 12–12 Sun 12–11) **Bar Meals** L served all week 12–2 D served all week 5.30–8 (Sun 12–8) Av main course £7 **Restaurant** L served all week 12–2 D served all week 5–8 (Sun 12–8) Av 3 course à la carte £14 Free House Belhaven Best, McEwans 60-. **Facilities** Garden Dogs allowed Parking

NEW GALLOWAY MAP 20 NX67

Cross Keys Hotel

High St DG7 3RN ☎ 01644 420494 01644 420672
e-mail: enquiries@crosskeys-newgalloway.co.uk
dir: *At N end of Loch Ken, 10m from Castle Douglas*

An 18th-century coaching inn with a beamed period bar, where food is served in restored, stone-walled cells (part of the hotel was once the police station). The à la carte restaurant offers hearty food with a Scottish accent, chicken stuffed with haggis and served with whisky sauce being a prime example. Real ales are a speciality, and there's a good choice of malts in the whisky bar.

Open 12–11 (Apr–Oct all wk 12–12) **Bar Meals** L served all week 12–2 D served all week 6–8 (Nov–Mar no food Mon–Tue, Sun 5.30–7.30) Av main course £7 **Restaurant** L served Sun 12–2 D served Apr–Oct, Tue–Sun 6.30–8.30 (Sun 5.30–7.30. Nov–Mar Thu–Sun) Av 3 course à la carte £17.50 Av fixed price £12.50 Houston real ales, Guest ales. **Facilities** Garden

NEWTON STEWART MAP 20 NX46

Pick of the Pubs

Creebridge House Hotel

Minnigaff DG8 6NP ☎ 01671 402121 01671 403258
e-mail: info@creebridge.co.uk
dir: *A75 into Newton Stewart, right over river bridge, 200yds on left*

A listed building dating from 1760, this family-run hotel is set in three acres of idyllic gardens and woodland at the foot of Kirroughtree forest. It was formerly the Earl of Galloway's shooting lodge and part of his estate. The newly refurbished Bridge's bar and brasserie offers malt whiskies, real ales and an interesting menu, perfect for an informal lunch. For a candlelit dinner the alternative dining venue is the Creebridge Garden Restaurant. The emphasis is on fresh Scottish produce, and both menus feature Kirkcudbrightshire beef, hung for 14 days, and an award-winning house speciality: best loin of lamb with creamed kale and roulade of braised shin. Fish dishes range from local sea bass set on chive mash with dill butter sauce, to the restaurant's seared Solway salmon served with lemon risotto and chive velouté.

Open 12–2.30 6–11 (Sun all day) **Bar Meals** L served all week 12–2 D served all week 6–8.45 Av main course £8.50 **Restaurant** L served all week 12–2 D served all week 6–9 Av 3 course à la carte £25 Av 5 course fixed price £25 Free House Fuller's London Pride, Tennents, Deuchers & Guinness. **Facilities** Children's licence Garden Dogs allowed Parking **Rooms** 18 bedrooms en suite S£45 D£65 (★★★ SH)

PORTPATRICK MAP 20 NW95

Crown Hotel

9 North Crescent DG9 8SX
☎ 01776 810261 01776 810551
e-mail: crownhotel@supanet.com
web: www.crownportpatrick.com
dir: *7m from Stranraer*

Just a few yards from the water's edge in one of the region's most picturesque villages, The Crown Hotel has striking views across the

CONTINUED

Scotland

PORTPATRICK continued

Irish Sea. The rambling old bar has seafaring displays and a warming winter fire. Naturally, seafood is a speciality, from a lunchtime seafood pancake to an evening meal of lobster thermidor. Other choices include pan-fried venison in a rich port and redcurrant game jus; and Scotch fillet steak garni.

Open 11–12 **Bar Meals** L served all week 12–6 D served all week 6–9.30 Av main course £7.95 **Restaurant** L served all week 12–2.30 D served all week 6–9.30 Av 3 course à la carte £22 Av 4 course fixed price £21.95 Free House John Smith's, McEwans 80/-, McEwans 70/-, Guinness. **Facilities** Children's licence Garden Dogs allowed Parking

CITY OF DUNDEE

BROUGHTY FERRY MAP 21 NO43

Fisherman's Tavern

10–16 Fort St DD5 2AD ☎ 01382 775941 01382 477466
e-mail: bookings@fishermans-tavern-hotel.co.uk
dir: *From Dundee A930 to Broughty Ferry, right for hotel*

Tucked down a side street off the waterfront, this pub occupies three pastel-washed cottages. The lounge is decorated in art deco style while the bar boasts a wood gantry that dates to 1873. There's a good selection of snacks and lighter meals that won't impede a post-prandial beach walk, while those preferring something heartier might opt for curry, burger and chips or steak and Guinness pie.

Open 11–12 (w/ends 11am–1am) **Bar Meals** L served all week 11.30–2.30 D served all week 5.30–7.30 Av main course £6.75 Free House Belhaven, Inveralmond Ossian's Ale, Caledonain Deuchers IPA,Timothy Taylor Landlord. 26 **Facilities** Children's licence Garden Dogs allowed Play Area **Rooms** 11 bedrooms en suite (★★ SH)

The Royal Arch Bar

285 Brook St DD5 2DS ☎ 01382 779741 01382 739174
dir: *3m from Dundee, 0.5 mins from Broughton Ferry Station*

In Victorian times, the jute industry made Broughty Ferry the 'richest square mile in Europe'. Named after the Masonic Arch, demolished to make way for the Tay road bridge, the pub dates from 1856. In the 1930s the landlady, Mrs Cardwell, sold her own label whisky, bottles of which are still displayed. An extensive selection of bar meals ranges from light snacks to three-course meals, served in the bar, lounge or pavement cafe.

Open 11–12 (Sun 12.30–12) Closed: 1 Jan **Bar Meals** L served all week 11.30–2.30 (Sun 12.30–2.30) D served all week 5–8 (Fri–Sat 11.30–7.30, 5–8) Av main course £6.50 **Restaurant** L served all week 11.30–2.30 (Sun 12.30–2.30) D served all week 5–8 (Fri–Sat 11.30–7.30, Sun 5–8) Free House Scottish Courage McEwans 80/-, Belhaven Best, Guinness, Clark Caledonian. 12 **Facilities** Children's licence Garden Dogs allowed

EAST AYRSHIRE

DALRYMPLE MAP 20 NS31

The Kirkton Inn NEW

1 Main St KA6 6DF ☎ 01292 560241 01292 560835
e-mail: kirkton@cqm.co.uk
dir: *6m SE from centre of Ayr just off A77*

This inn's motto is, 'There are no strangers here, only friends who have never met', and the welcoming atmosphere makes it easy to feel at home. It's a stoutly traditional setting, with open fires and polished brasses, set in the village of Dalrymple. A meal might include haggis with a dram of Drambuie, cream and redcurrants, followed by the chef's home-made steak pie.

Open 11–12 **Bar Meals** L served all week 12–4 D served all week 12–9 Av main course £9 **Restaurant** L served all week 12–4 D served all week 12–9 Av 3 course à la carte £18 Free House Belhaven Best, Tennents. **Facilities** Children's licence Garden Dogs allowed Parking **Rooms** 3 bedrooms en suite S£45 D£50

GATEHEAD MAP 20 NS33

The Cochrane Inn

45 Main Rd KA2 0AP ☎ 01563 570122
dir: *From Glasgow A77 to Kilmarnock, then A759 to Gatehead*

The emphasis is on contemporary British food at this village centre pub, just a short drive from the Ayrshire coast. There's a friendly, bustling atmosphere inside. Good choice of starters may include soused herring and grilled goats' cheese, while main courses might feature stuffed pancake, pan-fried trio of seafood with tiger prawns, or smoked haddock risotto.

Open 12–2 6–11 (Fri–Sat 6–12.30, Sun all day) **Bar Meals** L served all week 12–2 D served all week 6–9 (wknds 5.30–9) Av main course £10 **Restaurant** L served all week 12–2 D served all week 6–9 (wknds 5.30–9) Av 3 course à la carte £17 Free House John Smith's. 20 **Facilities** Garden Parking

SORN MAP 20 NS52

The Sorn Inn ★★★★ RR

35 Main St KA5 6HU ☎ 01290 551305 01290 553470
e-mail: craig@sorninn.com

This late 18th-century coaching inn is located in the heart of Ayrshire. It has two dining options: the chop house, which offers steaks, burgers, baguettes and simple meals such as cod and chips or goats' cheese tart; and the smart, award winning restaurant where the modern British fare could include pan-fried halibut with baby spinach and curried mussel chowder; and roast Ayrshire partridge with root vegetables and fondant potatoes.

Open 12–2.30 6–11 (Fri–Sat 6–12, Sun 12.30–11) Closed: 2 wks Jan **Bar Meals** L served Tue–Sun 12–2.30 D served Tue–Sun 6–9 (Sun 12.30–8.30) Av main course £9 **Restaurant** L served Tue–Sun 12–2.30 D served Tue–Sun 6–9 (Sun 12.30–6.30) Av 3 course fixed price £21.95 Free House John Smiths, McEwans 60/-. 12 **Facilities** Children's licence Parking **Rooms** 4 bedrooms en suite S£35 D£70 (U)

EAST LOTHIAN

EAST LINTON — MAP 21 NT57

The Drovers Inn

5 Bridge St EH40 3AG ☎ 01620 860298 📠 01620 860205

dir: *Off A1, 5m past Haddington, under rail bridge, then left*

Herdsmen used to stop here as they drove their livestock to market. Those old drovers are long gone but the bar, with wooden floors, beamed ceilings and half-panelled walls, retains an old-world charm. Upstairs, though, is more sumptuous with rich colours, low-beamed ceilings and antique furniture. The menus change every six weeks or so, but may include the likes of grilled halibut and black tiger prawns with chervil and garlic butter. The bistro downstairs next to the bar offers a more informal dining choice.

Open 11.30–11 **Bar Meals** L served all week 12.30–2.30 D served all week 6–9.30 Av main course £10 **Restaurant** L served all week 12–2.30 D served all week 6–9.30 (Sun all day) Av 3 course à la carte £22.50 Free House Adnams Broadside, Deuchars IPA, Old Speckled Hen, Burton Real Ale. **Facilities** Garden Dogs allowed

CITY OF EDINBURGH

EDINBURGH — MAP 21 NT27

Bennets Bar

8 Leven St EH3 9LG ☎ 0131 229 5143

Bennets is a friendly pub, popular with performers from the adjacent Kings Theatre, serving real ales, over 120 malt whiskies and a decent selection of wines. It's a listed property dating from 1839 with hand-painted tiles and murals on the walls, original stained glass windows and brass beer taps. Reasonably priced home-made food ranges from toasties, burgers and salads to stovies, steak pie, and macaroni cheese. There's also a daily roast and traditional puddings.

Open 11–12.30 (Thu–Sat 11–1 Sun 12.30–11.30) Closed: 25–26 Dec **Bar Meals** L served all week 12–2 D served Mon–Sat 5–8.30 (Sun 11.30–4) Scottish & Newcastle Caledonian Deuchars IPA, McEwans 80/-. Miller, Guinness. 14

The Bow Bar

80 The West Bow EH1 2HH ☎ 0131 226 7667

e-mail: helen@bowbar.com

dir: *Telephone for directions*

Located in the heart of Edinburgh's old town, the Bow Bar reflects the history and traditions of the area. Tables from decommissioned railway carriages and a gantry from an old church used for the huge selection of whiskies create interest in the bar, where 150 malts are on tap, and eight cask ales are dispensed from antique equipment. Bar snacks only are served, and there are no gaming machines or music to distract from conversation.

Open 12–11.30 (Sun 12.30–11) Closed: 25–26 Dec, 1–2 Jan Free House Deuchars IPA, Belhaven 80/-, Taylors Landlord, Harviestown Bitter & Twisted. 6 **Facilities** Dogs allowed

Pick of the Pubs

Doric Tavern

15–16 Market St EH1 1DE

☎ 0131 225 1084 📠 0131 220 0894

e-mail: info@mowco.co.uk

dir: *Opposite Waverly Station & Edinburgh Dungeons*

Built in 1710 as a private house by a writer who lived to the grand old age of 107, it became a pub in the mid–1800s, Around that time Waverley station was conveniently built nearby, and Princes Street and Edinburgh's famous castle are also only a short walk away. Public rooms include the regular bar, a wine bar and the bistro, all of which stay open until 1am seven days a week. In these pleasantly informal surroundings a wide choice of fresh, locally sourced food is available. The bistro offers an individually priced lunch and evening menu, with dishes such as steamed fillets of lemon sole with queen scallop and dill mousse; and haggis, neeps and tatties with a whisky jus. Food in the bars is lighter – bangers and mash, cheese and oatcakes, chilli con carne, and pastrami on rye, for instance.

Open 12–1am Closed: 25–26 Dec, 1 Jan **Bar Meals** L served Mon–Sun 12–11 Av main course £4.60 **Restaurant** L served all week 12–5 D served all week 5–11.30 Free House Deuchars IPA, Tennents, Fosters, Becks Vier. 13

The Shore Bar & Restaurant

3 Shore, Leith EH6 6QW

☎ 0131 553 5080 📠 0131 553 5080

e-mail: enquiries@the.shore.ukf.net

Part of this historic pub was a 17th-century lighthouse and, befitting its location beside the Port of Leith, it has a fine reputation for fish and seafood. The carte changes at every sitting during the day to ensure the freshest produce is on offer. A typical meal could be pan-fried pigeon breasts and pancetta followed by sautéed monkfish tail with a fennel and orange sauce. The bustling bar hosts regular live Latin-jazz and folk sessions.

Open 11–12 (Sun 11–11) Closed: 25–26 Dec, 1–2 Jan **Bar Meals** L served all week 12–2.30 (Sat–Sun 12–3) D served all week 6.30–10 Av main course £15 **Restaurant** L served all week 12–2.30 (Sat–Sun 12–3) D served all week 6.30–10 Av 3 course à la carte £26 Av 3 course fixed price £15.50 Free House Belhaven 80/-, Deuchars IPA, Guinness, Amstel. 14 **Facilities** Dogs allowed

RATHO — MAP 21 NT17

Pick of the Pubs

The Bridge Inn

27 Baird Rd EH28 8RA

☎ 0131 333 1320 📠 0131 333 3480

e-mail: info@bridgeinn.com

dir: *From Newbridge B7030 junction, follow signs for Ratho*

In 1822 the Union Canal reached to the door of this former farmhouse, which seized the opportunity of increased traffic to become an inn. Unfortunately, a century or so later the barge

CONTINUED

Scotland

RATHO continued

traffic declined and the rot set in. In 1971 the inn was transformed once again, becoming the lively multi-function establishment that still thrives today. The informal Pop Inn Lounge serves snacks and bar meals all day – to be eaten while gazing out over the canal. In the award-winning waterways-themed restaurant you can enjoy the likes of pan-fried chicken breast stuffed with haggis, and served with Drambuie, cream and mushroom sauce; poached smoked haddock and salmon with creamy prawn sauce; casserole of Highland venison, cooked with a whisky and port sauce; and pappardelle pasta with spring onion sauce. The Edinburgh Canal Centre arranges three-hour cruise dinners from here.

Open 12-11 (Sat 11-12, Sun 12.30-11) Closed: 26 Dec, 1-2 Jan **Bar Meals** L served all week 12-9 D served all week 12-9 (Sun 12.30-9) Av main course £8 **Restaurant** L served all week 12-2.30 D served all week 6.30-9 (Sun 12.30-9) Av 3 course à la carte £20 Free House Belhaven, Deuchars IPA, Tennents, Stella Artois. **Facilities** Children's licence Garden Parking

FIFE

ANSTRUTHER MAP 21 NO50

The Dreel Tavern

16 High St West KY10 3DL

☎ 01333 310727 Fax 01333 310577

e-mail: dreeltavern@aol.com

Complete with a local legend concerning an amorous encounter between James V and a local gypsy woman, the 16th-century Dreel Tavern has plenty of atmosphere. Its oak beams, open fire and stone walls retain much of the distant past, while home-cooked food and cask-conditioned ales are served to hungry visitors of the present. Expect to savour steak pie, roast beef and Yorkshire pudding, and plenty of local fish dishes including smoked fish pie, and local crab. Peaceful gardens overlook Dreel Burn. Beers changed weekly.

Open 11-12 (Sun 12.30-12) **Bar Meals** L served all week 12-2 (Sun 12.30-2) D served all week 5.30-9 Av main course £6.50 **Restaurant** L served all week 12-2 D served all week 5.30-9 Free House Tetley's Bitter, Harviestoun Bitter & Twisted, Greene King IPA, London Pride. **Facilities** Garden Dogs allowed Parking

BURNTISLAND MAP 21 NT28

Burntisland Sands Hotel

Lochies Rd KY3 9JX ☎ 01592 872230 Fax 01592 872230

e-mail: clarkelinton@hotmail.com

dir: *Towards Burntisland on A921, on right before Kinghorn*

This small, family-run hotel, just 50 yards from an award-winning sandy beach, was once a highly regarded girls' boarding school. Reasonably priced breakfasts, snacks, lunches and evening meals are always available, with a good selection of specials. Try breaded haddock and tartare sauce; gammon steak Hawaii; or crispy shredded beef. Desserts include hot naughty fudge cake, and banana boat. There is also an excellent choice of hot and cold filled rolls, and a children's menu.

Open 12-12 **Bar Meals** L served all week 12-2.30 D served all week 6-8.30 (Sat-Sun 12-8.30) Av main course £5.95 **Restaurant** L served all week 12-2.30 D served all week 5-8.30 (Sat-Sun all day) Av 3 course à la carte £15 Free House Scottish Courage Beers, Guinness, Carling & Guest ales. **Facilities** Children's licence Garden Parking Play Area

CRAIL MAP 21 NO60

The Golf Hotel

4 High St KY10 3TD ☎ 01333 450206 Fax 01333 450795

e-mail: enquiries@thegolfhotelcrail.com

dir: *On corner of High Street*

Reputedly one of the oldest licensed inns in Scotland, the present day Golf Hotel occupies an 18th-century Grade I-listed building, but the first inn on the site opened its doors 400 years earlier. In 1786, the Crail Golfing Society was established here, although the pub's present name appeared only in the mid-1800s. The pub is known for home-cooked meals such as smoked haddock and poached salmon fishcakes; and high teas with home-made scones.

Open 11-12 **Bar Meals** L served all week 12-7 D served all week 7-9 Av main course £8 **Restaurant** L served all week 12-7 D served all week 7-9 Av 3 course à la carte £18 Free House Scottish Courage McEwans 60/-, 80/-, 70/-, Belhaven Best & Real ale. **Facilities** Garden Dogs allowed Parking **Rooms** 5 bedrooms en suite S£40 D£58 (★★ SH)

ELIE MAP 21 NO40

The Ship Inn

The Toft KY9 1DT ☎ 01333 330246 Fax 01333 330864

e-mail: info@ship-elie.com

dir: *Follow A915 & A917 to Elie, then signs to Watersport Centre & The Toft*

Run by the enthusiastic Philip family for over two decades, this lively free house stands right on the waterfront at Elie Bay. The Ship has been a pub since 1838, and there's still plenty going on. The cricket team plays regular fixtures on the beach; there's also live music, and a programme of summer Sunday barbeques. Local bakers, butchers and fishmongers featured in the pub's colourful brochure provide many of the ingredients for featured dishes.

Open 11-11 Closed: 25 Dec **Bar Meals** L served all week 12-2 D served all week 6-9 **Restaurant** L served all week 12-2 D served all week 6-9 Free House Caledonian Deuchars IPA, Belhaven Best, Tetleys Xtra Cold, Caledonian 801. 7 **Facilities** Garden Dogs allowed Play Area

KINCARDINE MAP 21 NS98

Pick of the Pubs

The Unicorn

15 Excise St FK10 4LN ☎ 01259 739129

e-mail: info@theunicorn.co.uk

dir: *Cross Kincardine Bridge, go left, then 1st left, then sharp left at rdbt*

This 17th-century pub-restaurant in the heart of the historic port of Kincardine used to be a coaching inn. And it was where, in 1842, Sir James Dewar, inventor of the vacuum flask, was born. Leather sofas and modern décor blend in well with the older parts of the building. There is a comfortable lounge bar, a grillroom, and a more formal dining room upstairs. Food quality is everything to owners Tony and Liz, whose alliances with top local suppliers include Liz's own brother, who rears beef cattle on the Buccleuch estate, and Finlay 'The Fish' Finlayson, who sends smoked salmon from his home-built kiln in Fort William. Specialities include sea bass roasted in mustard and lemon butter; red pepper and spinach lasagne; and marinated lamb with seared hand-dived king scallops and sweet potato and lemon thyme sauce. In decent weather, have a drink by the old well in the walled garden.

Open 12–2 5.30–12 Closed: 1st wk in Jan & 3rd wk in July **Bar Meals** L served Tue–Sat 12–2 D served Tue–Sat 5.30–9 **Restaurant** D served Fri–Sat 7–9 Av 3 course à la carte £23.95 Extra Cold Guinness, Belhaven Best, Bitter & Twisted. 8 **Facilities** Parking

KIRKCALDY MAP 21 NT29

Pick of the Pubs

The Old Rectory Inn

West Quality St, Dysart KY1 2TE
01592 651211 01592 655221
dir: *A955 to Dysart, right at National Trust sign*

Built as a gentleman's residence by prominent Dysart merchant James Reddie in 1771, the Old Rectory Inn has been an inn only since the 1980s. It is a splendid Georgian building, retaining its period features, including moulded eaves, cornices, panelled chimneys and a Roman Doric door piece. Outside there is a large oval garden sheltered by a high stone wall, with seats for fine weather use. The lunch menu offers a good choice of pasta, cold table and vegetarian dishes, main courses like large Yorkshire pudding filled with chilli con carne. The supper line-up features hot and cold starters (deep-fried mushrooms, stilton mousse), fresh fish options (fish stew), pastas and vegetarian choices, curries and steaks. From the à la carte menu come salmon moutard; duck with three fruits; and pork with green ginger wine. Don't miss the home-made puddings – hot sticky toffee pudding with butterscotch sauce, bread and butter pudding, and cold sweets from the trolley.

Open 12–3 7–12 (Sun 12.30–3.30) Closed: 1wk Jan, 2wks mid-Oct & 1 wk early July **Bar Meals** L served Tue–Sun 12–2 (Sun 12.30–2.30) D served Tue–Sat 7–9.30 Av main course £8.75 **Restaurant** L served Tue–Sun 12–2 (Sun 12.30–2.30) D served Tue–Sat 7–9.30 Av 3 course à la carte £24.75 Av 4 course fixed price £15.50 Free House Calders Cream Ale. **Facilities** Garden Parking

LOWER LARGO MAP 21 NO40

The Crusoe Hotel

2 Main St KY8 6BT 01333 320759 01333 320865
e-mail: relax@crusoehotel.co.uk
dir: *A915 to Lundin Links, then right to Lower Largo*

This historic inn is located on the sea wall in Lower Largo, the birthplace of Alexander Selkirk, the real-life castaway immortalised by Daniel Defoe in his novel, *Robinson Crusoe*. In the past the area was also the heart of the once-thriving herring fishing industry. Today it is a charming bay ideal for a golfing break. A typical menu may include 'freshly shot' haggis, Pittenweem haddock and a variety of steaks.

Open 11–12 (Fri 11am–1am, Sun 12–12) **Bar Meals** L served all week 12–9 Av main course £6 **Restaurant** D served all week 6.45–9 Free House Belhaven 80/-, Best, Deuchars. **Facilities** Dogs allowed Parking Play Area **Rooms** 17 bedrooms en suite S£55 D£75 (★★★ SH)

ST ANDREWS MAP 21 NO51

The Inn at Lathones NEW ★★★★ INN

Largoward KY9 1JE 01334 840494 01334 840694
e-mail: lathones@theinn.co.uk
dir: *5m from St Andrews on A915*

This is St Andrews' oldest inn, and parts of the building date back over 400 years. Up to fifteen Scottish real ales are served in pewter tankards in the bar lounge, with its big leather sofas and log burning fires. The finest fresh, local produce features on the daily changing menus: typical dishes include oven-roasted salmon with pesto crust, shallots and cherry tomatoes; and roast Perthshire black-faced lamb with lemon and mint stuffing.

Open 7–12.30 Closed: 1st 2 wks in Jan **Bar Meals** L served all week 12–2.30 D served all week 6–9.30 **Restaurant** L served all week 12–2.30 D served all week 6–9.30 Av 3 course à la carte £45 Av 3 course fixed price £17.50 Stella, Becks, Boddingtons, Miller. 11 **Facilities** Garden Dogs allowed Parking **Rooms** 13 bedrooms en suite S£120 D£180

CITY OF GLASGOW

GLASGOW MAP 20 NS56

Rab Ha's

83 Hutchieson St G1 1SH
0141 572 0400 0141 572 0402
e-mail: management@rabhas.com

In the heart of Glasgow's revitalised Merchant City, Rab Ha's takes its name from Robert Hall, a local 19th-century character known as 'The Glasgow Glutton'. This hotel, restaurant and bar blend Victorian character with contemporary Scottish décor. Pre-theatre and set menus show extensive use of carefully sourced Scottish produce in starters like poached egg on grilled Stornoway black pudding, and pan-seared Oban scallops, followed by mains like roast saddle of Rannoch Moor venison.

Open 12–12 (Sun 12.30–12) **Bar Meals** L served all week 12 D served all week 8 Av main course £8 **Restaurant** L served all week 12–2.30 D served all week 5–10 Av 3 course à la carte £25 Av 3 course fixed price £13.95 Free House Tennents, Budvar, Stella, Belhaven Best. **Facilities** Children's licence Dogs allowed

Pick of the Pubs

Ubiquitous Chip

12 Ashton Ln G12 8SJ
0141 334 5007 0141 337 6417
e-mail: mail@ubiquitouschip.co.uk
dir: *In West End of Glasgow, off Byres Rd. Beside Hillhead subway station*

The Ubiquitous Chip opened in 1971 with the intention of bringing Scotland's endangered cuisine out of the home and into the restaurant, though in this case the restaurant is actually a glass-covered mews with cobbled floor, water fountains and enough greenery to fill an arboretum. Traditional draught beers, over a

CONTINUED

Scotland

GLASGOW continued

hundred malt whiskies and excellent wines by the glass are served from a bar that is reputed to be the smallest in Scotland; they could also be drunk on the new and sheltered roof terrace. Today's award-winning menus continue the founding philosophy of using locally sourced ingredients, intelligently presented and prepared. A typical dinner might start with vegetarian haggis, neeps and tatties, followed by baked Orkney organic salmon marinated in honey and tamari; or asparagus and pea custard with pea and mint vinaigrette. Desserts might include lemon meringue parfait, and Seville orange steamed pudding.

Open 11–12 (Sun 12.30–12) Closed: 25 Dec, 1 Jan **Bar Meals** L served all week 12–4 D served all week 4–11 (Sun 12.30–4) Av main course £5.50 **Restaurant** L served all week 12–2.30 D served all week 5.30–11 (Sun 12.30–2.30, 6.30–11) Av 3 course à la carte £20 Free House Caledonian 80, Chip 71 Ale. 21

HIGHLAND

ACHILTIBUIE — MAP 22 NC00

Summer Isles Hotel & Bar

IV26 2YG ☎ 01854 622282 01854 622251

e-mail: info@summerisleshotel.co.uk

dir: *A835 N from Ullapool 10m, Achiltibuie signed on left, 15m to village, hotel 1m on left*

Located in a stunningly beautiful and unspoilt landscape, it would be hard to discover a more individual and relaxing place in which to drink and unwind. The emphasis here is on locally caught and home-produced quality food, with a wide choice of malts and real ale. Seafood platter, seared local scallops, fresh lobster and dressed crab are popular favourites, as well as vegetarian dishes, steaks, casseroles and freshly made sandwiches.

Open 11–11 **Bar Meals** L served all week 12–2.30 D served all week 5.30–8.30 Av main course £10 **Restaurant** L served all week 12.30–2 D served all week 8 Av 5 course fixed price £51 Free House Red Cuillin, Misty Isle, Hebridean Gold, Young Pretender & IPA Deuchars. **Facilities** Garden Dogs allowed Parking

ALTNAHARRA — MAP 23 NC53

Altnaharra Hotel

IV27 4UE ☎ 01549 411222 01549 411222

e-mail: office@altnaharra.co.uk

dir: *A9 to Bonar Bridge, A836 to Lairg & Tongue*

Originally a drover's inn understood to date back to the late 17th century, the Altnaharra is located in the beautiful Flow Country of Scotland, with endless views over timeless moorland. Interesting items of fishing memorabilia decorate the walls, including some fine historical prints and fishing records. The imaginative menu features the best of Scottish produce and options might include scallops in a brandy and cream sauce, Aberdeen Angus roast rib of beef, whole baked sea bass, Kyle of Tongue oysters, and Scottish rack of lamb.

Open 11–12.45 **Bar Meals** L served all week 12–10 D served all week 12–10 Av main course £7 **Restaurant** D served all week 7–10 Av 3 course à la carte £32.50 Av 5 course fixed price £45 Scottish & Newcastle No real ale. **Facilities** Garden Dogs allowed Parking Play Area

APPLECROSS — MAP 22 NG74

Pick of the Pubs

Applecross Inn

Shore St IV54 8LR ☎ 01520 744262 01520 744400

e-mail: applecrossinn@globalnet.co.uk

dir: *From Lochcarron to Kishorn then left onto unclassifed road to Applecross, over 'Bealach Na Ba'*

To reach the Applecross Inn, you must climb over 2,000ft to traverse Bealach na Bo, the highest mountain pass in Britain, before descending onto a wild peninsula that overlooks the Isle of Skye. The traditional white-painted inn nestles on a sandy cove – an idyllic situation in anybody's book. Once a temperance hotel, the recently refurbished inn is now a thriving hub of the local community, and has also become something of a dining destination. The bar maintains its Highland character, with slate floors, a wood burning stove and a choice of over 50 malt whiskies. Head chef Clare Mansfield aims to source much of her ingredients from top quality local producers. Typical selections include king scallops in garlic butter; curried monkfish on mussels; and confit lamb niçoise with spinach and spiced aubergine.

Open 11–11 (Sun 12.30–11) Closed: 25 Dec, 1 Jan **Bar Meals** L served all week 12–9 D served all week Av main course £8.95 Free House Isle of Skye cask ales, Guinness, Fosters, McEwans 80 & Kronenbourg. **Facilities** Children's licence Garden Dogs allowed Parking Play Area

AVIEMORE — MAP 23 NH81

The Old Bridge Inn

Dalfaber Rd PH22 1PU ☎ 01479 811137 01479 810270

e-mail: nigel@oldbridgeinn.co.uk

dir: *A9 to Aviemore, 1st left to Ski Rd, 1st left again 200mtrs*

Cosy and friendly Highland pub overlooking the River Spey. Dine in the relaxing bars, the comfortable restaurant, or in the attractive riverside garden. A tasty chargrill menu includes lamb chops in redcurrant jelly, Aberdeen Angus sirloin or rib-eye steaks, and butterflied breast of chicken marinated in yoghurt, lime and coriander. Seafood specials include monkfish pan fried in chilli butter, mussels poached in white wine, and seafood crumble. Large selection of malt whiskies.

Open 11–11 **Bar Meals** L served all week 12–2 (Sun 12.30–2) D served all week 6–9 **Restaurant** L served all week 12–2 (Sun 12.30–2) D served all week 6–9 Free House Caledonian 80/-, Cairngorm Highland IPA. 18 **Facilities** Children's licence Garden Parking Play Area

BADACHRO MAP 22 NG77

The Badachro Inn

IV21 2AA ☎ 01445 741255 01445 741319
e-mail: Lesley@badachroinn.com
dir: *Off A832 onto B8056, right onto Badachro after 3.25m, towards quay.*

A commanding position on the cusp of Badachro Bay, one of Scotland's finest anchorages, makes this atmospheric local in the north Highlands very popular in summer with yachting folk. Log fires burn cheerily in the bar in winter as the sea laps against the windows in high tides. Seals and otters can also be seen from the pub. Local seafood is, unsurprisingly, a speciality, and includes hot-smoked salmon, marinated herring, and Gairloch prawns.

Open 12–12 Closed: 25 Dec **Bar Meals** L served all week 12–3 (Sun 12.30–3) D served all week 6–9 **Restaurant** L served all week 12–3 (Sun 12.30–3) D served all week 6–9 Free House Red Cullen, Anceallach, Blaven, 80/-. 11 **Facilities** Children's licence Garden Dogs allowed Parking

CAWDOR MAP 23 NH85

Pick of the Pubs

Cawdor Tavern

The Lane IV12 5XP ☎ 01667 404777 01667 404777
e-mail: cawdortavern@btopenworld.com
dir: *A96 take B9006 & follow Cawdor Castle signs. Tavern in village centre.*

Standing close to the famous castle in a beautiful conservation village, the Tavern was formerly a joinery workshop for the Cawdor Estate. Oak panelling from the castle, gifted by the late laird, is used to great effect in the bar. Roaring log fires keep the place cosy and warm on long winter evenings, while the garden patio comes into its own in summer. One menu is offered in the bar or restaurant, alongside the choice of real ales and 100 malt whiskies. The pub's reputation for seafood draws diners from some distance for dishes like steamed mussels with white wine and garlic; and smoked sprats on bruschetta with plum tomato and rocket. Other favourites include roast vegetable stack with mozzarella and balsamic reduction; and Scottish venison burger with red onion marmalade. Finish with brandy snap basket and ice cream; or a trio of Scottish cheeses with savoury biscuits.

Open 11–3 5–11 (May–Oct 11–11) Closed: 25 Dec, 1 Jan **Bar Meals** L served all week 12–2 (Sun 12.30–3) D served all week 5.30–9 Av main course £6.95 **Restaurant** L served all week 12–2 D served all week 6.30–9 (Sun 12.30–3, 5.30–9) Free House Tennents 80/-, Cairngorm, Tradewinds & Stag. 8 **Facilities** Children's licence Garden Dogs allowed Parking

CONTIN MAP 23 NH45

Achilty Hotel ★★★ SHL

IV14 9EG ☎ 01997 421355 01997 421923
e-mail: info@achiltyhotel.co.uk
dir: *On A835, at N edge of Contin*

The original stone walls and log fire keep this former drovers' inn warm when the Highlands weather closes in. On the edge of the village near a fast-flowing mountain river, the cosy Achilty Hotel serves good Scottish food made from fresh local produce. The bar/restaurant menu offers an extensive choice with a seafood slant: bouillabaisse (Scottish style), scampi provençal, seafood thermidor, halibut and monkfish, plus chicken with haggis in a creamy whisky and onion sauce, duck breasts, mushroom stroganoff, and a large selection of steaks and home-made desserts.

Open 11–2.30 5–11 (Sun 12.30–11 Apr–31 Oct 11–11) **Bar Meals** L served all week 12–2 D served all week 5–9 Av main course £8 **Restaurant** L served all week 12–2 D served all week 5–9 Free House Calders Cream, Calders 70/-. 8 **Facilities** Children's licence Garden Parking **Rooms** 12 bedrooms en suite S£39.95 D£61

DUNDONNELL MAP 22 NH08

Pick of the Pubs

Dundonnell Hotel ★★★ HL

IV23 2QR ☎ 01854 633204 01854 633366
e-mail: trish@dundonnellhotel.co.uk
dir: *From Inverness W on the A835, at Braemore junct take A382 for Gairloch*

The Dundonnell is one of the leading hotels in the Northern Highlands. Originally a small inn accommodating the occasional traveller to Wester Ross, it has been considerably extended and today offers many special facilities: its own petrol station (the next one is 26 miles away), showers and drying room for walkers and climbers, even a midge-killing machine in the garden. Sheltered beneath the massive An Teallach range (one of 21 Munros in the area), the views down Little Loch Broom are superb. An Teallach is also the name of the brewery sited a couple of miles down the road, which supplies five real ales for the Broom Beg bar. This

CONTINUED

Scotland

Scotland

DUNDONNELL continued

is the 'local', where casual dining ranges from sandwiches and salads to pizzas and lasagne. The Cocktail Bar is the place for a quiet aperitif while mulling over what to eat in the spacious restaurant. Expect soup or sautéed field mushrooms to start, followed by steak and ale pie, venison pie, or succulent steaks cooked to your liking.

Open 11–11 Part time opening 1 Dec–28 Feb **Bar Meals** L served all week 12–2 D served all week 6–8.30 (Sun 12–2.30, 6–8) Av main course £8 **Restaurant** D served all week 7–8.30 Av 3 course à la carte £18 Free House Kronenbourg, John Smiths, Fosters, An Teallach Ale Company (5 different varieties). **Facilities** Children's licence Garden Dogs allowed Parking **Rooms** 32 bedrooms en suite S£35 D£70

FORT WILLIAM MAP 22 NN17

Moorings Hotel ★★★ HL

Banavie PH33 7LY ☎ 01397 772797 01397 772441
e-mail: reservations@moorings-fortwilliam.co.uk
dir: *A82 signs for Mallaig, left onto A830 for 1m. Cross canal bridge then 1st right signed Banavie*

This modern hotel lies alongside Neptune's Staircase, on the coast-to-coast Caledonian Canal. The canal is a historic monument, its eight locks able to raise even sea-going craft a total of 64 feet. Most hotel bedrooms and the Upper Deck lounge bar have good views of Ben Nevis (1344m) and Aonach Mor (1219m). A range of eating options includes Mariners cellar bar, and the Caledonian split-level lounge bar overlooking the canal, plus the fine-dining Jacobean Restaurant.

Open 12–11.45 (Thu–Sat 12–1am) **Bar Meals** L served all week 12–9.30 D served all week Av main course £9 **Restaurant** D served all week 7–9.30 Av 3 course à la carte £28 Free House Calders 70/-, Tetley Bitter, Guinness. **Facilities** Children's licence Garden Dogs allowed Parking **Rooms** 27 bedrooms en suite S£41 D£82

Please see walk on opposite page

GAIRLOCH MAP 22 NG87

Pick of the Pubs

The Old Inn ★★★ INN

IV21 2BD ☎ 01445 712006 01445 712044
e-mail: info@theoldinn.net
dir: *Just off A832, near harbour at south end of village*

See Pick of the Pubs on page 706

GARVE MAP 23 NH36

Inchbae Lodge Guesthouse

IV23 2PH ☎ 01997 455269 01997 455207
e-mail: inchbae.lodge@tesco.net
dir: *A835 from Tore rdbt*

Situated on the banks of the River Blackwater, this was originally a 19th-century hunting lodge and today makes an ideal base for walkers wishing to take on Ben Wyvis and the Fannich Hills. Inside you'll find a bistro and a conservatory dining room with panoramic views. The menu might include Scotch fillet steak with all the trimmings; battered cod and French fries; and a choice of curries.

Inchbae Lodge Guesthouse

Open all day **Bar Meals** L served all week 9 D served all week 9 Av main course £5 **Restaurant** L served all week 9 D served all week 9 Free House Devanha, Guinness, Isle of Skye Red Cullin & Tennents. **Facilities** Garden Parking

GLENELG MAP 22 NG81

Glenelg Inn

IV40 8JR ☎ 01599 522273 01599 522283
e-mail: christophermain7@glenelg-inn.com
dir: *From Shiel Bridge (A87) take unclassified road to Glenelg*

The inn is a conversion of 200-year-old stables set in a large garden stretching down to the sea, with stunning views across the Sound of Sleat. Musicians are frequent visitors to the bar, where at times a ceilidh atmosphere prevails. Menus offer traditional Scottish fare based on local produce, including plenty of fresh fish and seafood, hill-bred lamb, venison and seasonal vegetables. In the bar are seafood casserole and pies, while the dinner menu offers West Coast turbot with fennel and new potatoes.

Open 12–11 (Bar closed lunch in winter) **Bar Meals** L served all week 12.30–2 D served all week 6–9.30 **Restaurant** 12.30–2 7.30–9 Free House **Facilities** Garden Dogs allowed Parking

INVERIE MAP 22 NG70

The Old Forge NEW

PH41 4PL ☎ 01687 462267 01687 462267
e-mail: info@theoldforge.co.uk
dir: *Take ferry from Mallaig to Inverie*

The remotest pub in mainland Britain, The Old Forge is only accessible by boat and stands 'between heaven and hell' – Loch Nevis is Gaelic for heaven and Loch Hourn is Gaelic for hell. It's a mecca for musicians (there are plenty of instruments for impromptu use) and an ideal place to sample local fish and seafood – especially the inn's renowned platters of Loch Nevis langoustine. Other treats include home-made soup with organic bread.

Open 10.30am–1am (Sun 12–11.45) (Open at 5 Tue & Thu from Dec–Mar) **Bar Meals** L served all week 12–3 D served all week 6.30–9.30 Av main course £8.50 **Restaurant** 12–3 6.30–9.30 Free House Carlsberg extra cold, 80 Shilling, Guinness, Black Cuillin & Red Cuillin. **Facilities** Children's licence Garden Dogs allowed Parking Play Area

Moorings Inn

Walk information

Distance: 4.5 miles (7.2km)
Map: OS Explorer 392 Ben Nevis & Fort William
Start/finish: Kilmallie Hall, Corpach; grid ref NN 097768
Ascent/gradient: 2
Paths: wide towpaths
Landscape: banks of wide canal, shore of tidal loch

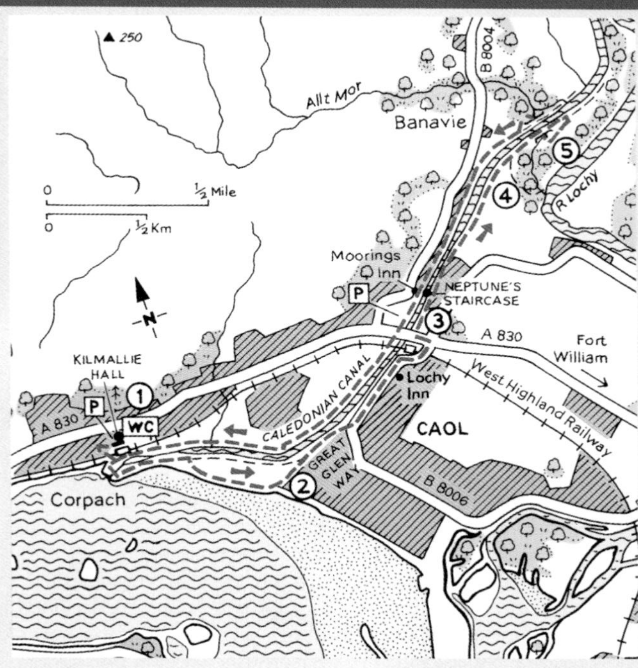

Walk directions

Ⓐ Go down past Corpach Station to the canal and cross the sea lock that separates salt water from fresh water. Follow the canal (on your left) up past another lock, where a path on the right has a blue footpath sign and a Great Glen Way marker. It passes under tall sycamores to the shore. Follow the shoreline path past a football pitch and then turn left, across damp grass to a road sign that warns motorists of a nearby playground. A path ahead leads up a wooded bank to the towpath.

Ⓑ Turn right along the towpath, for 1/2 mile (800m). Just before the Banavie swing bridge, a path down to the right has a Great Glen Way marker. Follow waymarkers on street signs to a level crossing, then turn left towards the other swing bridge, the one with the road on it.

Ⓒ Just before the bridge, turn right at signs for the Great Glen Way and the Great Glen Cycle Route and continue along the towpath to Neptune's Staircase (the Moorings Hotel on the opposite bank is encountered on the return route). The fanciful name was given to the group of eight locks by Thomas Telford himself. It takes about 90 minutes for boats to work through the system. As each lock fills, slow boiling currents come up from underneath, like bath water emptying but in reverse.

Ⓓ A gate marks the top of the locks. About 200 yards (183m) later, a grey gate on the right leads to a dump for dead cars; ignore this one. Over the next 100 yards (91m) the canal crosses a little wooded valley, with a black fence on the right. Go through a second grey gate to a track turning back sharp right and descending to ford a small stream.

Ⓔ On the right, the stream passes right under the canal in an arched tunnel, and alongside is a second tunnel which provides a walkers' way to the other side. Water from the canal drips into the tunnel – try not to think of the large boats sailing directly over your head! At the tunnel's end, a track runs up to join the canal's northern towpath. Turn right, back down the towpath. After passing the Moorings Hotel by Neptune's Staircase, cross the A830 to a level crossing without warning lights. Continue along the right-hand towpath. After a mile (1.6km) the towpath track leads back to the Corpach lock.

While there

Much to Telford's distress, the canal was a loss-making enterprise from the day it opened. One reason was the coming of the railways. At Banavie, the West Highland Railway is Britain's most beautiful. During the summer, the steam-powered Jacobite Steam Train runs daily to Mallaig and back.

Look for

From Fort William, Britain's biggest hill appears as a mere hump. The canalside, however, gives the best view into the great Northern Corrie of Ben Nevis. On its right-hand side, ranged one behind the other, rise the buttresses of the country's largest crag. Across the back runs a narrow edge of granite, linking it to Carn Mor Dearg.

The Old Inn

On a good day, you might be able to spy the Outer Hebrides from this attractive inn, though the setting is pretty fabulous whatever the weather. The pub sits at the foot of the Flowerdale Valley, looking out across Gairloch Harbour to the isles of Rona, Raasay and Skye.

Among the many activities in the area are walking, fishing, golf, birdwatching and boat trips from the adjacent harbour to see whales, porpoises and, if you are lucky, bottlenose dolphins. The inn provides a comfortable base for exploring these activities, or simply resting and lolling about on the golden beaches. The 14 bedrooms are named after famous pipers, and the atmosphere is friendly and hospitable. In the two bars you'll find the inn's own beer, the Blind Piper of Gairloch, which was created by the landlord and enthusiastic locals, alongside a good range of real ales. An extensive range of Highland malt whiskies is also available. Seafood will be the main draw in an area where Gairloch lobster, Loch Ewe scallops, Minch langoustines, mussels, brown crab and fresh fish are regularly landed. Tuck into the traditional Cullen Skink, a soup of smoked haddock, potato and cream, or steamed langoustine tails with aioli and salsa, before launching into cod and monkfish bakes; pan-seared scallops with smoked bacon mash and tamarind sauce, or grilled seafood platter with shoestring fries. Those less inclined towards the fruits of the sea might like pheasant and venison game casserole; or vegetable stuffed cannelloni topped with sherry cream. A large grassy area by the pretty stream with picnic tables is an attractive place to eat and enjoy the views. Dogs are more than welcome, with bowls, baskets and rugs to help them feel at home.

★★★ INN 🍷
MAP 22 NG87
IV21 2BD
☎ 01445 712006
📠 01445 712044
e-mail: info@theoldinn.net
dir: *Just off A832, near harbour at south end of village*

Open 11–12 (Winter eve & wkends only)
Bar Meals L served all week 12–2.30 D served all week 5–9.30 Av main course £8
Restaurant L served all week 12–5 D served all week 5–9.30 Av 3 course à la carte £22.50
Free House
Adnams Broadside, Isle of Skye Red Cullin, Blind Piper, Houston. 🍷 8
Facilities Children's licence Garden Dogs allowed Parking Play Area
Rooms 14 bedrooms en suite S£35 D£45

KYLESKU MAP 22 NC23

Pick of the Pubs

Kylesku Hotel

IV27 4HW ☎ 01971 502231 📠 01971 502313
e-mail: info@kyleskuhotel.co.uk
dir: *A894 into Kylesku to end of road at Old Ferry Pier*

A former coaching inn dating from 1680, the hotel stands by the ferry slipway between Loch Glencoul and Loch Glendhu in the Highlands of Sutherland. The Kylesku is now at the centre of Scotland's first designated Global Geopark, a 2,000 square kilometre area of loch, mountain and coastal scenery with an abundance of wildlife and wide range of outdoor activities. Real beers, 50 malt whiskies and 40 wines are served in the bar, along with bar meals and cream teas. The restaurant has panoramic views of Loch Glendhu and the mountains beyond, but wherever you eat local seafood is a speciality of the house, plus venison in season. Dishes include home-smoked salmon, crab cake with sweet chilli sauce, and ramekin of haggis to start. For the main event try moules marinière, Lochinver haddock with lemon butter, or fillet of Scottish lamb with redcurrant and rosemary sauce.

Open 11–11 Closed: 1 Nov–28 Feb **Bar Meals** L served all week 12–2.30 D served all week 6–9 Av main course £10 **Restaurant** D served Tue–Sun 7–8.30 Av 3 course fixed price £28.50 Free House Tennents Ember 80/-, Selection of Black Isle Brewery and Skye Cuillin bottled beers. **Facilities** Children's licence Garden Dogs allowed **Rooms** 6 bedrooms en suite S£40 D£70 (★★★ SH)

LYBSTER MAP 23 ND23

Portland Arms

KW3 6BS ☎ 01593 721721 📠 01593 721722
e-mail: manager.portlandarms@ohiml.com
dir: *A9 signed Latheron, A99 to Wick. 12m to Lybster*

This 19th-century coaching inn has evolved into a comfortable modern hotel. The bar and dining areas feature the best of fresh Scottish produce in settings that range from farmhouse to formal. The extensive menus cater for all tastes, with everything from a simple cheese ploughman's to chargrilled haunch of venison with haggis and black pudding. There's a children's menu too, and the home-made puddings include a tempting oat-baked fruit crumble.

Open 7.30–11 Closed: Dec 31-Jan 3 **Bar Meals** L served all week 12–3 D served all week 5–9 (Sat–Sun 12–9) Av main course £8.50 **Restaurant** L served all week 12–3 D served all week 5–9 (Sat–Sun 12–9) Av 3 course à la carte £20 Free House McEwans 70/-, Tennents Lager, Guinness & Stella Artois. **Facilities** Children's licence Dogs allowed Parking **Rooms** 22 bedrooms en suite S£60 D£70

NORTH BALLACHULISH MAP 22 NN06

Loch Leven Hotel

Old Ferry Rd PH33 6SA ☎ 01855 821236 📠 01855 821550
e-mail: reception@lochlevenhotel.co.uk
web: www.lochlevenhotel.co.uk
dir: *Off A82, N of Ballachulish Bridge*

With its relaxed atmosphere, beautiful lochside setting, and dramatic views, this privately owned hotel lies in the heart of Lochaber, 'The Outdoor Capital of the UK'. It began life over 300 years ago accommodating travellers from the adjacent Ballachulish ferry. Food is available in the restaurant and the bar, both of which offer spectacular views over the fast-flowing narrows to the mountains. Home-cooked meals are built around local produce, especially fresh seafood, game and other traditional Scottish dishes.

CONTINUED

Open 11–12 (Sun 12.30–11.45) (Closed Winter afternoons) **Bar Meals** L served all week 12–3 D served all week 6–9 Av main course £9.50 **Restaurant** L served all week 12–3 (Sun 12.30–3) D served all week 6–9 Av 3 course à la carte £20 Free House John Smith's Extra Smooth, McEwan's 80/-, Guinness, Tennent's Lager. **Facilities** Garden Dogs allowed Parking Play Area

See advert on page 707

PLOCKTON — MAP 22 NG83

Pick of the Pubs

The Plockton Hotel ★★ HL

Harbour St IV52 8TN ☎ 01599 544274 01599 544475

e-mail: info@plocktonhotel.co.uk

dir: *A87 to Kyle of Lochalsh turn at Balmacara. Plockton 7m N*

See Pick of the Pubs on opposite page

Pick of the Pubs

Plockton Inn & Seafood Restaurant

Innes St IV52 8TW ☎ 01599 544222 01599 544487

e-mail: info@plocktoninn.co.uk

dir: *On A87 to Kyle of Lochalsh take turn at Balmacara. Plockton 7m N*

See Pick of the Pubs on page 710

SHIELDAIG — MAP 22 NG85

Pick of the Pubs

Shieldaig Bar ★ SHL

IV54 8XN ☎ 01520 755251 01520 755321

e-mail: tighaneilean@kerne.co.uk

dir: *From Torridon take A896, 5m to Shieldaig. Bar on loch front*

See Pick of the Pubs on page 712

TORRIDON — MAP 22 NG95

Pick of the Pubs

The Torridon Inn ★★★ CHH

IV22 2EY ☎ 01445 791242 01445 712253

e-mail: Inn@thetorridon.com

dir: *From Inverness take A9 N, then follow signs to Ullapool. Take A335 then A832. In Kinlochelne take A896 to Annat. Pub 200yds on right after village*

On the shores of Loch Torridon, this is an ideal base for exploring Inverewe Gardens, Applecross Peninsula, and the road to Skye. The inn was created by converting the stable block, buttery and farm buildings of nearby Ben Demph House in 1996. Five real beers include the inn's own Torridon Ale, there's a good selection of wines by the glass, and malts numbered over 80 at the last count. The owners pride themselves on the local sourcing of their food; 90% comes from suppliers within an hour's drive. Delicious shellfish including Loch Ewe scallops are joined by sea bass, lemon sole, halibut and mackerel on the seafood list. Scottish meats from the butcher in Gairloch include wild boar, game and prime beef, while many fruit and vegetables originate in the kitchen garden. Even afternoon tea is memorable – don't forget to ask for the chocolate fruit cake recipe. Live music most weekends from May to September.

Open 11–11 (Mar 3–11) Closed: Nov–Feb **Bar Meals** L served all week 12–2 D served all week 6–8.45 Av main course £11.95 **Restaurant** L served all week 12–2 D served all week 6–8.45 Av 3 course à la carte £20 Isle of Skye Red Cullen, Cairngorm Brewery Stag, Torridon Ale, Blaven & Tradewinds. 8 **Facilities** Children's licence Garden Dogs allowed Parking Play Area **Rooms** 12 bedrooms en suite S£50 D£80

Scotland

The Plockton Hotel

The stone-built Plockton Hotel stands in an incomparable location just fifty metres from the gently lapping waters of Loch Carron, a sheltered sea loch that is warmed by the Gulf Stream and fringed with palm trees.

It is the only waterfront hostelry in this lovely National Trust village, surrounded by a bowl of hills, which makes an ideal base for visiting the nearby Isle of Skye. The view across the bay from the hotel to the castle and the Applecross Hills is simply breathtaking, and unlikely to be forgotten. Plockton itself was the location for both The Wicker Man in the 1970s and the fishing village of Lochdubh in the 1990s Hamish Macbeth TV series. The hotel building was converted from a ship's chandlery in 1913; now run by the Pearson family and their staff, it has been extended into the adjoining house in recent years. Menus are based on the freshest local produce, traditionally cooked and simply presented with fresh vegetables and seasonal salads. Naturally, fish and seafood – chalked on the blackboard – are a strength. Typical examples include Skye mussels, dressed crab and hand-dived Hebridean scallops. Lunchtime options range from a selection of filled white or wholemeal baps to a full meal. The evening brings an extensive menu in which local specialities are the stars. Begin with the likes of Plockton smokies (flaked smoked mackerel layered with creme fraiche, mozzarella and tomatoes and baked); or home-made whiskey paté with red onion marmalade. Follow with baked monkfish in Serrano ham served with wild rice; a casserole of Highland venison; or a selection from the grill, and be sure to leave room for home-made sweets like butterscotch and apple steamed pudding or lemon tart. A fine range of malts is available to round off that perfect Highland day.

★★ HL

MAP 22 NG83
Harbour St IV52 8TN
☎ 01599 544274
01599 544475
e-mail: info@plocktonhotel.co.uk
dir: *A87 to Kyle of Lochalsh turn at Balmacara. Plockton 7m N*

Open 11–11.45 (Sun 12.30–11)
Bar Meals L served all week 12–2.15 (Sun 12.30–2.15) D served all week 6–9.15 Av main course £6
Restaurant L served all week 12–2.15 D served all week 6–9.15 Av 3 course à la carte £23.50
Free House
Caledonian Deuchars IPA, Hebridean Gold – Isle of Skye Brewery, Harvieston Blonde Beer, Tennents Emper. 6
Facilities Garden
Rooms 15 bedrooms en suite S£45 D£100

Plockton Inn & Seafood Restaurant

This attractive stone-built free house stands just 100 metres from the harbour in the fishing village of Hamish Macbeth fame. It was originally built as a manse by the great grandfather of proprietors Mary Gollan and her brother Kenny, who were born and bred in Plockton.

Mary and Kenny, together with Kenny's partner Susan Trowbridge, bought the inn in 1997 and have since built it up to award-winning status. Mary and Susan cook and Kenny runs the bar. The atmosphere is relaxed and friendly, with winter fires in both bars, and more than 50 malt whiskies to sample. Taking pride of place on the regular and daily changing specials menus in the two eating areas, the Dining Room and the Lounge Bar, are fresh West Coast fish and shellfish, West Highland beef, lamb and game. Starters include a platter of smoked fish from the house's own smokery, accompanied by a garlic mayonnaise dip, or oyster shooters – fresh oysters served in a glass with vodka, tomato juice and herbs. Haggis and clapshot is another speciality (including a vegetarian version), served with home-made pickled beetroot. Seafood main dishes take in creel caught langoustines from the waters of Loch Carron served hot with garlic butter or cold with Marie Rose sauce; and skewers of hand dived king scallops wrapped in bacon. Crannachan ice cream is an interesting variation on the popular Scottish dessert – a creamy whipped ice cream with raspberries, honey and a dash of whisky. The National Centre of Excellence in Traditional Music is based in Plockton, which is why the inn's public bar resonates with fantastic sounds twice a week.

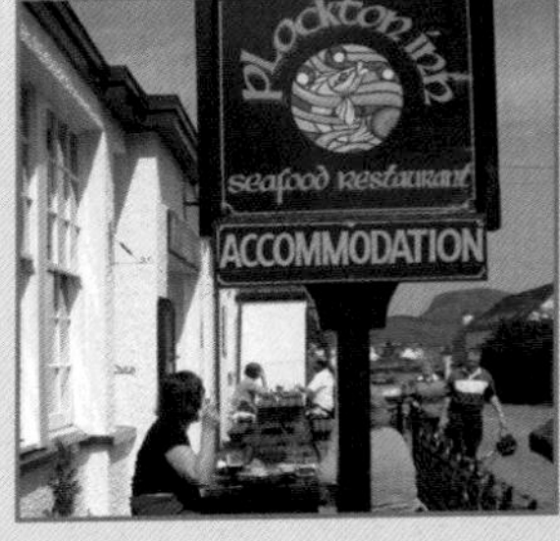

MAP 22 NG83
Innes St IV52 8TW
☎ 01599 544222
01599 544487
e-mail: info@plocktoninn.co.uk
dir: *On A87 to Kyle of Lochalsh take turn at Balmacara. Plockton 7m N*

Open 11–1am (Sun 12.30–11)
Bar Meals L served all week 12–2.30 D served all week 6.30–9.30 (Winter hrs 6–8.30/9) Av main course £10
Restaurant L served all week 12–2.30 D served all week 6.30–9.30 (Winter hrs 6–8.30/9) Av 3 course à la carte £17.50
Free House
Greene King Abbot Ale & Old Speckled Hen, Fuller's London Pride, Isle Of Skye Blaven, Caledonian 80/-.
Facilities Children's licence Garden Dogs allowed Parking Play Area
Rooms 13 en suite S£42 D£84 (★★★ INN)

ULLAPOOL MAP 22 NH19

Pick of the Pubs

The Ceilidh Place

14 West Argyle St IV26 2TY
01854 612103 01854 613773
e-mail: stay@theceilidhplace.com
dir: *On entering Ullapool, along Shore Street, pass pier, take 1st right to top of hill*

Organic growth has seen this old boatshed café metamorphose over 37 years into an all-day bar, coffee shop, restaurant, bookshop and art gallery. The late founder Robert Urquhart had aspirations for a place for serious writing – life histories, not postcards; a place for eating, meeting, talking and singing. This all came to pass and it is now known mostly for live traditional Scottish music, although some jazz slips in. The heart of The Ceilidh Place is the café/bar, with its big open fire and solid wooden furniture. It's a place to stay all day, and some do. Simple delights conjured up by the menu include mince and tatties, kedgeree, homity pie, and bone-warming cullen skink. Among the main dishes are braised venison chop; pan-roasted whole Loch Broom prawns; and seafood platter. A specials board offering seasonally available fish, meat, vegetables and fruits complements the printed menu.

Open 11–11 Closed: 2nd wk in Jan for 2 wks **Bar Meals** L served all week 12–6 D served all week 6.30–9 **Restaurant** L served all week D served all week 6.30–9.30 Av 3 course à la carte £20 Free House Belhaven Best, Guinness, Scottish ales. 8 **Facilities** Children's licence Garden Dogs allowed Parking

MIDLOTHIAN

PENICUIK MAP 21 NT25

The Howgate Restaurant

Howgate EH26 8PY 01968 670000 01968 670000
e-mail: peter@howgate.com
dir: *10m N of Peebles*

This long, low building has in the past been a racehorse stables and a dairy, but these days it makes a warm and welcoming bar and restaurant. The regularly changing menus feature a good range of dishes, from taglioni pasta with a salmon and dill sauce to braised Scotch lamb shank on chive mash with roasted root vegetables and a red wine sauce. For a vegetarian alternative try risotto of wild mushrooms and asparagus.

Open 12–2 6–11 Closed: 25–26 Dec, 1 Jan **Bar Meals** L served all week 12–2 D served all week 6–9.30 **Restaurant** L served all week 12–2 D served all week 6–9.30 Av 3 course à la carte £25 Free House Belhaven Best, Hoegaarden, Wheat Biere & Tennents Lager. 12 **Facilities** Children's licence Garden Parking

MORAY

FOCHABERS MAP 23 NJ35

Gordon Arms Hotel

80 High St IV32 7DH 01343 820508 01343 820300
e-mail: info@gordonarms.co.uk
dir: *A96 between Aberdeen and Inverness, 9m from Elgin*

This 200-year old former coaching inn, close to the River Spey and within easy reach of Speyside's whisky distilleries, is understandably popular with salmon fishers, golfers and walkers. Its public rooms have been carefully refurbished, and the hotel makes an ideal base from which to explore this scenic corner of Scotland. The cuisine makes full use of local produce: venison, lamb and game from the uplands, fish and seafood from the Moray coast, beef from Aberdeenshire and salmon from the Spey – barely a stone's throw from the kitchen!

Open 11–3 5–11 (Sun 12–3, 6–10.30) **Bar Meals** L served all week 12–2 D served all week 5–6.45 **Restaurant** L served all week 12–2 D served all week 7–9 Free House Caledonian Deuchars IPA, Scottish Courage John Smith's Smooth, Marstons Pedigree. **Facilities** Children's licence Dogs allowed Parking

NORTH LANARKSHIRE

CUMBERNAULD MAP 21 NS77

Castlecary House Hotel ★★ HL

Castlecary Rd G68 0HD 01324 840233 01324 841608
e-mail: enquiries@castlecaryhotel.com
web: www.castlecaryhotel.com
dir: *Off A80 onto B816 between Glasgow & Stirling*

Run by the same family for over 30 years, this friendly hotel is located close to the historic Antonine Wall and Forth and Clyde Canal. Meals in the lounge bars plough a traditional furrow with options such as home-made lasagna; oven-roasted Scottish salmon fillet with a cherry tomato and spring onion hollandaise; and a range flame-grilled burgers. More formal restaurant fare is available in Camerons Restaurant.

Open 11–11.30 **Bar Meals** L served all week 12–9 D served all week 12–9 Av main course £7.25 **Restaurant** D served Mon–Sat 6–9.45 (Sun high tea 12.30–6.45) Av 3 course à la carte £20 Av fixed price £20 Free House Arran Blonde, Harviestoun Brooker's Bitter & Twisted, Inveralmond Ossian's Ale, Housten Peter's Well. 10 **Facilities** Children's licence Garden Dogs allowed Parking **Rooms** 55 bedrooms en suite S£70 D£70

Scotland

Shieldaig Bar

You can enjoy stunning views across Loch Torridon to the sea beyond from this popular loch-front bar. Set in a charming fishing village, it comes alive on summer weekend nights with the sound of local musicians, among them owner Chris Field, playing guitar, banjo or pipes.

In fact, all over Wester Ross you are likely to find music like this being played somewhere. Throughout the day a full range of alcoholic and non-alcoholic beverages is served to suit the hour, and there's always a ready supply of newspapers and magazines to read. The pub has a fine reputation for its bar meals – sandwiches, home-made soups, burgers and bangers and mash – and for its daily-changing specials, such as Shieldaig crab cakes with tarragon mayonnaise; moules marinière; whole loch Torridon langoustines with a lemongrass, chilli and coriander dipping sauce; and the speciality Shieldaig bar seafood stew. All the seafood is caught locally, some from local prawn-fishing grounds which have won a sustainable fishery award. Alternatives might be local venison sausages with mash and a red wine and onion gravy; haggis with neeps and tatties; bigos (a Polish stew of mixed game and other meats) with pickled vegetables and home-made bread; or a shallot and goats' cheese tart with salad and new potatoes. Food is now served all day in summer, when you can also dine in the lochside courtyard, warmed, if necessary, by patio heaters. A good range of real ales is on tap from the Isle of Skye Brewery and Black Isle Ales, plus malt whiskies and a choice of wines by the glass. It's the sort of place you'll want to linger, so take note that the Fields also own the Tigh an Eilean Hotel next door

★ SHL ◎◎ ⇨ 🍷
MAP 22 NG85
IV54 8XN
☎ 01520 755251
🖷 01520 755321
e-mail:
tighaneilean@kerne.co.uk
dir: *From Torridon take A896, 5m to Shieldaig. Bar on loch front*

Open 11–11 Closed: 25 Dec, 1 Jan
Bar Meals L served all week 12–2.30 D served all week 6–8.30 Av main course £8.75
Restaurant D served all week 7–8.30 Av 3 course fixed price £42.50
Free House
Isle of Skye Brewery Ales, Tennents Superior Ale, Black Isle Ales. 🍷 12
Facilities Children's licence Garden Dogs allowed Parking
Rooms 11 bedrooms en suite S£70 D£150

PERTH & KINROSS

GLENDEVON

MAP 21 NN90

Pick of the Pubs

The Tormaukin Country Inn and Restaurant ★★★★ INN

FK14 7JY ☎ 01259 781252 01259 781526
e-mail: enquiries@tormaukin.co.uk
dir: *Exit at Yelts of Muckhard onto A823/Crieff*

This attractive whitewashed free house was built in 1720 as a drovers' inn, at a time when Glendevon was frequented by cattlemen making their way from the Tryst of Crieff to the market place at Falkirk. The name Tormaukin, which in Gaelic means hill of the mountain hare, reflects the inn's serene, romantic location in the midst of the Ochil Hills. The inn has been sympathetically refurbished throughout, but still bristles with real Scottish character and charm; original features like the stone walls, exposed beams and blazing winter fires in the cosy public rooms ensure a warm and welcoming atmosphere. The dinner menu is impressive and includes a good range of fish dishes like smoked haddock chowder, scallops with black pudding, and langoustines in garlic butter. Live music is a regular feature at the inn, and golfing breaks are available.

Open 12–11 **Bar Meals** L served all week 12–3.30 D served all week 5.30–9.30 (all day wknds) Av main course £14.95 **Restaurant** L served all week 12–3 D served all week 5.30–9 Av 3 course à la carte £30 Av 3 course fixed price £12.95 Free House Bitter & Twisted. 8 **Facilities** Garden Parking **Rooms** 12 bedrooms en suite S£85 D£100

GLENFARG

MAP 21 NO11

The Famous Bein Inn

PH2 9PY ☎ 01577 830216 01577 830211
e-mail: enquiries@beininn.com

Many famous musicians have performed in this inn's lively Bistro Bar, and the memorabilia collection in the Basement Bar rivals anything to be seen in a Hard Rock Café. It has been welcoming guests since 1861, and the atmosphere is enhanced by a log fire and a wood burning stove. House specialities include noisettes of Scottish lamb; and vegetables Bonnie Prince Charlie (cooked in Drambuie and mushroom sauce, and served with rice and noodles).

The Famous Bein Inn

Open 11–2.30 5–11 (Sat–Sun all day) **Bar Meals** L served all week 12–2 D served all week 5–9 Av main course £9 **Restaurant** L served Sat–Sun 12–2 D served all week 5–9 (Sat–Sun all day) Av 3 course à la carte £20 Free House Independence, Ossian, Guinness, Boddingtons & Tennents. **Facilities** Dogs allowed Parking **Rooms** 11 bedrooms S£45 D£70 (★★ INN)

KILLIECRANKIE

MAP 23 NN96

Pick of the Pubs

Killiecrankie House Hotel

PH16 5LG ☎ 01796 473220 01796 472451
e-mail: enquiries@killiecrankiehotel.co.uk
dir: *B8079 N from Pitlochry. 3m after NT Visitor Centre*

This long-established hotel, restaurant and bar is set in four sprawling acres of wooded grounds at the northern end of the historic Killiecrankie Pass. Built in 1840 as a dower house, it was converted to a hotel in 1940. It stands near the site of the Battle of Killiecrankie and overlooks the intriguingly named Soldier's Leap. It holds such a special place in Scottish history that it has a National Trust Visitor Centre dedicated to its history and current wildlife. The menu offers the best local produce, including seasonal vegetables, fruits and herbs from the garden. The conservatory makes an ideal spot for informal eating, while dinner is served in the elegant dining room. An excellent choice of light lunches includes open sandwiches and home-made salmon fishcakes, while more substantial supper dishes may offer traditional cock-a-leekie followed by home-made Aberdeen Angus cheeseburger with side salad and chips.

Open 12–2.30 6–11 Closed: Jan & Feb **Bar Meals** L served all week 12.30–2 D served all week 6.30–9 Av main course £9 **Restaurant** D served all week 6.15–8.30 Av 3 course à la carte £28 Free House Tennents Velvet Ale, Red McGregor, Becks, Deuchers IPA. 8 **Facilities** Children's licence Garden Dogs allowed Parking **Rooms** 10 bedrooms en suite S£65 D£130 (★★★★ SH)

Moulin Hotel

French-speakers might instinctively pronounce Moulin as they do in France. After all, it looks like their word for mill, but Moulin is actually derived from the Gaelic 'maohlinn', meaning either smooth rocks or calm water – a tad confusing, but presumably the locals know.

This old inn faces Moulin's square, a rewarding three-quarters of a mile from the busy tourist centre of Pitlochry. Awarded the accolade of AA Scottish Pub of the Year 2006, its popularity is partly due to the fact that it opened its own microbrewery in 1995 to celebrate the building's tercentenary. Since the area is known as the Vale of Atholl, don't be too surprised to find that the name of one of the house beers is the same. A major refurbishment of the building in the 1990s opened up old fireplaces and beautiful stone walls that had been hidden for many years, and lots of cosy niches were created using timbers from the old Coach House (now the brewery). The courtyard garden is lovely in summer, while blazing log fires warm the Moulin's innards in winter. Menus partly reflect the inn's Highlands location, and although more familiar dishes are available such as seafood pancake, lamb shank, and trio of salmon, you also have the opportunity to try something more ethnic, such as deep-fried haggis; venison Braveheart; Scotsman's bunnet, which is a meat and vegetable stew-filled batter pudding; or a plate of sauté potatoes, smoked bacon and fried egg, otherwise known as vrackie grostel. You might then round off your meal with ice cream with Highland toffee sauce, or bread and butter pudding. A specials board broadens the choice further. Around 20 wines by the glass and more than 30 malt whiskies are available.

★★ HL 🍷
MAP 23 NN95
11–13 Kirkmichael Rd, Moulin
PH16 5EH
☎ 01796 472196
01796 474098
e-mail:
enquiries@moulinhotel.co.uk
dir: *From A924 at Pitlochry take A923. Moulin 0.75m*

Open 12–11 (Fri–Sat 12–11.45)
Bar Meals L served all week 12–9.30 D served all week 12 Av main course £6.95
Restaurant D served all week 6–9 Av 3 course à la carte £25 Av 4 course fixed price £22.50
Free House
Moulin Braveheart, Old Remedial, Ale of Atholl & Moulin Light. 🍷 20
Facilities Garden Parking
Rooms 15 bedrooms en suite S£45 D£60

KINNESSWOOD MAP 21 NO10

Pick of the Pubs

Lomond Country Inn

KY13 9HN ☎ 01592 840253 01592 840693
e-mail: info@lomondcountryinn.co.uk
dir: *M90 junct 5, follow signs for Glenrothes then Scotlandwell, Kinnesswood next village*

A small, privately owned hotel on the slopes of the Lomond Hills that has been entertaining guests for more than 100 years. It is the only hostelry in the area with uninterrupted views over Loch Leven to the island on which Mary Queen of Scots was imprisoned. Cosy public areas offer log fires, a friendly atmosphere, real ales and a fine collection of single malts. If you want to make the most of the loch views, choose the charming restaurant, a relaxing room freshly decorated in country house style. Specials may include supreme of guinea fowl on creamed mash with Calvados sauce, roast sirloin of beef, or strips of chicken with a leek and stilton sauce. A selection of grills is also available.

Open 11–11 (Fri–Sat 11–12.45, Sun 12.30–11) Closed: Dec 25 **Bar Meals** L served all week 12.30–2 D served all week 6–9 Av main course £7 **Restaurant** L served all week 12–2.30 D served all week 6–9.30 (Sun all day) Av 3 course à la carte £25 Free House Deuchers IPA, Calders Cream, Tetleys, Orkney Dark Island. 6 **Facilities** Garden Dogs allowed Parking Play Area

PITLOCHRY MAP 23 NN95

Pick of the Pubs

Moulin Hotel ★★ HL

11–13 Kirkmichael Rd, Moulin PH16 5EH
☎ 01796 472196 01796 474098
e-mail: enquiries@moulinhotel.co.uk
dir: *From A924 at Pitlochry take A923. Moulin 0.75m*

See Pick of the Pubs on opposite page

RENFREWSHIRE

HOUSTON MAP 20 NS46

Fox & Hounds

South St PA6 7EN
☎ 01505 612448 & 612991 01505 614133
e-mail: jonathan@foxandhoundshouston.co.uk
dir: *A737, W from Glasgow. Johnstone Bridge off Weir exit, signs for Houston to village centre*

Beer lovers flock to this 18th-century village inn, home to the award-winning Houston Brewing Company. Alongside an impressive list of international bottled beers are two equally appealing bar and restaurant menus. Try smoked trout, rocket and potato salad in the bar; followed by Irish stew with creamy mash. Alternately, in the restaurant sample crayfish and tomato bisque, and a main course of chicken breast stuffed with tomato and basil.

Open 11–12 (Fri–Sat 11–1am, Sun 12.30–12) **Bar Meals** L served all week 12–10 D served all week 12–10 Av main course £9 **Restaurant** L served all week 12–10 D served all week 12–10 Av 3 course à la carte £22 Free House St Peters Well, Killelan, Warlock Stout, Texas & Jock Frost. 10 **Facilities** Children's licence Garden Dogs allowed Parking

Scotland

SCOTTISH BORDERS

ALLANTON — MAP 21 NT85

Allanton Inn

TD11 3JZ ☎ 01890 818260

e-mail: info@allantoninn.co.uk

dir: *From A1 at Berwick take A6105 for Chirnside (5m). At Chirnside Inn take Coldstream Rd for 1m to Allanton.*

Highly acclaimed for its food, this award-winning establishment is housed in an 18th-century coaching inn. Outside is a large lawned area with fruit trees overlooking open countryside. Inside are two restaurants and a cosy bar serving real ales and a range of malt whiskies. Daily changing menus may offer braised beef and Guinness casserole with a puff pastry crust at lunch, and monkfish tail sautéed onto a risotto of asparagus, mussels and rocket for dinner.

Open 12–2 6–10.30 **Bar Meals** L served Wed–Sun 12–1 D served all week 6–8.30 **Restaurant** L served Wed–Sun 12–1 D served all week 6–8.30 Free House Ossian, Bitter and Twisted, Latitude, Deuchars & Wylam. **Facilities** Children's licence Garden Dogs allowed Parking

ETTRICK — MAP 21 NT21

Tushielaw Inn

TD7 5HT ☎ 01750 62205 01750 62205

e-mail: robin@tushielaw.fsnet.co.uk

dir: *At junction of B709 & B711 (W of Hawick)*

An 18th-century former toll house and drovers' halt on the banks of Ettrick water, making a good base for trout fishing and those tackling the Southern Upland Way. An extensive menu is always available with daily changing specials. Fresh produce is used according to season, with local lamb and Aberdeen Angus beef regular specialities, and gluten-free and vegetarian meals. Home-made steak and stout pie and sticky toffee pudding rate among other popular dishes.

Open 12–2.30 6.30–11 **Bar Meals** L served all week 12–2 D served all week 7–9 **Restaurant** L served all week 12–2 D served all week 7–9 Free House **Facilities** Children's licence Dogs allowed Parking **Rooms** 3 bedrooms en suite S£34 D£54 (★★ INN)

GALASHIELS — MAP 21 NT43

Kingsknowes Hotel ★★★ HL

1 Selkirk Rd TD1 3HY ☎ 01896 758375 01896 750377

e-mail: enquiries@kingsknowes.co.uk

dir: *Off A7 at Galashiels/Selkirk rdbt*

In over three acres of grounds on the banks of the Tweed, a splendid baronial mansion built in 1869 for a textile magnate. There are lovely views of the Eildon Hills and Abbotsford House, Sir Walter Scott's ancestral home. Meals are served in two restaurants and the Courtyard Bar, where fresh local or regional produce is used as much as possible. The impressive glass conservatory is the ideal place to enjoy a drink.

Open 12–12 **Bar Meals** L served all week 11.45–2 D served all week 5.45–9.30 Av main course £8.50 **Restaurant** L served all week 11.45–2 D served all week 5.45–9.30 Free House McEwans 80/-, Scottish Courage John Smith's. **Facilities** Garden Dogs allowed Parking Play Area **Rooms** 12 bedrooms en suite S£65 D£95

INNERLEITHEN — MAP 21 NT33

Corner House NEW

1 Chapel St EH44 6HN ☎ 01896 831181 01896 831182

e-mail: cornerhouse@hotmail.com

dir: *From Galashiels take A72 W. Innerleithen in 12m*

This family-run hotel occupies a characterful street-corner building in the heart of Innerleithen and is a great place to relax after a day spent walking or biking at Glentress or Innerleithen. With well-equipped rooms and a generous menu in the restaurant, it may tempt you to stay longer than you first intended.

Open 11–12 **Bar Meals** L served all week 12–8.45 D served all week 12–8.45 Av main course £6 **Restaurant** L served all week 12–8.45 D served all week 12–8.45 Belhaven Belhaven Best, Carlsberg, Guinness, Strongbow. **Facilities** Children's licence Garden Dogs allowed Parking

LAUDER — MAP 21 NT54

Pick of the Pubs

The Black Bull ★★★★ INN

Market Place TD2 6SR

☎ 01578 722208 01578 722419

e-mail: enquiries@blackbull-lauder.com

dir: *In centre of Lauder on A68*

See Pick of the Pubs on opposite page

LEITHOLM — MAP 21 NT74

The Plough Hotel NEW

Main St TD12 4JN ☎ 01890 840252 01890 840252

e-mail: theplough@leitholm.wanadoo.co.uk

dir: *5m N of Coldstream on A697. Take B6461, Leitholm in 1m*

The only pub remaining in this small border village (there were originally two), the Plough dates from the 17th century and was once a coaching inn. A programme of major refurbishment and expansion is highlighting the building's historic features. Locally bred Aberdeen Angus beef is a speciality of the menu, along with fresh fish from Eyemouth. Frequent barbecues in the summer make the most of the long south facing beer garden, complete with decking.

Open 12–12 (Fri–Sat 12–1am) **Bar Meals** L served Tue–Sun 12–2 D served Tue–Sun 6–9 Av main course £7.95 **Restaurant** L served Tue–Sun 12–2 D served Tue–Sun 6–9 Free House Tennents, Guinness, Real Ale, Stella & Westons Cider. 8 **Facilities** Children's licence Garden Parking

The Black Bull

Dazzlingly white in the sun, a three-storey coaching inn dating from 1750. The large dining room was once a chapel, and the church spire remains in the roof! Proprietor Maureen Rennie bought the hotel in a decrepit state but has transformed it into a cosy, characterful hotel with lots of interesting pictures and artefacts.

She has gone on to win a host of prestigious awards, including AA Pub of the Year for Scotland a few years ago. Maureen uses only the best quality local beef, lamb, fish and seasonal game, all, of course, prepared to order. Lunch could begin with that hearty fish and potato soup, cullen skink; a platter of Belhaven smoked salmon with lemon and granary bread; or Italian-style meatballs with tomato sauce, spaghetti and fresh parmesan. Scottish fare is prominent among the mains too, with Wedderlie (a farm) Aberdeen Angus beef, Guinness and mushroom pie; grilled Stichill (a nearby village) cream cheese croutons with mixed leaves and balsamic vinaigrette; and wholetail Scottish scampi.

Bar suppers echo lunch, although again don't expect everything to be Scottish. Perhaps terrine of pheasant, duck and pistachios with tomato chutney to start; grilled fillet of salmon with sun-blushed tomato and olive crust; or lamb and spinach curry with cucumber raita, poppadom and steamed basmati rice. A selection of specials might include breast of duck with puy lentils and teriyaki vegetables; or corn-fed chicken breast with herbed mascarpone, pea and pancetta risotto. For hotel guests who have had a successful day on the Leader Water, a tributary of the Tweed, the kitchen will happily prepare your catch for dinner.

★★★★ INN 🍷
MAP 21 NT54
Market Place TD2 6SR
☎ 01578 722208
📠 01578 722419
e-mail:
enquiries@blackbull-lauder.com
dir: *In centre of Lauder on A68*

Open 12–2.30 5–9 (Winter 12–2, 5.30–9) Closed: 1st 3 wks in Feb
Bar Meals L served all week 12–2.30 D served all week 5–9
Av main course £9.50
Restaurant L served all week 12–2.30 D served all week 5–9
Av 3 course à la carte £18.50
Free House
Broughton Ales, Carling Lager, Guinness, Worthington & Caffreys.
🍷 16
Facilities Children's licence Dogs allowed Parking
Rooms 8 bedrooms en suite
S£55 D£80

The Wheatsheaf at Swinton

In the past few years, the award-winning Wheatsheaf has built up an impressive reputation as a dining destination. Run by husband and wife team Chris and Jan Winson, this popular venue is tucked away in the picturesque village of Swinton.

The surrounding area has much to offer tourists and travellers. The former county town of Duns – a short drive away – is a great starting point for ramblers keen to explore walking trails on the 190-acre Duns Castle nature reserve. The Jim Clark Museum is also nearby, devoted to the late world champion racing driver from Chirnside. Golfers will do well to invest in a 'freedom of the fairways' passport, which gives access to 21 superb golf courses throughout the region, including The Roxburghe championship golf course at Kelso. All that fresh air makes for good appetites, and thoughts will quickly turn to food. The Wheatsheaf's secret is to use carefully sourced local ingredients, used in imaginative combinations. The lunch menu offers the likes of sautéed Paris brown mushrooms with bacon in filo pastry with glazed Tobermory cheddar to start; and wild mushroom and spinach risotto with roast asparagus to follow. The dinner menu has similar dishes, offering perhaps pheasant, pork, chestnut and raisin terrine, to be followed by seared salmon with a gruyere and herb crust, or fillet of Scotch beef on an oyster mushroom, shallot and white truffle oil sauce. Desserts are not to be missed: iced poppy seed and cinnamon parfait with spiced roast plums, or warm apple crepes with Roquefort and mascarpone cheese and honey ice cream are two of several appealing options. The wine list provides useful tasting notes, and there are lots of malt whiskies to try for an after-dinner tipple. Ten comfortably furnished en suite bedrooms await the weary guest.

★★★★ RR ◎◎ 🍷
MAP 21 NT84
Main St TD11 3JJ
☎ 01890 860257
📠 01890 860688
e-mail: reception@wheatsheaf-swinton.co.uk
dir: *From Edinburgh A697 onto B6461. From E Lothian, A1 onto B6461.*

Open 11–3 6–11 (Closed Sun eve in winter) Closed: 25–27, 31 Dec, 1 Jan
Bar Meals L served all week 12–2 D served all week 6–9 (Sun 6–8.30) Av main course £8
Restaurant L served all week 12–2 D served all week 6–9 (Sun 6–8.30) Av 3 course à la carte £27
Free House
Deuchers IPA, Broughton Greenmantle Ale, Belhaven Best, Carlsberg. 🍷 10
Facilities Children's licence Parking
Rooms 10 bedrooms en suite S£69 D£102

MELROSE MAP 21 NT53

Pick of the Pubs

Burts Hotel ★★★ HL

Market Square TD6 9PL

01896 822285 01896 822870

e-mail: burtshotel@aol.com

dir: *A6091, 2m from A68 3m S of Earlston*

This very civilised hotel, which overlooks the picturesque market square in the historic town of Melrose, was built in 1722 as a townhouse for a local dignitary. For some time it was a temperance hotel, but with today's selection of several real ales, over 60 single malt whiskies and half a dozen wines by the glass, there's no danger of running dry. Graham and Anne Henderson have been running the award-winning business for over 35 years, more recently supported by their son Nicholas and wife Trish. Their personal attention ensures the highest standards of comfort, service and cuisine. For a true taste of the Borders, dinner might start with smoked haddock, potato and shrimp chowder; follow perhaps with a breast of chicken coated in oatmeal stuffed with haggis, served on a bed of pesto mash with a Drambuie cream sauce; and finish with sticky toffee pudding, vanilla ice cream and butterscotch sauce.

Open 11–2.30 5–11 **Bar Meals** L served all week 12–2 D served all week 6–9.30 Av main course £9.95 **Restaurant** L served all week 12–2 D served all week 7–9 Av 3 course à la carte £35 Av 3 course fixed price £32.50 Free House Caledonian 80/-, Deuchars IPA, Timothy Taylor Landlord, Fullers London Pride. 7 **Facilities** Children's licence Garden Dogs allowed Parking **Rooms** 20 bedrooms en suite S£60 D£112

ST BOSWELLS MAP 21 NT53

Buccleuch Arms Hotel ★★ HL

The Green TD6 0EW 01835 822243 01835 823965

e-mail: info@buccleucharms.com

dir: *On A68, 10m N of Jedburgh. Hotel on village green*

'Relax, unwind, enjoy' is the exhortation of this smart and friendly country house hotel. Built in the 16th century, it boasts a spacious garden and children's play area. Lunch might take in steak and ale pie, club sandwiches or home-made beef lasagne, while diners can sample coconut sweet potato curry; chargrilled lamb cutlets, or grilled fillet of sea bream from the extensive menus. The nineteen en suite bedrooms are well appointed and luxurious.

Open 7.30–11 Closed: 25 Dec **Bar Meals** L served all week 12–8.30 D served all week Av main course £10 **Restaurant** 12–2 D served all week 6–9 (Sun 12–8.30) Free House John Smiths, Guinness, Broughton. 8 **Facilities** Children's licence Garden Dogs allowed Parking Play Area **Rooms** 19 bedrooms en suite S£55 D£95

SWINTON MAP 21 NT84

Pick of the Pubs

The Wheatsheaf at Swinton

★★★★ RR

Main St TD11 3JJ 01890 860257 01890 860688

e-mail: reception@wheatsheaf-swinton.co.uk

dir: *From Edinburgh A697 onto B6461. From E Lothian, A1 onto B6461*

See Pick of the Pubs on opposite page

TIBBIE SHIELS INN MAP 21 NT22

Pick of the Pubs

Tibbie Shiels Inn

St Mary's Loch TD7 5LH

01750 42231 01750 42302

dir: *From Moffat take A708. Inn is 14m on right*

On the isthmus between St Mary's Loch and the Loch of the Lowes, this waterside Inn is named after the woman who first opened it in 1826 and expanded the inn from a small cottage to a hostelry capable of sleeping around 35 people, many of them on the floor! Famous visitors during her time included Walter Scott, Thomas Carlyle and Robert L. Stevenson. Tibbie Shiels herself is rumoured to keep watch over the bar, where the selection of over 50 malt whiskeys will sustain you for ghost watching! Meals can be enjoyed either in the bar or the non-smoking dining room; the inn also offers packed lunches for your walking, windsurfing or fishing expedition (residents fish free of charge). The menu offers a wide range of vegetarian options as well as local fish and game: highlights include Yarrow trout and Tibbies mixed grill.

Open 11–11 (Sun 12.30–11) Rest: 1Nov–Easter closed Mon, Tue & Wed **Bar Meals** L served all week 12.30–8 D served all week 12.30–8 Av main course £6.50 **Restaurant** L served all week 12.30–8 D served all week 12.30–8 Av 3 course à la carte £11.25 Free House Broughton Greenmantle Ale, Belhaven 80/-. **Facilities** Children's licence Garden Parking

WEST LINTON MAP 21 NT15

The Gordon Arms NEW

Dolphinton Rd EH46 7DR

01968 660208 01968 661852

e-mail: info@thegordon.co.uk

Set in the pretty village of West Linton but within easy reach of the M74, this 17th-century inn has a real log fire in the cosy lounge bar, and a lovely sun-trap beer garden. One of the pub's aims is to support the Scottish microbrewery industry as much as possible, so expect a changing selection of excellent ales. A meal might include Jamaican jerked chicken, followed by grilled sea bass with an orange sauce.

CONTINUED

Scotland

WEST LINTON continued

Open 10–12 (Winter 10–11, Fri–Sat 10–1am) **Bar Meals** L served all week 12–3 D served all week 6–9 (Sat–Sun 12–9) **Restaurant** L served all week 12–3 D served all week 6–9 (Sat–Sun 12–9) Av 3 course fixed price £25 Scottish & Newcastle Pub Enterprises Tennents, John Smiths, Guinness, Real Ales. **Facilities** Children's licence Garden Dogs allowed Parking **Rooms** 4 bedrooms en suite S£40 D£65 (★★★ INN)

SOUTH AYRSHIRE

SYMINGTON — MAP 20 NS33

Wheatsheaf Inn

Main St KA1 5QB ☎ 01563 830307 01563 830307

dir: *Telephone for directions*

This 17th-century inn lies in a lovely village setting close to the Royal Troon Golf Course, and there has been a hostelry here since the 1500s. Log fires burn in every room and the work of local artists adorns the walls. Seafood highlights the menu – maybe pan-fried scallops in lemon and chives – and alternatives include honey roasted lamb shank; haggis, tatties and neeps in Drambuie and onion cream, and the renowned steak pie.

Open 11–12 (Sun 11–11) Closed: 25 Dec, 1 Jan **Bar Meals** L served all week 12–9.30 Av main course £8 **Restaurant** D served all week 12–9.30 Belhaven Belhaven Best, St Andrews Ale, Tennents & Stella. **Facilities** Garden Parking

STIRLING

ARDEONAIG — MAP 20 NN63

The Ardeonaig Hotel NEW

South Lock Tay Side FK21 8SU

☎ 01567 820400 01567 820282

e-mail: info@ardeonaighotel.co.uk

dir: *On South Lock Tay road 1m from Killin, 10m from Kenmore*

Good food and wine are an important part of life at Ardeonaig, which is set within ten acres of private grounds on the shores of Loch Tay. Home-grown vegetables and locally produced ingredients feature strongly on the modern British menus in both the bistro and the restaurant. Dishes like Loch Tarbert lobster risotto; roasted wood pigeon with sweet potato and caramelised onion; and Highland beef, wild mushrooms and Marsala sauce are typical choices.

Open 12–11 (Fri–Sat 12–12) **Bar Meals** L served all week 11–10 D served all week 11–10 Av main course £11 **Restaurant** L served wknds 11–10 D served all week 11–10 Av 3 course à la carte £35.50 Av 3 course fixed price £26.50 Free House Arran Blonde, Tusker, Castle Larger, Windhoek Larger. **Facilities** Garden Dogs allowed Parking

BALQUHIDDER — MAP 20 NN52

Pick of the Pubs

Monachyle Mhor

FK19 8PQ ☎ 01877 384622 01877 384305

e-mail: info@monachylemhor.com

dir: *On A84, 11m N of Callender, turn right at Kingshouse. Establishment in 6m (between 2 lochs)*

Dramatic loch and mountain views are standard at this small, award-winning farmhouse hotel. Romantically located within 2,000 acres of Scotland's first National Park, Monachyle Mhor stands not far from Rob Roy's final resting place. The interiors are resplendent with open fires, antique furniture and country fabrics, as well as sporting prints and original modern art. Excellent menus change daily to reflect the seasons, with ingredients from the hotel's own organic garden as well as the rivers, lochs and hills of the estate. Starting with roasted cauliflower soup with truffle oil topping, lunchtime diners might move on to fillet of red fish in coconut and Shetland mussel broth with green Asian vegetables and coriander; or roasted Perthshire beef with creamed potatoes and hazelnut-crusted fennel gratin. Home-made puddings include chocolate and pear tart with praline ice cream.

Open 12 Closed: Jan–14 Feb **Bar Meals** L served all week 12–3 D served all week 7–8.45 Av main course £20 **Restaurant** L served all week 12–1.45 D served all week 7–8.45 Free House Heather Ale, Guinness, Organic Red Rite, Black Isle Porter & Tennents Lager Velvet. **Facilities** Garden Parking **Rooms** 11 bedrooms en suite S£85 D£95 (★★★★ SH)

CALLANDER — MAP 20 NN60

The Lade Inn

Kilmahog FK17 8HD ☎ 01877 330152

e-mail: info@theladeinn.com / frank@theladeinn.com

dir: *A821 towards Aberfoyle. Pub on right*

Built in 1935 as a tearoom serving the Trossachs National Park area, the Lade Inn was licensed in the 1960s, taking its name from the river that feeds the local woollen mills. It's a family-friendly traditional Scottish pub/restaurant, committed to providing value for money while supporting regional food producers and caring for the environment. The real ales certainly don't travel far – the Trossachs Craft Brewery is on site; its shop offers over 100 bottled Scottish varieties.

Open 12–11 (Sat 12–1am, Sun 12.30–10.30) (New year open to 4am) **Bar Meals** L served all week 12–9 D served all week 12–9 (Sun 12.30–9) Av main course £8 **Restaurant** L served all week 12–9 D served all week 12–9 (Sun 12.30–9) Av 3 course à la carte £16 Free House Local ales: Waylade, Lade Back, Lade Out, Guinness. 9 **Facilities** Children's licence Garden Dogs allowed Parking Play Area

DRYMEN — MAP 20 NS48

The Clachan Inn

2 Main St G63 0BG ☎ 01360 660824

Quaint, white-painted cottage, believed to be the oldest licensed pub in Scotland, situated in a small village on the West Highland Way, and once owned by Rob Roy's sister. Locate the appealing lounge bar for freshly-made food, the varied menu listing filled baked potatoes, salads, fresh haddock in crispy breadcrumbs, spicy Malaysian lamb casserole, vegetable lasagne, a variety of steaks, and daily specials.

Open 11–12 (Sun 12.30–12) Closed: 25 Dec & 1 Jan **Bar Meals** L served all week 12–4 D served all week 6–10 (Sun 12.30–4, 5–10) **Restaurant** L served all week 12–4 D served all week 6–10 (Sun 12.30–4, 5–10) Free House Caledonian Deuchars IPA, Belhaven Best, Tennents Lager, Budvar & Guinness. **Facilities** Dogs allowed Parking

KIPPEN MAP 20 NS69

Cross Keys Hotel

Main St FK8 3DN ☎ 01786 870293

e-mail: crosskeys@kippen70.fsnet.co.uk

dir: *10m W of Stirling, 20m from Loch Lomond off the A811*

The village of Kippen in the Fintry Hills overlooking the Forth Valley has strong associations with Rob Roy. The pub dates from 1703, retains its original stone walls, and enjoys real fires in winter. Nearby Burnside Wood is managed by a local community woodland group, and is perfect for walking and nature trails. An excellent range of home-made dishes includes Scottish smoked salmon platter; creamy smoked haddock omelette; and steak and mushroom pie. There's no food on Mondays in winter.

Open 12–2.30 5.30–11 (Fri 5.30–12, Sat 12–12, Sun 12.30–11) Closed: 25 Dec, 1 Jan **Bar Meals** L served all week 12–2 D served all week 5.30–9 (Sun 12.30–9, winter 5.30–8.30) Av main course £8.50 **Restaurant** L served all week 12–2 D served all week 5.30–9 (Sun 12.30–9) Free House Belhaven Best, IPA, 80/-, Harviestoun Bitter & Twisted. **Facilities** Children's licence Garden Dogs allowed Parking

Pick of the Pubs

AA PUB OF THE YEAR FOR SCOTLAND 2007-8

The Inn at Kippen

Fore Rd FK8 3DT ☎ 01786 871010 01786 871011

e-mail: info@theinnatkippen.co.uk

dir: *From Stirling take A811 to Loch Lomond. Take 1st left at Kippen station rdbt, then 1st right onto Fore Road. Inn on left*

Previously the Crown, the Inn at Kippen was taken over five years ago by James Fletcher and Laurie Newlands, who refurbished it to create a chic yet cosy country inn. The pretty beer garden now has an authentic wood-fired oven where Italian pizzas with a Scottish twist are cooked in the spring and summer months; a small beer festival with hog roast also takes place here in August or September. The stylish interior includes a fine dining restaurant where fresh local produce is carefully prepared – the beef and lamb come from Kippen itself. You may also find smoked salmon from the Outer Hebrides, scallops from Scrabster, and delicious bread baked in the nearby village of Fallin. The 'Old Favourites' include Aberdeen Angus beefburger with hand-cut chips, and Cameron's pork sausages on creamy mash. A very satisfactory menu for children also offers real food, or half portions from the main menu are happily served.

Open 11–1am (Mon–Thu 11–11) Closed: 25 Dec, 1–2 Jan **Bar Meals** L served all week 12–2.30 D served all week 6–9 (Nov–Feb Sun 5–7) Av main course £11.95 **Restaurant** L served all week 12–2.30 D served all week 6–9 (Nov–Feb Sun dinner 5–7.30) Av 3 course à la carte £25 Av 2 course fixed price £9.95 Free House Kronenbourg, Thrappledouser, Ossian, Baltika & John Smiths. 7 **Facilities** Children's licence Garden Dogs allowed Parking

WEST LOTHIAN

LINLITHGOW MAP 21 NS97

Pick of the Pubs

Champany Inn - The Chop and Ale House

Champany EH49 7LU

☎ 01506 834532 01506 834302

e-mail: reception@champany.com

If you want to sample the best Scottish beef, this place is not to be missed: it has been described as the 'Rolls Royce of steak restaurants'. A collection of buildings dating from the 17th century houses the Chop and Ale House and its superior sister, the main restaurant. The whole place is full of traditional charm and atmosphere, not to mention wine bottles, with one of the two extensive cellars visible from the bar. Food-wise, there are starters such as home-smoked chorizo sausage or marinated herring fillets before the main event: several choices of Aberdeen Angus steaks, and an extensive range of Champany burgers made from the same meat as the steaks and cooked medium rare. Other choices include Scottish lamb chops, home-made sausages, chargrilled chicken, and cod and chips.

Open 12–2 6.30–10 (Fri–Sun all day) Closed: 25–26 Dec, 1–2 Jan **Bar Meals** L served all week 12–2 D served all week 6.30–10 (Fri–Sun all day) Av main course £18.95 **Restaurant** L served Mon–Fri 12.30–2 D served Mon–Sat 7–10 Av 3 course à la carte £49.50 Av 2 course fixed price £19.50 Free House Belhaven. **Facilities** Garden Parking

SCOTTISH ISLANDS

COLL, ISLE OF

ARINAGOUR MAP 22 NM25

Pick of the Pubs

Coll Hotel NEW

PA78 6SZ ☎ 01879 230334 01879 230317

e-mail: info@collhotel.com

dir: *Ferry from Oban. Located at head of Arinagour Bay, 1m from Pier (collections by arrangement)*

The Isle of Coll only has 170 inhabitants, making it the perfect spot for a holiday away from it all. The Coll Hotel is the only inn on the island, and commands stunning views over the sea to Jura and Mull. In the winter, the hotel is a centre for local activities, while in the summer tourists flock in for the fabulous seafood and lively bar. Simple, well-prepared dishes make the most of excellent local produce, with spankingly fresh fish coming straight from the boats. Try seared scallops in garlic butter; or Thai-spiced Coll crab and prawn cakes with sweet chilli dressing. Main courses run along surf and turf lines: Scottish monkfish with tomato and basil sauce; and organic local sirloin with Loval garlic prawns give an indication of the style. If you're in the market for dessert, cranachan and shortbread is a regional delight that should not be missed.

Open 11–12 (Winter 11–2, 5–10) **Bar Meals** L served all week 12–2 D served all week 6–9.30 (Winter 12–2, 6–8.30) Av main course £8 **Restaurant** L served all week 12–2 D served all week 6–9.30 (Winter 12–2, 6–8.30) Free House Loch Fyne Ale, Pipers Gold, Guinness, Staropramen. **Facilities** Garden Parking **Rooms** 6 bedrooms en suite S£35 D£70 (★★★ INN)

SKYE, ISLE OF

ARDVASAR MAP 22 NG60

Ardvasar Hotel ★★ HL

IV45 8RS ☎ 01471 844223 01471 844495

e-mail: richard@ardvasar-hotel.demon.co.uk

dir: *From ferry terminal, 50yds & turn left*

An early 1800s white-painted cottage-style inn, the second oldest on Skye, renowned for its genuinely friendly hospitality and informal service. Sea views over the Sound of Sleat reach the Knoydart Mountains beyond. Malt whiskies are plentiful, but beer drinkers will not be disappointed. Food is served in the informal lounge bar throughout the day and evening, with a sumptuous four-course dinner in the dining room during high season. Local produce figures prominently, particularly freshly-landed seafood, venison, and Aberdeen Angus beef.

Open 12–12 **Bar Meals** L served all week 12–2.30 D served all week 5.30–9 Av main course £11.50 **Restaurant** D served all week 7–9 Av 3 course à la carte £23 Free House 80/-, Deuchars, IPA, Isle of Skye Red Cuillin. 6 **Facilities** Children's licence Garden Dogs allowed Parking **Rooms** 10 bedrooms en suite S£65 D£90 (★★★ INN)

CARBOST MAP 22 NG33

The Old Inn

IV47 8SR ☎ 01478 640205 01478 640325

e-mail: reservations@oldinn.f9.co.uk

Two-hundred-year-old free house on the edge of Loch Harport with wonderful views of the Cuillin Hills from the waterside patio. Not surprisingly, the inn is popular with walkers and climbers (inn and bunkhouse accommodation is available). Open fires welcome winter visitors, and live music is a regular feature. The menu includes daily home-cooked specials, with numerous fresh fish dishes, including local prawns and oysters and mackerel from the loch.

Open 11am–1am **Bar Meals** L served all week 12–3 D served all week 6–9 **Restaurant** L served all week 12–3 D served all week 6–9 Free House Red Cuillin, Black Cuillin, Hebridean Beer & Cuillin Skye Ale. **Facilities** Children's licence Garden Dogs allowed Parking

ISLE ORNSAY MAP 22 NG71

Pick of the Pubs

Hotel Eilean Iarmain ★★ SHL

IV43 8QR ☎ 01471 833332 01471 833275

e-mail: hotel@eileaniarmain.co.uk

dir: *A851, A852 right to Isle Ornsay harbour front*

An award-winning Hebridean hotel with its own pier, overlooking the Isle of Ornsay harbour and Sleat Sound. The old-fashioned character of the hotel remains intact, and décor is mainly cotton and linen chintzes with traditional furniture. More a small private hotel than a pub, the bar and restaurant ensure that the standards of food and drinks served here – personally chosen by the owner Sir Iain Noble – are exacting. The head chef declares: 'We never accept second best, it shines through in the standard of food served in our restaurant.' Here you can try dishes like Eilean Iarmain estate venison casserole, pan-seared sirloin steak, or grilled fillet of cod with hollandaise sauce. If you call in at lunchtime, a more humble range of baked potatoes, sandwiches and toasties is also available. Half portions are served for children, or the chef can usually find chicken wings, fish fingers, sausages and baked beans.

Open 11–1am (Sun 12.30–1am) **Bar Meals** L served all week 12–2.30 D served all week 6–9.30 Av main course £8.50 **Restaurant** L served all week 12–2 D served all week 6.30–9 Av 5 course fixed price £31 Free House McEwans 80/-, Guinness & Isle of Skye real ale. **Facilities** Children's licence Garden Dogs allowed Parking **Rooms** 16 bedrooms en suite S£65 D£90

STEIN MAP 22 NG25

Stein Inn

Macleod's Ter IV55 8GA ☎ 01470 592362

e-mail: angus.teresa@steininn.co.uk

dir: *A87 from Portree 5m, A850 15m. Right onto B886, 3m to junc and left*

The oldest inn on the island, set in a lovely hamlet right next to the sea, the Stein Inn provides a warm welcome, fine food, and an impressive selection of drinks: fine wines, real ales and no fewer than a hundred malt whiskies. Highland game and local seafood feature strongly on daily-changing menus that range from lunchtime toasties and jacket potatoes to moules marinière, venison pie, and salmon in a vermouth and tarragon sauce.

Open 11–12 (Sun 12.30–11. Winter 4–11) **Bar Meals** L served all week 12–4 (Sun lunch 12.30–4) D served all week 6–9 Av main course £7 **Restaurant** D served all week 6–9 Av 3 course à la carte £15 Free House Red Cuillin, Trade Winds, Reeling Deck, Deuchars IPA. 8 **Facilities** Children's licence Garden Dogs allowed Parking **Rooms** 5 bedrooms en suite S£26 D£52 (★★★ INN)

SOUTH UIST

LOCHBOISDALE MAP 22 NF71

The Polochar Inn

Polochar HS8 5TT ☎ 01878 700215 01878 700768

e-mail: polocharinn@btconnect.co.uk

dir: *W from Lochboisdale & take B888. Hotel at end of road*

Overlooking the sea towards the islands of Eriskay and Barra, this superbly situated 18th-century inn enjoys beautiful sunsets. The bar menu offers fresh seafood dishes and steaks with various sauces, while restaurant fare includes venison, fresh scallops or steak pie.

Open 11–11 (Thu–Sat 11–1am, Sun 12.30–11) **Bar Meals** L served all week 12.30–2.30 D served all week 6–9 Av main course £8 **Restaurant** L served all week 12–2.30 D served all week 6–9 Av 3 course à la carte £17 Free House Syke Ales. **Facilities** Garden Parking

Scotland

Wales

Snowdonia National Park, Conwy

ANGLESEY, ISLE OF

BEAUMARIS MAP 14 SH67

Pick of the Pubs

Ye Olde Bulls Head Inn ★★ HL ֍֍ 🍷

Castle St LL58 8AP ☎ 01248 810329 📠 01248 811294

e-mail: info@bullsheadinn.co.uk

dir: *From Brittannia Road Bridge A545 to town centre*

Situated a stone's throw from the gates of imposing Beaumaris castle, The Bull (as it is commonly known) is inextricably linked to Anglesey's history. Built in 1472 as a coaching house, it has welcomed such distinguished guests as Samuel Johnson and Charles Dickens. Inside there's a traditional bar leading on to the popular brasserie which offers modern European cuisine – perhaps shredded duck salad with plum sauce, followed by pork saltimbocca with celeriac purée and Marsala sauce. Or it's up the stairs to the smartly modern, first-floor Loft restaurant which offers a more formal menu. Try a terrine of wild rabbit, foie gras and Parma ham, followed by fillet of Anglesey black beef with spinach, red wine, shallots, ceps, fine beans, pancetta, fondant potatoes and madeira jus. Delectable desserts like caramelised hazelnut and sweet apple semifreddo with Bramley apple fritters and hazelnut tuile will be hard to resist.

Open 11–11 (Sun–12–10.30) Closed: 25 Dec **Bar Meals** L served all week 12–2 (Sun 12–3) D served all week 7–9 Av main course £9.35 **Restaurant** D served Mon–Sat 7–9 (Sun on BH wknds 12–1.30) Av 3 course fixed price £37.50 Free House Bass, Hancocks, Guest beers. 🍷 16 **Facilities** Parking **Rooms** 13 bedrooms en suite S£80 D£102

RED WHARF BAY MAP 14 SH58

Pick of the Pubs

The Ship Inn 🍷

LL75 8RJ ☎ 01248 852568 📠 01248 851013

Wading birds in their hundreds flock to feed on the extensive sands of Red Wharf Bay, making the Ship's waterside beer garden a birdwatcher's paradise on warm days. Before the age of steam, sailing ships landed cargoes here from all over the world; now the boats bring fresh Conwy Bay fish and seafood to the kitchens of this traditional free house. A single menu is served to diners in the bars and restaurant. Lunchtime sandwiches are a cut above the usual: choose from the likes of Perl Wen cheese and bacon, or seared strips of Welsh beef fillet with horseradish crème fraîche. Starters such as ham hock and leek terrine on toasted crumpet with poached free range egg is almost a meal in itself. Main courses may include rabbit and root vegetable casserole, or grilled fillets of lemon sole. If not quite replete, round off with banana custard and strawberry jam tart.

Open 11–11 **Bar Meals** L served all week 12–2.30 D served all week 6–9 (Sun 12–9) **Restaurant** D served Fri–Sat 7–9.30 Free House Brains SA, Adnams, Guest Beers. 🍷 16 **Facilities** Garden Parking Play Area

BRIDGEND

KENFIG MAP 09 SS88

Prince of Wales Inn 🍷

CF33 4PR ☎ 01656 740356

e-mail: prince-of-wales@bt.connect.com

dir: *M4 junct 37 into North Cornelly. Left at x-rds, follow signs for Kenfig & Porthcaw. Pub 600yds on right*

Dating from the 16th century, this stone-built inn has been many things in its time including a school, guildhall and courtroom. Why not sup some real cask ale in the bar by an inviting log fire? Typical menu includes steak and onion pie, lasagne, chicken and mushroom pie, and a variety of fish dishes. Look out for today's specials on the blackboard. The current landlords are only the sixth in 230 years!

Open 11–11 **Bar Meals** L served Tue–Sun 12–3 D served Tue–Sun 6–9 **Restaurant** L served all week 12–9 (Sun 12–3) D served Tue–Sun 7–9 Free House Bass Triangle, Worthington Best, Guest Ales. 🍷 20 **Facilities** Garden Dogs allowed Parking

CARDIFF

CREIGIAU

Pick of the Pubs

Caesars Arms

Cardiff Rd CF15 9NN
☎ 029 2089 0486 📠 029 2089 2176
e-mail: caesarsarms@btconnect.com
dir: *1m from M4 junct 34*

Though it's only ten miles out of Cardiff, the Caesars Arms is reached through a network of winding country lanes that make city life feel light years away. The heated patio and terrace, both boasting views over the surrounding countryside, attract a well-heeled clientele. The inn prides itself on the vast selection of fresh fish, seafood, meat and game which is enticingly displayed in shaven-ice display cabinets. Start with fresh Pembroke dressed crab; tiger prawns in garlic; or scallops with leek and bacon. Hake, salmon, John Dory and crevettes may follow, with Dover sole, lobster, lemon sole and crawfish tails priced by weight. For a real showstopper, order sea bass baked in rock salt: it will be theatrically cracked open and filleted at your table. Carnivores needn't worry though – naturally reared Welsh Black beef shows up in fillets, steaks and roasts.

Open 12–2.30 6–10.30 (Sun 12–4) Closed: 25 Dec **Bar Meals** L served all week 12–2.30 (Sun 12–4) D served Mon–Sat 6–10.30 **Restaurant** L served all week 12–2.30 (Sun 12–4) D served Mon–Sat 6–10.30 Free House Felinfoel. **Facilities** Garden Parking

CARMARTHENSHIRE

ABERGORLECH MAP 08 SN53

The Black Lion

SA32 7SN ☎ 01558 685271
e-mail: michelle.r@btinternet.com
dir: *A40 E from Carmarthen, then B4310 signed Brechfa & Abergorlech*

A 17th-century coaching inn in the Brechfa Forest, with a beer garden overlooking the Cothi River, and an old packhorse bridge. Flagstone floors, settles and a grandfather clock grace the antique-furnished bar, while the modern dining room is welcoming in pink and white. Try home-made chicken and leek pie, home-made curry of the day, or a fresh salmon steak. Miles of forest and riverside walks are easily reached from the pub.

Open 12–3.30 7–11 (Sat 12–11, Sun 12–10) **Bar Meals** L served Tue–Sun 12–2 D served Tue–Sat 7–9 (Sun 7–8.30) Av main course £6.50 **Restaurant** L served Sun 12–2 D served Sat 7–9 Av 3 course à la carte £12 Free House Brains SA, Buckley's Best, Spitfire, Young's Bitter. **Facilities** Garden Dogs allowed Parking

LLANDDAROG MAP 08 SN51

White Hart Thatched Inn & Brewery

NEW
SA32 8NT ☎ 01267 275395
dir: *6m E of Carmarthen towards Swansea, just off A48 on B4310, signed Llanddarog*

The White Hart's thick stone walls, heavy beams and thatched roof have stood in this rural Welsh village since 1371. Now, the Coles family invites you to sit by a cosy log fire with a pint from the on-site microbrewery, or eat out on the summer patio. Expect snacks and sandwiches, as well as specials such as duck breast in red wine and plum sauce; and sizzling marlin with garlic, wine and mushrooms.

Open 11.30–3 6.30–11 (Sun 12–3, 7–10.30) **Bar Meals** L served all week 11.30–2 D served all week 6.30–10 (Sun 12–2, 7–9.30) Av main course £6 **Restaurant** L served all week 11.30–2 D served all week 6.30–10 (Sun 12–2, 7–9.30) Av 3 course à la carte £20 Free House Roasted Barley Stout, Llanddarog Ale, Bramling Cross. **Facilities** Garden Parking Play Area

LLANDEILO MAP 08 SN62

The Angel Hotel

Rhosmaen St SA19 6EN ☎ 01558 822765 📠 01558 824346
e-mail: capelbach@hotmail.com

This popular pub in the centre of Llandeilo has something for everyone. Real ales are available in the bar area, which hosts regular live music nights. Upstairs, the Yr Eglwys function room ceiling is decorated with soaring frescoes inspired by Michelangelo's Sistine Chapel, and at the rear is an intimate bistro, where dishes might include butternut squash ravioli, followed by rack of salt marsh lamb with a blueberry and port jus and a nut crust.

Open 11–3.30 6.30–12 **Bar Meals** L served Mon–Sat 11.30–2.30 D served Mon–Sat 7–9.30 Av main course £6.50 **Restaurant** L served Mon–Sat 11.30–2.30 D served Mon–Sat 7–9.30 Av 3 course à la carte £23 Av 3 course fixed price £16.95 Free House Evans Evans Ales, Tetleys, Speckled Hen, CWRW & Youngs. 12 **Facilities** Garden **Rooms**

The Castle Hotel

113 Rhosmaen St SA19 6EN
☎ 01558 823446 📠 01558 822290

A 19th-century Edwardian-style hotel within easy reach of Dinefwr Castle and wonderful walks through classic parkland. A charming, tiled and partly green-painted back bar attracts plenty of locals, while the front bar and side area offer smart furnishings and the chance to relax in comfort over a drink. A good range of Tomas Watkins ales is available, and quality bar and restaurant food is prepared with the finest of fresh local ingredients.

Open 12–11 (Sun 12–10.30) **Bar Meals** L served Wed–Sun 12–2.30 D served Wed–Sun 6.30–9 Av main course £6.95 **Restaurant** L served all week 12–2.30 D served Mon–Sat 6.30–9 Celtic Inns Tomas Watkins, Hancocks Bitter, Archers Golden, London Pride. **Facilities** Garden Parking

NANTGAREDIG MAP 08 SN42

Pick of the Pubs

Y Polyn

SA32 7LH ☎ 01267 290000

e-mail: ypolyn@hotmail.com

dir: *From A48 follow signs to National Botanic Garden of Wales. Then follow brown signs to Y Polyn*

A 250-year-old inn, once a tollhouse, set in a lovely spot in the verdant Towy Valley. Its name means 'pole', probably after the original barrier across the road. It is handily placed by a fork in the roads, with Aberglasney in one direction and the National Botanic Garden of Wales in the other. Though drinkers are undoubtedly welcome to prop up the bar, or in reality sit by the fire in the squashy armchairs, it is as a food destination that Y Polyn continues to make its name. Dinner could comprise bruschetta of goats' cheese and sweet red onion marmalade as a starter; or perhaps Black Mountain smoked salmon and potato salad; followed by sea bass with pak choi and soy dressing; or crispy belly pork with caramelised apples. Puddings bring their own reward, in the guise of home-made warm pear and frangipane tart, or white chocolate cheesecake with cherry compote. Welsh real ales and cider and a wide-ranging wine list. Outside is a patio area and raised lawn.

Open 12-2 7-11 **Bar Meals** L served Tue-Fri & Sun D served Tue-Fri & Sat **Restaurant** L served Tue-Fri & Sun 12-2 D served Tue-Sat 7-9 Av 3 course à la carte £27.50 Av 3 course fixed price £27.50 Free House Tomos Watkins OSB, Tomos Watkins Cwrw Braf, Taffy Apples Cider, Staropramen Lager & Tomas Watkins Cwrw Haf. 7 **Facilities** Garden Parking

PONT-AR-GOTHI MAP 08 SN52

The Salutation Inn

SA32 7NH ☎ 01267 290336 01267 290111

e-mail: salutation.inn@virgin.net

dir: *5m from Carmarthen on A40*

Stripped floors, bare tables and candles are the defining features of both the bar and restaurant, with cosy little rooms tucked away from the main areas. Of interest to ghost hunters are the several friendly spirits that inhabit the place, and the spooky goings-on have been recorded by paranormal experts. The blackboard choices are based on the abundant local produce, and traditional Sunday lunches are always served. New owners – reports please.

Open 11-3 5-11 (All day Jun-Sep) **Bar Meals** L served all week 12-2.30 D served all week 6-10 **Restaurant** L served all week 12-2.30 D served all week 6-10 Felinfoel Felinfoel – Double Dragon, Dragon Bitter, Fosters, Stowford Press. 12 **Facilities** Garden Dogs allowed Parking Play Area

RHANDIRMWYN MAP 09 SN74

The Royal Oak Inn ★★★ INN

SA20 0NY ☎ 01550 760201 01550 760332

e-mail: royaloak@rhandirmwyn.com

dir: *From A483 turn left 7m N of Llandovery. Village on same road as RSPB Reserve & Llyn Brianne*

This comfortable inn with its stone floors and log fires was originally built as a hunting lodge in 1850. Local brews from Wye Valley and Evan Evans supplement better-known beers like Wadworth and Greene King, whilst whisky drinkers can sample from around fifty single malts. In summer, far-reaching views make the garden ideal for al fresco dining. Expect lunchtime sandwiches, as well as hot dishes like black beef curry, vegetable goulash, or grilled trout.

Open 12-2 6-11 (Sun 7-10.30) **Bar Meals** L served all week 12-2 D served all week 6-9.30 Av main course £6.50 **Restaurant** L served all week 12-2 D served all week 6.30-9.30 (Sun 7-9.30) Av 3 course à la carte £20 Free House Greene King Abbot Ale, Wadworth 6X, Burtons, Wye Valley. **Facilities** Children's licence Garden Dogs allowed Parking **Rooms** 3 bedrooms en suite S£22.50 D£50

CEREDIGION

ABERAERON MAP 08 SN46

Pick of the Pubs

Harbourmaster Hotel ★★★★★ INN

Pen Cei SA46 0BA ☎ 01545 570755

e-mail: info@harbour-master.com

dir: *From A487, follow signs for town centre tourist information centre.*

Originally the harbourmaster's residence as well as his office, this chic blue-painted hotel provides an imposing full-stop to the range of buildings on the Aberaeron quayside. Built in 1811, the four-storey listed building offers a commanding view of both the harbour and the open sea. The light, tasteful decor is complemented by original features like the Welsh slate masonry and listed spiral staircase. Real ale and draught beers are served in the popular bar, which also offers up to ten wines by the glass. The food is modern in style but substantial in character, with plenty of opportunities to sample fresh local produce in the restaurant. Typical choices range from chargrilled pheasant, rosemary and fennel tagliatelle, and pan-fried fillet of Gower sea bass with wild mushroom rice, to desserts like poached pear with honey ice cream. The menu, a fascinating insight into the Welsh language, offers Welsh cheeses such as Caerphilly and Perl Las.

Open 11-11 Closed: 25 Dec-9 Jan **Bar Meals** L served Tue-Sun 12-2 D served Mon-Sat 6-9 **Restaurant** L served Tue-Sun 12-2 D served Mon-Sat 6.30-9 Av 3 course à la carte £27.50 Free House Buckleys Best Bitter, Brains, Tomas Watkin & Stella Artois. 10 **Facilities** Children's licence Parking **Rooms** 9 bedrooms en suite S£60 D£110

CARDIGAN MAP 08 SN14

Webley Waterfront Inn & Hotel

Poppit Sands SA43 3LN ☎ 01239 612085

e-mail: webleyhotel@btconnect.com

dir: *A484 from Carmarthen to Cardigan, then to St Dogmaels, turn right in village centre to Poppit Sands on the B4546*

The inn offers outstanding views across the River Teifi and Poppit Sands to Cardigan Bay from its spectacular location at the start of the Pembrokeshire Coast National Park. It is perfect for walkers at the start or finish of the coastal path. Home-made food and a selection of local ales are served, which can be enjoyed in the beer garden at the water's edge. This is a SSSI with many interesting birds to be seen.

Open 9–11 **Bar Meals** L served all week 12-3 D served all week 6–9 Av main course £7.95 **Restaurant** L served all week 12–2.30 D served all week 6–8.30 Av 3 course à la carte £15.20 Free House Brains Buckleys Bitter, Carling, Worthington, Rev James. 8 **Facilities** Children's licence Garden Dogs allowed Parking

LLWYNDAFYDD MAP 08 SN35

The Crown Inn & Restaurant

SA44 6BU ☎ 01545 560396 01545 560857

dir: *Off A487 NE of Cardigan*

A traditional Welsh longhouse dating from 1799, with original beams, open fireplaces, and a pretty restaurant. A varied menu offers a good selection of dishes, including sautéed ballottine of chicken supreme; roast monkfish wrapped in Parma ham; and warm spiced couscous. Blackboard specials and bar meals are available lunchtimes and evenings. Outside is a delightful, award-winning garden. An easy walk down the lane leads to a cove with caves and NT-owned cliffs.

Open 12–3 6–11 (Fri–Sat all day Etr–Sep) Closed Sun eve (winter) **Bar Meals** L served all week 12–2 D served all week 6–9 Av main course £8 **Restaurant** D served all week 6.30–9 Av 3 course à la carte £30 Free House Interbrew Flowers Original & Flowers IPA , Greene King Old Speckled Hen, Honey Beers Envill Ale, Fullers London Pride. **Facilities** Children's licence Garden Dogs allowed Parking Play Area

CONWY

BETWS-Y-COED MAP 14 SH75

Pick of the Pubs

Ty Gwyn Inn ★★★ INN

LL24 0SG ☎ 01690 710383 & 710787 01690 710383

e-mail: mratcl1050@aol.com

dir: *At junct of A5 & A470, 100yds S of Waterloo Bridge*

Built in 1636, the Ty Gwyn used to be a coaching inn on the London to Holyhead road. It sits opposite the Waterloo Bridge, an impressive cast iron bridge, built by Thomas Telford in 1815. Set in the heart of the Snowdonia National Park, it overlooks the Conwy River, and enjoys some beautiful views of the mountains, and is understandably popular with walkers. The bar features the expected exposed beams, so minding your head is recommended. Home-cooked food is prepared from local produce. Bar dishes include lasagne verdie, cottage pie with melted cheese, and real ale battered fish, while the restaurant offers trimmed rack of Conwy Valley lamb; roast suckling pig; local smoked cod, mushroom and stilton bake or lobster thermidor among the daily specials. There are twelve bedrooms, eight with en suite bathrooms, some with four-poster beds, and including a honeymoon suite.

Open 12–3 6–11 Closed: 1 week in Jan **Bar Meals** L served all week 12–2 D served all week 6.30–9 **Restaurant** L served all week 12–2 D served all week 6.30–9 Free House Adnams Broadside, Reverend James, Old Speckled Hen, Bombardier & IPA, Orms Best. **Facilities** Parking **Rooms** 10 bedrooms en suite S£40 D£48

See advert on page 730

Wales

BETWS-Y-COED continued

White Horse Inn ★★★ INN

Capel Garmon LL26 0RW
☎ 01690 710271 📠 01690 710721
e-mail: r.alton@btconnect.com
dir: *Telephone for directions*

Picturesque Capel Garmon perches high above Betws-y-Coed, with spectacular views of the Snowdon Range a good 20 kilometres away. To make a detour to find this cosy 400-year-old inn, is to be rewarded by a menu featuring fresh local produce.

Open 6–11 (Sat–Sun 12–2.30) Closed: 25 Dec **Bar Meals** L served Sat–Sun 12–2.30 D served all week 4.30–8 (Fri–Sat 6.30–9.30, Sun 6.30–9) Av main course £8.85 **Restaurant** L served Sat–Sun 12–2.30 D served all week 9–9 Av 3 course à la carte £19 Free House Tetley Imperial, Tetley Smoothflow, Hob Goblin, Carlsberg Lager. **Facilities** Dogs allowed Parking **Rooms** 5 bedrooms en suite S£35 D£66

BETWS-YN-RHOS MAP 14 SH97

The Wheatsheaf Inn

LL22 8AW ☎ 01492 680218 📠 01492 680666
e-mail: perry@jonnyp.fsnet.co.uk
dir: *A55 to Abergele, take A548 to Llanrwst from High Street. 2m turn right B5381, 1m to Betws-yn-Rhos*

This 13th-century alehouse was licensed as a coaching inn in 1640. Splendid oak beams, old stone pillars and an original hayloft ladder combine to make this an ideal spot to enjoy a pint of John Smiths or one of the Wheatsheaf's special malt whiskies. A single menu serves the lounge bar and restaurant with dishes that may include grilled halibut with prawns; royal game pie and madeira sauce; or mushroom stroganoff.

Open 12–3 6–11 **Bar Meals** L served all week 12–2 D served all week 6–9 (Sun 12–3) Av main course £10 **Restaurant** L served all week 12–2 D served all week 6–9.30 (Sun 12–3) Av 3 course à la carte £17 Enterprise Inns John Smiths, Brains, Hobgoblin, Conwy Castle. **Facilities** Garden Parking Play Area

CAPEL CURIG MAP 14 SH75

Cobdens Hotel ★★ SHL

LL24 0EE ☎ 01690 720243 📠 01690 720354
e-mail: info@cobdens.co.uk

Situated in a beautiful mountain village in the heart of Snowdonia, this 250-year-old inn offers wholesome, locally sourced food and real ales. Start with local rabbit and pancetta carbonara; or leek and potato

terrine. Mains include roasted Welsh lamb with garlic and thyme mash; Welsh beef steaks; and pasta with roasted courgette, blue cheese and chestnut. Try bara brith parfait for pudding! Snacks and sandwiches also available.

Open 11–11 Closed: 6–26 Jan **Bar Meals** L served all week 12–2.30 D served all week 6–9 Av main course £10 **Restaurant** L served all week 12–2 D served all week 6–9 Av 3 course à la carte £22 Free House Conwy Castle Beer, Cobdens Ale & Guest Ale. **Facilities** Children's licence Garden Dogs allowed Parking **Rooms** 17 bedrooms en suite S£29.50 D£59

COLWYN BAY — MAP 14 SH87

Pick of the Pubs

Pen-y-Bryn

Pen-y-Bryn Rd LL29 6DD
☎ 01492 533360 & 535808 Fax 01492 536127
e-mail: pen.y.bryn@brunningandprice.co.uk

From the front, this 1970s pub looks a bit like a medical centre. Inside, though, you'll find lovely oak floors, open fires, bookcases, rugs and old furniture: it all looks very handsome and just has to be one of the country's finest doctor's waiting rooms (and no stroppy receptionist, either). Outside is a stunning garden and terrace with panoramic views over the sea and looming headland known as the Great Orme. The modern British menu opens with a good selection that includes black pudding fritter with poached egg and mustard sauce; home-cured duck breast with fennel and orange salad; and tempura battered tiger prawn cocktail. Among the main courses are braised shoulder of Welsh lamb; beer-braised pheasant with Madras sauce; smoked haddock and salmon fishcakes; Old Colwyn free-range pork sausages; and butternut squash risotto. For something lighter, sandwiches, 'bread things', Chinese-style chicken pancakes, and Menai mussels should do the trick.

Open 11.30–11 (Sun 12–11, 25 Dec 12–2) **Bar Meals** L served all week 12–9.30 D served all week 12–9.30 (Sun 12–9) **Restaurant** L served Mon–Sat 12–9.30 D served Mon–Sat 12–9.30 (Sun 12–9) Brunning & Price Timothy Taylors Landlord, Thwaites Original, Brag D.Y.R Bryn, Ormes Best & Weetwoods Eastgate. 14 **Facilities** Garden Parking

CONWY — MAP 14 SH77

Pick of the Pubs

The Groes Inn ★★★ HL

LL32 8TN ☎ 01492 650545 Fax 01492 650855
e-mail: reception@groesinn.com
dir: *Off A55 to Conwy, left at mini rdbt by Conwy Castle onto B5106, 2.5m inn on right*

See Pick of the Pubs on page 732

LLANDUDNO JUNCTION — MAP 14 SH77

The Queens Head

Glanwydden LL31 9JP ☎ 01492 546570 Fax 01492 546487
e-mail: enquiries@queensheadglanwydden.co.uk
dir: *From A55 take A470 towards Llandudno. At 3rd rdbt right towards Penrhyn Bay, then 2nd right into Glanwydden*

A country pub and restaurant just outside Llandudno retaining much of its original styling. The bar, fire-warmed when it's cold, is the perfect pre-prandial rendezvous. Among the extensively used local produce are Conwy mussels and queenie scallops from the Isle of Man. Hearty mains include Jamaican chicken curry; grilled pork and leek sausages; braised lamb shank; and roasted butternut squash and chestnut risotto.

Open 11–3 6–11 (Sun 11–10.30) **Bar Meals** L served all week 12–2 D served all week 6–9 (Sun 12–9) Av main course £9.50 **Restaurant** L served all week 12–2 D served all week 6–9 (Sun 12–9) Av 3 course à la carte £20 Free House Carlsberg-Tetley, Weetwood Ales, Great Orme Brewery. 7 **Facilities** Garden Parking

LLANNEFYDD — MAP 14 SH97

The Hawk & Buckle Inn

LL16 5ED ☎ 01745 540249 Fax 01745 540316
e-mail: hawkandbuckle@btinternet.com

A 17th-century coaching inn 200m up in the hills, with wonderful views to the sea beyond. Traditional dishes using local produce – shoulder of Welsh lamb, chicken breast stuffed with Welsh cheese or duck breast with port and redcurrant sauce, sit comfortably alongside international flavours – lamb pasanda, beef and Guinness casserole or chicken tikka masala, for example.

Open 12–2 6–11 Closed: 25–26 Dec **Bar Meals** L served Wed & Sun 12–2 D served Tue–Sat 6–9 (Sun 7–10.30) Av main course £8.50 **Restaurant** L served Sun D served Sat–Sun 6–9 Av 3 course à la carte £16 Free House Brains Bitter, Interbrew Boddingtons Bitter, Bass Bitter. **Facilities** Parking

Wales

The Groes Inn

Built as a small two-storey house in the 15th century, and first recorded as an inn in 1573. The location is stunning, with a panorama over the River Conwy and the surrounding hills from the front, and slopes rising towards Snowdonia at the rear.

Rambling rooms, beamed ceilings and historic settles – this inn has them all. For centuries it has maintained a tradition of welcoming travellers; drovers would rest here while drying their wet clothes in front of a blazing fire. Today it makes a great base for exploring the mountains, coastline, castles and gardens of North Wales. Owners Dawn and Justin Humphreys have decorated the interior with stone cats, military hats, saucy Victorian postcards, historic cooking utensils and old advertisements. You can eat in the bar or more stylishly in the award-winning restaurant. Dishes using fresh local produce reflect traditional tastes with some European influences. You can choose a small meal that doubles as a starter in the bar, from choices like butternut squash and sage ravioli; grilled kippers and crispy bacon with brown bread and butter; and fresh linguini with smoked chicken and carbonara sauce. Or perhaps plump for the favourites such as haddock, prawn and mushroom mornay; thick juicy Anglesey gammon and eggs; poached salmon with hollandaise sauce; and chicken curry. From the restaurant set menu come starters like deep-fried devilled whitebait with garlic mayonnaise; and salad of smoked chicken fillets with crispy bacon and avocado pear. Move on to chilli bean casserole; seafood platter; pot-roast widgeon stuffed with herbs, bacon and chestnuts; or steak and mushroom pie. For dessert try bara brith (Welsh fruit bread), white chocolate and vanilla bean panacotta; toffee and banana pie; or orange and rosemary jelly with roasted apricots and orange and Cointreau ice cream.

★★★ HL ⊛ 🍷
MAP 14 SH77
LL32 8TN
☎ 01492 650545
📠 01492 650855
e-mail: reception@groesinn.com
dir: *Off A55 to Conwy, left at mini rdbt by Conwy Castle onto B5106, 2.5m inn on right*

Open 12-3 6.30-11
Bar Meals L served all week 12-2.15 D served all week 6.30-9
Restaurant L served all week 12-2.15 D served all week 6.30-9
Av 3 course à la carte £28
Av 4 course fixed price £28
Free House
Tetley, Burton Ale. 🍷 10
Facilities Garden Parking
Rooms 14 bedrooms en suite S£85 D£103

ST GEORGE — MAP 14 SH97

Pick of the Pubs

The Kinmel Arms ★★★★★ RR

LL22 9BP ☎ 01745 832207 01745 822044
e-mail: info@thekinmelarms.co.uk
dir: *From Bodelwyddan towards Abergele take slip road at St George. 1st left and Kinmel Arms on left at top of hill*

Nestling in the foothills of the stunning Elwy valley, this rural free house offers ready access to the coast, mountains and cwms of beautiful North Wales. Despite its neo-Elizabethan style, the Kinmel Arms dates from the last decade of the Victorian era. It was built to replace the Dinorben Arms, which was demolished to make way for a new village hall in 1899. The building has been stylishly renovated by owners Lynn and Tim Watson, who have decorated the rooms with their own mountain photography. Good fresh food is offered from an à la carte menu at dinner, with a brasserie-style choice at lunchtime. Fish features strongly with dishes such as Menai mussels served with a cream and white wine sauce; and roast halibut fillet with braised fennel and red chicory in a lemon and thyme, balsamic peppers and rocket salad.

Open 12–3 6.30–11 (Sun 12–5, BH Sun–Mon all day) Closed: 25 Dec, 1–2 Jan **Bar Meals** L served Tue–Sun 12–2 (Sun 12–3) D served Tue–Thu 7–9.30 (Fri–Sat 6.30–9.30) Av main course £15 **Restaurant** L served Tue–Sun 12–2 (Sun 12–3) D served Tue–Thu 7–9.30 (Fri–Sat 6.30–9.30) Av 3 course à la carte £25 Free House Carlsberg, San Miguel, Guinness, Leffe Blond & 4 Real Ales (change weekly). 16 **Facilities** Garden Parking **Rooms** 4 bedrooms en suite D£115

DENBIGHSHIRE

PRESTATYN — MAP 15 SJ08

Nant Hall Restaurant & Bar

Nant Hall Rd LL19 9LD ☎ 01745 886766 01745 886998
e-mail: mail@nanthall.com
dir: *E towards Chester, 1m on left opposite large garage*

Nant Hall, a Grade II listed Victorian country house in seven acres of grounds, operates as a gastro-pub with a great variety of food, beers and wines. Dawsons Bar Cuisine menu offers local and regional dishes alongside recipes from around the world: Conwy award-winning pork and leek sausages with mash and onion gravy, vegetarian fajitas, lamb koftas with couscous, and sweet and sour king prawns. The large outdoor eating area is great in summer.

Open 11–12 (Oct–Mar Mon–Thu 11–3, 6–12) **Bar Meals** L served all week 12 D served all week 6–9.30 (Sun 12–6) Free House Stella Artois, 4X, Boddingtons, Welsh Smooth Bitter & Conwy Bitter. 14 **Facilities** Garden Parking Play Area

RHEWL — MAP 15 SJ16

The Drovers Arms, Rhewl

Denbigh Rd LL15 2UD ☎ 01824 703163 01824 703163
e-mail: Allen_Given@hotmail.com
dir: *1.3m from Ruthin on the A525*

A small village pub whose name recalls a past written up and illustrated on storyboards displayed inside. Main courses are divided on the menu into poultry, traditional meat, fish, grills and vegetarian; examples from each section are chicken tarragon; Welsh lambs' liver and onions; Vale of Clwyd sirloin steak; home-made fish pie; and fresh mushroom stroganoff. Desserts include treacle sponge pudding, and Black Forest gateau.

Open 12–3 5–11 (Times vary Summer & Winter) **Bar Meals** L served all week 12–2 (Sun 12–2.30) D served all week 5–8 (Fri–Sat 6–9) **Restaurant** L served all week 12–2 (Sun 12–2.30) D served Mon–Sun 5–8 (Fri–Sat 6–9) Free House London Pride, Youngs, Tetley Smooth. **Facilities** Children's licence Garden Parking Play Area

RUTHIN — MAP 15 SJ15

Ye Olde Anchor Inn

Rhos St LL15 1DY ☎ 01824 702813 01824 703050
e-mail: hotel@anchorinn.co.uk
dir: *At junction of A525 and A494*

Built in 1742, this impressive-looking inn has 16 windows at the front alone – all with award-winning window boxes. Choose starters of chicken satay; or mushrooms with spinach and cream cheese. Then, breast of chicken stuffed with a herbed cream cheese; or a classic French chateaubriand steak. Home-baked bread comes with the meal. A varied selection of freshly prepared desserts is available.

Open 11–11 **Bar Meals** L served all week 12–2 (Sun 12–3) D served all week 6–9.30 Av main course £7 **Restaurant** L served all week 12–2 D served all week 6–9.30 Av 3 course à la carte £13 Free House Timothy Taylor, Worthington, Carling, Guest ales. **Facilities** Dogs allowed Parking

Pick of the Pubs

White Horse Inn

Hendrerwydd LL16 4LL ☎ 01824 790218
e-mail: vintr74@hotmail.com
dir: *A494 10m, left opposite The Griffin pub to Llandyrnog. Through Gellifar to Hendrerwydd*

See Pick of the Pubs on page 734

Wales

White Horse Inn

A whitewashed, 400-year-old inn in the lovely vale of Clwyd, where you will find some of the prettiest scenery in Wales. Several years ago the building was extended to take in what was originally the village shop.

The inn used to be much frequented by sheep drovers traversing the Clwydian Range on their way to markets in England, but today's visitors tend to be unencumbered by ovine companions and are able to relax in one of several different rooms in front of a log fire, with newspapers and local publications. Outside is an attractive decked patio and garden with views of distant Snowdonia. The bar serves a regularly changing selection of real ales, as well as a wide variety of malts and some unusual spirits. Meals are served at anytime, the speciality of the house being farm-cured ham and fresh farm eggs, although sandwiches and dishes such as Irish stew and steak and ale pie are always available from the bar menu. The main menu includes starters of seared duck breast with smoky paprika salsa; local sliced belly pork roasted in curry spices served with mascarpone and mixed leaves; and garlic mushrooms. Typical main courses are extra mature Welsh rib-eye steak; fillet of smoked haddock, wilted spinach and bacon and smoked cheese sauce; slow-roasted Llanbedr spring lamb with olive oil, garlic and red wine and rosemary gravy; and pan-fried chicken breast wrapped in smoked bacon topped with a homemade barbecue sauce and Llandyrnog cheddar. For dessert, home-made apple and cinnamon crumble; warm chocolate fudge cake; and banoffee pie, all with cream. The interesting wine list is reasonably priced, and there's also a more expensive Cellar Selection.

🍷
MAP 15 SJ15
Hendrerwydd LL16 4LL
☎ 01824 790218
e-mail: vintr74@hotmail.com
dir: *A494 10m, left opposite The Griffin pub to Llandyrnog. Through Gellifar to Hendrerwydd*

Open 12–2.30 6–11
Bar Meals L served all week 12–2.30 D served all week 6–9.15
Restaurant L served all week 12–2.30 D served all week 6–9.15
Free House
Regular changing guest ales. 🍷 7
Facilities Garden Dogs allowed Parking

ST ASAPH — MAP 15 SJ07

The Plough Inn 🍷

The Roe LL17 0LU ☎ 01745 585080 📠 01745 585363

dir: *Rhyl/St Asaph turning from A55, left at rdbt for 200yds*

An 18th-century former coaching inn, the Plough has been transformed. The ground floor retains the traditional pub concept, cosy with open fires and rustic furniture, while upstairs there are two very different restaurants: an up-market bistro and an Italian-themed art deco restaurant, divided by a wine shop. All the kitchens are open so you can see the food being prepared. Desserts are a great strength throughout.

Open 12–11 (Fri–Sat 12–1) **Bar Meals** L served all week 12–9.30 D served all week Av main course £8.50 **Restaurant** L served all week 12–3 D served all week 6–10 Free House Greene King Old Speckled Hen, Shepherds Neame Spitfire, Plassey Brewery. 🍷 9 **Facilities** Garden Parking

FLINTSHIRE

BABELL — MAP 15 SJ17

Black Lion Inn

CH8 8PZ ☎ 01352 720239

dir: *Holywell B5121 towards A541 & 2nd right to Babell*

The paved patio at the front of this listed 13th-century free house is the ideal place to enjoy a meal or a quiet pint. Expect braised steak in red wine and mustard; short crust country pie; and grilled Dover sole. Home-made puddings include profiteroles and fresh cream. New licensees Jane and Andy are now in charge here.

Open 6–11 (Sat–Sun all day) **Bar Meals** L served Sat–Sun D served Thu–Mon 6–9 **Restaurant** L served Sat–Sun 12–2 D served Thu–Mon 6.30–9 Av 3 course à la carte £18 Free House Thwaites Lancaster Bomber, Thwaites Smooth Bitter, Guest Cask, Bragdyr Bryn. **Facilities** Garden Parking

CILCAIN — MAP 15 SJ16

White Horse Inn

CH7 5NN ☎ 01352 740142 📠 01352 740142

e-mail: christine.jeory@btopenworld.com

dir: *From Mold A541 towards Denbigh 6m, left*

A 400-year-old pub, which is the last survivor of five originally to be found in this lovely hillside village – no doubt because it was the centre of the local gold-mining industry in the 19th century. Today the White Horse is popular with walkers, cyclists, and horse-riders. The dishes are home made by the landlord's wife using the best quality local ingredients, including filled omelettes, grilled ham and eggs, breaded fillet of trout, cig oen Cymraeg (Welsh lamb pie), and various curries.

Open 12–3 6.30–11 (Sat–Sun 12–11) **Bar Meals** L served all week 12–2 D served all week 7–9 Free House Marston's Pedigree, Bank's Bitter, Timothy Taylor Landlord, Draught Bass. **Facilities** Garden Dogs allowed Parking

MOLD — MAP 15 SJ26

Pick of the Pubs

AA PUB OF THE YEAR FOR WALES 2007-8

Glasfryn 🍷

Raikes Ln, Sychdyn CH7 6LR

☎ 01352 750500 📠 01352 751923

e-mail: glasfryn@brunningandprice.co.uk

dir: *From Mold signs to Theatre Glwyd, 1m town centre*

Built as a judge's residence in around 1900, later a farm and then divided into bedsits, this building was rescued by the present owners in 1999 and transformed into a wonderful pub. It attracts a variety of visitors from farmers and business people to holiday makers along the north Wales coast. Outside, the newly landscaped garden is maturing well, while inside the bright open space there are lots of polished wooden tables and chairs. Puddings and cheeses are not to be missed. The comprehensive daily menu runs from sandwiches and snacks through to meals such as beetroot gravad lax followed by crab and prawn noodles with lime and chilli; or perhaps Welsh lamb sausage with braised tomato beans followed by beer battered haddock with chips.

Open 11.30–11 (Sun 12–10.30) Closed: 25–26 Dec **Bar Meals** L served all week 12–9.30 D served all week 12–9.30 (Sun 12–9) Av main course £10.50 **Restaurant** L served all week 12–9.30 D served all week 12–9.30 (Sun 12–9) Brunning & Price Timothy Taylor, Thwaites, Flowers, Deuchars IPA & Bryn Bitter. 🍷 20 **Facilities** Children's licence Garden Dogs allowed Parking

NORTHOP — MAP 15 SJ26

Stables Bar Restaurant 🍷

CH7 6AB ☎ 01352 840577 📠 01352 840382

e-mail: info@soughtonhall.co.uk

dir: *From A55, take A119 through Northop village*

This destination pub is housed in the magnificent setting of the 17th-century Soughton Hall stables. Fortunately, it has kept many of original features intact, including the cobbled floors, stalls and roof timbers. The tables are named after famous racecourses and their winners. Menus continue the racing theme. Try pan-seared scallops with bacon polenta, followed by grilled sea bass and shellfish chowder. 'Final Furlong' sweets make for a spectacular finish.

Open 11–11.30 **Bar Meals** L served all week 12–3 D served all week 7–9.30 (Sun 4–9.30) **Restaurant** L served all week 12–3 D served all week 7–10 (Sun 1–3, 7–10) Free House Shepherds Neame Spitfire, Shepherd Neame Bishops Finger, Coach House Honeypot, Dick Turpin. 🍷 6 **Facilities** Garden Parking

Wales

GWYNEDD

ABERDYFI MAP 14 SN69

Pick of the Pubs

Penhelig Arms Hotel & Restaurant

★★ SHL 🏵 🐟 🍷

Terrace Rd LL35 0LT ☎ 01654 767215 📠 01654 767690

e-mail: info@penheligarms.com

dir: *On A493 W of Machynlleth*

The Penhelig Arms has been in business since the late 18th century. It enjoys glorious views over the tidal Dyfi estuary, and is idyllically placed for breezy sea strolls or hill walks. Cader Idris and a variety of majestic mountains and historic castles are within easy reach. Locals and visitors alike experience a warm welcome in the wood-panelled Fisherman's bar, where they find a choice of traditional ales; many customers relax on the sea wall opposite during fine weather. Owner Robert Hughes' passion for good food and wine is reflected in inventive brasserie-style cooking and a legendary list of over 300 wines. A speciality in the contemporary restaurant is fresh seafood, which features in up to five starters and seven main courses during high season. Welsh Black beef and lamb are other regional favourites, ably supported by that wine list which proffers around 30 served by the glass.

Open 11.30-3.30 5.30-11 (Sun 12-3.30, 6-11) Closed: Dec 25-26 **Bar Meals** L served all week 12-2.30 D served all week 6-9.30 Av main course £11.95 **Restaurant** L served all week 12-2.30 D served all week 7-9.30 Av 3 course fixed price £28 ⊕ Free House ◀ Speckled Hen, Greene King Abbot Ale, Adnams Broadside, Brains Reverend James & SA. 🍷 30 **Facilities** Children's licence Garden Dogs allowed Parking **Rooms** 16 bedrooms en suite S£49 D£79

BLAENAU FFESTINIOG MAP 14 SH74

The Miners Arms

Llechwedd Slate Caverns LL41 3NB

☎ 01766 830306 📠 01766 831260

e-mail: quarrytours@aol.com

dir: *From Llandudno take A470 south. Through Betwys-Y-Coed, 16m to Blaenau Ffestiniog*

Slate floors, open fires and staff in Victorian costume emphasise the heritage theme of this welcoming pub nestling in the centre of a Welsh village. On the site of Llechwedd Slate Caverns, one of the country's leading tourist attractions, it caters for all comers and tastes: expect steak and ale casserole, pork pie and salad, various ploughman's lunches, and hot apple pie, as well as afternoon tea with scones and cream.

Open 11-5.30 Closed: Oct-Easter **Bar Meals** L served all week 11-5 ⊕ Free House **Facilities** Garden Dogs allowed Parking Play Area

LLANBEDR MAP 14 SH52

Victoria Inn ★★★★ INN 🍷

LL45 2LD ☎ 01341 241213 📠 01341 241644

e-mail: junevicinn@aol.com

dir: *Telephone for directions*

Heavily beamed and wonderfully atmospheric, the Victoria is perfect for the pub connoisseur seeking authentic features such as flagged floors, an unusual circular wooden settle, an ancient stove and a grandfather clock. Good food in the bars and restaurant includes honey roast ham, sausage in onion gravy, Japanese torpedo prawns served with a lemon mayonnaise dip, and Welsh dragon tart. Relax with a leisurely drink in the pub's well-kept garden.

Open 12-11 (Fri-Sat 12-12, Sun 12-10.30) **Bar Meals** L served all week 12-9 D served all week 6-9 (Sun 12-8) Av main course £7.95 **Restaurant** L served all week 12-3 D served all week 6-9 Av 3 course à la carte £18 ⊕ Frederic Robinson ◀ Robinson's Best Bitter, Hartleys XB. 🍷 10 **Facilities** Garden Dogs allowed Parking Play Area **Rooms** 5 bedrooms en suite S£40 D£70

LLANDWROG MAP 14 SH45

The Harp Inn 🍷

Tyn'llan LL54 5SY ☎ 01286 831071 📠 01286 830239

e-mail: management@theharp.globalnet.co.uk

dir: *A55 from Chester bypass, signed off A487 Pwllheli Rd*

This old free house stands in the centre of a lovely village. There used to be a secret passage to the ancient churchyard across the road, and the building is said to be haunted. Nowadays you'll find real ale a peaceful garden. New licensees due to take over late 2007 – reports welcome.

Open 12-3 6-11 (Sat 12-11) (Times vary, ring for details) Closed: 1 Jan **Bar Meals** L served Tue-Sun 12-2 D served Tue-Sun 6.30-8.30 **Restaurant** L served Tue-Sun 12-2 D served Tue-Sun 6.30-8.30 ⊕ Free House ◀ Guest Welsh Ales. 🍷 8 **Facilities** Garden Dogs allowed Parking

Please see cycle ride on opposite page

The Harp Inn

Cycle information

Distance: 14 miles/22.8km (2h30)
Map: OS OL Explorer 17 Snowdonia _ Snowdon & Conwy Valley
Start/Finish: Slate Quay car park, Caernarfon; grid ref: SH 477627
Trails/Tracks: gravel cycle trail, quiet country lanes
Landscape: gently undulating farmland, level coastline, views of mountains
Public toilets: Slate Quay, Dinas Dinlle
Tourist information: Caernarfon, tel 01286 672232
Cycle hire: Beics Menai Cycles, Slate Quay, Caernarfon, tel: 01286 676804
The Pub: The Harp Inn, Llandwrog
Short stretch of busy road linking Slate Quay and the start of the cycle trail. A few short climbs and a couple of blind bends on the lanes. An easy ride for older children

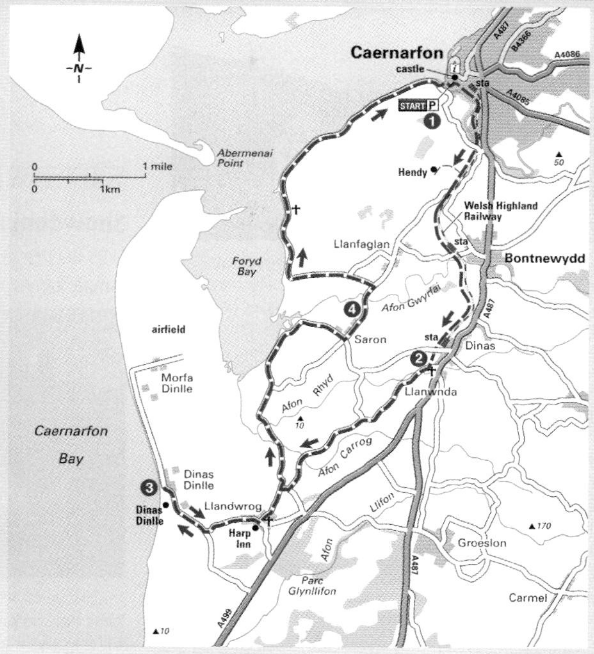

Cycle directions

1. From Slate Quay car park, pass the Harbour Offices to join a road between the railway line and warehouses. In 300 yards (274m) join the old trackbed on the left and pass beneath the impressive Lon Eifion cycle route sign. With the Welsh Highland railway to your left, gradually climb above the harbour and leave the town. Cross a lane by a house, signposted 'Hendy', continue to cross another road and keep to the trail to reach Bontnewydd, where you cross the Afon Gwyrfai. Gently ascend through a cutting, pass Dinas station to reach a road at Llanwnda, with the village church to your left.

2. Go right along the narrow lane for two miles (3.2km), ignoring a turning on the right and soon drop down to the waters of the Afon Carrog. Climb to a junction, go right and then left at the next junction to reach Llandwrog. Turn right by the Harp Inn; the road descends to a junction in 0.5 mile (0.8km). Go right for Dinas Dinlle and soon reach the seafront.

3. Retrace your route to Llandwrog and turn left before the Harp Inn, still on your outward route. Keep to this lane for 0.75 mile (1.2km) to cross the Afon Carrog and pass a small cluster of buildings (telephone box). Continue to a sharp right bend and bear off left along a quiet narrow road leading to Foryd Bay. The lane bears right close to the water's edge, eventually reaching a crossroads. Go left here through the hamlet of Saron.

4. The road descends to a bridge at Pont Faen, crossing the Afon Gwyrfai, and rises to a junction, just before the Llanfaglan village sign. Turn left and continue for less than 0.5 mile (0.8km) to the water's edge at Foryd Bay, with excellent views across to the Isle of Anglesey. This delightful lane hugs the coast and passes the small windswept Llanfaglan church, isolated in a field to your right. The road bears right and runs along the front of the harbour at Caernarfon. Wheel your cycle across the Aber footbridge and return to the castle and the start point of the ride.

Where to go from here

Just a short ride away from the Harp Inn is Parc Glynllifon, a 70-acre country park with exotic gardens, 18th-century follies, contemporary sculptures, a restored steam engine, a craft centre and signed walks. It is also home to a rich and diverse wildlife, including the largest roost in Europe for the Lesser Horse Shoe Bat.

MALLWYD MAP 14 SH81

Pick of the Pubs

Brigands Inn ★★★★ INN

SY20 9HJ ☎ 01650 511999 🖷 01650 531208

dir: *On A487 between Dolgellau and Machynlleth*

At the heart of the Cambrian Mountains, on the upper banks of the gin-clear River Dovey, lies the Brigands Inn, a renowned 15th-century coaching establishment. The pub's impressive setting makes it a popular base for exploring this scenic, spectacular corner of Wales. Fly fishing is a much-loved activity here, as is walking, and one well-worn route offers the chance to stroll up Camlan Mountain to inspect the site of King Arthur's last battle. Alternatively, or afterwards, opt for a glass of wine in the pub's sunny garden with its fine country views. The chef sources the finest local produce to create a fusion of contemporary and classic Welsh cuisine. The menus reflect the changing seasons with a good selection of fish, meat and game. A typical example is grilled fillet of sea bass with sun-dried tomato and pesto; grilled sirloin steak with tomato, mushrooms and onions; and loin of venison on caramelised red onions with a port and juniper sauce.

Open 10–11 **Bar Meals** L served all week 12–2.30 D served all week 6–9 **Restaurant** L served all week 12–2.30 D served all week 6–9 Worthington Cream, Worthington Cask, Archers Guest Ale. **Facilities** Garden Parking **Rooms** 11 bedrooms en suite S£50 D£80

NANTGWYNANT MAP 14 SH65

Pen-Y-Gwryd Hotel

LL55 4NT ☎ 01286 870211

dir: *A5 to Capel Curig, left on A4086 to T-junct.*

This slate-roofed climbers' pub and rescue post in the heart of Snowdonia has long been the home of British mountaineering. The 1953 Everest team used it as their training base, and etched their signatures on the ceiling. The appetising and inexpensive menus make good use of Welsh lamb and local pork; other options include home-made pâté with pickles, salad and crusty bread; or ham and cannellini bean spaghetti with home-made olive and herb flatbread.

Open 11–11 Closed: Nov–1 Jan **Bar Meals** L served all week 12–2 D served all week **Restaurant** D served all week 7.30–8 Av 5 course fixed price £26 Free House Interbrew Bass & Boddingtons Bitter. **Facilities** Garden Dogs allowed Parking Play Area

TUDWEILIOG MAP 14 SH23

Lion Hotel

LL53 8ND ☎ 01758 770244 🖷 0871 256 5207

dir: *A499 from Caernarfon, B4417 Tudweiliog*

The beach is only a mile away from this friendly inn, run by the Lee family for over 30 years. The large garden and children's play area makes the pub especially popular with the cyclists, walkers and families who flock to the Lleyn Peninsula. The bar features an extensive list of over 80 malt whiskies. A typical menu might consist of Tuscan bean soup, Welsh lamb bake, and rice pudding.

Open 11.30–11 (Sun 12–2) (Winter 12–2, 7–11) **Bar Meals** L served all week 12–2 D served all week 6–9 Av main course £8 **Restaurant** L served 12–2 D served 6–9 Free House Wye Valley Brewery, Purple Moose Brewery Ales, Becks & Carling. 6 **Facilities** Garden Parking Play Area

WAUNFAWR MAP 14 SH55

Snowdonia Parc Brewpub & Campsite

LL55 4AQ ☎ 01286 650409 & 650218 🖷 01286 650409

e-mail: karen@snowdonia-park.co.uk

This pub stands 400 feet above sea level at Waunfawr Station on the Welsh Highland Railway. There are steam trains on site (the building was originally the station master's house), plus a micro-brewery and campsite. All around is pleasant mountain scenery. Expect standard pub food such as sausage and mash; steak and ale pie; home-made curries; and filled jacket potatoes. Children and dogs are welcome, and a children's playground is provided.

Open 11–11 (Open late Summer wkends) **Bar Meals** L served all week 11–8.30 D served all week 5–8.30 **Restaurant** L served all week 11–8.30 D served all week 11–8.30 Free House Marston's Bitter & Pedigree, Welsh Highand Bitter (ownbrew), Mansfield Dark Mild. **Facilities** Garden Dogs allowed Parking Play Area

MONMOUTHSHIRE

ABERGAVENNY MAP 09 SO21

Pick of the Pubs

Clytha Arms

Clytha NP7 9BW ☎ 01873 840209 🖷 01873 840209
e-mail: theclythaarms@tiscali.co.uk
dir: *From A449/A40 junction (E of Abergavenny) follow signs for 'Old Road Abergavenny/Clytha'*

At one time a dower house, this family-run free house functions successfully as both informal pub and outstanding restaurant. A truly extensive and innovative list of bar snacks includes mussels in Belgian beer; spaghetti with bacon and cockles; and salmon burger with fennel coleslaw. Fish and shellfish are plentiful, including baked Pembrokeshire crab with Thai chilli sauce; carpaccio of tuna; salmon, brill and sole plait; and brodetto, Italy's version of bouillabaisse. Apart from fish, the frequently changing restaurant menu might offer wild boar in Rioja and chorizo; chargrilled vegetable soufflé; and roast herbed guinea fowl. Felinfoel and Hook Norton ales are joined by an ever-changing selection of guest beers, and there's also a good choice of wines by the glass. The inn is surrounded by two acres of lawns and gardens, perfect for an al fresco supper in the sun.

Open 12–3 6–12 (Fri–Sat 12–12, Sun 12–10.30) Closed: 25 Dec **Bar Meals** L served Tue–Sun 12.30–2.15 D served Mon–Sat 7–9.3 Av main course £14 **Restaurant** L served Tue–Sun 12.30–2.30 D served Mon–Sun 7–9.30 Av 3 course à la carte £30 Av 3 course fixed price £19.95 Free House Felinfoel Double Dragon, Hook Norton, Rhymer Bitter & 3 Guest beers. 10 **Facilities** Garden Parking Play Area

Llanwenarth Hotel & Riverside Restaurant ★★ HL

Brecon Rd NP8 1EP ☎ 01873 810550 🖷 01873 811880
e-mail: info@llanwenarthhotel.com
dir: *On A40 between Abergavenny & Crickhowell*

Not long ago, the owners of this part 16th-century inn and restaurant featured in Channel 4's *No Turning Back*, a programme about major lifestyle change. The views from its elevated position above the River Usk are splendid, as those who watched the programme may recall. The mostly locally-sourced, all home-made, dishes are available throughout the two bars, conservatory, dining room and patio. Fish choices include salmon, hake, bream and gurnard, while among the meats are duck, lamb, and fillet and rib-eye steaks.

Open 12–2 5.30–9.30 Closed: 26 Dec & 1 Jan **Restaurant** L served all week 12–2 D served all week 5.30–9.30 Av 3 course à la carte £25 Free House Braines Smooth. **Facilities** Garden Parking Play Area **Rooms** 17 bedrooms en suite S£63 D£75

CHEPSTOW MAP 04 ST59

Castle View Hotel

16 Bridge St NP16 5EZ ☎ 01291 620349 🖷 01291 627397
e-mail: castleviewhotel@btconnect.com
dir: *Opposite Chepstow Castle*

This hotel was built as a private house some 300 years ago, and has solid walls up to five feet thick in places. It stands opposite the castle, alongside the River Wye, and has a lovely secluded walled garden. Food choices include cold options such as sandwiches, ploughman's and baguettes, plus omelettes and full meals – perhaps duck and orange paté with chilli dressing followed by lamb cutlets with parsnip purée.

Bar Meals L served all week 12–2.30 D served all week 6.30–9.30 (Sun 12–3, 7–9) Av main course £9 **Restaurant** D served all week 6.30–9.30 Free House Wye Valley Real Ale, Double Dragon, Felinfoel Best Bitter. **Facilities** Garden Dogs allowed Parking **Rooms** 13 bedrooms en suite S£55 D£77

LLANTRISANT MAP 09 ST39

Pick of the Pubs

The Greyhound Inn

NP15 1LE ☎ 01291 672505 & 673447 🖷 01291 673255
e-mail: enquiry@greyhound-inn.com
dir: *A449 towards Monmouth, 1st junct to Usk, left onto Usk Sq. 2nd left signed Llantrisant 2.5m*

During the 17th century this traditional Welsh longhouse oversaw a 400-acre farm estate; then in 1845 the milk parlour was converted into an inn. Over the decades land was sold off, and by 1980 the whole complex was in a sorry state, as pictures hanging in the Cocktail and Llangibby lounges bear witness. Today, after a quarter of a century in the same family's hands, the Greyhound has two acres of award-winning gardens, a four-acre paddock, and an array of restored outbuildings. Owner Nick Davies heads the kitchen team, serving customers in the relaxed lounges or more formal candle-lit dining room. The regular menu is complemented by a daily specials blackboard offering unusual and seasonal dishes. Otherwise choose from well-prepared standards such as

CONTINUED

Wales

LLANTRISANT continued

deep-fried breaded brie wedges or whitebait; home-made chicken curry, or chilli con carne; and fish in the form of grilled local trout or battered plaice.

Open 11–11 (Sun 12–4, 7–11) Closed: 25, 31 Dec, 1 Jan **Bar Meals** L served all week 12–2.15 D served Mon–Sat 6–10 (Sun 12–2.15) Av main course £8 **Restaurant** L served all week 12–2.15 D served Mon–Sat 6–10.30 Av 3 course à la carte £20 Free House Interbrew Flowers Original & Bass, Greene King Abbot Ale & Guest Beer. 10 **Facilities** Garden Parking **Rooms** 10 bedrooms en suite S£56 D£76 (★★★ INN)

LLANVAIR DISCOED MAP 09 ST49

Pick of the Pubs

The Woodland Restaurant & Bar

NP16 6LX ☎ 01633 400313 01633 400313

e-mail: lausnik@aol.co.uk

This old inn has been extended to accommodate a growing number of diners, but remains at heart a friendly, family-run village local serving a good range of beers. The pub is located close to the Roman fortress town of Caerwent and Wentworth's forest and reservoir. Its nickname, 'the war office' recalls the fact that Irish navvies building the reservoir used to hold bare-knuckle fights here. A varied menu of freshly prepared dishes caters for all tastes from ciabatta bread with various toppings to seared fillets of sea bream, crayfish risotto and buttered samphire; and devilled Cornish mackerel with tomato, onion and basil salad. Meat is sourced from a local butcher who slaughters all his own, and the fish is mostly from Cornwall. Various guest ales back up a regular supply of Felinfoel Double Dragon and Tomas Watkins OSB. Outside there's a large, well-equipped garden with plenty of bench seating.

Open 11–3 6–11 (Sun 12–3, closed Sun eve/Mon) **Bar Meals** L served Tue–Sat 12–2 (Sun 12–3) D served Tue–Sat 6–10 Av main course £10.50 **Restaurant** L served Tue–Sun 12–2 (Sun 12–3) D served Tue–Sat 6–9.30 Av 3 course à la carte £20 Av 2 course fixed price £9.25 Free House Brains, Felinfoel Double Dragon,Tomas Watkins OSB, Guest ales. 8 **Facilities** Garden Dogs allowed Parking

PENALLT MAP 04 SO51

The Boat Inn

Lone Ln NP25 4AJ ☎ 01600 712615 01600 719120

dir: *From Monmouth take A466. In Redbrook, pub car park signed. Access by foot across rail bridge over River Wye*

Dating back over 360 years, this riverside pub has served as a hostelry for quarry, mill, paper and tin mine workers, and even had a landlord operating a ferry across the Wye at shift times. The unspoilt slate floor is testament to the age of the place. The excellent selection of real ales and local ciders complements the menu well, with choices ranging from various ploughman's to lamb stiffados or the charmingly-named pan haggerty. Ideal for walkers on the Offa's Dyke or Wye Valley walks.

Open 11–11 (Sun 12–10.30) **Bar Meals** L served all week 12–2.30 (Sun 12–3 Winter) D served all week 6–9 (Sat–Sun 12–9 Summer) Av main course £5 Free House Freeminer Bitter, Wadworth 6X, Abbot Ale & Old Speckled Hen, Wye Valley Butty Bach. **Facilities** Garden Dogs allowed Parking

RAGLAN MAP 09 SO40

Pick of the Pubs

The Beaufort Arms Coaching Inn & Restaurant ★★ HL

High St NP15 2DY ☎ 01291 690412 01291 690935

e-mail: enquiries@beaufortraglan.co.uk

dir: *0.5m junct A40 and A449*

This atmospheric inn, nestling between the Wye Valley and the Usk, dates from the 15th century. It was used by Parliamentarian soldiers during the Siege of Raglan Castle in 1646, and was later an important staging post on the London to Fishguard road. The beautifully refurbished interior still resonates with history: the large stone fireplace in the lounge allegedly came from the castle, and locals believe a stash of vintage champagne lies hidden in tunnels beneath the inn. Expect excellent ales, continental lagers and food served in the bar, lounge and restaurant. The daytime menu offers paninis, sandwiches, prime Welsh steak, beer battered catch of the day, wild mushroom risotto, and seared leg of chicken with chorizo mousse and braised lentils. There are light meals in the evening too, doubling as starters (chicken caesar salad, salmon and smoked haddock fishcakes), and mains like slow roasted herb crusted loin of pork.

Open 7–11 (Sat 8–11, Sun 8–10.30) **Bar Meals** L served all week 12–5 D served all week 6–9 (Fri–Sat 6–9.30, Sun 6–8.30, Summer all day) Av main course £8.95 **Restaurant** L served all week 12–3 D served all week 6–9 (Fri–Sat 6–9.30, Sun 6–8.30) Av 3 course à la carte £22.50 Free House London Pride, Reverend James, Budweiser & Warsteiner, Old Speckled Hen. 12 **Facilities** Garden Parking **Rooms** 15 bedrooms en suite S£60 D£70

SHIRENEWTON MAP 09 ST49

The Carpenters Arms

Usk Rd NP16 6BU ☎ 01291 641231 01291 641231

dir: *A48 to Chepstow then A4661, B4235. Village 3m*

A 400-year-old hostelry, formerly a smithy and carpenter's shop, with flagstone floors, open fires and antiques. It's set in a pleasant wooded location in the valley of the Mounton Brook which lies between the bigger valleys of the Wye and Usk. Straightforward bar food is typified by steak and mushroom pie, smoked haddock and potato pie, guinea fowl in orange sauce, and lamb rogan josh.

Open 11–11 **Bar Meals** L served all week 12–2 D served all week 7–9.30 Av main course £6.95 **Restaurant** L served all week 12–9.30 D served all week 12–9.30 Av 3 course à la carte £12 Punch Taverns Fuller's London Pride, Wadworth 6X, Marston's Pedigree,Theakston Old Peculier. **Facilities** Children's licence Dogs allowed Parking

Wales

SKENFRITH MAP 09 SO42

Pick of the Pubs

The Bell at Skenfrith ★★★★★ RR

NP7 8UH ☎ 01600 750235 01600 750525

e-mail: enquiries@skenfrith.co.uk

dir: *A449 onto A40, through tunnel & lights. At rdbt 1st exit, right at lights onto Hereford Rd. Left onto B4521 towards Abergavenny, 3m on left*

From its setting by the historic arched bridge over the River Morrow, this 17th-century coaching inn has views of Skenfrith Castle. An oak bar, flagstone floors, comfortable sofas and old settles provide plenty of character, and there are eight well-equipped bedrooms, some with four-poster beds. The pub flies the flag for superb food and drink. Guest real ales, hand-pumped local cider and wines by the glass are a treat in themselves. Locally sourced and mainly organic ingredients are used in dishes offered from a daily menu. One day's selection might include roast local woodcock with pancetta and mushroom dumplings, sautéed spinach and winter vegetable broth, followed by pan-roasted fillet of sea bass with green olive and herb crushed new potatoes, baby leeks, fine ratatouille and basil pesto. Hot chocolate fondant with vanilla ice cream and crème anglaise would be a fitting finale, or a selection of Neal's Yard cheeses.

Open 11-11 Closed: Last wk Jan & 1st wk Feb **Bar Meals** L served all week 12-2.30 D served all week 7-9.30 (Sun 7-9) Av main course £16 **Restaurant** L served all week 12-2.30 D served all week 7-9.30 (Sun 7-9) Av 3 course à la carte £27 Free House Freeminer Best Bitter, Golden Valley,Timothy Taylor Landlord. 13 **Facilities** Garden Dogs allowed Parking **Rooms** 8 bedrooms en suite S£75 D£105

TINTERN PARVA MAP 04 SO50

Fountain Inn

Trellech Grange NP16 6QW

☎ 01291 689303 01291 689303

e-mail: thefountaininn@msn.com

dir: *In Tintern turn by George Hotel for Raglan. Bear right, inn at top of hill*

A fire nearly destroyed this fine old inn, but the thick 17th-century walls survived the flames, and its character remains unspoilt. It enjoys views of the Wye Valley from the garden, and is close to Tintern Abbey. Home-cooked food includes grilled sardines with balsamic vinegar and cherry tomatoes; leek and Caerphilly sausages with onion gravy; and beef and Guinness pie. Also a good selection of steaks, omelettes, and seafood choices.

Open 12-3 6.30-11 **Bar Meals** L served all week 12-2.30 D served all week 7-9.15 **Restaurant** L served all week 12-2.30 D served all week 7-9.15 Free House Hook Norton, Spinning Dog, Ring of Bells, Interbrew Bass. **Facilities** Garden Dogs allowed Parking

TREDUNNOCK MAP 09 ST39

Pick of the Pubs

The Newbridge ★★★★ RR

NP15 1LY ☎ 01633 451000 01633 451001

e-mail: thenewbridge@tinyonline.co.uk

dir: *Usk towards Llangybi. 0.5m, left for Tredunnock. Pub in 800yds*

See Pick of the Pubs on page 742

TRELLECH MAP 04 SO50

Pick of the Pubs

The Lion Inn

NP25 4PA ☎ 01600 860322 01600 860060

e-mail: debs@globalnet.co.uk

dir: *From A40 S of Monmouth take B4293, follow signs for Trellech. From M8 junct 2, straight across rdbt, 2nd left at 2nd rdbt, B4293 to Trellech*

Once an Elizabethan stone pig cot, this multi-award-winning pub has also been a coaching inn and a brewhouse. Much effort has been made to preserve that authentic sense of history. There are beams and open fires in both bar and restaurant, and all the accoutrements of the traditional English pub have been maintained: hearty wholesome grub, traditional beers, ciders and games, and no plastic flowers, jukebox, or gaming machines. But homage to tradition is not total, since authentic Hungarian dishes are also served, like Kecskemét stuffed chicken, in which chicken breast is stuffed with apricots, cherries and cheese, then wrapped in bacon. Keep an eye out too for the Back to the Earth board, which touts such hedgerow-foraged foodstuffs as nettle soup; wild mushroom stroganoff; or pan-fried puffball and bacon. Unusual spirits are a house speciality: look out for absinthe and Hungarian plum brandy.

Open 12-3 6-11 (Thu-Sat 6-12, Mon 7-11) (Summer all day Sat) **Bar Meals** L served all week 12-2 (Sat-Sun 12-2.30) D served Mon-Sat 6-9.30 Av main course £9 **Restaurant** L served all week 12-2 (Sat-Sun 12-2.30) D served Mon-Sat 6-9.30 Av 3 course à la carte £23 Free House Bath Ales, Wadworth 6X, Wye Valley Butty Bach, Archers. **Facilities** Garden Dogs allowed Parking

The Newbridge

The Newbridge has commanded the bridge over the River Usk since 1800. This particular structure dates back to 1850, although it was totally renovated in the 1980s. The inn occupies an idyllic location: to be there in the early morning and watch the mist over the river is magical.

A few minutes' drive away is the historic town of Caerleon, site of one of Britain's three Roman legionary fortresses and what many believe to be the location of King Arthur's Camelot. The decor is warm and welcoming, with comfortable sofas and subtle lighting; in the Gallery is the work of Graham Knuttel, probably the most important painter to come out of Ireland and the first to find universal acceptance. Head Chef Iain Sampson has worked in some of the country's finest kitchens and the quality and consistency of his modern British with Mediterranean-influenced food is well reflected in exciting seasonal menus, based extensively on local produce. Expect therefore a typical meal of Welsh oak-smoked haddock risotto with parmesan wafer and herb oil; mustard-crusted rack of local Penperlleni lamb with fondant potatoes and carved vegetables; and banana Tatin with caramel ice cream. Dinner could be watercress, spinach and goats' cheese tart with beetroot coulis; Gloucestershire Old Spot pork loin with potato cake, baby vegetables and buttered tarragon jus; and home-made ice cream. The day's catch, purchased from the quayside in Cornwall, is displayed on the specials board. Wines are carefully chosen to complement the menu, a good number being served by the glass.

★★★★ RR 🏵 ⟴ 🍷

MAP 09 ST39

NP15 1LY

☎ 01633 451000

🖷 01633 451001

e-mail: eatandsleep@thenewbridge.co.uk

dir: *M4 junct 24/26 from Usk towards Llangybi. 0.5m, left for Tredunnock. Pub in 800yds*

Open 12–2.30 6.30–9.30 (Sun 12–3, 6.30–8.30)

Bar Meals L served all week 12–2.30 D served all week

Restaurant L served all week 12–2.30 D served all week 6–9.30 (Sun 12–3, 6.30–8.30)

Free House

Coor's Hancock's HB, Brains Rev James, Brains Smooth & Guest Ale. 🍷 12

Facilities Garden Parking

Rooms 6 bedrooms en suite

USK MAP 09 SO30

The Nags Head Inn

Twyn Square NP15 1BH ☎ 01291 672820 01291 672720

dir: *On A472*

This 15th-century coaching inn overlooks the square just a short stroll from the River Usk, and boasts magnificent hanging flower baskets. The traditional bar is furnished with polished tables and chairs, and decorated with collections of horse brasses, farming tools and lanterns hanging from exposed oak beams. Game in season figures strongly among the speciality dishes, including whole stuffed partridge (one of the hardest birds to shoot), pheasant in port, and wild boar steak with apricot and brandy sauce.

Open 10–3 5.30–11 Closed: 25 Dec **Bar Meals** L served all week 10–2 D served all week 5.30–10.30 (Sun 12–2, 6–9.30) **Restaurant** L served all week 11.30–2 D served all week 5.30–10.30 Free House Brains Bitter, Dark, Buckleys Best, Reverend James & Bread of Heaven. 8 **Facilities** Garden Dogs allowed Parking

Raglan Arms NEW

Llandenny NP15 1DL ☎ 01291 690800 01291 690155

e-mail: raglanarms@aol.com

dir: *Monmouth A449 to Raglan, left in village*

Giles, Charlott and Sebastien have put their own stamp on the Raglan Arms since taking over in 2006, offering well-cooked modern British food from local ingredients. Whilst the choice of dishes is fairly small, menus are changed daily and a good selection of Welsh and English cheeses supports a well-chosen range of starters, mains and puddings. At lunchtime, expect open sandwiches, too: slow-roast pork with apples, perhaps, or smoked salmon with rocket and horseradish.

Open 12–3 6.30–9.30 **Bar Meals** L served Tue–Sun 12–3 D served Tue–Sat 6.30–9.30 Av main course £13.50 **Restaurant** L served Tue–Sun 12–3 D served Tue–Sat 6.30–9.30 Av 3 course à la carte £23 Av 3 course fixed price £20.50 Wye Valley Bitter, Butty Bach, Guinness. 12 **Facilities** Garden Parking

PEMBROKESHIRE

AMROTH MAP 08 SN10

The New Inn

SA67 8NW ☎ 01834 812368

dir: *A48 to Carmarthen, A40 to St Clears, A477 to Llanteg then left*

A 400-year-old inn, originally a farmhouse, belonging to Amroth Castle Estate. It has old world charm with beamed ceilings, a Flemish chimney, a flagstone floor and an inglenook fireplace. It is close to the beach, and local lobster and crab are a feature, along with a popular choice of home-made dishes including steak and kidney pie, soup and curry. Enjoy food or drink outside on the large lawn complete with picnic benches.

Open 11.30–3 5.30–11 Closed: Nov–Mar **Bar Meals** L served all week 12–2 D served all week 6–9 (Summer all day) **Restaurant** L served all week 12–2 D served all week 6–9 (Summer all day) Free House Brains, Carlsberg-Tetley Tetley Bitter, Speckled Hen & Guest ales. **Facilities** Garden Dogs allowed Parking **Notes**

Temple Bar Inn

SA67 8ND ☎ 01834 812486

Overlooking the beach and the sea, this popular family pub is handy for both the coast and the countryside. Nearby is the famous Pembrokeshire Coast Path which offers miles of unspoilt walking. Very extensive menu offers grills, curries, fish and Sunday roast dishes, as well as filled jacket potatoes, giant salad rolls, sandwiches, burgers and ploughman's lunches. Other fare ranges from Welsh ham and steak and kidney pudding to pork sausages and sliced turkey.

Open 11–11 **Bar Meals** L served all week 11–9 D served all week 11–9 Av main course £6 Worthingtons, Brains Ales. **Facilities** Children's licence Garden Dogs allowed Parking

CAREW MAP 08 SN00

Carew Inn

SA70 8SL ☎ 01646 651267

e-mail: mandy@carewinn.co.uk

dir: *From A477 take A4075. Inn 400yds opp castle & Celtic cross*

A traditional stone-built country inn situated opposite the Carew Celtic cross and Norman castle. Enjoy the one-mile circular walk around the castle and millpond. A good range of bar meals includes Welsh black steak and kidney pie; chilli con carne; Thai red chicken curry; and seafood pancakes. Fruit crumble and old favourite jam roly poly feature among the puddings. Live music every Thursday night under the marquee.

Open 11–11 Closed: Dec 25 **Bar Meals** L served all week 11.30–2 D served all week 5.30–9 Av main course £8.50 **Restaurant** L served all week 11.30–2 D served all week 5.30–9 Av 3 course à la carte £15 Free House Worthington Best, SA Brains Reverend James & Guest Ales. **Facilities** Garden Dogs allowed Parking Play Area

CILGERRAN MAP 08 SN14

Pendre Inn

Pendre SA43 2SL ☎ 01239 614223

dir: *Off A478 south of Cardigan*

Dating back to the 14th century, this is a pub full of memorabilia and featuring exposed interior walls, old beams, slate floors and an inglenook fireplace. An ancient ash tree grows through the pavement in front of the white stone, thick-walled building. Typical menu includes lamb steaks with red wine and cherries, rump and sirloin steaks, pork loin with honey and mustard glaze, and salmon with hollandaise sauce.

Open 12 –11 **Bar Meals** L served Wed–Sun 12–2 D served Wed–Sun 6–8.30 Av main course £6 **Restaurant** L served Wed–Sun 12–2 D served Wed–Sun 6–8 Av 3 course à la carte £12 Free House Tomas Watkins, OSB, Murphys, Worthington. **Facilities** Garden Parking

HAVERFORDWEST MAP 08 SM91

Pick of the Pubs

The Georges Restaurant/Cafe Bar

24 Market St SA61 1NH

☎ 01437 766683 📠 01437 760345

e-mail: llewis6140@aol.com

dir: *In town centre*

Formerly George's Brewery, this remarkable 18th-century building incorporates many original features in its restored vaulted cellar and eating areas. Its delightful walled garden, with spectacular views over the ruins of 12th-century Haverfordwest Castle, has outdoor heating for chillier days and evenings. Genuine local character is a feature of the all-day café bar and cellar bistro, where freshly-prepared food and sheer enthusiasm sets it apart from the norm. An extensive range of home-made dishes is served all day in the Celtic-themed restaurant. Given the proximity of the sea, there are plenty of fish dishes including crab cakes, black bream, poached turbot and scallops. Locally-sourced meat appears in choices such as Welsh venison steak with a rich port and berry sauce; Welsh lamb-steak with red wine, mushroom and fresh mint sauce; and Pembrokeshire sausage pie with mashed potatoes and rich onion gravy topped with toasted cheese. For those whose tastebuds are tickled by the exotic, George's Creole rump steak is marinated in Cajun spices with a hot chilli and ginger sauce.

Open 10–5.30 (Sat 10.30–11) Closed: 25 Dec, 1 Jan **Bar Meals** L served Mon–Sat 12–5.30 D served Fri–Sat 6–9.45 Av main course £7 **Restaurant** L served Mon–Sat 12–2.30 D served Fri–Sat 6–9.30 Av 3 course à la carte £20 Free House Marston's Pedigree, Wye Valley Bitter, Adnams Broadside, Brains Bitter. 10 **Facilities** Garden

LAMPHEY MAP 08 SN00

The Dial Inn

Ridegway Rd SA71 5NU ☎ 01646 672426 📠 01646 672426

dir: *Just off A4139*

The Dial started life around 1830 as the Dower House for nearby Lamphey Court, and was converted into a pub in 1966. It immediately established itself as a popular village local, and in recent years the owners have extended the dining areas. Food is a real strength, and Pembrokeshire farm products are used whenever possible. You can choose from traditional bar food, the imaginative restaurant menu, or the daily blackboard.

Open 11-3 6–12 **Bar Meals** L served all week 12–3 D served all week 6.30–9.30 **Restaurant** L served all week 12–3 D served all week 6.30–9.30 Free House Coors Beer, Runmey Bitter. 8 **Facilities** Children's licence Garden Parking

LETTERSTON MAP 08 SM92

The Harp Inn

31 Haverfordwest Rd SA62 5UA

☎ 01348 840061 📠 01348 840812

dir: *On A40*

This 15th-century free house was once a working farm, as well as home to a weekly market. After remaining largely unchanged for 500 years, the inn is now firmly grounded in the 21st century with new disabled facilities and a 130-seater restaurant. Two comprehensive menus and a chalkboard offer dishes ranging from grilled sea bass to tenderloin pork in red plum sauce; and Welsh steaks garni to stir-fried vegetables in black bean sauce.

Open 11–3 6–11 (Sun 12–3, 6–10.30) **Bar Meals** L served all week 12–2.30 D served all week 6–9.30 **Restaurant** L served all week 12–2.30 D served all week 6.30–9.30 Av 3 course à la carte £20 Free House Tetleys, Greene King, Abbot Ale. 8 **Facilities** Garden Parking Play Area

NEWPORT MAP 08 SN03

Salutation Inn

Felindre Farchog, Crymych SA41 3UY

☎ 01239 820564 📠 01239 820355

e-mail: JohnDenley@aol.com

dir: *On A487 between Cardigan and Fishguard*

Set right on the banks of the River Nevern, this 16th-century coaching inn stands in a quiet village in the heart of the Pembrokeshire Coast National Park. Travellers will find a comfortable bar, a lounge and a restaurant. The varied menu might include potted asparagus and smoked Cerwyn cheese, or rustic game paté to start, with perhaps prime fillet of Welsh Black beef on rôsti and roasted shallots to follow.

Open 12–12 **Bar Meals** L served all week 12.30–2.30 D served all week 6.30–9.30 **Restaurant** L served all week 12.30–2.30 D served all week 6.30–9.30 Free House Local guest ales, Felinfoel, Brains. **Facilities** Garden Dogs allowed Parking **Rooms** 8 bedrooms en suite S£50 D£70 (★★★ INN)

The Stackpole Inn

A now-famous phrase sums up this 17th-century inn – location, location, location. It stands in beautiful gardens within the Pembrokeshire Coast National Park, just 15 minutes walk from the coastal path, Stackpole Quay and Barafundle Bay – described by the Sunday Times as 'a desert island dream beach in Wales'.

In the mellow stone wall outside is a rare King George V post box, a hangover from when one of the two original stone cottages was a post office. It's a freehouse, so there's always a guest beer from elsewhere in the UK to accompany three Welsh ales. The bar surface is made from slate, while the wood for the ceiling beams came from ash trees grown on the estate. Warmth is provided by a wood-burning stove set within the stone fireplace. Local produce from the surrounding countryside and fish from the nearby coast play a major part in the home-cooked menu. From its snack section might come battered cod, chips and peas, a home-made cheeseburger, prawn masala, or a filled baguette. On the lunch and dinner menu starters include toasted goats' cheese with red onion marmalade; deep-fried whitebait; and creamy garlic mushrooms. Among the main courses are provençale chicken in rich tomato and Mediterranean vegetable sauce on pesto linguine; confit of duck with orange and sage sauce and red lentil purée; rack of Welsh lamb with redcurrant and rosemary jus; and a daily vegetarian dish. Finish with a dessert such as Black Forest torte, or fresh raspberry brûlée. Specials, which are always available, might include whole foil-baked Thai-style sea bass; or Welsh Black fillet steak with Madeira sauce. The wine list is short, but well chosen. Bed and breakfast accommodation consists of four high-quality twin/double bed en suite rooms in a separate building in the grounds.

🍷

MAP 08 SR99
SA71 5DF
☎ 01646 672324
📠 01646 672716
e-mail: info@stackpoleinn.co.uk
dir: *From Pembroke take B4319 & follow signs for Stackpole, 4m.*

Open 12-2.30 6-11 (Summer 12-3, 5.30-11)
Bar Meals L served all week 12-2 D served all week 6.30-9 (Summer Sat-Sun 12-3, 5.30-9)
Restaurant L served all week 12-2 D served all week 6.30-9 (Summer Sat-Sun 12-3, 5.30-9)
Free House
Brains Reverend James, Felinfoel, Double Dragon, Best Bitter & Guest Ale. 🍷 12
Facilities Children's licence Garden Dogs allowed Parking
Rooms 4 bedrooms en suite S£37.50 D£60 (★★★★ INN)

Wales

PEMBROKE DOCK MAP 08 SM90

Ferry Inn

Pembroke Ferry SA72 6UD ☎ 01646 682947

e-mail: ferryinn@aol.com

dir: *A477, off A48, right at garage, signs for Cleddau Bridge, left at rdbt*

There are fine views across the Cleddau estuary from the terrace of this 16th-century free house. Once the haunt of smugglers, the riverside inn has a nautical-themed bar with a 'great disaster' corner highlighting pictures of local catastrophes! The pub is also said to be haunted. Fresh fish features strongly on the menu: favourites include locally caught trout; salmon fillet with dill butter; and brill with cherry tomatoes and crème fraiche.

Open 11.30-2.45 7-11 (Summer all day) Closed: 25-26 Dec **Bar Meals** L served all week 12-2 D served all week 7-9.30 (Sun 12-1.30, 7-9) Av main course £10 **Restaurant** L served all week 12-2 D served all week 7-9.30 (Sun 12-1.30, 7-9) Free House Worthington, Bass, Felinfoel Double Dragon, Weekly Guest Ale. **Facilities** Garden Parking

PORTHGAIN MAP 08 SM83

The Sloop Inn

SA62 5BN ☎ 01348 831449 01348 831388

e-mail: matthew@sloop-inn.freeserve.co.uk

A mere 100 metres from the harbour side at Porthgain, this is the ideal place for watching village activity on the green including fishermen landing the fish you may well eat for dinner. The Sloop Inn has been in the same hands for 20 years, and the landlord catches most of his own crab, lobster and scallops.

Open 9.30-11 **Bar Meals** L served all week 12-2.30 D served all week 6-9.30 **Restaurant** L served all week 12-2.30 D served all week 6-9.30 Free House Reverend James, Brains Draught & Felinfoel. 8 **Facilities** Children's licence Garden Parking

ROSEBUSH MAP 08 SN02

Tafarn Sinc NEW

Preseli SA66 7QT ☎ 01437 532214

High in the Preseli Hills, the looming presence of this large red corrugated-iron free house stands testament to its rapid construction in 1876. Now deserted by the railway it was built to serve, Tafarn Sinc boasts woodburning stoves, a sawdusted floor, and a charming garden. This idiosyncratic establishment is popular with walkers, who can stoke up on traditional favourites like faggots with onion gravy, and Preseli lamb burgers.

Open 12-12 **Bar Meals** L served all week 12-2 D served Tue-Sat 6-9 Av main course £11.90 Worthington, Tafarn Sinc, Guest ale. **Facilities** Garden Dogs allowed Parking

SOLVA MAP 08 SM82

The Cambrian Inn

Main St SA62 6UU ☎ 01437 721210 01437 720661

e-mail: thecambrianinn@btconnect.com

dir: *13m from Haverfordwest on St David's road*

Something of an institution in this pretty fishing village is a Grade II listed 17th-century inn that attracts local and returning visitors alike. A sample bar menu offers Welsh black beef curry, vegetable pancakes topped with melted cheese or Welsh sirloin steak, while the carte dinner menu offers lots of fresh fish dishes plus perhaps duckling with orange and Grand Marnier sauce, mushroom stroganoff, and pork fillet in honey and mustard sauce. Sandwiches, jackets, salads and ploughman's also available.

Open 10 -11 (Sun 10-10.30) **Bar Meals** L served all week 12-3 D served all week 6-9 **Restaurant** L served all week 12-2 D served all week 6-9 Free House Tomas Watkins OSB, Guest Ale. 15 **Facilities** Garden Parking

STACKPOLE MAP 08 SR99

Pick of the Pubs

The Stackpole Inn

SA71 5DF ☎ 01646 672324 01646 672716

e-mail: info@stackpoleinn.co.uk

dir: *From Pembroke take B4319 & follow signs for Stackpole, 4m.*

See Pick of the Pubs on page 745

WOLF'S CASTLE MAP 08 SM92

The Wolfe Inn

SA62 5LS ☎ 01437 741662 01437 741676

dir: *On A40 between Haverfordwest & Fishguard*

The Wolfe is an oak-beamed, stone-built property in a lovely village setting. The bar-brasserie and restaurant comprise four interconnecting but distinctly different rooms: the Victorian Parlour, Hunters' Lodge, the Brasserie and a conservatory. The inn uses mainly local produce in its 'robust, real food'. Example dishes are fillet of beef bordelaise, lamb all'aglio e menta, chicken piccante, salmon fillet with cream and Pernod sauce, and mussels in garlic, white wine and cream. Award-winning local cheeses and scrumptious home-made desserts follow.

Open 12-2 6-11 **Bar Meals** L served all week 12-2 D served all week 7-9 Av main course £12 **Restaurant** L served all week 12-2 D served all week 7–9 Av 3 course à la carte £25 Av 3 course fixed price £15 Free House Interbrew Worthington Bitter, Monthly Guest Beer. 11 **Facilities** Garden Parking

POWYS

BERRIEW MAP 15 SJ10

The Lion Hotel

SY21 8PQ 01686 640452 01686 640604
e-mail: patrick@okeeffe.demon.co.uk
dir: *5m from Welshpool on A483, right to Berriew. Centre of village next to church.*

Behind the black and white timbered grid of this 17th-century coaching inn lie bars and dining areas where yet more old timbers testify to its age. Menus include loin of venison with pan-fried wild mushrooms and redcurrant jus; slow-roasted Welsh lamb shoulder with red wine mint gravy; leek and mozzarella-filled crêpe with spiced tomato sauce; and a fish board with sea bream, halibut, red snapper and salmon based dishes.

Open 12–3 6–11 (Sat 12–11, Sun 7–10.30) Closed: Dec 24, 25 **Bar Meals** L served all week 12–2 D served all week 7–8.45 **Restaurant** L served all week 12–2 D served all week 7–8.45 Banks Bitter/Mild, Pedigree, Old Empire. **Facilities** Children's licence Garden Dogs allowed Parking

BRECON MAP 09 SO02

Pick of the Pubs

The Felin Fach Griffin ★★★★ INN

Felin Fach LD3 0UB 01874 620111 01874 620120
e-mail: enquiries@eatdrinksleep.ltd.uk
dir: *4.5m N of Brecon on the A470*

This country inn on the edge of the Brecon Beacons exemplifies owner Charles Inkin's uncompromising belief in 'simple things done well'. Under the EatDrinkSleep label, the ethos is applied to food, wines, beers and bedrooms, and a further pub, the Gurnard's Head has been acquired in West Cornwall. In the Griffin's bar are deep leather sofas surrounding a large newspaper-strewn table and an open fire; and food is served in the deep red dining room or the blue and yellow bar. The garden supplies the kitchen with a wide range of organic produce, and the freshest seafood is available in the form of two starters (scallops, crab) and two or three mains, like wild sea bass fillet with crushed potatoes and spinach and creamed girolles. An alternative might be local venison with winter fruits, butternut squash purée and thyme jus. Private parties can be accommodated in the Aga or Tack Rooms.

Open 12–3 6.30–11 (Sun 12–11) Closed: 24–25 Dec **Bar Meals** L served Tue–Sun 12.30–2.30 D served Mon–Sat 6.30–9.30 (Sun 6.30–9) Av main course £16 **Restaurant** L served Tue–Sun 12.30–2.30 D served Mon–Sat 7–9.30 (Sun 6.30–9) Av 3 course à la carte £30 Free House Breckonshire Breweries, Tomas Watkin OSB & Evan Evans. 10 **Facilities** Garden Dogs allowed Parking **Rooms** 7 bedrooms en suite S£67.50 D£97.50

Pick of the Pubs

The Usk Inn ★★★★ INN

Talybont-on-Usk LD3 7JE
01874 676251 01874 676392
e-mail: stay@uskinn.co.uk
dir: *6m E of Brecon, just off A40 towards Abergavenny*

The inn was established in the 1840s, just as the Brecon to Merthyr Railway arrived. In 1878 the locomotive Hercules failed to stop at the former station opposite and crashed into the street, seriously disrupting conversations and beer consumption in the bar. The owner Andrew Felix is making sure you can still partake of interesting food like fried haggis and chilli dressing. This haggis, by the way, is prefixed by the all-important word Celtic. Alternatively, opt for risotto of smoked garlic and porcini mushrooms, then half a honey-roast duck with apricot and tarragon, or a fish special, and home-made treacle tart to finish. The Brecon to Monmouth Canal runs through the village, in some places at rooftop level.

Open 8am–11pm Closed: Dec 25–26 **Bar Meals** L served all week 12–3 D served all week 6.30–9 **Restaurant** L served all week 12–3 D served all week 6.30–9 Free House Hancocks HB, Brains, Guinness, Worthington. 11 **Facilities** Garden Parking **Rooms** 11 bedrooms en suite S£50 D£80

Wales

BRECON continued

Pick of the Pubs

The White Swan Inn

Llanfrynach LD3 7BZ

☎ 01874 665276 01874 665362

dir: *3m E of Brecon off A40, B4558 and Llanfrynach signs*

The long, white-painted stone frontage of the White Swan overlooks St Brynach's churchyard in the heart of the Brecon Beacons National Park. With its exposed oak beams, stone walls and inglenook fireplace, the stamp of character and atmosphere is everywhere. The theme here is unpretentious gastro-pub food with the emphasis on fish and modern dishes characterised by a distinct European flavour. Expect venison with port and cranberry sauce, or, perhaps, lamb with sweet potato. Other options include trio of mullet, sea bass and salmon; Caesar salad; Gressingham duck breast; and asparagus mousse gateau with crepes. Traditional afternoon tea with clotted cream is a perennial favourite. The White Swan is especially popular with walkers and cyclists, and there's trout fishing on the nearby River Usk, while the Monmouthshire and Brecon Canal runs close by. Brains SA and Smooth, and Reverend James, are served.

Open 12-2 6.30-11 Closed: 25-26 Dec, 1 Jan **Bar Meals** L served Tue-Sun 12-2 D served Tue-Sun 7-9.30 (Sun 12-2.30, 7-9) Av main course £14.95 **Restaurant** L served Tue-Sun 12-2 D served Tue-Sun 7-9.30 (Sun 12-2.30, 7-9) Av 3 course à la carte £25 Free House HB, Brains SA, Brains Smooth, Guinness. 8 **Facilities** Garden Parking

CAERSWS MAP 15 SO09

Pick of the Pubs

The Talkhouse ★★★★★ RR

Pontdolgoch SY17 5JE

☎ 01686 688919 01686 689134

e-mail: info@talkhouse.co.uk

dir: *A470 through Caersws, inn on left after 1m*

From the outside this traditional stone coaching inn, low-roofed and whitewashed, has the appearance of a typical country pub. Inside, the relaxing sitting room is furnished with comfortable armchairs and sofas, while the bar with its beams and log fire offers a welcoming atmosphere. Indeed a warm welcome, good food, quality wines and great service are what the Talkhouse owners are passionate about. The varied menu of classical seasonal cooking is based on Welsh ingredients where possible. French windows open from the restaurant on to a private garden for romantic alfresco summer dining. A meal may start with a home-made venison terrine, or cream of mushroom soup. Main course examples are local Welsh fillet of beef served on a horseradish rôsti, or rack of local lamb with dauphinoise potatoes. In addition to classic desserts such as lemon tart or vanilla pod crème brûlée, the Welsh cheeseboard offers tastes of four different varieties: Snowdonia cheddar, Cambrian brie, Perlas blue and Pantysgawn goats' cheese would be typical.

Open 12-1.30 6.30-8.45 (Winter hours vary, pre-book essential) Closed: 1st 2 weeks in Jan **Bar Meals** L served Wed-Sun 12-1.30 D served Tue-Sat 6.30-8.45 Av main course £14.95 **Restaurant** L served Wed-Sun 12-1.30 D served Tue-Sat 6.30-8.45 Av 3 course à la carte £22 Free House Brains, Barcud Coch, Chimay, Leffe & Ddraig Aur. 6 **Facilities** Garden Parking **Rooms** 3 bedrooms en suite S£70 D£95

COEDWAY MAP 15 SJ31

The Old Hand and Diamond Inn

SY5 9AR ☎ 01743 884379 01743 884379

e-mail: moz123@aol.com

web: www.oldhandanddiamond.co.uk

dir: *9m from Shrewsbury*

A 17th-century inn close to the Powys/Shropshire border and the River Severn. It retains much of its original character and open log fires crackle warmly in winter. Outside there's a large car park, children's play area and beer garden, plus a patio with plenty of seating. The 100-seat restaurant provides a popular lunchtime carvery and many supper favourites, augmented by specials such as fruity coronation chicken, and braised duck breast with buttered pear.

Open 11-11 **Bar Meals** L served all week 12-2 D served all week 6-9.30 (Fri-Sun 12-9.30) **Restaurant** L served all week 12-2 D served all week 6-9.30 (Fri-Sun - 12-9.30) Av 3 course à la carte £18 Free House Bass, Worthington, Shropshire Lad & Guest beers. **Facilities** Garden Dogs allowed Parking Play Area

CRICKHOWELL MAP 09 SO21

Pick of the Pubs

The Bear Hotel ★★★ HL

Brecon Rd NP8 1BW ☎ 01873 810408 01873 811696

e-mail: bearhotel@aol.com

dir: *On A40 between Abergavenny & Brecon*

See Pick of the Pubs on opposite page

Wales

The Bear Hotel

By 2008, Stephen and Judith Hindmarsh will have been at The Bear for 30 years – so that's three decades of building and maintaining a sound reputation for good food and value for money. But that time is as the blink of an eye for this atmospheric country inn, looking after travellers on the road between London and Fishguard since 1432.

Its low-beamed, antique-filled bars are popular, making the Bear very much the hub of the community. Well-behaved dogs are welcomed, apparently to the dismay of the resident canines. There are two dining rooms, one with oak beams, stone walls and flag floor; the other smaller, with candles, flowers and lace tablecloths. The kitchen uses as much fresh local produce and home-grown herbs as it can lay its hands on, and the head chef specialises in delicious natural sauces. Welsh lamb is always a favourite and fish, such as Usk and Wye salmon, and local game are used to exceptionally good advantage. No surprises then that the food has won awards. In addition to a wide range of starters and light meals, there are bar specials of Hungarian chicken paprika with sp‰tzle; baked cauliflower cheese; and grilled lemon sole with capers. In the restaurants try braised beef in ale; baked cod on spinach topped with grilled Welsh cheddar; ham hock off the bone; or a Welsh Black steak with one of those fine sauces. Among the mouth-watering desserts are lemon posset with cream; damson custard tart with berry coulis; and apple and raspberry crumble. A revamped wine list has house bottles at a modest £11 as well as rare vintages from Australia to Tuscany. While not surrounded by acres of lawns, the Bear does have a delightful small garden where you can sit with a drink and listen to the birds.

★★★ HL

MAP 09 SO21

Brecon Rd NP8 1BW

☎ 01873 810408

01873 811696

e-mail: bearhotel@aol.com

dir: *On A40 between Abergavenny & Brecon*

Open 11-3 6-11 (Sun 12-3, 7-10.30)

Bar Meals L served all week 12-2 D served all week 6-10 (Sun 12-2, 7-9.30) Av main course £8.95

Restaurant L served Tue-Sun 12-2 D served Tue-Sat 7-9.30 (Closed Sun-Mon) Av 3 course à la carte £30

Free House

Interbrew Bass, Ruddles Best, Evans & Jones (Premium Welsh), Brains Reverend James. 12

Facilities Garden Dogs allowed Parking

Rooms 35 bedrooms en suite S£68 D£84

The Old Black Lion

Expect a warm welcome and a tranquil atmosphere at this charming old inn, close to the centre of Hay-on-Wye. Parts of this historic building date back to the 1300s, but structurally most of it is 17th century. It stands on Lion Street, near the site of the Lion Gate, one of the original entrances to the walled town of Hay-on-Wye.

With the Brecon Beacons to the west and the Black Mountains to the south, Hay is the world's largest second-hand book centre, with bookshops at every turn. It also hosts a renowned annual literary festival and marks the crossing point of the Offa's Dyke Path and the Wye Valley Walk. Oliver Cromwell is reputed to have stayed at the inn during the siege of Hay Castle, although he would not have found a teddy bear in his room as guests do today. The oak-timbered bar is furnished with scrubbed pine tables and comfy armchairs – an ideal setting in which to enjoy beers from Brains and Wye Valley Breweries (including Wye Valley's Old Black Lion) beside the log-burning stove. The inn has a long-standing reputation for its food, and the pretty dining room overlooking the garden terrace provides a perfect environment for the enjoyment of meals. Lunchtime snacks include filled baguettes with chips and salad; and sausages and mash with onion and seed mustard gravy. Other menus include 'bar favourites' (calves' liver with bacon, onion and Madeira gravy with creamed potatoes; baked loin of cod on braised leeks and fennel with a light cheese sauce and new potatoes); and an à la carte offering the likes of confit of duck on spicy noodles with a plum sauce followed by fillet of fallow venison with a quenelle of parsnip and spring onion purée with a pink peppercorn sauce.

★★★ INN ◎
MAP 09 SO24
HR3 5AD
☎ 01497 820841
01497 822960
e-mail: info@oldblacklion.co.uk
dir: *Town centre*

Open 11–11 Closed: 24–26 Dec
Bar Meals L served all week 12–2.30 D served all week 6.30–9.30
Restaurant D served all week 6.30–9 Av 3 course à la carte £22.50
Free House
Old Black Lion Ale, Wye Valley, Rev James – Brains.
Facilities Garden Parking
Rooms 10 bedrooms en suite S£42.50 D£80

CRICKHOWELL continued

Pick of the Pubs

Nantyffin Cider Mill

Brecon Rd NP8 1SG ☎ 01873 810775 01873 810986

e-mail: info@cidermill.co.uk

dir: *At junct of A40 & A479, 1.5m west of Crickhowell*

Originally a drovers' inn, located at the foot of the Black Mountains between Crickhowell and Brecon, the Nantyffin dates from the 16th century. It became well known for the cider it produced in the 19th century and the original cider press, fully working until the 1960s, has been incorporated into the main dining room. These days the place is renowned for its successful pairing of traditional pub values with acclaimed French bistro-style food. The bars are full of character and offer a range of ales, a comprehensive wine list, and house specialities of mulled cider and home-made lemonade. Menus are based on carefully sourced local produce, featuring organically reared, free-range meat and poultry from the proprietor's family farm in Llangynidr. Dishes include half a roast home-reared Aylesbury duck with honey and spices, and confit of Uncle Martin's home-reared Welsh mountain lamb with rosemary garlic sauce and mashed Maris Pipers.

Open 12-2.30 6-9.30 **Bar Meals** L served Tue-Sun 12-2.30 D served Tue-Sun 6.30-9.30 **Restaurant** L served Tue-Sun 12-2.30 D served Tue-Sun 7-9.30 Av 3 course à la carte £25 Free House Uleys Old Spot, Felinfoel Best Bitter, Marston's Pedigree, Hancocks HB. 8 **Facilities** Garden Dogs allowed Parking

DYLIFE MAP 14 SN89

Star Inn ★★ INN

SY19 7BW ☎ 01650 521345 01650 521345

dir: *Between Llanidloes & Machynlleth on mountain road*

Situated at 1300 feet in some of Wales' most breathtaking countryside, the inn is in an area favoured by Dylan Thomas and Wynford Vaughn Thomas; red kites swoop overhead, and the magnificent Clywedog reservoir is close by. A varied choice of wholesome pub fare includes cottage pie, big banger and chips, chicken in mushroom cream sauce, and gammon with egg or pineapple. Between November and March the inn is not open for weekday lunch.

Open 12-2.30 7-11 Rest: (Winter, Nov- Mar) **Bar Meals** L served all week 12-2.30 D served all week 7-10 **Restaurant** L served 12-2 D served 7-10 (Sun 7-9) Free House Tetley Smooth, Abbots. **Facilities** Children's licence Dogs allowed Parking **Rooms** 2 bedrooms en suite S£25 D£22

GLADESTRY MAP 09 SO25

The Royal Oak Inn NEW

HR5 3NR ☎ 01544 370669 & 370342

dir: *4m W of Kington, 10m from Hay-on-Wye on B4594*

The huge inglenook fireplace, heavily beamed ceilings and a flagstone floor set a scene befitting a 300-year-old inn that once welcomed drovers travelling between Kington and Painscastle. The Offa's Dyke footpath is nearby, and Hay-on-Wye is a 12-mile trek away. Meals include home-made soup; steak and stout pie; three bean chilli; and Greek salad pizza.

Open 12-3 7-11 **Bar Meals** L served Tue-Sat 12-2 D served Tue-Sat 7-9 Av main course £8 **Restaurant** L served Tue-Sun 12-2 D served Tue-Sat 7-9 Av 3 course à la carte £16 Free House Hancocks HB, Reverend James, Butty Bach, Brains S A. 8 **Facilities** Garden Dogs allowed Parking

HAY-ON-WYE MAP 09 SO24

Kilverts Hotel

The Bullring HR3 5AG ☎ 01497 821042 01497 821580

e-mail: info@kilverts.co.uk

dir: *From A50 take A49, then L onto B4348 into Hay-on-Wye. In town centre near Butter Market*

A timber-framed, olde worlde style bar, offering a range of local beers as well as Black Fox organic cider. The gardens have lawns and flower beds with a pond and fountain, as well as a pavement terrace at the front. Pizza and pasta menus are supplemented by daily specials offering fresh fish and local lamb dishes, as well as the carte. Try pan-fried loin of new season lamb with a rich Cumberland sauce for example.

Open 9-11 (Sun 12-10.30) Closed: 25 Dec **Bar Meals** L served all week 12-2 D served all week 7-9.30 Av main course £9.75 **Restaurant** D served all week 7-9.30 Free House Wye Valley Butty Bach, Brains Cream Flow & Hancock's HB, The Reverend James. 10 **Facilities** Garden Dogs allowed Parking **Rooms** 12 bedrooms en suite S£50 D£80 (WTB) (★★ HL)

Pick of the Pubs

The Old Black Lion ★★★ INN

HR3 5AD ☎ 01497 820841 01497 822960

e-mail: info@oldblacklion.co.uk

dir: *Town centre*

See Pick of the Pubs on opposite page

LLANDRINDOD WELLS MAP 09 SO06

The Gold Bell Country Inn

Llanyre LD1 6DY ☎ 01597 823959

dir: *1.5m NW of Llandrindod Wells on the A4081*

This free house has recently changed its name from the Bell Country Inn to the Gold Bell Country Inn. It's a former drovers' inn set in the hills above Llandrindod Wells, right at the centre of Wales with most attractions within an hour's drive. Food is served in the dining room,

CONTINUED

Wales

LLANDRINDOD WELLS continued

lounge bar and restaurant, including local specialities and traditional dishes. In summer meals are also served outside on the patio area.

Open 7am–1.30am **Bar Meals** L served all week 12–2.15 D served Mon–Sat 6.30–9.30 Av main course £10 **Restaurant** L served all week 12–2 D served Mon–Sat 6.30–9.30 Free House Brain's, Hancock's, Guest ales. 12 **Facilities** Garden Parking Play Area

LLANFYLLIN MAP 15 SJ11

Cain Valley Hotel ★★ HL

High St SY22 5AQ ☎ 01691 648366 01691 648307

e-mail: info@cainvalleyhotel.co.uk

dir: *From Shrewsbury & Oswestry follow signs for Lake Vyrnwy & onto A490 to Llanfyllin. Hotel on right*

Family-run coaching inn dating from the 17th century, with a stunning Jacobean staircase, oak-panelled lounge bar and a heavily beamed restaurant with exposed hand-made bricks. A full bar menu is available at lunchtime and in the evening. Local lamb steak with red wine and rosemary sauce, vegetable risotto, prime steak braised in real ale, or salmon fillet in a dill butter and lemon sauce may be on the menu.

Open 11.30–12 (Sun 12–10) Closed: 25 Dec **Bar Meals** L served all week 12–2 D served all week 7–9 Av main course £7.50 **Restaurant** L served all week 12–2 D served all week 7–9 Av 3 course à la carte £16 Free House Worthingtons, Ansells Mild, Guinness, Carling & Tetleys. **Facilities** Dogs allowed Parking **Rooms** 13 bedrooms en suite S£42 D£67

The Stumble Inn

Bwlch-y-Cibau SY22 5LL

☎ 01691 648860 01691 648955

dir: *A490 to Bwlch-y-Cibau*

Located opposite the church in a peaceful farming community in unspoilt mid-Wales countryside close to Lake Vyrnwy, this popular stone-built 18th-century inn offers a traditional pub atmosphere. Ideal base for walkers and cyclists. The menu changes frequently and might feature duck with orange sauce, lamb shank, whole Dover sole, pork with lemon and mustard sauce, sizzling Chinese steak, mushroom stroganoff, and Mediterranean risotto.

Open 11–11 **Bar Meals** L served all week 12 D served all week 6–9 Av main course £5.95 **Restaurant** L served all week 12–2 D served all week 6–10 Free House Coors Worthington's, Hook Norton, Guest ales. **Facilities** Garden Parking

LLANGATTOCK MAP 09 SO21

The Vine Tree Inn

The Legar NP8 1HG ☎ 01873 810514

dir: *A40 W from Abergavenny then A4077 from Crickhowell*

A pretty pink pub on the River Usk, at the edge of the National Park and within walking distance of Crickhowell. The large garden overlooks the river, bridge and Table Mountain. It is predominantly a dining pub serving a comprehensive menu, with traditional roast lunches on Sundays. Tuesdays now feature the weekly Mexican evening, when authentic Latin dishes cooked to order include nachos, spicy bean soup, a choice of fajitas and enchiladas, and chilli con carne.

Open 12–3 6–11 (Sun 12–3, 6.30–9) **Bar Meals** L served all week 12–3 D served all week 6–10 (Sun 6.30–9) **Restaurant** L served all week 12–3 D served all week 6–10 Av 3 course à la carte £15 Free House Fuller's London Pride, Coors Worthington's, Golden Valley. 8 **Facilities** Garden Parking

LLANGYNIDR MAP 09 SO11

The Coach & Horses NEW

Cwmcrawnon Rd NP8 1LS ☎ 01874 730245

dir: *A40 from Brecon to Abergavenny, 12m from Brecon. Through village of Bwlch, after bend turn right*

Real ales from local breweries are a feature of this free house, which stands just two minutes' walk from the nearby canal moorings. Local ingredients including Welsh black beef are the basis for the seasonal menus: look out for local lamb on crushed new potatoes with sautéed bacon and white pudding; salmon, prawn and coriander fishcakes with Thai chilli jam; and pasta with spinach, chargrilled vegetables and parmesan shavings.

Open 12–11.30 **Bar Meals** L served all week 12–2.30 D served all week 7–9 **Restaurant** L served all week 12.30–2 D served all week 7–9 Av 3 course à la carte £22.50 Free House **Facilities** Children's licence Garden Parking

LLOWES MAP 09 SO14

The Radnor Arms

HR3 5JA ☎ 01497 847460 01497 847460

e-mail: brian@radnorsarms.freeserve.co.uk

dir: *A438 between Glasbury & Clyro*

This Grade II, 400-year-old former drovers' inn provides outstanding views from the garden, looking over the Wye Valley to the Black Mountains, to the west of the Brecon Beacons. Local Felinfoel bitter is amongst the beers served beside blazing winter fires in the cosy bar. The extensive blackboard menus offer French and English cuisine, with good vegetarian options and a selection of fish dishes, including sardines and monkfish. Long wine list.

Open 11–2.30 6.30–11 (Sun 12–3) **Bar Meals** L served Tue–Sun 12–2.30 (Sun 12–3) D served Tue–Sun 6.30–9 (Sat 6.30–10) **Restaurant** L served Tue–Sun 12–2.30 D served Tue–Sun 6.30–9 Av 3 course à la carte £18 Free House Felinfoel, Worthington, Bitburger. 9 **Facilities** Garden Dogs allowed Parking

MACHYNLLETH MAP 14 SH70

Pick of the Pubs

Wynnstay Hotel NEW ★★★ HL

SY20 8AE ☎ 01654 702941 01654 703884

e-mail: info@wynnstay-hotel.com

See Pick of the Pubs on opposite page

Wales

Wynnstay Hotel

In the middle of Machynlleth, once the capital of Wales, the Wynnstay is an attractive old coaching inn dating from 1780. Sheila and Charles Dark have been here 10 years and have created a genuinely warm and friendly atmosphere.

This explains why people are just as likely to drop in to the lively bars for tea, coffee and cakes, as others are for something alcoholic or more substantial to eat. Gareth Johns flies the flag for Wales at home and abroad, and here he and his team have created a menu based firmly on good Welsh produce, with influences from France and Italy. The influences are notable in the traditional wood-fired pizzeria, which appeals to lovers of good food at all levels. Lunch is a mix of lighter snacks and more substantial fare, whilst at dinner the daily-changing carte might encompass such dishes as griddled asparagus with crayfish and lemon butter, or goats' cheese and nettle malfatti, followed by Dyfi sewin with wild garlic and rhubarb relish, or a plate of Welsh lamb. To finish, perhaps a pannacotta lightened with Llaeth-y-llan yoghourt, and seved with ginger bara brau (shortbread). In the autumn and winter the surrounding hills often echo to the sound of gunfire - it could be the patron bagging some game for the table. Fresh fish, lobster and crab are landed daily at Borth, Aberdovey and other little Cardigan Bay ports, but catch your own if you prefer and the kitchen will cook it for you. A selection of Welsh cheeses – hard, soft, blue, cows', sheep's or goats' – is always served, occasionally joined by a guest from Italy.

NEW ★★★ HL ◎
MAP 14 SH70
SY20 8AE
☎ 01654 702941
📠 01654 703884
e-mail:
info@wynnstay-hotel.com

Open 12–2.30 6–11 (Sun 6–10.30)
Bar Meals L served all week 12–2 D served all week 6.30–9
Restaurant L served all week 12–2 D served all week 6.30–9
Av 5 course fixed price £25
Av 3 course à la carte £20
Free House
Greene King IPA, Carlsberg, Reverend James, Old Speckled Hen & Guinness.
Facilities Dogs allowed Children Licence Parking
Rooms 22 bedrooms en suite S£55 D£80
Notes

MONTGOMERY MAP 15 SO29

Pick of the Pubs

Dragon Hotel ★★ HL ®

SY15 6PA ☎ 01686 668359 📠 0870 011 8227

e-mail: reception@dragonhotel.com

dir: *A483 toward Welshpool, right onto B4386 then B4385 & behind the town hall*

A strikingly attractive, black and white timber-framed coaching inn with a unique enclosed patio created from the former coach entrance. The bar, lounge and most bedrooms contain beams and masonry reputed to have been removed from the ruins of the castle destroyed by Oliver Cromwell in 1649. Today the hotel prides itself on the quality of its kitchen, where fresh local produce is prepared to a high standard. The head chef describes his approach to food as modern English and Welsh with a Mediterranean influence. In addition to daily blackboard specials and soups, the bar menu includes starters such as grilled sardines or tangy barbecued chicken, followed by main courses ranging from seafood spaghetti to a choice of fajitas and steaks. Dinner menus may include leek-laced Welsh cakes (savoury cakes topped with Perl Las cheese sauce) to start, followed by roast loin of venison with an apricot and honey stuffing.

Open 11-11 **Bar Meals** L served all week 12-2 D served all week 7-9 Av main course £6.95 **Restaurant** L served bookings only 12-2 D served bookings only 7-9 Av 3 course à la carte £27.50 Av 3 course fixed price £22.50 Free House Wood Special, Interbrew Bass & Guest. **Facilities** Children's licence Garden Parking **Rooms** 20 bedrooms en suite S£51 D£87.50

NEW RADNOR MAP 09 SO26

Pick of the Pubs

Red Lion Inn

Llanfihangel-nant-Melan LD8 2TN

☎ 01544 350220 📠 01544 350220

e-mail: theredlion@aol.com

dir: *A483 to Crossgates then right onto A44, 6m to pub*

Old habits die hard here: this ancient drover's inn still provides water, though nowadays it's for hosing down the bike. Next door is one of four churches named after St Michael that encircle the burial place of the last Welsh dragon. According to legend, should anything happen to them the dragon will rise again. The inn has a lounge and a locals' bar, two small restaurants and a sun-trap garden. A broad menu draws extensively on local produce, including herbs from the garden. Mussels, usually served as a starter in white wine, garlic and cream, come from the River Conwy up north. Main courses might include game terrine with cognac and grape preserve; Welsh Black beef fillet with béarnaise sauce; organic salmon fish cakes; and leek, wild mushroom and chestnut gateau. Round off with Welsh cheeses and home-made walnut bread.

Open 12-2.30 6-11 (Summer all day) **Bar Meals** L served Wed-Mon 12-2 D served Wed-Mon 6-9 Av main course £7 **Restaurant** L served Wed-Mon 12-2 D served Wed-Mon 6-9 Av 3 course à la carte £17.50 Free House Parish (Woods), Springer (Spinning Dog Brewery). **Facilities** Garden Dogs allowed Parking **Rooms** 7 bedrooms en suite S£35 D£55 (★★★ INN)

OLD RADNOR MAP 09 SO25

Pick of the Pubs

The Harp

LD8 2RH ☎ 01544 350655

e-mail: info@harpinnradnor.co.uk

dir: *Old Radnor signed off A44*

There are spectacular views over the Radnor countryside from this seemingly untouched village inn, just yards from Old Radnor's fine parish church of St Stephen. The building is a Welsh longhouse made from local stone and slate, and dating back to the 15th century. Open the simple wooden door and you'll step in to a cosy lounge and bars with oak beams, open log fires, semi-circular wooden settles, flagstone floors, and lots of guide books to browse through. Pictures of local history adorn the walls. A changing menu is served in the two dining rooms, and two bar areas, and dining here is a casual, relaxing experience. Look out for steaks with a selection of sauces, and home-made pies, and there are real ales to help wash it all down: Timothy Taylor, Three Tons, Hopback and Guinness are all kept in good condition.

Open 6-11 (Sat-Sun 12-3) **Bar Meals** L served Sat-Sun 12-2 D served Tue-Sun 6.30-9 Av main course £8 **Restaurant** L served Sat-Sun 12-2 D served Tue-Sun 7-9 Free House Timothy Taylor, Guinness, Three Tuns, Hopback. **Facilities** Garden Parking Play Area

TALGARTH MAP 09 SO13

Castle Inn

Pengenffordd LD3 0EP ☎ 01874 711353 📠 01874 711353

e-mail: castleinnwales@aol.com

dir: *4m S of Talgarth on the A479*

Located in the heart of the Black Mountains, in the Brecon Beacons National Park, the Castle takes its name from nearby Castell Dinas, the highest Iron Age fort in England and Wales. Substantial pub food includes gammon steak, sausage and mash, fisherman's pie, and chick pea tagine, with apple and blackberry crumble, and chocarocka pie with cream or ice cream to follow. The pub also offers bunkhouse accommodation and a camping field.

Open 12-11 Closed Mon Nov-Etr **Bar Meals** L served Sat-Sun 12-3 D served Tue-Fri 6-9 (Sat-Sun 6-9.30) Av main course £7 **Restaurant** L served Sat-Sun 12-3 D served Tue-Fri 6-9 (Sat-Sun 6-9.30) Av 3 course à la carte £13.50 Free House Butty Bach, Rumney Bitter, Guest ales. **Facilities** Garden Parking

The Castle Coaching Inn

A Georgian coaching inn on the old London to Carmarthen coaching route, now the main A40 trunk road. Family-owned and run, the hotel has been carefully restored in recent years, and has lovely old fireplaces and a remarkable bow-fronted bar window.

The inn also offers a peaceful terrace and garden. Food is served in the bar or more formally in the restaurant, and landlord John Porter continues to maintain high standards. Bar lunches consist of freshly-cut sandwiches (roast beef, turkey, stilton or tuna), ploughman's with tuna, duck and port pate perhaps, and hot filled baguettes (steak with melted stilton, bacon with mushrooms and melted mature cheddar). Specialities include mature Welsh 12oz sirloin steak served with mushrooms and onion rings; home-made lasagne with parmesan cheese; and supreme of chicken with a Marsala and mascarpone sauce. Other options range from battered haddock fillet to chilli con carne. Complete your meal with a dessert of strawberry crush cake, hot jaffa puddle pudding (an irresistible chocolate sponge with a Jaffa orange centre, topped with a milk chocolate sauce), and Dutch chunky apple flan. Alternatively, sample the selection of Welsh farmhouse cheeses. From the bar you can wash it all down with Red Dragon or Timothy Taylor Landlord real ales, or try one of nine malts. A separate children's list runs through the usual favourites – turkey dinosaurs, fish stars, or jumbo sausage, all served with chips and baked beans.

MAP 09 SN82
LD3 8UH
☎ 01874 636354
🖷 01874 636457
e-mail:
guest@castle-coaching-inn.co.uk
dir: *On A40 W of Brecon*

Open 12–3 6–11
Bar Meals L served Mon–Sun 12–2 D served Mon–Sat 6.30–9 (Sun 7–9) Av main course £10
Restaurant L served Mon–Sun 12–2 D served Mon–Sat 6.30–9 (Sun 7–9) Av 3 course à la carte £16
Free House
Fuller's London Pride, Breconshire Brewery Red Dragon, Timothy Taylor Landlord.
Facilities Children's licence Garden Parking

Blue Anchor Inn

Dating from around 1380, the Blue Anchor has been trading as a pub virtually non-stop for over 600 years. The only break came in 2004 when a serious fire destroyed the top half of this medieval building, forcing its closure for restoration.

It's a stone-built inn, heavily thatched, and legend has it that an underground passage leads down to the shore; it would have been used by wreckers and smugglers who roamed this wild Bristol Channel coastline. The interior comprises a warren of small rooms separated by thick walls, with low, beamed ceilings and a number of open fires including a large inglenook. The inn was part of the Fonmon estate until 1941 when it was acquired by the grandfather of the present owners, Jeremy and Andrew Coleman. A good selection of regional real ales plus guest beers from around the country are always on tap. An enticing range of food is offered by both the bar menu and the upstairs restaurant carte. Down in the bar expect starters such as duck and sour cherry spring roll, or Glamorgan cheese sausage; follow these with a main course of braised pork belly with celeriac purée; or calves' liver and onions with dauphinoise potatoes. In the restaurant may be found home-cured gravadlax with sweet pickled beetroot and candied lemons to start, followed by roast Merthyr Mawr pheasant on a sauté of wild mushrooms, spinach and baby onions. Fresh fish dishes may include whole lemon sole with a mussel and clam chowder; pan-fried fillet of red bream with pickled courgettes and sautéed potatoes; seared fillet of salmon on a lemon and crab risotto; and grilled fillet of wild sea bass on aromatic Chinese greens. Desserts follow classic lines, with chocolate orange and honeycomb parfait, or sticky toffee pudding with rum sauce.

MAP 09 ST06
CF62 3DD
☎ 01446 750329
01446 750077

Open 11–11
Bar Meals L served Mon–Sat 12–2 D served Sun–Fri 6–8
Restaurant L served Sun 12–2.30 D served all week 7–9.30
Free House
Theakston Old Peculier, Wadworth 6X, Wye Valley Hereford Pale Ale, Brains Bitter.
Facilities Garden Parking

TALYBONT-ON-USK MAP 09 SO12

Star Inn

LD3 7YX ☎ 01874 676635

dir: *Telephone for directions*

With its pretty riverside garden, this traditional 250-year-old inn stands in a picturesque village within the Brecon Beacons National Park. The pub, unmodernised and with welcoming fireplace, is known for its constantly changing range of well-kept real ales, and hosts quiz nights on Monday and live bands on Wednesday. Hearty bar food with dishes such as chicken in leek and stilton sauce, Hungarian pork goulash, traditional roasts, salmon fish cakes, and vegetarian chilli.

Open 11–3 6.30–11 (Sat all day) **Bar Meals** L served all week 12–2.15 D served all week 6.30–9 Av main course £6.50 Free House Felinfoel Double Dragon, Theakston Old Peculier, Hancock's HB, Bullmastiff Best. **Facilities** Garden Dogs allowed

TRECASTLE MAP 09 SN82

Pick of the Pubs

The Castle Coaching Inn

LD3 8UH ☎ 01874 636354 01874 636457

e-mail: guest@castle-coaching-inn.co.uk

dir: *On A40 W of Brecon*

See Pick of the Pubs on page 755

UPPER CWMTWRCH MAP 09 SN71

Lowther's Gourmet Restaurant and Bar

SA9 2XH ☎ 01639 830938

dir: *2m from Ystalyfera rdbt at Upper Cwmtwrch, next to the river*

A traditional family-owned pub and restaurant, which occupies a scenic riverside location at the foot of the Black Mountains. Relax by the cosy wood-burner on a cold winter's day or, in summer, make use of the colourful garden and patio for alfresco dining. The pub brews its own beers and offers wholesome fare made from Welsh produce wherever possible. Traditional roasts, sizzling bass in garlic, and Welsh black beef feature on the extensive menu.

Open 12–4 6–11 (Sun 12–3, 6–10.30) Closed: 26 Dec Rest: 1 Jan **Bar Meals** L served 11.30–2.30 D served 6–10 **Restaurant** L served all week 12–3 D served all week 6–9 Av 3 course à la carte £25 Free House **Facilities** Garden Parking Play Area

SWANSEA

REYNOLDSTON MAP 08 SS48

King Arthur Hotel

Higher Green SA3 1AD ☎ 01792 390775 01792 391075

e-mail: info@kingarthurhotel.co.uk

dir: *Just N of A4118 SW of Swansea*

A traditional country inn, with real log fires, in a village lying at the heart of the beautiful Gower Peninsula. Eat in the restaurant, main bar or family room, choosing main menu or specials board dishes including seasonal game, Welsh Black beef, locally caught fish and vegetarian options. Try whole trout with cockle and laverbread sauce; crisp garlicky chicken Kiev; or tuna and bean salad. Tastefully furnished bedrooms all have en suite bathrooms.

Open 11–11 Closed: 25 Dec **Bar Meals** L served all week 12–6 D served all week 6–9 **Restaurant** L served all week 12–2.30 D served all week 6–9 Free House Felinfoel Double Dragon, Worthington Bitter & Bass & Tomas Watkins OSB, King Arthur Ale. 9 **Facilities** Garden Parking **Rooms** 19 bedrooms en suite S£50 D£65 (★★★ INN)

VALE OF GLAMORGAN

COWBRIDGE MAP 09 SS97

Victoria Inn

Sigingstone CF71 7LP ☎ 01446 773943 01446 776446

dir: *Off the B4270 in village of Sigingstone*

A quiet, attractively furnished old village inn with a fine reputation for good quality home-prepared food. The beamed interior, decorated with old photographs, prints and antiques, has a good feel about it. The daily menu is extensive, with some 40 different dishes on offer, plus specials and vegetarian boards, and the likes of red snapper, sea bass, salmon and more. Tomas Watkin Bitter is brewed in Swansea.

Open 11.45–3 6–11 **Bar Meals** L served all week 11.45–2 D served all week 6.30–9.30 (Sun 11.45–2.30, 7–9) **Restaurant** L served Mon–Sat D served Mon–Sat 6.30–9.30 (Sun 11.45–2.30, 7–9) Free House Tomas Watkins Best Bitter, Hancocks HB, Worthington Creamflow. **Facilities** Garden Parking

EAST ABERTHAW MAP 09 ST06

Pick of the Pubs

Blue Anchor Inn

CF62 3DD ☎ 01446 750329 01446 750077

See Pick of the Pubs on opposite page

MONKNASH MAP 09 SS97

The Plough & Harrow

CF71 7QQ ☎ 01656 890209

e-mail: info@theploughmonknash.com

dir: *M4 junct 35 take dual carriageway to Bridgend. At rdbt follow St Brides sign, then brown heritage signs. Pub 3m NW of Llantwit Major*

In a peaceful country setting on the edge of a small village with views across the fields to the Bristol Channel, this low, slate-roofed, 14th-century building was originally built as the chapter house of a monastery, although it has been a pub for 500 of its 600-year existence. Expect an atmospheric interior, open fires, up to eight guest ales on tap, and home-cooked food using fresh local ingredients. Great area for walkers.

Open 12–11 (Sun 12–10.30) **Bar Meals** L served all week 12–2.30 D served Mon–Sat 6–9 Av main course £6.95 **Restaurant** L served all week D served Mon–Sat 6–9 Av 3 course à la carte £20 Free House Archers Golden, Shepherds Neame Spitfire, Hereford Pale ale, Sharps IPA. **Facilities** Garden Parking

ST HILARY

MAP 09 ST07

Pick of the Pubs

The Bush Inn ♀

CF71 7DP ☎ 01446 772745

dir: *S of A48, E of Cowbridge*

This is a thatched pub in a picturesque village in the Vale of Glamorgan, with seating at the front overlooking the 14th-century church. It has been a meeting place for people for over two hundred years, and one of the earlier ones remains in the form of a resident ghost, a highwayman who was caught close to the pub and hung on the downs. His presence notwithstanding, The Bush is a warm, friendly and happy pub with enthusiastic owners. An inglenook fireplace, flagstone floors and a spiral staircase are features of the cosy interior, and the pretty restaurant has French windows leading out to the garden. There is a separate bar and restaurant menu which, between them, will give you choices like light bites, sandwiches and salads, chargrilled steaks, the fresh fish special of the day, and vegetarian options. There is a selection of desserts on the blackboard menu.

Open 11.30–11 (Sun 12–10.30) **Bar Meals** L served all week 12–2.30 (Sun 12.15–3.30) D served Mon–Sat 6.45–9.30 **Restaurant** L served all week 12–2.30 (Sun 12.15–3.30) D served Mon–Sat 6.45–9.30 ⊕ Punch Taverns ◀ Hancock's HB, Greene King Abbot Ale, Interbrew Worthington Bitter & Bass, Guest Beer. ♀ 10 **Facilities** Children's licence Garden Dogs allowed Parking

WREXHAM

ERBISTOCK

MAP 15 SJ34

The Boat Inn

LL13 0DL ☎ 01978 780666 🖹 01978 780607

e-mail: info@theboatinn.co.uk

dir: *A483 Whitchurch/Llangollen exit, towards Whitchurch on A539. After 2m turn right at signs for Erbistock & The Boat Inn*

A 16th-century pub in a great spot on the Dee, where you can still see the landing stage for the one-time ferry and windlass that wound it across the river. Lunch includes pasta, home-made pie of the day, and beer-battered cod and chips. In the evening, pan-fried fillet of salmon with puy lentils, fresh asparagus and mustard, cream and chive sauce; and chargrilled veal chop with parsnip purée and red wine, orange and garlic sauce.

Open 12–11 (Sun 12–10.30) **Bar Meals** L served all week 12–9 (Sun: Winter 12–5, Summer 12–9) **Restaurant** L served all week 12–2.30 D served all week 6.30–9 (Sun: Winter Sun 12–5, Summer 12–9) ⊕ Free House ◀ Tetleys, Export, Addlestones, Guinness. **Facilities** Children's licence Garden Dogs allowed Parking

GRESFORD

MAP 15 SJ35

Pant-yr-Ochain NEW ♀

Old Wrexham Rd LL12 8TY

☎ 01978 853525 🖹 01978 853505

e-mail: pant.yr.ochain@brunningandprice.co.uk

dir: *From Chester take exit for Nantwhich. Holt off A483. Take 2nd left, also signed Nantwhich Holt. Turn left at 'The Flash' sign. Pub 500yds on right*

A sweeping drive leads to this 16th-century manor house overlooking a small lake and a sculpted, tree-dotted landscape. Its interior delivers on the promise of its picture-perfect exterior, with an inglenook fireplace and a wealth of nooks and crannies. Food choices range from sandwiches to main meals such as five spice roasted belly pork, followed by fillet of haddock with pea and bacon risotto and mustard butter. Ask the staff about the ghostly sightings.

Open 12–11 (Sun 12–10.30) Closed: 25–26 Dec **Bar Meals** L served all week 12–9.30 D served all week 12–9.30 Av main course £8.95 **Restaurant** 12–9.30 ⊕ Brunning & Price ◀ Timothy Taylor Landlord, Interbrew Flowers Original, Thwaites Original, Weetwood eastgate. ♀ 22 **Facilities** Children's licence Garden Parking

LLANARMON DYFFRYN CEIRIOG

MAP 15 SJ13

The Hand at Llanarmon ★★ SHL ♀

LL20 7LD ☎ 01691 600666 🖹 01691 600262

e-mail: reception@thehandhotel.co.uk

dir: *Turn off A5 at Chirk, follow B4500 for 11m. Through Ceiriog Valley to Llanarmon D C. Pub straight ahead*

Old world charm and modern comforts blend easily at this 16th-century free house, located at the head of the beautiful Ceiriog Valley. This is a good base for walking and pony trekking, and David Lloyd George once described the area as 'a little bit of heaven on earth'. Seasonal, home-cooked dishes include game broth with warm crusty bread; Ceirog trout with lemon, olive and capers; and Welsh beef with red wine, rosemary and lentils.

Open 8–12 **Bar Meals** L served all week 12–2.30 (Sun 12.30–2.45) D served all week 6.30–9 **Restaurant** L served 12–2.30 (Sun 12.30–2.45) D served 6.30–9 Av 3 course à la carte £22.50 Av 3 course fixed price £17 ⊕ Free House ◀ Coors, Worthington Cream Flow, Guinness, Guest ale & Carling. ♀ 7 **Facilities** Garden Dogs allowed Parking **Rooms** 13 bedrooms en suite S£50 D£80

Wales

Pick of the Pubs

The West Arms Hotel ★★★ HL @@ 🍷

LL20 7LD ☎ 01691 600665 📠 01691 600622
e-mail: gowestarms@aol.com
dir: *Leave A483 at Chirk, follow signs for Ceiriog Valley B4500, 11m from Chirk*

Take slate-flagged floors, ancient timberwork, inglenooks and open fires. Add some period furniture and warm hospitality, and the precious traditions of this 17th-century drovers' inn are kept well and truly alive. Long ago the drovers would come down from the Welsh hills by way of three tracks that converged here. After resting for the night they continued their slow, arduous journeys to markets in Chirk, Oswestry, Wrexham and as far away as London. Award-winning chef Grant Williams has travelled too, working in kitchens around the world, appearing on several TV cookery programmes, and even cooking for Prince Charles. Grant's seafood dishes are sheer indulgence: grilled fillets of Dover sole with thyme-roasted asparagus; truffled scallops with Anglesey lobster; grilled rosettes of sole and wild River Dee smoked salmon. Or you can simply relax outside with a pint, view the Berwyn mountains, and lose track of time as the Ceiriog River burbles away in the valley.

Open 8-11 **Bar Meals** L served all week 12-2 D served all week 7-9 Av main course £10.95 **Restaurant** L served Sun 12-2 D served all week 7-9 Av 3 course fixed price £32.90 Free House Interbrew Flowers IPA, Double Dragon, Carlsberg, Tetleys Smooth. 🍷 10 **Facilities** Garden Dogs allowed Parking **Rooms** 15 bedrooms en suite S£53.50 D£125

MARFORD MAP 15 SJ35

Trevor Arms Hotel 🍷

LL12 8TA ☎ 01244 570436 📠 01244 570273
e-mail: info@trevorarmsmarford.fsnet.co.uk
web: www.trevorarmshotel.com
dir: *Off A483 onto B5102 then right onto B5445 into Marford*

The reputedly haunted early 19th-century coaching inn takes its name from Lord Trevor of Trevallin, who was killed in a duel. Grisly past notwithstanding, the Trevallin is a charming inn, offering a varied menu. Starters range from prawn cocktail to Cajun chicken strips with chilli salsa, and mains from darne of poached salmon with smoked bacon and tarragon cream sauce, to slowly braised beef bourguignon. Chargrilled steaks are a house speciality.

Open 11-11.30 (Fri-Sat 11-12) **Bar Meals** L served all week 11-10 D served all week 6-10 (Sun 12-8.30) Av main course £7.50 **Restaurant** L served all week 11-10 D served all week 11-10 (Sun 12-8.30) Av 3 course à la carte £15.50 Av 3 course fixed price £9.75 Scottish Courage Greenalls, Scottish Courage, Bombardier & John Smiths, Morland Old Speckled Hen & 2 Guest beers. 🍷 12 **Facilities** Garden Parking Play Area

How to Find a Pub in the Atlas Section

Pubs are located in the gazetteer under the name of the nearest town or village. If a pub is in a small village or rural area, it may appear under a town within fives miles of its actual location. The black dots and town names shown in the atlas refer to the gazetteer location in the guide. Please use the directions in the pub entry to find the pub on foot or by car. If directions are not given, or are not clear, please telephone the pub for details.

Key to County Map

The county map shown here will help you identify the counties within each country. You can look up each county in the guide using the county names at the top of each page. Towns featured in the guide use the atlas pages and index following this map.

England

1 Bedfordshire
2 Berkshire
3 Bristol
4 Buckinghamshire
5 Cambridgeshire
6 Greater Manchester
7 Herefordshire
8 Hertfordshire
9 Leicestershire
10 Northamptonshire
11 Nottinghamshire
12 Rutland
13 Staffordshire
14 Warwickshire
15 West Midlands
16 Worcestershire

Scotland

17 City of Glasgow
18 Clackmannanshire
19 East Ayrshire
20 East Dunbartonshire
21 East Renfrewshire
22 Perth & Kinross
23 Renfrewshire
24 South Lanarkshire
25 West Dunbartonshire

Wales

26 Blaenau Gwent
27 Bridgend
28 Caerphilly
29 Denbighshire
30 Flintshire
31 Merthyr Tydfil
32 Monmouthshire
33 Neath Port Talbot
34 Newport
35 Rhondda Cynon Taff
36 Torfaen
37 Vale of Glamorgan
38 Wrexham

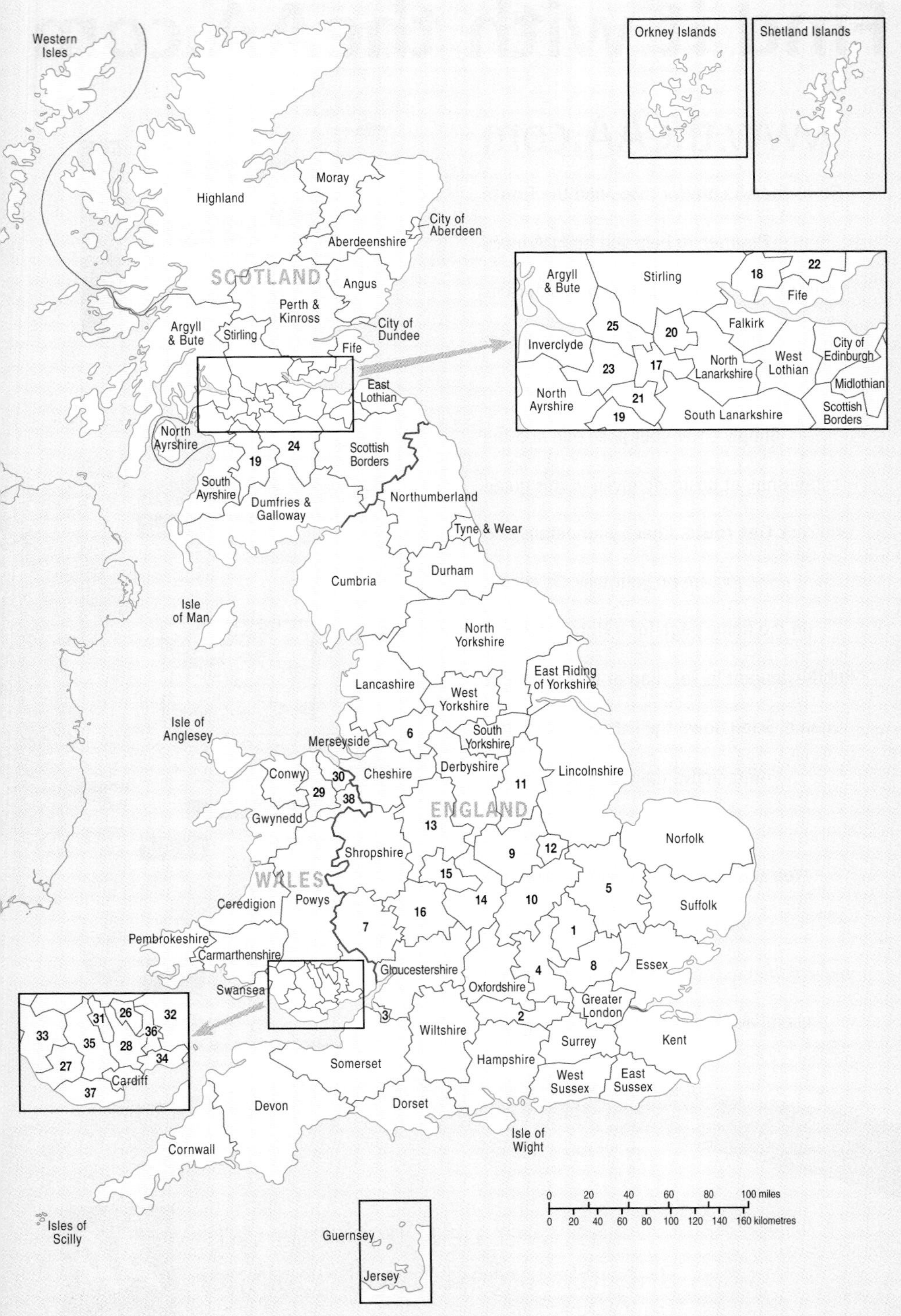

Western Isles
Orkney Islands
Shetland Islands
Highland
Moray
City of Aberdeen
Aberdeenshire
SCOTLAND
Angus
Perth & Kinross
Argyll & Bute
Stirling
City of Dundee
Fife
East Lothian
North Ayrshire
24
19
Scottish Borders
South Ayrshire
Dumfries & Galloway
Argyll & Bute
Stirling
18
22
Fife
25
20
Falkirk
Inverclyde
City of Edinburgh
23
17
North Lanarkshire
West Lothian
Midlothian
North Ayrshire
21
19
South Lanarkshire
Scottish Borders
Northumberland
Tyne & Wear
Durham
Cumbria
Isle of Man
North Yorkshire
East Riding of Yorkshire
Lancashire
West Yorkshire
Isle of Anglesey
6
South Yorkshire
Merseyside
Conwy
30
Cheshire
Derbyshire
Lincolnshire
29
38
11
ENGLAND
Gwynedd
13
Norfolk
Shropshire
9
12
WALES
15
5
Ceredigion
Powys
14
10
Suffolk
16
7
1
Pembrokeshire
Carmarthenshire
4
8
Essex
Gloucestershire
Swansea
Oxfordshire
Greater London
33
31
26
32
36
35
28
34
27
Cardiff
37
3
2
Wiltshire
Surrey
Kent
Somerset
Hampshire
West Sussex
East Sussex
Devon
Dorset
Isle of Wight
Cornwall
0 20 40 60 80 100 miles
0 20 40 60 80 100 120 140 160 kilometres
Isles of Scilly
Guernsey
Jersey

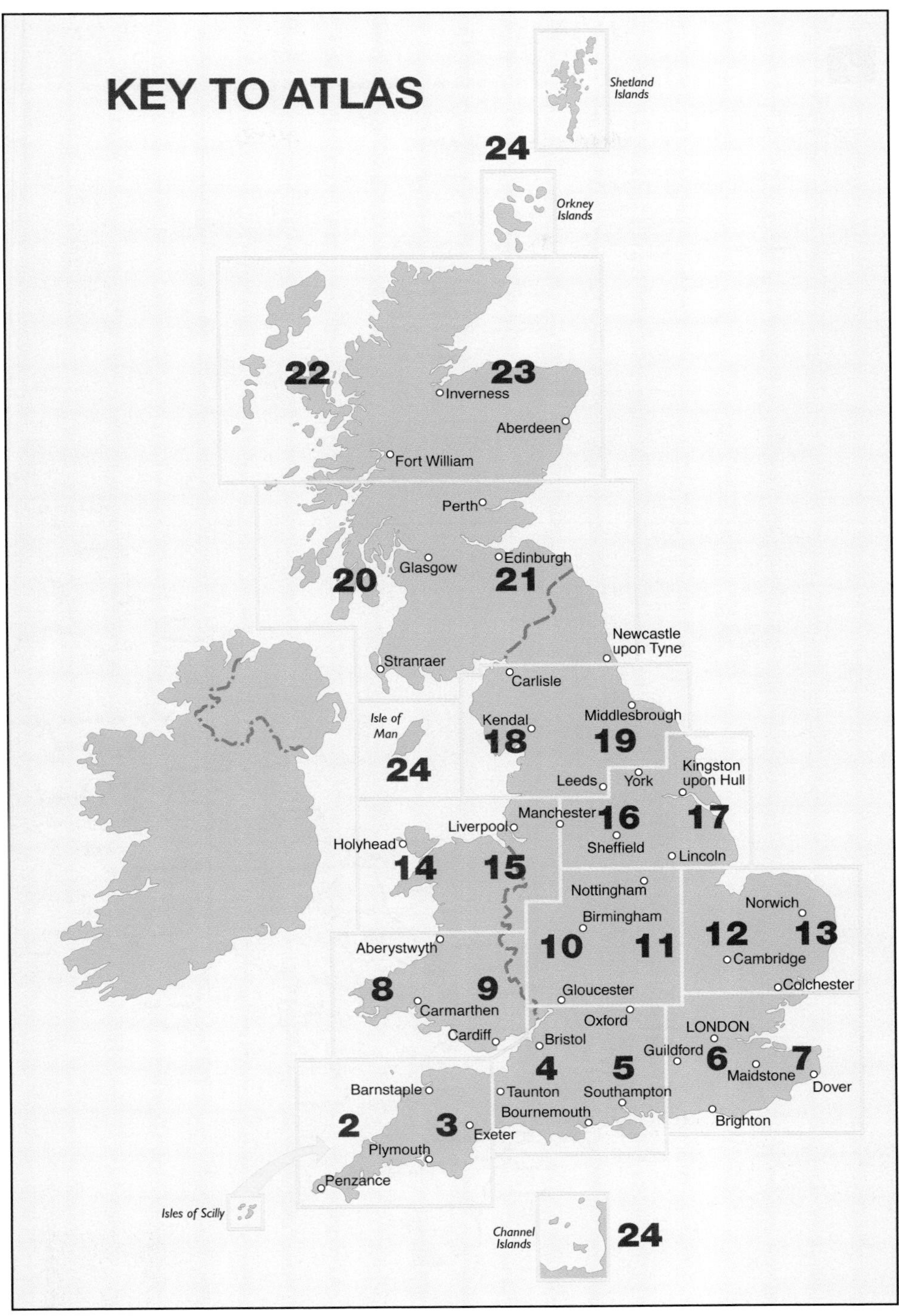
KEY TO ATLAS
Shetland Islands
24
Orkney Islands
22
23
Inverness
Aberdeen
Fort William
Perth
Glasgow
Edinburgh
20
21
Newcastle upon Tyne
Stranraer
Carlisle
Isle of Man
Kendal
Middlesbrough
18
19
24
Leeds
York
Kingston upon Hull
Manchester
16
17
Liverpool
Holyhead
Sheffield
Lincoln
14
15
Nottingham
Norwich
Birmingham
12
13
10
11
Aberystwyth
Cambridge
8
9
Gloucester
Colchester
Carmarthen
Oxford
LONDON
Cardiff
Bristol
Guildford
6
7
4
5
Maidstone
Dover
Barnstaple
Taunton
Southampton
Bournemouth
Brighton
2
3
Exeter
Plymouth
Penzance
Isles of Scilly
Channel Islands
24

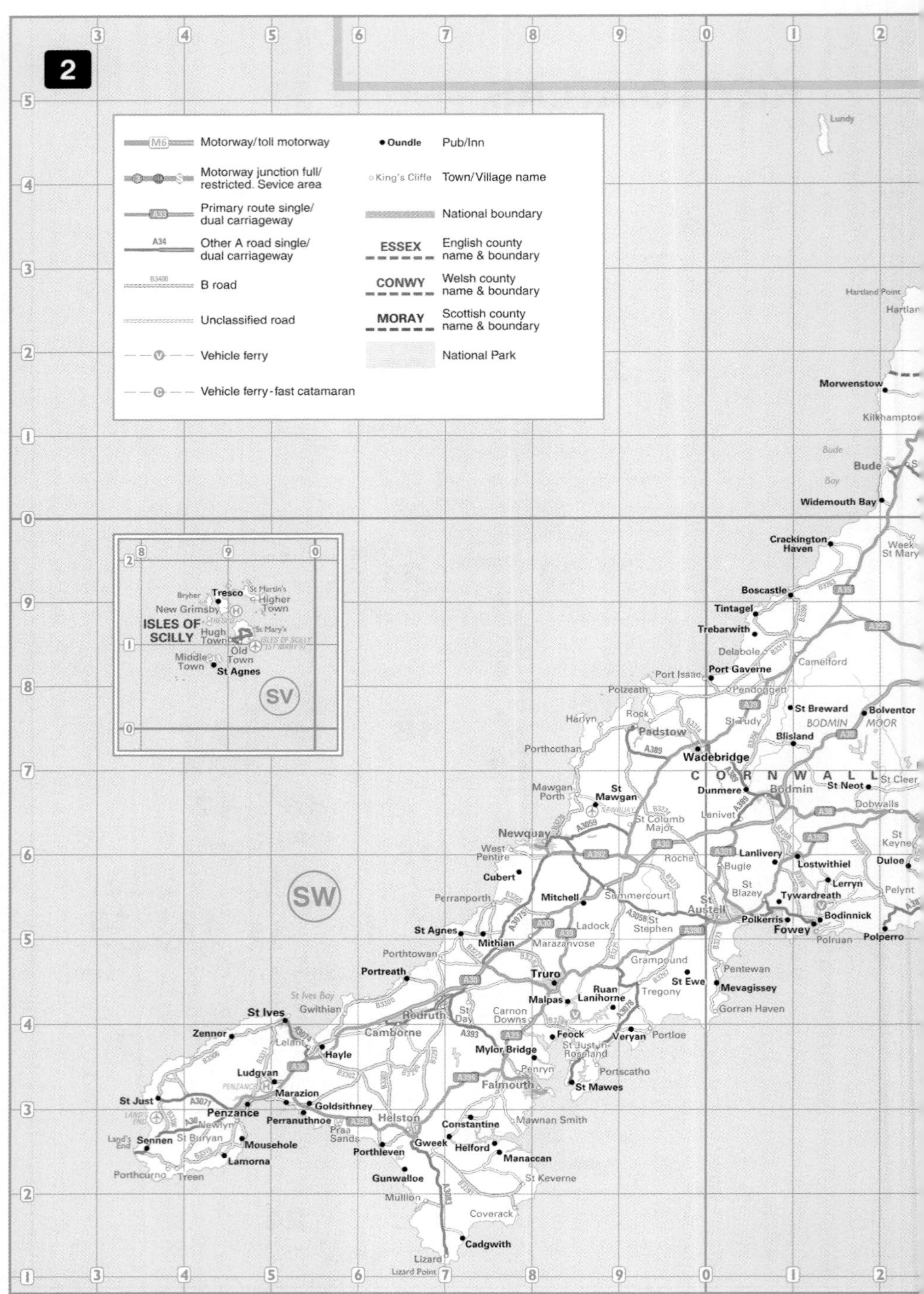

2
Motorway/toll motorway
Motorway junction full/ restricted. Sevice area
Primary route single/ dual carriageway
Other A road single/ dual carriageway
B road
Unclassified road
Vehicle ferry
Vehicle ferry - fast catamaran
Oundle
Pub/Inn
King's Cliffe
Town/Village name
National boundary
ESSEX
English county name & boundary
CONWY
Welsh county name & boundary
MORAY
Scottish county name & boundary
National Park
ISLES OF SCILLY
Bryher
Tresco
St Martin's
Higher Town
New Grimsby
Hugh Town
St Mary's
Old Town
Middle Town
St Agnes
SV
SW
Lundy
Hartland Point
Morwenstow
Kilkhampton
Bude
Widemouth Bay
Crackington Haven
Week St Mary
Boscastle
Tintagel
Trebarwith
Delabole
Camelford
Port Isaac
Port Gaverne
Polzeath
Pendoggett
St Breward
Bolventor
BODMIN MOOR
Harlyn
Rock
St Tudy
Blisland
Padstow
Porthcothan
Wadebridge
CORNWALL
St Cleer
Mawgan Porth
St Mawgan
Dunmere
Bodmin
St Neot
Dobwalls
Lanivet
St Columb Major
Newquay
West Pentire
Roche
Lanlivery
Lostwithiel
St Keyne
Duloe
Bugle
Cubert
St Blazey
Lerryn
Pelynt
Perranporth
Mitchell
Summercourt
St Austell
Tywardreath
Ladock
St Stephen
Polkerris
Bodinnick
Fowey
Polruan
Polperro
St Agnes
Mithian
Marazanvose
Porthtowan
Grampound
Pentewan
Portreath
Truro
St Ewe
Mevagissey
Ruan Lanihorne
Tregony
St Ives Bay
Gwithian
Malpas
Gorran Haven
St Ives
Redruth
St Day
Carnon Downs
Zennor
Camborne
Feock
Veryan
Portloe
Lelant
Hayle
Mylor Bridge
St Just-in-Roseland
Penryn
Ludgvan
Portscatho
Falmouth
St Mawes
Marazion
St Just
Penzance
Goldsithney
Helston
Mawnan Smith
Newlyn
Perranuthnoe
Constantine
Praa Sands
Land's End
Sennen
St Buryan
Mousehole
Porthleven
Gweek
Helford
Manaccan
Lamorna
Porthcurno
Treen
Gunwalloe
St Keverne
Mullion
Coverack
Cadgwith
Lizard
Lizard Point
For continuation pages refer to numbered arrows

3
9
4
SUPER-MARE
Bridgwater Bay
Burnham-on-Sea
West Huntspill
Ilfracombe
Lynton
Lynmouth
Combe Martin
Barbrook
Brendon
Porlock Weir
Porlock
Minehead
Mortehoe
Lee
Woolacombe
Parracombe
EXMOOR
Wootton Courtenay
Dunster
Blue Anchor
Watchet
Kilve
Stogursey
Georgeham
Challacombe
NATIONAL
Carhampton
Sampford Brett
Croyde
Bratton Fleming
Wheddon Cross
Washford
Bicknoller
Cannington
Barnstaple
Saunton
Muddiford
Simonsbath
Exford
Luxborough
Monksilver
Stogumber
Nether Stowey
or
Braunton
Brayford
Withypool
PARK
Crowcombe
Bridgwater
Bideford Bay
Barnstaple
Winsford
Elworthy
Triscombe
QUANTOCK HILLS
Appledore
Instow
Brompton Regis
Goathurst
North Petherton
Westward Ho!
Northam
North Molton
Molland
Langley Marsh
Bishops Lydeard
ST
SOM
Lyng
Clovelly
Horns Cross
Bideford
SS
South Molton
Dulverton
Wiveliscombe
Fitzhead
Waterrow
Milverton
North Curry
Umberleigh
Exbridge
Petton
Taunton
Monkleigh
Great Torrington
Chittlehamholt
Bampton
Appley
Bradford-on-Tone
Wellington
Hatch Beauchamp
Sampford Arundel
Corfe
Slough Green
Little Torrington
Burrington
Rackenford
Taunton Deane
Staple Fitzpaine
Ashill
Stibb Cross
Beaford
Chulmleigh
Witheridge
Culmstock
Clayhidon
Bradworthy
Merton
Dolton
Chawleigh
Horton
Ilminster
Milton Damerel
Eggesford
Tiverton
Halberton
Uffculme
Willand
Hemyock
Shebbear
Meeth
Lapford
Butterleigh
Yarcombe
Black Torrington
Sheepwash
Winkleigh
Morchard Bishop
Cheriton Fitzpaine
Upottery
Cullompton
Hatherleigh
Bickleigh
Chardstock
Highampton
Copplestone
Silverton
Clyst Hydon
Stockland
Halwill Junction
Coleford
Crediton
Tytherleigh
Clawton
Beaworthy
Stoke Canon
Fenny Bridges
Honiton
Dalwood
D E V O N
Spreyton
Newton St Cyres
Whimple
Wilmington
Broadclyst
Shute
Axminster
Ashwater
Okehampton
Tedburn St Mary
Cheriton Bishop
South Zeal
Rockbeare
Ottery St Mary
Colyton
Bratton Clovelly
Crockernwell
EXETER
Colyford
Uplyme
Whiddon Down
Clyst St Mary
Axmouth
Sourton
Drewsteignton
Bridestowe
Dunsford
Topsham
Woodbury Salterton
Branscombe
Seaton
Chagford
Beer
Lewdown
DARTMOOR
Doddiscombsleigh
Kenford
Exminster
Exton
Sidmouth
Lifton
Lydford
Moretonhampstead
Lower Ashton
Lympstone
Otterton
North Bovey
Kenton
Budleigh Salterton
Milton Abbot
Bovey Tracey
Chudleigh
Cockwood
Horndon
Exmouth
Lamerton
Mary Tavy
Postbridge
Widecombe in the Moor
Haytor Vale
Ideford
Treburley
Luton
Dawlish
Tavistock
NATIONAL
Chudleigh Knighton
Bishopsteignton
Horsebridge
Princetown
Teignmouth
Kingsteignton
Gunnislake
Hexworthy
Buckland Monachorum
Horrabridge
Ashburton
Newton Abbot
Dousland
Holne
Denbury
Maidencombe
Bere Alston
Yelverton
PARK
Broadhempston
Kingskerswell
Meavy
Buckfastleigh
Ipplepen
Pillaton
Clearbrook
Marldon
SY
Bere Ferrers
Shaugh Prior
Dartington
Landrake
Littlehempston
TORQUAY
Rattery
Cornwood
South Brent
Totnes
Paignton
Saltash
Wrangaton
Avonwick
Stoke Gabriel
Tor Bay
Plympton
Harberton
Torpoint
Ivybridge
Harbertonford
Churston Ferrers
Cornworthy
Tuckenhay
Dittisham
Brixham
PLYMOUTH
Ugborough
Crafthole
Millbrook
Halwell
Kingsand
Heybrook Bay
Brixton
Yealmpton
Modbury
Kingswear
Cawsand
Dartmouth
Newton Ferrers
Aveton Gifford
Wembury
Holbeton
Stoke Fleming
Noss Mayo
Kingston
Strete
SX
Slapton
Bigbury-on-Sea
Kingsbridge
Bigbury Bay
Chillington
Stokenham
Start Bay
Thurlestone
South Pool
Torcross
Hope
Malborough
Salcombe
Hallsands
Start Point
East Prawle
0
10 miles
0
10
20 kilometres
4
5
6
7
8
9
0
1
2
3

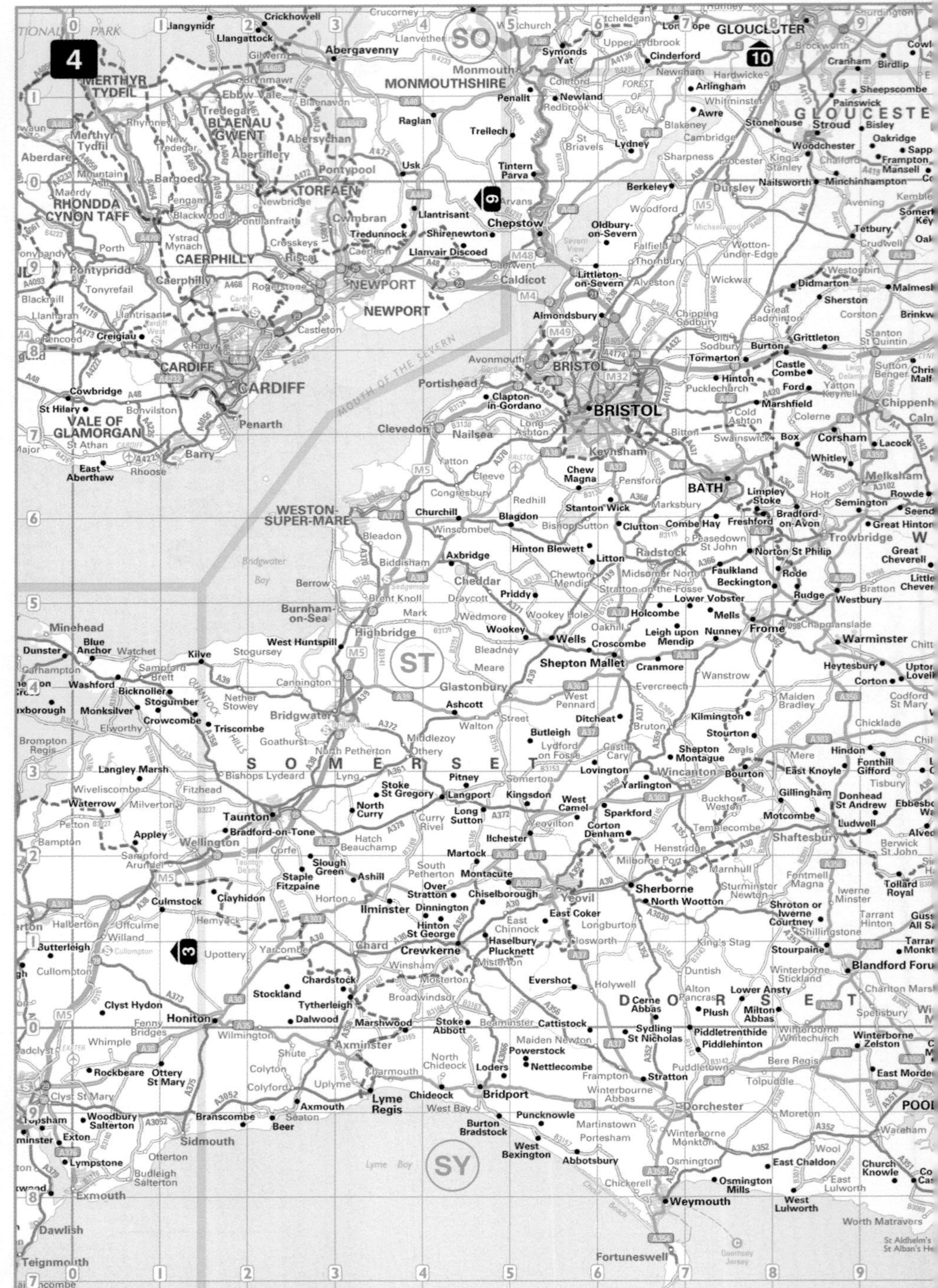

For continuation pages refer to numbered arrows

5
OXFORDSHIRE
BERKSHIRE
HAMPSHIRE
SURREY
WEST SUSSEX
ISLE OF WIGHT
SP
SU
SZ
OXFORD
READING
SWINDON
BASINGSTOKE
SOUTHAMPTON
PORTSMOUTH
BOURNEMOUTH
GUILDFORD
MAIDENHEAD
SLOUGH
HIGH WYCOMBE
CAMBERLEY
WOKING
WATERLOOVILLE
FAREHAM
GOSPORT
HAVANT
EASTLEIGH
BOGNOR REGIS
HEMEL HEMPSTEAD
Aylesbury
Thame
Abingdon
Didcot
Wantage
Newbury
Hungerford
Marlborough
Andover
Salisbury
Winchester
Romsey
Petersfield
Midhurst
Chichester
Haslemere
Farnham
Alton
Henley-on-Thames
Marlow
Windsor
Lymington
Christchurch
Ringwood
Cowes
Newport
Ryde
Shanklin
LAMBOURN DOWNS
NEW FOREST NATIONAL PARK
SOUTH DOWNS NATIONAL PARK (Proposed Area)
The Solent
Pub/Inn
Town/Village name
10 miles
0 10 20 kilometres

For continuation pages refer to numbered arrows

Halstead
Gosfield
Earls Colne
Chappel
Aldham
COLCHESTER
Pattiswick
Marks Tey
Coggeshall
Copford Green
Wivenhoe
Ardleigh
Elmstead Market
Wix
13
Thorpe-le-Soken
Walton on the Naze
Harwi
Feering
Silver End
Kelvedon
Fingringhoe
Thorrington
Little Clacton
Frinton-on-Sea
Little Braxted
Tiptree
Brightlingsea
St Osyth
CLACTON-ON-SEA
TM
Great Braxted
Tolleshunt D'Arcy
West Mersea
Wickham Bishops
Goldhanger
Tollesbury
Woodham Mortimer
Maldon
River Blackwater
Bradwell-on-Sea
Steeple
Cold Norton
Latchingdon
Southminster
North Fambridge
South Woodham Ferrers
Burnham-on-Crouch
Hockley
Rayleigh
Rochford
Great Wakering
SOUTHEND-ON-SEA
Canvey Island
Grain
Sheerness
Minster
Hoo St Werburgh
Eastchurch
Leysdown-on-Sea
Isle of Sheppey
Iwade
GILLINGHAM
Herne Bay
Reculver
MARGATE
Broadstairs
Ramsgate
Whitstable
Boyden Gate
Sarre
Minster
Sittingbourne
Teynham
Faversham
Ospringe
Hernhill
Blean
Sturry
Hersden
Upstreet
Bredhurst
Fordwich
Ash
Sandwich
Doddington
Newnham
Boughton Street
Littlebourne
Canterbury
Wingham
Eastry
Hollingbourne
Selling
Chartham
Bridge
Chillenden
Lenham
Chilham
Harrietsham
Challock
Aylesham
Deal
TR
Sutton Valence
Charing
Bossingham
K E N T
Kingsdown
Pluckley
Wye
Wingmore
Headcorn
Elham
St Margaret's at Cliffe
Staplehurst
Smarden
Ashford
Brabourne
Lyminge
Densole
Alkham
DOVER
Bethersden
CHANNEL TUNNEL TERMINAL
Hawkinge
Biddenden
High Halden
Kingsnorth
Sellindge
Sissinghurst
Cranbrook
Woodchurch
Lympne
FOLKESTONE
Channel Tunnel (Rail)
Benenden
Tenterden
Hythe
Hamstreet
Rolvenden
Wittersham
Appledore
Dymchurch
St Mary's Bay
Brookland
Brenzett
Northiam
New Romney
STRAIT OF DOVER
Peasmarsh
Lydd
Rye
Camber
Brede
Icklesham
Winchelsea
Dungeness
Westfield
Guestling Green
Fairlight
HASTINGS
A12
A120
A133
A414
A13
A127
A228
A2
A249
M2
M20
A20
A28
A251
A299
A256
A258
A259
A260
A261
A268
A2070
A257
A290
A291
A2990
A255
A274
8
9
0
1
2
3
4
5
6
7
• Pub/Inn
○ Town/Village name
0
10 miles
0
10
20 kilometres

For continuation pages refer to numbered arrows

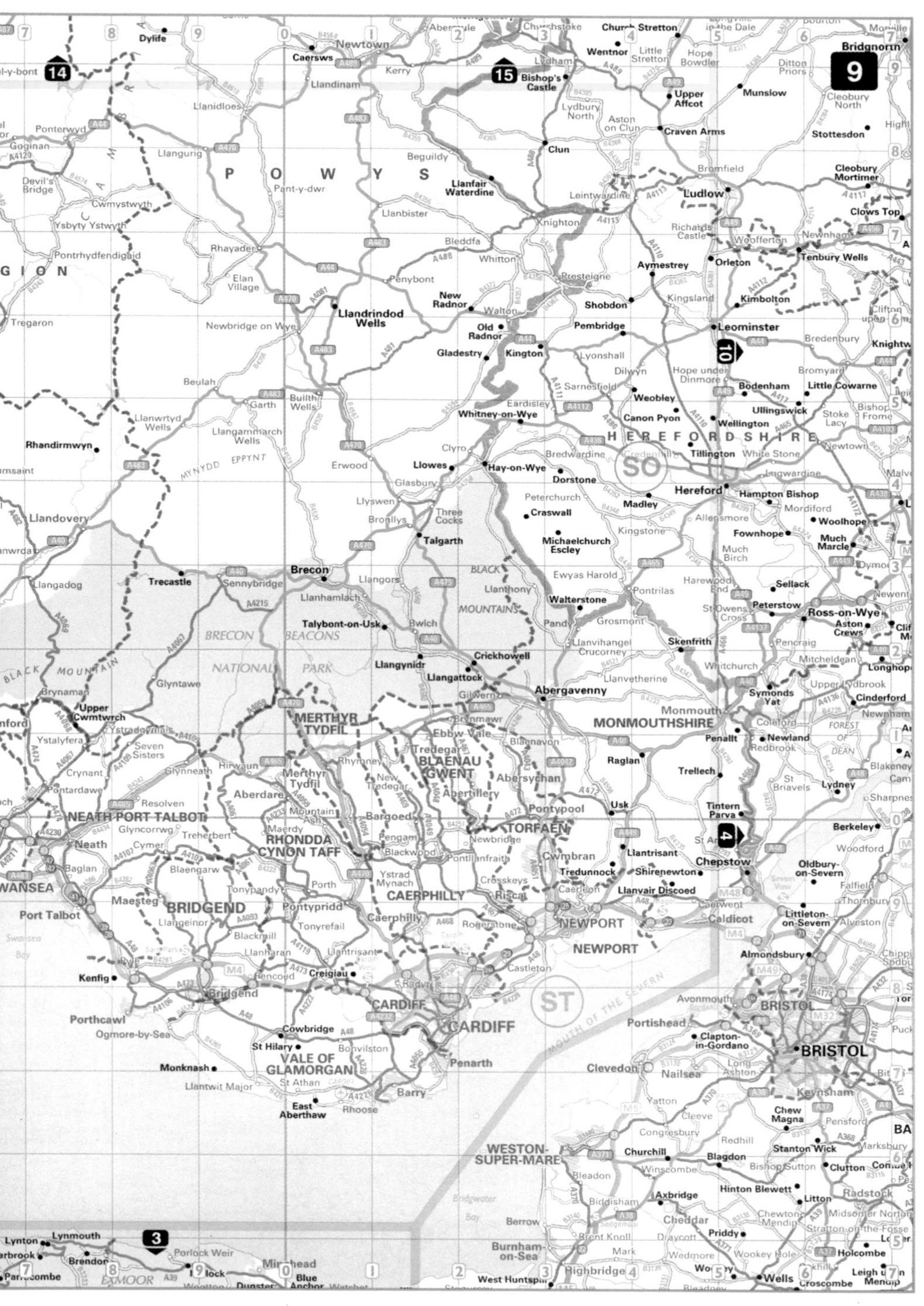

9
14
15
3
4
10
Dylife
Caersws
Newtown
Kerry
Llandinam
Llanidloes
Bishop's Castle
Lydham
Church Stretton
Wentnor
Little Stretton
Hope Bowdler
Ditton Priors
Bridgnorth
Upper Affcot
Munslow
Cleobury North
Stottesdon
Lydbury North
Aston on Clun
Craven Arms
Clun
Ponterwyd
Goginan
Devil's Bridge
Cwmystwyth
Ysbyty Ystwyth
Llangurig
P O W Y S
Pant-y-dwr
Beguildy
Llanfair Waterdine
Llanbister
Bromfield
Ludlow
Leintwardine
Cleobury Mortimer
Clows Top
Knighton
Richards Castle
Woofferton
Newnham
Tenbury Wells
Pontrhydfendigaid
Rhayader
Elan Village
Bleddfa
Whitton
Penybont
Presteigne
Aymestrey
Orleton
Kingsland
Kimbolton
Tregaron
Newbridge on Wye
Llandrindod Wells
New Radnor
Walton
Old Radnor
Shobdon
Pembridge
Leominster
Gladestry
Kington
Lyonshall
Dilwyn
Bredenbury
Hope under Dinmore
Bromyard
Bodenham
Little Cowarne
Beulah
Garth
Builth Wells
Llanwrtyd Wells
Llangammarch Wells
Sarnesfield
Weobley
Eardisley
Whitney-on-Wye
Canon Pyon
Ullingswick
Wellington
Stoke Lacy
Bishop's Frome
Rhandirmwyn
MYNYDD EPPYNT
Erwood
Clyro
Llowes
Hay-on-Wye
Bredwardine
H E R E F O R D S H I R E
Tillington
White Stone
Newtown
SO
Dorstone
Glasbury
Peterchurch
Hereford
Hampton Bishop
Mordiford
Madley
Llyswen
Bronllys
Three Cocks
Craswall
Kingstone
Allensmore
Fownhope
Woolhope
Much Marcle
Llandovery
Talgarth
Michaelchurch Escley
Much Birch
Llangadog
Trecastle
Sennybridge
Brecon
Llangors
BLACK MOUNTAINS
Llanthony
Ewyas Harold
Pontrilas
Harewood End
Sellack
Llanhamlach
Walterstone
Peterstow
Ross-on-Wye
Talybont-on-Usk
Bwlch
St Owens Cross
Aston Crews
BRECON BEACONS
NATIONAL PARK
Pandy
Grosmont
Llanvihangel Crucorney
Skenfrith
Pencraig
BLACK MOUNTAIN
Crickhowell
Llangynidr
Llangattock
Whitchurch
Mitcheldean
Longhope
Glyntawe
Llanvetherine
Brynaman
Upper Cwmtwrch
Gilwern
Abergavenny
Symonds Yat
Upper Lydbrook
Cinderford
MERTHYR TYDFIL
Brynmawr
Ebbw Vale
Monmouth
MONMOUTHSHIRE
Coleford
Newnham
FOREST OF DEAN
Ystradgynlais
Ystalyfera
Seven Sisters
Tredegar
BLAENAU GWENT
Blaenavon
Penallt
Newland
Redbrook
Crynant
Hirwaun
Rhymney
Raglan
Trellech
Blakeney
Glynneath
Merthyr Tydfil
New Tredegar
Abersychan
St Briavels
Lydney
Pontardawe
Resolven
Aberdare
Abertillery
NEATH PORT TALBOT
Mountain Ash
Bargoed
Pontypool
Usk
Tintern Parva
Sharpness
Glyncorrwg
Treherbert
Maerdy
Pengam
TORFAEN
Berkeley
Neath
Cymer
RHONDDA CYNON TAFF
Blackwood
Newbridge
Cwmbran
Llantrisant
St Arvans
Chepstow
Woodford
Baglan
Blaengarw
Pontllanfraith
Tredunnock
Shirenewton
Oldbury-on-Severn
SWANSEA
Porth
Ystrad Mynach
Crosskeys
Caerleon
Llanvair Discoed
Falfield
Maesteg
Tonypandy
CAERPHILLY
Risca
Caerwent
Port Talbot
BRIDGEND
Pontypridd
Caldicot
Thornbury
Llangeinor
Tonyrefail
Caerphilly
Rogerstone
NEWPORT
Littleton-on-Severn
Alveston
Blackmill
Llanharan
Llantrisant
Almondsbury
Kenfig
Pencoed
Creigiau
Castleton
Bridgend
Radyr
CARDIFF
ST
MOUTH OF THE SEVERN
Avonmouth
BRISTOL
Porthcawl
Ogmore-by-Sea
Cowbridge
Portishead
Clapton-in-Gordano
St Hilary
VALE OF GLAMORGAN
Bonvilston
Monknash
Penarth
Clevedon
Nailsea
Long Ashton
Keynsham
Llantwit Major
St Athan
Barry
East Aberthaw
Rhoose
Yatton
Cleeve
Chew Magna
Pensford
Congresbury
Redhill
Stanton Wick
Marksbury
WESTON-SUPER-MARE
Churchill
Blagdon
Bishop Sutton
Clutton
Bleadon
Winscombe
Hinton Blewett
Litton
Radstock
Bridgwater Bay
Biddisham
Axbridge
Berrow
Cheddar
Chewton Mendip
Midsomer Norton
Stratton-on-the-Fosse
Lynton
Lynmouth
Brendon
Porlock Weir
Brent Knoll
Draycott
Priddy
Holcombe
Burnham-on-Sea
Mark
Wedmore
Wookey Hole
Minehead
Blue Anchor
Parracombe
EXMOOR
West Huntspill
Highbridge
Wells
Croscombe
Leigh upon Mendip

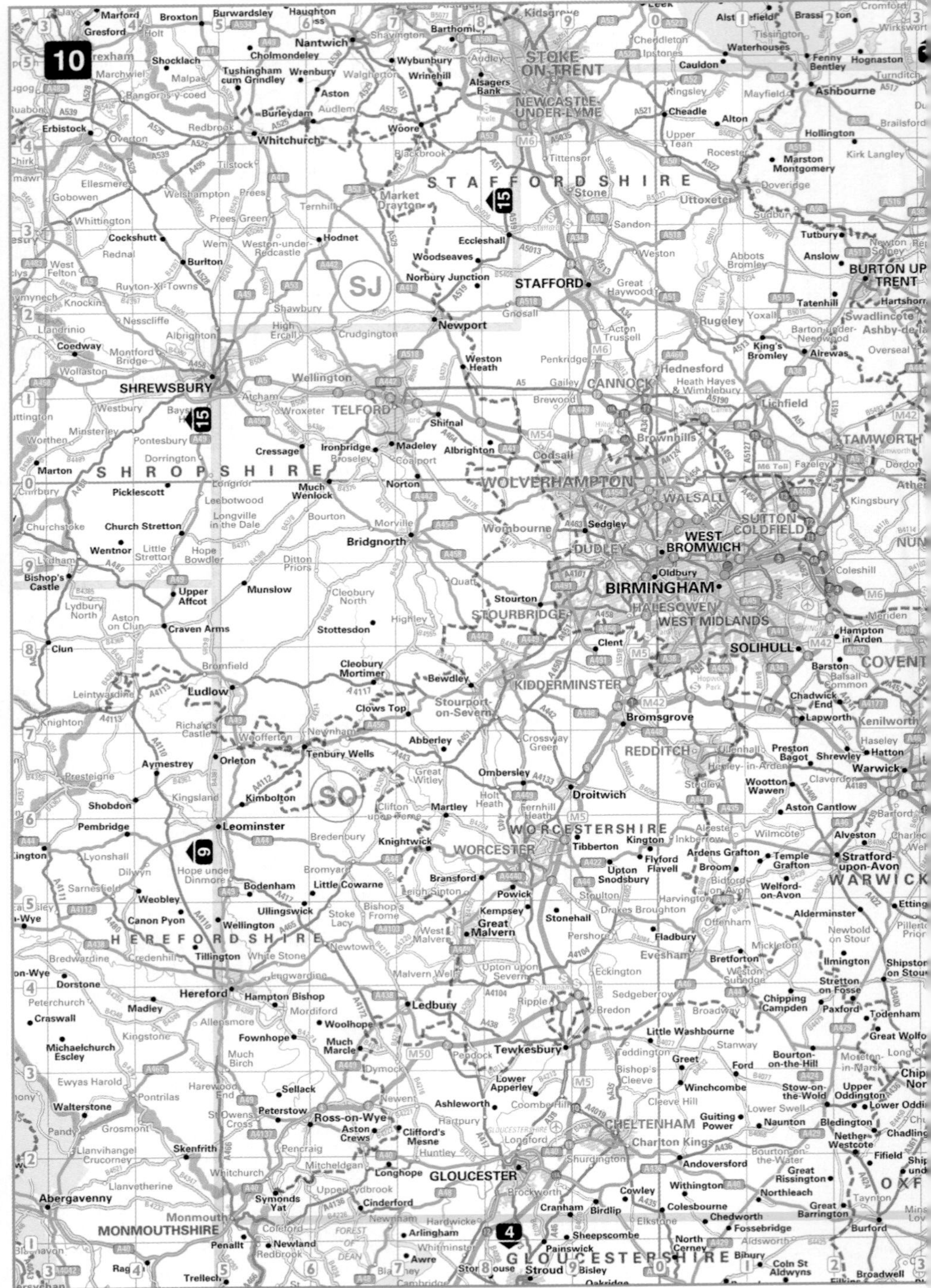

For continuation pages refer to numbered arrows

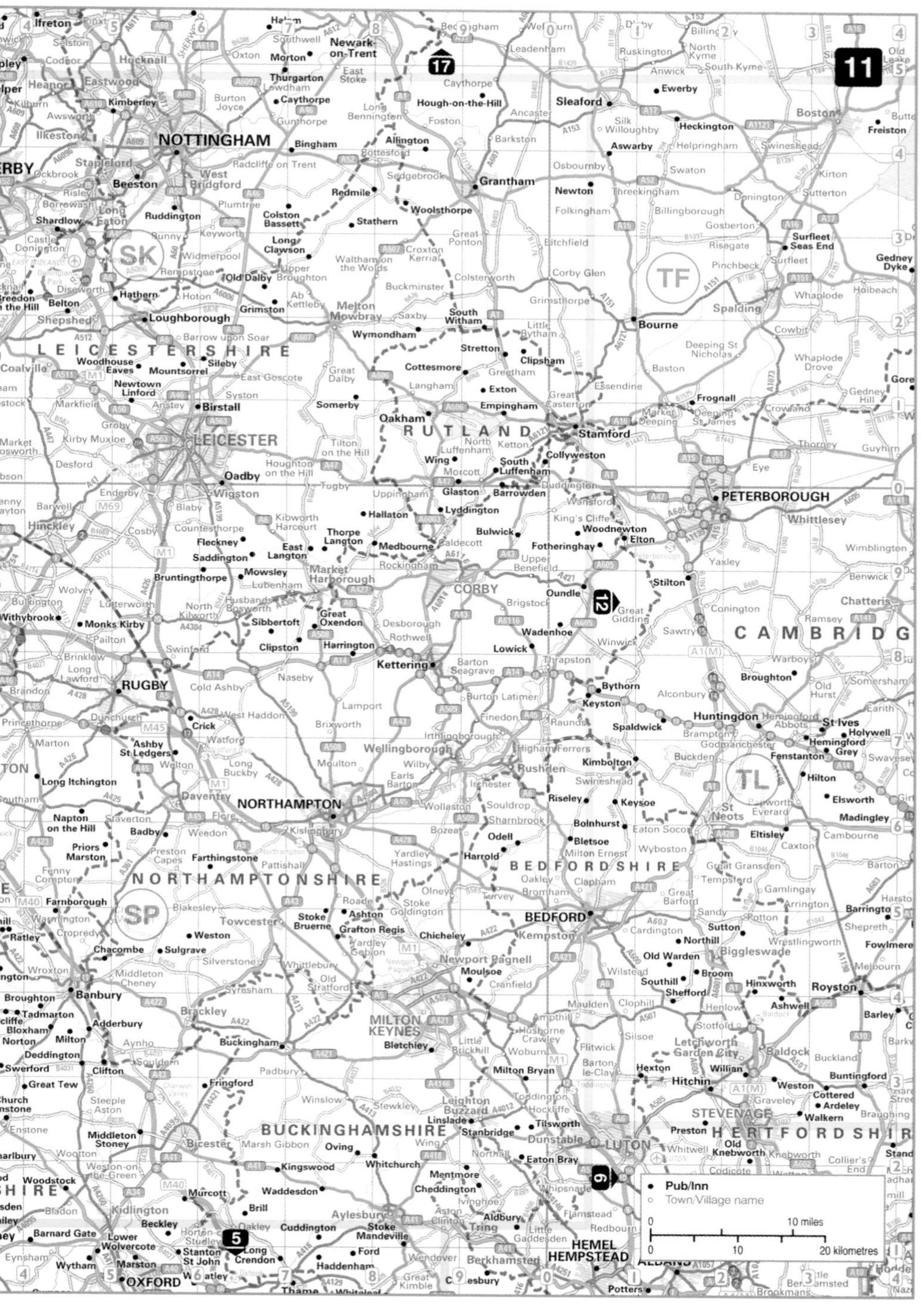
11
Pub/Inn
Town/Village name
0
10 miles
0
10
20 kilometres
SK
TF
SP
TL
LEICESTERSHIRE
RUTLAND
NORTHAMPTONSHIRE
BEDFORDSHIRE
BUCKINGHAMSHIRE
HERTFORDSHIRE
CAMBRIDG
NOTTINGHAM
LEICESTER
PETERBOROUGH
NORTHAMPTON
BEDFORD
MILTON KEYNES
LUTON
HEMEL HEMPSTEAD
OXFORD
RUGBY
CORBY
Newark-on-Trent
Grantham
Sleaford
Boston
Stamford
Oakham
Loughborough
Melton Mowbray
Market Harborough
Kettering
Wellingborough
Huntingdon
St Neots
Biggleswade
Hitchin
Stevenage
Royston
Banbury
Bicester
Aylesbury
Buckingham
Daventry
Oundle
Spalding
Bourne
Hinckley
Kimberley
Beeston
Ruddington
Colston Bassett
Long Clawson
Old Dalby
Grimston
Hathern
Belton
Woodhouse Eaves
Mountsorrel
Sileby
Newtown Linford
Birstall
Oadby
Somerby
Cottesmore
Exton
Empingham
Stretton
Clipsham
Wymondham
South Witham
Redmile
Stathern
Woolsthorpe
Allington
Hough-on-the-Hill
Bingham
Morton
Thurgarton
Caythorpe
Ewerby
Heckington
Asworby
Newton
Freiston
Surfleet Seas End
Gedney Dyke
Frognall
Collyweston
South Luffenham
Barrowden
Glaston
Lyddington
Hallaton
Wing
Medbourne
Thorpe Langton
East Langton
Fleckney
Saddington
Bruntingthorpe
Mowsley
Sibbertoft
Great Oxendon
Clipston
Harrington
Monks Kirby
Withybrook
Crick
Ashby St Ledgers
Long Itchington
Napton on the Hill
Priors Marston
Badby
Farthingstone
Farnborough
Ratley
Weston
Sulgrave
Chacombe
Stoke Bruerne
Ashton
Grafton Regis
Chicheley
Moulsoe
Odell
Harrold
Bletsoe
Bolnhurst
Riseley
Keysoe
Kimbolton
Spaldwick
Keyston
Bythorn
Lowick
Wadenhoe
Fotheringhay
Woodnewton
Elton
Stilton
Bulwick
Broughton
Hemingford Grey
Holywell
St Ives
Fenstanton
Hilton
Elsworth
Madingley
Eltisley
Barrington
Fowlmere
Northill
Old Warden
Southill
Shefford
Broom
Hinxworth
Ashwell
Barley
Buntingford
Cottered
Ardeley
Walkern
Weston
Hexton
Preston
Old Knebworth
Milton Bryan
Tilsworth
Eaton Bray
Stanbridge
Linslade
Mentmore
Cheddington
Aldbury
Oving
Whitchurch
Kingswood
Waddesdon
Brill
Cuddington
Haddenham
Long Crendon
Ford
Stanton St John
Murcott
Fringford
Beckley
Barnard Gate
Wytham
Woodstock
Middleton Stoney
Clifton
Great Tew
Swerford
Deddington
Adderbury
Tadmarton
Broughton
Bloxham
Milton

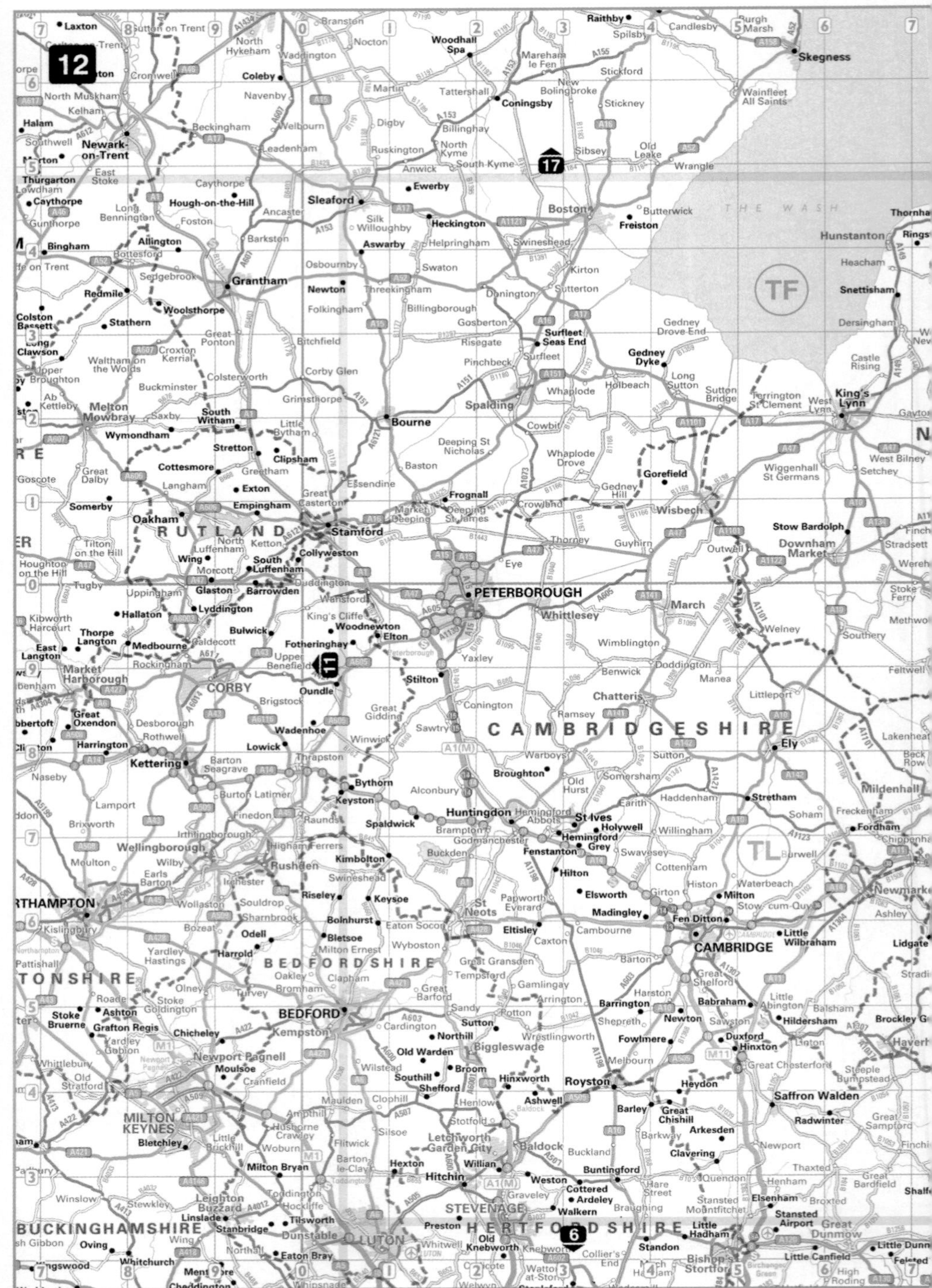

For continuation pages refer to numbered arrows

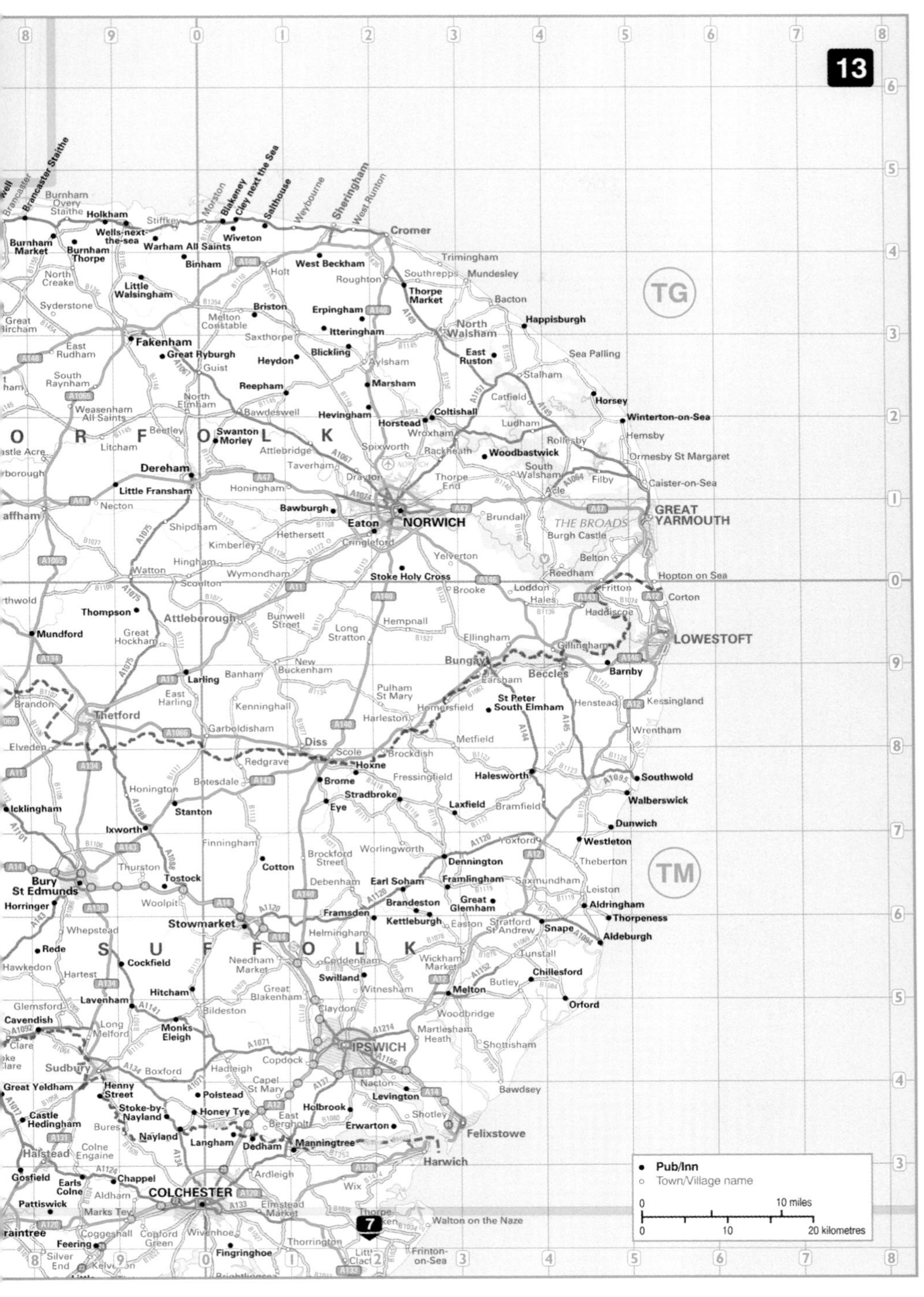
13
TG
TM
N O R F O L K
S U F F O L K
Brancaster
Brancaster Staithe
Burnham Overy Staithe
Holkham
Stiffkey
Morston
Blakeney
Cley next the Sea
Salthouse
Weybourne
Sheringham
West Runton
Cromer
Burnham Market
Burnham Thorpe
Wells-next-the-sea
Warham All Saints
Wiveton
Binham
Holt
West Beckham
Trimingham
Southrepps
Mundesley
Roughton
North Creake
Little Walsingham
Thorpe Market
Bacton
Syderstone
Briston
Erpingham
Great Bircham
Melton Constable
Itteringham
North Walsham
Happisburgh
Saxthorpe
Fakenham
Great Ryburgh
East Rudham
Guist
Heydon
Blickling
Aylsham
East Ruston
Sea Palling
Stalham
South Raynham
Reepham
Marsham
Catfield
Horsey
North Elmham
Weasenham All Saints
Bawdeswell
Hevingham
Coltishall
Horstead
Winterton-on-Sea
Ludham
Hemsby
Beetley
Swanton Morley
Wroxham
Rollesby
Litcham
Attlebridge
Spixworth
Rackheath
Woodbastwick
Ormesby St Margaret
Castle Acre
Taverham
South Walsham
Dereham
Drayton
Thorpe End
Acle
Filby
Caister-on-Sea
Honingham
Little Fransham
Necton
Bawburgh
Eaton
NORWICH
Brundall
GREAT YARMOUTH
Swaffham
THE BROADS
Shipdham
Hethersett
Burgh Castle
Kimberley
Cringleford
Yelverton
Belton
Hingham
Watton
Wymondham
Stoke Holy Cross
Reedham
Hopton on Sea
Scoulton
Brooke
Loddon
Fritton
Corton
Hales
Haddiscoe
Thompson
Attleborough
Bunwell Street
Hempnall
Long Stratton
Mundford
Great Hockham
Ellingham
Gillingham
LOWESTOFT
New Buckenham
Bungay
Beccles
Barnby
Larling
Banham
Earsham
East Harling
Pulham St Mary
St Peter South Elmham
Henstead
Kessingland
Brandon
Kenninghall
Homersfield
Thetford
Harleston
Wrentham
Garboldisham
Elveden
Diss
Metfield
Scole
Brockdish
Redgrave
Hoxne
Fressingfield
Halesworth
Southwold
Brome
Botesdale
Honington
Stradbroke
Walberswick
Eye
Laxfield
Bramfield
Mildenhall
Icklingham
Stanton
Dunwich
Ixworth
Yoxford
Westleton
Finningham
Worlingworth
Brockford Street
Dennington
Theberton
Thurston
Cotton
Tostock
Bury St Edmunds
Debenham
Earl Soham
Framlingham
Saxmundham
Leiston
Woolpit
Brandeston
Great Glemham
Aldringham
Horringer
Framsden
Kettleburgh
Easton
Stratford St Andrew
Snape
Thorpeness
Stowmarket
Whepstead
Helmingham
Aldeburgh
Rede
Cockfield
Coddenham
Wickham Market
Tunstall
Hawkedon
Hartest
Needham Market
Swilland
Chillesford
Witnesham
Butley
Hitcham
Great Blakenham
Melton
Glemsford
Lavenham
Orford
Bildeston
Claydon
Woodbridge
Cavendish
Long Melford
Monks Eleigh
Martlesham Heath
Clare
Shottisham
IPSWICH
Sudbury
Boxford
Hadleigh
Copdock
Great Yeldham
Henny Street
Polstead
Capel St Mary
Nacton
Levington
Bawdsey
Castle Hedingham
Stoke-by-Nayland
Honey Tye
Holbrook
Shotley
Bures
Nayland
East Bergholt
Erwarton
Felixstowe
Colne Engaine
Langham
Dedham
Manningtree
Halstead
Harwich
Gosfield
Earls Colne
Chappel
Ardleigh
Aldham
COLCHESTER
Wix
Pattiswick
Marks Tey
Elmstead Market
Thorpe-le-Soken
Walton on the Naze
Braintree
Coggeshall
Copford Green
Wivenhoe
Feering
Thorrington
Frinton-on-Sea
Silver End
Kelvedon
Fingringhoe
Little Clacton
Brightlingsea
7
A148
A1065
A1067
A140
A149
A1151
A1062
A1064
A47
A1074
A146
A143
A11
A1075
A1066
A134
A1088
A1101
A14
A1120
A12
A1094
A1152
A1214
A1156
A137
A1071
A1092
A131
A1124
A120
A133
A1017
A1095
A144
A145
A1117
B1155
B1105
B1110
B1149
B1354
B1145
B1150
B1159
B1135
B1108
B1172
B1113
B1077
B1106
B1111
B1527
B1136
B1074
B1332
B1134
B1116
B1118
B1117
B1123
B1125
B1126
B1127
B1119
B1121
B1078
B1069
B1084
B1083
B1070
B1115
B1071
B1068
B1080
B1352
B1035
B1414
B1034
B1027
B1029
B1022
B1024
B1508
B1058
B1054
B1115
B1106
B1355
B1454
B1153
B1146
B1140
B1122
0
1
2
3
4
5
6
7
8
9
● Pub/Inn
○ Town/Village name
0
10 miles
0
10
20 kilometres

For continuation pages refer to numbered arrows

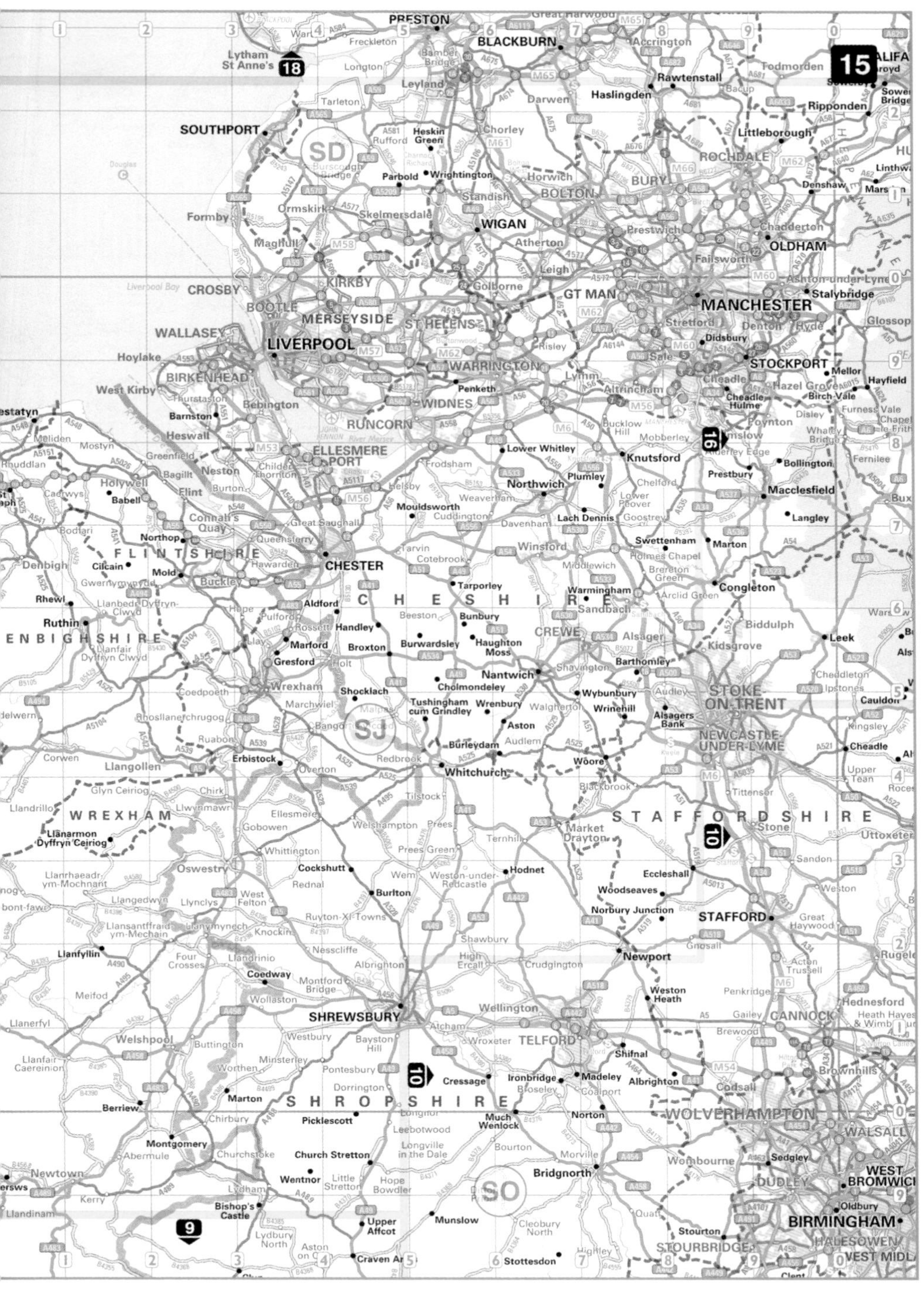

15
18
16
10
10
9
SD
SJ
SO
PRESTON
BLACKBURN
Lytham St Anne's
Freckleton
Longton
Leyland
Bamber Bridge
Accrington
Rawtenstall
Haslingden
Darwen
Todmorden
Ripponden
Littleborough
ROCHDALE
SOUTHPORT
Tarleton
Rufford
Heskin Green
Chorley
Burscough Bridge
Parbold
Wrightington
Horwich
BOLTON
BURY
Denshaw
Formby
Ormskirk
Skelmersdale
Standish
WIGAN
Atherton
Prestwich
Chadderton
OLDHAM
Maghull
Leigh
Failsworth
Ashton-under-Lyne
Liverpool Bay
CROSBY
KIRKBY
Golborne
GT MAN
MANCHESTER
Stalybridge
BOOTLE
MERSEYSIDE
ST HELENS
Stretford
Denton
Hyde
Glossop
WALLASEY
LIVERPOOL
Risley
Didsbury
Hoylake
BIRKENHEAD
WARRINGTON
Sale
STOCKPORT
Mellor
Hayfield
West Kirby
Thurstaston
Penketh
Lymm
Altrincham
Cheadle
Cheadle Hulme
Hazel Grove
Birch Vale
Bebington
WIDNES
Barnston
RUNCORN
Poynton
Disley
Furness Vale
Prestatyn
Heswall
Meliden
Mostyn
Bucklow Hill
Mobberley
Wilmslow
Whaley Bridge
Rhuddlan
Greenfield
ELLESMERE PORT
Lower Whitley
Alderley Edge
Knutsford
Bollington
Fernilee
Holywell
Bagillt
Neston
Childer Thornton
Frodsham
Helsby
Northwich
Plumley
Prestbury
Macclesfield
Babell
Flint
Burton
Mouldsworth
Weaverham
Chelford
Lower Peover
Cuddington
Lach Dennis
Goostrey
Langley
Bodfari
Connah's Quay
Great Saughall
Queensferry
Davenham
Northop
FLINTSHIRE
Tarvin
Cotebrook
Winsford
Swettenham
Holmes Chapel
Marton
Denbigh
Cilcain
Hawarden
CHESTER
Middlewich
Brereton Green
Mold
Buckley
Gwernymynydd
Tarporley
Congleton
Rhewl
Llanbedr-Dyffryn-Clwyd
Hope
Aldford
CHESHIRE
Warmingham
Sandbach
Arclid Green
Ruthin
Pulford
Beeston
Bunbury
Biddulph
DENBIGHSHIRE
Rossett
Handley
Llanfair Dyffryn Clwyd
Marford
Broxton
Burwardsley
Haughton Moss
CREWE
Alsager
Kidsgrove
Leek
Gresford
Holt
Nantwich
Shavington
Barthomley
Wrexham
ShockLach
Cholmondeley
Wybunbury
Audley
STOKE-ON-TRENT
Cheddleton
Ipstones
Cauldon
Coedpoeth
Marchwiel
Tushingham cum Grindley
Wrenbury
Walgherton
Wrinehill
Alsagers Bank
Rhosllanerchrugog
Malpas
Bangor
Aston
NEWCASTLE-UNDER-LYME
Kingsley
Ruabon
Burleydam
Audlem
Cheadle
Corwen
Erbistock
Redbrook
Overton
Whitchurch
Woore
Llangollen
Upper Tean
Glyn Ceiriog
Chirk
Blackbrook
Tittensor
Llandrillo
WREXHAM
Llwynmawr
Tilstock
Ellesmere
Llanarmon Dyffryn Ceiriog
Gobowen
Welshampton
Prees
Tern Hill
Market Drayton
STAFFORDSHIRE
Stone
Uttoxeter
Whittington
Prees Green
Oswestry
Cockshutt
Wem
Weston-under-Redcastle
Hodnet
Eccleshall
Sandon
Llanrhaeadr-ym-Mochnant
Rednal
Burlton
Woodseaves
Weston
Llangedwyn
West Felton
Llynclys
Norbury Junction
Llansantffraid-ym-Mechain
Ruyton-XI-Towns
Llanymynech
Knockin
STAFFORD
Great Haywood
Shawbury
Gnosall
Llanfyllin
Nesscliffe
Llandrinio
High Ercall
Newport
Four Crosses
Albrighton
Crudgington
Acton Trussell
Coedway
Montford Bridge
Meifod
Weston Heath
Penkridge
Wollaston
Hednesford
SHREWSBURY
Wellington
Gailey
CANNOCK
Llanerfyl
Atcham
Brewood
Welshpool
Buttington
Westbury
Bayston Hill
Wroxeter
TELFORD
Shifnal
Llanfair Caereinion
Minsterley
Worthen
Pontesbury
Cressage
Ironbridge
Madeley
Albrighton
Brownhills
Dorrington
Broseley
Coalport
Codsall
Berriew
Marton
SHROPSHIRE
Much Wenlock
Norton
WOLVERHAMPTON
Chirbury
Picklescott
Longnor
WALSALL
Montgomery
Leebotwood
Bourton
Abermule
Churchstoke
Church Stretton
Longville in the Dale
Morville
Wombourne
Sedgley
Newtown
Wentnor
Little Stretton
Hope Bowdler
Bridgnorth
DUDLEY
WEST BROMWICH
Lydham
Kerry
Bishop's Castle
Quatt
Oldbury
Llandinam
Upper Affcot
Munslow
Cleobury North
Stourton
BIRMINGHAM
Lydbury North
STOURBRIDGE
HALESOWEN
Aston on Clun
Craven Arms
Stottesdon
Highley
WEST MIDLANDS
M65
M61
M66
M62
M58
M60
M57
M56
M6
M53
M54
A59
A580
A49
A41
A5
A483
A458
A442
A34
A50
A54
A51
A53
A523
A525
A534
A500
A530
A556
A57
A6
A56

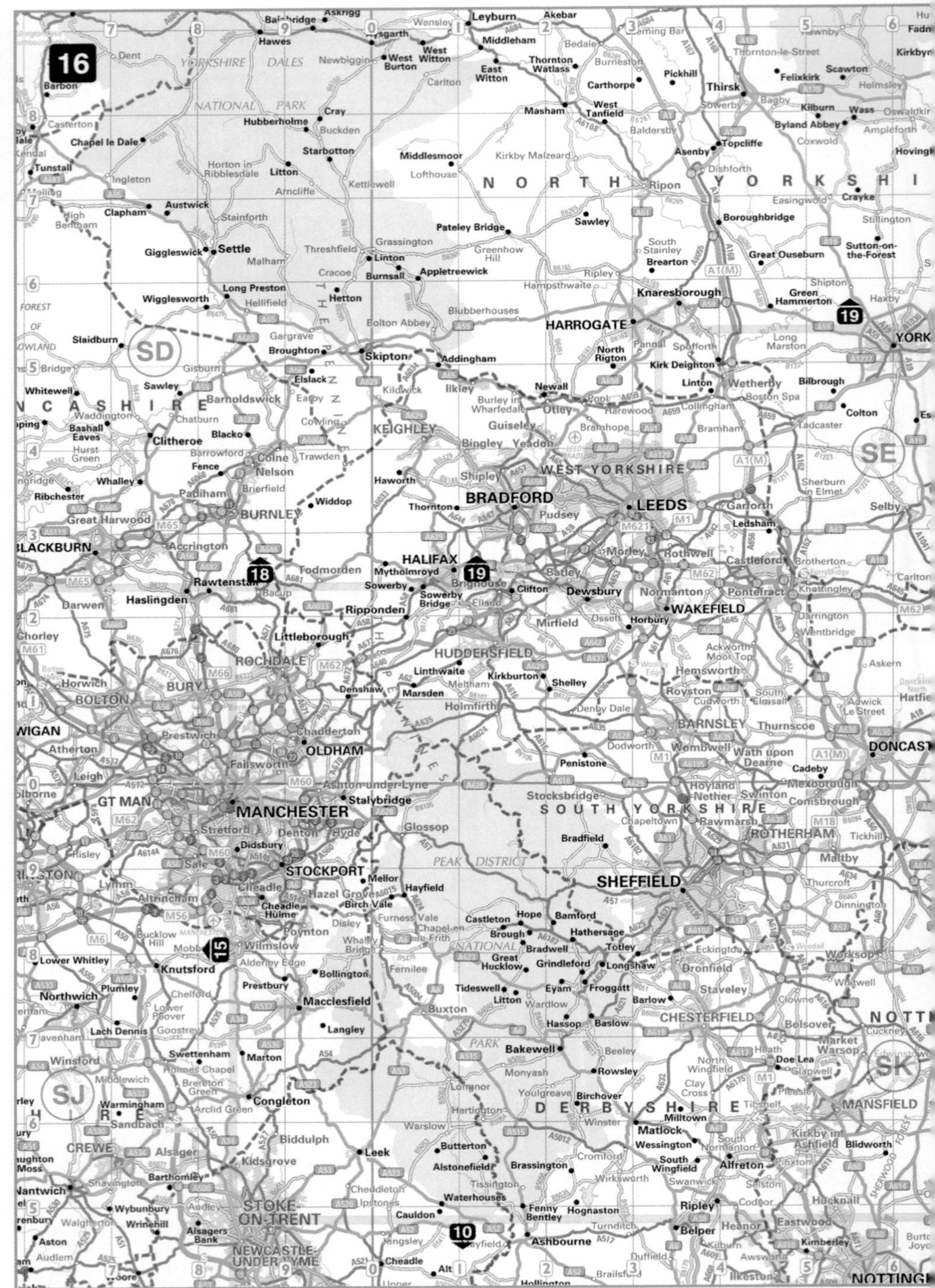

For continuation pages refer to numbered arrows

17
Pub/Inn
Town/Village name
0
10 miles
0
10
20 kilometres
TA
TF
EAST RIDING
OF YORKSHIRE
LINCOLNSHIRE
HAMSHIRE
Lastingham
Cropton
Appleton-le-Moors
Wrelton
Middleton
Marton
Pickering
Thornton le Dale
Lockton
Hackness
Sawdon
East Ayton
Seamer
Snainton
Brompton
Scarborough
Cayton
Flixton
Filey
Staxton
Kirby Misperton
Sherburn
Hunmanby
Reighton
Bempton
Flamborough Head
Flamborough
Rillington
Malton
Norton
Weaverthorpe
North Grimston
Burton Fleming
Rudston
Carnaby
Bridlington
Kirkham
Westow
Sledmere
Langtoft
Kilham
Burton Agnes
Fridaythorpe
Wetwang
Driffield
Barmston
Skipsea
Stamford Bridge
Low Catton
Huggate
North Dalton
Bainton
North Frodingham
Beeford
Atwick
Wilberfoss
Barmby Moor
Pocklington
Middleton on the Wolds
Lund
Brandesburton
Hornsea
Sutton upon Derwent
South Dalton
Leven
Shiptonthorpe
Market Weighton
Holme upon Spalding Moor
Beverley
Walkington
Aldbrough
Coniston
North Cave
South Cave
Cottingham
Sproatley
Howden
Elloughton
Hessle
KINGSTON UPON HULL
Hedon
Withernsea
Goole
Melton
North Ferriby
New Holland
Patrington
Winteringham
Barton upon-Humber
Goxhill
Easington
Burton upon Stather
Winterton
Immingham Dock
River Humber
Wootton
Ulceby
Immingham
Crowle
Gunness
SCUNTHORPE
Broughton
Wrawby
Keelby
GRIMSBY
Spurn Head
Althorpe
Barnetby le Wold
Cleethorpes
Belton
Brigg
Laceby
Humberston
Scawby
Waltham
Epworth
Messingham
Swallow
Holton le Clay
Hibaldstow
Caistor
Barnoldby le Beck
Tetney
North Cotes
Scotter
Haxey
Kirton in Lindsey
Grainthorpe
North Somercotes
Ludborough
Misterton
Blyton
Binbrook
Saltfleet
Gringley on the Hill
Gainsborough
Middle Rasen
Glentham
Market Rasen
Louth
Saundby
Faldingworth
Legbourne
Mablethorpe
Ingham
Lissington
Donington on Bain
Sutton on Sea
Retford
East Barkwith
Withern
Torksey
Sturton by Stow
Wragby
Scamblesby
Gamston
Alford
Huttoft
Elkesley
Newton on Trent
Saxilby
Langworth
Belchford
Bilsby
Markham Moor
Baumber
Tetford
Chapel St Leonards
Skellingthorpe
LINCOLN
Edlington
Hogsthorpe
Tuxford
Washingborough
Bardney
Horncastle
Hagworthingham
Ingoldmells
Partney
Laxton
Sutton on Trent
Branston
Raithby
Candlesby
Burgh le Marsh
Spilsby
Carlton-on-Trent
North Hykeham
Nocton
Woodhall Spa
Mareham le Fen
Skegness
Waddington
Caunton
Cromwell
Coleby
Stickford
Martin
Tattershall
New Bolingbroke
North Muskham
Navenby
Coningsby
Wainfleet All Saints
Kelham
Stickney
Beckingham
Welbourn
Digby
Billinghay
Newark-on-Trent
Leadenham
North Kyme
Ruskington
Sibsey
Old Leake
Wrangle
Anwick
South Kyme
East Stoke
Caythorpe
Ewerby
Hough-on-the-Hill
Sleaford
Boston
Long Bennington
Ancaster
Silk Willoughby
Heckington
Butterwick
THE WASH
Thornham
Foston
Freiston
Allington
Barkston
Aswarby
Helpringham
Swineshead
Hunstanton
Ringstead
Bingham
Caythorpe
Thorpe
M62
M181
M180
A1
A15
A16
A17
A18
A46
A52
A57
A63
A64
A156
A158
A165
A614
A631
A1033
A1079
11
12
19

For continuation pages refer to numbered arrows

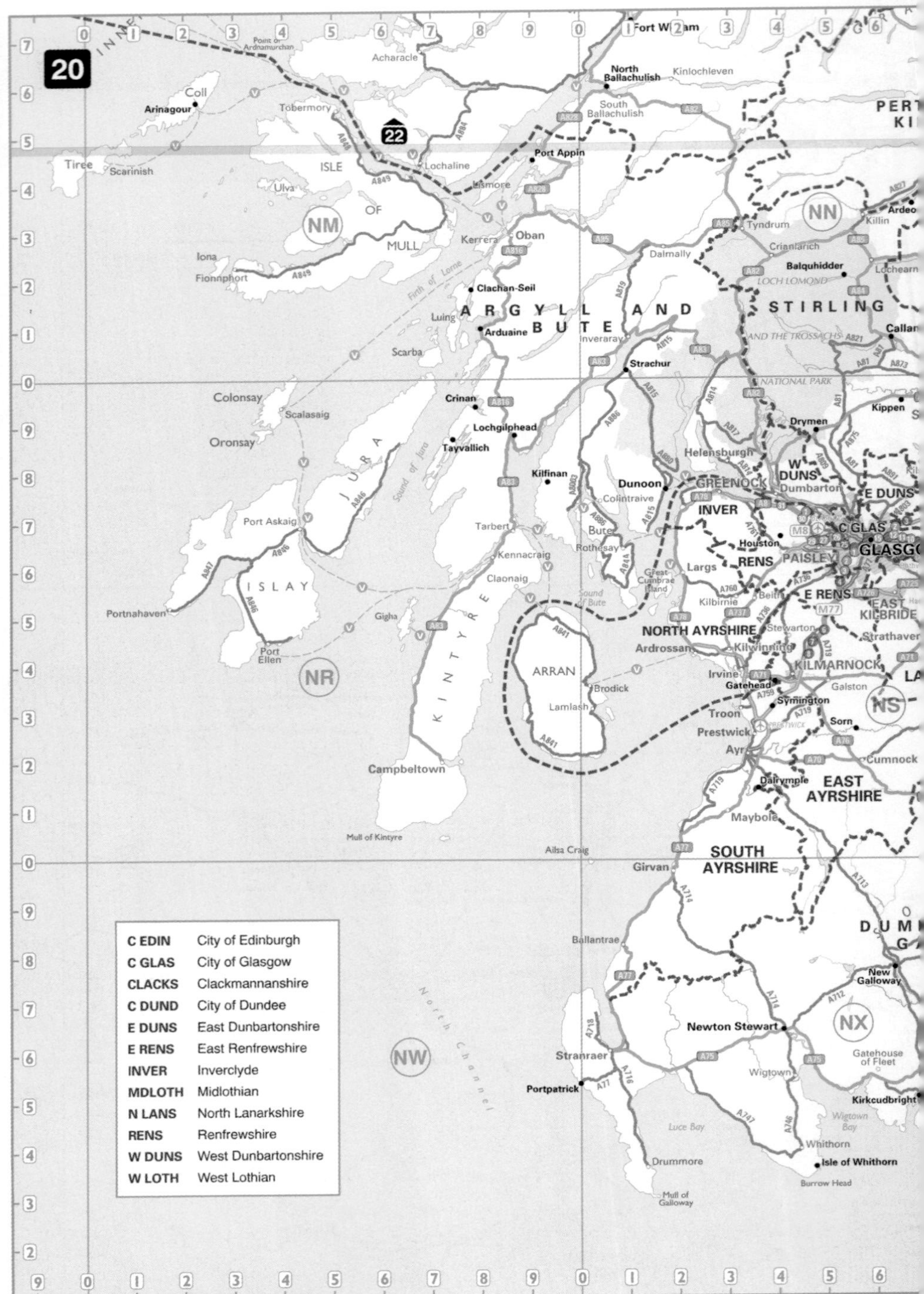

For continuation pages refer to numbered arrows

21
Pub/Inn
Town/Village name
0 10 20 miles
0 10 20 30 kilometres
ANGUS
Blair Atholl
Pitlochry
Brechin
Montrose
Kirriemuir
Forfar
Blairgowrie
Coupar Angus
Arbroath
SIDLAW HILLS
C DUND
DUNDEE
Carnoustie
Broughty Ferry
Newport-on-Tay
St Andrews Bay
Perth
Crieff
Newburgh
Auchtermuchty
St Andrews
Cupar
Auchterarder
Glenfarg
FIFE
Fife Ness
Crail
Glendevon
Falkland
Kinnesswood
Lower Largo
Anstruther
Pittenweem
Kinross
Glenrothes
Leven
Elie
CLACKS
Dollar
Alloa
Kincardine
Kirkcaldy
Burntisland
DUNFERMLINE
NORTH SEA
North Berwick
FIRTH OF FORTH
Falkirk
FALKIRK
Linlithgow
W LOTH
East Linton
Dunbar
EDINBURGH
C EDIN
Haddington
Ratho
Dalkeith
EAST LOTHIAN
St Abb's Head
LIVINGSTON
Eyemouth
MDLOTH
Penicuik
LAMMERMUIR HILLS
PENTLAND HILLS
NT
Duns
Berwick-upon-Tweed
Allanton
West Linton
Lauder
Swinton
Greenlaw
Leitholm
NU
Holy Island
Lanark
Biggar
Peebles
Coldstream
Etal
Innerleithen
Galashiels
Melrose
Bamburgh
Belford
Seahouses
Kelso
St Boswells
Selkirk
Wooler
Chatton
Warenford
Low Newton by the Sea
SCOTTISH BORDERS
Tibbie Shiels Inn
Jedburgh
Eglingham
Craster
SOUTHERN UPLANDS
Ettrick
Hawick
Alnwick
CHEVIOT HILLS
NORTHUMBERLAND
Newton on the Moor
Netherton
Amble
Moffat
Longframlington
NATIONAL PARK
Thornhill
Longhorsley
NORTHUMBERLAND
DUMFRIES AND GALLOWAY
Lochmaben
Langholm
Falstone
Morpeth
Ashington
Lockerbie
Whalton
Bedlington
Blyth
NZ
Dumfries
NY
Great Whittington
Whitley Bay
Longtown
North Shields
Tynemouth
New Abbey
Annan
Gretna
Haltwhistle
Haydon Bridge
Warden
Corbridge
NEWCASTLE UPON TYNE
SOUTH SHIELDS
Dalbeattie
Brampton
Hexham
TYNE AND WEAR
Rowfoot
GATESHEAD
SUNDERLAND
18
CARLISLE
19
WASHINGTON
Consett
Chester-le-Street
Seaham
Wigton
Solway Firth
Alston
Durham
Peterlee
Maryport
Crook
HARTLEPOOL
Cockermouth
Penrith
DURHAM
Workington
Bishop Auckland
Redcar
Newton Aycliffe
Whitehaven
Keswick
Appleby-in-Westmorland
STOCKTON-ON-TEES
LAKE DISTRICT
CUMBRIA
Barnard Castle
MIDDLESBROUGH
St Bees
Egremont
Brough
DARLINGTON
Guisborough

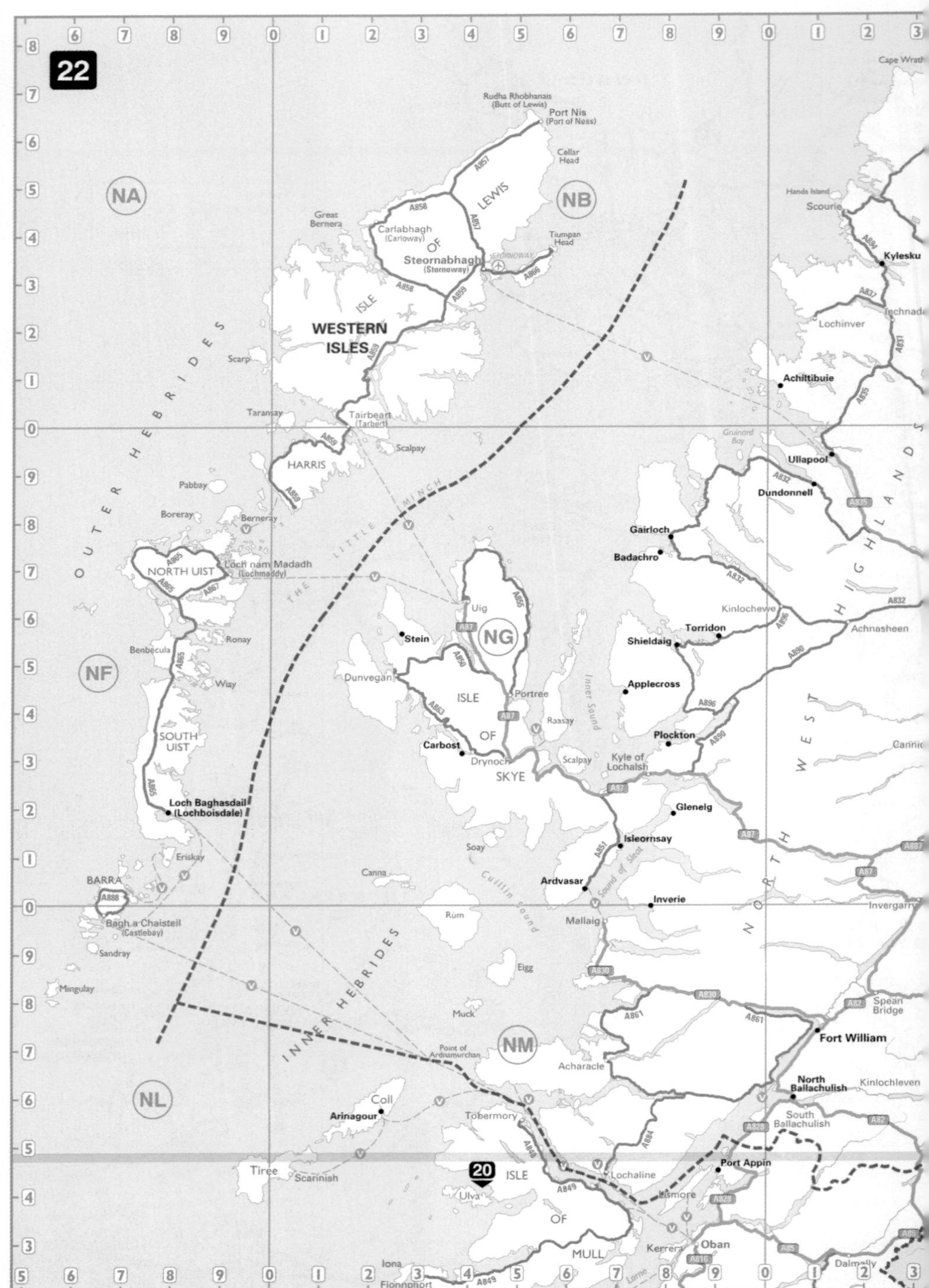

For continuation pages refer to numbered arrows

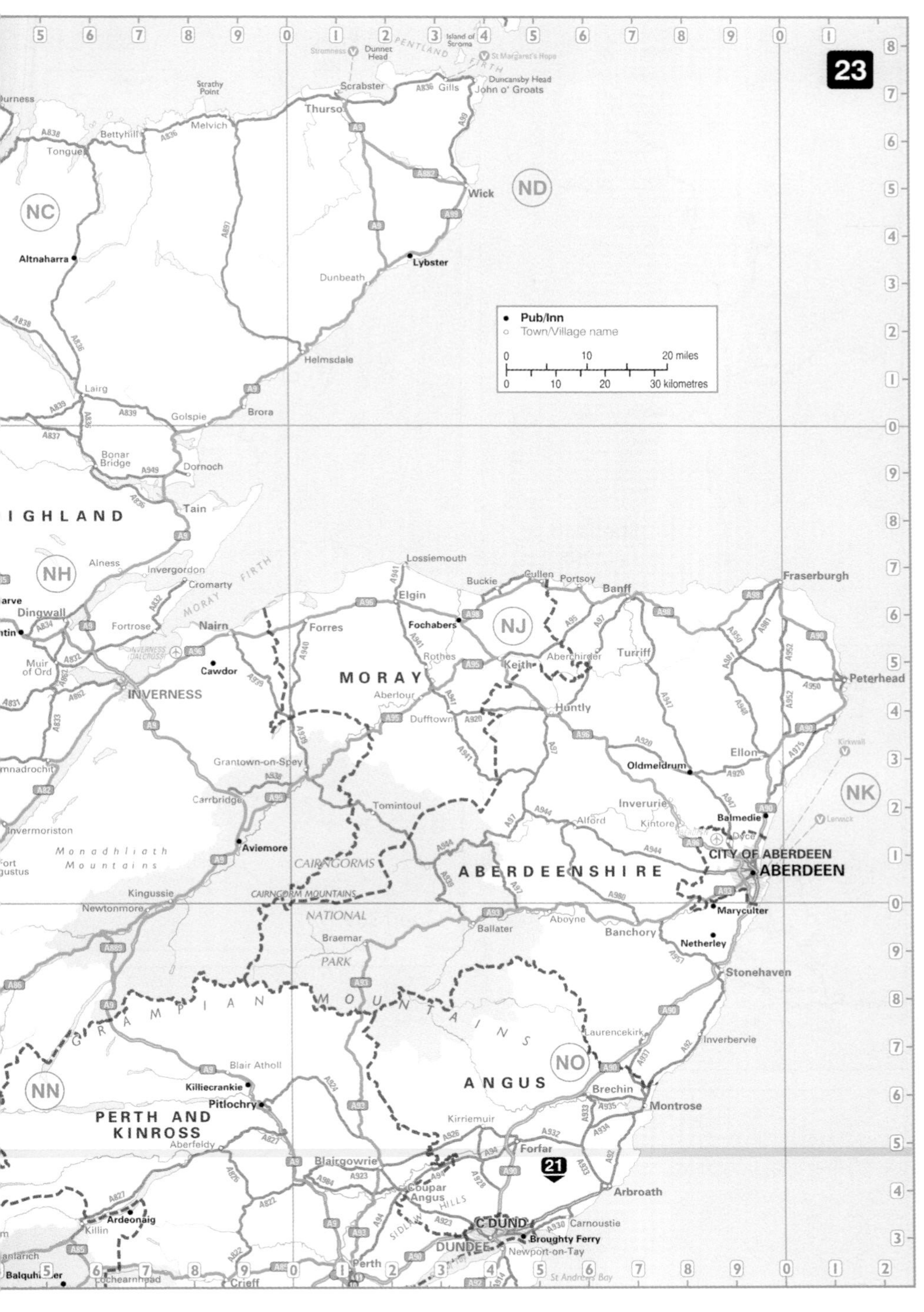

23
Pub/Inn
Town/Village name
0 10 20 miles
0 10 20 30 kilometres
Dunnet Head
PENTLAND FIRTH
Island of Stroma
St Margaret's Hope
Stromness
Duncansby Head
John o' Groats
Scrabster
Gills
Strathy Point
Thurso
Melvich
Bettyhill
Tongue
Wick
ND
NC
Altnaharra
Lybster
Dunbeath
Helmsdale
Lairg
Brora
Golspie
Bonar Bridge
Dornoch
Tain
HIGHLAND
NH
Alness
Invergordon
Cromarty
MORAY FIRTH
Dingwall
Fortrose
Nairn
Muir of Ord
INVERNESS
Cawdor
Forres
Lossiemouth
Elgin
Buckie
Cullen
Portsoy
Banff
Fraserburgh
Fochabers
NJ
Rothes
Keith
Aberchirder
Turriff
Peterhead
MORAY
Aberlour
Dufftown
Huntly
Grantown-on-Spey
Carrbridge
Tomintoul
Oldmeldrum
Ellon
Kirkwall
NK
Inverurie
Balmedie
Kintore
Dyce
Alford
Lerwick
Aviemore
Monadhliath Mountains
Invermoriston
CAIRNGORMS
CAIRNGORM MOUNTAINS
NATIONAL PARK
ABERDEENSHIRE
CITY OF ABERDEEN
ABERDEEN
Kingussie
Newtonmore
Aboyne
Maryculter
Ballater
Braemar
Banchory
Netherley
Stonehaven
GRAMPIAN MOUNTAINS
Laurencekirk
Inverbervie
NO
NN
Blair Atholl
Killiecrankie
Pitlochry
ANGUS
Brechin
Montrose
PERTH AND KINROSS
Kirriemuir
Aberfeldy
Forfar
Blairgowrie
21
Coupar Angus
SIDLAW HILLS
Arbroath
Ardeonaig
Killin
DUNDEE
Carnoustie
Broughty Ferry
Newport-on-Tay
Perth
St Andrews Bay
Lochearnhead
Crieff

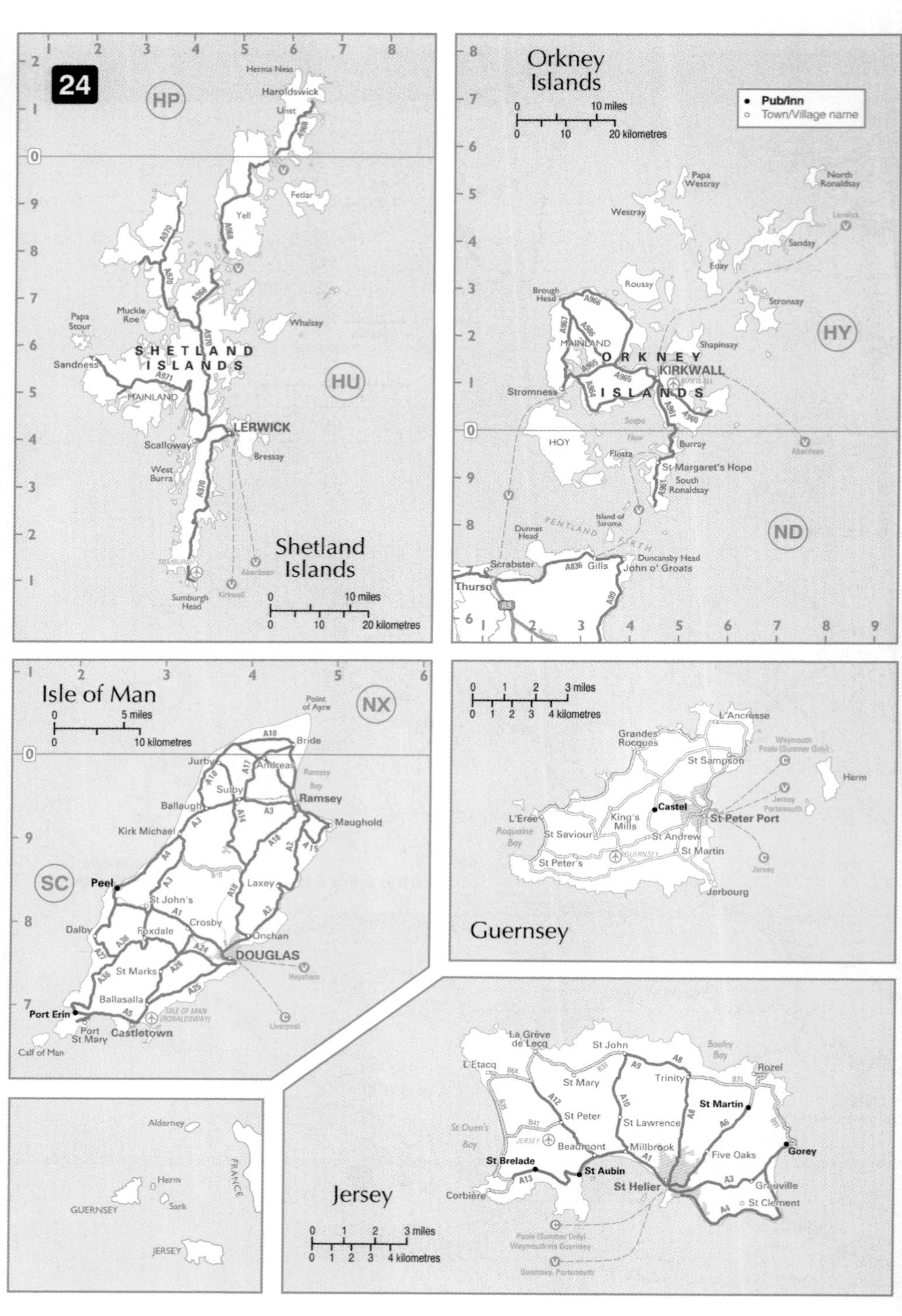
24
Shetland Islands
0 10 miles
0 10 20 kilometres
HP
HU
Herma Ness
Haroldswick
Unst
Fetlar
Yell
Papa Stour
Muckle Roe
Whalsay
SHETLAND ISLANDS
Sandness
MAINLAND
LERWICK
Scalloway
Bressay
West Burra
Sumburgh Head
Kirkwall
Aberdeen
Orkney Islands
0 10 miles
0 10 20 kilometres
Pub/Inn
Town/Village name
Papa Westray
North Ronaldsay
Westray
Sanday
Eday
Rousay
Stronsay
Brough Head
MAINLAND
Shapinsay
ORKNEY ISLANDS
KIRKWALL
Stromness
HOY
Scapa Flow
Flotta
Burray
St Margaret's Hope
South Ronaldsay
Island of Stroma
Dunnet Head
PENTLAND FIRTH
Duncansby Head
Scrabster
Gills
John o' Groats
Thurso
HY
ND
Aberdeen
Isle of Man
0 5 miles
0 10 kilometres
NX
SC
Point of Ayre
Bride
Jurby
Andreas
Sulby
Ramsey
Ramsey Bay
Ballaugh
Maughold
Kirk Michael
Peel
Laxey
St John's
Crosby
Dalby
Foxdale
Onchan
DOUGLAS
Heysham
St Marks
Ballasalla
Port Erin
Port St Mary
Castletown
ISLE OF MAN (RONALDSWAY)
Calf of Man
Liverpool
Guernsey
0 1 2 3 miles
0 1 2 3 4 kilometres
L'Ancresse
Grandes Rocques
Weymouth Poole (Summer Only)
St Sampson
Herm
Castel
L'Eree
King's Mills
St Peter Port
Jersey Portsmouth
Rocquaine Bay
St Saviour
St Andrew
St Martin
St Peter's
Jersey
Jerbourg
Alderney
Herm
Sark
GUERNSEY
JERSEY
FRANCE
Jersey
0 1 2 3 miles
0 1 2 3 4 kilometres
La Grève de Lecq
St John
Bouley Bay
L'Etacq
Rozel
Trinity
St Mary
St Martin
St Peter
St Lawrence
St Ouen's Bay
Beaumont
Millbrook
Five Oaks
Gorey
St Brelade
St Aubin
St Helier
Corbière
Grouville
St Clement
Poole (Summer Only) Weymouth via Guernsey
Guernsey, Portsmouth

Central London

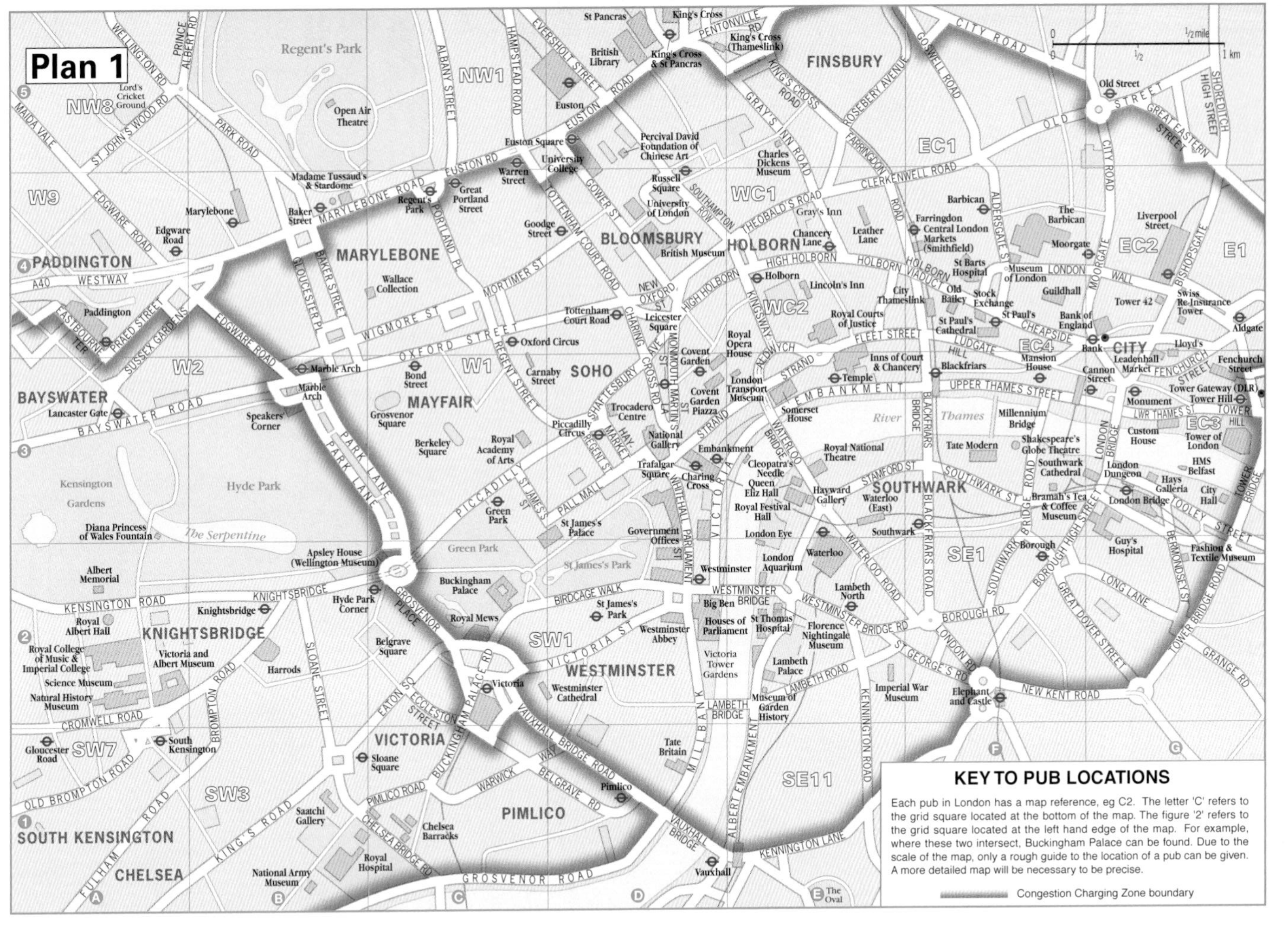

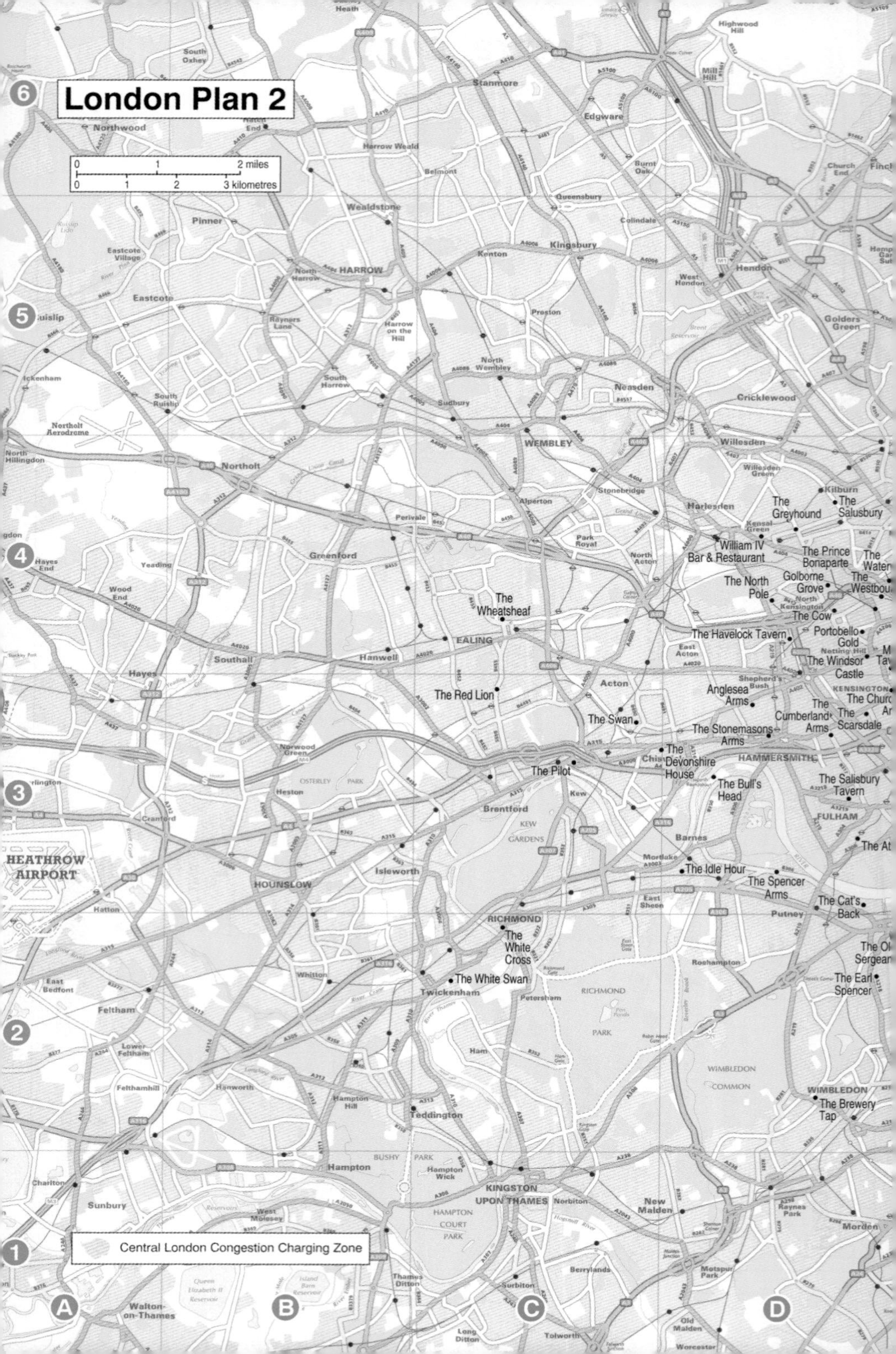
London Plan 2
0 1 2 miles
0 1 2 3 kilometres
Central London Congestion Charging Zone
A
B
C
D
1
2
3
4
5
6
Heath
South Oxhey
Highwood Hill
Mill Hill
Stanmore
Edgware
Northwood
Harrow Weald
Belmont
Burnt Oak
Church End
Queensbury
Wealdstone
Pinner
Colindale
Kingsbury
Kenton
Hendon
West Hendon
Eastcote Village
North Harrow
HARROW
Eastcote
Ruislip
Rayners Lane
Harrow on the Hill
Preston
Golders Green
Ickenham
South Harrow
North Wembley
Neasden
Cricklewood
South Ruislip
Sudbury
Northolt Aerodrome
WEMBLEY
Willesden
North Hillingdon
Northolt
Willesden Green
Stonebridge
Kilburn
Alperton
Harlesden
The Greyhound
The Salusbury
Perivale
Kensal Green
Park Royal
William IV Bar & Restaurant
The Prince Bonaparte
Hayes End
Yeading
Greenford
North Acton
The North Pole
Golborne Grove
Wood End
The Wheatsheaf
North Kensington
The Cow
EALING
The Havelock Tavern
Portobello Gold
Southall
Hanwell
East Acton
Notting Hill
The Windsor Castle
Hayes
Acton
Shepherd's Bush
Anglesea Arms
KENSINGTON
The Red Lion
The Swan
Cumberland Arms
The Scarsdale
The Stonemasons Arms
Norwood Green
The Devonshire House
HAMMERSMITH
OSTERLEY PARK
The Pilot
Heston
Kew
The Bull's Head
The Salisbury Tavern
Cranford
Brentford
FULHAM
HEATHROW AIRPORT
KEW GARDENS
Barnes
Isleworth
Mortlake
The Idle Hour
HOUNSLOW
The Spencer Arms
East Sheen
The Cat's Back
Hatton
RICHMOND
Putney
The White Cross
Roehampton
East Bedfont
Whitton
The White Swan
The Earl Spencer
Twickenham
Feltham
Petersham
RICHMOND PARK
Lower Feltham
Ham
WIMBLEDON COMMON
Felthamhill
Hanworth
WIMBLEDON
The Brewery Tap
Hampton Hill
Teddington
BUSHY PARK
Hampton
Hampton Wick
Charlton
KINGSTON UPON THAMES
Norbiton
New Malden
Raynes Park
Sunbury
West Molesey
HAMPTON COURT PARK
Morden
Berrylands
Motspur Park
Thames Ditton
Surbiton
Walton-on-Thames
Long Ditton
Tolworth
Old Malden
Worcester

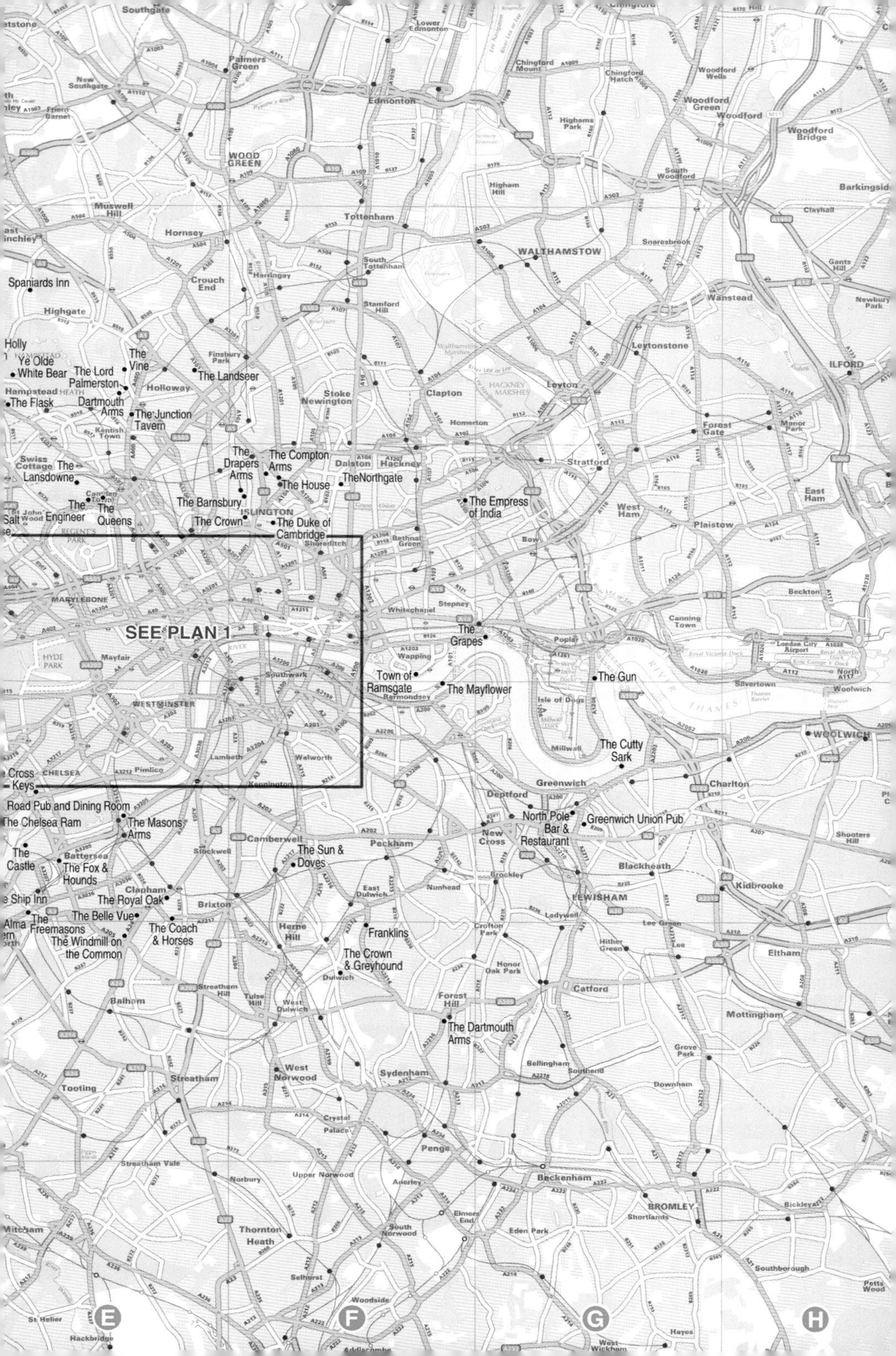

Southgate
Palmers Green
Lower Edmonton
Edmonton
Chingford Mount
Chingford Hatch
Woodford Wells
Woodford Green
Woodford
Woodford Bridge
New Southgate
Friern Barnet
WOOD GREEN
Highams Park
South Woodford
Higham Hill
Barkingside
Muswell Hill
Hornsey
Tottenham
WALTHAMSTOW
Snaresbrook
Clayhall
Crouch End
Harringay
South Tottenham
Gants Hill
Spaniards Inn
Highgate
Stamford Hill
Wanstead
Newbury Park
Holly
Ye Olde White Bear
The Vine
The Lord Palmerston
Finsbury Park
The Landseer
Leytonstone
ILFORD
Hampstead Heath
The Flask
Dartmouth Arms
Holloway
The Junction Tavern
Kentish Town
Stoke Newington
Clapton
HACKNEY MARSHES
Leyton
Forest Gate
Manor Park
Homerton
Swiss Cottage
The Lansdowne
The Drapers Arms
The Compton Arms
Dalston
Hackney
Stratford
The House
TheNorthgate
The Engineer
The Queens
The Barnsbury
ISLINGTON
The Crown
The Duke of Cambridge
The Empress of India
West Ham
Plaistow
East Ham
REGENT'S PARK
Shoreditch
Bethnal Green
Bow
MARYLEBONE
Whitechapel
Stepney
Beckton
Canning Town
SEE PLAN 1
The Grapes
Poplar
HYDE PARK
Mayfair
Wapping
London City Airport
Southwark
Town of Ramsgate
Bermondsey
The Mayflower
The Gun
Isle of Dogs
Silvertown
Woolwich
WESTMINSTER
RIVER THAMES
Thames Barrier
Millwall
The Cutty Sark
WOOLWICH
Lambeth
Walworth
CHELSEA
Pimlico
Cross Keys
Kennington
Greenwich
Charlton
Road Pub and Dining Room
The Chelsea Ram
The Masons Arms
Deptford
North Pole Bar & Restaurant
Greenwich Union Pub
Camberwell
Peckham
New Cross
Shooters Hill
The Castle
Battersea
The Fox & Hounds
Stockwell
The Sun & Doves
Brockley
Blackheath
Nunhead
East Dulwich
LEWISHAM
Kidbrooke
Ship Inn
Clapham
The Royal Oak
Brixton
The Freemasons
The Belle Vue
The Coach & Horses
Herne Hill
Franklins
Crofton Park
Ladywell
Lee Green
Lee
Hither Green
Eltham
The Windmill on the Common
The Crown & Greyhound
Dulwich
Honor Oak Park
Catford
Balham
Streatham Hill
Tulse Hill
West Dulwich
Forest Hill
Mottingham
The Dartmouth Arms
Grove Park
Bellingham
Southend
Tooting
Streatham
West Norwood
Sydenham
Downham
Crystal Palace
Penge
Streatham Vale
Norbury
Upper Norwood
Anerley
Beckenham
BROMLEY
Bickley
Elmers End
Shortlands
Mitcham
Thornton Heath
South Norwood
Eden Park
Selhurst
Southborough
Petts Wood
Woodside
St Helier
Hackbridge
Addiscombe
West Wickham
Hayes
E
F
G
H

Index

Highlighted entries are Pick of the Pubs

G

H

I

K

N

The Automobile Association would like to thank the following photographers, companies and picture libraries for their assistance in the preparation of this book.

Abbreviations for the picture credits are as follows: (t) top; (b) bottom; (l) left; (r) right; (AA) AA World Travel Library.

1 AA/A Baker; 2l AA/S Watkins; 3tr, 3bl AA/C Sawyer; 3br AA/D Foster; 4tl AA/C Sawyer; 5tr AA/C Sawyer; 5br AA/K Paterson; 6tl AA/C Sawyer; 7tr, 7b AA/C Sawyer; 8tl AA/C Sawyer; 9tr AA/C Sawyer; 10tl, 10br AA/C Sawyer; 11tr, 11c AA/C Sawyer; 12tl AA/C Sawyer; 13tr AA/C Sawyer; 14 AA/S L Day; 688 AA/R Elliott; 724 AA/S Watkins.

Other credits;
8t The White Swan, Pickering
10bl Royal Oak, Poynings
12tr, 12bl, 12br, 13bl, 13br Rose Cottage Inn, Alciston

Every effort has been made to trace the copyright holders, and we apologise in advance for any accidental errors. We would be happy to apply the corrections in the following edition of this publication.

Please send this form to:
Editor, The Pub Guide,
Lifestyle Guides,
The Automobile Association,
Fanum House,
Basingstoke RG21 4EA

or fax: 01256 491647
or e-mail: lifestyleguides@theAA.com

Please use this form to tell us about any pub or inn you have visited, whether it is in the guide or not currently listed. We are interested in the quality of food, the selection of beers and the overall ambience of the establishment.

Feedback from readers helps us to keep our guide accurate and up to date. However, if you have a complaint to make during a visit, we do recommend that you discuss the matter with the pub management there and then, so that they have a chance to put things right before your visit is spoilt.

Please note that the AA does not undertake to arbitrate between you and the pub management, or to obtain compensation or engage in protracted correspondence.

Date: ....

Your name (block capitals) ....

Your address (block capitals) ....

....

....

.... Post Code.......................

e-mail address: ....

Name of pub: ....

Location ....

Comments ....

....

....

....

(please attach a separate sheet if necessary)

Please tick here if you DO NOT wish to receive details of AA offers or products ☐

PTO

	YES	NO
Have you bought this guide before?	☐	☐

Do you regularly use any other pub, accommodation or food guides? If yes, which ones?

....

....

What do you find most useful about The AA Pub Guide?

....

....

....

....

Do you read the editorial features in the guide?..

Do you use the location atlas? ....

Have you tried any of the walks included in this guide?...............................

Is there any other information you would like to see added to this guide?

....

....

....

....

....

What are your main reasons for visiting pubs (tick all that apply)

food	☐	business	☐	accommodation	☐
beer	☐	celebrations	☐	entertainment	☐
atmosphere	☐	leisure	☐	other	....

How often do you visit a pub for a meal?

more than once a week	☐
one a week	☐
once a fortnight	☐
once a month	☐
once in six months	☐

Notes